CORPORATE FINANCE AND THE SECURITIES LAWS

Third Edition

Charles J. Johnson, Jr.

Joseph McLaughlin

ASPEN
PUBLISHERS

1185 Avenue of the Americas, New York, NY 10036
www.aspenpublishers.com

This publication is designed to provide accurate and authoritative information in regard to the subject matter covered. It is sold with the understanding that the publisher is not engaged in rendering legal, accounting, or other professional services. If legal advice or other professional assistance is required the services of a competent professional person should be sought.

> —From a *Declaration of Principles* jointly adopted by a Committee of the American Bar Association and a Committee of Publishers and Associations

© 2004 Aspen Publishers, Inc.
A Wolters Kluwer Company
www.aspenpublishers.com

All rights reserved. No part of this publication may be reproduced or transmitted in any form or by any means, electronic or mechanical, including photocopy, recording, or any information storage and retrieval system, without permission in writing from the publisher. Requests for permission to reproduce content should be directed to the Aspen Publishers website at *www.aspenpublishers.com*, or fax a letter of intent to the permissions department at 646-728-3048.

Library of Congress Cataloging-in-Publication Data

Johnson, Charles J., 1932–
  Corporate finance and the securities laws / Charles J. Johnson, Jr., Joseph McLaughlin.—3rd ed.
    p. cm.
  Includes index.
  ISBN 0-7355-2332-0
    1. Corporations—Finance—Law and legislation—United States.
    2. Securities—United States. I. McLaughlin, Joseph, 1941– II. Title.

KF1428.J58 2004
346.73'0666–dc22

2004055066

Printed in the United States of America

1 2 3 4 5 6 7 8 9 0

About Aspen Publishers

Aspen Publishers, headquartered in New York City, is a leading information provider for attorneys, business professionals, and law students. Written by preeminent authorities, our products consist of analytical and practical information covering both U.S. and international topics. We publish in the full range of formats, including updated manuals, books, periodicals, CDs, and online products.

Our proprietary content is complemented by 2,500 legal databases, containing over 11 million documents, available through our Loislaw division. Aspen Publishers also offers a wide range of topical legal and business databases linked to Loislaw's primary material. Our mission is to provide accurate, timely, and authoritative content in easily accessible formats, supported by unmatched customer care.

To order any Aspen Publishers title, go to *www.aspenpublishers.com* or call 1-800-638-8437.

To reinstate your manual update service, call 1-800-638-8437.

For more information on Loislaw products, go to *www.loislaw.com* or call 1-800-364-2512.

For Customer Care issues, e-mail *CustomerCare@aspenpublishers.com;* call 1-800-234-1660; or fax 1-800-901-9075.

Aspen Publishers
A Wolters Kluwer Company

*For Chris
and
to the memory of
J. Courtney Ivey*

C.J.J., Jr.

*For
Joseph Nicholas McLaughlin
and
Genevieve Lardiere McLaughlin*

J.McL.

TABLE OF CONTENTS

Chapter 1

OVERVIEW OF THE SECURITIES ACT OF 1933 AND THE INTEGRATED DISCLOSURE SYSTEM................1
Market Crashes and Securities Legislation 1
History of the 1933 Act 3
The Securities and Exchange Commission 6
Operation of the 1933 Act...7
- *Disclosure Philosophy*..7
- *Definition of Security* 8
- *Registration and Prospectus Delivery Requirements*..11
  - *Registration for a Purpose*...............................12
  - *Operation of the Registration Requirement* 13
    - *Contents of the Registration Statement* 14
    - *Development of the Integrated Disclosure System* 15
    - *SEC Staff Review of the Registration Statement* 18
    - *"Effective Date" of the Registration Statement* 18
    - *Offers and Sales of the Registered Securities* 19

- - Operation of the Prospectus Delivery Requirement 20
  - - - Preliminary Prospectus 21
  - - - Delivery of Final Prospectus with Confirmation 21
  - - - "Free-Writing" Privilege 24
  - - - Delivery of Final Prospectus with Registered Security 25
  - - - Dealers' Delivery of Final Prospectus in Connection with After-Market Transactions 25
  - - - Unsold Allotments and Updating the Prospectus 27
  - - - Market-Makers' Delivery of Prospectus When Affiliated With Issuer 29
  - - - Electronic Delivery of Prospectus 30
- Communications During the Offering Process ("Gun-jumping") 30
  - - Source of the Problem 31
- Notices of Proposed Registered Offerings (Rule 135) 33
- Notice of Proposed Unregistered Offerings (Rule 135c) 35
- Offshore Press-Related Communications (Rule 135e) 36
- Communications Not Deemed a Prospectus (Rule 134) 36
- Research Reports 38
- Certain Offers and Sales 39
  - - Spin-offs 39
  - - Rule 145 40
- Exempted Transactions 42
  - - Private Placements 42
  - - Trading Transactions 42
  - - Transactions by Underwriters 44
  - - Rule 144 47
  - - Offers and Sales to Employees 49

- *Exempted Securities* 49
  - • *U.S. Government Obligations* 49
  - • *Municipal Obligations* 51
  - • *Bank Securities* 54
  - • *Thrift Institutions* 57
  - • *Commercial Paper* 57
  - • *Railroad Equipment Trust Certificates* 57
  - • *Insurance Contracts* 58
  - • *Exchanges with Existing Securityholders* 58
  - • *Court or Government Approved Exchanges* 59
  - • *Bankruptcy* 60
  - • *Other Exemptions* 60
- **The Future of the 1933 Act** 60

Chapter 2

SYNDICATE PROCEDURES AND UNDERWRITING DOCUMENTS 65

Underwriting Syndicates 66
- *Pre-1933 Act Procedures* 68
- *Post-1933 Act Procedures* 70

The Agreement Among Underwriters 72
- *Underwriters' Questionnaire* 73
- *Manager's Authority* 74
- *Price Maintenance* 74
- *Retentions and "Pot" Sales* 75
- *Proposed Restriction on First-Day Market Orders in IPOs* 76
- *Shares Returned to Underwriters* 76
- *Overallotment and Stabilization Authority* 77
- *Control of the Syndicate* 78
- *Trading Restrictions* 78
- *Penalty Bids* 79
- *Components of the Spread* 80
- *Payment and Delivery* 82
- *Authority to Borrow* 82
- *NASD Provisions* 83
- *Claims Against Underwriters* 83

- *Miscellaneous Provisions* 84
- *Termination of Price and Other Restrictions* 85

The Underwriting Agreement 86
- *Several Commitments* 87
- *Rule 430A* 87
- *Timing and Risk* 88
- *"Green Shoe" Option* 88
- *Representations and Warranties* 91
- *Representations by Selling Securityholders* 94
- *Delayed Delivery Contracts* 94
- *Proposed Enhancement of Issuer's Role in Pricing IPOs* 96
- *Covenants* 97
- *Lock-Up Agreements* 99
- *Closing Conditions* 101
- *Comfort Letters* 104
- *Purchase and Sale; Closing* 106
- *Indemnification* 107
- *Contribution* 111
- *Termination of Underwriting Agreement at Underwriters' Election* 112
- *Default and Step-Up* 116

The Selected Dealers Agreement 117
Competitive Bidding 118

Chapter 3

SELECTED ISSUES IN THE REGISTRATION AND DISTRIBUTION PROCESS 121
Selecting the Investment Banker 122
Getting Organized and Other Preliminary Matters 125
- *Form of Registration Statement* 127
- *Gun-Jumping Questions* 131
  - • *Websites* 132
  - • *Product Advertisements* 133
  - • *Annual Reports* 134
  - • *Presentations to Securities Analysts* 134

TABLE OF CONTENTS

- • Restricted Lists 136
- Stock Exchange Listing; "Blue Sky"
  Considerations 137
- Issuer-Directed Shares 138

Preparation of the Registration Statement..................141
- "Plain English" 141
- Risk Factors..143
- Prospectus Summary..145

Other Selected Issues..146
- Role of the Securities Analyst in Securities
  Offerings 146
- Management's Discussion and Analysis 150
- MD&A:Taking a "Fresh Look" 152
  - • MD&A Presentation....................................152
  - • MD&A Content and Focus 153
    - • • "Key Indicators" 153
    - • • Materiality 154
    - • • Material Trends and Uncertainties 154
    - • • Analysis 155
  - • Significance of Additional Information
      Available to Management 155
  - • Responsibility for Preparing MD&A..............157
  - • Liquidity and Capital 159
  - • Results of Operations 160
  - • Off-Balance Sheet Arrangements 161
  - • Tabular Disclosure of Contractual
      Obligations..162
  - • Critical Accounting Estimates 162
  - • Forward-Looking Focus of MD&A 164
  - • Caterpillar Proceeding..................................164
- Projections and Other Forward-Looking
  Information 166
- Initial Public Offerings 171
- "Online" Offerings 174
- Electronic Auctions 179
- "Deal Sites" 181
- Guarantees and Credit Enhancement 184
- Requests for Confidential Treatment 185

The SEC Review Process 185
  • *Selective Review* 186
  • *SEC Comments* 188
  • *Responding to Comments* 188
  • *Recirculation* 190
Post-Filing Issues 191
  • *Roadshows (Electronic and Otherwise)* 191
  • *Dealing with Gun-Jumping Problems* 195
    • • *E-Mail and Other Electronic Communications* 198
    • • *Press Coverage* 200
    • • *Rating Agencies* 202
    • • *Research Coverage* 203
  • *Regulation M Problems* 208
  • *Changes in Deal Size (Rule 430A)* 208
  • *"T+3" Settlement Date and Prospectus Delivery Problems* 211
  • *The Electronic Prospectus* 214
Chinese Walls 218
Inadvertent and Transient Investment Companies 219
Extension of Credit—(Section 11(d)(1)) 223

Chapter 4

MANIPULATIVE PRACTICES AND MARKET ACTIVITIES DURING DISTRIBUTIONS 231
Early Prohibitions of Manipulative Practices 232
  • *Fletcher Committee Investigation* 233
  • *Wall Street's Response* 235
  • *Prohibition of Manipulation (Section 9)* 236
  • *Effects of Section 9* 238
  • *The Next Twenty Years* 239
    • • *Over-the-Counter Manipulations* 240
    • • *Meaning of the Term "Transactions"* 241
    • • *Inference of Motive.* 241
    • • *Stabilization Before Rule 10b-7* 242

TABLE OF CONTENTS

- Adoption of the Original Trading Practice Rules 244
- Subsequent Revisions of the Trading Practice Rules 244
- Adoption of Regulation M 246

Regulation M 247
- Rule 101—Basic Outline 248
- Rule 101—Basic Prohibitions 248
- Distributions 251
  - • The 1983 Definition 252
  - • The 1994 Concept Release 253
  - • Shelf Registrations 255
- Distribution Participant 255
- Affiliated Purchasers 257
- Beginning of Restricted Period 259
- Termination of Restricted Period 259
  - • Successful Offering 260
  - • Unsuccessful Offering 263
    - • • Investment Account 264
- Covered Securities 266
- Excepted Securities 268
- Excepted Activities 270
  - • Research 270
  - • Passive Market-Making and Stabilization Transactions 271
  - • Odd-Lot Transactions 271
  - • Exercises of Securities 271
  - • Unsolicited Transactions 271
    - • • Unsolicited Brokerage Transactions 271
    - • • Unsolicited Purchases 272
  - • Basket Transactions 273
  - • De Minimis Transactions 274
  - • Transactions Among Distribution Participants 274
  - • Transactions in the Securities Being Distributed or Securities Offered as Principal 275

- - *Transactions in Rule 144A Securities* 277
- - *Transactions in Foreign Sovereign Bonds* 277
- *Disclosure, SRO Notification and Recordkeeping* 278

Passive Market-Making 278
Stabilization and Related Activities 279
- *Excepted Securities* 280
- *Mechanics* 281
- *General Requirements* 282
- *Prices at Which Stabilization May Take Place* 283
  - - *Initiating Stabilization When There Is No Market for the Security* 284
  - - *Initiating Stabilization When the Principal Market Is Open* 284
  - - *Initiating Stabilization When the Principal Market Is Closed* 285
  - - *Initiating Stabilization Before the Offering Price Is Determined* 287
  - - *Maintaining or Carrying Over a Stabilizing Bid* 288
  - - *Increasing or Reducing a Stabilizing Bid* 288
  - - *Effects of Exchange Rates* 289
  - - *Adjustments to Stabilizing Bid* 289
- *Stabilization Outside the United States* 289

Disclosure, SRO Notification and Recordkeeping 290
Trading Restrictions for Issuers and Selling Securityholders (Rule 102) 292
Dealing with Problems Under the Trading Practice Rules 295
Covering Short Sales with Registered Securities (Rule 105) 296
Manipulation Outside the Trading Practice Rules 300

Chapter 5

LIABILITIES AND DUE DILIGENCE 305
  Statutory Bases for Liability..307
    • *Section 11* 308
    • *Section 12(a)(2)*..314
    • *Rule 10b-5* 317
    • *Controlling Persons*..320
  SEC and Judicial Interpretations Concerning
    Due Diligence 321
    • *SEC Administrative Proceedings* 322
    • *The* BarChris *Case* 323
    • *The* Leasco Data Processing *Case* 325
    • *The* Chris-Craft *Case* 326
    • *Summary Judgment* 328
    • *Few Judicial Decisions* 328
  Due Diligence Standards 329
  Due Diligence Procedures 331
    • *Integrity of Management*..331
    • *Effect of the Transaction on the Issuer's*
      Financial Statements 332
    • *Corporate Governance* 334
    • *Staffing*..335
    • *Checklists* 337
    • *Legal Review—Opinion Matters*............................337
    • *Legal Review—Disclosure Matters*........................339
    • *Review of Industry* 341
    • *Role of Analysts in Due Diligence*.........................342
    • *Issuer's Website and Basic Documents* 344
    • *Questionnaire from Officers, Directors and Other*
      Persons 346
    • *Review of Registration Statement*...........................347
    • *Maximizing "Expertization"* 351
    • *Visits to Principal Facilities* 352
    • *Meetings with Principal Officers* 352
    • *Negotiation of Underwriting Agreement* 353
    • *Review of Confidential or Bulky Documents*..........354
    • *Accounting Matters* 354

- - *Preparing for Financial Statement Due Diligence* 355
- - *Meeting Focused on Financial Statement Due Diligence* 357
  - - - *SEC's Formal Requirements for Financial Statements* 359
  - - - *Revenue Recognition* 360
  - - - *Derivatives and Market Risk* 361
  - - - *Non-GAAP Financial Measures* 364
  - - - *Segment Disclosure* 365
  - - - *Related Party Transactions* 366
  - - - *Other Areas for Inquiry* 366
  - - - *MD&A Adequacy* 366
  - - - *Critical Accounting Estimates* 367
  - - - *Off-Balance Sheet Entities* 367
- *Negotiation of Comfort Letters* 367
- *"Bring-Down" Due Diligence* 371
- *Documentation* 372

The Penn Central Affair 374
The Hughes Tool Company Initial Public Offering 382

Chapter 6

RULES OF THE SELF-REGULATORY ORGANIZATIONS 391
Review of Corporate Financing (Rule 2710) 397
- *Filing Requirements* 398
- *Exemptions* 401
- *Request for Underwriting Activity Report* 403
- *Submission of Pricing Information* 403
- *Items of Value.* 403
- *Lockup Agreements* 406
- *"Included in Underwriting Compensation"* 408
  - - *"Profit-Sharing" Allegations* 411
- *Standards of Fairness* 412
- *Unfair Underwriting Arrangements* 413
- *Proceeds Directed to a Member* 414

TABLE OF CONTENTS

- *Applications for Exemptions* 415
- *Antitrust Immunity* 415
- *Proposed Enhancements of Issuer's Role in Pricing IPOs* 416

Underwritings Involving Conflicts of Interest (Rule 2720) 417

Potential Liabilities of Qualified Independent Underwriters 420

Free-Riding and Withholding (Rule 2790) and Other Ways of Exploiting "New Issues" 423

- *Early NASD and SEC Responses to Free-Riding* 424
- *Free-Riding and Withholding Interpretation* 426
  - • *Definition of Hot Issue* 427
  - • *Restricted Persons and "Normal Investment Practice"* 428
- *Rule 2790* 429
  - • *Applicable to "New Issues" Rather Than "Hot Issues"* 430
  - • *Prohibitions of Rule 2790* 431
  - • *Restricted Persons* 432
  - • *Preconditions for Sale* 434
  - • *General Exemptions* 434
  - • *Issuer-Directed Securities* 436
  - • *Antidilution Provisions* 436
  - • *Stand-by Purchasers* 437
  - • *IPO Distribution Manager* 437
  - • *Other Exemptive Relief* 437
- *Proposed Restrictions on "Spinning"* 437
- *Proposed Restrictions on Excessive Compensation for Other Services* 439

The *Papilsky* Rules (Rules 2740, 2730 and 2750) 440

- *Background* 442
  - • *Pressures by Institutions* 443
  - • *The* Papilsky *Case* 446
- *Analysis of the Papilsky Rules* 448
  - • *Selling Commissions, Discounts and Other Allowances (Rule 2740)* 448

xviii   CORPORATE FINANCE & THE SECURITIES LAWS

- • *Securities Taken in Trade (Rule 2730)* 454
- • *Transactions with Related Persons (Rule 2750)* 457

Chapter 7

PRIVATE PLACEMENTS 459
   Legislative History 461
   Early Administrative Interpretations 463
   The *Ralston Purina* Case 467
   The *Crowell-Collier* Case 471
   Pre-Rule 146 Developments 474
   Rule 146 476
   Regulation D 481
     • *General Solicitation or Advertising* 482
       • • *Express Exclusions* 482
       • • *Internet Offerings and Notices* 483
       • • *Newsletters, Media and Interviews* 487
       • • *Number of Offerees* 488
       • • *Future of the General Solicitation Prohibition* 489
     • *"Accredited Investors"* 490
     • *Informational Access and Disclosure* 493
     • *Anti-Underwriter Precautions* 493
       • • *Restrictive Legends* 494
     • *Resales* 495
     • *Notice, Disqualification, Blue Sky Requirements* 495
     • *Integration* 497
     • *The Substantial Compliance Rule* 500
   Rule 144A 501
     • *QIB Status* 502
     • *Screen-Based and Other "Offers"* 505
     • *"Fungibility"* 506
     • *Information Requirement* 507
     • *Notice Requirement* 508
     • *Resales, PORTAL and DTC* 509
   Private Placement Procedures 510
     • *Rule 144A Private Placement* 511

TABLE OF CONTENTS

- - *Rule 144A Debt Offering* 511
- - *Rule 144 Offering of Equity Securities* 514
- *Continuous Private Placement Programs* 516
  - - *Continuous Offering Procedures for Restricted Commercial Paper* 516
  - - *Integration* 524
  - - *Extendible Commercial Paper* 527
  - - *Continuous Offering Procedures for Restricted MTNs* 528
- *Stand-Alone Institutional Placements* 531
  - - *Procedures* 533
  - - *Investment Representations* 534
  - - *Availability of Section 4(2) Exemption* 535
  - - *Secondary Private Placements* 536
- *Regulation D Placements with Individual Investors* 537
  - - *Potential Ineligibility of Certain Reporting Companies* 538
  - - *General Solicitation and Prior Relationships* 538
  - - *Procedures and Controls* 541
    - - *Designation of Qualified Sales Representatives* 542
    - - *Designation of Qualified Offerees* 542
    - - *Solicitation of Qualified Offerees* 543
    - - *Processing of Subscription Agreements* 543

Related Private Placements and Public Offerings 543
- *Private Offering Followed by Public Filing* 544
- *Public Filing Followed by Private Offering* 549
- *Private Offering with Concurrent or Future Registration* 552
- *Registration Rights Agreement* 553
- *Private Offering Followed by "Exxon Capital" or "A/B" Exchange Offer* 555
- *Private Offering Followed by Short Sales Into Public Market* 557

Private Investment Companies (Section 3(c)(7)) 558
Credit on New Issues (Section 11(d)(1)) 560

Chapter 8

SHELF REGISTRATION (RULE 415)..............................561
The Evolution of Shelf Registration......................564
- *Traditional Shelf Registration*..............................565
  - • *Continuous Acquisition Programs*................566
  - • *Sales Following Private Placements*..............567
  - • *Shares Issued on Conversions of Privately Placed Securities*...............................568
  - • *Underwriters' Stock and Warrants*................569
  - • *Resales Following Rule 133 Transactions*......569
  - • *Stock Option Plans*...................................572
  - • *Pledged Securities*...................................572
- *"90-Day Undertakings"*......................................573
- *The Hazel Bishop Case*......................................574
- *Guide 4*..578
- *Further Developments*..579

The Adoption of Rule 415.....................................579
Expansion of Eligibility to Use Form S-3 and Form F-3..584
The Impact of Rule 415......................................586
How Rule 415 Works..590
- *Securities Covered by Rule 415*............................590
- *Amount of Securities Registered*..........................592
- *Type of Securities Registered ("Unallocated," "Generic" or "Universal" Shelf)*......................594
- *Documentation*...596
- *Incorporation by Reference of 1934 Act Reports*...597
- *Use of Offering Material*....................................601
- *Undertaking to File Post-Effective Amendments in Certain Situations*...................................602

Shelf Filings by Foreign Governments or Political Subdivisions..................................606
Conventional Debt and Preferred Stock Shelf Registration..609
- *Securities To Be Registered; "Convenience Shelf" Problem*..610
- *Plan of Distribution*..611

- *The Indenture and the Description of the Securities* 614
- *Preferred Stock* 617
- *Board Authorization* 617
- *Underwriting Documents* 618
- *Use of Preliminary Prospectus* 620
- *Disclosure and Due Diligence* 621

Medium-Term Note Programs 632
- *Documentation* 634
- *Registration Under Rule 415* 636
- *Procedures* 639
- *Disclosure and Due Diligence* 640
- *Section 11(d)(1)* 642

Common Stock Shelf Registration 643
- *Primary Offerings* 643
- *At-the-Market Equity Offerings* 644
- *Investment Companies* 644
- *Non-Underwritten Registered Equity Secondaries* 646

The Presumptive Underwriter Problem 652
Regulation M 654
Deep Discount and Zero Coupon Obligations 656
- *Tax Considerations* 656
  - • *Definition of OID* 656
  - • *Consequences of OID* 657
  - • *Reporting of OID* 658
- *Bankruptcy and Events of Default* 659
- *Accounting Treatment* 659
- *Deep Discount Obligations* 660
- *Zero Coupon Obligations* 660

"Reopenings" 661

Chapter 9

INTERNATIONAL FINANCINGS 665
Offshore Offerings and the 1933 Act 667
- *Interest Equalization Tax* 667
- *Release 33-4708* 669
- *Debt Financings After Elimination of IET* 671

xxii   CORPORATE FINANCE & THE SECURITIES LAWS

- *Dissatisfaction with Release 33-4708* 674
- *Evolution of a Territorial Approach*........................677
- *Adoption of Regulation S* 679
  - *Subsequent SEC Concerns with "Abusive" Regulation S Transactions*............................680
  - *General Statement* 681
  - *Safe Harbors*..682
  - *Offshore Transaction* 682
  - *Directed Selling Efforts* 683
    - *Internet Postings* 683
    - *Foreign Press-Related Activity* 685
    - *Notices of Unregistered Offerings* 688
    - *Advertising* 688
    - *Quotations* 689
    - *Research* 689
    - *Miscellaneous Activities*........................690
    - *Registered or Exempt Offers Excluded* 690
    - *Duration of Prohibition* 691
  - *Issuer Safe Harbor* 691
    - *Category 1 Transactions* 691
    - *Category 2 Transactions* 693
    - *Category 3 Transactions* 698
  - *New Rule 905* 701
  - *Convertible Securities*....................................702
  - *Private Placements in United States Concurrent with Public Offerings Abroad* 702
  - *Resale Safe Harbor* 704
  - *Resales in the United States* 705
- **Tax Considerations in Offshore Debt Offerings** 706
  - *TEFRA Issuer and Holder Sanctions*.....................707
    - *TEFRA D Rules* 708
    - *TEFRA C Rules* 709
  - *Withholding Taxes and Gross-Up Obligations* 710
- **Foreign Private Issuers and the U.S. Securities Laws** 710
  - *Status as a "Foreign Private Issuer"* 712
  - *American Depositary Receipts* 713

TABLE OF CONTENTS

- - *Types of ADR Facilities* 715
- - *1933 Act Status of ADR Facilities* 717
- - *Form F-6* 720
- *1934 Act Reporting Obligations of Foreign Companies* 721
  - - *Development of a Regulatory Compromise* 722
  - - *Current "Trigger" for 1934 Act Registration* 728
  - - *Obtaining the Rule 12g3-2(b) Exemption* 728
- *Form 20-F* 731
- *Financial Statement Requirements* 733
  - - *Formal Requirements* 733
  - - *Reconciliation to U.S. GAAP*........................734
  - - *Geographic Market and Industry Segments*..736
- *Continuous Reporting Under the 1934 Act* 737
- *Listing on a U.S. Exchange or NASDAQ* 738
- *Sarbanes-Oxley Consequences for Foreign Reporting Companies* 738
- *Exiting the Continuous Reporting System* 739
- *Multijurisdictional Disclosure System* 740
- *1933 Act Registration for Foreign Private Issuers* 742
- *1940 Act Exemptions for Foreign Banks, Insurance Companies and Finance Subsidiaries* 743

Rights Offerings...744
Global Offerings by Foreign Corporations 749
- *1933 Act Registration* 749
- *Form and Delivery of Prospectus* 751
- *Section 11 Liability* 752
- *Underwriting Practices* 753
- *Foreign Publicity* 756
- *Foreign Research*..757
- *Regulation M* 759
- *Installment Payment Offerings* 759

Sales in the United States by Foreign Governments and Their Political Subdivisions...............................760
- *1933 Act Registration* 761
- *Consent to Service and Sovereign Immunity*..........764
- *1934 Act Registration and Reporting*......................767

Chapter 10

COMMERCIAL PAPER 769
Characteristics of the Market...771
Credit Quality and the "Orderly Exit" 773
Dealers' Role 776
Mechanics 777
1933 Act Considerations 778
- *Section 3(a)(3) Commercial Paper Exemption* 778
  - • *SEC Release No. 33-4412* 779
  - • *The Prime Quality Standard* 779
  - • *Offers to the Public* 780
  - • *Eligibility for Discounting* 783
  - • *The Current Transaction Test* 783
  - • *The Concept of Commercial Paper Capacity*..784
  - • *Role of No-action Letters.* 787
  - • *Financing of Inventories and Accounts Receivable* 787
  - • *Payment of Operating Expenses* 788
  - • *Carrying Finance Company Receivables* 789
  - • *Lending Activities of U.S. Bank Holding Companies and Foreign Banks*....................789
  - • *Financing of Leasing and Related Activities*...790
  - • *Financing of Insurance Operations*................792
  - • *Financing of Broker-Dealer Operations* 792
  - • *Investments in Money Market Obligations* 794
  - • *Interim Construction Financing*.....................796
  - • *Financing of Public Utility Operations*..........798
  - • *Nuclear Fuel Financing* 799
  - • *Acquisition Financing*....................................801

TABLE OF CONTENTS   XXV

- - *Issuer's Repurchase of Securities* 802
- - *Financing by Foreign Governmental Entities* 802
- *Section 3(a)(2) Bank Support Exemption* 805
- *Section 4(2) Continuous Private Placement Programs*..808

1940 Act Considerations 809
- *Foreign Banks and Insurance Companies* 810
- *Finance Subsidiaries* 811

Liabilities on Default 813
- *Section 12(a)(1)*..814
- *Antifraud Remedies* 816
  - - *Section 12(a)(2)* 817
  - - *Rule 10b-5* 822

Chapter 11

INNOVATIVE FINANCING TECHNIQUES 825
Regulation Under the Commodity Exchange Act 828
- *Evolution of the Regulatory Structure* 829
- *The Commodity Futures Modernization Act of 2000*...831

Debt Securities with Embedded Options 834
Inflation-Indexed Debt Securities..................................837
Retail-Oriented Issuer Debt Programs 838
Trust Preferred Securities..839
- *1933 Act Considerations*......................................842
- *1934 Act Considerations*......................................843
- *1939 Act Considerations*......................................843
- *1940 Act Considerations*......................................843
- *Effects of Deconsolidation* 843
- *"Securitization" of Trust Preferred Securities* 844

Custody Receipts (Old Bottles Waiting for New Wine) 845
Remarketings..851
"Equity Line" Financing Arrangements.....................855
- *1933 Act Issues* 855
- *1934 Act Issues* 856

Short Sales and Equity Derivatives 856

Chapter 12

CONVERTIBLE, EXCHANGEABLE AND "LINKED" SECURITIES; WARRANTS 865
Convertible Securities 867
- *Current Return* 867
- *Conversion Price* 869
- *Puts by Holder* 873
- *Cash or Stock on Conversion* 874
- *Redemption* 874
- *M&A Transactions* 874
- *1933 Act Considerations* 875
- *1934 Act Issues* 878
- *Rule 144A Convertible Securities* 880

Exchangeable Securities 880
- *Registration of the Underlying Securities* 881
- *Avoiding Registration in Control Situations* 882
- *Disclosure About Issuer of Underlying Securities* 885
- *Liabilities and Due Diligence* 887
- *Communications with Underlying Issuer* 888
- *Listing; State Preemption; CEA Considerations* 889
- *Regulation M* 889

Mandatorily Convertible or Exchangeable or Case-Settled Securities 890
- *Conversion into Company's Own Common Stock* 891
- *Exchange for Another Company's Common Stock* 892
- *1933 Act Registration* 892
- *Rule 144A* 893
- *Disclosure* 893
- *Cash-Settled Equity-Linked Notes* 893
- *Third-Party Monetizations (STRYPES)* 894
  - • *1933 Act Considerations* 895
  - • *Liability Considerations* 896
  - • *Listing; State Preemption; CEA Considerations* 896

TABLE OF CONTENTS

Debt/Stock Units 896
Stock Purchase Warrants 897
- *Units of Debt Securities and Warrants* 897
- *Units of Common Stock and Warrants* 898

Calls for Redemption to Force Conversions 902
- *Standy Arrangements* 904
- *1933 Act Considerations* 905
- *Redemptions and Regulation M* 908
- *Lay-Offs* 908

Expiring Warrants 909

Chapter 13

TRANSACTIONS WITH SECURITYHOLDERS: STOCK REPURCHASES, DEBT RESTRUCTURINGS AND RIGHTS OFFERINGS 911

Stock Repurchases 912
- *Corporate Law Considerations* 913
- *Rule 10b-5 Considerations* 914
- *Purchases in the Open Market* 914
  - • • *Avoiding a "Tender Offer"* 915
  - • • *Rule 10b-18* 917
    - • • • *"Rule 10b-18 Purchases"* 918
    - • • • *Scope of Safe Harbor* 920
    - • • • *Conditions to Availability of Safe Harbor* 921
    - • • • *Relaxed Conditions During Marketwide Trading Suspensions* 924
    - • • • *Purchases Outside the Safe Harbor* 924
    - • • • *Short Sales by Broker-Dealers* 925
- *Using Derivatives* 925
- *Disclosure of Stock Repurchases* 928
- *Cash Tender Offers* 929
  - • • *Tender Offer Mechanics* 929
  - • • *Regulation of Issuer Tender Offers* 931
  - • • *Going Private Transactions* 936
  - • • *Short Tendering of Securities; Rule 14e-4* 938

Debt Restructurings 940
- *Redemptions* 941
- *Open Market Purchases* 945
- *Cash Tender Offers* 946
- *Fixed-Spread Cash Tender Offers* 950
- *Premium Payable to Tendering Holder* 952
- *Issuer Recommendation* 952
- *Exchange Offers* 953
  - • • *Section 3(a)(9)* 954
    - • • • *Issuer Identity Requirement* 954
    - • • • *Exclusivity Requirement* 957
    - • • • *No Paid Solicitation* 958
    - • • • *Shareholder Votes; Trust Indenture Act; Resales of Exchanged Securities* 964
  - • • *Tender Offer and Going Private Rules* 964
  - • • *Regulation M and 14e-5* 967
- *Consent Solicitations* 968

When-Issued Trading and Arbitrage 975
- *When-Issued Trading* 976
- *Borrowing Stock from Control Persons* 978

Rights Offerings 979
- *Mechanics* 980
- *The Role of the Investment Banker* 982
- *1933 Act Registration* 984
- *Shields Plan* 985
- *Dealer-Manager Plan* 986

Chapter 14

ASSET-BACKED SECURITIES 987
Basic Structure of an Asset-Backed Transaction 990
- *Conventional Securitizations* 990
- *Asset-Backed Commercial Paper* 992
- *New Asset Classes* 992

1933 Act Considerations 993
- *Who Is the Registrant?* 993
- *Definition of ABS* 994

- *Form S-1 and Form S-3* 997
- *Registration of Underlying Pool Assets* 998
- *Disclosure Requirements* 1000
- *Offering Materials* 1006
  - *ABS Informational and Computational Materials* 1006
  - *Access to Loan Files* 1011
- *Prospectus Delivery Considerations* 1012
  - *Rule 15c2-8(b)* 1012
  - *Post-Offering Delivery Requirements; Availability of Materials through Electronic Media* 1013
  - *Market-Maker Prospectuses* 1014
- *Research Materials* 1015
- *Integration* 1019
- *Due Diligence* 1019
- *Rule 144A(d)(4) Information* 1021

1934 Act Considerations 1021
1940 Act Considerations 1025
Other Considerations 1030
- *Bankruptcy* 1030
- *Accounting Issues* 1031
- *Tax Issues* 1031
- *1939 Act* 1031
- *SMMEA* 1032
- *Legal Investment Considerations* 1033
- *Preemption of State Securities Registration* 1033
- *Underwriting* 1034
- *NASD Considerations* 1034

Index 1035

ABOUT THE AUTHORS

Charles J. Johnson, Jr. is one of the country's most experienced securities lawyers. A graduate of Yale College and Harvard Law School, he began the practice of law at Brown & Wood in 1956 and became a partner in 1967. He is now a Retired Partner of Sidley Austin Brown & Wood LLP. During his last ten years as a member of the firm, he was head of its corporate and securities practice.

Mr. Johnson has acted as counsel to issuers and investment banking firms in hundreds of major financial transactions, including public offerings of debt and equity securities, leveraged buyouts, issuer tender offers, underwritten calls and institutional private placements. Among the transactions in which he has played a major role are the initial public offering by Communications Satellite Corporation and numerous first mortgage bond financings by Duke Power Company and Public Service Electric and Gas Company. He represented Merrill Lynch, Pierce, Fenner & Smith Incorporated when it went public in 1971 and subsequently worked on the public offerings of several other securities firms. He has represented the underwriters in a large number of securities offerings by money center banks and bank holding companies.

The author has written many articles for legal journals, including "Application of Federal Securities Laws to International Securities Transactions," which appeared in the *Albany Law Review*. He contributed a chapter on legal considerations in the establishment of a United States commercial paper program for a book published by *Euromoney*. The *Review of Securities & Commodities Regulation* has published articles by him on former Rules 10b-6 and 10b-7, on underwritten calls, and on Rule 415 and the integrated disclosure system.

Mr. Johnson has been an active participant in continuing legal education programs, including Practicing Law Institute seminars on the mechanics of underwriting, international finance transactions, and the 10b series of rules. He has also been a regular speaker at the Practicing Law Institute's *Annual Institute on Securities Regulation* where he has lectured on such matters as the regulations of the National Association of Securities Dealers, Inc., innovative financial products, and special disclosure problems. He has spoken at conferences sponsored by the Institute for International Research on Law in the Euromarkets and on Eurocommercial paper.

Mr. Johnson also has presented papers or participated in programs sponsored by the American Bar Association, the Southwest Legal Foundation, the Securities Industry Association, the New York Society of Securities Analysts, and the Fordham Corporate Law Institute.

Mr. Johnson is an elected member of the American Law Institute. He served a three-year term as a member of the Committee on Securities Regulation of The Association of the Bar of The City of New York, the final year as Chairman of its Subcommittee on the Issue and Distribution of Securities.

Joseph McLaughlin is a partner of Sidley Austin Brown & Wood LLP in New York City, where he has one of the country's most diversified securities practices. A graduate of Columbia College and Columbia Law School, he was also a Jervey Fellow of the Parker School of Foreign and Comparative Law at Columbia Law School and did post-graduate work at the University of Munich. He practiced with Sullivan & Cromwell for seven years, where he worked on a wide variety of securities transactions.

Mr. McLaughlin became general counsel of Goldman, Sachs & Co. in 1976. He worked closely for many years with the firm's investment banking departments, as well as with its equity and fixed-income research, sales and trading areas. He was active in securities industry matters, including the Federal Regulation Committee of the Securities Industry Association, the Corporate Financing Committee of the National Association of Securities Dealers, Inc. and the Legal Advisory Committee of the New York Stock Exchange, Inc. During this period. Mr. McLaughlin contributed to industry and SEC initiatives involving securities research, trading practices, short sales, the new capital rule, margin regulations, underwriters' liability, the "Papilsky rules" and shelf registration. Many of these subjects are discussed in this book.

After experimenting with a teaching career, Mr. McLaughlin joined Brown & Wood LLP, a predecessor firm of Sidley Austin Brown & Wood LLP, where he is a member of the corporate and securities group as well as the broker-dealer regulatory group. He works on domestic and international public offerings and private placements and spends a significant part of his time on regulatory and litigation matters for securities industry associations and more than 20 major broker-dealer clients. He also represented two of the leading groups responsible for the SEC and legislative initiatives that produced the Private Securities Litigation Reform Act of 1995.

ABOUT THE AUTHORS

Mr. McLaughlin is a leading writer and speaker on the subject of electronic communications and the securities laws, the listing of foreign securities on U.S. exchanges, and the future of U.S. securities regulation. He also co-chaired an American Bar Association committee's Task Force on Sellers' Due Diligence and Similar Defenses Under the Federal Securities Laws as well as its Task Force on Rule 10b-6.

Mr. McLaughlin is an elected member of the American Law Institute. He is a frequent speaker at programs sponsored by the Practicing Law Institute and The Federalist Society.

PREFACE TO THE THIRD EDITION

Like its previous editions, this book is about doing deals—transactions in which companies raise funds in the U.S. and international capital markets. We do not intend this book as a complete treatise on the U.S. federal securities laws, nor do we intend it as an investor's or issuer's guide to the capital markets. Rather, we are trying to explain the legal environment in which capital markets transactions take place, just as we are trying to explain the capital markets transactions to which that environment is always trying to adapt. What we are describing in this book is in many ways just as much an ecosystem as a tropical rain forest—and, unfortunately, sometimes just as impenetrable.

There were signs when the previous edition appeared that the jungle canopy might be thinning. As a result in part of a revolution in information technology and communication, the Securities and Exchange Commission had requested public comment on possible fundamental changes under the Securities Act of 1933. Unfortunately, the SEC followed up on this initiative with the ill-fated "aircraft carrier release" of 1998, which combined some sensible reform proposals with impractical innovations that would have delayed offerings and increased the potential for litigation.

After the 2000 elections, there were signs that the SEC might again be interested in proposing much-needed reforms. Enron and other corporate scandals, and the herculean rulemaking effort needed to implement the Sarbanes-Oxley Act of 2002, once again forced the SEC to put Securities Act reform aside.

As of this writing, there are signs that the SEC is again considering reform proposals. But experience tells us that it would be a mistake to imagine that these will be adopted without controversy and delay.

We have tried to retain the book's practical orientation, which we believe was responsible for the previous editions' considerable success. We caution, however, that the pace of change in the capital markets is still accelerating. Many of the topics discussed in this book may need to be revisited within a relatively short time.

As in the previous editions, our focus has remained the raising of capital by business entities. We have not discussed public finance—the sale of securities by federal or state governmental entities or their instrumentalities—or the corporate and specialized securities aspects of mergers and acquisitions. Nor have we devoted space to the parallel structure of SEC rules and forms that are designed specifically for the needs of "small business."

As in the case of the previous editions, we have had the full support of our colleagues at Sidley Austin Brown & Wood. Many of them provided us with valuable insights into their areas of special expertise.

A special debt is owed to Norman D. Slonaker, who is really one of the preeminent transactional lawyers in the United States.

We also thank Michael Hyatte, who joined Sidley Austin Brown & Wood after many years in the SEC's Division of Corporation Finance and possesses a unique knowledge and understanding of the Securities Act of 1933.

Renwick D. Martin, Jack M. Costello, Jr. and Giselle M. Barth reviewed the chapter on asset-backed securities. Thomas

PREFACE TO THE THIRD EDITION

R. Smith, Jr., John A. MacKinnon, Frank P. Bruno and Brian J. Kaplowitz were generous with their help on Investment Company Act issues.

Barbara J. Endres reviewed the chapter on manipulation, and Michael S. Sackheim was patient in explaining the Commodity Exchange Act and the Commodities Futures Modernization Act. Thomas A. Humphreys, Marc J. Tibaldi, Jacob J. Amato III and Shelley Howard Grant provided help on tax issues.

Joseph W. Armbrust, L. Markus Wiltshire, Daniel M. Rossner, Edward F. Petrosky, Howard G. Godwin, Jr., Michael T. Kohler, Jonathan B. Miller, Barbara J. Endres, David M. Katz, Vivian A. Root, Benjamin L. Nager, Robert Mandell and Edward D. Ricchiuto read certain chapters and provided important suggestions.

Much expertise that used to be taken for granted at large Wall Street law firms has migrated into the legal, compliance and capital markets departments of the investment banking firms. We are therefore grateful for the help of John W. Curtis, Elizabeth J. Ford, Randolph Stuzin and Victoria Bridges of Goldman, Sachs & Co., Sarah Leah Whitson (formerly of Goldman, Sachs & Co.), Mitchell B. Kleinman of Keefe, Bruyette & Woods, Inc. and Ranada R. Fergerson of Banc of America Securities LLC. We also thank Richard N. Doyle, Jr. of Merrill Lynch & Co., Dr. Alexander Georgieff of Deutsche Bank AG and A. Post Howland of New York Life Investment Management LLC.

Any errors or omissions are, of course, the sole responsibility of the authors.

We are grateful to Louis Vitale, who supervised a team of associates that cite-checked the third edition. For their help on this project, we acknowledge the efforts of David Anziska, Lynette Ashby, Farrah Chu, Christina Gmiterek, Jeffrey Kurzon, William Lyman, Celia Mitchell and Daniel Schiffer.

We also thank Birgit Berkow, Danielle R. Francis, Christa M. Lange and Teresa Tully of Sidley Austin Brown & Wood's library staff for their patient and diligent support.

Charles J. Johnson, Jr.
Joseph McLaughlin
New York
June 2004

PREFACE TO THE FIRST EDITION

This book is about doing deals—structuring them, shepherding them through the regulatory process, keeping them out of trouble, and getting them closed. It is about the Federal securities laws, those laws and regulations administered by the Securities and Exchange Commission that have a direct impact on every aspect of corporate finance and that must be complied with if a deal is to get done.

A corporation that decides to go public or to raise additional funds to finance a growing business must comply with the Securities Act of 1933 and the applicable provisions of the Securities Exchange Act of 1934. If debt securities are being sold to the public, the Trust Indenture Act of 1939 will be applicable. If securities are being issued by a public utility holding company or one of its operating subsidiaries, then competitive bidding may be required under the Public Utility Holding Company Act of 1935. An obscure provision of the Investment Company Act of 1940 may come into play when least expected.

The securities laws regulate other types of financial transactions such as corporate restructurings, offers to exchange new securities for existing securities, and stock repurchase programs. At the same time, corporate financial officers and investment bankers must contend with regulations administered by state securities commissions, the National Association of Securities Dealers, Inc., and the Federal Reserve Board. In the case of a hybrid instrument—a security tied to the performance of a commodity, a stock or bond index, a foreign currency, or the rate of inflation—care must be taken to assure that the transaction does not run afoul of the Commodity Exchange Act.

Guiding their clients through this morass of regulation are lawyers of a special breed known as securities lawyers. I have been one for over 33 years, practicing in New York City with Brown & Wood. In writing this book, I have called upon my experiences as a securities lawyer to flesh out the descriptions of the statutes and rules with some practical observations on how they are applied in real-life situations and how they can best be coped with when a crisis arises in the course of a financial transaction. I have described the mechanics and practices of corporate finance in addition to the legal principles that govern them. I have not hesitated to insert editorial comment where I have thought it appropriate.

This book places securities regulation in an historical perspective. I believe that the law can be understood more fully and applied more effectively with a knowledge of its development over the years. Also, the history of the securities laws and the development of investment banking practices are a part of the culture of the financial community. A knowledge of the way that these laws and practices have evolved adds zest to an already fascinating business.

This book is directed primarily to lawyers working in the field of corporate finance, members of the "green goods" bar to use a Wall Street term. By discussing the law in the context of specific types of transactions, my objective is a book that will be useful to experienced securities lawyers as well as those just learning the law of corporate finance. Also, the lawyer whose practice is not devoted primarily to securities regulation may find it helpful to read through the relevant chapters if a client is about to engage in a financial transaction such as a public offering of convertible debentures or the establishment of a commercial paper program.

I hope this book will be useful to businessmen as well. I hope it will be read by corporate officers responsible for financial transactions—the chief executive officer, the chief financial officer, and those who assist them. It also can provide insights to investment bankers. The legal aspects of corporate finance are so intertwined with the business aspects that a businessman cannot fully perform his functions without some knowledge of securities regulation.

The practice of securities law is a fascinating occupation. Equally fascinating is the work of the corporate financial officer and the investment banker. The intellectual challenge of corporate finance is a source of constant stimulation to the securities lawyer and the financial experts that he represents. There is a camaraderie in the practice of securities law. I value the relationships that I have developed over the years with investment bankers, corporate financial officers, and members of the accounting profession, to say nothing of the scores of other securities lawyers with whom I have worked on hundreds of financial transactions. I have learned from all of them, and many have become my close friends.

There is some drudgery in the work, particularly for the younger lawyer. There is little to challenge the intellect in marking up an indenture for a "plain-vanilla" debenture offering. The work is hard. "All nighters" at the printer take their toll. But it is exciting to work on a deal, especially an important deal with national or worldwide visibility, and the feeling of satisfaction at the closing of a successful financing can be one of the securities lawyer's greatest rewards.

I have always believed that it is the job of the securities lawyer to get the deal done. Closing the deal should be the objective foremost in his mind, as it is in the mind of the businessman that he represents. Clients appreciate a "businessman's lawyer," one that can cut through to the core of a problem to accomplish the client's objective. In the thick of a deal, decisions must be made quickly. There are times when a lawyer must be willing to stick his neck out and take a position, even though the law and its application are less than clear. This is not to say that a financial transaction must not be approached with the greatest care. Someone once said that to be a good securities lawyer you don't have to be very smart, but you do have to be very very careful.

There are times when a lawyer simply must say "No," no matter how unhappy it may make his client. But there are real problems and manufactured problems, and it is the job of the securities lawyer to solve problems, not to create them. He must distinguish between the important issues and those that are more theoretical than real. The real problems should be raised early in the transaction and not at the eleventh hour. There are few legal problems that cannot be solved with the proper approach, but it is frustrating to a client for a legal issue to be raised on the eve of the closing when it should have been raised before the deal was put in motion.

There is nothing worse than over-lawyering on a deal, unless it is a combative approach to a transaction. Most financial transactions should be viewed as cooperative endeavors, not adversary proceedings, and the lawyer who attempts to score points for the sake of his ego renders a disservice to his client. Counsel for the underwriters in a public offering should always remember that the issuer is his client's client and that the managing underwriter has worked hard to secure this relationship. The issuer's officers and lawyers should be treated accordingly.

By working shoulder to shoulder, rather than nose to nose, the participants in a financial transaction can best accomplish the objective of getting the deal done. The aim of this book is to provide some help and guidance to the lawyers, corporate executives, and investment bankers who share this goal.

Charles J. Johnson, Jr.
New York
June 1990

ABBREVIATIONS AND TERMS FREQUENTLY USED IN SECURITIES LAW PRACTICE

1933 Act	Securities Act of 1933
1934 Act	Securities Exchange Act of 1934
1939 Act	Trust Indenture Act of 1939
1940 Act	Investment Company Act of 1940
AAU	Agreement among underwriters
ADR	American depositary receipts
ADS	American depositary shares
ADTV	Average daily trading volume
AICPA	American Institute of Certified Public Accountants
Aircraft carrier release	SEC Release No. 33-7606A (November 13, 1998)
AMEX	American Stock Exchange
CEA	Commodity Exchange Act
CFMA	Commodity Futures Modernization Act of 2000
CFTC	Commodity Futures Trading Commission
EBITDA	Earnings before interest, taxes, depreciation and amortization
ECN	Electronic communications network
EDGAR	Electronic Data Gathering, Analysis and Retrieval
DTC	The Depository Trust Company
FASB	Financial Accounting Standards Board

ERISA	Employee Retirement Income Security Act of 1974
ESOP	Employee stock ownership plan
GAAP	U.S. generally accepted accounting principles
GAAS	U.S. generally accepted auditing standards (effective May 20, 2004, as determined by the PCAOB)
IAS/IFRS	International accounting standards/International financial reporting standards
IET	Interest equalization tax
Improvement Act	National Securities Markets Improvement Act of 1996
IPO	Initial public offering
MAAU	Master agreement among underwriters
M&A	Mergers and acquisitions
MD&A	Management's Discussion and Analysis of Financial Condition and Results of Operations
MJDS	Multijurisdictional disclosure system
MSRB	Municipal Securities Rulemaking Board
MTN	Medium-term notes
NASD	National Association of Securities Dealers, Inc.
NASDAQ	National Association of Securities Dealers Automated Quotation System
NGFM	Non-GAAP financial measure
NRSRO	Nationally recognized statistical rating organization
NYSE	New York Stock Exchange, Inc.
PCAOB	Public Company Accounting Oversight Board
OID	Original issue discount
PIPE transaction	Private investment in public equity

ABBREVIATIONS AND TERMS USED IN THIS BOOK

PORTAL	Private Offering, Resale and Trading Through Automated Linkages
QIB	Qualified institutional buyer
Reform Act	Private Securities Litigation Reform Act of 1995
Reporting Company	Company obligated to file periodic reports with the SEC
SAB	Staff Accounting Bulletin
Sarbanes-Oxley	Sarbanes-Oxley Act of 2002
SAS	Statement on Auditing Standards
SEAQ	Stock Exchange Automated Quotation System
SEC	Securities and Exchange Commission
SFAS	Statement of Financial Accounting Standards
SPV	Special purpose vehicle
SRO	Self-regulatory organization
SUSMI	Substantial U.S. market interest
UAR	Underwriting activity report
VaR	Value at risk

Authors' note on SEC no-action letters: Thanks to electronic search engines, it has become far easier to locate relevant no-action letters. We have therefore refrained from extensive citations of no-action letters except in those areas where most of the available law is based on such letters. Also, the most frequently used method of electronically locating a no-action letter is to refer to the name of the requesting party and the date of the SEC staff's response. At one time, the date of the SEC staff's response was not the same as the date on which the response became "available" to the public, and citations to no-action letters therefore used the latter date. In this edition, we have omitted references to the "available" date, even for earlier letters.

Chapter 1

OVERVIEW OF THE SECURITIES ACT OF 1933 AND THE INTEGRATED DISCLOSURE SYSTEM

Market Crashes and Securities Legislation

History has a way of repeating itself.

The bursting of the 1998–2000 "Internet Bubble" was accompanied by a decline in the value of equity securities that may have reached as much as $7.4 trillion.[1] Investor confidence was shaken not only by the decline in equity prices but by revelations of accounting failures, corporate fraud and malfeasance, and by a failure by some securities analysts to live up to professional standards.

Congress reacted by enacting in 2002 the Sarbanes–Oxley Act, which many observers describe as the most significant federal legislation affecting the securities markets since the 1930s.

Fortunately, the events that produced Sarbanes–Oxley did not lead to a collapse of economic activity in the United States. By way of contrast, when Franklin Delano Roosevelt took the presidential oath of office in March 1933, the country was still

---

1. Estimates of market losses vary widely, but the aggregate market value of the securities in the Wilshire 5000 index declined from $14.7 trillion in March 2000 to $7.3 trillion in October 2002.

reeling from the impact of the 1929 market crash and the ensuing deep depression. The market value of stocks listed on the New York Stock Exchange (NYSE) had declined between 1929 and 1932 by $74 billion, a loss for which "the annals of finance" up to that time "present[ed] no counterpart."[2]

Initial public offerings (IPOs) accounted for a significant part of the losses associated with the bursting of the "Internet Bubble," but investors also suffered losses in established companies. By way of contrast, some $50 billion of new securities had been floated in the United States during the decade following World War I, of which fully half had proved to be worthless.[3] The House committee report placed much of the blame on the securities industry:

> The flotation of such a mass of essentially fraudulent securities was made possible because of the complete abandonment by many underwriters and dealers in securities of those standards of fair, honest, and prudent dealing that should be basic to the encouragement of investment in any enterprise. Alluring promises of easy wealth were freely made with little or no attempt to bring to the investor's attention those facts essential to estimating the worth of any security.[4]

Although the 73d Congress only a year later got around to legislation that would improve disclosure about companies whose securities were trading in the secondary markets, the legislative priority in 1933 was the new-issue market.[5]

---

2. S. Rep. No. 1455, 73d Cong., 2d Sess., *Stock Exchange Practices, Report of the Senate Banking and Currency Committee Pursuant to S. Res. 84 (72d Cong.) and S. Res. 56 and S. Res. 97 (73d Cong.)* (June 16, 1934), at 7. Of course, $74 billion may have represented in 1929 a larger portion of the U.S. gross domestic product than did $7.4 trillion at the end of the century.

3. H.R. Rep. No. 85, 73d Cong., 1st Sess., at 2 (1933) [hereafter *H.R. Rep. No. 85*].

4. *Id.* at 2.

5. There are two widely used repositories of the legislative history of the Securities Act of 1933 and the Securities Exchange Act of 1934. The first,

History of the 1933 Act

Since 1911, when the first blue sky law was enacted in Kansas, new-issue securities regulation had been the exclusive province of the states. In the aftermath of the crash, however, state securities laws were perceived to be inadequate.

In his speech accepting the presidential nomination of his party, Franklin Roosevelt promised not only a "new deal" for the American people but also called for the "letting in of the light of day on issues of securities, foreign and domestic, which are offered for sale to the investing public."[6] As one of his first acts as president, Mr. Roosevelt delivered to the Congress on March 29, 1933 a message proposing remedial legislation:

> I recommend to the Congress legislation for Federal supervision of traffic in investment securities in interstate commerce.
>
> In spite of many State statutes the public in the past has sustained severe losses through practices neither ethical nor honest on the part of many persons and corporations selling securities.
>
> Of course, the Federal Government cannot and should not take any action which might be construed as approving or guaranteeing that newly issued securities are sound in the sense that their value will be maintained or that the properties which they represent will earn profit.
>
> There is, however, an obligation upon us to insist that every issue of new securities to be sold in interstate commerce shall be accompanied by full publicity and

---

which is limited to the original legislation, is the 11-volume compilation prepared by J. S. Ellenberger and Ellen P. Mahar, librarians at Covington & Burling in Washington, D.C., and published in 1973 for the Law Librarians' Society of Washington, D.C. by Fred B. Rothman & Co., South Hackensack, N.J. The second, *Federal Securities Laws: Legislative History*, was prepared by the Securities Law Committee of the Federal Bar Association and is published by The Bureau of National Affairs, Inc. It covers each of the federal securities laws in four volumes and supplements and has been updated through 1990.

6. Quoted in J. Seligman, *The Transformation of Wall Street* 19 (1982).

information, and that no essentially important element attending the issue shall be concealed from the buying public.

This proposal adds to the ancient rule of caveat emptor, the further doctrine "let the seller also beware." It puts the burden of telling the whole truth on the seller. It should give impetus to honest dealing in securities and thereby bring back public confidence.[7]

The drafting of legislation to carry out this message had been assigned to Huston Thompson, a former member of the Federal Trade Commission.[8] The bill drafted by Thompson called for more than disclosure. It gave to the federal government extensive powers to control the issuance of securities. Sam Rayburn, chairman of the House Committee on Interstate and Foreign Commerce, became convinced that the Thompson bill did not provide a sound basis for federal securities legislation. In response to Mr. Rayburn's concern, Raymond S. Moley, the head of the president's "brain trust," turned for help to Harvard professor Felix Frankfurter who, in turn, called on the skills of James M. Landis, Benjamin V. Cohen and Thomas G. Corcoran.

This team determined to prepare a draft based on the English Companies Act, stressing the theme of disclosure expressed in the president's message. The first draft was completed over a weekend. It went through a number of revisions, with the assistance of Middleton Beaman, the chief legislative draftsman for the House of Representatives.

By the time the bill was ready to be reported to the full committee, agitation had built up on Wall Street, and Mr. Rayburn consented to a meeting between the draftsmen and a delegation of New York lawyers comprised of John Foster Dulles and Arthur H. Dean

---

7. H.R. Rep. No. 85, *supra* note 2, at 1–2.

8. J. M. Landis, *The Legislative History of the Securities Act of 1933*, 28 Geo. Wash. L. Rev. 29 (1959) [hereafter *Landis*]. The brief account that follows is taken principally from this article, which is required reading for anyone interested in the history of federal securities regulation. *See also* Schlesinger, *The Coming of the New Deal* 440–42 (1959). For a detailed account of the drafting process, see Seligman, *supra* note 6, at 50–72.

of Sullivan & Cromwell and A. I. Henderson of the Cravath firm. Landis reports that Dulles launched an inadequately prepared attack to the annoyance of Rayburn, but that Dean and Henderson were far better acquainted with the details of the bill, and that their technical comments had merit. Ultimately, the Securities Act of 1933 (1933 Act) became law on May 27, 1933 as part of the New Deal's 100 days legislation.

The essential elements of the 1933 Act consisted of (a) mandatory full disclosure in a registration statement filed with the Federal Trade Commission (later the Securities and Exchange Commission (SEC)), (b) SEC review during a "waiting period," at the end of which sales could commence, (c) mandatory delivery of a prospectus at or before the delivery of the security and (d) civil liabilities for untrue statements and for certain omissions.

Contemporaneous concern about the 1933 Act[9] focused primarily on the new civil liabilities that were to be imposed on "those who have participated in . . . [the] distribution either knowing of such untrue statement or omission or having failed to take due care in discovering it."[10] In this connection, Section 11(c) specified that the applicable standard of "due care" was to be "that of a person occupying a fiduciary relationship." The securities industry understandably opposed the application of a "fiduciary" standard of "due care" as a measure of underwriters' responsibility for an issuer's untrue statements or omissions. This opposition, which extended to other provisions of the new

---

9. The reactions to the 1933 Act varied. Some thought that it would retard economic recovery and bring an end to firm commitment underwriting. A. H. Dean, *The Federal Securities Act: I*, Fortune 50, 106 (August 1933). Some felt that it was of secondary importance in a comprehensive program of social control over finance. A. A. Berle, Jr. *High Finance: Master or Servant*, 23 Yale Rev. 20 (1933). Others adopted a more positive attitude and, recognizing that the principles embodied in the 1933 Act "have become a permanent and integral part of our legal system," stressed the need to find "ways and means of accomplishing expeditiously and efficiently their avowed purposes." W. O. Douglas & G. E. Bates, *The Federal Securities Act of 1933*, 43 Yale L.J. 171, 173 (1933).

10. H.R. Rep. No. 85, *supra* note 3, at 9.

statute relating to underwriters' liabilities, led to amendments in 1934 that provided, among other things, that the standard of care was to be that of "a prudent man in the management of his own property." In addition, the new Securities Exchange Act of 1934 (1934 Act) created an agency to administer both statutes, the SEC.

The Securities and Exchange Commission

The SEC is an independent agency in the executive branch of the federal government. It consists of five commissioners appointed by the president with the advice and consent of the Senate. Commissioners hold office for a term of five years. No more than three may be members of the same political party.

The SEC is presided over by a chairman who has the sole power to assign SEC personnel to perform such functions as may have been delegated to them. The chairman sets the tone for the SEC during his or her tenure.

On the staff level, the SEC is organized into four divisions:

- Corporation Finance, which administers the 1933 Act, the Trust Indenture Act of 1939 and the disclosure-related requirements of the 1934 Act;

- Market Regulation, which administers those parts of the 1934 Act that relate to the regulation of securities markets and broker-dealers;

- Investment Management, which regulates investment companies, investment advisers and public utility holding companies; and

- Enforcement, which initiates formal and informal investigations, leading in many cases to injunctive actions in the federal courts or to administrative proceedings before the SEC. In administrative proceedings, the SEC carries out an important quasi-judicial function that in turn is subject to review in the courts.

Other important SEC staff departments include the Offices of the General Counsel and the Chief Accountant as well as other staff offices, including Economic Analysis and Compliance Inspections and Examinations.

The SEC accounting staff maintains a Codification of Financial Reporting Policies and has also for many years issued periodic Staff Accounting Bulletins. These sources are indispensable for the preparation of the financial statements included in a prospectus. The Division of Corporation Finance and the Division of Market Regulation also publish "staff legal bulletins" on current topics. All of these, together with a wealth of other information helpful to the preparation of disclosure documents, are included on the SEC's website at www.sec.gov.

The staffs of the Division of Corporation Finance, Market Regulation and Investment Management also issue "no-action" letters that assure a requesting party that the staff will not recommend any enforcement action to the SEC if the requesting party proceeds with a described transaction. Neither the SEC itself nor much less the courts are bound by the staff's no-action letters, but they are usually accorded significant respect. No-action letters are issued on a fact-specific basis, but securities lawyers frequently cite these letters as precedents. From time to time, the SEC staff also issues interpretive letters that are intended to be relied on by a broader group of persons and that may have significantly greater precedential value.

The SEC's principal office is in Washington, D.C. It has regional offices that are located in major cities throughout the country.

Operation of the 1933 Act

- *Disclosure Philosophy*

It cannot be emphasized too often that the 1933 Act is a disclosure statute. Its principal purpose, as set forth in its preamble, is to provide "full and fair disclosure of the character of securities sold in interstate and foreign commerce and through the mails. . . ." As explained in 1933 by Professor Frankfurter:

> Unlike the theory on which state blue-sky laws are based, the Federal Securities Act does not place the government's

imprimatur upon securities. It is designed merely to secure essential facts for the investor, not to substitute the government's judgment for his own.[11]

Sarbanes–Oxley represents a major departure from the 1933 Act's original emphasis on disclosure, as it thrusts the SEC into areas of corporate governance that were formerly the responsibility of the states and the securities markets such as the NYSE and the National Association of Securities Dealers (NASD). It also involves the SEC, as a result of its oversight authority over the Public Company Accounting Oversight Board, in the regulation of the accounting profession.

- *Definition of Security*

An important threshold question under the 1933 Act is whether a financing vehicle is a "security." The term is broadly defined in Section 2(a)(1) as well as in Section 3(a)(10) of the 1934 Act.[12]

According to the U.S. Supreme Court's leading decision in *Reves v. Ernst & Young*,[13] Congress "did not attempt precisely to cabin the scope of the Securities Acts" but rather "enacted a

---

11. F. Frankfurter, *The Federal Securities Act: II*, Fortune 53, 108 (August 1933). It cannot be denied that disclosure also has a prophylactic effect. For example, a chief executive officer is less likely to engage in self-dealing with his corporation if he knows that his conduct will be exposed to public scrutiny. As Louis Brandeis put it, "Publicity is justly commended as a remedy for social and industrial diseases. Sunlight is said to be the best of disinfectants; electric light the most efficient policeman." Brandeis, *Other People's Money* 92 (1914).
12. The U.S. Supreme Court has consistently held that the scope of coverage of the 1933 Act and the 1934 Act, insofar as it depends on the two "virtually identical" definitions in the two statutes, "may be considered the same." *Reves v. Ernst & Young*, 494 U.S. 56, 61 n.1 (1990). In practice, however, attempts to characterize an instrument as a security are more likely to succeed where the effect is to preserve holders' federal antifraud remedies under the 1934 Act than where it would lead to rescission rights under the 1933 Act.
13. 494 U.S. 56 (1990).

definition of 'security' sufficiently broad to encompass virtually any instrument that might be sold as an investment." In deciding which transactions are covered by the federal securities laws, "legal formalisms" are less important than "the economics of the transaction." Some instruments, on the other hand, are "obviously within the class Congress intended to regulate because they are by their nature investments." For example, "stock is, as a practical matter, always an investment if it has the economic characteristics traditionally associated with stock."

In *Reves*, the Court adopted a rebuttable presumption that all notes are "securities." To rebut the presumption would require a showing that the note bears a strong resemblance to those categories of notes held by lower courts not to be securities, for example, notes delivered in consumer financing, notes secured by home mortgages, notes evidencing unsecured bank loans to individuals, and short-term notes secured by business assets. The required "resemblance" would depend on four factors: the motivations of the parties, whether the instrument is traded, the expectations of the investing public and the presence or absence of an alternative regulatory scheme for the public's protection.

The term "security" includes a guarantee of a security. If a subsidiary corporation makes a public offering of debentures guaranteed by its parent, the guarantee must therefore be registered under the 1933 Act along with the primary obligations.

Is an orange grove a security? Hardly. But the U.S. Supreme Court has held that a security was indeed involved in an offer of land sales contracts covering plots planted with citrus trees along with service contracts giving the promoter discretion and authority over the cultivation of the groves and the harvest and marketing of the crops.[14] The Section 2(a)(1) definition includes among the types of securities subject to the 1933 Act a "certificate of interest or participation in any profit-sharing agreement," an "investment contract" and "any interest or instrument commonly known as a security." In *SEC v. Howey*, Justice Murphy said that an investment contract is "a contract, transaction or scheme whereby a person invests his money in

---

14. *SEC v. W. J. Howey Co.*, 328 U.S. 293 (1946).

a common enterprise and is led to expect profits solely from the efforts of the promoter or a third party . . . ." Investments following the *Howey* pattern appear irresistibly attractive to some classes of promoters. Pay telephones are a common medium for recent versions of these arrangements. The Eleventh Circuit in 2002 rejected the SEC's characterization of pay telephone lease arrangements as investment contracts, but the Supreme Court had little difficulty concluding that the SEC was right and the Eleventh Circuit wrong.[15]

The Supreme Court has held that a bank certificate of deposit is not a security.[16] However, the Court of Appeals for the Second Circuit, applying the *Howey* analysis, concluded that Merrill Lynch's then existing "CD Program" involving the sale of certificates of deposit selected by Merrill Lynch, including some specifically created for the program, involved investment contracts and therefore securities for purposes of the antifraud provisions of the 1933 Act and the 1934 Act because a significant portion of the customer's investment depended on Merrill Lynch's managerial and financial expertise.[17]

In the early days of derivatives, a corporation that was a party to certain interest rate and currency swaps argued that these were securities for purposes of the 1933 Act, the 1934 Act and a state's blue sky law. The court rejected the argument.[18] It held that the swaps were not investment contracts because they lacked the element of a "common enterprise." Even if viewed as notes, they fell outside each of the four parts of the *Reves* "family resemblance" test. Neither were they "evidences of indebtedness" because they lacked the essential element of an obligation to pay principal, and they were not "options" on securities because they did not give either counterparty the right to take possession of any security. The

---

15. *SEC v. Edwards,* 124 S. Ct. 892 (2004), *rev'g SEC v. ETS Payphones, Inc.*, 300 F.3d 1281 (11th Cir. 2002).

16. *Marine Bank v. Weaver*, 455 U.S. 551 (1982).

17. *Gary Plastic Packaging Corp. v. Merrill Lynch, Pierce, Fenner & Smith Inc.*, 756 F.2d 230 (2d Cir. 1985).

18. *Procter & Gamble Co. v. Bankers Trust Co.*, 925 F. Supp. 1270 (S.D. Ohio 1996).

court was careful to point out that it was not holding that all swaps or leveraged derivative instruments were not securities.

Most swap transactions, at least those between eligible participants, were excluded from the definition of security by the Commodity Futures Modernization Act of 2000. Questions still arise, however, concerning the "investment contract" part of the definition. Apart from the pay telephone arrangements mentioned above, for example, the First Circuit held in 2001 that the SEC had alleged sufficient facts to go to trial on whether an investment contract had been created from the opportunity to purchase "virtual shares" in "virtual companies" on an Internet-based "virtual stock exchange."[19]

- *Registration and Prospectus Delivery Requirements*

At the heart of the 1933 Act are the registration and prospectus delivery requirements set forth in Section 5. These are the only requirements of the 1933 Act that can be violated, except for the antifraud prohibitions of Section 17 and (in a loose sense) the disclosure-based remedies provided by Sections 11 and 12(a)(2). The remainder of the 1933 Act consists of definitions, exemptions and other provisions that implement Section 5.

Section 5 requires that its registration and prospectus delivery requirements be complied with in connection with any offer or sale of a security in interstate commerce or through the use of the mails. The SEC vigorously enforces Section 5 through administrative and court proceedings, but the primary reason for complying with Section 5 is that a violation entitles a buyer to return the security to the seller—no questions asked—at any time during the year following the sale.[20] There is nothing wrong with selling "puts" to customers, but it is a major mistake to do so inadvertently and without getting paid for them!

Of course, not every transaction in securities must be registered with the SEC or be the subject of a prospectus.

---

19. *SEC v. SG Ltd.*, 265 F.3d 42 (1st Cir. 2001).

20. Section 12(a)(1) permits a purchaser of securities offered or sold in violation of Section 5 to put the securities back to the seller, and Section 13 provides for a one-year period within which to exercise the put. *See P. Stolz Family Partnership L.P. v. Daum*, 355 F.3d 92 (2d Cir. 2004).

Important exemptions are available, based either on the nature of the security (Section 3) or the nature of the transaction (Sections 3 and 4).

An important limitation on the transactional exemptions under Section 4 is that they are not available, for the most part, to anyone who is an "underwriter." The scope of this term is discussed below in this chapter and elsewhere in this book.

In all cases, the burden of proving the availability of an exemption is on the person who claims it.

• • *Registration for a Purpose.* Before considering in more detail the operation of the 1933 Act, a common misconception should be laid to rest—the misconception that there is something bad about securities that are not registered and something good about securities that are. A report appears in the business section of the morning newspaper to the effect that a broker has been sanctioned by the SEC for selling "unregistered securities." The reader thereby assumes that, on the one hand, there are nice registered securities with wings and halos and, on the other hand, there are bad unregistered securities with forked tails and horns. Many people, even in the securities industry, believe that if a person sells unregistered securities he will go to jail, but that if he can find some good registered securities to deliver in the transaction he will remain a free man. This is not the way that the 1933 Act operates.

Billions of shares of common stock are traded on the NYSE that have never been the subject of a registration statement. They may have been issued before the adoption of the 1933 Act; they may have been issued in a private placement and resold in accordance with Rule 144 (to be discussed below); or they may have been sold in an offshore offering or issued as a stock dividend.

Conversely, if a company reacquires for its treasury shares that had once been the subject of a registration statement, it must register them again before it may sell them to the public. Similarly, if a person in a control relationship with a company acquires that company's registered securities in the open market, the securities must be registered again before they may be resold through a broker-dealer in a public offering outside of the limits of Rule 144.

A sale of securities in violation of the 1933 Act cannot be remedied by filing a registration statement after the fact, except for the purpose of a rescission offer. Securities issued in a private placement cannot be made freely tradable by registering them after the fact, except for the purpose of resale with the use of a current prospectus. (It is also possible under certain circumstances, as discussed in Chapter 7, to conduct a registered exchange offer that gives holders of privately placed securities the opportunity to exchange them for registered securities.)

Although the 1933 Act speaks of registering securities, it is more accurate to think in terms of registering a transaction, or at least of registering securities for the purpose of sale in a particular transaction. This characterization flows from a comparison of Section 5, prohibiting offers before filing and sales before effectiveness, and Section 6(a), permitting registration only of such specified securities as are "proposed to be offered." A registration statement is filed and becomes effective not to place a stamp of approval on the securities but to provide persons being offered securities in a non-exempt transaction with sufficient information on which to base an informed investment decision. Part of the ambiguity must be laid to somewhat faulty draftsmanship. As one of the principal draftsmen of the 1933 Act acknowledged, the bill "came close to accurately carving out a differentiation between the registration of securities and the registration of offerings of securities" but was "far from perfect on this point as well as in many of its other provisions."[21]

• • *Operation of the Registration Requirement.* Assume that a commercial or industrial corporation (not a bank or other issuer of exempted securities) proposes to sell to the public 10 million shares of common stock through an underwriting syndicate. The 1933 Act requires such an issuer to provide potential investors with extensive information concerning its business and finances. This information is made available in the first instance to the SEC by the filing of a registration statement, nearly always

---

21. Landis, *supra* note 8, at 36.

in electronic form.[22] Once filed, this is a public document available for examination on the SEC's EDGAR (Electronic Data Gathering, Analysis and Retrieval) system.

As discussed below, the 1933 Act also requires the principal part of the registration statement—the prospectus—to be delivered to purchasers of the registered securities.[23]

• • • *Contents of the Registration Statement.* Section 7 of the 1933 Act requires that our hypothetical issuer's registration statement contain the information specified in Schedule A to the 1933 Act except as otherwise required by the SEC. Using its extensive rulemaking authority, the SEC has adopted registration forms[24] that together with Regulation S-K (narrative disclosure) and Regulation S-X (financial statements) specify the required contents of the registration statement. These forms and related rules make Schedule A obsolete for most intents and purposes.[25]

There are two basic types of registration forms under the 1933 Act. The first (Form S-1 or its counterpart for foreign companies, Form F-1) is a stand-alone document that contains all the required information, including a full description of the business and financial condition of the issuer. The second (Form S-3 or its counterpart for foreign companies, Form F-3)[26] is a document that "incorporates by reference" information from the

---

22. If debt securities are to be offered, in addition to filing under the 1933 Act, it is necessary to qualify an indenture under the Trust Indenture Act of 1939.

23. The statement in the text is something of an exaggeration. Nothing in the 1933 Act requires the delivery of a prospectus. As we shall see, however, a sale cannot be legally completed without delivering a prospectus.

24. Rule 130 provides that the term "rules and regulations" as used in Section 7 includes the forms for registration of securities and the related instructions.

25. Registration statements filed by a foreign government, or a political subdivision thereof, are governed by Schedule B to the 1933 Act. No forms have been adopted for these registration statements. As described in Chapter 9, however, the disclosures have become fairly well standardized.

26. There is a third pair of forms, Form S-2 and Form F-2, but these are rarely used.

issuer's periodic reports filed with the SEC under the 1934 Act.[27] As one might expect, the ability to incorporate by reference is conditioned (among other things) on the issuer's having a minimum reporting history. This was once 36 calendar months, but the required period is now 12 calendar months.

• • • *Development of the Integrated Disclosure System.* From its beginning, the 1933 Act operated on a sporadic basis—that is, whenever an issuer decided to make a public offering of securities. Even after the passage of the 1934 Act, which required issuers of exchange-listed securities to file periodic reports with the SEC, the two statutes operated independently. A 1933 Act registration statement and the related prospectus delivered the information considered necessary for persons buying a particular distribution of securities. On the other hand, the periodic reports filed under the 1934 Act provided the

---

27. The 1934 Act also requires the "registration" of securities, but primarily for the benefit of persons who purchase securities in the secondary markets. Section 12(b) of the 1934 Act requires registration of securities listed on a national securities exchange. Section 12(g) extends the registration requirement to any securities traded in interstate commerce if the issuer has total assets exceeding $1 million (increased by SEC rule to $10 million) and a class of equity securities held of record by 500 or more persons. (Such a class can include outstanding employee stock options, but the SEC staff has granted relief from the registration requirement under certain circumstances. See SEC Division of Corporation Finance, *Current Issues and Rulemaking Projects* 10 (March 31, 2001 update).)

An initial application for registration under the 1934 Act is made on Form 10, and additional classes of securities are registered on Form 8-A. Section 13 of the 1934 Act requires issuers of registered securities to keep their Form 10 current through the filing of annual reports on Form 10-K and quarterly reports on Form 10-Q. Form 8-K is used for any current updating, including the disclosure of acquisitions. Any issuer that has filed a 1933 Act registration statement that has become effective is required by Section 15(d) of the 1934 Act to file the same periodic reports as are required of an issuer with securities registered under the 1934 Act. An issuer can relieve itself of 1934 Act reporting requirements, generally by certifying to the SEC that fewer than 300 persons are holders of record of the registered security. The corresponding requirements for foreign private issuers are discussed in Chapter 9.

information considered necessary for persons buying securities traded on securities exchanges.

There was never a good reason—other than historical—for the differences between the forms and instructions that governed the content of periodic reports filed under the 1934 Act and those that governed registration statements filed under the 1933 Act. The information required for a decision to purchase or sell securities on an exchange or in the over-the-counter market is, after all, substantially the same as the information required for a decision whether to purchase securities being distributed in a registered public offering. Even so, until the SEC's adoption of the integrated disclosure system the disclosure requirements on any given subject were likely to vary depending on whether the document was being prepared for filing under the 1933 Act or 1934 Act. As Milton H. Cohen stated in his seminal article, *"Truth in Securities" Revisited*,[28] the combined disclosure requirements of the 1933 and 1934 Acts probably would have been quite different if they had been enacted in the opposite order.

With the extension in 1964 of the periodic reporting requirements of the 1934 Act to substantial issuers of securities traded over-the-counter, the "efficient market hypothesis" began to gain recognition. For purposes of the federal securities laws, the efficient market hypothesis is that all the information that an issuer disseminates—whether by means of its 1934 Act reports, communications with shareholders or press releases—is absorbed into the market through the activities of the financial press, securities analysts and other professionals, thereby causing the market price of the issuer's securities to reflect this information. Thus, it may be presumed in the case of an offering of new securities by a widely followed public company that the prospective investors in the new securities have already received and discounted the information previously made public by the issuer. Accordingly, it should not be necessary to disclose it to them again.

The *Wheat Report*,[29] published in 1969, suggegsted improvements to the SEC's disclosure requirements that were compatible

---

28. 79 Harv. L. Rev. 1340 (1966).

29. This report, *Disclosure to Investors—A Reappraisal of Administrative Policies Under the '33 and '34 Acts*, was prepared under the direction of Commissioner Francis M. Wheat.

with the efficient market hypothesis. It recommended expanded periodic disclosure under the 1934 Act and coordination of the disclosure requirements of the 1933 Act and the 1934 Act. In accordance with the report's recommendations, the SEC adopted in late 1970 a short form of registration statement, called Form S-16, which provided for incorporation by reference of reports filed under the 1934 Act.[30] As originally adopted, Form S-16 was available only for securities issued on the conversion of convertible securities or the exercise of warrants as well as for securities being sold "in the regular way" on a national securities exchange by persons other than the issuer. The form was amended in 1972 to make it available for any kind of secondary offering[31] and in 1978 to make it available for firm commitment primary offerings where issuer's "float" was at least $50 million.[32]

In 1977, the SEC adopted Regulation S-K, then consisting of two items, "Description of Business" and "Description of Property." For the first time, the principal disclosure items were made uniform for annual reports on Form 10-K and 1933 Act registration statements. In time, full consistency was achieved, and the various registration and reporting forms under the 1933 Act and the 1934 Act now specify the required information by references to Regulation S-K.

In March 1982, the SEC announced significant changes in the forms and rules governing registration statements under the 1933 Act.[33] This action represented the final stage of the SEC's program to implement an integrated disclosure system under the 1933 Act and the 1934 Act. New Forms S-1, S-2 and S-3 were adopted to replace Forms S-1, S-7 and S-16, and the abbreviated Form S-3 (unlike its predecessor, Form S-16) was made available

---

30. SEC Release No. 33-5117 (December 23, 1970). Form S-16 had an antecedent in Form S-7, which for many years allowed qualified issuers to omit from their 1933 Act registration statements information relating to management compensation and transactions that was set forth in the issuer's 1934 Act filings.

31. SEC Release No. 33-5265 (June 27, 1972).

32. SEC Release No. 33-5923 (April 11, 1978).

33. SEC Release No. 33-6383 (March 3, 1982).

for primary offerings of securities even where there was no firm commitment underwriting.[34] Later in 1982, the SEC adopted an integrated disclosure system for foreign private issuers, with registration forms (Forms F-1, F-2 and F-3) that correspond to their domestic counterparts.[35]

• • • *SEC Staff Review of the Registration Statement.* One of the principal purposes of registration is to give the SEC staff the opportunity to review and comment on the registration statement's compliance with the requirements of the statute, the rules and the forms. As discussed throughout this book, however, compliance with the disclosure requirements is not a "check the boxes" exercise. The objective is to achieve a full and fair disclosure that will enable an investor to make an intelligent investment decision.

• • • *"Effective Date" of the Registration Statement.* By the terms of Section 8(a) of the 1933 Act, a registration statement becomes effective by operation of law on the 20th day after filing. In practice, it does not become effective until declared effective by the staff of the SEC under delegated authority. This works through the magic of a "delaying amendment" under Rule 473, which prevents the registration statement from becoming effective until our hypothetical issuer has responded to any SEC staff comments on the contents of the registration statement and is ready to price and sell its securities. At that time, and on request of the issuer and its underwriters, the staff "accelerates" the effectiveness of the registration statement by issuing the requisite order.

The registration statement may become effective without pricing information if the issuer follows the requirements of Rule 430A (discussed in Chapters 2 and 3), thus mitigating somewhat the problem of being unable to predict exactly when the staff will act. Also, as discussed in Chapter 8, one of the advantages of shelf registration is that it eliminates the

---

34. *See* Chapter 3 for a discussion of registration forms for U.S. issuers. As discussed in Chapter 8, the availability of Form S-3 for primary offerings on a delayed or continuous basis was the driving force behind the growth of shelf registration.

35. SEC Release No. 33-6437 (November 19, 1982). *See* Chapter 9 for a discussion of registration forms for foreign private issuers.

1933 ACT OVERVIEW

uncertainty and delay sometimes associated with staff review and acceleration on a transaction-by-transaction basis.

• • • *Offers and Sales of the Registered Securities.* In examining how the 1933 Act governs the offering process for our hypothetical offering, it is important to keep in mind the three stages of the registration process described above: (i) the period prior to the filing of the registration statement with the SEC, (ii) the period between the time the registration statement is filed and the time it is declared effective and (iii) the period after the registration statement is effective. It is also important to distinguish between sales, including contracts to sell, on the one hand, and offers, on the other hand. With respect to offers, it is important to distinguish between oral offers and written offers.

Prior to the time that the registration statement is filed, Section 5(c) prohibits any offer of the securities, whether written or oral.[36] Once the registration statement is filed, the securities may be offered for sale, but Section 5(a)(1) prohibits any sale or contract to sell the securities until the SEC declares the registration statement effective. (As discussed in Chapter 3 under "Online Offerings," the SEC construes this prohibition as extending to an underwriter's premature receipt of payment from a customer.) During the so-called "waiting period" prior to effectiveness, while the SEC staff may be reviewing the registration statement and the underwriters may be marketing the issue, there is no restriction on oral offers, but no written[37] offering material

---

36. Thanks to the definitions in Section 2(a)(3), the prohibition does not extend to "preliminary negotiations or agreements" among issuers, underwriters and selling shareholders. On the other hand, the prohibition applies in full to securities firms that will act as dealers rather than underwriters.

37. Are e-mails "written" for this purpose? There is considerable interest among underwriters in finding a way to permit their sales personnel to inform customers by means of e-mail of the availability of a new offering. While an e-mail message may consist of "magnetic impulses" within Rule 405's elaboration on Section 2(a)(9)'s definition of "written" as including any form of "graphic communication," it would seem more logical to analyze e-mail messages on the basis of whether they are being used as substitutes for oral (e.g., telephone) conversations. After all, voice mail messages also consist of "magnetic impulses," and no one has yet suggested that a voice mail message is a "prospectus." The use of e-mail for this purpose is further discussed in Chapter 3.

is permitted other than the preliminary or "red herring" prospectus[38] permitted by Rule 430, even if the material is accompanied by the preliminary prospectus.[39] Thus, during the period between filing and effectiveness, it would be a violation of Section 5(b)(1) for an underwriter to send a preliminary prospectus to a customer with a cover letter, e-mail or any other written message pointing out the merits of the proposed investment.[40]

The making of pre-filing offers in violation of Section 5(c) is sometimes referred to as "gun-jumping." After the filing of the registration statement, the term "gun-jumping" is used—somewhat illogically—to describe the distribution of written offering material other than the preliminary prospectus.

Once the registration statement is declared effective, the securities may continue to be offered and actual sales may be made. Written offers may be made only by means of the final prospectus, except that other offering material (sometimes referred to as "supplementary selling literature") may be used if preceded or accompanied by the final prospectus.

• • *Operation of the Prospectus Delivery Requirement.* As noted above, it is something of an exaggeration to state that the 1933 Act requires delivery of a prospectus. On the other hand, it is illegal to confirm a sale or to deliver a security in a registered public offering without delivering a prospectus that meets the statutory requirements. Also, as mentioned above and as further discussed below, it may be illegal gun-jumping to offer the

---

38. So called for the legend (formerly required to be in red ink) that must be printed on the cover of every preliminary prospectus. Item 501(b)(10) of Regulation S-K.

39. Rule 482 permits investment companies to use certain limited supplemental selling literature during this period. Also, as discussed below, certain communications are deemed under SEC rules not to be offers or prospectuses.

40. In *Franklin, Meyer & Barnett,* 37 S.E.C. 47 (1956), a broker-dealer was sanctioned because, among other transgressions, a registered representative enclosed with a preliminary prospectus his business card on which he wrote "Phone me as soon as possible as my allotment is almost complete on this issue." An oral statement to this effect would not have violated Section 5. *See also Diskin v. Lomasney & Co.,* 452 F.2d 871 (2d Cir. 1971).

securities by means of any written communication other than the preliminary or final prospectus.

• • • *Preliminary Prospectus.* There is no 1933 Act requirement that a preliminary prospectus be provided to investors, but Rule 15c2-8(b) under the 1934 Act states that it is a deceptive practice for a broker-dealer participating in an issuer's initial public offering not to send copies of the preliminary prospectus to investors at least 48 hours prior to the expected time of mailing of confirmations. The 48-hour requirement does not apply to securities of reporting companies. A preliminary prospectus is distributed other than for Rule 15c2-8 purposes only to the extent that the underwriters believe it will be useful as a marketing tool for the offering.

Rule 15c2-8(b) has no further application once the final prospectus is available. In other words, an underwriter or dealer may confirm a sale immediately to a customer who turns up after the deal is priced.

Rule 15c2-8(e) requires a broker-dealer to take reasonable steps to make available a copy of the preliminary prospectus to each registered representative who is expected to solicit customers' orders and also to make available a copy of any amended preliminary prospectus. The purpose of this requirement is to provide the salesperson with a reasonable basis on which to advise customers on the investment merits of the security.

• • • *Delivery of Final Prospectus with Confirmation.* The 1933 Act does not in so many words require delivery of the final prospectus to the buyer of the registered security, but it does make it illegal to confirm the sale unless the final prospectus is provided to the buyer.

The way this works is complex. Section 5(b)(1) provides that after a registration statement has been filed, it is unlawful to transmit a prospectus unless it meets the requirements of Section 10. Such a prospectus is one that contains all the information required by the 1933 Act, including price terms. Section 5(b)(1) does not prohibit the use of a preliminary prospectus, even though a preliminary prospectus does not include price terms, because Rule 430 deems a preliminary prospectus to meet the requirements of Section 10 if it is used prior to the effective date.

When securities are sold after the effective date, Rule 10b-10 under the 1934 Act requires that broker-dealers send out a written confirmation. But a confirmation is a prospectus under Section 2(a)(10), and a confirmation clearly does not meet the requirements of Section 10. This means that sending the confirmation to the customer would violate Section 5(b)(1).

The magic solution? Section 2(a)(10)(a) excludes from the definition of "prospectus" a communication that is "sent or given" after the effective date of a registration statement if, prior to or at the same time as such communication, a prospectus meeting the requirements of Section 10(a) (i.e., a "final prospectus," which is a prospectus that contains all the information required by the 1933 Act)[41] is "sent or given" to the person to whom the communication is made. Thus, even though the confirmation is a prospectus that does not meet the requirements of Section 10 and whose transmittal by itself would constitute a violation of Section 5(b)(1), simply preceding or accompanying the confirmation with the final prospectus converts the confirmation into a communication that is no longer a prospectus.

The underwriter does not bear the risk of nondelivery of the prospectus; it is sufficient if he can prove that he sent the prospectus together with or earlier than the confirmation. The established practice, however, is to include a copy of the final prospectus in the same envelope as the confirmation.[42]

A copy of the final prospectus must therefore precede or accompany each confirmation of sale. However, except as provided in Rule 15c2-8, there is no requirement that a prospectus be given to an investor before he makes an investment decision. The result is that, except in the case of an IPO, a purchaser of securities may never see an offering document until

---

41. In the SEC's view, a Rule 430A prospectus does not meet the requirements of Section 10, and neither does a base prospectus included in a shelf registration statement.

42. Chronic delays in printing the final prospectus and in delivering it to underwriters in sufficient quantities have frequently caused delays in the mailing of confirmations. *See* Chapter 3 for a discussion of this problem in the context of the introduction in 1995 of "T+3" settlements.

after he purchases the securities and subsequently receives a confirmation. If he makes a written request for a preliminary prospectus, it must be furnished to him (if one has been prepared), but if he does not, it is likely that he will not see an offering document until after his purchase has been made.

If the purchaser reads the prospectus that he receives with his confirmation and decides that he does not want the security, he has no right to renege on his purchase. Although many securities firms will not attempt to hold a customer to his agreement under these circumstances, there is nothing in the 1933 Act that gives a purchaser a right to change his mind after reading the prospectus. If the prospectus is misleading or contains false statements, the purchaser has the remedies described in Chapter 5. But there is nothing in the 1933 Act that affords a purchaser a reasonable time to read a prospectus before being bound.[43]

These conclusions may on the surface appear inconsistent with the statutory objective of full and fair disclosure as the basis for an informed investment decision. But this is the law, and the courts have so held. In *Byrnes v. Faulkner, Dawkins & Sullivan*,[44] Judge Werker had this to say on the matter:

> The defendant's Fifth Affirmative Defense is unique; Faulkner asserts the right to cancel the contract and rescind the purchase on the receipt of the prospectus. No authority has been cited for this proposition, and this

---

43. A customer's receipt of a confirmation is related to the possible availability to the customer of a statute of frauds defense under Section 8-319 of the former version of the Uniform Commercial Code, which requires a party to an oral contract for the purchase or sale of securities to object within ten days to the contents of the confirmation. As a practical matter, the statute of frauds defense has very seldom been asserted as a defense by customers or other participants in the organized securities markets, even in periods of abrupt moves in securities prices. Moreover, the 1994 revision of Article 8 of the Uniform Commercial Code, as approved by the National Conference of Commissioners on Uniform State Laws and the American Law Institute, deletes former Section 8-319 and specifically makes the statute of frauds inapplicable to such contracts.

44. 413 F. Supp. 453 (S.D.N.Y. 1976), *aff'd* 550 F.2d 1303 (2d Cir. 1977).

court has been unable to find any. Acceptance of this defense would stretch the provisions of the [1933 Act] far beyond their intended scope.

The defendant argues that inherent in the prospectus delivery requirement is an implied right to rescind. Otherwise, so the argument goes, the purpose of the delivery requirement would be defeated. That reading flies in the face of the statute and ignores already far-reaching, remedial provisions.

Section 5(b)(2) of the 1933 Act makes it unlawful for anyone to send a registered security through the mail "for the purpose of sale or for delivery after sale, unless accompanied or preceded by a prospectus." It was clearly within the contemplation of the drafters of the statute that a purchaser might not see the prospectus covering the security he purchased until after the sale had been completed. Yet no provision of the statute either permits rescission upon receipt of the prospectus or prevents the parties from binding themselves to the terms of a contract prior to that receipt.

Furthermore, Section 12 of the 1933 Act explicitly provides for rescission in two specific circumstances: where a person offers or sells securities (a) in violation of Section 5 of the Act or (b) through the use of a material misrepresentation. The defendant would have this section judicially amended to include a third situation, i.e., where a person, in conformity with the statute[,] delivers a final prospectus and the purchased securities simultaneously. This the court refuses to do.[45]

• • • *"Free-Writing" Privilege.* If a confirmation can be rescued from the status of an illegal prospectus by accompanying or preceding it by a final prospectus, then so can any other written offering material. Glossy brochures and other

---

45. *Id.* at 472–73. The SEC proposed in the 1998 Aircraft Carrier Release (SEC Release No. 33-7606A (November 13, 1998)) to require that prospectus information be delivered to an investor prior to an investment decision. Issuers and underwriters were strongly opposed to the proposal, and it was not adopted.

"supplementary selling literature" are sometimes distributed to investors in connection with an offering, but only if accompanied or preceded (more likely, for safety's sake, accompanied in the same envelope or folder) by the final prospectus. (The "final" prospectus for this purpose means a prospectus that meets the requirements of Section 10(a) of the 1933 Act, i.e., a prospectus that contains all the information required by the 1933 Act, including the price terms. This means that a preliminary prospectus cannot be relied upon for this purpose.) The distribution of offering material in this manner is sometimes referred to as "free-writing."

• • • *Delivery of Final Prospectus with Registered Security.* Section 5(b)(2) prohibits the use of the mails or any means of interstate commerce to "carry" any 1933 Act–registered security for the purpose of sale or for delivery after sale unless the security is "accompanied or preceded" by a final prospectus. Unlike the requirement of Section 5(b)(1) that the final prospectus be "sent or given" with or before the confirmation, Section 5(b)(2) appears to require that the prospectus "accompan[y] or precede" the delivery of the security. In more leisurely times, one could usually assume that the prospectus had been delivered to the customer (with the confirmation) prior to the settlement date on which the security was delivered to the customer's account. Under a T+3 settlement regime, such an assumption is more hazardous. This subject is discussed in greater detail in Chapter 3.

• • • *Dealers' Delivery of Final Prospectus in Connection with After-Market Transactions.* In principle, all dealers must deliver final prospectuses to persons who buy in the after-market for a specified period of time after a registration statement becomes effective. The existence and duration of this obligation is the subject of a boldface notice required by Item 502(b) of Regulation S-K to appear on the outside back page of the prospectus. The obligation extends to dealers who did not participate in the offering, and it also applies to underwriters who are no longer acting as such.

The obligation arises from the terms of the "dealer's exemption" in Section 4(3)(B) of the 1933 Act, which states in effect that the exemption is not available during a period of 40 or 90 days following the later of the effective date of the registration statement or the first bona fide offering of the security. It is therefore necessary for the dealer to deliver a prospectus in order to avoid its confirmation constituting an illegal prospectus violating Section 5(b)(1) of the 1933 Act.

The applicable statutory prospectus delivery period is generally 90 days, but the SEC's Rule 174(b) reduces the period to zero if immediately prior to the filing of the registration statement the issuer was subject to the reporting requirements of the 1934 Act. In the case of an IPO, Rule 174(d) terminates the delivery obligation "after the expiration of 25 calendar days after the offering date" if the securities are listed on an exchange or quoted in NASDAQ as of their offering date. For this purpose, the "offering date" is the later of the effective date of the registration statement or the date of the first bona fide offering of the security.

The prospectus delivery obligation applies to transactions between dealers, as well as between a dealer and a customer. In the case of "face-to-face" transactions between members of a national securities exchange on the floor of the exchange, Rule 153 permits a "constructive delivery" procedure by which a member firm is deemed to have received a copy of a prospectus that has been delivered to the exchange by the issuer or any underwriter. No such procedure exists for transactions between dealers in the over-the-counter market, despite suggestions that such a procedure should be adopted.[46] Of course, if the SEC approves NASDAQ's application to become registered as a national securities exchange, Rule 153 should become applicable to interdealer transactions effected through NASDAQ.

For 1933 Act purposes, the expiration of the after-market period during which a prospectus must be delivered also determines when a broker-dealer may commence the publication of research reports on the security covered by the prospectus.[47] Confusion sometimes

---

46. Joseph McLaughlin, *"Ten Easy Pieces" for the SEC*, 18 Rev. Sec. & Commodities Reg. 200, 201 (1985).

47. Research reports are generally "prospectuses" within the meaning of Section 2(10) of the 1933 Act, but they do not meet the requirements

arises on this point because of the unfortunate wording of the legend prescribed by Item 502(b) of Regulation S-K, which requires the insertion of the "expiration date" of the prospectus delivery period into a sentence that states that dealers must deliver a prospectus "until" that date. In other words, if the prospectus delivery period "expires" on June 15, the legend will require delivery of a prospectus "until" June 15. A research analyst relying on the legend may therefore understandably assume that a report may be mailed on June 15, but this would be one day too early.

• • • *Unsold Allotments and Updating the Prospectus.* In any event, underwriters and dealers are required to comply with the prospectus delivery obligation with respect to their unsold allotments. If an issue is difficult to sell (a "sticky deal" in the vernacular of Wall Street), the underwriters and dealers may require a substantial period of time to complete the distribution. Indeed, it is not uncommon for the managing underwriter to take back all of the securities not sold by the syndicate, place them in its own investment account for purposes of Regulation M (see Chapter 4) and resell them at a later date when market conditions have improved.

Unsold allotments do not lose their status as registered securities, however long they are retained by an underwriter and whether or not they are placed in an investment account. On the

---

of Section 10 of the statute. It would therefore be illegal under Section 5(b)(1) to deliver a research report unless an exemption were available, and as we have seen the Section 4(3)(B) exemption is not available for the period during which the "official" prospectus must be delivered. SRO rules adopted in 2002 impose a "blackout" period of 40 days on managers or co-managers of an IPO, i.e., 15 days longer than the usual 1933 Act prospectus delivery period. The SRO rules also impose a ten-day blackout period on managers or co-managers of a "secondary" offering, i.e., offerings for which there is no 1933 Act prospectus delivery period, with an exception for research that meets the standards of Rule 139 (discussed in Chapter 3) and that relates to "actively traded" securities within the meaning of Rule 101 of Regulation M (discussed in Chapter 4). There is also an exception under certain circumstances for research responding to "significant news or events." NYSE Rule 472(f); NASD Conduct Rule 2711(f).

other hand, a current prospectus must be delivered when the securities are sold. The original prospectus may have to be updated because of Section 10(a)(3), which provides that if a prospectus is used more than nine months after the effective date of a registration statement, the information contained therein must be as of a date not more than 16 months prior to its use. This requirement applies in particular to the audited financial statements included in the prospectus. The original prospectus may also have to be updated because statements in the prospectus may no longer be true or may have become misleading because of the passage of time.

Underwriting agreements generally require the issuer to update the prospectus in order to protect the underwriter against liability for delivering an out-of-date prospectus or one that is no longer accurate.[48] Typically, the issuer will bear the expense of updating for a period of nine months after the effective date of the registration statement. Thereafter, updating is at the underwriter's expense.

As discussed above, research material may ordinarily not be distributed during the prospectus delivery period because Section 4(3)(B) makes the dealer's exemption unavailable during this period. Section 4(3)(C) also makes the dealer's exemption unavailable, however, at any time—even after expiration of the prospectus delivery period—in respect of "[t]ransactions as to securities constituting the whole or a part of an unsold allotment." On its face, this means that a dealer with an unsold allotment may not distribute research on the registered securities, at least where the dealer is actively trying to sell the unsold allotment. On the other hand, it should be permissible to distribute research if the dealer has placed the unsold securities into an investment account as discussed in Chapter 4. Also, such

---

48. Delivery of a defective prospectus does not cause a violation of Section 5 (as opposed, for example, to a violation of Section 12(a)(2)). *But see SEC v. Manor Nursing Centers, Inc.*, 458 F.2d 1082 (2d Cir. 1972), *criticized in* Richard W. Jennings, Harold Marsh, Jr., John C. Coffee, Jr. & Joel Seligman, *Securities Regulation: Cases and Materials* 172–73 (8th ed. 1998). The argument for a Section 5 violation may be barely credible where the delivered prospectus on its face does not conform to Section 10(a)(3)'s express updating requirement.

1933 ACT OVERVIEW

research may be entitled to the Rule 139 exemption discussed in Chapter 3.

• • • *Market-Makers' Delivery of Prospectus When Affiliated with Issuer.* Except during the prospectus delivery period discussed above, a dealer may sell a recently registered security in the secondary market without delivering a prospectus. The dealer may never have been an underwriter, or the dealer may no longer be acting as an underwriter, and the Section 4(3) dealer's exemption will apply.

One type of dealer, however, is not so lucky. When a financial services holding company issues debt securities in a registered public offering, investors expect the issuer's broker-dealer affiliate to make a market in the new securities. The SEC takes the position, however, that the Section 4(3) dealer's exemption is not available for a transaction in which the dealer is an affiliate of the issuer. This position applies generally, not just to financial services holding companies and their affiliated broker-dealers. On the other hand, non–financial services issuers seldom have affiliated broker-dealers.

The theory of the SEC position is that a dealer, according to the definition in Section 2(a)(12) of the 1933 Act, is a person who deals in securities issued "by another person;" an issuer is not deemed by the SEC to be "another person;" with respect to its affiliates.[49] While this analysis is less than persuasive as a technical matter, the practice developed of preparing a "market-maker prospectus" to be included in the registration statement and that would state on its cover page that it would relate to any resales in market making transactions by an affiliated broker-dealer. It is often more convenient to use the original prospectus supplement and base prospectus for this purpose, stripped of time sensitive information so as to avoid the need to file updates, and the prospectus supplement or base prospectus will include a statement to this effect. There is no additional SEC registration fee for the market-making resales.[50]

---

49. Aircraft Carrier Release, text at nn.132–38.

50. The 1996 report of the Task Force on Disclosure Simplification recommended elimination of the market-making prospectus requirement. The Aircraft Carrier Release acknowledged that the requirement was a "burden"

The market-maker prospectus problem seldom arises in connection with equity securities because the NYSE regards its Rule 312(g) as in effect precluding market-making in a parent company's equity securities, thus forcing the affiliated broker-dealer to execute customer orders as agent in reliance on Section 4(4) of the 1933 Act.

• • • *Electronic Delivery of Prospectus.* Beginning with the *Brown & Wood* letter[51] in 1995 and continuing in a series of releases, the SEC has recognized that the 1933 Act obligation to deliver a prospectus may be satisfied by the delivery of an electronic prospectus. The ability to deliver a prospectus electronically would alleviate some of the burden of the various prospectus delivery obligations described above. The conditions under which electronic delivery may be relied on are discussed in Chapter 3.

- *Communications During the Offering Process ("Gun-jumping")*

As we have seen, it is a violation of Section 5(c) of the 1933 Act to make offers in advance of the filing of the registration statement. After the filing of the registration statement, it is a violation of Section 5(b)(1) of the 1933 Act to make written offers other than by means of a prospectus that meets the requirements of Section 10 of the 1933 Act, for example, the preliminary prospectus. Both types of violation are referred to as "gun-jumping."

There is no area of 1933 Act practice that is subject to regulation as outmoded and as difficult to apply as that involving communications from the issuer or underwriters at or about the time of a registered public offering.

The statutory basis for regulating communications during the offering process is nearly 50 years old. As the SEC acknowledged in its 1998 Aircraft Carrier Release, the securities markets

---

and proposed rules that it said would alleviate the burden. The proposals were not adopted.

51. SEC Interpretive Letter, *Brown & Wood* (February 17, 1995).

have changed significantly as a result of major advancements in technology and communications media and by increased cross-border activity. These changes, it acknowledged, "have increasingly created conflicts between communications mechanisms to which markets have become accustomed and the restrictions placed by the . . . [1933] Act on communications around the time of a registered offering."[52]

The SEC has, to be sure, adopted some rules and issued some advice in this area. But it admitted in the Aircraft Carrier Release that its traditional "facts and circumstances" test was difficult to apply and had led to significant restrictions on communications. It also confessed that its guidance had been "vague" and "general" and difficult to apply in practice.

The Aircraft Carrier Release proposed no fewer than nine separate new or amended "safe harbor" rules for communications made in the context of a registered public offering. The price of these reforms was very high, however, and the proposals were not adopted.

• • *Source of the Problem.* When the 1933 Act prohibits "offers" prior to the filing of a registration statement and limits the type of written offers that are permitted after filing, the prohibition is not limited to communications that constitute an offer in the common law contract sense or that on their face purport to offer to sell the security to be registered. The term "offer to sell" is broadly defined in Section 2(a)(3) of the 1933 Act to include "every attempt or offer to dispose of, or solicitation of an offer to buy . . . for value." The SEC has long cautioned that publicity efforts made in advance of a proposed offering "may in fact contribute to conditioning the public mind or arousing public interest in . . . [an] issuer or in . . . [its] securities . . . in a manner which raises a serious question whether the publicity is not in fact part of the selling effort."[53]

Starting a selling effort prior to the filing of a registration statement is called "gun-jumping." Those who "jump the gun" on a forthcoming offering, whether by interviews with newspaper

---

52. SEC Release No. 33-7606A (November 13, 1998), text at nn.273–74.
53. *See* SEC Release No. 33-3844 (October 8, 1957).

or magazine reporters, speeches, market letters or otherwise, violate the basic prohibitions of the 1933 Act.

In *Carl M. Loeb, Rhoades & Co.*,[54] the managing underwriters of an initial public offering were disciplined by the SEC for issuing a press release providing details of the proposed offering and holding a press conference at which the release was distributed and questions were answered. The SEC found that, in the two days following the release of this publicity, over 100 securities firms had contacted Loeb, Rhoades expressing interest in the offering. During the same period, the managing underwriters received numerous indications of interest from the public. In its opinion, the SEC stated its belief that it had a mandate from Congress to prevent issuers, underwriters and dealers from "initiating a public sales campaign prior to the filing of a registration statement by means of publicity efforts which, even though not couched in terms of an express offer, condition the public mind or arouse public interest in . . . particular securities."

At the same time, the SEC recognized that "difficult and close questions of fact" might arise in distinguishing between an "item of publicity" that is "part of a selling effort" or part of "legitimate disclosure to investors unrelated to such an effort." It identified as relevant circumstances in this regard "the nature, source, distribution, timing, and apparent purpose and effect of the published material."[55]

Another way of putting it might be to focus on the audience, timing and content of a publication. If the communication is

---

54. *In re Carl M. Loeb, Rhoades & Co.*, 38 S.E.C. 843 (1959).

55. The SEC also concluded in *Loeb, Rhoades* that pre-filing publicity by prospective underwriters "must be *presumed* to set in motion or to be a part of the distribution process," and therefore involve prohibited offers to sell (emphasis added). This "presumption" was almost immediately qualified in *First Maine Corp.*, Release No. 34-5898 (March 2, 1959), where the SEC observed that "broker-dealers in the ordinary course of their business commonly furnish to customers and prospective customers a considerable volume of business and financial information," and that the *Loeb, Rhoades* "presumption" would not necessarily apply to "incidental mention of an issuer or a security in financial information distributed by broker-dealers through the mails."

directed to an audience that is different from prospective purchasers of securities (e.g., an ad or article directed at issuers of securities rather than purchasers of securities), it might not constitute gun-jumping. If the timing is long before the commencement of an offering (e.g., 30 days as suggested in the Aircraft Carrier Release), the effects of the communication might be so attenuated at the time of commencement of the offering that it could no longer be said that the communication had conditioned the market for the securities to be offered. And the content of the communication—while this is the most difficult factor for the securities lawyer to evaluate—might as a practical matter not make the securities more attractive in the eyes of the investor (e.g., a negative research piece could hardly be construed as part of a marketing effort). These considerations are discussed at greater length in Chapter 3.

Gun-jumping can have severe business and legal consequences. If the SEC becomes aware of activity that it regards as improper, it can hold up effectiveness of the registration statement until such time as it believes the effects of the improper activity have dissipated. It can require that an underwriter be excluded from the offering, and it has on occasion insisted that facts contained in gun-jumping communications be included in the registration statement. The SEC can also assess administrative penalties against any of the persons it believes to be responsible for the improper activity. Finally, even if the offering is successfully completed, any purchaser who has been the recipient of an illegal offer may be able for a period of one year to "put" his securities to the offending seller at the original purchase price.

- *Notices of Proposed Registered Offerings (Rule 135)*

The SEC has long considered it appropriate to permit advance notice of certain offerings of securities. In 1955, it adopted Rule 135 to permit a brief notice to be sent to existing securityholders to inform them of the proposed issuance of rights to subscribe to additional securities.[56] Rule 135 was subsequently amended to permit a similar notice to be sent to the securityholders of the issuer or of another issuer advising them

---

56. SEC Release No. 33-3568 (August 29, 1955).

of a proposed exchange offer and to permit a notice of offerings to employees.[57] Finally, at the urging of the *Wheat Report* and certain securities exchanges, Rule 135 was amended in 1970 to permit the publication of a brief notice relating to any cash offering of securities to be registered under the 1933 Act.[58]

A proposed stock offering may be a material fact from the standpoint of existing shareholders. For example, an equity financing may result in the dilution of their holdings. Rule 135 seeks to accommodate the interests of existing shareholders and the interests of the SEC in prohibiting gun-jumping. It provides that for purposes of Section 5 a notice by an issuer that it proposes to make a public offering of securities to be registered under the 1933 Act will not be deemed an offer of the securities if the notice states that the offering will be made only by means of a prospectus and contains no more than the name of the issuer, the title, amount and basic terms of the securities to be offered, and a brief statement of the manner and purpose of the offering without naming the underwriters. The notice may take the form of a news release or a written communication directed to holders of the issuer's securities.

A major point to be stressed in the case of a Rule 135 notice is that *it may not identify the managing underwriters.* In the pre-filing period, not only are underwriters prohibited from offering the securities for sale, but also dealers are prohibited from offering to buy the securities. The SEC has said that the announcement of the underwriter's identity should be avoided during this period because "experience shows that such announcements are very likely to lead to illegal offers to buy."[59]

In 1969, Bangor Punta Corporation issued a press release announcing a proposed exchange offer of its securities for shares of Piper Aircraft Corporation. The announcement was made prior to the filing of the registration statement and stated that there

---

57. SEC Release No. 33-4099 (June 16, 1959).

58. SEC Release No. 33-5101 (November 19, 1970). Rule 135 was amended in SEC Release No. 33-7760 (October 26, 1999) to include certain information regarding business combinations.

59. SEC Release No. 33-4697 (May 28, 1964).

would be offered for the Piper shares "a package of Bangor Punta securities to be valued in the judgment of The First Boston Corporation at not less than $80 per Piper share." In a proceeding by Chris-Craft Industries, Inc. seeking to enjoin the exchange offer, Judge Waterman held that the categories of information permitted under Rule 135 are exclusive and that the statement that the package of securities would be valued at $80 made the press release an offer to sell that violated Section 5.[60]

- *Notice of Proposed Unregistered Offerings (Rule 135c)*

The purpose of Rule 135 was to permit existing securityholders to be informed of an issuer's forthcoming registered offering in a manner that did not condition the market for that offering. Existing securityholders may also have an interest in an issuer's forthcoming *non-registered* offering, for example, a private placement or an offshore offering that might have a dilutive effect on outstanding common stock. The SEC's interest in this situation is to prevent any news about the unregistered offering from arousing interest in the offering among the issuer's securityholders. As discussed in Chapter 9, a listed U.S. company that had completed in the early 1990s an offshore convertible debt offering in reliance on the SEC's new Regulation S filed a report of the transaction on Form 8-K. The SEC staff criticized the issuer in strong terms on the theory that the report amounted to an attempt to condition the U.S. market for the convertible securities. The staff position was untenable and eventually resulted in the adoption of Rule 135c,[61] which permits a reporting issuer (or a foreign issuer that files "home country" information with the SEC) to give a notice—which may consist of a news release, a written communication to securityholders or employees or "other published statements"—about an unregistered offering. The notice is limited to specified facts about the offering and may not be "used for the purpose of conditioning the market in the United States for any of the

---

60. *Chris-Craft Industries, Inc. v. Bangor Punta Corp.*, 426 F.2d 569, 574 (2d Cir. 1970).

61. SEC Release No. 33-7053 (April 19, 1994).

securities offered." It must be filed with the SEC as part of a report on Form 8-K or 6-K or as part of a non-reporting foreign issuer's "home country" information.

- *Offshore Press-Related Communications (Rule 135e)*

Foreign issuers may take advantage of Rule 135e to permit journalists to attend offshore press conferences and meetings with issuer or underwriter representatives and to receive press-releases and other communications. Rule 135e is discussed in Chapter 9.

- *Communications Not Deemed a Prospectus (Rule 134)*

Once a registration statement is filed, certain limited written communications are permitted if they are deemed not to be a prospectus under the "safe harbor" of Rule 134.

Rule 134 deems a communication not to be a prospectus if it contains no more than the name of the issuer, the title of the securities, a brief indication of the general type of business of the issuer, the offering price or its method of determination, the yield or probable yield range in the case of a debt security, the name and address of the sender of the communication, the names of the managing underwriters, the approximate date of the proposed sale to the public, and legal investment, tax and rating information. Certain other information may be included in the case of a rights offering. The SEC staff tends to take a very narrow view of Rule 134, and even direct quotations from the prospectus are not safe if they contain embellishments that go beyond what is literally permitted by the rule.

Unfortunately, Rule 134 was designed for a simpler world. In particular, it has not kept pace with the development of increasingly complex fixed-income securities and the need to convey relevant non-oral information to investors during the offering period. On the other hand, a considerable amount of relevant information about fixed-income securities can be communicated in reliance on Rule 134. The "title" of fixed-income securities, for example, invariably includes the maturity or maturities. Weighted-average coupon and maturity information, prepayment speeds and similar information is relevant to both maturity and yield.

If the registration statement is not effective, Rule 134(b) requires that the communication include a legend to the effect that a registration statement has been filed but has not yet become effective, that the securities may not be sold prior to effectiveness, and that the communication does not constitute an offer. This legend is not required, however, if the communication is accompanied or preceded by a preliminary prospectus *or* does no more than state from whom a written prospectus meeting the requirements of Section 10 may be obtained, identify the security, state its price, and state by whom orders will be executed.

If the registration statement has become effective, there is no guidance in the rule on how to modify the Rule 134(b) legend. It is probably safe, however, simply to omit the reference to the registration statement's not having become effective.

The rule does not by its terms require that a prospectus meeting the requirements of Section 10 (e.g., a preliminary prospectus permitted by Rule 430) be available, but the SEC staff took the position during the Internet Bubble that underwriters could not rely on Rule 134 unless such a prospectus were available and, moreover, in the case of an IPO a prospectus that contained a bona fide estimated price range.[62] The availability of a so-called "pink herring," that is, a preliminary prospectus without an estimated price range, would be insufficient. It is doubtful that this staff position can prevent reliance on Rule 134 in other contexts, such as offerings of fixed-income securities where the underwriters wish to communicate to investors written information about anticipated price, yield and maturity.

During the period between filing and effectiveness, Rule 134 permits a "tombstone" advertisement to be published to advertise the availability of the preliminary prospectus. In the usual case, however, the Rule 134 tombstone advertisement is published after the registration statement becomes effective, more for the purpose of recording the transaction and enhancing the status of the managing underwriter than for generating interest in the

---

62. SEC Division of Corporation Finance, *Current Issues and Rulemaking Projects* (November 14, 2000), at 51.

securities. A tombstone advertisement derives its name from its stark appearance.

Any press release that is issued after the filing of a registration statement must remain within the confines of Rule 134, as must any pre-effective notices to shareholders to whom subscription rights are proposed to be issued. The press release must set forth the Rule 134 legend. Some public relations firms print the legend on the stationery on which pre-effective press releases are published.

As discussed above, there is interest among underwriters in permitting their sales personnel to use e-mail messages to inform customers of the availability of new offerings. Even if an e-mail message is assumed to be a "written" communication, it will still be permitted if its content is kept within the limits prescribed by Rule 134.

In connection with electronic underwritings, the SEC staff took the position during the Internet Bubble that "communications on an e-broker's (as well as on the issuer's) web site" that were "merely instructional and . . . not designed to generate interest in a particular offering typically are unobjectionable even if they do not fall within the safe harbor of Rule 134." This would include, for example, "general information on how to use the web site, how the brokerage service operates and how to open an account."[63]

Chapter 3 discusses the applicability of Rule 134 to online offerings.

- *Research Reports*

Gun-jumping problems are particularly acute for a securities firm with an active research department and a retail sales system. The difficulty is that, depending on their timing and content and the audience to whom they are addressed, research reports may be viewed by the SEC as illegal offers of the securities proposed to be sold under a registration statement. As research reports are written documents (or the equivalent thereof, as in the case

---

63. *Id.* at 50, citing SEC No-action Letter, *Wit Capital* (available July 14, 1999).

of research that is distributed electronically), the problem exists both prior to the filing of the registration statement and after filing but prior to completion of the distribution of the registered securities.

Research problems in this context are discussed in detail in Chapter 3.

- *Certain Offers and Sales*

The registration and prospectus delivery requirements of Section 5 come into play only when there is an "offer" or a "sale" of a security. Section 2(a)(3) defines a "sale" to include any disposition of a security for value and an "offer" to include any offer or attempt to dispose of a security for value, including the solicitation of an offer to buy. For there to be a sale, the person to whom the security is issued or delivered must give some consideration or "value" in return. Thus, an ordinary stock dividend does not involve a sale.[64]

- - *Spin-Offs.* In a spin-off, a corporation distributes to its shareholders shares of a subsidiary corporation. Logic would dictate that such a transaction does not involve a sale any more than does a stock dividend. But in the late 1960s the SEC became concerned with the whole spin-off phenomenon and issued a release in which it referred to a pattern involving "the issuance by a company, with little, if any, business activity, of its shares to a publicly-owned company in exchange for what may or may not be nominal consideration" followed by a spin-off of these shares to shareholders of the public company "with the result that active trading in the shares begins with no information on the issuer being available to the investing public."[65] The SEC brushed aside the "theory" that no sale was involved in the spin-off on the basis that the distribution "does not cease at the point of receipt by the initial distributees of the shares but continues into the trading market involving sales to the investing public

---

64. This is true even though the shareholder has the right to choose stock or cash so long as the choice is not made after the "vesting" of the right to receive the cash. SEC Release No. 33-929 (July 29, 1936).

65. SEC Release No. 33-4982 (July 2, 1969).

at large." The SEC simply did not wish to see trading markets spring up where there was no public information concerning the issuer.

Prior to September 1997, the SEC staff frequently took no-action positions with respect to unregistered spin-offs. In Staff Legal Bulletin No. 4, the Division of Corporation Finance announced that it would no longer respond to inquiries regarding spin-offs unless a transaction presented "novel or unusual" issues. It then set forth its views on the conditions under which a spin-off could be characterized as not involving a sale, that is, that the parent company shareholders did not provide consideration for the spun-off shares, that the spin-off be pro rata to the parent company shareholders, that the parent provide "adequate information" about the transaction and the spun-off company to its shareholders and the trading markets, that the parent have "a valid business purpose" for the transaction and that, in the case of a spin-off of "restricted shares," the parent have held them for at least two years.

Notwithstanding the SEC staff's views, whether there is "a valid business purpose" for the spin-off should be irrelevant for 1933 Act purposes so long as adequate public information is available regarding the newly public company. The point is seldom a significant one since such a purpose is sometimes important to the tax consequences of the spin-off.

• • *Rule 145.* The question whether the issuance of securities in a merger or similar transaction involves a sale has had a long history culminating in the adoption of Rule 145. If a company seeks to acquire another company in a statutory consolidation or merger in which the stock of the company to be acquired will become or be exchanged for securities of the acquiring company, or if a company seeks to acquire all or substantially all of the assets of another company in exchange for its securities to be followed by a statutory liquidation, the transaction will require the affirmative vote or consent of the holders of a majority or more of the voting stock of the company to be acquired. A shareholder vote will also be required in the case of a reclassification that involves the substitution of one security for another security. The required vote is governed by state law.

In transactions of this type, unlike a voluntary exchange of one security for another, a change in the shareholder's status occurs by operation of law and not because he makes an individual investment decision. Thus, during the first 39 years of the 1933 Act's operation, the SEC took the position that no "offer" or "sale" was involved where, pursuant to statutory provisions or provisions contained in the certificate of incorporation of the company to be acquired, there is submitted to a vote of shareholders a proposal for a transfer of assets or a merger or consolidation if the vote of a required favorable majority would bind all shareholders except for those asserting appraisal rights. This "no-sale theory" was codified in Rule 133, adopted by the SEC in 1951.[66] In 1972 the SEC did a complete about-face. Based on a recommendation of the *Wheat Report*, it adopted Rule 145, which provides that such a transaction does indeed involve an offer and sale. Accordingly, in the absence of an exemption, when a company submits such a transaction to a shareholder vote, it must mail a joint proxy statement and prospectus to its shareholders. The SEC has made Form S-4 available for the registration of securities to be issued in business combinations of this type.

With respect to resales of securities issued in a registered Rule 145 transaction, a person who is an affiliate of the company to be acquired at the time the transaction is submitted to a vote will be deemed an underwriter and must deliver a prospectus in connection with a resale of the registered securities, unless the securities are sold in accordance with the public information, limitation on the amount of securities sold, and manner of sale provisions of Rule 144. (The holding period condition does not apply.) If the affiliate of the acquired corporation does not become an affiliate of the acquiring corporation and holds his securities for two years, he may sell without limitation. If he holds the securities for one year, he may sell free of all but the current public information requirement.[67] The SEC has taken

---

66. SEC Release No. 33-3420 (August 2, 1951).

67. In early 1997, the SEC proposed to eliminate the presumption that an affiliate of the acquired company is deemed to be an underwriter on resale of the registered securities. SEC Release No. 33-7391 (February 20, 1997).

the position that the resale provisions of Rule 145 also apply to securities acquired in exchanges exempted under Section 3(a)(9) or Section 3(a)(10).[68]

- *Exempted Transactions*

In general, Section 4 exempts certain types of transactions from the registration and prospectus delivery requirements of Section 5, and Section 3 exempts certain types of securities. The transaction exemptions set forth in Section 4 appear on their face to be rather complicated. What they boil down to, however, is that Section 4(2) exempts private placements, which are the subject of Chapter 7. Subsections (1), (3) and (4) of Section 4 exempt trading transactions as opposed to distributions.

• • *Private Placements.* Corporate financing by means of private placements has been revolutionized in recent years by the SEC's adoption of Rule 144A. The history of the private placement exemption set forth in Section 4(2) of the 1933 Act and its culmination in Rule 144A are described in Chapter 7.

• • *Trading Transactions.* To understand the exemptions from the registration and prospectus delivery requirements of Section 5 available for trading transactions, it is necessary to analyze the separate subsections of Section 4, their relationship to certain definitions in Section 2, and the refinements to the Section 4 exemptions spelled out in Rule 144.

Section 4(1) exempts from the provisions of Section 5 "transactions by any person other than an issuer, underwriter, or dealer." This is the exemption that allows an ordinary investor to sell 100 shares of common stock on an exchange or in the over-the-counter market without going through the futile exercise of asking the issuer to file a registration statement to cover the sale. Without the Section 4(1) exemption, the trading markets simply could not operate. The ordinary investor, of course, is not the "issuer" of the securities. As will be seen, if he bought the securities in the open market or in a registered offering, he

---

68. *See* J. William Hicks, *Resales of Restricted Securities* §3:30 (2004 ed.).

will not be deemed an "underwriter." Nor is he a "dealer."[69] He will be selling through a dealer, however, and the securities firm through which he sells his 100 shares must find its own exemption under Section 4.

A dealer that is selling for a customer will usually rely on the dealer's exemption under Section 4(3). This section exempts transactions by a dealer (including an underwriter no longer acting as an underwriter in respect of the securities involved in the transaction), except under three circumstances:

- paragraph (A) removes the exemption for transactions taking place prior to the expiration of 40 days after the first date on which the security was bona fide first offered to the public by the issuer or by or through an underwriter;
- as discussed above, paragraph (B) removes the exemption for transactions by a dealer taking place prior to the expiration of a specified number of days following a registered public offering; and
- paragraph (C) removes the exemption for transactions in securities constituting a part of a dealer's unsold allotment as a participant in a distribution of the securities.

The reasons for the exceptions are fairly obvious. Paragraph (A) permits the development of a market in securities that may have been the subject of an *illegal* unregistered distribution in the United States or a legal distribution outside the United States. It is the origin of the 40-day period following an offshore offering during which U.S. dealers will not make a market in the new security. Paragraph (B) was discussed above, and its prospectus delivery requirement was historically intended to encourage

---

69. Section 2(a)(12) of the 1933 Act defines the term "dealer" to mean "any person who engages either for all or part of his time, directly or indirectly, as agent, broker, or principal, in the business of offering, buying, selling, or otherwise dealing or trading in securities issued by another person." An ordinary private investor should not be considered a "dealer," even though he may trade in securities on a regular basis.

dissemination of the prospectus that was used to sell the new offering. Finally, paragraph (C) is intended to prevent reliance on the dealer's exemption *at any time* at which the dealer is trying to sell part of an unsold allotment from the offering.

A securities dealer unable to rely on Section 4(3) to execute a sell order for his customer—for example, because prospectuses are unavailable to fulfill a delivery requirement or because the transaction takes place within the first 40 days following an offshore offering—may be able to execute the transaction in reliance on Section 4(4). This exemption applies to "brokers' transactions executed upon customers' orders on any exchange or in the over-the-counter market but not the solicitation of such orders." The SEC construes the exemption as being available only where the sell order is unsolicited and the dealer acts as agent and does not solicit the buy side of the transaction.

• • *Transactions by Underwriters.* Except for certain brokers' transactions under the limited circumstances of Section 4(4),[70] an exemption under Section 4 is not available for transactions by an "underwriter." If an underwriter is involved in a transaction, registration is required unless the securities are exempted securities under Section 3. The term "underwriter" applies not only to a securities professional, whether acting as principal or agent, but also to any other person who comes within the statutory definition. Such a person is commonly known as a "statutory underwriter" to distinguish him from a professional.[71]

Section 2(a)(11) defines the term "underwriter" to mean

> any person who has purchased from an issuer with a view to, or offers or sells for an issuer in connection with, the distribution of any security, or participates or

---

70. For a discussion of Section 4(4), *see* 7B J. Williams Hicks, *Exempted Transactions Under the Securities Act of 1933* (2003), at ch. 13.

71. One of the authors was once required to explain the statutory underwriter concept to counsel for a person in this position who argued that his client obviously was not an underwriter because he operated a dry cleaning business.

has a direct or indirect participation in any such undertaking, or participates or has a participation in the direct or indirect underwriting of any such undertaking.

For the purpose of this definition only, and for no other purpose, the term "issuer" includes, in addition to the actual issuer of the securities, "any person directly or indirectly controlling or controlled by the issuer, or any person under direct or indirect common control with the issuer."[72] In other words, an intermediary who distributes securities for a control person of the issuer is treated as though the distribution had been made for the issuer itself.

Cutting through to the essence of this wordy definition, it covers not only conventional underwriters, investment banking firms underwriting a public offering of securities for an issuer or a control person, but also individuals who buy securities from an issuer in a private placement (called "restricted securities" under Rule 144) and redistribute them to the public under circumstances that lead to the conclusion that they purchased the securities "with a view to distribution." A statutory underwriter problem often arises when a person sells a privately owned business to a larger publicly owned company in exchange for its stock and then decides to liquidate his holdings. The issue must also be addressed in connection with any resale of privately placed securities.

There is a lot at stake in whether or not a person is acting as an underwriter. Not only are the Section 4 exemptions for the most part not available to underwriters, but as we will see in Chapter 5 underwriters who sell securities registered under the 1933 Act are exposed to significant liabilities. For this reason, and also to encourage registration and prospectus delivery in as many transactions as possible, the SEC and its staff tend to see underwriters lurking about in many transactions where no one is performing a traditional underwriting role. Problems in identifying underwriting status are discussed in Chapters 7, 8 and 11.

---

72. This would include a controlling shareholder, a subsidiary of the issuer, or a sister subsidiary in a holding company structure. Even though an issuer may "control" a low-level employee, he is not considered a person "controlled by the issuer."

Is an ordinary member of the public an underwriter if he purchases securities from an issuer in a registered public offering with a view to their resale? If read literally, Section 2(a)(11) covers any purchase from an issuer with a view to distribution. But Section 2(a)(11) cannot be read literally in this context. Manuel F. Cohen, when chief counsel of the SEC's Division of Corporation Finance, explained it this way in a speech delivered to the Association of the Bar of the City of New York:

> The Commission has not construed Section 2[a](11) to identify as underwriters public stockholders who intend to distribute shares acquired in a registered rights or other public offering, or in a transaction exempt under Sections 3(a)(9), 3(a)(10), or 3(b). In some of these situations, substantial blocks of securities, amounting to a "distribution" by any test, are in fact redistributed. It would be an inversion of the purposes and provisions of the Act, however, to subject members of the public, for whose protection the Act is designed, to the duties, responsibilities and liabilities of an underwriter.[73]

A person may have a statutory underwriter problem if he purchases securities from a shareholder in a "control" relationship with the issuer, a person that Rule 144 calls an "affiliate." As noted above, a control person is an issuer solely for the purpose of the Section 2(a)(11) definition. Thus, a Section 4(1) exemption would be available to a control person owning non-restricted securities who stood on a street corner and hawked his securities to the public. It would not be available, however, if he sold his securities through an intermediary, such as a securities firm, in a transaction that constituted a distribution. Under these circumstances, the intermediary would be considered an underwriter.

Who is a control person? Rule 405 under the 1933 Act defines "control" as "the possession, direct or indirect, of the

---

73. M. F. Cohen, *Rule 133 of the Securities and Exchange Comm'n*, 14 *The Record of the Association of the Bar of the City of New York* 162, 178 (1959).

power to direct or cause the direction of the management and policies of a person, whether through the ownership of voting securities, by contract or otherwise." Obviously, this means that whether or not a person is a control person requires a fact-intensive analysis that must take into account the size of the person's holdings, his position with the issuer and other objective and subjective considerations (e.g., it is often useful to discover that someone else is clearly in control of the company).[74] Red flags should fly if a person is a director or an executive officer of the issuer, but the analysis cannot stop there.[75] Precisely because of the fact-intensive nature of the question, the SEC staff will not issue no-action letters on whether or not a person is a control person. Lawyers are sometimes asked to render legal opinions as to whether a person is a control person, but the subtle dynamics of how companies are run makes it very difficult—especially for outside counsel—to opine on control questions. It goes without saying that the 1933 Act has been construed to recognize the concept of the "control group," such as a controlling family.[76]

• • *Rule 144.* A person who sells securities for the account of an "affiliate" or a person who sells "restricted securities" for his own account may claim a Section 4(1) or 4(3) exemption if the transaction does not constitute a distribution so that the seller is not an underwriter.

Rule 144 under the 1933 Act spells out those transactions that are not deemed to be distributions and that accordingly may be effected without registration. It provides that any affiliate (i.e., a control person) or any person who sells restricted securities of an issuer for his own account, or any person who sells restricted or any other securities of the issuer for the account

---

74. *See* J. William Hicks, *Resales of Restricted Securities* §§4.25 to 4.31 (2004 ed.).

75. The SEC proposed in 1997 to exclude as control persons anyone who was *none* of the following: a 10% beneficial owner of any class of the company's equity securities, an officer or a director. SEC Release No. 33-7391 (February 20, 1997). The proposal has not been adopted.

76. *See, e.g.*, *SEC v. Culpepper*, 270 F.2d 241 (2d Cir. 1959).

of an affiliate, will be deemed not to be engaged in a distribution of such securities and therefore not to be an underwriter thereof within the meaning of Section 2(a)(11) if all of the conditions of the rule are met. Rule 144 defines "restricted securities" as including securities that are "acquired directly or indirectly from the issuer, or from an affiliate of the issuer, in a transaction or chain of transactions not involving any public offering."

In general, Rule 144 permits an affiliate or a holder of restricted securities to sell without registration in ordinary brokerage transactions, or to a market-maker, an amount of securities that, together with his other sales during the preceding three months (other than pursuant to a registration statement or a private placement), does not exceed the greater of one percent of the amount of securities of that class outstanding or the average weekly volume of trading in those securities during the preceding four weeks.

To rely on Rule 144 for a sale of restricted securities, a minimum of one year must have elapsed between the acquisition of the securities from the issuer or an affiliate of the issuer and the date of their resale under the rule by the acquirer or any subsequent holder.

Under Rule 144(k), a holder of restricted securities who is not and has not been an affiliate of the issuer during the three months preceding the sale may sell free of any Rule 144 limitations if two years have elapsed from the time that the securities were acquired from the issuer or an affiliate of the issuer.[77]

In most cases, a Form 144 must be filed with the SEC before the sale is made. Also, there must be available adequate current

---

77. This brief summary of Rule 144 does not do justice to its many nuances. For further information, see the current edition of J. William Hicks, *Resales of Restricted Securities.* In early 1997, the SEC proposed to eliminate the requirement that sales be limited to ordinary brokerage transactions or to sales to a market-maker, to link the volume of sales exclusively to a percentage of shares outstanding and to increase the threshold requirements for filing Form 144. It also invited comment on proposals to address the application of the 1933 Act to the hedging of restricted securities. SEC Release No. 33-7391 (February 20, 1997). It took no action on these proposals.

public information with respect to the issuer of the securities, which means either that the issuer has been a reporting company for 90 days and has been current for 12 months in its reporting obligations (with a limited exception for certain Form 8-K reports) or, in the case of a non-reporting issuer, that specified information about the issuer is otherwise publicly available.

• • *Offers and Sales to Employees.* Under the SEC's Rule 701, a non-reporting issuer (i.e., a U.S. or foreign issuer not subject to the SEC's reporting requirements under the 1934 Act) may offer and sell its securities "in compensatory circumstances" and pursuant to a written compensatory benefit plan to its employees, officers, directors, consultants and advisers without registration under the 1933 Act. Sales in reliance on the rule may not exceed the greatest of $1 million or 15 percent of the issuer's assets or 15 percent of the outstanding securities of the same class (calculated as prescribed by the rule). Securities sold in reliance on the rule are restricted securities and may be resold only pursuant to 1933 Act registration or an exemption. A limitation on the usefulness of Rule 701 is that it provides no exemption from the registration or qualification requirements of the various states where the employees may be located.

• *Exempted Securities*

Whether or not a Section 4 exemption is available for a particular transaction, the securities involved in the transaction may be offered and sold without compliance with Section 5 if an exemption is available under Section 3. An exemption under Section 3 may be available because of the nature of the issuer or the nature of the securities or, in another example of the untidiness of the 1933 Act, because of the nature of the transaction.

• • *U.S. Government Obligations.* Section 3(a)(2) exempts securities issued or guaranteed by the United States or any person "controlled or supervised by and acting as an instrumentality" of the U.S. government pursuant to statutory authority. Securities exempted by Section 3(a)(2) include not only direct U.S. Treasury obligations, but also obligations issued or guaranteed by the various federal agencies that finance in the public markets. Section 3(a)(2) is used most often to exempt debt securities, but it can also apply to equity securities of instrumentalities of the United States.[78]

The exemption is available for the great variety of obligations that are guaranteed by the federal government. For example, the securities of Chrysler Corporation that were guaranteed by the federal government when that company was encountering financial difficulties were exempt from registration. Certificates representing interests in a pool of mortgages are exempted when guaranteed by the Government National Mortgage Association. Securities of foreign governments, however, are not exempt from registration.

The SEC staff has taken a no-action position with respect to debt securities issued by the Private Export Funding Corporation where the payment of interest is guaranteed by Eximbank and the payment of principal is secured by the pledge of securities guaranteed by Eximbank or by other instruments backed by the full faith and credit of the United States.[79]

In determining the availability of an exemption under Section 3(a)(2), the SEC will look to the substance of a transaction and not just its form. Thus, the staff has permitted reliance on this exemption where a limited partnership, organized for the sole purpose of renovating and redeveloping the City Post Office in Washington, D.C., proposed to issue non-recourse obligations to finance the project. These obligations were to be guaranteed by the U.S. Postal Service during the construction period and thereafter backed by a lease obligation of the United States acting through the Administrator of General Services (GSA). The Postal Service is an instrumentality of the United States, and thus its guarantee provided an exemption for the bonds during the construction period. When the GSA lease obligation came into effect, the holders of the bonds would be relying solely upon the credit of the GSA, and thus the bonds would be the economic equivalent of U.S. government obligations. In taking a no-action

---

78. *See, e.g.,* SEC No-action Letter, *Federal Agricultural Mortgage Corp.* (available October 5, 1988).

79. SEC No-action Letter, *Private Export Funding Corporation* (June 9, 1975).

position, the staff particularly noted that both the guarantee and the lease obligation could be enforced directly by a bondholder.[80]

The securities of certain international organizations are exempted securities under the 1933 Act pursuant to federal enabling statutes. For example, a 1949 amendment to the Bretton Woods Agreements Act provides that securities issued or guaranteed by the International Bank for Reconstruction and Development (the World Bank) are deemed to be exempted securities within the meaning of Section 3(a)(2).[81] The statutes relating to the Inter-American Development Bank Act,[82] the African Development Bank[83] and the Asian Development Bank Act[84] contain similar exemptions for securities issued or guaranteed by these entities. The SEC has authority to suspend or impose conditions on these exemptions and, acting under this authority, has adopted regulations that require the filing of certain periodic and transaction-related reports.[85]

The statutes that created Fannie Mae and Freddie Mac also exempted their securities from the 1933 Act.[86] There have been suggestions in recent years from within and from outside Congress that these exemptions should be modified.

• • *Municipal Obligations.* Section 3(a)(2) also exempts securities issued or guaranteed by the states and territories, their

---

80. SEC No-action Letter, *Postal Square Limited Partnership* (May 24, 1990). See also SEC No-action Letter, *Tennessee Valley Authority Office of Power Headquarters Building Project* (February 18, 1983), where non-recourse obligations backed by a TVA lease were permitted to be issued in reliance on Section 3(a)(2).

81. 22 U.S.C. §286k-l(a) (1990).

82. 22 U.S.C. §283h(a) (1990).

83. 22 U.S.C. §290i-9(a) (1990).

84. 22 U.S.C. §285h(a) (1990).

85. Regulations BW (World Bank), IA (Inter-American Development Bank), AFDB (African Development Bank) and AD (Asian Development Bank).

86. 12 U.S.C. §1723c (Supp. 1996) (Fannie Mae); 12 U.S.C. §1455(g) (Freddie Mac). The exempt status of these issuers' securities is not affected by their voluntary registration of their securities under the 1934 Act. SEC No-action Letter, *Federal Home Loan Mortgage Corp.* (July 12, 2002).

political subdivisions and public instrumentalities, or the District of Columbia. It also exempts certain industrial development bonds the interest on which is tax-exempt under Section 103(a) of the Internal Revenue Code. In the late 1960s, the SEC attempted to subject industrial development bonds to 1933 Act registration requirements by adopting Rule 131.[87] Rule 131 provided that any part of an obligation evidenced by a bond issued by a governmental entity specified in Section 3(a)(2), "which is payable from payments to be made in respect of property or money which is or will be used, under a lease, sale, or loan arrangement, by or for industrial or commercial enterprise," would be deemed a "separate security" issued by the industrial or commercial enterprise that is the obligor under the lease, sale or loan arrangement. The separate non-municipal security would, of course, not be entitled to the Section 3(a)(2) exemption. Congress quickly responded by enacting Section 401 of the Employment Security Amendments of 1970 to amend Section 3(a)(2) to override Rule 131 in the case of tax-exempt industrial development bonds.[88] Changes in the tax law have restricted the purposes for which industrial development bonds may be issued.

As discussed in Chapter 5, securities exempt under Section 3(a)(2) are not covered by the remedy provided to investors by Section 12(a)(2) of the 1933 Act. Does the SEC's Rule 131 mean that an investor may sue an underwriter of a tax-exempt industrial revenue bond under Section 12(a)(2) because of the "separate security" represented by the underlying obligation? So far, the courts appear to be dismissing these cases.[89]

Tax law changes have led to the issuance of taxable bonds by municipalities and their instrumentalities. The taxable or tax-exempt status of interest on these securities does not affect the availability of the Section 3(a)(2) exemption.

Although municipal bonds are exempt from 1933 Act registration, many official statements used in connection with

---

87. SEC Release No. 33-4921 (August 28, 1968).
88. *See* SEC Release No. 33-5103 (November 6, 1970).
89. A recent case is *Lieberman v. Cambridge Partners, LLC et al.*, 2003 U.S. Dist. LEXIS 23732 (E.D. Pa. 2003).

municipal offerings are as complete and as well prepared as any 1933 Act prospectus. Nonetheless, the SEC continues to express concern over the adequacy of disclosure in the area of municipal finance. Its jurisdiction in this area is limited to some extent by Section 15B(d)(1) of the 1934 Act, which prohibits the SEC or the Municipal Securities Rulemaking Board (MSRB) from requiring that any municipal issuer make any filing prior to the sale of municipal securities. In addition, Section 15B(d)(2) (the "Tower Amendment") prevents the MSRB from requiring any issuer to furnish any information either to the MSRB or to any prospective purchaser.

Notwithstanding Section 15B(d), the SEC has extensively regulated disclosure practices in the municipal securities field by means of its authority over broker-dealers and its power to define fraudulent conduct. Rule 15c2-12[90] thus makes it unlawful, as a means "reasonably designed" to prevent fraud, for a broker-dealer to act as underwriter of a primary offering of municipal securities in a principal amount of $1 million except in compliance with the rule's requirements. These requirements include obtaining and reviewing an official statement that the issuer "deems final" (with certain authorized omissions), and delivering to potential customers preliminary and final official statements. The rule also requires an underwriter to "reasonably determine" that the issuer or any "obligated person" has agreed to provide annual financial information and notice of specified occurrences (if material) (e.g., delinquencies, defaults, unscheduled draws, substitution of credit enhancers or liquidity providers). Finally, the rule prohibits any broker-dealer from recommending the purchase or sale of a municipal security unless the broker-dealer has procedures in place that provide "reasonable assurance" that it will receive prompt notice of the specified occurrences.

The SEC has released three interpretive statements on the disclosure obligations of underwriters, broker-dealers and issuers

---

90. SEC Release No. 34-26985 (June 28, 1989). The rule was originally proposed in SEC Release No. 34-26100 (September 22, 1988) at the same time as the SEC released to Congress the results of its investigation of the default of the Washington Public Power Supply System.

in the municipal securities markets.[91] Insofar as underwriters are concerned, the SEC takes the position (without citing any authority) that "[b]y participating in an offering, an underwriter makes an implied recommendation about the securities."[92] Moreover, the SEC also believes that "most situations" in which a broker-dealer "brings a municipal security to the attention of a customer involve an implicit recommendation of the security to the customer."[93] From these premises, it is easy for the SEC to invoke prior precedents to the effect that a broker-dealer that recommends a security must have a reasonable basis for doing so. The broker-dealer can establish such a basis, in the SEC's view, by reviewing the issuer's disclosures in connection with a public offering and by taking into account available continuing disclosure in the case of securities traded in the secondary market.

When the SEC adopted Rule 15c2-12, it was by no means clear that it was correct in asserting that a broker-dealer "recommends" a security for purposes of triggering the "reasonable investigation" requirement merely because the broker-dealer acts as an underwriter. There is no apparent historical support for this proposition. There is even less basis for the proposition that the requirement is triggered merely by "bringing a security to the attention of a customer." The SEC's position to this effect obliterates any distinction between a mere solicitation and a recommendation. Exactly what obligations a broker-dealer assumes in a given situation should depend, as they historically have, on all the facts and circumstances of the transaction. Nevertheless, the consequences under Rule 10b-5 of the SEC's position remain to be determined.

• • *Bank Securities.* Section 3(a)(2) exempts securities issued or fully guaranteed by a national bank or any banking institution organized in a U.S. jurisdiction. Securities of foreign banks are not exempt, but the SEC has long regarded securities issued or guaranteed by foreign banks' branches or agencies in

---

91. SEC Release No. 34-26100 (September 22, 1988), *modified in* Release No. 34-28985 (June 28, 1989); Release No. 34-33741 (March 9, 1994).

92. SEC Release No. 34-26100 (September 22, 1988).

93. SEC Release No. 34-34961 (November 10, 1994) at note 143.

the United States as entitled to the Section 3(a)(2) exemption so long as each branch or agency is subject to regulation that is "substantially equivalent" to that of U.S. banks in the same jurisdiction.[94] Section 3(a)(2) does not exempt securities of bank holding companies, but Section 3(a)(12) exempts the formation of a bank holding company where the shareholders of a bank receive stock of the holding company in accordance with specified criteria that seek to ensure a continuity of ownership, assets and liabilities.

The SEC staff has taken the position that a bank that is being newly organized may not offer its stock to the public without compliance with the registration requirements of the 1933 Act unless the invested funds are placed in escrow, or investors are otherwise fully protected against loss, until the bank is authorized to commence operations under applicable state law.[95] Escrows are not practical in underwritten transactions since underwriters will be reluctant to place their compensation in escrow and return it to investors in the event that the certificate of authority is not forthcoming.

For this reason, some banks during organization have registered their IPOs under the 1933 Act. To avoid this problem, in several instances involving new Connecticut banks, arrangements were made with the chartering authority in the State of Connecticut to issue the requisite final certificate of authority at the closing. The transaction was structured so that receipt of the funds and regulatory approval were conditions concurrent. Although no request was made to the SEC for approval of this procedure, investors clearly were not at risk prior to the issuance of the final certificate of authority, and the conditions of prior no-action letters were fully satisfied.

---

94. SEC Release No. 33-6661 (September 23, 1986).

95. *See, e.g.,* SEC No-action Letter, *County First Bank* (March 31, 1989); SEC No-action Letter, *Commerce Bank Corporation* (September 19, 1988); SEC No-action Letter, *The Springs Bank* (June 15, 1987); SEC No-action Letter, *Constitution Bank* (April 21, 1986); SEC No-action Letter, *First Allied Bank of Baton Rouge* (July 24, 1985); SEC No-action Letter, *Bank of World* (June 6, 1983).

Section 3(a)(2) is not the end of the story for national banks or federally licensed U.S. branches and agencies of foreign banks. Regulations adopted by the Office of the Comptroller of the Currency (OCC)[96] require—unless an exemption is available—that these institutions not offer and sell their securities until a registration statement has been filed with and declared effective by the OCC. (The exemptions under the regulations incorporate, in general, the 1933 Act's non-bank exemptions.) The OCC regulations generally require the offering documents for nonexempt offerings to conform to the SEC form that would have applied if 1933 Act registration were required. An abbreviated registration system is available for offers and sales of investment grade nonconvertible debt by bank subsidiaries of SEC-reporting bank holding companies if the debt is offered in minimum denominations of $250,000 to accredited investors.[97]

The federal regulators for state banks and state-licensed branches and agencies of foreign banks have not imposed registration requirements.[98] Some states have adopted registration or filing requirements relating to securities of institutions subject to their jurisdiction.

Of course, as discussed above under the definition of "security," not every instrument issued by a bank is a security. Conversely, not every security issued by a bank is an exempt security. As discussed in Chapter 9, American Depositary Receipts (ADRs) must be registered under the 1933 Act in a special procedure that is more form than substance. And, as discussed in Chapter 14, asset-backed securities do not enjoy

---

96. 12 C.F.R. Part 16 (1996).

97. 12 C.F.R. Section 16.6 (1996). *See* the letter dated May 31, 1995 from Ellen Broadman, Director, Securities and Corporate Practices Division, OCC, to Daniel M. Rossner of Brown & Wood, [1994–95 Transfer Binder] Fed. Banking L. Rep. (CCH) ¶83,610.

98. The FDIC has adopted a Statement of Policy on the Use of Offering Circulars that sets forth standards for the offer and sale of securities by insured state banks that are not members of the Federal Reserve System. 61 Fed. Reg. 46,807 (1996). The statement reminds banks of the applicability of the antifraud provisions of the federal securities laws and suggests the type of information that should be included in an offering circular of a state non-member bank.

the Section 3(a)(2) exemption just because a bank passes through to investors the principal and interest on the underlying assets.

Banks often issue certificates of deposit (CDs) or notes the return on which is linked to the performance of an index such as the S&P 500 Index or to other financial assets, and they do so in reliance on the Section 3(a)(2) exemption. Many of these instruments are "principal protected" by the bank to a significant degree, thus strengthening the case that the investor is still relying on the credit of the bank. There may be situations, of course, where what is nominally a bank obligation turns out to be an investment in a non-bank enterprise. In those cases, the availability of the exemption might not be clear.

• • *Thrift Institutions.* An exemption is provided under Section 3(a)(5) for securities issued by savings and loan associations and similar institutions. The exemption is not applicable to securities issued by these institutions' holding companies. As in the case of banks, however, Section 3(a)(12) exempts under certain circumstances the formation of a savings association holding company.

Again, however, the 1933 Act exemption is not the end of the story. Regulations adopted by the Office of Thrift Supervision (OTS)[99] require OTS registration of securities offerings of OTS-regulated thrifts unless an exemption is available. Certain states have also adopted registration requirements for securities offerings by their state-chartered thrift institutions.

• • *Commercial Paper.* Section 3(a)(3) exempts notes with maturities of nine months or less where the proceeds are to be used for current transactions. This is the so-called "commercial paper" exemption. Commercial paper is discussed in greater detail in Chapter 10.

• • *Railroad Equipment Trust Certificates.* Section 3(a)(6) exempts any interest in a railroad equipment trust. The exemption

---

99. 12 C.F.R. 563g (1996). For further guidance on these regulations, see a release of the Office of General Counsel of the Federal Home Loan Bank Board (the predecessor to the OTS) entitled *Questions and Answers on Part 563g: Securities Offering Regulations.*

originally applied to securities of railroads and motor carriers, the issuance of which was subject to the approval of the Interstate Commerce Commission. The exemption for railroad securities was removed in 1976 as a result of the Penn Central bankruptcy (see Chapter 5), and the motor carrier exemption was removed in 1982.

• • *Insurance Contracts.* Section 3(a)(8) exempts "any insurance or endowment policy or annuity contract or optional annuity contract" issued by a corporation subject to regulation by an insurance commissioner of a state, territory or the District of Columbia. The statement is made in the *House Committee Report* that insurance policies and similar contracts were not regarded in the commercial world as securities offered to the public for investment purposes.[100]

Insurance products are no longer so simple, and certain hybrid products will not qualify for the Section 3(a)(8) exemption. Thus, a "variable annuity," where the payout will depend on the performance of a portfolio of securities, may not be offered without registration.[101] The SEC has attempted to provide guidelines in its Rule 151, stressing that for the exemption to be available the insurer must assume the investment risk and the contract must not be marketed primarily as an investment.

• • *Exchanges with Existing Securityholders.* Section 3(a)(9) exempts any securities exchanged by an issuer exclusively with its existing securityholders where no commission or other remuneration is paid for soliciting the exchange. This is the exemption that permits a company to have convertible securities outstanding without maintaining a current prospectus (see Chapter 12). If not for this exemption, a prospectus would have to be delivered on every conversion of a convertible security. This exemption is frequently relied on in connection with recapitalizations where a company makes an offer to exchange new debt securities for existing debt securities (see Chapter 13).

The exemption provided by Section 3(a)(9) is in the nature of a transaction exemption in that it is not based on the characteristics of the securities exchanged or of the issuer of the

---

100. H.R. Rep. No. 85, *supra* note 3, at 15.
101. *SEC v. Variable Annuity Life Insurance Co.*, 359 U.S. 65 (1959).

securities. This exemption originally was set forth in Section 4. It was moved to Section 3 when the 1933 Act was amended in 1934 in order to clarify that dealers could trade immediately in securities issued in an exempt exchange.[102]

• • *Court or Government Approved Exchanges.* Exchanges of securities are exempt under Section 3(a)(10) if the terms and conditions of the exchange are approved after a fairness hearing by any U.S. or non-U.S. court or authorized government entity. The SEC's Division of Corporation Finance originally published its views on the exemption in 1997 in Staff Legal Bulletin No. 3, and it revised this bulletin on October 20, 1999. In the staff's view, the following conditions must be met before an issuer may rely on the exemption:

– the securities must be issued in exchange for securities, claims or property interests (i.e., not for cash);

– a court or authorized government entity must approve the fairness of the terms and conditions of the exchange;

– the reviewing court or government entity must hold a hearing prior to approving the transaction; it must be "expressly authorized by law" to hold the hearing (without necessarily being required to do so); it must be advised prior to the hearing that the issuer will rely on the hearing as a basis for the Section 3(a)(10) exemption; and the court or government entity must find, before approving the transaction, that its terms and conditions are fair to those to whom securities will be issued; and

– the hearing must be open "without improper impediments" to everyone to whom securities would be issued in the proposed exchange, and such persons must receive adequate notice of the hearing.

The exemption can be useful in connection with acquisitions involving regulated companies such as banks or insurance companies. It is not available in connection with securities being

---

102. *See* SEC Release No. 33-646 (February 3, 1936).

issued as part of a plan of reorganization under Title 11 of the U.S. Bankruptcy Code.

Like Section 3(a)(9), Section 3(a)(10) is in substance a transaction exemption and was originally contained in Section 4 and moved to Section 3 as part of the 1934 amendments to the 1933 Act.

• • *Bankruptcy.* Originally, Section 3(a)(10) exempted securities issued in exchange for claims in a bankruptcy proceeding. It now specifically excepts from the exemption securities exchanged for claims in a case under Title 11 of the U.S. Bankruptcy Code. This is because the Bankruptcy Reform Act of 1978 set forth in Section 1145 its own exemptions for securities issued in a bankruptcy proceeding.

• • *Other Exemptions.* Certain other exemptions are contained in Section 3, including an exemption for securities issued by charitable organizations, intrastate offerings (elaborated upon in Rule 147), and certain small issues (Regulation A offerings and those made in compliance with Rule 504 of Regulation D).

The Future of the 1933 Act

After the first 25 years of experience with the 1933 Act, two observers could write that "[t]he controversies over fundamental concepts which were prevalent in the 30's are now almost forgotten, and such disagreements as now arise between the SEC and the industry are mostly over matters of detail and technique."[103] It is rare to find such complacency in the early years of the new millennium.

The last 25 years alone have seen developments that would have astounded the drafters of the 1933 and 1934 Acts. These developments, which have had a profound effect on the way securities are distributed, include the following:

- a great expansion of publicly held companies' periodic disclosure obligations under the 1934 Act;

---

103. T. A. Halleran & J. N. Calderwood, *Effect of Federal Regulation on Distribution of and Trading in Securities,* 28 Geo. Wash. L. Rev. 86, 118 (1959).

1933 ACT OVERVIEW

- progress in technology and communications that has revolutionized the dissemination and retrieval of information about reporting companies;
- drastic changes in the SEC's administration of registration procedures under the 1933 Act, particularly in regard to the "integrated disclosure system" and shelf registration;
- increased executive officer responsibility and accountability for their companies' disclosure and internal controls over financial reporting;
- unprecedented institutionalization and globalization of the securities markets; and
- radical changes in the techniques and economics of the distribution of securities.

In March 1996 the SEC published a report of the Task Force on Disclosure Simplification (Task Force Report), and in July 1996 it published a report of the Advisory Committee on the Capital Formation and Regulatory Processes. These reports provided part of the basis for the SEC's publication in July 1996 of its concept release on Securities Act Concepts and Their Effects on Capital Formation[104] and for the publication in November 1998 of the Aircraft Carrier Release[105] proposing far-reaching reforms. As noted above, the price of the Aircraft Carrier reforms was high, and adverse public comment led to the shelving of most of the proposals.

These reports and releases raised important questions for issuers, underwriters and investors. They evidenced an openness on the part of the SEC to reexamine such fundamental securities law concepts as the following:

- Whether current SEC procedures permit issuers to have predictable and reliable access to the U.S. public markets in a way that enables them to take advantage of market opportunities.

---

104. SEC Release No. 33-7314 (July 25, 1996).
105. SEC Release No. 33-7606A (November 13, 1998).

- To the extent that this is not the case, should the current system be abandoned or is it capable of improvement?
- Whether technology and the "information explosion" have made obsolete any attempt to regulate "offers," and whether there is any longer a basis for a distinction between written and oral communications.
- Whether, assuming that improvements could be made in the current system, public companies would still need to retain the "safety valve" of being able to do private and/or offshore transactions.
- Whether investors are seriously disadvantaged by having to make investment decisions without the benefit of actual or constructive prior receipt of an offering document.
- Whether the role of underwriters as "gatekeepers" has so diminished that their liabilities for issuers' disclosure deficiencies need to be readdressed. For example, are issuers acting in effect as their own gatekeepers and, if so, should they be required or encouraged to adopt "disclosure enhancements" such as management certifications or disclosure committees of outside directors?

Each of the authors of this book has questioned the continuing need for 1933 Act registration for reporting companies.[106] As radical as such a proposal may have appeared at one time, it may no longer be radical enough. Elimination of 1933 Act registration for reporting companies—or even mandated 1933 Act registration for all their transactions, as contemplated by the Advisory Committee's proposal for "company registration"— would still preserve too many restrictions for too many issuers and too many transactions. And simple changes to permit "on-demand registration," as proposed in the Aircraft Carrier Release, would accomplish even less.

---

106. E.g., Joseph McLaughlin, *1933 Act's Registration Provisions: Is Time Ripe for Repealing Them?*, Nat'l L.J., August 18, 1986.

The SEC should continue, of course, to require that mandated information be available to public investors, and, thanks in part to Sarbanes-Oxley, it will be reviewing every public company's periodic filings at least once every three years. SEC administrative sanctions and the private antifraud remedies should also continue to apply to information on which investors rely in making investment decisions. But in the midst of what a former SEC chairman has called the "age of information," it is simply unrealistic for the SEC to continue to base its regulatory approach on a "command-and-control" philosophy that regards information with fear and suspicion. The absurdities of the current system are amply highlighted by some of the "gun-jumping" episodes discussed in Chapter 3, including the consequences resulting from the publication in *Playboy* of an interview with Google's founders just prior to the pricing of the Google IPO. It is time for the SEC to use its new exemptive authority under the Improvement Act to relax the 1933 Act's stranglehold on the timing and content of securities-related information and the means by which it is distributed, and there were indications in late 2004 that the SEC might again be ready to consider more flexibility in permitted communications prior to and during securities offerings registered under the 1933 Act.[107]

---

107. *See* Joseph McLaughlin, *The SEC's Coming Regulatory Retreat*, wallstreetlawyer.com (January 1999). *See also* William J. Williams, Jr., *Securities Act Reform Proposals*, The Securities Reporter 22 (Spring 2004).

Chapter 2

SYNDICATE PROCEDURES AND UNDERWRITING DOCUMENTS

Apart from the registration statement, the basic documents governing underwritten offerings of securities are the following:

- the agreement among underwriters (AAU), which establishes the relationship among the managing underwriter, the co-managers (if any) and the other members of the underwriting syndicate, and governs the mechanics of the distribution;
- the underwriting agreement (or "purchase agreement," as it is frequently called), in which the underwriters commit to purchase the securities from the issuing corporation or the selling securityholders; and
- the selected dealers agreement, in which dealers that are not members of the syndicate (the selling group) agree to certain provisions relating to the distribution.

Each of the major investment banking firms has its own form of underwriting documents, but basic similarities have developed over the years, reflecting the "Street" practices that have evolved in the management of underwriting syndicates. In addition, most firms have a master agreement among underwriters (MAAU) that applies to all transactions that they lead manage and that is pre-signed by other firms likely to participate in their deals.

If the securities are underwritten by a small group of managers, there may be no AAU or only a short memorandum of understanding. In that case, the only underwriting documents will be the underwriting agreement and the selected dealer's agreement (if any). If the offering is being made on an agency or "best efforts" basis, then an agency agreement, rather than a purchase agreement, will be entered into between the issuer and the securities firm handling the offering.[1] Continuous medium-term note programs may also be handled on an agency basis (see Chapter 8).

If there are separate U.S. and international underwriting syndicates, the efforts of the two groups may be the subject of an Intersyndicate Agreement (see Chapter 9). For traditional syndicated fixed-price offerings, however, the structural framework for the distribution is provided by the AAU, the underwriting agreement and the selected dealer's agreement.

Underwriting Syndicates

The standard method of distributing securities has been through a syndicate of investment banking firms that engage in a marketing and "book building" process and then agree, on a firm commitment basis, to purchase the securities at a discount from the public offering price and resell them to investors. This traditional method of distribution has come under pressure from two directions.

In the weeks preceding the adoption of Rule 415 (discussed in Chapter 8), the investment banking community became concerned about the potential effect of shelf registrations on

---

1. If a best efforts underwriting is made on an "all-or-none" basis, or on any other basis that contemplates that payment is not to be made to the person on whose behalf the distribution is being made until some further event or contingency occurs, Rule 15c2-4 under the 1934 Act requires that the funds received by the broker-dealer from investors be placed in an escrow account with a bank. Rule 10b-9 under the 1934 Act prohibits the description of an offering as being on an "all-or-none" or similar basis unless the offering contemplates a prompt refund in the event that specified conditions are not met.

SYNDICATE PROCEDURES

traditional syndicate practices. Morgan Stanley & Co. Incorporated stated in a 1982 letter to the SEC that the proposed rule "could substantially impair the process by which most of the long-term private capital has been raised in this century—fixed-price public offerings by syndicates of securities firms."[2] The financial press joined in the controversy. An article in *The Wall Street Journal* commented:

> Now it appears that the gentlemanly art of syndication may be supplanted by a sort of financial roller derby in which gutsy Wall Street risk-takers bid for big blocks of new securities on a moment's notice. In lieu of the old mystique will be a sharpshooter's sense of timing and a heightened readiness to commit huge amounts of capital quickly.[3]

The frequent use of shelf registration statements, principally those covering debt securities of major issuers that finance on a regular basis, has resulted in an increase in "bought deals" in which a single firm or a small group of firms, in competition with other firms bidding for the securities, will take down an entire tranche for their own account without first attempting to market the securities to investors. As discussed in Chapters 8 and 9, shelf registration statements also make possible what amounts to "continuous offerings" by issuers, particularly of investment-grade debt securities.

The other source of pressure on the traditional model comes from those who believe that securities can be priced and allocated more fairly by taking advantage of electronic communication methods, for example, by conducting a "Dutch auction" in which pricing and allocation are removed from issuer and underwriter discretion. As discussed in Chapter 3, Google Inc. conducted its IPO in 2004 as a modified Dutch auction.

But traditional underwriting syndicates continue to be used to distribute initial public offerings (IPOs) and even many common stock and debt offerings by "seasoned" issuers.

---

2. Letter dated February 2, 1982. *See also* January 7, 1982 letter from Goldman, Sachs & Co.

3. T. Carrington, *Proposed SEC Rule on New Financings May Kill Gentlemanly Art of Syndication*, Wall St. J., Feb. 12, 1982, at 8.

- *Pre–1933 Act Procedures*

According to Professor Louis Loss, Jay Cooke is credited with first using the syndicate method of distribution in an 1870 underwriting of Pennsylvania Railroad bonds.[4] The most common method of distribution during the latter part of the 19th century was for issuers to offer their securities directly to potential investors and for underwriters to stand by with a commitment to purchase any securities that were not subscribed for as a result of the issuer's efforts. Syndicate practices evolved during the latter part of the 19th century and the early years of the 20th century as corporations sought to raise the vast amounts of capital that were required to build the country's railroads and to finance the growth of American industry.[5] By the turn of the century, as the banking houses gained prestige, it became common for them to purchase issues and to be responsible for their sale, rather than merely agreeing to purchase the securities should the issuer not succeed in marketing them itself.[6] The increase in the size of financings strained the risk-bearing capacity of the individual investment banking firms. Thus, it became necessary for firms to join together in syndicates to share the underwriting risk.

Some of the early syndicate arrangements grew out of friendships and close business relationships, as charmingly described by Judge Medina in his opinion in the government's post–World War II antitrust case against the major investment banking firms:

> When the opportunity arose in the year 1906 for Goldman, Sachs & Co. to underwrite the financing of United Cigar Manufacturers, it was unable to undertake the entire commitment alone, and could not get the additional funds which it needed to underwrite from commercial banks or other underwriters, as they would

---

4. 1 L. Loss & J. Seligman, *Securities Regulation* (rev. 3d ed. 1998), at 329, citing H. Larson, *Jay Cooke*, 314 (1936) [hereinafter Loss & Seligman].

5. *See* V. P. Corosso, *Investment Banking in America* (1970), at ch. 3, "The Development of the Syndicate to 1914."

6. *Id.* at 53.

not at that time underwrite this type of securities. Henry Goldman prevailed upon his friend Philip Lehman of Lehman Brothers to divert some of his capital from the commodity business and to take a share in the underwriting. The result was that the two firms, Goldman, Sachs & Co. and Lehman Brothers, became partners in the underwriting of the financing of United Cigar Manufacturers. When the opportunity arose in that same year for Goldman, Sachs & Co. to underwrite the financing of Sears, Roebuck & Co., it was perfectly natural for it again to turn to Lehman Brothers for assistance, and the two firms became partners in that enterprise. Thus it was through this oral arrangement between two friends, Henry Goldman and Philip Lehman, through this informal partnership, that Goldman, Sachs & Co. was able to obtain the capital which it needed to underwrite these two security issues in the year 1906. Without such capital, it would have been unable to enter the business of underwriting securities. The events which occurred in the year 1906 set the pattern for subsequent financings which Goldman, Sachs & Co. underwrote prior to the First World War. In the period from the year 1906 to the year 1917, although Goldman, Sachs & Co. occasionally underwrote financings with other partners, notably Kleinwort Sons & Co., merchant bankers of London, its principal partner was Lehman Brothers.[7]

Judge Medina went on to describe syndication practices during the period prior to World War I.[8] During this period, it was common for an investment banking firm, the "originating banker" or "house of issue," to purchase an entire issue of securities directly from the issuer and to immediately resell them at

---

7. Corrected opinion of Harold R. Medina in *United States v. Morgan* at 19–20 (filed February 4, 1954) [hereinafter Medina Opinion]. The original opinion is reported at 118 F. Supp. 621 (S.D.N.Y. 1953).

8. *Id.* at 25. Much of Judge Medina's description is based on the historical account of investment banking practices set forth in *National Association of Securities Dealers, Inc.*, 19 S.E.C. 424 (1945).

a "step-up" in price to a relatively small number of firms comprising the so-called "purchase syndicate," which would in effect sub-underwrite the risk. The originating banker would be one of the members and the manager of the purchase syndicate. As American businesses grew in size and required greater amounts of capital, it became customary to form a second group, more numerous than the purchase syndicate, to further share the risk. The purchase syndicate would sell the securities at a further step-up in price to this larger group known as the "banking syndicate." The originating banker and the other firms that were members of the purchase syndicate usually became members of the banking syndicate, and the originating banker acted as its manager.

In the period following World War I, it became customary to form an additional group called the "selling syndicate."[9] Initially, the members of a selling syndicate performed an underwriting function in that they assumed the obligation to purchase pro rata any securities that the members of the selling syndicate were unable to sell. This was known as the "unlimited liability selling syndicate." Subsequently, a second type of syndicate developed, known as the "limited liability selling syndicate," in which the obligation of each member was limited to the amount of its commitment. When it distributed that amount, it was relieved of further liability. Out of the limited liability selling syndicate evolved the "selling group," in which the financial liability of each member was restricted to selling or taking up the amount of securities for which it subscribed. This arrangement is similar to the way that selected dealers operate today.

- *Post–1933 Act Procedures*

The Revenue Act of 1932 imposed for the first time a tax on the transfer of bonds. It also increased the amount of the stock transfer tax. The amendments to the 1933 Act adopted in 1934 limited an underwriter's liability to the offering price of the securities underwritten by it. Thus, the old purchase and banking syndicates with successive sales at increasing prices disappeared as a matter of economic necessity. Instead, it became

---

9. Medina Opinion, *supra* note 7, at 30.

SYNDICATE PROCEDURES

the practice to have a single underwriting syndicate and for each underwriter to be in privity of contract with the issuer. Each would severally agree to purchase from the issuer a specified amount of securities.[10] This is the structure used today.

Where securities are distributed through an investment banking syndicate, one or more firms will be designated by the issuer as the managing or lead underwriter or underwriters. If there are co-managers, one will be designated as the book-running manager and its name will usually appear first on the left side of the prospectus and in the same position as on the tombstone advertisement. (Sometimes a firm will be willing to give up the honor of the left-hand position if it can run the books.)

Recently, issuers have been applying pressure to have multiple firms designated as "joint book-runners," where fees and "league table" credit are divided among them. Considerable imagination may be applied to this exercise. In one recent very large Rule 144A note offering involving three different maturities, one firm was designated as "Transaction Coordinator and Joint Book-Running Manager on All Series of Notes," while three different firms were designated as "Joint Book-Running Managers" for each maturity (with a "Co-Lead Manager" added for two of the maturities). In an SEC-registered deal, the staff comment letter may object to or request clarification of overly imaginative designations.

There generally is no written agreement between or among the managers as such other than the AAU. The prospectus is usually printed in the distinctive typeface (and sometimes ink color)[11] of the book-running manager, and that firm usually

---

10. *Id.* at 41. *See also* P. P. Gourrich, *Investment Banking Methods prior to and since the Securities Act of 1933*, 4 Law & Contemp. Probs. 44 (1937).

11. Certain colors of ink are strongly identified with certain underwriters. In a recent deal with three co-managers, great pains had been taken to avoid identifying which of the three firms was acting as the book-running manager, including the use of a generic typeface. When the printer delivered the offering documents to the underwriters, it was discovered that the printer had (on its own) used the ink color identified with the firm that was in fact the book-running manager. The other firms strongly objected, and the offering documents were destroyed and reprinted (in black ink).

selects counsel for the underwriters. As shelf registration has evolved, underwriters' counsel may in effect be named by the issuer. However selected, underwriters' counsel's responsibility is to represent the entire syndicate.

The size of underwriting syndicates grew in the years following World War II. Ford's 1956 IPO, valued at almost $660 million, was underwritten by a syndicate of 722 investment banking houses. This was the largest public stock offering up to that time, and the size of the syndicate set a record. Throughout the 1960s and 1970s, it was standard practice for an average-size common stock offering to be underwritten by a syndicate of between 50 and 100 underwriters. Since the early 1980s, syndicates have become smaller, and it has become increasingly common for a single investment banking firm to underwrite an entire issue without forming a syndicate or for the underwriting group to be limited to two or three firms that will appear on the cover page of the prospectus as managing underwriters. These are referred to as "one-handed" or "two- or three-handed" deals.

The Agreement Among Underwriters

The AAU is essentially a power of attorney authorizing the managing underwriter to enter into an underwriting agreement with the issuer or the selling securityholders and to otherwise manage the distribution of the securities. The AAU will be addressed to the co-managers, if there is more than one, unless the book-running manager's master AAU is relied on. The manager's authority is broad and sweeping, and it is considered bad form for a syndicate member to question the decisions of the firm running the deal.

Prior to the early 1970s, it was the practice for officers or partners of the various syndicate members to meet at the office of the book-running manager on the morning that the registration statement was scheduled to become effective for the purpose of reviewing and signing the AAU. Snowstorms and train delays could result in panic, because the price amendment to the registration statement could not be filed until all of the underwriters had signed the AAU. It had long been the practice for

SYNDICATE PROCEDURES

regional firms to provide the managing underwriter with powers of attorney authorizing it to sign the AAU on their behalf. The practice then evolved for all members of the syndicate, even those with a local office, to provide the book-running manager with written authority to sign the AAU on their behalf. Early morning meetings to sign the AAU were thus eliminated.

As underwriting procedures further evolved, many of the leading investment banking firms developed master AAUs, which were broadly structured to govern any and all future underwritten offerings managed by them. The firms distributed their master AAUs to the members of the underwriting community, and those that expected to participate in syndicates managed by them signed and returned to them their master AAUs. Thereafter, for a specific transaction, the managing underwriter would send by telex or otherwise to the prospective syndicate members an invitation containing information regarding the principal terms of the securities to be offered, the expected offering date and the amount of the underwriter's proposed underwriting participation. Acceptance of the invitation could be made orally or by telex, and the acceptance would remain in effect unless withdrawn in writing prior to a time specified in the invitation. In one or more subsequent communications, the underwriter would be informed of the amount of securities that would be allocated to it for purposes of resale, the initial public offering price, the interest or dividend rate in the case of fixed income securities, the conversion price of any convertible securities, the underwriting discount, the management fee, the selling concession and the reallowance. The master AAU would be deemed supplemented by these communications.

There have been recent efforts to standardize AAUs as among several investment banking firms.

- *Underwriters' Questionnaire*

A number of disclosure and other aspects of an underwritten offering depend on the accuracy of information concerning the underwriters. These include the existence of any material relationships between the issuer and any underwriter (Item 508(a) of Regulation S-K), any undisclosed arrangements to overallot or stabilize the securities being offered, any undisclosed discounts or commissions or other arrangements that might present NASD problems, any relationships (in the case of debt offerings) that might present problems under the Trust Indenture Act of 1939 and whether the underwriter intends to confirm any sales to discretionary accounts. These items are the subject of an Underwriters' Questionnaire that is customarily made part of a master AAU and that may be supplemented by the invitation. An underwriter is obligated to note any exceptions in writing prior to the time specified in the invitation.

- *Manager's Authority*

Whether a separate AAU is used for a particular transaction or the transaction is governed by a master AAU as supplemented by the communications constituting the invitation, the basic terms of the AAU will be the same. First, and most fundamentally, the AAU authorizes the managing underwriter to execute on behalf of the participating underwriters an underwriting agreement in such form as the managing underwriter determines. The AAU authorizes the manager to take such action as it deems necessary to carry out the underwriting agreement and the purchase, sale and distribution of the securities. The manager is authorized to overallot and to stabilize within limits and to exercise any overallotment option to the extent that it deems advisable. The manager should also be authorized to agree to any waiver or modification of any provision in the underwriting agreement (subject to limitations on the amount by which an underwriter's commitment may be increased). If, for example, a condition to the underwriters' obligations cannot be satisfied at the closing, then the managing underwriter should be in a position to waive the condition, whether or not it considers it to be material.

- *Price Maintenance*

The AAU will contain an agreement on the part of the underwriters that, when the securities are released for sale by the managing underwriter, they will offer to the public, in conformity with the terms of offering set forth in the prospectus, such of the securities as are not reserved for sale to selected dealers and others. Of the offering terms, the most important is the public offering price specified on the cover page of the prospectus.

SYNDICATE PROCEDURES

Most underwritten offerings are fixed price offerings in which the underwriters are obligated to offer the securities to the public at the specified public offering price, at least until such time as the managing underwriter otherwise determines. There is no legal requirement that offerings be conducted in this manner, but it would not be workable to have many firms trying to sell the securities at different prices.

In the environment of Rule 415, there have been instances of public offerings at varying prices based on the market or on terms negotiated with individual purchasers. In some cases, the underwriter has provided a volume discount to purchasers of a large amount of the securities being offered. If the offering is structured as a fixed price offering, however, the manager will control the price and will have the sole authority to lower the price if it finds it necessary to do so. Where there is a fixed price offering, the rules of the NASD prohibit discounts or selling concessions to nonmembers (see Chapter 6).

- *Retentions and "Pot" Sales*

As permitted by the AAU, the syndicate manager will determine the amount of securities that will be available for sale by each of the underwriters. It has absolute discretion in this respect. It will reserve some of the securities for sale to institutional investors that prefer to deal directly with the syndicate manager, rather than with individual underwriters or dealers, and a portion for sale to selected dealers that are not members of the underwriting syndicate. These securities are held in a syndicate account known as the "pot." There are various methods of allocating or directing sales credits on pot orders. The method chosen will reflect the syndicate manager's judgment about what it takes, given the circumstances of the offering, to create the optimum combination of cooperation and competition among the co-managers and underwriters.[12] In recent years, issuers have been exercising a greater influence on the allocation of sales credits, by insisting on the inclusion in the syndicate of small and more specialized firms as well as a tying of sales credits to

---

12. *See* Securities Industry Association, *Capital Markets Handbook* 168–73 (John C. Burch, Jr. and Bruce S. Foerster eds., 5th ed. 2004).

actual sales (not orders). However sales credits are allocated, syndicate members will try to convince the issuer that it was principally through their efforts that the offering was a success, always with a view to getting "the books" on the next deal.

The amount of securities allotted to any particular underwriter for sale to its customers will depend on its distribution power. AAUs speak in terms of securities "retained" by an underwriter for direct sale and those "reserved" for sale to selected dealers and others. In the actual operation of a syndicate, a substantial portion of the underwritten securities will be allocated according to the expectations or tacit understandings of the participating firms, while the remainder will be allocated on the basis of customer orders. In the real world, the managers will sell most of the issue.

As discussed below, underwriters and dealers may receive selling credit for securities purchased by institutions out of the pot to the extent that the institutions designate them for that purpose.

- *Proposed Restriction on First-Day Market Orders in IPOs*

In response to reports of investors' losses during the Internet Bubble, when they entered market orders for IPO stocks on the first day of trading only to see them filled at prices many times in excess of the initial public offering price, the NYSE/NASD IPO Advisory Committee recommended that market orders be prohibited for the first trading day following the IPO. It cautioned that limit orders far above the initial public offering price might "in effect amount to market orders," and it recommended that broker-dealers pay special attention in this regard to their "know your customer" and suitability obligations.[13]

The NASD proposed such a ban in November 2003.[14]

- *Shares Returned to Underwriters*

The NASD also proposed in November 2003 that the AAU establish specific procedures for the disposition of any shares

---

13. NYSE/NASD IPO Advisory Committee, *Report and Recommendations* 6 (May 2003).
14. NASD Notice to Members 03-76.

returned by a customer to any member of the syndicate after secondary market trading commences. The returned shares would have to be allotted to the syndicate's existing short position (thus reducing the amount of the "Green Shoe" option that can be exercised) or, if the market price is greater than the IPO price, sold in the open market. Any profit on sales of shares in the open market must be returned to the issuer. If the market price is less than the IPO price, the syndicate member may either sell the shares or retain them in an investment account.[15]

The NASD states that the new procedures are intended to ensure that reneged IPO allocations are not used to benefit an underwriter's favored clients.

- *Overallotment and Stabilization Authority*

The AAU will authorize the managing underwriter to overallot for the account of the syndicate—that is, to create a syndicate short position by accepting orders for more securities than are to be sold. It will authorize the manager to effect stabilizing bids and purchases for the account of the syndicate (see Chapter 4). Overallotments and stabilizing purchases are made for the accounts of the underwriters as nearly as practicable in proportion to their respective underwriting commitments. The AAU will provide that at the close of business on any day an underwriter's net commitment, either for long or short account, resulting from overallotments and stabilizing purchases may not exceed a specified percentage, usually 15% or 20%, of its underwriting commitment.

Overallotments are made to provide for purchasers who renege on their commitments but, more importantly, to create buying power in the after-market. This has hardly been a secret to the SEC. A 1943 opinion of the director of the SEC's Trading and Exchange Division "start[ed] with the premise that a syndicate overallotment is customarily made for the purpose of facilitating the orderly distribution of the offered securities by creating buying power which can be used for the purpose of supporting the market price."[16]

---

15. NASD Notice to Members 03-76.
16. SEC Release No. 34-3506 (November 16, 1943).

Overallotments are in effect short sales, and they must be covered sooner or later. They may be covered through stabilization while the distribution is still in process. After completion of the distribution, the syndicate short position may also be covered through open market purchases. Covering through stabilization or open market purchases is discussed in Chapter 4. As discussed below in connection with the underwriting agreement, the syndicate short position may also be covered through the exercise of the "Green Shoe" or overallotment option, which is granted to the underwriters by the issuer or the selling securityholders allowing them to purchase additional securities during a specified period (usually 30 days) after the offering.

- *Control of the Syndicate*

The manager will monitor closely the performance of the syndicate members in selling the securities allocated to them. Indeed, the 1943 SEC staff opinion referred to earlier stated that the manager has an obligation to be in a position to know whether the underwriters and selling group members have securities remaining unsold and to require them to make these available to permit the covering of the syndicate short position.

The authors do not believe that the SEC opinion means that unsold securities must be used to cover the syndicate short position, but the AAU will ordinarily require each underwriter to advise the manager of the amount of securities remaining unsold. The AAU will also require the underwriter to release to the manager on its request all or any part of such unsold securities.

- *Trading Restrictions*

In 1943, prior to the adoption of Rule 10b-6 (since superseded by Regulation M, as discussed in Chapter 4), the director of the SEC's Trading and Exchange Division expressed the opinion that an underwriter may not trade in securities of a class that are the subject of a distribution, through a trading department or otherwise, so long as the syndicate agreement remains in effect.[17] It then became the practice to include trading restrictions in AAUs. These restrictions are discussed in Chapter 4.

---

17. SEC Release No. 34-3505 (November 16, 1943).

- *Penalty Bids*

A failure to place IPO securities with bona fide investors, followed by "flipping" or resales into the syndicate bid, is not a new problem. AAUs have traditionally provided that, in recognition of the importance of distributing IPO securities to bona fide investors, if any securities sold by an underwriter are purchased by the syndicate in the open market or otherwise during the distribution period, that underwriter must repurchase the securities at the syndicate's cost, or its account will be charged with an amount not in excess of the concession to selected dealers. The theory is that under these circumstances the underwriter has not earned the selling concession.

This so-called "penalty" clause has sometimes been difficult to enforce. The difficulty increased with the use of DTC to make deliveries and to settle syndicate accounts. Some underwriting firms resorted to physical delivery in order to enhance their ability to police the penalty clause. Since physical delivery is hardly consistent with the desire of the SEC and other regulators to promote the use of securities depositories, DTC worked with the industry to develop its automated "IPO Tracking System." This system allows managing underwriters to track deliveries of IPO securities by syndicate members to identify securities sold back during the underwriting stabilization period.

A syndicate bid pursuant to the penalty clause of an AAU is known as a "penalty bid." As discussed in Chapter 4, such bids are now the subject of disclosure and recordkeeping obligations.

Following the Internet Bubble, there were allegations that underwriters had abused the penalty bid to the disadvantage of retail investors. The NYSE/NASD IPO Advisory Committee stated that individual syndicate members—even where penalty bids were not imposed pursuant to the AAU—had "apparently . . . imposed penalties on individual brokers in connection with flipping by the broker's small retail customers, while not imposing penalties in connection with flipping by other categories of IPO participants [e.g., institutions]."[18] It recommended that the

---

18. Advisory Committee, *supra* note 13, at 7.

SEC and the SROs address this "discrimination" and endorsed the NASD's proposed Rule 2712(d), which would prohibit a member firm from imposing a penalty on a salesperson "unless the managing underwriter has assessed a penalty bid on the member." Firms would also be required to keep records of any "penalty or disincentive" assessed on salespersons in connection with a penalty bid.[19]

Neither the NYSE/NASD committee nor the NASD's proposed Rule 2712(d) takes issue with the syndicate manager's imposition of a penalty bid. Rather, the allegation appears to be that individual firms will create incentives for their retail brokers to discourage retail customers from reselling IPO shares while not creating such incentives in the case of sales by institutional customers. Presumably, the committee and the NASD believe that individual firms are willing to bear the cost of the reversed sales credits in the case of flipping by institutions but not in the case of flipping by retail (or at least "small retail") customers. The effect of the proposed NASD rule is that the individual firm will only be able to penalize the individual broker when, as and if the syndicate manager imposes a penalty on the individual firm.

It has been reported that there has been some recent slippage from what had been long-standing "industry-wide agreement that the lead manager must also penalize itself and assess and allocate penalties for all institutional pot shares" that are repurchased.[20]

- *Components of the Spread*

There are three components of the underwriting spread, that is, the gross spread between the initial public offering price and the price paid by the underwriters for the securities being underwritten. These are the management component and the selling component, which are specified in the AAU or in the invitation to underwriters, and the remainder, which is called the underwriting component. Approximately 20% of the spread is paid by the syndicate members to the managing underwriter as compensation for its services in the management of the distribution.

---

19. NASD Notice to Members 02-55 (August 2002).
20. *Capital Markets Handbook, supra* note 12, at 201.

SYNDICATE PROCEDURES 81

It is paid out of the spread, and not by the issuer or selling securityholders, to avoid a claim that the manager had received a benefit not shared by all other underwriters similarly situated, thus precluding it from having the benefit of the hold-down provision in Section 11(e) of the 1933 Act (see Chapter 5). Neither the AAU nor the invitation telex customarily specifies how the management fee is to be split among the co-managers. The allocation of this fee is often a matter of intense dispute among the managing underwriters.

The selling portion of the spread, known as the "selling concession," is the amount paid to dealers for actually selling the securities. As a rule of thumb, the selling concession will be 60% of the gross spread, although the amount may vary depending on how difficult it is to sell the securities. This amount is retained by an underwriter in respect of securities that it actually sells to its own customers. Institutions that purchase securities directly from the syndicate will designate the underwriters and other dealers that are to receive selling concession credit for the securities that they purchase. The term used in this context is "designated orders."

Money managers and institutions designate dealers to receive credit for securities purchased in underwritten offerings in order to compensate them for providing research services. The rules of the NASD governing this practice are discussed in Chapter 6. Some syndicate managers complain that institutions misuse designated orders. They will enter an order solely for the purpose of providing a selling concession to a dealer to whom they are obligated and will immediately resell the securities, thereby disrupting the distribution.

Dealers who purchase securities at the public offering price less the selling concession may resell them to other dealers at the public offering price less a so-called "reallowance," perhaps 25% of the selling concession (or as much as 50% on some debt transactions). Underwriters may do the same with respect to their retained securities. Some AAUs permit resales to reallowance dealers only with the specific consent of the manager, thus permitting the manager to retain tighter control of the distribution process.

The remaining portion of the spread, roughly 20% depending on the size of the selling concession, theoretically is the compensation that the underwriters earn for committing their capital and taking an underwriting risk. Syndicate expenses, however, are paid out of this portion of the spread. Thus, the fees and expenses of underwriters' counsel, the cost of the tombstone advertisement, the managers' road show expenses and the like must be paid before an underwriter will be compensated for its underwriting risk. In some cases, the lion's share of the underwriting portion of the spread will go to the payment of expenses. In other cases, expenses may exceed that portion of the spread.

- *Payment and Delivery*

The AAU provides that payment for the securities must be made on such date as the manager specifies, usually the morning of the closing date. The closing usually is scheduled for the third or fourth business day after the date of the initial public offering to correspond to the normal settlement period between dealers and their customers. The amount that each underwriter agrees to pay to the manager is the public offering price less the selling concession, not the public offering price less the underwriting discount. The effect of this is that an underwriter will not receive its share of the underwriting portion of the spread until final settlement of its account. This makes it unnecessary, in most cases, for the manager to call on the underwriters to pay their share of the syndicate expenses. These expenses will simply be deducted from the final payment.

The AAU provides that securities retained by an underwriter for direct sale will be delivered to it as soon as practicable after receipt of the securities at the closing. Settlement and delivery will ordinarily be effected through the facilities of DTC.

- *Authority to Borrow*

The AAU authorizes the manager to advance its own funds for the accounts of the underwriters, charging current interest rates, or to arrange loans for their account, as the manager deems necessary or advisable for the purchase, carrying, sale and distribution of the securities. The manager is authorized to execute any notes or other instruments required in connection therewith and, in this connection, to hold or pledge the securities that the underwriters have agreed to purchase.

- *NASD Provisions*

To be a member of an underwriting syndicate, a securities firm must represent in the AAU that it is a member in good standing of the NASD. Alternatively, it must represent in the AAU that it is a foreign dealer ineligible for such membership (i.e., because it is not registered with the SEC as a broker-dealer) and agree to make no sales within the United States (except that it may participate in syndicate sales to selected dealers and others).

U.S. underwriters customarily agree in the AAU to comply with the NASD's Conduct Rules, including the free-riding and withholding interpretation and the *Papilsky* rules discussed in Chapter 6. Foreign underwriters must agree in the AAU to comply with the free-riding and withholding interpretation in making sales outside the United States and also with the *Papilsky* rules insofar as they apply to foreign broker-dealers.

In turn, the managing underwriter agrees to make the required NASD filings, for example, under the Corporate Financing Rule discussed in Chapter 6.

In early 2003, the Federal Reserve Board issued an interpretation of its Regulation K to the effect that foreign banks subject to the U.S. Bank Holding Company Act (i.e., those foreign banks with a U.S. commercial banking presence) could not participate in underwriting securities that are distributed in the United States unless they had a U.S. affiliate that was authorized to underwrite securities in the United States.[21] The interpretation appears to be limited to the underwriting of securities that are distributed in the United States. It would not prevent a covered bank from acting as an underwriter in a global offering where the securities underwritten by the bank are actually distributed outside the United States, including securities that the bank itself sells outside the United States.

- *Claims Against Underwriters*

The AAU contains a provision relating to claims against any underwriter arising out of alleged misstatements or omissions in the registration statement or prospectus or any act or omission

---

21. Codified at 12 C.F.R. §211.605 (February 7, 2003).

by the manager or by the underwriters in connection with or in preparing for the offering. This provision will stipulate that any such claims may be settled by the manager, usually with the approval of a majority in interest of the underwriters, and that each underwriter will pay its proportionate share (based on its underwriting commitment) of all expenses, including legal fees, incurred in investigating and defending against the claim as well as its proportionate share of the aggregate liability incurred by all underwriters with respect to the claim. The manager is authorized to retain counsel for the underwriters, but any underwriter may retain separate counsel at its own expense.

One of the primary reasons for this provision is that litigation based on alleged misstatements or omissions in a registration statement or prospectus will often be brought against the manager without naming the entire underwriting syndicate. This provision in the AAU provides in effect that all of the underwriters will share in the expenses and liabilities even if they are not actually named in the complaint.

The AAU also customarily contains a provision exculpating the manager, except for obligations expressly assumed or for the manager's lack of good faith, from any liability to the underwriters for misstatements or omissions in the prospectus or any other matter in connection with the underwriting. The exculpation provision is sometimes qualified by reference to limitations imposed by the 1933 Act.

The AAU also provides that each underwriter will indemnify each other underwriter to the same extent as each underwriter agrees in the underwriting agreement to indemnify the issuer or selling securityholder. As discussed below, this indemnity is limited to information furnished by the underwriter for use in the prospectus. Accordingly, each underwriter also agrees to indemnify its fellow underwriters for any false statements or omissions in such information.

- *Miscellaneous Provisions*

The AAU will contain a number of representations by members of the underwriting syndicate, such as their familiarity with the prospectus delivery requirements of the securities laws and their compliance with the net capital rule. It will authorize the manager to increase the underwriters' commitments to the limited extent provided in the underwriting agreement in the event of default by one or more of the underwriters.

The AAU will also outline the mechanism for the settlement of syndicate accounts. In this connection, Rule 11880 of the NASD's Uniform Practice Code requires that the syndicate manager finally settle the syndicate account within 90 days of the closing date and provide each underwriter with an itemized statement of syndicate expenses.[22]

- *Termination of Price and Other Restrictions*

The manager may terminate at any time by notice to the underwriters any or all of the provisions in the AAU regarding the price at which the securities may be sold, the time that the penalty clause will remain in operation, the manager's authorization to stabilize and overallot, and applicable trading restrictions. In practice, the manager will usually terminate price and trading restrictions within hours after the commencement of the offering. It is unusual, except in a weak market, for these restrictions to continue in effect for more than a few days.

The AAU also provides that the foregoing provisions will automatically terminate at a specified time (perhaps between 30 and 45 days) after the commencement of the offering. One of the principal reasons for specifying an automatic termination date is to avoid an allegation that the price maintenance provisions of the AAU constitute a violation of the Sherman Act. This issue was considered by the SEC in reviewing an NASD disciplinary proceeding decision that found that certain underwriters and dealers had violated the NASD's *Rules of Fair Practice* when they failed to comply with the price maintenance agreement in a 1939 underwriting of $38 million of first mortgage bonds of Public Service Company of Indiana managed by Halsey, Stuart & Co., Inc.[23] At the close of the hearing before the hearing examiner,

---

22. On the subject of syndicate expenses, *see Capital Markets Handbook, supra* note 12, at 203–05.

23. *National Association of Securities Dealers, Inc.*, 19 S.E.C. 424 (1945).

the Antitrust Division of the Department of Justice intervened and filed a brief attacking the price maintenance, penalty, stabilization, uniform concession and reallowance, and other clauses of the AAU as unlawful *per se* under the Sherman Act. The same position was taken by counsel for the Trading and Exchange Division of the SEC. In effect, this constituted an antitrust attack on the fixed price method of distributing securities.

The SEC found on technical grounds that the NASD did not have power to impose sanctions in this instance, but nevertheless went on to discuss the antitrust implications of fixed-price offerings. The SEC observed that "because of the nature of the securities markets, price maintenance as to one security during a relatively short period of distribution may be distinguished from schemes affecting the long-term marketing of consumers' goods."[24] It concluded that agreements containing provisions for a fixed-offering price, price maintenance, and stabilization are not *per se* unlawful, but, like many other contracts, may be entered into and performed under circumstances that amount to an unlawful suppression of competition. The SEC stated that among the factors to be taken into account in determining the lawfulness of this type of distribution are "the size of the group in relation to the size of the issue, the suppression of competition in bidding or negotiating for the business, and the duration of a syndicate dictated by the manager and major underwriters."[25] Judge Medina discussed this case at length in his opinion in the investment banking antitrust case, and in general agreed with the SEC's conclusions.[26]

The Underwriting Agreement

The underwriting agreement, or purchase agreement, is the document under which the underwriters commit to purchase at a specified price, or at a price to be determined, the securities that are the subject of the underwriting. In addition to the basic

---

24. *Id.* at 451.
25. *Id.* at 464.
26. Medina Opinion, *supra* note 7, at 149.

purchase and sale commitment, the underwriting agreement contains representations and warranties, covenants, conditions, indemnification provisions, and other terms governing the relationship between the issuer or the selling securityholders and the underwriters.

- *Several Commitments*

It is important to note that U.S. underwriting commitments are always several, and not joint and several, when they relate to securities other than municipal bonds. Where there is a syndicate, a schedule to the underwriting agreement will set forth the specific number of shares or principal amount of debt securities that each underwriter has committed to purchase. Each underwriter also will agree to purchase its proportionate share of any securities to be purchased pursuant to the exercise of the overallotment option.

One reason why underwriting commitments are several is to limit the amount of the charge against the underwriters' net capital. Another important reason is to ensure the availability of the hold-down provision in Section 11(e) of the 1933 Act, which limits an underwriter's liability to the total price at which the securities underwritten by it and distributed to the public are offered to the public. If all underwriters were jointly liable for the full underwritten amount, the hold-down provision would not be effective. To limit the liability of underwriters, joint and several commitments were abandoned after the hold-down provision was enacted in 1934.[27] Joint commitments are still used in underwriting municipal bonds, which are not subject to the 1933 Act.

- *Rule 430A*

The form of the underwriting agreement depends on whether the issuer and the managing underwriter have elected to rely upon Rule 430A under the 1933 Act. As discussed in Chapter 3, Rule 430A permits a registration statement that covers a cash securities offering to become effective without pricing and related information, provided that the omitted information is

---

27. *Id.* at 42.

included in a supplemented prospectus filed under Rule 424(b).[28] Pursuant to an undertaking required by Item 512(i) of Regulation S-K, the omitted information when filed will be deemed to be part of the registration statement as of the time of effectiveness. This is to ensure that the omitted information becomes subject to the liabilities imposed by Section 11.

- *Timing and Risk*

In a firm commitment underwriting, at least one not involving shelf-registered securities, the underwriting agreement is not entered into until after the final amendment to the registration statement is filed (or immediately before it is filed in the case of offerings that do not rely on Rule 430A). While some underwriters will enter into agreements in principle or letters of intent early in the registration process, these are not ordinarily intended to be binding agreements, except to the extent that they provide for the reimbursement of underwriters' expenses if the transaction does not go forward. Thus, the underwriters are not committed until the very last minute. By this time, except in the case of a bought deal taken off the shelf, they will have completed their marketing efforts and will have reasonable assurances that they will be able to sell the securities to be underwritten and to build an acceptable short position. If, at the time of pricing, the underwriters are not comfortable that all of the securities can be sold, the size of the transaction may be cut back, the offering price may be reduced to a level more consistent with indications in the "book" or the offering may be postponed. Although underwriters do run risks and commit their capital, the risk is tempered by the timing of their final commitment and their knowledge of how well the deal has been accepted in the marketplace (the "size of the book") at the time that they do commit.

- *"Green Shoe" Option*

As noted above, the underwriters may overallot or sell more securities to their customers than they have the right to purchase

---

28. Rule 430A procedures provide the same benefits as so-called "formula pricing," which was used frequently prior to the adoption of the rule.

SYNDICATE PROCEDURES

under the underwriting agreement. Overallotments are short sales and must be covered. Rather than take the risk of having to cover in the open market or through stabilization transactions, underwriters will often bargain with the issuer or the selling shareholders for an option to purchase additional securities during a specified period (usually 30 days) after the offering.

An option of this kind is generically referred to as the "overallotment option" but more colorfully as the "Green Shoe" option, or simply "the shoe." It is so named because it was first used in connection with a 1963 secondary offering of shares of common stock of The Green Shoe Manufacturing Company, the Boston-based manufacturer of Stride Rite shoes (not green shoes for leprechauns as some have supposed). The original filing in that offering had not specified the purpose of the option. In its letter of comment, the SEC staff requested the inclusion in the prospectus of a statement of the conditions under which the option could be exercised. The final prospectus contained the statement, "It is the intention of the Underwriters to exercise this option only for the purpose of covering any short position which may be incurred in the initial distribution."

The term "overallotment option" implies that the option will be used to cover overallotments, and it is common for both underwriting agreements and prospectuses to describe the option as being intended for that purpose. There is no apparent reason why the option should be so limited, however, and it is believed that there have been several recent offerings where the purpose of the option was not so limited.

There is also no legal requirement that overallotments be limited to a certain percentage of the offering. The AAU may set a percentage limit on the manager's authority to overallot, but this is solely for the purpose of limiting the risk to the members of the syndicate. The Green Shoe option is designed to protect the underwriters against loss if they overallot and the price of the securities rises in the aftermarket. Rather than purchasing securities in the open market to cover overallotments, the managing underwriter can exercise the Green Shoe option and cover overallotments by purchasing from the issuer or the selling securityholders additional securities at the original public offering price less the underwriting discount. The size of the Green Shoe option, however, is limited by the rules of the NASD to 15% of the firm commitment securities.[29] Any overallotments in excess of the amount of the Green Shoe option are "naked shorts."

In a successful deal, the underwriters may decide to exercise the Green Shoe option immediately. As noted above, the option must usually be exercised within 30 days. It is not clear whether there is or why there should be a legal reason to limit the option to 30 days. Some securities lawyers believe the SEC would object to a longer option as tending to violate the spirit of Section 6(a) of the 1933 Act, which limits the registration process to those securities "proposed to be offered." Under that theory, a longer option would cause the transaction to be recharacterized as one that should be conducted under the shelf registration rules discussed in Chapter 8.

In recent years, the practice has been to overallot in an amount that substantially exceeds the Green Shoe option. The reason for this is to build a large short position that can be used to purchase securities sold into the syndicate bid by "flippers," that is, hedge funds and other speculators who buy in underwritings not as investors but to turn a quick profit. This is a serious and ever-present problem. To permit larger short positions, the contractual limitation on net commitments has tended to increase, and whatever limitation is imposed by the AAU has been construed by syndicate managers to be a percentage of the amount of securities offered plus the amount of the overallotment option.

If underwriters overallot in excess of the Green Shoe option, they do so expecting to repurchase the excess securities in the open market, with all of the risk that that entails. One issuer, Borden Chemicals and Plastics Limited Partnership, did manage in connection with a 1987 offering to persuade the SEC staff that it should be permitted to register additional securities under a separate registration statement for the purpose of issuing additional securities to the underwriters to enable them to cover excess overallotments. The offering came just after the October 1987 sell-off in the equity markets, and it is not believed

---

29. NASD Conduct Rule 2710(c)(6)(B)(ix).

SYNDICATE PROCEDURES 91

that other issuers have been permitted to make use of a similar "extra-wide" shoe.

The securities covered by the Green Shoe option must, of course, be registered under the 1933 Act in order for the underwriters to be able to use them to cover their overallotments. It is therefore customary for the registration statement for the offering to include the full amount of the shoe. If the option is not exercised in full, the remaining securities can be deregistered by a post-effective amendment, and nothing is lost except the SEC registration fee for those securities.

As discussed in Chapter 4, Item 508(l) of Regulation S-K requires a description in the prospectus of any transaction that an underwriter intends to conduct during the offering that stabilizes, maintains or otherwise affects the market price of the offered securities. The item specifically calls for information on stabilizing transactions, syndicate short covering transactions and penalty bids.

- *Representations and Warranties*

    Underwriting agreements traditionally contain representations and warranties running from the issuer (and in some cases the selling securityholders) to the several underwriters. Unlike representations and warranties contained in agreements relating to the sale of a business, those contained in underwriting agreements have never, to the knowledge of the authors, been the subject of litigation or otherwise enforced. They are nevertheless customary and in some cases become the subject of fierce negotiations. As discussed in Chapter 5, the real importance of representations and warranties is that they cause the issuer, the managing underwriter, and their counsel to focus on potential problem areas. The negotiation of representations and warranties can be viewed as a part of the due diligence process.

    A basic representation that is included in all underwriting agreements for SEC-registered public offerings is the issuer's representation to the effect that, at the time it becomes effective, the registration statement will comply in all material respects with the requirements of the 1933 Act and the regulations thereunder and will not contain an untrue statement of a material fact or omit to state a material fact required to be stated therein or necessary to make the statements therein not misleading and that, at the time the registration statement becomes effective and at the time of closing, the prospectus will not include an untrue statement of a material fact or omit to state a material fact necessary in order to make the statements therein, in the light of the circumstances under which they were made, not misleading. This representation tracks the language of Section 11 of the 1933 Act with respect to the registration statement and the language of Section 12(a)(2) with respect to the prospectus. The representation traditionally will carve out misstatements or omissions made in reliance on information furnished to the issuer by the underwriters. For the most part, this is a meaningless exception since the underwriters take responsibility for very little information included in the registration statement.[30] The issuer's representation with respect to the registration statement and prospectus in effect embraces all of the subsequent representations customarily found in underwriting agreements.

If the registration statement incorporates by reference documents filed with the SEC under the 1934 Act, the underwriting agreement will contain a representation with respect to the adequacy and accuracy of these documents. Other representations that frequently are included in underwriting agreements are those that go to the independence of the accountants certifying the financial statements, the fair presentation in the financial statements of the issuer's financial position and results of operations and the preparation of the financial statements in accordance with GAAP. Another representation will relate to the absence of any material adverse change in the condition, financial or otherwise, or in the earnings, business affairs or business prospects[31] of the issuer and its subsidiaries considered

---

30. The underwriters will specify in a so-called "blood letter" delivered prior to the closing that they have provided only certain information relating to their intention to reoffer the securities, to stabilize the price of certain securities and to allocate the underwriting discount in a specified manner. All other information in the registration statement is the responsibility of the issuer, including information reflected in the underwriting agreement itself (for which the issuer can justifiably be expected to take responsibility, since it is a party to that agreement).

31. Issuers often object to representing as to their "business affairs or business prospects" or, alternatively, to the absence of any development

as a whole since the respective dates as of which information is given in the registration statement, as well as the absence since those dates of any material transactions entered into by the issuer other than in the ordinary course of business.

Other representations of a legal nature are frequently included in underwriting agreements, such as those that relate to the due incorporation and good standing of the issuer and its principal subsidiaries, their qualification as foreign corporations in the states in which this is required, the due authorization of the securities, compliance with material contracts, the filing of all required exhibits and the absence of material lawsuits or governmental proceedings other than those disclosed in the registration statement.

Additional representations may be included depending on the nature of the issuer's business. For example, in the case of a high technology company, it may be appropriate to include a representation with respect to its patents. In the first major class action brought under Section 11, a claim was made that the issuer had failed to disclose that it had been placed on notice that it was allegedly infringing the patent of a competitor.[32] In preparing the registration statement, the issuer had simply forgotten that it had received a letter making this claim. If a representation had been included in the underwriting agreement to the effect that the issuer had not received any notices of patent infringement, then it might have focused upon the problem, and some reference to the claim might have been made in the prospectus.

New representations will be added from time to time to the leading investment banking firms' standard forms of underwriting agreements as a result of legal developments. For example, it will undoubtedly become standard for issuers to represent that they have paid their "accounting support fees" to the PCAOB.

---

involving a "prospective material change" in various specified areas. As discussed in Chapter 5, the process of negotiating acceptable wording can be an important part of due diligence.

32. *Cherner v. Transitron Electronic Corp.*, 201 F. Supp. 934 (D. Mass. 1962).

As noted below under "Closing Conditions" and "Termination," the issuer will be expected to update its representations as of the closing date.

- *Representations by Selling Securityholders*

Where there are selling securityholders, each of them must make special representations that are not joined in by the issuer. Principally, these representations relate to each seller's authority to enter into the underwriting agreement and its good title to the securities being sold. The most important of these representations is that each of the underwriters will receive good and marketable title to the securities purchased by it, free and clear of any pledge, lien, encumbrance, claim or equity.

Where there are many selling securityholders, it is customary, for administrative purposes, for each of them to enter into a custody agreement and power of attorney with one of the principal selling securityholders or some other satisfactory person. The attorney-in-fact signs the underwriting agreement on behalf of all the sellers. The custodian delivers the stock certificates at the closing. The underwriting agreement will contain representations by the sellers to the effect that these arrangements have been entered into.

These powers of attorney are drafted in such a way that it can be argued that they survive the death of the seller. They purport to be powers "coupled with an interest." Whether they will indeed survive has not been tested.

- *Delayed Delivery Contracts*

Where non-convertible debt securities or preferred shares are being underwritten, provision has sometimes been made for the underwriters to satisfy their commitments by delivering to the issuer at the closing delayed delivery contracts entered into by institutional investors. Under a delayed delivery contract, the investor agrees to purchase the securities at the public offering price on a specified date subsequent to the closing. The reason for permitting a portion of the securities to be issued on a delayed basis is to facilitate their marketing by accommodating institutions that wish to invest but do not expect to have funds available for investment until some months in the future (e.g., in the next calendar or fiscal year). It may also be the case that the issuer does not immediately need all of the proceeds of the offering.

Delayed delivery contracts have been used only rarely in the recent past. Where they are used, however, the issuer authorizes the underwriters to solicit offers by institutions to enter into delayed delivery contracts. There is a contractual limit on the amount of securities that can be covered by such contracts, and each contract must be for a specified minimum amount. Each institution must be approved by the issuer. The issuer pays the underwriters a commission, equal to the spread, with respect to delayed delivery contracts delivered at the closing.

The contracts are not subject to any conditions, except that the purchase of the securities not be prohibited under the laws of the jurisdiction to which the purchaser is subject and that the sale of the securities to be purchased by the underwriters have been consummated. The principal amount of securities to be purchased by the underwriters is reduced by the principal amount of securities covered by the delayed delivery contracts. Once the contracts have been delivered, the underwriters have no responsibility in respect of their validity or performance.

In 1970, questions were raised by the SEC and the staff of the Federal Reserve Board as to whether the solicitation of delayed delivery contracts by underwriters constituted an arrangement of credit in violation of Regulation T. This came as a total surprise to the securities bar. A number of New York City law firms participated in the preparation of a written submission to the Federal Reserve Board to the effect that an issuer should not be viewed as extending credit to an institution when it enters into a delayed delivery contract. The Board responded[33] to the effect that, while in this type of transaction the issuer may be regarded as extending credit to the institutional purchaser at the time of closing when the obligations of both become fixed, Regulation T as then constituted provided that if a security when purchased is an unissued security, the time required for payment

---

33. 1971 Fed. Res. Bull. 127; 12 C.F.R. §220.123 ¶5862.

was seven days after the date on which the security is made available by the issuer for delivery to the purchaser. The Board concluded that non-convertible debt and preferred stock subject to delayed delivery contracts should not be regarded as having been issued until delivered to institutional purchasers pursuant to the contracts.

Regulation T no longer prohibits most "arranging" of credit by a broker-dealer, but the Federal Reserve Board's position on delayed delivery contracts is instructive for purposes of Section 11(d)(1) of the 1934 Act. Section 11(d)(1) prohibits a broker-dealer from extending or arranging credit "on" a security that was part of a new issue in the distribution of which the broker-dealer participated within the past 30 days. Section 11(d)(1) has no application, however, unless the credit is secured by the new issue. If the security that is the subject of a delayed delivery contract is an "unissued" security, the broker-dealer can hardly be said to be extending or arranging credit that is secured by that security.[34]

- *Proposed Enhancement of Issuer's Role in Pricing IPOs*

During the Internet Bubble, the immediate after-market for many IPOs resulted in dramatic run-ups of the public offering price. On the theory that the issuers in these offerings must have left far more money on the table than had ever been the case before, an NYSE/NASD IPO Advisory Committee convened by the SEC recommended in May 2003 that each IPO issuer be required—presumably as a condition of listing—to establish a "pricing committee" of its board of directors to "oversee the pricing process." The NASD proposed rules in November 2003[35] that would require a provision in the underwriting agreement to

---

34. Section 11(d)(1) expressly exempts bona fide delayed delivery contracts that settle within 35 days. The exemption applies, of course, to delayed delivery contracts between a broker-dealer and a customer involving *issued* securities that are executed within 30 days after the completion of the broker-dealer's participation in the distribution. The exemption does not imply that delayed delivery contracts involving *unissued* securities should be limited to 35 days.

35. NASD Notice to Members 03-72.

the effect that the book-running lead manager must furnish the issuer's pricing committee (or its board of directors) with

- a regular report of indications of interest, including the names of interested investors and the number of shares indicated by each; and
- after the closing date, a final allocation report including the names of purchasers and the number of shares purchased by each.

The NASD proposal does not mandate the creation of a pricing committee, which would require a change in listing standards.

The NASD also requested comment in November 2003 on what it called "additional regulatory steps that might be adopted to promote transparency in IPO pricing." These steps included requiring underwriters to

- retain an independent broker-dealer to opine as to the reasonableness of the initial offering range and the final price;
- use an auction or other system to collect indications of interest to help establish the final price; or
- include a "valuation disclosure" section in the prospectus with information about how the underwriters and the issuer arrived at the initial price range and the final IPO price, such as the issuer's one-year projected earnings or price-earnings ratios and share price information of comparable companies.

- *Covenants*

The issuer customarily will covenant with the managing underwriter to notify it of any communications received from the SEC with respect to the registration statement. It will agree not to file any amendment to the registration statement or any supplement to the prospectus to which the managing underwriter or its counsel may reasonably object.

Other customary covenants relate to the payment of expenses, the furnishing of sufficient copies of the prospectus to the underwriters and to filings under state blue sky laws.

Underwriting agreements will obligate the issuer to make generally available to its securityholders, as soon as practicable, an earnings statement (in form complying with the provisions of Rule 158 under the 1933 Act) covering a 12-month period beginning not later than the first day of the fiscal quarter next following the effective date of the registration statement. The purpose of this covenant is to call into play at the earliest possible date the provision of Section 11(a) of the 1933 Act that states that if a person acquires a security after the issuer has made generally available to its securityholders an earnings statement covering a period of at least 12 months beginning after the effective date of the registration statement, then the right of recovery is conditioned on proof that such person acquired the security relying on the alleged untrue statement in the registration statement or relying on the registration statement and not knowing of the alleged omission.

Rule 158 contains provisions relating to the adequacy of the earnings statement and provides that the earnings statement shall be deemed to be made generally available to the issuer's securityholders if it is required to file reports under the 1934 Act and has filed its reports on Form 10-K, Form 10-Q or Form 8-K or has supplied to the SEC copies of its annual report containing such information. Prior to the adoption of Rule 158, it was customary to make the earnings statement "generally available" by publishing a notice of its availability in *The Wall Street Journal.*

The underwriting agreement will obligate the issuer, even after the closing, to amend or supplement the prospectus as necessary to maintain it as a document that the underwriters may deliver in connection with the sale of the registered securities. This obligation applies for such period as the delivery of the prospectus is required for this purpose. For example, as discussed in Chapter 4, the underwriters may have placed a portion of the offered securities in an investment account. If the underwriters then decide to sell these securities four or five months after the original offering, it may be necessary to amend the prospectus to reflect material developments concerning the issuer or to include updated financial statements. The cost of amending the prospectus is usually borne by the issuer for the first nine months after the effective date of the registration statement (which is the period of time prescribed by Section 10(a)(3) of the 1933 Act after which the financial statements may become "stale"), while the underwriters bear the cost of any necessary amendments beyond the nine-month period.

The announcement by an issuer of a material business acquisition can sometimes complicate an underwriter's disposition of securities held in its investment account. For example, an issuer that announces an agreement to acquire a significant business may have no practical way of immediately filing the acquired company financial statements required by Rule 3-05 of Regulation S-X and the pro forma financial statements required by Article 11 of Regulation S-X. Item 11 of Form S-3 requires that the prospectus include this information. The instructions to Item 7 of Form 8-K also state that, with certain exceptions, "offerings should not be made pursuant to effective registration statements" until the filing of the required financial statements. Even though the SEC has recently relaxed the financial statement requirements for acquired businesses, a material acquisition can still prevent the issuer from updating the prospectus and an underwriter from selling securities from its investment account.

- *Lock-Up Agreements*

In the case of an offering of equity securities, the underwriters customarily will insist that the issuer, as well as certain of its officers, directors, founders, venture capital investors and other principal securityholders, enter into agreements to the effect that they will not sell any additional securities of the same class, or any securities into which they may be convertible, for a specified period of time after the date of the prospectus. The time periods most frequently seen are 180 to 270 days for IPOs and shorter periods for follow-on offerings. The "lock-up" agreements are designed to provide investors with some assurance that the market for an IPO security will find its own level before having to absorb the additional supply that is the subject of the lock-up agreements. In a follow-on offering, the agreements facilitate the distribution by preventing large blocks of securities from being dumped in the market while the distribution is in process. The managing underwriter has the right to consent to any sales or to terminate the lock-up agreements at any time. The manager normally will agree to any sales that will not disrupt the distribution or have an adverse effect on the aftermarket for the securities.

Lock-up agreements became a subject of public scrutiny during the Internet Bubble, to the point where the financial press commenced publishing on a regular basis the expiration dates of the lock-up agreements related to recent IPOs. There were also allegations of abuse, particularly regarding the terms on which underwriters released insiders from their obligations. The NYSE/NASD IPO Advisory Committee recommended in May 2003 that the prospectus more fully inform investors about the terms of lock-up agreements, including whether the agreements permitted the hedging or collaring of the locked-up shares without the manager's consent and also about any preexisting plans to exempt a director or officer from a lock-up agreement. The Committee also recommended that underwriters be required to notify the issuer before granting any exemption to a lock-up and that the issuer and the underwriter both be required to make a public announcement of the exemption prior to any sale by the person to whom the exemption was granted. Separately, SEC staff comment letters on IPOs have recently been requesting a description of the factors that underwriters would consider in deciding to modify lock-up agreements, including whether the underwriters would consider in this connection their own positions in the issuer's securities.

The NASD proposed rules in November 2003 that would require that underwriting agreements state that any lock-up or other restriction on the transfer of the issuer's shares by officers and directors of the issuer would apply also to any issuer-directed shares. In addition, the underwriting agreement would have to require the book-running lead manager to notify the issuer at least two business days before the release or waiver of any lock-up and announce the impending release or waiver through a national news service.

The NASD's proposed rules should be viewed in the light of amendments to NYSE and NASD rules approved by the SEC in July 2003 that prohibit research activity by managers or co-managers within 15 days before or after the expiration, waiver or termination of a lock-up. The intent is to prevent the so-called "booster shot" at or about the time an insider is freed up to sell.

Exceptions apply for Rule 139 research on issuers whose stocks are actively traded as defined for Regulation M purposes as well as where legal or compliance personnel have approved a statement in response to significant news or events.[36] Notwithstanding these exceptions, some underwriters have been trying to ensure the continuity of their research coverage by bargaining for an extension of the lock-up if it would otherwise expire or terminate at or about the time of an earnings announcement by the issuer.

- *Closing Conditions*

The underwriting agreement will specify conditions precedent to the obligations of the underwriters to purchase the securities at the closing. These generally include the receipt of opinions from issuer's and underwriters' counsel (and selling securityholder's counsel, if any), a comfort letter from the independent accountants, and certificates of officers of the issuer.

The agreement will spell out in considerable detail the matters to be covered by company or selling securityholder counsel and the conclusions to be expressed. As discussed in Chapter 5, the underwriters should consider at an early stage whether the issuer needs to involve separate outside counsel with special expertise.

Sometimes the agreement includes complete drafts of the legal opinions, but more often the agreement simply states the matters to be covered and the conclusions to be reached. As in the case of the issuer's representations and warranties, negotiating the substantive coverage of the opinion or opinions can contribute to the underwriters' due diligence. A great deal can be learned about the issuer during these discussions.

For example, the discussions may lead to a better understanding of the division of legal work between the company's legal department and its outside counsel. This may result in a division of opinion responsibility between the company's inside and outside counsel. Internal counsel usually will have greater familiarity with its day-to-day legal affairs than the outside law firm that has been retained for the financing. Outside counsel may have been hired primarily for its expertise in the securities laws. In these cases, internal counsel will usually opine on due incorporation, good standing, qualification as a foreign

---

36. SEC Release No. 34-48252 (July 29, 2003).

corporation, matters relating to subsidiaries, material contracts and litigation. Outside counsel will usually pass on matters relating to the securities, the validity of their issuance and the accuracy of their description in the registration statement. Outside counsel's opinion will also cover securities law matters, such as the effectiveness of the registration statement, the availability of any exemptions and the registration statement's compliance as to form with the requirements of the 1933 Act and the SEC's rules.

The underwriting agreement will require both inside and outside counsel (or, in many cases, only outside counsel) to give negative assurance, with customary disclaimers, that "nothing has come to their attention" that has caused them to believe that the registration statement or prospectus is false or misleading in any material respect. The vehicle for this negative assurance is sometimes referred to as the "10b-5 opinion." In the case of a registered public offering, of course, the "opinion" is expressed in terms of Section 11 as to the registration statement as of its effective date and in terms of Section 12(a)(2) as to the prospectus as of its date and as of the closing date. Many lawyers resist characterizing their negative assurance on disclosure matters as an "opinion."

It is customary to carve out from the negative assurance the issuer's financial statements contained in the prospectus, both audited and unaudited. For these, the underwriter relies on the expertization defense in Section 11 and upon the comfort letter. The carve-out usually also extends to financial schedules and financial data, and some counsel also disclaim responsibility for statistical information. Underwriters differ in their response to these carve-outs. Management's discussion and analysis (MD&A) may contain "financial data," for example, but it would not be reasonable to allow issuer's counsel to disclaim responsibility for the entire MD&A. On the other hand, as discussed in Chapter 5, portions of the market risk discussion depend heavily on statistical analyses (e.g., VaR calculations), and few lawyers would wish to take responsibility for those analyses. In some transactions, both sides may be content to live with ambiguity. In others, an explicit dialogue is required.

The opinions requested of company counsel can sometimes lead to controversy even after their coverage has been negotiated. If the underwriting agreement does not contain a complete draft of the opinion, then it is a good idea to obtain one at an early date. More than once, an opinion delivered at the closing has covered *in haec verba* every matter contemplated by the underwriting agreement, but it has also contained an equal number of pages setting forth assumptions and qualifications that call into question the value of the opinion. Understanding and negotiating these assumptions and qualifications can take time, and the atmosphere can become thick when issuer's counsel insists that only a particular form of opinion will do because this is the form decreed by the firm's opinion committee. A law firm does not serve its client well if the partner negotiating the terms of the underwriting agreement does not have the authority to agree to a form of opinion preferred by the underwriters that is not substantively different from that preferred by his own firm. On the other hand, counsel for the underwriters should be reasonable in their requests for opinions from company counsel. No lawyer should ask another to render an opinion that he or she would not be comfortable giving if standing in the other lawyer's shoes.

The underwriting agreement will also make the closing conditional on the underwriters' receipt of an opinion from their own counsel. The contents of this opinion are described in more general terms than in the case of the opinion of issuer's or selling securityholder's counsel.

Because the opinions are negotiated well in advance of closing, few transactions fail to close because of counsel's inability to deliver the required opinion. There are exceptions that prove the rule, however, such as a $160 million common stock offering by a real estate investment trust that failed to close after pricing in February 2004 when counsel discovered a flaw in the issuer's tax status.

Another customary condition to closing is the delivery of an officers' certificate with respect to the company's performance of all of its obligations under the underwriting agreement, the absence of any material adverse changes and to the effect that the representations and warranties in the underwriting agreement are true and correct with the same effect as though made at the time of closing. Underwriting agreements sometimes specify which officers should deliver the certificates, with a view to having an operating officer and a financial officer both sign each certificate.

- *Comfort Letters*

The underwriters will often have received a comfort letter from the issuer's accountants at the time of execution of the underwriting agreement.[37] The underwriting agreement will also require a bring-down letter from the accountants as a condition to closing. Comfort letters are now governed by the accounting profession's Statement on Auditing Standards No. 86, which is codified as AU ¶634 of the AICPA's *Codification of Statements on Auditing Standards*. The conditions for obtaining a comfort letter are discussed in Chapter 5.

A typical comfort letter will confirm that the accountants are independent public accountants within the meaning of the 1933 Act and the SEC's rules. It will also express the accountants' opinion whether the audited financial statements included in the prospectus comply as to form in all material respects with the applicable accounting requirements of the 1933 Act and the SEC's rules. There is no need for the comfort letter to reiterate the accountants' report on the audited financial statements, since that report (which speaks as of its date) appears or is incorporated by reference in the prospectus and the accountant has consented to such appearance or incorporation by reference.

If unaudited interim financial statements are included in the prospectus, the comfort letter may express "negative assurance" as to whether these statements comply as to form with SEC requirements and also as to whether any material modifications should be made to these statements for them to be in conformity with generally accepted accounting principles. The negative assurance may extend to financial information included or incorporated by reference in the prospectus because of specific requirements of Regulation S-K (e.g., selected financial data to the extent not expertized as discussed in Chapter 5, supplementary financial information, executive compensation and any presentation of the issuer's ratio of earnings to fixed charges). The letter may also express negative assurance as to changes in

---

37. *The Comfort Letter* (1975), by Philadelphia lawyer-novelist Arthur R. G. Solmssen, is a delightful fictional account of what happens when the conditions to the closing of an acquisition transaction are not satisfied.

SYNDICATE PROCEDURES 105

the issuer's capital stock, long-term debt or other specified financial statement or items during a specified period (the "change period") beginning immediately after the date of the latest audited financial statements in the prospectus and ending on a "cut-off" date that may be three business days before the date of delivery of the letter.

A comfort letter may also comment on tables, statistics and other financial information that appears in the registration statement and that is derived from the issuer's accounting records. As discussed in Chapter 5, any comment on this information will be expressed not as "negative assurance" but rather as findings based on the application of limited procedures set forth in the letter. Counsel for the underwriters should ensure that the accountants provide comfort with respect to all numbers and computations that can be checked without unreasonable effort. But counsel and its clients should not resort to overkill. An accountant cannot be expected to provide comfort with respect to any number that cannot be derived from the accounting records of the issuer.

As in the case of legal opinions, it is a good idea to obtain a draft of the comfort letter in advance and to confirm the level of clearance that the letter has received. A comfort letter is subject to multiple layers of review at the accounting firm that issues it, and a national office SEC partner may disagree at the last minute with the conclusions reached by the local office. The danger of such a last-minute problem is especially acute in the case of transactions involving foreign issuers.

Accountants have been frequent targets of litigation and are understandably reluctant to risk liability for activities that are outside the scope of their normal audit engagements. Strictly speaking, as discussed in Chapter 5, comfort letters are for the benefit of the underwriters as a means of helping to establish their "due diligence" defense under Section 11 or comparable provisions. The authors are not aware of any litigation against accountants arising out of any comfort letter delivered to underwriters, but the accounting profession has nevertheless been trying for some time to standardize the procedural and substantive aspects of comfort letters. In particular, there appears to be a concern that—at least on some transactions not registered with the SEC—"no one is doing any due diligence except the accountants." These concerns and their consequences for underwriters are discussed in Chapter 5.

- *Purchase and Sale; Closing*

The underwriting agreement will specify a price that the underwriters will pay for the securities. This will be the public offering price less the agreed underwriting discount.

One exception is where the securities are preferred stock with a fixed par value carrying a dividend calculated to have the public offering price be equal to par. An example is preferred stock with a par value of $100 per share that will be offered to the public at that price. As a matter of corporate law in certain states, stock may not be issued for a consideration having a value less than its par value.[38] Accordingly, if shares of the preferred stock were issued to the underwriters at $100 per share less the underwriting discount, questions could be raised as to the validity of the issuance of the shares. To avoid this issue, the practice in these circumstances is to have the underwriters buy the preferred stock at par and to compensate them with a separate check covering what is then called their underwriting "commission."

The underwriting agreement will specify the date and place of closing. Rule 15c6-1 sets "T+3" as the standard settlement cycle for most transactions in non-exempted securities, but a "T+4" cycle is permitted for firm commitment offerings that are priced after 4:30 P.M. Eastern time. (See Chapter 3 for a discussion of other exceptions to the T+3 requirement.)

Prior to 1996, purchase agreements provided for payment in "next-day" clearing house funds rather than same-day funds. When DTC moved to same-day funds settlement in 1996, underwriters changed their policy accordingly.

When a debt closing takes place through the facilities of DTC, one or more global certificates will be signed by the company's officers and delivered to the trustee acting as authentication agent for the issuer. They will then be delivered to DTC or DTC's custodian. When counsel for the issuer and the

---

38. E.g., Delaware General Corporation Law §153(a).

SYNDICATE PROCEDURES 107

underwriters agree that all closing conditions have been met, they will initiate a conference call among themselves, the company, DTC and the managing underwriter. DTC will confirm the aggregate amount of securities being released to the underwriters, and the company will confirm its receipt of funds. The closing is then complete. Subsequently, DTC will credit the securities to the accounts of the individual underwriters in accordance with the managing underwriter's instructions.

In an equity offering, if the underwriters exercise the Green Shoe option on or before the closing date, the closing for the additional shares will usually take place simultaneously with the closing for the "original" or "firm" shares. If the Green Shoe option is exercised after the closing date, the underwriting agreement will provide for a second closing for the additional shares. Some underwriters require only that they receive at the second closing assurance as to the validity of the additional shares. Other underwriters insist that the issuer or other person providing the additional shares fulfill at the second closing all of the conditions that they were required to fulfill at the time of the first closing. The first practice seems preferable when the Green Shoe option is exercised for the purpose of covering overallotments, since in this situation the underwriters sold all of the shares—the "firm" shares and the additional shares—at the outset of the offering on a fungible basis and with delivery of the same prospectus. The time for due diligence is long since gone, and the only matter on which the underwriters logically require assurance is the validity of the additional shares.

- *Indemnification*

The issuer, and in appropriate cases the selling securityholders, will agree to indemnify each underwriter and each controlling person of an underwriter against liabilities and expenses arising out of alleged misstatements or omissions in the registration statement and prospectus. The indemnity agreement should make it clear that litigation expenses, including fees of counsel, will be reimbursed as incurred. The underwriting agreement will contain a cross indemnity from each underwriter with respect to information furnished by it. (As discussed above in note 30, such information is very limited.)

Issuers often will insist that the indemnity agreement, insofar as it relates to any untrue statement or omission made in a preliminary prospectus but remedied in the final prospectus, will not be available to any underwriter from whom the person asserting the claim purchased the securities if a copy of the final prospectus was not given to such person and the receipt thereof would have constituted a defense to the asserted claim. In theory, this is not an unreasonable position for an issuer to take, but the fact is that underwriters are already required under Section 5 of the 1933 Act to deliver a final prospectus with the confirmation. Moreover, there is seldom any significant difference between the last preliminary prospectus and the final prospectus. If there are significant differences, the issuer was presumably involved in the discussion not to recirculate an amended preliminary prospectus. The point is hardly worth the hours of discussion it sometimes generates, since the fact is that very little litigation arises that is based upon misstatements in preliminary prospectuses.

The *Globus* case, decided in 1969,[39] raised questions as to the validity of indemnity agreements insofar as they relate to underwriters who have actual knowledge of a misstatement or omission in a registration statement. This led to concern about the enforceability of indemnity agreements in general, and many courts have held indemnity agreements to be invalid as contrary to public policy even where the underwriter was not aware of the misstatement or omission.[40] Doubts about enforceability notwithstanding, indemnity provisions are routinely—probably invariably—included in underwriting agreements, and issuers routinely honor their commitments (except in some cases where the issuer is insolvent or close to insolvency). Because of these doubts, however, counsel often opines only that the underwriting agreement has been duly authorized, executed and delivered and not that it is a valid and binding agreement enforceable in accordance with its terms.

---

39. *Globus v. Law Research Services, Inc.*, 418 F.2d 1276 (2d Cir. 1969), *aff'g* 287 F. Supp. 188 (S.D.N.Y. 1968), *cert. denied,* 397 U.S. 913 (1970).
40. *See, e.g., Eichenholtz v. Brennan*, 52 F.3d 478 (3d Cir. 1995).

In the case of a secondary offering by a selling securityholder, there is often an issue as to whether indemnification by the issuer is permitted as a matter of corporate law. The concern is that providing such a benefit to a securityholder without receiving any valuable consideration in return might be viewed as a waste of corporate assets. If the securities are being registered pursuant to an agreement that provides for registration rights, then indemnification by the issuer probably is enforceable. Indemnification may be deemed to be incidental to the obligation to register. To avoid any question on this issue, agreements providing for registration rights should contain a specific agreement on the part of the corporation that it will agree to indemnify underwriters through whom the securities are sold.

The argument has been made that there is justification for a corporate indemnity where shareholders are selling and the secondary offering enables the corporation to meet the listing requirements of an exchange or otherwise creates a more liquid market for its shares. In the case of an IPO, the pre-offering shareholders are sometimes requested to consent to the issuer's indemnification with respect to the selling shareholders' portion of the offering.

The sellers in the secondary offering should also be required to provide indemnity, but where the sellers are individuals, there is frequently concern as to whether they will have funds available to honor their indemnity if this should prove necessary. Perhaps the proceeds of the secondary offering will be frittered away. In the past, underwriters sometimes required individual selling securityholders to purchase an indemnity insurance policy, at least for a portion of the offering, naming the underwriters as beneficiaries. These policies are expensive, and they generally have not been required in recent years.

Even where there is a question as to the enforceability of the issuer's indemnification for the benefit of selling securityholders, underwriters will require it for what it is worth. So long as the underwriters understand that the indemnity may not be enforceable, this approach is not objectionable.

The question has also arisen as to whether a trustee, executor or other fiduciary should indemnify in the absence of specific authority in the governing instrument or a court order. Banks and other fiduciaries fear that if they do so they may be held liable in their individual capacities and not as fiduciaries. One way of handling this problem is to have an indemnitor, such as the principal beneficiary, indemnify on behalf of the trust or estate.

The SEC considers it to be contrary to public policy for a registrant to indemnify any of its directors, officers or controlling persons against liabilities arising under the 1933 Act. Item 512(h) of Regulation S-K requires an undertaking to be included in the registration statement to the effect that if a claim for indemnification is made against the issuer by a director, officer or controlling person, the issuer will, unless in the opinion of its counsel the matter has been settled by controlling precedent, submit the question to a court and be governed by a final adjudication of the question. It should be noted that Item 512(h) does not apply to the issuer's agreement to indemnify the underwriters except in the increasingly rare situation where a controlling person of an underwriter is also a director of the issuer. In that case, the underwriting agreement should state that, insofar as the indemnity agreement applies to such person, it is subject to the issuer's undertaking pursuant to Item 512(h).

The indemnity section of the underwriting agreement will specify the procedures to be followed if a claim is made. Looking at these procedures from the standpoint of the underwriter,[41] each underwriter must notify the issuer of any action commenced against it. Many underwriting agreements provide that an issuer may assume the defense of an action with counsel chosen by it and approved by the underwriters, unless the underwriters reasonably object on the grounds that they may have legal defenses that are different from or in addition to those available to the issuer. In that case, the underwriters may be represented by their own counsel at the issuer's expense.

---

41. The underwriting agreement provides for indemnity in both directions, but the underwriters indemnify the issuer for very limited information. Also, control persons are also entitled to indemnity, but they seldom participate in any litigation on an independent basis. The discussion in the text therefore assumes that the underwriters are seeking indemnity from the issuer.

Over the years, it has become evident that underwriters must always have separate counsel in an action based on a registration statement because their interests and defenses always are different from those of the issuer (even at those stages of the litigation where the due diligence defense is not yet relevant). As the exception to the rule always applies, many modern underwriting agreements simply state—again, from the standpoint of the underwriter—that the underwriters may not be required without their consent to accept the issuer's counsel as their counsel. Alternatively, the agreement will recognize the underwriters' right to select their own defense counsel (perhaps with the issuer's consent, not to be unreasonably withheld) on condition that there will not be more than one counsel for all of the underwriters in connection with any single action (plus any local counsel required to be retained under local rules).

Underwriting agreements have also in recent years prohibited any indemnifying party from settling any action in respect of which an indemnified party may seek indemnification unless the settlement includes an unconditional release of the indemnified parties and does not contain any admission of fault or liability on the part of the indemnified parties. This is designed to prevent an issuer—usually one in financial distress—from entering into a sweetheart settlement that will help finance the plaintiffs' ongoing litigation against the deep-pocket underwriters. The prohibition does not usually extend to settlements by the issuer's officers and directors, including a settlement financed by insurance proceeds.

- *Contribution*

Section 11(f) of the 1933 Act provides that every person who becomes liable under Section 11 may "recover contribution as in cases of contract from any person who, if sued separately, would have been liable to make the same payment, unless the person who has become liable was, and the other was not, guilty of fraudulent misrepresentation." The provision is not a model of legislative draftsmanship. In order to resolve some of the ambiguities and open questions about how contribution would be applied in the event that the issuer's indemnity agreement were held to be unenforceable, underwriters customarily include contribution clauses in their forms of underwriting agreement.

These clauses state that if the indemnity agreement is for any reason held to be unavailable to the underwriters, then the issuer (and the selling securityholders, if any) and the underwriters will contribute to the aggregate losses of the nature contemplated by the indemnity agreement in such proportions that the underwriters will be responsible for that portion represented by the percentage that the underwriting discount bears to the initial public offering price; the issuer (and the selling securityholders, in the proportions that they have agreed to indemnify) will be responsible for the balance. The agreement should specify that the underwriters' obligation to contribute will be several and not joint and in proportion to their respective underwriting obligations. Of course, it is also specified that no person guilty of fraudulent misrepresentation within the meaning of Section 11(f) of the 1933 Act will be entitled to contribution from any person who is not guilty of such fraudulent misrepresentation.

Many underwriting agreements go on to provide that if this contribution formula is not enforceable, then contribution will be made on the basis of such factors as relative fault and relative benefit. The point of all of this is to provide an alternative to full indemnification based on the statutory underpinnings of Section 11(f), in the event that the indemnity agreement is not upheld.

Indemnity agreements sometimes provide that indemnity will not be available if the person seeking indemnity fails to give any required notice of a claim, at least where the failure to give notice is materially prejudicial to the person providing indemnity. Issuers sometimes seek to insert a similar condition into the contribution agreement. Since the underwriters are already entitled to contribution as a result of Section 11(f), the insertion of procedural conditions may have the effect of leaving them worse off for having an express agreement than if they had no agreement at all. This is clearly not a rational result, and procedural conditions to the issuer's contribution obligation should be avoided.

- *Termination of Underwriting Agreement at Underwriters' Election*

Underwriting agreements routinely permit the managing underwriter to terminate the obligations of the syndicate if events occur prior to the closing date (other than events described in the prospectus) that involve any change in the issuer's general affairs, management, financial condition or results of operations that in the managing underwriter's judgment is so material and adverse as to make it inadvisable to proceed with the offering on the contemplated terms.[42] The agreement may refer expressly to "any development involving a prospective change" and may include a reference to the issuer's "business prospects." As noted above, issuers sometimes object to making representations about their business prospects, but this is a separate issue from the underwriters' right to terminate their obligation if an event occurs prior to closing that has a material adverse effect on the business prospects and therefore the investment merits of the underwritten securities. There is probably little difference between "general affairs" and "business prospects."

At one time, the material adverse change "out" was limited to matters relating to the actual condition of the issuer and did not cover its business prospects or developments involving a "prospective" change. The term "business prospects" was introduced into many underwriting agreements shortly after Fidel Castro came to power in Cuba. In connection with a convertible debenture offering by a company with substantial business interests in that country, there was an announcement between pricing and closing that Castro intended to impose a confiscatory tax that would have a material impact on the issuer's overall operations. Because there had not been any change in the issuer's actual condition or in its earnings, it was not clear whether the material adverse change clause could be invoked. If the words "business prospects" had been included, then the clause clearly would have been applicable.[43]

In the case of an offering of fixed-income securities, it is also common for the underwriters to reserve the option to terminate their obligations in the event of a downgrading in the

---

42. Formerly in the judgment of a majority in interest of the underwriters but now more often in the "judgment," "sole judgment" or even "absolute discretion" of the managing underwriter.

43. The securities in question became known in the financial community as "Castro Convertibles."

company's ratings by a nationally recognized statistical rating organization (such as Moody's or Standard & Poor's). The option usually extends to the placement of the issuer's ratings on a "watch" or similar list for surveillance or review where this is announced as having "possible negative implications."

Underwriting agreements also often provide for a material adverse change "out" in the event of any loss or interference with the issuer's business from "fire, explosion, flood or other calamity." Labor disputes and adverse governmental action are sometimes also specified, often over the issuer's objection that the risk of these events is described in the prospectus and therefore already discounted in the price of the issuer's securities.

It is also customary to permit the managing underwriter to terminate in the event of an external calamity that, in the managing underwriter's judgment, makes it inadvisable or impracticable to proceed with the offering (sometimes also "to enforce contracts for the sale of the securities"). Some of these calamities are spelled out. Thus, the manager may be permitted to terminate the underwriting agreement "if there has occurred any new outbreak of hostilities or any calamity or crisis the effect of which on the financial markets of the United States [or, in the case of international offerings, any other relevant markets] is such as to make it, in the judgment of the managing underwriter, impracticable to market the securities or enforce contracts for the sale of the securities." Recently, terrorist activity has been separately specified.

When there are pending or threatened hostilities at the time of pricing, an issuer may try to exclude those specific hostilities from the calamity out (sometimes in the absence of a "major escalation") on the theory that the market has already discounted the effects of the pending or threatened hostilities. These attempts do not often succeed.

Other specified events will normally include a suspension or material limitation in trading generally on the NYSE (sometimes on NASDAQ or other designated markets) or in the issuer's securities in its principal market, the declaration of a banking moratorium or the establishment of minimum or maximum prices in the securities markets. Some of these events have their roots in the disruptions of the early 1930s.

From time to time, the typical calamity out has been modified in anticipation of specific events that could adversely affect the financial markets. For example, at one point during the 1960s, the financial markets anxiously anticipated a devaluation of the pound sterling. During this period, some underwriting agreements specified that devaluation would provide a basis for termination. In the spring of 1975, when The City of New York was facing a financial crisis, it became quite common to include a termination provision that would operate in the event of bankruptcy of a state or a major city or a default by it on its debt obligations. After the crisis passed in mid-June of that year, provisions of this type became less common.

Underwriting agreements often also refer to more generalized market disruptions such as "any other calamity or crisis," "any change [sometimes any material adverse change] in financial, political or economic conditions" or "any material adverse change in the financial markets." Market collapses such as the crash of October 19, 1987 would appear to be covered by such language, but in fact many underwritten public offerings that had been priced before that crash were routinely closed afterward, notwithstanding a dramatic fall in the market price of the underwritten security.

In practice, underwriters do not walk away from deals because of external calamities. It has been reported, for example, that there is no evidence that any underwriters invoked these provisions as a result of the terrorist attacks of September 11, 2001.[44] Also, the August 2003 electrical blackout in the Northeast led only to a few postponements of scheduled closings.

An underwriter does not have a free hand in describing the market conditions that will excuse its performance in a firm commitment underwriting. First of all, the SEC or the NASD may view a loose "market out" provision—for example, one based on "nonmaterial events affecting the issuer or the securities markets in general" that is triggered by an inability to market the underwritten securities—as making the underwriting arrangement a "best efforts" arrangement rather than a firm

---

44. *Capital Markets Handbook, supra* note 12, at 81 n.8.

commitment.[45] Second, the NASD may view an unjustifiable failure to complete a firm commitment underwriting as a violation of just and equitable principles of trade within the meaning of the Conduct Rules.[46]

- *Default and Step-Up*

As stated above, the commitments of the underwriters are several. Thus, if one of the underwriters were to default, the issuer would receive less funds than it wished to raise unless some provision were made for a limited step-up by the remaining underwriters.

Underwriting agreements typically provide that if one or more of the underwriters fails at the closing to purchase the securities that it or they are obligated to purchase, then the manager has 24 hours to make arrangements for one or more of the non-defaulting underwriters, or any other underwriters, to purchase all, but not less than all, of the defaulted securities. If such arrangements are not completed within that period, and if the amount of defaulted securities does not exceed 10% of the total, then the non-defaulting underwriters are obligated to purchase the full amount in the proportions that their respective underwriting commitments bear to the underwriting commitments of all non-defaulting underwriters. If the amount of defaulted securities exceeds 10% of the total, the underwriting agreement terminates without liability on the part of any non-defaulting underwriter.

---

45. SEC No-action Letter, *The First Boston Corporation* (September 3, 1985).

46. *See* NASD Regulatory & Compliance Alert, "Members Reminded to Complete Firm-Commitment Underwritings" (November 1996). The NASD recently penalized a member firm and one of its registered principals for failing to comply with just and equitable principles of trade by unjustifiably canceling a firm commitment offering. *Security Capital Trading, Inc. et al.*, NASD Disciplinary Actions 91 (February 2003). Rule 11880 of the NASD's Uniform Practice Code obligates a managing underwriter to notify the NASD of any delay in the closing of a firm commitment underwriting. Among other things, the cancellation of an underwriting usually means that a large number of "when-issued" trades must be unwound under the NASD's Uniform Practice Code.

The default provision almost never comes into play. Investment banking firms simply do not default on their obligations. It stands as backup insurance to the issuer while preserving the principle that underwriting commitments are several and not joint. One occasion on which it was necessary to operate under a default clause occurred in May 1973 when Weis Securities, Inc. was placed in liquidation under the Securities Investor Protection Act between the signing of the underwriting agreement and the closing of a public offering of 6.5 million shares of common stock of Consolidated Edison Company of New York, Inc. On the afternoon after the underwriting agreement was signed, the SEC applied to the court for the appointment of a temporary receiver of Weis Securities' assets, and the Securities Investor Protection Corporation applied for the appointment of a trustee for the firm's liquidation. Weis resisted, and it remained uncertain until shortly before the closing whether it would be able to honor its underwriting commitment. A trustee was appointed the day before the closing, and it became evident that it would be impossible for the trustee to honor Weis' commitment. Weis defaulted on the morning of the closing, and at the closing the non-defaulting underwriters purchased, pro rata, the shares that Weis had agreed to purchase. The book-running manager's form of underwriting agreement did not permit the managers to purchase the defaulted securities themselves or to substitute other underwriters, and thus it was necessary to apply the pro rata step-up provision. Most underwriting agreements have now been amended to permit a substitution of underwriters and not merely an across-the-board step-up.

The SEC has sometimes taken the position that a step-up is necessary in order for the issuer and the underwriters to be able to represent that all of the offered securities will be sold if any are sold. The step-up may also be a source of comfort regarding the issuer's expectations that it will receive the full amount of the offering for the purposes described under "Use of Proceeds."

The Selected Dealers Agreement

The underwriting document that generally gets the least attention is the selected dealers agreement. This document, which is also known as the "selling agreement," permits dealers who are not also members of the underwriting syndicate to purchase securities from the underwriters at the public offering price less a discount called the "concession." They will agree to maintain the public offering price in their resales, except that they may sell to other dealers at the public offering price less a discount called the "reallowance." Selected dealers will make the same representations as the underwriters with respect to their membership in, and good standing with, the NASD and will agree to comply with NASD rules. They will confirm their awareness of the prospectus delivery requirements of the securities laws.

In the case of an IPO, the selling agreement may contain a penalty clause requiring the repayment of the selling concession if securities sold by the dealer are purchased by the syndicate in the open market. The agreement contains other provisions of a routine nature relating to the distribution.

The practice of requiring dealers to enter into selling agreements in connection with specific transactions has all but disappeared, as the major investment banking firms have adopted master selling agreements that have been signed by the dealers that participate in their offerings and that govern all underwritings that they manage.

Some master agreements between underwriters and dealers cover a wide range of transactions that go far beyond public offerings of SEC-registered securities. The desire of underwriting firms to extend their distribution capabilities has led some of them to form alliances with "regional" broker-dealers who use their sales forces to sell products originated by the underwriting firm. These products can include commercial paper, private placements and various types of derivative products. The form of agreement generally calls for the dealer to agree that it will observe applicable selling restrictions, deliver required documents and assume responsibility for making suitability determinations.

Competitive Bidding

Competitive bidding is required by the public utility laws or utility commission regulations of several states, particularly in the case of fixed-income securities. In some of these states exemptions will be granted quite readily, but in others the public utility commission will insist that bidding procedures be adhered to. In addition, until 1994, the SEC's Rule 50 under the Public Utility Holding Company Act of 1935 also required public utility holding companies and their operating subsidiaries to sell their securities through competitive bidding.

The SEC rescinded Rule 50 in 1994[47] because of the dwindling number of companies still subject to the Public Utility Holding Company Act, the many exceptions to which the competitive bid requirement was subject and, perhaps most important, the extensive disclosure requirements imposed by the other federal securities laws. The SEC anticipated that the rescission of the rule would permit companies in a registered public utility holding company system to choose the marketing method for their securities, including shelf registration, that offered the most advantageous terms.

Some public utilities have adopted streamlined bidding procedures. One public utility with an effective shelf registration statement covering its first mortgage bonds has been able to satisfy the requirements of its state public utilities commission without publishing a bidding notice. Instead it sends letters to those investment banking firms that have participated in its prior financings inviting them to submit bids. As set forth in these letters, provision is made for telephonic bids confirmed in writing within one hour after the close of bidding. Written confirmations are provided by facsimile, and the winning bid is accepted by the public utility's execution of the fax of the bid. Following Rule 415 procedures, rather than traditional competitive bidding procedures, a post-effective amendment is not required, but rather a prospectus supplement is filed with the SEC pursuant to Rule 424(b).

---

47. SEC Release No. 35-26031 (April 20, 1994).

Chapter 3

SELECTED ISSUES IN THE REGISTRATION AND DISTRIBUTION PROCESS

The process of bringing a securities offering to market may extend over several months in the case of an IPO. It may also be completed in as little as a few days in the case of a "drive-by" offering such as a shelf takedown of debt securities.[1] Some deals run like clockwork. Others are plagued by problems. In some cases, a stock offering will be a blowout. In others, it will be necessary for the underwriters to cut back on the size of the offering to get the deal done. Timing is crucial to many transactions. A favorable market climate may evaporate overnight; or the financing must be closed by the end of the year, and if the SEC does not produce its comments by the end of the day, the underwriters will be forced to come to market during the week before Christmas.

---

1. For many years, the usual pattern was that the underwriters were ready to price and sell the securities but could not do so because the SEC staff had not completed its review. While this still happens, the usual pattern in the case of issuers that have registered their securities "on the shelf" on Form S-3 is that the SEC formalities are (or can be) resolved well before the marketing effort is even commenced. Even in the case of non-shelf transactions, Rule 430A makes it possible to resolve staff comments prior to pricing.

The working group must be prepared to deal with surprises. A deal may be rolling along smoothly when "up jumps the devil." The SEC's accounting staff raises a major issue on revenue recognition. A co-manager informs counsel that an e-mail intended for dissemination to its sales force has inadvertently been sent to one or more investors. An underwriter's research department unexpectedly initiates coverage of the issuer.

Most of these problems get solved, and the key to their solution is a cooperative working relationship among the representatives of the issuer, the lead underwriter, their respective counsel and the issuer's accounting firm.

Selecting the Investment Banker

If a privately held issuer decides to "go public," its first item of business will be to select the investment banking firm that will manage the transaction. If an SEC-reporting issuer decides to raise additional funds through the sale of securities, its first item of business will probably be to determine the type of security to be offered and whether the transaction should take the form of an SEC-registered public offering, a private placement or an offering in the offshore markets. The issuer's choice in this regard may influence its choice of investment banker to handle the transaction, since many investment bankers are perceived as having more expertise in one of these areas than in others.

It is often the case, of course, that various investment banking firms will have been soliciting the issuer's business for a considerable period of time.

In the days when relationship banking was far stronger than today, when most major corporations did business with only one investment bank, the issuer's president or chief financial officer would simply call on the senior officer in the investment banking firm responsible for the relationship. Through a joint effort, a decision would be made as to the type of securities most appropriate to meet the company's financial requirements. The choice might depend on the issuer's capital structure, its debt to equity ratio, the market price of its common stock, prevailing interest rates, and the market's current appetite for specific types of securities. Frequently, the offering would be a part of a carefully devised financial plan worked out well in advance by the issuer and its regular investment bank.

Today, investment banking relationships are less close than in the past. Few corporations that finance on a regular basis rely on the services of only one investment bank. Some corporations have a strong relationship with an investment banking firm that will handle most of their business and a significant relationship with a number of other firms that they will call on from time to time to manage one or more transactions. Other corporations have an equally strong relationship with a core group of firms, with no one relationship reaching the level found in a single bank or dominant bank relationship.[2]

The result is a reduced flow of information from the corporation to the firms providing it with financial services.[3] The tendency now is for a corporation to rely more heavily than in the past on its own internal financial staff and for the chief financial officer to have a greater say in the selection of the type of transaction and of the investment bank that will manage the transaction. All but gone are the days when a firm was chosen because it was run by the issuer's chief executive's college roommate.

When the time comes to choose a lead underwriter, the chief financial officer may have arrived at his own decision as to the nature of the financing, having relied on the analysis of his own staff. He may then consult with a number of investment banking firms to discuss such issues as the probable price terms (including underwriting spread), whether the marketing focus should be primarily retail or institutional, and the firms' distribution capacity in the relevant market. Based on these considerations and other factors, tangible and intangible, one or more managing underwriters will be chosen.[4] Sometimes a prospective issuer will hold

---

2. For ease of presentation, this chapter deals primarily with offerings by issuers, but the issues are essentially the same for registered secondary offerings.

3. For an extensive discussion of the different levels of investment banking relationships, *see* R. Eccles & D. Crane, *Doing Deals* (1988), particularly ch. 4.

4. The firm that expects to be selected as book-running manager will usually argue against the need for co-managers. In some common stock offerings, however, the book-running manager may suggest that a regional firm be brought in as co-manager if it is expected that there will be interest for the

a "beauty contest." A corporation that has no real tie with any investment bank may interview a number of firms and choose among competing underwriters on the basis of its perception of the firms' responsiveness to the corporation's needs, their understanding of its business model and the chemistry that develops between the investment bankers and their counterparts at the corporation. This process frequently is used for IPOs, particularly by quality issuers being courted for their business. In the case of investment-grade shelf takedowns, the process more closely resembles competitive bidding on price terms alone. It is frequently alleged, however, that underwriters who are affiliated with large commercial banks reap an advantage from "tying" the underwriting business to loan facilities provided by the commercial bank affiliate.

The quality of a firm's research coverage has been and undoubtedly remains an important factor in getting new business, particularly in the case of IPOs. Notwithstanding the new SRO rules adopted over the past few years that mandate a separation between investment banking and research, and notwithstanding the 2003 "global settlement" among various regulators and ten major investment banking firms, an issuer planning an IPO would be foolish not to take into consideration the research capabilities of the firms it is considering to lead the transaction. IPO candidates know their competition among publicly held companies in their industry, and they often know which analysts most capably cover these companies. They also know that newly public companies worry constantly about "getting lost in the crowd," and they understand that they will be dependent after their own IPO on analysts for disseminating news and developments about their company. It is logical that an analyst that has already successfully covered companies in the same industry, and who has a substantial institutional following, will be able to do the same thing for the IPO candidate. It also stands to reason that an analyst will be more willing to cover a newly public company if the banking side of the firm has played a significant role in bringing the IPO to market and many of the firm's customers have taken positions in the stock.

---

securities in a particular area of the country. In other cases, a co-manager may be brought in to compensate for the book-running manager's relative weakness in covering institutional or retail customers, as the case may be.

Some investment bankers believe that it is easier to obtain the mandate for an initial public offering than for the financing that follows it. The expectations that are created in the minds of the issuer's management through the investment banking firm's efforts to sell itself are so high that they can seldom be met. The issuer's disappointment may be fanned by the firms that were not selected. If the deal is not going well, these firms will not hesitate to call the chief financial officer to say, "We told you so."

Occasionally a firm having no prior relationship with an issuer will earn the job of managing an underwriting because it brought to the company a creative idea that met its financial needs. To compete effectively in an environment in which traditional relationships have declined in importance, investment bankers must be innovative. The major firms have formed product development departments to create new financial instruments, both debt and equity, that are marketed to potential issuers, whether or not they are historical clients of the firm. The firm that convinces a chief financial officer to issue its own brand of innovative security expects to be awarded the business of selling the issue.

Getting Organized and Other Preliminary Matters

Once the issuer has given an investment banker a mandate[5] to proceed with an SEC-registered public offering (other than a shelf-registered takedown of investment-grade debt securities,

---

5. Should the mandate be memorialized in a "letter of intent"? Many investment banking firms would not dream of commencing work on an M&A assignment or a private placement without an engagement letter that spells out their fee and provides for indemnification, but the same firms will seldom if ever enter into a letter of intent in connection with a public securities offering. Some issuers may press for a letter of intent for the sake of its symbolic value, i.e., a letter signed by a reputable investment banking firm—even a letter that states that it is not legally binding—may be comforting to investors or creditors. Some bankers may press for a letter of intent for the sake of up-front or continuing fees or in order to discourage competing proposals. Unfortunately, letters of intent often lead to litigation based on claims that they contained discrete provisions intended to be binding or that they created "fiduciary" obligations. *See, e.g., Café La France, Inc. v. Schneider Securities, Inc.*, 281 F. Supp. 2d 361 (D.R.I. 2003).

as discussed in Chapter 8), it is time for the parties to get together to plan a course of action. The kickoff of a public offering is the organizational meeting or conference call, in which all hands participate to set the underwriting process in motion. The participants will include the managing underwriter, underwriters' counsel, the issuer's principal officers and representatives of its accounting firm and the law firm that will act as issuer's counsel.[6] On this occasion, a timetable will be reviewed and the responsibility for the various documents will be assigned to the members of the working group.

The job of preparing a first draft of the registration statement usually is assigned to the issuer's lawyers and the company officers responsible for gathering the required factual data. The preparation of the financial statements to be included in the registration statement will be supervised by the issuer's chief financial officer, who will be assisted by the issuer's accounting staff and its independent public accountants. The first draft of the underwriting documents will be prepared by underwriters' counsel. Preparation of the blue sky survey and the making of any necessary state and NASD filings generally is the responsibility of underwriters' counsel. The fee of underwriters' counsel for performing this function and any blue sky or NASD filing fees customarily are paid by the issuer.

Many substantive issues will be considered at the first meeting, or reviewed with those present if already decided. Must the amount of authorized common stock be increased? Should the stock be split to facilitate the offering? Is it "probable" that the company will make a significant acquisition that might require additional financial statements? Are the financial statements about to become "stale"? Are there accounting or disclosure issues that should be the subject of a pre-filing conference with the SEC staff? Are there portions of contracts subject to the exhibit filing requirements that the issuer wishes to make the subject of an application for confidential treatment?

---

6. In many cases, particularly if the issuer is a major corporation, the issuer's legal work will be handled by its inside counsel. The underwriters, however, are always represented by an independent law firm whose client is the syndicate as a whole and not just the book-running manager.

In the case of an IPO, what, if any, anti-takeover provisions should be adopted to ward off an unfriendly takeover attempt? If the transaction involves the sale of a minority interest in a subsidiary, what operating and tax-sharing agreements should be put into place? What plans does the company have for granting stock options to key employees? Will the filing of the registration statement trigger registration rights held by shareholders who acquired stock in a private placement? Other substantive issues to be considered at the organizational meeting are discussed below.

Housekeeping matters will be dealt with as well, such as the selection of a financial printer, an indenture trustee if debt securities are to be issued and a transfer agent if the shares are not publicly traded. At this meeting or shortly thereafter, the issuer will be given a list of documents that the managing underwriter and counsel will need to review. Due diligence visits will be scheduled. (Due diligence is considered in more detail in Chapter 5.)

- *Form of Registration Statement*

In the case of an IPO, the issuer will file its registration statement using Form S-1. This is the all-purpose form for issuers that do not meet the requirements for the use of a more convenient form such as Form S-3.[7] If the issuer is already an SEC-reporting company, the issuer's counsel will by the time of the organizational meeting have made a determination as to whether the issuer is eligible to use Form S-3.

Form S-3 is an abbreviated document required to include information about the securities being registered, the plan of distribution and similar matters. All other disclosures may be provided through incorporation by reference of the issuer's latest

---

7. Form S-2 is a general purpose form that is not generally used. Other forms are available for specialized types of issuers or transactions. For example, Form S-8 may be used for the registration of securities to be offered to employees (including consultants or advisers) under certain employee benefit plans. Registration statements on Form S-8 become effective automatically on filing, and they can therefore be abused. The SEC has found it necessary to emphasize that Form S-8 is not intended to be used in connection with the offer or sale of securities in capital-raising transactions. *See e.g.*, SEC Release No. 33-8407 (April 15, 2004).

annual report on Form 10-K and any subsequent quarterly report on Form 10-Q or current report on Form 8-K. Any 1934 Act reports or proxy statements filed after the effective date of the registration statement and prior to the termination of the offering are deemed to be incorporated by reference. The ability to amend and update the prospectus through subsequent 1934 Act filings (without the need to reprint or sticker the prospectus itself) is important for Rule 415 shelf registration programs, which are discussed in Chapter 8.

An issuer may file a registration statement on Form S-3 if it meets all of the following *registrant requirements*:

- it is organized under the laws of the United States or any state or territory or the District of Columbia and has its principal operations in the Untied States or its territories;

- it has a class of securities registered pursuant to Section 12(b) or Section 12(g) of the 1934 Act or is required to file reports pursuant to Section 15(d) of the 1934 Act;

- it has been subject to the 1934 Act filing requirements and has made all required 1934 Act filings (including EDGAR filings) for a period of at least 12 calendar months, and all filings during the immediately preceding 12 calendar months (and any fraction of a month) have been made on a timely basis;[8] and

- neither it nor any of its subsidiaries has failed to make a required preferred stock dividend or sinking fund payment

---

8. When the SEC expanded in 2004 the number of items required to be reported on Form 8-K, it amended Form S-3 to excuse late Form 8-K filings triggered "solely" by specific events that it ackowledged required the making of "rapid materiality and similar judgments within the compressed . . . filing timeframe" introduced by the 2004 amendments. SEC Release No. 33-8400 (March 16, 2004). The events are listed in General Instruction I(A)(3)(b) to Form S-3. The late filing is excused, however, only until the due date of the next Form 10-Q. Moreover, the issuer must be current in its Form 8-K reports as of the time it files the S-3 registration statement. As discussed in Chapter 8, late filings do not necessarily make an effective registration statement unavailable for "shelf takedowns."

The timely and current requirement is not affected by a finding by management or the auditors that the issuer's internal control over financial

or defaulted on payment of any material indebtedness or long-term lease rentals since the end of the most recent fiscal year for which a Form 10-K annual report has been filed.

A foreign private issuer satisfying all of the foregoing conditions other than the first condition is eligible provided the 1934 Act reports filed were the same as those required of a U.S. registrant.

Issuers of investment-grade ABS need not meet the 1934 Act registration or reporting history requirements.

Use of Form S-3 is also conditioned on the offering meeting at least one of the following *transaction requirements*:

- a primary or secondary offering of securities for cash if the issuer has a "float" of at least $75 million (float is computed by reference to the market value of the issuer's voting and non-voting common equity held by non-affiliates);
- a primary offering for cash of non-convertible debt or preferred securities that are rated investment grade;
- any secondary offering of a security that is either listed on a stock exchange or quoted on NASDAQ;

---

reporting is not effective so long as the issuer has timely satisfied its other reporting obligations. Office of the Chief Accountant and Division of Corporation Finance, *Frequently Asked Questions* (June 22, 2004), Question 4.

Before EDGAR, it was necessary to worry about whether a 1934 Act report had been delivered to the SEC on time. Even with EDGAR, timeliness should not be assumed but should be checked. Note that Rule 12b-25 under the 1934 Act provides that an issuer that fails to file certain specified reports on time must file a Form 12b-25 by the business day after the due date. The form must disclose the issuer's inability to file the report in a timely fashion and the reasons therefor in reasonable detail. The report will be deemed to have been filed on the prescribed due date if the Form 12b-25 represents that the delay could not have been prevented except by means of unreasonable effort or expense and that any late annual report will be filed within 15 calendar days or that any quarterly report will be filed within five calendar days; it is also necessary, of course, that the report actually be filed within such periods. By following this procedure, the registrant may retain its eligibility to use Form S-3 once the filing is made; it may not use the form, however, until the filing is actually made.

- dividend reinvestment plans, rights offerings and securities offered on conversion of outstanding convertible securities or on the exercise of outstanding warrants; or
- investment grade asset-backed securities.

Several other important points should be noted about the Form S-3 transaction requirements. First, Form S-3 may be used to register non-convertible debt or preferred securities rated investment-grade even if the issuer does not meet the float test. Second, the form may be used for secondary offerings of listed or NASDAQ securities even if the issuer does not meet the float or investment-grade tests. Third, because of the requirement that primary offerings on Form S-3 be "for cash," the form may not be used for exchange offers. (Form S-4 is used for exchange offers and similar transactions.)

Form S-3 may be used to register securities issued by a majority-owned subsidiary that does not itself meet the registrant and transaction tests if

- the parent meets the registrant requirements and the subsidiary is registering straight debt or preferred securities rated investment-grade; or
- the parent meets the registrant requirements and the applicable transaction requirement (e.g., the "float" test) and fully and unconditionally guarantees the securities being registered (which may not be convertible securities).

The form of signature page for a registration statement on Form S-3 requires a certification by the issuer that it has reasonable grounds to believe that it meets all of the requirements for filing on that form. The officer signing on behalf of the issuer must be in a position to make this certification, and the issuer's counsel should make sure that the certification properly can be made.

On occasion, a discussion with the SEC staff may result in the staff acquiescing in the issuer's use of Form S-3 notwithstanding its failure to meet one or more technical conditions. The question may be raised whether staff concurrence is sufficient. If an issuer does not strictly comply with the registrant requirements of Form S-3, can a purchaser of the securities claim a 1933 Act violation on the basis that there was no effective registration statement in that it was filed on the wrong form? Rule 401(g) under the 1933 Act puts this issue to rest. It provides that any registration statement or any amendment thereto "shall be deemed to be filed on the proper form" unless the SEC raises an objection prior to the effective date.

Can counsel rely on Rule 401(g) to opine that the registration statement complies as to form in all material respects with the requirements of the 1933 Act? This may be a closer question.

- *Gun-Jumping Questions*

It is important at the organizational meeting to discuss the need for the issuer and the managing underwriters to avoid any conduct that would constitute an illegal "offer" of the registered securities. As discussed in Chapter 1, any offer of the securities prior to the filing of the registration statement constitutes "gun-jumping." Even after filing, it is illegal to make any written offer of the registered securities except by means of the preliminary prospectus. The common ingredient in these various types of illegal offer is a communication that attempts to "condition the market" for the new offering. As discussed in Chapter 1, it is sometimes helpful in this regard to analyze a communication in terms of its audience, timing and content.

It is clear, however, that management should be carefully warned to exercise caution in any discussions with the press or with analysts and above all to avoid references to the forthcoming issue. Indeed, unless there is to be a Rule 135 announcement of the proposed financing, knowledge of the prospective offering should be confined to those who "need to know." The fact that a financing is in the works should be assumed to be a material fact (although arguably a prospective debt financing may not be), and those in the know should not purchase or sell any of the issuer's securities until the financing is disclosed to the public.[9] If the company employs a financial public relations

---

9. Whether or not prohibited by antimanipulation rules (*see* Chapter 4) or insider trading restraints, it is usually not a good idea for individuals involved in the registration process to trade in the issuer's equity securities during this period of time. For example, if a senior officer were to sell shares during the preparation of a common stock offering, the required Form 4 disclosure could have a chilling effect on the underwriter's marketing efforts. If an investment banker were to buy

firm, its activities must be carefully monitored. If the company has an in-house publication distributed to employees, this must also be monitored. (Such publications are often of value in connection with the due diligence investigation.)

As discussed below under "Dealing with Gun-Jumping Problems," the press is often persistent in trying to report on forthcoming IPOs. This is unavoidable, but all participants in the offering must be cautioned not to initiate or facilitate press coverage. Given the frequency of problems in this area, perhaps the T-shirt worn by a Google officer at a June 2004 technology conference—which carried "Quiet Period" on the front and "Can't answer questions" on the back—should become a standard handout at organizational meetings.

• • *Websites.* Most companies maintain a website as a means of facilitating communication with shareholders, customers, suppliers and others. The website may contain 1934 Act reports, annual and quarterly reports to shareholders, transcripts of officers' speeches, new product announcements, press releases or transcripts or summaries of shareholders' or analysts' meetings. Some companies even include the text of broker-dealer research reports, although this practice—especially if only selected reports are included—involves some risk of the issuer becoming "entangled" with the report in a way that could result in liability for the report's contents.

In a 2000 release,[10] the SEC cautioned that it was necessary for an issuer "in registration" to consider the gun-jumping consequences of all of its communications with the public, including information on the issuer's own website as well as on any third-party website to which the issuer has established a hyperlink. The release also stated that such issuers "should maintain communications with the public as long as the subject matter of the communications is limited to ordinary-course business

---

shares of an issuer while working on a financing for that issuer, it may be difficult for him to convince his superiors, or indeed the SEC, that he did not buy on the strength of favorable information uncovered in his due diligence investigation. In this context, it is best to be like Caesar's wife.

10. SEC Release No. 33-7856 (April 28, 2000).

SELECTED ISSUES 133

and financial information," which might include the following:
- advertisements concerning the issuer's products and services;
- 1934 Act reports required to be filed with the SEC;
- proxy statements, annual reports and dividend notices;
- press announcements concerning business and financial developments;
- "answers to unsolicited telephone inquiries concerning business matters from securities analysts, financial analysts, security holders and participants in the communications field who have a legitimate interest in the issuer's affairs;" and
- security holders' meetings and responses to security holder inquiries relating to these matters.[11]

The release also advised that an IPO issuer that had established "a history of ordinary course business communications through its web site should be able to continue to provide business and financial information on its site," but it advised more caution if the issuer were establishing the website contemporaneously with its preparations for its IPO.

In other words, so long as the issuer's website has been maintained with reasonable regularity and does not contain any references to the offering (at least none that would not be permissible if made in written form), there should be no need for the issuer to "purge" its website just because a securities offering is in the works.

Issuers, underwriters and counsel should keep in mind that the SEC staff will often visit the issuer's website as a routine part of its review of the registration statement. In the case of IPOs, this has become standard practice.

• • *Product Advertisements.* When beginning work on a registration statement, it is advisable to review the issuer's

---

11. The items enumerated in the release have their antecedents in prior SEC releases, e.g., SEC Release Nos. 33-5992 (November 7, 1978), 33-5180 (August 16, 1971), 33-5009 (October 7, 1969), 33-4697 (May 28, 1964) and 33-3844 (October 8, 1957).

advertising program. As the SEC has observed on many occasions, there is no reason why a company should stop advertising its products or services merely because it is about to go into registration. No one would suggest otherwise. But the type of advertisements that stress a company's strength and growth, which are sometimes seen in the financial press in proximity to the stock quotations, may well raise problems if the issuer has no track record of publishing such advertisements and they begin to appear at or about the time of an offering. As discussed in Chapter 9, it was this concern that motivated Deutsche Telekom AG, prior to its 1996 global IPO, to obtain no-action relief from the SEC staff regarding "image" advertising and certain other publicity.

• • *Annual Reports.* If the annual report to shareholders is scheduled to be released while the company is in registration, early drafts and final proofs should be reviewed by counsel to ensure that no statements are made that could raise questions under the 1933 Act (or that might be inconsistent with statements in the registration statement or documents incorporated by reference). The SEC has taken the position that annual reports should not present a 1933 Act problem if they are of the character and content normally published by a company and do not contain material designed to assist in a proposed offering.[12] Editing of the report to make sure that it does not contain statements that could be so construed may be advisable under these circumstances.

• • *Presentations to Securities Analysts.* An officer of an SEC-reporting company may ask whether there is any problem with his or her scheduled appearance at a meeting of securities analysts. The question is usually a polite way of stating that there had better not be a problem. In fact, there is not likely to be much of a problem if the issuer is offering its debt securities. Even in the case of a common stock offering, the SEC's staff recognizes the importance of ongoing communications with analysts and will not object to them while an issuer is in registration so long as it has a consistent history of these activities.[13] It is not a

---

12. SEC Release No. 33-3844 (October 8, 1957).
13. *See* SEC No-action Letter, *William E. Chatlos; Georgeson & Co.* (February 3, 1977).

good idea, however, to schedule such an appearance after work has begun on a common stock offering.

If the meeting is scheduled for a date prior to the filing of a registration statement for a common stock offering, then a press release meeting the requirements of Rule 135 should be issued several days in advance of the meeting. The officer cannot in good conscience make his or her presentation without advising the analysts that a financing is imminent. But even before Regulation FD, a company that informed analysts of a proposed financing would have been expected to inform the public as well.

Cancellation of a scheduled appearance is not without its risks. Analysts may speculate that the cancellation is a sign that the issuer is involved in preparations for a public offering or even an acquisition. Or the analysts may downgrade the stock because they fear that the issuer has "nothing good to talk about."

Although a scheduled speech to analysts may be permitted, hard copies of the speech should not be distributed during the registration period. This created a serious problem for a transaction in the mid-1950s. Two weeks prior to the filing of a registration statement, the president of the issuer delivered a prepared address before the New York Society of Security Analysts. His talk had been scheduled several months earlier at a time when the registered offering had not been contemplated. In his speech, he discussed his company's operations and expansion program, its sales and its earnings. The speech included a forecast of sales and referred to the issuer's proposal to file with the SEC later in the month a registration statement with respect to a proposed offering of convertible debentures. Copies of the speech were distributed to approximately 4,000 analysts. The matter was discussed with the staff of the SEC. Because the speech had been booked months in advance, the staff agreed that the offering could proceed.

That was not the end of the story. At that time, acceleration of the effectiveness of a registration statement required action at a formal meeting of the SEC. The commissioners would meet every morning and declare registration statements effective. Despite the staff's affirmative recommendation, the commissioners decided at the last minute to deny acceleration until after the company had distributed copies of its preliminary prospectus to all persons who had been sent copies of the speech. In this case, the SEC was not concerned with the speech itself but rather with the widespread distribution of the hard copy. The result was a disaster. The market took a bad turn, and when the deal was later revived, it was on far less favorable terms.[14]

The analysts who attend a company presentation may be subject to their own restrictions about what they can report about the meeting. If their firms are prospective underwriters, they will be subject to the restrictions on research coverage discussed later in this chapter.

• • *Restricted Lists.* The managing underwriter that has a handshake agreement with an issuer to proceed with a financing must implement compliance procedures to avoid gun-jumping violations, Rule 10b-5 violations (based on trading the issuer's securities on the basis of material non-public information) and Regulation M violations. Members of the underwriting syndicate must do likewise when they decide to accept the manager's invitation to participate in the financing.

Before announcement of an offering, many underwriters will place the issuer's securities on a "gray" or "watch" list. This is a highly confidential list of securities whose market price could be affected by material unannounced transactions in which the underwriter is involved. The primary purpose of the list is to enable the underwriter's compliance department to monitor proprietary and employee trading to be on the alert for possible "leaks." In some firms, the list also serves as a means of prohibiting arbitrage activity and as a means of triggering special review procedures for research material.

Once a transaction has been announced (or, in some cases, when the firm's involvement in a previously announced transaction is publicly disclosed), the affected securities may be moved from the "gray" or "watch" list to a "restricted" list. While still a confidential document, the restricted list is much more widely distributed within a securities firm. It generally identifies securities in which a compliance officer's prior approval is required for any proprietary or employee transaction (and, in some cases,

---

14. This incident was the subject of Example No. 7 in SEC Release No. 33-3844 (available October 8, 1957). *See also id.*, Example No. 6.

even customer transactions). Securities on the restricted list are also subject to special procedures that require that all related research be approved by a compliance officer (or, in some firms, a person designated by the director of research). See the discussion in Chapter 4 regarding Regulation M.

It is a good idea for underwriters' counsel to be familiar with the managing underwriters' "gray" or "watch" list or restricted list procedures and how (and by whom) they are implemented. Underwriters' counsel should also be familiar with the managing underwriters' "Chinese Wall" procedures (discussed later in this chapter).

- *Stock Exchange Listing; "Blue Sky" Considerations*

In the case of an IPO, an issue that will be raised at the first meeting is whether the stock should be listed on the NYSE (assuming the listing requirements can be met) or whether the over-the-counter NASDAQ market will best serve the interests of the company and its shareholders. Some investment bankers will advise that NASDAQ can provide as deep and as liquid a market as the NYSE's floor-based auction market. Some issuers will opt for NASDAQ because they believe it to be more "modern" and "high-tech." Other issuers may opt for an NYSE listing because they conclude that the opportunity for price improvement is important to their shareholders and more likely to be available on the NYSE. Others list on the NYSE simply because they believe it provides more prestige. Recently, some companies have elected to have their securities trade in both markets.

If the securities are to be listed on an exchange or quoted on NASDAQ, it will be necessary to "register" the class of securities under the 1934 Act as well as to register the offered securities under the 1933 Act. In the case of an IPO, the relevant filings can incorporate the 1933 Act documents.

For many years, most state securities or "blue sky" laws provided an exemption from state registration requirements for public offerings of securities that were listed on the NYSE or the American Stock Exchange (as well as certain securities of senior or equal rank). Most of these states extended the exemption to IPOs that were to be listed at the time of the offering. Some states also exempted securities that were quoted on the NASDAQ National Market. The exemption was extremely useful since the blue sky hurdles for a non-exempt offering could be formidable in terms of time, expense and possible inability to offer the shares in some states.

The blue sky situation has been considerably simplified by the National Securities Markets Improvement Act of 1996 (Improvement Act). That statute amended Section 18 of the 1933 Act to preempt state registration requirements for securities listed "or authorized to be listed" on the NYSE or the American Stock Exchange or "listed" on the NASDAQ National Market (or, in either case, securities of equal or senior ranking). It is presumably safe to rely on this preemption once a letter has been received from the NYSE or the American Stock Exchange confirming that the security will be listed, as is customary, "upon notice of issuance."[15] The preemption also extends, however, to a security that will be so listed "upon completion of the transaction." This is probably intended to permit underwriters to commence their marketing efforts before the issuer has received a listing "authorization" from the exchange. Reliance on the extended preemption to make offers in a given state may involve some risk in the event that the authorization is not forthcoming. Indeed, if an offering were abandoned, would a state seek administrative penalties against an underwriter for making illegal offers? This would presumably be contrary to the spirit of the Improvement Act.

- *Issuer-Directed Shares*

A topic of discussion that frequently arises in the early planning stages of an initial public offering is whether a portion of the offering should be reserved for sale to employees, customers,

---

15. It is not clear whether Congress intended the apparent distinction between listed and NASDAQ securities insofar as "authorization" is concerned. The NASD and at least one state securities regulator have been reported as having different views on this point. A further ambiguity arises because of the absence of a definition of the term "authorized." It is not clear, for example, whether a listing approval would be sufficient for purposes of the Improvement Act if it is conditioned not only on issuance of the securities but also on compliance with the market's distribution or governance requirements.

SELECTED ISSUES

suppliers and other "friends and family" of the company. The founder and chief executive officer is proud of the company that he has built and that he now plans to take public. He is convinced beyond question that his company's shares will be a terrific investment, that they surely will soar in value as the business continues to grow, strengthened by the new capital raised in the public offering. Shouldn't those employees who worked so hard through the difficult early years, those customers whose loyalty has been a key factor in the company's success and those suppliers who were so generous with their credit terms in the days when cash was tight be assured that they will be able to buy shares in the public offering?

It can be persuasively argued that issuer-directed shares are not a good idea. Employees, in particular, can get in over their heads in an effort to demonstrate their loyalty to the company. Even for customers and suppliers, the goodwill that will prevail if the price of the stock does go up will never exceed the ill will resulting from a decline in the market price.

All of these arguments notwithstanding, underwriters will often defer to the wishes of the issuer and agree to reserve a specified portion of an initial public offering for sale to persons designated by the issuer. In almost all cases, the shares are reserved for sale to these persons at the public offering price. Any suggestion that they be sold at a discount should be resisted.[16] These shares are in fact being underwritten. The managing underwriter must find a home for any of the reserved shares that are not purchased and paid for by the issuer's designees. For the most part, the designees will not be established customers of the managing underwriter. Thus, the manager must incur the considerable expense of opening an account for what may well be a single trade. With no broker-customer relationship at stake, the issuer's designees may be the first to renege on their purchases if the price of the shares falls below the public offering price before the settlement date. The underwriters are entitled to be compensated for incurring these risks.

---

16. The rules of the NASD do not prohibit two-tier pricing (*see* Chapter 6), so this is a business issue rather than a legal one.

In some cases where issuer-directed shares have been offered at a discount, the offer was made directly by the issuer and not through the underwriters. This is not a very satisfactory procedure. Most issuers are simply not equipped to handle the record-keeping details involved in the process of issuing shares and collecting payment from a substantial number of people. Moreover, it must bear the risk of an unsuccessful offering. In some states a direct sale by an issuer may require registration as a dealer in securities.

The requirement that a registration statement describe the plan of distribution mandates that the arrangements for reserving shares for persons designated by the issuer be fully disclosed in the prospectus. The letter or other notice directed to the persons for whom shares are being reserved can itself constitute gun-jumping and should therefore be drafted so as to come within the safe harbor of Rule 134. The SEC staff will often request information about the directed-share program in order to satisfy itself that there is no Section 5 violation.

During the Internet Bubble, the amount of an IPO reserved for "friends and family" increased dramatically from traditional levels to as much as 10% of the offering. An NYSE/NASD advisory committee[17] concluded in 2003 that "[w]hen misused or overused, an issuer's 'friends and family' program may compromise the IPO process." The committee recommended that the SEC and the SROs establish reasonable parameters for such programs by imposing a 5% ceiling and requiring that any lock-up applicable to insider shares be extended to the shares purchased by "friends and family."

The committee also recommended additional disclosure in the prospectus regarding "friends and family" sales, including the number of persons participating, the largest, smallest, and average purchase, the minimum percentage being allocated to employees, the categories of recipients and allocations over a specified threshold. Some of the additional disclosure recommended by the committee would be difficult to include in the final prospectus on a timely basis.

---

17. NYSE/NASD IPO Advisory Committee, *Report and Recommendations* 13 (May 2003).

Preparation of the Registration Statement

In the days following the organizational meeting, the company and its counsel will begin the preparation of the registration statement. If the registration statement is on Form S-3, a decision will have been made as to whether the prospectus is to be "bare bones" or "beefed up"—that is, whether it is to contain virtually no information as permitted by Form S-3 or whether for marketing reasons the underwriters would prefer to include a description of the issuer's business and at least summary financial data. Generally speaking, a more extensive description of the issuer will be found in prospectuses for large common stock offerings, for "high yield" bonds and for securities issued by companies that have been the subject of recent restructurings or involved in material acquisitions or divestitures.

The drafting of the registration statement requires far more than responding to the items of the applicable form and Regulation S-K. While the financial statements constitute the skeleton on which the registration statement is built, the management's discussion and analysis of financial condition and results of operations (the MD&A) and the business description provide the muscle and flesh, whether they are set forth in the document itself or incorporated by reference to the annual report on Form 10-K.

- *"Plain English"*

The business description should be factual and non-technical. The company's officers must be made to realize that the terms that they use in their daily business conversation may be incomprehensible to the average investor and thus may require clarification in the text of the registration statement.

Prospectuses have frequently been criticized as being unreadable or, even worse, as being drafted "to obscure, rather than reveal, in plain English, the critical elements of a proposed business deal. . . ."[18] There are certainly horrible examples of badly

---

18. *Feit v. Leasco Data Processing Equip. Corp.*, 332 F. Supp. 544, 549 (E.D.N.Y. 1971) (Weinstein, D.J.).

written prospectuses, but good securities lawyers have always taken pains to avoid ambiguous or obscure statements in their disclosure documents. At the same time, it cannot be denied that many companies and transactions are complex or that disclosure documents are read primarily by professional investors or their advisers.

In 1998, the SEC adopted a new Rule 421(d) that requires the use of "plain English" writing principles when drafting the front and back cover pages and the summary and risk factor sections of a prospectus.[19] It also amended Rule 421(b), which had already required the entire prospectus to be "clear, concise and understandable," to require

- the presentation of information "in clear, concise sections, paragraphs, and sentences" and the use, whenever possible, of "short, explanatory sentences and bullet lists;"
- the use of descriptive headings and subheadings;
- avoiding frequent reliance on glossaries or defined terms as the primary means of explaining information in the prospectus; and
- avoiding legal and highly technical business terminology.

Later that year, the SEC also published *A Plain English Handbook: How to Create Clear SEC Disclosure Documents* as further assistance for lawyers and others responsible for preparing prospectuses. In 1999, the staff updated Staff Legal Bulletin No. 7 on this subject. The bulletin contains sample staff comments on plain English disclosure in the body of the prospectus as well as on the cover pages and in the risk factors and summary sections. Both the handbook and the bulletin are in need of update to reflect current staff policies.

---

19. SEC Release No. 33-7497 (January 28, 1998). The techniques spelled out in Rule 421(d) include short sentences, "definite, concrete, everyday words," active voice, "tabular presentation or bullet lists for complex material, whenever possible," no legal jargon or highly technical business terms and no multiple negatives.

The adjustment to plain English disclosure required a considerable effort on the part of the SEC in reviewing and commenting on 1933 Act disclosure documents and an even greater effort on the part of the securities bar. By now, the adjustment process has been largely completed, even though the staff will from time to time make an unexpected request.

Plain English principles have come to be widely applied, even where not strictly required by the SEC rules. For example, 1934 Act reports are customarily written in plain English even though the rules apply only to 1933 Act filings. The SEC staff has never formally insisted on the use of plain English principles in drafting 1934 Act documents that are incorporated into Form S-3 registration statements, but it strongly favors plain English and often encourages in a forceful manner its use on a general basis.

- *Risk Factors*

The persons preparing a prospectus must anticipate the problems that the company may face in the future and set them forth as possible risks for the investor. This is not to say that every prospectus must have a section containing a litany of "risk factors." This is required only where there are factors, as described in Item 503(c) of Regulation S-K, "that make the offering speculative or risky." But every prospectus should point out where appropriate those factors that could have a negative impact on the business.

Some issuers and underwriters tried in the past to straddle the question whether an offering involved high risk by including a section with a heading such as "Certain Investment Considerations." The SEC amended what are now Items 501(b), 502(a) and 503(c) in 1995 to require that any discussion required by that item be captioned "Risk Factors," that it be included immediately following the summary section or cover page and that a specific reference to it (by page number) be included on the cover page of the prospectus and in the table of contents.[20]

---

20. SEC Release No. 33-7168 (May 11, 1995).

It is unfortunate that issuers and underwriters, sometimes (but not always) at the urging of SEC examiners, have expanded the list of risk factors in many offerings to the point where the reader has difficulty distinguishing the real risks from the remote risks. For example, the prospectus for a 2004 IPO—admittedly for a large and complex company—described 55 risk factors in more than 30 pages! Issuers and underwriters should exercise self-restraint in this regard and, where necessary, should not hesitate to argue to an SEC examiner checking off a list of favorite risk factors that the inclusion of boilerplate in the risk factor section will distract attention from the real risks that should be focused on by potential investors and their financial advisers. Indeed, the SEC cautioned in its 1998 plain English adopting release against the use of boilerplate and the discussion of risk "in purely generic terms." It also advised issuers to place any risk factor in context so investors can understand the specific risk as it applies to a particular issuer and its operations.

All this being said, reasonable people can obviously disagree over which risks are real and which are remote or obvious. For example, the authors would regard "the lack of an established trading market" for an IPO as an obvious risk that does not need to be stated in the prospectus. On the other hand, Item 503(c) expressly refers to the absence of a previous trading market as a factor to be disclosed *if* it makes the offering "speculative" or "risky." This need not be the case, however, if the issuer's common stock is to be listed on the NYSE or the co-managers have a good track record of making a market in their IPO stocks.

Some of the problems associated with "risk factor" disclosure were addressed in the SEC's 1997 release proposing the adoption of plain English requirements.[21] Two of the SEC's suggestions were to require a prioritization of risk factors, that is, that they be discussed in the order of their importance, and to limit the number of risk factors. Neither suggestion was adopted.

As noted above, Staff Legal Bulletin No. 7 contains sample staff comments on risk factors.

---

21. SEC Release No. 33-7380 (January 14, 1997).

SELECTED ISSUES 145

- *Prospectus Summary*

Item 503(a) of Regulation S-K advises issuers to include a summary of the information contained in the prospectus where the length or complexity of the prospectus makes a summary useful. Some securities lawyers resisted for a time the inclusion of summaries in prospectuses because of their concern that something important might be omitted. It is a fact, however, that many investors and securities professionals will read only the summary section of the prospectus. For that reason, summaries are customary in IPOs and other offerings (e.g., complex structured securities) that require an increased marketing effort.

As part of its 1997 plain English proposals, the SEC emphasized that a prospectus summary should "provide investors with a clear, concise and coherent 'snapshot' description of the most significant aspects of the offering." It criticized "summaries" that ran 10 to 30 pages and asked for comment on whether prospectus summaries should be limited to a specific number of pages. The SEC eventually decided not to pursue this idea.

As noted above, Staff Legal Bulletin No. 7 contains sample staff comments on the summary section of the prospectus.

One of the most important parts of the summary—and sometimes the most difficult to write—is the capsule description of the issuer's business. This description should explain to the reader in as few words as possible just what it is that the company does and what makes it different from its competitors. Frequently, this includes a brief discussion of the company's business strategy. The summary should also include a reference to significant risks associated with the company's business but without attempting to enumerate all of the risk factors set forth in the document.

These are simple goals, but they are often not easily achieved. For one thing, the underwriters and their counsel improve their understanding of the issuer's business as work on the transaction progresses. For another, the issuer's managers usually have strong (and sometimes conflicting) opinions about just what makes their company special. For these reasons, the business summary often ends up being revised more than any other part of the prospectus.

Other Selected Issues

No book can provide adequate instructions on the preparation of a registration statement. This is an art that can be learned only by experience. A few additional points, however, may be worth mentioning: the role of the securities analyst in connection with IPOs, the preparation of the MD&A section of the prospectus, the role of projections and other forward-looking information, the SEC's special disclosure and other requirements for IPOs, online offerings, Internet auctions, "deal sites," the treatment of guarantees and other credit enhancement and the making of requests for confidential treatment.

As noted earlier, due diligence is discussed in Chapter 5.

- *Role of the Securities Analyst in Securities Offerings*

During the Internet Bubble, securities analysts from the major investment banking firms played a major role in IPOs and, less frequently, in other securities offerings. A highly ranked industry analyst gave his or her firm an important advantage in competing to "run the books" on an IPO. The analyst would also participate in due diligence, help to come up with an earnings estimate for use in the IPO and would participate in the roadshow. In addition, the analyst would publish a research report on the IPO as soon as the post-offering prospectus delivery period expired.

Following the collapse of the Internet Bubble, there were sensational revelations about how some analysts had permitted investment banking considerations to obscure their true views on the investment merits of many stocks. These revelations were followed by SRO rules that mandated a separation between investment banking and securities research and also by a "global settlement" by ten major investment banking firms with the SEC, state law enforcement authorities and the SROs.

In May 2002, the SEC approved SRO rules designed to address conflicts of interest in connection with the preparation

SELECTED ISSUES **147**

and publication of research reports and public appearances relating to equity securities.[22] The most important elements of the 2002 rules include

- a prohibition on offering favorable research to induce issuers to award investment banking business;

- structural reforms to increase analyst independence, including a prohibition on investment banking personnel supervising analysts or approving research reports;

- a prohibition on tying analyst compensation to a specific investment banking transaction;

- a prohibition on submitting a research report to the issuer prior to the report's publication, with a narrow exception for verifying facts;

- mandated "quiet periods" of 40 calendar days and ten calendar days for managers and co-managers following IPOs and follow-on offerings, respectively,[23] with exceptions for significant news or events and (in the case of follow-on offerings) for securities that meet the average daily trading volume (ADTV) test in Rule 101 of Regulation M and that also meet the requirements of Rule 139;

- increased disclosures of conflicts of interest in research reports and public appearances by analysts;

- restrictions on personal trading by analysts; and

- disclosure in research reports of data and price charts showing a firm's ratings track record.

---

22. SEC Release No. 34-45908 (May 10, 2002). The SRO research rules are located in NYSE Rules 472, 344 and 351 and in NASD Rule 2711.

23. As discussed in Chapter 1, Section 4(3)(B) of the 1933 Act in combination with Rule 174 mandates a "quiet period" of only 25 days following most IPOs and does not require any quiet period at all in the case of a follow-on offering of a reporting issuer.

After the enactment of Sarbanes–Oxley, which mandated further rulemaking, the SROs proposed rules that the SEC approved in July 2003.[24] These rules require the following additional steps to increase analyst independence:

- eliminating investment banking influence or control over analyst compensation by mandating the creation of an independent compensation committee to review and approve analyst compensation, with specific criteria that must be considered and other criteria (e.g., the analyst's contributions to the firm's investment banking business or a specific investment banking transaction) that must not be considered;
- prohibiting analyst participation in efforts to solicit investment banking business (with an exception for communications "the sole purpose of which is due diligence");
- extending the quiet periods following IPOs and follow-on offerings to views expressed by analysts in public appearances;
- introducing a 25-day IPO quiet period for all participating underwriters and dealers other than managers or co-managers;
- introducing a 15-day quiet period prior to or following the expiration, waiver or termination of a lock-up agreement (with exceptions for significant news or events and for research reports or public appearances regarding securities that meet the ADTV test in Rule 101 of Regulation M and that also meet the requirements of Rule 139);
- publishing a notice to customers in the event of termination of coverage of a company, with a final research report, recommendation and rating;

---

24. SEC Release No. 34-48252 (July 29, 2003).

– prohibiting any non-research personnel reviewing or approving, with a narrow exception for reviews for the purpose of checking factual accuracy; and

– prohibiting a firm's direct or indirect "retaliation" against an analyst because of an unfavorable research report or public statement about an investment banking client.

Other SRO rules regulate personal trading by analysts and specify additional disclosures in research reports.

The SROs published a joint memorandum in March 2004 that discussed and interpreted the new research rules.

In February 2003, the SEC also approved its Regulation AC.[25] This rule requires that broker-dealers include in research reports a statement by the research analyst certifying that the views expressed in the report accurately reflect his or her personal views and that no part of his or her compensation was, is or will be directly or indirectly related to the specific recommendations or views contained in the report. If the certification would not be true, specified disclosure must be provided.

In April 2003, the SEC, state law enforcement authorities and the SROs announced the settlement of enforcement actions against ten major investment banking firms.[26] The settlement included an agreement by the firms to implement structural changes to promote analyst independence, to provide additional disclosure regarding potential conflicts and to make available to their customers "independent" research. Relevant parts of the settlement include

– mandated separation of research and investment banking as business units, with separate reporting lines, separate legal and compliance staff and overall physical separation of the functions;

---

25. SEC Release No. 34-47384 (February 20, 2003).

26. Joint Press Release dated April 28, 2003 at www.sec.gov/news/press/2003-54.htm. The substantive terms of the global settlement are set forth in Addendum A to each of the individual settlements. The settlement was approved by a federal court on October 31, 2003. *See* www.sec.gov/litigation/litreleases/lr18438.htm.

- further safeguards against investment banking control or influence over research compensation, budget and coverage decisions;
- mandated "firewalls" between research and investment banking designed to prohibit all communications between the two functions, with exceptions that include (i) seeking or providing research views on the "merits" of a proposed transaction or on market or industry trends, conditions or developments, (ii) assisting "in confirming the adequacy of disclosure in offering or other disclosure documents" based on communications with the company "and other vetting" conducted outside the presence of investment banking personnel, where any views are expressed in the presence of counsel and (iii) expressing views to the firm's equity capital markets group on the "structuring and pricing" of an investment banking mandate or block bid or similar transaction; and
- a prohibition on research personnel participation in roadshows relating to a public offering or other investment banking transaction and on investment banking personnel's "directing" research personnel to engage in marketing or selling efforts to investors.

The terms of the global settlement apply literally only to the ten settling firms, and by its own terms it will be superseded by any SEC or SRO rules or interpretations that have the "stated intent" to supersede any provision of the global settlement. The SEC staff stated in late 2003 that it was considering whether any of the provisions of the global settlement should be applied to the industry more broadly—for example, by means of an SEC rule that would incorporate into one single federal standard all of the rules applicable to research analysts, including the SRO rules and certain provisions of the global settlement. The staff also noted that it was working with foreign regulators in an attempt to harmonize the U.S. and foreign rules dealing with research analyst conflicts of interest.

- *Management's Discussion and Analysis*

One of the most challenging assignments in the preparation of an SEC prospectus or other disclosure document, but particularly an IPO prospectus, is the preparation of the "Management's Discussion and Analysis of Financial Condition and Results of Operations."

The requirements for MD&A are set forth in Item 303 of Regulation S-K and the related instructions. The express requirements of the item have not changed significantly in many years, with the notable exception of recently added requirements regarding a company's off-balance sheet arrangements and tabular disclosure regarding its contractual obligations. But MD&A cannot be drafted solely on the basis of the literal requirements and instructions. The SEC's views on how companies should respond to the MD&A requirements are largely set forth in a series of interpretive releases, the most recent of which appeared in December 2003.[27]

As a disclosure discipline, MD&A has evolved far beyond its original limits, and its evolution is by no means complete. In the December 2003 Release, the SEC described the evolved purpose of MD&A as "not complicated," but rather as intended to provide readers with information "necessary to an understanding of [a company's] financial condition, changes in financial condition and results of operations." The MD&A requirements are intended to satisfy three principal objectives:

- to provide a narrative explanation of a company's financial statements that enables investors to see the company through the eyes of management;
- to enhance the overall financial disclosure and provide the context within which financial information should be analyzed; and
- to provide information about the quality of, and potential variability of, a company's earnings and cash flow, so that investors can ascertain the likelihood that past performance is indicative of future performance.

---

27. SEC Release No. 33-8350 (December 19, 2003) (December 2003 Release). In addition to the December 2003 Release, see the SEC's 1981 interpretive release on MD&A, SEC Release No. 33-6349 (September 29, 1981), and its 1989 interpretive release, SEC Release No. 33-6835 (May 18, 1989). Unless otherwise attributed, quotations in this discussion of MD&A are from the December 2003 Release.

- *MD&A: Taking a "Fresh Look"*

The SEC and its staff have frequently criticized the quality of companies' responses to the MD&A requirements.[28] In the December 2003 Release, the SEC cautioned that MD&A should not be "a recitation of financial statements in narrative form or an otherwise uninformative series of technical responses to MD&A requirements," neither of which provides any insight into management's "unique perspective on its business."

Accordingly, the SEC encouraged companies in the December 2003 Release to take a "fresh look" at their MD&A disclosures with a view to enhancing the quality of disclosure. The SEC also encouraged "early top-level involvement by a company's management in identifying the key disclosure themes and items that should be included in a company's MD&A."

• • *MD&A Presentation.* In the December 2003 Release, the SEC observed that the MD&A presentation of many companies had become unnecessarily lengthy, difficult to understand and confusing. It emphasized that it understood that complex companies and situations require disclosure of complex matters and that it was not in any way seeking over-simplification or "dumbing down" of MD&A. It also believed, on the other hand, that companies could improve the clarity and understandability of MD&A by using language that was "clearer and less convoluted." In this connection, it recommended that companies consider

- tabular presentations of relevant financial or other information;
- additional headings; and
- the use of a "layered" approach to disclosure (i.e., starting out with the most important information and following up with additional explanation).

---

28. *See, e.g.,* the Summary by the Division of Corporation Finance of Significant Issues Addressed in the Review of the Periodic Reports of the Fortune 500 Companies (February 27, 2003), available on the SEC's website.

The SEC also stated its belief that the MD&A of many companies could benefit from adding an introduction, executive overview or summary that would provide a balanced, executive-level discussion that identified the most important themes or other significant matters that management relied on in evaluating the company's financial condition and operating results.[29]

• • *MD&A Content and Focus.* According to the December 2003 Release, MD&A should emphasize material information that is required or that promotes understanding and deemphasize (or, if appropriate, delete) immaterial information that is not required and does not promote understanding. Specifically, companies should focus on the following:

• • • *"Key Indicators."* Companies should consider disclosing the key "variables" or "indicators" and other factors that management uses to manage the business. While financial measures are generally the "starting point" for such disclosure, companies should also consider whether disclosure of non-financial factors "would be material to investors, and therefore required."[30] In determining what information is material for this purpose, companies should take into account the information they disclose to investors and other persons by means other than

---

29. In response to some lawyers' concern about the potential of increased civil liability arising from an executive overview or summary of MD&A, a senior SEC staff person advised them in late 2003 to "get over it."

30. Note 27 of the December 2003 Release suggested that such other factors might include, depending on a particular company's circumstances, manufacturing plant capacity and utilization, backlog, trends in bookings and employee turnover rates. The same note suggested that companies should also consider disclosing information "that may be peripheral to the accounting function, but is integral to the business or operating activity," e.g., measures "based on units or volume, customer satisfaction, time-to-market, interest rates, product development, service offerings, throughput capacity, affiliations/joint undertakings, market demand, customer/vendor relations, employee retention, business strategy, changes in the managerial approach or structure, regulatory actions or regulatory environment, and any other pertinent macroeconomic measures." Because these measures are generally non-financial in nature, the SEC did not believe that their disclosure would "generally" trigger the NGFM requirements.

SEC-filed reports (e.g., earnings releases, publicly accessible analysts' calls or companion website postings). The December 2003 Release also pointed to academic and other studies of "the types of information, outside of financial statement measures, that would be helpful to investors and other users." Such information might include external or macroeconomic matters as well as those specific to a company or industry.

The December 2003 Release also encouraged companies to provide "a balanced view of the underlying dynamics of the business, including not only a description of a company's successes, but also of instances when it failed to realize goals, if material. Good MD&A will focus readers' attention on these key matters."

• • • *Materiality.* Companies should take the December 2003 Release as an opportunity to delete information in their MD&A that has become stale or otherwise no longer material or useful. Segment information should also be reviewed to avoid unnecessary duplication and immaterial detail. Changes in line items should be discussed only where material and necessary to promote understanding. In the case of quarterly reports, materiality should be assessed in the context of the interim results.

• • • *Material Trends and Uncertainties.* Like prior SEC interpretations, the December 2003 Release emphasized the importance of a discussion and analysis of known trends, demands, commitments, events and uncertainties ("known material trends and uncertainties"). It reminded companies that disclosure in this area is required unless a company is able to conclude either that it is not reasonably likely that the trend, uncertainty or other event will occur or come to fruition, or that a material effect on the company's liquidity, capital resources or results of operations is not reasonably likely to occur.[31] It also advised companies, in

---

31. In other words, the SEC considers the Supreme Court's "probability/magnitude" test in *Basic Inc. v. Levinson*, 484 U.S. 224, 238–41 (1988) to be "inapposite to Item 303 disclosure." SEC Release No. 33-6835 (May 31, 1989) [hereinafter 1989 Interpretive Release], at note 27. In making this distinction, the SEC is presumably stating its views as to the standard that should govern companies' disclosure decisions regarding MD&A and not the standard that a court would apply for civil liability purposes, e.g., under Rule 10b-5.

the course of identifying such known material trends and uncertainties, to make use of the substantial amount of financial and non-financial information available to them. It also recommended that companies consider quantifying the material effects of known material trends and uncertainties and advised that such quantification may be required to the extent material if quantitative information is reasonably available.

• • • *Analysis.* The December 2003 Release emphasized that MD&A requires analysis as well as discussion. Identifying the "intermediate effects" of a known material trend and uncertainty might not be sufficient unless the company also provides the reasons underlying those intermediate effects. The release offered the illustration of a decline in sales and suggested that MD&A should identify the underlying material causes of the decline, including for example difficulties in production, decline in quality, loss of competitive position or a combination of these. In the event of restructuring or impairment charges, the release suggested that MD&A should analyze the underlying reasons such as the inability to realize economies of scale, a failure to renew or secure key customer contracts or inefficiencies resulting from aging equipment.

• • *Significance of Additional Information Available to Management.* An important indicator of the future direction of MD&A may be the SEC's and its staff's frequent observations in the recent past that "[c]ompanies have access to and use substantially more detailed and timely information about their financial condition and operating performance" than they did when MD&A requirements were first imposed. This information includes non-financial information that, in the SEC's view, also has a bearing on companies' financial condition and operating performance as well as on the identification and disclosure of known material trends and uncertainties.

In the December 2003 Release, the SEC pointed to "[c]hanges in business enterprise systems, communications and other aspects of information technology" as having significantly increased the amount of information available to management as well as the speed with which management receives and is able to use such information. "There is therefore a larger and more up-to-date universe of information, financial and non-financial alike, that companies have and should evaluate in determining whether disclosure is required." In addition, advances in technology can be expected to lead to even greater quantities of more up-to-date information, which can lead management to rely on different factors for operating and analyzing the business. "As this occurs, the discussion in MD&A should change over time to maintain an appropriate focus on material matters."

The SEC said in the December 2003 Release that it believed that this increased availability of information to management was relevant to the preparation of MD&A for three reasons:

- in evaluating an increased amount of information to determine which information is to be disclosed, companies should "avoid the information overload for investors that can result from disclosure of information that is not required, is immaterial, and does not promote understanding;"

- "in identifying, discussing and analyzing known material trends and uncertainties, companies are expected to consider all relevant information, even if that information is not required to be disclosed;" and

- "with advances in technology contributing to increasing amounts and currency of information, the factors relied upon by companies to operate and analyze the business may change," and as this occurs the MD&A should "change over time to maintain an appropriate focus on material factors."

Companies and underwriters should not overlook the litigation implications of the SEC's emphasis on the additional information now available to management. For many years, plaintiffs' lawyers' decisions whether to bring actions under Rule 10b-5 against a company or courts' decisions on motions to dismiss have been influenced by what a company might reasonably have been expected to know about adverse developments in its business. Information known to "the assistant controller in Dubuque" might not be communicated immediately to top management, or top management might not immediately appreciate its significance as evidence of a known material trend or uncertainty.

SEC references to the additional information available to management are generalizations, of course, and do not mean that top management in any particular instance should have been aware at the time of an MD&A filing of a material trend or uncertainty. The SEC's references are nevertheless likely to result in more inquiry, both in SEC enforcement actions and in private litigation, about "what management knew and when it knew it."

The SEC's references to additional information also have significance for the usefulness of the statutory safe harbors for forward-looking information (discussed below). The SEC has justified the forward-looking emphasis of MD&A in part on the basis that companies have available to them the statutory safe harbors where forward-looking information is accompanied by "meaningful cautionary statements." The courts have made it clear that the safe harbor is not available where an adverse event described as possible has already occurred. One can reasonably expect that the SEC's expansive view of the information available to management will be cited by plaintiffs' lawyers as diminishing the availability of the safe harbors.

It is therefore important for companies and underwriters in drafting and reviewing MD&A to be aware of any information available to top management that might later be cited as evidence that management was aware of undisclosed adverse developments.

• • *Responsibility for Preparing MD&A.* A company's financial reporting staff obviously plays an important role in drafting the company's MD&A. During the years when MD&A principally focused on "elevator music," it may have received only cursory review by top management or the company's audit committee. The SEC's expanded view of the role of MD&A and its emphasis on non-financial as well as financial "value drivers" probably means that, for many companies, the financial reporting staff must ensure that top management becomes involved in MD&A at an early stage of the drafting process. This is important, first, for the purpose of identifying the relevant information. For example, what are the key performance indicators that should be highlighted in MD&A? What information does top management review for the purpose of making decisions about allocation of resources? On the other hand, what information is top management likely to resist including in the MD&A? For example, what competitive concerns should be recognized? What are other companies in the industry likely to be emphasizing as their value drivers? Are there definitional issues that need to be addressed? What are analysts saying about the variables that affect the company's performance? What is in the company's own files, including Treasury, Human Resources and "board books," that might be inconsistent with the proposed MD&A? How much time should be allocated for review of MD&A by the company's independent accountants?

Indeed, the major themes of MD&A should have been identified at the time of the company's earnings release for the year or the quarter and reflected as necessary in that press release. It might otherwise be too late to prepare a responsive MD&A without appearing to have saved the "bad news" for the periodic report or, even worse, appearing to contradict what was said in the earnings release.

Disclosure committees are useful vehicles for coordinating a company's response to MD&A and for preparing for a presentation to the audit committee prior to the earnings release and often again prior to the filing of the offering document or periodic report. Companies should at least consider memorializing their significant decisions about what they include or do not include in MD&A.

Caution should be taken to avoid any inadvertent release of information that contains NGFM.

In the case of IPOs, it is important that the underwriters and underwriters' counsel participate actively in the development, review and revision of the MD&A. Not only does such participation improve the quality of the disclosure, but it is an important due diligence tool in identifying areas for further inquiry. The individuals involved in this assignment should obviously be familiar with the issuer's industry and have sufficient experience in financial and accounting matters to be able to carry out this responsibility.

In the case of follow-on offerings by reporting companies, it is more difficult for underwriters and their counsel to bring about changes in MD&A. This does not mean that underwriters should not attempt to assess the strengths and weaknesses of a

SELECTED ISSUES   159

company's MD&A on file with the SEC and, if necessary, encourage the company to supplement the filed MD&A with additional disclosures.

• • *Liquidity and Capital.* MD&A has for many years required a discussion and analysis of a company's liquidity and capital resources. A company must identify "any known trends or any known demands, commitments, events or uncertainties that will result in or that are reasonably likely to result in the registrant's liquidity increasing or decreasing in any material way." It must also describe its material commitments for capital expenditures and the anticipated source of funds needed to fulfill these commitments. Any material changes in the mix and relative cost of capital resources must also be described.

Some of the spectacular collapses of major companies that led up to the enactment of Sarbanes–Oxley demonstrated that the MD&A requirements were not preventing the market from being surprised by the amount of a company's obligations, including off-balance sheet obligations, the timing and other terms of those obligations, the availability of cash to satisfy those obligations and the access of the company to capital resources or other sources of liquidity. The SEC and its staff quickly concluded that the MD&A of too many companies was not informative when it came to liquidity and cash flow. "Too many companies merely repeat the information that is already apparent from the face of the statement of cash flows. There is clearly not enough analysis. The time has come to reverse that direction."[32]

In the December 2003 Release, the SEC emphasized that companies were required to evaluate separately their ability to meet upcoming cash requirements over both the short and the long term. Also, companies should consider whether their liquidity would be materially affected by the cash requirements necessary to maintain current operations, to complete projects under way and to achieve stated objectives or plans, as well as to meet any cash requirements associated with known trends or uncertainties (and an indication of the time periods in which the resolution of such

---

32. Alan L. Beller, "Remarks at The Bond Market Association, Corporate Credit Markets" (April 10, 2003) (speech available on SEC website).

uncertainties is anticipated). The release suggested starting with the tabular disclosure of contractual obligations discussed below, supplemented with additional information material to an understanding of the company's cash requirements, including disclosures regarding the effect of specific loss contingencies on cash and liquidity. MD&A should also focus on the primary drivers of and other material factors necessary to an understanding of the company's cash flows and the indicative value of historical cash flows from operations and financing. If a company has incurred debt in material amounts, it should explain the reasons for incurring debt and the use of proceeds and analyze how the incurrence of debt fits into its overall business plan. Future debt or equity financing should be discussed, if material.[33] MD&A should also disclose any limitations on a company's ability to access the cash flow and financial assets of any consolidated entities such as foreign or partially owned affiliates.

A company should consider discussing and analyzing the material financial covenants relating to its outstanding debt or to its contingent obligations such as guarantees, including any limitations on its ability to obtain financing and the impact of a reasonably likely inability to meet the terms of such covenants.

• • *Results of Operations.* The discussion of results of operations must focus on "unusual or infrequent events or transactions or any significant economic changes" that have materially affected income from continuing operations. In addition, the MD&A must describe "any known trends or uncertainties that have had or that the registrant reasonably believes will have a material favorable or unfavorable impact on net sales or revenues or income from continuing operations." If the issuer has experienced material increases in sales or revenues, it must explain the degree to which the increases are attributable to price increases or increased volume of sales or the introduction of new products or services.

---

33. The SEC offered its view that such disclosure would not necessarily result in "gun-jumping" in violation of Section 5, citing Rule 135c as an available safe harbor.

Instruction 4 to Item 303(a) of Regulation S-K requires a discussion of "material changes from year to year in one or more line items" in the financial statements, but only to the extent necessary for an understanding of the company's business as a whole. The instruction explicitly warns against repeating numerical changes easily identifiable from the financial statements, a technique that the SEC staff has often dismissed as "elevator music." Rather, as noted above, the emphasis should be "on explaining a company's financial results and condition by identifying key elements of the business model and the drivers and dynamics of the business, and also addressing key variables."[34]

• • *Off-Balance Sheet Arrangements.* Pursuant to Section 401(a) of Sarbanes–Oxley, the SEC in January 2003 amended MD&A to require disclosure of an issuer's off-balance sheet arrangements. "Off-balance sheet arrangements" include arrangements with unconsolidated entities where the issuer has (a) obligations under guarantee contracts requiring recognition and measurement under FIN 45,[35] (b) a retained or contingent interest in transferred assets where the effect is for the issuer to provide support to the transferee, (c) obligations under certain derivative contracts except for those related to the issuer's own stock and (d) obligations arising out of a variable interest (as described in FIN 46)[36] in an unconsolidated entity that provides certain support to or engages in certain activities with the issuer.

MD&A calls for a discussion in a separate section of the nature and business purpose of the arrangements, their significance for the company's liquidity, capital resources, market or credit risk, their magnitude, and the known events, demands,

---

34. SEC Release No. 33-8098 (May 10, 2002).

35. The FASB issued FIN 45 in November 2002. FIN 45 requires a guarantor to recognize a liability for the fair value of the obligation undertaken in issuing the guarantee, and it also requires the guarantor to make certain disclosures in its annual and interim financial statements.

36. The FASB issued FIN 46 in January 2003 and a revision ("FIN 46R") in December 2003. FIN 46 requires the consolidation under certain circumstances of variable interest entities with which the issuer is involved.

commitments, trends or uncertainties that might limit their future availability to the company. An instruction to Item 303(a)(4) states that the discussion of off-balance sheet arrangements may cross-refer to specific information in the relevant footnotes to the financial statements if the "substance of the footnotes" is "integrate[d] . . . into such discussion in a manner designed to inform readers of the significance of the information that is not included within the body of such discussion." The instruction is not very helpful in avoiding duplicative disclosure.

Some of the required disclosures call for forward-looking information. To encourage companies to provide the type of information and analysis necessary for investors to understand the impact of off-balance sheet arrangements, the SEC included an express safe harbor for these disclosures in order "to remove possible ambiguity" about whether they would be eligible for the statutory safe harbors. Under Item 303(c), all of the required disclosures (except for "historic facts") are deemed to be forward-looking statements within the meaning of the statutory safe harbors, and the "meaningful cautionary statements" element of the safe harbors is deemed to be satisfied if the company satisfies all requirements for MD&A disclosure.

• • *Tabular Disclosure of Contractual Obligations.* Also in January 2003, the SEC added a new item to MD&A that requires a tabular presentation of the company's known contractual obligations, with specific reference to long-term debt obligations, capital and operating lease obligations, purchase obligations and other long-term obligations reflected on the company's balance sheet under GAAP. The tabular presentation is also eligible for an express safe harbor, but, unlike the safe harbor for off-balance sheet arrangements, it is still necessary to provide meaningful cautionary statements.

• • *Critical Accounting Estimates.* The SEC requested in December 2001 that companies include in their MD&A an explanation of the effects of the critical accounting policies applied by the company. The SEC's chief accountant followed up on this request in a January 2002 speech about MD&A's role in conveying the importance of accounting methods, assumptions and

SELECTED ISSUES

estimates. The SEC proposed formal rules in May 2002 as an "initial step" in improving the "transparency" of financial statements with a focus on estimates, uncertainties and subjectivity.

The SEC referred in the December 2003 Release to the May 2003 proposals as still being under consideration. In the meantime, it advised issuers to disclose critical accounting estimates or assumptions where

- the nature of the estimates or assumptions is material due to the levels of subjectivity and judgment necessary to account for highly uncertain matters or the susceptibility of such matters to change; and
- the impact of the estimates and assumptions on the company's financial condition or operating performance is material.

In the SEC's view, the disclosure should provide greater insight into the quality and variability of information regarding financial condition and operating performance. Disclosure should not supplement the accounting policy notes in the financial statements. These notes describe the accounting principles used to prepare the financial statements, while the MD&A discussion should present the company's analysis of the uncertainties involved in applying a principle at a given time or the variability that is reasonably likely to result from its application over time. In this connection, companies should explain the reasons for the risk of change, how they arrive at a given estimate or assumption, how accurate it has been in the past, how much it has changed and whether it is reasonably likely to change in the future. If a change is reasonably likely to occur and would have a material effect, the company should provide a sensitivity analysis.

For example, if reasonably likely changes in the long-term rate of return used in accounting for a company's pension plan would have a material effect on the company's financial condition or operating performance, the company should quantify and disclose the impact that could result from the range of reasonably likely outcomes.

• • *Forward-Looking Focus of MD&A.* The SEC acknowledged for many years that MD&A had a forward-looking aspect, but perhaps because of its once having prohibited such information from appearing in filed documents it was somewhat reluctant to admit that MD&A sometimes required such information. By the time of its 1989 Interpretive Release, however, it described the purpose of MD&A as being "to give investors an opportunity to look at the registrant through the eyes of management by providing a historical and prospective analysis of the registrant's financial condition and results of operations, with particular emphasis on the registrant's prospects for the future." The SEC emphasized the forward-looking function of MD&A when, as discussed in Chapter 5, it proposed in 2002 to require that issuers identify and discuss in MD&A their "critical accounting estimates." Some of the proposed disclosure, according to the SEC, would require a company to make forward-looking statements. In light of the forward-looking statements that would be required, the SEC proposed to delete the instruction to Item 303(a) to the effect that issuers are "encouraged, but not required, to supply forward-looking information." Although the SEC has not yet adopted the 2002 proposals, it deleted the relevant instruction in early 2003 when it adopted amendments to MD&A to require disclosure regarding a company's off-balance sheet arrangements and contractual obligations.

• • *Caterpillar Proceeding.* As we have seen, the SEC's view of the purpose of MD&A is to "give the investor an opportunity to look at the company through the eyes of management." As illustrated by the SEC's 1992 proceeding against Caterpillar, Inc.,[37] even management's vision may be blurred on critical issues relating to disclosure of prospective events.

In 1989, Caterpillar's subsidiary in Brazil contributed an exceptional 23% of the parent company's net earnings, greatly disproportionate to its contribution of 5% to the parent company's revenues. By mid-February 1990, Caterpillar management had recognized that there were substantial uncertainties as to

---

37. *In re Caterpillar, Inc.*, SEC Release No. 34-30532 (March 31, 1992).

whether the subsidiary would repeat its 1989 performance in 1990. By the end of the first quarter, management had recognized that the subsidiary's 1990 profit would be "substantially lower than in 1989." The MD&A in the company's 1989 10-K did not disclose the subsidiary's disproportionate contribution to net earnings in that year, and neither that document nor the 10-Q for the first quarter of 1990 disclosed the risk of lower earnings in 1990 or the possible magnitude of such a shortfall.

The SEC seized upon certain corporate events as indicating failure to comply with MD&A requirements: it noted that management had started to break out the subsidiary's results for purposes of presentations to the board of directors; also, the board received reports in February and April 1990 indicating the magnitude of the subsidiary's 1989 contribution and the unlikelihood that it would match this performance in 1990. The SEC brought cease and desist proceedings based on MD&A violations in both the 1989 10-K and the 10-Q filed for the first quarter of 1990.

Caterpillar consented to the entry against it of a cease and desist order barring it from future violations of Section 13(a) of the 1934 Act and Rules 13a-1 and 13a-13 thereunder and ordering it to "implement and maintain procedures designed to ensure compliance with Item 303 . . . ." The release stated that Caterpillar had already voluntarily adopted such procedures but did not state what they were.

The SEC made no findings as to Caterpillar's having violated any antifraud statute or rule (such as Rule 10b-5), and it has often limited its findings to 1934 Act reporting and record-keeping violations in the many MD&A proceedings that it has brought against issuers that allegedly failed to meet the requirements of Item 303.

In the case of a registered public offering, however, both the issuer and the underwriters face the prospect of civil liability if the registered securities decline in value after the offering because of unexpected negative news about the issuer's earnings or liquidity. The intriguing question for underwriters and other persons with a due diligence defense (e.g., the issuer's outside directors) is what level of inquiry into the issuer's procedures and underlying judgments would be "reasonable" for purposes of a defense under Section 11 or Section 12(a)(2). It is difficult, after all, for outsiders to second-guess management's determinations as to what trends or other events are "known" or even as to the degree to which they are likely to occur.

- *Projections and Other Forward-Looking Information*

A company's stock price can be dramatically affected by earnings disappointments. Such reverses are often quickly followed by litigation alleging that the issuer's prospectus or 1934 Act reports or public statements failed to disclose the "likelihood" or "probability" of lower earnings.

In the case of IPOs, underwriters face a difficult choice. Investors in these offerings insist on being supplied with earnings estimates. On the other hand, issuers generally refuse to include projections in the prospectus (the most common exceptions being certain high-yield securities, restructurings and M&A transactions). The dilemma is generally solved by a lead underwriter's orally providing projections to investors at road show presentations or, more commonly, by means of the underwriters' sales force.

At least until the 2003 "global settlement" between regulators and ten large investment banks, these projections were often made by the lead underwriter's analyst on the basis of discussions with management and sometimes access to management's internal projections. Despite the global settlement's ban on analyst participation in roadshows and its imposition of "firewalls" between analysts and bankers, it is still permissible for analysts to "confirm the adequacy of disclosure in offering or other disclosure documents for a transaction based on the analysts' communications with the company and other vetting conducted outside the presence of [i]nvestment [b]anking personnel." Any communication by the analyst to the bankers working on the transaction must be chaperoned by underwriters' counsel or internal legal or compliance staff. Even under these confining ground rules, it remains possible for underwriters to make use of their analyst's expertise in the issuer's industry to test management's assumptions in the light of problems common to the industry. At least in the case of IPOs, it remains possible to permit the analyst to have access to the issuer's internal projections.

In the case of non-IPOs, there may be "consensus" views on the issuer's future earnings. Ratings agencies or fixed-income analysts may have expressed views about the issuer's improving, stable or declining creditworthiness.

To avoid surprises and investor disappointment (and possible lawsuits), underwriters—with or without an analyst's assistance—will typically make extensive inquiry of management about its earnings projections for succeeding quarters, the next fiscal year and farther out into the future. They will closely examine management's assumptions, particularly with regard to such variables as competition.

In the case of debt offerings, the underwriters will make similar inquiries of the issuer. They will also ask about recent communications or visits with the ratings agencies, and the underwriters will probably insist on a reconfirmation of the ratings as a condition to closing the deal.

Issuers' fear of litigation arising out of "earnings surprises" was a principal factor in the enactment of the Private Securities Litigation Reform Act of 1995 (the Reform Act), which became effective over President Clinton's veto on December 22, 1995. Among other things, the Reform Act creates in Section 27A of the 1933 Act and Section 21E of the 1934 Act a multichannel safe harbor for forward-looking statements.

The first channel of the safe harbor provides that a person will not be liable for a forward-looking statement, whether oral or written, if the statement is

- identified as a forward-looking statement and
- accompanied by meaningful cautionary statements identifying important factors that could cause actual results to differ materially from those in the forward-looking statement.

As noted in the Conference Report,[38] this first channel of the safe harbor on its face does not require identification of "all" important factors that could cause results to differ materially.

---

38. H. Conf. Rep. No. 104-369 (1995).

It still remains to be seen, however, how the courts will deal with the Conference Report's further statements that the safe harbor will not be lost by a "[f]ailure to include the particular factor that ultimately causes the forward-looking statement not to come true" or that plaintiffs should not have an opportunity to conduct discovery on what factors were known to the issuer at the time the statement was made or on the speaker's state of mind. It also remains to be seen how the courts will deal with the much-discussed situation where an issuer omits reference to a factor that may be the most likely factor to undermine the forward-looking statement.

Under the second channel of the safe harbor, a person is protected against liability if the forward-looking statement is immaterial. This preserves the ability of a defendant, for example, to argue that a statement was immaterial under the "bespeaks caution" doctrine, even if the statement does not meet the new test referred to above.

Finally, even if a statement does not fit into either of the channels described above, the plaintiff loses unless it can prove that the forward-looking statement

- if made by a natural person, was made with the actual knowledge by that person that the statement was false or misleading; or

- if made by a business entity, was made by or with the approval of an executive officer of the entity with actual knowledge by that officer that the statement was false or misleading.

This third channel of the safe harbor flatly requires a plaintiff to demonstrate "actual knowledge" on the part of the speaker that the statement was false or misleading. Since the safe harbor applies to 1933 Act liability for prospectus disclosures, the Reform Act modifies to this extent the 1933 Act's private remedies by imposing liability based on actual intent to defraud rather than on a failure to act reasonably. The third channel also contemplates that a company may be able to escape liability for a projection by a senior officer even though a more junior officer

SELECTED ISSUES

may have known facts tending to undermine the projection (the so-called "pipeline" problem).[39]

A fourth channel of the Reform Act's safe harbor applies to oral forward-looking statements by or on behalf of issuers that are subject to the reporting requirements of the 1934 Act. In these cases (e.g., statements made at roadshows), reference could be made to a "readily available written document" (e.g., a 1934 Act report) for information about the factors that could cause actual results to differ from the forward-looking statement.

The safe harbor can be relied on by an issuer reporting under the 1934 Act, any person acting on its behalf, an "outside reviewer" or an underwriter (but only with respect to information provided by the issuer or information derived by the underwriter from such information). The safe harbor is not available for forward-looking statements that are included in financial statements prepared in accordance with GAAP (but it is available for statements included in MD&A), made in connection with IPOs or tender offers or 13D or similar ownership statements or that relate to issuers that have been sanctioned for securities violations during the past three years or that are blank check companies, partnerships or similar entities, investment companies, issuers of penny stock or issuers that are engaged in rollup or going-private transactions.

The Reform Act gives the SEC authority to expand the safe harbor, and the Conference Report recommends that the SEC

---

39. *See, e.g., In re Kulicke & Soffa Industries Inc. Securities Litig.* [1990–91 Transfer Binder] Fed. Sec. L. Rep. (CCH) ¶95,721 (E.D. Pa. Oct. 2, 1990); *In re The Ultimate Corp. Securities Litigation*, [1989 Transfer Binder] Fed. Sec. L. Rep. (CCH) ¶94,522 and ¶94,523 (S.D.N.Y. June 30, 1989). But see the discussion above ("Significance of Additional Information Available to Management") regarding the SEC's view that companies today have available to them much more extensive and up-to-date information about their operations than used to be the case. Also, Item 307 of Regulation S-K requires chief executive and financial officers to include in 1934 Act reports their evaluation of the effectiveness of the issuer's "disclosure controls and procedures," a term that includes the communication of information to top management within a time frame that permits the timely filing of 1934 Act reports.

do so "for established and reputable entities who are excluded from the safe harbor" under the Reform Act. The Conference Report refers to the Reform Act's safe harbor as a "starting point" and states its expectation that the SEC will continue its rulemaking proceedings in this area.[40]

Reporting companies are providing more earnings guidance today than ever before, but not primarily because of the Reform Act's safe harbor. Rather, the SEC's adoption of Regulation FD required reporting companies to adopt a more orderly and systematic approach to the dissemination of earnings guidance.

The Reform Act's safe harbor does not cover projections in those cases where they are most needed—namely, IPOs. In addition, Regulation FD does not apply to disclosures made in connection with IPOs and most other SEC-registered public offerings. For these reasons, earnings estimates during IPOs are likely to continue to be disseminated to investors at roadshows and in conversations between investors and the underwriters' sales representatives. Given the concern that the SEC often expresses about unequal disclosure of projections, it is unclear why it has not exercised its power to make the safe harbor available for IPOs.

Issuers and underwriters and their counsel should seek to take advantage of the statutory safe harbors whenever possible and, where the safe harbors are by their terms not available, of the "bespeaks caution" doctrine. To succeed in this effort, however, the "meaningful cautionary statements" must be *meaningful*: they cannot be boilerplate or borrowed from other issuers' disclosure documents or even represent an uncritical markup of last year's disclosure. Also, issuers and underwriters must keep in mind that the statutory safe harbors and the "bespeaks caution" doctrine protect only for forward-looking statements. All the cautionary language in the world will not protect an issuer

---

40. Only a few days after the Reform Act became law, the SEC stated that in light of the Reform Act it would propose safe harbor relief for certain of the additional disclosures proposed to be required of issuers in its release on derivatives. SEC Release No. 33-7250 (December 28, 1995). It adopted such relief in SEC Release No. 33-7386 (January 31, 1997).

SELECTED ISSUES

or underwriter from misrepresentations or omissions relating to historical or current facts.

- *Initial Public Offerings*

In the case of an IPO, the outside front cover page of the preliminary prospectus must set forth bona fide estimates of the range of the maximum offering price of the shares to be offered and of the maximum number of securities to be offered.[41] The prospectus also must include a description of the various factors considered in determining the public offering price.[42]

An initial filing with the SEC will often not include a price range. The SEC staff will review such a filing, but the preliminary prospectus included in the filing may not be distributed to investors. The staff will not allow a registration statement to become effective unless a preliminary prospectus has been distributed that includes a bona fide price range. The staff informally considers a $2 range to be bona fide if the upper limit of the range is $20 or less, and a range of up to 10% if the upper limit is more than $20. The SEC staff believes that it is important for it to know the proposed price range in order for it to provide comments on important parts of the prospectus (e.g., use of proceeds or MD&A), and it is therefore a good idea to inform the staff as soon as possible what the price range is likely to be.

A question sometimes raised is whether it is necessary to recirculate an amended preliminary prospectus if the deal is downsized or the price that is ultimately fixed is below the range set forth in a previously circulated preliminary prospectus. Assume that the first preliminary prospectus that is circulated sets forth a deal size of 10 million shares and a price range of $18 to $20 per share. In the final few days before pricing, the managing underwriter reluctantly concludes that the only way to make the deal a success is to drop the size to 8 million shares and the offering price to $16. Can a final pre-effective amendment to the registration statement be filed with the reduced deal

---

41. Regulation S-K, Instruction 1(A) to Item 501(b)(3).
42. Regulation S-K, Item 505.

size and the $16 price (or without a price pursuant to Rule 430A), or will it be necessary first to circulate a revised preliminary prospectus showing the $16 price? Unless the proceeds of the offering are earmarked for a specific purpose and the price reduction materially affects the issuer's ability to achieve this purpose, it should be possible simply to insert the 8 million shares and the $16 offering price in the Rule 424(b) prospectus without circulating a revised preliminary prospectus. The SEC staff has sometimes requested the managing underwriter to represent that it and the other underwriters will notify purchasers of the new size and price prior to confirming sales.

As discussed below under "Post-Filing Issues," Rule 430A permits a registration statement to become effective without price information. If the issuer and the underwriters subsequently agree to a deal size and price (e.g., 8 million shares and $16) that is lower than as last disclosed in a preliminary prospectus, an instruction to Rule 430A(a) states that the changes may be disclosed in the Rule 424(b) prospectus "as long as the decrease in the volume or change in the price range would not materially change the disclosure contained in the registration statement at effectiveness." The instruction goes on to say that, "[n]otwithstanding the foregoing," any change in deal size or price (whether above or below the previously disclosed range) may be disclosed in the Rule 424(b) prospectus if the changes in volume and price represent in the aggregate no more than a 20% change in the maximum aggregate offering price set forth in the effective registration statement. The instruction is not clearly drafted, but it presumably does not mean that changes within the percentage limits need not be reflected in a post-effective amendment if they indeed have a material effect on the disclosure in the effective registration statement (e.g., an adverse effect on the issuer's use of proceeds or the liquidity of the market in the offered securities). If the changes require the registration of additional securities within the 20% limit (which may depend on whether the registration fee was calculated pursuant to Rule 457(a) or Rule 457(o)), this may be accomplished by means of an abbreviated registration statement that is filed and that becomes effective automatically pursuant to Rule 462(b).

The prospectus for an IPO must identify any principal underwriter that intends to sell to any account over which it exercises discretionary authority and must include an estimate of the amount of securities so intended to be sold.[43] This information must be contained in a pre-effective amendment that is circulated if the information is not available when the registration statement is filed. To comply with this requirement, many managing underwriters include in the AAU or MAAU an undertaking not to sell to discretionary accounts more than 5% of an underwriter's allotment and recite this limitation in the prospectus.

Where, as in the case in any IPO, there is no established public trading market in the United States, the prospectus must disclose the amount of common stock subject to outstanding options, warrants or convertible securities and the amount of common stock that could be sold pursuant to Rule 144 under the 1933 Act or that the issuer has agreed to register for sale by securityholders.[44] The purpose of this disclosure is to indicate the possibility that future sales of a substantial number of shares by existing shareholders could have an adverse impact on the market price of the stock being offered.

If equity securities are being registered for an IPO, the registration statement must include an undertaking by the registrant to provide to the underwriter at the closing certificates in such denominations and registered in such names as required by the underwriter to ensure prompt delivery to each purchaser.[45] This requirement was designed to deal with abuses during the "hot issue" markets of 1959–61, when certificates sometimes were withheld from investors to inhibit the resale of their shares.[46] This is less of a problem, of course, in an environment where DTC book-entry closings are the rule.

---

43. Regulation S-K, Item 508(j).
44. Regulation S-K, Item 201(a)(2).
45. Regulation S-K, Item 512(f).
46. *See Securities and Exchange Commission, Special Study of Securities Markets*, H.R. Doc. No. 95, pt. 1, at 527 (1963).

- *"Online" Offerings*

During the Internet Bubble, a number of non-traditional securities firms (sometimes referred to as "e-brokers" or "e-dealers") announced their intention to use the Internet as their primary means of distributing SEC-registered securities. Because many of the IPOs during this period involved companies in Internet-related businesses, it was not surprising that even the more established investment banking firms announced their own plans to use the Internet or began to include firms in their syndicates that did so (sometimes to the extent of including these firms on the front page of the prospectus, in which case they were sometimes referred to as "e-managers").

One of the identifying characteristics of the e-brokers was that they depended on electronic communication with their customers and therefore lacked the sales force to perform two essential underwriting tasks traditionally carried out by telephone: soliciting customers to place "indications of interest" for the registered securities and then, after pricing, to track customers down for the purpose of confirming sales. As we have seen, written solicitations other than the preliminary prospectus would run the risk of violating Section 5(b)(1), and any attempt to enter into agreements to sell the securities prior to the effective date of the registration statement would run the risk of violating Section 5(a)(1).

In a 1999 no-action letter[47] limited to firm commitment IPOs, the SEC staff agreed that it would not recommend enforcement action to the SEC if Wit Capital Corporation followed Internet-based procedures designed to prevent Section 5 violations. Essentially, Wit Capital made two general proposals. First, it would inform customers and non-customers about a new IPO by means of an e-mail designed to comply with Rule 134 that would contain a hyperlink to a "cul de sac" dedicated to that IPO. The cul de sac would contain a preliminary prospectus. E-mail recipients could hyperlink from the cul de sac to other web pages to open an account or to obtain procedural information. Non-customers could reach the prospectus and submit a "conditional

---

47. SEC No-action Letter, *Wit Capital Corp.* (July 14, 1999).

offer to buy" only after opening an account with Wit Capital through its clearing firm, but no account could be opened without the customer consenting to the electronic delivery of prospectuses and depositing at least $2,000. In addition to reaching the cul de sac by means of the hyperlink embedded in the e-mail, a person could reach the cul de sac by means of a "Look at New Issues" page on Wit Capital's general website. The information provided to the customer by means of this procedure would therefore, according to Wit Capital, not violate Section 5(b)(1) since it would consist only of the preliminary prospectus, information covered by Rule 134 and other information relating to "procedural" matters.[48]

Second, Wit Capital proposed to solicit and accept "conditional offers to buy" IPO shares, either with or without a maximum price that the customer was willing to pay. Approximately two business days prior to the expected effective date of the registration statement, Wit Capital would transmit to each person who had submitted a conditional offer to buy an e-mail requesting that the customer affirmatively reconfirm the offer. An affirmative reconfirmation would remain effective for five business days, but the customer could withdraw the conditional offer to buy at any time prior to acceptance by Wit Capital (which could not take place until after effectiveness and pricing). A customer would have to reconfirm an offer in the event of a recirculation of the preliminary prospectus, a change in the expected price range or a pricing of the IPO outside the expected price range. After effectiveness, Wit Capital would send each reconfirming customer a notice of effectiveness and of Wit Capital's right to accept the conditional offer within a stated time after the IPO is priced. During the period between effectiveness and pricing, investors would have the opportunity to withdraw their offers. After pricing, Wit Capital would allocate its available IPO shares on the basis of a modified first-come,

---

48. In the November 2000 edition of *Current Issues and Rulemaking Projects*, the staff referred to communications "that are merely instructional and not designed to generate interest in a particular offering" as unobjectionable even if they did not fall within the safe harbor of Rule 134.

first-served system and send customers an e-mail notice stating whether or not they had received an allocation. Wit Capital's clearing firm would send confirmations together with hard copies of the final prospectus. The procedure would, according to Wit Capital, not violate Section 5(a)(1) because it would not result in a "sale" prior to effectiveness.

In its legal analysis of the "conditional offer to buy" procedure, Wit Capital's request letter depended on Rule 134(d), which provides that a Rule 134 communication that is accompanied or preceded by a preliminary prospectus may solicit an offer to buy the security or request the recipient to indicate, on an enclosed or attached coupon or card or in some other manner, whether he might be interested in the security. The communication must contain substantially the following statement:

> No offer to buy the securities can be accepted and no part of the purchase price can be received until the registration statement has become effective, and any such offer may be withdrawn or revoked, without obligation or commitment of any kind, at any time prior to notice of its acceptance given after the effective date. An indication of interest in response to this advertisement will involve no obligation or commitment of any kind.

Prior to Wit Capital's use of Rule 134(d), the rule was not well known to the securities bar and was relied on infrequently. It had proved useful in the 1964 IPO of Communications Satellite Corporation. By statute, communications common carriers were entitled to purchase half of the 10 million shares being offered. Any unpurchased shares were to be underwritten and included in the shares sold to the public. It was essential, therefore, for the underwriters to know the number of shares for which they would be responsible prior to the effectiveness of the registration statement. The solution was to rely upon Rule 134(d). A document inviting orders was sent to the eligible common carriers along with a preliminary prospectus. This document was kept within the confines of Rule 134 and contained the statement required by Rule 134(d). It was stipulated that orders must be received by a specified date prior to the proposed effective date of the registration statement. The carrier offering was fully subscribed, and, as there was great demand for the shares, there was virtual certainty that no orders would be withdrawn. A notice of acceptance in accordance with Rule 134(d) was given to the carriers immediately after the registration statement became effective, and the underwriters proceeded with the public offering.

After the issuance of the Wit Capital no-action letter, many other e-brokers adopted similar but not necessarily identical procedures. Many of these firms submitted their procedures to the SEC staff for informal review. Because of its concern, as expressed in the 2000 Internet Release, that online offering procedures might be unfamiliar to retail investors and might lead them to make "hasty, and perhaps uninformed, investment decisions," the staff during the height of the Internet Bubble launched an aggressive campaign to encourage underwriters to submit their "electronic underwriting procedures" for staff review. To avoid last-minute delays, issuers and managing underwriters sometimes excluded non-complying underwriters from participation in IPOs. Even today, comment letters on registration statements still request a description of such procedures or confirmation that they have been approved by the staff.

In the November 2000 update of its *Current Issues and Rulemaking Projects*,[49] the Division of Corporation Finance noted that it had been issuing comments "to get information on what procedures the different e-brokers are using to assure compliance with Section 5 . . . and specifically, to avoid pre-effective sales of securities violative of Section 5(a)." It also noted its effort to "actively contact[ ] e-brokers to review their procedures outside the context of a particular offering to avoid timing concerns." It noted that its review focused on how conditional offers to buy are solicited, how and when they are accepted and how these purchases are funded. It also focused on whether e-brokers had procedures in place to reconfirm after the effective date any traditional indications of interest, to the extent these were also solicited.

---

49. SEC Division of Corporation Finance, *Current Issues and Rulemaking Projects* 49–52 (November 14, 2000).

The staff summarized its comments on online offering procedures as follows:

- conditional offers to buy must be received or reconfirmed not more than seven days before acceptance, and acceptance cannot take place until after effectiveness, pricing and "a meaningful opportunity to withdraw" (at least one hour after the customer is notified of effectiveness, but customers must be able to withdraw their offers at any time up to notice of acceptance);
- e-brokers must notify customers and obtain new conditional offers to buy or reconfirmations of prior offers if there is a material change in the prospectus that requires recirculation, the offering price range changes before effectiveness or the agreed-on offering price is outside the range;
- e-brokers are "asked" to treat conditional offers to buy at a price above the range in the prospectus as limit orders at the top of the range;
- if the only available preliminary prospectus does not include a price range, it may not be used to solicit customers or as a basis for the availability of Rule 134;
- e-brokers may not require customers to "certify" that they have read the prospectus because this could lead customers to believe that they have waived rights that they have under the federal securities laws (it is acceptable to encourage customers to read the prospectus and to ask them to certify that they have received or accessed the prospectus); and
- an e-broker may require a customer to make a small deposit (e.g., $2,000) to open an account, but the amount may not be tied to the purchase price of the securities and the funds must remain under the customer's control at least until the acceptance of the customer's conditional offer to buy (these conditions are intended to avoid a premature "sale" in violation of Section 5(a)(1) of the 1933 Act).

In the prior edition of this book, the authors cautioned that it should not be assumed that Rule 134(d)'s reference to "notice of . . . acceptance" is intended to make it possible for underwriters to set up "automatic acceptance" arrangements. As the SEC staff's cautious advice to e-brokers indicates, the staff still takes seriously the prohibition in Section 5 of "sales" prior to the effective date. Unless a particular procedure falls squarely within prior SEC staff advice or has been reviewed by the staff without objection, care must be taken to avoid an arrangement that amounts in effect to a contract of sale that is subject to conditions subsequent.

- *Electronic Auctions*

The SEC staff issued three interpretive letters in July 2000[50] that address "live" online auctions of securities registered under the 1933 Act by SEC-reporting companies. The auctions were to take place subsequent to the effective date of the registration statement, and the letters did not rely on Rule 134.

The three underwriting firms that requested the interpretive letters wished to conduct "live" and transparent auctions by means of which investors would determine the price of the registered securities. The auction screens by which the auction would be conducted, if they constituted offering material for the securities, would not themselves meet the requirements of Section 10 and therefore risked becoming illegal prospectuses under Section 5(b)(1). The base prospectus contained in the effective registration statement, even with a preliminary prospectus supplement describing the securities to be sold and the auction process, could not be used to take the auction screens out of illegal prospectus territory pursuant to Section 2(a)(10)(a) because the prospectus, although it met the requirements of Section 10, lacked pricing information and therefore did not meet the requirements of Section 10(a).

The solution to the problem was to make the auction screens accessible only by means of a hyperlink contained in the electronic version of the prospectus posted on the auction site. Consistent with the 2000 Internet Release, this procedure made the auction screens part of that prospectus. After the completion of the

---

50. SEC No-action Letters, *W.R. Hambrecht & Co.* (July 12, 2000), *Wit Capital Corp.* (July 20, 2000), and *Bear Stearns & Co., Inc.* (July 20, 2000).

auction, the issuer would file with the SEC pursuant to Rule 424(b) a final prospectus supplement that would present the final terms of the offering, interim information describing bidding activity (either periodic "screen shots" or a summary) and interim information evidencing a substantive change in the information already on file at the SEC.[51]

In the November 2000 update of its *Current Issues and Rulemaking Projects*,[52] the Division of Corporation Finance referred to the interpretive letters discussed above and stated that making the auction site available through the electronic prospectus was not the exclusive method of making a document part of an electronic prospectus. For example, the auction site could be made available by means of a hyperlink from the corresponding caption in the table of contents of the electronic prospectus, or it could be presented on a web page next to the electronic prospectus along with a statement that the auction web page is part of the prospectus.

The staff also cautioned that the plan of distribution disclosure in the electronic prospectus must describe the auction process in a manner sufficient to satisfy Item 508 of Regulation S-K. This would include a description of the terms to be established by the auction (e.g., price), a summary of the auction process and a fair and accurate description (or screen shots) of the web pages that participating investors would see prior to the auction. If a base prospectus in a shelf registration statement did not provide for auctions, it would have to be updated by means of a post-effective amendment.

The staff also reiterated that the final prospectus must include the results of the auction and "a fair and accurate representation of the electronic auction presentation." Although the auction

---

51. The 2000 Internet Release contemplated that hyperlinked information would be filed as part of the prospectus in the effective registration statement and would be subject to Section 11 liability. The July 2000 interpretive letters contemplated only the filing of Rule 424(b) prospectuses and therefore left open the question of Section 11 liability for the auction-related disclosures. *See* Chapter 8.

52. SEC Division of Corporation Finance, *Current Issues and Rulemaking Projects* 52–54 (November 14, 2000).

screens would be constantly changing during the auction, and notwithstanding that in the staff's view "every different view of the auction screens is a separate prospectus," it would not be necessary to make a filing for each change to the screens. Rather, the final prospectus should contain screen shots or summaries "at sufficiently small intervals to capture all substantive changes in the bidding process."

Until 2004, only a handful of U.S. companies had conducted IPOs by means of electronic auctions, with modest after-market price performance. In some foreign markets, electronic auctions were reported to have led to speculative excess. None of this deterred Google Inc. from announcing in early 2004 that the "principal factor" in pricing its IPO would be the clearing price determined by means of an electronic auction. Unlike as in a true auction, however, Google reserved the right to agree with its underwriters on a lower initial public offering price. Investors did not have access to the master order book in which bids were collected, thus making it unnecessary for auction screens to be filed as contemplated by the 2000 no-action letters.

Google conducted its IPO in a manner substantially consistent with the "online offering" procedures discussed above (e.g., notices to investors regarding effectiveness of the registration statement, investors' opportunity to withdraw bids and the circumstances under which investors would be required to reconfirm their bids). The electronic auction aspects of the offering attracted a great deal of media and investor attention, but because Google ended up pricing the deal at the bottom of the price range established on the day of effectiveness (which was itself considerably lower than the previously-disclosed range), it is difficult to predict the extent to which future IPO issuers will rely on a similar approach.

The electronic auction process contemplated by the 2000 no-action letters has been used for debt and equity offerings of SEC-reporting companies as well as for IPOs.

- *"Deal Sites"*

One reason for the "cul de sac" procedure described in the 1999 Wit Capital no-action letter was the concern that information that an investor could access from the Wit Capital website might be construed as offering material that could therefore constitute an illegal prospectus and/or that such information might be deemed to have become part of the electronic prospectus on the website. The SEC's 1995 release on electronic communication provided some justification for this concern, since it had stated there in several illustrations that documents in close proximity to one another (or to the links which are in close proximity) would be deemed to have been delivered together.[53]

The premise underlying the 1995 illustrations has come to be known as the "envelope" theory: documents in the same "virtual envelope" may be considered to have been delivered together. Notwithstanding that the 1995 guidance was offered in the context of determining when linked documents might be deemed to have been delivered as required by the 1933 Act, it came to be viewed by some market participants as suggesting that if a Section 10 prospectus were posted on a website then everything on the website would become part of that prospectus. Also, it was feared that all of the information on the website outside the corners of the Section 10 prospectus but in close proximity to it might be deemed to be written offering material and therefore an illegal prospectus.

In the 2000 Internet Release, the SEC attempted to alleviate these concerns. First, it stated that information on a website would become part of a posted Section 10 prospectus only if the issuer or underwriter acted to make it part of the prospectus, for example, by including a hyperlink within the prospectus to other information. Second, whether or not information on a website was in proximity to a posted prospectus was not conclusive in determining whether such information was an illegal prospectus; rather, "[r]egardless of whether or where the Section 10 prospectus is posted, the web site content must be reviewed in its entirety to determine whether it contains impermissible free writing."

The 2000 Internet Release was more successful in alleviating concern over whether information was deemed to be part of a prospectus than it was on the related issue of when information

---

53. SEC Release No. 33-7233 (October 6, 1995).

accessible from a "deal site" would be deemed to be written offering material and therefore an illegal prospectus. Nevertheless, it was recently suggested that "the cul-de-sac structure used today is often less restrictive than it once was"[54] and that underwriters frequently link directly to information outside the deal site such as news and market commentary and deal calendars without requiring the user to go back to the deal site portal.

Underwriters would frequently like to be able to provide prospective investors with price-related information such as the outstanding debt securities they might be willing to accept in exchange for newly offered debt securities and the prices at which they might be willing to engage in such "swaps."[55] Or underwriters might wish to assist investors in determining the price they might be willing to pay for the newly offered securities by identifying "comparable" securities of the same or other issuers and by providing relevant information about these securities (e.g., rating and yield). There are good reasons not to consider such information an "offer" in the first place since it is difficult to see how it would "condition the market" for the newly offered securities. Rule 134 permits a written communication containing information about the "yield" or the "probable yield range" of the offered security as well as its "price" or "the method of its determination or the probable price range," and many firms have relied on Rule 134 to provide information about swaps and comparables.[56]

One popular third-party site provider is Market Axess Inc., which is typically described in prospectuses as "an Internet-based communications technology provider" that provides its system as a "conduit" for communications between underwriters and their customers but does not become a party to any transactions.

---

54. David Harms, *The 2000 Internet Release, One Year Later*, 6 The Securities Reporter 3, 6 (Summer 2001).

55. *See* Chapter 6 regarding the NASD rules that apply where securities are taken "in trade."

56. *But see* Harms, *supra* note 54, at 6 (suggesting that the Internet auction letters discussed above "make it clear that there are limits on the scope of price-related information permitted under Rule 134").

- *Guarantees and Credit Enhancement*

In many transactions, some form of guarantee or other credit enhancement is necessary in order for the securities to be sold at an acceptable price. A guarantee of a security is a separate security under Section 2(a)(1) of the 1933 Act that must be registered—as a security issued by the guarantor—along with the security that it supports. Registration is not required, of course, if an exemption is available. As discussed in Chapter 10, a guarantee of commercial paper is subsumed into the commercial paper and has the benefit of that instrument's exemption under the 1933 Act. Also as discussed in Chapter 10, a guarantee in the form of a letter of credit issued by a U.S. bank is not only exempt in its own right but bootstraps into exempt status the security that it supports.

The SEC's requirements for separate financial statements of guarantors of registered securities and issuers of registered securities that are guaranteed by other persons are set forth in Rule 3-10 of Regulation S-X.

There are many forms of credit enhancement that fall short of outright guarantees. The key difference is that credit enhancement generally takes the form of an agreement (often referred to as a "support agreement") between a third party and the issuer (or a trustee) where the agreement does not run directly to the securityholders. The SEC generally does not require a third-party credit enhancer to register its obligations under the support agreement, but this does not mean that no disclosure need be provided about the third party. The staff takes the position that if an investor's return is materially dependent on the third-party credit enhancer, the issuer must provide sufficient information about the third party to enable an investor to assess the ability of the third party to meet the obligations undertaken in the support agreement.

The factors considered by the SEC staff as relevant in assessing the adequacy of disclosure in this area are discussed in Chapter 14.

The financial statement, disclosure and related issues raised by third-party guarantees and credit enhancement must be addressed at an early stage of the preparation of the registration statement.

- *Requests for Confidential Treatment*

Item 601 of Regulation S-K sets forth the requirements for filing exhibits to the registration statement. One of the requirements that is often troublesome mandates filing every "contract not made in the ordinary course of business which is material to the registrant and is to be performed in whole or in part at or after the filing of the registration statement . . . or was entered into not more than two years before such filing." Although the filing requirement is subject to numerous exceptions, issuers often object to filing particular contracts or portions of contracts because of competitive or related concerns.

Item 30 of Schedule A to the 1933 Act contemplates that the SEC may grant confidential treatment to "contracts" where disclosure "would impair the value of the contract and would not be necessary for the protection of investors." The Freedom of Information Act (FOIA) narrows the authority of federal agencies to withhold "agency records," which include materials provided to the SEC, from public disclosure. Rule 406 sets forth the substantive and procedural requirements for requesting confidential treatment for documents filed under the 1933 Act, and Rule 24b-2 does the same for 1934 Act documents. Under both rules, an application for confidential treatment must make the case that the information in question is immune from public disclosure based on an FOIA exemption. Guidance on these requirements is provided in the Division of Corporation Finance's Staff Legal Bulletin No. 1 dated February 28, 1997 with an addendum dated July 11, 2001.

The SEC Review Process

Once a working draft of the registration statement has been prepared by the issuer and its counsel, it will be reviewed by the managing underwriters and counsel for the underwriters and a number of drafting sessions will be held to work on the disclosure. The managing underwriters, with the assistance of counsel, will complete their due diligence investigations (see Chapter 5), and the results of their investigations will be reflected in the disclosure document.

During this period, various parts of the body of the prospectus may be on underwriters' or issuer's counsel's word processing system, while the financial statements will be on the issuer's accountants' system. Some or all of these systems may be compatible with the printer's system, but this cannot always be assumed.

After the customary "all nighter" at the printer, when the final changes are made and proof pages are checked and rechecked, the registration statement and accompanying documents such as the transmittal letter will be filed in electronic form pursuant to the SEC's Regulation S-T by means of the Electronic Data Gathering, Analysis and Retrieval (EDGAR) system.[57]

- *Selective Review*

The SEC's Division of Corporation Finance reviews registration statements on a selective basis. A registration statement on Form S-1 covering an IPO will almost always be selected for full review by the staff. Registration statements on Form S-3 are less likely to be reviewed, particularly where the issuer's 1934 Act reports have recently been reviewed by the staff. If the registration statement covers a security that is "novel and unique," this will increase the chances for review (although the review may be less than a full review). The issuer's industry, whether or not it has been involved in a recent restructuring and whether or not its filing presents "hot button" disclosure issues (e.g., derivatives, environmental liabilities, regulatory problems) will also affect the chances for review.

Section 408 of Sarbanes–Oxley requires the SEC to review companies' 1934 Act reports on a "regular and systematic basis,"

---

57. Instructions relating to the preparation of documents for electronic filing and the procedures to be followed in making such filings are set forth in the SEC's EDGAR Filing Manual. The 1933 Act registration fee is currently $126.70 per million dollars of securities to be acquired. (The SEC posts its current filing fees on its website at http://www.sec.gov/info/edgar/feeamt.htm.) Registration fees in connection with electronic filings must be made to the SEC's "lockbox" depository. There are verification and timing advantages in paying these fees by wire transfer.

not less frequently than once every three years. The SEC is required to consider, for purposes of scheduling such reviews, whether companies have issued material restatements of their financial results, have experienced relatively higher stock price volatility, are among the companies with the largest capitalizations, are emerging companies with "disparities" in their price-earnings ratios, or have operations that may significantly affect any material sector of the economy. The SEC has recently added staff to meet these additional responsibilities, and the staff of the Division of Corporation Finance has stated that it is developing "more substantive preliminary selective review criteria" to identify issuers at higher risk of "disclosure failure" in registration statements and periodic reports. Despite the additional staff, it is still possible that fewer 1933 Act registration statements will be reviewed as a result of the mandated focus on 1934 Act reports. As noted in Chapter 5, it is essential that underwriters and their counsel inquire about the last SEC staff review of a reporting company's 1934 Act documents and whether there are any unresolved comments. They also must verify that the issuer has followed through on any undertakings to the SEC staff to comply with its comments on a prospective basis.

It should be noted that all SEC examiners have direct Internet access for the express purpose of enabling them to retrieve public information about the issuers whose registration statements they are reviewing. Careful counsel will not allow themselves to be surprised by an SEC comment based on an Internet report of which they were unaware.

Oral advice that a registration statement will or will not be reviewed generally can be obtained from the SEC's staff within a few days after filing. If there is to be no review, the staff will confirm its telephonic advice by letter. If there is to be a full review, it is usually safe to assume under current staff policies that comments will be forthcoming in about 30 days. SEC staffing and workload sometimes lengthen the average time for full review. In any event, the managing underwriter should plan its marketing efforts accordingly. If marketing begins too soon, investor interest may cool while the deal is hung up at the SEC.

- *SEC Comments*

Any questions that the Division of Corporation Finance may have with respect to the registration statement and any suggestions that it may have for improving disclosure will be set forth in a "letter of comments," a term that has come to replace the former pejorative term, "deficiency letter." Accounting comments will often be made in a separate letter prepared by the SEC's accounting staff.

A lengthy comment letter is not necessarily an indication that a registration statement has been poorly prepared. While counsel is always pleased to receive a brief letter of comments, and even more pleased to receive no comments at all, he or she has no right to brag to the client if the SEC's comments are light. The length or complexity of a comment letter depends primarily on the perceptions of the examiner. Experience proves that a skillfully drafted registration statement may draw heavy comments, particularly if the transaction is a highly visible one, while a registration statement that is no better prepared may receive few, if any, comments.

Some comments will take the form of questions designed to elicit assurance that certain disclosures have been adequately made. Some will seek supplemental information pursuant to Rule 418 to support the disclosure or lack of disclosure of a particular matter. Others will simply indicate a lack of understanding on the examiner's part or a failure to read the document with sufficient care. Most comments, however, are well thought out, and some will lead to a substantial improvement in the registration statement. Counsel should welcome any suggestion made by the examiner to which he or she can respond, "That's a good comment."

The SEC staff disclosed in early 2004 that comment letters were regularly discussed at meetings of the SEC's chief accountant and the chief accountants of the Divisions of Corporation Finance, Investment Management and Enforcement. Disclosure issues frequently identified in comment letters could potentially be used by the Division of Enforcement to identify high-risk financial reporting issues.

- *Responding to Comments*

Some comments should be discussed with the examiner by telephone, if only to clarify their meaning and intent. But lengthy arguments should be avoided. The comment in dispute may have come from—or at least been authorized by—the examiner's superior, and the examiner will often not have the authority to concede the point in question without the superior's approval. The usual response will be, "Put it in your letter of transmittal, and we'll consider your argument." It is sometimes possible to resolve open items by the informal submission of draft language.

Each comment should be addressed in the issuer's transmittal letter to the SEC, even if the issuer has responded to the comment in full. This will speed up the review process by leading the examiner to the place in the registration statement where the particular comment has been dealt with. It takes little effort to state in the transmittal letter, "As requested by comment 12, the word 'excellent' has been changed to 'good' on page 34 of the prospectus." The change will have been black-lined, as will have been all changes made in the registration statement.[58]

One of the most vexing problems that can arise during a financing is the 11th-hour comment from the SEC. Even after the examiner has signed off and the offering has been priced, there is always the possibility of a phone call relating one last comment from the examiner's supervisor. This may result in an even later night at the printer. Even worse is the comment that is made after the price amendment has been filed or the registration statement has become effective pursuant to Rule 430A. Such a comment usually can be handled in the prospectus filed under Rule 424 without filing a further amendment to the registration statement.[59]

SEC staff comment letters and responses to such letters were discoverable for many years under FOIA, but it still came as a shock to many companies, underwriters and securities lawyers when in late 2003 a database vendor began to make these

---

58. Rule 472(a) requires the filing of at least five copies of each amendment to a registration statement marked to indicate, by underlining or in some other appropriate manner, the changes made. On the other hand, Rule 310 of Regulation S-T provides that for EDGAR filings all marking requirements must be satisfied by electronic "tags." These tags are much less helpful than precise black-lined hard copies or PDF files of amended filings, but it is understood that SEC policy discourages its staff reviewers from requesting precise black-lined hard copies or PDF files. Accordingly, many practitioners volunteer these as a routine matter.

59. This procedure usually requires consultation with the SEC's staff.

letters available through its website. In June 2004 the SEC staff announced that it would begin publicly releasing, free of charge and without the need for an FOIA request, staff comment letters and responses relating to disclosure filings made after August 1, 2004.[60] In appropriate cases, a request for confidential treatment may be made relating to such correspondence, but the SEC staff has cautioned that it would view blanket requests for confidential treatment as "abusive."[61]

- *Recirculation*

In the case of an IPO, the initial filing will often be "quiet," that is, the preliminary prospectuses will not be printed and distributed until after the SEC staff's comments on the initial filing have been dealt with and any necessary amendment to the registration statement has been filed. The managing underwriter will then be able to commence the marketing effort. It is possible to start the marketing effort with the preliminary prospectus included in the original filing, but this raises the risk that extensive SEC staff comments may lead to such extensive changes that "recirculation" of the amended preliminary prospectus will be required.

"Recirculation" is a somewhat misunderstood term. It should be used only to refer to a requirement imposed by the SEC staff that the amended preliminary prospectus be delivered to each person who received a copy of the preliminary prospectus as originally filed. SEC staff comments may impose such a requirement, but staff may also only ask for assurances that investors will be orally informed of certain changes before they are asked to commit to a purchase. On the other hand, securities lawyers will often err on the side of caution where there have been extensive changes to the initially distributed preliminary prospectus and advise the underwriters to recirculate the amended document. One reason for this advice in the case of IPOs may be that there will otherwise be doubt whether the distribution of the original preliminary prospectus satisfied the 48-hour distribution requirement of Rule 15c2-8 under the 1934 Act.

---

60. SEC Press Release 2004-89 (June 24, 2004).

61. The procedures are set out in Rule 83 under the SEC's Rules on Information and Requests.

In some cases, the change may be so material, such as an accounting change that requires a reduction in stated earnings per share, that the underwriters would be ill advised to price the issue before the preliminary prospectus containing the change has received wide distribution in the marketplace. Here the issue is not whether the underwriters need to "recirculate," but to what extent must the revised information be disseminated to protect the underwriters from the possibility of complaints from purchasers who learn of the change only on receipt of the final prospectus.

Post-Filing Issues

Once the registration statement has been filed and the underwriters are ready to market the issue, there are legal issues to be considered that are different from those that arise in the pre-filing period. It is during this later period that the difficult problems frequently arise. This is when counsel may be called upon to put out a fire that threatens the success of the deal.

- *Roadshows (Electronic and Otherwise)*

As part of its efforts to sell the securities, the managing underwriter will organize a "roadshow"—a series of meetings throughout the country, and frequently abroad, at which the company's management will make presentations to invited groups of institutional investors, money managers and securities salesmen. Where appropriate, the manager may arrange for the company's chief executive officer or another corporate official to have "one-on-one" meetings with important prospective investors. These marketing efforts may legally begin only after the registration statement has been filed.

The pitch to prospective investors at roadshow presentations or "one-on-ones" clearly constitutes an offer of the subject securities. The purpose of the presentation is to solicit interest from major potential investors. These offers are permissible because oral offers are permitted once the registration statement is filed. Just as registered representatives of the underwriters may solicit interest from their customers once the registration statement is filed, so too may company officers solicit interest from other prospective purchasers.

In preparing for a roadshow, corporate officers will sometimes be told by their counsel that they cannot say anything that is not in the preliminary prospectus. This is overly conservative advice. There is nothing in the 1933 Act that states that oral statements made in an effort to market securities must be limited to statements contained in the registration statement. A roadshow presentation would be stilted indeed if the chief executive officer were not permitted to range beyond the factual statements in the prospectus and discuss with potential investors his or her own views as to the company's prospects, the prospects for the industry in which it operates, and the economic factors affecting its business.

Regulation FD, which normally requires SEC-reporting companies to make simultaneous public disclosure of material non-public information disclosed to security holders and other persons, has an exception for information disclosed in connection with most public offerings registered under the 1933 Act. In the case of IPOs, of course, the issuer is not yet an SEC-reporting company and therefore not yet subject to Regulation FD.

The only written document that should be distributed at a roadshow presentation is the preliminary prospectus. The documents incorporated by reference into a Form S-3 prospectus may be distributed as well, although it is not customary to do so. Although shareholder reports may be distributed during the registration period in accordance with the company's normal schedule, they should not be used as part of a selling effort.

Videos,[62] power points and charts and graphs customarily are used as part of the roadshow presentation. Do these become

---

62. It is true that Section 2(a)(10) of the 1933 Act defines the term "prospectus" to include an offer that is "written or by radio or television." A radio or television advertisement broadcast to the public clearly is a prospectus for purposes of Section 5 of the 1933 Act, but it should be equally clear that this definition was not intended to extend to a video presentation at a roadshow simply because it appears on a screen.

written offers that make them illegal prospectuses, resulting in violations of Section 5? No one has ever taken the position that this is the case, but it would risk a Section 5(b)(1) violation to distribute to investors hard copies of the presentations. This applies to investors who are physically present at the roadshow as well as to those who are not. As for distributing hard copies to investors at the roadshow on condition that they be returned before the investors leave the room, this may or may not prevent a violation of Section 5, but in reality one or more of the distributed copies always slips through.

It would be acceptable, of course, to distribute roadshow materials if the issuer and the underwriters were willing to file them with the SEC as part of the registration statement. Google Inc. did this in connection with its 2004 IPO. This means accepting Section 11 liability for such materials, and not all issuers and underwriters are willing to go that far.

Beginning in early 1997, the SEC staff issued a series of no-action letters on the subject of electronic roadshows.[63] Issuers and underwriters were not willing to proceed with such roadshows absent the SEC's or its staff's assurance that they would not be considered as written communications in violation of Section 5.[64] The letters were issued to third-party contractors who wished to provide issuers and underwriters with a service that would provide for the recording and electronic transmission of roadshow presentations, but there is no reason why an issuer or underwriter may not rely on the letters without using a third-party contractor (subject to the usual caveat that no-action letters may formally be relied on only by the person to whom they are issued).

According to the Division of Corporation Finance's November 2001 compilation of *Current Issues and Rulemaking*

---

63. The first such letter was *Private Financial Network* (March 12, 1997). Other letters include *Net Roadshow, Inc.* (July 30, 1997), *Bloomberg L.P.* (October 27, 1997), *Thomson Financial Services, Inc.* (September 4, 1998) and *Activate.net Corp.* (September 21, 1999).

64. Section 2(a)(9) of the 1933 Act defines "written" as including "any means of graphic communication," and Rule 405 defines "graphic communication" as including "magnetic impulses or other forms of computer data compilation."

Projects, the letters have the following common conditions:

- an entire "live" roadshow, including any questions and answers from the audience, would be recorded after the filing of the registration statement for transmission on a real-time or subsequent basis; there would be no editing, except for "housekeeping" changes to eliminate dead airtime and to correct mistakes (the staff's intention here is to preserve the spontaneous nature of the live roadshow and to avoid slick studio-type productions amounting to "infomercials" for the securities; at the same time, it is probably sufficient to meet the "live" requirement that the roadshow be recorded before sales representatives rather than actual investors);

- the electronic roadshow would not be made "widely available;" rather, access would be restricted by password to a "limited audience" of persons "customarily invited by the underwriter to attend a 'live' roadshow" (the staff's intention here is again to preserve the elements of the traditional live roadshow);

- any investor given a password would be limited to viewing the presentation twice in connection with a particular offering or an unlimited number of times within a single 24-hour period;

- a copy of the prospectus in the registration statement would be delivered in paper or electronic form to each viewer before or contemporaneously with obtaining access to the roadshow (unfortunately, compliance with this condition sometimes requires issuers and underwriters to prepare a preliminary prospectus where they would otherwise have not done so);

- viewers would have the ability to download and print any electronic prospectus; on the other hand, they would have to agree not to copy, download or further distribute the roadshow transmission, and a visual statement or "crawl" would be included in each transmission to emphasize this prohibition;

SELECTED ISSUES

- material developments occurring after the taping of the original or "live" roadshow would be presented pursuant to a "periodic textual crawl;" and

- information provided in the electronic roadshow would "not be inconsistent" with the filed prospectus (this condition has not been taken to mean that the roadshow cannot contain information that does not appear in the prospectus).

More recently, the SEC staff permitted a securities firm to make electronic roadshows available to a highly qualified and high net worth "segment" of its retail customer base that, according to anecdotal evidence at the time, might have amounted to as many as 500,000 accounts.[65]

- *Dealing with Gun-Jumping Problems*

Counsel for the underwriters must be prepared to deal promptly with any gun-jumping problems[66] that arise during the course of a registered public offering. In some cases, a problem may be dealt with independently without involving the SEC staff. Given that the staff is likely to be monitoring news and events about the issuer by means of the Internet, "going it alone" should probably be reserved for those situations that have the strongest factual and legal arguments about why there has been no Section 5 violation. It is a matter of judgment.

The staff response to a gun-jumping problem is difficult to predict. It may listen to counsel's arguments and agree that there has been no Section 5 violation. On the other hand, it may insist on a postponement of the offering. The duration of a postponement can be negotiated, depending on the source of the problem. An issuer might argue that it should not be punished

---

65. SEC No-action Letters, *Charles Schwab & Co., Inc.* (November 15, 1999 and February 9, 2000).

66. After the filing of the registration statement, "gun-jumping" refers to the dissemination of written offering material other than the preliminary prospectus.

by having to take the market risk of a postponement when it was an underwriter that created the problem. In these situations, the underwriter may "volunteer" to drop out of the deal. A postponement of more than 30 days would be unusual, particularly given the SEC's proposal in the Aircraft Carrier Release to ignore any communications made more than 30 days prior to commencement of an offering.[67]

If the gun-jumping problem involved the dissemination of information that the SEC staff considers material and that does not appear in the prospectus, for example, earnings projections or estimates, the staff may insist that the information be included in the prospectus. This means that the issuer and all of the underwriters must bear Section 11 liability for information that would otherwise have created a Rule 10b-5 risk only for the underwriter that disseminated the information. There will undoubtedly be discussions about who should indemnify whom for such information.

Even if the staff permits the offering to proceed, there is no guarantee that a purchaser will not subsequently seek rescission under Section 12(a)(1) because of an alleged Section 5 violation. Obviously, one can hope to argue to the court that the staff's permitting the deal to proceed—together with whatever curative steps it demanded—is evidence that there was no Section 5 violation. In some cases, it may be advisable to foreclose Section 12(a)(1) liability by excluding from the offering any prospective purchasers who received offending communications (e.g., e-mails).

In extreme cases, the SEC staff may insist that the prospectus contain a risk factor describing the potential Section 5 violation and stating that the issuer may be at risk in the event of rescission claims. The staff was fond of using this technique during the Internet Bubble so as to impress on issuers the importance of monitoring what their underwriters were doing in the way of "electronic underwriting." Given the privity requirements of Section 12(a)(1), of course, it would be an unusual case in which an issuer would be responsible for an underwriter's gun-jumping violation.

---

67. SEC Release No. 33-7606A (November 13, 1998).

In pre-Internet days, it was somewhat easier to deal with gun-jumping problems without involving the SEC staff. In a bizarre episode, the registration statement for a large note offering was about to become effective when the office manager of one of the co-manager's retail branch offices discovered that one of his registered representatives had prepared a one-page flyer urging purchases of the notes, had taken a supply of them to the local Bloomingdale's parking lot and had stuffed them under the windshield wipers of all of the cars on the lot.

The initial reaction of underwriters' counsel was to call the SEC staff. It was the view of the other law firm that staff involvement so close to pricing could disrupt the financing. There was not sufficient time to explain the situation to the staff without risking a delay. Both firms finally agreed that under the circumstances the matter could be handled internally. The problem was confined to one office, and the co-manager withdrew that office's allocation of notes. The office was instructed that it could not refer customers to any other office. Later, a compliance visit was made to the office, and a seminar was held on the restrictions imposed by the securities laws during a distribution. Also, the guilty registered representative was fired. The action taken was documented in a memorandum to underwriters' counsel.

In this and in other cases, as we have already discussed, it may not be so clear whether a communication constitutes an offer and whether a document constitutes a prospectus. A determination will depend as much on the context of a communication—timing and audience—as its content. For example, a retailer of electronic equipment had filed a registration statement for a common stock offering but had delayed the offering to close an acquisition that had been presented to it after the filing. Once the deal was closed, it had every intention of amending the registration statement to reflect the acquisition and of proceeding with the sale of the common stock.

The company not only operated its own retail outlets but also had numerous franchisees. Its relationships with the manufacturers of the products that it sold were also important to its business. Management decided that as soon as the acquisition was completed it would write to its franchisees and suppliers to assure them that the acquisition would strengthen the company and would make their business relationships with the company even more desirable. Counsel for the underwriters was asked whether the distribution of this written material in the manner proposed would raise problems under the 1933 Act in view of the pending public offering.

The material would contain strong positive statements that indeed would create problems if used in the context of a public offering. But, in this case, the statements were to be directed exclusively to franchisees and suppliers for the sole purpose of strengthening existing business relationships. Any of these persons might incidentally buy shares in the offering, but the communications were in no way designed to generate interest in the common stock. They were not intended to result in the sale of one additional share. Underwriters' counsel advised that they did not expect that they would object to the use of the material in this particular business context.

• • *E-mail and Other Electronic Communications.* More recent episodes illustrate the dangers of e-mail and other electronic communications. For example, the financial press reported in October 1996 the postponement because of "market conditions" of an "Internet-media" company's "long-awaited" IPO. There was also speculation, however, that the deal had been pulled because of an e-mail memorandum sent by the issuer's chief executive officer "to the company's 334 employees in the wake of news reports skeptical about the company's IPO prospects." The memo found its way onto an online service with 10,000 subscribers with the result that the sender's optimistic views were sent around the world just before the pricing of the planned IPO.

The company denied that the e-mail message had anything to do with the withdrawal of the offering. If it had been otherwise, one could have argued that the original communication was proper and that the issuer should not be penalized for a recipient's unauthorized public dissemination of the message. An analogy might have been made to an institutional investor who, despite warnings to the contrary, commented on a roadshow presentation to the press. On the other hand, the e-mail message was sent to a fairly large and possibly unsophisticated (at least when it comes to the securities laws) audience, and there is no indication that there were warnings to the employees that the message was to be treated confidentially. One might anticipate that the SEC staff's reaction would be that the issuer should not benefit from an employee's widespread dissemination of an upbeat message not in conformity with the securities laws, and that the staff might well require a reasonable postponement of the commencement of the offering.

There have been numerous situations where one or more underwriters have discovered that their sales representatives had sent e-mails to prospective investors about a proposed offering. Where these e-mails have contained material information not in the prospectus, the SEC staff has frequently required that the offending information be added to the prospectus.

For example, a preliminary prospectus for a follow-on common stock offering disclosed in March 2004 that employees of one of the lead underwriters had sent e-mails to 223 persons with whom the underwriter "has or is seeking an investment banking relationship . . . for the intended purpose of cultivating investment banking business" and not in connection with selling efforts for the offering. Also, an employee of one of the other lead underwriters had sent an e-mail about the offering—before the filing of the registration statement—to the firm's sales force, trading desk and other departments. Before the compliance department could intervene, one salesperson had orally disclosed the offering to two customers.

The underwriters undertook not to sell in the offering to the 223 addressees or to the two customers who had been informed about the offering. A risk factor was added to the prospectus describing the circumstances and stating that the e-mails may have constituted an illegal prospectus and an impermissible pre-filing offer, respectively, and that if this were the case, then the recipients of the e-mails and the pre-filing disclosure might have rescission rights if they were able to purchase stock in the offering despite the underwriters' undertaking not to sell to such persons. Each underwriter agreed to indemnify the issuer for losses, costs and expenses that it might incur as a result of the e-mails or the pre-filing disclosure.[68]

---

68. The e-mails to the 223 prospective investment banking clients might not have constituted gun-jumping at all if their purpose was not to offer or sell securities but to drum up additional investment banking business.

Without making excuses for sales representatives who should know better,[69] it is admittedly difficult to explain why a communication that could have safely been read over the telephone to a customer becomes a Section 5 violation when it is incorporated into an e-mail.[70]

Underwriters have a general obligation to supervise their employees with a view to preventing violations of the securities laws, including Section 5 violations arising from e-mail or other communications. The SEC fined a major firm $2 million in mid-2004 for what it called "confusing and incomplete" guidance and training to a sales desk, resulting in e-mail communications to customers that violated Section 5 in connection with four separate IPOs of foreign issuers. The SEC also ordered the firm to cease and desist from future violations of Section 5(b) or 5(c). SEC Release No. 33-8434 (July 1, 2004).

Even the best supervision and training can be in vain. One major firm had admonished its sales force against forwarding to customers the Bloomberg reports on a series of new issues. A few days later, the head of the relevant desk asked for relief from the restriction, complaining that "it's a pain in the neck to have to retype all those Bloomberg reports."

• • *Press Coverage.* Communications with the press frequently lead to difficult problems. Prior to the filing of the registration statement for the 2004 IPO of Google Inc., its two founding stockholders were interviewed by *Playboy.* Perhaps because of unanticipated delays in the IPO, the interview appeared in the September 2004 issue of the magazine at a time

---

69. Sales personnel have been warned for years not to send written communications to customers in connection with public offerings. The pre-Internet version of the problem was the faxing to customers of retail sales memos prepared (and clearly labeled as) for "internal use only."

70. One of the authors suggested a few years ago that the SEC should simply exempt from the definition of "prospectus" any e-mail of 200 words or less. Joseph McLaughlin, *"Booting" the Federal Securities Laws into the 21st Century,* 11 InSights 21, 22 (July 1997). The same suggestion was made by Professor John C. Coffee in his article *Brave New World?: The Impact(s) of the Internet on Modern Securities Regulation,* 52 Bus. Law. 1195, 1208 (August 1997).

just prior to the IPO's pricing. The SEC required the IPO prospectus to include the full text of the *Playboy* interview. Some modifications and updates were included in a risk factor, but this is the first instance known to the authors where an issuer and underwriters assumed Section 11 liability for material included in *Playboy*.

Other communications with the press have raised similar problems. For example, three weeks before the planned pricing of a 1990 common stock offering for a major company, the "Heard on the Street" column of *The Wall Street Journal* reported earnings projections on the issuer that had been confirmed to the author of the column by an analyst for one of the co-managers. The SEC staff immediately demanded an explanation from the underwriters, and it was eventually agreed that the projections would be included in the prospectus and identified as having been confirmed by the co-manager's analyst. The transaction proceeded on schedule, but the underwriters had to live with Section 11 liability for estimates that would ordinarily have been communicated only in verbal form.

A high-profile IPO was stopped in its tracks in May 2004 after The New York Times published an article that included descriptions of the company with quotations from its chief executive officer about its development and business strategy. The article was based on the reporter's having spent "most of a full day" with the chief executive officer. According to the final prospectus, it could therefore have been expected that a lengthy article would be published. A risk factor noted that the article as well as other publicity regarding the IPO had presented statements about the company "in isolation" and without disclosure of the related risks and uncertainties described in the prospectus. The risk factor stated that the company had "stopped" the offering shortly after the publication of the article to allow a "cooling off period" so that the effects of the article and other publicity could be "dissipated." It also referred to the risk of a Section 5 violation and the possibility—which the company would "contest vigorously"—that investors could seek to rescind their purchases within a period of one year.

In another situation, two representatives of the lead manager for an SEC-registered offering of "trust preferred" securities (see

Chapter 11) permitted themselves to be interviewed by a reporter for a banking industry publication. The interview was published with highly positive statements about the merits of trust preferred securities for issuers and investors alike just before the launch of several new transactions involving different issuers. After making inquiries about the publication's readership, counsel concluded that the interview was likely to be seen only by other issuers who might be interested in effecting similar transactions and not by potential investors in such transactions. The published interview was therefore not thought to constitute gun-jumping for the new transactions.

Another transaction—slated to be the largest collateralized mortgage-backed securities offering of 2000—had to be terminated because an officer of one of the co-lead managing underwriters was quoted in an industry newsletter about the deal's ten-year tranche being a "compelling trade."

Also, during the Internet Bubble, it was a common occurrence for the chief executive of a newly public high-technology company to be interviewed by the electronic financial press shortly after the pricing of the IPO and the commencement of trading. The SEC staff began to monitor these interviews and objected on occasion to statements that it believed were in violation of Section 5.

No one can prevent the press from covering a pending IPO or other offering, but the SEC staff's reaction is likely to be influenced considerably by the degree to which the issuer or an underwriter initiated or otherwise facilitated the coverage.

• • *Rating Agencies.* In advance of an offering of debt, asset-backed or "structured" securities, the issuer and the underwriters will often send relevant information to the rating agencies for the purpose of enabling the agencies to assign a rating to the securities. There is no problem with doing so, nor with publication or dissemination of the rating when it is issued. Some of the agencies take the process a step farther, however, by publishing a "pre-sale report" on the forthcoming transaction. Even if the reports would be impermissible if published by an underwriter, they should not present a Section 5 problem if the underwriter took reasonable steps to caution the agency that the information was being provided for rating purposes only.

SELECTED ISSUES 203

• • *Research Coverage.* Research material often presents problems under the 1933 Act because of the prohibition in Section 5(b)(1) against the dissemination of any prospectus unless it meets the requirements of Section 10 of the 1933 Act. Research material may constitute a prospectus as defined by Section 2(a)(10) of the 1933 Act, but research material seldom meets the requirements of Section 10. Accordingly, the dissemination of research material must rely on an exemption from Section 5(b)(l).

In addition, as discussed above under "Role of the Securities Analyst in Securities Offerings," recently adopted rules of the SROs may inhibit research coverage after the completion of an IPO or even a follow-on offering by an SEC-reporting company.

It is understandable that analysts wish to maintain the continuity of their coverage, and it is certainly true that customers expect to receive continuous coverage. For this reason, the SEC in 1970 adopted a series of rules designed to minimize the number and scope of restrictions on research.[71] The rules were originally proposed in the *Wheat Report*.[72]

Rule 137 states in substance that a dealer is not an "underwriter" in respect of a registered offering of a reporting issuer if the dealer distributes research in the regular course of business and is not and does not propose to be a member of the underwriting syndicate or the dealer group. The rule also requires, as might be expected, that the dealer not receive any direct or indirect consideration from anyone participating in the offering and that the dealer not be distributing the research pursuant to any arrangement with any such person. The effect of Rule 137 is to make a dealer eligible for the Section 4(3) exemption as a dealer who is not an underwriter. In the case of a reporting company, this means that the dealer may distribute research to its customers without limitation. In the case of an IPO, however, such a dealer is unable to obtain any research advantage over an underwriter. First, the dealer cannot rely on Rule 137 to conclude that it is not an "underwriter." Second, even a non-underwriter dealer is subject to the post-offering

---

71. SEC Release No. 33-5101 (November 19, 1970).

72. *Disclosure to Investors—A Reappraisal of Administrative Policies Under the '33 and '34 Acts* (1969).

prospectus delivery requirement (usually for a period of 25 days) discussed in Chapter 1. (Of course, any dealer—whether or not it acted as an underwriter in the IPO—can commence research coverage immediately following the IPO if it is willing to have the research treated as "free writing," i.e., by linking an electronic final prospectus to electronically-delivered research or by delivering a copy of the final prospectus in the same envelope with hard-copy research.)

Rule 138 provides that, if a qualified issuer has filed or proposes to file a registration statement relating to non-convertible debt securities or nonconvertible preferred stock, the publication in the regular course of business by a dealer of information, opinions or recommendations relating solely to the issuer's common stock or convertible securities will not be deemed to constitute an "offer" of the securities being registered, even though the dealer is a member of the underwriting syndicate. The reverse is also true: if the registration statement covers common stock or convertible securities, a dealer acting as an underwriter of those securities may continue to publish information and opinions solely with respect to the issuer's non-convertible debt securities or preferred stock.

A qualified issuer for purposes of Rule 138 is any issuer that meets both the registrant and transaction requirements of Form S-2 or the registrant requirements of Form S-3 or, in addition, any foreign private issuer that meets the registrant requirements of Form F-3 (except for the reporting history requirements) and meets the minimum float or investment-grade conditions of the form and has had its securities traded for at least 12 months on a "designated offshore securities market" (see the discussion in Chapter 9 relating to Regulation S).

An instruction to Rule 138 makes clear that a dealer may rely on the rule to distribute research on the issuer's equity or debt securities notwithstanding its participation as an underwriter in discrete "takedowns" of debt or equity securities, respectively, from a "generic" or "universal" shelf registration statement (see Chapter 8).

The most important rule in the series was Rule 139, which permitted an underwriter or prospective underwriter to publish in the regular course of business certain information, opinions or recommendations about registered securities issued by reporting companies under the 1934 Act. As adopted by the SEC in 1970, however, the rule in effect required that references to the registered securities had to be accompanied by references to other securities, and that any opinion or recommendation could not be more favorable than a previous opinion or recommendation.

Notwithstanding the adoption of Rule 139 and its companion rules, the task of separating "normal" research from forbidden "gun-jumping" remained difficult. In addition, it became apparent in the early 1980s that the SEC's integrated disclosure system would not work without a broader involvement by securities analysts and the financial press.

Increasing conflicts between research and underwriting activity led many broker-dealers by the early 1980s to request more specific standards from the SEC on the bounds of permissible research. Some of these requests were supported by appeals to the First Amendment, which the Supreme Court had begun in the 1970s to apply to "commercial speech."[73]

The SEC accommodated these requests to some degree in 1984, when it adopted a major liberalization of Rule 139.[74] As modified, Rule 139(a) permits considerable latitude for research relating to (1) those companies that meet the registrant requirements of Form S-3 or Form F-3 as well as the minimum float or investment-grade securities provisions of that form or (2) foreign private issuers that meet the requirements specified above for Rule 138. For these companies and their securities, the only condition is that the research be "contained in a publication which is distributed with reasonable regularity in the normal course of business." An instruction to the rule states that a publication has not been distributed with "reasonable regularity" if it contains information, an opinion or a recommendation concerning a company with respect to which the dealer "currently is not publishing research." The significance of the instruction

---

73. *Virginia State Bd. of Pharmacy v. Virginia Citizens Consumer Council, Inc.*, 425 U.S. 758 (1976). *See also* the Washington Legal Foundation's *Petition for Rulemaking* (December 20, 1995) filed with the SEC.

74. SEC Release No. 33-6550 (September 19, 1984).

is not always clear. It obviously means that a dealer that hopes to be an underwriter in a forthcoming offering by a particular issuer cannot rely on the rule to initiate coverage of that issuer's securities. On the other hand, assume that a dealer proposes to initiate coverage of a new steel company by including it in a quarterly industry survey just prior to *another* steel company's registered offering. It would be unreasonable to read the instruction as requiring that the dealer exclude the new company from the survey and publish its views in a stand-alone report.

Securities research has come to be distributed more frequently in electronic form. It hardly deserves mention that screen-based research (which by its nature is made available to the investor rather than "distributed") is nonetheless eligible to qualify as a "publication" that is "distributed with reasonable regularity in the normal course of business."

When the issuer does not satisfy the requirements specified in Rule 139(a), the research material may still be permitted under Rule 139(b) if it is contained in a publication that meets the "reasonable regularity" test of Rule 139(a) and "includes similar information, opinions or recommendations with respect to a substantial number of companies in the registrant's industry or sub-industry, or contains a comprehensive list of securities currently recommended" by the dealer. In this case, the information, opinion or recommendation may be given no "materially greater space or prominence" in the publication than that given to other securities or issuers. Also, an opinion or recommendation "as favorable or more favorable" as to the company or its securities must have been published by the dealer in its last publication addressing the issuer or its securities prior to the commencement of the dealer's participation in the distribution. The "space or prominence" and "as favorable or more favorable" requirements are extremely difficult to apply in practice, particularly with respect to fixed-income securities.

An instruction to Rule 139(b) states that a publication that contains projections of an issuer's sales or earnings cannot meet the rule's conditions unless the projections (1) were previously published on a regular basis, (2) are included with respect to a substantial number of companies in the issuer's industry or sub-industry or all companies in a comprehensive list contained in

SELECTED ISSUES

the publication and (3) are not more favorable than previously published projections.

Rule 139 did not anticipate the degree to which fixed-income research has become an important market factor. Given the number of issuers of fixed-income securities, it is much more difficult for broker-dealers in these securities to meet the "reasonable regularity" test of Rule 139. On the other hand, the standard has to be a flexible one. "Reasonable regularity" of coverage for a common stock probably implies coverage over a period of at least several quarters. For a fixed-income security, however, it is probably fair to conclude that "reasonable regularity" can be established with a single report if it is published at a time when no underwriting is in sight and with the intention to maintain continuous coverage (as evidenced, perhaps, by continuous coverage of similar securities or products).

The provisions of Rule 139 can never be satisfied in the case of an IPO as there will have been no prior history of research coverage. Thus, the blackout period on research reports will extend through the 25-day or longer prospectus delivery period, and the initial research report may not be published until this period is over as well as (in the case of a manager or co-manager of the IPO) the additional period of 15 days mandated by recently adopted SRO rules.[75]

Despite these rules, questions with respect to research reports and similar material published by securities firms frequently arise in connection with underwritten offerings. Often the resolution of the question turns on timing. Research material should not be a problem if distributed by a managing underwriter prior to reaching an understanding with the issuer that it will manage a financing. In the case of a non-managing underwriter, the restriction on research reports will not apply until it decides to accept an invitation to participate in the underwriting.

Gun-jumping problems, whether of the press coverage or research variety, are among the types of problems that can arise in connection with any financing. Dealing with such issues is

---

75. See the discussion above under "Role of the Securities Analyst in Securities Offerings."

one of the most important tasks that must be performed by lawyers representing securities firms. The staff of the SEC makes every effort to be helpful when problems of this type arise so long as it is convinced that the problem arose through human error and with no intention of violating the securities laws.

All this being said, the SEC's rules on research are in need of a major overhaul. Investors require continuous in-depth research from broker-dealer firms in order to be able to cope with the volatility of securities markets, the complexity of financial instruments and the amount of information released by issuers. Increasingly, investors are receiving this research material by electronic means that cannot be easily interrupted when the issuer of the research finds itself participating in a distribution. The SEC concept release of mid-1996 cited "the deregulation of offers" as a possible means of resolving these conflicts. The SEC's Aircraft Carrier Release in late 1998[76] proposed several useful changes to the research rules, but these have not been adopted.

- *Regulation M Problems*

In the case of equity offerings where the same securities are trading in the secondary market, an underwriter may inadvertently enter a bid for or purchase the security during the restricted period contemplated by Rule 101 under Regulation M. The response of underwriters' counsel to this type of situation is discussed in Chapter 4.

- *Changes in Deal Size (Rule 430A)*

Traditionally, the final pricing of an offering would take place after the close of the market on the day before the registration statement was to become effective. The underwriting agreement would be signed and held in escrow until the following morning just prior to the filing of the price amendment—that is, the amendment to the registration statement that reflected the pricing terms. The price information would be inserted in the registration statement and checked and rechecked at the printer.

---

76. SEC Release No. 33-7606A (November 13, 1998).

Delays at the SEC in declaring the price amendment effective sometimes led to serious inconvenience on the part of the underwriters, who could not confirm sales until the registration statement became effective. The SEC addressed this problem in 1987 by adopting Rule 430A.

Rule 430A permits a registration statement that covers a cash securities offering to become effective without pricing and related information, provided that the omitted information is included in a supplemented prospectus filed under Rule 424(b).[77] Pursuant to an undertaking required by Item 512(i) of Regulation S-K, the omitted information when filed will be deemed to be part of the registration statement as of the time of effectiveness. This is to ensure that the omitted information becomes subject to the liabilities imposed by Section 11.

The supplemented prospectus must be filed within 15 business days after the effectiveness of the registration statement. If this deadline is missed, then the supplemented prospectus must be filed as part of a post-effective amendment.[78] Pursuant to Rule 462(c), however, the post-effective amendment will become effective on filing if it contains no substantive information other than the omitted price-related information. An issuer may also rely on Rule 462(c) to "re-start the 15-business-day period in which pricing must occur under Rule 430A(a)(3)," that is, the post-effective amendment need not contain the final price terms.[79]

A decrease in the amount of securities offered or a change in the estimate of the price range from that indicated in the form of prospectus included in the registration statement at the time of effectiveness may be reflected in the Rule 424(b) prospectus—rather than in a post-effective amendment—if the decrease in amount or change in price range would not materially change the disclosure contained in the registration statement at effectiveness.

---

77. Rule 430A procedures provide the same benefits as so-called "formula pricing," which was used frequently prior to the adoption of the rule.

78. The "pricing" period had been five business days until May 1995, when the SEC adopted various amendments designed to facilitate the new "T+3" standard settlement cycle.

79. SEC Division of Corporation Finance, *Manual of Publicly-Available Telephone Interpretations* (July 1997), at 42–43.

An increase in the amount or price of securities offered may also be reflected in the Rule 424(b) prospectus if it does not result in an increase of more than 20% in the maximum aggregate offering price set forth in the registration statement.

If an increase requires the registration of additional securities within the 20% limit, this may be accomplished under Rule 462(b) by means of an abbreviated registration statement consisting of a facing page, a statement incorporating by reference the contents of the earlier registration statement relating to the offering, all required consents and opinions, and the signature page. The abbreviated registration statement must be filed prior to the time sales are made and confirmations are sent or given. The abbreviated registration statement will be effective automatically on filing with the SEC.

The NYSE/NASD IPO Advisory Committee observed in May 2003 that the need to file a post-effective amendment in the event of changes of more than 20% in the amount of offered securities tended to discourage increases to the offering price or number of shares offered for the purpose of meeting "excess investor demand" for an IPO.[80] It recommended an increase to 40% without the need for SEC staff review or the need to delay the offering unless the increase resulted in "a material change to the prospectus disclosure beyond that related to price or number of shares offered." Presumably the committee had in mind a material effect on the issuer's use of proceeds, for example, by turning the offering into a "blind pool" offering.

It should come as no surprise that the Rule 430A prospectus, because it contains no price terms, has the same status as a preliminary prospectus notwithstanding the effectiveness of the registration statement, that is, it is not considered a "final" prospectus that can accompany or precede supplementary selling literature without causing a Section 5(b)(1) violation.

Whether the price information is inserted into a price amendment or a prospectus supplement, the greatest care is required. This can be illustrated by an incident that occurred some years ago in connection with an offering of capital notes by a large New York City bank. The preliminary offering circular contained a statement on its cover to the effect that the initial optional

---

80. NYSE/NASD IPO Advisory Committee, *supra* note 17, at 8–9.

redemption price of the notes was their "principal amount plus a premium of ____%." The blank was to be filled in when the interest rate and the initial redemption premium were finally set. Negotiations resulted in a figure of, let us assume, 8%. When the final offering circular arrived on the chairman's desk the following morning, he noticed that the figure that appeared in the blank was "108%," the initial redemption *price* rather than the initial redemption *premium*. The notes were stated to be redeemable at their "principal amount plus a premium of 108%." None of the 20 people who had worked so carefully at the printer the previous evening had caught the error. Faces were red, and the circular was reprinted. The senior author obtained a copy of the erroneous circular and kept it in his desk for many years as a reminder that "there but for the grace of God go I."

- *"T+3" Settlement Date and Prospectus Delivery Problems*

As discussed in Chapter 1, a copy of the final prospectus must precede or accompany each confirmation of sale. For years, chronic delays in printing the final prospectus and in delivering it to underwriters in sufficient quantities have frequently caused delays in the mailing of confirmations. Historically, these delays especially affected underwriters located outside New York, thus giving rise to references to the "Texas problem" or the "California problem." The situation has been improved, however, as the major printing firms have improved their capability to print in multiple locations.

On the other hand, the problem threatened to become worse with the SEC's adoption in 1995 of its Rule 15c6-1. This rule requires "T+3" settlements in lieu of the historical "T+5" settlement convention in all securities transactions, including SEC-registered public offerings as well as private placements. There are exceptions for government or municipal securities and certain money market instruments.

In response to underwriters' concerns about T+3 settlement, the SEC simultaneously adopted amendments to its rules and registration forms to facilitate the delivery of prospectuses.[81] These amendments included (1) a package of changes to rules and registration forms designed to speed up the process of preparing full prospectuses for delivery to customers with

---

81. SEC Release No. 33-7168 (May 11, 1995).

confirmations and (2) a new Rule 434 designed to reduce the amount of paper involved in the confirmation process by permitting the use of "term sheets" as supplements to previously delivered preliminary or base prospectuses.

Rule 15c6-1 itself contains some useful exceptions that provide needed flexibility:

- It permits routine settlement on a T+4 basis of transactions in connection with firm commitment underwritings priced after the close of the market, that is, 4:30 P.M. Eastern time.

- It permits a managing underwriter and an issuer to "expressly" agree to a longer settlement at the time of the transaction. The SEC has cautioned, however, that this "override provision" is intended to be used only in those circumstances where T+3 settlement is not "feasible." Underwriters' counsel should therefore be satisfied that there are important business reasons for a longer settlement.

- It permits a longer settlement date—whether or not a T+3 settlement date would be "feasible"—if the longer settlement date is "expressly agreed to by the parties at the time of the transaction." In this case, the required agreement to a longer settlement date includes not only the managing underwriter and the issuer but also the other underwriters, dealers and customers. It is simple enough to commit the parties in the underwriting documents (including the non-managing underwriters and dealers) to a specific settlement date, but what about the customers? Fortunately, nothing in the rule requires that the customers' agreement be in writing. For example, an implied agreement should be sufficient where the customer has agreed to buy after receiving a preliminary prospectus that specifies a longer settlement date. Alternatively, an underwriter could rely on its sales representatives to obtain the customers' oral agreement. This would appear to be a satisfactory practice if the firm has a high degree of confidence in the ability of its sales people to follow prescribed procedures. It is certainly satisfactory in the case of offerings of fixed-income securities, where the settlement date is inevitably a part of the conversation between the salesperson and the customer.

The SEC has urged issuers and underwriters to ensure that all interested parties are informed of non-standard settlements, including not only customers but also any affected depositaries and trading markets. Also, customers should be informed in the prospectus of any likely impact of a non-standard settlement, for example, that secondary market trades may settle earlier than the new offering.

Experience since the 1995 amendments suggests that underwriters are coping with T+3 principally by attempting to accelerate the prospectus production process at the printer and by making greater use of PDF prospectuses transmitted by e-mail. Issuers' and underwriters' counsel and printers are under greater pressure than ever to put prospectuses into the hands of the underwriters at the earliest possible time.

As noted in Chapter 1, the availability of the prospectus for delivery to the customer has a significance that goes beyond its linkage to the mailing of a confirmation. Unlike the confirmation requirement, which the underwriter can meet simply by enclosing a copy of the prospectus in the same envelope with the confirmation, Section 5(b)(2) of the 1933 Act requires that the prospectus "accompan[y] or precede[ ]" the *delivery* of the security to the customer.

An underwriter will normally debit a customer's account on the settlement date and deposit the security in the customer's account. Section 5(b)(2) says nothing about the underwriter's receiving payment from the customer. It appears to say, however, that the underwriter cannot deliver the security to the customer unless the customer has *received* the prospectus (not merely that it has been mailed or otherwise sent or given to the customer). The question therefore arises whether Section 5(b)(2) is violated if settlement occurs before the customer has actually received the prospectus.

It is hard to see how a customer is disadvantaged by the delivery to his account of a purchased security prior to the customer's actual receipt of the prospectus. Presumably, underwriters have been relying for many years on the assumption that confirmations were ordinarily sent out (with prospectuses) in time to provide reasonable assurance that they would be received by the customer on or before the T+5 settlement date. In a T+3 environment, of course, this is less certain.

Rule 434(a), discussed above as part of the SEC's T+3 initiative, provides that the "term sheet" procedure may be relied on to permit not only the sending of the confirmation but also the delivery of the registered security. This procedure is seldom followed, however, and it would be preferable for the SEC to act under the Improvement Act to clarify the Section 5(b)(2) situation.

In the meantime, it should be kept in mind that Section 5(b)(2) antedates the age of electronic settlements. It is therefore logical to interpret its requirements in the context of physical deliveries. A requirement that the security not be "carried through the mails or in interstate commerce . . . unless accompanied or preceded by a prospectus" could therefore be interpreted as requiring only that the prospectus has already been deposited in the mail or otherwise sent on its way.

- *The Electronic Prospectus*

Printing efficiencies can go only so far, of course, and no efficiencies will be adequate to the task if the SEC eventually moves (as some expect) to a T+1 standard settlement cycle. One of the authors of this book suggested some years ago that the prospectus delivery problem could easily be solved, at least for offerings registered on Form S-3, by permitting an underwriter or dealer to incorporate the prospectus into the confirmation.[82] More recently, attention has been focused on the electronic delivery of the prospectus. In a February 1995 interpretive letter[83] and in interpretive releases published in October 1995[84] and April 2000,[85] the SEC discussed the circumstances under which an

---

82. Joseph McLaughlin, *"Ten Easy Pieces" for the SEC*, 18 Rev. Sec. & Commodities Reg. 200, 201 (1985).

83. SEC Interpretive Letter, *Brown & Wood* (February 17, 1995).

84. SEC Release No. 33-7233 (October 6, 1995). *See also* SEC Release Nos. 33-7289 (May 9, 1996) and 34-37182 (May 9, 1996).

85. SEC Release No. 33-7856 (April 28, 2000).

SELECTED ISSUES

electronic prospectus could be used as a means of satisfying the requirements of Section 5.

"Electronic" media for this purpose includes audiotapes, videotapes, facsimiles, CD-ROM, DVD, electronic mail, bulletin boards, Internet websites and computer networks. The 1995 release states that the SEC, as a general matter, would view "information distributed through electronic means as satisfying the delivery or transmission requirements of the federal securities laws if such distribution results in the delivery to the intended recipients of substantially equivalent information as these recipients would have had if the information were delivered to them in paper form." Whether an electronic communication is "delivered" or "transmitted" for purposes of this general statement will depend on (1) giving notice to the recipient that information is available in electronic form, (2) providing the recipient with access to the required disclosure and (3) following procedures that evidence delivery of the information.

The release elaborated on these three considerations as follows:

– Notice of the availability of electronic information may be provided, for example, by a supplemental communication (presumably a trailer on a confirmation would suffice).

– Access to the electronic information must not be burdensome; in particular, it must not involve too many steps or require the downloading of a separate software program. The recipient must also have an opportunity to retain the information or to have ongoing access equivalent to personal retention. In addition, recipients must retain the right to receive a paper version of any required document.

– Delivery may be evidenced by (a) an investor's "informed consent" to receive information through a particular electronic medium, (b) evidence of actual receipt (e.g., electronic mail return-receipt or confirmation of accessing, downloading or printing), (c) facsimile, (d) hyperlink or (e) inference from the investor's response in a particular format.

The 2000 release elaborated on the permissible means of obtaining a customer's "informed consent." Although many lawyers had already understood the 1995 release to permit oral consents, the 2000 release confirmed that this was permissible so long as a record of that consent was retained. The release also cautioned that broker-dealers had to obtain consents in a manner that ensured "authenticity."

The 2000 release also confirmed that "global consents" were permissible—that is, consents relating to all documents of any issuer in any specified media—so long as the consent was "informed." The release stated that this meant that "intermediaries should take particular care to ensure that the investor understands that he or she is providing a global consent to electronic delivery." For example, the release encouraged the obtaining of a global consent through a document separate from an account-opening agreement or by means of a second signature in such an agreement. It also stated the SEC's belief that a global consent would not be "informed" if the opening of a brokerage account were conditioned on providing the consent (except in the case of "online" brokers). Finally, a global consent could permit the addition of further issuers without the need for a subsequent consent (but not for the addition of new media).

Consents may be revoked, in which case a provider of information would presumably need to find a different method of evidencing the delivery (or, alternatively, justifying the presumption of delivery) of the required information. According to the 2000 release, a broker-dealer could require a person to revoke his or her consent on an "all-or-none" basis—all issuers or none—so long as this policy was adequately disclosed when the consent was given.

The SEC's 1995 release expressly contemplated offerings that are made *exclusively* through electronic means. This would suggest that an investor who revokes his consent just before pricing may be summarily dropped from the offering. In 2001, two SEC commissioners permitted an issuer to go even further albeit over a dissent by the third sitting SEC commissioner.[86]

---

86. *In the Matter of The American Separate Account 5 of The American Life Insurance Company of New York*, SEC Release No. 33-8027 (October 25, 2001).

The American Life Insurance Company of New York proposed to offer variable annuity contracts to investors who were willing to consent to electronic delivery of the prospectus and all subsequent reports and other documents. Revocation of consent resulted in a surrender of the contract. A few years later, the May 21, 2004 preliminary prospectus for Google Inc.'s IPO stated that investors would be permitted to participate in the IPO auction only if they agreed to accept electronic delivery of the preliminary prospectus, any amended prospectus and the final prospectus.

The 2000 release also confirmed underwriters' ability to use PDF documents as a means of fulfilling prospectus delivery obligations if the underwriters informed investors of the relevant requirements at the time of the investors' consent and provided investors with "any necessary software and technical assistance at no cost."

Electronic communications obviously pose interesting challenges for securities lawyers. Both underwriters' and issuer's counsel will need to be alert to all electronic communications used in connection with the offering and to be in a position to verify that all communications are either not "offers" of the registered securities, are entitled to a 1933 Act exemption, or are made a part of the registration statement filed with the SEC.

The use of electronic prospectuses is not yet common for the purpose of permitting a confirmation to be sent to a customer. This will likely remain the case for as long as the SEC is paralyzed by its fear of the "digital divide" and unwilling to entertain the presumption that all investors have access to a computer or other terminal (as it does, e.g., in presuming that each investor has a mailbox).[87] The absence of such a presumption means that an underwriter will have to obtain the customer's "informed consent" in order to rely on electronic delivery. Even if a significant number of customers so consent, it is obviously less expensive and more reliable to send a paper prospectus to all purchasers.

---

87. The 2000 release requested comment on such "technological" issues as "access-equals-delivery" and implied consent to the delivery of electronic documents.

Electronic prospectuses are much more popular for the purpose of posting or sending electronic information about a security during a prospectus delivery period. As discussed in Chapter 1, it would violate Section 5 to send written offering material to investors during a prospectus delivery period unless the material were accompanied or preceded by a final prospectus. Posting the final prospectus on a website or delivering it as a PDF document by e-mail allows the simultaneous posting or sending of research material or (in the case of asset-backed securities) performance information relating to the underlying collateral. The electronic prospectus can take the form of a hyperlink to the EDGAR version of the prospectus.

Chinese Walls

In the course of working on a securities offering, investment bankers may learn of material information, favorable or unfavorable, that is to be included in the disclosure document but has not yet been disclosed to the public. This is not a problem so long as the banker does not trade on the information personally and does not disclose it to anyone likely to trade on the information, especially the research, trading or sales arms of his or her firm. To ensure compliance with this principle, an underwriting firm's written procedures will provide for an information barrier between investment banking and the other parts of the firm as impregnable as the Great Wall of China.[88]

The concept of the Chinese Wall grew out of the settlement of an administrative proceeding brought by the SEC against Merrill Lynch, Pierce, Fenner & Smith Incorporated and certain of its officers and employees in connection with a 1966 underwriting of convertible debentures of Douglas Aircraft Co., Inc.[89] Two weeks after the filing of the registration statement, Merrill

---

88. For a general discussion of Chinese Walls, *see* Report of SEC Division of Market Regulation, *Broker-Dealer Policies and Procedures Designed to Segment the Flow and Prevent the Misuse of Material Nonpublic Information* (March 1990). For reasons of political correctness, the term "information barriers" has lately come into greater use.

89. SEC Release No. 34-8459 (November 25, 1968).

Lynch, in its capacity as managing underwriter, received non-public information from Douglas to the effect that it expected to report little or no profit for the fiscal year and that it had substantially reduced its projection of earnings for the following fiscal year. The SEC charged that Merrill Lynch had disclosed this information to certain of its institutional and other large customers prior to its dissemination to the public and that these customers had traded on the basis of this information. As part of the settlement negotiated with the SEC, Merrill Lynch adopted a statement of policy that prohibited the disclosure of material non-public information obtained during the course of an investment banking transaction to any person other than persons involved in the transaction or senior executives of the firm and members of its Legal Department.

All investment banking firms have now adopted similar policies, which are supplemented by restricted list and "gray" or "watch" list procedures (discussed earlier in this chapter). It should be noted that Section 15(f) of the 1934 Act imposes an affirmative duty on all broker-dealers to "establish, maintain and enforce written policies and procedures reasonably designed . . . to prevent the [illegal] misuse . . . of material, nonpublic information."

The legal effect of Chinese Wall and similar procedures was unclear for many years except in the area of tender offers, where Rule 14e-3 contained an express Chinese Wall defense for securities firm. In 2000, however, the SEC adopted Rule 10b5-1. Among other things, this rule provides a Chinese Wall defense similar to that contained in Rule 14e-3 but applicable to all charges under Rule 10b-5 of trading "on the basis of" material non-public information.

Inadvertent and Transient Investment Companies

The "inadvertent investment company" problem can be a trap for the unwary. Although not often encountered, it is always lurking in the bushes ready to spring out and create its mischief. Section 3(a)(1)(C) of the Investment Company Act of 1940 (the 1940 Act) defines the term "investment company" to include any issuer that

[i]s engaged or proposes to engage in the business of investing, reinvesting, owning, holding, or trading in securities, and owns or proposes to acquire investment securities having a value exceeding 40 per centum of the value of such issuer's total assets (exclusive of Government securities and cash items) on an unconsolidated basis.

The key words are "owning" and "holding." No active investing, reinvesting or trading is required to fall within this definition, unlike the more conventional definition in Section 3(a)(1)(A). The term "investment securities" is defined to include all securities except (as here relevant) U.S. government securities and securities of subsidiaries, 50% or more of whose voting securities are owned by the issuer. Section 3(b)(1) provides that, notwithstanding the Section 3(a)(1)(C) definition, an issuer is not an investment company if it is "primarily engaged," directly or through wholly owned subsidiaries, in a business other than owning or holding securities. An issuer may also be excluded under Section 3(b)(2) if the SEC finds that it is primarily engaged in such a business directly or through majority-owned subsidiaries or controlled companies. If it does not exceed the limitations on securities ownership and income set forth in Rule 3a-1, it may be able to take advantage of the safe harbor provided by that rule.

There are statutory exclusions for domestic banks and insurance companies, as well as for broker-dealer firms and finance companies. Rules adopted by the SEC exempt certain foreign banks and foreign insurance companies (Rule 3a-6), certain finance subsidiaries of U.S. and foreign companies (Rule 3a-5) and certain issuers of asset-backed securities (Rule 3a-7). Some of these exemptions are discussed elsewhere in this book.

A company with no more than 100 securityholders (in addition to holders of its short-term paper) that does not propose to make a public offering of its securities is excluded under Section 3(c)(1). Also, the Improvement Act added a new Section 3(c)(7) that excludes a company whose securities are owned exclusively (but with certain exceptions) by "qualified purchasers" and that does not propose to make a public offering of its securities.

The difficulty is that a manufacturing company or one engaged in any other business may find that it is inadvertently an investment company. The solution is not registration under the 1940 Act, for such a company could not possibly operate within the strictures of that statute. But under Section 7 an unregistered investment company may not engage in any business in interstate commerce or sell its securities in interstate commerce, and under Section 47(b) its contracts may be unenforceable. It may seek an exemption from the SEC under Section 6(c), but this requires a lengthy application process.

Take the case of a company that, with funds raised in a private placements, successfully develops a product, later transfers the business to a subsidiary, and then sells substantially all of the subsidiary's shares to a third party while retaining a small interest for itself. Time goes by, and the former subsidiary becomes a public company. Its shares increase in value, and the company now holds a valuable asset, its sole asset other than cash items and a small amount of equipment. It uses its funds on research and development and reaches a point where it wishes to engage in its own IPO to raise the funds required to begin manufacturing its new product and to build a sales force.

Out of the bush pops the inadvertent investment company problem. The shares representing a minority interest in the company's former subsidiary are "investment securities." In terms of their value, they constitute over 90% of its assets, far more than the 40% stipulated in Section 3(a)(1)(C) of the 1940 Act. The company proposes to make a public offering and thus cannot rely on Section 3(c)(1) or Section 3(c)(7), even if it had fewer than 100 securityholders or were owned exclusively by "qualified purchasers," neither of which happens to be the case. It is loathe to approach the SEC for a Section 6(c) exemption or even for a Section 3(b)(2) determination. It does not come close to meeting the thresholds permitted under Rule 3a-1.

The company might try to take advantage of Rule 3a-8, which the SEC adopted in 2003[90] for the express purpose of relieving the 1940 Act problem for companies engaged in

---

90. SEC Release No. IC-26077 (June 16, 2003).

research and development. That rule exempts a company whose income from investments in securities for the past four quarters does not exceed two times the amount of its research and development expenses for that period. The rule also limits investment management and related expenses to 5% of total expenses and restricts investments to "capital preservation assets" (as defined) and certain investments related to research and development.

If the conditions of Rule 3a-8 cannot be met, perhaps the company's counsel can opine that it is primarily engaged in a business other than that of holding the shares. On the other hand, it is just getting started on its new venture; not a single widget has been manufactured to date, and it has no operating earnings. Even if counsel is willing to render the opinion, will it be acceptable to underwriters' counsel when the problem goes to the very core of the underwriting, the validity of the issuance of the shares? This is an instance where the underwriters may be well advised to take no chances and to refuse to go forward with the financing in the absence of a Section 6(c) exemptive order.

An issue may arise under the 1940 Act as the result of any event that provides the issuer with a substantial amount of liquid assets—for example, an IPO or the making of substantial divestitures. The issuer may well intend to invest the assets in majority-owned subsidiaries or other purposes that would not make it an investment company. To deal with these "transient investment companies," the SEC in 1981 adopted Rule 3a-2.[91] This rule provides that an issuer is deemed not to be engaged in the business of investing, reinvesting, owning, holding or trading in securities during a period of time not to exceed one year, provided that the issuer has a bona fide intent to be engaged primarily in another business as soon as is reasonably possible (in any event by the termination of such period of time), such intent to be evidenced by its business activities and a board resolution or comparable documents. This rule is viewed by the SEC as a safe harbor, and the staff has been willing in appropriate cases to provide no-action relief to transient investment companies after the expiration of the one-year period specified in Rule 3a-2.

---

91. SEC Release No. IC-11552 (January 14, 1981).

Extension of Credit (Section 11(d)(1))

Counsel for the underwriters frequently will be asked by the managing underwriter whether the security being underwritten is "marginable." The answer to this question depends in the first instance, of course, on whether the security is marginable (or has "loan value") under Regulation T. Generally speaking, Regulation T assigns loan value only to exempted securities or "margin securities" (which include listed or NASDAQ securities, "nonequity securities," "OTC margin stock" and certain other securities).

The answer to the question also depends, however, on an analysis of Section 11(d)(1) of the 1934 Act and Rule 11d1-1 thereunder. A securities firm that acts both as a broker and a dealer (and there are few if any firms that do not perform this dual function) may not sell to a customer on margin any security that is part of a "new issue" in which it is participating as an underwriter or a member of the selling group. Section 11(d)(1) provides that, subject to certain exceptions, such a broker-dealer may not effect

> any transaction in connection with which, directly or indirectly, he extends or maintains or arranges for the extension or maintenance of credit to or for a customer on any security (other than an exempted security) which was part of a new issue in the distribution of which he participated as a member of the selling syndicate or group within 30 days prior to such transaction.

One of the concerns of the Congress in 1934 was the apparent conflict of interest inherent in acting as a dealer trading for its own account and acting as a broker or agent for customers. There were those who called for the segregation of these functions, while others argued for the status quo. As a compromise, the 1934 Act directed the SEC to investigate the question of completely segregating the activities of brokers and dealers and to report to the Congress by a specified date. By prohibiting the extension of credit on new issues, the Congress believed that it was striking a blow at "one of the greatest potential evils inherent in the combination of the broker and dealer function in the same person, by assuring that he will not induce his customers to buy on credit securities which he has undertaken to distribute to the public."[92]

Although the segregation of broker and dealer activities is no longer a significant issue, Section 11(d)(1) continues to operate. The restrictions apply not only to transactions that are part of the initial distribution but also to certain transactions in the after-market during a 30-day period after the broker-dealer's completion of its participation in the distribution. As originally enacted in 1934, the restriction continued for six months. Rule 11d1-1(e) provides significant relief from the 30-day restriction insofar as it would otherwise be applicable to the shares of companies that are widely traded. When the new issue in which the broker-dealer has participated constitutes 50% or less of all securities of the same class to be outstanding after the completion of the distribution, the broker-dealer may extend credit on the security if it sells the security to the customer or buys it for the customer's account on a day when it is not participating in the distribution of the new issue. This exemption is almost always available for transactions in the shares of major corporations.

Rule 11d1-1(e) spells out when a broker-dealer will be deemed to be participating in a distribution of a new issue. It will be deemed to be a participant if it "owns, directly or indirectly, any undistributed security of such issue" or if it is engaged in stabilizing activities or is a party to a syndicate agreement (an AAU) under which stabilizing activities are being or may be undertaken. Unlike Rule 101 (discussed in Chapter 4), Rule 11d1-1(e) does not adopt the concept that securities taken by an underwriter into an investment account are deemed to have been distributed. Thus, if new issue securities are placed by an underwriter in its own investment account, the underwriter presumably cannot take advantage of the Rule 11d1-1(e) exemption until it has sold those securities. A broker-dealer also will be considered a participant in the distribution of a new issue if it "is a party to an executory agreement to purchase or

---

92. H.R. Rep. No. 1383, 73d Cong., 2d Sess. 22 (1934), 5 Leg. Hist., Item 18.

distribute such issue." An underwriting agreement remains executory until the closing, and accordingly credit may not be extended on purchases in the after-market in reliance on Rule 11d1-1(e) until (at the earliest) after the closing date.[93]

Rule 11d1-1 contains other exemptions. Although it has participated in the new issue, a broker-dealer may receive securities from a customer and place them in the customer's margin account if it has not sold the security to the customer or bought the security for the customer's account. It may take into a margin account securities that have been acquired by a customer in exchange with the issuer for an outstanding security of the same issuer on which credit was lawfully maintained for the customer at the time of the exchange. Also, the restrictions of Section 11(d)(1) do not apply to securities acquired by a customer on the exercise of rights issued to that customer in a subscription offer to the issuer's shareholders where the subscription period does not exceed 90 days.

Section 11(d)(1) applies only to "new issues." It does not prohibit the extension of credit in the case of the normal secondary distribution of outstanding securities, no matter how large the distribution or how great the incentive to the underwriters to get the deal done.[94] The SEC has placed an administrative gloss on this concept, however. If the shares to be sold were acquired from the issuer shortly before the offering, for example in connection with an acquisition, then the offering may be

---

93. The "executory agreement" language presents problems in the context of continuous or delayed offerings. The SEC staff had at one point taken the position that an agency agreement relating to a medium-term note program was an executory agreement that would preclude the extension of credit to purchase outstanding notes. SEC No-action Letter, *Goldman, Sachs & Co.* (December 4, 1986). It subsequently reversed this position and permitted an agent under a similar program to extend credit on notes of a particular series after the notes had been owned by the customer for at least 30 days. SEC No-action Letter, *Kidder, Peabody & Co. Incorporated* (August 16, 1990). The staff appears to have accepted the theory for this purpose that the terms of each note issuance under the program were independently negotiated and unique.

94. SEC No-action Letter, *Hewlett-Packard Co.* (February 23, 1978); SEC No-action Letter, *Golden West Mobile Homes, Inc.* (November 15, 1976).

viewed as a new issue. Thus, where the sellers exercised their registration rights four months after acquiring their shares, the staff of the SEC took the position that the acquisition was sufficiently close to the offering to make the secondary distribution a new issue.[95]

In another instance, however, shares acquired four months prior to an offering were considered to be marginal.[96] Where selling shareholders acquired their shares on December 31, 1975, on the automatic conversion of convertible preferred stock, a secondary offering under a registration statement filed on October 6, 1976, some ten months later, was not viewed as a new issue.[97]

But where debentures proposed to be sold by a person in a control relationship with the issuer had been acquired in an exchange offer 15 months before a proposed sale, the staff refused to take a no-action position "particularly" because of the control relationship.[98] This emphasis on control is a misapplication of the statute, and the relationship between the seller and the issuer does not appear to have been a factor in any other instance where the staff refused to take a no-action position. Also, the 15-month time span would appear to be sufficiently great to take the transaction out of the coverage of Section 11(d)(1).

Credit may not be extended on shares sold in a secondary offering if a stock split has been effected under circumstances that the staff views as intended to facilitate the distribution. In this case, the split shares would be considered a new issue. The staff refused to take a no-action position with respect to a secondary offering scheduled to take place on April 6, 1972, where on December 10, 1971, the issuer declared a 3% stock dividend payable January 14, 1972 to shareholders of record on December 23, 1971, and a three-for-two stock distribution payable

---

95. SEC No-action Letter, *Geon Industries, Inc.* (May 26, 1973).
96. SEC No-action Letter, *Flowers Industries, Inc.* (December 4, 1976).
97. SEC No-action Letter, *Goldman, Sachs & Co.* (December 27, 1976).
98. SEC No-action Letter, *Metro-Goldwyn-Mayer Inc.* (November 29, 1975).

SELECTED ISSUES 227

February 1, 1972 to shareholders of record on January 6, 1972.[99] It mattered not that it was represented to the staff that the dividend and distribution were not intended to facilitate the offering. Nor did it matter that the shares to be sold were to be taken from shares owned prior to the corporate action. The time span of only four months may have been enough to lead to the staff's refusal, or it may have been influenced by the fact that the sellers were directors who voted in favor of the stock dividend and stock split.

Pursuant to a consent decree entered in September 1971, International Telephone & Telegraph Company was required within three years to divest its wholly owned subsidiary, Avis, Inc. In May 1972, Avis increased its 1,000 outstanding shares to six million by means of a stock split. In June 1972, ITT took the first step in the divestiture by selling 1.4 million shares to the public. In December 1972, a registration statement was filed covering a second secondary offering, this time a proposed sale of 1.5 million shares. The staff took the position that the June 1972 stock split created a new issue that was sufficiently close to the proposed sale to have the practical effect of facilitating the distribution. It refused to express a view as to any future sales made in connection with the divestiture.[100] Here it may be argued that the size of the split (6,000-for-1) and the circumstances under which it was made demonstrated that it could have had no purpose other than to facilitate the divestiture, no matter when the specific sales were made. Under these circumstances, proximity in time may not be a significant factor.

In another case, where a two-for-one stock split was approved by the board of directors of a company on March 31, 1977, prior to the seller's decision to make a secondary offering, the staff took the position that Section 11(d)(1) was not applicable, even though the registration statement covering the sale was filed on July 26, 1977, just four months later.[101] The

---

99. SEC No-action Letter, *Leaseway Transportation Corp.* (May 11, 1972).
100. SEC No-action Letter, *Avis, Inc.* (February 7, 1973).
101. SEC No-action Letter, *Tektronix, Inc.* (September 9, 1977).

staff also issued a no-action letter where a two and one-half-for-one split was authorized five months prior to a non-registered secondary offering, although it was not effected until two months prior to the offering.[102] Nor was Section 11(d)(1) found to be applicable where a two-for-one stock split was effected one year prior to a secondary offering where it was represented that the purpose of the split was to qualify the common stock for listing on the NYSE.[103] The same position was taken where the last of a series of stock splits, a two-for-one split, was effected one year and eight months prior to the offering.[104] Similarly, a three-for-one split of the common stock of Johnson & Johnson effected one year and ten months prior to the filing of a registration statement did not raise Section 11(d)(1) problems, even though the sellers were J. Seward Johnson and the Robert Wood Johnson Foundation, shareholders in a control relationship with the issuer.[105]

In another case, an October 1972 recapitalization in which the company's 15 million shares of common stock were reclassified into three million shares of preferred stock and six million shares of new common stock, did not make Section 11(d)(1) applicable to a June 1977 secondary offering where the shares to be sold had been purchased in the open market subsequent to the recapitalization.[106] In this instance, it is difficult to see why counsel felt it appropriate to approach the staff, for the stock clearly was marginable. The same can be said where the most recent split was four years before the offering[107] or even two and one-half years,[108] particularly, in the latter case, where the split was suggested by the NYSE.

Although stock dividends theoretically could raise new issue problems, a 5% or 10% stock dividend is far less likely to be viewed as facilitating a distribution than a split of substantially

---

102. SEC No-action Letter, *Metro-Goldwyn-Mayer Inc.* (June 22, 1975).
103. SEC No-action Letter, *Corroon & Black Corp.* (May 22, 1978).
104. SEC No-action Letter, *Eli Lilly & Co.* (May 23, 1973).
105. SEC No-action Letter, *Johnson & Johnson* (April 14, 1972).
106. SEC No-action Letter, *Source Capital Inc.* (June 15, 1977).
107. SEC No-action Letter, *S.S. Kresge Co.* (May 8, 1976).
108. SEC No-action Letter, *The Lubrizol Corp.* (March 29, 1971).

greater magnitude. The staff of the SEC has consistently taken no-action positions where asked to do so with respect to stock dividends. Thus, where a registration statement covering a secondary offering was filed on September 26, 1978, 10% stock dividends paid in each of the preceding three years, the most recent of which was three months prior to filing, did not create a problem under Section 11(d)(1).[109] The staff also was willing to take a no-action position where a 5% stock dividend was paid three and one-half months prior to the filing of a registration statement covering a secondary offering.[110]

In the case of a combination offering, where both secondary and newly issued shares are being sold in a single underwriting, none of the shares being offered should be considered marginable for purposes of Section 11(d)(1), for as a practical matter it is impossible to distinguish between the outstanding shares and the new shares.

Counsel should avoid the trap of concluding that shares are marginable after a careful Section 11(d)(1) analysis only to find that they are not "margin securities" and thus not marginable under Regulation T.

---

109. SEC No-action Letter, *Oakwood Homes Corp.* (November 11, 1978).

110. SEC No-action Letter, *Applied Magnetics Corp.* (August 2, 1982).

Chapter 4

MANIPULATIVE PRACTICES AND MARKET ACTIVITIES DURING DISTRIBUTIONS

A basic goal of the federal securities laws, rivaling in importance the principle of full and fair disclosure, is the prevention of manipulation. As the SEC has observed, "[m]anipulation impedes the securities markets from functioning as independent pricing mechanisms, and undermines the integrity and fairness of those markets."[1]

In the 1934 Act, Congress prohibited certain conduct as manipulative. It also granted the SEC broad rulemaking authority to combat manipulative abuses. In exercising this authority, the SEC has especially focused on the market activities of persons participating in a securities offering. It has done so on the assumption that "securities offerings present special opportunities and incentives for manipulation that require specific regulatory attention."[2]

For more than 40 years, the SEC's principal antimanipulation rules in the area of securities offerings consisted of Rules 10b-6, 10b-7 and 10b-8 (known collectively as the "Trading

---

1. SEC Release No. 34-38067 (December 20, 1996) (adopting Regulation M) (Regulation M Release). Certain technical amendments were adopted on the same day in SEC Release No. 34-38363 (March 4, 1997).
2. *Id.*

Practice Rules"). The most important of these rules was Rule 10b-6, which prohibited underwriters, issuers and other persons involved in a "distribution" from engaging in secondary market activity that might raise the price of the security to be distributed. Rule 10b-7 regulated stabilizing activities in connection with a securities offering, and Rule 10b-8 regulated certain trading activities in connection with rights offerings.

From their adoption in 1955, the Trading Practice Rules gave rise to frequent interpretive questions. These questions even extended to the most basic question of all: when does a securities offering constitute a "distribution" that triggers the application of the rules? Many securities lawyers considered the rules to be among the most arcane administered by the SEC.

Rule 10b-6 received a major overhaul in 1983 and was further amended in 1987. Following a comprehensive review by the SEC in the 1990s of its antimanipulation regulations in the context of securities offerings,[3] the Trading Practice Rules were reborn in late 1996 in the form of a new Regulation M.[4]

Before discussing the application of Regulation M to securities offerings, it might be useful to review some of the history in this area.

Early Prohibitions of Manipulative Practices

Long before the SEC's adoption of the Trading Practice Rules, Congress had taken action to prohibit specific manipulative practices, whether or not related to a distribution of securities. Section 17(b) of the 1933 Act prohibited "touting," that is, the description of a security for an undisclosed "consideration" received directly or indirectly from an issuer, underwriter or dealer. More direct prohibitions were included in the 1934 Act, and the experience gained by the SEC over a 20-year period

---

3. The SEC's review included the publication in April 1994 of a concept release on the subject. SEC Release No. 34-33924 (April 19, 1994).

4. Regulation M became effective on March 4, 1997. Related notice and recordkeeping changes became effective on April 1, 1997.

MANIPULATIVE PRACTICES

in enforcing these antimanipulative provisions played a major role in its adoption in 1955 of the Trading Practice Rules.

- *Fletcher Committee Investigation*

In 1934, the Congress was not concerned specifically with trading activities during distributions. It was interested rather in out-and-out fraud, blatant market manipulations that some believed were at the root of the 1929 crash.[5] The Fletcher–Rayburn bill, which became the 1934 Act, contained provisions outlawing manipulative practices on stock exchanges. These provisions were designed to prohibit in clear and specific terms the types of abuses exposed by the Senate Committee on Banking and Currency chaired by Senator Duncan U. Fletcher of Florida (Fletcher Committee).

In April 1932, a subcommittee of the Fletcher Committee began an exhaustive investigation into stock exchange practices in the context of the 1929 market crash. In January 1933, Ferdinand D. Pecora was retained as counsel to the subcommittee and began what has been called "one of the most extraordinary shows ever produced in a Washington committee room."[6] Under Pecora's direction, the subcommittee revealed to the public extensive manipulative practices that had been conducted on the exchanges and particularly on the NYSE.[7]

Of particular significance was the exposure of pool operations in which speculators, often stock exchange members or partners in member firms, would form a group to trade in a stock and engage in fictitious transactions for the purpose of raising

---

5. Statement of Representative Adolph J. Sabath, *Stock Exchange Regulation: Hearings Before the House Interstate and Foreign Commerce Committee*, 73d Cong., 2d Sess. 826 (1934) [hereafter *House Hearings*].

6. F. L. Allen, *Since Yesterday—The 1930s in America, September 3, 1929–September 3, 1939* 168 (1940).

7. The subcommittee's findings are summarized in S. Rep. No. 1455, 73d Cong., 2d Sess., *Stock Exchange Practices, Report of the Senate Banking and Currency Committee Pursuant to S. Res. 84 (72d Cong.) and S. Res. 56 and S. Res. 97 (73d Cong.) (June 16, 1934)* [hereafter S. Rep. No. 1455]. Pecora later recounted his experiences in *Wall Street Under Oath* (1939).

its price to enable them to unload their holdings at a profit. The Fletcher Committee found that pools would most frequently be organized in stocks that had attracted public attention, such as the "alcohol" or "repeal" stocks in which there was speculative interest during the summer of 1933 because of the expected repeal of the Eighteenth Amendment to the Constitution. Before beginning their operations, pool participants would often obtain options at fixed or graduated prices on substantial blocks of the stock. These options frequently were obtained from the corporation itself or from officers or large shareholders who might also participate in the pool. In some cases, the pool would drive down the price through short selling and the dissemination of false rumors and then accumulate blocks in the market at artificially reduced prices.

Trading activity on the exchange would then be instituted for the purpose of raising the price of the stock. These transactions included "wash sales" in which a person would simultaneously purchase and sell a like number of shares, a transaction in which, in effect, he would buy from and sell to himself, leading others to believe that a real trade had taken place. Another type of fictitious transaction was the matched order in which one manipulator would make an arrangement with another to buy and sell at the same time so that their orders would meet and be crossed on the floor of the exchange. As part of a pool operation, puts and calls frequently would be granted to other speculators to induce them to buy or sell a stock. In addition, the pool operators would cause market letters and tip sheets to be distributed to attract public attention to a security.

Officials of the NYSE played down or closed their eyes to the evils of pool operations. Following a sharp drop in stock prices in July 1933, led by the repeal stocks, Pecora requested the NYSE to institute an inquiry to determine whether pool operations had been conducted in repeal stocks during the preceding months.[8] The NYSE responded with a report concluding that "there were no material deliberate improprieties in connection with transactions in these securities" and that there was no

---

8. S. Rep. No. 1455 at 56.

evidence of "activities which might have stimulated improperly the activity of these stocks."[9] Pecora caused an independent inquiry to be made by his staff. This resulted in the exposure of manipulative practices that the NYSE had failed to uncover.

- *Wall Street's Response*

The introduction of the Fletcher–Rayburn bill elicited a strong negative reaction from Wall Street. The opposition was led by NYSE President Richard Whitney, who in a letter dated February 14, 1934 to all members of the NYSE protested with patrician indignation that the bill "contains sweeping and drastic provisions which affect seriously the business of all members and which may have very disastrous consequences to the stock market resulting in great prejudice to the interests of investors throughout the country."[10] He went on to attack the section dealing with the manipulation of securities prices, although with less vigor than the other sections of the bill.

Senator Fletcher responded in a statement published in *The New York Times* on February 22, 1934:

> The propaganda released by the exchange officials is intended to persuade the people that regulation of that exchange and the other exchanges by the Federal Government will hurt business. Whose business? Only that of brokers who have lined their pockets by disregarding the interest of their customers.[11]

Despite Whitney's initial objections, the NYSE did not launch a major attack on the antimanipulative provisions of the bill. At the hearings, there was vigorous debate as to whether stabilization was a legitimate practice, but when it came to hardcore pool manipulations, the NYSE's objections were limited to the argument that the rules of the NYSE and existing law were

---

9. *Stock Exchange Practices: Hearings Before the Senate Committee on Banking and Currency*, 73d Cong., 1st Sess. 6613 (1934) [hereafter *Senate Hearings*].
10. 4 Ellenberger & Mahar, Leg. Hist., Item 6.
11. *Id.* at Item 7.

adequate to deal with the problem and some minor drafting issues.[12] In general, the events bore out the observation of Thomas G. Corcoran at the House Hearings that the control of manipulation was not one of the "real battlegrounds of this act."[13]

Except for the provision on stabilization, which was left entirely to SEC rulemaking, the provisions of the bill designed to control manipulation passed virtually unchanged from the original draft.

- *Prohibition of Manipulation (Section 9)*

As ultimately enacted, Section 9 of the 1934 Act bore the title "Prohibition of Manipulation of Securities Prices." Section 9(a)(1) prohibited wash sales, where there is no change in beneficial ownership, and matched purchase or sell orders, where one confederate places a buy or sell order intended to meet on the exchange floor a sell or buy order placed by the other confederate.

In the House report on the Fletcher–Rayburn bill, it was noted that "the most subtle manipulating device employed in the security markets is not simply the crude form of a wash sale or a matched order" but rather "the conscious marking up of prices to make investors believe that there is a constantly increasing demand for stock at higher prices, or a conscious marking down of stocks to make investors believe that an increasing number of investors are selling as prices recede."[14] To this end, Section 9(a)(2) provided that it was unlawful

> [t]o effect, alone or with one or more other persons, a series of transactions in any security registered on a national securities exchange creating actual or apparent active trading in such security, or raising or depressing the price of such security, for the purpose of inducing the purchase or sale of such security by others.

---

12. *See* Statement of Richard Whitney, Senate Hearings at 6624. *See also* discussion between Roland L. Redmond, counsel to the NYSE, and Thomas G. Corcoran, one of the draftsmen of the bill, *id.* at 6506.
13. House Hearings at 85.
14. H.R. Rep. No. 1383, 73d Cong., 2d Sess. (1934), at 10.

The House report recognized that "any extensive purchases or sales are bound to cause changes in the market price of the security" and stressed that such transactions are unlawful "only when they are made for the purpose of raising or depressing the market price."[15]

Section 9(a)(3) made it unlawful for sellers or buyers of securities to circulate information to the effect that the price of a security registered on a national securities exchange is likely to rise or fall because of market operations conducted for the purpose of raising or depressing the price of such security.

Section 9(a)(4) made it unlawful for persons selling or offering for sale or purchasing or offering to purchase a security registered on a national securities exchange, for the purpose of inducing the purchase or sale of the security, to make any false or misleading statement of a material fact.

Section 9(a)(5) made it unlawful, for a consideration received from a person purchasing or selling a security, to circulate predictions of price changes of securities registered on a national securities exchange for the purpose of raising or depressing the price.

Sections 9(a)(3) and 9(a)(5) were aimed at tip sheets and the spreading of rumors with respect to pool operations.[16]

Section 9(a)(6) made unlawful stabilizing transactions in contravention of such rules as the SEC might adopt. In this way, the Congress delegated to the SEC the task of prescribing such rules "as may be necessary or appropriate to protect investors and the public from the vicious and unsocial aspects of these practices."[17]

Sections 9(b) and 9(c) gave to the SEC the power to regulate transactions in puts, calls, straddles or other options.

It should be noted that Section 9(a) was made applicable only to securities registered on a national securities exchange. It did not specifically address manipulation in the over-the-counter market. The reason for this was concern by the draftsmen of the bill as to its constitutionality if it had a broader scope.[18]

---

15. *Id.* at 20.
16. *Id.* at 21.
17. S. Rep. No. 1455 at 55.
18. Senate Hearings at 6507.

- *Effects of Section 9*

Although it was essential as a political matter for the Congress to have adopted Section 9 in response to the manipulations exposed by the Fletcher Committee, it has been suggested that the provisions of that section did little more than codify the substantive law existing at that time.[19] The decision of Judge Woolsey in *United States v. Brown*,[20] denying a motion to quash a mail fraud and conspiracy indictment of the operators of a pool in the NYSE listed stock of Manhattan Electric Supply Company, had demonstrated that the existing criminal law could be applied to stock manipulation.[21]

Judge Woolsey based his decision on 19th-century English cases,[22] including *Rex v. Berenger*[23] (which involved a conspiracy to raise the price of British government funds and other government securities by circulating a false report of the death of Napoleon Bonaparte and predicting that peace would soon be concluded between England and France) and *Scott v. Brown*[24] (which related to a conspiracy to purchase shares in a company in order to induce persons who might subsequently purchase shares to believe, contrary to fact, that there was a bona fide market for the shares and that the shares were trading at a real premium). In upholding the indictment, Judge Woolsey stated:

> It is obvious that, when two or more persons, by a joint effort, raise the price of a listed stock artificially, they are creating a kind of price mirage which may lure an outsider into the market to his damage.

---

19. This point is made in A. A. Berle, Jr., *Stock Market Manipulation*, 38 Colum. L. Rev. 393 (1938).

20. 5 F. Supp. 81 (S.D.N.Y. 1933).

21. *See also Harris v. United States*, 48 F.2d 771 (9th Cir. 1931).

22. The opinion should be read, if for no other reason, for its in-depth review of the English cases. Professors Louis Loss and Joel Seligman also discuss these decisions. 8 Loss & Seligman, *Securities Regulation* 3942–47 (3d ed. 1991). *See also* James Wm. Moore & Frank M. Wiseman, *Market Manipulation and the Exchange Act*, 2 U. Chi. L. Rev. 46, 57 (1934).

23. 3 Maule & Selwyne's Reports 67 (1814).

24. 2 Q.B. 724 (1892).

In my opinion, such a procedure would of itself constitute a fraud on the public—just as was held in *Scott v. Brown* [citation omitted]. *A fortiori,* when such a procedure is accompanied by active propaganda seeking to interest the public in the shares thus artificially raised in price, it becomes the grossest kind of fraud. That is what I find set forth in the indictment before me.

A. A. Berle, Jr. has suggested that it was Section 17(a) of the 1933 Act, the general antifraud provision of that statute, rather than the 1934 Act, that brought the SEC (or more precisely its predecessor, the Federal Trade Commission) into the enforcement arena "as investigator, plaintiff in an injunction suit, or stimulator of a criminal action," and that in the early years, even after passage of the 1934 Act, the SEC's chief enforcement vehicle had been Section 17(a) of the 1933 Act.[25] Nonetheless, as will be seen, during the 20-year period prior to the adoption of the Trading Practice Rules, Section 9(a)(2) provided a major statutory underpinning for the SEC's attacks on manipulation and for the development of its views on the restrictions that should be imposed on market activities during distributions.

- *The Next Twenty Years*

The 20-year period between the enactment of the 1934 Act and the adoption of the original Trading Practice Rules was marked by extensive enforcement activity aimed at market manipulation[26] as well as efforts by the SEC to develop and

---

25. Berle, *supra* note 19, at 399. In the early years of the 21st century, the SEC appears to be returning to its earlier frequent reliance on Section 17(a).

26. For example, in its *Fourth Annual Report*, covering the fiscal year ended June 30, 1938, the SEC reported on thirteen Section 9 cases resulting in injunctions, stock exchange expulsions or suspensions from membership or criminal convictions.

In its *Seventeenth Annual Report*, covering its fiscal year ended June 30, 1951, the SEC believed itself able to state (at page 38) that as a result of its administration of the 1934 Act "manipulation has been reduced to a point

refine the principles that would be embodied in the rules ultimately adopted in 1955.

• • *Over-the-Counter Manipulations.* In an administrative proceeding against Barrett & Company and two other broker-dealers to determine whether they should be suspended or expelled from the NASD for manipulating the price of a security in the over-the-counter market, the SEC held, citing *United States v. Brown* and several law review articles, that practices that would be illegal under Section 9(a)(2), if effected on a securities exchange, would likewise be fraudulent under the 1934 Act if conducted in the over-the-counter market.[27] The SEC said that there is no reasonable distinction between the manipulation of over-the-counter prices and the manipulation of prices on a national securities exchange and that both are condemned as fraudulent by the 1934 Act and, in fact, were fraudulent at common law. The SEC went on to state that the 1934 Act contemplates that Section 15(c)(1), which was adopted as an amendment to the 1934 Act in 1936, affords to the over-the-counter market at least as great a degree of protection as is afforded to the exchange market by Section 9(a).

Section 15(c)(1), as then in effect, made it unlawful to effect a transaction in a security otherwise than on a national securities exchange "by means of any manipulative, deceptive, or other fraudulent device or contrivance." In 1937, the SEC adopted Rule X-15C1-2, which in paragraph (a) defined the term "manipulative, deceptive, or other fraudulent device or contrivance" to include "any act, practice, or course of business which operates or would operate as a fraud or deceit upon any person." In *Barrett,* the SEC found that the activities in question constituted an "act, practice or course of business" that operated as a "fraud or deceit" and that Barrett & Company and the other respondents had violated Section 15(c)(1) and paragraph (a) of Rule X-15C1-2 thereunder.

---

where it is no longer an appreciable factor in our markets." As Loss and Seligman aptly point out, "[t]his sanguine belief was not retained for long." 8 Loss & Seligman, *supra* note 22, at 3984.

27. *Barrett & Company,* 9 S.E.C. 319 (1941).

• • *Meaning of the Term "Transactions."* In *Kidder Peabody & Co.*,[28] counsel for the respondents argued that the term "transactions" as used in Section 9(a)(2) meant "completed purchases or sales." The SEC disagreed, pointing to the legislative history that demonstrated that the original bill sought to prohibit "transactions for the purchase and sale" for manipulative purposes while Section 9(a)(2) as finally enacted contained broader phrasing. The SEC stated that Section 9(a)(2) prohibits the manipulation of prices on a securities exchange by means of the placing of bids on the exchange and that in an auction market the placing of bids, although not met by sellers, may be as effective an influence on price as a completed sale.

• • *Inference of Motive.* To be in violation of Section 9(a)(2), the transactions in question must be "for the purpose of inducing the purchase or sale" of the security by others. Thus, motive is an ingredient of the offense. But the required statutory motive may be inferred from the facts of the case.[29]

The issue of intent in the context of an underwritten offering of securities was addressed in an opinion of James A. Treanor, Jr., director of the SEC's Trading and Exchange Division,[30] rendered in response to an inquiry whether prior to the completion of sales of debentures at the fixed public offering price, an underwriter, through its trading department, could buy and sell debentures at prices that might exceed the price at which debentures were being offered at retail. The opinion stated, "[w]hen an underwriter is engaged in the distribution of a security, he obviously has the purpose of inducing the purchase of that security by others." It went on to state, in effect, that even though an underwriter may have sold all of the securities

---

28. 18 S.E.C. 559 (1945).

29. *Michael J. Meehan*, 2 S.E.C. 588 (1937). In this case, the SEC stated, "As to the respondent's motive, there is no direct testimony. The existence or nonexistence of the required statutory motive must thus be a matter of inference from the voluminous testimony introduced in the case." *See also Russell Maguire & Co.*, 10 S.E.C. 332 (1941); *Halsey, Stuart & Co.*, 30 S.E.C. 106, 112 (1949).

30. SEC Release No. 34-3505 (November 16, 1943).

retained by or allotted to it in the distribution, it may not trade in the securities, through a trading department or otherwise, so long as the syndicate agreement remains in effect. As a result of this opinion, it became the practice to include in agreements among underwriters absolute prohibitions against trading during distributions.[31]

• • *Stabilization Before Rule 10b-7.* In 1936, in response to an inquiry on the question of stabilization during an underwritten public offering of securities, the general counsel of the SEC rendered an opinion to the effect that Section 9(a)(6) of the 1934 Act, in making unlawful stabilizing in contravention of SEC regulations, "seems conclusively to indicate that stabilization not in contravention of such rules, or in the absence of [SEC] rules, as in the present case, is not illegal."[32] He went on to state:

> Turning to your second question, I may further state that, in my opinion, the accepted concept of stabilization does not require that the price of the security be held to one particular quotation. Of course, activities designed substantially to raise or lower stock exchange prices are clearly manipulative, and therefore within the prohibition of Section 9(a)(2).

The SEC adopted no rules on stabilization until 1939, when it adopted Rule 17a-2 under the 1934 Act (requiring reports of stabilizing activity) and a rule under the 1933 Act requiring a notice in the prospectus of any intention to overallot or stabilize.[33] In 1940, however, the SEC adopted Rule X-9A6-1, which regulated stabilization in connection with "at the market" offerings of listed securities.[34] As offerings of this type soon became virtually extinct, the rule had no effect.

---

31. Foshay, *Market Activities of Participants in Securities Distributions*, 45 U. Va. L. Rev. 907, 911 (1959).
32. SEC Release No. 34-605 (April 17, 1936).
33. SEC Release No. 34-2008 (February 9, 1939). The current disclosure requirements are discussed below under "Disclosure, SRO Notification and Recordkeeping."
34. SEC Release No. 34-2363 (January 3, 1940).

Shortly after the adoption of Rule X-9A6-1, the SEC issued a statement on the question of regulating stabilization.[35] In this statement, the SEC said that it was faced with three choices. It could permit stabilization to continue unregulated; it could adopt a program for the regulation of stabilization in an effort to eliminate particular abuses; or, finally, it could decide that stabilization is inherently so detrimental to the interest of investors that the SEC should recommend to Congress that all stabilization be prohibited. After reviewing the pros and cons of stabilization, the SEC stated that one of the major deterrents to earlier action on the adoption of rules regulating stabilization had been its reluctance to adopt any program of comprehensive regulation on which competent representatives of the securities industry could not reach substantial agreement. The release ended inconclusively with a discussion of new Rule X-9A6-1. Commissioner Healy entered a sharp dissent arguing that stabilization should be outlawed.

Following the issuance of its statement of policy in 1940, rather than promulgating specific rules in connection with stabilizing practices, the SEC depended on informal interpretations, some of which were issued in the form of releases, but most of which were rendered individually by letter or telephone in answer to specific requests.[36]

In a 1948 report on an investigation of an offering of common stock of Kaiser-Frazer Corporation, the SEC said that stabilization for the sole purpose of preventing or retarding a decline in the price of a security does not violate Section 9(a)(2) or any other provision of the 1934 Act so long as the purchases are effected at the lower of "a *bona fide* independent market price for the security being stabilized" or the public offering price and that "within these restrictions there is no limit under existing statute and rules on the amount of securities which may be purchased in the stabilizing process."[37]

---

35. SEC Release No. 34-2446 (March 18, 1940).
36. For examples of these informal interpretations, *see* Foshay, *supra* note 31, at 911–13.
37. SEC Release No. 34-4163 (September 16, 1948).

In 1949, two members of the SEC's staff published a law review article of major significance bringing together in one place the principles and interpretations governing stabilization in connection with fixed-price offerings.[38] This article became the principal reference for securities lawyers advising clients as to permitted stabilization practices and continued to be a useful interpretative guide even after the adoption of the Trading Practice Rules.

- *Adoption of the Original Trading Practice Rules*

Despite its earlier reluctance to act, in 1954 the SEC finally took steps to formalize its positions with respect to market activities during distributions and stabilization practices. This required some congressional prodding. As reported in the SEC's *Twentieth Annual Report,* the Committee on Interstate and Foreign Commerce of the House of Representatives recommended in a report dated December 30, 1952 that "the Commission should earnestly and expeditiously grapple with the problem of stabilization with the view either of the early promulgation of rules publicly covering these operations or of recommending to the Congress such changes in legislation as its experience and study show now to be desirable."[39]

After intensive study by the staff and review by the SEC, the proposed rules, designated Rules X-10B-6, X-10B-7 and X-10B-8, were circulated for public comment in May 1954.[40] A revised proposal was published for comment in April 1955,[41] and the SEC adopted the final rules in July 1955.[42]

- *Subsequent Revisions of the Trading Practice Rules*

By 1983, the securities markets had changed considerably. The SEC and its staff had attempted for many years to accommodate Rule 10b-6 to changing markets and underwriting

---

38. George S. Parlin & Edward Everett, *The Stabilization of Security Prices,* 49 Colum. L. Rev. 607 (1949).
39. H.R. Rep. No. 2508, 82d Cong., 2d Sess. 3 (1952).
40. SEC Release No. 34-5040 (May 18, 1954).
41. SEC Release No. 34-5159 (April 19, 1955).
42. SEC Release No. 34-5194 (July 5, 1955).

practices by granting exemptive relief and issuing no-action and interpretive letters. In many cases, underwriters and issuers were required to make time-consuming identical applications for substantially the same relief. It was probably no coincidence that Rule 10b-6's first major overhaul occurred in 1983[43] on the occasion of the introduction of shelf registration. The 1983 amendments introduced a definition of the term "distribution." They also exempted nonconvertible investment-grade debt and preferred securities, relaxed prohibitions on research, dealt with the relatively new phenomenon of exchange-traded options and reduced the rule's applicability to "affiliated purchasers."

Just as important, the 1983 amendments relaxed various trading prohibitions, including delaying certain prohibitions of the rule until the start of a "cooling-off" period beginning two business days prior to the commencement of a distribution in the case of stock with a minimum price of $5 per share and a minimum float of 400,000 shares or beginning nine business days prior to such commencement in the case of other securities. (Previously, the trading restrictions began for a prospective underwriter when it reached an understanding with the issuer or selling securityholder that it would participate in the distribution, except that over-the-counter trading was permitted through the tenth business day prior to the offering.)

In 1987 the SEC further amended the rule[44] to permit underwriters to engage in solicited brokerage transactions prior to the "cooling-off" period, to adjust further the concept of "affiliated purchaser" and to permit the exercise at any time throughout a distribution of previously established standardized call option positions.

Until 1987, the preamble to Rule 10b-6 had stated that violations of the rule were violations of Section 10(b) of the 1934 Act, which prohibits the use of any "manipulative or deceptive device or contrivance" in violation of SEC rules. As part of the 1987 amendments, the SEC modified the preamble to state that violations of the rule were "unlawful." In so doing, the SEC intended "more completely [to] reflect the prophylactic scope of the Rule,

---

43. SEC Release No. 34-19565 (March 4, 1983).
44. SEC Release No. 34-24003 (January 16, 1987).

the authority for the Rule's provisions, and the Commission's intention to use its full statutory authority, including the authority to adopt rules that are reasonably designed to prevent fraudulent, deceptive, or manipulative acts and practices."[45] The SEC's action was undoubtedly based on Division of Enforcement concerns that action in compliance with the various exceptions to the rule might be impervious to attack even if there was clear evidence of manipulative intent; it was probably also based on concern that the SEC might have to prove scienter or other elements of a Rule 10b-5 proceeding.[46] In any event, the SEC position was that Rule 10b-6 was based on its authority under at least Sections 2, 3, 9(a)(6), 13(e), 15(c) and 23(a) of the 1934 Act.

The 1987 amendments also made explicit the SEC's position that the exceptions to Rule 10b-6's prohibitions could not be relied on as "safe harbors" from charges of manipulation. They did so by providing that transactions in reliance on the exceptions could not be "for the purpose of creating actual, or apparent, active trading in or raising the price of any such security."

In 1993 the SEC adopted Rule 10b-6A[47] to permit "passive market making" during a distribution and also amended Rule 10b-6[48] to exempt transactions in certain Rule 144A–eligible securities of foreign issuers offered and sold in the United States exclusively to qualified institutional buyers (QIBs). The SEC also continued its efforts to accommodate the Trading Practice Rules to innovative securities market products such as "baskets" of securities, as well as to international securities offerings.

- *Adoption of Regulation M*

In April 1994 the SEC published a Concept Release on its antimanipulation regulation of securities offerings. In the release,

---

45. In support of this contention, the SEC cited Section 13(e)(1) of the 1934 Act (applicable to issuer repurchases) and Section 15(c)(2) of the 1934 Act (applicable to OTC transactions). *Id.* at note 51.

46. It is true that some courts held that scienter had to be alleged and proved as one element of a Rule 10b-6 violation, but this is of more relevance to a litigator than to an advisor to issuers and underwriters.

47. SEC Release No. 34-32117 (April 8, 1993).

48. SEC Release No. 34-33138 (November 3, 1993).

it invited comment on whether certain classes of securities, transactions or investors needed the protection of the Trading Practice Rules. It noted changes in the securities markets that it believed might make manipulation less likely to occur in many situations. These included the role of institutions, whose sophistication and "bargaining power" could be expected to provide protection against abusive conduct on the "sell-side" of an offering, the increased transparency and liquidity of secondary markets and the more sophisticated surveillance techniques employed by SROs.

Based on responses to the Concept Release, the SEC proposed in April 1996 to adopt a new Regulation M that would supersede the original Trading Practice Rules. After a relatively short comment period, made possible in part by the significant response solicited by the Concept Release, the SEC adopted Regulation M in late December 1996. The new rules became effective on March 4, 1997.

Regulation M

Regulation M represents the most significant overhaul of the Trading Practice Rules since the adoption of Rules 10b-6, 10b-7 and 10b-8 in 1955. Its format differs significantly from that of the original Trading Practice Rules:

– Rule 100 defines terms used in the rules.
– Rules 101 and 102 restrict the activities of (a) distribution participants such as underwriters and (b) issuers or selling securityholders, respectively.
– Rule 103 permits "passive market-making" in NASDAQ securities during all distributions (except best efforts or at-the-market offerings or at any time when a stabilizing bid is in effect).
– Rule 104 governs stabilization activities.
– Rule 105 governs the covering of short sales with securities purchased in a public offering.

- *Rule 101—Basic Outline*

Rule 101 prohibits *distribution participants* (such as underwriters)[49] and their *affiliated purchasers* from directly or indirectly *bidding* for, *purchasing* or *attempting to induce* any person to bid for or purchase specified securities at specified times during a "distribution."

A *distribution* is defined as "an offering of securities, whether or not subject to registration under the Securities Act, that is distinguished from ordinary trading transactions by the magnitude of the offering *and* the presence of special selling efforts and selling methods" (emphasis added). The definition is the same as in the original Trading Practice Rules.

Rule 101 applies, however, only to *"covered securities,"* which are defined as the security being distributed and any *"reference security."* In turn, "reference security" means any security into which the security being distributed may be converted, exchanged or exercised or that may significantly determine the value of the security being distributed.

Rule 101 does not apply at all to certain *actively traded*[50] or *investment-grade* or *exempted* securities, and it applies to other securities only during certain *restricted periods* that begin one or five business days prior to pricing. Even during such restricted periods, the rule permits *ten specified categories of activity* that are discussed below under "Excepted Activities."

- *Rule 101—Basic Prohibitions*

Unless an exception applies, Rule 101 prohibits underwriters and other covered persons from directly or indirectly

---

49. Issuers and selling securityholders can also be distribution participants within the meaning of Rule 101, but they are subject to Rule 102 discussed below.

50. As discussed below, the exception for actively traded securities is not available to any underwriter or other distribution participant that is affiliated with the issuer of the security.

- bidding for,
- purchasing, or
- attempting to induce another person to bid for or purchase a covered security during a restricted period for a distribution.

There is seldom any doubt about what constitutes a bid or a purchase. A market-maker's quotations are bids, for example, and the NASD's Rule 4619(d) specifies the procedure for a market-maker facing Rule 101 restrictions to obtain "excused withdrawal status" or passive market-maker status. As for purchases, the SEC staff has noted that the 1934 Act defines "purchase" to include an agreement to purchase, with the result that an agreement reached during the restricted period can violate Rule 101 even though it is not to be executed until a later time.[51] And the staff has confirmed that a purchase prior to the commencement of a restricted period may be settled in routine fashion during the restricted period.[52]

The prohibition on "attempts to induce" would be difficult to apply, given its subjective nature, if not for the specific exceptions discussed below that are adequate to avoid most practical problems.

One area of lingering difficulty, however, relates to after-market purchases. The staff has taken the position at least since 1961 that a "tie-in" agreement—that is, an agreement by an underwriter to allocate IPO shares to a customer only on condition that the customer agrees to purchase additional shares in the after-market—violates Rule 101 and its predecessors.[53] In Staff Legal Bulletin No. 10, published in 2000, the staff referred to complaints about such tie-in agreements (often referred to as "laddering") and emphasized that such agreements violate Rule

---

51. Staff Legal Bulletin No. 10 at n.2 (August 25, 2000).
52. Staff Legal Bulletin No. 9 at 7 (October 27, 1999 as revised April 12, 2002).
53. SEC Release No. 34-6536 (April 24, 1961).

101 and also risk rising to the level of "fraudulent devices . . . because they facilitate material omissions in connection with the offer or sale of securities."[54]

Staff Legal Bulletin No. 10 also stated, however, that "solicitations or other inducements by distribution participants during the distribution to generate purchases in the aftermarket" are equally prohibited. And in October 2003, the SEC announced the filing and settlement of a civil injunctive action against a prominent investment banking firm for violating Rule 101 in attempting to induce customers to place orders for IPO shares in the after-market.[55] The complaint alleged that the firm, while acting as managing underwriter for IPOs, had solicited customers to provide information about their after-market intentions, had communicated to certain customers that expressions of after-market interest would help them obtain allocations in "hot" IPOs, had encouraged customers to increase the level of their after-market interest and had solicited after-market interest from customers who had no interest in being long-term holders of the IPO shares. Various internal communications had referred to the customers' after-market interest as "promises, obligations or commitments," and the firm had made follow-up calls to customers and had tracked their after-market activity. The complaint alleged that the firm's activity had nothing to do with "a customer's desired position size or whether a customer intended to be a long-term holder," suggesting that such a motivation might justify at least the solicitation of information about customers' after-market intentions. More likely, the SEC complaint will tend to chill an important area of discussion during the allocation period, namely, whether a particular institutional investor will provide a "good home" for the securities as evidenced by, among other things, the investor's intentions

---

54. In the staff's view, an agreement by the customer to sell his shares back to the underwriter at the beginning of after-market trading was equally likely to operate as a fraud on the market. SEC Staff Legal Bulletin No. 10 at n.6.

55. SEC Litigation Release No. 18385, *SEC v. J.P. Morgan Securities Inc.* (October 1, 2003). The firm agreed to be enjoined from violating Rule 101 as well as the NASD's Conduct Rule 2110 relating to just and equitable principles of trade and to pay a $25 million civil penalty.

regarding after-market purchases. For example, some investors need to accumulate a position of sufficient size to justify the assignment of an internal analyst to cover the security, and the investor's needs in this respect (and how the investor plans to satisfy those needs) are a legitimate topic of discussion.

Rule 101 and its companion rules do not provide for "safe harbors," that is, they do not provide that conduct permitted under the rules is therefore in compliance with the antifraud and antimanipulation prohibitions of Sections 9(a) and 15(c)(1) of the 1934 Act and Rule 10b-5. Commenters on the proposed version of Regulation M urged the SEC to take this approach, but nothing in the comments changed the SEC's view expressed in the proposing release that "[a] safe harbor from manipulation charges is inappropriate in contexts where it is reasonable to infer that manipulative incentives are present, such as during securities distributions." See the discussion below of "Manipulation Outside the Trading Practice Rules."

- *Distributions*

As noted above, the definition of "distribution" in Regulation M is the same as in the original Trading Practice Rules: an offering of securities, whether or not subject to registration under the Securities Act,[56] "that is distinguished from ordinary trading transactions by the magnitude of the offering *and* the presence of special selling efforts and selling methods" (emphasis added).

Understanding the definition requires a discussion of how it evolved under the former rules.

As originally adopted, Rule 10b-6 did not contain a definition of the key term "distribution." It had been recognized from the outset, however, that the rule applied to all distributions

---

56. In 1970, the SEC held that any offering under a 1933 Act registration statement constitutes a "distribution" regardless of the size of the offering or the manner in which the sale is made. *Jaffee & Co.*, SEC Release No. 34-8866 (April 20, 1970), *aff'd in relevant part sub nom. Jaffee & Co. v. SEC*, 446 F.2d 387 (2d Cir. 1971). In 1975, the SEC came to its senses and abandoned this position. *Collins Securities Corp.*, SEC Release No. 34-11766 (October 23, 1975), *remanded on other grounds sub nom. Collins Securities Corp. v. SEC*, 562 F.2d 820 (D.C. Cir. 1977).

whether or not registered under the 1933 Act and whether or not underwritten.

The *Bruns, Nordeman* case established, although in broad terms, the standard for determining whether or not there was a distribution for Rule 10b-6 purposes.[57] The SEC there stated that the determination should be made "upon the basis of the magnitude of the offering and particularly upon the basis of the selling efforts and selling methods utilized."[58]

• • *The 1983 Definition.* In March 1982, the SEC proposed a number of amendments to Rule 10b-6, including the adoption of a definition of the term "distribution."[59] The proposed definition, which purported to codify existing case law, provided that the term "distribution" means

> an offering of securities, whether or not subject to registration under the Securities Act of 1933, which is distinguished from ordinary trading transactions by the magnitude of the offering or the presence of either special selling efforts and selling methods or the payment of compensation greater than that normally paid in connection with ordinary trading transactions.

The proposed definition went on to set forth, with unfortunate negative implications, the proviso that

> the sale of securities will not constitute a distribution for purposes of this section if the sale has been made in compliance with both the volume limitations and the manner of sale provisions contained in paragraphs (e) and (f) of Rule 144 under the Securities Act of 1933.

A year later, the SEC adopted the Rule 10b-6 amendments in somewhat altered form after receiving comments from members of the securities industry and others.[60] The definition of

---

57. *Bruns, Nordeman & Co.*, 40 S.E.C. 652 (1961).
58. *Id.* at 660.
59. SEC Release No. 34-18528 (March 3, 1982).
60. SEC Release No. 34-19565 (March 4, 1983).

"distribution," as finally adopted, came closer to the *Bruns, Nordeman* test than the definition originally proposed. Instead of applying a three-pronged test, expressed disjunctively through the use of "or," the revised definition simply stated that the term means

> an offering of securities, whether or not subject to registration under the Securities Act of 1933, that is distinguished from ordinary trading transactions by the magnitude of the offering and the presence of special selling efforts and selling methods.

The SEC stated in a footnote to the adopting release:

> The presence of special selling efforts and selling methods may be indicated in a number of ways, including the payment of compensation greater than that normally paid in connection with ordinary trading transactions.

The proposed Rule 144 proviso, referred to for the first time in the adopting release as a "safe harbor," was not adopted in deference to objections from commentators that it was unnecessary and might become a prescriptive standard.

The adoption of a definition served the useful function of codifying the *Bruns, Nordeman* test in the rule itself, thus making it readily apparent to lawyers who might not be familiar with the prior case law. The definition, through the use of the conjunctive "and," made it clear that size alone is not the determining factor.

• • *The 1994 Concept Release.* In its 1994 Concept Release, the SEC referred to the 1983 definition as a "functional" one that was intended "to provide a greater degree of guidance on, and certainty to, the types of offerings that would give rise to an incentive to artificially condition the market for the offered security." The reference to an "incentive" to manipulate is unfortunate, of course, because it harks back to a time when the Division of Enforcement saw a "distribution" whenever it perceived a "temptation to manipulate" on the part of a broker-dealer. The objective of a definition, of course, should be to minimize the subjective element.

In the Concept Release, the SEC noted that a "distribution" must have both elements—"magnitude" and "special selling efforts and selling methods":

> Factors relevant to the magnitude element are: the number of shares to be registered for sale by the issuer, and the percentage of the outstanding shares, public float, and trading volume that those shares represent. The Commission has indicated that providing greater than normal sales compensation arrangements pertaining to the distribution of a security, delivering a sales document, such as a prospectus or market letters, and conducting "road shows" are generally indicative of "special selling efforts and selling methods." Based upon an analysis of their individual characteristics, the following transactions, among others, have been viewed as involving distributions under this definition: registered public offerings, private placements, Rule 144A transactions, rights offerings, warrant exercise solicitations, dividend reinvestment and stock purchase plans, the issuance of securities in connection with a merger or exchange offer, "major sales campaigns" by a broker-dealer, and sales made pursuant to a shelf registration statement. [Footnotes omitted.]

While the foregoing is a useful compendium of factors that the SEC deems relevant, it is hardly conclusive. It overlooks the fact that the rule's definition of "distribution" really has *three* elements: (1) magnitude, (2) special selling efforts and selling methods *and* (3) whether the transaction because of the presence or absence of the first two elements resembles or does not resemble an "ordinary trading transaction." For example, two different firms might execute the same transaction in entirely different ways depending on the depth and efficiency of their block trading desks. This is not to suggest that there is a special definition of "distribution" for certain large block trading firms, but it is surely relevant that a given trade—say, a block equal to five days' trading volume—would be executed by a particular broker-dealer in a routine fashion similar to its other "ordinary trading transactions."

• • *Shelf Registrations.* Under early SEC staff interpretations of Rule 10b-6, any shelf registration that constituted a distribution was considered a "single distribution" for purposes of the rule, that is, each takedown was subject to Rule 10b-6 regardless of its magnitude or other circumstances. Under the SEC's interpretation of Regulation M, on the other hand, "each takedown off a shelf is to be individually examined to determine whether such offering constitutes a distribution," based on its size or "magnitude" and whether "special selling efforts and selling methods" will be used.[61] Contrary to another early interpretation, the Regulation M Release states that the mere description in a shelf registration statement of various potential selling methods (some of which might constitute "special selling methods") would not require a broker-dealer to consider itself involved in a distribution unless it in fact used special selling efforts or methods in connection with particular sales off the shelf and the sales met the magnitude test.

The Regulation M Release states that a broker-dealer would "likely" be subject to Rule 101 if it entered into a "sales agency agreement that provides for unusual transaction-based compensation for the sales, even if the securities are sold in ordinary trading transactions." Unless one is willing to assume that "unusual compensation" always means "special selling efforts and selling methods" (a proposition that is not self-evident), this statement would appear to be contrary to the plain language of the rule.

• *Distribution Participant*

Assuming that an offering involves a distribution, Rule 101's prohibitions apply to any person who is a "distribution participant" (and that person's "affiliated purchasers," as discussed below). Under the definition in Rule 100, the term "distribution participant" means an underwriter, a "prospective underwriter" or a broker-dealer "or other person who has agreed to participate or is participating in a distribution."[62]

---

61. Regulation M Release (text at n.46).

62. Again, issuers and selling securityholders can also be distribution participants within the meaning of Rule 101, but they are subject to Rule 102 discussed below.

A "prospective underwriter" means a person who has either (1) "submitted a bid to the issuer or selling securityholder, and who knows or is reasonably certain that such bid will be accepted" or (2) "reached, or is reasonably certain to reach, an understanding with the issuer or selling securityholder ... or managing underwriter that such person will become an underwriter," in either case "whether or not the terms and conditions of the underwriting have been agreed upon."

A person who is participating in a distribution remains subject to Rule 101's prohibitions until he has completed his participation. This is discussed below.

Identifying the commencement of a person's participation in a distribution is less often an important task under Rule 101 than used to be the case under Rule 10b-6. This is because the prohibitions of Rule 101 apply only during specified "restricted periods," while the prohibitions of Rule 10b-6 applied from the moment of commencement of a person's participation in the distribution (subject, to be sure, to a number of exceptions). Even under Rule 101, however, it can be important to identify the commencement of a person's participation in a distribution. For example, it is possible that such participation may commence during the applicable restricted period where a securities firm receives an invitation to bid from an issuer or an invitation to join a syndicate from a managing underwriter.

The SEC's traditional view in this situation has been that "there is frequently some point prior to when a bid actually has been accepted, or a broker-dealer has been told that it will be an underwriter, when it is reasonably certain that such person will be an underwriter, and that the incentive to facilitate the distribution is present at that point."[63] Rule 10b-6 therefore measured the commencement of a broker-dealer's participation from the time it decided to submit a bid to a person who had requested bids or from the time it reached an understanding that it would become an underwriter. This was replaced in the proposed Regulation M by reference to the broker-dealer's "reasonabl[e] expect[ation]" and, in turn, in the final Regulation M by reference

---

63. Regulation M Release (text following n.16).

MANIPULATIVE PRACTICES

to the broker-dealer's "reasonabl[e] certain[ty]."[64] The Regulation M Release admitted that the final definition did not provide "a bright line test" but anticipated that its "practical effect should be to reduce the circumstances in which a broker-dealer will be a prospective underwriter."

Broker-dealers who become "prospective underwriters" or "distribution participants" often maintain "restricted" or "watch" lists for the purpose, among other things,[65] of monitoring (and, within the restricted periods, preventing) bids for or purchases of covered securities or the publication of certain research relating to covered securities.

Rule 101 also applies to dealers who are not acting as underwriters, that is, members of the selling group, but only to the extent that they have agreed to participate or are participating in the distribution. Like Rule 10b-6, the new rule does not speak of a "prospective" participating dealer as it does of a "prospective underwriter," only of a dealer who has agreed to participate or is participating in the distribution.

- *Affiliated Purchasers*

Consistent with the SEC's traditional position that the Trading Practice Rules should extend to persons whose relationship with a distribution participant might be perceived as providing an incentive to condition the market to facilitate the distribution of the offered security,[66] Rule 101 applies to the "affiliated purchasers" of distribution participants.

Regulation M defines an "affiliated purchaser" as any person[67] who acts "in concert" with a distribution participant, issuer

---

64. One way in which a broker-dealer may be "reasonably certain" that it would participate in a shelf distribution would be on the basis of a "continuing agreement" regarding its participation in takedowns off the shelf. Regulation M Release at n.116.

65. E.g., to prevent any actual or perceived misuse of material nonpublic information received in a capacity of trust or confidence. See the discussion in Chapter 3.

66. *See SEC v. Burns,* 816 F.2d 471, 474–75 (9th Cir. 1987).

67. In the staff's view, persons outside the United States can fall under the definition of "affiliated purchaser." Staff Legal Bulletin No. 9 at 11 (October 27, 1999 as revised April 12, 2002).

or selling securityholder in connection with the acquisition or distribution of a covered security. The term also includes any affiliate (including a separately identifiable department or division) whose purchases are under the control of (or whose purchases are controlled by or under common control with) a distribution participant, issuer or selling securityholder.

In addition, an affiliated purchaser includes any other affiliated person "that regularly purchases securities for its own account or for the account of others, or that recommends or exercises investment discretion with respect to the purchase or sale of securities." In order to accommodate underwriters that are part of organizational complexes that provide diversified financial services, this part of the definition then excludes affiliates (including a separately identifiable department or division) where the underwriter establishes, maintains and enforces written information barriers between itself and the affiliate and obtains an annual independent assessment of the operation of such information barriers. The affiliate must not, however, act during the applicable restricted period as a market-maker (other than as a specialist) or as a broker-dealer in solicited transactions or proprietary trading activities in covered securities.[68]

Distribution participants are ordinarily subject to Rule 101, but a distribution participant that is simultaneously an affiliated purchaser of an issuer or selling securityholder can also be subject to Rule 102. Regulation M resolves the possible overlap by providing that a distribution participant is subject to Rule 101 under these circumstances.[69] On the other hand, if the securities in distribution are issued by the distribution participant or any

---

68. Regulation M does not perpetuate the additional requirements of Rule 10b-6 that, in order to be excluded from the definition, distribution participants and their affiliates would have to have separate compensation arrangements, separate and distinct organizational structures and no common officers or non-ministerial employees (except that Regulation M does not permit common officers or employees who direct, effect or recommend transactions in securities).

69. Rules 101(a) and 102(a). The Regulation M Release notes that the variety and complexity of organizational structures in the financial services industry may cause Regulation M to apply to some affiliates that it may be

of its affiliates, the distribution participant may not take advantage of the actively traded security exception discussed below.[70]

- *Beginning of Restricted Period*

Rule 101 imposes restrictions only during a "restricted period," which is defined in Rule 100. The length of the restricted period depends on the trading volume and "public float" of the security being distributed.

First, Rule 101 does not apply at all to securities with an "average daily trading volume" (ADTV) of at least $1 million *and* whose issuer—unaffiliated with the underwriter—has common equity securities with a public float value of at least $150 million. (The computation of ADTV and public float are discussed below.)

Second, where the securities meet an ADTV standard of $100,000 and the issuer meets a float test of $25 million, Rule 101 imposes restrictions during a restricted period that begins one business day[71] prior to the determination of the price of the security to be distributed.[72]

Third, in the case of all other securities, the restricted period begins five business days prior to such determination.

The definition of "restricted period" in Rule 100 specifies that a restricted period does not start for a distribution participant until that person actually becomes a distribution participant.

- *Termination of Restricted Period*

The restricted period ends when a person completes its participation in a distribution. This is determined under

---

appropriate to exclude. In those cases, the SEC's Division of Market Regulation will entertain exemption requests.

70. Rule 101(c)(1).

71. Rule 100, as amended in SEC Release No. 34-38363 (March 4, 1997), defines "business day" as a 24-hour period that includes an entire trading session in the principal market for the security to be distributed.

72. In the staff's view, "[t]he determination of the offering price occurs when the parties agree on the price, whether or not the agreement is memorialized in writing." Staff Legal Bulletin No. 9 at 5 (October 27, 1999 revised April 12, 2002).

Regulation M in the same manner as under Rule 10b-6—namely, when an underwriter has sold its participation (including other securities of the same class acquired in connection with the distribution, e.g., those acquired in stabilization) and when "stabilization arrangements and trading restrictions"[73] in connection with the distribution have been terminated.[74] Other persons, including dealers, are no longer subject to Rule 101 when they have distributed their participations.

A person, including an underwriter or dealer, is deemed for this purpose to have distributed securities acquired "for investment" as discussed below.

Although not stated in the rule, an affiliated purchaser should be viewed as standing in the shoes of the underwriter or other person with whom it has the affiliation that gave rise to its affiliated purchaser status.

• • *Successful Offering.* How do these principles apply in the context of a successful underwritten offering? Assume that the syndicate manager is satisfied shortly after the pricing and release of the securities that the offering has gone extremely well. There may be a syndicate short position created through overallotments in an amount that the manager considers adequate and prudent in light of the strength of the "book," the market price of the securities and the availability of a "Green Shoe" option to purchase additional securities from the issuer.[75] There may be a stabilizing bid maintained at the public offering price, and stabilizing purchases may have been made in moderate amounts, thus reducing somewhat the original syndicate short position. The syndicate members have assured

---

73. "Trading" restrictions for this purpose means "price" restrictions—the agreement among the underwriters to offer the securities at a fixed price.

74. These provisions are contained in the AAU as discussed in Chapter 2. A "lockup" agreement, under which an issuer, selling securityholders and other securityholders agree to refrain from making additional sales for a specified period following the effectiveness of a registration statement, is not a trading restriction for this purpose.

75. *See* Chapter 2 for a discussion of the purpose and effect of overallotments and the use of overallotment, or Green Shoe, options.

MANIPULATIVE PRACTICES 261

the manager that they have sold all securities retained by them for direct sale.[76]

At this point, the manager may pull the stabilizing bid and inform the syndicate members of the termination of trading restrictions.[77] The distribution has at this point been completed for purposes of Rule 101, and the underwriters are no longer subject to the rule's prohibitions (assuming that they have in fact sold all of their participation or, as discussed below, acquired the unsold portion "for investment"). They may now participate in a two-way trading market for the securities.

The syndicate manager may now go into the market and cover the syndicate short position free of the restrictions of Rule 101.[78] Prior to this time, the short position could have been reduced only through stabilizing purchases or through otherwise "excepted" purchases (discussed below). Of course, the syndicate manager may cover the short position at any time by exercising the Green Shoe option. In deciding whether to cover the short position in the market or by exercising the Green Shoe option, the manager will be guided in part by the current market price of the underwritten securities.

It used to be suggested that it might be prudent for the manager to wait for the mailing of confirmations, for the receipt of payment from customers or for the closing with the issuer or selling securityholder (now usually three business days after the offering) before considering the distribution completed. The delay was presumably to guard against the possibility of

---

76. The manager should be entitled to accept at face value "all sold" assurances received from members of the syndicate. Of course, syndicate members may be reluctant to admit that they have unsold shares even if in fact they do. Under these circumstances, the syndicate member with an unsold allotment remains subject to Rule 101.

If a syndicate member does have unsold shares, the manager should take these back and apply them against the syndicate short position before covering purchases are made in the market.

77. Pursuant to the AAU, these restrictions may be terminated by the managing underwriter at any time (*see* Chapter 2).

78. SEC Release No. 34-3506 (November 16, 1943) contains certain pre–Rule 10b-6 guidelines to be followed in covering overallotments. These no longer need to be taken into consideration.

reneging customers. Nothing in the rule requires any such delay, provided that the underwriter or dealer is relying in good faith on the customer's agreement to purchase.

At one time, the SEC took the position that the Green Shoe option must either be exercised or irrevocably terminated before the managing underwriter would be permitted to go into the market to cover the syndicate short position. Rule 10b-6 was amended in 1983 to provide, as does Regulation M, that bids and purchases are permitted even while the Green Shoe option remains unexercised, provided that the option is not exercised for an amount in excess of the *net* syndicate short position at the time of exercise (the short position at the time the distribution is terminated as reduced by subsequent purchases for the account of the syndicate). If the Green Shoe option is exercised for securities in excess of the amount necessary to cover the syndicate short position, the distribution will not be deemed to have been completed, and any open market bids or purchases prior to the exercise of the option could in theory constitute a retroactive violation of Rule 101.

Suppose, however, that the managing underwriter has purchased shares for the account of the syndicate and resold those shares without applying them against the syndicate short position? To exercise the Green Shoe option under these circumstances for the net short position at the time of exercise, a practice referred to as "refreshing the Shoe," is thought by some underwriters and lawyers to be the same as exercising the option for an amount in excess of the short position.

In the course of an underwriting, the syndicate manager and other underwriters may have sold to customers more securities than retained or allotted to them for that purpose, that is, they will have created a short position in the accounts out of which they sell to customers. Like the syndicate short position, these short positions may not be covered until trading restrictions and stabilization authority have been terminated. In addition, of course, the underwriter must have sold its participation or applied it against its short position. If these conditions have been met, there is no reason why a non-managing underwriter may not cover a short position in its customer accounts or make a two-way market in the covered securities without limitations other than those imposed by general antimanipulative principles.

In the case of the syndicate manager, however, it can be argued that it should not trade in the securities for its own account or cover its own short position until the syndicate short position has been covered. The manager is an agent for the rest of the underwriting group, and, under general agency principles, it should not take any action for its own benefit that might conflict with the interests of the members of the syndicate. Securities professionals have taken the position, however, that in many if not all cases, it may actually be to the benefit of the syndicate for the manager to make a two-way market while the syndicate still has a short position. It is correct that this would not be prohibited by Rule 101. As a matter of prudence, however, if the manager does make a market under these circumstances, it should consider applying any long position existing at the end of any business day against any remaining short position in the syndicate account and not covering the short position in its customer accounts until the syndicate short position has been covered.

• • *Unsuccessful Offering.* Assume next a sticky deal, an unsuccessful underwriting. The offering may have been reduced in size, but the securities are still not all sold. The market is in a state of flux. The stabilizing bid may be hit in force, and the syndicate manager may be buying more securities for the syndicate than it would like. Several members of the syndicate may be having trouble disposing of their securities. If the securities are traded over-the-counter rather than on an exchange, there may be great pressure from the issuer and from customers for the underwriters to commence participation in a regular two-way market. What are the options in the context of Rule 101?

The manager could try to hold the syndicate together and perhaps raise the selling concession. He could maintain price restrictions and lower the public offering price, as authorized under the AAU and under the language of the typical prospectus.[79] He could maintain the original terms of the offering and engage in

---

79. The prospectus should state, "After the initial public offering, the public offering price, concession and discount may be changed." If it does, the price may be reduced or the concession increased without stickering the prospectus.

purchase and sale transactions in reliance on exceptions 5 and 9 to Rule 101 as discussed below under "Unsolicited Purchases."

Another option is to terminate the syndicate and turn over to the underwriters the unsold securities that they are committed to purchase. In this case, the manager would terminate price and trading restrictions, pull the stabilizing bid and let each of the underwriters sell its securities as best it can into an unsettled market. After each underwriter disposes of its participation, probably at a loss, it may commence regular trading activity. (Of course, if an individual underwriter with an unsold allotment does not wish to sell at a loss, it may place the unsold allotment in an investment account (as discussed below) and immediately commence regular trading activity.)

When stabilization and trading restrictions are terminated prior to the completion of the distribution, the Rule 101 restrictions apply on an underwriter-by-underwriter basis, so that if a particular underwriter has distributed its participation, it may make a market even though other members of the now-disbanded syndicate are still distributing securities. That is not the case if the syndicate is being held together and trading restrictions have not been terminated. However, breaking the syndicate and leaving the underwriters to distribute the securities as best they can is not a very satisfactory way to handle an unsuccessful offering.

Occasionally, in a sticky deal, if there is not too much unsold stock, the managing underwriter will take back securities from members of the syndicate and sell them to an institution that has made a so-called "clean-up bid." This approach may work if the manager is able to find an institution that is willing to buy all of the remaining unsold securities at a price somewhat below the public offering price.

• • • *Investment Account.* Another alternative is for the manager to stand behind the deal and purchase "for investment" for its own account the securities taken back from the syndicate. As previously noted, Rule 101 specifically states that a distribution is deemed to have been completed as to any securities that are acquired by an underwriter for investment. As the distribution is deemed to have been completed at this point, the manager and all other members of the syndicate may trade in the securities free of Rule 101 restrictions.

Of course, even if the syndicate manager does not take securities back from the syndicate, any syndicate member with an unsold participation may place the securities into its own investment account and commence trading.

Under what circumstances and subject to what restrictions may an underwriter later sell securities acquired for investment? The SEC does not apply the same tests under the 1934 Act as it does under the 1933 Act in determining when a person may sell securities acquired for investment. The best advice one can give is that there is no magic holding period, but securities should ordinarily be held for several months, rather than several weeks, to demonstrate that they were actually acquired for investment. An earlier rather than a later sale might be justified by an unexpected and significant change of circumstances affecting the underwriter, the issuer or the market for the securities. The theory in that situation is that the early sale was not inconsistent with an investment intent because of the intervention of the change of circumstances.

At such time as an underwriter decides to sell securities out of its investment account, the provisions of Rule 101 may again apply, depending on whether the sale involves a "distribution" at the time. This will again depend on the magnitude of the unsold allotment and the selling efforts and selling methods that will be employed in connection with its sale. Of course, the security may in the meantime have qualified for the $1 million ADTV/$150 million public float test so that Rule 101 will not apply to the distribution of the unsold allotment. If this is not the case, the underwriter will be required to stop making a market during the applicable period of one or five business days before the determination of the offering price.

The Rule 101 principle that a distribution has been completed when an underwriter acquires securities for investment is not relevant to a 1933 Act analysis. For purposes of the 1933 Act, the distribution will be viewed as continuing, and the prospectus delivery requirements must be met at such time as the underwriter sells its securities. A sale of securities from an investment account must therefore be made in accordance with the prospectus delivery requirements of the 1933 Act, and the prospectus, when delivered to a purchaser, must meet the updating requirements of Section 10(a) of the 1933 Act as well as not violate the disclosure requirements of Section 12(a)(2) of the 1933 Act or Rule 10b-5 under the 1934 Act.

Before the underwriter sells the securities out of its investment account, it must therefore satisfy itself that the prospectus does not need to be amended to replace "stale" financial statements or to reflect changes in the issuer's business. Of course, the underwriting agreement should provide (as discussed in Chapter 2) that the issuer will amend the prospectus as necessary for this purpose. This obligation applies, however, only during any period when a prospectus is required to be delivered. For this reason, it will usually be necessary for the underwriter to take the initiative and check with the issuer about any need for amendments to the prospectus. Underwriters dislike making this inquiry because it may come as a surprise to the issuer that the deal was not as successful as it had been led to believe.

It is generally not necessary to amend the prospectus merely to reflect the fact that the underwriter is selling securities from the investment account.[80]

- *Covered Securities*

Regulation M applies to "covered securities," which are defined in Rule 100 to include only the security being distributed (the "subject security") and any "reference security," which is defined in turn as a security into which the subject security may be converted, exchanged or exercised or which, under the

---

80. The question is sometimes raised whether an underwriter selling securities from an investment account should be regarded as resuming its participation in the original distribution (and thus be subject to Rule 101) or as a selling securityholder (and thus subject to Rule 102, which does not have an ADTV exception). It seems self-evident that Rule 101 should apply. First, it was the uniform practice under the original Trading Practice Rules for an underwriter in this position to act as if it were an underwriter rather than as if it were any other participant in the distribution. Second, the fact that the underwriter is obligated to deliver a prospectus and still has Section 11 and 12(a)(2) liabilities in connection with post-investment account sales should be conclusive evidence that it is acting as an underwriter in connection with the original distribution. As to this last point, of course, the SEC staff in applying Regulation M is perfectly willing to reject 1933 Act considerations when it suits its purpose.

terms of the subject security, may in whole or significant part determine the value of the subject security.

Derivative securities (those that derive all or part of their value from a security being distributed) are therefore not subject to the prohibitions of Rule 101. Thus, bids for or purchases of options, warrants, rights, convertible securities, or equity-linked securities are not restricted during a distribution of the related common stock because, according to the Regulation M Release, "while they derive their value from the security being distributed, they do not by their terms affect the value of the security in distribution." The SEC specifically rejected an NASD suggestion that it limit the exclusion to derivative securities "not likely to present manipulative risk, such as 'out-of-the-money' options."

On the other hand, Rule 101 does apply to the underlying security in the case of a distribution of a derivative security the return on which is a function of the value of the underlying security. This could include an issuer's common stock underlying the same issuer's convertible debt offering or the common stock underlying a different issuer's cash-settled equity-linked security offering. In many cases, of course, the underlying security will be eligible for the $1 million ADTV/$150 million float exception.

Under Rule 101, it is not necessary (as it was under the original Trading Practice Rules) to make judgments about whether an outstanding debt security is of the same "class and series" as a new debt security. According to the Regulation M Release, an issuer's outstanding debt securities would be restricted only where they are "identical in all of [their] terms" to the debt securities being distributed. This means, according to the release, that identity is destroyed by "a single basis point" difference in coupon rates or "a single day's difference" in maturity dates. This change has particular importance to transactions in which an underwriter and a customer "swap" newly distributed securities for outstanding securities of the same issuer.[81] Underwriters must still keep in mind, however, the NASD's "Papilsky" requirements (discussed in Chapter 6) that are

---

81. On the other hand, the release states that voting and non-voting equity securities will be treated as the *same* security for Rule 101 purposes.

applicable to "securities taken in trade" in connection with a fixed-price public offering.

The new rules also mean the end of SEC interpretations that had treated standardized call options as "rights to purchase" the underlying security and standardized put options as continuing "bids" for the underlying security.[82]

- *Excepted Securities*

    Three types of securities are excepted entirely from Rule 101:

    – exempted securities under the 1934 Act (e.g., municipal bonds);

    – nonconvertible debt or preferred securities (including asset-backed securities as defined for purposes of Form S-3) if they are rated investment-grade by at least one nationally recognized statistical rating organization;[83] and

    – ADTV securities.

    An ADTV security is any security that has an "average daily trading volume" of at least $1 million *and* whose issuer—unaffiliated with the underwriter—has common equity securities with a public float value of at least $150 million. ADTV means "the worldwide average daily trading volume during the two full calendar months immediately preceding, or any 60 consecutive calendar days ending within the 10 calendar days preceding, the *filing* of the registration statement" (emphasis added). (In the case of unregistered distributions or "the sale of securities on a

---

82. SEC Release No. 34-17609 (March 6, 1981).

83. Shortly after Rule 10b-6 was amended in 1983 to exclude investment-grade debt and preferred securities, the staff took the position that the exclusion did not apply to preferred stock that was offered by means of an auction process. The staff position has been much criticized as inconsistent with the plain meaning of the exclusion, and it is not referred to in the Regulation M Release. It is hard to see how the staff position can be regarded under the circumstances as anything other than a dead letter.

delayed basis pursuant to Rule 415,"[84] the relevant periods are measured from the time of determination of the offering price.)

According to the Regulation M Release, the SEC decided against designating "acceptable information sources" for determining ADTV; rather, distribution participants have flexibility in determining ADTV from information that is publicly available (if the participant "has a reasonable basis for believing that the information is reliable"). Also, "any reasonable and verifiable method" may be used to calculate ADTV (e.g., by multiplying the number of shares by the price in each trade, or by multiplying each day's total volume of shares by the closing price on that day). Public float is determined in the same manner as provided in Form 10-K (even if the issuer is not required to file Form 10-K).[85]

It should be reiterated that ADTV is calculated on a worldwide basis. In the case of a publicly held foreign issuer that is making its first distribution of securities into the U.S. market, the trading volume in the home country may be taken into account for purposes of the ADTV test.

Note that it is the ADTV of the security being distributed that decides whether the exception applies to that security, not the ADTV of a reference security. In the case of a convertible security, for example, the ADTV of the underlying reference security determines the restricted period for that underlying

---

84. The question sometimes arises, where a significant amount of time has elapsed between the filing of a shelf registration statement and its effectiveness, whether the first takedown from the newly effective shelf constitutes a sale "on a delayed basis" pursuant to Rule 415. If the transaction qualifies under Rule 415(a)(x), i.e., if it is effected by means of a prospectus supplement rather than a post-effective amendment, it should qualify as a delayed sale for ADTV purposes even if it immediately follows effectiveness. This approach also avoids relying on a "stale" ADTV.

85. Form 10-K requires an issuer to disclose the aggregate market value of voting stock held by non-affiliates. If a determination as to whether a particular person or entity is an affiliate cannot be made without involving unreasonable effort and expense, an instructional note to Form 10-K permits information to be disclosed on the basis of "assumptions reasonable under the circumstances."

reference security but not the restricted period for the convertible security.[86] This leads to the odd result that there may be no Rule 101 exception for convertible securities, even if they are investment-grade and the underlying reference securities meet the ADTV test.

Before relying on the ADTV exception, an underwriter should verify that the AAU does not contain any restriction that prevents syndicate members from taking advantage of the exception.

- *Excepted Activities*

Rule 101 excepts ten specified activities from its prohibitions. These are designed to facilitate an orderly distribution of securities or to limit disruptions of the trading market for the securities being distributed.

- - *Research.* Exception 1 to Rule 101 permits the publication or dissemination of any information, opinion or recommendation relating to a covered security if the conditions of either Rule 138 or Rule 139 under the 1933 Act are satisfied. A proposed requirement that the material be published or distributed "in the ordinary course of business" was deleted as redundant. The Regulation M Release also clarifies that if a distribution participant in the normal course of its business provides research to independent research services that make such reports available to their subscribers electronically, whether or not the subscribers are customers of or have previously received research from the distribution participant, such research is still excepted from Rule 101. (This clarification presumably applies also to hard-copy research that is distributed by third parties.) "Similarly, a distribution participant may update its mailing list (i.e., new persons may be added) where it is intended that they receive all future research sent to others on the list, and not just the research related to the security in distribution."

Rules 138 and 139 apply by their terms to the dissemination of research during registered offerings. The Regulation M Release states, however, that the exception from Rule 101 will

---

86. Staff Legal Bulletin No. 9 at 5, 6 (October 27, 1999 revised April 12, 2002).

be available during distributions that are not registered under the 1933 Act so long as all of the other conditions of either rule are met. The release also states that Rules 138 and 139 "define the appropriate parameters" even for research disseminated outside the United States during a global offering, whether or not in conformity with local rule or custom, if securities are to be distributed in the United States.

• • *Passive Market-Making and Stabilization Transactions.* Passive market-making transactions in compliance with Rule 103 and stabilization transactions in compliance with Rule 104 are excepted (exception 2) from the prohibitions of Rule 101. Passive market-making and stabilization are discussed below.

• • *Odd-Lot Transactions.* Exception 3 to Rule 101 permits a distribution participant to purchase odd-lots during a restricted period. Among other things, this exception permits a distribution participant to engage in activities in connection with issuer odd-lot tender offers conducted pursuant to Rule 13e-4(h)(5) under the 1934 Act, including effecting purchases necessary to permit odd-lot holders to "round up" their holdings to 100 shares.

• • *Exercises of Securities.* Exception 4 to Rule 101 permits distribution participants to exercise any option, warrant, right or any conversion privilege set forth in the instrument governing a security. This exception does not distinguish call options acquired prior to becoming a distribution participant from those acquired afterward. In addition, the exception covers the exercise of non-standardized call options. The broadened exception is based on the SEC's belief that exercises or conversions of derivative securities generally have an uncertain and attenuated manipulative potential and, for that reason, do not need to be subject to the prohibitions of Regulation M.

• • *Unsolicited Transactions.*

• • • *Unsolicited Brokerage Transactions.* The first part of exception 5 to Rule 101 permits brokerage transactions not involving solicitation of the customer's order. In the case of a customer's unsolicited buy order, it could be argued that this exception is not necessary because such a transaction would not involve a bid or purchase by the broker for an account in which it has a beneficial interest. It would also not constitute an inducement to purchase.

The exception makes it clear, however, that although it is participating in a distribution, a broker may continue to execute on an agency basis unsolicited buy orders received from customers. It may also execute unsolicited sell orders for a customer even though this requires the solicitation of buy orders on the other side of the transaction.

Suppose that a registered representative of an underwriter participating in an offering of common stock listed on the NYSE solicits a customer to purchase stock in the offering. After discussing with the customer the merits of the stock and the timing of the offering, the broker sends the customer a preliminary prospectus. Two days later—during the restricted period—the customer calls and says that he has read the document, that he likes the stock and wishes to buy 5,000 shares immediately. Without any suggestion from the broker, the customer places an order to buy 5,000 shares on the NYSE. Can the broker fill the order in reliance on the unsolicited brokerage exception?

Under one school of thought, the exception should be available because the broker intended to solicit the customer to buy on the offering and not in the secondary market. This approach involves difficult compliance problems, however, and it is probably more common for underwriters to consider the exception as not being available where the customer has been solicited to participate in the offering. The SEC staff endorsed the latter position in 1999.[87]

• • • *Unsolicited Purchases.* The second part of exception 5 permits "unsolicited purchases" of a security that are not effected from or through a broker or dealer, on a securities exchange, or through an inter-dealer quotation system or electronic communications network (ECN).

This part of exception 5, when used in conjunction with exception 9, can be extremely useful to a syndicate manager. Assume that a substantial block of common stock is shown to a managing

---

87. Staff Legal Bulletin No. 9 at 10 (October 27, 1999 revised April 12, 2002).

underwriter during a restricted period and just before the pricing of a common stock offering. The existence of this block overhanging the market could have a depressing effect on the price of the stock. The manager can purchase the block as principal at a negotiated price relying on exception 5 and resell it as part of the distribution, or otherwise, relying on exception 9.

The exception is also useful during the period following a less-than-successful offering, particularly of high-yield securities, where the syndicate manager is maintaining trading restrictions and trying to sell the rest of the offering. Customers who have already bought the securities may be insisting on a bid or even that they be taken out of their position. Exception 5 permits the syndicate manager to purchase the customer's securities in this situation, while exception 9 permits the manager to seek buyers for the securities (and the unsold remainder of the offering) in as aggressive a fashion as the manager chooses. This is not quite the same as making a regular two-way market, but it relieves the pressure while the manager is trying to complete the distribution.

Questions can arise because of the restrictions in exception 5 on the manner in which purchases may be made. Purchases in reliance on the exception may not take place on an exchange (thus reinstating a condition that the SEC dropped in 1983). They may also not be effected from or through a broker or dealer, thus excluding such systems as Instinet. The condition that purchases not be effected "through an inter-dealer quotation system" is stated in the Regulation M Release to apply only to NASDAQ.

• • *Basket Transactions.* Distribution participants often wish to purchase a large number of stocks at the same time, usually where the stocks are part of either a standardized or customized index (a "basket transaction"). For example, an underwriter may have sold a futures contract on a standardized index and wish to purchase the stocks in the index in order to lock in an arbitrage profit. If the index includes a covered security as defined in Regulation M, then purchases of the stock during a restricted period would violate Rule 101 unless an exception were available.

Exception 6 to Rule 101 permits bids for or purchases of a covered security in the ordinary course of business, in connection with the purchase of a basket of securities consisting of at least 20 stocks, where the covered security constitutes 5% or less of the value of the basket. The basket may be index-related or "customized," but the Regulation M Release cautions that the requirement that the purchase be "in the ordinary course of business" means that the decision to include the covered security in the basket must be "independent of the existence of the distribution" of the covered security.

Bids and purchases are also permitted in order to adjust a basket position to reflect changes in the composition of any standardized index; in the case of a customized basket, however, similar adjustments would be permitted only if the basket met the 20 security/5% test.

• • *De Minimis Transactions.* Exception 7 to Rule 101 permits purchases during a restricted period that total less than 2% of the ADTV of the security being purchased. It also permits unaccepted bids. In either case, however, the person making the purchase or bid must be maintaining and enforcing written policies and procedures reasonably designed to achieve compliance with the rule. The Release explains the requirement of policies and procedures as arising out of the SEC's intention that the exception cover only "inadvertent" violations. The Release states that "[o]nce inadvertent transaction(s) are discovered, subsequent transaction(s) would not be covered by this exception." Moreover, "repeated reliance on the exception would raise questions about the adequacy and effectiveness of a firm's procedures." The Release states that "upon the occurrence of *any* violation, a broker-dealer is expected to review its policies and procedures and modify them as appropriate" (emphasis added). Also, *any* purchase—even if the trade is "broken"—must be considered a purchase (and a violation) for purposes of the exception.

The de minimis exception is not available in the case of NASDAQ passive market-making transactions.

• • *Transactions Among Distribution Participants.* Exception 8 to Rule 101 excepts transactions among distribution participants in connection with a distribution and purchases of securities from an issuer or selling securityholder in connection with a distribution that are not effected on a securities exchange or through an inter-dealer quotation system or ECN.

Without this exception, the underwriters technically would be prohibited from purchasing the securities from the issuer or selling securityholders pursuant to the underwriting agreement prior to the completion of the distribution and dealers would be prohibited from purchasing from the underwriters. This exception also permits the syndicate manager to allocate and reallocate securities among underwriters and dealers.

• • *Transactions in the Securities Being Distributed or Securities Offered as Principal.* The first part of exception 9 to Rule 101 permits "offers to sell or the solicitation of offers to buy the securities being distributed (including securities or rights acquired in stabilizing)...." Without this exception, the inducement of customers to purchase the securities being distributed would violate the rule, an absurd result that the exception prevents.

The second part of exception 9 permits offers to sell or the solicitation of offers to buy "securities or rights offered as principal by the person making such offer to sell or solicitation." Thus, if a prospective underwriter has a long position in a security when the Rule 101 restrictions become applicable, it may close out its long position, even though this may involve the solicitation of buy orders. Also, as discussed above, an underwriter can rely on exception 9 to offer and sell securities that it has purchased during a restricted period in reliance on the second part of exception 5.

On rare occasions, an issuer may conduct different but concurrent distributions of the same security, for example, an offering of its common stock for cash while it is offering its common stock to securityholders of another company in connection with a merger or exchange offer. The question has arisen in these situations whether selling activity in one distribution would be deemed an impermissible inducement to purchase in the other distribution. The SEC staff has stated that exception 9 in Rule 101 and the corresponding exception in Rule 102(b)(5) do not extend to inducements to purchase in one distribution while the issuer or distribution participant is engaged in another distribution of the same security or a reference security. On the other hand, the staff recognizes that solicitation activity for one offering does not necessarily create an impermissible inducement to purchase in the concurrent offering. "Therefore, absent additional factors, bona fide offers to sell or the solicitation of offers to buy the securities being distributed in one distribution would not be impermissible inducements with respect to a concurrent distribution. . . . However, a distribution may rise to the level of an impermissible inducement to purchase when a distribution participant engages in sales efforts that go beyond bona fide offers to sell or the solicitation of offers to buy the securities in distribution."[88]

Exception 9 permits sales to anyone, so long as the securities sold are part of the offering or offered as principal, including sales to distribution participants or their affiliated purchasers. But are these persons permitted to *buy* these securities? As for distribution participants, exception 8 (discussed above) permits transactions among distribution participants in connection with a distribution that are not effected on an exchange or through an inter-dealer quotation system or ECN. As for affiliated purchasers (keeping in mind the transaction-oriented definition of this term discussed above), exception 5 on its face permits purchases *on an unsolicited basis* and if the purchases are not effected through a broker-dealer or on an exchange or through an inter-dealer quotation system or ECN. But the SEC staff stated generally in a 1983 no-action letter[89] under the original Trading Practice Rules that "purchases in a distribution of the securities being distributed . . . are not the type of purchases prohibited" by the Trading Practice Rules. The facts presented to the staff in that letter included the intention of the affiliated purchasers to purchase for investment without any present intention to resell the securities. Since that no-action letter, the staff has stated at least twice[90] that an investment intent is necessary for affiliated purchasers to buy the distribution securities, but it has explained this condition as resulting

---

88. *Id.* at 10–11.

89. SEC No-action Letter, *VLI Corp.* (November 16, 1983).

90. Regulation M Release at n.20; Staff Legal Bulletin No. 9 at 2 (October 27, 1999 revised April 12, 2002).

from the definition of "completion of the distribution." That definition, as discussed above, merely makes it clear that an underwriter may resume normal trading activities if it places its unsold allotment in an investment account, and it would seem to have nothing to do with whether an affiliated purchaser should be able to buy distribution securities in the offering. The conditions on which affiliated purchasers may buy distribution securities therefore remain unsettled, but it seems that the SEC staff had it right when it said in the 1983 no-action letter that purchases of distribution securities are not the type of transaction prohibited by the Trading Practice Rules.

It is sometimes overlooked that exception 9 permits short sales. To be sure, a distribution participant might be prevented from covering the short sale by a purchase during a restricted period. The fact that a transaction is permitted under exception 9 does not, of course, mean that it is immune from attack by the SEC under general antimanipulation or antifraud principles. See the discussion below of "Manipulation Outside the Trading Practice Rules."

• • *Transactions in Rule 144A Securities.* Exception 10 permits transactions in Rule 144A-eligible securities (and their reference securities) offered and sold in the United States solely to QIBs in transactions exempt from 1933 Act registration pursuant to Rule 144A, Section 4(2) or Regulation D or to persons not deemed to be "U.S. persons" for purposes of Regulation S. The SEC did not accept comments urging it to expand the exception to transactions that involve offerings to institutional accredited investors as well as QIBs.

The Rule 144A-eligible securities must be *offered as well as sold* only to the classes of buyers specified above. It will not do to offer them to a wider audience but to limit sales to eligible buyers.

Exception 10 of Rule 101 applies to Rule 144A-eligible securities of U.S. issuers as well as non-U.S. issuers.

• • *Transactions in Foreign Sovereign Bonds.* Many foreign sovereign bonds are not rated investment-grade and would not qualify for the investment-grade exception from Rule 101. The SEC granted exemptive relief in 2000 to permit the lead underwriters or dealer managers of an offering of foreign sovereign bonds to bid for or purchase those bonds and any reference securities during the applicable restricted period for the distribution of the bonds. The exemptive relief was conditioned on the issue size being at least $500 million, the sovereign's outstanding bonds aggregating at least $1 billion and the bonds' having a minimum rating of Ba3 from Moody's or BB- by Standard & Poor's. Other conditions included minimum levels of market-making by dealers not covered by the exemption, a limitation of bids and purchases to market-making activity, availability of bid and ask prices and daily transaction reports to the Division of Market Regulation.[91] The staff has granted similar relief in other situations on a case-by-case basis.

- *Disclosure, SRO Notification and Recordkeeping*

As part of the adoption of Regulation M, the SEC increased the prospectus disclosure, SRO notification and recordkeeping obligations associated with stabilizing activity, "syndicate covering transactions"[92] and "penalty bids."[93] These obligations are discussed below under "Disclosure, SRO Notification and Recordkeeping."

Passive Market-Making

Rule 103 permits "passive market-making" during a distribution of a NASDAQ security where the market-maker's bids and purchases would otherwise violate Rule 101. The exception permits passive market-making in *all* NASDAQ securities throughout the applicable restricted period and extends to all distributions (*except* best efforts or at-the-market offerings or at any time when a stabilizing bid is in effect).

---

91. SEC No-action Letter, *Goldman, Sachs & Co., J.P. Morgan & Co.* (January 12, 2000).

92. Rule 100 defines a syndicate covering transaction as the placing of any bid or the effecting of any purchase to reduce a syndicate short position.

93. Rule 100 defines a penalty bid as an arrangement that permits a managing underwriter to reclaim a selling concession from a syndicate member when the securities originally sold by the member are purchased in syndicate covering transactions. *See* the discussion in Chapter 2.

Rule 103 generally limits a passive market-marker's bids and purchases to the highest current independent bid (i.e., a bid of a NASDAQ market-maker who is not participating in the distribution). It also limits the amount of net purchases that a passive market-maker can make on any day to the greater of (a) 30% of the market-maker's ADTV in that security during a "reference period" of two full calendar months or (b) 200 shares, except that a market-maker may purchase all of the securities that are part of a single order even if this would equal or exceed its purchase limitation.

The Regulation M Release preserves certain earlier interpretations relating to contemporaneous transactions,[94] including one to the effect that if a passive market-maker is involved in a contemporaneous purchase and sale of a security, the market-maker can "net" the transactions for purposes of the ADTV calculation so long as the two transactions are reported within 30 seconds of each other. Another such interpretation permits offsetting two customer orders received within 15 minutes of each other without affecting net purchasing capacity.

Rule 103 limits the bid size a passive market-maker may display and contains requirements relating to notification, identification and disclosure of passive market-making.

Rule 103 allows passive market makers to make bids or purchases at a price higher than the highest independent bid where necessary to comply with any SEC or NASD rule relating to the execution of customer orders.

As noted above, the NASD's Rule 4619(d) specifies the procedure for a market-maker to obtain passive market-maker status. Before doing so, the market-maker should verify that the AAU does not contain any restriction that prevents syndicate members from taking advantage of Rule 103.

Stabilization and Related Activities

As discussed above, the SEC adopted Rule 10b-7 in 1955 to implement Section 9(a)(6) of the 1934 Act. The rule for many

---

94. Regulation M Release, text at n.115.

years had two independent functions. First, stabilizing transactions effected in compliance with Rule 10b-7 were excepted from Rule 10b-6. Second, the rule declared it to be a "manipulative or deceptive device or contrivance" as used in Section 10(b) of the 1934 Act to effect any transaction in violation of Rule 10b-7.

Like transactions effected in compliance with Rule 103, transactions effected in compliance with Rule 104 are excepted from Rule 101. Unlike Rule 103, however, Rule 104 is a "self-operating" and "stand-alone" rule that applies to stabilizing transactions even when the prohibitions of Rule 101 do not apply (e.g., in the case of an offering of actively traded or non-convertible investment-grade securities). Also, transactions in violation of Rule 104 are "unlawful." This is consistent with the SEC's view that the Trading Practice Rules are based on a broader SEC authority than that available to it under Section 10(b).

In addition, unlike Rules 101 and 102, the conduct governed by Rule 104 relates to "offerings" of securities. This is a term that, according to the Regulation M Release, has broader application than "distributions."

Stabilization is defined in Rule 100 as "the placing of any bid, or the effecting of any purchase, for the purpose of pegging, fixing or maintaining the price of a security."[95] Rule 104 applies to the stabilization of the price of a security "in connection with an offering," not as in the case of Rule 10b-7 to stabilization "to facilitate an offering." The only subjective element relevant to the application of Rule 104 is therefore the intent to affect the price of a security, rather than to do so for the purpose of facilitating the offering.

- *Excepted Securities*

It is important to note that there is no exception in Rule 104 comparable to Rule 101's exceptions for actively traded or non-convertible investment-grade securities. This means that stabilization of actively traded or investment-grade securities must

---

95. The reference to "maintaining" the price of a security replaces Rule 10b-7's somewhat circular definition that included a bid or purchase for the purpose of "stabilizing" a security.

comply with Rule 104.[96] The rule does not, however, apply to exempted securities under the 1934 Act (e.g., municipal bonds). Like Rule 101, it also does not apply to transactions in Rule 144A–eligible securities (or their reference securities)[97] of a foreign or domestic issuer, where the securities are offered or sold in the United States only to QIBs or to persons deemed not to be U.S. persons for Regulation S purposes.

- *Mechanics*

As a practical matter, stabilization generally takes place only in connection with an offering of common stock. Although underwriters reserve the right to stabilize in connection with distributions of many debt securities or preferred stock, it would be highly unusual for the manager to stabilize in this type of transaction. It would also be unusual (although not unheard of) for an underwriter to stabilize outstanding common stock to facilitate an offering of convertible securities.

In practice, stabilizing transactions are effected exclusively by the managing underwriter. In the usual AAU, the manager reserves the right to stabilize on behalf of the syndicate.[98] Centralized control of stabilizing is required by Rule 104, which prohibits a syndicate from maintaining more than one stabilizing bid in any one market at the same price at the same time.

---

96. It would be difficult to stabilize investment-grade securities in compliance with Rule 104. For example, a bid would have to be disclosed as a stabilizing bid, and it is not clear that the bid could follow changes in Treasury rates or in the spread over Treasury rates that was used to fix the initial price of the security. On the other hand, not every bid placed to gauge or get a feel for the market is intended for the purpose of stabilization and has the effect of triggering Rule 104.

97. The reference to "reference securities" does not appear in Rule 104, but the authors understand the omission to be inadvertent.

98. Rule 104 eliminated a provision of Rule 10b-7 that in effect protected a syndicate manager from liability for a syndicate member's stabilizing violations if the manager had no knowledge of such violations. The elimination of the provision is probably harmless since it is hard to imagine how the manager could violate the rule under those circumstances.

The AAU limits the net commitments of the underwriters resulting from overallotments and stabilization to a fixed percentage, usually 15% or 20% of the amount of securities being offered. This limitation is for the purpose of limiting the underwriters' risk and is not required by SEC rules. The issuer or a selling securityholder normally does not effect stabilization transactions in connection with an underwritten offering, and any attempt to do so would violate Rule 102 since stabilization is not an exception to the prohibitions of that rule.

A managing underwriter may have its representative on the exchange floor hold a stabilizing bid in reserve to be placed when certain market conditions occur. A managing underwriter who is not an exchange member could have the stabilization bid held in reserve for its account by an exchange member. On an exchange, a stabilizing bid is placed with the specialist. In the over-the-counter market, stabilization bids are placed with dealers.

- *General Requirements*

Rule 104 contains a number of general requirements applicable to all stabilization transactions. No stabilizing bid or purchase may be made except for the purpose of preventing or retarding a decline in the market price of a security. In addition, stabilization may not be effected at a price that the stabilizer knows or has reason to know is the result of activity that is fraudulent, manipulative or deceptive under the securities laws "or any rule or regulation." The effect of this provision is that if the market for a security has been manipulated at any time during the course of stabilization, it is improper for the underwriters (if they know or have reason to know of such activity) to initiate or continue stabilization transactions even if they had nothing to do with the manipulation.[99] Of course, if an underwriter has reason to believe that the market has been manipulated for a security that it plans to distribute, it has more serious problems than whether it may enter a stabilizing bid. There is no way that it can go forward with such an offering.

---

99. Rule 10b-7 literally applied this prohibition only to the "initiation" of stabilizing activity, not to its continuation.

When a stabilization bid is placed, it must be disclosed as such. In other words, the specialist or the over-the-counter dealers with whom the bid is placed must be told that the bid is a stabilizing bid. In addition, notice must be given to the market on which stabilizing will be effected.[100] The prospectus or other offering document must contain a legend similar to that required by Item 508(l) of Regulation S-K relating to stabilization activity.

Priority must be given to non-stabilizing bids "to the extent permitted or required by the market where stabilizing occurs." The stabilizer is a reluctant buyer, and independent bids at the same price must be filled before the stabilizer's bid. The size of the independent bid is irrelevant. On the other hand, the stabilizer's bid should not be larger than necessary to effect its purpose.

A person may not effect any stabilizing transaction to facilitate an offering "at the market," that is, an offering at other than a fixed price.[101] For example, there may be no stabilization in connection with the type of shelf registration where securities are offered from time to time at prices current at the time of sale. On the other hand, there is no prohibition against stabilizing a best efforts offering.

- *Prices at Which Stabilization May Take Place*

Rule 104 regulates the prices at which stabilizing bids may be initiated and continued. A stabilizing bid may never exceed the lower of the offering price of the security or the stabilizing bid in the principal market.[102] Subject to this condition, the rule

---

100. NASD Rule 4614 requires market-makers who intend to initiate stabilization in NASDAQ securities to request permission to do so. Stabilizing bids are then identified by a symbol on the NASDAQ quotation display.

101. Rule 10b-7 defined an at-the-market offering as one in which it was contemplated that any offering price set in any calendar day would be increased more than once during such day.

102. The "principal market" is defined as the "single securities market with the largest aggregate reported trading volume for the class of securities during the 12 full calendar months immediately preceding the filing of the registration statement." If there is no registration statement or if the securities

permits a stabilizing bid to be initiated in any market based on independent prices in the principal market for the security. Subject to the same condition, the bid may then be maintained, reduced or raised to follow the independent market.

According to the Regulation M Release, "Rule 104 incorporates a knowledge-based standard to avoid imposition of an undue burden on underwriters to discover the prices of obscure transactions, whether reported or not."[103]

• • *Initiating Stabilization When There Is No Market for the Security.* If there is no market for the security being distributed (as would be the case in an IPO), stabilizing may be initiated at a price not in excess of the offering price.

Example: Offering price is 20. Stabilizing bid may be entered at 20 or less.

• • *Initiating Stabilization When the Principal Market Is Open.* Assume that the NYSE is the principal market for a security. The underwriters may initiate stabilization after the NYSE opening at a price no higher than the last independent transaction price for that security on the NYSE. This price level applies, however, only if the security traded on the NYSE on the day stabilizing was initiated (or on the preceding business day) (i.e., the last sale price must not be "stale") *and* the current asked price on the NYSE is equal to or greater than the last independent transaction price (i.e., the last sale price must not be "obsolete").

Example: Offering price is 20. Security has not yet opened on NYSE. Previous day's close was 20, and current asked price is 20.25. Stabilizing bid may be entered on NYSE at 20 (i.e., not higher than the offering price and also not higher than last independent transaction price).

Example: Same as above, except that offering price is 20.25. Stabilizing bid may not exceed 20 (i.e., last

---

are registered on a shelf basis, the relevant period is 12 full calendar months immediately preceding the determination of the offering price.

103. Regulation M Release at n.122.

independent transaction price). This is a good reason not to price offerings at a price higher than the last sale.

It would be unusual for the last sale price on the NYSE to ever be "stale"; however, that price could become "obsolete" if the market moves down. In that case, stabilizing may be initiated after the NYSE opening at a price no higher than the highest current independent bid for the security on the NYSE.

Example: Offering price is 20. Security has not yet opened on NYSE. Previous day's close was 20, but current independent asked price is now 19.75 (which makes the last sale "obsolete"). If current independent bid price is 19.50, stabilizing bid may be entered on NYSE at no more than 19.50. (This would be an unusual situation, since the underwriters should have entered a stabilizing bid at 20 *before* the market moved down.)

Assume now that another market is the principal market for the security and that that market is open at the time the underwriters wish to initiate stabilization. The rule permits stabilization on the NYSE at a price no higher than the last independent transaction price for that security on the principal market (assuming that the price is neither "stale" nor "obsolete"). If the last independent transaction price is either stale or obsolete, stabilization may be initiated on the NYSE at a price no higher than the highest current independent bid in the principal market.

Example: Offering price is 20. Principal market is Frankfurt Stock Exchange, where security recently traded at equivalent of 20. Current asked price in Frankfurt is above 20. Stabilizing bid may be entered on NYSE at 20.

Example: Same as above, except that current market in Frankfurt is 19.75 bid and 19.85 asked. Stabilizing bid in New York may not exceed 19.75.

• • *Initiating Stabilization When the Principal Market Is Closed.* Assume that the NYSE is the principal market for a security and that the offering price is established just after the close of trading. Stabilizing may be initiated after the security starts to trade in the over-the-counter market at a price no higher than the *lower* of

- the price at which stabilizing could have been initiated at the close of trading on the NYSE (see above), or
- the last independent transaction price for the security in the over-the-counter market before stabilizing began, but only if the security has traded on that day or the previous day (the price must not be "stale") and if the current asked price in the over-the-counter market is not less than the last independent transaction price (the price must not be "obsolete"). If either condition is not met, stabilizing may be initiated at a price no higher than the highest current independent bid for the security in the over-the-counter market.

Example: Closing price on NYSE is 20, and offering price is 20. Stabilizing may be initiated after the security starts to trade in the over-the-counter market at 20 (assuming that neither the last independent transaction price in that market nor the current asked price is less than 20).

If the underwriters initiate stabilization before the security starts to trade in the over-the-counter market (or if they wait until just before the security starts to trade the following morning on the NYSE), they may enter a bid at a price no higher than the *lower* of

- the price at which stabilizing could have been initiated at the close of trading on the NYSE, or
- the most recent price at which an independent transaction in the security has been effected in any market since the close of trading on the NYSE (assuming that the person stabilizing knows or has reason to know of such transaction).

Example: Offering price is 20. Stabilizing could have been initiated at previous day's NYSE close at 20, and managing underwriter has no reason to know of any intervening independent transaction in the security at a lower price. Stabilizing bid may be entered at 20.

Example: Same as previous example, but underwriter knows of an intervening transaction at 19.90. Stabilizing bid may be entered at no more than 19.90.

Assume that the Frankfurt Stock Exchange is the principal market for the security and that stabilizing is initiated on the NYSE after the close in Frankfurt. Under these circumstances, stabilization may be initiated after the NYSE opening at a price no higher than the *lower* of

- the price at which stabilizing could have been initiated in Frankfurt at its previous close, or
- the last independent transaction price for the security on the NYSE if the security has traded in that market on the day stabilizing is initiated (or on the last preceding business day) *and* the current asked price in that market is equal to or greater than the last independent transaction price. If either condition is not satisfied, then stabilizing may be initiated at a price no higher than the highest current independent bid on the NYSE.

Example: German stock is priced at 20 before close of trading in Frankfurt. Last trade of day in Frankfurt was at 19.90. Last NYSE trade was at 19.90, and current NYSE market is 19.85 bid and 19.95 asked. Stabilizing bid may be entered on NYSE at the equivalent of 19.90. (Of course, the underwriters could have prevented the trade at 19.90 by entering a stabilizing bid in the German over-the-counter market at the equivalent of 20.)

• • *Initiating Stabilization Before the Offering Price Is Determined.* Stabilizing may be initiated on rare occasions before the offering price is determined. In these cases, stabilization may be continued after the determination of the offering price at the price at which stabilizing then could be initiated.

Example: Underwriters stabilize stock at 20 on NYSE prior to pricing of offering. Stock then trades up and closes on NYSE at 20.25. Offering is priced at 20.25. Stabilization may be resumed in over-the-counter market at 20.25, assuming that current asked price is not less than 20.25.

• • *Maintaining or Carrying Over a Stabilizing Bid.* A stabilizing bid initiated at a permissible price level and that has not been discontinued may be maintained, or carried over into another market, without regard to changes in the independent bids or transaction prices for that security. The Regulation M Release states that the end of a trading session will not be deemed to discontinue a stabilizing bid in effect at the close. Rather, a stabilizing bid in effect at the market's close may be maintained between trading sessions and used to establish a stabilizing bid just prior to the market's opening on the next trading day.

Example: German stock is priced at 20 before close of trading in Frankfurt, which is its primary market. Last trade in Frankfurt was at 20, and stabilization could have been initiated at this price. Stabilizing bid entered on NYSE at the equivalent of 20 may be carried over on the next day onto Frankfurt Stock Exchange and maintained at 20 notwithstanding any decline in the price of the stock.

• • *Increasing or Reducing a Stabilizing Bid.* In what the SEC thought was the most significant change from the prior rule, Rule 104 permits a stabilizing bid to be increased to a price no higher than the highest current independent bid for the security in the principal market if the principal market is open. If the principal market is closed, then the bid may be increased to a price no higher than the highest independent bid in the principal market at its previous close.

It is still the case, however, that the stabilization bid may never exceed the offering price.

A stabilizing bid may be reduced, or carried over into another market at a reduced price, without regard to changes in the independent bids or transaction prices for the security.

If stabilizing is discontinued, it may not be resumed at a price higher than the price at which stabilizing could then be initiated.

• • *Effects of Exchange Rates.* If a stabilizing bid is expressed in a currency other than the currency of the principal market for the security, it may be initiated, maintained or adjusted to reflect the current exchange rate. If it is necessary for this purpose to round up or down to a trading differential (e.g., one-eighth), the bid must be rounded down.

• • *Adjustments to Stabilizing Bid.* If a security goes ex-dividend, ex-rights or ex-distribution, the stabilizing bid must be reduced by an amount equal to the value of the dividend, right, or distribution. If it is necessary for this purpose to round up or down to a trading differential (e.g., one-eighth), the bid must be rounded down.

- *Stabilization Outside the United States*

The SEC took the position in 1991 that it interpreted the former Rule 10b-7 as applying only where an offering was made at least in part in the United States. This was without prejudice to the possible application of the U.S. antifraud provisions to fraudulent or manipulative activity occurring outside of the United States if such activity had an effect in the United States.[104]

Many offerings take place in part in the United States and in part outside the United States. To accommodate these transactions, Rule 104(g) provides that the rule does not apply to stabilization outside the United States during an offering in the United States if

- there is no stabilization in the United States;
- the foreign stabilization is not conducted above the U.S. offering price; and
- the foreign stabilization is conducted in a jurisdiction with comparable regulation of stabilization activities.

---

104. SEC Release No. 34-28732 (January 3, 1991).

The Regulation M Release stated that the SEC recognized as comparable the stabilization regulations of the U.K. Securities and Investments Board and invited appropriate requests to recognize other markets as having comparable regulations for purposes of this provision. The SEC has not acted on any such requests.

In many offerings, it is necessary to stabilize outside the United States in a manner that exceeds the limits of Rule 104(g). In these cases, the SEC's staff may be prepared to grant general or specific exemptive relief.[105]

Disclosure, SRO Notification and Recordkeeping

Item 508(l) of Regulation S-K calls for a brief description of any transaction that an underwriter intends to conduct during the offering that stabilizes, maintains or otherwise affects the market price of the offered securities. The item specifically calls for information on stabilizing transactions, syndicate short covering transactions and penalty bids. It requires a clear description of the transactions and an explanation of how they will affect the offered security's price. If true, it must be disclosed that the underwriter may discontinue these transactions at any time. Whether or not a security is offered in a registered public offering, Rule 104(h) requires that a similar statement be provided to each purchaser (e.g., in an offering memorandum or confirmation) if the price of the security has been or may be stabilized.[106]

---

105. *See, e.g.*, SEC No-action Letter, *Nippon Telegraph and Telephone Corp.* (November 8, 1999) (class exemption to permit stabilization in Japan in conformity to local regulations, at a level higher than offering price, after completion of distribution in the United States and subject to other conditions).

106. The SEC considered in connection with the adoption of Regulation M a requirement of similar disclosure to purchasers of securities that are the subject of syndicate short covering activities or penalty bids. It decided against such disclosure for the time being but stated that it intended to reconsider the need for such disclosure as it reviewed developments relating to after-market activity.

If stabilization began prior to the effective date of the registration statement (or the determination of the public offering price in the event of a Rule 430A offering), the amount of securities bought, the price at which bought, and the periods within which they were bought must be disclosed in the prospectus. This information may be set forth immediately following the stabilization legend or, perhaps more appropriately, as a final paragraph under the heading "Price Range of Common Stock." If necessary, it may be set forth in a sticker.

There is no reason to make excuses for pre-effective or pre-pricing stabilizing purchases, as was done, to the amusement of Wall Street, in a supplement to a March 11, 1982 prospectus covering an offering of common stock by The Washington Water Power Company:

> Because of fog problems in the Washington, D.C., area on March 11, 1982, the filing of the price amendment to, and the effectiveness of, the Registration Statement, were delayed. Kidder, Peabody & Co. Incorporated and Dean Witter Reynolds Inc., as Representatives of the Underwriters, have advised the Company that on March 11, 1982, prior to the effectiveness of the Registration Statement, they made stabilizing purchases of 11,700 shares of the Company's Common Stock at 18-1/4.

Rule 104(h) requires prior notice to the relevant SRO by any person who displays or transmits a stabilizing bid or who effects a syndicate short covering transaction[107] or imposes a penalty bid.[108] In 1999, the SEC staff stated that notices of penalty bids need be furnished only when the penalty bid will be assessed.

---

107. The exercise of a Green Shoe or overallotment option is not a syndicate short covering transaction for this purpose. Staff Legal Bulletin No. 9 at 12 (October 27, 1999 revised April 12, 2002).

108. The SEC issued an exemption in late 1997 dispensing with the SRO notice requirement for syndicate covering transactions and penalty bids in connection with non-convertible investment-grade debt, preferred and asset-backed securities. SEC No-action Letter, *The Bond Market Association* (December 10, 1997).

"If notice of a penalty bid is given at the time of pricing because an agreement among the underwriters contains a penalty bid provision, but the penalty bid is not in fact imposed, an amended notice should be filed to reflect that no assessments were made."[109] Both the NYSE (Rule 392) and the NASD (Rule 4614 for stabilizing of NASDAQ securities, Rule 4624 for penalty bids and syndicate covering transactions for NASDAQ securities and Rule 6540 for OTC Bulletin Board securities) have prescribed procedures for this purpose. Rule 104(h) does not require that the notice to the SRO be a public notice, but the SEC stated in the Regulation M Release that it might revisit this issue if circumstances were to indicate that a public notice was warranted.

Rule 17a-2 under the 1934 Act has long provided that the manager effecting stabilization transactions must maintain records of his activities. As amended with the adoption of Regulation M, the rule also applies to syndicate short covering transactions[110] and the imposition of penalty bids. The rule applies to registered and Regulation A transactions and to other transactions where the aggregate offering price exceeds $5 million.[111]

Trading Restrictions for Issuers and Selling Securityholders (Rule 102)

Rule 102 covers bids, purchases and related activity in connection with distributions of securities "effected by or on

---

109. SEC Staff Legal Bulletin No. 9 at 12 (October 27, 1999 revised April 12, 2002).

110. The NASD adopted a rule in 1997 that would have supplemented Rule 17a-2 by requiring the manager to retain information on the amount of the syndicate short position, including whether it was no greater than the overallotment option or, if greater, the size of any naked short position. NASD Notice to Members 97-80. The rule expired pursuant to its terms on January 1, 2000.

111. Such other transactions could literally include private placements that amount to distributions for purposes of Regulation M, but it would be unusual for private placements to be accompanied by stabilization, syndicate short covering or penalty bids.

behalf" of an issuer or selling securityholder. A primary distribution is clearly by or on behalf of the issuer, but not every distribution by or on behalf of a selling securityholder is also by or on behalf of the issuer.[112]

The rule's prohibitions also apply to the "affiliated purchasers" of issuers and selling securityholders, but this term is defined by reference to conduct as discussed above. In addition, any affiliated purchaser that is a distribution participant may comply with Rule 101 rather than with Rule 102 (unless the distribution participant is itself the issuer or the selling securityholder).[113]

Rule 102 is similar in format to Rule 101, but it contains fewer exceptions than Rule 101 because of the SEC's belief that issuers and selling securityholders "have the greatest interest in an offering's outcome and generally do not have the same market access needs as underwriters."

Exceptions to Rule 102 permit transactions in non-convertible investment-grade securities, transactions during Rule 144A distributions, unsolicited purchases and exercises of options and other securities (including rights). Closed-end investment companies that engage in continuous offerings of securities may conduct certain tender offers for those securities during such distributions.

Rule 102 applies during a restricted period that begins one or five business days prior to pricing, depending as in the case of Rule 101 on the ADTV and public float of the securities in

---

112. Rule 102 therefore does not limit an issuer's activities during a distribution effected solely by or on behalf of a selling securityholder who is not an "affiliated purchaser" of the issuer. Regulation M Release, text at n.81.

113. Directors, officers, and controlling persons of an issuer may be "affiliates" of the issuer, but they are less likely to be "affiliated purchasers" under Regulation M's more narrow definition of the term. They are therefore usually free to purchase the underwritten securities. As noted above, the Regulation M Release refers approvingly to a no-action letter in which the staff stated that "purchases [by directors of an issuer] in a distribution of the securities being distributed . . . are not the type of purchases prohibited by Rule 10b-6." SEC No-action Letter, *VLI Corp.* (November 16, 1983), cited in Regulation M Release at n.20.

distribution. There is, however, no general exception under Rule 102 for securities meeting the $1 million ADTV/$150 million public float test; even these securities are subject to a restricted period that begins one business day prior to pricing. There is a limited exception for certain actively traded reference securities, for example, in the case of equity-linked notes, where the reference security is issued by an unaffiliated entity.

The restricted period ends when the distribution is complete. In a somewhat circular fashion, Rule 100 defines this as occurring in the case of an issuer or selling securityholder "when the distribution is completed." The question often arises whether an issuer may consider itself free of Rule 102's restrictions when the distribution has been priced, that is, when the economic risk has been shifted to the underwriters pursuant to the underwriting agreement. This would not be sufficient under the definition if the underwriters are still engaged in the distribution, for example, because they still have unsold allotments or if stabilization arrangements or price restrictions are still in effect. On the other hand, if the underwriters have sold out and terminated stabilization arrangements and price restrictions, the issuer should be able to resume stock repurchases without waiting for the closing.

Rule 102 divides stock-issuance plans[114] into three categories: (a) plans limited to employees and shareholders, (b) plans not limited to employees and shareholders where securities are purchased in the open market or in privately negotiated transactions by an agent independent from the issuer ("open market plans")[115] and (c) plans not so limited where securities are purchased from the issuer ("direct issuance plans"). Rule 102 makes available an exception for the first two categories, but the rule applies fully to direct issuance plans. Of course, it is still

---

114. Plans offered by bank transfer agents and registered broker-dealers qualify for the plan exception.

115. Under the Rule 100 definition of "agent independent of the issuer," the issuer may not specify the broker-dealer who makes purchases for the plan, and it may not change more than once every three months the source of the securities or certain other elections.

necessary that a plan involve a "distribution" in order for Rule 102 to apply. In this connection, the Regulation M Release describes the factors that should be considered in determining the magnitude of a direct issuance plan and whether or not it involves special selling efforts or selling methods.

As noted in the Regulation M Release, Regulation M supersedes prior SEC releases and staff no-action letters insofar as these related to issuer stock plans and Rule 10b-6, but the prior advice remains in effect insofar as it addressed other securities law issues such as Section 5 under the 1933 Act.

In connection with the adoption of Rule 102, the SEC also amended Rule 10b-18. That rule, which is discussed in Chapter 13, provides a safe harbor from manipulation liability for issuers or affiliated purchasers who repurchase the issuer's common stock. The safe harbor is not available when the issuer or an affiliated purchaser is in a Rule 102 restricted period for a distribution of the issuer's common stock or any security for which the common stock is a reference security.

Dealing with Problems Under the Trading Practice Rules

In the Rule 10b-6 era, the timing of a securities offering or even the membership of the underwriting syndicate could occasionally be threatened by the discovery of an inadvertent violation. These problems have become far less frequent under Rule 101, given that rule's shorter restricted periods, the de minimis exception and the many securities to which the rule has no application.

If a transaction occurs that violates Regulation M, the SEC staff may acquiesce in all or a combination of doing nothing, disclosing the violation in the prospectus, excluding the offending underwriter from the transaction or delaying the offering. Obviously, the first two outcomes are preferable.

In some cases, a transaction by a co-manager or other member of the underwriting syndicate may be entirely permissible, but the firm will be required by the book-running manager to clear the transaction with the staff of the SEC. This will usually be the result of genuine concern on the part of the firm running the books. In one case, a co-manager's purchase of a large block of stock, as permitted by exception (ii) of Rule 10b-6, was questioned by the book-running manager. It insisted on SEC approval if the co-manager was to continue as such. Fortunately, it agreed that oral clearance with a confirmatory letter to the SEC from the co-manager's counsel would be sufficient and that a no-action letter from the staff would not be necessary. The Division of Market Regulation had no problem with the purchase, and the confirmatory letter from counsel, which spelled out in great detail the transaction and its legal justification, was viewed as sufficient by the manager and underwriters' counsel. The time required to obtain a no-action letter could have effectively forced the co-manager out of the financing.

The staff of the Division of Market Regulation has been helpful to underwriters and their counsel on many occasions in resolving problems under the Trading Practice Rules and their predecessors. Based on this experience, it is advisable to have two items of information available when calling the staff regarding possible violations of Regulation M. The first consists of detailed factual information on the bids or purchases or other conduct that appears to have violated the rule, for example, the number of shares traded, the trade price and the time of the trade, together with contemporaneous volume and price information for the security. This information enables the staff to form a view as to whether the violations may have affected the market for the security. The second category of information is simply an explanation of how the violation occurred and what steps are being taken to prevent a repetition.

Covering Short Sales with Registered Securities (Rule 105)

Syndicate managers face many problems in bringing a stock offering to market. For many years, one of the principal reasons for their sleepless nights was the practice engaged in by hedge funds and other institutions of entering indications of interest for shares to be distributed in an underwriting, selling short aggressively prior to the effective date of the registration statement in an effort to drive down the market price of the shares, and covering their short position with shares purchased in the underwriting. Persons selling short in anticipation of a public offering are not subject to the usual market risk accompanying the covering transaction, but are assured of covering with offered securities purchased in the public offering at a fixed, and generally lower, price.

In 1972, the SEC published a staff opinion that addressed short selling prior to a public offering.[116] The release observed that this short selling may be "disruptive of fair and orderly markets in [the] securities" and, where the short sales are intended to depress the market price of the security so that the short position can be covered at a lower price, the activity violates the antimanipulative provisions of the 1934 Act.

Then, in 1974, the SEC proposed for adoption Rule 10b-21,[117] and the following year reproposed the rule in revised form.[118] A third version of the rule was published for comment at the end of 1976.[119]

On the same date that the SEC first proposed Rule 10b-21, it commenced a proceeding against the brokerage firm of A.P. Montgomery & Co., Inc., charging that, for its own account or for the accounts of customers, it made short sales of securities prior to the effective dates of several registration statements that caused, or contributed to, a decline in the market price for the securities and affected the pricing of the offering. This was alleged by the SEC to be a manipulative practice. Montgomery subsequently consented to SEC sanctions.[120] A few years later, the SEC brought a similar proceeding against another broker-dealer.[121]

The underwriting community was delighted at the prospect that Rule 10b-21 would be adopted, but years passed and nothing happened. The sharks continued to circle the boat, darting in with their short sales at the most inopportune times. Syndicate managers continued to have sleepless nights. The problems of

---

116. SEC Release No. 34-9824 (October 16, 1972).
117. SEC Release No. 34-10636 (February 11, 1974).
118. SEC Release No. 34-11328 (April 2, 1975).
119. SEC Release No. 34-13092 (December 21, 1976).
120. SEC Release No. 34-10909 (July 9, 1974).
121. *J.A.B. Securities Co., Inc.*, SEC Release No. 34-15948 (June 25, 1979).

Wall Street were not high on the SEC's agenda in the post-Watergate era.

In 1987, the SEC once again proposed Rule 10b-21, this time in response to a petition for rulemaking filed by the NASD.[122] A number of commentators responded to the SEC's request for comment regarding the extent of pre-offering short selling and its impact on the costs to issuers of completing an offering. Most of these commentators described firsthand experiences with the adverse effects of short selling activity, which caused them to cancel proposed offerings or to complete offerings even though the issuer was deprived of proceeds that would have been realized had the market not been adversely affected by this activity.

The NASD submitted information relating to investigations of three separate public offerings, and stated that, based on these investigations and others involving similar circumstances, it believed that the practice of short selling before a public offering with the intention of covering with shares purchased in the public offering was not uncommon. The investigations revealed substantial short selling activity by certain firms after the filing of the registration statement and a decline in the price of the stock prior to the effective date. In each instance, the short sellers covered their positions at a profit immediately after the offering with shares purchased from entities that had obtained them in the public offering.

In August 1988, Rule 10b-21(T) finally was adopted, although on a temporary basis.[123] The rule was made permanent as of March 1994,[124] and it was amended and "recodified" as Rule 105 when the SEC adopted Regulation M in 1997.

Rule 105 quite simply states that it is unlawful to cover a short sale with securities purchased from an underwriter or broker participating in a firm commitment offering for cash that is registered under the 1933 Act (or exempt under Regulation A) if "such" short sale occurred during the period of five business days preceding the pricing of the offering (or, if shorter, the

---

122. SEC Release No. 34-24485 (May 20, 1987).
123. SEC Release No. 34-26028 (August 25, 1988).
124. SEC Release No. 34-33702 (March 2, 1994).

period between the filing of the registration statement and the pricing of the offering).[125]

The SEC expressed little sympathy in the Regulation M Release for the short seller's potential difficulties in identifying the correct five-business-day period. It simply observed that "short sellers contemplating a covering transaction will be in a position to know if any of their short sales were made within that . . . period" and that if a short sale turned out to have been made during this period—which could happen, of course, because of an acceleration of the offering date—then the short seller will not be able to cover the short sale with securities purchased in the offering.

The SEC declined in 1997 to expand the rule to include options and other derivatives or to add an express reference to "indirect" covering transactions. It observed in the Regulation M Release that "[a]ny manipulative short sales involving derivatives transactions continue to be addressed by the general anti-manipulation provisions, including Section 9(a)(2) of and Rule 10b-5 under the . . . [1934] Act," and it had earlier stated in the adopting release for Rule 10b-21 that Section 20(b) of the 1934 Act would prohibit covering purchases effected by prearrangement with other purchasers in the offering.

As adopted, Rule 105 did not apply to shelf offerings under Rule 415 because of the SEC's belief that investors' lack of prior notice of such offerings made it less likely that such offerings could be used as a vehicle for manipulative or disruptive short sales. The SEC cautioned in the Regulation M Release that it might revisit the shelf registration exclusion if the offering of shelf-registered equity securities became more common. Simultaneously with its adoption of Regulation SHO in July 2004,[126] the SEC rescinded the shelf registration exclusion on

---

125. Although the rule clearly states that "such" short sale, i.e., a short sale effected within the relevant period, cannot be covered with securities from the offering, the SEC staff in Staff Legal Bulletin No. 9 (1999) stated that a person could not use offered securities to cover any short sale—even one made long before the beginning of the relevant period—if the person makes a single short sale within the relevant period.

126. SEC Release No. 34-50103 (July 28, 2004). In the same release, the SEC criticized "sham transactions" designed to give the "appearance" of covering

the ground that shelf offerings had taken on many of the characteristics of non-shelf offerings, including roadshows and other special selling efforts that provided investors with prior notice of such offerings. In addition, it found that equity shelf offerings had become more common since the adoption of Rule 105.

Notwithstanding the SEC's emphasis in the Regulation M Release and in the July 2004 rulemaking on the frequency of shelf-registered *equity* offerings as bearing on the continued viability of shelf registration exclusion, it rejected in July 2004 a commenter's suggestion that it amend Rule 105 to exclude debt offerings. The rule therefore continues to apply to short sales prior to registered offerings of debt securities, which the SEC said "continue to . . . present a potential for manipulation."

Manipulation Outside the Trading Practice Rules

As discussed above, the SEC rejected suggestions that Regulation M should be regarded as establishing safe harbors against violations of the general antifraud and antimanipulation provisions of the 1934 Act. The preliminary note to Rule 100 makes this explicit. This means that a transaction that is not in violation of Regulation M may still be held to have violated the 1934 Act or, more generally, an SRO's rules regarding "just and equitable principles of trade."

For example, it has been noted that Rule 101—like Rule 10b-6 before it—does not prohibit an underwriter from engaging in short sales during the restricted period. Some traders had to learn this the hard way. In November 1990, for example, Shearson Lehman Brothers Inc. was the sole underwriter of a 4.4 million share offering of common stock of ConAgra Inc., a major food company.[127] By November 20, it had obtained indications of interest to purchase the entire block at prices up to $33.25. ConAgra's stock traded at that price during most of the afternoon, but 5,900 shares traded during the last minute of trading on the NYSE at

---

with open market securities. It cited as an example the transactions involved in *Ascend Capital, LLC*, SEC Release No. 34-48188 (July 17, 2003).

127. The facts regarding this matter are taken from NYSE, *Hearing Panel Decision 92-84* (May 21, 1992); NYSE, *Hearing Panel Decision 92-85* (May 22, 1992); and press reports.

$33.375. Following the NYSE close, several prospective purchasers informed Shearson Lehman that they were not willing to buy at $33.375. Shearson Lehman suggested to ConAgra that the offering price of the 4.4 million shares be lowered to $33.25, but ConAgra took the position that it did not want the offering to appear to have been priced at a discount. A decision was postponed until the close of trading on the Pacific Stock Exchange.

A senior trader for Shearson Lehman issued instructions to a specialist and a floor broker on the Pacific Stock Exchange (both employees of Shearson Lehman) that resulted in the short sale by a "$2 broker" of 100 shares of ConAgra at $33.25. This was the closing transaction in the stock on that day. Shearson Lehman and ConAgra then agreed to price the 4.4 million share offering at $33.25.

Upon discovering the facts, Shearson Lehman conducted an internal investigation and reported its results to the NYSE. It also suspended certain of the employees involved in the Pacific Stock Exchange transaction and paid $550,000 to ConAgra, this being the additional amount that ConAgra would have received if the offering had been priced at $33.375. Without referring to the word "manipulation," an NYSE hearing panel found Shearson Lehman and its co-head equities trader to have violated just and equitable principles of trade. It censured both the firm and the trader, fined Shearson Lehman the sum of $500,000 and the trader $100,000, suspended the trader for four months and accepted an undertaking from Shearson Lehman regarding improvements in its internal procedures.

In a similar incident that occurred earlier but required more time to be resolved, a trader/salesman for Drexel Burnham Lambert Inc. and a trader for one of its hedge fund clients ended up suffering more serious consequences than the Shearson Lehman trader. According to SEC proceedings,[128] Drexel Burnham was to price an underwritten offering of $25 million offering of convertible debentures of C.O.M.B. Co. on April 11,

---

128. *In the Matter of Charles M. Zarzecki*, SEC Release No. 34-31764 (January 26, 1993); *In the Matter of Bruce L. Newberg* (Admin. Proc. File No. 3-7651) (September 1, 1993). See also Steve Thel, *$850,000 in Six Minutes—The Mechanics of Securities Manipulation*, 79 Cornell L. Rev. 219, 273–74 (1994).

1985. Michael Milken of Drexel Burnham was upset about the strong performance of the C.O.M.B. common stock and may even have believed that it was being manipulated upward. A higher price for the C.O.M.B. common stock would, of course, make it harder to sell the convertible securities. A trader/salesman for Drexel Burnham called one of his accounts, a trader at a hedge fund, and expressed his desire that the C.O.M.B. stock not be at "16 bid" but rather that it be "down to at least 15-3/4, and hopefully lower." He added that the hedge fund would be "indemnified." The hedge fund trader then sold short two blocks of C.O.M.B.

Unfortunately for the two individuals, their conversations were taped and eventually made public as part of the notorious "sleaze bag" tapes. The government used the tapes to support its *criminal* prosecution of the two individuals on a variety of charges, including securities fraud. Both individuals were convicted and eventually sentenced to three months imprisonment, two years probation on release and fines of $155,000. The convictions on securities fraud and certain other counts were upheld on appeal, while certain other convictions were vacated and remanded.[129] On remand, Judge Carter of the Southern District of New York expressed displeasure that other persons he regarded as "major actors" in the case were getting off "scott free." He accordingly vacated the two individuals' sentences, not least because of the relatively mild non-criminal punishment handed out in the Shearson Lehman case by the NYSE (and presumably acquiesced in by the SEC). Judge Carter's views did not stop the SEC, however, from permanently barring the two individuals from the securities industry.

At the time of the ConAgra and C.O.M.B. offerings, of course, Rule 10b-6 would have prevented Shearson Lehman and Drexel Burnham, respectively, from purchasing shares of the two issuers in the open market or from inducing others to do so. As noted above, however, it would not have prohibited either prospective underwriter from engaging in short sales of the shares. These sales would have been expressly permitted by exception (vi) of

---

129. *United States v. Regan*, 937 F.2d 823 (2d Cir.), *modified*, 946 F.2d 188 (2d Cir. 1991), *cert. denied*, 504 U.S. 940 (1992).

Rule 10b-6 as "securities ... offered as principal," an exception that is carried forward into exception 9 of Rule 101.

At the time of the two proceedings, however, the SEC's and the U.S. government's theory was that all investors are under a "general duty" not to manipulate. Moreover, manipulation could be found whenever an investor—who did not need to be a fiduciary or an insider of an issuer—engaged in securities transactions in the open market "with the sole intent to affect the price of the security" (i.e., without an "investment purpose").[130] In decisions rendered only two weeks apart, one panel of the Second Circuit expressed "doubt" and "misgivings" about the government's view of the law,[131] while another—the panel reviewing the convictions of the Drexel Burnham and hedge fund traders—accepted it without serious reservation.

The hedge fund trader asked the Supreme Court to review the Second Circuit's affirmance of his convictions. The U.S. government (with the SEC's participation) declined to submit its broad theory to the Court and argued instead that the trader's convictions should be affirmed because he had sold the C.O.M.B. stock on Drexel Burnham's behalf. Since an underwriter such as Drexel Burnham "has a duty to both 'the issuer and the investing public,'" the trader's conduct would be criminal even under a narrower theory than the government's.[132]

Under the government's modified theory, therefore, the underwriter has a duty to the issuer as well as to the "investing public." Under the circumstances of the ConAgra and C.O.M.B. offerings, however, it is hard to see how any duty to the "investing public" is violated by action that results in the public's paying less for a security. It is much easier, of course, to see how an underwriter might violate a duty to an issuer under these circumstances. Even here, however, much depends on the particular facts. ConAgra, for example, might have been perfectly happy to have the offering priced at $33.25 so long as it did not appear that the stock was being sold at a discount.

---

130. *United States v. Mulheren*, 938 F.2d 364, 368 (2d Cir. 1991).
131. *Id.*
132. Brief for the United States in Opposition, *Zarzecki v. United States*, No. 91-1223 (S. Ct.), at 12–13.

There is no suggestion in the record, of course, that ConAgra knew what Shearson Lehman's trader was doing. But would there have been a violation if it had been informed of the facts and agreed to the short sale?

Persuasive arguments have been made that "real" (i.e., not sham) trades should not be prohibited as manipulative regardless of the intent of the trader,[133] and it remains to be seen how the SEC's aggressive theory of manipulation would be treated in the Supreme Court.

---

133. Daniel R. Fischel & David J. Ross, *Should the Law Prohibit "Manipulation" in Financial Markets?*, 105 Harv. L. Rev. 503 (1991).

Chapter 5

LIABILITIES AND DUE DILIGENCE

The term "due diligence" does not appear in the federal securities laws, but securities lawyers generally understand it as referring to the "reasonable investigation" defense against civil liability made available by Section 11(b)(3)(A) of the 1933 Act or to the "reasonable care" defense made available by Section 12(a)(2) of the 1933 Act.

More broadly, due diligence is understood in the capital markets as including the entire process by which an underwriter or other marketer of securities reaches the conclusion that its comfort level regarding the premises of a securities offering is sufficiently high to justify proceeding with the transaction and selling the securities to its customers.

Litigation risk is obviously one of the factors considered in reaching this conclusion, but so is the underwriter's concern for its reputation and the good will of its customers.

Traditionally, a managing underwriter of an SEC-registered securities offering was thought of as a "gatekeeper" or "reputational intermediary" on whom investors relied to reduce their information costs. Members of the underwriting syndicate, who could not as a practical matter conduct their own due diligence, also relied on the managing underwriter for similar purposes.

Under the traditional arrangement, an investment banking firm that placed its name on a prospectus necessarily had a vital reputational interest in the soundness of the issuer's business plan and in a disclosure document that completely and accurately described the risks associated with that plan. Moreover, generally uniform high standards of due diligence among other underwriters—and the likelihood of detailed SEC comments on the registration statement—meant that even the most recalcitrant issuer was likely to cooperate with the underwriter in this exercise.

The traditional model is alive and well but has been threatened from two directions.

First, due diligence in connection with debt or follow-on equity offerings by public companies has come under pressure as a result of the SEC's introduction of the "integrated disclosure system" and the expansion of incorporation-by-reference and shelf registration. Volatile markets have also led to the increasing compression of time schedules for these offerings. The effect of these changes on underwriters' due diligence was described in a 1993 report prepared by a task force of the Federal Regulation of Securities Committee of the Section on Business Law of the American Bar Association.[1] That report focused on the shelf takedown of investment-grade debt, the medium-term notes (MTN) offering and the non-underwritten registered equity secondary offering. These transactions are discussed in Chapter 8.

Second, due diligence generally suffers in a time of rising stock prices. During the Internet Bubble from 1998 until 2000, due diligence was to some degree crowded out as investors' demand for new offerings and sharp competition among investment bankers led to the churning out of one high-tech or Internet IPO after another, often under conditions—such as the issuer's brief or non-existent operating history, the untested nature of its

---

1. *Report of the Task Force on Sellers' Due Diligence and Similar Defenses Under the Federal Securities Laws*, 48 Bus. Law. 1185 (1993) (ABA Task Force Report). One of the authors of this book served as co-chair of the task force.

business plan and the absence of significant sales or earnings—that made traditional due diligence procedures difficult.

Even for established companies, the quality of disclosure often suffered as management cut corners or took advantage of technical accounting rules to meet ever-higher "Street" expectations. And for a large part of this period, the SEC allowed itself to be distracted from pursuing a diligent review of issuers' periodic reports by less relevant issues, such as a fixation on "plain English."

To a large degree, the pendulum has swung back in the direction of better due diligence. We have been reminded that investors can lose money, and underwriters can suffer damaged reputations, in transactions involving securities of established companies as well as in IPOs. Many of the Sarbanes–Oxley disclosure and corporate governance enhancements apply to IPO issuers as well as to companies already public, and investment banks have become reluctant to participate in transactions that can expose them to additional criticism and financial risk. All of this means a resurgence in due diligence, both before and after the lawyers are brought into a transaction.

As noted above, due diligence in connection with shelf takedowns, MTNs and certain other transactions is discussed in Chapter 8. Certain other types of transactions—commercial paper offerings, private placements (including Rule 144A offerings), securitization transactions and international offerings—present unique due diligence problems that are treated in the chapters devoted to those transactions.

The remainder of this chapter deals with "general principles" of due diligence as they apply to "traditional" transactions—especially IPOs—and as they apply to important aspects of the non-traditional offerings discussed elsewhere.

Statutory Bases for Liability

Section 11 of the 1933 Act provides the principal basis for civil liability in connection with registered public offerings of securities. Section 12(a)(2) imposes civil liability for certain sellers of securities in the public markets, whether or not the security is registered under the 1933 Act, unless the security is exempted by Section 3(a)(2). Rule 10b-5 under Section 10(b) of the 1934 Act lurks in the background, but for reasons to be discussed it is a less effective remedy for a purchaser of securities in a public offering.

- *Section 11*

Section 11(a) of the 1933 Act provides that a person acquiring a security covered by a registration statement may recover damages on a joint and several basis from the issuer,[2] its directors, its officers who sign the registration statement, accountants and other experts named in the registration statement with their consent, and every underwriter of the security if "any part of the registration statement, when such part became effective, contained an untrue statement of a material fact or omitted to state a material fact required to be stated therein or necessary to make the statements therein not misleading."[3]

There is no requirement of privity. Also, the remedy is not limited to persons who purchase directly in the offering. Aftermarket purchasers can also sue under Section 11, so long as they can demonstrate compliance with the statutory requirement that they bought registered securities and not securities that were outstanding prior to the public offering or that were issued after

---

2. Section 6(a) requires the registration statement to be signed by the issuer as well as by the issuer's principal executive officer, its principal financial officer and its comptroller or principal accounting officer. A majority of the directors must also sign the registration statement, but each director has potential Section 11 liability whether or not he or she actually signs the document.

3. Rule 405 under the 1933 Act provides:

The term "material," when used to qualify a requirement for the furnishing of information as to any subject, limits the information required to those matters to which there is a substantial likelihood that a reasonable investor would attach importance in determining whether to purchase the security registered.

See *TSC Indus. v. Northway*, 426 U.S. 438, 440–64 (1976).

the public offering.[4] The required "tracing" is sometimes not so easy. On the one hand, a plaintiff who can produce a confirmation of a purchase of IPO shares from an underwriter at the initial public offering price might be able to meet the burden. On the other hand, a plaintiff who purchased shares in the secondary market might have a more difficult task. Shares purchased in the secondary market are fungible, and even after an IPO a large number of unregistered shares may have "leaked" into the market as lock-ups expired and holders of control or restricted shares began to sell in the secondary market under Rule 144. The courts have not been consistent in what they have required of Section 11 plaintiffs in this regard, but we can safely leave this topic to the litigators.

It goes without saying, however, that a purchaser can bring a Section 11 claim only if he or she knows or at least suspects that the purchased securities are part of a registered public offering. Purchasers in the secondary market on any given day may have no idea that they are purchasing shares that the issuer has registered for resale by holders of control or restricted shares.

What are the defenses to a Section 11 claim? First, a defendant can try to prove that the plaintiff, at the time he or she acquired the securities, knew of the alleged untruth or omission. This is a difficult defense to sustain, particularly in the context of a class action—and virtually all Section 11 claims are asserted as class actions. On the other hand, a proposed class representative who had some unique insight might not be typical of the class and could be subject to challenge on that ground.

Also, if the defendants can prove that any portion or all of the "depreciation in value" of the registered security did not result from the registration statement's being false or misleading—the so-called "negative causation" defense—then Section 11(e) provides that such portion or all of plaintiff's damages are not recoverable. Thus, if the market price of the securities

---

4. *Barnes v. Osofsky*, 373 F.2d 269 (2d Cir. 1967); *DeMaria v. Andersen*, 318 F.3d 170 (2d Cir. 2003); *Lee v. Ernst & Young*, 294 F.2d 969 (8th Cir. 2002).

declined solely because of general market conditions, then the plaintiffs could not recover damages.[5]

In Section 11 actions based on misstatements or omissions relating to "forward-looking statements" contained in the registration statement, the Reform Act makes available to all defendants a safe harbor defense if the forward-looking statement was identified as such and accompanied by "meaningful cautionary statements identifying important factors that could cause actual results to differ materially . . . ." Another safe harbor defense is available under the Reform Act if the plaintiffs are unable to prove that a forward-looking statement in the registration statement was made with actual knowledge that it was false or misleading. The safe harbor defenses for forward-looking statements are not available in IPOs and in certain other circumstances, but the court-created "bespeaks caution" doctrine may be helpful in achieving a similar result.

An additional defense, more in the nature of a limitation on damages, is available only to underwriters. As noted above, the usual rule in Section 11 cases is joint and several liability for all defendants. Section 11(e) contains a so-called "hold-down" provision, however, that modifies the joint and several rule for underwriters. Under Section 11(e), which was part of the 1934 amendments to the 1933 Act, an underwriter cannot be held liable under Section 11 for damages in excess of the total price at which the securities underwritten by it and distributed to the public were offered to the public *unless* that underwriter knowingly received from the issuer for acting as an underwriter some benefit, directly or indirectly, in which all the other underwriters similarly situated did not share in proportion to their

---

5. *See Akerman v. Oryx Communications, Inc.*, 810 F.2d 336 (2d Cir. 1987) (decline in price found to have occurred prior to corrective disclosure); *In re Fortune Systems Securities Litig.*, [1988–1989 Transfer Binder] Fed. Sec. L. Rep. (CCH) ¶93,390 (N.D. Cal. July 30, 1987) (defendants argued that price decline of registered shares was due to "poor management of the IPO" and resulting cancellation of orders); *Beecher v. Able*, 435 F. Supp. 397 (S.D.N.Y. 1977) ("value" of registered shares held not necessarily to be same amount as market price where latter was influenced by "panic selling").

LIABILITIES AND DUE DILIGENCE 311

respective interests in the underwriting. Thus, an underwriter's exposure is ordinarily limited to the aggregate public offering price of the securities that constituted its underwriting commitment. This is the principal reason why the commitments of members of an underwriting syndicate are several and not joint and several.[6]

The Reform Act introduced another deviation from the joint and several rule, this time for the benefit of "outside directors" of the issuer who did not "knowingly" commit a violation of the securities laws. The liability of these persons under Section 11 is proportionate based on fault and other factors rather than joint and several.[7]

Another defense arises only if the plaintiff acquired the securities after the issuer has made generally available to its securityholders an earnings statement covering a period of at least 12 months beginning after the effective date of the registration statement. In this case, the plaintiff's right of recovery is conditioned on proof that he or she relied on the untrue statement in the registration statement or that he or she relied on the registration statement without knowing about the alleged omission. It is for this reason that underwriting agreements contain a covenant requiring the issuer to make such an earnings statement available at the earliest practicable date. Rule 158 under the 1933 Act permits an issuer's 1934 Act reports to serve as the earnings statement contemplated by Section 11.

---

6. In the usual case, the managing underwriter does not receive any special benefits from the issuer. The management fee is not paid by the issuer, but rather by the syndicate out of the underwriting spread. If the managing underwriter were to receive warrants or cheap stock from the issuer—to the exclusion of the other underwriters—then it could be argued that the managing underwriter would not be entitled to the benefits of the hold-down provision. Under these circumstances, the managing underwriter would presumably argue that it had received the additional benefit in consideration of advisory or other services that it had provided to the issuer, i.e., that it was not "similarly situated" with the other underwriters in respect of the additional benefit.

7. See Section 11(f)(2) of the 1933 Act and Section 21D(f) of the 1934 Act. The SEC has yet to adopt rules defining who is an "outside director" for the purpose of these provisions.

Section 13 of the 1933 Act provides that the statute of limitations for an action under Section 11 is one year after the untrue statement or omission was discovered or should have been discovered by the person asserting the action or, at the outside, three years after the public offering. Section 804 of Sarbanes–Oxley in 2002 amended the general statute of limitations for civil actions arising under federal statutes to provide that a private right of action involving a claim of fraud, deceit, manipulation or contrivance in violation of a regulatory requirement concerning the federal securities laws would have to be brought within two years after discovery or five years after the violation. There is no indication that Congress intended in Sarbanes–Oxley to override the express statute of limitations contained in Section 13 of the 1933 Act. Also, Section 11 creates a negligence-based remedy that would not appear to be included within the reference to claims based on fraud, deceit, manipulation or contrivances.[8]

The principal defense under Section 11, however, is the so-called "due diligence" defense. This defense is available to all defendants other than the issuer.[9]

In specifying when the due diligence defense is available, Section 11 distinguishes between that portion of a registration statement that is covered by the opinion of an expert, such as

---

8. *See, e.g.*, *In re WorldCom, Inc. Securities Litig.*, 294 F. Supp. 2d 431 (S.D.N.Y. 2003). Notwithstanding the negligence-based nature of the Section 11 remedy, several Courts of Appeal have held that the heightened pleading requirements of Rule 9(b) of the Federal Rules of Civil Procedure apply to claims under Sections 11 and 12(a)(2) to the extent that the claims "sound in fraud." See, e.g., *Rombach v. Chang*, 355 F.3d 164 (2d Cir. 2004).

9. *But see In re The Ultimate Corp. Securities Litig.*, CCH Fed. Secs. L. Rep. [1989 Transfer Binder] Fed. Sec. L. Rep. (CCH) ¶¶94,522, 94,523 (S.D.N.Y. 1989), where Judge Haight granted an issuer's summary judgment motion notwithstanding plaintiffs' objection that the issuer's liability under Section 11 was "virtually absolute." Judge Haight held that the issuer was under no obligation to disclose in its prospectus that two senior officers had decided to leave the issuer where the issuer did not learn of the officers' decision until several weeks later.

the certified financial statements or information covered by an opinion of a petroleum engineer, and that portion that is not expertized.

As to *non-expertized* portions of the registration statement, Section 11(b)(3)(A) permits an underwriter to avoid liability if he can sustain the burden of proof that "he had, *after reasonable investigation*, reasonable ground to believe and did believe, at the time such part of the registration statement became effective, that the statements therein were true and that there was no omission to state a material fact required to be stated therein or necessary to make the statements therein not misleading" (emphasis added). The concept of due diligence derives from the words "reasonable investigation." Section 11(c) provides that, in determining what constitutes reasonable investigation and reasonable grounds for belief, "the standard of reasonableness shall be that required of a prudent man in the management of his own property."[10]

As to *expertized* portions of the registration statement, Section 11(b)(3)(C) dispenses with the reasonable investigation requirement. Expertized portions of the registration statement are those portions made on the authority of "experts" (i.e., any accountant, engineer, appraiser or "any person whose profession gives authority to a statement made by him" who consents to be named as such). Similarly, Section 11(b)(3)(D) dispenses with the reasonable investigation requirement insofar as the registration statement contains statements made by public officials or extracts from public official documents. In order to sustain a defense in these situations, a defendant need only prove that he or she had no reasonable ground to believe, and did not believe, that the expertized portions of the registration statement contained materially untrue statements or omissions or did not fairly represent the expert's or public official's statement or the contents of the public official document.

---

10. In 1982, the SEC attempted in Rule 176 under the 1933 Act to identify circumstances "relevant" to the reasonableness of the conduct of a person other than the issuer for the purposes of the due diligence defense in Section 11. The rule does not apply to the reasonableness of care under Section 12(a)(2).

Accountants are the quintessential experts when it comes to registration statements, but it is important to keep in mind that any interim *unaudited* financial information contained in a registration statement is by definition not "expertized" material. Nor does such information become "expertized" because the accountant performs a review of such information or covers it in a comfort letter. Moreover, there are many reasons for underwriters to focus with great care on the issuer's financial statements—audited and unaudited—included in the registration statement. These reasons, and the subject of due diligence in relation to accounting matters, are discussed below.

- *Section 12(a)(2)*

Section 12(a)(2) imposes liability on any person who offers or sells a security by means of a prospectus or oral communication "which includes an untrue statement of a material fact or omits to state a material fact necessary in order to make the statements in the light of the circumstances under which they were made, not misleading." Liability, which may be for rescission, or for damages if the security is no longer owned, extends to any person who sells a security—whether or not that person is an underwriter. Liability under Section 12(a)(2) may be incurred whether or not the securities are exempt from registration, except in the case of United States government, municipal, and bank securities exempted under Section 3(a)(2), as to which there is no Section 12(a)(2) liability.

According to a relatively recent decision of the U.S. Supreme Court, *Gustafson v. Alloyd Co.*,[11] Section 12(a)(2) applies only in the case of public offerings by an issuer or a controlling securityholder. This decision came as a surprise to many securities lawyers, who had long assumed that an investment banker had Section 12(a)(2) liability in connection with private placements and even in connection with certain secondary market transactions. The most important category of non-registered securities offering remaining subject to Section 12(a)(2) liability after *Gustafson* would appear to be commercial paper programs,

---

11. *Gustafson v. Alloyd Co.*, 513 U.S. 561 (1995).

which are neither registered nor exempt under Section 3(a)(2). On the other hand, it is possible that purchasers of securities in an overseas offering (including an offering pursuant to Regulation S) might claim rights under Section 12(a)(2) if they could show that their purchase involved the use of the U.S. mails or other "jurisdictional means."[12]

In the case of a registered public offering, a securities firm that acts as a dealer, but not as an underwriter, may have liability under Section 12(a)(2), even though it will not have liability under Section 11. Section 2(a)(11) excludes a member of the dealer group from the definition of the term "underwriter" by stating that the term "shall not include a person whose interest is limited to a commission from an underwriter or dealer not in excess of the usual and customary distributors' or sellers' commission." Rule 141 provides that the term "commission" as used in Section 2(a)(11) includes "such remuneration, commonly known as a spread, as may be received by a distributor or dealer as a consequence of reselling securities bought from an underwriter or dealer at a price below the offering price of such securities" so long as the spread is not in excess of what is usual and customary in the distribution and sale of issues of similar type and size. Thus, a dealer, even though it does not have underwriters' liability under Section 11, does have potential liability under Section 12(a)(2) if the prospectus used by it in selling the securities is materially false or misleading.

Under Section 12(a)(2), unlike Section 11, the seller of the security is liable only to "the person purchasing such security from him." In this respect, Section 12(a)(2) is very unlike Section 11, which permits any purchaser of securities to sue any person on whom Section 11 imposes liability. On the other hand, Section 12(a)(2) does not limit liability to the person who transfers title to the security. A person who solicits the purchase will

---

12. *See, e.g., Sloane Overseas Fund, Ltd. et al. v. Sapiens Int'l Corp., N.V. et al.*, 941 F. Supp. 1369, 1374–75 (S.D.N.Y. 1996). Any purchaser located abroad might have difficulty persuading a U.S. court to exercise its subject matter jurisdiction over such a claim, even if the requisite jurisdictional means could be shown to be present.

be considered to be among those "from" whom the buyer "purchased" the security if the person did so for his or her own financial benefit or that of the seller.[13] Under this approach, several courts have held that Section 12(a)(2) does not reach the issuer in a typical firm commitment underwriting, since the solicitation effort is conducted by the underwriters and dealers.[14] The result might be different if the issuer's representatives were to engage in direct solicitation, for example, by appearing at investors' meetings or roadshows.

The reference in Section 12(a)(2) to "oral communication" must be taken in context. Not every oral communication will provide a basis for relief under Section 12(a)(2). The Supreme Court in *Gustafson* noted that the lower courts were in agreement that the term "oral communication" in Section 12(a)(2) is restricted to oral communications that relate to a prospectus, which the Court held in *Gustafson* meant a document relating to a public offering by an issuer or its controlling shareholders. This at least suggests that isolated oral statements—those, for example, by a salesperson in connection with a registered public offering—may not be actionable under Section 12(a)(2) unless they relate to the contents of the prospectus for the offering.

Defendants under Section 12(a)(2) have the same defenses as defendants under Section 11 based on the plaintiff's knowledge of the alleged untrue statement or omission and on the Reform Act's safe harbors for forward-looking statements.

As in the case of Section 11, the seller's principal defense under Section 12(a)(2) is to demonstrate due diligence, which under Section 12(a)(2) requires proof "that he did not know, and in the exercise of reasonable care could not have known," of the untruth or omission. The language of the statute suggests that the defendant need not prove that he in fact exercised due diligence but only that if he had exercised due diligence, he could not have discovered the untruth or omission in the prospectus. The Court of Appeals for the Seventh Circuit, however, has

---

13. *Pinter v. Dahl*, 486 U.S. 622 (1988).

14. *See, e.g., Rosenzweig et al. v. Azurix Corp. et al.*, 332 F.3d 854, 870–71 (5th Cir. 2003).

read this language as requiring affirmative due diligence—even in connection with audited financial statements—in order to sustain the defense.[15] The ABA Task Force Report criticized the Seventh Circuit decision and concluded that it should be confined to its facts.[16]

Section 12(a)(2) does not refer to expertization (e.g., of financial statements) as a part of a seller's defense, but presumably reliance on an expert is a factor to be considered in determining whether the seller has acted with "reasonable care." And, until recently, it was also unclear under Section 12(a)(2) whether a defendant could benefit from "negative causation" as in the case of a Section 11 claim, that is, to be able to reduce the amount of damages by showing that the reduction in value of the purchased security resulted from factors not relating to a misstatement or omission. As amended by the Private Securities Litigation Reform Act of 1995, Section 12(a)(2) claims are now subject to such a "negative causation" defense.

Section 13 of the 1933 Act provides that an action under Section 12(a)(2) must be brought within the same time frame as required for actions brought under Section 11. As discussed above in connection with Section 11, the Sarbanes–Oxley provisions dealing with the statute of limitations for certain claims should not affect the Section 13 periods applicable to Section 12(a)(2) claims.

- *Rule 10b-5*

Section 12(a)(2) by its terms does not apply to securities exempt from 1933 Act registration pursuant to Section 3(a)(2).

---

15. *Sanders v. John Nuveen & Co.*, 619 F.2d 1222 (7th Cir. 1980), *cert. denied*, 450 U.S. 1005 (1981). Justices Powell and Rehnquist dissented from the denial of *certiorari* on the ground that the Court of Appeals had improperly imposed the "higher duty" of inquiry contemplated by Section 11 without giving the defendants the opportunity to assert the "expertization" defense permitted by the same section.

16. ABA Task Force Report, *supra* note 1, at 1238. It would be easier to disregard the Seventh Circuit decision if it had not been written by Judge John Paul Stevens, subsequently elevated to the Supreme Court.

Also, according to the Supreme Court's *Gustafson* decision, Section 12(a)(2) does not apply to private placements.[17] For many years, however, the federal courts have implied a private remedy from the SEC's Rule 10b-5 that is applicable to all purchases and sales of securities. Persons who sue under Rule 10b-5 enjoy some advantages and face a number of disadvantages. The major advantage of Rule 10b-5 is that it reaches all persons who commit a disclosure violation "in connection with the purchase or sale of any security." It is not limited, like Section 11 or Section 12(a)(2), to specific categories of defendants. The reach of the rule has been somewhat curtailed, to be sure, by a U.S. Supreme Court decision that rejected the ability of plaintiffs to use Rule 10b-5 to reach persons who merely "aided and abetted" another person's violation of Rule 10b-5.[18]

As an implied remedy based on common law deceit, Rule 10b-5 has been held to require proof that the defendant acted with scienter—that is, that he intentionally or at least recklessly acted to cause a disclosure violation. Also, the Reform Act requires a plaintiff to state facts in the complaint that "giv[e]

---

17. This should be the case notwithstanding that the offering memorandum in the private placement contains the same information that one would find in a 1933 Act prospectus, that the private placement contemplated a subsequent registered exchange offer or resale registration statement or that the offering memorandum was distributed to a large number of eligible purchasers. *See, e.g., Hayes Lenmerz Securities Litig.*, 271 F. Supp. 2d 1007, 1026–28 (E.D. Mich. 2003), referring also to an SEC letter filed in a separate litigation stating the SEC's view that the "more likely reading" of *Gustafson* is that there is no Section 12(a)(2) liability for a Rule 144A private placement even where it is to be followed by a registered exchange offer.

18. *Central Bank of Denver v. First Interstate Bank of Denver*, 511 U.S. 164 (1994). The SEC has recently persuaded at least one federal court that a law firm could be sued as a "primary violator" of Rule 10b-5 where it "created" or acted as a "co-author" of misrepresentations drafted for inclusion in documents to be given to investors. *In re Enron Corp. Securities, Derivative and ERISA Litig.*, 235 F. Supp. 2d 549, 587 (S.D. Tex. 2002). Many observers would have viewed the law firm's conduct as amounting to no more than "aiding and abetting," conduct that *Central Bank* had said would not support a private right of action under Rule 10b-5.

rise to a strong inference that the defendant acted with the required state of mind." The appellate courts are split on the degree to which the Reform Act raised the pleading standard.[19]

A claim under Rule 10b-5 also requires proof of reliance, although the courts often apply the "fraud-on-the-market" theory to provide a rebuttable presumption of reliance on information disclosed by an issuer in an efficient securities market. The courts have also held, and the Reform Act confirmed, that Rule 10b-5 requires that the plaintiff's loss be "caused" by the alleged disclosure violation. Some courts also require "transaction causation," that is, that the plaintiff would not have entered into the purchase or sale of securities but for the alleged fraud.

Defendants under Rule 10b-5 have the same defenses as defendants under Sections 11 and 12(a)(2) based on the Reform Act's safe harbors for forward-looking statements and on the court-created "bespeaks caution" doctrine.

Rule 10b-5 claims are typically thrown into complaints arising out of securities offerings along with claims based on Section 11, Section 12(a)(2), state securities law remedies and common law remedies. Because of the scienter requirement, Rule 10b-5 is generally thought to represent a "fraud-based" remedy, unlike Section 11 or Section 12(a)(2), which are generally regarded as "negligence-based" remedies. It is difficult to see how an underwriter or other defendant who has performed sufficient due diligence to prevail under Section 11 or Section 12(a)(2) could

---

19. The Ninth Circuit reads the pleading standard as calling for allegations of "deliberately reckless or conscious misconduct . . . that strongly suggests an actual intent" (e.g., *In re Silicon Graphics Inc. Securities Litig.*, 183 F.3d 970, *reh'g en banc denied*, 195 F.3d 521 (9th Cir. 1999)). One court in the Ninth Circuit has compared the required defendant state of mind to that of "a driver that attempts to speed across railroad tracks in front of a rapidly approaching and visible oncoming train." *In re Southern Pac. Funding Corp. Securities Lit.*, 83 F. Supp. 2d 1172, 1177 (D. Or. 1999). The Second Circuit takes the position that the Reform Act merely codified that Circuit's pre–Reform Act willingness to accept allegations of either motive and opportunity or "strong circumstantial evidence of conscious misbehavior or recklessness." *Novak v. Kasaks*, 216 F.3d 300 (2d Cir. 2000).

possibly be found to have acted with scienter so as to be exposed on a Rule 10b-5 claim.

As noted above, the remedy provided by Rule 10b-5 has been implied by the courts. Understandably, there is therefore no specific federal statute of limitations (such as Section 13 of the 1933 Act) applicable to claims brought under Rule 10b-5. At one time, plaintiffs were able to rely on state statutes of limitations—which are frequently longer than those set forth in Section 13 of the 1933 Act—to provide the period within which a claim had to be brought. This advantage disappeared in 1991 when the U.S. Supreme Court decided that the appropriate statute of limitations for a Rule 10b-5 claim was that found in Section 9(e) of the 1934 Act: "one year after the discovery of the facts constituting the violation and within three years after such violation."[20] And in 2002, Section 804 of Sarbanes–Oxley extended these periods to two years and five years, respectively, for proceedings commenced on or after the date of enactment of the statute.[21]

Nearly all recent court decisions have refused to imply a private right of action from Section 17(a) of the 1933 Act;[22] however, Section 17(a) remains available to the SEC as a basis for enforcement proceedings, and the SEC appears to be making more frequent use of Section 17(a) for this purpose.

- *Controlling Persons*

Section 15 under the 1933 Act provides that every person who controls any person liable under Section 11 or Section 12 shall also be liable jointly and severally with and to the same

---

20. *Lampf, Pleva, Lipkind, Prupis & Petigrow v. Gilbertson*, 501 U.S. 350, 364 (1991).

21. At least one court has held that Section 804 of Sarbanes–Oxley does not have the effect of reviving claims that were time-barred at the date of enactment. *In re Enterprise Mortgage Acceptance Co. Securities Litig.*, 295 F. Supp. 2d 307 (S.D.N.Y. 2003).

22. *See* Richard W. Jennings, Harold Marsh, Jr. & John C. Coffee, Jr., *Securities Regulation: Cases and Materials* 836–39 (7th ed. 1992) (collecting cases).

extent as such controlled person unless the controlling person "had no knowledge of or reasonable ground to believe in the existence of the facts by reason of which the liability of the controlled person is alleged to exist." Section 20(a) of the 1934 Act contains a similar provision that could render a controlling person liable for a Rule 10b-5 violation by a person it controls "unless the controlling person acted in good faith and did not directly or indirectly induce the act or acts constituting the violation or cause of action." Both of these provisions are sometimes used to expand the scope of a lawsuit to include persons such as parent companies and major holders of voting securities.

SEC and Judicial Interpretations Concerning Due Diligence

There have been relatively few interpretations by the SEC or the courts as to the type of investigation that will satisfy the due diligence standard applicable to a particular offering.[23]

Of course, the SEC prescribes the contents of registration statements under the 1933 Act by its adoption of registration forms and disclosure rules such as Regulation S-K. It also administers the public offering process by reviewing and commenting on registration statements and 1934 Act periodic reports, and it has the ability to capture issuers' and underwriters' attention by its public pronouncements about the kind of disclosure that it deems to be responsive to its requirements and the needs of investors.

For example, the SEC has warned underwriters that the level of due diligence required in connection with new high-risk ventures is particularly high. In its view, a "thorough and intensive underwriters' investigation is especially important in an initial public offering by companies in the developmental stage or those dealing with 'high technology' products or processes."[24] This was in 1972!

---

23. *See generally*, on the subject of underwriters' due diligence, the ABA Task Force Report, *supra* note 1.

24. SEC Release No. 33-5275 (July 26, 1972).

On the other hand, the SEC has no formal role in private civil actions brought under Section 11 or Section 12(a)(2) or even under Rule 10b-5. It seldom files amicus briefs on due diligence questions, for example, in support of or in opposition to motions to dismiss or for summary judgment. With the exception of Rule 176 adopted in 1982, it has steadfastly declined to lay down specific rules or safe harbors that might constrain a court's assessment of the reasonableness of an underwriter's conduct.

The SEC has, however, made clear in several key enforcement proceedings its view that due diligence is not just an affirmative defense that underwriters may or may not choose to assert if they happen to be sued under Section 11 or Section 12(a)(2) case. Rather, due diligence in its view may be an affirmative obligation arising out of an underwriter's general obligation to deal fairly with its customers.

- *SEC Administrative Proceedings*

As early as 1953, the SEC found that an underwriter "owe[d] a duty to the investing public to exercise a degree of care reasonable under the circumstances of th[e] offering to assure the substantial accuracy of representations made in the prospectus . . . ."[25] In a 1963 stop order proceeding, *In re The Richmond Corp.*,[26] the SEC criticized an underwriter for failing to perform a reasonable investigation. The SEC stressed that reliance on the representations of management does not satisfy the obligations imposed on an underwriter. It noted critically that the underwriter's investigation of the issuer's business consisted of visits to two of its three tracts of land, an examination of a list of its shareholders, and obtaining a credit report, and that, as to all other matters in connection with the registration statement, the underwriter relied only on representations of management. The SEC concluded that this did not constitute the "investigation in accordance with professional standards" that an underwriter impliedly represents that it has made when it associates

---

25. *In re Charles E. Bailey & Co.*, 35 S.E.C. 33, 41 (1953).
26. *In re The Richmond Corp.*, 41 S.E.C. 398 (1963).

itself with an offering. "The underwriter who does not make a reasonable investigation is derelict in his responsibilities to deal fairly with the investing public."

The SEC has often embraced the idea expressed in *Richmond* that an underwriter has an *affirmative obligation* to perform a reasonable investigation—that is, that an underwriter is not free simply to "take its chances" whether it will need to invoke a due diligence defense. Apart from the "shingle theory" approach in *Richmond*, it has also based this idea on the theory that by participating in an offering an underwriter makes an implied recommendation of the securities being offered, and that under general antifraud principles it must have an "adequate basis" for such a recommendation.[27]

In connection with the 1992 settlement of an administrative proceeding involving municipal securities, the SEC issued a report in which it summarized its views about an underwriter's affirmative obligation to make a reasonable investigation.[28] It found the underwriter to have violated Section 17(a) of the 1933 Act and Rule 10b-5 in not following up on information known to the underwriter that called into question the legitimacy of certain key transactions. Significantly, it found that the presence of underwriter's counsel at some of the key meetings did not excuse the underwriter from its obligation "to adequately explore questions concerning the business and financial aspects of the offering which were raised during the due diligence process."

- *The* BarChris *Case*

The first extended discussion by a court of the due diligence defense was Judge McLean's opinion in *BarChris*.[29] BarChris was engaged in the construction and installation of bowling alleys, an industry that had experienced dramatic growth after

---

27. *See, e.g.*, SEC Release No. 34-26100 (September 22, 1988).

28. *In re Donaldson, Lufkin & Jenrette Securities Corp.*, SEC Release No. 34-31207 (September 22, 1992).

29. *Escott v. BarChris Construction Corp.*, 283 F. Supp. 643 (S.D.N.Y. 1968).

automatic pinsetters were first introduced in 1952. The company's sales had increased over the years and, to meet its need for working capital, it sold subordinated debentures under a registration statement that became effective in 1961. Drexel & Co. was the managing underwriter.

In 1961 and 1962, it became apparent that the industry was overbuilt, and BarChris filed for bankruptcy in 1962. Judge McLean found that the registration statement covering the debentures was false and misleading and that Drexel & Co. had not satisfied the due diligence standard.

In the course of their investigation, the managing underwriter and its counsel reviewed only a limited range of materials. They read the annual reports and prospectuses of other bowling alley builders, a prior prospectus and earlier reports of the company, minutes of the company's board of directors and executive committee, and minutes of certain subsidiaries. They contacted BarChris's banks and James Talcott Inc., its factor, inquired about the company, and received favorable replies. They also obtained a Dun & Bradstreet report. A series of meetings was held with several BarChris officers at which the registration statement was considered and reviewed. Several of the points that later became the subject of the lawsuit were discussed at these meetings. As to these matters, representatives of the company assured the managing underwriter and its counsel that there were no problems.

The court found that the managing underwriter and its counsel had not made an adequate review of documents. They did not insist on the preparation of missing minutes, nor did they inspect the notes of meetings for which no minutes were available. They failed to ask for a schedule of customer delinquencies or for copies of such delinquencies and correspondence from Talcott. They did not review contracts with Talcott or the company's customers. Many of these documents contained information that would have alerted them to the problems facing the company.

Judge McLean expressed his views on the proper relationship between underwriters and management as follows:

> In a sense, the positions of the underwriter and the company's officers are adverse. It is not unlikely that

statements made by company officers to an underwriter to induce him to underwrite may be self-serving. They may be unduly enthusiastic. As in this case, they may, on occasion, be deliberately false.[30]

For the underwriters' participation in an offering to be of any value to investors, it was therefore necessary for the underwriters to "make some reasonable attempt to verify the data submitted to them. They may not rely solely on the company's officers or on the company's counsel. A prudent man in the management of his own property would not rely on them."[31]

Not surprisingly, Judge McLean refused to be specific as to the degree of effort required in order to perform a "reasonable investigation." It was impossible to lay down a rigid rule. Rather, "[i]t is a question of degree, a matter of judgment in each case."[32]

- *The* Leasco Data Processing *Case*

In *Leasco Data Processing*,[33] the court found that the dealer managers for a registered exchange offer had "just barely" satisfied the due diligence standard and were accordingly not liable under Section 11. The case involved an exchange offer by Leasco for the outstanding shares of Reliance Insurance Company. A major factor in Leasco's decision to seek to acquire Reliance was the latter's "surplus surplus," that portion of its surplus not required to support its insurance operations. The exchange offer prospectus did not quantify the amount of surplus surplus.

Prior to acting as dealer-managers in this transaction, White Weld & Co. and Lehman Brothers examined the report of an actuary and several other reports that specifically dealt with surplus surplus. Meetings were held with Leasco officers, at which time the surplus surplus issue was explored. Uncertainty existed as to the exact amount of Reliance's surplus surplus in that there

---

30. *Id.* at 696–97.
31. *Id.* at 697.
32. *Id.*
33. *Feit v. Leasco Data Processing Equip. Corp.*, 332 F. Supp. 544 (E.D.N.Y. 1971).

were several methods of calculation and the basic data for the calculation were in the possession of Reliance and the Pennsylvania Insurance Commission.

A key element in the underwriters' due diligence defense was their lack of access to the information necessary to calculate surplus surplus. The underwriters were unable to review the data primarily because of the hostility of the members of Reliance's management and their refusal to cooperate in the preparation of the registration statement. Several weeks prior to the effectiveness of the registration statement, however, Reliance and Leasco entered into an agreement of which the dealer-managers were aware. This agreement provided for the cooperation of Reliance's management. Even after this agreement was signed, however, counsel for the dealer-managers received a copy of a letter from Leasco's counsel to the SEC stating that the Reliance management still declined to furnish any information.

The weakness in the due diligence of the dealer-managers was, first, that they did not attempt to contact directly third parties having the necessary information and, second, that they failed after the agreement was signed to insist that Leasco press its new advantage in order to obtain the surplus surplus data from Reliance. The court described the dealer-managers' role as being "to exercise a high degree of care in investigation and independent verification of the company's representations"; in this connection, they must play "devil's advocate." The court concluded, however, that "on balance" the dealer-managers had "just barely" managed to establish the reasonableness of their investigation, including the verification of Leasco's representations that access to Reliance's management was not available.[34]

- *The* Chris-Craft *Case*

The Second Circuit's decision in *Chris-Craft*[35] also discussed the due diligence obligation of underwriters, albeit in the somewhat unusual context of Section 14(e) of the 1934 Act. The

---

34. *Id.* at 583.
35. *Chris-Craft Industries, Inc. v. Piper Aircraft Corp.*, 480 F.2d 341 (2d Cir.), *cert. denied*, 414 U.S. 910 (1973).

following excerpt from Judge Timbers' opinion relates to the liability of First Boston, as dealer-manager of a registered exchange offer, for the lack of disclosure in the registration statement of a proposed disposition by Bangor-Punta Corp. to Amoskeag Corp. of its interest in the Bangor & Aroostook Railroad:

> Since we already have concluded that the BPC [BangorPunta Corp.] registration statement and prospectus were materially deficient, the remaining issue to be determined is First Boston's culpability. First Boston is a skilled, experienced and well respected dealer-manager and underwriter. It had an obligation with respect to the BPC exchange offer to reach a careful, independent judgment based on facts known to it as to the accuracy of the registration statement. Moreover, if it was aware of facts that strongly suggested, even though they did not conclusively show, that the registration materials were deceptive, it was duty-bound to make a reasonable further investigation.
>
> We hold that First Boston did not adequately perform its duty in these respects. . . . First Boston did not seek verification of the officials' answer that a sale [of the Bangor & Aroostook Railroad to Amoskeag] was not anticipated at that time. . . . It did not make a more careful search of BPC's records, nor did it talk to officials at Amoskeag after it discovered from the minutes that Amoskeag was the likely buyer. Under these circumstances, First Boston's certification of the BPC registration statement carrying the BAR [Bangor & Aroostook Railroad] at $18.4 million amounted to an almost complete abdication of its responsibility to potential investors, to CCI [Chris-Craft Industries], and to others who relied upon it to detect misrepresentations.[36]

---

36. *Id.* at 371–73. Of course, there was then and is now no such concept as "certification" of a registration statement, particularly by an underwriter.

- *Summary Judgment*

Because the adequacy of due diligence is so oriented to the facts and circumstances of a particular offering, underwriters have seldom been able to prevail on motions for summary judgment. In recent years, however, courts appear to be more willing to dispose of cases at an early stage. In one decision,[37] the Ninth Circuit affirmed most of the trial court's grant of a summary judgment motion in favor of underwriters. On one issue, however, it deemed summary judgment to be inappropriate. This issue involved the issuer's booking of large consignment sales at the end of the most recent quarter. The Ninth Circuit found that the underwriters, despite the presence of "red flags" as to these sales, had done little more for their due diligence investigation than to rely on the issuer's assurances that these sales were legitimate. It was, therefore, inappropriate to grant summary judgment on the adequacy of due diligence on this issue.[38]

- *Few Judicial Decisions*

As noted in the ABA Task Force Report, one of the major reasons that cases such as *BarChris* still loom large in any discussion of underwriters' due diligence is that there have been so few judicial opinions on the subject. The fact is that defendants in Section 11 litigation tend to settle cases without proceeding to trial for a full development of relevant facts that can then be analyzed in a judicial opinion.[39] It has even been

---

37. *In re Software Toolworks Inc. Securities Litig.*, 50 F.3d 615 (9th Cir. 1994).

38. Other decisions involving successful underwriter motions for summary judgments based at least in part on the due diligence defense include *Weinberger v. Jackson*, [1990–1991 Transfer Binder] Fed. Sec. L. Rep. (CCH) ¶95,693 (N.D. Cal. 1990); *In re International Rectifier Securities Litig.*, [1997 Transfer Binder] Fed. Sec. L. Rep. (CCH) ¶99,469 (C.D. Cal. 1997); *Picard Chemical Inc. Profit Sharing Plan v. Perrigo Co.*, 1998 U.S. Dist. LEXIS 11783 (W.D. Mich. 1998); and *Lilley v. Charren*, 1999 U.S. Dist. LEXIS 23061 (N.D. Cal. 1999), *aff'd*, 17 Fed. Appx. 603, 2001 U.S. App. LEXIS 19430 (9th Cir. 2001).

39. ABA Task Force Report, *supra* note 1, at 1210–12, 1229–30.

asserted on the basis of an admittedly incomplete collection of data that the pressures to settle are so great that the merits of a Section 11 claim appear to have little to do with the amount for which a case is settled.[40]

Due Diligence Standards

The discussion in this chapter about due diligence as a defense to liability should not obscure the fact that the more important function of due diligence is to verify the premises underlying the transaction and to minimize reputational risk to the underwriter and financial loss to the investor. In this sense, the best due diligence is that which prevents a bad transaction from getting done in the first place.

It follows that effective due diligence cannot take place if the persons conducting due diligence are in the dark about the premises of the transaction. This applies to underwriters' counsel, issuer's counsel and anyone else advising on disclosure matters. The client must be made to understand that disclosure is too important to leave to the lawyers!

What are the strengths and weaknesses of the issuer's business plan? Is its management capable of executing it? What internal or external events or trends could jeopardize success? What is the state of the issuer's technology? Who are the current and potential competitors? What is it, with the benefit of hindsight, that we might be wishing we had done a year or two from now?

Only a frank discussion between lawyer and client can answer these questions and identify potential disclosure problems. And only a frank discussion can address the question of resources. Time and money are always in short supply in securities transactions, and every transaction—even the largest IPO—requires a sensible allocation of resources and establishment of priorities. Again, this cannot be successfully accomplished without communication and cooperation.

---

40. Janet C. Alexander, *Do the Merits Matter? A Study of Settlements in Securities Class Actions*, 43 Stan. L. Rev. 497 (1991).

When an investment banker is dealing with an established and "seasoned" client, the amount of due diligence required in connection with a particular offering may be substantially less than in the case of a new client or one that has only recently become an SEC-reporting company. In some cases, the investment banker may be engaged in a continuous due diligence process through its day-to-day work with the client. Its knowledge of the client may be so extensive that an update is all that is required. In most cases, however, the amount of due diligence that must be exercised will fall somewhere between the two extremes.

The standard of due diligence is especially unclear in connection with an offering of securities registered on a "shelf" basis, usually by means of a registration statement on Form S-3, which incorporates by reference the issuer's most recent Form 10-K and subsequent filings under the 1934 Act. Investment bankers and their counsel have been concerned that the underwriters could be held liable for inadequate disclosure in the Form 10-K and other documents incorporated by reference in the Form S-3 prospectus, documents that the underwriters and their counsel had no role in preparing. These concerns are magnified when securities are "taken down" on short notice from the shelf. Even where the underwriters and their counsel have reviewed the documents incorporated by reference and identified areas of concern, they may find the issuer reluctant to amend the filed documents. Due diligence concerns in the context of shelf registration statements and Form S-3 are discussed in Chapter 8.

As indicated above, courts have criticized underwriters for relying on representations by an issuer's management without independent verification. But it would be unreasonable to expect underwriters to verify every statement that appears in a prospectus. The extent to which underwriters should independently verify factual statements depends on the importance of the information being disclosed and whether management has the motivation and opportunity to misstate the facts.

In other words, a rule of reason must be applied in deciding which facts provided by management should be made the subject of independent verification. The process of verifying facts, however, should not obscure the real thrust of due diligence, which is understanding and verifying the premises underlying the transaction.

Due Diligence Procedures

Not all of the due diligence procedures discussed in this chapter are called for in every securities offering. And many desirable procedures simply cannot be performed given the available time and resources. Shelf takedowns and IPOs are very different transactions. We therefore discuss in this section the procedures that might be applied to a hypothetical transaction where time and resources are plentiful and where the issuer has the requisite degree of patience. For convenience, we discuss these procedures as they might be considered chronologically in the context of the underwriting process.

- *Integrity of Management*

Before committing to underwrite securities for a client, a securities firm should be satisfied as to the integrity of the client's management. Many financial scandals involving inadequate disclosure in registration statements or other SEC filings, including some of those preceding the enactment of Sarbanes–Oxley, have involved outright fraud on the part of management. No amount of due diligence can ensure an accurate registration statement if the issuer's officers are prepared to withhold or falsify information. Nor are there any due diligence procedures guaranteed to identify such persons.

In the case of a long-standing investment banking client, the relationships that have developed over the years can provide a high degree of assurance of management integrity. These relationships are becoming fewer and fewer, with the decline in relationship-based investment banking and the increase in management turnover. But especially in the case of a new client, or an existing client with new and unknown management, it may be in order to make inquiries to determine whether the company is being run by people on whom the investment banker is willing to stake its reputation. Such inquiries may be difficult at times, particularly if it is important to maintain the confidentiality of a proposed financing. Also, there may be legitimate concern that the very fact that inquiries are being made would, in the eyes of management, imply a lack of trust.

In some instances, it may be appropriate to go no further than to rely on a LexisNexis or Google check or on the judgment of persons within the securities firm such as a knowledgeable branch office manager or research analyst. If there is any hint of sharp practices, questionable accounting, previous difficulties with the SEC or litigation that reflects on the integrity of management, more probing inquiries will be necessary. For example, specialized firms may be retained to conduct background checks. In some cases, it may be appropriate, with the consent of management, to speak with the company's commercial bankers and with some of its major suppliers and customers.

Of course, management's choice of underwriters, counsel, outside directors and accountants can sometimes speak loudly about its business standards. One should resist the assumption that management must be honest and capable simply because they had the good sense to retain one's client!

Management integrity goes hand in hand with confidence, patience, determination, resourcefulness and the other qualities that enable management—without taking shortcuts—to pursue a business model and to adapt it to changed circumstances. Nothing can destroy investors' confidence in a company more surely than revelations of disclosure or accounting irregularities, which quickly send the market a strong signal that the business model is not working.

Many underwriters have a formal procedure for approving their participation in securities offerings, particularly as managing underwriter. The procedure ordinarily involves written reports to a commitment committee by those of the underwriter's personnel who are supporting the establishment of a relationship with the issuer. These reports are part of the underwriter's due diligence just as much as the comfort letter and legal opinions. They should be prepared with a commensurate degree of care.

- *Effect of the Transaction on the Issuer's Financial Statements*

Until recently, most investment bankers would have assumed that it was exclusively the responsibility of the issuer and its accountants to worry about the accounting consequences of a transaction. While this is still true, at least in a formal sense, it would be foolish not to recognize that the SEC, banking regulators and the criminal prosecutors have recently and emphatically taken the position that financial intermediaries cannot "turn a blind eye" to the consequences of the transactions that they arrange for their issuer clients. In 2003, a number of financial institutions entered into settlements with the SEC and federal and state banking authorities and criminal prosecutors arising out of their participation in transactions for Enron Corp., Dynegy Inc., and other companies that allegedly helped these companies mislead their investors by characterizing what were essentially loan proceeds as cash from operating activities. Three bank holding companies paid $135 million, $120 million and $80 million as disgorgement, penalties and interest, respectively.[41] A major securities firm paid $80 million, and a major insurance holding company paid $10 million.[42]

Two of the bank holding companies also entered into an agreement with the Federal Reserve Bank of New York in which each of them agreed to submit an acceptable legal and reputational risk management program that would, among other things, identify transactions in which the counterparty relationship or the nature of the transaction with the counterparty would pose heightened legal or reputational risk. The program would include a requirement that thorough assessments of legal and reputational risks be incorporated into the institution's "transactional approval process" as well as its "transactional monitoring activities," with emphasis on "complete and accurate disclosure of the counterparty's purpose in entering into the particular transaction" and on obtaining complete and accurate information about the

---

41. SEC Litigation Release No. 18252 (July 28, 2003) (J.P. Morgan Chase & Co.); SEC Release No. 34-48230 (July 28, 2003) (Citigroup, Inc.); SEC Litigation Release No. 18517 (December 22, 2003) (Canadian Imperial Bank of Commerce).

42. SEC Litigation Release No. 18038 (March 17, 2003) (Merrill Lynch & Co. et al.); SEC Litigation Release No. 18340 (September 11, 2003) (American International Group et al.).

counterparty's proposed accounting treatment of the transaction and the effect of the transaction on the counterparty's financial disclosures. The program would call for a higher level review in all instances that present heightened risk, "in particular where the counterparty's primary purpose, goal or objective in entering into a transaction is to achieve an accounting or tax effect." A third bank holding company entered into a similar agreement that contained a three-year bar on its entering into any "structured finance" transactions on behalf of any third party.[43]

It hardly pays to earn a fee or league table credit for a transaction that later explodes into a legal and reputational disaster.

- *Corporate Governance*

Until recently, underwriters also paid relatively little attention to an issuer's corporate governance standards. If investors didn't like the way the company was run, they didn't have to buy the company's securities. This has changed with the corporate governance reforms introduced by Sarbanes–Oxley and the widespread belief that good corporate governance practices go hand in hand with good management. Even some analysts and rating agencies now rank companies at least in part based on corporate governance considerations. Underwriters are therefore taking into consideration a company's governance when deciding whether to undertake a transaction, with special emphasis on the quality, independence and engagement of the company's audit committee. Management compensation and related party transactions are other considerations likely to play an increasing role.

"Good" corporate governance does not always translate into good disclosure, and even companies ranked low in the corporate governance surveys may have exemplary disclosure. But it is hard to overlook the fact that many recent corporate scandals have involved companies with passive audit committees and

---

43. The agreements are available on the Federal Reserve Board's website at www.federalreserve.gov. *See also* the related discussion in Chapter 11 and the proposed Interagency Statement of Sound Practices Concerning Complex Structures Finance Activities, SEC Release No. 34-49695 (May 14, 2004).

boards, highly compensated management and significant related party transactions. At some point, corporate governance "deficiencies" rise to the level of red flags that require more careful investigation.

- *Staffing*

It is important for the investment bankers and their counsel to assign people to the transaction who are sufficiently prepared to carry out their responsibilities. This includes anticipating the need for bankers or lawyers with specialized expertise in areas such as intellectual property, real estate, pensions, employment law and the various regulatory disciplines (food and drug, communications, banking, insurance, tax, securities, etc.). Statistical expertise may be relevant to the issuer's required disclosures relating to market risk.

All the expertise in the world will count for little if the members of the team are poorly instructed or managed. Securities lawyers should remember the adverse inference drawn by Judge McLean in *BarChris* from the fact that a junior associate[44] had failed to identify important information during the course of reading minutes. It is vital that each member of the team understand his or her responsibilities and how these relate to the underwriters' overall objective of conducting a reasonable investigation.

In particular, members of the legal team (especially junior ones) should understand why due diligence is important to the achievement of their clients' objectives of completing a transaction with an intact reputation, happy customers and no prospect of litigation in the future.

Each member of the legal team should also understand who is and who is not the client. In representing an underwriter, the client is not the banker on the transaction but rather the underwriter as an entity.

Team members should understand the role of other members of the team in order to minimize the likelihood of duplication

---

44. "Stanton was a very junior associate. He had been admitted to the bar . . . some three months before. This was the first registration statement he had ever worked on." 283 F. Supp. at 694 n.23.

of effort or—often worse—the erroneous assumption that someone else is handling an important task. In the view of the authors, junior lawyers who read minutes and review corporate documents should also participate in drafting sessions. Such participation provides a context for their other work, and they may be better prepared than anyone else in the room to spot an issue that relates to their work.

Team members should understand the documentation policies that will govern the transaction. They should be encouraged to work in an organized fashion and to memorialize their work on a contemporaneous basis. Records are more convincing when written close to the fact, and prompt preparation of written memoranda facilitates their circulation to other persons involved in the transaction.

It goes without saying that junior team members should be encouraged to ask questions and raise potential problems. One of the authors is fond of observing that "there are no dumb questions, only dumb assumptions." After all, as *BarChris* illustrates, some issuers have sought to mislead underwriters in the past, and some will undoubtedly continue to do so in the future. Persons working on due diligence should therefore be encouraged to develop what the accountants call "professional skepticism," that is, "neither assum[ing] that management is dishonest nor assum[ing] unquestioned honesty" and not being satisfied "with less than persuasive evidence because of a belief that management is honest."[45]

Team members should also be warned of the dangers of complacency, of "tunnel vision," and of losing objectivity. They should be encouraged to stay informed, budget their time and regard their efforts as an indispensable learning experience.

A lawyer engaged in due diligence must have faith in his or her instincts and be willing to withstand attempts at intimidation. See the discussion below of the "The Penn Central Affair."

---

45. AICPA, *Codification of Statements on Auditing Standards* AU §230A.09 (2003).

- *Checklists*

Many underwriters and their counsel use checklists as a tool in organizing their due diligence efforts. The danger in relying on a checklist, of course, is that a checklist cannot be devised that will cover all situations. Moreover, checklists can be dangerous in that they may lead the person performing due diligence to believe that the job has been completed if all items on the list are covered. As one of the authors has put it, most checklists are worth no more than one's neighbor's shopping list: they may be interesting, and there may be some overlap, but they cannot be relied on as a guide for prudent behavior. Also, checklists can distract the participants in an offering from the essential due diligence function, which is to understand fully the business of the issuer, to identify the problems it faces and may face in the future, and to ensure that the registration statement is complete and accurate.

These comments should not be understood as a recommendation against the use of checklists. On the contrary, professionals in many critical disciplines such as aviation and health care find them indispensable. But no one securities transaction is exactly like another, and the lawyer must be careful not to be lulled into complacency by reliance on a checklist.

- *Legal Review—Opinion Matters*

Counsel must conduct a legal review of the issuer in order to be able to deliver at the closing the opinions required by the underwriting agreement. Often, as discussed below, the legal review also turns up disclosure issues.

The contents of the legal opinions required at the closing are discussed in Chapter 2. The legal review must be planned with a view to establishing a foundation for these opinions.

In the case of an issuance of stock, for example, counsel will be expected to opine that the shares being delivered at the closing have been duly and validly authorized and issued and are fully paid and non-assessable and that the shares conform to the description of the issuer's common stock contained in the prospectus. In the case of an issuance of debt securities, counsel will be expected to opine that the debt securities have been duly authorized, executed, authenticated, issued and delivered and represent valid and legally binding obligations of the issuer. An opinion covering these matters must be based on a review of the issuer's certificate of incorporation and by-laws and the minutes of the meetings at which the board or its committees took relevant action.

Minutes of meetings of the issuer's board of directors should be reviewed for at least three years and possibly five years. The minutes of the board's significant committees should be reviewed for the same period. Which committees are "significant" will vary from company to company, but the reviewing lawyer should try to form some independent understanding of how the board delegates authority rather than rely entirely on what he or she is told by the custodian of the corporate records. It is hard to imagine that the lawyer will not be reviewing in every case the minutes of the executive committee (if one has been established) and the audit committee.

The minutes of shareholders' meetings may also need to be reviewed to confirm the absence or adequacy of action taken that bears on the company's ability to offer securities. Subsidiaries' board and committee meeting minutes may also have to be reviewed, particularly if the subsidiary has a role in the transaction but also (as discussed below) for disclosure purposes.

The lawyer assigned to read minutes should know what he or she is looking for in terms of the corporate action to be verified for opinion purposes and in terms of the important disclosure issues for the offering. The lawyer should be on the alert for gaps in the minute books, any evidence of alterations in the written record or any signs that material transactions have occurred without corporate authorization.

Underwriters' counsel is seldom requested any longer to opine on the validity of all of the issuer's outstanding stock. The time and effort required to do so are simply too great, except in the case of recently organized companies. Opining on the stock to be issued is a more straightforward matter. Are there any preemptive rights? Does the company have enough authorized stock? Has the issuance of the stock been properly authorized?

A number of years ago, a major company had restated its certificate of incorporation in a way that inadvertently prevented it

LIABILITIES AND DUE DILIGENCE 339

from declaring dividends on its common stock. It is better to identify such problems before the transaction rather than afterward.

In the case of debt offerings, counsel should verify that the offering will not violate regulatory requirements or covenants in the issuer's other indentures or loan agreements.

Counsel may be required to opine that the issuer is not an "investment company" within the meaning of the Investment Company Act of 1940. This issue is discussed in Chapter 3.

Closing opinions also confirm the accuracy of the description of tax matters contained in the prospectus. It is important to line up one's tax colleagues at an early date in order to be sure that they are aware of the opinion that will be required. It is particularly important to keep them informed about any changes in the transaction.

Finally, it goes without saying that counsel must ensure that the description of the securities in the prospectus is a faithful summary of the actual terms and conditions of the documents constituting the securities. It should be recalled that the closing opinions of both issuer's counsel and underwriters' counsel customarily state that the description of securities contained in the prospectus is an accurate, complete and fair summary of the terms of the securities.

There have been situations where the description of securities in the prospectus has deviated from the constituent documents. Such deviations often arise because different lawyers are responsible for the description and the documents and there is insufficient communication between them as the deal changes. Regrettably, such deviations also occur because the description and the documents are based on "precedents" from two different transactions that were carelessly thought to be identical but contained variations that turned out to be significant. Or sometimes a word processor simply drops a paragraph from an indenture and the red-lining software is defective (this has happened) and the lawyer reviewing the document does not notice the deletion.

- *Legal Review—Disclosure Matters*

The legal review has an important role in the effort to ensure that the prospectus is free of material misstatements and omissions.

Many companies tried over the past few decades to streamline their corporate minutes so that they were often limited to the "bare bones" of corporate housekeeping. At one point, the reading of minutes for disclosure purposes might have become the exception rather than the rule if the minutes of BarChris Construction Corp. and its subsidiaries had not played such a large role in the litigation that bears that company's name.[46] Even before the recent heightened concern about corporate governance, however, sufficient "nuggets" turned up here and there, particularly at the operating division or subsidiary level, to justify continued efforts in this area.

For example, references to a loan to a corporate officer or other related party transaction would frequently trigger the need for additional disclosure. Also, the SEC in a 1992 administrative proceeding against Caterpillar, Inc. relied in part on references in Caterpillar's board minutes to argue that Caterpillar's MD&A should have been expanded to highlight the disproportionate contribution to earnings of its Brazilian subsidiary.[47]

Board minutes have in more recent years become more detailed as boards and their advisers seek to document important decisions in order to demonstrate good corporate governance and also to guard against litigation. Audit committee minutes, in particular, are also becoming more thorough. The review of board and committee minutes is therefore taking on even more importance than in the recent past.

Minute-reading may also shed light on the issuer's view of its litigation or regulatory exposure. There are two tasks here. The first is to verify what litigation or government proceedings have been or may be brought against the issuer. The second is to assess the significance of the proceedings for the issuer, not just in terms of the adequacy of disclosure but also in terms of the issuer's ability to carry on with its business plan. Reports

---

46. In *BarChris,* counsel was criticized for failing to review the minutes of certain subsidiaries and for failing to insist that the minutes of certain recent meetings be prepared.

47. *In re Caterpillar, Inc.*, SEC Release No. 34-30532 (March 31, 1992). See the discussion in Chapter 3.

LIABILITIES AND DUE DILIGENCE 341

to the board on litigation and government proceedings are frequently far more informative on these issues than generalized comments by the issuer's general counsel or the SFAS 5 letters written by the issuer's defense counsel to its auditors.

In assessing the significance of litigation and government proceedings, it may also be helpful to review analysts' reports and the SEC reports or public statements of companies that are similarly situated or that are on the other side of civil actions.

It may be desirable in some situations to review pleadings, but this is seldom cost-effective. In some instances, it may be appropriate to meet with the issuer's outside counsel handling material litigation.

Counsel should review key contracts (especially those referred to in the prospectus or the notes to the financial statements)—including supply and sales agreements, stock option plans and pension and profit sharing plans, employment contracts, leases and license agreements—to the extent material. The purpose is to confirm the accuracy of the references in the prospectus as well as to identify documents that must be filed as exhibits to the registration statement. Sufficient time should be set aside for the making of any application to the SEC for confidential treatment of exhibits that the issuer believes to be eligible for such treatment.[48]

Sometimes, documentary evidence will not suffice to confirm important facts relating to the transaction, and a lawyer will have to go to extraordinary lengths to verify facts that under normal circumstances are not open to question. See the discussion at the end of this chapter regarding the 1972 IPO of Hughes Tool Company, where the entire transaction depended on verifying Howard Hughes' identity and competency.

- *Review of Industry*

A company is much more easily understood against the background of the industry in which it operates. Both the investment bankers and their counsel should therefore become familiar with the industry by means of a study of prospectuses, Form 10-Ks

---

48. *See* Staff Legal Bulletin No. 1A (CF), as amended July 11, 2001.

and annual reports prepared by other companies in the industry. Research reports on the industry and major companies in the industry should be reviewed, including those prepared by other securities firms.

If the industry is subject to a particular system of regulation, as, for example, transportation, banking, insurance or communications, the investment bankers should verify that they are current on any new developments.

The investment bankers should be familiar with relevant trade publications, which may identify environmental problems, litigation exposures or labor difficulties that are of concern to the industry.

- *Role of Analysts in Due Diligence*

The previous edition of this book commented on the then-increasing contribution of research analysts to the success of investment banking transactions, particularly IPOs.[49] It was noted that analysts were playing a major role in helping their firms solicit IPO issuers for the purpose of being named as the managing underwriter of the offering. They also played a major role in the underwriter's due diligence investigation, particularly in the case of high-technology companies where an analyst familiar in general terms with the issuer's products or services could often better analyze the subtle competitive, managerial and technological advantages that make the issuer's securities a good investment. Just as important, the analyst could spot weaknesses in the issuer's strategy or program that need to be investigated as a matter of due diligence and perhaps disclosed in the issuer's IPO prospectus.

Unfortunately, it became clear during and after the Internet Bubble that many analysts had no better idea than anyone else of why some high-technology companies were selling at such high prices. And some analysts allowed investment banking considerations to interfere with their rating judgment.

To curb some of the abuses, NYSE and NASD rules now mandate certain organizational and functional separations

---

49. *See also* Joseph McLaughlin, *The Changing Role of the Securities Analyst in Initial Public Offerings*, 8 Insights 6 (August 1994).

LIABILITIES AND DUE DILIGENCE 343

between investment banking and research personnel. In addition, a "global settlement" announced in 2003 among various regulators and ten large investment banking firms went even farther in separating the two functions. It prohibited analysts from participating in "pitches" for investment banking business or having other communications with issuers for the purpose of soliciting investment banking business, and it prohibited analysts from participating in roadshows relating to public offerings or other investment banking transactions. Analysts' participation in investment banking transactions was limited to providing their views about the merits of a proposed transaction or a candidate for a proposed transaction but only with certain safeguards, and any assistance "in confirming the adequacy of disclosure in offering or other disclosure documents" had to be provided outside the presence of investment banking personnel. After the firm received a mandate, an analyst could communicate his or her views on structuring and pricing the transaction but only to the firm's equity capital markets group, and they could participate with that group in preparing internal-use memoranda and other efforts to educate the sales force.

Notwithstanding these restrictions and subject to an underwriter's Restricted List and other compliance procedures, there is nothing to prevent underwriters' counsel on a transaction from requesting access to the analyst to obtain his or her general views on the industry, including the strengths and weaknesses of competing companies and technologies, and on the issuer and its management. In this connection, it should be kept in mind that the SEC staff often reviews analyst reports on a company or an industry in preparation for reviewing a prospectus or other disclosure document.[50]

Also, IPOs usually cannot be marketed without an earnings estimate. The logical person to prepare such an estimate for use

---

50. The SEC staff also cooperates with other government agencies on matters of corporate disclosure. For example, the SEC and the Food and Drug Administration announced in February 2004 a continuation and enhancement of their cooperative efforts. SEC Press Release 2004-13 (February 5, 2004) (available on SEC website).

by persons engaged in selling the registered securities is the underwriter's own analyst. See the discussion below regarding "Forward-Looking Statements." The "global settlement" leaves it unclear whether such an estimate can still be used at a roadshow, but there appears to be no prohibition against using it in internal sales memoranda and other communications or from passing it on to customers other than in a roadshow setting.

The "global settlement" provisions are to be superseded if and when the SEC adopts a rule or approves an SRO rule or interpretation with the stated intent of superseding any or all of the provisions of the settlement.

- *Issuer's Website and Basic Documents*

Immediately after the investment banking firm decides to proceed with a securities offering, its counsel should check the issuer's website! As noted in Chapter 3, the issuer's website may contain information that could be considered "gun-jumping" in connection with the offering. It may also contain information relevant to the disclosure in connection with the offering, and it is a good idea to check for such information at the earliest opportunity.

Counsel must also consider what basic documents regarding the issuer will need to be reviewed for disclosure purposes. The issuer's 1934 Act filings will be available through the SEC's EDGAR system if the issuer is a reporting company. They may also be available on the issuer's website, but it is a better practice to obtain 1934 Act filings directly from EDGAR. The issuer's website may be relied on for such items as communications to shareholders not sent to the SEC. Other documents must be requested from the issuer.

Documents customarily reviewed include all documents filed with the SEC since the issuer became a reporting company under the 1934 Act or during its past five fiscal years, whichever is less, and all reports and other communications sent to shareholders during this period. Documents filed with the SEC include reports on Form 10-K, Form 8-K and Form 10-Q, registration statements relating to the sale of other securities, and any proxy statements for annual meetings, acquisitions or other transactions requiring a shareholder vote. Documents sent to shareholders include the

LIABILITIES AND DUE DILIGENCE 345

company's annual reports, its quarterly reports, any follow-up reports on its annual meeting, and shareholder letters and press releases.

In the case of an IPO, of course, there will be no alternative but to request many documents from the issuer. Care should be taken to tailor the document request to the specific circumstances of the offering. Nothing can get an offering off to a worse start than sending the issuer a lengthy request for documents that has clearly been generated by a word processor without the application of common sense, including an understanding of what documents are publicly available, or an appreciation of the difficulties and cost that the issuer might experience in attempting to comply with the request.

In reviewing annual and quarterly reports, particular attention should be directed to the chief executive officer's letter to shareholders. Employees' newsletters often contain useful information "from the inside."

In appropriate cases, a LexisNexis, Google or other electronic data base search should be performed to verify product announcements, litigation developments, regulatory proceedings or even personnel changes. If there is a recent private placement memorandum or a written rating agency presentation, this should also be reviewed.

Underwriters' counsel should review all indentures and loan agreements to which the issuer or any subsidiary is a party, primarily for the purpose of evaluating any restrictive covenants and analyzing the impact that they may have on the company's operations and the prospective financing.

As the SEC implements the Sarbanes–Oxley requirement that it review every issuer at least once every three years, there will be fewer and fewer issuers that will not have received recent comments from the SEC on their periodic filings. It is therefore important to verify that there are no open disclosure issues with the SEC staff, either on the accounting or on the disclosure side. For this purpose, it may be necessary to request and to review the issuer's correspondence to and from the SEC, such as comment letters on previous prospectuses or on the issuer's periodic reports and the issuer's response to such comments. As noted in Chapter 3, it is also important to verify that the issuer has made its 1934 Act reports on a timely basis.

- *Questionnaires from Officers, Directors and Other Persons*

A registration statement on Form S-1 must include information on the company's officers and directors, their remuneration and employee benefits, holdings of voting securities and material transactions that they have had or currently have with the company. Information must also be included regarding persons who own more than 5% of any class of voting securities and regarding any arrangements that might result in a change of control of the company. This information need not be included in a registration statement on Form S-3, but it must be included in the issuer's documents incorporated by reference.

If securities are being registered for resale, the registration statement must include specified information on the selling securityholders.

It is standard procedure for issuer's counsel to prepare one or more questionnaires addressed to these disclosure requirements. In the case of a registration statement on Form S-3, underwriters' counsel could—but seldom do—request access to the questionnaires completed in connection with the most recent Form 10-K and proxy statement incorporated by reference. This may become a more frequent request as underwriters' counsel seek to confirm that the form of questionnaire includes all the new information required by Sarbanes–Oxley.

At least in the case of a registration statement on Form S-1, counsel for the underwriters should review the completed questionnaires and compare the responses with the disclosure in the registration statement. This is not an exercise that should be put off until the last minute.

In most cases, questionnaires serve a backstop function since the company probably has more reliable information on the matters required to be disclosed. This is more the case, of course, for officers and directors than it may be for securityholders. It goes without saying that blind reliance on questionnaires is unwarranted, and underwriters' counsel should be alert to any evidence in company documents or the public record that might contradict responses to the questionnaires.

An effort should be made to encourage the use of questionnaires that are in "plain English." There are forms of questionnaires now in use that contain language that is even

LIABILITIES AND DUE DILIGENCE 347

more complex and obscure than the SEC rules on which the questionnaires are based. A director, officer or selling security-holder should not have to consult counsel to figure out what information is being requested.

- *Review of Registration Statement*

After receiving the first draft of the registration statement, underwriters and their counsel should read it carefully for content and against the items of the applicable form and Regulation S-K (to the extent covered by the applicable form), and should note any questions or suggestions for improved disclosure. They should then meet with the officers of the company responsible for the registration statement, the company's counsel and a representative of the issuer's accountants for the purpose of reviewing the registration statement on a line-by-line basis.

As the issuer's accounting firm will have general knowledge of all aspects of the issuer's business, not only its financial reporting, it can be helpful for a representative of the accountants to be present at all review sessions, not just those relating to the financial statements. Accountants sometimes resist this suggestion, for liability as well as cost reasons.

During the review process, the disclosure in the registration statement will be discussed in depth, and invariably the registration statement will be revised in an effort to improve on the disclosure. The give-and-take over a period of days or weeks in working on a registration statement—if one is lucky enough to have that amount of time—is an effective means for performing due diligence and ensuring full and accurate disclosure. Probing inquiry will often lead management to take a fresh look at the company's business, to recall items of disclosure that may have been overlooked, to focus on problem areas, and to revise those portions of the registration statement that can be improved on.

Every effort should be made to avoid regarding any portion of the document as "boilerplate." A close examination and analysis of proposed risk factors and "meaningful cautionary statements" relating to forward-looking information can yield important dividends in understanding the issuer and the adequacy of its disclosure. The time spent in exploring and perfecting a rider for the MD&A can be the most important time spent in the entire registration process. During the course of the review, officers who were previously interviewed may be called on again to concentrate on particular points discussed in the registration statement.

One of the purposes of a thorough pre-filing review of the registration statement, especially in those offerings where there is a high probability of a full review by the SEC staff, is to anticipate staff comments based on counsel's experience with other SEC filings, recent SEC releases and recent speeches and presentations by SEC officials.

At the same time, it is important to verify whether the issuer's prior reports have been the subject of SEC comments and whether there are any open disclosure issues with the staff. This includes whether the issuer has followed through on any undertakings to comply with staff comments for the purpose of future filings.

In preparing a registration statement, it is not sufficient to follow to the letter the requirements of Form S-1 or any other applicable form. Rule 408 under the 1933 Act makes explicit what Section 11 in any event implies:

> [i]n addition to the information expressly required to be included in a registration statement, there shall be added such further material information, if any, as may be necessary to make the required statements, in the light of the circumstances under which they are made, not misleading.

The most difficult part of the disclosure process is drawing out the information that has not been volunteered but that may have to be disclosed to avoid a misleading impression. An inevitable part of this process is that the issuer and underwriter will often have different views about the materiality of the additional information. Some underwriters and their counsel follow the "two-minute" rule in resolving these differences of view: "If we have to discuss it for more than two minutes, it's material." This is obviously too simplistic. The issuer knows its business better than the underwriters (and certainly better than underwriters' counsel), and it may take some time and effort for it to persuade the underwriters and their counsel that an apparently significant point is really not important.

Rule 405 under the 1933 Act defines materiality for the purpose of determining what is required to be disclosed in the prospectus as relating to those matters as to which "there is a substantial likelihood that a reasonable investor would attach importance in determining whether to purchase the security . . . ." This definition, which is based on one of the Supreme Court's tests in *TSC Indus. v. Northway*,[51] requires a broad perspective. Arbitrary numerical cutoffs will not do.

The SEC's staff made this point convincingly in its Staff Accounting Bulletin No. 99, which it issued in August 1999. While the bulletin focused on materiality judgments in the financial statements, it has broader application. The staff stated, for example, that it was impermissible in making judgments about materiality to place exclusive reliance on a percentage or numerical test (e.g., 5%). Rather, issuers and their accountants had to assess "all relevant circumstances" that might shed light on what an investor might consider important." These circumstances included "qualitative factors" that might "well render material a quantitatively small misstatement of a financial statement item." Such qualitative factors might include, but were not limited to, whether a misstatement

- arises from an estimate or an item capable of precise measurement;
- masks a change in earnings or other trends;
- hides a failure to meet analysts' consensus expectations;
- changes a loss into income or vice versa;
- concerns a segment important to operations or profitability;
- affects compliance with regulatory requirements, covenants, etc.;
- has the effect of increasing management's compensation;

---

51. 426 U.S. 438, 449 (1976).

- involves concealment of an illegal transaction;
- may be expected (based on a "pattern of market performance" or other information) to have a significant market reaction; or
- appears to be for the express purpose of "earnings management."

It goes without saying that the prospectus should be written so as to be comprehensible to the average investor. The information should be presented in clear, understandable prose. As discussed in Chapter 3, the SEC rules now expressly require the use of "plain English" in lieu of the standard that Judge Weinstein described some years ago:

> In at least some instances, what has developed ... is a literary art form calculated to communicate as little of the essential information as possible while exuding an air of total candor. Masters of this medium utilize turgid prose to enshroud the occasional critical revelation in a morass of dull, and—to all but the sophisticates—useless financial and historical data.[52]

Care should be taken that the due diligence record not leave any questions unresolved. One of the authors vividly recalls receiving, as a young lawyer, a kick in the foot from a senior partner at a drafting session for a registration statement. The author had prepared diligently for the session, including inserting handwritten comments and questions in the margin of the draft of the document. The session went well, with the issuer's management responding candidly to the comments and questions, until the young lawyer failed to record a response. The senior partner's action was well-taken: if a question is important enough to be written down, the record should show that the question was asked and answered. Anything else might be interpreted, years later and with the benefit of hindsight, as casual

---

52. *Feit v. Leasco Data Processing Equip. Corp.*, 332 F. Supp. 544, 565 (E.D.N.Y. 1971).

LIABILITIES AND DUE DILIGENCE 351

or reckless indifference to the completion or accuracy of the document.[53]

When the participants in the offering are generally satisfied with a draft of the registration statement, it should be distributed to all directors and key officers. The investment bankers should satisfy themselves that the company has established adequate procedures for collecting and evaluating comments on the document from those persons to whom it has been furnished. This is particularly important for Management's Discussion and Analysis (MD&A) and any forward-looking statements that are included in the registration statement.

- *Maximizing "Expertization"*

As discussed above, underwriters are more easily able to assert a due diligence defense under Section 11(b) in connection with portions of the registration statement that have been expertized. Underwriters should therefore try to identify opportunities to maximize the extent to which statements in the registration statement can be expertized, for example, by recommending in appropriate cases that the issuer retain engineers, actuaries, appraisers or other experts to pass on relevant disclosure matters.

Accountants are normally "experts" only as to the audited financial statements. In some cases, however, financial information outside the audited financial statements can also be expertized. For example, SAS 42 contemplates a report by the issuer's accountants on parent company condensed financial statements required to be included in the registration statement as well as on the issuer's "selected financial data" required by Item 301 of Regulation S-K. Both categories of information are derived from the issuer's audited financial statements but would not be covered by the routine audit report. But if the audit report is expanded as contemplated by SAS 42 to cover this information, and if corresponding changes are made in the "Experts"

---

53. *See, e.g., Kronfeld v. Trans World Airlines, Inc.*, 832 F.2d 726, 736 (2d Cir. 1987) (investment banking associate's notes held to constitute evidence that reorganization was a "live" option and to raise issues of fact sufficient to reverse grant of summary judgment).

section of the prospectus and in the accountants' consent, the information should be considered to be expertized. In that case, it will not be necessary to cover the information in the comfort letter.

The accountants' attestation report on management's assessment of the issuer's internal control over financial reporting, which is discussed below, would also appear to constitute an expertization of the issuer's internal control. The attestation report does not appear to be required in the case of a registration statement on Form S-1, but it seems inevitable that it would have to become part of a registration statement on Form S-3 as a result of its being incorporated by reference from the issuer's Form 10-K. The SEC staff muddied the waters somewhat by suggesting in its June 2004 FAQ that such incorporation by reference was optional, and it remains to be seen whether accountants will object to such incorporation by reference or whether they will refuse consents.

It should be noted that the underwriters' experization defense in Section 11(b)(C), unlike an expert's own liability under Section 11(a)(4), is not expressly conditioned on the expert's providing the consent required by Section 7.

- *Visits to Principal Facilities*

In the case of a manufacturing enterprise, it can be useful to visit one or more of the company's principal plants, if for no other reason than to get a feel for the company's products and the manner in which they are produced. For example, after a visit to the principal plant of a South American producer of packaged foods, one of the authors had a considerably improved understanding of the state of the company's technical, labor, environmental and logistical challenges and how it was meeting them.

The extent to which an issuer's facilities should be inspected will depend on the particular circumstances, especially whether the offering is an IPO or a repeat offering. In all cases, a rule of reason must be applied.

- *Meetings with Principal Officers*

If appropriate under the circumstances, individual meetings should be held with company officers responsible for significant aspects of the company's business. In the case of an IPO, these meetings might include all of the company's principal operating and staff officers. In the case of repeat offerings, these meetings might be limited to those officers with responsibility for particularly sensitive areas of the business, for example, the chief financial officer and, possibly, the chief environmental officer in the case of a battery manufacturer, the chief risk manager or loan officer in the case of a bank or the head of intellectual property in the case of a high-technology company. Except for IPOs, it is unusual to obtain direct access to the chief executive officer for these purposes, but there are occasions when this is indispensable.

The thrust of these interviews should be to obtain a deeper understanding of the company's business and prospects and particularly regarding any challenges that have not previously been identified. Here a review of other companies in the same industry and a list of questions prepared in advance can be helpful in focusing the discussions.

No matter how much homework has been done, it is important to resist the temptation to show off one's recently gained knowledge about the company, its products or its industry. As in so many other areas, one learns more by listening than by talking.

It is not unreasonable to ask the same questions of different corporate officers in order to evaluate the answers received and to obtain different perspectives on potential problems. It is a good idea, however, to clarify with one's colleagues that this is to be done. A few years ago, one of the authors was asking the same question of a second company officer when the author's colleague—undoubtedly trying to prove that he was paying attention—interrupted to observe that the question had already been asked of the first officer and to repeat the answer given by that person!

- *Negotiation of Underwriting Agreement*

As discussed in Chapter 2, the process of negotiating the representations, warranties and legal opinions required by the underwriting agreement is a further opportunity for performing due diligence. As management focuses on the representations and opinions requested by the underwriters, problems may be identified that should be discussed in detail and possibly disclosed in the registration statement.

354   CORPORATE FINANCE & THE SECURITIES LAWS

- *Review of Confidential or Bulky Documents*

In the course of working on the transaction at the company's headquarters, time should be allocated for the study of documents not previously furnished to the underwriters, including those of a confidential nature that the company would prefer not to be taken from its offices. These would include such documents as multi-year plans, financial forecasts, budgets, periodic reports by operating units to senior management or the board of directors, and at least the most recent management letter prepared by the accountants in connection with their audit. The opportunity may be worth taking on a visit to corporate headquarters to review such bulky documents as product catalogs and operating manuals, although these may be more conveniently reviewed on the Internet if the issuer will permit access for this purpose.

- *Accounting Matters*

To paraphrase Clemenceau, accounting matters are too important to be left to the accountants.

As noted above, Section 11 does not expressly require a "reasonable investigation" as to "expertized" material such as certified financial statements. This does not mean, however, that an underwriter should not understand the issuer's financial statements and the choices that were made in preparing them.

- First of all, the market impact when companies disclose accounting irregularities, earnings restatements or SEC inquiries is often out of all proportion to the actual numbers involved. Something else is going on. The market tends to assume that if management is playing games with the numbers, then the company's prospects for success must be worse—perhaps much worse—than the market has assumed.

- Second, even as to expertized material, Section 11(b)(3)(C) still requires an underwriter to show that it had "no reasonable ground to believe" that the material was false or misleading. Moreover, as noted above, Section 12(a)(2) contains no express expertization defense.

- Third, interim financial statements and other unaudited financial information are not expertized. It is difficult to

LIABILITIES AND DUE DILIGENCE 355

understand interim financial statements without close examination of the audited financial statements. Any deficiencies in the audited or interim financial statements are likely to render misleading at least some of the disclosure in the prospectus outside the financial statements, e.g., MD&A.

– Fourth, financial statement analysis plays a major role in an underwriter's decision to underwrite an issuer's securities in the first place, in marketing the securities to customers and in comparing the issuer's performance to the performance of other companies for pricing purposes. Liability aside, an underwriter will not want to risk embarrassment and reputational damage because it failed to understand the issuer's accounting.

• • *Preparing for Financial Statement Due Diligence.* It is not necessary to be trained as an accountant in order to perform effective due diligence on financial statements. Experience in reviewing financial statements certainly helps, but as in other areas effective financial statement due diligence is principally a matter of preparation, focus and common sense. Accounting expertise is not required to form conclusions as to whether financial statements are too old, whether additional statements need to be filed or whether MD&A disclosures are responsive to the SEC's requirements. The Division of Corporation Finance also makes available on its section of the SEC's website a variety of useful information regarding accounting, financial reporting and disclosure issues.

Underwriters and their counsel should therefore prepare for financial statement due diligence as carefully as they would for due diligence in regard to any other part of the offering document.

The issuer's audited and interim financial statements for the past few years should be reviewed in advance and compared with those of other issuers in the same industry. The questions in the reviewer's mind should include the following:

– Have there been accounting failures in the industry? Has the industry's accounting come under public criticism from the SEC, regulators or others?

- How does the issuer's choice of accounting principles compare to that of other companies in the same industry? Does the issuer's explanation of its accounting principles appear to explain adequately the nature of the choices that should be highlighted?
- Has the issuer made a recent significant change in accounting policy or principles? Is the change in the direction of greater or lesser clarity?
- Are there expectations built into the company's stock price or debt rating that depend on the company meeting certain levels of reporting earnings or other performance measure, i.e., is management under pressure to "make the number"?[54] In the case of oper-ations, what are investors focusing on: net earnings, operating earnings, EBITDA or some other performance measure?
- Are there any new accounting standards, proposed or adopted, that might have a disproportionate effect on the issuer or its industry? Does the issuer's industry present issues that are the subject of study by the Emerging Issues Task Force of the FASB?
- What are the issuer's "critical accounting estimates" and how do they compare to those identified by other companies in its industry?
- Has the company recently changed auditors? Were there any indications, whatever may have been said at the time, of disagreements between management and the former accountants?
- If the issuer has published non-GAAP financial measures (NGFM), do other companies and investors in the same industry regard such measures as useful guides to performance? Does the issuer appear to have complied with SEC requirements for reconciling and explaining these measures?

---

54. Warren Buffett is reported to have said that "managers that always promise to 'make the number' will at some point be tempted to make up the number." Obviously, this is the exception rather than the rule.

LIABILITIES AND DUE DILIGENCE

• • *Meeting Focused on Financial Statement Due Diligence.* This preliminary review should be followed by a meeting among the issuer's accounting personnel, the outside auditors, counsel and the underwriters. Obviously, the scope and duration of such a meeting will vary from issuer to issuer and from offering to offering, but it is important that some time be set aside in the time schedule to permit a focus on the financial statements and the related disclosure.

In any discussion of financial statements, it is necessary to cover broad themes as well as what might appear to be minor details. Since it is almost always the case that the persons essential to the discussion have limited time (and even more limited patience at putting up with questions), it is often advisable to cover both broad themes and minor details in one pass through the financial statements and MD&A. This requires planning, organization and discipline on the part of the person running the meeting, who must ensure that time is not wasted and that all the important points are covered.

It would be useful before such a meeting to review relevant SEC guidance on accounting matters, including SAB 99 discussed below regarding the concept of materiality as it applies to financial statements and other disclosure matters.

The broad themes that should be explored include the following:

- Does the issuer's audit committee consist of independent and qualified persons? Is there a financial expert on the audit committee? If not, why not? Is the committee actively engaged in the responsibilities assigned to it by its charter? What resources are available to it? How often does it meet?
- Are there any independence issues regarding the issuer's accountants? Have the accountants communicated all required matters to the issuer's audit committee? Have all of the accountants' audit and non-audit services to the issuer been approved by the audit committee?
- Have the CEO and CFO filed all certifications and reports required by the SEC's rules adopted pursuant

to Section 302 of Sarbanes–Oxley? Have all the certifications and reports required by Section 906 been filed? How have the CEO and the CFO prepared themselves to make the required certifications?

- What "disclosure controls and procedures"[55] has the issuer implemented in response to the SEC's rules adopted pursuant to Section 302 of Sarbanes–Oxley? What is management's level of confidence in the effectiveness of those controls and procedures?

- What "internal control over financial reporting"[56] has the issuer implemented in response to the SEC's rules under Section 404 of Sarbanes–Oxley? How does management go about reporting on and assessing the effectiveness of that control, and how do the issuer's accountants go about the required *audit* of the issuer's internal control over financial reporting as required by rules adopted by the PCAOB in early 2004?[57] In particular, how do the accountants and the audit committee go about distinguishing control problems or irregularities that are "significant deficiencies" from those that are "material weaknesses"?

- When were the issuer's 1934 Act reports, particularly its financial statements, last reviewed by the SEC staff? Did the staff request any amendments or request that the issuer make any adjustments in future reports? Has the issuer complied with any undertakings that it made to the staff?

---

55. Rule 13a-15(e) defines this term in part as "controls and other procedures ... designed to ensure that information required to be disclosed" in 1934 Act reports "is recorded, processed, summarized and reported, within the time periods specified" by SEC rules.

56. Rule 13a-15(f) defines this term in part as "a process ... to provide reasonable assurance regarding the reliability of financial reporting and the preparation of financial statements for external purposes" in accordance with GAAP.

57. The PCAOB's rules adopted on March 9, 2004 were approved by the SEC on June 17, 2004. SEC Release No. 34-49884 (June 17, 2004). *See* the PCAOB and SEC websites for staff responses to frequently asked questions about internal control over financial reporting.

LIABILITIES AND DUE DILIGENCE

- Are the issuer's most recent audited financial statements the subject of a PCAOB inspection? (Depending on the progress of such an inspection, the outside accountants may be the only persons in a position to answer this question.)
- Is the issuer's performance obscured by period-to-period non-operating revenues or profits (e.g., pension accounting, currency gains or losses, fair value accounting)?
- What is the issuer's plan for implementing any new accounting standards? What effect will implementation have on the issuer's financial condition and results? Will the new standards affect the issuer's ability to comply with its financial covenants?

The meeting should then turn to a line-by-line review of the financial statements and the related disclosure. It is likely that the following topics will deserve particular attention.

• • • *SEC's Formal Requirements for Financial Statements.* An issuer's financial statements may be prepared in perfect conformity with U.S. GAAP and yet be entirely unacceptable for inclusion in an SEC filing.

SEC rules (primarily Regulation S-X) specify the form and content of, and the periods for which, companies must file balance sheets and statements of income and cash flow. They also specify which statements must be audited in accordance with "generally accepted auditing standards" (which now means auditing standards as specified by the PCAOB), how old these statements may be as of the date of filing and when they become "stale"—that is, when they must be updated with more recent financial statements. SEC rules also specify when issuers must furnish financial statement information regarding significant business acquisitions or dispositions. The SEC will not permit a registration statement to become effective if the issuer does not comply with these requirements.

Various SEC forms, for example, Form 10-K for annual reports and Form S-1 for registration statements, require the inclusion of a five-year table setting forth the "selected financial information" specified in Regulation S-K.

SEC rules also specify the financial statements that must be included if the issuer's securities are being guaranteed by another issuer, including an affiliate of the issuer.

It is undoubtedly fair to expect the accountants in the first instance to pass upon the formal adequacy for SEC purposes of the financial statements included in the issuer's filing. It is small comfort, however, to find after the filing that the accountants were wrong about what was required and that the transaction will be significantly delayed. Compliance with the SEC's formal requirements as to financial statements should be the subject of an early discussion.

• • • *Revenue Recognition.* Assuming that the auditors' report is "clean" or unqualified, the first topic for discussion is often the issuer's sales or revenues. This is usually the first line of the issuer's income statement. The discussion of this one line has in the authors' experience consumed hours, particularly with the heightened concern in recent years about revenue recognition.

In December 1999, the SEC staff released SAB 101 for the purpose of providing guidance on how to apply generally accepted accounting principles to revenue recognition issues. According to SAB 101, in order for an issuer to recognize revenue, it is necessary for there to be (a) persuasive evidence of an arrangement (e.g., an agreement to sell products or services), (b) delivery of the product or the rendering of a service, (c) a price that is fixed or determinable and (d) reasonable assurance of collectibility.[58]

Notwithstanding SAB 101, revenue recognition issues continue to be responsible for many of the accounting restatements announced by public companies, and they remain at the top of the SEC staff's list of the most frequently issued comments. In its summary of the Fortune 500 review, the SEC staff noted that it had encouraged issuers "to provide additional company-specific disclosure about the nature, terms and activities from

---

58. SAB 101 and interpretive guidance issued in October 2000 by the Office of the Chief Accountant ("Frequently Asked Questions About SAB 101") were incorporated by SAB 104 (December 17, 2003) into Topic 13 of the SEC's Codification of Staff Accounting Bulletins.

which revenue is generated and the accounting policies for each material revenue generating activity."[59]

There is often a blurred line between impermissible "channel stuffing" and legitimate incentives to customers to purchase additional products or services. Even if the revenues may be recognized under SAB 101, additional disclosure may be required in MD&A.

The Fortune 500 Review Issues Summary noted common revenue recognition disclosure and comment themes in certain industries, including computer software, services and hardware, communications equipment, capital goods, semiconductors, electronic instruments and controls, energy, and pharmaceutical and retail.

In addition to gaining a complete understanding of the issuer's revenue recognition policies, the meeting's goal should be to determine whether these policies are consistent with the expectations of the underwriters, analysts and investors. Also, how do the company's policies compare to those of other companies in the same industry? Have they attracted criticism from investors or regulators?

It goes without saying that underwriters should be alert to significant transactions that take place at the end of a reporting period. Companies have been accused of loading trucks on the last day of a reporting period and recording revenues as the trucks left the dock, even where the trucks were later "lost in traffic" or otherwise unable to reach their intended destinations.

Also, there have been recent allegations about the misuse of rebates, promotion allowances and similar devices to enable retail companies to inflate their revenues.

• • • *Derivatives and Market Risk.* As in other areas, due diligence in respect of an issuer's exposure arising from derivatives and market risk has two objectives. The first is the immediate objective of verifying that the issuer's disclosure and accounting presentation are in conformity with applicable rules.

---

59. "Summary by the Division of Corporation Finance of Significant Issues Addressed in the Review of the Periodic Reports of the Fortune 500 Companies," available at www.sec.gov/divisions/corpfin/fortune500rep.htm (February 27, 2003).

The second is the more general objective of understanding how the issuer's derivative activity relates to its overall management of market risk.

The accounting rules for derivative instruments require that they be recorded on the balance sheet at fair value. The effect of changes in value depends on whether they are used for trading purposes or qualify for hedge accounting. In the latter case, the relevant risk management strategy and objective must be documented along with the method of assessing effectiveness. For those issuers with significant exposure to derivatives, it is reasonable to ask the issuer and its accountants how these determinations are made.

The accounting rules result at best in a snapshot of the issuer's exposure to market risk. In 1997, the SEC adopted a new Item 305 of Regulation S-K that requires both quantitative and qualitative information about risk exposure.

Quantitative information must be set forth separately for instruments held for trading purposes and for non-trading purposes in each market risk exposure category (e.g., interest rate risk, foreign currency exchange risk, commodity price risk and other relevant market risks such as equity price risk).

The three available disclosure alternatives for quantitative information are (a) a tabular presentation of information sufficient to determine related cash flows for the next five years, (b) a sensitivity analysis expressing potential losses resulting from selected hypothetical changes in market rates or prices and (c) value at risk (VaR) disclosures that express potential losses over a selected period of time, with a selected likelihood of occurrence, resulting from changes in market rates or prices. In the case of VaR disclosures, the issuer must describe its VaR model and the relevant assumptions and limitations. In addition, it must provide information either on the range or distribution of VaR amounts during the reporting period, actual changes in fair values, earnings or cash flows during the reporting period or on the frequency with which actual changes exceeded VaR amounts during the reporting period.

Underwriters and their counsel face a significant challenge in performing due diligence on an issuer's disclosure of quantitative information on market risk in response to the SEC rules. In particular, lawyers seldom have enough statistical expertise to be in a position to evaluate a VaR model, the adequacy of the issuer's back-testing or stress testing of the model or to be able to identify limitations in a model that call for further inquiry or additional disclosure.

The accounting profession takes the position that accountants should not make any comments or perform any procedures related to the sensitivity analysis or VaR disclosures required by Item 305. Accountants are permitted to perform limited procedures related to the issuer's tabular presentations.[60]

The SEC rules also call for a qualitative description of the issuer's primary market risk exposures and how those exposures are managed. The accounting profession takes the position that accountants should not comment on the qualitative disclosures.

Underwriters should consider in appropriate cases designating a person with relevant expertise to assist in assessing the issuer's sensitivity analysis or VaR disclosure as well as its description of the objectives, general strategies and procedures related to its management of market risk.

In this connection, it may be a good idea for underwriters and their counsel to meet with the issuer's employees in charge of risk management. The following areas of inquiry should be considered:

- What is the issuer doing and why? Is the activity authorized by board action? It should not be assumed that there is no risk associated even with "plain vanilla" derivatives.
- What are the issuer's controls? Is there someone who is competent and independent to oversee what is being done, including pricing of positions?
- Who is conducting the activity, i.e., who are the highly compensated traders responsible for derivative activities? Who supervises them? Do the supervisors understand what the traders are doing?
- Are compensation schemes geared to reward "bet-the-company" activity? It should be noted that some

---

60. AICPA, *Codification of Statements on Auditing Standards* AUI ¶634.13-29 (2003).

regulators may be considering guidelines that will focus on whether banks have compensation policies that encourage hazardous trading practices.

- Are credit criteria established to control counterparty risk? Who monitors limits? Who tracks authorization and suitability issues?

- What are the cash requirements under various stress scenarios? Have actual cash movements been consistent with what would be expected to result if the issuer's stated risk tolerance was being observed?

• • • *Non-GAAP Financial Measures.* Pursuant to Section 401(a) of Sarbanes–Oxley, the SEC in January 2003 amended its disclosure and accounting regulations and Form 8-K and adopted a new Regulation G to deal with the perceived problem of non-GAAP financial measures (NGFM).[61] The new rules cover any financial measure that deviates from the issuer's GAAP disclosure. It does not include operating measures, and it does not include financial measures that are required to be disclosed.

Regulation G applies to all public disclosures of material information that includes NGFM (e.g., press releases). It requires that such public disclosures be accompanied by a presentation of the most directly comparable GAAP measure and a reconciliation of the differences.

If an issuer includes NGFM in a document filed with the SEC, Item 10(e) of Regulation S-K requires that the document include the comparable GAAP number "with equal or greater prominence" as well as a reconciliation. The document must also include an explanation of why the NGFM is useful to investors and to the issuer's management. This explanation should be convincing. As a senior SEC staffer stated in May 2004, " 'analysts want to see it' is no longer a sufficient explanation."

---

61. The SEC staff also released in June 2003 "Frequently Asked Questions Regarding the Use of Non-GAAP Financial Measures." The document is available on the SEC's website.

The goal of a meeting to review the registration statement should be to identify any NGFM included in the issuer's periodic reports that are among those adjustments and presentations flatly prohibited by Item 10(e) or that may have to be included or incorporated by reference into the registration statement and for which the underwriters may have to assume liability. It should also be to confirm that the issuer has complied with all of the other requirements of Regulation G and Item 10(e). Finally, the meeting should determine whether investors have formed any expectations based on NGFM, whether the company has published such NGFM and whether and how the issuer and the underwriters can confirm the reasonableness of those expectations.

• • • *Segment Disclosure.* An area identified in the Fortune 500 review that should be discussed at the meeting is the company's response to the requirements for disclosure about operating segments. The relevant definition of an operating segment in SFAS 131 focuses on a company component whose operating results are regularly reviewed by the "chief operating decision maker" to make decisions about resources to be allocated to the segment and to assess its performance. Segments may be aggregated only on a limited basis, and any aggregation must be disclosed. The SEC staff has stated that it has

> "[o]n a few occasions . . . requested copies of all reports furnished to the chief operating decision maker if the company's reported segments did not appear realistic for management's assessment of a company's performance or conflicted with that officer's public statements describing the company. The staff has also reviewed analysts' reports, interviews by management with the press, and other public information to evaluate consistency with segment disclosures in the financial statements. Where that information revealed different or additional segments, amendment of the registrant's filing to comply with SFAS 131 was required."[62]

---

62. SEC Division of Corporation Finance, *Current Issues and Rulemaking Projects* 86-87 (November 14, 2000).

• • • *Related Party Transactions.* The officers' and directors' questionnaires discussed above are designed in part to identify related party transactions that must be disclosed under SEC rules or included to avoid any part of the offering document becoming misleading. The SEC's statement issued in January 2002 regarding MD&A also focused on the subject of related party transactions. The SEC noted that MD&A should include discussion of material related party transactions to the extent necessary for an understanding of the issuer's current and prospective financial position and operating results. It emphasized a realistic view of this requirement, focusing on whether arrangements might involve terms or other aspects that might differ from those that might be negotiated with clearly independent parties. It then provided illustrations of the disclosure that might be required in this respect, emphasizing that its understanding of "related parties" went beyond that called for by U.S. GAAP and included anyone with whom the company had a relationship that "enabled the parties to negotiate terms of material transactions that may not be available from other, more clearly independent parties on an arm's-length basis."

• • • *Other Areas for Inquiry.* Other areas identified in the Fortune 500 Review Issues Summary that should be discussed at the meeting include restructuring charges, impairment charges, pension plan funding assumptions and environmental and product liability disclosures. Underwriters and their counsel should also be alert for potential tax issues,[63] indications of operational risk[64] and accounting for self-insurance activity (e.g., for worker' compensation claims). It goes without saying that these areas should be explored for a company's international operations if these are material.

• • • *MD&A Adequacy.* Chapter 3 describes the SEC's expectations for companies' MD&A disclosures. The goal of a

---

63. *See* Speech by Donald T. Nicolaisen, SEC Chief Accountant, "Remarks at the Tax Council Institute Conference on the Corporate Tax Practice: Responding to the New Challenges of a Changing Landscape" (February 11, 2004) (available on SEC website).

64. *See, e.g.*, the Basel Committee on Banking Supervision's Working Paper on the Regulatory Treatment of Operational Risk (September 2001), available at www.bis.org/publ/bcbs_wp8.pdf.

meeting focused on the financial statements should be to explore the company's approach to MD&A, keeping in mind that the Fortune 500 Review Issues Summary stated that the staff had issued more comments on MD&A than on any other topic.

Has the company taken a recent "fresh look" at its MD&A, as the SEC has urged? Is the presentation clear and informative? Does it focus on the key variables or indicators relevant to the company's business? Does it identify and evaluate known material trends and uncertainties? Are disclosure and analysis balanced and responsive to Item 303 of Regulation S-K and the SEC's guidance?

Does the disclosure reflect the information available to management? What is the involvement of management in the preparation of MD&A? The audit committee? The disclosure committee, if any? The outside accountants?

• • • *Critical Accounting Estimates.* Chapter 3 describes the SEC's expectations regarding companies' disclosure and explanation of the effects of the critical accounting estimates used in the preparation of their financial statements. The goal of a meeting focused on the financial statements should be to determine the reasonableness of the issuer's identification of its critical accounting estimates and its response to the SEC's disclosure requirements. A comparison of the issuer's situation with that of other companies in the same industry is often instructive and may suggest areas for further inquiry.

• • • *Off-Balance Sheet Entities.* Chapter 3 describes the new MD&A requirements, inspired by Sarbanes–Oxley, relating to disclosure of an issuer's off-balance sheet arrangements and its contractual obligations and commitments. The meeting should focus on whether the issuer has identified all of its significant off-balance sheet arrangements, whether or not explicitly covered by the MD&A requirements, and also on whether or not the MD&A disclosure sets forth a complete picture of the effect of the arrangements.

- *Negotiation of Comfort Letters*

The negotiation of the accountants' comfort letter often can bring out matters for possible disclosure. The process is less effective than in the past, however, because of the accounting profession's adoption of standards that have steadily reduced accountants' freedom of action in this area. Also, individual firms' concern about liability has in recent years led them on occasion to resist providing even as much comfort as the professional standards allow. This is especially regrettable since comfort letters, which are usually thought of as exclusively the underwriters' concern (apart from questions of cost to the issuer), are also commonly addressed to the issuer and often to the issuer's directors. They therefore serve an important verification function that can be valuable to the issuer's directors and officers who have potential Section 11 liability in a registered offering. They can also provide "comfort" to the issuer and its directors and officers in the case of an unregistered offering such as a private placement or Regulation S transaction.

Nevertheless, accountants have been concerned for some time that on certain transactions "no one is doing any due diligence but the accountants." Effective June 30, 1993, therefore, the accounting profession adopted a new Statement on Auditing Standards No. 72, *Letters for Underwriters and Certain Other Requesting Parties*. SAS 72 was subsequently amended and superseded by SAS 76 and SAS 86, which is now codified as AU ¶634 of the AICPA's *Codification of Statements on Auditing Standards*.

The AICPA standards permit the giving of negative assurance on interim financial information only if the accountants have performed an interim review in accordance with SAS 100, *Interim Financial Information*. Moreover, negative assurance on subsequent changes in specific financial statement items is available only within 135 days from the end of the most recent period for which the accountants performed an SAS 100 review. (The 135-day cutoff can create problems for foreign issuers who do not normally report on a quarterly basis.)

In addition, a traditional negative assurance comfort letter will be available to a person other than a "named underwriter" in a registered transaction only if a legal opinion is delivered to the effect that the person has a due diligence defense under Section 11 of the Act. This requirement will apply, for example, to agents in MTN offerings. If the opinion is not or cannot be delivered, the agent must be content with a "procedures letter" (discussed below) as in the case of unregistered offerings.

In connection with unregistered offerings, financial intermediaries such as underwriters or agents will have to make a choice as to the kind of "comfort" they wish to receive on the transaction.

The first alternative for unregistered transactions, which results in a traditional "negative assurance" comfort letter, requires compliance with the SAS 100 conditions described above. In addition, the recipient must represent in writing that it has conducted a "review process ... substantially consistent" with the due diligence process that would be performed if the transaction were registered under the Act.[65] It also requires a representation that the requesting person is "knowledgeable with respect to the due diligence review process that would be performed if this placement of securities were being registered pursuant to the Act."

If, for whatever reason, the foregoing representation letter cannot be given, the underwriter or agent in an unregistered transaction is limited to requesting that the accountants follow agreed-on procedures as to specified elements of financial statement information contained in the offering document and that the accountants report on these procedures in a "procedures letter" issued under AU ¶634. (An example of such a letter is included in AU ¶634 as Example Q.) Such a letter may "not provide negative assurance on the financial statements as a whole, or on any of the specified elements, accounts, or items thereof."

Neither option is completely satisfactory. The AU ¶634 representation letter calls for a characterization of due diligence performed on an unregistered transaction for which there may not be a registered analogue (e.g., there are not many SEC-registered offerings of municipal securities or bank securities). Also, the standard of care required under Section 11 is generally thought

---

65. AU ¶634 n.4 purports to recognize that "what is 'substantially consistent' may vary from situation to situation and may not be the same as that done in a registered offering of the same securities for the same issuer; whether the procedures being, or to be, followed will be 'substantially consistent' will be determined by the requesting party on a case-by-case basis."

to be more demanding than under Section 12(a)(2) (which applies to public unregistered offerings of non-exempt securities).

The alternative of the "procedures letter" is thought by some investment bankers to provide less in the way of comfort than a negative assurance letter. It also requires a detailed discussion among investment banking personnel, counsel and the issuer's accountants as to which items of information should be the subject of investigation by the accountants and the procedures that the accountants should follow. (The accountants will insist that the underwriters take responsibility for the interpretation of the findings and the adequacy of the procedures, but they are usually prepared to assist in suggesting appropriate procedures.) There is a school of thought to the effect that a procedures letter can be as valuable as a negative assurance letter, particularly because it encourages the kind of inquiry and discussion that is the foundation of the traditional due diligence process.

All this being said, public offerings under modern conditions often leave little time for inquiry and discussion. This is where the AICPA's original comfort letter standards introduced in 1993 played a useful role insofar as they mandated SAS 100 reviews as a prerequisite for obtaining negative comfort on interim financial statements. Despite the cost factor, many issuers and their outside directors took comfort from having their independent accountants perform these reviews as part of the comfort letter process, and the SEC since 2000 has mandated SAS 100 reviews as part of the routine process of preparing the quarterly report on Form 10-Q. And there is no question but that routine performance of SAS 100 reviews has facilitated the due diligence process when the time comes to offer securities.

The issuer's accountants are permitted to include in a comfort letter references to an examination or review of the issuer's MD&A included in annual or quarterly reports to the SEC and to attach to the comfort letter copies of such examinations or reviews.[66] An examination results in a statement that the MD&A includes the required elements of the SEC's rules, that the

---

66. AICPA, *Codification of Statements on Auditing Standards* AU ¶634.64 (Example R) (2003).

historical financial amounts have been accurately derived from the financial statements and that "the underlying information, determinations, estimates, and assumptions of the [company] provide a reasonable basis for the disclosures contained therein." A review provides negative assurance to the same effect.

AU ¶634 makes useful suggestions relating to the timely issuance of the comfort letter. It properly notes the limitations on what accountants can do in respect of interim financial statements and other information that has not been the subject of an audit in accordance with generally accepted auditing standards. It emphasizes the value of an early meeting regarding the subject matter of the letter and the procedures to be followed, as well as the desirability of the accountants' producing a draft letter on which the underwriters may comment.

The contents of the comfort letter are discussed in Chapter 2.

- *"Bring-Down" Due Diligence*

Particularly in the better-managed transactions, where the bulk of due diligence is done before the filing date, there is an inevitable tendency to relax after the filing and the response to staff comments (if any). The underwriters start to think about the next deal (while the syndicate and sales functions attend to the marketing effort), and counsel may confine its efforts to thinking about the closing documents required by the underwriting agreement.

Relaxing can be a major mistake. It is important to continue due diligence down to the effective date of the registration statement (if applicable), the pricing date and the closing date. The comfort letter can be useful in this connection if it covers increases or decreases in specific balance sheet or income statement items down to the "cutoff" date, which is usually a few days before closing, but it is equally important to confer just before pricing and just before closing with management in order to verify that nothing has occurred that would materially change the premises on which the transaction is based.

For example, a preferred stock offering by Digital Equipment Corp. closed on March 28, 1994. The fiscal quarter closed a few days later, and the issuer less than three weeks later announced an operating loss for the quarter that sent the market priced of the newly distributed preferred stock in one day from $25 to less than $21. In the subsequent Section 11 litigation,[67] plaintiffs appealed from a dismissal of the complaint. The First Circuit stated that it "reject[ed] any bright-line rule that an issuer engaging in a public offering is obligated to disclose interim operating results for the quarter in progress whenever it perceives a possibility that the quarter's results may disappoint the market." On the other hand, in response to the defendant issuer's argument that there could never be a duty to disclose internally known, pre-end-of-quarter financial information, the court responded that if an issuer "is in possession of nonpublic information indicating that the quarter in progress at the time of the public offering will be an extreme departure from the range of results which could be anticipated based on currently available information, it is consistent with the basic statutory policies favoring disclosure to require inclusion of that information in the registration statement." In view of the early stage of the litigation, the court could not conclude as a matter of law that the information known to the issuer was not subject to mandatory disclosure under the heading of "material changes" referred to in Item 11(c) of Form S-3.

Underwriters' and issuer's counsel are often asked to deliver a disclosure opinion or letter that speaks as of the closing date. The issuer's representations and warranties in the underwriting agreement will normally be updated to the date of the closing, but counsel should consider what other steps are appropriate as a foundation for the "bring-down" opinion.

- *Documentation*

An underwriter has the burden of proving its due diligence defense under Section 11. Reasonable care may have been exercised by the managing underwriter in accordance with the statutory standard, but if a lawsuit is brought on the registration statement and the managing underwriter is unable to prove in court that it did in fact exercise due diligence, its efforts will be wasted.

---

67. *Shaw v. Digital Equip. Corp.*, 82 F.3d 1194 (1st Cir. 1996).

It is difficult to prove due diligence unless the investigation is adequately documented. Some underwriters take the position that "the best evidence of our due diligence is the prospectus" or other offering document. It is undoubtedly true that a carefully prepared prospectus and the usual closing documents such as officers' certificates, legal opinions and comfort letter constitute persuasive evidence of due diligence. It would be preferable in most situations, however, to have a more complete record of the numerous verification issues that arose during the course of the transaction and the manner in which they were resolved.

There is no single right answer on the documentation that should be retained by the underwriters or their counsel following the closing of a securities transaction. At one time, it was customary for one of the investment bankers working on the financing to be responsible for maintaining a due diligence file. This file would contain a list of documents reviewed and notes taken at visits to corporate facilities, at interviews of corporate officers, and at meetings held to review the registration statement. It might also contain drafts of the prospectus and other disclosure documents. Above all, however, the person responsible for the file would try to prune it of material that reflected careless speculation, the presence of unresolved disclosure issues or comments that contained gratuitous and unflattering characterizations of the issuer or its management. Such material is sure to be disclosed in the event of litigation, and it can and has prejudiced the underwriters' legal defense even where the highest due diligence standards were applied.

For some investment bankers, the "complete file" approach is still feasible. Given the faster pace of modern securities transactions, however, that approach requires intense effort and places a severe burden on the person or persons charged with responsibility for the task. If the file is carelessly put together, without review of its contents and without verification that all necessary documents (including computer files and e-mail records) are included, the file will work against the underwriter in the event of litigation.

Some underwriters follow the practice of retaining a complete file only on IPOs and not on other transactions. This is a defensible practice and is preferable to making *ad hoc* decisions about which transactions should receive the complete file treatment.[68] It is important, however, to make sure that all participants in the transaction follow the same policy. For example, printers may retain drafts of the registration statement and prospectus unless requested not to do so.

Electronic copies of final documents may contain "hidden text" or comments or a record of all changes made to the document. These should not be inadvertently retained.

A modified approach to document retention is to rely more on underwriters' counsel for this purpose. Counsel will already have prepared and retained summaries of key corporate documents, including minutes. It is usually feasible also to request counsel to memorialize important aspects of the transaction. These may include notes of any visits to principal facilities, meetings with management and registration statement review sessions, as well as summaries of discussions at which disclosure or accounting issues were resolved or earnings estimates were developed.

The Penn Central Affair

One of the most celebrated examples of effective due diligence is the job performed by William J. Williams, Jr., of

---

68. Rule 17a-4(b)(4) under the 1934 Act requires the preservation of communications relating to a broker-dealer's "business as such," including inter-office memoranda and communications. In the authors' experience, the rule has not been thought to apply to underwriters' due diligence files. In any event, drafts and notes are hardly "communications." In late 2002, however, the SEC imposed cease-and-desist orders and fines against five large investment banking firms for failing to preserve e-mail communications, which in the SEC's view were as much covered by Rule 17a-4(b)(4) as paper communications. SEC Release No. 34-46937 (December 3, 2002). In July 2003, the NASD announced that members' recordkeeping obligations extended in its view to instant messaging. Notice to Members 03-33 (July 2003). As a result, some firms might choose to follow the policy of retaining electronic communications that relate to an offering while eliminating nonessential drafts, notes, and other documents. In particular, there is no reason to retain unsent *drafts* of e-mail and other communications.

LIABILITIES AND DUE DILIGENCE

Sullivan & Cromwell in representing the underwriters of a proposed $20 million debenture offering in the Euromarket by a subsidiary of the Penn Central Company.

The Penn Central Transportation Co. was formed on February 1, 1968 by the merger of the Pennsylvania and the New York Central railroads. At the time, there were fanfares of optimism. The merged railroad was expected to be more efficient and to produce substantial earnings for its shareholders. Moreover, diversification into real estate development and other areas was seen as the beginning of a major conglomerate enterprise. The price of the stock soared following the merger. Two and one-half years later the railroad was bankrupt, at the time the largest bankruptcy in the nation's history. In September 1970, the SEC commenced an investigation of the Penn Central collapse, and almost two years later it published a report on its findings.[69]

The SEC's report includes the story of how the scrutiny applied and disclosure required by investment bankers and their counsel thwarted the efforts of a failing company to stay afloat by selling its securities to the investing public. Pennsylvania Co. (Pennco), a wholly owned subsidiary of the transportation company, had as its principal assets large holdings of the stock of the Norfolk & Western and Wabash railroads and the stock of its "diversification" subsidiaries, Buckeye Pipeline Corporation and two real estate development corporations, Great Southwest Corporation and Arvida Corporation. In December 1969, Pennco had a successful $50 million offering of debentures exchangeable for common stock of Norfolk & Western, its most valuable asset from the standpoint of underlying value and income production. This offering was underwritten by First Boston Corporation and Glore Forgan, Wm. R. Staats, Inc. It was not registered with the SEC because the issuance of Pennco's securities was subject to the jurisdiction of the Interstate Commerce Commission and at the time Section 3(a)(6) of the 1933 Act provided an exemption for such securities.

---

69. *Staff Report of the Securities and Exchange Commission to the Special Subcommittee on Investigations of the House of Representatives Committee on Interstate and Foreign Commerce on the Financial Collapse of the Penn Central Company*, Subcommittee Print (1972).

In February 1970, Jonathan O'Herron, who in November 1969 had become the principal assistant to David Bevan, Penn Central's chief financial officer, contacted N. Gregory Doescher of First Boston to explore the possibility of another debenture offering for Pennco, a $100 million offering that would include warrants to purchase the stock of the Penn Central Company (the holding company for the enterprise that had been organized in October 1969) and Great Southwest Corporation. The SEC observed in its report that the fact that this proposal was made less than two months after Pennco had completed a similar offering "was a clear indication of the serious cash drain and the limited financing possibilities."[70] One complication was encountered immediately. Penn Central had proposed the use of Great Southwest warrants despite the fact that Great Southwest had been forced to abandon a proposed public offering in late 1969 because of the adverse disclosure that would have been required in a registration statement. Penn Central had hoped to avoid the disclosure problem by delaying the registration of the warrants until their proposed exercise date on July 1, 1971. Great Southwest and its outside counsel were not happy with this approach. Even if registration could be delayed, Great Southwest would have a registration commitment hanging over its head, and its affairs were deteriorating. Sullivan & Cromwell had serious legal reservations as to whether registration could be delayed, and ultimately the plan to issue warrants was abandoned.

At the same time as it was pursuing the Pennco debenture offering, the Penn Central management was gearing up for a simultaneous offering in Europe of $20 million of debentures of a newly formed subsidiary, Penn Central International Corp. First Boston and Pierson, Heldring & Pierson of Amsterdam were to be the underwriters. In the course of preparing the offering circular, concerns arose as to the company's cash flow. As described in the SEC's report:

> The preparation of the circulars proceeded routinely, except for the warrant question, until mid-March. At that

---

70. *Id.* at 110.

time, the underwriters began receiving materials, including financial statements, from Penn Central. The underwriters' counsel had indicated that the preparation of financial information should take the SEC standards into consideration even though the circulars would not be filed with the SEC. Counsel had also asked for cash flow information. The information began to alarm the underwriters and counsel for the underwriters. They were also concerned about whether the company was making full disclosure to them. On March 18 Bevan and O'Herron met with the underwriting group working on the domestic issue. Bevan stated that budget projections showed break-even results in third quarter of 1970 and a profit in fourth quarter. The statement was not based on fact. The railroad had already lost as much as was projected for all of 1970 and there was no indication of a reversal. The underwriters knew or should have known that these projections were not founded on fact because Penn Central did not have established forecasts or budgets.[71]

Doescher testified to the SEC that he was surprised that the transportation company had not prepared budgets. The reason given to him was the size of the railroad and the lack of financial controls. Bevan, however, gave the underwriters his own forecast of the railroad's results for 1970. The investment bankers at First Boston were "uncomfortable" about the international offering but decided that they would go along because of its small size. Williams, however, was not satisfied:

> At the same time that the underwriters were being appeased by Bevan, William Williams, counsel to the underwriters on the international issue, was becoming increasingly concerned about what he was seeing. He was particularly concerned about the cash situation at Penn Central. In light of the excess of current liabilities, debt due within 5 years and the growing losses, Williams concluded that "there was a risk, perhaps a significant

---

71. *Id.* at 112.

risk, that some time within the next 1 or 2 years that the railroad could end up in bankruptcy whether they obtained $120 million or not." On March 19 Williams spoke with John Arning, counsel to the underwriters on the domestic offering, and then with the working group members representing the underwriters on the international offering. He told the working group members to bring to the attention of the senior underwriting representatives the adverse information that was being uncovered.

The following day, Williams and other members of the International offering working group were in Philadelphia for a regular session on the circular. As a routine question in light of large writeoffs in 1969 the underwriters asked the Penn Central representatives whether any additional writeoffs were contemplated for 1970. The comptroller, [Charles] Hill, stated that a major writeoff of track was being contemplated. Hill produced a book describing the writeoff plans. He also submitted a draft of the 1969 annual report to shareholders which was to be issued shortly and which contained the following statement:

> *Redesign of System Trackage.*—We have launched a project to streamline our railroad by eliminating 5,800 miles of surplus track from our total of 40,000 miles. This could bring benefits of $90 million of equivalent capital and save $9 million annually in operating expenses.
>
> Efficiency of our remaining plant will be enhanced through disposition of these unneeded freight facilities, seldom-used branch lines, excess yard trackage, and duplicate lines.

Williams indicated that the writeoff against earnings that would result should be disclosed in the circulars and that a press release should be issued no later than the issuance of the circular if such a writeoff was imminent. E.K. Taylor, Penn Central's house counsel who was working on the offering, then suggested that this be taken up with Bevan. After Hill had briefed Bevan, the working group was called to Bevan's office. Bevan was annoyed about this question of disclosure. He stated that much of any writeoff would be covered by the merger reserve and would not have to be reflected in earnings. He said the abandonment plan was subject to constant change. When asked why the abandonment was mentioned in the annual report he said he did not know of it and considered such reference to be stupid. He left the room to consult with Saunders and returned to assure the working group that there were no plans for abandonment "in the foreseeable future." Williams pressed Bevan on the meaning of "foreseeable future." Bevan finally indicated that it would not take place in 1970. Hill agreed with Bevan. [Footnotes omitted.][72]

Williams was troubled by the inconsistency between Bevan's position and the earlier statements made by Hill. With some reluctance, Williams testified to the SEC that it was his impression that Bevan was being evasive. He also testified that he considered the possibility that a writeoff had been contemplated, but that Bevan was denying it to avoid a damaging disclosure in the offering circular. Denial of a proposed course of action is not an unusual reaction by a corporate officer who is seeking to avoid disclosure. Where, as in this case, the contemplated action had gelled sufficiently as to be the subject of a paragraph in a draft annual report, denial can be given little credence. A strong reaction to a problem and the use of terms such as "stupid" in an effort to intimidate are indications of the seriousness of a problem.

The only response to intimidation is increased diligence. Williams, of course, continued to pursue the matter:

Arning was out of the country from March 21 to April 4 during which time Williams covered the work on both the Pennco and the International offering. On March 23, Williams informed Arthur Dean, senior partner of Sullivan & Cromwell, about what he had told the junior members working on the International offering, including

---

72. *Id.* at 112–13.

the possibility of bankruptcy of the railroad. Dean advised him to be sure the senior underwriting officers were aware of the problem. Williams then contacted the senior members to say that Sullivan & Cromwell would not go along with the International offering unless the underwriters were fully aware of the facts.

Doescher of First Boston then reviewed the International circular and, after speaking with a representative of Pierson, Heldring & Pierson, decided to recommend postponing the International offering because the "disclosures are very severe and [the underwriters] did not want to be in a position of appearing to sell something abroad which could not be sold at home" according to a note made by Doescher. On the 24th and 26th, further conferences involving the underwriters, counsel, accountants, and officers of Penn Central took place. At about this time, Dean decided to call a meeting of the top officers of each of the underwriters to make certain that they understood the facts. The meeting was set for March 31. This was acknowledged to be an extraordinary meeting which resulted in part from Williams' growing concern that "someday this whole thing would blow up, and I wanted to make sure that the firm was focusing on it at the stage where we could do something about it, focusing on it at the highest levels. . . ."

Bevan was growing increasing [*sic*] concerned for his own reasons. Every probe was uncovering embarrassing information that was contradicting his representations, which he knew were false. On March 27 Dean met with Bevan at Bevan's request. Bevan criticized Williams and asked that Williams be removed. In response, Dean noted that Williams belonged to a younger generation and that certain duties were imposed by a case known as *BarChris*. [Footnotes omitted.][73]

An attempt by a corporate officer to have underwriters' counsel removed from a deal is the ultimate sign of weakness

---

73. *Id.* at 114–15.

and desperation. In this case, Bevan's attempt to remove Williams was a strong indication that Penn Central's financing efforts would ultimately fail. Williams continued to question Bevan and elicited an admission that losses for the first quarter of 1970 would be greater than those for the comparable period in 1969. Bevan also stated that there were assets that could be sold. When Williams referred to the negative pledge clause in the revolving credit agreement, Bevan said that he was negotiating with First National City Bank to get a release of the assets.

On March 28, 1970, Williams wrote a memorandum to Arthur Dean outlining some of his concerns, including the fact that substantially all of the railroad's system lines were mortgaged or otherwise encumbered, the pledge of a substantial portion of Pennco's investments, the extremely large losses from railroad operations, the uncertainty of Penn Central's earnings prospects, the company's accelerated efforts to exchange stock of the Wabash railroad for stock of Norfolk & Western, which would result in a large paper profit in the first quarter, and the fact that Penn Central had arranged financings through a convicted defrauder of the U.S. government. At Williams's request, First Boston contacted First National City Bank to review the credit position of the company. They were informed that the railroad could be in trouble if there was not a turnaround, that the bank had turned down Bevan's request for a bridge loan, which later was made by a group of banks led by Chemical Bank, and that one of the Penn Central subsidiaries, Executive Jet Aviation, was in default on certain of its obligations to the bank.

A meeting of the underwriters and their counsel was held at the offices of Sullivan & Cromwell on March 31, 1970. The leaders of the investment banking firms were there along with Dean and Williams. Williams's March 28 memorandum was distributed to those in attendance. There was a discussion of the possible bankruptcy of the railroad, and, in response to a question from the underwriters, counsel expressed the view that, as a legal matter, Pennco would withstand the bankruptcy of the railroad. This danger most directly affected the international offering, and it was decided that it would be "postponed." It was also decided that work on the Pennco offering would continue on the understanding that Sullivan & Cromwell would include any disclosures needed to protect the underwriters from liability. The underwriters knew that they were running a risk, but they were unwilling to be known in the financial community as the cause of the collapse of the Penn Central.

A major hurdle to the Pennco offering was encountered on April 22, 1970, when Penn Central released its results for the first quarter. The reported loss was greater than Bevan had previously indicated to the underwriters. In the accompanying press release, management attempted to play down the losses, which were lessened on a consolidated level by a $51 million profit on the acceleration of the Wabash exchange and on the transportation company level by the sale of a coal company to Pennco. The significance of the railroad losses was a cause of their being set forth in the offering circular for the first time. On April 27, 1970, the application for the Pennco offering was filed with the Interstate Commerce Commission, and the next day copies of the offering circular were mailed to prospective selling group members, selected institutions and certain publications. The reaction to the offering was poor. On May 15, 1970, Pennco's rating was downgraded from BBB to BB, thereby effectively eliminating the institutional market. Following the announcement of the first quarter loss, there was a runoff of the company's commercial paper. The price ideas floated by the underwriters on May 15, 1970 failed to generate any interest in the issue. On May 21, 1970, the underwriters were told that the company did not intend to go forward with the offering. They were relieved that at last they were off the hook.

A month later, the transportation company filed for bankruptcy. Through the diligence of the lawyers, supported by their investment banking clients, the investing public was spared the losses that would have been sustained if the proposed deals had gone forward. As a result of the Penn Central collapse, Section 3(a)(6) of the 1933 Act was amended to bring railroad securities under the jurisdiction of the SEC.

The Hughes Tool Company Initial Public Offering

There are times when a managing underwriter and its counsel must go to extraordinary lengths to perform the diligence

LIABILITIES AND DUE DILIGENCE

required for a public offering of securities. This was true in the case of the December 7, 1972 initial public offering of common stock of Hughes Tool Company managed by Merrill Lynch, Pierce, Fenner & Smith Incorporated.

The company was formed to acquire the business and assets of the oil tool division of Summa Corporation, which prior to the offering was known as Hughes Tool Company. The company's business had been founded in 1908 to develop, manufacture and distribute a rock drilling bit that had been patented by Howard R. Hughes, Sr. The bit was a significant factor in the development of the oil and gas well drilling industry, and its success had been the foundation of the Hughes family fortune. All of the stock of Summa Corporation was owned by Howard R. Hughes, the billionaire recluse and the son of the founder of the business.

At the time that the offering was conceived, Hughes was ensconced on the seventh floor of the Intercontinental Hotel in Managua, Nicaragua, a country ruled at the time by the dictator Anastasio Somoza. The only persons who had seen Hughes in many years were his Mormon attendants, who maintained a 24-hour-a-day vigil. There were rumors as to Hughes's mental state and appearance. He was said to have an obsessive fear of germs and to have foot-long finger- and toenails.

Merrill Lynch and its counsel had been presented with a document bearing the signature "Howard R. Hughes," acknowledged by two witnesses, Howard Eckersley and James H. Rickard. The document constituted a consent to the transfer of the assets of the oil tool division to the new company and the sale of the shares of the new company to underwriters managed by Merrill Lynch. It contained certain indemnities and appointed Raymond M. Holliday as proxy and attorney-in-fact to carry out all matters relating to the conveyance of the assets and the sale of the securities. Holliday was to be the chairman of the board and chief executive officer of Hughes Tool Company.

Was the document real? No one had any reason to doubt Holliday's integrity, but he had an interest in the transaction and millions of dollars were at stake. No one was absolutely sure that Hughes was alive (there had been rumors of his death). If he was alive, was he competent to act? A few months before, a purported autobiography of Howard Hughes, which actually turned out to be authored by one Clifford Irving, had been exposed as a fraud to the great embarrassment of the distinguished publishing house that had accepted it for publication. Merrill Lynch and its counsel would face even worse embarrassment, to say nothing of monetary exposure, if they participated in an initial public offering of shares worth close to $150 million and it turned out that the transaction had not been authorized by the sole owner of the business.

J. Courtney Ivey, the senior partner of Brown, Wood, Fuller, Caldwell & Ivey, the firm acting as underwriters' counsel, had met Howard Hughes on two previous occasions. He felt certain that he would know Hughes if he saw him again. Julius H. ("Dooley") Sedlmayr, the head of investment banking at Merrill Lynch, had spoken by telephone with Hughes on at least one occasion. The two men determined that the only way that the deal would be done was for them to fly to Nicaragua, meet with Hughes, and actually see him sign a certificate confirming the instrument authorizing the transaction. This, of course, was strongly resisted by Hughes's people. Mr. Hughes simply did not see outsiders. There was no way that he would consent to such a meeting. Ivey and Sedlmayr persisted. There was too much at stake. This was a matter that went to the very heart of the deal. If they did not meet with Howard Hughes, there would be no public offering managed by Merrill Lynch.

Time passed, and there was no affirmative response. The deal was in danger of cratering. Finally, Ivey and Sedlmayr received word that Hughes would see them. They were to go to Nicaragua on September 22, 1972. Ivey related the story of the trip in a sworn statement prepared shortly after his return:

> Re: Discussion with Howard R. Hughes on Monday morning, September 25, 1972 at the Intercontinental Hotel, Managua, Nicaragua
>
> On Friday, September 22, Mr. Julius H. Sedlmayr, Group Vice President of Merrill Lynch, and I flew to Managua, Nicaragua, for the purpose of seeing Mr. Howard R. Hughes and obtaining from him a signed certificate regarding the power of attorney which he had

executed on Saturday, September 16. We arrived at the Intercontinental Hotel in Managua around 6:30 P.M. The next day, Saturday, September 23, Mr. Raymond Holliday, Executive Vice President of Hughes Tool Company, and Mr. Milton H. West, Jr., a partner in the firm of Andrews, Kurth, Campbell & Jones, of Houston, Texas, counsel for Hughes Tool Company, arrived in Managua. We talked to them Saturday morning and Raymond Holliday thought our appointment with Mr. Hughes would be around 8:00 P.M. Sunday evening, September 24. Around lunch time on Sunday, Mr. Holliday advised that the meeting had been postponed until around 11:00 P.M.

After dinner on Sunday, the four of us went to Mr. Holliday's room on the third floor of the hotel and we waited there. During the evening Mr. Holliday called Mr. Hughes' quarters for a progress report and we got little encouragement until around 3:30 A.M., when Mr. Holliday was advised that the meeting would take place in an hour or an hour and a half. At this point, Mr. Sedlmayr and I returned to our respective rooms and made preparations for leaving on the 6:45 A.M. plane for New York.

A little after 5:00 A.M., Mr. Holliday called Mr. Sedlmayr's room and advised us to meet on the seventh floor at the elevator doors. We then proceeded to the seventh floor, met Messrs. Holliday and West and then the four of us went into the living room of Mr. Hughes' quarters. We sat there for five or ten minutes. Mr. Clarence A. Waldron and Mr. George A. Francom were in and out of the room, and around 5:40 A.M., Mr. Waldron advised us Mr. Hughes was ready to see Mr. Sedlmayr and myself. We went into another room and there we were introduced to Mr. Hughes. Mr. Hughes was seated in a chair with a footrest. He wore a beard from ear to ear and a mustache. He had a blanket spread over him up to his waist and was bare from waist up except a light jacket was draped around his shoulders. Mr. Waldron sat on Mr. Hughes' right and Mr. Francom on his left. Mr. Sedlmayr and I sat in two straight armchairs directly in front of Mr. Hughes and only about two or three feet away from him.

Mr. Hughes stated that he thought he had talked to Mr. Sedlmayr before on the telephone, which Mr. Sedlmayr confirmed, and Mr. Sedlmayr also stated that I had seen Mr. Hughes some years ago with Mr. Maury Bent. I proceeded to tell Mr. Hughes the occasion of our previous visit, but was not able to finish because he was not able to hear me. He was then handed his hearing aid and proceeded to manipulate the batteries, and finally was given a new set of batteries by Mr. Waldron and inserted them in the hearing aid.

Mr. Hughes recalled the TWA stock financing in 1966 and stated he was very pleased with it; that he was glad that the stock went up after the offering, and, in accordance with the advice given him many years before by Mr. Randolph Hearst, Sr., a very good friend of his, he did not wish to get the last dollar but would let someone else make that. Mr. Sedlmayr reminded Mr. Hughes that Merrill Lynch had had two deals with him—referring to the approximately $100,000,000 debenture issue with warrants of TWA which were publicly offered in 1963. Mr. Hughes told Mr. Sedlmayr that he hoped Merrill Lynch would be able to get him a good price, but that he was not satisfied with any of the figures which had been given him to date. In the course of this discussion, Mr. Hughes stated that of course this was not the purpose of the meeting, that is, the fixing of the price for the stock of the Tool Company. Mr. Sedlmayr advised Mr. Hughes that Merrill Lynch would get the best price it possibly could. Mr. Hughes further stated that if he were Merrill Lynch, he would sell the stock to customers at the most favorable price he could get for the customers because Mr. Hughes was getting along and very probably there would be no more deals to go to Merrill Lynch from Mr. Hughes. Mr. Sedlmayr advised him that was not the way Merrill Lynch operated, that Merrill Lynch would get the best price it could that would be fair to both Mr. Hughes and Merrill Lynch's customers. Mr. Hughes also told Mr. Sedlmayr that he wanted him to go back and tell Mr. [Winthrop R.] Smith and others that he wanted a good price.

In the course of our discussion, Mr. Hughes wanted to know if Mr. Sedlmayr and I had missed our plane and stated that if we had, he would have one sent down from Miami to take us back.

He reminisced about his acquisition of the Tool Company through inheritance and purchase of parts of the stock from other relatives who had also inherited from Mr. Hughes' father. He further reminisced about his father's participation in World War I and described a tool that his father had invented to bore a hole under the ground parallel to the surface that could be used to place bombs near the enemy's trenches and then detonated. There was also some discussion about an Army colonel who came to work for Hughes Tool during his father's life and later took over the operations on his father's death. Mr. Hughes stated that the Army colonel was let go as a result of claims of fraud made by Mr. Noah Dietrich. I gather that Mr. Dietrich made a federal case of the incident but Mr. Hughes stated that it was nothing more than taking a company truck to haul manure to his farm. He stated that it was a trivial matter—like a man using the company car to go to the movies instead of his own car. There was also some by-play about the handwriting experts in the recent Irving debacle.

During the discussions Mr. Hughes told us of a new hearing aid that a doctor had given him and he described it in some detail. He stated that the entire instrument, including the batteries, was inserted in the ear and it was really a good instrument but he continued to use his old one. He further stated that he thought the scientists at Hughes Aircraft would be able to design a hearing aid that would be the best ever. I am not sure that he stated that Hughes Aircraft was at the present time working on such a device, but I received the impression that they were or would be.

During the many discussions with Mr. Raymond Holliday, we were told a good deal about the eight or nine people that customarily worked in Mr. Hughes' quarters. I think all are Mormons and are married. They shuttle back and forth from their homes in Salt Lake or Los Angeles on a fixed schedule basis—so many days off and so many days on. At least one and possibly two men are present on a 24 hour day, three eight hour shifts. At one point Mr. Holliday stated that Clarence Waldron had been with Mr. Hughes for approximately fifteen years and I gather that all of them had been with him for several years.

After testing two pens, Mr. Hughes picked one and in our presence and in the presence of Mr. Waldron and Mr. Francom, signed the certificate we had brought with us to Managua, and Mr. Waldron and Mr. Francom witnessed the signature. A xerox copy of the signed certificate is attached hereto.

The foregoing is my best present recollection of the conference with Mr. Hughes, although the items mentioned above probably did not occur in the order given.

In 1954 in connection with the possible sale of approximately 25% of the stock of the Hughes Tool Company, Mr. Winthrop Smith, Mr. George Leness and Mr. Maury Bent and I had about a two hour conference with Mr. Hughes and Mr. Tom Slack, his attorney at the time and a former partner of Andrews, Kurth, Campbell & Jones, at the Beverly Hills Hotel. I also saw Mr. Hughes for about fifteen minutes with Messrs. Smith, Leness and Bent outside the Beverly Wilshire Hotel before we departed for the airport for our return trip to New York. The conference in 1954 with Mr. Hughes was unusual even at that time in that few people, other than his personal staff, ever saw him. Because of the unusual nature of the conference, the events that occurred before, during and after the conference were inscribed on my memory much more than a run of the mill business conference would be. Also, I have described many times since 1954 the things that occurred and this has helped in my recollections of Mr. Hughes.

Prior to going to Los Angeles, Mr. Ralph L. Jones, one of my partners, and I spent at least a week in Houston working on a registration statement. Off and on during the 1960s I spent considerable time in California regarding a possible underwriting of stock of Hughes Aircraft and later in New York on the two underwritings of TWA securities. This involved a great deal of contact with trusted representatives of Mr. Hughes and as a result I learned a good deal about Mr. Hughes and his financial operations.

Although the previous conference with Mr. Hughes took place approximately eighteen years ago, because of the unusual nature of the conference as mentioned above, and reinforced by numerous pictures that I have seen over a considerable period of time, particularly in the recent past, and, notwithstanding the addition of a beard, the man we had our discussions with on September 25 did resemble the Mr. Hughes I saw in 1954.

From these recollections and our discussions summarized above, together with knowledge gained over the years, I am convinced that the man with whom we talked and who signed the certificate was the real Howard R. Hughes. I was also convinced that Mr. Hughes was capable of making decisions and mentally competent.

It was difficult to get away from Mr. Hughes after he had signed the certificate and I believe if time had permitted he would have talked to us for two or three hours—he was in a talking mood. As we left, Mr. Hughes shook hands with each of us with a firm hand grip.

We left Mr. Hughes' rooms around 6:15 A.M. and after picking up our baggage on the eighth floor left for the airport. We caught the 6:45 A.M. plane back to New York.

Mr. Ivey's statement failed to relate the fact that he and Mr. Sedlmayr each ordered a double martini before breakfast on the return flight to New York.

Chapter 6

RULES OF THE SELF-REGULATORY ORGANIZATIONS

The major investment banking firms in the United States are generally members of the New York Stock Exchange, Inc. (NYSE) as well as of the National Association of Securities Dealers, Inc. (NASD). The NASD and the NYSE and the other national securities exchanges in the United States are "self-regulatory organizations," or SROs, within the meaning of the 1934 Act. As such, they are subject to the SEC's oversight.

Membership in the NYSE is elective and requires purchasing or otherwise obtaining the rights to use a NYSE "seat," but membership in the NASD is generally mandatory.[1]

In the case of a securities firm that is a member both of the NYSE and the NASD, the firm will ordinarily have the NYSE as its designated examining authority for purposes of ensuring its compliance with applicable financial responsibility and other rules. This is the case for more than 250 firms that deal with the

---

1. Section 15(b)(8) of the 1934 Act requires a broker or dealer registered with the SEC under Section 15 to be a member of the NASD unless it deals exclusively in commercial paper, bankers' acceptances or commercial bills or it effects transactions in securities solely on a national securities exchange of which it is a member. Rule 15b9-1 further exempts certain other exchange members who carry no customer accounts.

public and account for more than 85% of the public customer accounts handled by broker-dealers in the United States.[2]

In addition to regulating its member firms, the NYSE operates the world's largest auction equity market. Accordingly, the NYSE exercises direct regulatory authority over its listed companies, its trading floor and its member firms.

Until 1996, the NASD also operated and regulated NASDAQ, the world's largest dealer equity market.[3] A Department of Justice investigation of NASD market-makers and an SEC investigation of the NASD's enforcement of NASDAQ's trading rules led in 1994 to the appointment of a committee to review NASD governance and oversight. The committee recommended that the NASD's relationship with NASDAQ be restructured so as to put substantial "daylight" between the membership association and the market.

Accordingly, the NASD was reorganized in early 1996 as a parent company with two operating subsidiaries. One of the subsidiaries operated NASDAQ. The other—NASD Regulation, Inc. (NASDR)—had the primary authority to regulate NASD member firms. This authority included the development and administration of the NASD Rules of Fair Practice (subsequently redesignated as "Conduct Rules"), membership rules and operational requirements for member firms.

In 2000, the NASD decided to sell NASDAQ and to assume the regulatory responsibilities of NASDR.[4]

By setting and enforcing their respective listing standards, the NYSE and NASDAQ also exercise a very significant influence over the corporate governance practices of their listed companies.

---

2. *See* the NYSE's website at www.nyse.com. The NASD's website is at www.nasd.com.

3. NASDAQ's current formal name is The NASDAQ Stock Market Inc. It consists of two distinct market "tiers," including the NASDAQ National Market and the NASDAQ SmallCap Market.

4. The NASD operates other markets such as the PORTAL system and the OTC Bulletin Board Service. It also controls the American Stock Exchange but announced in late 2003 its plans to transfer that exchange to its members.

The NYSE and the NASD have examination and investigation responsibility for member firms and their "associated persons" as well as enforcement and disciplinary authority. The fact that the NYSE and the NASD are "self-regulatory organizations" does not mean that they are inclined to go easy on their members. (As many in the industry have had cause to observe, "there is not much 'self' left anymore in 'self-regulation.' ") Support for this proposition can easily be obtained by a casual glance at the NYSE's and NASD's monthly published lists of disciplinary proceedings or at the annual surveys of SRO disciplinary practices and proceedings published by the ABA's Section of Litigation.

Since the SEC's approval in 1988 of the elimination of the previous ceilings on disciplinary fines imposed by the NYSE and the NASD,[5] the SROs have aggressively pursued monetary fines as a means of tailoring sanctions to fit the facts and circumstances of individual cases. Sanctions can also include suspensions of member firms or their employees for shorter or longer periods as well as, in extreme cases, expulsion from the NYSE or the NASD. Disciplinary actions by the SROs are subject to review by the SEC.

As noted above, underwriting activities in the United States are not conducted through the facilities of the stock exchanges. Nor, for that matter, are they conducted through NASDAQ. Rather, securities that are the subject of registered underwritten public offerings are sold directly to customers of the underwriters and the dealers participating in the distribution. Thus, to the extent that underwriting practices are regulated by the SROs, that regulation is imposed and administered by the NASD (and to a lesser extent the NYSE) as regulators of their member firms.

NYSE rules have little impact on underwritten securities offerings as such, particularly since the practical abolition of prohibitions against "off-board trading" of listed securities. In the case of a "follow-on" offering of a listed security, however,

---

5. SEC Rel. No. 34-25999 (August 6, 1988).

the issuer is required to apply for the NYSE listing of the additional securities, while Rule 392 requires the lead underwriter to notify the NYSE of the offering and to provide certain specified information about the offering.[6] In addition, there are NYSE requirements of a technical nature applicable to rights offerings (see Chapter 13).

Finally, NYSE Rule 312(g) prevents member firms from effecting or recommending customer transactions in their own securities or securities of their affiliates.[7]

The NASD has a much more direct role than the NYSE in regulating important aspects of the underwriting process. Its role in this area goes back to the Investment Bankers Code adopted in 1932 by the investment banking industry pursuant to the National Industrial Recovery Act (NIRA). The code was amended in 1934 to incorporate certain rules of fair practice. When NIRA was declared unconstitutional in 1935,[8] the securities industry continued on a voluntary basis to meet the standards of the code under the direction of the Investment Bankers Conference Committee, which later became the Investment Bankers Conference, Inc. (IBCI).

In 1938, the Maloney Act amended the 1934 Act by adding Section 15A to provide for regulation of the over-the-counter market by national securities associations registered with the SEC.[9] The statutory objective was to establish a mechanism to

---

6. NASDAQ requires its issuers to provide it with 15 days prior notice of any transaction that may result in the issuance of common stock greater than 10% of the total shares or voting power outstanding and with notice within 10 days after the fact of any aggregate increase or decrease of any class of securities included in NASDAQ that exceeds 5% of the amount outstanding. Both the NYSE and NASDAQ also require their issuers to obtain shareholder approval in the case of certain large follow-on offerings.

7. The NASD considered in 1987 adopting a rule to restrict its members' market-making or trading in securities issued by their affiliates. It decided to take no action for the time being. NASD Notice to Members 87-62 (September 22, 1987).

8. *A.L.A. Schecter Poultry Corp. v. United States,* 295 U.S. 495 (1935).

9. Pub. L. No. 719, 75th Cong., 3d Sess. (June 25, 1938). *See* Comment, *Over-the-Counter Trading and the Maloney Act,* 48 Yale L.J. 633 (1939).

regulate brokers and dealers operating in the over-the-counter market comparable to that provided by the national securities exchanges.[10] The congressional reports on the bill pointed out that "the primary operations of the great underwriting houses take place over the counter" and that, accordingly, the over-the-counter market provided the principal channel by which savings flowed into new financing.

The Maloney Act was designed, among other things, "to cope with those methods of doing business which, while technically outside the area of definite illegality, are nevertheless unfair both to customer and to decent competitor, and are seriously damaging to the mechanism of the free and open market."[11] The underlying principle was "cooperative regulation" performed by representative organizations of investment bankers, dealers and brokers, with the federal government, acting through the SEC, exercising appropriate supervision and exercising supplementary powers of direct regulation.[12]

After the adoption of the Maloney Act, the IBCI appointed a drafting committee to draw up the necessary organizational documents, rules of fair practice and a code of procedures. After approval by the IBCI membership and the SEC, the NASD succeeded to the IBCI in the summer of 1939.

The NASD's Rules of Fair Practice were reorganized in 1996 as part of an overall reorganization of the NASD *Manual.* The Rules of Fair Practice now form part of the NASD's "Conduct Rules." Rule 2110 (formerly Article III, Section 1) still establishes the basic overriding principle: "A member, in the conduct of his business, shall observe high standards of commercial honor and just and equitable principles of trade."[13] This broad and sweeping statement is implemented by a number of rules

---

10. S. Rep. No. 1455, 75th Cong., 3d Sess. 1 (1938).
11. *Id.* at 3.
12. *Id.* at 4–5.
13. The NASD construes this "fundamental rule of ethical practice" in broad fashion. For example, it interprets the rule to prohibit "abusive communications" with customers or with employees of other broker-dealers. *See* Notice to Members 96-44 (July 1996).

and interpretations administered by the NASD Regulation staff subject to oversight by its board of directors.

Rule 2710 provides for NASD review of underwriting terms and arrangements and is concerned primarily with the fairness of such terms and arrangements. It requires that a filing be made in connection with most public offerings of securities to enable the Corporate Financing Department of the NASD to determine that the proposed underwriting compensation and other arrangements are not unfair or unreasonable.

Rule 2720 (formerly Schedule E to the NASD's by-laws) regulates the participation by a member in a public offering of securities issued by that member or its affiliates *or* where the member has a "conflict of interest" with respect to the offering (defined as beneficial ownership by the member and certain related persons of more than 10% of specified securities of the issuer).

Rule 2790, a new rule based on a long-standing interpretation of Rule 2110, relates to "free-riding and withholding." It is based on the premise that NASD members have an obligation to make a bona fide public distribution of IPOs at the public offering price. In other words, underwriters should not be permitted to exploit for their own benefit their control over IPO allocations.

Unfortunately, events during the Internet Bubble demonstrated that there were other ways for underwriters to exploit their control over IPO allocations. Pending rule proposals by the NASD seek to close off some of these more recently discovered opportunities such as "spinning" or excessive compensation for other services.

Since 2002, the NYSE and the NASD both regulate the involvement of research analysts in securities offerings. Rule 2711 is the applicable NASD rule, and Rule 472 is the NYSE's rule. These rules are discussed in Chapter 3.

Rules 2730, 2740 and 2750—the so-called "*Papilsky* rules"— are designed to prevent rebates of selling concessions in fixed-price offerings. Rule 2420 prohibits transactions with non-member broker-dealers (other than certain foreign dealers) except on the same terms accorded to the general public.

These are the principal SRO rules that apply to public offerings of securities, other than "exempted securities" (as defined in

Section 3(a)(12) of the 1934 Act).[14] Because they are rules that govern the conduct of the underwriters and selected dealers, rather than rules relating to the overall transaction, the responsibility for ensuring compliance rests with the managing underwriter and its in-house legal or transactional staff, assisted by underwriters' counsel. Underwriters' counsel needs to ensure that the requisite filings are made, that the underwriting documents contain the necessary provisions to ensure compliance, and that the underwriters are aware of their responsibilities as members of the NASD.

Review of Corporate Financing (Rule 2710)

Rule 2710, the "Corporate Financing Rule," is based on the premise that it would be contrary to high standards of commercial honor and just and equitable principles of trade for an NASD member to participate in a distribution of securities if the underwriting or other arrangements are unfair or unreasonable.[15] The rule therefore prohibits participation in such offerings and requires NASD members to file specified information about offerings, which may not proceed until the NASD has given its clearance. An offering may be exempt from the filing requirement but not from the rule's standards of fairness and reasonableness.

The NASD first became concerned with unfair underwriting arrangements in the wake of the hot-issue market that existed from 1959 through 1961. In late 1961, it established a standing committee on underwriting arrangements to review offerings of securities of unseasoned companies to determine whether the underwriting arrangements were fair and consistent with just and equitable principles of trade.[16] The corporate financing

---

14. Rule 2810 regulates public offerings of direct participation programs, that is, limited partnerships and similar entities that provide for flow-through tax consequences.

15. Underwriting compensation also is regulated by certain state securities laws, although the significance of such laws in this respect has diminished since the passage of the Improvement Act. *See* Chapter 3.

16. NASD Notice to Members (December 26, 1961).

interpretation was adopted in 1970[17] and became a rule in 1992.[18] The rule was significantly amended in 2004, primarily for the purposes of modernization and simplification and to take account of the more varied activities of financial services firms.[19]

- *Filing Requirements*

Unless one of the exemptions discussed below is available, specified documents and information must be filed with the NASD for every "public offering" for the purpose of enabling the Corporate Financing Department to pass upon the fairness and reasonableness of the underwriting arrangements.

"Public offering" is defined in Rule 2720(b)(14), and this definition is incorporated by reference into Rule 2710. The term includes any registered or non-registered primary or secondary distribution, and it excludes private placements effected pursuant to specified 1933 Act provisions and rules. The definition also excludes public offerings of "exempted securities" (as defined in the 1934 Act, not as defined in the 1933 Act). Accordingly, an NASD filing may be required for a public offering even where it is exempt from registration under the 1933 Act—for example, public offerings by banks, intrastate offerings and certain exchange offers.

In the case of an underwritten public offering, the managing underwriter is responsible for ensuring that the filing is made. Since July 2002, the filing takes the form of an electronic communication—often by underwriters' counsel—through the NASD's Web-based COBRADesk System (Corporate Offerings Business Regulatory Analysis System). Firms must be registered to use the COBRADesk System, and passwords for individuals using the system on behalf of a firm must be renewed every 60 days.[20] The rule provides that the registration statement and other

---

17. NASD Notice to Members (March 10, 1970).
18. NASD Notice to Members 92-28 (May 1992).
19. The SEC approved the amendments at the end of 2003. SEC Release No. 34-48989 (December 23, 2003). The amendments became effective on March 22, 2004. NASD Notice to Members 04-13 (February 2004).
20. Information on the use of the CobraDesk System is available on the NASD's website.

documents filed with the SEC through the EDGAR system are treated as filed with the NASD.

The filing must be made not later than one business day after filing with the SEC or any other regulatory authority or, if there is no filing with the SEC or any other regulatory body, at least 15 business days prior to the anticipated offering date.[21] The NASD imposes a filing fee of $500 plus .01% of the proposed maximum aggregate offering price of the offering, not to exceed a fee of $30,500.[22] The fee may (but need not) be paid by wire transfer to the NASD.

The original filing with the NASD must set forth an estimate of the maximum public offering price and the maximum underwriting discount or commission, information as to any arrangement for the reimbursement of underwriters' expenses, including the fees of underwriters' counsel, the maximum financial consulting and/or advisory fees to the underwriter and related persons, maximum finder's fees, and a statement of any other type and amount of compensation that may accrue to the underwriter and related persons.

For purposes of the rule, the term "underwriter and related person" comprises "underwriter's counsel, financial consultants and advisors, finders, any participating member, and any other persons related to any participating member." The term "participating member" means "any NASD member that is participating in a public offering, any associated person of the member, any members of their immediate family, and any affiliate of the member."[23]

---

21. Offerings submitted to the SEC for confidential review, e.g., in the case of certain foreign issuers as discussed in Chapter 9, are considered to be filed with the SEC *as of the date of the confidential submission.* NASD Notice to Members 04-13 (February 2004), at 119.

22. Section 7 of Schedule A to the NASD's by-laws.

23. A "person associated with a member" or an "associated person of a member" includes every "sole proprietor, partner, officer, director, or branch manager of a member, or other natural person occupying a similar status or performing similar functions, or a natural person engaged in the investment banking or securities business who is directly or indirectly controlling or controlled by a member." NASD By-laws, Article I(dd).

The term "immediate family" is broadly defined in Rule 2720(b)(9) and incorporated by reference in Rule 2710.

The filing must identify and provide information regarding any association or affiliation between any NASD member and any officer or director or 5% beneficial owner of any class of the issuer's securities or any beneficial owner of any of the issuer's unregistered equity securities acquired during the six months preceding the required filing date (except for purchases pursuant to a qualified compensation plan). In the case of securities ownership, the filing must identify the amount of securities owned and the acquisition date and price. The filing must also include a "detailed explanation" of any arrangements during the preceding six months involving the issuer's transfer to the underwriter and related persons of any "items of value" or warrants, options or other securities. Certain debt securities and derivatives are excluded from the filing requirement or require only a brief description.

If it is claimed that certain items of value do not constitute underwriting compensation, the filing must include a statement demonstrating compliance with all of the criteria for any relevant exception.

To discourage "spinning," a practice discussed later in this chapter, the NASD proposed in August 2002 to add the requirement that the filing include information regarding the book-running managing underwriter's sale during the preceding six months of any IPO shares to any executive officer or director of the issuer.[24] If such a sale took place, the filing would have to disclose whether the officer or director participated in any capacity in the selection of the book-running managing underwriter for the issuer's public offering for which the filing is being made. A similar statement would have to be filed within 15 days of the close of the six-month period following the public offering for which the filing is being made.

Information necessary for the filing under the Corporate Financing Rule will ordinarily be obtained by underwriters' counsel from questionnaires completed by the underwriters and

---

24. NASD Notice to Members 02-55 (August 2002).

RULES OF THE SELF-REGULATORY ORGANIZATIONS 401

by the issuer's officers, directors and substantial securityholders. These questionnaires are usually based on standard forms used by major law firms, but it is necessary, as in the case of any standard form, to consider what revisions are required for the particular transaction. Persons who receive questionnaires must be encouraged to complete them in time to permit a timely NASD filing.

Rule 461(b)(6) under the 1933 Act states that the SEC may refuse to accelerate the effective date of a registration statement where the NASD has not signed off on the fairness of the underwriting arrangements. The NASD's opinion of no objections will eventually be reduced to writing, but the registration statement will usually be declared effective based on a telephone call from the NASD examiner to his or her counterpart at the SEC.

- *Exemptions*

Certain offerings are subject to the rule but are exempt from its filing requirements, unless they are subject to Rule 2720 (discussed below). One of the most important exemptions from the filing requirements applies to securities (debt or equity, but *not* an IPO of equity securities) offered by an issuer that has unsecured non-convertible debt with a term of at least four years, or unsecured non-convertible preferred stock, rated by a nationally recognized statistical rating agency in one of its four highest generic rating categories. An offering of investment-grade non-convertible debt securities or preferred stock is also exempt from the filing requirement even though the issuer has no outstanding securities that have an investment-grade rating.

Because of these exemptions, offerings by many major issuers are not required to be filed with the NASD. The assumption is that issuers of this caliber have the sophistication and economic clout to ensure that the underwriting spread will be reasonable.

Another exemption from filing applies to securities registered with the SEC on Form S-3 or Form F-3 and offered pursuant to the shelf registration provisions of Rule 415.[25] Shelf takedowns under Rule 415 could not be effected on an expeditious basis if it were necessary to seek NASD approval each time an issue is taken off the shelf.

In the case of non-exempt shelf registrations, the issuer may make the filing. The NASD will issue a conditional or unconditional no-objections opinion, depending on whether underwriters are named. There were reports in mid-2004 that the NASD would propose rule changes that would formalize this procedure but require a new underwriter to obtain its own no-objections opinion (which would, however, be good for the life of the shelf assuming a maximum level of underwriting compensation was disclosed and there were no material changes in the information included in the filing).

No filing is required in connection with offerings of asset-backed securities that are rated in one of the four highest generic rating categories or for certain redemption standby arrangements.

Although the foregoing offerings are exempt from the filing requirements, the rule's substantive fairness requirements for underwriting arrangements are still applicable. On the other hand, offerings of certain securities are exempt from the rule itself and not just the filing requirement. These include securities sold in private placements (including Rule 144A offerings), U.S. government and municipal and other "exempted" securities, certain open-end and closed-end investment company shares, and securities issued pursuant to competitive bidding arrangements that meet the requirements of the Public Utility Holding Company Act of 1935. Commercial paper is not a "security" within the meaning of the 1934 Act (unlike the 1933 Act), and NASD filings are not made for commercial paper programs. Tender offers made pursuant to Regulation 14D under the 1934 Act are also exempt from the rule.

---

25. Somewhat stubbornly, the NASD for this purpose applies the standards for Form S-3 and Form F-3 that applied prior to October 21, 1992. An issuer must therefore have a 1934 Act reporting history of 36 months rather than 12 months. A U.S. issuer must have a public float of $150 million (or $100 million and an annual trading volume of three million shares) rather than the $75 million that the SEC requires, and a non-U.S. issuer must have a float of $300 million rather than $75 million. Separate criteria apply for Canadian issuers.

The NASD also takes the position that the shelf exemption is not available in a "convenience" context, i.e., where all of the registered securities are distributed in a traditional underwriting arrangement shortly after effectiveness. SEC Releases No. 34-32316 (May 17, 1993), 34-33185 (November 10, 1993). *See also* NASD Notice to Members 93-88 (December 1993).

- *Request for Underwriting Activity Report*

Even where an exemption is available from the rule's filing requirements, Rule 2710(b)(10) requires the managing underwriter of an offering that is subject to Rule 101 (the SEC's antimanipulation rule discussed in Chapter 4) or that involves an "actively traded" security under Rule 101 to submit a request to the NASD's Market Regulation Department for an Underwriting Activity Report (UAR) relating to the offered securities. The requirement to obtain a UAR does not apply if the securities are listed on the NYSE or another national securities exchange. As noted above, the NYSE's Rule 392 requires the lead underwriter to notify it of any offering in a listed security.

The stated purpose of the UAR requirement is to enable the NASD to provide information to the managing underwriter regarding the trading volume and public float of the relevant securities, thus facilitating compliance with Rule 101 and related rules. As discussed in Chapter 4, a managing underwriter may at its option also use the UAR to submit a request to stabilize a NASDAQ security and to provide notice of its intent to impose a penalty bid or to conduct syndicate covering transactions.

- *Submission of Pricing Information*

If the offering involves listed securities that are subject securities or reference securities subject to Rule 101 or actively traded securities under Rule 101 or any other securities that are actively traded securities under Rule 101, then Rule 2710(b)(11) requires the managing underwriter to notify the NASD's Market Regulation Department "no later than the close of business the day the offering terminates" of the date and time of the offering's pricing, the offering price and the time the offering terminated. The notice may be submitted on the UAR.

- *Items of Value*

The items to be included in determining the total amount of underwriters' compensation for purposes of the rule are all items of value received or to be received from any source "in connection with or related to the distribution of the public offering," and "whether in the form of cash, securities or any other item of value," including without limitation: the underwriting discount or commission, any reimbursed underwriters' expenses, the fees and expenses of underwriters' counsel, finder's fees, "wholesalers' fees," financial consulting and advisory fees, stock, options, warrants and other equity securities received as payment for services or purchased in a private placement, "special sales incentive items," rights of first refusal, compensation received during the 12 months following the offering as the result of exercise of warrants, options or similar securities, QIU fees and any "busted deal" expense reimbursement.

An underwriter or related person may not receive securities as underwriting compensation unless they are (a) identical to the securities being offered to the public or to a security with a bona fide independent market or (b) "can be accurately valued." Securities without an exercise or conversion price that are received as underwriting compensation are valued by taking into consideration the difference between their cost to the underwriter and the proposed public offering price or, if there is a market for the stock, the market price on the date of acquisition. The rule also sets forth a formula for valuing options, warrants, or convertible securities received as underwriting compensation.

A right of first refusal to underwrite future offerings is an item of compensation that will be valued at 1% of the offering proceeds or that dollar amount, if any, contractually agreed to by the issuer and the underwriter as the price for a waiver or termination of the right of first refusal. The rule also imposes certain substantive restrictions on rights of first refusal (see below).

"Items of value" for purposes of the rule do not include reimbursement of expenses customarily borne by an issuer, cash compensation for certain investment banking services, "listed securities" purchased in public market transactions,[26] securities

---

26. The definition of "listed securities" in the rule refers to securities that meet the listing standards of the "national securities exchanges" identified in Rule 146 under the 1933 Act. NASDAQ's National Market System is referred to in Rule 146 but is not a national securities exchange. Notwithstanding, the NASD takes the position that NSM securities are "listed" for purposes of Rule 2710.

acquired through a qualified equity compensation plan and securities acquired by an investment company registered under the Investment Company Act of 1940.

In addition, certain debt securities and derivatives are excluded as items of value. These must be acquired or entered into for a fair price, in the ordinary course of business and in transactions unrelated to the public offering. The "fair price" requirement means that the underwriter or related person must price the debt security or derivative in good faith, on an arm's length, commercially reasonable basis and in accordance with pricing methods and models and procedures used in the ordinary course of their business for pricing similar transactions. Debt securities and derivatives received in exchange for services or providing credit are deemed not to have been acquired or entered into for a fair price.

The exclusion for debt securities and derivatives applies only where they are entered into or acquired in transactions "unrelated to the public offering." According to the NASD, transactions occurring during the "review period" (i.e., from 180 days prior to the required filing date up to the commencement of sales) that are negotiated by personnel in a member's investment banking department generally would not be considered to be unrelated to the public offering.[27] In that case, information relating to the debt securities or derivatives must be filed with the NASD if the offering is subject to the filing requirements of the rule. The NASD's Notice to Members provides the illustration of "a derivative transaction designed to hedge the interest rate risk in a non-investment grade rated debt offering." The information initially filed may be limited to a brief description of the transaction and a representation that the transaction was or will be entered into at a fair price. The NASD will evaluate the submitted information on a case-by-case basis and will determine that the debt security or derivative has compensation value "only if facts and circumstances indicate that the transaction is structured

---

27. The NASD recognizes an exception to this "general principle" in the case of a put option or other derivative instrument that is entered into by an issuer with an underwriter or related person in connection with a publicly disclosed share repurchase program.

so that the risk to the underwriter or related person and the benefit to the customer is minimal, in comparison to the benefit received by the underwriter or related person."

In the case of a debt security or derivative related to a public offering that is exempt from the rule's filing requirement (e.g., investment-grade debt or shelf offerings by issuers with a 36-month reporting history and a $150 million public float), the NASD cautions that the substantive requirements of the rule must still be met. Specifically, "[i]f a participating member has entered into a fair price derivative transaction in connection with an offering that is exempt from the Rule's filing requirements, members or their counsel must evaluate the facts and circumstances and reasonably determine that the transaction was executed at a fair price and, therefore, has no compensation value." In making this determination, members or their counsel would be guided by the same test applied by the NASD in connection with filed transactions.

Swaps are common in connection with debt offerings, and even many equity offerings may be accompanied by or be for the purpose of unwinding derivative transactions. Counsel should keep in mind that Item 508(e) of Regulation S-K requires disclosure of all items considered by the NASD to be underwriting compensation.

- *Lockup Agreements*

Except in the case of securities of an issuer that meets the NASD shelf eligibility criteria (36 months reporting history and $150 million public float), any unregistered[28] equity securities acquired by an underwriter during the six months prior to the required filing date or after filing and deemed to be underwriting compensation are subject to a six-month lockup—that is, they may not be sold, transferred, assigned, pledged or hypothecated for a period of six months after the offering. The lockup's

---

28. The NASD takes the position that "unregistered" in this context means unregistered under both the 1933 Act and the 1934 Act. In other words, the lockup requirement applies to securities acquired in private placements but not to securities that are acquired in the public trading markets such as an underwriter's market-making or trading positions at the time of an offering.

prohibitions extend to short sales, hedges or derivatives that would result in the "effective economic disposition" of the securities.

The lockup requirement does not apply to dispositions by operation of law or as a result of the issuer's reorganization or transfers to officers or partners of the firm receiving the compensation or to another firm participating in the offering or its officers or partners (provided that the lockup follows the securities). Also, the lockup does not apply for an underwriter and its related persons to the extent that they do not own in the aggregate more than 1% of the securities being offered. Other underwriters and their related persons may take advantage of their own 1% exception. The lockup also does not apply to securities owned by certain investment funds, to securities not deemed to be items of value because they were acquired through a qualified equity compensation plan or by an investment company registered under the Investment Company Act of 1940 or to securities acquired in Rule 144A transactions subsequent to the issuer's IPO.

The lockup requirement does not apply to fair price derivatives excluded from the definition of items of value or eligible to be briefly described in the initial filing, but it does apply to any "unregistered equity securities" of the issuer acquired as a result of the settlement of such a fair price derivative. Commenters requested the NASD to exempt such acquisitions from the lockup requirement, noting that issuer puts in connection with share repurchase programs and certain shareholder hedging transactions could be adversely affected when settled in unregistered equity securities during the 180-day period. The NASD declined to provide a blanket exemption but held out the possibility of case-by-case relief on the basis of whether or not the lockup requirement would interfere with "bona fide hedging activity that benefits an issuer and its shareholders."[29]

Securities eligible for the five exceptions described below from treatment as underwriting compensation are nevertheless subject to the lockup requirement.

---

29. NASD Notice to Members 04-13 (February 2004), at 119.

Longer lockups can provide a benefit under the rule, which for the purpose of arriving at a value for the securities permits a 10% discount for every six additional months by which the lockup period extends beyond the usual six months.

Lockups required by the Corporate Financing Rule do not trigger the recommended or proposed disclosure and notice requirements or the research restrictions associated with the underwriter-imposed lockups discussed in Chapter 2.

- *"Included in Underwriting Compensation"*

Prior to the 2004 amendments to Rule 2710, it was necessary to determine whether compensation had been received "in connection with" the offering. This determination was one of the most difficult and unpredictable determinations to be made in connection with the Corporate Financing Rule. The NASD itself noted in April 2000 that the rule as then in effect required the staff to weigh as many as ten different factors on a case-by-case basis to determine whether an item of value was received in connection with the public offering and therefore included in the calculation of underwriting compensation. It suggested that this "subjective, factor-weighing process" was an "inefficient method" for achieving the rule's purposes and hampered the staff's ability to provide clear and predictable guidance to members.[30]

The NASD also acknowledged that the "in connection with" element of the rule had become more unwieldy because many NASD members had expanded the variety of services that they provided to their investment banking clients and also because the time period between many issuers' private financing activity and their IPOs had been shortened.

As finally amended in 2004, the rule considers all items of value received and all arrangements entered into for the future receipt of items of value during the six months preceding the required filing date and until the commencement of the offering to be underwriting compensation in connection with the offering. Any items and arrangements not disclosed to the NASD,

---

30. SEC Release No. 34-42619 (April 4, 2000) (notice of NASD rulemaking), text at nn.13–17.

including items received subsequent to the public offering, are subject to "post-offering review" by the NASD to determine whether the items of value in question are underwriting compensation for the public offering.

The 2004 amendments also provide for five new exceptions, intended to cover bona fide capital-raising transactions, that have the effect of excluding certain items of value from underwriting compensation. The exceptions are available in the case of:

- securities of the issuer (in the aggregate, up to 25% of the issuer's total equity securities on a post-transaction basis) purchased before the filing date in a private placement or received as compensation for a loan or credit facility or placement activity if the related recipient[31] is a money manager, insurance company or bank meeting certain conditions and if there are specified elements of separation between the investing activity and the member's underwriting activity;

- securities of the issuer (for each transaction, up to 25% of the issuer's total equity securities on a post-transaction basis) purchased before the filing date in a private placement or received as compensation for a loan or credit facility or placement activity if the related recipient[32] is a money manager meeting certain conditions, including specified elements of separation between the investing activity and the member's underwriting activity, and the issuer is owned to the extent of at least 33% prior to the transaction by institutional investors and the transaction is approved by a majority of the issuer's board and a majority of any institutional investors or their designees who are members of the board;

---

31. A recipient may consist of more than one person if such persons are "contractually obligated to make co-investments and have previously made at least one such investment" or if they have filed a Schedule 13D or 13G with the SEC. A single investor (but not a group) may invest through a wholly owned subsidiary.

32. *See* the preceding footnote.

410 CORPORATE FINANCE & THE SECURITIES LAWS

- securities purchased in or received as placement agent compensation for a private placement if institutional investors[33] buy at least 51% of the total offering, an unaffiliated institutional investor is the lead negotiator (or the lead investor) and underwriters and related persons (other than qualified related investors under the first exception described above) do not receive more than 20% of the total offering;

- securities acquired pursuant to certain preemptive rights, stock splits, rights or similar offerings and certain conversions, but only where other investors have similar rights and the underwriter's percentage interest does not increase (except in the case of conversions or passive increases resulting from other investors' failure to exercise their own rights); and

- securities acquired on the basis of a prior investment history, that is, where an initial purchase of the issuer's securities was made at least two years and a second purchase more than 180 days before the filing date, and where the purchase does not increase the underwriter's percentage interest in the issuer.

The exceptions are not available if the underwriter conditions its participation in the public offering on the receipt of the securities pursuant to an exception or where any securities purchased are not purchased at the same price and with the same terms as securities purchased by all other investors.

The NASD considered but ultimately rejected an additional exception that would have applied to securities acquired in connection with financial consulting and advisory services. The NASD will analyze on a case-by-case basis in light of all the

---

33. An "institutional investor" for purposes of the exception has at least $50 million invested or under management. Participating members may not direct or otherwise manage such investments or have an equity interest, individually or in the aggregate, that exceeds 5% for a publicly owned entity or 1% for a nonpublic entity.

facts and circumstances whether securities or cash acquired in connection with financial consulting and advisory services constitute underwriting compensation.

As noted above, securities acquired pursuant to the five exceptions are not "items of value," but they are subject to the lockup requirements.

• • *"Profit-Sharing" Allegations.* The allegation was made following the collapse of the Internet Bubble that some underwriters had sought to exploit their ability to allocate "hot" IPOs by conditioning an allocation on the customer's agreement to pay excessive compensation for other services. For example, a customer might agree in exchange for an allocation to pay commissions of $1 or more per share for secondary market transactions where the usual commission for such transactions might be only pennies per share. Some underwriters were alleged to have kept meticulous records of customers' profits on allocated IPOs and to have insisted that the customers "rebate" to the underwriter a specified portion of such profits.

As discussed below under "Free-Riding and Withholding," the NASD and other regulators eventually alleged that these arrangements amounted to "profit sharing" on hot IPOs and therefore to an impermissible albeit indirect violation of the free-riding and withholding interpretation. Purchasers of IPO securities also eventually alleged in private litigation that the related IPO registration statements had contained misstatements and omissions in violation of Section 11 of the 1933 Act because the excessive compensation amounted to undisclosed "underwriting compensation" within the meaning of the NASD's Corporate Financing Rule and therefore Item 508(e) of Regulation S-K, and this claim was held to have been properly pled.[34]

As noted above, the definition of "underwriting compensation" includes items of value received "from any source." On the other hand, and without condoning an underwriter's attempt in this fashion to exploit its control over the allocation process, the

---

34. *In re Initial Public Offering Securities Litig.*, 241 F. Supp. 2d 281, 336–51 (S.D.N.Y. 2003).

Corporate Financing Rule is clearly designed to protect the *issuer* against unreasonable underwriting arrangements. Also, underwriters have been deriving collateral benefits for decades from their role as underwriter. If nothing else, customers who are well treated in the allocation process are likely to be good customers and to become better customers. Also, success breeds success, as underwriters capitalize on one deal's contribution to their "league table" standings as a means of winning business from other issuers. The NASD has never attempted to collect data on these collateral benefits, much less tried to quantify them. Nor is it clear that customers' commissions on secondary markets transactions bear anything but the most superficial connection to the underwriting.

Whether or not the excessive compensation arrangements violated the Corporate Financing Rule or were otherwise unlawful (firms have been allocating hot issues to their best customers for decades based in part on the profitability of the customer relationship), they were clearly abusive and not based on sound business practice. After all, an occasional customer should not be allowed to become an "instant best customer" by paying excessive compensation on a few transactions and thereby obtain an advantage over a customer that has been paying customary compensation in good times and bad.

- *Standards of Fairness*

The NASD has not published standards as to the amount of underwriting compensation that will be considered unfair or unreasonable. It does have internal guidelines, however, and the maximum permissible percentage compensation will vary inversely with the overall size of the deal and directly with the amount of risk borne by the underwriters. The NASD staff has not formally disclosed these guidelines.

The rule states that, in reaching a determination of fairness, the factors to be taken into consideration include the size of the offering (the smaller the offering, the greater the proportion of compensation to offering size that may be reasonable), the amount of risk being assumed by participating members (which is deemed to be a function of whether the underwriting is a firm commitment or "best efforts" arrangement and whether it is a primary or secondary offering) (greater risk justifies greater compensation) and the type of securities being offered. In addition, "any other relevant factors and circumstances shall . . . be taken into consideration."

The net result is that filing and NASD clearance under the Corporate Financing Rule is a routine procedure for most offerings underwritten by major investment banking firms, assuming that filing is required at all.

- *Unfair Underwriting Arrangements*

The rule sets forth certain arrangements that it deems to be unfair on their face. These include:

- non-accountable expense reimbursement allowances in excess of 3% and accountable expense allowances that cover the underwriter's general overhead or similar expenses;
- rights of first refusal that have a duration of more than three years, that provide more than one opportunity to waive or terminate the right in consideration of any payment or fee, or that provide for waiver or termination fees that are either non-cash or that exceed specified guidelines;
- the receipt of options, warrants or convertible securities as underwriting compensation where they are exercisable or convertible for a period of more than five years, or where the option, warrant or convertible security does not meet the specific standards relating to registration rights, antidilution provisions and other matters set forth in the rule;
- the receipt of items for which a value cannot be determined at the time of the offering;
- the receipt of an overallotment or "Green Shoe" option in connection with a firm commitment underwriting if the option is in excess of 15% of the amount of securities

being offered[35] (such an option calls into question, in the view of the NASD, whether the underwriting is really on a firm commitment basis);[36] and

– receipt from an issuer of non-cash sales incentives, including travel bonuses, prizes and awards in excess of $100 per person per issuer annually.[37]

The 2004 amendments eliminated as an unreasonable term and arrangement a 10% limitation on the amount of securities deemed to be underwriting compensation.

• *Proceeds Directed to a Member*

During the late 1980s, the NASD became concerned that NASD members were underwriting securities the proceeds of which would be used in whole or in part to pay off "bridge loans" extended to the issuer by the NASD member or an affiliate. In

---

35. Computed on the basis of the "firm" shares, not on the basis of the "grossed up" number of shares. In the case of global offerings, there are reports that the NASD believes that the 15% limit should be computed on the basis of the number of shares sold in the United States.

36. As discussed in Chapter 2, the NASD's 15% cap on an issuer's Green Shoe option does not mean that the underwriters may not overallot in an amount in excess of 15% of the offering. If they do so, they are creating a "naked short" position that must be covered by purchases in the open market.

37. NASD Conduct Rule 2710(i)(2). There are two additional prohibitions not related to the rule's general purpose of promoting fair and reasonable underwriting arrangements. One of these states that a member may not participate with an issuer in a public non-underwritten distribution if the issuer has hired persons primarily for the purpose of distributing or assisting in the distribution of the securities. An exception to the prohibition suggests that its purpose is to prevent NASD members from collaborating with issuer employees that may be acting as unregistered broker-dealers. The exception states that the prohibition does not apply if the issuer's personnel are in compliance with "applicable state law" (presumably broker-dealer registration requirements) and with the SEC safe harbor rule (Rule 3a4-1 under the 1934 Act) relating to issuer's employees. NASD Conduct Rule 2710(f)(2)(L).

The other prohibition unrelated to the rule's general purpose states that a member may not participate in a distribution of securities of a real estate investment trust unless the trustee is obligated to disclose in annual reports to investors certain information relating to the per share estimated value of the trust's securities. NASD Conduct Rule 2710(f)(2)(M).

order to reduce the NASD member's perceived conflict of interest and possible disincentive to conduct adequate due diligence, the NASD amended the predecessor of the Corporate Financing Rule to address those underwritings where more than 10% of the proceeds are intended to be paid to members participating in the distribution (or their related persons). In these cases, described in Rule 2710(h), the securities offered to the public must be priced as if there were a conflict of interest subject to Rule 2720 (see below), including the possible involvement of a "qualified independent underwriter" (QIU). Certain offerings are exempted from this requirement, including offerings by real estate investment trusts, various non-profit institutions and certain direct participation programs (unless the proceeds are to be used to repay loans used to acquire an interest in a preexisting company). Also, as discussed below, a QIU need not price the securities if such pricing is not required under Rule 2720.

- *Applications for Exemptions*

An underwriter may apply to the Corporate Financing Department for an exemption from the Corporate Financing Rule. The underwriter must show "good cause" for the requested exemption. If the exemption is denied, the underwriter may appeal under Rule 9630 of the NASD's Code of Procedure to the NASD's National Adjudicatory Council.

- *Antitrust Immunity*

Despite the NASD's rigorous monitoring over many years of the reasonableness of underwriting arrangements, there were allegations during the late 1990s that a remarkable number of IPOs were accompanied by gross "spreads" of 7%. The NASD confirmed in 1998 that it had noticed "a high degree of price uniformity in gross spreads charged by underwriters in initial public offerings of corporate equity securities" and admonished its members to ensure that the pricing of their services resulted from appropriate negotiation with the issuer free of anticompetitive conduct.[38] It also censured a major firm in 2000 and fined it $100,000 for failing to adhere to high standards of

---

38. Notice to Members 98-88 (October 1998).

commercial honor and just and equitable principles of trade by allegedly pressuring a co-manager to accept a 7% gross spread on an IPO.[39]

Following the collapse of the Internet Bubble, separate class actions on behalf of issuers and purchasers in mid-sized IPOs were brought against two large groups of underwriters. The complaints alleged the fixing of underwriting compensation in violation of the antitrust laws. Citing the regulation of underwriting compensation by the SEC and the NASD, the defendants moved to dismiss based on an implied repeal of the antitrust laws. The court found that there was no actual or potential conflict between the antitrust claims and the SEC's and the NASD's regulatory scheme, and denied the motion to dismiss.[40] It concluded that the NASD's failure to object to the underwriters' compensation in any of the IPOs before the court could have been based on "numerous reasons, . . . including the NASD being unaware of defendants' alleged behavior." Such inaction was, however, "clearly not evidence of . . . [the NASD's] having the authority to permit the fixing of IPO fees by underwriters."

- *Proposed Enhancements of Issuer's Role in Pricing IPOs*

Economists and financial analysts have observed for many years that some securities offerings, particularly IPOs, appear to be consistently "underpriced." Explanations for such underpricing include the possible desire of underwriters to build in a "cushion" for liability purposes or the joint desire of the issuer and the underwriters to "leave some money on the table" so that investors can enjoy a slight increase in the value of their investment.

During the Internet Bubble, however, the immediate aftermarket for many IPOs resulted in dramatic run-ups of the public offering price. On the theory that the issuers in these offerings must have left far more money on the table than had ever been

---

39. NASD Press Release, March 9, 2000.

40. *In re Public Offering Fee Antitrust Litig.*, 2003 WL 21496795 (S.D.N.Y. 2003). By contrast, broader antitrust attacks on practices such as "laddering" or "tie-in" arrangements have been rejected on the basis of implied immunity. *In re Initial Public Offering Antitrust Litig.*, 287 F. Supp. 2d 497 (S.D.N.Y. 2003).

the case before, an NYSE/NASD IPO Advisory Committee convened by the SEC recommended in May 2003 that each IPO issuer be required—presumably as a condition of listing—to establish a "pricing committee" of its board of directors to "oversee the pricing process." The NASD proposed rules in November 2003 that would implement certain of the Advisory Committee recommendations by mandating corresponding provisions in the underwriting agreement. These enhancements are discussed in Chapter 2.

Underwritings Involving Conflicts of Interest (Rule 2720)

Rule 2720 imposes a number of special requirements when a member of the NASD participates in a public offering that is deemed to present a particular kind of conflict of interest. The rule's predecessor came into being in the early 1970s shortly after the groundbreaking IPOs by Donaldson, Lufkin & Jenrette, Inc. and Merrill Lynch, Pierce, Fenner & Smith Incorporated. It was clear by this time that securities firms needed permanent capital—that is, capital that could not be withdrawn if a large shareholder died or decided to leave the firm. But introducing the concept of public ownership of securities firms required changing long-entrenched rules and philosophies at both the NYSE and the NASD.[41] One of the chief stumbling blocks to public ownership was the "conflict of interest" believed to exist when a securities firm participated in the underwriting of its own IPO.

Rule 2720 applies to NASD members' participation in their own and their affiliates' public offerings of debt or equity securities as well as to offerings as to which they or their affiliates have a "conflict of interest." (A "conflict of interest" is deemed to exist where an NASD member and its associated persons and affiliates beneficially own 10% or more of the issuer's common or preferred stock or subordinated debt.)

---

41. An excellent account of this critical period in the history of the securities industry can be found in D. T. Regan, *A View From the Street* (1972), particularly ch. 7. The DLJ and Merrill Lynch IPOs and the NYSE and NASD background are also discussed in the previous editions of this book.

In addition, as discussed above under "Proceeds Directed to a Member," NASD members are also required in the situations described in Rule 2710(h) to follow Rule 2720's QIU procedures.

The core of Rule 2720 is the requirement that if a member participates in the distribution of its own securities or those of an affiliate (as defined), the offering price may be no higher, or the yield on debt securities no lower, than that recommended by a QIU. In the case of an offering of securities by a member of the NASD that has not been actively engaged in the investment banking or securities business for at least the past five years, a QIU must manage the offering. A member may not participate in the distribution of its own or an affiliate's securities unless a majority of its board of directors or general partners have been actively engaged in the investment banking or securities business for at least five years.

To be a QIU, a firm must meet the detailed requirements set forth in Rule 2720(b)(15). It must not be an affiliate of the issuer or own 5% or more of specified classes of the issuer's outstanding securities. The firm, as well as a majority of its board of directors or general partners, must have been actively engaged in the investment banking or securities business for at least five years. The firm must also have been actively engaged in the underwriting of public offerings of securities of a similar size and type during that period. The firm will not be acceptable as a QIU if any person associated with it in a supervisory capacity responsible for organizing, structuring or performing due diligence with respect to corporate public offerings of securities has within the past five years been convicted, enjoined or subject to certain disciplinary action as a result of a violation of the antifraud provisions of federal or state securities laws.

The QIU can be a co-manager or a firm not otherwise participating in the offering. It must participate in the preparation of the offering document and must exercise the usual standards of due diligence with respect to the offering. As originally adopted, the predecessor of Rule 2720 required that the QIU be represented by independent legal counsel. This is no longer a requirement, although QIUs not otherwise acting as underwriters often retain counsel to assist them in the transaction.

Rule 2720 contains certain disclosure requirements. It also requires that all proceeds from an offering by an NASD member (i.e., a broker-dealer subject to the SEC's net capital rule) be placed in escrow, whether or not the member participates in the distribution. The funds cannot be released from escrow until the member has satisfied the NASD that it meets certain net capital standards. If it does not, the funds must be returned to the investors. Escrow is not required for the sale of securities of a member's holding company parent. Most securities firms that tap the public market on a regular basis do so through a holding company, and accordingly the escrow provision of Rule 2720 has not presented a problem.

A member or a parent of a member that makes a public offering of securities must establish an audit committee within 12 months thereafter and within that period must cause to be elected to its board of directors a public director who serves as a member of the audit committee. A member that makes a distribution to the public of an issue of its securities must send to investors quarterly summary statements of operations and annual certified financial statements. These requirements apply even if the member does not participate in the distribution.

Rule 2720(k) sets forth additional suitability requirements for members underwriting their own securities or those of an affiliate. The suitability determination must be based on information furnished by the customer, and the member must maintain in its files the basis for its suitability determination. Also, Rule 2720(l) states that a transaction in securities of a member or an affiliate of a member may not be executed in a discretionary account without the customer's prior written approval. This prohibition is not limited to a member selling its own or its affiliate's securities. It is also applicable to a member selling securities of another member or that member's affiliate.

The term "affiliate" as used in Rule 2720 is defined as a company that controls, is controlled by, or is under common control with the member. Ownership of a 10% interest creates a presumption of control. Excluded from the category of affiliates are registered investment companies, real estate investment trusts, direct participation programs and entities issuing financing instrument-backed securities rated investment-grade.

Rule 2720(c) does not require independent pricing by a QIU if the offering is of a class of equity securities for which a bona fide independent market exists both on the date that the registration statement is filed and the date that it becomes effective. Nor is it required if the offering is of a class of securities rated Baa or better by Moody's or BBB or better by Standard & Poor's or is rated in a comparable category by another rating service acceptable to the NASD.

Potential Liabilities of Qualified Independent Underwriters

A footnote to Rule 2720 states that, in the opinion of the NASD and the SEC, "the full responsibilities and liabilities of an underwriter" under the 1933 Act attach to a QIU performing the functions called for by the rule. Many practitioners have doubted that a QIU should be liable under Section 11, particularly where the firm performing the pricing function was not a member of the underwriting syndicate and did not otherwise participate in the distribution of the securities. The contrary conclusion would require a considerable stretch of the Section 2(a)(11) definition of "underwriter" to bring within its terms a firm that does no more than recommend the price, perform due diligence and participate in the drafting of the registration statement.

Even assuming that the pricer is an underwriter with Section 11 liability, there remains the question of the extent of this liability. The SEC and the NASD presumably believe that the pricer may be liable for the entire offering. This position would have to ignore, of course, the provision in Section 11(e) to the effect that an underwriter may not be held liable for damages "in excess of the total price at which the securities underwritten by him and distributed to the public were offered to the public." The pricer would argue that it has not "underwritten" any securities in the sense contemplated by Section 11(e).

The Notice to Members announcing the adoption of the predecessor of Rule 2720 stated that the SEC "has expressed the view that the most important factor involved in its authorization of self-underwritings by members is that the responsibilities and liabilities of underwriters under the Securities Act attach to qualified independent underwriters." For this reason, and because of its recognition that the question had never been adjudicated, the SEC required that a footnote expressing its views be included in the predecessor of Rule 2720 as a condition to not disapproving the self-underwriting proposal. Another condition was that the NASD propose to its membership an amendment to the rule that would bring a firm within the definition of "qualified independent underwriter" only if it "has agreed in connection with the offering in respect to which he is acting as such to undertake the full legal responsibilities and liabilities of an underwriter under the Securities Act of 1933, specifically including those inherent in the provisions of Section 11 thereof."

A provision to this effect is now included in the definition of "qualified independent underwriter" appearing in Rule 2720(b). Investment banking firms have become accustomed to the requirement that they enter into such an agreement as a condition to acting as a QIU. The agreement is filed as an exhibit to the registration statement. A QIU not otherwise acting as an underwriter might try to qualify its acceptance of Section 11 liability as follows:

> [W]e undertake the legal responsibilities and liabilities of an "underwriter" under the Securities Act of 1933, specifically including those inherent in Section 11 thereof. It is specifically understood, however, that we will bear such legal responsibilities and liabilities only to the extent, if any, that a court of competent jurisdiction rules in a judgment which has become final, and not subject to further appeal, that we, in our capacity as a "qualified independent underwriter," bear the legal responsibilities and liabilities of an "underwriter." We understand that views expressed by the NASD and the Securities and Exchange Commission indicate that, in acting as a "qualified independent underwriter," we may be deemed to be an "underwriter" within the meaning of the Securities Act of 1933. These are, however, questions of statutory interpretation regarding the underwriter status of a "qualified independent underwriter" that have not yet been judicially determined.

Many prospectuses will state that the QIU may be deemed to be an "underwriter" within the meaning of the 1933 Act, and that the amount paid to it may be underwriting compensation but that these are questions that have not yet been judicially determined. Other prospectuses are silent on the issue.

Unfortunately for the QIU, a Seventh Circuit decision provides strong support for the SEC and NASD position. In *Harden v. Raffensperger, Hughes & Co., Inc.*,[42] an NASD member had retained Raffensperger, Hughes & Co. (Raffensperger) to act as its QIU for a $20 million note offering by one of its subsidiaries. Raffensperger did not join the underwriting syndicate and did not offer or sell any notes. Following the offering and the issuer's subsequent bankruptcy, Raffensperger was sued in a class action under Section 11 and related provisions of federal law. The Seventh Circuit affirmed the trial court's denial of Raffensperger's motion for summary judgment.

First, the court held that a QIU is an "underwriter" subject to Section 11 liability even where it is not a syndicate member. The court relied on Section 2(a)(11)'s reference to an underwriter as including anyone who "participates or has a direct or indirect participation" in a registered offering. The court found that Raffensperger had "participated" in the offering even though it had not purchased, offered or sold any securities.

Raffensperger also argued that because it was not a syndicate member and did not underwrite or sell any securities, its pro rata share of the offering for Section 11(e) purposes was zero. The court found, however, that Raffensperger had acted as a QIU with respect to the entire note offering, thus "perform[ing] the protective function envisioned by the 1933 Congress with respect to the entire . . . distribution." In essence, then, Raffensperger had underwritten and incurred Section 11 liability for all the notes.

If the Seventh Circuit is correct in its holding that a QIU incurs Section 11 liability for the entire offering, then such an underwriter needs to assess this additional risk in making its decision to assume this responsibility and in determining its requirements with respect to compensation and indemnity protection.

---

42. 65 F.3d 1392 (7th Cir. 1995), *reh'g denied,* 1995 U.S. App. LEXIS 29723 (7th Cir. 1995).

Free-Riding and Withholding (Rule 2790) and Other Ways of Exploiting "New Issues"

To the extent that a new issue is "hot," i.e., one that investors are willing to buy in the after-market at a price in excess—sometimes dramatically in excess—of the initial public offering price, the underwriters have the ability to use their control over the distribution to realize profits over and above the agreed-upon underwriting spread.

Hot issues occur for various reasons, but some common denominators are suggested by a casual look at what some observers identify as the four distinct "hot-issue markets" of the last 40 years. Each of these markets involved what the SEC Special Study in 1963 referred to as IPOs by companies in "glamour" industries. In 1959–1962, it was largely electronics companies. In 1967–1971, it was fast food and space-age technology. In 1979–1983, it was robotics, medical products, computers, video games and entertainment. And in 1998–2000, it was the Internet and Silicon Valley.[43]

Each of these hot-issue markets involved emerging technologies and emerging industries that captured the public imagination. At the same time, it is obviously difficult to price IPOs where there are no standard comparables such as balance sheet strength or an earnings history. The sales effort may emphasize the issuer's relative advantages in technology, competition and management, but investors' enthusiasm for these relatively subjective attributes is hard to predict. Particularly during the Internet Bubble, media focus on IPOs encouraged after-market bids by many less sophisticated investors who would not normally have participated in IPOs during past cycles.

Obviously, an underwriter might be tempted when it becomes clear that an IPO is a hot issue to cancel its customers' orders and retain its participation for itself or for its insiders—that is, *withhold* the shares from the market—and subsequently resell them for an easy profit—that is, get a *free ride*? The NASD has for more than 50 years condemned such a practice as

---

43. Judge Scheindlin briefly describes these markets in *In re Initial Public Offering Securities Litig.*, 241 F. Supp. 2d 281, 300–08 (S.D.N.Y. 2003).

inconsistent with "high standards of commercial honor and just and equitable principles of trade." Not only is such conduct inconsistent with the underwriter's obligation to make a bona fide public distribution of the shares at the public offering price, but withholding the shares can create a further imbalance in the after-market between investors' demand for the shares and the supply available to members of the public.

What else might the underwriter be tempted to do, given that the ability to control the allocation of a hot issue is in some ways like being able to make a gift of cash? During the most recent hot-issue market, there were allegations that underwriters tried to profit from hot issues in two ways: first, by charging customers excessive commissions on routine trades as a quid pro quo for making a hot-issue allocation to those customers; and second, by allocating hot issues to insiders of actual or potential investment banking clients as a means of obtaining additional investment banking business.

In 2003, the NASD abandoned its longstanding focus on hot issues and replaced its regulatory structure with a new Rule 2790 that applies equally to all "new issues" of common stock. Before analyzing the new rule, we will discuss the history of the NASD's efforts to control abuses in this area as well as some underwriters' more recent and imaginative attempts to profit from their power to allocate new issues.

- *Early NASD and SEC Responses to Free-Riding*

In 1950, the NASD adopted its initial free-riding and withholding interpretation. This interpretation stated that it was a violation of what was then Article III, Section 1 of the *Rules of Fair Practice* for any member, directly or indirectly, to withhold a portion of any public offering for its own account or to sell any such portion to persons connected with it, members of their immediate families, or accounts in which such member or such persons had a beneficial interest. Securities taken for investment were exempted from the interpretation if the allotment was in accordance with the purchaser's *normal investment practice.* In 1959, the interpretation was amended to include the additional requirement that any stock taken by insiders not be *disproportionate* in amount to allotments made to the public.

In the following year, the NASD further amended the interpretation to require that aggregate sales made to insiders be *insubstantial.*

In connection with each of the hot-issue markets mentioned above, the SEC encouraged the NASD to take steps to strengthen the free-riding interpretation, to take more effective enforcement measures against violators and to impose more severe penalties in flagrant cases. The SEC's landmark *Special Study of Securities Markets,* published in 1963, analyzed the 1959–1962 hot issue market in depth and described the adverse effects of free-riding.

In addition to free-riding, the *Special Study* pointed to other practices designed to drive up the price of stock by artificially restricting the supply in the after-market while at the same time fanning the demand.[44] It found that many distributors of new issues adopted a policy of allotting stock only to customers who would not immediately resell in the after-market. They implemented this policy by such measures as making allotments only to customers with a record of not reselling new issues, allotting to discretionary accounts or to a relatively small number of customers who customarily relied on their advice or penalizing salesmen whose customers sold their allotments in the immediate after-market. Sometimes customers would be advised of a "requirement" or "expectation" that they would not immediately resell or that immediate resale would reduce their chances of being considered for future new issues. Some underwriters would simply refuse to execute customers' sell orders in the after-market. Others would delay the delivery of stock certificates so that the customer would find it difficult to sell through another broker.

Following a study of the hot issue market of 1968–1969, the SEC issued a series of proposals.[45] These fell into two principal categories. The first group was characterized by the SEC as "initial steps to help curtail excesses of hot issues." They were directed toward the character of the after-market, the quality of underwriters' due diligence, suitability standards for hot issues sold in the after-market, sales of hot issues to discretionary

---

44. *Special Study* Pt. 1 at 555.
45. SEC Release No. 33-5274 (July 26, 1972); SEC Release No. 33-5275 (July 26, 1972); SEC Release No. 33-5276 (July 26, 1972).

accounts and prompt delivery of certificates. The second group of proposals related to improved prospectus disclosure.

The two areas most directly related to hot-issue abuses, namely, the quality of the after-market and suitability standards, were left to the NASD for further study. The question of due diligence standards, which related only tangentially to the problem of hot issues, likewise was referred to the NASD for further consideration. Apart from these matters, the SEC made only two specific proposals in the July 1972 releases, one relating to disclosure of expected sales to discretionary accounts and the other relating to a registration statement undertaking with respect to certificate delivery. The SEC eventually adopted these two proposals.

To deal with the matters that the SEC had referred to it, the NASD established an ad hoc committee to recommend appropriate rule changes. This committee submitted its recommendations to the NASD's Board of Governors, which in March 1973 submitted to the NASD membership proposed new rules relating to due diligence, suitability standards and the qualifications of members engaged in underwriting.[46] The proposed rules relating to due diligence standards and rules relating to the qualification of members engaged in underwriting were hotly debated, and the NASD finally was convinced that it should not try to impose standards in this area. The NASD did adopt suitability provisions relating specifically to speculative low-priced issues.[47]

- *Free-Riding and Withholding Interpretation*

By 2003, the NASD's interpretation on free-riding and withholding was more than 50 years old. It was then part of the NASD's "Interpretive Material" to its Conduct Rule 2110 and

---

46. NASD Notice to Members 73-17 (March 14, 1973).

47. The principal relevant provision is now designated as Rule IM-2310-2(b)(1) ("Fair Dealing With Customers—Recommending Speculative Low-Priced Securities"), which condemns the recommendation of speculative low-priced securities to customers without having or attempting to obtain relevant information regarding the suitability of such securities for the customers to whom the recommendations were made. Of course, as demonstrated by the Internet Bubble, securities can be speculative without being low-priced.

was designated as "IM-2110-1." The interpretation stated that it was

> based upon the premise that members have an obligation to make a bona fide public distribution at the public offering price of securities of a public offering which trade at a premium in the secondary market whenever such secondary market begins (a "hot issue") regardless of whether such securities are acquired by the member as an underwriter, as a selling group member, or from a member participating in the distribution as an underwriter or a selling group member, or otherwise.

It will come as no surprise that, like any set of rules more than half a century old, the interpretation presented a number of problems in its practical application.

• • *Definition of Hot Issue.* One of the most troublesome aspects of the interpretation was that it applied to "hot issues," which were defined as offerings that traded at a premium over the public offering price at the time that the secondary market began.[48] As recently as 2000, the NASD had reasserted its view that "any premium, no matter how small, makes an offering a hot issue. Thus, under the current [i]nterpretation, a security that prices at $15 per share and begins trading at $15 1/32 is a 'hot issue.' "[49]

During the period before a registration statement becomes effective, underwriters may have an expectation that an issue will be hot, but this will not be known as a fact until the stock begins to trade in the after-market. Accordingly, underwriters and dealers

---

48. The interpretation formerly defined a hot issue as one that trades at a premium "immediately after the distribution process is commenced." It was amended as a result of the SEC's decision in *Lowell H. Listrom & Co.,* SEC Release No. 34-19414 (January 10, 1983), where the NASD's findings were set aside because it was not clear that the free-riding interpretation was violated where a best efforts offering took three months to sell, was closed with shares in the hands of restricted accounts, and the shares then traded at a premium. NASD Notice to Members 83-26 (June 1, 1983).

49. SEC Release No. 34-42325 (January 10, 2000), text at n.4 (footnote omitted).

for many years incurred a risk when they took indications of interest from customers of the type restricted under the interpretation (unless the transaction qualified under the exception discussed below relating to a customer's "normal investment practice"). Sales to these persons might easily be confirmed after pricing in routine fashion notwithstanding that the securities began to trade at a premium in the after-market, and this would result in a violation of the interpretation.

The NASD attempted to mitigate these difficulties, first by permitting the NASD member to cancel a sale when it became clear that a hot issue was involved and allowing the member to reallocate the security to an unrestricted account before the end of the first day of trading.[50] The NASD also introduced in 1996[51] a new regulatory service called "Compliance Desk" under which it would monitor trading in the immediate after-market to determine (based on an "analysis of all the facts and circumstances surrounding the first day of trading") whether a new issue is a hot issue, in which case it would issue a "hot-issue notification" wire to the participants in the distribution. The participants would then be obligated to review their customer allocations to determine whether sales had been made to restricted persons or accounts; if so, they would have to cancel those trades and reallocate the securities at the public offering price to unrestricted persons or accounts.

Notwithstanding these attempts at relief, many firms chose to treat all IPOs as if they were subject to the interpretation. In so deciding, they avoided the risk that a given IPO would become "hot" and cause them to have to bear the administrative costs of tracking, canceling and reallocating sales and the ill will generated by having to cancel a customer's allocation.

• • *Restricted Persons and "Normal Investment Practice."* The interpretation identified as restricted persons those individuals who were insiders of the underwriter or any other broker-dealer or who were in a position to direct reciprocal securities business to the underwriter and provided that such persons, together with a wide range of related persons and accounts in which any of them had a beneficial interest, could not participate

---

50. NASD Notice to Members 95-7 (February 1995).
51. NASD Notice to Members 96-18 (March 1996).

in a hot issue. The broad scope of the restriction created particular problems for underwriters in connection with investment corporations and partnerships and other collective vehicles.

In addition, difficulties arose in connection with the long-standing exception for transactions consistent with the "normal investment practice" of customers other than insiders of broker-dealers and their related persons. Sales could be made to such customers if the underwriter could demonstrate that the sales were "in accordance with their *normal investment practice*, that the aggregate of the securities so sold was *insubstantial* and *not disproportionate in amount* as compared to sales to members of the public and that the amount sold to any one of such persons is insubstantial in amount" (emphasis added).[52]

- *Rule 2790*

In 1999, the NASD submitted to the SEC a proposed rule change to deal with "hot issues" and to supersede the free-riding

---

52. Under the interpretation, a customer's previous one-year period of securities activity—whether at the underwriter or at one or more other firms—was the usual basis for determining the adequacy of a restricted person's investment history. In analyzing a restricted person's investment history, the NASD specified that the factors to be considered included the frequency of transactions in the account, the nature and size of the investments, and a comparison of the dollar amount of previous transactions with the dollar amount of the hot-issue purchase. The example was given in the interpretation that, if a restricted person purchased $1,000 of a hot issue and his or her account revealed a series of purchases and sales in $100 amounts, the $1,000 purchase would not be consistent with the restricted person's normal investment practice. The interpretation stated that the practice of purchasing mainly hot issues would not constitute a normal investment practice.

With respect to the determination of what constituted a disproportionate allocation, the interpretation referred to a guideline of 10% of the member's participation in the issue. The interpretation cautioned that the 10% guideline was only a guideline, and it specified other relevant factors that should be taken into account. The requirement of insubstantiality was separate and distinct from the requirement relating to disproportionate allocations and normal investment practice. No specific guidance was given as to what is considered an insubstantial allocation, but the interpretation pointed out that the term applied both to the aggregate of the securities sold to restricted accounts and to each individual allocation.

and withholding interpretation. The proposal was amended on several occasions until its approval by the SEC in October 2003.[53] In the NASD's view, Rule 2790 is better designed to further the purposes of the former interpretation and is easier to understand.

• • *Applicable to "New Issues" Rather Than "Hot Issues."* Rule 2790 eliminates the interpretation's 50-year linkage to "hot issues." Rather, the rule applies to all "new issues," which are defined as any IPO of an equity security "made pursuant to a registration statement or offering circular."[54]

Secondaries and follow-on offerings are therefore not subject to the rule. The definition of "new issue" also excludes private placements, rights offerings, exchange offers or offerings pursuant to business combinations as well as offerings of exempt securities, convertible securities (but not warrants or exchangeable securities), preferred securities or any offering of securities that already have a market outside the United States. Investment-grade asset-backed securities are also specifically excluded, but lower-rated ABS would not appear to be subject to the rule unless they represent the equivalent of equity securities. New issues effected pursuant to Regulation S are covered by the rule, but many underwriters will conduct such offerings through their offshore affiliates that are not NASD members.[55]

Rule 2790 is therefore principally applicable to IPOs involving common stock or warrants.

---

53. SEC Release No. 34-48701 (October 24, 2003). The new rule became effective on March 23, 2004. NASD Notice to Members 03-79 (December 2003). For a general discussion, see Suzanne Rothwell, *The NASD Revises Its Regulation of IPO Sales,* 18 *Insights* 8 (January 2004).

54. The reference to an offer "made pursuant to a registration statement" is significant in determining when Rule 2790 ceases to apply to a given offering. Nothing in the rule states, as it perhaps should, that the rule ceases to apply when syndicate restrictions are terminated. The prospectus delivery period under Section 4(3)(B) of the 1933 Act and Rule 174 should set the outer boundary for the rule's applicability.

55. The NASD states that the rule applies to "members and their associated persons with respect to foreign offerings," but the term "associated person" as defined in the NASD's by-laws is limited to natural persons.

• • *Prohibitions of Rule 2790.* The rule prohibits the sale of a new issue to an account in which a "restricted person" has a beneficial interest.[56]

It also prohibits an underwriter from continuing to hold a new issue. It would be safe to assume that, as under the interpretation, the prohibition on continuing to hold a new issue is absolute and does not disappear just because an underwriter has allocated all of its participation to customers. It would also be safe to assume that the underwriter continues to be required to have procedures for dealing with customer cancellations of IPO allocations.[57]

The rule allows for exceptions related to the conduct of public offerings. It expressly permits sales within a selling group that are incidental to the distribution of the new issue to non-restricted persons at the public offering price. It also permits sales or purchases at the public offering price "as part of an accommodation to a non-restricted customer." An underwriter may also, "pursuant to an underwriting agreement," place a portion of a public offering in an investment account "when it is unable to sell that portion to the public."[58]

---

56. "Beneficial interest" is defined in the rule as "any economic interest, such as the right to share in gains or losses." A management or performance based fee for operating a collective investment account is not considered a beneficial interest in the account.

57. In May 2003 the NASD announced that it had fined a broker-dealer $250,000, including disgorgement of profits of $125,000, for placing cancelled customer allocations into proprietary error accounts and selling the related shares at a profit. The NYSE/NASD IPO Advisory Committee recommended in May 2003 that the SROs establish "clear parameters" for handling returned IPO shares, including that such shares be used first to reduce the syndicate short position and that any remaining shares be sold on the open market with the profits returned to the issuer. The NASD proposed such a rule in November 2003. NASD Notice to Members 03-72 (November 2003).

58. It is not clear what is meant by the requirement that the placement of the securities in an investment account must be "pursuant to an underwriting agreement." Underwriting agreements do not ordinarily address whether or not an underwriter may take such action. Rather, they customarily state only that the underwriters intend to make a public offering of the shares at the initial public offering price.

There is also an exception for purchases by a broker-dealer (or an owner of a broker-dealer) organized as an investment partnership if the purchases are credited to the capital accounts of the partners and if restricted persons do not have more than a 10% interest in such accounts. This exception is intended to cover purchases by "joint back office" or "JBO" broker-dealers of the kind customarily formed by hedge funds, although the rule does not expressly refer to JBOs as such.[59]

The rule also prohibits a member or a person associated with a member from purchasing a new issue in any account in which any of them has a beneficial interest.

• • *Restricted Persons.* Restricted persons under Rule 2790 include:

- any NASD member or other broker-dealers;[60]

- associated persons of an NASD member or any other broker-dealer, agents of an NASD member or any other broker-dealer engaged in the investment banking or securities business, or an immediate family member[61] of any of the foregoing if the associated person or agent materially supports or receives material support from the immediate family member, is employed by or associated with the member or an affiliate of the member that is selling the new issue to the immediate family member or has "an" ability to control the allocation of the new issue.

- with respect to the security being offered, a finder or any person acting in a fiduciary capacity to the managing

---

59. The JBO or JBO owner may also be organized as a limited liability company or corporation. NASD Notice to Members 03-79 (December 2003), at n.5.

60. The reference to "other broker-dealer" includes foreign broker-dealers who are not members of the NASD.

61. "Immediate family member" means a person's parents, mother-in-law or father-in-law, spouse, brother or sister, brother-in-law or sister-in-law, son-in-law or daughter-in-law, and children, and any other individual to whom the person provides material support (i.e., more than 25% of a person's income in the prior calendar year or living in the same household).

underwriter (including but not limited to lawyers, accountants and financial consultants) or any immediate family member of a finder or fiduciary who provides or receives material support;

- portfolio managers, that is, persons who have authority to buy or sell securities for a bank, savings and loan institution, insurance company, investment company, investment advisor or collective investment account,[62] as well as their immediate family members if the portfolio manager materially supports or receives material support from the immediate family member; and

- persons owning a broker-dealer, that is, persons listed or required to be listed in a schedule to a broker-dealer's Form BD or persons (other than publicly traded companies) who own more than specified amounts of publicly traded companies that are listed in a schedule to a broker-dealer's Form BD, as well as such persons' immediate family members unless the listed person does not materially support or receive material support from the immediate family member, is not an owner of the member or an affiliate of the member that is selling the new issue to the immediate family member and has no ability to control the allocation of the new issue.[63]

Certain individuals who are restricted persons because of their relationship to a broker-dealer are excluded from this status if the broker-dealer is a "limited business broker-dealer," which is a broker-dealer authorized only to buy and sell investment company/variable contract securities and direct participation program securities.

---

62. For this purpose, "collective investment account" means any hedge fund, investment partnership or corporation or any other collective investment vehicle that is engaged primarily in the purchase and/or sale of securities. The term does not include a "family investment vehicle" or an "investment club."

63. U.S. and foreign broker-dealers not registered with the SEC do not file a Form BD, so their owners are not restricted persons.

In a major departure from the interpretation, there are no "conditionally restricted" persons, which is to say persons who would be restricted but for their "prior investment history."

• • *Preconditions for Sale.* Before selling a new issue to any account, an underwriter must in good faith have obtained within the previous 12 months a representation from (a) the beneficial owner of the account or an authorized representative that the account is eligible to purchase new issues in compliance with the rule or (b) a bank, foreign bank, broker-dealer or investment advisor or other conduit that all purchases of new issues are in compliance with the rule.

The underwriter may not rely on any representation that it believes or has reason to believe is inaccurate. It must maintain a copy of all relevant records and documents for at least three years. The NASD stated that the initial such representation must consist of a positive affirmation by the customer but that it intended to permit annual verifications to be by means of negative consents. The NASD also stated that it would allow the use of electronic communications for "eligible customers" but that oral verifications would not be permitted.

The NASD's Office of General Counsel issued a letter in February 2004[64] approving an underwriter's reliance on a third-party service to "assist" in determining the status of a particular account under the rule, but the member "remains directly and fully responsible for compliance" with the rule. An industry association has developed a uniform customer questionnaire to simplify the process of complying with the rule.

• • *General Exemptions.* The prohibitions of the rule do not apply to sales to certain persons or accounts in which they have a beneficial interest:

- investment companies registered under the 1940 Act;
- common trust funds or similar funds, provided that the fund has investments from at least 1,000 accounts and it does not limit beneficial interests in the fund principally to trust accounts of restricted persons;

---

64. *Dealogic* (February 27, 2004). The letter is on the NASD's website.

RULES OF THE SELF-REGULATORY ORGANIZATIONS 435

- an insurance company's general, separate or investment account funded by premiums from at least 1,000 policyholders[65] and where the insurance company does not limit the relevant policyholders principally to restricted persons;
- an account if the beneficial interests of restricted persons do not exceed 10% of such account (the de minimis exemption);[66]
- a publicly traded entity (other than a broker-dealer or an affiliate of a broker-dealer where the broker-dealer is authorized to engage in the offering of new issues) that is listed on an exchange or the NASDAQ National Market or, in the case of a foreign entity, would meet those markets' quantitative listing standards;
- a foreign investment company listed on a foreign exchange or authorized for sale to the public[67] by a foreign regulatory authority, provided that no person owning more than 5% of its shares is a restricted person;
- an ERISA plan that is not sponsored solely by a broker-dealer;
- a public benefits plan subject to state and/or local regulation;
- a Section 501(c)(3) organization; and
- a church plan under Section 414(e) of the Internal Revenue Code.

---

65. In the case of a general account, the insurance company must have at least 1,000 policyholders.

66. "Carve-outs" continue to be available under Rule 2790 and on a more flexible basis than under the interpretation. Accordingly, a collective investment account in which restricted persons hold an interest of 10% or more may continue to invest in new issues, provided that restricted persons receive no more than 10% of the notional pro rata proceeds of the new issue. The NASD intends to offer detailed guidance regarding carve-outs in a forthcoming Notice to Members.

67. According to the NASD, this exception "is intended to extend benefits to foreign investment entities that are similar to U.S. mutual funds." It is not intended to cover foreign investment companies that are limited to high net worth individuals. NASD Notice to Members 03-79 (December 2003), at 838.

The NASD declined to include in Rule 2790 a blanket exemption for foreign employee benefit plans but held out the possibility of issuing additional guidance regarding such plans as its staff becomes more familiar with the various types of foreign investment plans. The NASD issued an exemption in 2001 to a pension fund operated by a Canadian province, explaining this action on the basis of the large number of plan participants and the small notional pro rata allocation of each of the fund's assets to any individual participant.

• • *Issuer-Directed Securities.* Rule 2790 does not apply to securities that are specifically directed by the issuer to restricted persons, provided that

- the securities may not be purchased by an account in which an associated person of a broker-dealer or a finder or fiduciary with respect to the securities has a beneficial interest unless the associated person, finder or fiduciary (or a member of his or her immediate family) is an employer or director of the issuer or one of its affiliates;[68] or

- the directed sales are part of a program sponsored by the issuer or an affiliate that is offered to at least 10,000 participants each of whom is offered the opportunity to purchase an equivalent number of shares (or a specified number of shares pursuant to a formula);[69] or

- the directed sales are in connection with a conversion offering effected in accordance with the standards of the competent governmental agency or instrumentality.

• • *Antidilution Provisions.* Rule 2790 does not apply to sales to an account in which a restricted person has a beneficial

---

68. Affiliation is established for this purpose by the power to vote 50% or more of a company's class of voting security or "to sell or direct [the sale of] 50% or more" of such a class.

69. If not all participants receive shares, the allocation must be based on a random or other non-discretionary method. Also, the class may not contain a disproportionate number of restricted persons as compared to the investing public generally.

interest if the account has held equity securities in the issuer (or a company acquired by the issuer within the past year) for at least one year prior to the effective date of the offering, the sale does not increase the account's percentage interest in the issuer above the level as of three months before the offering, the sale does not include any special terms and the newly purchased securities are locked up for three months after the offering.

• • *Stand-by Purchasers.* Rule 2790 does not apply to sales pursuant to a "formal" written stand-by agreement that is disclosed in the prospectus for the new issue, where the managing underwriter "represents in writing that it was unable to find any other purchasers for the securities" and where the newly purchased securities are locked up for three months.

• • *IPO Distribution Manager.* As part of the implementation of Rule 2790, the NASD replaced its Compliance Desk system discussed above with a new IPO Distribution Manager that member firms would use to file initial and final lists of distribution participants and their commitment and retention amounts.

• • *Other Exemptive Relief.* The NASD's staff may issue exemptions from any and all provisions of Rule 2790. Staff decisions may be appealed under Rule 9630 of the NASD's Code of Procedure to the National Adjudicatory Council.

• *Proposed Restrictions on "Spinning"*

As noted above, free-riding and withholding are not the only ways for underwriters to exploit hot issues. During the most recent hot-issue market in 1998–2000, there were frequent allegations that underwriting firms allocated hot issues to the private accounts of officers and directors of investment banking clients as an inducement for those individuals to attempt to persuade the issuer to use the underwriting firm for future investment banking business. Such a practice, of course, could amount to a personal gratuity to the officer or director to cause the issuer to select an investment banker that might not offer the best service or performance on a given transaction.[70]

---

70. In early 2004, the Delaware Chancery Court denied motions to dismiss complaints alleging that corporate officers had usurped corporate opportunities and breached their duty of loyalty by engaging in "spinning"

Also as noted above, the NASD in August 2002[71] proposed amendments to the Corporate Financing Rule to require the filings under that rule to disclose whether any executive officer or director of the issuer acquired any IPO shares from the book-running managing underwriter during the six month periods preceding and following the offering for which the filing is made. If such purchases took place, the filing would have to disclose whether the officer or director participated in any capacity in the selection of the book-running managing underwriter for the issuer's public offering for which the filing is being made.

At the same time, the NASD proposed a new Conduct Rule 2712(c) that would specifically prohibit member firms from allocating IPO shares to an executive officer or director of a company "on the condition that the executive officer or director, on behalf of the company, direct future investment banking business to the member," or as consideration for directing investment banking services previously rendered by the member to the company. The NASD explained that allocating IPO shares on such a basis "divide[d] the loyalty of the agents of the company (i.e., the executive officers and directors) from the principal (i.e., the company) on whose behalf they must act. This practice is inconsistent with just and equitable principles of trade."

In May 2003, the NYSE/NASD IPO Advisory Committee endorsed the NASD's proposed Rule 2712 but also recommended a complete ban on the allocation of IPO shares to officers and directors (and their immediate families) of companies that have an investment banking relationship with the underwriter. The committee believed that a complete ban was necessary because of the "appearance of impropriety" that would otherwise attach to allocations, and it encouraged the SEC and the SROs to consider whether the existence of "a previous

---

transactions and that a securities firm had aided and abetted these breaches. The court described the complaint as alleging in effect that the securities firm had "bribed certain eBay insiders, using the currency of highly profitable investment opportunities—opportunities that should have been offered to, or provided for the benefit of, eBay rather than the favored insiders." *In re Ebay, Inc. Shareholders Litig.*, 2004 Del. Ch. LEXIS 4 (Ct. Ch. Del. 2004).

71. NASD Notice to Members 02-55 (August 2002).

investment banking relationship" should trigger similar restrictions on allocations to officers and directors. The committee also proposed that public companies consider including in their codes of ethics specific policies regarding the receipt of IPO allocations by the companies' officers and directors.

In the "global settlement" reached in 2003 among various regulators and ten large investment banking firms, the latter agreed to a "voluntary initiative" by which they undertook for a period of five years (or until the earlier adoption of an applicable SEC or SRO rule) not to allocate securities in an IPO "in exchange for or for the purpose of obtaining investment banking business," not to allocate securities in a "hot" IPO to the account of an executive officer or director of a U.S. public company or any public company for which the United States is the principal equity trading market and not to permit their investment banking personnel to influence the allocation of IPO securities to specific non-institutional customer accounts.[72]

- *Proposed Restrictions on Excessive Compensation for Other Services*

Another way in which it was alleged that underwriters during the Internet Bubble sought to exploit their ability to allocate "hot" IPOs was to condition an allocation on the customer's agreement to pay excessive compensation for other services. For example, a customer might agree in exchange for an allocation to pay commissions of $1 or more per share for secondary market transactions where the usual commission for such transactions might be only pennies per share. Some underwriters were alleged to have kept meticulous records of customers' profits on allocated IPOs and to insist that the customers "rebate" to the underwriter a specified portion of such profits.

The NASD and other regulators alleged that these arrangements amounted to "profit sharing" on hot IPOs and therefore to an impermissible albeit indirect violation of the free-riding and withholding interpretation.

---

72. *See* www.sec.gov/news/press/globalvolinit.htm (April 28, 2003).

In any event, the NASD proposed in August 2002[73] a new Rule 2712(a) that would prohibit firms from offering or threatening to withhold allocations in any IPO (whether or not "hot") as consideration or inducement for the firm's receipt of "compensation that is excessive in relation to the services provided by the member." The NASD explained that the proposed rule would not prohibit an allocation of IPO shares on the basis of a customer's separate retention of the firm for other services, when such services do not involve excessive compensation in relation to those services. The NYSE/NASD IPO Advisory Committee in May 2003 endorsed the NASD's proposal, with the caveat that an underwriter should be able "to allocate IPO shares to customers as it chooses, including to its retail and institutional clients."

Without waiting for the adoption of the proposed rule, the NASD in May 2004 announced that it had censured three major investment banking firms and imposed more than $15 million in fines because of the firms' receipt of "unusually high commissions" from certain customers on listed agency trades within one day of allocating "hot" IPOs to the same customers. The NASD described the firms' conduct as inconsistent with the high standards of commercial honor and just and equitable principles of trade demanded by NASD rules.

The *Papilsky* Rules (Rules 2740, 2730 and 2750)

Rule 2740 and its companions, Rules 2730 and 2750, are designed to preserve the integrity of the fixed-price distribution system that for many years has been the established method of selling securities in underwritten public offerings. These are known as the *Papilsky* rules in honor of Mrs. Paulette Papilsky, the plaintiff in a case that held that, in the absence of a ruling from the SEC or the NASD, an investor's indirect recapture of underwriting discounts and commissions was legal under an earlier version of Rule 2740.

---

73. NASD Notice to Members 02-55 (August 2002).

In 1980, the predecessors of Rules 2740 and 2730 were amended and the predecessor of Rule 2750 was adopted as a result of the uncertainties created by this decision. In its current form, Rule 2740 provides in effect that a member of the NASD may not grant or receive selling concessions, discounts or other allowances in connection with the sale of securities that are part of a fixed-price offering except as "consideration for services rendered in distribution" and may not grant such concessions, discounts or other allowances to anyone other than a broker or dealer "actually engaged in the investment banking or securities business." A purchaser of the securities, however, may designate that selling credit be given to a broker or dealer that has provided or will provide it with "bona fide research."

Rule 2730 provides that a member engaged in a fixed-price offering who purchases or arranges the purchase of securities "taken in trade" must either purchase the securities "at a fair market price" at the time of purchase or act as agent in the sale of the securities and charge "the normal commission" for the sale. A failure to do so is known as "overtrading." Purchasing the securities at a higher price or selling with a less than normal commission can be an indirect means of granting a discount to the customer. In order to prevent institutional purchasers from recapturing selling concessions by designating an affiliated NASD member to purchase securities for it in a fixed-price offering, Rule 2750 provides that a member participating in a fixed-price offering may not sell the securities to a "related person."

It should be noted at the outset that the *Papilsky* rules do not require that distributions of securities be structured as fixed-price offerings. Rather, as noted by the SEC in the release approving the rules pursuant to Section 19(b), "the provisions of the proposed rule change come into play only after the underwriters have themselves agreed to distribute securities through a fixed price offering."[74]

The SEC has specifically stated that the rule does not prohibit multiple price arrangements. For example, an underwriter may agree with an issuer to offer securities at different prices

---

74. SEC Release No. 34-17371 (December 12, 1980).

depending on the amount of securities that the customer is willing to purchase.[75] But if the underwriters voluntarily enter into a price maintenance agreement, the NASD rules require that the agreement be adhered to and that it not be undermined through some subterfuge.

- *Background*

Prior to its amendment in 1980, the predecessor of Rule 2740 provided:

> Selling concessions, discounts, or other allowances, as such, shall be allowed only as consideration for services rendered in distribution and in no event shall be allowed to anyone other than a broker or dealer actually engaged in the investment banking or securities business; provided, however, that nothing in this rule shall prevent any member from selling any security owned by him to any person at any net price which may be fixed by him unless prevented therefrom by agreement.

The rule traces its origin to the Investment Bankers Code approved by President Franklin Roosevelt acting under the authority of the National Industrial Recovery Act, as amended in 1934 to include fair practice provisions.[76] Included among the code's rules of fair practice was a rule establishing one price for all investors regardless of the size of the transaction or the importance of the purchaser. In 1935, the rules of fair practice were amended to require an investment banker who received a selling concession to certify that his purchase was solely for the account of clients or, if for his own account, that he intended to redistribute the securities to his clients in the ordinary course of business. This rule was based on the principle that an investment banker is entitled to a selling concession only if it actively participates in the distribution of the securities to others. The original rules of fair practice adopted by the NASD included a

---

75. *Id.*
76. *Id.*

provision virtually identical to the predecessor of Rule 2740 as it existed prior to its amendment in 1980.

Prior to its amendment, the predecessor of Rule 2730 provided:

> A member, when a member of a selling syndicate or a selling group, shall purchase securities taken in trade at a fair market price at the time of purchase, or shall act as agent in the sale of such securities.

This rule was designed to prevent overtrading, but as stated by the SEC, as then-drafted it "provides little guidance to members or to the NASD in its enforcement efforts in differentiating between a permissible swap and a prohibited overtrade."[77] The predecessor of Rule 2750 was a new provision that had no counterpart in the then-existing rules of fair practice, although it was the position of the NASD that the predecessor of Rule 2740 itself prohibited the use of affiliates to recapture selling concessions.

• • *Pressures by Institutions.* In the release requesting public comment on the proposed *Papilsky* rules,[78] the SEC recognized that the growth of institutional participation in the securities markets had exerted increasing pressure on the fixed-price offering system. In the release approving the rules, the SEC observed that when the securities laws were passed in the early 1930s, individual retail investors were the principal customers of securities firms. At that time, the securities industry "performed an intermediation function that, in many cases, extended all the way from the individual investor to the corporate issuer, in the case of securities distributions, and to the specialist's post, in the case of exchange trading."[79] By the 1960s, however, it had become clear that institutional investors, including bank trust departments, insurance companies, mutual funds and pension funds, had made serious inroads, capturing a substantial portion

---

77. *Id.*
78. SEC Release No. 34-15807 (May 9, 1979).
79. SEC Release No. 34-17371 (December 12, 1980).

of the intermediation function in that a large portion of the securities issued by corporations, both debt and equity, were being bought by institutional investors acting as financial intermediaries for the individuals whom the securities industry previously had served.

The SEC stated that one of the reasons for this was that "fiduciaries gradually became interested in achieving economic growth in the portfolios they managed instead of concentrating primarily on safety and income." Accordingly, "it became possible for savers to invest in the stock market through a financial intermediary either by creating a trust or by establishing an account managed by a bank or other institutional investor." The SEC stated that the growth of tax-exempt pension funds created large new pools of money available for investment in the securities markets. Bank trust departments, investment advisors and insurance companies began to play a major role in managing the assets of those who received a portion of their compensation in the form of tax-deferred pension benefits. In addition, the SEC noted that the explosive growth in mutual funds "brought into the market many investors who, if they had invested directly, would not have been able to achieve a diversified portfolio." The growth in mutual fund investments magnified the trend toward the institutionalization of the securities market.

The desire of institutional investors to lower their transaction costs led to practices that undermined the fixed commission rate system established by the securities exchanges and finally led to the elimination of fixed commission rates on May 1, 1975, known in the industry as "May Day."[80] Institutions were

---

80. Rule 19b-3 under the 1934 Act, adopted by the SEC in January 1975 (SEC Release No. 34-11203 (January 23, 1975)) effective May 1, 1975, prohibits any national securities exchange from adopting or retaining any rule that requires its members to charge fixed commission rates for transactions effected on the exchange or by the use of exchange facilities. As stated in SEC Release No. 34-11203, the practice of fixed commission rates on stock exchanges in the United States originated in the so-called Buttonwood Tree Agreement of 1792, which provided:

We, the Subscribers, Brokers for the Purchase and Sale of Public Stock, do hereby solemnly promise and pledge ourselves to each other, that

unhappy with a system that required them to pay the same percentage commission on a 50,000-share trade as an individual investor on a 500-share trade. The transaction cost to the broker was substantially the same regardless of the number of shares involved. Thus, exchange members were willing to submit to competitive pressures and to cooperate with their institutional customers in devising methods to evade the antirebate rules of the exchanges.

The customer-directed give-up was one device that undermined the fixed-rate system. Institutions such as mutual fund managers would direct the executing broker to share its commission with another exchange member that had provided benefits to the manager by selling fund shares or furnishing research or statistical or advisory services. Reciprocal commission business between exchange members and non-member firms was another device that undermined the system. Then there were exotic schemes such as the "end run" and the "incorporated give-up pocket," where a subsidiary of a mutual fund manager gained membership on a regional exchange in order to recapture commissions.[81]

Schemes used to evade the fixed commission rate structure also were employed in the context of underwritten fixed-price offerings. These schemes had the economic effect of affording to institutional and other large purchasers a rebate of some portion of the selling concession. As stated by the SEC:

> Such practices include both direct discounting techniques, such as "overtrading" in swap transactions and certain types of underwriting fee recapture, and indirect compensation arrangements, such as the provision of goods and services in return for so-called "syndicate soft dollars."

---

we will not buy or sell from this day for any person whatsoever, any kind of Public Stock at a less rate than one-quarter percent Commission on the Specie value, and that we will give a preference to each other in our Negotiations. In Testimony whereof we have set our hands this 17th day of May, at New York, 1792.

81. The various schemes to evade the antirebate rules of the stock exchanges are described in Richard W. Jennings, Harold Marsh, Jr. & John C. Coffee, Jr., *Securities Regulation* 556–62 (7th ed. 1992).

In swap transactions, securities are taken in trade from a customer, in lieu of cash, in exchange for the offered securities. A discount from the fixed offering price may be granted to the purchaser of the offered securities where the syndicate member purchases the securities taken in trade at a price exceeding their market value. This "overtrade" is economically equivalent to paying less than the stated offering price for the securities being distributed.

A customer may seek to recapture underwriting fees by designating a broker-dealer affiliate to be included in the selling group. The customer may then purchase the offered security through its affiliate, thereby recapturing the selling concession. Such concession payments to an affiliate enable the customer to obtain direct discounts from the fixed offering price.

A broker-dealer providing research or other services to a customer may be compensated for those services, at least in part, through purchases by the customer in a fixed price offering. The customer can either purchase the securities directly through the broker-dealer or can contact the managing underwriter and "designate" the dealer to receive credit for the order. In these instances, the dealer is compensated indirectly by receiving "soft dollar" concessions for the research or other services it has provided.[82]

• • *The* Papilsky *Case.* In 1976, Judge Frankel handed down his decision in *Papilsky v. Berndt.*[83] The plaintiff, an owner of 40 shares of Affiliated Fund, Inc., then one of the largest mutual funds in the country, brought a derivative suit against the fund and its management company, Lord, Abbett & Co., charging violations of fiduciary duties in failing to recapture brokerage commissions, underwriting commissions and tender offer fees

---

82. SEC Release No. 34-15807 (May 9, 1979).

83. [1976–1977 Transfer Binder] Fed. Sec. L. Rep. (CCH) ¶95,627 (S.D.N.Y. 1976).

for the fund and its shareholders. With respect to the recapture of selling concessions, the plaintiff alleged that Affiliated Fund should have designated Lord Abbett, a NASD member, to receive selling credit when the fund purchased securities in underwritten offerings and that the selling concession so received by Lord Abbett should have been applied to reduce its management fee. Counsel had advised that this would have violated NASD regulations, but Judge Frankel found that, in the absence of a contrary ruling from the SEC or the NASD, underwriting recapture in this manner was available and legal under the predecessor of Rule 2740. He held that a mutual fund advisor would be liable for unrecaptured underwriting discounts unless it established that it fully disclosed to the fund's independent directors that recapture was a possible alternative to other uses of the fees, and that the directors, as a matter of reasonable business judgment, determined not to seek recapture.

As a result of *Papilsky*, a number of requests were made to the NASD on behalf of mutual fund managers for a ruling on the propriety of recapture under the predecessor of Rule 2740. The NASD responded to these requests in November and December of 1976 by stating that, in its opinion, that rule prohibited underwriting recapture. The SEC wrote to the NASD in February 1977, stating that this interpretation of the rule raised important issues, and that, accordingly, it should be filed as a proposed rule change. After a public meeting with the SEC in May 1977, the NASD agreed to do so.

In July 1978, the NASD made the so-called *Papilsky* filing after first circulating two exposure drafts to its membership. The SEC held hearings on the proposal, and on July 3, 1980 it sent to the NASD a letter requesting that it consider amending the proposals in certain respects.[84] The NASD amended the proposed rule changes, and they were then approved by the membership. The NASD filed its final amended version on September 4, 1980. The proposal was approved by the SEC on December 12, 1980.[85]

---

84. SEC Release No. 34-16956 (July 3, 1980).
85. SEC Release No. 34-17371 (December 12, 1980).

448 CORPORATE FINANCE & THE SECURITIES LAWS

• *Analysis of the* Papilsky *Rules*

Having reviewed the circumstances leading up to their adoption and the purpose that they are intended to accomplish, the *Papilsky* rules and interpretations can now be examined in detail.

• • *Selling Commissions, Discounts and Other Allowances (Rule 2740).* The basic operative provision designed to ensure the integrity of the fixed-price distribution system is Rule 2740. This rule provides that, *in connection with the sale of securities that are part of a fixed-price offering*:

> A member may not grant or receive selling concessions, discounts, or other allowances except as consideration for services rendered in distribution and may not grant such concessions, discounts or other allowances to anyone other than a broker or dealer actually engaged in the investment banking or securities business; provided, however, that nothing in this Rule shall prevent any member from (1) selling any such securities to any person, or account managed by any person, to whom it has provided or will provide bona fide research, if the stated public offering price for such securities is paid by the purchaser; or (2) selling any such securities owned by him to any person at any net price which may be fixed by him unless prevented therefrom by agreement.

A related rule, Rule 2420 (Dealing with Non-Members), prohibits NASD members from allowing selling concessions, discounts or other allowances to non-member broker-dealers, except for foreign dealers who make the undertakings discussed below.[86] Thus, the broker-dealers referred to in Rule 2740 must be NASD members or non-member foreign dealers who satisfy the requirements of Rule 2420. An interpretation of Rule 2420, IM-2420-1(d)(2), states that NASD members participating in the distribution of securities may not allow any selling concession, discount or other allowance in connection with the sale of such

---

86. Rule 2420 also prohibits a member from joining in any syndicate or group with a non-member broker-dealer in connection with a public offering.

RULES OF THE SELF-REGULATORY ORGANIZATIONS 449

securities to any bank or trust company.[87] This interpretation is necessary because banks and trust companies are excluded from the relevant definitions of "broker" and "dealer" in the NASD's by-laws.

Of course, the purpose, history and language of Rule 2740 make it clear that the rule does not apply to a payment unless it is made to a person *who purchases a security and in a manner that results in a discount from what purports to be a fixed-price offering.* Thus, the NASD's Office of General Counsel has written a letter stating that Rule 2740 would not be violated if an NASD member firm paid a portion of its underwriting fees to another broker-dealer as a referral or advisory fee.[88] Nor should the rule apply where, for example, a broker-dealer has a profit-sharing agreement with a bank (e.g., in connection with subordinated loan arrangements) or any other person that is neither a registered broker-dealer nor required to be so registered.

Rule 2740 applies to reallowances as well as to selling concessions. The NASD's interpretation of Rule 2740—IM-2740—provides:

> A broker or dealer who has received or retained a selling concession, discount or other allowance may not grant or otherwise reallow all or part of that concession, discount or allowance to anyone other than a broker or dealer engaged in the investment banking or securities business and only as consideration for services rendered in distribution.

A member is not his or her brother's keeper, however. The interpretation goes on to state:

> A member granting a selling concession, discount or other allowance to another person is not responsible for

---

[87]. Keeping in mind that Rule 2740 and related rules are intended to ensure the integrity of the fixed-price distribution system, profit-sharing agreements with banks (e.g., in connection with subordinated loan arrangements) are not prohibited except where the bank is the purchaser of securities being distributed.

[88]. *Dana Fleischman* (November 24, 2003). The letter is on the NASD's website.

determining whether such other person may be violating Rule 2740 by granting or reallowing that selling concession, discount or other allowance to another person, unless the member knew, or had reasonable cause to know, of the violation.

Rule 2740 is applicable only to a "fixed-price offering," which term is defined as follows in NASD Rule 0120:

> The term "fixed price offering" means the offering of securities at a stated public offering price or prices, all or part of which securities are publicly offered in the United States or any territory thereof, whether or not registered under the Securities Act of 1933, except that the term does not include offerings of "exempted securities" or "municipal securities" as those terms are defined in Sections 3(a)(12) and 3(a)(29), respectively, of the [Securities Exchange] Act [of 1934] or offerings of redeemable securities of investment companies registered pursuant to the Investment Company Act of 1940 which are offered at prices determined by the net asset value of the securities.

Offerings of exempted securities and municipal securities are excluded because they are largely outside of the NASD's jurisdiction. Mutual fund shares are excluded because Section 22(d) of the 1940 Act expressly prohibits dealers from selling such securities at prices below the public offering price.[89] Wholly foreign offerings are not covered. Thus, in a Eurobond offering made exclusively abroad (even where a portion of the securities are privately placed in the United States), a NASD member participating in the offering may follow the European practice of reallowing a portion of the selling concession to banks that are purchasing for the account of customers.

IM-2740 states that a dealer has rendered services in distribution "if the dealer is an underwriter of a portion of that offering, has engaged in some selling effort with respect to the sale or has provided or agreed to provide bona fide research to

---

89. *See Spiro Sideris,* 44 S.E.C. 212 (1970).

RULES OF THE SELF-REGULATORY ORGANIZATIONS 451

the person to whom or at whose direction the sale is made." The interpretation makes the same point in slightly different terms where it states that "nothing in Rule 2740 prohibits a member from providing bona fide research to a customer who also purchases securities from fixed price offerings from the member whether or not there is an express or implied agreement between the member providing the research and the recipient that the member will be compensated for the research in cash, brokerage commissions, selling concessions or some other form of consideration."

The key term is "bona fide research," which is defined as follows in Rule 2740(b):

> The term "bona fide research," when used in this Rule means advice, rendered either directly or through publications or writings, as to the value of securities, the advisability of investing in, purchasing, or selling securities, and the availability of securities or purchasers or sellers of securities, or analyses and reports concerning issuers, industries, securities, economic factors and trends, portfolio strategy, and performance of accounts; provided, however, that investment management or investment discretionary services are not bona fide research.

The meaning of the term "bona fide research" is elaborated on in IM-2740. It is noted in that interpretation that the Rule 2740(b) definition of bona fide research is substantially the same as the definition of the term "research" in Section 28(e)(3) of the 1934 Act.[90] Interpretations concerning the definition of "research" under Section 28(e) are referred to for guidance, including SEC Release No. 34-23170 (April 30, 1986).

---

90. Section 28(e), which was enacted in 1975 following the elimination of fixed stock exchange commissions, provides that a mutual fund advisor or other fiduciary may cause an account with respect to which it exercises investment discretion to pay a commission in excess of that which another broker would have charged if it determines in good faith that the commission paid is reasonable "in relation to the value of the brokerage and research services provided." Thus, fiduciaries may "pay up" for research.

IM-2740 goes on to make the following observations:

> Moreover, while the provisions in Rule 2740 concerning bona fide research are intended to permit money managers to receive bona fide research from persons from whom securities are purchased, it is not intended to enable a money manager, who is also a member, to view its money management services as bona fide research. Accordingly, the performance of money management or investment discretionary services themselves are expressly excluded from the definition of bona fide research.
>
> Another factor relating to bona fide research is that the research must be "provided by" the member who receives or retains the selling concession, discount or other allowance. Under Section 28(e) of the [Securities Exchange] Act [of 1934], the Commission has stated that the "safe harbor" provided by Section 28(e) only extends to research that is "provided by" the broker to whom brokerage commissions are paid. In determining whether the exclusion for bona fide research under Rule 2740 is available in any given instance, members should refer to the interpretations of the Commission and its staff of the similar requirement applicable to Section 28(e).

A member who, directly or through an affiliate, supplies another person with services or products that fail to qualify as bona fide research, or that, in the case of services or products other than bona fide research, are provided to customers for cash or for some other consideration, and also retains or receives selling concessions, discounts or other allowances from purchases by that person, is improperly granting a selling concession, discount or other allowance to that person unless it has been, or has arranged and reasonably expects to be, fully compensated for such services or products from sources other than the selling concession, discount or allowance. The net effect of this is that NASD members simply should not provide these products or services to their customers unless they are prepared to demonstrate that they have been fully compensated for them with consideration other than selling concessions, discounts or other allowances received or retained on the sale of securities in fixed-price offerings.

RULES OF THE SELF-REGULATORY ORGANIZATIONS 453

The interpretation states that, in order to demonstrate that the cash or other consideration is full consideration, records should be kept that identify the recipient of the services or products and the amount of cash or other consideration paid or to be paid. The interpretation also states that, unless the amount of cash or other consideration agreed on appears on its face to be unreasonably low, it will not be necessary to demonstrate that the agreed-on price represented fair market price. There is no requirement that the member charge the same amount to each person to whom it provides the same or similar services or products.

Rule 2740(d) imposes quarterly reporting requirements on members receiving an order designating another broker or dealer to receive credit for a sale. Rule 2740(e) imposes similar record keeping requirements on designees.

NASD rules require that certain agreements be entered into by dealers participating in a distribution. Rule 2740(c) provides:

> A member who grants a selling concession, discount or other allowance to another person shall obtain a written agreement from that person that he will comply with the provisions of this Rule, and a member who grants such selling concession, discount or other allowance to a non-member broker or dealer in a foreign country shall also obtain from such broker or dealer a written agreement to comply, as though such broker or dealer were a member, with the provisions of Rules 2730 and 2750 and to comply with Rule 2420 as that Rule applies to a non-member broker/dealer in a foreign country.

Rule 2420(c) requires that, if concessions are allowed to foreign dealers not eligible for NASD membership, "a member shall as a condition of such transaction secure from such foreign broker or dealer an agreement that, in making any sales to purchasers within the United States of securities acquired as a result of such transactions, he will conform to the provisions of paragraphs (a) and (b) of this Rule to the same extent as though he were a member of the [NASD]." It should be noted that any foreign dealer that is registered with the SEC under Section 15 of the 1934 Act is eligible for membership in the NASD.

As discussed in Chapter 2, the practice is to include the agreements required by Rule 2740(c) and Rule 2420(c) in the AAU and the selected dealers agreement.

The approval by the SEC of the predecessor of amended Rule 2740 put to rest any question as to whether the NASD is authorized to bring disciplinary proceedings based on violations of the price maintenance provisions of an AAU. In 1945, the SEC had determined that the NASD did not have this power on the basis that an NASD interpretation specifically requiring adherence to price maintenance agreements would be contrary to the provisions of what is now designated as Section 15A(b)(6) of the 1934 Act.[91] This section provides that the rules of the NASD shall not be designed to "impose any schedule or fix rates of commissions, allowances, discounts, or other fees to be charged by its members."

In connection with the adoption of amended Rule 2740, the SEC stated that, regardless of the merits of its analysis in 1945, it was now required to review rules proposed by the NASD under a different standard than was then in effect and that it could now weigh the beneficial purposes of an NASD rule against any burdens on competition. The SEC concluded that it was no longer correct to follow the *per se* approach that it followed in 1945 when it considered irrelevant any beneficial aspects of the NASD's interpretation of its rules.

• • *Securities Taken in Trade (Rule 2730).* The improper grant or reallowance of a selling concession or discount may be made indirectly by the use of such devices as "overtrading." This is precisely what Rule 2730 is designed to prevent.

"Swapping" is a legitimate technique in the sale of underwritten securities. In a swap transaction, securities are taken "in trade" from a customer in exchange for the underwritten securities. This allows an underwriter or dealer to reduce its risk by diversifying its holdings if it is unable to sell the underwritten securities for cash. It permits an institution to purchase securities being offered where it does not have available cash to pay

---

91. *National Association of Securities Dealers, Inc.,* 19 S.E.C. 424 (1945).

for them or where for other reasons it prefers not to pay cash. Swaps are seldom, if ever, used in connection with common stock offerings. In practice, they are limited to offerings of debt securities or other securities that trade on the basis of yield. In making the trade, if the underwriter or dealer places a higher value on the swapped securities than they are actually worth, then this may be viewed as an indirect rebate of the selling concession. Rule 2730 has provided for many years that securities may be taken in trade only at their fair market price at the time of purchase. It also provides guidance as to what constitutes a fair price.

Rule 2730(a) provides:

> A member engaged in a fixed price offering, who purchases or arranges the purchase of securities taken in trade, shall purchase the securities at a fair market price at the time of purchase or shall act as agent in the sale of such securities and charge a normal commission therefor.

Rule 2730(b)(1) defines "taken in trade" to mean "the purchase by a member as principal, or as agent for the account of another, of a security from a customer pursuant to an agreement or understanding that the customer purchase securities from the member which are part of a fixed price offering." The term "fair market price" is defined to mean a price not higher than the price at which the securities would be purchased in the ordinary course of business by a dealer in such securities in transactions of similar size and having similar characteristics but not involving a security taken in trade. The term "normal commission" is defined in a similar manner.

Rule 2730(c) and its interpretation IM-2730 together establish certain benchmarks, presumptions and recordkeeping obligations relating to what is the fair market price of common stocks and securities other than common stocks. With respect to common stocks, a member is "presumed," and with respect to other securities is "deemed," to have taken them in trade at a fair market price when the price paid is not higher than the highest independent bid at the time of purchase, if bid quotations are readily available. A member is "presumed" to have taken a security in trade at a price higher than the fair market price when the price paid is higher than the lowest independent offer for the securities at the time of purchase, if offer quotations are readily available. If bid and offer quotations are not readily available for the security taken in trade, a member may rely on quotations for comparable securities. In instances where a member takes securities in trade at a price higher than the highest independent bid and not higher than the lowest independent offer, or when bid and offer quotations are not readily available, there is no safe harbor and there is neither a presumption of compliance nor of non-compliance. If the securities taken in trade are common stocks that are traded on an exchange or quoted in NASDAQ, the quotations must be obtained from the exchange or the NASDAQ screen. Quotations for all other securities must be obtained from at least two other dealers. The quotations must be for a transaction of a size corresponding generally to the amount of securities taken in trade.

As of when is the fair market value of the securities taken in trade to be determined? IM-2730 states the NASD's view that swap transactions "that are arranged before the effectiveness of a fixed price offering are not generally viewed as being legally consummated until effectiveness of the fixed price offering." It goes on to state that the fair market price of the securities taken in trade is nonetheless "normally determined at the time of the pricing of the fixed price offering, which occurs on the day before effectiveness usually in the afternoon, and the swap is arranged on the basis of that price." In such cases, according to IM-2730, the determination of the fair market price of the securities taken in trade "may be made as of the time of pricing of the fixed price offering."

The foregoing guidelines obviously predate the use of shelf registration and Rule 430A prospectuses, which make the effective date of the registration statement irrelevant as a guide to the enforceability of a swap. They are clearly correct, however, in focusing on the pricing of the new securities as a better guide to the proper time of valuation than the time of "effectiveness." On the other hand, it is clearly open to a securities firm and a customer to agree that the trade date for the purchase of securities by the securities firm will be a date other than the date of pricing of the new issue. In such a case, the fair market price on the trade date should control for purposes of Rule 2730. The interpretation implies as much when it states that when swaps are agreed to after the effectiveness of the offering (i.e., after pricing), then the fair market price of the swapped securities "must be determined as of the time the transaction is legally consummated," which is the trade date.

• • *Transactions With Related Persons (Rule 2750).* One method that an institution would use to recapture selling concessions was to establish an affiliate as a member of the NASD and to designate the affiliate as the dealer to receive credit for the selling concession. This is what the plaintiff in *Papilsky* claimed that Affiliated Fund should have done.

The predecessor of Rule 2750 was adopted specifically to prohibit recapture through affiliated NASD members. Rule 2750 provides that no NASD member engaged in a fixed-price offering of securities shall sell the securities to, or place the securities with, any person or account that is a "related person" of the member unless such related person is itself subject to Rule 2750 or is a non-member foreign broker or dealer who has entered into the agreements required by Rule 2740. A "related person" of a member includes any person or account which directly or indirectly owns, is owned by, or is under common ownership with the member. A person is deemed to own another person if it has the right to participate to the extent of more than 25% in the profits of the other person or owns beneficially more than 25% of the outstanding voting securities of that person. On the other hand, it seems clear that a person (e.g., an investment fund) is not a related person merely because the NASD member is an affiliate of the person's advisor.

Because of Rule 2750, an NASD member may not participate in an underwriting and sell any of the securities to an institution with which it is affiliated. A member may place securities with a related person, however, if it has made a bona fide public offering of the securities. There is a presumption that the member has not made a bona fide public offering if the securities immediately trade at a premium in the secondary market.

An interpretation to Rule 2750 makes it clear that a sponsor of a unit investment trust will not violate Rule 2750 if it accumulates securities with respect to which it has acted as a member of the underwriting syndicate or selling group if, at the time of accumulation, it intends in good faith to deposit the securities into the unit investment trust at the public offering price and intends to make a public offering of the units. The logic of the interpretation would appear to extend to situations involving the accumulation of debt securities in anticipation of a CDO or similar securitization of such securities.

Chapter 7

PRIVATE PLACEMENTS

Section 4(2) of the 1933 Act exempts from the registration and prospectus delivery requirements of Section 5 all "transactions by an issuer not involving any public offering." This is the so-called "private offering" or "private placement" exemption. Issuers rely on the exemption for a wide variety of transactions, ranging from the initial sale of "founders' stock" by a new business to a billion-dollar sale of investment-grade debt securities by a "world-class" issuer to literally hundreds of institutional investors. The exemption may also be used for venture capital investments, for acquisitions of closely held corporations where all or part of the consideration is securities of the acquiring corporation, or for sales of limited partnership interests to individual investors.

As in the case of other exemptions from the requirements of Section 5, the person claiming an exemption has the burden of establishing that the exemption is available for the particular transaction. If securities are sold without registration and without a valid exemption, Section 12(a)(1) of the 1933 Act gives the purchaser a right to rescind the transaction for a period of one year after the sale. This right may be exercised against anyone who "sold" the security, which certainly means the selling broker-dealer and may include the issuer.[1] The seller's good faith belief that the exemption was available is irrelevant, as is the fact that the seller may have provided the purchaser with full and fair disclosure.

The procedures appropriate to establish the exemption will depend on the nature of the transaction. Section 4(2) is self-executing and may be relied on by an issuer—and its financial intermediaries, if any—on the basis of many decades of court cases, SEC rulings and "lore." In the case of many transactions, however, issuers and financial intermediaries will prefer to rely on SEC rules that provide more certainty than Section 4(2).

Regulation D is the SEC's general purpose set of rules governing private placements by issuers. When the purchasers are accredited investors, as we will see, Regulation D permits an offering to a potentially indefinite number of persons.

The field of institutional private placements has been revolutionized since 1990, however, by an SEC rule that does not even apply to a private placement by an issuer. Rule 144A by its terms only permits persons *other than the issuer* to resell "restricted" securities, that is, securities that they have purchased directly or indirectly from the issuer (or an affiliate of the issuer) in a transaction or series of transactions not involving a public offering. Rule 144A's powerful influence on the market arises from the fact that a financial intermediary can purchase securities from an issuer as principal on a "firm commitment" basis and rely on Rule 144A to resell those securities, subject to a few easily verified conditions, to a potentially indefinite number of "qualified institutional buyers" or "QIBs."

This chapter will describe the history of the Section 4(2) exemption, including the early administrative emphasis on the number of offerees and the Supreme Court's shift of emphasis in *Ralston Purina*[2] to the ability of offerees to "fend for themselves." It will describe how the SEC—usually yielding only

---

1. *See* the discussion of *Pinter v. Dahl*, 486 U.S. 622 (1988), in Chapter 5.
2. *SEC v. Ralston Purina Co.*, 346 U.S. 119 (1953).

reluctantly to the pressure of market realities but sometimes leading the charge—built on the statutory exemption in ways that would likely have astounded the drafters of the 1933 Act. The SEC's efforts culminated with the adoption of Regulation D in 1982 and Rule 144A in 1990. These rules, which established for all intents and purposes a reliable exemption for sales to institutional investors (not unlike that found in state blue sky statutes), can best be understood in the light of the circumstances that led to their adoption.

Legislative History

The original bill introduced in the House and Senate in 1933, as drafted by Houston Thompson,[3] did not include a private offering exemption as such.[4] It did include an exemption for "the issuance of additional capital stock of a corporation sold or distributed by it among its own stockholders exclusively," where no commission or other remuneration was paid in connection with the sale or distribution. It provided an exemption for isolated transactions, similar to that found in state blue sky laws, which removed from the coverage of the statute:

> Isolated transactions in which any security is sold, offered for sale, subscription, or delivery by the owner thereof, or by his representative solely for the owner's account, such sale or offer for sale, subscription, or delivery not being made in the course of repeated and

---

3. *See* Chapter 1.
4. H.R. 4314 as introduced by Mr. Rayburn and referred to the House Interstate and Foreign Commerce Committee on March 29, 1933, 73d Cong., 1st Sess. (1933), *reprinted in* 3 *Legislative History of the Securities Act of 1933 and Securities Act of 1934,* Item 22 (J. S. Ellenberger & Ellen P. Mahar eds. 1973), and §875 as introduced by Mr. Robinson and referred to the Senate Judiciary Committee on March 29, 1933, 73d Cong., 1st Sess. (1933), *reprinted in* 3 *Legislative History,* Item 28. Section 875 was subsequently discharged from the Judiciary Committee and referred to the Banking and Currency Committee on March 30, 1933.

successive transactions of a like character by such owner for the purpose of engaging in the purchase and sale of securities as a business, and such owner or representative not being the underwriter of such security.

The inadequacy of such an approach is evident today, and it soon became evident to James M. Landis, Benjamin V. Cohen and Thomas G. Corcoran, the draftsmen recruited by Professor Felix Frankfurter to revise the Thompson bill. As Landis recalled in 1959, it was the probing of Middleton Beaman, the chief legislative draftsman for the House of Representatives, that led to the Section 4 transaction exemptions:

> "[P]ublic offerings" as distinguished from "private offerings" proved to be the answer. The sale of an issue of securities to insurance companies or to a limited group of experienced investors, was certainly not a matter of concern to the federal government. That bureaucracy, untrained in these matters as it was, could hardly equal these investors for sophistication, provided it was only their own money they were spending. And so the conception of an exemption for all sales, other than by an issuer, underwriter, or dealer came into being, replacing the concept of "isolated transactions" theretofore traditional to blue sky legislation.[5]

The substitute bill introduced in May 1933, as drafted by Landis, Cohen and Corcoran,[6] contained an exemption for "transactions by an issuer not with or through an underwriter." The bill as reported by the House Committee added to this phrase the words "and not involving any public offering."[7] In

---

5. J. M. Landis, *The Legislative History of the Securities Act of 1933*, 28 Geo. Wash. L. Rev. 29, 37 (1959).

6. H.R. 5480 as introduced by Mr. Rayburn and referred to the House Interstate and Foreign Commerce Committee on May 3, 1933, 73d Cong., 1st Sess. (1933), *reprinted in* 3 *Legislative History*, Item 24.

7. *See* H.R. Rep. No. 85, *supra* Chapter 1, note 3, at 1.

1934, the exemption was amended to delete the words "not with or through an underwriter." The Conference Report on this legislation stated clearly the reason for this deletion:

> The Commission has recognized by its interpretations that a public offering is necessary for distribution. Therefore there can be no underwriter within the meaning of the act in the absence of a public offer and the phrase eliminated in the second clause is really superfluous.[8]

Congress provided no meaningful guidance as to what was contemplated by the term "public offering." A House report stated that the clause in question "exempts transactions by an issuer unless made by or through an underwriter so as to permit an issuer to make a specific or an isolated sale of its securities to a particular person, but insisting that if a sale of the issuer's securities should be made generally to the public that that transaction shall come within the purview of the act."[9] Referring to the exemptions generally, the report stated that the bill "carefully exempts from its application certain types of securities and securities transactions where there is no practical need for its application or where the public benefits are too remote."[10] The Conference Report on the 1933 Act contained a statement that sales of stock to stockholders are subject to the 1933 Act "unless the stockholders are so small in number that the sale to them does not constitute a public offering."[11]

Early Administrative Interpretations

In the first few years following the adoption of the 1933 Act, the number of offerees was emphasized in applying the

---

8. H.R. Rep. No. 1838, 73d Cong., 2d Sess. (1934), *reprinted in* 5 *Legislative History,* Item 20, at 41. This was the Conference Report accompanying H.R. 9323, 73d Cong., 2d Sess. (1934).

9. H.R. Rep. No. 85, *supra* Chapter 1, note 3, at 15–16.

10. *Id.* at 5.

11. H.R. Rep. No. 152, 73d Cong., 1st Sess. (1933), 2 *Legislative History,* Item 19, at 25.

private offering exemption. At some point, the number 25 became the test. As early as 1934, Arthur H. Dean made the flat statement that registration is required if securities "are to be sold through the use of interstate commerce or the mails, and are to be offered to more than twenty-five people."[12] Although Dean did not indicate the basis for this statement, it is evident that this well-known securities lawyer had come to believe that this was the test.

The first SEC reference to the number 25 appears in a 1935 release quoting an opinion of the SEC's office of general counsel rendered in the case of a proposed offering of preferred stock to 25 offerees:

> The opinion has been previously expressed by this office that an offering of securities to an insubstantial number of persons is a transaction by the issuer not involving any public offering, and hence an exempted transaction under the provisions of Section [4(2)] of the Securities Act. Furthermore, the opinion has been expressed that under ordinary circumstances an offering to not more than approximately twenty-five persons is not an offering to a substantial number and presumably does not involve a public offering.[13]

In the same release, after setting forth the 25-person safe harbor, the SEC's general counsel made the point that in no sense was the question of what constitutes a public offering to be determined exclusively by the number of prospective offerees, although this was one factor to be considered. He stressed in this context that the number of offerees "does not mean the number of actual purchasers, but the number of persons to whom the security in question is offered for sale." Other factors considered to be significant were the relationship of the offerees to each other and to the issuer, the number of units offered, the size of the offering and the manner of offering. The general

---

12. A. H. Dean, *As Amended: The Federal Securities Act,* Fortune, Sept. 1934, at 82.

13. SEC Release No. 33-285 (January 24, 1935).

counsel stated that the basis on which the offerees are selected is of the greatest importance:

> Thus, an offering to a given number of persons chosen from the general public on the ground that they are possible purchasers may be a public offering even though an offering to a larger number of persons who are all the members of a particular class, membership in which may be determined by the application of some pre-existing standard, would be a non-public offering.

On the other hand, the general counsel stated that he had "no doubt but that an offering restricted to a particular group or class may nevertheless be a public offering if it is open to a sufficient number of persons." He stated that "an offering to the members of a class who should have special knowledge of the issuer is less likely to be a public offering than is an offering to members of a class of the same size who do not have this advantage." An example would be a group of "high executive officers."

The number of units offered was considered significant because where many units are offered in small denominations, there is "some indication that the issuer recognizes the possibility, if not the probability, of a distribution of a security to the public generally." The size of the offering was considered significant in that small offerings "are less likely to be publicly offered even if redistributed." Finally, the general counsel stated that transactions that are effected "by direct negotiation by the issuer are more likely to be non-public than those effected through the use of machinery of public distribution." With all of these generalities floating about, it is no wonder that in the early years the best conservative advice was to limit the number of offerees to 25.

The same release stated that there appeared to be developing a general practice on the part of issuers desiring to avoid registration of their securities to seek to dispose of them to insurance companies or other institutions that at the time of purchase state that they are acquiring the securities "for investment and not with a view to distribution." This was the genesis of the "investment letter"—the representation obtained from purchasers in private placements assuring the issuer that they have not, in the words of Section 2(a)(11), purchased the securities "with a view to" their distribution. The representation that the securities have been acquired "for investment" has no statutory underpinnings and, as we will see, can lead to confusion.

In a subsequent release, the SEC's general counsel, after reaffirming that the test for determining whether securities acquired in connection with a private offering could be sold without registration is whether or not they had been acquired with a view to distribution, went on to set forth the factors to be considered in making that determination:

> I wish to make clear, however, that I do not believe the fact that the initial purchaser has stated that his original purchase was for investment and not for resale is necessarily conclusive on this question. In my opinion there should be considered such other factors as: (1) the relation between the issuer and the initial purchaser; (2) the business of the latter, as for example, whether such purchaser is an underwriter or dealer in securities, and, if not, whether the purchase of such a block of securities for investment is consistent with its general operations; and (3) the length of time elapsing between the acquisition of the securities by the initial purchaser and the date of their proposed resale.[14]

In commenting on Rule 142, an obscure rule still on the books that was designed to exclude from the category of underwriters persons whose connection with a distribution of securities is confined to supplying secondary capital by purchasing "for investment" any securities remaining unsold in the hands of underwriters at the conclusion of a public offering,[15] the general counsel made the following observations:

> Although it is not impossible to conceive of a situation in which a person who had purchased securities for

---

14. SEC Release No. 33-603 (December 16, 1935).

15. As far as the authors are aware, Rule 142 and Regulation M under the 1934 Act are the only 1933 Act or 1934 Act rules that use the term "for investment."

investment changed his mind in good faith on the next day, and proceeded to dispose of the securities, it must nevertheless be remembered that a state of mind can ordinarily be ascertained only by weighing evidentiary factors, and that a person's actions may be of far greater evidentiary significance than his statements as throwing light on what his state of mind was at a given time. Thus, self-serving statements that a particular purchase was made for investment would carry very little weight in the face of more concrete facts and circumstances inconsistent with such an intention.

Most prominent among the relevant evidentiary factors would undoubtedly be the length of time elapsing between the acquisition of the securities and their proposed resale. Although retention of the securities for any given length of time would in no event be conclusive, it is obvious that the longer they were held the easier it would be to maintain that they had originally been purchased for investment; and it is my opinion that if they were retained for a period as long as a year that fact would be sufficient, if not contradicted by other evidence, to create a strong inference that they had been purchased for investment. However, such an inference would be rebuttable; for example, it would fall in the face of evidence of a pre-arranged scheme to effect a distribution at the end of the year.[16]

This statement was the source of the one-year holding period rule of thumb that was applied by securities lawyers well into the 1950s.

The *Ralston Purina* Case

The 1953 decision of the U.S. Supreme Court in *Ralston Purina*[17] had the effect of shifting the emphasis from numbers to the ability of the offerees to fend for themselves.

---

16. SEC Release No. 33-1862 (December 14, 1938).
17. 346 U.S. 119 (1953).

As described by the district court, the facts of the case were not in dispute.[18] A manufacturer of mixed feeds for poultry and livestock and cereal for human consumption, Ralston Purina Company had been organized in 1894. Since 1942, it had offered stock ownership to employees who could meet its test of "key employees." The company had, from time to time, paid a bonus to certain key employees, and with rare exceptions they had used their bonuses to purchase stock offered to them. The company would make known to managers and heads of departments that stock was available, and the managers were depended on to select the key employees to whom stock would be made available. The company had approximately 7,000 employees. Purchases were made in 1947 by 243 employees, in 1948 by 20, in 1949 by 414, and in 1950 by 411. For 1951, there were applications to purchase by 165 employees. Although no record was kept of those to whom offers were made and who did not purchase, it was estimated that the offering for the year 1951 had been made to approximately 500 key employees.

The stock was traded in the over-the-counter market, but apparently it was a thin market. One reason given for selling stock directly to employees was that if they attempted to purchase in the open market, the demand would force up the price artificially. At no time was stock sold to employees to procure needed financing. The district court was sympathetic to Ralston Purina's program of stock ownership:

> The sole purpose of the "selection" is to keep part stock ownership of the business within the operating personnel of the business and to spread ownership throughout all departments and activities of the business. No greater tie, to secure loyalty, could be forged between the corporation and its employees than part ownership in the business by the employees. It is an appeal to the employees' self-interest, but a commendable one. Defendant could confine stock offerings to those high in the executive positions but that would not accomplish its long range

---

18. 102 F. Supp. 964, 965 (E.D. Mo. 1952).

purpose of bringing from the ranks those who represent good prospects for company management.[19]

The district court held that the private offering exemption had been satisfied.

The Court of Appeals affirmed.[20] In doing so, it was obviously moved by the statement of management as to the reasons for selling stock to employees:

> We feel, sir, that that creates a greater efficiency with the company, because it draws employees of the company closer together. Many of our people come from the rural area, where proprietorship is a matter of great pride to them. The fact that they feel that they are owners, at least part owners, in the company, contributes to the morale, and we feel that the idea of breaking down the gap between the ownership and management is something that is highly desirable and something that contributed substantially to the success of the company.[21]

In conclusion, the Court of Appeals stated:

> We sympathize with the efforts of the Commission to restrict the exemption granted by Section [4(2)] to the narrowest possible scope, but we do not think that the intra-organizational offerings of stock by the Company, unaccompanied by any solicitation, which have resulted in a limited distribution of stock, for investment purposes, to a select group of employees considered by the management to be worthy of retention and probable future promotion, is to be excluded from the exemption of nonpublic offerings granted by Congress. There is, we think, virtually no possibility that these offerings, if continued, will frustrate or impair the purpose of the Act.[22]

---

19. *Id.* at 968–69.
20. 200 F.2d 85 (8th Cir. 1952).
21. *Id.* at 87–88.
22. *Id.* at 93.

The Supreme Court disagreed. In his landmark decision, Justice Clark emphasized that among those responding to the offers "were employees with the duties of artist, bakeshop foreman, chow loading foreman, clerical assistant, copywriter, electrician, stock clerk, mill office clerk, audit credit trainee, production trainee, and veterinarian." He quoted the observation of Judge Denman in *Sunbeam Gold Mine*.[23]

> In its broadest meaning the term "public" distinguishes the populace at large from groups of individual members of the public segregated because of some common interest or characteristic. Yet such a distinction is inadequate for practical purposes; manifestly, an offering of securities to all red-headed men, to all residents of Chicago or San Francisco, to all existing stockholders of the General Motors Corporation or the American Telephone & Telegraph Company, is no less "public," in every realistic sense of the word, than an unrestricted offering to the world at large.

The district court and the Court of Appeals in *Ralston Purina* had purported to apply the reasoning of *Sunbeam Gold Mines*. The district court stated that this reasoning was "more in harmony with the statute" than the numbers test urged by the SEC in its *Ralston Purina* brief.[24]

Justice Clark stated that the applicability of the private offering exemption should turn on "whether the particular class of persons affected needs the protection of the Act." The basic test, as he saw it, was whether the offerees were "able to fend for themselves." He rejected a numbers test, stating that "the statute would seem to apply to a 'public offering' whether to few or many." He recognized that numbers might have some relevance and could be used for enforcement purposes:

> It may well be that offerings to a substantial number of persons would rarely be exempt. Indeed nothing prevents

---

23. *SEC v. Sunbeam Gold Mines Co.*, 95 F.2d 699 (9th Cir. 1938).
24. 102 F. Supp. at 968.

the commission, in enforcing the statute, from using some kind of numerical test in deciding when to investigate particular exemption claims. But there is no warrant for superimposing a quantity limit on private offerings as a matter of statutory interpretation.

He agreed that some employee offerings may come within the exemption, for example, one made to executive personnel who because of their position have access to the same kind of information that the 1933 Act would make available in the form of a registration statement. But in this case, he concluded that the Ralston Purina employees were not shown to have access to the kind of information that registration would disclose.

Although one may sympathize with the Ralston Purina management, shaking their heads in frustration over the need to terminate a stock purchase program that had been advantageous to the employees, it is hard to quarrel with Justice Clark's analysis. A movement away from the number of offerees as the principal determinant of a private offering made eminent good sense, although one may question Justice Clark's suggestion that an offering to two persons may be public. Based on the reasoning in *Ralston Purina,* it became easier to render opinions on private placements where the number of purchasers was substantially in excess of 25.

The *Crowell-Collier* Case

The next major event in the development of the private offering exemption was the publication of the SEC's comments on its investigation of a purported private placement of convertible debentures by The Crowell-Collier Publishing Company.[25]

---

25. SEC Release No. 33-3825 (August 12, 1957). This transaction also led to disciplinary action under Sections 15(b) and 15A of the 1934 Act against the broker-dealers that participated in the sale of the securities. *See, e.g., Elliott & Company,* SEC Release No. 34-5688 (May 7, 1958); *Gilligan, Will & Co.,* SEC Release No. 34-5689 (May 7, 1958); *Dempsey & Company,* SEC Release No. 34-5690 (May 7, 1958).

During 1955 and 1956, Crowell-Collier sold $4 million principal amount of convertible debentures through Elliott & Company, a broker-dealer firm. Crowell-Collier was in need of funds and was being pressured by its banks. In June or early July of 1955, Elliott & Company proposed a plan that contemplated the sale of $3 million of debentures in a private placement and the purchase of another $1 million principal amount by the company's controlling stockholder. On July 6 and 7, Elliott secured commitments from 27 persons, including four broker-dealer firms. It testified in the SEC investigation that no prospects were called who did not purchase. Each of the 27 purchasers represented that it was purchasing the debentures for investment with no present intention of distributing the same. The SEC pointed out that the representation did not run to the underlying common stock as it clearly should have.

Prior to the closing on August 10, 1955, approximately one-third of the 27 purchasers had secured others to join them as participants in their commitments or had secured purchasers of portions of their commitments. The result was that the number of purchasers totaled 88. In February 1956, shortly after the expiration of six months from the closing date, holders of the debentures began to convert them and to sell the common stock on the American Stock Exchange. The remaining $1 million principal amount of debentures was not purchased by the controlling stockholder, but was sold by Elliott in May and June of 1956 to 22 purchasers, including three broker-dealer firms, that made the same investment representations as were made in the 1955 transaction. The SEC found that, as a result of these transactions, in the space of 12 months, Crowell-Collier effected a wide distribution of its debentures and common stock.

In the *Crowell-Collier* release, the SEC made a point that in general had been tacitly understood but that previously had not been articulated:

> It has been and is the Commission's position that an issuer or an underwriter may not separate parts of a series of related transactions comprising an issue of securities and thereby seek to establish that a particular part

is a private transaction if the whole involves a public offering of the securities.

In this case, the transaction as a whole involved a public offering. The principle can be applied conversely. If all resales are limited to persons who could have been participants in the original placement, then the original transaction is entitled to the Section 4(2) exemption.

The *Crowell-Collier* release presented the securities bar with the challenging assignment of advising their clients as to when privately placed securities could be resold—that is, when such a sale would not cause the holder of the securities to be deemed an "underwriter" whose presence in the original transaction would vitiate the Section 4(2) exemption. The release contained a statement, however, that the bar came to rely on for this purpose:

> An exemption under the provisions of Section [4(2)] is available only when the transactions do not involve a public offering and is not gained by the formality of obtaining "investment representations." Holding for the six months' capital gains period of the tax statutes, holding in an "investment account" rather than a "trading account," holding for a deferred sale, holding for a market rise, holding for sale if the market does not rise, or holding for a year, does not afford a statutory basis for an exemption and therefore does not provide an adequate basis on which counsel may give opinions or businessmen rely in selling securities without registration. Purchasing for the purpose of future sale is nonetheless purchasing for sale and, if the transactions involve any public offering even at some future date, the registration provisions apply unless at the time of the public offering an exemption is available.

After the *Crowell-Collier* release, the one-year rule of thumb, which had been suggested by the SEC's general counsel, became a two-year rule of thumb that was generally applied by the securities bar in advising with respect to resales of securities initially issued in a private placement.[26]

Pre–Rule 146 Developments

During the 1960s, issuers continued to make private placements, and lawyers continued to grapple with resale issues, with limited interpretive guidance from the SEC. Lawyers worried about such matters as holding periods for privately placed securities and sales motivated by unforeseen changes in circumstances. In 1962, "an increasing tendency to rely upon the exemption for offerings of speculative issues to unrelated and uninformed persons" prompted the SEC to issue a release pointing out the limitations on the availability of the private offering exemption.[27] This release contained little more than a rehash of statements previously made by the SEC, but it did flesh out the change in circumstances doctrine that was then an important consideration in determining when resales could be made:

> An unforeseen change of circumstances since the date of purchase may be a basis for an opinion that the proposed resale is not inconsistent with an investment representation. However, such claim must be considered in the light of all of the relevant facts. Thus, an advance or decline in market price or a change in the issuer's operating results are normal investment risks and do not usually provide an acceptable basis for such claim of changed circumstances. Possible inability of the purchaser

---

26. This was based in part on the following statement by Judge Sugarman:

> The passage of two years before the commencement of distribution of any of these shares is an insuperable obstacle to my finding that Sherwood took these shares with a view to distribution thereof, in the absence of any relevant evidence from which I could conclude he did not take the shares for investment. No such evidence was offered at the trial.

United States v. Sherwood, 175 F. Supp. 480, 483 (S.D.N.Y. 1959).
27. SEC Release No. 33-4552 (November 6, 1962).

PRIVATE PLACEMENTS

to pay off loans incurred in connection with the purchase of the stock would ordinarily not be deemed an unforeseeable change of circumstances. Further, in the case of securities pledged for a loan, the pledgee should not assume that he is free to distribute without registration. The Congressional mandate of disclosure to investors is not to be avoided to permit a public distribution of unregistered securities because the pledgee took the securities from a purchaser, subsequently delinquent.

In late 1970, the SEC issued a pronouncement to the effect that it would regard the presence or absence of an appropriate legend and stop-transfer instructions as a factor in considering whether the circumstances surrounding an offering were consistent with the Section 4(2) exemption.[28] By this time, the staff of the SEC was taking the position that no-action letters would not be issued unless the securities had been held for three years or there was a compelling change of circumstances.

In 1972, the SEC adopted Rule 144,[29] which brought objective standards to the question of resales of privately placed securities. Under Rule 144, a holder of "restricted securities" could begin to sell in "brokers' transactions" after two years, but only in limited amounts and only upon giving public notice of a proposed resale. It was no longer necessary to identify a "change in circumstances."[30]

In the early 1970s, a number of judicial decisions were handed down that appeared to limit the availability of the Section 4(2) exemption. In *Lively v. Hirschfeld*,[31] the Court of Appeals

---

28. SEC Release No. 33-5121 (December 30, 1970).

29. SEC Release No. 33-5223 (January 11, 1972).

30. The rule stated explicitly that it was "not the exclusive means" for reselling restricted securities. Over the years, Rule 144 has been amended in important respects. The volume limitation has been increased; the two-year "holding period" has become a one-year period and is now measured from the time the securities were sold by the issuer or its affiliate (rather than from the time of each acquisition by a holder); and all restrictions lapse under certain conditions after the expiration of a two-year holding period. *See* the discussion in Chapter 1.

31. 440 F.2d 631 (10th Cir. 1971).

for the Tenth Circuit read *Ralston Purina* as including within a private offering "only persons of exceptional business experience" who are in "a position where they have regular access to all the information and records which would show the potential for the corporation."

In *Hill York Corp. v. American International Franchises, Inc.*,[32] the court said that the fact that the purchasers were sophisticated businessmen was not sufficient to establish the exemption and cited with approval an article indicating that the exemption was limited to those instances "where the number of offerees is so limited that they may constitute a class of persons having such a privileged relationship with the issuer that their present knowledge and facilities for acquiring information about the issuer would make registration unnecessary for their protection."[33]

In *SEC v. Continental Tobacco Co.*,[34] the court required that the defendant demonstrate "that each offeree had a relationship with Continental giving access to the kind of information that registration would have disclosed." The judicial insistence on a preexisting relationship between the offerees and the issuer raised substantial questions as to the availability of the exemption, at least where individual investors were concerned.

These cases involved offers and sales of equity securities to individual investors. Institutional private placements continued with little concern for these decisions, but reliance on Section 4(2) for tax-shelter programs and similar transactions was viewed by some as extremely risky.

Rule 146

Pressure from the financial community, which believed that the judicial trend had impaired the ability of issuers to safely

---

32. 448 F.2d 680 (5th Cir. 1971).

33. Andrew D. Orrick, *Non-Public Offerings of Corporate Securities: Limitations on the Exemption Under the Federal Securities Act,* 21 U. Pitt. L. Rev. 1, 8 (1959).

34. 463 F.2d 137 (5th Cir. 1972).

effect private placements, led the SEC in 1974 to adopt Rule 146, which was designed to provide a safe harbor for reliance on the private placement exemption.[35]

Rule 146 was designed to create greater certainty in the application of the Section 4(2) exemption. While stressing that a failure to satisfy all of the conditions of the rule did not raise a presumption that the Section 4(2) exemption was not available and that attempted compliance with the rule did not operate as an election, in that the issuer also could claim the availability of Section 4(2) outside of the rule, the SEC provided in Rule 146 that the private placement exemption would be available if specified conditions were met relating to the manner of offering, the nature of the offerees and purchasers, access to or furnishing of information, limitations on the number of purchasers, and procedures designed to limit subsequent resales.

With respect to the manner of offering, the rule precluded general advertising or general solicitation, including promotional seminars or meetings. The rule, however, did not preclude meetings with qualified offerees to discuss the terms of and to impart information about the offering.

In order to ensure that the offerees could fend for themselves (the basic test established by *Ralston Purina*), the rule provided that prior to making any offer the issuer and those acting on its behalf must reasonably believe either that the offeree "has such knowledge and experience in financial and business matters that he is capable of evaluating the merits and risks of the prospective investment" or that he is "a person who is able to bear the economic risk of the investment." In the jargon of Wall Street, the offeree was required to be either "smart" or "rich." It was not necessary to be both.

The rule imposed somewhat stricter requirements with respect to purchasers as distinguished from offerees. It provided that, prior to making any sale, there must be reasonable belief either that the offeree had the requisite knowledge and experience or that he and his offeree representative together had the requisite knowledge and experience and that, in the latter case, he could

---

35. SEC Release No. 33-5487 (April 23, 1974).

bear the economic risk of the investment. Thus, the SEC imposed the requirement that a purchaser be able to bear the economic risk of the investment where it was necessary for him to be guided by the knowledge and experience of an offeree representative. The number of purchasers was limited to 35, but there could be excluded from this number any person who purchased or agreed to purchase for cash, in a single payment or installments, securities in the aggregate amount of $150,000 or more.

It was required that prior to the sale each offeree have access to the same kind of information that would be provided in a 1933 Act registration statement or that he be furnished with that information. A note to the rule made clear that access could exist only by reason of the offeree's "position with respect to the issuer" and that "position" means "an employment or family relationship or economic bargaining power that enables the offeree to obtain information from the issuer in order to evaluate the merits and risks of the prospective investment." A reporting company could satisfy this requirement by delivering to a prospective purchaser its most recent 1934 Act filings. Most issuers that relied on Rule 146 opted for the procedure of delivering 1934 Act materials to prospective purchasers rather than relying on the more subjective access test.

The rule required that the issuer make available to each offeree or its offeree representative the opportunity to ask questions of and receive answers from the issuer or any person acting on its behalf concerning the terms and conditions of the offering and to obtain additional information. A statement to this effect customarily was included in the private placement memorandum. The procedures specified to ensure that purchasers were not statutory underwriters included reasonable inquiry to determine whether the purchaser was acquiring the securities for his own account or on behalf of other persons; legends referring to restrictions on transferability; stop transfer instructions; and a written agreement that the securities would not be sold without registration or an exemption therefrom.

As originally adopted, Rule 146 had no reporting requirement. But in 1977, the SEC, referring to abuses of Rule 146, particularly in connection with offerings of oil and gas partnership interests, proposed that reports be required in connection with Rule 146 offerings.[36] The amendment was adopted and a filing on Form 146 was required at the time of the first sale of securities in any offering effected in reliance on the rule.[37]

Two years after the effectiveness of Rule 146, the SEC made a public request for empirical information regarding its operation.[38] The SEC stated that it was "aware of criticism that the Rule is hindering the investment of venture capital, and that as an experiment the Rule is a failure and should be rescinded." The SEC went on to state that, on the other hand, Rule 146 had been criticized by some "as facilitating the fraudulent offering of certain types of securities."

In response to the SEC's request for information, the Committee on Securities Regulation of The Association of the Bar of the City of New York (of which the senior author was then a member) stated, "It is the consensus of this Committee that Rule 146 is serving its purpose well." The committee stated that it was unaware that the rule was hindering the investment of venture capital and failed to see how Rule 146 could facilitate "the fraudulent offering of certain types of securities." The committee's letter went on to describe how different lawyers viewed Rule 146 in the context of private placements of corporate debt securities with institutional investors:

> It is true that certain lawyers experienced in this area believe that Rule 146 provides no substantial benefits and prefer to rely on the traditional standards for private placements developed prior to the adoption of the Rule. See *Section 4(2) and Statutory Law,* 31 Business Lawyer 483 (November, 1975). Other experienced lawyers, including a number of members of this Committee, believe that Rule 146 helps to provide certainty, even in the case of an institutional private placement. Their practice is to render opinions in reliance on Section 4(2), without reference to Rule 146, but to attempt to structure

---

36. SEC Release No. 33-5822 (April 18, 1977).
37. SEC Release No. 33-5912 (March 3, 1978).
38. SEC Release No. 33-5779 (December 6, 1976).

transactions so that they comply with the Rule in all material respects.

The letter also described certain practices that had developed in the investment banking community following the adoption of Rule 146:

> Certain investment banking firms that act as private placement agent follow procedures designed to comply with Rule 146. These firms maintain a list of qualified offerees consisting of institutional investors who, in their opinion, have such knowledge and experience in financial and business matters as to be capable of evaluating the merits and risks of an investment in corporate debt securities and, in addition, are able to bear the economic risk of the investment. Under Rule 146, there is no limit on the number of offerees, provided that each meets this standard. Institutions may be added to or deleted from the list, but, of course, any additional institutions must have the necessary qualifications. To avoid the necessity for limiting the number of actual purchasers, the securities are offered to qualified offerees in minimum amounts of $150,000 for any single purchaser. If the issuer is a reporting company, as is normally the case, before an institution purchases any of the securities, it is furnished with a copy of the issuer's most recent Annual Report on Form 10-K and each definitive proxy statement, and each report on Form 8-K or Form 10-Q, required to be filed by the issuer since the filing of the Form 10-K. It is also furnished with a description of any material changes in the issuer's affairs which are not disclosed in the above documents. Other information and statements required by Rule 146, such as use of proceeds and a description of the securities, are included in a private placement memorandum. Each offeree is advised by the placement agent that it is afforded the opportunity, prior to purchasing any of the securities, to ask questions of, and receive answers from, the issuer concerning the terms and conditions of the offering and to obtain any additional

information, to the extent the issuer possesses the same or can acquire it without unreasonable expense, necessary to verify the accuracy of the information in these documents. Appropriate restrictions are placed on the transfer of the securities.

In addition to providing substantial comfort in traditional types of institutional private placements, Rule 146 procedures of the type described above have facilitated certain types of private placements that were not usually made prior to the adoption of the Rule. For example, since the adoption of Rule 146, there have been an increasing number of continuous offerings of corporate notes which do not meet the requirements of Section 3(a)(3) made to pre-cleared groups of institutional investors in minimum denominations of $150,000 and in conformity with the other requirements of Rule 146.

Regulation D

In view of mixed comments regarding Rule 146, the SEC proposed in 1981 that the rule be superseded by a new Regulation D.[39] Seven months later, Regulation D was adopted in substantially the form originally proposed.[40] Since its adoption, Regulation D has been amended on several occasions to broaden its scope and improve its operation,[41] and it continues to operate as an important safe harbor.

Rule 501 of Regulation D defines key terms such as "accredited investor." Rule 502 sets forth general conditions to the exemption, such as integration of other transactions, requirements for the furnishing of specified information, a prohibition of "any form of general solicitation or general advertising" and

---

39. SEC Release No. 33-6339 (August 7, 1981).
40. SEC Release No. 33-6389 (March 8, 1982).
41. SEC Release No. 33-6437 (November 19, 1982); SEC Release No. 33-6663 (October 2, 1986); SEC Release No. 33-6758 (March 3, 1988); SEC Release No. 33-6825 (March 14, 1989).

a requirement that the issuer "exercise reasonable care to assure that the purchasers of the securities are not underwriters" (together with a specification of actions that will establish such reasonable care). Rule 503 provides for a public notice of sales in reliance on the exemption.

For the purposes of this chapter, the most important exemption under Regulation D is that provided by Rule 506. Significantly, Rule 506 eliminates the offeree qualification requirement of Rule 146 in favor of a general permission to offer and sell to a potentially indefinite number of persons who come within the definition of "accredited investor."

For the sake of completeness, we will note that Rules 504 and 505 provide exemptions from registration under Section 3(b) of the 1933 Act rather than Section 4(2).[42] Rules 504 and 505 are useful to small businesses and relate to offerings of securities not exceeding $1 million and $5 million, respectively.

- *General Solicitation or Advertising*

If an offering is to be made in reliance on Regulation D, then Rule 502(c) requires that "neither the issuer nor any person acting on its behalf" may offer or sell the securities by any form of "general solicitation or general advertising."[43] The rule defines the prohibited activities as including, but not limited to, advertisements, articles, notices or other communication published in newspapers, magazines or similar media or broadcast over television or radio. It also includes any seminar or meeting whose attendees have been invited by any general solicitation or general advertising.

- - *Express Exclusions.* Rule 502(c) expressly excludes certain communications from the definition of general solicitation.

First, the rule expressly excludes a notice under Rule 135c. As discussed in Chapter 1, Rule 135c permits an issuer that files

---

42. Section 3(b) permits the SEC to adopt regulations exempting issues in the amount of $5 million or less.

43. Private placements are seldom advertised as such, and references in this chapter to "general solicitation" should be understood as including "general advertising."

reports under the 1934 Act (as well as certain foreign issuers) to publish a notice of an unregistered offering of securities. The purpose of the rule is to permit issuers that have public reporting responsibilities to give notice of an unregistered offering that may be material to its securityholders. The rule provides that the notice may not be used "for the purpose of conditioning the market in the United States for any of the securities offered." Given this condition, it may be advisable for the issuer to publish the notice only after the completion of the solicitation phase of the offering or, in the alternative, to take steps to exclude from the offering any potential investors who initiate communication with the issuer or its placement agent after the publication of the notice. On the other hand, it is neither possible nor desirable to lay down rigid rules in this regard. If the private placement is indeed material to public securityholders, then an announcement should not be delayed. In fact, Regulation FD may require a press release to be issued prior to the commencement of the solicitation phase. The type of security being offered is also relevant. Potential purchasers of debt securities are less likely to be "conditioned" by a press release directed to public shareholders.

Second, the rule expressly excludes communicative activity covered by Rule 135e. As discussed in Chapter 1, such activity includes providing any journalist with access to press conferences held outside of the United States, meetings with issuer representatives conducted outside of the United States and written press-related materials released outside the United States.

• • *Internet Offerings and Notices.* Placing offering materials on the Internet relating to a Regulation D offering may result in a general solicitation. The SEC took this position in October 1995 in response to its own hypothetical involving an issuer's posting of Rule 506 offering materials on the issuer's website, access to which was conditioned on a user's providing unspecified information to the issuer.[44]

Soon after, the SEC staff issued interpretive guidance[45] to a broker-dealer and its affiliate that planned to invite previously

---

44. SEC Release No. 33-7233 (October 6, 1995) (Example 20).
45. SEC No-action Letter, *IPONET* (July 26, 1996).

unknown prospective investors to complete a questionnaire posted on the affiliate's IPONET website "as a means of building a customer base and data base of accredited and sophisticated investors" for the broker-dealer. A password-restricted web page permitting access to private offerings would become available to a prospective investor only after the affiliated broker-dealer determined on the basis of the questionnaire that the investor was "accredited" or "sophisticated" within the meaning of Regulation D. Also, a prospective investor could buy securities only in offerings that were posted on the restricted web page after the investor had been qualified as an accredited or sophisticated investor and had been added to the broker-dealer's customer and data base.

In the SEC's interpretive statement of April 2000 on the "Use of Electronic Media," the SEC explained the IPONET advice as having been based on the "important and well-known principle [that] . . . a general solicitation is not present when there is a pre-existing, substantive relationship between an issuer, or its broker-dealer, and the offerees." It referred in this connection to the fact that the SEC staff's prior interpretations in this area had been limited to procedures established by broker-dealers regarding their customers "because traditional broker-dealer relationships require that a broker-dealer deal fairly with, and make suitable recommendations to, customers, and, thus, implies that a substantive relationship exists between the broker-dealer and its customers."

The April 2000 release also stressed, however, that the presence or absence of a general solicitation is always dependent on the facts and circumstances of each particular case and that the SEC was not suggesting that the a prior relationship was the only way to avoid a general solicitation. Moreover, there could be facts and circumstances in which a third party, other than a broker-dealer, could establish a preexisting substantive relationship sufficient to avoid a general solicitation.[46]

---

46. The April 2000 release also expressed reservations about persons other than broker-dealers making the determination about an investor's status as an accredited or sophisticated investor, and it criticized some website

Even with the April 2000 release's reference to broker-dealers and prior relationships, the IPONET letter would still appear to permit a broker-dealer to use a website to invite previously unknown investors to complete a questionnaire and then, after determination of their accredited investor status, to rely on Regulation D to offer them subsequently offered securities, all without triggering a general solicitation.

From this, it would be but a short step to permitting a broker-dealer to make information about pending Regulation D offers available, by means of e-mail or a password-protected website, to non-customers who it knows to be eligible investors.[47] Whether this is permissible might depend on *how* the broker-dealer "knows" the non-customers to be eligible investors. In the case of institutions, for example, the broker-dealer might persuasively argue that it has at least a potential relationship with every institution in the country that may be willing at some point to buy or sell securities, and their names and qualifications as accredited investors are readily available from public sources.[48]

Such an argument is more difficult to make in the case of individuals, but its strength would depend on who the investors

---

operators for permitting investors to self-certify their status. In this connection, it limited to their facts previous no-action letters (*Lamp Technologies* (May 29, 1997 and May 29, 1998)) that permitted hedge funds to conduct online private offerings on the basis of procedures similar to the IPONET procedures. Moreover, the 2000 release and subsequent no-action letters (*see* David B. Harms, *The 2000 Internet Release One Year Later*, ABA Section of Business Law, 6 The Securities Reporter 3, 9 (Summer 2001)) suggest that screening investors for eligibility to participate in private offerings might be "broker-dealer" activity requiring an unregistered person to register with the SEC as a broker-dealer. It may therefore be academic whether non-broker-dealers can troll for investors without triggering a general solicitation.

47. *Id.*

48. Apart from suitability concerns, the foregoing distinction between institutional and individual accredited investors is undoubtedly the reason why many offers are made available only to "institutional accredited investors" rather than to accredited investors as such.

were and how they had been identified. Also, the IPONET request letter cited a 1987 SEC no-action letter[49] that permitted the use of a generic hard copy questionnaire to qualify investors where "sufficient time would elapse between the respondents' initial completion of the Questionnaire and the inception of any particular offering, so that the circulation of the Questionnaire is not deemed to be a solicitation with regard to such particular offering." The 1987 letter and similar pre-Internet letters are discussed below under "Regulation D Placements with Individual Investors," and they clearly suggest the value of building in some delay or waiting period between qualification and the opportunity to participate in a particular offering.[50]

A waiting period would not be practical in the case of continuous offerings, but it has been suggested that "efforts to solicit investor to purchase particular securities are arguably less intense [in a continuous offering] than in a single, market offering," and that a waiting period for that reason would appear to be less important in breaking the link between the solicitation and the offering.[51] In the case of institutions, of course, a waiting period should be entirely unnecessary.

And it should go without saying that an issuer that provides updated information about outstanding securities for the benefit of their holders—without providing offering material for the benefit of prospective new purchasers—should not be deemed to be involved in a general solicitation even if the website is not password-protected. In such a case, even if the updated

---

49. SEC No-action Letter, *H.B. Shaine & Co., Inc.* (May 1, 1987).

50. In its 2003 report on "Implications of the Growth of Hedge Funds," the SEC staff stated at page 16 that the "relationship must be established at a time prior to the commencement of the private offering or, in the case of a hedge fund, 30 days before the investor can make an investment." The 30-day period for hedge funds derives from the *Lamp Technologies* no-action letters (May 29, 1997 and May 29, 1998), which approved the use of a website to identify eligible hedge fund investors. The SEC staff report on hedge funds is available on the SEC website at www.sec.gov/news/studies/hedgefunds0903.pdf.

51. Harms, *supra* note 46, at 10.

information motivates an investor to seek out a broker-dealer who can effect a purchase of a new or outstanding security, the primary purpose of the website is to inform existing investors rather than to attract new ones. Also, the broker-dealer will have the responsibility of determining the investor's eligibility to purchase. Like many other questions involving the Internet and private placements, however, this one remains in doubt.[52]

• • *Newsletters, Media and Interviews.* Investment newsletters often publish detailed and highly accurate information on Regulation D offerings while they are in the solicitation stage. The information may even include the name of the placement agent, one or more of the lead investors and the range of "price talk." The information is usually obtained from persons who have been solicited to participate in the offering or who are actually purchasing in the offering. Rule 502(c), as noted above, prohibits general solicitation or general advertising only by the issuer or any person acting on its behalf. Assuming that the publisher of the information relating to the Regulation D offering is not acting in concert with—and has not obtained the information from—the issuer or any person acting on its behalf, there should be no problem under Rule 502(c).

Occasionally, an investment newsletter will publish an interview of an investment banker working on a private placement that is in the active marketing stage. A banker should never consent to an interview without obtaining clearance from counsel working on the transaction, in addition to the firm's own internal counsel. Even where the published interview contains details of the transaction, the interview may not be fatal if the overall effect—the subscriber base of the newsletter, the degree of innovation involved in the transaction, the interest of other issuers in executing a similar transaction and the content of the banker's remarks—is not to condition the market for the securities being offered but rather to encourage other issuers to consider executing a similar transaction.

---

52. There may be less doubt where the securities are eligible to be purchased only by QIBs. *See* text below at note 78.

The same problem arises, of course, where the banker is interviewed by the electronic financial media. In these cases, it is difficult to argue that the interview will have no marketing effect. Counsel has sometimes permitted a transaction to proceed under these circumstances where the placement agent agreed to close the "book" as of a date before the interview is shown. Alternatively, a placement agent may offer to obtain a certificate from each purchaser to the effect that it did not see the offending interview. Few investors will want to sign such a certificate if it means that they cannot review information that may turn out to be material. It may be satisfactory to require such certificates only from persons who have agreed to buy in the private placement, with the understanding that they may drop out after looking at the interview.

• • *Number of Offerees.* As discussed below, Rule 506 imposes no explicit limitation on the number of offerees or purchasers if they are limited to accredited investors. Some securities lawyers have occasionally expressed concern that offers to "too many" accredited investors might result in a general solicitation. In a footnote to the release proposing Regulation D, the SEC warned that, although offers could theoretically be made to an unlimited number of persons, offers to a large number of potential purchasers might involve a violation of the prohibitions against general solicitation and general advertising.[53]

This footnote does not appear in the release adopting Regulation D, but the warning was reiterated in the SEC staff's 2003 report *Implications of the Growth of Hedge Funds.*[54] It would be unwise to assume that the number of potential investors is irrelevant to the concept of general solicitation. Some securities firms follow the policy of placing a limit on the number of offerees in all Regulation D transactions, while others follow this policy only where individual investors are to be solicited.

---

53. SEC Release No. 33-6339 (August 7, 1981).
54. SEC Staff Report, *Implications of the Growth of Hedge Funds* 15 n.44 (September 2003). The report is available on the SEC website at www.sec.gov/news/studies/hedgefunds0903.pdf.

On the other hand, as discussed above under "Internet Offerings and Notices," it is also relevant to ask *how* an offer came to be made to a very large number of accredited investors. There should be no general solicitation, for example, if a broker-dealer makes an offer to a very large number (e.g., 25,000 or more) of its existing customers who it knows to be accredited investors and who it pre-selects on the basis of whether or not the offered security would be suitable for their circumstances.

• • *Future of the General Solicitation Prohibition.* Given the large amount of information that is readily available about private transactions, whether from Internet websites, investment newsletters, communications exempt under Rules 135c or 135e and the large number of persons who may be solicited or even participate in a Regulation D offering, it may be that the general solicitation prohibition is simply proving unworkable.

Indeed, the SEC requested comment in June 1995 and again in July 1996 on whether it should modify the general solicitation prohibition.[55] It noted that an ability on the part of issuers to broadly disseminate offering materials to locate potential investors might not compromise investor protection interests in view of the fact that all purchases would continue to meet the requirements of Regulation D. The SEC also requested comment on whether, in view of the language of Section 4(2), it had the statutory authority to eliminate this prohibition. This was, of course, prior to the Improvement Act's grant to the SEC of broad exemptive authority under the 1933 Act.

An ABA subcommittee in December 1996, responding to the SEC's request for comments, called the general solicitation prohibition a "vestige of private placement lore" and urged the SEC to eliminate or narrow the prohibition.[56]

In its 2003 report on hedge funds, the SEC staff stated that it would be reluctant to ease or eliminate the prohibition on

---

55. SEC Release No. 33-7185 (June 27, 1995); SEC Release No. 33-7314 (July 25, 1996).

56. The letter is on the SEC's website at www.sec.gov/rules/concept/s71996/liftin2.htm.

general solicitation in transactions that are offered to accredited investors. On the other hand, it concluded that permitting a general solicitation in transactions offered to investors that met "a higher standard" could facilitate capital formation without raising significant investor protection concerns. One example it cited of such a higher standard was that of "qualified purchasers" for purposes of Section 3(c)(7) of the 1940 Act.[57]

- *"Accredited Investors"*

On its face, Rule 506(b)(2)(i) limits the number of purchasers to 35. On the other hand, Rule 501(c)(1)(iv) excludes for purposes of "calculating the number of purchasers under . . . Rule 506(b)" any purchaser who is an accredited investor. This somewhat inelegant drafting technique is the basis for Rule 506's permitting offers and sales to a potentially indefinite number of persons so long as they are "accredited investors."

The term "accredited investor" is defined to include virtually every type of institution that participates in the private placement market, as well as individual investors with substantial income or a large net worth. Thus, the term includes:

- Any bank as defined in Section 3(a)(2) of the 1933 Act or any savings and loan association or other institution as defined in Section 3(a)(5)(A) of the 1933 Act, whether acting in its individual or fiduciary capacity.

- Any broker or dealer registered under the 1934 Act.

- Any insurance company as defined in Section 2(13) of the 1933 Act.

- Any investment company registered under the 1940 Act or a business development company as defined in Section 2(a)(48) of the 1940 Act.

- Any small business investment company licensed by the U.S. Small Business Administration.

---

57. *Implications of the Growth of Hedge Funds, supra* note 54, at 100–01.

- Any plan established and maintained by a state, its political subdivisions, or any agency or instrumentality thereof, for the benefit of its employees, if such plan has total assets in excess of $5 million.

- Any employee benefit plan within the meaning of the Employee Retirement Income Security Act of 1974 if the investment decision is made by a plan fiduciary that is either a bank, savings and loan association, insurance company, or registered advisor, or if the plan has total assets in excess of $5 million or, if a self-directed plan, with investment decisions made solely by persons that are accredited investors.

- Any private business development company as defined in the Investment Advisers Act of 1940.

- Any corporation, partnership, business trust or Section 501(c)(3) organization, not formed for the specific purpose of acquiring the securities offered,[58] with total assets in excess of $5 million. A 1996 no-action letter permits a limited liability company to qualify as an accredited investor under this heading.[59] States and their incorporated political subdivisions should qualify as "corporations" under this heading, but the status of other governmental entities may be more ambiguous.

---

58. This limitation does not mean that an entity cannot be formed for the purpose of purchasing private placements in general, only that it cannot be formed for the purpose of buying a particular private placement and no other. When it wants to, the SEC knows how to disqualify an entity formed for the general purpose of buying unregistered securities (e.g., Rule 902(k)(1)(viii)(B) of Regulation S). Obviously, every entity formed for the purpose of buying private placements has to make its first such purchase, and the definition does not stand in the way of its doing so. On the other hand, if the facts may suggest a lack of any real intention to make future purchases of private placements, the entity's status as an accredited investor may be doubtful.

59. SEC No-action Letter, *Wolfe, Block, Schorr and Solis-Cohen* (December 11, 1996).

- Any director, executive officer, or general partner of the issuer of the securities being offered or of a general partner of the issuer.
- Any natural person whose individual net worth, or joint net worth with that person's spouse, at the time of purchase exceeds $1 million.
- Any natural person who has an individual income in excess of $200,000 in each of the two most recent years or joint income with that person's spouse in excess of $300,000 in each of those years and has a reasonable expectation of reaching the same income level in the current year.
- Any trust with total assets in excess of $5 million, not formed for the specific purpose of acquiring the securities offered, whose purchase is directed by a person who has such knowledge and experience in financial and business matters that he is capable of evaluating the merits and risks of the prospective investment.
- Any entity in which all of the equity owners are accredited investors.[60]

This litany of accredited investors covers a wide range of prospective purchasers. Certainly, in the case of an institutional placement, there is no reason to dip into the 35-purchaser pool, for there are few institutional investors that would not qualify as an accredited investor. In this respect, Regulation D introduced into the 1933 Act a *de facto* institutional investor exemption similar to that found in state blue sky laws.

For suitability and state securities law reasons, private placements under Regulation D are often limited to "institutional accredited investors," that is, those categories specified above except for natural persons. In the case of sales of limited

---

60. It seems obvious, but it bears mentioning, that the interpositioning of one or more entities between a purchaser and its ultimate parent company does not disqualify the purchaser as an accredited investor so long as the ultimate parent company is an accredited investor.

partnership interests or similar investments that are directed to individuals, Regulation D's net worth or income levels to qualify natural persons as accredited investors are hardly restrictive (particularly since these levels have not been changed since the regulation's adoption in 1988).

Accredited investors need not satisfy any standard of sophistication on the theory that such investors either are presumably sophisticated or have the means to fend for themselves. On the other hand, Rule 506(b)(2)(ii) requires that any non-accredited investor who participates in the transaction must, either alone or with a purchaser representative, have such knowledge and experience in financial and business matters to be capable of evaluating the merits and risks of the prospective investment.

- *Informational Access and Disclosure*

Rule 502(b) does not require that any specific information be furnished if sales are made only to accredited investors. Presumably, such investors have either the sophistication or the means to fend for themselves and to demand and receive such information as they consider necessary. If a sale is made to a person who is not an accredited investor, however, that person must be furnished with the information specified in Rule 502(b) not later than "a reasonable time prior to sale." The information required to be furnished depends on whether the issuer is subject to the reporting requirements of the 1934 Act and on the size of the offering.

In addition, the non-accredited investor must be afforded the opportunity to ask questions of and receive answers from the issuer regarding the offering and to obtain any additional information that the issuer possesses or can acquire without unreasonable effort or expense that is necessary to verify the accuracy of the information furnished under Rule 502(b).

- *Anti-Underwriter Precautions*

Rule 502(d) requires the issuer to exercise reasonable care to ensure that the purchasers are not underwriters. It also sets up a "safe harbor" by specifying means by which such reasonable care may be demonstrated. These are *"reasonable inquiry* to determine if the purchaser is acquiring the securities for himself or for other persons," *"written disclosure . . . that the securities have not been registered"* and therefore cannot be resold without registration or an exemption, and placement of a *restrictive legend* on the certificate or other document that evidences the securities (emphasis added).

Rule 502(d) states expressly that "[o]ther actions by the issuer may satisfy" the requirement to exercise reasonable care that purchasers are not underwriters.

• • *Restrictive Legends.* Participants in Regulation D transactions often find it necessary to devise "other actions" to substitute for the "safe harbor" ingredient of a restrictive legend. In the case of offerings of investment-grade fixed-income securities to accredited institutional investors, many securities lawyers believe that an issuer is taking "reasonable care" by obtaining representations from the original purchasers and by making written disclosure that the securities cannot be transferred without an exemption. These lawyers undoubtedly take considerable comfort from the fact that holders of these securities, as a practical matter, generally seek to resell them through broker-dealers who almost invariably inquire as to the origin of the securities and take steps to ensure the availability of an exemption when they effect a resale.[61]

Also, given the increasing preference of issuers and investors alike for book-entry securities, it is obviously ineffective to place a restrictive legend on a global security that disappears into the vault of The Depository Trust Company (DTC) or a similar institution. Indeed, the SEC in 1993 approved changes to DTC's rules to permit it to make Rule 144A-eligible securities eligible for DTC's book-entry settlement services, on the basis of representations from issuers and transfer agents, if the securities were investment-grade debt or were included in an SRO transfer system such as PORTAL.[62] The SEC approved the rule changes on the basis of findings that, among other things, the proposal reduced

---

61. *See* the discussion later in this chapter of "Secondary Private Placements."

62. SEC Release No. 34-33672 (February 23, 1994).

(presumably to its satisfaction) the potential for unlawful transfers of restricted securities. This finding was in turn based on the representations and undertakings that would be required of issuers and transfer agents when they applied for deposit and book-entry eligibility for a new privately placed security. It is difficult to conclude that the SEC was not also finding that these procedures were sufficient to constitute reasonable care on the part of the issuer, when it made the initial sale to a placement agent, that the purchasers were not underwriters.

It is probably true that there is no book-entry transaction—even one involving equity securities—where procedures cannot be devised that would constitute "reasonable care" on the part of the participants that the purchasers are not underwriters. Whether these procedures would be acceptable to all participants is, of course, another question.

- *Resales*

However they are communicated to the holder, resale restrictions commonly permit resales in reliance on an exemption under the 1933 Act. The restrictions vary as to the formal requirements that a holder may have to fulfill (e.g., furnishing a legal opinion) before selling in reliance on an exemption.

Rule 506 does not provide an exemption for resales of securities sold in a Rule 506 offering. Rule 506 applies only to transactions by issuers. Of course, an investor may be able to sell in a "secondary private placement" as discussed below. As noted in Chapter 1, Rule 144 is available for the resale of restricted securities that have been outstanding for at least one year, but the volume limitations of that rule make it of little use for securities that do not have a public trading market. On the other hand, Rule 144(k) permits a holder of restricted securities who is not and has not been an affiliate of the issuer during the three months preceding the sale to sell free of any Rule 144 limitations if two years have elapsed from the time that the securities were acquired from the issuer or an affiliate of the issuer.

- *Notice, Disqualification, Blue Sky Requirements*

Rule 503 requires an issuer selling securities in reliance on Regulation D to file with the SEC five copies of a notice on

Form D no later than 15 days after the first sale of the securities. In the case of institutional private placements, the Form D filing requirement was often cited as a reason to prefer reliance on Section 4(2) rather than Rule 506. As a result of the 1989 amendments to Regulation D, however, the filing of a Form D is no longer a condition to the establishment of an exemption under Regulation D.

This does not mean that the filing requirement is optional. Rule 507 contemplates that the SEC may seek a temporary or permanent injunction against an issuer's violations of the filing requirement. An injunction is a drastic remedy, of course, that a court would be likely to grant for Rule 503 violations only in unusual circumstances. If an injunction were granted, Rule 507 would disqualify the issuer from future reliance on Regulation D. The SEC could waive such a disqualification on a showing of good cause.

The North American Securities Administrators Association, Inc., an association of securities administrators from each of the 50 states, the District of Columbia, Puerto Rico, and several of the Canadian provinces, has adopted as an official policy guideline for administering the blue sky laws the "Uniform Limited Offering Exemption." Regulation D has served as the core of the exemption, and Form D was designed to be a uniform notification form that could be filed with the states as well as with the SEC.

On the other hand, the Improvement Act exempted from state blue sky registration and qualification requirements (but not from state notice filing or fee requirements) any security exempted from Section 5 of the 1933 Act pursuant to SEC "rules or regulations issued under section 4(2)."[63] The result is that state blue sky laws cannot require the registration or qualification of a private placement that is effected in reliance on Rule 506 of Regulation D.[64]

---

63. Section 18(b)(4)(D) of the 1933 Act.

64. As noted above, Rules 504 and 505 are Section 3(b) exemptions rather than Section 4(2) exemptions.

The Improvement Act also exempted securities offered and sold in transactions that are exempt from Section 5 pursuant to Section 4(1) or 4(3), but only if the issuer files reports under the 1934 Act.[65] Among other things, this exemption covers Rule 144A transactions. It should cover secondary private placements, which are sometimes referred to as "Section 4(1-1/2) transactions" but are more properly analyzed as being effected in reliance on Section 4(1) or Section 4(3), depending on whether the seller is a securities dealer.

Traditional "Section 4(2)" transactions do not appear entitled to the Improvement Act's benefits, unless the securities are equal in seniority or senior to the issuer's NYSE- or Amex-listed[66] or NASDAQ NMS securities, but even if this is not the case the participating dealers and institutions will in most states be entitled to rely on the regular institutional exemption.

- *Integration*

Rule 502(a) states that all sales that are part of the "same" Regulation D offering must meet all of the terms and conditions of Regulation D. It also sets forth a safe harbor, which is that offers and sales made more than six months before the start of a Regulation D offering or more than six months after completion of a Regulation D offering will not be considered part of the Regulation D offering, so long as during those six-month periods there were no offers or sales of securities by or for the issuer that are of the same or a similar class as those offered or sold under Regulation D, other than offers or sales of securities under an employee benefit plan. The six-month rule is merely a safe harbor, and the fact that another offering is made within six months of the Regulation D offering does not necessarily indicate that it is part of that offering. Whether or not separate offerings of securities will be viewed as a single offering (i.e., will be "integrated") depends on the particular facts and circumstances.

---

65. This includes an issuer that has completed a 1933 Act registered offering even if it has not yet filed any reports under the 1934 Act. SEC No-action Letter, *Sidley & Austin* (April 24, 1997).

66. Rule 146 under the 1933 Act specifies certain additional exchanges.

The integration problem is not a new one, and it is not unique to Regulation D. In a 1962 release dealing with the Section 4(2) private offering exemption,[67] the SEC stated that a determination whether an offering is public or private will also include a consideration of the question whether it should be regarded as part of a larger offering made or to be made. In the release, the SEC articulated the factors that it considered relevant to the question of integration: whether (i) the different offerings are part of a single plan of financing, (ii) the offerings involve issuance of the same class of security, (iii) the offerings are made at or about the same time, (iv) the same type of consideration is to be received, and (v) the offerings are made for the same general purpose. These same factors are repeated in a note to Rule 502(a) that also makes clear that a private placement in the United States will "generally" not be integrated with simultaneous public offerings being made outside the United States effected in compliance with Regulation S.[68]

The five factors stated in SEC Release No. 33-4552 and in the note to Rule 502(a) are not always helpful in applying the integration doctrine. The SEC has provided no formal advice as to the weight to be afforded to each of the enumerated factors. Certainly, whether the same type of consideration is received is a meaningless factor. Except in the context of an acquisition, private placements are almost always made for cash. The first and last factors seem to overlap: if the sales are part of a "single plan of financing," then it would appear that they are "made for the same general purpose." If the "sales have been made at or about the same time," it is also likely that they are "part of a single plan of financing."[69] The second factor—namely, whether the transactions "involve issuance of the same class of

---

67. SEC Release No. 33-4552 (November 6, 1962).

68. The SEC took the same position in SEC Release No. 33-4708 (July 9, 1964).

69. There have been indications that the SEC staff considers the "single plan" and "general purpose" tests to be somewhat more important than the other three tests. As noted, these are often two sides of the same coin. Together with the "at or about the same time" test, they would make a three-sided coin.

securities"—would seem self-evident. There is no basis for integrating a private placement of debt securities with a public offering of common stock. Similarly, if an issuer is having a public offering of subordinated debentures, there should be no reason why it may not concurrently make a private placement of senior debt with a group of insurance companies, even though both offerings are part of a single plan of financing, are made at the same time, involve the same type of consideration and are made for the same general purpose. As stated by the late Linda Quinn, who was then the director of the SEC's division of Corporation Finance:

> [I]t should be clear why recent structured financing involving side-by-side private and registered offerings do not require integration. In these cases, for example, a single purchaser—a financial institution—buys the entire unregistered senior debt; the senior subordinated unregistered debt is sold to 10 insurance companies and the subordinated debt offered to the public is registered. The validity of the nonregistered offering should be clear but, unfortunately, it is not under current law.[70]

The result may not be clear if one gives too much credence to the SEC's five factors, but no experienced securities practitioner would doubt for a moment the availability of Section 4(2) or Regulation D for the sales to the financial institution and the ten insurance companies. These are simply not the types of transactions that the integration doctrine was designed to reach.

Realistically, integration problems seldom arise in the context of two or more institutional private placements. For example, if a private placement of debt securities is made to accredited investors and a second offering of the same type is made shortly thereafter for the same purpose, the two transactions—even if integrated—would still meet the requirements of Regulation D and Section 4(2).

---

70. L. C. Quinn, "Redefining 'Public Offering or Distribution' for Today," speech delivered on November 22, 1986.

The integration issue has arisen where a company is engaged in a continuous acquisition program, for example, a program by a motel chain to acquire franchisees in exchange for the issuer's common stock. One court refused to apply the integration doctrine where a company made ten acquisitions involving the issuance of approximately 1.6 million shares of its common stock over a relatively short period of time,[71] but a number of issuers have filed shelf registration statements to cover acquisition programs.

An integration issue may arise where a company is relying on Rule 505 and the question is whether the $5 million limit has been exceeded. This is one reason why it is preferable to structure offerings under Section 506 rather than Section 505. It also may arise where a company is relying on the 35-purchaser test under Regulation D. In this connection, integration was a real concern to promoters offering series of limited partnership interests in oil and gas, real estate and other tax driven ventures. During the period from 1971 through 1979, when the staff ceased giving interpretive advice for no-action rulings on integration questions, a number of conflicting positions were taken in no-action letters and interpretive responses to inquiries from the industry. Would drilling program *A* be integrated with drilling program *B* where portions of the properties overlapped?[72]

Challenging integration problems can arise where an offering starts out as a private placement but evolves into—or is followed by—a registered public offering, and *vice versa*. These problems are discussed below under *Related Private Placements and Public Offerings*.

- *The Substantial Compliance Rule*

The 1989 amendments to Regulation D included the adoption of Rule 508, which provides in effect that minor failures to comply with the technical requirements of Regulation D will

---

71. *Bowers v. Columbia General Corp.*, 336 F. Supp. 609 (D. Del. 1971).

72. For a detailed discussion of these issues, *see Integration of Partnership Offerings: A Proposal for Identifying a Discrete Offering,* 37 Bus. Law. 1591 (1982).

not necessarily cause a loss of the exemption. This so-called "innocent and immaterial" defense was long advocated by securities practitioners.

Rule 508 protects an issuer against civil liability under the 1933 Act for a failure to comply with Regulation D in the case of a sale to a particular person if (i) the failure to comply did not pertain to a requirement directly intended to protect that person, (ii) the failure to comply was insignificant with respect to the offering as a whole and (iii) a good faith and reasonable attempt was made to comply with all applicable requirements of the regulation.

Rule 508 deems the general solicitation prohibition and numerical purchaser limits of Rule 506 to be significant. Under Rule 508, if a provision designed to protect a particular investor is violated, that person could sue for rescission, but other investors in the offering would not have the same right of rescission, unless the violation was significant as to the offering overall.

As originally proposed, Rule 508 would have barred enforcement actions by the SEC. That element of the original proposal generated much opposition by state securities regulators and resulted in the SEC's staff holding joint meetings during the late summer and early fall of 1988 with representatives of the American Bar Association's Section of Business Law and of the North American Securities Administrators Association to seek a workable compromise to preserve federal–state coordination in the limited offering area. As adopted, Rule 508 specifically states that the failure to comply is actionable by the SEC.

Rule 144A

As noted above, the field of institutional private placements has been revolutionized since 1990 by an SEC rule that by its terms does not even apply to a private placement by an issuer. Rule 144A only permits persons *other than the issuer* to resell securities that they have purchased directly or indirectly from the issuer (or an affiliate of the issuer) in a transaction or series of transactions not involving a public offering. Rule 144A's powerful influence on the market arises from the fact that it permits a financial intermediary who has purchased securities from an issuer in a private placement—and is therefore often referred to as an "initial purchaser"—to make resales of those securities, subject to certain easily verified conditions, to a potentially indefinite number of "qualified institutional buyers" or QIBs.

The SEC adopted Rule 144A in April 1990.[73] The rule provides a non-exclusive safe harbor from the registration and prospectus delivery requirements of Section 5 of the 1933 Act for resales of certain restricted securities to QIBs. The rule provides that sales to QIBs in compliance with the rule are not distributions and that the seller is therefore not an "underwriter." If the seller is not the issuer or a dealer, it can rely on the Section 4(1) exemption. If the seller is a dealer, it can rely on the Section 4(3) exemption. Each transaction will be assessed individually. The exemption for an offer and sale under the rule is unaffected by transactions by other sellers.

Rule 144A contains four conditions that are normally subject to easy verification by the person relying on the exemption—the seller. These are that the restricted security be offered or sold only to QIBs or persons "reasonably believe[d]" to be QIBs; that the seller take "reasonable steps" to ensure that the purchaser is aware that the seller *may* be relying on Rule 144A in making the sale; that the securities not be "fungible" with certain exchange-listed or NASDAQ-quoted securities; and that the issuer—if it is not a 1934 Act reporting company, an "exempt" foreign private issuer or a foreign government—has committed itself to provide certain "reasonably current" information to a holder or a prospective purchaser. Notably, there is no prohibition relating to "general solicitation."

- *QIB Status*

QIBs are specified types of institutions, acting for their own account or the account of other QIBs, that in the aggregate own and invest on a discretionary basis at least $100 million in

---

73. SEC Release No. 33-6862 (April 23, 1990).

securities of non-affiliated issuers.[74] The specified types of institutions include business entities that are corporations, partnerships and business trusts.[75] They also include regulated entities that are insurance companies (including their separate accounts that are not investment companies), registered investment companies, business development companies, licensed small business investment companies, public employee benefit plans, ERISA employee benefit plans and not-for-profit organizations described in Section 501(c)(3) of the Internal Revenue Code.

Banks and savings and loan associations (and certain foreign counterparts) must meet the $100 million test *and* must also meet a $25 million net worth test. Trust funds may qualify as QIBs if their trustees are banks or trust companies and their participants include only public or ERISA employee benefit plans (other than individual retirement accounts or Keogh plans). While investment advisors and other entities may qualify as QIBs by aggregating their proprietary securities with the securities owned by managed accounts, it is still necessary for a managed account itself to meet the $100 million test in order to qualify as a QIB.

---

74. Securities are to be valued at cost, unless the institution reports its security holdings in its financial statements on the basis of market value and no current cost information has been published, in which case the determination may be based on market value.

The SEC requested comment in its 1998 Aircraft Carrier Release on whether "changes . . . in the markets" since 1990 should lead it to increase the $100 million requirement to as much as $200 million and also to increase the other numerical minimums in the rule. SEC Release No. 33-7606A (November 13, 1998), text at nn.101–05. It took no action on these proposals.

75. As in the case of "accredited investors," limited liability companies, states and their incorporated political subdivisions should also qualify as "corporations" for purposes of the QIB definition. Also, since the QIB definition is not qualified according to whether or not an entity is formed for the purposes of a Rule 144A transaction, it should be possible to have an "instant QIB," one that qualifies by making its initial investment of at least $100 million of securities in the Rule 144A transaction. But see SEC Division of Corporation Finance, *Manual of Publicly Available Telephone Interpretations* #6S (March 1999 Supplement).

Less stringent eligibility standards are applicable to broker-dealers registered under the 1934 Act. They are QIBs if on the relevant date they owned or managed on a discretionary basis at least $10 million in securities of nonaffiliated issuers (other than securities that are part of an unsold allotment in a public offering) or if they act in a "riskless principal transaction" on behalf of a QIB.[76] A dealer is deemed to own securities in a trading account as well as those in an investment account. Whether or not it comes within the definition of a QIB, a broker-dealer may act as agent in a sale to a QIB.

In order to rely on the rule, the seller and any person acting on its behalf must offer and sell the securities only to QIBs or to persons whom they reasonably believe to be QIBs. The rule specifies several non-exclusive methods of establishing the amount of securities owned and under investment management by a purchaser. These include the purchaser's most recent publicly available financial statements or the most recent information appearing in documents filed with the SEC or other governmental agencies or in a recognized securities manual, in each case if the information is not "stale" as prescribed by the rule. On the other hand, the adopting release states that a seller may rely on such information notwithstanding the existence of more current information that may show a lower amount of securities owned by the prospective purchaser.

The seller also may rely on a certification by an executive officer of the prospective purchaser as to the "amount" of securities owned or managed.

Many financial intermediaries have provided questionnaires to their customers who appear to be eligible for QIB status. This is an inefficient means of establishing "reasonable belief." At one point, it appeared that one or more of the rating agencies would list institutions that represented themselves as satisfying the QIB criteria. Such a listing would presumably qualify as

---

76. A "riskless principal transaction" is defined as "a transaction in which a dealer buys a security from any person and makes a simultaneous offsetting sale of such security to a qualified institutional buyer, including another dealer acting as riskless principal for a qualified institutional buyer."

either information contained in a "recognized securities manual" or as a "certification" by the investor. The SEC staff has also issued a no-action letter permitting sellers to rely on a third-party vendor's Internet-based list of QIBs.[77]

- *Screen-Based and Other "Offers"*

Rule 144A requires that offers as well as sales be made only to QIBs or to persons reasonably believed to be QIBs. Dealers will frequently want to use proprietary or Internet-based electronic communications to facilitate Rule 144A offerings. If the information is accessible only to QIBs (e.g., by means of a password), electronic display cannot constitute an "offer" to non-QIBs. As noted above, the SEC staff recently agreed that a password-restricted electronic display of information related to private placements would not constitute a "general solicitation." Since general solicitation is a broader concept than "offer," it would clearly follow that a password-protected display should be permissible under Rule 144A if the password is made available only to QIBs. The SEC staff has been unwilling to concede, however, that information may be displayed electronically on a non-password-protected basis even if the screen contains a legend to the effect that the information is not intended as an offer to any person who is not a QIB.

The SEC staff's caution regarding the accessibility of screen-based information to non-QIBs overlooks one of the basic distinctions between Rule 144A and Regulation D—namely, that Rule 144A permits *offers* only to QIBs but does not prohibit *general solicitations*. Even if an Internet communication available to all persons were deemed a general solicitation, it would appear to be a basic principle of contract law that a communication should not be construed as an "offer" if it clearly states that it is not an offer to anyone other than a QIB.[78]

---

77. SEC No-action Letter, *CommScan, LLC* (February 3, 1999).

78. *See* Harms, *supra* note 46, at 9. The SEC's 2000 interpretive release on "Use of Electronic Media" studiously limited its comments on online private offerings to those conducted under Regulation D as opposed to those made pursuant to Rule 144A.

In the case of ABS, the willingness of dealers to make bids on such securities may depend on the ready electronic availability of performance and related information. In fact, customers who would like the comfort of knowing that a bid will be available in the secondary market would be among those most adversely affected by a position that discourages the electronic availability of such information because of the bare possibility that it may be seen by non-QIBs as an incident to its screen-based delivery format. Indeed, it is difficult to see how Rule 144A could become unavailable for a transaction where the screen-based format is not the Internet but an expensive and professionally oriented medium such as Bloomberg and where the primary offering has long been completed.

An offering pursuant to Rule 144A is an unregistered offering within the meaning of Rule 135c, and an issuer that reports under the 1934 Act or is exempt under Rule 12g3-2(b) is entitled to rely on Rule 135c to publish a notice regarding a Rule 144A transaction. When it adopted Rule 135c, the SEC did not amend Rule 144A to exclude a notice pursuant to Rule 135c from the prohibition on offers and sales to persons other than QIBs (as it amended both Regulation D and Regulation S). On the other hand, a notice pursuant to Rule 135c is expressly deemed not to be an "offer" and should therefore not interfere with a Rule 144A transaction.

In its 1998 Aircraft Carrier Release, the SEC proposed amendments to Rules 138 and 139 that would have expressly permitted research about an issuer at or about the time of its Rule 144A transaction. The proposals were not adopted, but routine research—particularly where it covers an issuer's equity securities when the Rule 144A securities are debt securities—seldom rises to the level of an "offer" of the Rule 144A securities.

Some lawyers continue to recommend high minimum denominations, for example, $250,000, for Rule 144A securities. While high minimum denominations may serve a purpose in a Regulation D transaction, they are not necessary in a transaction relying on Rule 144A.

- *"Fungibility"*

Rule 144A is applicable to both debt and equity securities. It is not available, however, for transactions in securities that, when issued (as opposed to when sold), were of the same class as securities listed on a national securities exchange or quoted in an automated inter-dealer quotation system, such as NASDAQ. Securities quoted in the pink sheets or in the NASD's PORTAL system are not excluded. Securities issued by open-end investment companies and unit investment trusts are not covered by the rule.

Debt securities and preferred stock of different series generally will be viewed as different, non-"fungible" classes of securities for purposes of Rule 144A. Securities that are convertible into securities that are listed or quoted in NASDAQ are treated as securities of the same class as those into which they are convertible unless at the time of issuance the effective conversion premium was at least 10%. Warrants are treated as securities of the same class as the underlying securities unless at the time of issuance they had a term of at least three years and an effective exercise premium of at least 10%. Likewise, securities of the same class as those underlying ADRs that are listed or quoted in NASDAQ are not eligible for resale under the rule.

The SEC staff has taken the position that because mandatorily convertible securities (discussed in Chapter 12) in effect require the investor to make an investment decision on the underlying security, then the "fungibility" requirement of Rule 144A is not met if the underlying security is listed or quoted in an automated inter-dealer quotation system such as NASDAQ. Eligibility is not affected, however, if the underlying security was not so listed or quoted at the time of its issuance.[79]

- *Information Requirement*

If the issuer of the securities is not a reporting company under the 1934 Act and is not a foreign issuer exempt from reporting under Rule 12g3-2(b) (whether on a voluntary basis or otherwise) and is not a foreign government, the availability of Rule 144A is conditioned on the holder of the securities and the purchaser having the right to obtain specified information from the issuer, on request, and the purchaser having received

---

79. SEC No-action Letter, *Shearman & Sterling* (December 21, 1998).

that information, if requested. The information required to be furnished, if requested by the purchaser, is a "very brief" and "reasonably current" description of the business of the issuer and its products and services offered; the issuer's most recent balance sheet and profit and loss and retained earnings statements; and similar financial statements for such part of the two preceding fiscal years as the issuer has been in operation.

The rule does not specify the means of establishing the "right" to obtain this information, but the SEC release that adopted Rule 144A suggested that the issuer's obligation could be imposed, *inter alia,* in the terms of the security, by contract (e.g., the purchase agreement), by corporate law, by regulatory requirement or by the rules of applicable SROs. Presumably, a representation or undertaking in an offering document would also be sufficient. If reliance is placed on a purchase agreement between the issuer and the underwriters or placement agents where the agreement is governed by non-U.S. law, it would be advisable to determine whether third-party beneficiary rights are recognized under the applicable law.

The SEC staff has advised in several no-action letters that, where a Rule 144A issuer's securities are guaranteed by its parent company, the information requirement depends on the status of the guarantor.[80] Accordingly, the information requirement does not apply where the securities are guaranteed by a parent company that would itself be exempt from the information requirement. If the parent-guarantor would not be exempt, the information required to be supplied would be that of the parent-guarantor.

- *Notice Requirement*

Although Rule 144A imposes no resale restrictions, a seller or any person acting on its behalf must take reasonable steps to ensure that the buyer is aware that the seller may rely on the exemption from registration afforded by the rule. Since Rule 144A provides an exemption for what might otherwise be

---

80. See, e.g., SEC No-action Letters, *British Aerospace* (May 9, 1990) and *Schering-Plough Corp.* (November 21, 1991).

PRIVATE PLACEMENTS

an illegal *offer,* the notice should presumably be given to the prospective purchaser at the time of the offer and not be delayed, for example, until an offering memorandum or the confirmation of sale is forwarded to the purchaser.

- *Resales, PORTAL and DTC*

Since Rule 144A is a resale exemption, secondary market transactions in Rule 144A securities may obviously take place in reliance on Rule 144A exactly as in the case of their original placement by a financial intermediary. Rule 144A securities are also restricted securities within the meaning of Rule 144, but that rule's volume limitation seldom makes the rule of any practical value during the first years after the securities are sold. Thereafter, Rule 144(k) may permit unlimited public resales, but contractual restrictions may prevent reliance on that exemption.

At the same time that it adopted Rule 144A, the SEC approved rules establishing a new NASD marketplace called PORTAL (Private Offering, Resale and Trading through Automated Linkages) for the purpose of facilitating transactions in the Rule 144A market by the dissemination of trading information and the availability of an execution capability.[81] PORTAL is an electronic facility for transactions in securities that are eligible for resale pursuant to Rule 144A and that are (a) restricted securities as defined in Rule 144(a)(3) or (b) contractually required to be resold only pursuant to Regulation S, Rule 144A or Rule 144 or in secondary private placements.

The prospects for PORTAL's success were undermined from the start by a lapse in communications between the NASD and the SEC. The NASD appears to have anticipated that Rule 144A would *mandate* that resales pursuant to the rule take place in a "closed-loop" system such as PORTAL. As adopted by the SEC, however, Rule 144A contained no such requirement. During the next ten years, secondary market activity in Rule 144A securities expanded steadily, but without the benefit of PORTAL as institutional investors found alternative trading venues that offered greater liquidity. And in 2001, the SEC approved

---

81. SEC Release No. 34-27956 (April 27, 1990).

amendments to the rules that "delete[d] the remnants" of the closed-loop concept.[82]

Except for non-convertible investment-grade securities, inclusion in PORTAL is a precondition to the availability of DTC's book-entry settlement facilities.

Private Placement Procedures

The procedures appropriate for establishing the private placement exemption depend on the type of transaction being effected. The most common types of institutional private placement are the following:

– the stand-alone Rule 144A placement with U.S. institutional investors of a large amount of securities of a domestic or foreign issuer, where the methods used to negotiate terms and distribute the securities resemble closely those used in the case of a registered public offering;

– the continuous "Section 4(2)" or "restricted" program, following Regulation D or Rule 144A procedures, involving either commercial paper that does not qualify for the Section 3(a)(3) exemption or MTNs, which in either case are continuously sold to institutions; and

– the traditional stand-alone private placement of debt securities with a relatively small number of institutional purchasers.

The type of private placement that involves the most risk and requires the most carefully structured offering procedures is an offering pursuant to Regulation D of limited partnership interests or other equity securities in a market that consists largely of individuals rather than institutions.

---

82. SEC Release No. 34-44042 (March 6, 2001).

- *Rule 144A Private Placement*

There are two types of Rule 144A offering: Rule 144A-only offerings and Rule 144A-eligible offerings. Both commence as private placements from an issuer to an intermediary such as a securities dealer; the difference lies in the permitted resales of the securities.

Rule 144A-only offerings generally provide that any resales of the securities (until the securities become freely tradable under Rule 144 or registered under the 1933 Act) may be made only pursuant to Rule 144A. Rule 144A-only offerings also generally provide that investors that initially purchase the securities from the issuer or the intermediary must be QIBs, although some Rule 144A-only offerings permit accredited investors that are not QIBs to purchase securities in the initial placement.

In Rule 144A-eligible offerings, the terms of the securities are drafted to permit resales pursuant to Rule 144A. However, resales of the securities pursuant to some or all of the other available 1933 Act exemptions (e.g., Regulation S or a secondary private placement) are also available.

- - *Rule 144A Debt Offering.* Except for the fact that they are by definition directed at a more limited universe of investors, Rule 144A transactions in debt securities have come to resemble closely their SEC-registered counterparts. Indeed, it might not be an overstatement to assert that for at least some securities the public and Rule 144A markets have merged for all practical and economic purposes. Some investment banks have combined or closely aligned their public and private origination groups in order more effectively to compete for issuers' business. Even on the "buy side," many investors have become so accustomed to the after-market liquidity made possible by Rule 144A that they regard the security's designation as "Rule 144A-eligible" as more of a technicality than a distinction of economic importance.

As in a public offering, the issuer will work with its counsel, its investment banker and its counsel, and its independent accountants to prepare the purchase agreement and the offering materials. The purchase agreement's representations and warranties, covenants and agreements, closing conditions and indemnification and contribution arrangements will usually reflect the investment banker's standard format. Of course, the offering materials will not be subject to the regulatory review process involved in an SEC-registered public offering, but marketing considerations and the disclosure policies of the investment banker will raise many similar drafting issues. Also, the offering materials will be drafted to the same standard as SEC-filed documents if the issuer has agreed to file a resale registration statement or an "Exxon Capital" exchange offer.

In the case of a non-U.S. issuer, the investment banker will generally determine in consultation with the issuer what U.S. dollar convenience translations and what U.S. GAAP reconciliation items, if any, would be desirable for the marketing and sale of the security. In the case of high-yield debt, it may be desirable to include forecasts or projections in the offering materials.

With all the strengths and weaknesses inherent in the comparison, due diligence on a Rule 144A debt offering resembles in many ways the due diligence process followed on registered public offerings. If the debt is investment-grade, due diligence on a Rule 144A placement will parallel that associated with an investment-grade shelf takedown (see Chapter 8) with the important reservations that there will not have been an initial filing with the SEC nor an opportunity for designated purchasers' counsel to perform any "continuous due diligence" on the issuer. On the other hand, if the debt is less than investment-grade, due diligence may be quite extensive, depending on the investment banker's familiarity with the issuer and the rating agencies' views of trends in the issuer's credit standing.

As discussed in Chapter 5, an intermediary's liability for disclosure deficiencies in a private placement has been determined, since the Supreme Court's decision in *Gustafson,* under Rule 10b-5 rather than under Section 12(a)(2) of the 1933 Act. Rule 10b-5, of course, requires a demonstration of scienter on the part of the defendant—either intentional fraud or, according to most courts, "recklessness." Section 12(a)(2), on the other hand, which most investment bankers and securities lawyers assumed for many years would determine an intermediary's liability, is a "negligence-based" remedy because its due diligence defense requires the exercise of "reasonable care."

PRIVATE PLACEMENTS

For this reason, investment bankers' due diligence procedures for private offerings (including, since 1990, Rule 144A transactions) were established on the assumption that the securities firm would have to prove a lack of negligence, that is, that it had acted in the exercise of reasonable care. *Gustafson* meant that such firms now had to establish only the absence of intentional fraud or reckless misconduct. While this difference might appear to justify some modifications in traditional procedures, there are some downside risks:

- Plaintiffs' lawyers are skilled in alleging—with the benefit of hindsight—that securities firms were "reckless" in ignoring "red flags" or other indications that an issuer had undisclosed problems.

- The document alleged in *Gustafson* to be a "prospectus" was the purchase agreement itself rather than an offering document. This might be the basis for a factual distinction in future litigation, despite the majority opinion's strong language suggesting that its holding is of general application.

- Modifications to traditional procedures might make it more difficult to give the issuer's accountants the representation contemplated by AU ¶634 regarding the underwriter's use of due diligence procedures in a non-registered offering that are substantially equivalent to those used in a registered offering.

- All participants should be aware of the possibility that state law may provide remedies that go beyond Rule 10b-5.

The pressures on investment bankers to alter traditional due diligence procedures are, of course, external rather than internal. The premium placed on speed in order to lock-in a transaction means that there is often simply little time for the usual inquiries, opinions or comfort letters. Also, issuers often object to the cost or inconvenience of these basic due diligence methods.

The SEC staff takes the position that an offering of securities pursuant to Rule 144A may constitute a "distribution" for purposes of the SEC's antimanipulation rules under Regulation M if the transaction is distinguishable from ordinary trading transactions by reason of its "magnitude" and the presence of special selling efforts and selling methods. Distributions of investment-grade debt securities are not subject to the relevant rules, and neither are Rule 144A securities offered in the United States solely to QIBs. Since underwriters of non-investment-grade debt securities are eager to commence making a market in the new securities as soon as possible, even before the completion of the distribution, offerings of high-yield securities are almost invariably offered only to QIBs.

• • *Rule 144A Offering of Equity Securities.* As noted above, Rule 144A is not available for a security that is "fungible" with a security listed on a U.S. securities exchange or quoted in NASDAQ. This means that U.S. issuers have not been able to rely significantly on Rule 144A for the purpose of offering their common stock. They have, however, been able to rely on the rule for significant offerings of convertible securities, often on a "bought deal" or "overnight" basis, where the conversion premium is sufficiently high to overcome the fungibility problem.

Rule 144A convertible offerings have the advantage of being able to be launched and marketed quickly, often to hedge funds that intend to make short sales of the issuer's common stock. In the case of SEC-reporting companies, the issuer usually agrees to register the convertible securities for resale or to engage in an "Exxon Capital" or "A/B" exchange offer. The 1933 Act aspects of these transactions are discussed below under "Related Private Placements and Public Offerings."

Non-U.S. issuers may also rely on Rule 144A in making placements in the United States of convertible securities, ordinary shares or ADRs, either on a stand-alone basis or as part of a global offering.

Due diligence procedures in connection with a non-U.S. issuer's Rule 144A equity offering are quite similar to those followed in connection with registered public offerings. The offering document will normally not include a numeric or quantitative reconciliation of the issuer's financial statements to U.S. GAAP, since this will often have been the single most significant obstacle to the issuer's engaging in an SEC-registered transaction. It is common, however, for the document to provide a narrative description of the major differences between U.S. GAAP and the local accounting principles used to prepare the financial statements included in the document.

If ADRs are to be offered, the non-U.S. issuer will deposit its ordinary securities with the custodian bank, which will in turn issue its ADRs to the investment bank or banks engaged by the issuer to distribute the ADRs. This transaction usually relies on the Section 4(2) exemption. The investment bank or banks will then rely on Rule 144A in making resales of the ADRs.

There is no U.S. exchange listing in the case of a Rule 144A ADR offering, but the Rule 144A ADRs will typically be designated for trading in the PORTAL system in order to make them eligible for book-entry settlement.

Generally, Rule 144A ADR facilities permit new deposits of underlying ordinary shares by QIBs or offshore purchasers who have bought such shares in the secondary market and who are willing to accept restricted ADRs in exchange. As in the case of other "restricted" securities, Rule 144(k) will permit the ADRs to be publicly offered and sold without registration upon the lapse of two years from the sale of the ADRs by the issuer or its affiliate. For this reason, a Rule 144A ADR facility is generally structured to permit neither the issuer nor any affiliate to deposit additional shares into the facility following the offering.

The SEC has issued guidelines relating to the situation where an issuer has concurrent restricted and unrestricted ADR facilities. This might arise, for example, where an issuer completes a Rule 144A offering either before or after it establishes a "Level One" facility for the convenience of the public holders of the same class of the issuer's underlying securities. The SEC's concern arises from the possibility of "leakage" between a restricted and an unrestricted facility as well as from the prospect of "automatic fungibility," where depositary receipts offered outside the United States in reliance on Regulation S become eligible for resale into the United States. The guidelines were issued in *Depositary Receipts* (available April 14, 1993) and rely on the SEC's power to control whether and when a Form F-6 registration statement becomes effective. (As discussed in Chapter 9, a Form F-6 registration statement is required for an unrestricted program.)

The guidelines require that Rule 144A ADRs be distinguished from Regulation S depositary receipts and from unrestricted depositary receipts by a different name and CUSIP number. Deposits into and withdrawals from the restricted facility are subject to certification requirements. Depositors of securities into a Regulation S facility must certify that they are not an affiliate of the issuer and that the securities are not restricted securities. Finally, a Form F-6 registration statement may not be filed covering a new unrestricted facility or a new Regulation S facility until 40 days after consummation of the Regulation S offering.

- *Continuous Private Placement Programs*

Traditionally, institutional private placements were effected as discrete offerings with a single closing. In the mid-1970s, a number of commercial paper dealers began to sell commercial paper that did not qualify for the Section 3(a)(3) exemption (see Chapter 10) to institutional investors in ostensible reliance on Section 4(2). Because commercial paper programs require the continuous issuance of new notes to replace maturing notes, these "Section 4(2)" or "restricted" programs represented private placements made on a continuous basis over an extended period of time. "Section 4(2)" eventually came also to be relied on for continuous offerings of medium-term notes (see Chapter 8) where the Section 3(a)(3) exemption was not available because the notes had maturities in excess of 270 days.

- - *Continuous Offering Procedures for Restricted Commercial Paper.* Originally, these programs were effected in accordance with procedures designed to comply in all material respects with the provisions of Rule 146 other than the requirement that a report be filed on Form 146. (See the discussion above under "Rule 146.") Subsequently, these procedures could be simplified with the adoption of Regulation D. In either case, the dealer[83]

---

83. Most commercial paper programs are conducted by two or more dealers on behalf of an issuer, and references to "dealers" should be understood to include references to "co-dealers" unless the context otherwise requires.

did not sell the notes in reliance on Rule 146 or Regulation D or even Section 4(2) itself—all of which are issuers' exemptions—but in reliance on the dealer's exemption under Section 4(3). This analysis is based on the assumption that there is no "public offering" or "distribution" within the meaning of Section 4(3) when the dealer offers and sells the notes in accordance with Section 4(2), Rule 146 or Regulation D.

In contrast to other types of private placement, Rule 144A is not relied on as often as Regulation D in the case of continuous "restricted" commercial paper programs. Non-QIBs make up a significant part of the universe of buyers in these programs, and dealers are reluctant to give up this segment of the market.

At one time, many Section 3(a)(3) commercial paper programs were conducted without benefit of a formal agreement between the dealer and the issuer. From the early days of "restricted" programs, however, it was recognized that there should be a clear understanding between the issuer and the dealer as to the procedures to be followed in making offers and sales under the program. The procedures proposed to be followed by the dealer were therefore set forth in a formal "dealer agreement." Just as in the case of underwriting agreements (see Chapter 2), there are variations among the various dealers' standard form of agreement. The Bond Market Association, an industry trade group, has developed model forms of agreement for both Section 3(a)(3) and Section 4(2) programs.[84]

A dealer agreement will contain customary representations and warranties by the issuer, undertakings by the issuer to inform the dealers of material developments on an ongoing basis, indemnity and contribution undertakings by the issuer, and formal conditions to the commencement of the program.

The principal purpose of the dealer agreement in a "restricted" program is to formalize the procedures to be followed in offering and selling the issuer's notes. As noted above, the dealer will be relying on the Section 4(3) exemption and not on Regulation D.

---

84. The model forms, which were updated in February 2004, are posted on the association's website at www.bondmarkets.com/Market/corporate.shtml#comm. Model forms for guaranteed programs were added in May 2004.

Since the issuer will neither solicit investors nor pass title to the notes to investors, it would appear that the issuer has no real stake in whether or not the dealer has a good exemption. On the other hand, the issuer is relying on Regulation D to sell the notes to the dealer. The issuer will therefore want to know that it has exercised "reasonable care" to assure that the dealer will not be acting as an "underwriter" in reselling the notes.

The dealer will also want the issuer to agree to the reasonableness of the procedures that the dealer proposes to follow. Moreover, the issuer's counsel will customarily be asked to deliver an opinion *to the dealer* that the offer and sale of the notes in the manner contemplated by the dealer agreement will be exempt from the requirements of Section 5 of the 1933 Act. Finally, the dealer will want to demonstrate to the issuer great concern about the adequacy of the procedures to achieve the exemption if for no other reason than to head off a request from the issuer that the dealer indemnify it against any loss arising out of the exemption's proving to be unavailable. (Such a request would be rather pointless, of course, since the issuer's maximum exposure in that event would be the obligation to prepay its own short-term notes.)

The dealer agreement will usually specify that notes will be sold in minimum denominations or amounts of $250,000. In a book-entry settlement environment, of course, minimum denominations are a fiction. The useful purpose of the undertaking, however, is to reinforce the "non-public" nature of the program by requiring each investor's investment decision to be in a significant amount. In view of this purpose, the authors do not believe it is necessary to provide (as some agreements do) that each person for whom a fiduciary is acting must also be purchasing the minimum amount of notes, particularly if the fiduciary is a bank.

The universe of eligible buyers is a frequent source of confusion and disagreement. The commercial paper market is primarily institutional, and the dealer agreement will typically limit offers and sales to QIBs and institutional accredited investors. Some dealers, however, will want to be able to offer and sell notes to individual accredited investors who are "sophisticated." This is sometimes permitted in the agreement, but there is a lack of uniformity on who is deemed to be a "sophisticated" individual investor. Some agreements require only a minimum net worth (usually well in excess of the accredited investor minimum for "natural persons" of $1 million), while others require a preexisting relationship and a dealer determination of investment sophistication. The latter requirements deserve some discussion.

"Preexisting relationship" is a concept sometimes relied on to show the absence of a general solicitation in the context of a private offering directed at individual investors. As discussed above, however, the existence of a preexisting relationship is not the only means by which one can demonstrate the absence of a general solicitation. If a dealer wishes to offer "restricted" commercial paper to its *customers* who are high net worth individuals, this clearly satisfies the test (even on the assumption the test has any applicability in a private commercial paper program designed to comply with Regulation D).

The requirement that a dealer make a determination of investor sophistication is really a throwback to Rule 146. Unlike the requirements of that rule, however, it is irrelevant under Regulation D whether or not an investor is "sophisticated" so long as the investor is an "accredited investor." Moreover, sophistication has nothing to do with whether or not a general solicitation is taking place. To be sure, a judgment about sophistication is appropriate as part of the dealer's discharge of its obligation to its customer to recommend suitable investments, but this obligation does not concern the issuer and does not belong in the dealer agreement.

Dealers and issuers and their respective counsel no longer appear to disagree whether there should be a ceiling on the number of investors who can participate in the program. Like the "minimum denomination" requirement discussed above, a ceiling on the number of offerees serves the purpose of reducing the likelihood that a program will involve a general solicitation. In the context of a predominantly institutional offering, however, the analysis should focus on the manner of offering rather than on numbers. In the early days of restricted commercial paper programs, some dealer agreements provided for a flexible ceiling where the maximum number of offerees increased with the size of the program. For a $1 billion program, for example, the dealer could approach as many as 750 offerees. Such arbitrary limits are unnecessary in the context of a commercial paper program structured in accordance with Regulation D and directed at institutional accredited investors or high net worth individuals.

No one appears to contend any longer that dealers should be in a position at any given time to identify all persons to whom notes have been offered. Those lawyers who believed that this was necessary relied on court decisions and SEC statements in *amicus* briefs to the effect that an offering cannot qualify for a private placement exemption unless evidence can be produced of the exact number and identity of all offerees. The private placements under attack in the cited court decisions or SEC proceedings, however, usually involved somewhat careless large-scale solicitations of individual investors to purchase a speculative security. In addition, the availability of an exemption usually had to be tested under the subjective standards of Section 4(2), since the issuers or their agents had either not attempted to take advantage of Rule 146 or Regulation D or were held to have failed in the attempt. Under Regulation D, as discussed above, the *number* of offerees is arguably relevant to whether there is a general solicitation; on the other hand, arbitrary limits should be unnecessary in the context of a restricted commercial paper program directed at institutional accredited investors and high net worth individuals. (It follows that one should not have to be able to fix the exact number of offerees; the ability to approximate the number by reference to mailing, facsimile or courier records should suffice.) The *identity* of the offerees at any given time is, of course, relevant to whether the investors are accredited investors. Again, however, it should be possible to establish this fact without knowing the name and address of each offeree by reference to common business records such as standard mailing lists.

Dealer agreements customarily obligate the issuer to notify the dealer or dealers if the issuer will or may use the proceeds to purchase or carry securities. In that case, the dealer will be required to sell the restricted paper as principal only to QIBs and to make sales to other persons only as agent. The reason for the distinction arises out of the Federal Reserve Board's

Regulation T, which governs extensions of credit by broker-dealers and, among other things, prohibits broker-dealers from extending unsecured credit that is to be used for the purpose of purchasing, carrying or trading in securities. The problem arises most frequently where the issuer is using the proceeds of the program to finance a stock acquisition, a purpose for which restricted commercial paper programs are a swift and efficient vehicle. Traditionally, the Federal Reserve Board does not regard *public* offerings of commercial paper or debt securities (e.g., a firm commitment underwriting of an issuer's debt securities) as an extension of credit by the underwriter or dealer. The problem arises when the dealer wishes to act as principal in purchasing *restricted* commercial paper from the issuer for purposes of resale to the dealer's customers. This practice, while customary in the commercial paper market, was deemed by the staff of the Federal Reserve Board in 1984 to constitute a prohibited "extension" of credit because the dealer became the owner of the issuer's commercial paper for some period of time before it was sold to an investor.[85] The board modified this position somewhat in 1990 by permitting the dealer to act as principal if it purchased debt securities for resale pursuant to Rule 144A.[86] Dealer agreements may also leave it to the dealer to act in a manner consistent with Regulation T, which is interpreted by many dealers to permit principal purchases that are offset on the same day by principal sales.[87]

Commercial paper notes are traditionally issued in bearer form, and they are ordinarily negotiable instruments under the Uniform Commercial Code. One might, therefore, conclude that particularly stringent resale restrictions would be appropriate in order to demonstrate reasonable care that the dealer and subsequent purchasers were not acting as "underwriters." In fact, however, commercial paper presents few challenges arising out

---

85. Staff Opinion of December 11, 1984, Federal Reserve Regulatory Service ¶ 5-606.4.
86. Interpretation of the Federal Reserve Board of July 16, 1990, Federal Reserve Regulatory Service ¶ 5-470.1.
87. C. F. Rechlin, *Securities Credit Regulation* 2:28 (2003).

of resale activity. First of all, most investors hold notes until maturity. Second, in those cases where an investor has an unanticipated need for liquidity, it will almost invariably seek a bid from one of the dealers on the program. The dealers are the natural buyers for the paper in view of their familiarity with the issuer and the issuer's credit, and they have a natural outlet for the repurchased paper: they can simply resell under the program. Third, the fact that most commercial paper transactions are settled by book-entry rather than by the issuance of physical notes makes it difficult for an investor to sell or even pledge a note outside the program. These considerations should be of significant importance in deciding what resale restrictions are appropriate for a restricted commercial paper program.

In particular, the considerations mentioned above do have significance for a traditional device for preventing resales that might destroy the basis for the private placement exemption— namely, restrictive legends. In traditional private placements, prospective investors received warnings about restrictions on resale from three separate sources: the offering materials (the "private placement memorandum" or "PPM"), the purchase contract and the physical certificate relating to the security that was being offered and sold. In addition, the documents stated that the investor would be deemed to have agreed to the restrictions in the event that it purchased notes.

In restricted commercial paper programs, there is no written purchase contract that binds the purchaser of notes. Although it has become customary to place a restrictive legend on a "master" commercial paper note that is being deposited with DTC for purposes of facilitating book-entry settlement of notes, the efficacy of such a legend as a basis for a "deemed agreement" is doubtful because no purchaser of notes ever sees the legend. This leaves the private placement memorandum as the only effective vehicle for providing notice to the investor of restrictions on resale and for obtaining the investor's deemed agreement to abide by such restrictions.

The authors believe that it is sufficient to rely on the private placement memorandum as the vehicle for disclosing and obtaining agreements to restrictions on resale, but it is harmless for the same legend to appear on the note.

Wherever its location, the restrictive legend serves to reinforce that the notes are available only to specified categories of investor. In addition, the legend states that in the event the holder wishes to resell the note it must do so in accordance with specified procedures. At one time, legends often required the holder to resell the note only to the dealer from which it had been purchased. More recently, legends permit the holder to sell back to the issuer, to any dealer designated by the issuer or directly to a QIB in a Rule 144A transaction.

As in the case of the offering memorandum for Section 3(a)(3) commercial paper discussed in Chapter 10, the format of the private placement memorandum relating to restricted commercial paper has undergone significant change. Apart from the notice to the investor of restrictions on resale and the obtaining of the investor's deemed agreement to abide by such restrictions, many dealers' offering memoranda contain only "bare bones" information about the commercial paper program and refer the investor for further information to the issuer or its 1934 Act reports.

Unlike commercial paper offered under Section 3(a)(3), restricted commercial paper can have maturities that are longer than nine months. Such paper can become hard to distinguish from privately placed MTNs that are often sold with the benefit of a more complete offering document. The point at which a more complete offering document will be prepared depends on the issuer's and the dealers' preferences and most significantly on the issuer's creditworthiness.

Questions also arise from time to time relating to dealers' screen-based solicitation efforts. Many commercial paper dealers communicate with their commercial paper buyer customers by screen-based displays. These enable the potential buyer efficiently to examine the notes that the dealer is offering for sale. So long as the screens are available—by password or otherwise—only to investors who are eligible to purchase paper under the dealer agreement, the screens present no problem. If they are more broadly available, for example, to all Internet users, this can amount to a general solicitation under Regulation D in violation of the dealer agreement. This is not a sensible result, of course, particularly if the screen carries a legend to the effect that it is not intended as an offer to or solicitation of anyone who is not an eligible purchaser.

• • *Integration.* The question of integration must be faced when an issuer decides to commence a "restricted" program at the same time that it is issuing commercial paper in reliance on Section 3(a)(3). The problem can also arise in reverse order. In either case, it is likely that there will be an overlap in the maturities of the notes issued in the separate programs.

The staff of the SEC has issued a number of no-action letters permitting simultaneous offerings of commercial paper under Section 3(a)(3) and private placements of notes with overlapping maturities. In the first of these, the issuer represented that different securities dealers would be used in connection with the sale of the commercial paper and the private placement of notes with maturities ranging from 30 days to seven years.[88] The issuer also represented that controls would be established to ensure that proceeds from the sale of the commercial paper would be used to finance only current transactions and that the proceeds from the private placement would be used to finance only non-current transactions.

The staff has taken a similar no-action position with respect to the simultaneous sale through the same dealer of commercial paper and the private placement of notes with maturities ranging from 30 days to 270 days.[89] There the issuer represented that it had in effect controls to ensure that proceeds from the sale of its commercial paper would be used exclusively for current transactions and that the proceeds from the private placement would be used exclusively for transactions that were not current. The issuer agreed to deposit the proceeds from the private placement in a different bank from that utilized for the deposit of proceeds from the sale of its commercial paper. The issuer stated that it expected that the two offerings would have some overlap because of the sale of commercial paper to institutions that also participated in the private placement.

---

88. SEC No-action Letter, *Pittsburgh National Corp.* (August 15, 1977).
89. SEC No-action Letter, *NCNB Corp.* (April 27, 1978).

The SEC's staff also took a favorable no-action position where an issuer contemplated a simultaneous offering of commercial paper and a private placement of promissory notes with maturities ranging from 30 days to one year.[90] Again, the issuer represented that the proceeds from the two offerings would be used for current transactions and non-current transactions, respectively. The issuer represented that the private placement would be to major corporate and other institutional investors in the national market, whereas the commercial paper would be restricted primarily to a predominantly regional market.

Dealer agreements customarily address the integration problem by requiring the issuer to represent to the dealer or dealers that it will segregate the proceeds of the restricted commercial paper program from the proceeds of any Section 3(a)(3) program, that it will "institute appropriate corporate procedures" to prevent integration and that it will comply with the conditions of Section 3(a)(3) in selling commercial paper away from the restricted program.

An integration problem can arise if an issuer decides to convert a commercial paper program from a Section 3(a)(3) program to a Section 4(2) program. This occurred in the case of a joint venture that issued three series of commercial paper notes, each guaranteed by one of the three joint venturers. The notes were issued without registration in reliance on an opinion of counsel based on a number of no-action letters that recognized that the Section 3(a)(3) exemption would be available for commercial paper issued to provide interim financing of capital expenditures where permanent financing was to be obtained within a reasonable time after the completion of construction. The opinion was conditioned on the understanding that the commercial paper program would not be continued beyond a specified date. In view of the success of the commercial paper program and the then-existing relationship between interest rates in the commercial paper market and interest rates for long-term indebtedness, the issuer sought a means of extending the commercial paper program beyond the time originally contemplated.

---

90. SEC No-action Letter, *First & Merchants Corp.* (July 27, 1978).

The issuer's commercial paper dealer, Goldman Sachs Money Markets Inc., had established procedures under Section 4(2) designed to provide an exemption from registration for the sale of commercial paper that did not meet the requirements of Section 3(a)(3). These procedures were embodied in an agreement that Goldman Sachs proposed to enter into with the issuer. The decision was made to convert the program to one made in reliance on Section 4(2). The problem was integration. If the Section 4(2) program was merely a continuation of the Section 3(a)(3) program, the public nature of the Section 3(a)(3) program could taint the availability of Section 4(2).

The commercial paper market is essentially an institutional market. It was, therefore, possible that the Section 3(a)(3) program did not in fact involve a public offering. Counsel advised the issuer that, although the existing commercial paper program had been instituted in reliance on Section 3(a)(3), if, in fact, it had been conducted in a manner that satisfied Section 4(2), then it would not affect the availability of the private placement exemption for the notes proposed to be issued in accordance with Section 4(2) procedures.

Counsel reviewed the program as theretofore conducted and was able to conclude that the private placement exemption had in fact been available. This conclusion was based on the following findings set forth in its opinion letter:

> To determine whether, in our opinion, the XYZ commercial paper program has in fact been conducted as a private placement, we have examined records made available to us by Goldman setting forth the potential investors to whom offers of XYZ commercial paper were made and the identity of each purchaser of Notes of each series since the commercial paper program was instituted in April 1983. These records indicate that since the institution of the commercial paper program, 41 investors have owned Series A Notes, 23 investors have owned Series B Notes and 13 investors have owned Series C Notes. Each of these investors appears to be an "accredited investor" within the meaning of Regulation D under the Securities Act. Goldman has advised us that the only sales of less

than $200,000 of the Notes were made to the following investors: in Series A, to affiliates of two large insurance companies; in Series B, to a large union pension fund, to a university and to a large cash management fund; in Series C, to affiliates of a large union pension fund. Chemical Bank has advised us that there have been no exchanges of Notes for Notes of smaller denominations.

We have also discussed with representatives of Goldman the manner in which the Notes have been offered for sale. We are satisfied that the Notes have not been offered "by any form of general solicitation or general advertising" within the meaning of Regulation D under the Securities Act.

On this basis, the Section 4(2) program went forward as planned.

An integration problem can also arise if an issuer wishes to conduct simultaneously a "restricted" commercial paper program and a registered MTN program where the maturities of the MTNs overlap with those of the commercial paper notes. (The same problem can arise if an issuer conducts simultaneously a restricted MTN program and a Section 3(a)(3) commercial paper program.) Overlapping maturities should not in isolation present a problem if the programs can be distinguished in other ways, for example, by the use of proceeds. If this is not the case, the issuer should undertake that it will not issue MTNs with a maturity of less than a specified period at any time while it is issuing "restricted" commercial paper. The period should be specified with a view to establishing a reasonable distinction between the MTNs and the commercial paper in light of the investor base and market conditions.

• • *Extendible Commercial Paper.* As discussed in Chapter 10, most commercial paper issuers maintain unused bank lines in an amount equal to their outstanding paper in order to demonstrate to investors and the rating agencies their ability to liquidate their commercial paper obligations and effect an "orderly exit" should market conditions prevent financing through the issuance of new notes. Bank lines are no less important for the purpose of backing up restricted commercial paper.

The need to maintain expensive bank lines can be reduced by the use of "extendible commercial paper." While such paper has a stated maturity date, its terms give the issuer the unilateral right to extend the maturity date if it should choose to do so. Obviously, an issuer would resort to such a mandatory extension only if it found it difficult to roll over its regular commercial paper. In effect, the buyer of the extendible commercial paper is assuming the role of the banks that would normally back up the issuer's commercial paper, and the investors are compensated for this risk by a higher return on the paper.

The issuer's ability to extend the maturity date means that the extendible commercial paper cannot be said to have at the time it is issued a fixed maturity date of nine months or less. Extendible commercial paper therefore fails to qualify for the Section 3(a)(3) exemption and must be offered on a private placement basis.

• • *Continuous Offering Procedures for Restricted MTNs.* MTNs emerged during the 1980s as a major source of funding for U.S. and non-U.S. corporations. One reason for the growth of the market was the willingness of major U.S. investment banks to commit resources to assist in primary issuance and to provide secondary market liquidity. Another significant reason was the SEC's adoption of Rule 415 in March 1982 (see Chapter 8). Shelf registration made it possible for issuers to take advantage of brief "window periods" of attractive interest rates by selling registered securities on very short notice.

U.S. issuers will normally elect to set up their MTN programs on a shelf-registered basis. For non-U.S. issuers, however, registered public offerings are not so easy. It is true that non-U.S. issuers that wish to make an SEC-registered offering of investment-grade debt are not required to provide the geographic market and industry segment information normally associated with a registered public offering (see Chapter 9). They are still required, however, to reconcile certain financial statement information to U.S. GAAP. This requirement has served as an obstacle to many non-U.S. issuers who otherwise would have set up a public MTN program in the U.S. Also, for reasons related to the Investment Company Act of 1940, a public MTN program might not be possible for a non-U.S. issuer's

U.S. finance subsidiary where the parent company is unwilling or unable to provide an unconditional guarantee of the subsidiary's MTNs.

It is possible, of course, for non-U.S. issuers to avoid the reconciliation and related SEC disclosure requirements by selling MTNs on a private placement basis. Unlike the situation in the restricted commercial paper market with its shorter maturities, however, non-U.S. issuers for many years believed there would be a significant illiquidity premium associated with the private placement of MTNs.

Following the SEC's adoption of Rule 144A, an alternative market was effectively created that enabled non-U.S. corporations to access U.S. capital markets without having to comply with SEC accounting and related requirements and without having to pay a material liquidity premium. Non-U.S. issuers responded to Rule 144A by dramatically increasing their sale of MTNs in the U.S. private market.

Private MTN programs involve the initial issuance of MTNs (a) to a dealer acting as principal or (b) through a dealer, acting as agent, to QIBs or institutional accredited investors. As in the case of Rule 144A private placements discussed above, the issuer's exemption for its sales to or through dealers may be Section 4(2) or Regulation D, while the dealer buying as principal will resell to QIBs under Rule 144A and to institutional accredited investors under Section 4(3) by analogy to Regulation D. Investors who wish to resell will be able, of course, to do so in reliance on Rule 144A (or any other available exemption permitted under the terms of the program).

Given that the offering procedures for a private MTN program will generally restrict offerees and purchasers to QIBs or institutional accredited investors, no particular disclosure is required to be delivered to investors to perfect the private placement exemption. For marketing reasons, however, substantial disclosure about the issuer and, if the issuer is a U.S. finance subsidiary, the non-U.S. parent is customarily provided in a private placement memorandum. The disclosure in the memorandum about the issuer (or its parent) is normally greater than that required for a commercial paper program but less than that required for a registered offering and will depend on the business of the issuer (or its parent) and the credit ratings assigned to the notes. The SEC disclosure rules often serve as a guide to what is disclosed in the memorandum. The differences between the issuer's home country accounting and U.S. GAAP are usually described only in narrative form. The typical memorandum will also contain a general description of the MTNs (including any affirmative and negative covenants and the events of default), private placement legends and disclosure about resale and other transfer restrictions (including the availability of Rule 144A) and the availability of the issuer to answer questions and to provide further documents to the extent it can do so without unreasonable effort or expense. The memorandum will need to be updated from time to time, depending on the degree to which the MTN program involves a continuous offering. Pricing supplements reflecting the specific terms of an MTN takedown are generally delivered to investors.

If the MTNs are to be eligible for Rule 144A, of course, the issuer (and, in the case of a guaranteed U.S. finance subsidiary, the non-U.S. parent) will have to meet the information requirement of Rule 144A(d)(4). For non-reporting issuers, the information requirement will probably be met either by a contractual undertaking as contemplated by Rule 144A(d)(4) or by filings with the SEC under Rule 12g3-2(b).

Qualification of an indenture under the 1939 Act is not required for a private MTN program; however, issuers that expect to eventually register their programs under the 1933 Act may use an indenture that can be qualified under the 1939 Act so that all their U.S. MTN notes of the same rank will be offered on the same terms and provisions. Normally, issuers of private MTNs issue notes pursuant to an agreement with an issuing and paying agent that does not assume the fiduciary obligations of a trustee under the 1939 Act. These agreements are largely standardized. Because of the absence of express fiduciary obligations, the issuing and paying agents charge less for their services than trustees. The agreement will include guidelines to be followed by the issuing and paying agent in connection with transfers of outstanding MTNs; these procedures are designed to preserve the private placement exemptions on which the program is built.

The distribution agreement for a private MTN program will contain representations and warranties by the issuer about its business, its financial condition and the MTN program that will be deemed to be updated as of the time of each sale and issuance of MTNs. Closing conditions, including officers' certificates, comfort letters and opinions of counsel, as well as the requirement for periodic delivery of such documents, are also specified. The agreement will provide for indemnity and contribution by the issuer to the investment bank intermediary in the event of material misstatements or omissions in the disclosure document.

If the proceeds of the MTN program are to be used to finance the purchase or carrying of securities, the same Regulation T considerations apply as discussed above in connection with continuous offerings of restricted commercial paper.

Privately offered MTNs are eligible for DTC book-entry settlement if they are PORTAL-eligible or, if not PORTAL-eligible, if they are investment-grade.

In all other material respects, a private MTN program is administered in the same manner as a registered MTN program. As in the case of Rule 144A offerings, dealers will want to display information about the program on their private or common carrier screen-based information networks. If this is the case, steps must be taken to avoid a "general solicitation" (e.g., by making access dependent on a password) or an "offer" to non-QIBs.

- *Stand-Alone Institutional Placements*

Private placements with insurance companies and other institutional investors became the preferred method of financing in the years immediately following the adoption of the 1933 Act.[91] At that time, many companies were reluctant to register securities under the 1933 Act for fear of the liabilities that might be incurred under Section 11. They therefore resorted to transactions qualifying for the private offering exemption, and an institutional private placement market developed.

---

91. C. Rodgers, *Purchase by Life Insurance Companies of Securities Privately Offered,* 52 Harv. L. Rev. 773 (1939).

Traditional private placements declined in relative importance during the 1980s and 1990s for several reasons:

- In a Rule 415 environment, the registration of debt securities became a relatively easy procedure.
- Even where a registered public offering was not possible (e.g., because speed is particularly important or where SEC accounting requirements could not be immediately complied with), many issuers had the option of an offshore offering pursuant to Regulation S or an "underwritten" Rule 144A placement.
- There was increasing competition from loan syndication groups, which are housed not only at commercial banks but also at the major investment banking firms.
- Many issuers and investors became impatient with the delay, expense and inconvenience associated with negotiating the detailed terms and covenants that traditionally characterize this market.

Recently, the traditional private placement has enjoyed something of a renaissance. Issuers still value the flexibility and confidentiality that have traditionally characterized these transactions, as well as investors' willingness to entertain unrated "story" issuers (a sector of the market that does not generally appeal to the public markets). European issuers have recently become important issuers in this market as their banks have reduced their investment-grade fixed-rate lending.[92]

One additional reason for the revival of interest is very likely the buy side's success in overcoming the "delay, expense and inconvenience" problem mentioned above. In an effort to make the private placement process more efficient and attractive, a group of institutional investors and investment banks formed in 1993 the Private Placement Enhancement Project. The project's working group published in 1994 two model forms of note

---

92. *See* Alexander Georgieff, *Closing the Funding Gap* 16–20 (Deutsche Bank Global Corporation Finance 2003).

purchase agreement and in 1996 a *Financial Covenants Reference Manual.*

In 1996 the Council's Transaction Process Management Committee also published its *Private Placement Process Enhancements,* which includes recommendations for facilitating the documentation process. It also published in 1996 a *Guide to Amendments* brochure that sets forth recommended procedures and enhancements for the amendment process. The available documents also include term sheet checklists and legal due diligence guidelines.[93]

• • *Procedures.* An issuer that decides to make a private placement generally will work with an investment banker. After reviewing market conditions, the issuer and the investment banker's private placement department will agree on a tentative term sheet that will include the financial covenants that the purchasers are likely to require. The banker will contact insurance companies, public and private pension funds and other institutions in an effort to place the issue. Investors' counsel will be pre-selected from among a small group of law firms that specialize in acting in this capacity and that are known to be acceptable to the major investing institutions. A note purchase agreement will be drafted on the basis of the term sheet and one of the model forms mentioned above and circulated, with a copy marked to show changes from the model form, to the prospective investors.

A private placement memorandum will be prepared by the issuer with the assistance of the investment banker. If the issuer is an SEC-reporting company, the memorandum will consist of a term sheet and the issuer's 1934 Act reports. In the case of a privately held company, the memorandum may have to be drafted from scratch.

Depending on the creditworthiness of the issuer, it may be required to negotiate and agree to various financial covenants. Limitations may be placed on the amount of additional debt that it may incur, and the incurrence of funded debt on a subsidiary

---

93. All of these documents may be found on the website of the American College of Investment Counsel at www.aciclaw.org/forms_guides/default.asp.

level may be prohibited entirely. There may be limitations on the incurrence of liens and the disposition of assets. The payment of dividends may be limited to earnings subsequent to the date of the transaction plus a cushion in an amount to be negotiated. There may be limitations on the type of investments that the issuer may make.

The model note purchase agreement contains detailed representations by the issuer as well as affirmative covenants (e.g., to maintain the issuer's existence, to maintain its properties, to keep proper books and records and to comply with applicable laws). The issuer may be required to agree to deliver periodic financial information to the purchasers so long as the securities are outstanding. Private placements of this type were traditionally the subject of intense negotiation between counsel for the purchasers and counsel for the issuer, but the introduction of the model forms has ameliorated the process considerably.

A draft of the documents will be delivered to each of the prospective purchasers and in all likelihood will be reviewed by a member of the legal department of each. If there are 50 purchasers, comments on the documents can be expected from 50 different lawyers or lending officers. The job of collecting comments falls on special counsel for the purchasers. Prior to the introduction of the model forms, it was (and can still be) a time-consuming task. When all comments are received, there may be a further round of negotiations. A separate purchase agreement will be entered into with each purchaser, but their terms will be identical.

Since the investors are responsible for doing their own due diligence, the investment banker arranging the transaction will generally not be represented by counsel, and there will be no disclosure opinion from issuer's counsel.

• • *Investment Representations.* In an institutional private placement, it has been customary for the loan agreement to contain a representation by the purchaser that it is purchasing the securities for investment and not with a view to distribution but subject to the proviso that the disposition of its property shall at all times be within its control. More modern agreements, including the model forms, omit the reference to "investment" but also call for the purchasers to acknowledge that the securities may not be resold without an available exemption under the 1933 Act.

The reference to "control" of the purchasers' "property" had its origin in language that once appeared in Section 78 of the New York Insurance Law.[94] Institutional investors will resist any suggestion that a legend be placed on the notes that they purchase. Their investment portfolios may be subject to review by state regulatory authorities, and legends may be questioned by the state examiners. When Rule 146 required legends, some lawyers made efforts to overcome this resistance. But since the adoption of Regulation D, where a legend is only one means of demonstrating that a purchaser is not an underwriter, legends are generally thought to be unnecessary in an institutional placement of debt securities.

• • *Availability of Section 4(2) Exemption.* An institutional private placement will satisfy the requirements of Section 4(2) since the issuer will be selling securities directly to the investors or through a financial intermediary acting as agent. It generally will be able to satisfy the requirements of Regulation D as well. Each purchaser is a sophisticated investor. It has the bargaining power to fend for itself. Like the mutual funds in *Value Line Fund, Inc. v. Marcus,*[95] they are "sophisticated, knowledgeable, experienced institutional investors with great resources, and plainly [are] 'able to fend for themselves.' " The notes will be placed through direct negotiation, and there will be no general solicitation or general advertising. Although, as will be seen, a secondary market exists in privately placed debt securities, institutions do not generally purchase debt securities with a view to resale. Although counsel generally will obtain a representation

---

94. Prior to its amendment in 1984, Section 78 provided that an insurer could not enter into "any agreement to withhold from sale any of its property" and that "[t]he disposition of its property shall be at all times within the control of its board of directors, in accordance with its charter and by-laws." With the amendment of Section 78 (now recodified as Section 1411), the proviso is no longer necessary, if indeed it was ever required.

95. [1964–1966 Transfer Binder] Fed. Sec. L. Rep. (CCH) ¶91,523 at 94,970 (S.D.N.Y. 1965).

from the investment banker that placed the issue with respect to the number of offerees, numbers are not a significant factor in the case of an institutional placement. The opinion rendered at the closing with respect to the availability of the Section 4(2) exemption is a relatively easy opinion for counsel to give. The SEC has never challenged an issuer's reliance on Section 4(2) in the case of a private placement with insurance companies and other institutional investors, and the authors are not aware that the exempt status of such a transaction has ever been the subject of litigation under the 1933 Act.

• • *Secondary Private Placements.* A large and active secondary market exists for privately placed debt securities, whether issued in traditional stand-alone institutional placements or in Regulation D transactions. If an institution that has purchased debt securities in a private placement decides that it would like to sell all or part of its position, it will be relatively easy for it to find one or more other institutional investors to take over its position at a price related to the then current market price for similar debt securities. The "secondary private placement" is likely to be made through a securities dealer, frequently the firm that arranged the initial private placement, which is therefore familiar with its terms. If the dealer is not familiar with the transaction, it will have to obtain and review the relevant documentation in order to be sure of what it is buying (and what it will reoffer to its customers).

In reselling the securities to the dealer, the institution will rely on the exemption provided by Section 4(1) of the 1933 Act, which applies to "transactions by any person other than an issuer, underwriter or dealer." The seller is not an underwriter because the original transaction did not involve a distribution; in addition, the seller will represent to the dealer that it has not offered the securities for resale except to the dealer and, if applicable, a specified number of other institutions (i.e., it has not engaged in any "general solicitation"). The dealer will also obtain representations from the purchasing institution to the effect that it will not resell except in reliance on an exemption under the 1933 Act. The dealer itself will not engage in any general solicitation, and on this foundation it will rest its claim to the dealer's exemption provided by Section 4(3). Since the purchaser will be an institution that could have participated in the original private placement, the issuer's original Section 4(2) exemption remains intact when the transaction is viewed as a whole in a manner consistent with the *Crowell-Collier* analysis discussed earlier in this chapter.

Because the selling institution in a secondary private placement is relying on Section 4(1) by analogy to principles underlying Section 4(2), this type of transaction is sometimes referred to as a "Section 4(1-1/2)" transaction.[96] The use of the term "Section 4(1-1/2)" confuses the issue. The institutional seller has a clear Section 4(1) exemption, the intermediary has a Section 4(3) exemption, and the issuer retains its Section 4(2) exemption. There is no need to resort to "half measures" in making the 1933 Act analysis.

Even if the original transaction did not involve reliance on Rule 144A, it may be that the institutional seller and the intermediary dealer may be able to rely on Rule 144A as a basis for their respective sales if the requirements of that rule—particularly that the dealer and the new purchasers be QIBs—are met.

- *Regulation D Placements with Individual Investors*

Where the market for securities being sold in reliance on Regulation D is comprised of individuals rather than institutions, more elaborate procedures are required. For the most part, this has been the market for limited partnership offerings such as real estate syndicates, oil and gas drilling programs, research and development partnerships, and offerings involving investments in such assets as race horses and precious coins. At one time, most of these offerings provided some tax benefits. High net worth

---

96. C. W. Schneider, *Section 4(1-1/2)—Private Resales of Restricted or Control Securities*, Ohio St. L.J. 501 (1988); Christopher D. Olander & Margaret Jacks, *The Section 4(1-1/2) Exemption—Reading Between the Lines of the Securities Act of 1933*, 15 Sec. Reg. L.J. 339 (1988); ABA Committee Report, *The Section "4(1-1/2)" Phenomenon: Private Resales of "Restricted" Securities*, 34 Bus. Law. 1961 (1979).

individuals sought to shelter their income from taxation by investing in these programs. Even after tax reform eliminated most of the tax benefits, such individuals continued to invest in structured private placements promising potential economic benefits. More recently, hedge funds and venture capital and private equity investments have been directed at individual investors.

• • *Potential Ineligibility of Certain Reporting Companies.* A reporting company will most frequently resort to a private placement, whether under Rule 144A or Regulation D, if it is unable or unwilling to make a registered public offering. This will most often be the case if the issuer has no shelf registration statement on file (or has insufficient capacity to meet its needs), and it is unwilling to risk the loss of a market opportunity because of the unpredictable delays associated with the filing of a new registration statement. This can also be the case if the issuer has made a recent acquisition (or an acquisition is "probable"), and it is unable to file with the SEC the financial statements required by Regulation S-X and Item 9.01 of Form 8-K.

According to the instructions to Item 9.01 of Form 8-K, new registration statements and post-effective amendments will not be declared effective during the period in which a reporting issuer has not filed the required financial statements. In addition, "offerings should not be made pursuant to effective registration statements or pursuant to Rules 505 and 506 of Regulation D where any purchasers are not accredited investors" (with certain exceptions for non-financing transactions). Accordingly, takedowns from effective shelf registrations and Rule 505 and 506 offerings to non-accredited investors may not be possible during this period.

• • *General Solicitation and Prior Relationships.* As discussed above under "Regulation D—General Solicitation or Advertising," the existence of a preexisting relationship with prospective individual investors is not the only means by which one can demonstrate the absence of a general solicitation. On the other hand, it is a pretty reliable means of doing so.

Understandably, when it comes to individual investors, the SEC and its staff have underscored the existence and substance

PRIVATE PLACEMENTS   539

of preexisting relationships between the issuer, or the placement agent, and the persons being solicited.[97] In the pre-Internet days, the staff had taken the position that efforts by a broker-dealer to identify prospective offerees by arranging for third-party intermediaries to provide the names of persons believed to be suitable offerees would constitute a general solicitation.[98] Subsequently, however, the staff agreed that an unsolicited recommendation by a qualified offeree that an offer be made to another previously unidentified person and the subsequent solicitation of that person did not violate Rule 146; nor did receiving recommendations from intermediaries of prospective offerees for subsequent offerings not in progress or contemplated.[99]

A number of broker-dealers have sought the staff's blessing for programs designed to enable their registered representatives to identify and solicit prospective offerees in a manner consistent with the staff's views on prior relationships. A program devised by Bateman Eichler contemplated the mailing of an introductory letter and a questionnaire to no more than 50 professionals such as lawyers, accountants and corporate executives. If questionnaires were returned, the registered representatives would follow up to obtain additional financial and personal data. These people then would be considered eligible offerees in private placements of the type in which the person had indicated an interest and that were considered to be suitable for him. It was stipulated that no offering materials would be sent to a

---

97. *Kenman Corp.*, SEC Release No. 34-21962 (April 19, 1985) (administrative proceeding against a broker-dealer that made a promotional mailing in connection with two limited partnership offerings to a list of persons who had invested in prior offerings by the broker-dealer, a list of executive officers of fifty Fortune 500 companies, a list of physicians in California, and a list of presidents of certain listed companies); SEC No-action Letter, *Mineral Lands Research & Marketing Corporation* (December 4, 1985); SEC No-action Letter, *Woodtrails-Seattle, Ltd.* (August 9, 1982). See the SEC Staff Report, *Implications of the Growth of Hedge Funds* 16–17 (September 2003). The report is available on the SEC website at www.sec.gov/news/studies/hedgefunds0903.pdf.

98. SEC No-action Letter, *Arthur M. Borden* (September 15, 1977).

99. SEC No-action Letter, *Arthur M. Borden* (October 6, 1978).

prospective offeree for at least 45 days after the original mailing to him. The staff responded that the program itself did not constitute an offer to sell securities and that subsequent offers to persons identified through the program would not be viewed as a general solicitation "provided a substantive relationship has been established with the offeree between the time of the initial solicitation and the later offer." The staff said that such a relationship could be established if the information furnished to Bateman Eichler provided it with "sufficient information to evaluate the prospective offeree's sophistication and financial circumstances."[100]

On the same day, the staff responded to a request by E.F. Hutton & Company for confirmation that its procedures for the private placement of direct participation programs did not constitute a general solicitation.[101] The staff concluded that substantive relationships would be considered to have been created between Hutton and persons who within the preceding three years had invested in a public or private program sponsored by Hutton and for whom Hutton had on file a current completed suitability questionnaire and a new account form. It also agreed that substantive relationships could be established through responses to Hutton's suitability questionnaire if the response provided "sufficient information to evaluate the prospective offerees' sophistication and financial circumstances." In this case, the staff found Hutton's forms to be lacking. It went on to stress that the relationship must be established prior to the time that the broker-dealer begins participating in the particular Regulation D offering.

The staff has been reluctant to pass on the sufficiency of specific questionnaires submitted to it for approval. It has been willing to go no further than to say that "a satisfactory response by a prospective offeree to a questionnaire that provides a broker-dealer with sufficient information to evaluate the respondent's sophistication and financial situation will establish a substantive relationship."[102]

---

100. SEC No-action Letter, *Bateman Eichler, Hill Richards, Inc.* (December 3, 1985).
101. SEC No-action Letter, *E.F. Hutton & Co.* (December 3, 1985).
102. SEC No-action Letter, *H.B. Shaine & Co., Inc.* (May 1, 1987).

In 1989, the SEC conceded that "if an offering is structured so that only persons with whom the issuer and its agents have had a prior relationship are solicited, the fact that one potential investor with whom there is no such prior relationship is called may not necessarily result in a general solicitation." In the same release, however, the SEC stated that "[t]he staff has never stated, and it is not the case, that prior relationship is the only way to show the absence of a general solicitation."[103]

With the arrival of the Internet, broker-dealers and others have sought to use websites to qualify individual and institutional investors for participation in Regulation D offerings. The use of websites for this purpose has highlighted the question whether any substantial amount of time must elapse between identification of an eligible investor and the making of a solicitation. See the discussion above under "Regulation D–General Solicitation or Advertising."

• • *Procedures and Controls.* Private placements to high net worth individuals inevitably require the participation of the sales representatives who deal with these accounts on a daily basis. Securities firms commonly adopt elaborate procedures to ensure that the offering complies with Regulation D and other relevant requirements (e.g., Sections 3(c)(1) or 3(c)(7) under the 1940 Act and Rule 4.7 under the Commodity Exchange Act) and that the offered security is suitable for the investor.

It may be instructive to review the procedures and controls adopted by a major securities firm for Regulation D offerings of hedge fund securities to sophisticated high net worth individuals and smaller institutions. Of course, to the extent that the issuers rely on the Section 3(c)(7) exemption from the 1940 Act, then the standard for purchasers in these offerings is not the "accredited investor" standard under Regulation D but the higher "qualified purchaser" standard.

The firm's procedures emphasize the importance of avoiding a "general solicitation" in the offering of the securities. They also warn against "cold calls" or other "prospecting," the use of

---

103. SEC Release No. 33-6825 (March 14, 1989) (text at and in note 12).

financial intermediaries (except authorized purchaser representatives for approved offerees), the use of unauthorized "for internal use" materials or promotional materials, advertising, discussions at conferences or seminars, press interviews and unauthorized Internet postings. They also emphasize the importance of maintaining strict control over offering procedures.

The procedures describe four basic stages of an offering: (1) designation of qualified sales representatives, (2) designation of qualified offerees, (3) solicitation of qualified offerees and (4) processing of subscription agreements. Each stage of the offering is under the supervision of a designated staff unit. In addition, the firm's internal legal department is consulted on questions that arise during the offering. The staff unit maintains logs that record information relevant to each of the three stages.

• • • *Designation of Qualified Sales Representatives.* Sales representatives interested in participating in private offers must obtain permission to do so from their branch managers, who may act in consultation with more senior officers. Permission is granted, that is, the representative becomes "qualified," on the basis of the representative's prior experience and general familiarity with similar investments and other relevant factors.

Qualified sales representatives may receive a copy of the private placement memorandum, the subscription agreement and any other relevant documents on an "for information only" basis. The documents are identified by the name of the qualified sales representative and are numbered. A staff department maintains a log of all documents distributed to qualified sales representatives.

• • • *Designation of Qualified Offerees.* Interests may be offered only to existing customers who have been pre-qualified. If a qualified sales representative has a customer who has been a client of the firm for at least six months[104] and who meets the applicable suitability standards, the qualified sales representative completes an offeree qualification form as prescribed by the

---

104. Persons who have been clients for less than six months may be eligible to be qualified after consultation with the branch manager and internal counsel.

procedures. The form covers, among other things, the customer's financial resources, knowledge and sophistication. The offeree qualification forms are reviewed by designated staff personnel who determine whether the customers are designated as qualified offerees.

• • • *Solicitation of Qualified Offerees.* Qualified sales representatives may communicate orally with qualified offerees to determine whether they are likely to be interested in investing in the offering. If so, the qualified sales representative forwards to the qualified offeree a numbered copy of the private placement memorandum and an execution copy of the subscription agreement. The private placement memorandum and subscription agreement are valid only for the designated qualified offeree, and these and other documents are prohibited from being copied or reproduced in any manner. A copy of these and other documents may be provided to the qualified offeree's representative on request but only under the same conditions as such documents are made available to qualified sales representatives.

• • • *Processing of Subscription Agreements.* Designated staff personnel review subscription agreements for proper completion and execution, the consistency of the information therein with that provided on the offeree qualification form and other relevant requirements. The documents may then be forwarded to a separate staff function for final approval.

Related Private Placements and Public Offerings

We discussed above the integration problem in the context of two or more private offerings, where the object of analysis is to determine whether the offerings should be viewed as a single offering. The integration problem can also arise in the context of a private offering and a related registered public offering. The consequences of integration in this context are, of course, much more severe. Since it is unlikely that a private offering can survive being integrated with a public offering, the result may be that the private offering has lost its exemption. In addition, making private offers before the filing of a registration statement may be viewed as "gun-jumping."

With some exceptions, it has become more difficult to advise clients on when and how a private offering's exemption might be endangered because of a contemporaneous SEC-filed registration statement. There are two principal reasons for this development. First, as the discussion above should demonstrate, the traditional distinctions between the public and private markets are blurring. Investment bankers may act as agent today in selling a tranche of *registered* securities "off the shelf" to a single buyer, while tomorrow they may act as principal in making a private placement of *restricted* securities to a potentially indefinite number of investors. In addition, investors who used to be happy with "demand" or "piggyback" registration rights for their restricted securities are more often insisting on a currently effective resale registration statement or a covenant to file one within a specified period of time. Second, the SEC staff has abandoned to some degree its former flexibility and pragmatism in this area—an ability, as Professor Loss has observed, "to separate the big from the small potatoes"[105]—in an apparent effort to prevent "end runs" around the 1933 Act's liability provisions.

There are several frequently occurring situations in which it is necessary to decide whether a private offering's exemption is endangered by a related registered public offering. These include (1) an unsuccessful attempt at a private offering followed by a registered public offering, (2) an unsuccessful registered public offering followed by a private offering, (3) a private offering with immediate or delayed registration of the purchased securities for resale, (4) a private offering followed by the issuer's exchange offer of registered securities for the restricted securities and (5) a private placement accompanied or quickly followed by the purchasers' short sales of a related security for hedging purposes.

- *Private Offering Followed by Public Filing*

In a not infrequent situation, an issuer and its investment banker will commence work on a private offering and conclude,

---

105. L. Loss & J. Seligman, 2 *Securities Regulation* 1138.51 (rev. 3d ed. 1999).

after unsuccessful solicitation efforts, that the transaction can only be effected by means of a registered public offering. An SEC rule applicable to this situation has been around since 1935. Rule 152 provides:

> The phrase "transactions by an issuer not involving any public offering" in Section 4(2) shall be deemed to apply to transactions not involving any public offering at the time of said transactions although subsequently thereto the issuer decides to make a public offering and/or files a registration statement.

This rule was originally adopted to allow "those who have contemplated or begun to undertake a private offering to register the securities without incurring any risk of liability as a consequence of having first contemplated or begun to undertake a private offering."[106]

While the rule and its explanation appear simple enough on the surface, the SEC staff had taken the position that the rule does not apply where the private offering and the public offering are in effect the "same" transaction. According to the staff view, this would constitute "gun-jumping" in violation of Section 5.

There are two ways of making sure, of course, that a registered offering is not the "same" offering as a previous private offering. One way is to abandon the private offering, and the other is to complete it.

While the staff would not dispute that it is possible to abandon a private offering and start up a *new* registered offering, it has offered little guidance on what facts and circumstances would support this distinction. For example, how much time must elapse between the "abandonment" of the private offering and the filing of a registration statement? Must the issuer refuse to return the calls of the investors who indicated interest in participating in the transaction?

The SEC answered some of these questions in early 2001 when it adopted a new safe harbor.[107] Rule 155(b) provides that

---

106. SEC Release No. 33-305 (March 2, 1935).
107. SEC Release No. 33-7943 (January 26, 2001).

the abandoned private offering will not be considered part of an offering for which the issuer subsequently files a registration statement if

- the transactions are not part of a plan or scheme to evade the registration requirements of the 1933 Act;
- no securities were sold in the abandoned private offering;
- the issuer and any person acting on its behalf terminate all private offering activity before the registration statement is filed;
- the preliminary and final prospectus in the registered offering disclose information about the abandoned private offering, including its size and nature, the date on which it was abandoned, that any offers were rejected or otherwise not accepted and that the prospectus used in the registered offering supersedes any offering materials used in the private offering; and
- the issuer does not file the registration statement until 30 days after termination of all private offering activity (except activity that involved persons who were or who the issuer reasonably believes to have been accredited investors or certain sophisticated investors).

In the adopting release for Rule 155(b), the SEC described these conditions as intended to ensure that "there is a clean break between the private and registered offerings and that persons who were offered securities in the abandoned private offering understand this break as they consider an investment in the registered offering." It also cautioned that it would direct the staff to monitor the use of Rule 155(b) in order to prevent its abuse and that such monitoring might include requests for supplemental information regarding the termination of all offering activity in the private offering.

Rule 155(b) does not address the other way of ensuring that the registration statement represents a "new" offering, namely, to complete the private offering. But what is "completion"?

The SEC staff concurs that it is possible to plan a transaction from the beginning on the basis that investors will agree to purchase securities in a private offering on the condition that the issuer will file and cause to become effective a registration statement covering their resales (a so-called "PIPE" or "private investment, public equity" transaction). The staff will insist, however, that the purchasers be irrevocably bound to purchase the securities subject only to the filing or effectiveness of the resale registration statement or other conditions outside their control and that the purchase price be established at the time of the private placement.[108]

Suppose, however, that it has become clear to the issuer that the transaction must be registered but the issuer is unable—perhaps because of a shortage of time—to negotiate definitive purchase agreements before filing a registration statement. In the *Black Box* letter,[109] the SEC staff "for policy reasons" acquiesced in a financially troubled issuer's filing a registration statement before reaching definitive agreements with not more than 35 QIBs and seven other institutional investors. In a subsequent letter,[110] the staff explained *Black Box* as having been based not on the financial condition of the issuer but rather on "the nature and number of the offerees." It also stated that the *Black Box* "policy position" was "narrowly construed by the staff" and limited to situations where the unregistered offering was made only to QIBs and "no more than two or three large institutional accredited investors."[111]

What happens if the issuer is not willing to abandon its prospective investors, if it is not able to negotiate definitive agreements and if the investors are not of the "super-heavyweight" character involved in *Black Box*? It may be a sufficient indication of a "new" offering if the issuer genuinely intended to proceed with

---

108. SEC Division of Corporation Finance, *Manual of Publicly Available Telephone Interpretations*, Interpretation No. 51 at 11 (July 1997).

109. SEC No-action Letter, *Black Box Incorporated* (June 26, 1990).

110. SEC No-action Letter, *Squadron Ellenhoff* (February 28, 1992).

111. In the adopting release for Rule 155, the SEC referred again to *Black Box* as articulating a "policy position" and one that was unaffected by the new Rule 155. SEC Release No. 33-7943 (January 26, 2001), at n.22.

a private offering and only subsequently decided that it was necessary to turn to the public alternative. There is support in *Black Box* for this proposition, but the staff is reluctant for obvious reasons (relating to the SEC's Division of Enforcement not being fond of having to prove an issuer's state of mind) to confirm it.

What does one do, for example, in the situation where an issuer decides in effect to "test the waters" with investors under cover of a purported private placement, but where the real purpose is to lay the groundwork for a registered public offering? Notwithstanding that such offers might constitute "gun-jumping" if a registration statement covering the "same" offer is subsequently filed, the SEC has grudgingly admitted that such "test the waters" activity may be consistent with investor protection. Accordingly, it proposed in June 1995[112] the adoption of a rule that would expressly permit such activity by non-reporting companies. Solicitation activity would have to terminate on the filing of a registration statement, and sales of securities could not commence until 20 days after such termination. The release proposing the rule noted difficulties that might arise if the issuer decided to abandon a public offering in favor of a private offering where its "test the waters" activity had amounted to a general solicitation; in that event, the issuer might have to wait six months or restructure its offering to avoid "integration." That the rule has not been adopted is an indication of the SEC's caution in this area.

Where an issuer planned a registered public offering within four months after a private placement, the staff took a no-action position under Rule 152.[113] The staff has reaffirmed this position even where the issuer contemplated the subsequent public offering at the time of the private placement.[114]

---

112. SEC Release No. 33-7188 (June 27, 1995). Proposed new Rule 135d was based on a 1992 SEC initiative applicable to small offerings under Regulation A.

113. SEC No-action Letter, *Verticom, Inc.* (February 12, 1986).

114. See SEC No-action Letter, *Vintage Group*, Inc. (May 11, 1988); SEC No-action Letter, *Immune Response Corp.* (November 2, 1987); SEC No-action Letter, *Vulture Petroleum Corp.* (February 2, 1987); SEC No-action Letter, *BBI Associates* (December 29, 1986).

Of course, even where Rule 152 does not apply, the issuer may be able to fall back on the five-part "facts and circumstances" test (discussed above under "Regulation D—Integration") to support a conclusion that the private offering and the public offering are not the same transaction. Or the issuer can wait six months before filing the registration statement, since the SEC regards the six-month safe harbor in Rule 502(a) as immunizing a completed private placement from infection by the filing of a subsequent registration statement.[115]

- *Public Filing Followed by Private Offering*

For many years the SEC staff has taken the position that "[t]he filing of a registration statement for a specific securities offering (as contrasted with a generic shelf registration) constitutes a general solicitation for that securities offering, thus rendering Section 4(2) unavailable for the same offering."[116] Taken literally, the staff position would doom any attempt to withdraw a registration statement and proceed with a private offering of the same securities. Particularly for smaller companies, the staff position can amount to playing financial Russian Roulette: once it files its registration statement, it assumes the risk that if the public market becomes unavailable to it because of market conditions or disclosure problems, then it will not have the private markets available either (subject possibly to the *Black Box* "super-heavyweight" exception discussed above).

In an effort to address this problem in appropriate cases, the SEC adopted in early 2001 Rule 155(c).[117] The rule provides that an offering for which the issuer filed a registration statement will not be considered part of a subsequent private offering if

- the transactions are not part of a plan or scheme to evade the registration requirements of the 1933 Act;

---

115. *See* SEC Release No. 33-7606A (November 13, 1998) (Aircraft Carrier Release), text at n.482.

116. E.g., SEC Division of Corporation Finance, *Current Issues and Rulemaking Projects* 55 (July 1997).

117. SEC Release No. 33-7943 (January 26, 2001).

- no securities were sold in the registered offering;[118]
- the issuer applies to the SEC under Rule 477(c) for withdrawal of the registration statement, stating that it may undertake a subsequent private offering in reliance on Rule 155(c) (but "without discussing any terms of the private offering");
- the private offering is not begun until 30 days after the effective date of the withdrawal;
- the issuer notifies each offeree in the private offering that the offering is unregistered, that the securities will be restricted securities, that the liabilities imposed by Section 11 will not apply and that the registration statement for the abandoned public offering was withdrawn as of a specified date; and
- any disclosure document in the private offering discloses any material changes in the issuer's business or financial condition that occurred after the filing of the registration statement.

In the adopting release for Rule 155(c), the SEC explained these conditions as designed to ensure that the private offering is "separate and distinct" from the registered offering and that offerees in the private offering are aware that they will not be entitled to the "legal benefits and protections" of a registered offering. It also cautioned issuers against attempting to rely on the safe harbor by using a registered offering to generate publicity for the purpose of soliciting purchasers for the private offering. Such an effort would be considered a plan or scheme to avoid the registration requirements of the 1933 Act and would make the safe harbor unavailable.

The condition in Rule 155(c) that the private placement memorandum disclose any material changes is explained in the adopting release as "reduc[ing] concerns that private offerees will be influenced by outdated disclosure in the prospectus filed as part of the registration statement." The condition is not as

---

118. The adopting release makes clear that this includes the receipt of any funds, whether or not in escrow.

innocuous as it appears. It may seem obvious that the private placement memorandum will be updated to reflect the issuer's current condition, but a failure to do so may have consequences beyond the risk of giving purchasers a right to sue under Rule 10b-5. Since the availability of Rule 155(c) purports to depend on accurate current disclosure, a failure to comply with this condition may have been intended by the SEC as giving disappointed purchasers the additional right to rescind their purchases under Section 12(a)(1) of the 1933 Act.

Rule 155(c) does not cure all of the problems raised by the SEC staff position that the filing of a registration statement constitutes an "offer to the world." In the authors' view, the staff position elevates form over substance. Even though the public has constructive access to the 1933 Act filing by means of EDGAR and SEC copying facilities, the issuer should still be able to take into account such factors as the reason for the abandonment of the public offering, whether the registration statement is still on file, and—most important—whether the filing was a "quiet" filing, where no preliminary prospectuses were circulated and where no marketing efforts took place. In this last respect, the staff position is particularly unfair when one considers that U.S. IPO candidates are not permitted to make "confidential" filings of the kind available to every foreign issuer and to some U.S. issuers engaged in acquisitions.

Apart from Rule 155(c), there are several alternatives available to an issuer that finds itself in the position of having filed, but being unable to proceed with, a public offering. First, the issuer can try to structure a private offering that differs sufficiently from the offering contemplated by the registration statement to support advice from counsel that it is prudent to proceed with the private offering. Second, the issuer can wait for six months by analogy to Regulation D. Third, if the reason for the failure to proceed with the public offering is related to market conditions rather than SEC comments on the registration statement, the issuer can elect to proceed with a "private" offering on a registered basis. Under current staff positions,[119] even a small group of individual

---

119. *See, e.g.*, SEC No-action Letter, *American Council of Life Insurance* (June 10, 1983).

or institutional purchasers will not be deemed presumptive underwriters if and when they attempt to resell.

• *Private Offering with Concurrent or Future Registration*

It is commonplace today for purchasers of privately placed securities to bargain for the ability to make prompt resales of their securities pursuant to an effective registration statement. There are two conceptual problems under the 1933 Act in connection with the registration of the privately placed securities. The first is that there may be an integration problem if the private offering is not "complete" prior to the filing of the registration statement. Under the staff positions discussed above, however, integration will not be a problem—even where the private placement is not closed prior to the filing of the registration statement—so long as the only conditions to the investors' commitments are ones that are beyond their control.[120]

What conditions are beyond the investors' control? In the analogous situation of private "equity lines," the staff has stated that a "due diligence out" is sufficiently within the investors' control as to prevent the private placement from being regarded as "complete." On the other hand, it has no objection to "bring downs" of customary representations and warranties or to conditions relating to the absence of any material adverse changes affecting the issuer.

The second conceptual problem relates to the capacity in which the registered securities are to be sold. The staff takes the position that if offers are made and commitments obtained in reliance on the private placement exemption prior to the filing of the registration statement, then the registration statement should cover resales by the purchasers and not the initial issuance of securities to the purchasers. The significance of this distinction is that the securities are "restricted securities" in the hands of the purchasers and that the broker-dealers through whom they resell pursuant to the registration statement may therefore be acting as underwriters with corresponding Section 11 liabilities.

Of course, where the private placement investors are willing to close prior to the filing or effectiveness of a registration

---

120. SEC Division of Corporation Finance, *Current Issues and Rulemaking Projects* (March 31, 2001 update), at 11–12.

statement, they may bargain for terms that obligate the issuer promptly to file and obtain the effectiveness of a registration statement. The terms may also create an inducement for the issuer to follow through on this commitment, for example, additional shares or an increased interest rate if the registration statement is not filed or does not become effective within a stated period of time.

- *Registration Rights Agreement*

Investors have traditionally bargained for an agreement by the issuer to register the new securities as promptly as practicable or on a "demand" or "piggyback" basis. Under the typical registration rights agreement, the holders of a specified amount of the securities may demand registration at the company's expense ("demand" rights). There may be a cutoff period when the registration rights expire. In some cases, registration rights may be exercised only once, and in other cases, the holders will be entitled to demand registration on more than one occasion. The purchasers of the securities also may be granted incidental or "piggyback" registration rights, so that if the issuer files a registration statement covering securities of the same class, the holders will be entitled to include their shares in the registration statement. The agreement may require them to sell in the offering through the same underwriters that the issuer is using in order to ensure an orderly distribution. They may be required to refrain from making any sales until a specified period of time after the completion of the distribution. The issuer may agree to indemnify any brokers or dealers ("underwriters") through whom the holders may resell their securities. The terms of any registration rights agreement will vary from transaction to transaction.[121]

The registration statement filed by the issuer will state that the selling securityholders may sell from time to time on terms to be determined at the time of sale and that the selling securityholders and any broker-dealers that participate with them in the distribution of the securities may be deemed to be

---

121. For a thorough discussion, *see* Carl W. Schneider, *Registration Rights Agreements—Variables and Practical Considerations*, The Corporate Counsel (March–April 1996).

underwriters within the meaning of the 1933 Act. The holders of the securities at the time the registration statement becomes effective must be named in the prospectus. Exceptions to this requirement, and the subsequent addition and substitution of sellers, are discussed in Chapter 8.

One of the disadvantages of registration rights for an issuer is that the registration statement will have to be "evergreen" until the holders have completed their sales, in other words, the prospectus will have to be updated and the registration statement possibly amended in order to reflect new developments. For an issuer eligible to use Form S-3, of course, the burden will be considerably less.

Purchasers of privately placed warrants or convertible securities also commonly bargain for registration rights for the common stock underlying the warrants or convertible securities. Their expectation is that they will hold the warrants or convertible securities until it appears advantageous to exercise or convert and that they will then receive registered common stock that they may freely resell into the public market. The SEC staff does not appear to agree. The staff position is that an investor must receive *restricted* common stock on exercise or conversion of a restricted security.

The fact that the common stock is restricted does not necessarily mean that it is not eligible for public sale. In the case of a convertible security, the exchange is exempt under Section 3(a)(9) of the 1933 Act. It is therefore not necessary to repeat the formalities of the original private placement. In addition, because the holding period for the convertible security is "tacked" to the holding period of the common stock, the common stock will be eligible for sale under Rule 144(k) if the combined holding period is two years or more. The same result applies in the case of warrants that are "net settled," i.e., where common stock is issued without the payment of cash in an amount equal to the "in the money" value of the warrants. Where warrants are exercised for cash, however, a new private placement exemption must be established to support the issuance of the common stock. This may not be easy where the holders of the warrants are no longer accredited investors or otherwise do not measure up to private placement requirements. In addition, cash exercise starts a new Rule 144(d) holding period for the common stock.

Of course, the issuer may register the common stock for resale by the exercising or converting holder. The holder is no worse off as a result, but the issuer must maintain an "evergreen" registration statement as described above.

- *Private Offering Followed by "Exxon Capital" or "A/B" Exchange Offer*

The registration-for-resale procedure described above offers potential liquidity to the holder of privately placed securities, but it has the disadvantage that the securities are still "restricted securities" in the hands of the investor until they are actually sold pursuant to the registration statement. This has the effect of eliminating potential institutional investors who for legal or policy reasons may be unable to purchase restricted securities even with registration rights. On the other hand, a procedure that enabled the investors to *exchange* the restricted securities for registered securities would promote a broader institutional market and increase liquidity for the securities, thus resulting in cost savings to the issuer. Another advantage for the issuer would be that it would not have to maintain an "evergreen" shelf registration statement for the period of time it took for the investors to sell their securities.

In fact, the SEC staff has published several interpretive letters[122] that permit an issuer and the purchasers of its privately placed securities[123] to agree that the issuer will effect a post-closing exchange offer for the privately placed securities. These exchange offers have become known as "Exxon Capital" exchange offers after the first letter approving their use. More generically, they are also referred to as "A/B" exchange offers.

---

122. The original letter was *Exxon Capital Holdings Corp.* (May 13, 1988). Other significant letters include *Brown & Wood LLP* (February 7, 1997); *Grupo Financiero InverMexico, S.A.* (April 4, 1995); *K-III Communication Corp.* (May 14, 1993); *Corimon C.A. S.A.C.A.* (March 22, 1993); *Vitro S.A.* (November 19, 1991); *Epic Properties, Inc.* (October 21, 1991); *Warnaco, Inc.* (October 11, 1991); *Morgan Stanley & Co., Inc.* (June 5, 1991); and *Mary Kay Cosmetics, Inc.* (June 5, 1991).

123. The earlier letters were limited to debt and preferred stock. By 1993, the availability of the technique could be summarized as extending to non-convertible debt securities, investment-grade non-convertible preferred stock, unrated non-convertible preferred stock that is exchangeable into debt

The exchange offer will be registered on Form S-4 and will offer substantially identical securities that the purchasers will be able to resell without delivering a prospectus. The letters are generally conditioned on (a) the holder not being an affiliate of the issuer, (b) the holder having acquired the new securities in the ordinary course of its business, (c) the holder having no arrangement or understanding with any person to participate in a distribution of the new securities and (d) the holder not having purchased the "old" securities directly from the issuer to resell pursuant to Rule 144A or any other available exemption under the 1933 Act. The last condition, of course, essentially prevents a broker-dealer from taking advantage of the interpretive position to sell securities left over from the original placement ("unsold allotments").

Before effectiveness of the exchange offer registration statement, it is necessary to provide the staff with a supplemental letter stating that the exchange offer is being registered in reliance on the staff position set forth in the interpretive letters. The letter must also contain prescribed representations, including the absence of any arrangements for the distribution of the registered securities to be issued in the exchange offer.

The no-action letters take the position that the person acquiring the "new" securities from the issuer in the exchange offer is not an "underwriter" with respect to such securities even though the securities are "purchased from . . . [the] issuer with a view to . . . the distribution" thereof. Broker-dealers, however, are not so lucky. In 1993, the staff issued a letter[124] that required any broker-dealer participating in the exchange offer to be described in the exchange offer prospectus as possibly being a "statutory underwriter" and to deliver a prospectus on any resales of the

---

securities, broker-remarketed or auction preferred stock, and, in certain cases, equity securities of foreign issuers. SEC No-action letter, *Shearman & Sterling* (July 2, 1993). The justification for extending the technique to equity securities of non-reporting non-U.S. companies is that the exchange offer technique offers these companies a "stepping stone" approach to the U.S. public equity markets. The *Brown & Wood LLP* letter in early 1997 confirmed the availability of the technique for "capital securities" (also known as "trust" or "hybrid" preferred securities).

124. SEC No-action letter, *Shearman & Sterling* (July 2, 1993).

registered securities. The staff appears to be troubled by the absence of any financial intermediary with Section 11 liabilities in a transaction where a placement of securities pursuant to Rule 144A is followed quickly by a registered exchange offer.

In its 1998 Aircraft Carrier Release, the SEC stated its concurrence with the Division of Corporation Finance's belief "that the Exxon Capital line of interpretive letters should be repealed" on the adoption of proposed reforms to the registration process.[125] The proposed reforms were never adopted, and Exxon Capital exchanges continue to take place.

- *Private Offering Followed by Short Sales Into Public Market*

Many private placements of convertible securities are sold primarily to hedge funds. These purchasers may not have a fundamental view on the investment merits of the security; rather, they buy the securities with a view to hedging part or all of the equity risk of the instrument by making immediate short sales into the public trading market for the underlying common stock. Buyers in PIPE transactions may also seek to lay off part of their risk, either by short sales or swaps with dealers who engage in short sales.

From a 1933 Act point of view, the short sales are made in reliance on the Section 4(1) exemption, that is, sales by a person other than an issuer, dealer or underwriter. Clearly, if purchasers of the privately placed convertible securities were to make an immediate public resale of the convertible securities, they would risk being characterized as underwriters, but it is much harder to suggest that such purchasers may not immediately make a short sale of the underlying common stock without being characterized as underwriters. PIPE purchasers who make immediate short sales of the common stock might also look like underwriters, but this characterization is more difficult where they lay off risk through swaps.

Are there any limits on short sale activity in connection with a private placement? To the extent that the broker-dealer acting as placement agent is too closely involved with the purchasers' short sales (e.g., by executing the short sales or by lending stock for the purpose of completing the short sales or by entering into

---

125. SEC Release No. 33-7606A (November 13, 1998), text at nn.250–51.

a swap), this may cause the short sales to be viewed as being by or for the benefit of the issuer with a resulting violation of Section 5. The exact limits of what a broker-dealer can do for its customers in these situations has yet to be worked out.

Private Investment Companies (Section 3(c)(7))

As discussed in Chapter 3, an issuer may find to its surprise that it fits the definition of an "investment company" in the Investment Company Act of 1940 (the 1940 Act) and that, in order to complete a securities transaction (or, indeed, to conduct any business at all), it must register as an investment company (not a viable solution for operating companies or issuers involved in structured financings) or find an available exception or exemption.

One of the useful exceptions is that provided by Section 3(c)(1) of the 1940 Act, which applies to issuers "whose outstanding securities (other than short-term paper) are beneficially owned by not more than one hundred persons and which is not making and does not presently propose to make a public offering of its securities."

As interpreted by the SEC staff, the 100-owner limit is imposed differently depending on where the issuer is located. In the case of a U.S. issuer, the 100-owner limit applies to all holders. In the case of a non-U.S. issuer, the 100-owner limit applies to U.S. residents.[126]

The 100-owner limit is a continuing restriction, which requires the issuer to implement transfer restrictions and related procedures. When counting the number of securityholders, attribution rules apply to certain investors holding 10% or more of the issuer's voting securities.[127]

---

126. See, e.g., SEC No-action Letter, *Touche Remnant & Co.* (August 27, 1984).

127. Beneficial ownership by a company is considered beneficial ownership by one person unless the company (a) owns 10% or more of the issuer's outstanding voting securities and (b) is an investment company or would be considered an investment company but for the exceptions provided by Sections 3(c)(1) or 3(c)(7). If the company satisfies these two conditions and avoids the application of SEC-created attribution rules, the beneficial ownership is considered that of the holders of the company's outstanding securities (other than short-term paper).

Compliance with the 100-owner limit can be difficult, and Congress amended the 1940 Act in 1996 to add a new exception for issuers whose securities are held by "qualified purchasers." Under Section 3(c)(7), an issuer is not an investment company if its securities are beneficially owned exclusively by one or more persons who were "qualified purchasers" (QPs) at the time the securities were acquired and if the issuer "is not making and does not at that time propose to make a public offering of such securities." In the case of non-U.S. issuers, the QP requirement applies only to its U.S. securityholders.

Section 2(a)(51) defines a QP as (a) individuals and certain family companies that have not less than $5 million in "investments," (b) certain trusts if both the trustee or other person with investment discretion and all settlors or other contributors are QPs and (c) other persons that own and invest on a discretionary basis not less than $25 million in "investments." The SEC's Rule 2a51-1 defines "investments" for this purpose and also provides that persons reasonably believed to be QIBs will be deemed to be QPs (with certain exceptions for dealers and employee benefit plans). Rule 2a51-3 provides that any company may be deemed a QP if its securities are beneficially owned only by QPs; any other company will not be deemed a QP if it was formed for the specific purpose of acquiring securities issued by Section 3(c)(7) companies.

The QP test is a continuing test that applies to resales as well as to initial sales of securities. This means that, in order for the issuer to continue to be eligible for the Section 3(c)(7) exception, every buyer in the secondary market must be a person the issuer reasonably believes to be a QP. This requirement would have imposed a difficult burden on Section 3(c)(7) issuers and would as a practical matter have made it impossible for such issuers' securities to be deposited into DTC and other depositaries for the purpose of book-entry and settlement. The Bond Market Association, a trade group, has posted on its website procedures that are designed to enable Section 3(c)(7) issuers to form the required reasonable belief notwithstanding the deposit of those securities into DTC and other depositaries. The procedures, revised in early 2003, are designed to be used only for Rule 144A offerings by structured finance issuers such as

SPVs and CDOs and not "classic" private investment companies or hedge funds.[128]

Credit on New Issues (Section 11(d)(1))

Section 11(d)(1) of the 1934 Act restricts a broker-dealer's extension or arranging of credit on a security that is part of a "new issue" in the "distribution" of which the broker-dealer is participating or has participated as a member of a selling syndicate or group. (There is no reason to assume that a "selling syndicate or group" cannot consist of a single broker-dealer.) If Section 11(d)(1) applied to private placements, a broker-dealer could not extend or arrange credit for the purchaser and might be unable to arrange for delayed settlements beyond 35 days after purchase.

The term "distribution" is not defined in Section 11(d)(1) or the SEC's rules under that section, but it is generally agreed that the prohibition does not apply to private placements under Section 4(2) of the 1933 Act or Rule 506 of Regulation D.[129] The SEC took the position when it adopted Rule 144A that it would be prepared to consider providing "interpretive relief . . . in appropriate circumstances." Given the purpose of Section 11(d)(1), which is to prevent broker-dealers from dumping securities into customers' margin accounts, the authors do not believe that the SEC could successfully maintain that the prohibition applies to Rule 144A transactions.

---

128. *See* www.bondmarkets.com/market/3c7_recom_policies_final_2003.pdf. The association published in 2001 related procedures for book-entry settlement of "risk-linked securities," a subset of securities offered by Section 3(c)(7) vehicles. *See* www.bondmarkets.com/market/risk-linked_policies_and_procedures.pdf.

129. *See* Rechlin, *supra* note 87, at 8:4.

Chapter 8

SHELF REGISTRATION (RULE 415)

If an issuer expects to be making frequent public offerings of its securities, and especially if it is eligible to use Form S-3 or Form F-3, it will probably decide to file a shelf registration statement as permitted by Rule 415 under the 1933 Act. A shelf registration statement covers securities that are not necessarily to be sold in a single discrete offering immediately on effectiveness, but rather are proposed to be sold in a number of "takedowns" over a period of time or on a continuous basis.

If a qualified issuer decides to take the shelf route, it will register a specified dollar amount of securities pursuant to Rule 415. Since 1992, U.S. issuers eligible to use Form S-3 have been permitted to register both debt and equity securities on the same registration statement on an unallocated basis, that is, without specifying the principal amount of debt and the amount of shares of equity securities being registered.[1] (In 1994, this privilege was extended to non-U.S. issuers eligible to use Form F-3).[2] In

---

1. SEC Release No. 33-6964 (October 22, 1992).
2. SEC Release No. 33-7053 (April 19, 1994).

the aggregate, the amount of securities that may be registered is limited to that which "is reasonably expected to be offered and sold within two years from the initial effective date of the registration."

Issuers eligible to use Form S-3 or Form F-3 may offer their securities either on a continuous or delayed basis. For example, at some time after effectiveness, when market conditions appear favorable, the issuer may request proposals or bids from one or more underwriters for the sale of, for example, $500 million principal amount of debt securities of a specified maturity or range of maturities. The issuer weighs the various proposals and decides to accept terms that include, by way of illustration, a 6% coupon, a seven-year maturity and a specific price to public and underwriting discount. The securities are then "taken off the shelf": the issuer and the underwriters sign a terms agreement that is based on a full-scale underwriting agreement that was previously filed as an exhibit to the registration statement, and the terms of the securities and the underwriting arrangements are set forth in a supplement to the basic prospectus that is filed with the SEC under Rule 424(b)(2) by the close of business on the second business day after pricing. There is no need for the SEC to take any action.

A few months later, when the issuer needs funds or simply wishes to take advantage of a perceived "market window," it may repeat the process, this time ending up with a $100 million issue of five-year notes with a specified coupon, public offering price and underwriting discount. It may issue additional securities from time to time until all of the registered securities have been sold, at which time it may file a new shelf registration statement. With the availability of the unallocated shelf procedure, the issuer has the ability to move rapidly with great flexibility to take advantage of market opportunities.

After several offerings, the amount of securities remaining "on the shelf" may be insufficient—even taking into consideration the 20% "cushion" afforded by Rule 462(b)[3]—to meet the issuer's anticipated needs in the near term. In that case, the

---

3. *See* "Amount of Securities Registered" below.

issuer can "reload" the shelf by filing a new shelf registration statement. The newly registered securities, together with the remnant remaining from the old shelf, can be offered by means of a common prospectus under Rule 429. The market sometimes assumes that a significant "reloading" means that the issuer has acquisition plans, but most new shelf registrations are regarded— as one analyst put it in 2003—as being "like gasoline in the car. . . . When the tank gets low, you fill it up, and you don't know if you're going to use it Saturday morning or three weeks from now."

The use of Form S-3 or Form F-3 greatly simplifies a shelf registration program because the issuer can incorporate its 1934 Act reports by reference rather than amend or supplement the registration statement and prospectus each time a material event occurs. The rule does not require, however, that an issuer be eligible to use Form S-3 or Form F-3 in order to take advantage of shelf registration for purposes other than "delayed" offerings. For example, shelf registration is available to any issuer for "continuous" offerings of securities such as in the case of MTN programs, discussed below.

Shelf registrations were also used by issuers of mortgage related securities long before Rule 415, and the technique continues to be used to register billions of dollars of asset-backed securities each year. See Chapter 14.

Rule 415 specifically permits shelf registration of secondary offerings by selling securityholders from time to time on a securities exchange or otherwise at prices current at the time of sale. This technique also predates Rule 415 by many years.

Rule 415 permits shelf registration of securities offered under a dividend or interest reinvestment plan or an employee benefit plan; securities to be issued on the exercise of outstanding options, warrants or rights or on the conversion of other outstanding securities; securities that have been pledged as collateral; and ADSs registered on Form F-6.

Shelf registration has made it possible for issuers to reduce the cost of capital by ensuring prompt access to the public markets at the desired time, by reducing transaction costs and by facilitating the use of efficient methods of distributing securities. But Rule 415 did not come about without controversy. As will be seen, the SEC did not escape criticism and opposition as it sought to adapt its rules and policies to evolving practices in the securities markets.

The process by which the SEC sought to deal with registration "for the shelf" began in the 1930s. The way that the law has developed in this area is not unlike that described by Professor Lon Fuller in his jurisprudence classes at Harvard Law School. As an example of how the law responds to the realities of life, Professor Fuller would point to the flagstone paths laid out on the Cambridge Common. If the otherwise law-abiding citizens of Cambridge consistently strayed from the paths designated for their use, wearing away the grass as they followed a more convenient route from one point to another, the city fathers simply would pave over the paths that they had created. The SEC has followed similar pragmatic principles in coping with shelf registration, and Rule 415 can be viewed as a pavement that has been laid to widen and improve an already existing path.

The Evolution of Shelf Registration

Section 6(a) of the 1933 Act provides that "[a] registration statement shall be deemed effective only as to the securities specified therein as proposed to be offered."[4] Shortly after the adoption of the 1933 Act, the SEC had occasion to interpret this sentence and took the position that it permitted the registration only of securities intended to be offered presently (i.e., soon) and not those intended to be offered at some remote future date.[5] The SEC's theory was that, if securities are registered for future distribution, prospective investors relying on the registration statement may receive "stale" information. Among the amendments to the 1933 Act proposed in 1941[6] was a modification of

---

4. For a discussion of the legislative history of Section 6(a), *see* S. Hodes, *Shelf Registration: The Dilemma of the Securities and Exchange Commission,* 49 Va. L. Rev. 1106, 1108–15 (1963).

5. *United Combustion Corp.,* 3 S.E.C. 1062 (1938); *Shawnee Chiles Syndicate,* 10 S.E.C. 109 (1941).

6. H.R. 4344, 77th Cong., 1st Sess. (1941); S. 3985, 76th Cong., 3d Sess. (1940).

Section 6(a) to permit registration for the shelf. This amendment was opposed by the SEC and was never enacted.

- *Traditional Shelf Registration*

In time, the SEC backed away from a rigid interpretation of Section 6(a), and it had become established by the early 1960s that certain types of offerings could be covered by shelf registration statements.[7] For the most part, these were offerings that by their very nature were required to be put on the shelf. The following minute of a June 8, 1961 meeting of the SEC summarized the status at that time:

> Discussion also was had concerning the general problem involved in the registration of stock which was not to be made the subject of an offering in the immediate, foreseeable future. Mr. [Manuel F.] Cohen suggested that the Commission should continue the practice of permitting registration (a) in the American Marietta type of case in which a reasonable number of shares were being registered for future issuance under a continuing program for the issuance of stock in connection with the acquisition of other companies by purchase or merger; (b) in cases involving "private placements" under circumstances which suggest the necessity for registration; (c) where there was a likely distribution within the reasonable future upon conversion of privately placed debentures and similar situations in which the Commission insisted upon registration, including the issuance of options and stock to underwriters; (d) for sale of shares by "controlling" persons of acquired companies following transactions falling within Rule 133; and (e) where there was a representation that the shares were otherwise proposed for distribution within a reasonable period after the effective date of registration. However, he further suggested that registration for cash sale would not be in order, whether for

---

7. *See generally* C. Israels, *S.E.C. Problems of Controlling Stockholders and in Underwritings* 182 (Practising Law Institute Transcript 1962).

new or control shares, if there was no bona fide intention to sell within a reasonable period but only at some indefinite future period and eventuality.

Charles E. Shreve, chief counsel of the Division of Corporation Finance, described the SEC's position in somewhat more pragmatic terms:

> The policy of the Commission is to afford the opportunity for registration where it seems consistent with the Congressional intention of having you register offerings proposed to be made. Sometimes the line is not easy to draw. It is not possible under §6(a) to register all of the outstanding stock simply because someday somebody might want to sell it. On the other hand, it is recognized that sales are not always made by a conventional offering. Controlling persons who must register the securities when they want to sell to the public, may want to sell by normal market trading transactions. That may take a matter of months. If they seem to have a real present intention of selling a designated maximum amount of stock in that way, we say "All right; go ahead and register."[8]

One type of shelf transaction that the SEC had no intention of permitting was one in which an issuer, as opposed to a selling shareholder, sought to register a block of shares to be sold for cash from time to time in the future.[9] One that slipped through the cracks, however, was a prospectus dated August 5, 1966 of Industrial Electronic Hardware Corp. covering 100,000 shares of common stock offered by the issuer "from time to time, for a maximum period of two years, in brokerage transactions on the American Stock Exchange or otherwise at prices then current on that Exchange." As a rule, this type of transaction was not permitted.

• • *Continuous Acquisition Programs.* The use of shelf registration statements to cover shares of common stock to be issued

---

8. C. Israels & G. Duff, *When Corporations Go Public* 115–16 (1962).

9. Israels, *supra* note 7, at 208.

in future acquisitions was to all intents and purposes mandated by the SEC in the late 1950s and early 1960s. At that time, a number of companies launched programs that contemplated future acquisitions of privately owned companies on a more or less regular basis. Each separate acquisition might qualify as a private placement, but applying its integration doctrine (see Chapter 7), the SEC took the position that the transactions were sufficiently interrelated as to require registration of the shares to be issued. Of necessity, the registered shares were kept on the shelf until the closing of each particular transaction. One example of this type of shelf registration was the prospectus dated February 24, 1961 of American-Marietta Company covering nearly 5 million shares of common stock to be issued from time to time in the acquisition of other businesses. Prospectuses of this type came to be known as "American-Marietta-type" prospectuses, as indicated by Mr. Cohen's reference in the above quoted SEC minute.

Other early examples of shelf registrations designed for acquisitions were the February 28, 1961 prospectus covering 95,000 shares of common stock of Sports Arenas, Inc. and the May 14, 1963 prospectus of Holiday Inns of America, Inc., which stated, "The Common Stock is to be offered from time to time in connection with acquisition by the Company of licensee-owned Holiday Inns and in isolated instances for motel properties owned by non-licensees."

• • *Sales Following Private Placements.* The most common type of shelf registration was one covering securities issued in a private placement to persons wishing to be in a position to resell if they should choose to do so. Frequently, the transaction would have involved the acquisition of a privately owned company in exchange for the acquiring company's shares. The registration statement would be filed pursuant to a registration rights agreement or simply because the issuer was willing to accommodate the holders of the securities.

Prior to the adoption of Rule 144 in 1972,[10] there was substantial uncertainty as to when and under what circumstances a

---

10. SEC Release No. 33-5223 (January 11, 1972).

person acquiring securities in a private placement could resell them without being deemed a statutory underwriter. The holder may have signed an investment letter stating that he had not purchased the securities "with a view to distribution," the key words in the Section 2(a)(11) definition. But conduct inconsistent with this representation, such as a public sale shortly after the acquisition, could lead to the conclusion that the seller was indeed an underwriter and that accordingly the securities should have been registered to cover his sale.

In some private acquisition transactions, not all of the shareholders were willing to give investment representations. The solution in some cases was to register the securities for the shelf to enable the holders to sell from time to time at prices prevailing at the time of sale. The SEC was willing to allow these registration statements to become effective without any representation from the holders that they had an immediate intention to sell. The following excerpt from an October 4, 1961 prospectus of Universal Match Corporation is an apt illustration:

> On June 30, 1961, the Company acquired all the outstanding capital stock of Reflectone Electronics, Inc., a Connecticut corporation, in exchange for 120,000 shares of the Company's common stock. As to 84,000 of said shares, the recipients represented to the Company that they were acquiring said shares for investment and not for distribution. No such representation was made with respect to the remaining 36,000 shares which are covered by this Prospectus and which may be sold by the holders thereof as set forth on the cover page of this Prospectus.

• • *Shares Issued on Conversions of Privately Placed Securities.* Section 3(a)(9) of the 1933 Act exempts the issuance of common stock on the conversion of outstanding convertible debentures or preferred stock but does not exempt the resale of that stock. Rule 155, adopted by the SEC in 1962[11] but

---

11. SEC Release No. 33-4450 (February 7, 1962).

subsequently rescinded, provided in effect that the public sale of shares acquired on conversion of a privately placed security would require registration unless the shares were not acquired with a view to distribution. Unlike Rule 144, which now permits tacking in these circumstances, under Rule 155 the holding period for the underlying shares began on conversion and not when the convertible securities were purchased. In the 1960 release reproposing Rule 155, the SEC indicated its willingness to be flexible in its interpretation of Section 6(a) in the context of resales of privately placed convertible securities or the shares into which they were converted.[12]

• • *Underwriters' Stock and Warrants.* The SEC has consistently taken the position that cheap stock and immediately exercisable warrants sold to underwriters in connection with a public offering of securities should be registered at the same time as the securities to be offered to the public. In a published response to an inquiry regarding underwriters' warrants, where it was stated that for tax reasons none of the warrants or the underlying stock would be reoffered for at least six months after the effective date of the registration statement, the SEC said that, since it was not contemplated that the warrants or the underlying stock would be distributed immediately, the registration statement should contain an undertaking to file a post-effective amendment that would disclose the terms of the distribution.[13] Amended prospectuses covering the resale of underwriters' warrants or stock were permitted to provide for sales on a delayed or continuous basis.

• • *Resales Following Rule 133 Transactions.* Prior to the adoption of Rule 145 in 1972,[14] a merger or similar transaction requiring a vote of shareholders was not deemed to involve a "sale" of the securities issued in exchange for shares of the acquired corporation. The "no sale theory" was upheld by the

---

12. SEC Release No. 33-4248 (July 14, 1960). Rule 155 was originally proposed in SEC Release No. 33-4162 (December 2, 1959).

13. SEC Release No. 33-3210 (April 9, 1947).

14. SEC Release No. 33-5316 (October 6, 1972).

Court of Appeals for the Ninth Circuit[15] and was codified when Rule 133 was adopted in 1951.[16] But abuses arose. Controlling shareholders would arrange questionable mergers to "free up" large blocks of stock.

In *Great Sweet Grass*,[17] the SEC held that Rule 133 could not be relied on where there was a preexisting plan to use the shareholders of an acquired corporation as a conduit in distributing a block of stock to the public. In *SEC v. Micro-Moisture Controls, Inc.*,[18] the court held that, where the persons negotiating a merger had such control over the process as to make the stockholder vote a mere formality, there was no "corporate action" on which Rule 133 was premised, and registration would be required.

In 1959, the SEC amended Rule 133[19] to spell out the circumstances under which the shareholders of an acquired corporation would be deemed underwriters in reselling the securities received in the acquisition transaction. Registration of any resales would be required if the issuer had made arrangements with an underwriter to purchase the securities issued to the shareholders of the constituent corporation. Absent such arrangements, only the constituent corporation and its affiliates (those in a control relationship with it) would be considered underwriters if they acquired their securities with a view to distribution. The rule excluded from the term "distribution" brokerage transactions of the type then permitted by Rule 154, the predecessor to the current Rule 144.

At the same time as it amended Rule 133, the SEC adopted Form S-14, which permitted an issuer whose shares were listed on an exchange to file with a prospectus consisting of the proxy

---

15. *National Supply Co. v. Leland Stanford Junior Univ.*, 134 F.2d 689 (9th Cir. 1943), *rev'g* 46 F. Supp. 389 (N.D. Cal. 1942).

16. SEC Release No. 33-3420 (August 2, 1951).

17. *In re Great Sweet Grass Oils Ltd.*, 37 S.E.C. 683 (1957).

18. 148 F. Supp. 558 (S.D.N.Y. 1957) (preliminary injunction), 167 F. Supp. 716 (S.D.N.Y. 1958) (permanent injunction), *aff'd sub nom. SEC v. Culpepper*, 270 F.2d 241 (2d Cir. 1959). *See also United States v. Crosby*, 294 F.2d 928 (2d Cir. 1961).

19. SEC Release No. 33-4115 (July 16, 1959).

statement used in the acquisition transaction with a wraparound spelling out the plan of distribution. One issuer, Schering-White Laboratories, had been permitted to use this type of wraparound prospectus prior to the adoption of Form S-14.[20] Form S-14 required an undertaking to update the registration statement to comply with Section 10(a)(3) of the 1933 Act for a period of 24 months after its effective date. Implicit in the adoption of Form S-14 was a waiver in this context of any restriction that Section 6(a) might impose upon registration for the shelf.

In the years following the amendment of Rule 133, there were occasions when registration for the shelf was all but insisted on by the SEC. An Allied Chemical Corporation prospectus dated February 28, 1963—covering 2.5 million of the 6.3 million shares of common stock issued a year earlier on the acquisition of Union Texas Natural Gas Corporation—contained the following statement on its cover page:

> This Prospectus relates to an aggregate of 2,595,511 shares of the Common Stock of Allied issued upon the merger to the stockholders of Union Texas listed under the heading "Certain Stockholders of Union Texas" in this Prospectus. Such stockholders were unwilling to represent that they were acquiring such shares for investment. Allied understands that, under such circumstances, the Securities and Exchange Commission takes the position that such stockholders may be "underwriters" as such term is defined in the Securities Act of 1933; and, accordingly, such shares have been registered. Allied disclaims that such stockholders are "underwriters" under such Act or that sales of such shares by them will constitute a public offering of such shares by Allied.

Shelf-type prospectuses have been used to cover resales by certain shareholders of companies acquired in a registered exchange offer. The SEC has taken the position that those shareholders of the target company who negotiated the exchange offer

---

20. Israels, *supra* note 7, at 211–12. This is the transaction referred to in SEC Release No. 33-3846 (October 10, 1957).

will be considered underwriters in reselling the securities acquired by them in exchange for those of the acquired company. There are numerous examples of exchange offer prospectuses that contain a paragraph at the foot of the cover page to the effect that the prospectus may also "be used to cover resales of shares acquired in the exchange offer by those persons who may be deemed to be underwriters in making such sales."

• • *Stock Option Plans.* One type of shelf registration not referred to by Mr. Cohen in his June 8, 1961 presentation to the SEC was a Form S-8 registration statement covering shares that could be issued from time to time under an employee stock option plan or other type of employee benefit plan. By the very nature of these plans, the securities are registered for sale at some unspecified time in the future. With respect to resales of the registered shares, there always has been some question as to whether a prospectus principally focused on the operation of the plan is suitable to cover resales to the public. At one point, the SEC permitted the Form S-8 prospectus to be used for resales if augmented in certain respects. Instruction C to the form now provides that the Form S-8 prospectus is not available for this purpose but that resales under Rule 415 may be made with a separate prospectus filed as part of the Form S-8 registration statement. The prospectus may be prepared in accordance with the requirements of Form S-3. Resales are permitted without limitation if the issuer meets the registrant requirements of that form; if that is not the case, then the amount of securities proposed to be sold during any three-month period by any person may not exceed the amount provided for in Rule 144(e).

• • *Pledged Securities.* Another type of shelf registration not referred to by Mr. Cohen is one covering securities pledged by a control person or a statutory underwriter as collateral for a loan. Unless it makes a private sale or sells under Rule 144, the creditor foreclosing on the collateral may have to comply with the registration and prospectus delivery requirements of Section 5 of the 1933 Act.[21] A pledgee, of course, does not generally take

---

21. *SEC v. Guild Films Co., Inc.*, 178 F. Supp. 418 (S.D.N.Y. 1959), *aff'd*, 279 F.2d 485 (2d Cir. 1960); *In re Skiatron Electronics and Television Corp.*, SEC Release No. 33-4282 (October 3, 1960).

securities as collateral with a view to selling them. It makes a secured loan with the full intention that interest and principal will be paid at the required time. If, however, the borrower does not meet its obligations, the lender wishes to be in a position to foreclose on the collateral and to sell it promptly. Registration of pledged securities to deal with this contingency has been permitted by the SEC without question and with little, if any, concern over the limitations inherent in Section 6(a).

- *"90-Day Undertakings"*

In addition to the undertaking to update the registration statement specifically called for by former Form S-14, the SEC sometimes required similar undertakings to justify the use of shelf registration. In 1961, the SEC began to call for so-called "90-day undertakings." These undertakings required a registrant to file a post-effective amendment disclosing such current information as would have been required in the filing of a new registration statement if the first offering of the securities took place more than 90 days after the effective date of the registration statement.

In attempting to be flexible, the SEC received a certain amount of criticism from those who believed that Section 6(a) should be strictly construed. One writer complained that the SEC was in effect "disregarding the thrust of section 6(a), which ensures current information by prohibiting shelf registration; at the same time it is stepping outside the governing statute by administratively requiring the issuer to incorporate an undertaking to update the registration statement.[22] The same writer concluded that "[p]roper enforcement of the Securities Act requires that Section 6(a) not be emasculated by allowing the filing of post-effective amendments in lieu of strict adherence to congressional intent that securities not be registered unless they are presently intended to be offered for sale."[23] Other commentators questioned the SEC's authority to require undertakings in the absence of a statute conferring this power.[24]

---

22. Hodes, *supra* note 4, at 1140.
23. *Id.* at 1148.
24. A. H. Dean, *Twenty-Five Years of Federal Securities Regulation by the Securities and Exchange Commission,* 59 Colum. L. Rev. 697, 726 (1959).

- *The* Hazel Bishop *Case*

In June 1960, Hazel Bishop, Inc. filed a registration statement relating to 1.1 million shares of its outstanding common stock. This represented approximately 61% of the number of shares outstanding, and the registration statement named 70 selling shareholders who might offer shares from time to time at prices current at the time of sale through brokers on the American Stock Exchange, in the open market, or otherwise. An amendment filed in October 1960 increased the number of shares to 1.3 million and the number of selling shareholders to 112.

Shortly thereafter, the SEC initiated proceedings under Section 8(d) of the 1933 Act to determine whether a stop order should be issued suspending the effectiveness of the registration statement. In issuing a stop order, the SEC found that the registration statement contained numerous false and misleading statements, including deficiencies in the financial statements.[25] More significantly, the SEC raised fundamental questions with respect to a massive uncoordinated distribution of this type.

It first questioned the efficacy of Rule 153, which permits the prospectus delivery requirements of the 1933 Act to be satisfied as between brokers in a transaction on a national securities exchange by delivering copies of the prospectus to the exchange. The SEC noted that members of the exchange may or may not request copies for their own use or for delivery to customers and that there was a real danger that the information contained in the registration statement might not in fact come to the attention of brokers and dealers or buyers of the securities and that the public would not be aware of the material facts pertaining to Hazel Bishop and the circumstances of the distribution. The SEC stated:

> We believe that it would be highly prejudicial to the protection of investors and the public interest generally if the massive distribution here proposed by a large group which numbers among it the controlling persons of Hazel Bishop should be initiated through the facilities of the Exchange unless prior thereto facts of this case are given

---

25. *In re Hazel Bishop, Inc.*, SEC Release No. 33-4371 (June 7, 1961).

a much wider public distribution than is likely to result from the mere delivery of copies of the prospectus to the Exchange. Accordingly, it is our view that prior to the final effective date of this registration statement, the public interest requires the transmittal by registrant of our opinion accompanied by an adequate prospectus to all of the selling stockholders and the members of the Exchange community.

The SEC also noted that in a conventional distribution of securities the activities of underwriters are governed by the underwriting documents that provide "a controlled procedure designed to bring about an orderly marketing of the security free of practices prohibited by the statutes or rules as manipulative, deceptive or fraudulent, or otherwise unlawful." The SEC noted that here there were at least 112 selling shareholders and that no procedures had been established to coordinate their activities or guard against unlawful practices such as bids and purchases in violation of Rule 10b-6.

The SEC also expressed concern that there might be written communications that violated the prohibitions of Section 5 of the 1933 Act. It observed that one of the selling shareholders was the specialist in the common stock of Hazel Bishop and expressed skepticism as to how a specialist could properly discharge its function and at the same time comply with Rule 10b-6 and the other applicable provisions of the 1934 Act. The SEC concluded:

In summary, we think that under the factual situation here presented the potentialities for violations of the law, witting or unwitting, on the part of those who are about to offer their stock on the basis stated are so grave that consistent with our obligations under the Exchange Act, they should be called to the attention of the selling stockholders, the issuer, the Exchange, the existing stockholders of Hazel Bishop and the general public.

Shortly after this decision was handed down, the stop order was lifted and an amended registration statement became effective. In order to meet the problems raised by the SEC's opinion, the selling shareholders and Hazel Bishop entered into an agreement designed to prevent violations of the antimanipulation provisions under the 1934 Act, with particular reference to Rules 10b-2, 10b-6 and 10b-7. The company instructed its transfer agent to honor requests for transfer only for those selling shareholders who were signatories to this agreement. Hazel Bishop sent a copy of the SEC's opinion and the final prospectus to all members of the NASD and the American Stock Exchange and recommended that they not execute any orders without confirming that the selling stockholder had signed the requisite agreement. The notice to dealers stated that "any broker who acts for any of the selling shareholders named in the Registration Statement must be furnished by such selling shareholders with copies of the Prospectus to enable him to deliver a prospectus to the buying broker, who may be required to deliver a copy of its prospectus to its customer." The notice to dealers also contained warnings with respect to compliance with Rules 10b-2, 10b-6 and 10b-7.[26]

---

26. The following year, the SEC issued a stop order suspending the effectiveness of a registration statement filed by American Finance Co., Inc. covering an offering of units, on the basis of misleading statements and omissions with respect to, among other matters, a proposed offering by a group of selling shareholders, 17 in number. The prospectus disclosed that the Lomasney underwriting firm was to purchase 60,000 shares at an advantageous price for its own account and for the account of favored customers. These shares were included in the registration statement, and the prospectus stated that they would be reoffered subsequently pursuant to an appropriately supplemented prospectus furnishing additional information. "However," said the SEC, "the prospectus does not inform prospective investors of the possible effects on the market in the common stock, following the completion of the sale of the Units, of a subsequent distribution of the 60,000 shares, which is a very large number of shares in relation to the 75,000 shares that will be available for trading on the completion of the sale of Units." The SEC went on to say, "In view of the large number of shares proposed to be offered in relation to the limited floating supply of shares, the apparent lack of cohesiveness in the selling group and the absence of a prior market, the registration statement should have identified the sellers and their relationships to each other, registrant and Lomasney, and should have disclosed that such distribution would not be coordinated or controlled by a managing underwriter and that the selling group had not provided the contractual safeguards for the protection of buyers and sellers usually provided in a conventional distribution." *In re American Finance Co., Inc.,* 40 S.E.C. 103, 1050–51 (1962).

SHELF REGISTRATION (RULE 415)

In a subsequent shelf offering of outstanding shares of common stock of Thompson-Starrett Companies, Inc., additional steps were taken to coordinate the distribution. There it was provided in the agreement between the company and the selling shareholders that only a broker authorized by the issuer could be used to effect sales and that no sales could be made other than on the American Stock Exchange. The agreement also provided that all sell orders must be at a specified price or prices not lower than the last reported bid price nor higher than the higher of either the last reported asked price or the last reported sales price on the American Stock Exchange prior to the receipt of the order by the broker. The agreement further provided that neither a "market" nor a "stop loss" order could be entered and that an order could be given to a broker on a discretionary ("not held") basis.[27]

The SEC formalized its position with respect to uncoordinated distributions by publishing a speech delivered by Chairman William J. Cary to the Practising Law Institute in which he outlined the administrative procedures developed by the SEC to control offerings of this type.[28] These procedures were further codified when the SEC adopted its Guide 53.[29]

Guide 53 applied to a registered "at the market" offering by selling shareholders who included insiders or substantial holders, involving a substantial amount of securities in relation to the securities of the class outstanding (more than 10%), the absence of a professional underwriter to act for the group and the absence of a conventional underwriting agreement. The guide stated that where these elements were present and there was a limited group of selling shareholders or several groups of related shareholders, then the members of the respective groups and the issuer should enter into agreements requiring compliance with the SEC's antimanipulation rules.

---

27. *See* William L. Yerkes, *Shelf Registrations: The Role of the Broker-Dealer,* 29 Bus. Law. 397, 409 (1974).
28. SEC Release No. 33-4401 (August 3, 1961).
29. SEC Release No. 33-4936 (December 9, 1968).

The guide provided that, where there is a large group of unrelated sellers and agreements are thus not feasible, the issuer should notify the sellers of the applicable SEC rules and regulations. It also stated that, under a single registration statement, some shareholders might be required to enter into agreements while notification of others might be sufficient. These arrangements were required to be disclosed in the registration statement.

Guide 53 was ultimately replaced by the provision in Rule 461 that provides that one of the bases on which the SEC may refuse to accelerate the effectiveness of a registration statement is "[w]hether, in the case of a significant secondary offering at the market, the registrant, selling security holders and underwriters have not taken sufficient measures to insure compliance with Regulation M." As a general matter, the problem of uncontrolled or uncoordinated distributions has not been a significant issue in recent years.

- *Guide 4*

In 1968, the SEC codified its position with respect to shelf registration statements as Guide 4 to its guides for the preparation and filing of registration statements.[30] The circumstances under which shelf registrations would be permitted were those previously mentioned: a continuous acquisition program, Rule 155 situations, resales of securities acquired in a Rule 133 transaction, pledged securities, securities purchased by underwriters in connection with public offerings and securities to be offered pursuant to options, warrants or rights.

Guide 4 also permitted securities to be shelf-registered if a representation was made that they would be publicly offered within a reasonable period of time after the effective date of the registration statement or if, because of particular circumstances, effective control over the resale of the securities by other persons would be difficult to maintain. The guide noted that where securities are so registered they could not be sold at a time when the prospectus had not been kept up to date in accordance with

---

30. *Id.* These guides were initially proposed in SEC Release No. 33-4890 (December 20, 1967).

Section 10(a) of the 1933 Act. It also noted that registration statements of this character may involve questions arising under Rules 10b-2, 10b-6 and 10b-7 under the 1934 Act.

- *Further Developments*

The adoption of Form S-16, which originally was applicable only to brokerage transactions on an exchange, facilitated the development of shelf registrations for secondary offerings. The issuer could use a short-form registration statement that could be continuously updated by the filing of 1934 Act reports, thus easing the burden on the issuer and placing it in a position where it might be more inclined to accommodate selling security-holders. As previously noted, the SEC began in the mid-1970s to permit the registration on Form S-1 or Form S-7 of MTNs proposed to be offered on a continuous basis by finance companies and bank holding companies. Also, a number of institutions, including the Bank of America, were permitted to shelf-register mortgage pass-through securities to be sold in direct sales, sales on an agency basis, or offerings through syndicates organized by specified managing underwriters. The stage was set for the SEC to play out the drama that led to the adoption of Rule 415.

The Adoption of Rule 415

Rule 415 came into being as a result of efforts by the staff of the SEC to improve the integrated disclosure system. As part of that process, the SEC conducted a comprehensive review of all of the guides for the preparation and filing of registration statements. As a result of its reevaluation of Guide 4, the SEC published for comment, as proposed Rule 462A, a comprehensive position with respect to shelf registration statements.[31] In addition to blessing traditional shelf registrations, the proposed rule would have permitted shelf registration of primary offerings of debt and equity securities that an issuer reasonably expected to offer over the next two years.

---

31. SEC Release No. 33-6276 (December 23, 1980).

Proposed Rule 462A drew little attention, perhaps because it was buried in a release in which the SEC proposed for comment the reorganization of Regulation S-K, the elimination or incorporation of all the guides (except those pertaining to specific industries) into Regulation S-K or Regulation C and certain revisions to the general rules and regulations under the 1933 Act. It was a massive document of which the shelf rule was only a small part. Several of those who commented on the proposed shelf rule were concerned that it had not received widespread attention from issuers and investment bankers because it appeared in the middle of a lengthy release. These commentators recommended that the proposal be republished for comment in a separate release in order that it might receive the careful consideration that it deserved. Thus, the SEC reproposed Rule 462A in a separate release and in a somewhat revised form.[32]

As the investment banking community focused on the proposed shelf rule, a Chicken Little reaction set in. Here was a proposal that some believed could undermine the traditional manner in which securities had been distributed to the public—fixed-price offerings through underwriting syndicates. Efforts to persuade the SEC to postpone the rule's adoption were led by Morgan Stanley & Co. Incorporated, which stated in a letter to the SEC dated February 2, 1982: "Implementation of the Rule as proposed may produce fundamental structural changes in the capital raising process with undesirable consequences that have not been explored, either in the Commission's release or in the comment letters submitted." Morgan Stanley went on to predict that the proposed rule "could substantially impair the process by which most of the long-term private capital has been raised in this country—fixed price public offerings by syndicates of securities firms." Goldman, Sachs & Co., in a letter dated January 7, 1982 from its co-senior partner, John C. Whitehead, also expressed concern over the proposed shelf rule.

In recognition of the concerns expressed by the securities industry, the SEC adopted the shelf rule (redesignated Rule 415) in March 1982 on a temporary basis.[33] It proposed to experiment

---

32. SEC Release No. 33-6334 (August 6, 1981).
33. SEC Release No. 33-6383 (March 3, 1982).

with the rule's use and announced that during the period before November 1982 it would hold public hearings to explore the rule's impact and to give interested parties further opportunities to express their views.

The period immediately following the adoption of Rule 415 was marked by a flurry of activity on Wall Street. Each of the major investment banking firms produced its own thick brochure explaining how the rule would operate. These brochures were in the hands of clients and prospective clients within days following the announcement of the rule's adoption. Lawyers worked around the clock to produce standard forms of indentures, underwriting documents and prospectus disclosure that their investment banking clients could use to demonstrate to corporate issuers that they were ready to move full steam ahead in assisting them in establishing shelf programs. At the same time that they were seeking to persuade issuers that their services were essential in this new era, the investment banks were preparing for presentations at the SEC hearings, presentations that would raise concerns as to the rule's impact on the healthy functioning of the capital markets.

Some of the principal players under Rule 415 were among its most vocal critics. John Whitehead was quoted in *Fortune* as saying that he did not have any problem with Goldman Sachs' willingness to make use of the new rule. "We adapt to the ground rules whether or not we like them," he explained. "We've been very active under 415. That's where I get my information that it's bad for investors."[34] Firms with fewer blue chip clients than Morgan Stanley or Goldman Sachs welcomed Rule 415 as providing an opportunity to make inroads into their competitors' investment banking relationships.

In a March 1982 release, the SEC scheduled the hearings for June and framed the issues to be considered.[35] The SEC stated that it would examine the extent to which structural changes in public offerings were due to factors extrinsic to the

---

34. A. F. Ehrbar, *Upheaval in Investment Banking,* Fortune, Aug. 23, 1982. *See also* N. Osborn, *The Furor over Shelf Registration,* Institutional Investor, June 1982.

35. SEC Release No. 33-6391 (March 12, 1982).

adoption of Rule 415, such as volatile markets and interest rates, the role played by institutional investors in the securities markets, quick financings made possible by short-form registration statements and the significance of "market windows." The SEC stated that it would pay particular attention to the effects of Rule 415 on fixed-price public offerings and the practice of syndication. The entire tone of the release suggested that the SEC believed that the problems that concerned the investment banking community did not stem from Rule 415 but rather from other economic forces. This certainly was the view of certain key members of the staff.[36]

Written and oral presentations were made at the June 28 hearings. Issuers gave their strong support to Rule 415. Citicorp, which had filed the first registration statement under Rule 415 (a Form S-3 covering $500 million of notes), made a particularly eloquent presentation. A number of the major investment banking firms reiterated the concerns previously expressed, including the difficulty of performing due diligence and the impact of Rule 415 on syndicates and fixed-price offerings.

John H. Gutfreund, the chairman of Salomon Brothers, argued convincingly that knowledge of the calendar for debt financings is an important factor in pricing an issue. "The concept of a financing calendar, or some mechanism to provide notice to the market of imminent new issues," he said, "is central to the supply and demand judgments which all investors must undertake in securities evaluation." This information, according to Mr. Gutfreund, was almost as important as disclosure concerning the issuer itself. With respect to disclosure and due diligence, Mr. Gutfreund expressed the view that the effective due diligence that uncovered the problems of Penn Central before its demise in 1970 (see Chapter 5) would have been impossible in the context of an instantaneous shelf offering.

Several persons testifying at the hearing urged the SEC to increase the amount of information required to be included

---

36. *See* Remarks of Lee B. Spencer, Jr., Director, Division of Corporation Finance, before the University of Southern California School of Accounting's SEC and Financial Reporting Institute (May 7, 1982).

in an S-3 prospectus. In addition, the Securities Industry Association and others urged the SEC to relieve underwriters of responsibility for documents incorporated by reference. The most far-reaching relief urged at the hearings for the problems presented by fast time schedules, however, was the introduction of a mandatory "cooling-off" period for many primary distributions. Numerous regional firms appeared at the hearing and testified that as a result of Rule 415 they had been unable to participate in syndicates in which they normally would have been included. Also, the NASD was particularly concerned about the impact of the rule on fixed-price offerings, a method of distributing securities that had been strongly praised by the SEC in the *Papilsky* hearings.[37]

In September 1982, the SEC, with three commissioners sitting, voted to extend Rule 415's effectiveness through December 31, 1983.[38] Chairman John R. Shad had recused himself from the proceedings, and there was one vacancy at the time. The extension was intended to "provide a greater opportunity to study the operation and impact of Rule 415 through what might be a full financial cycle." Commissioner Barbara Thomas wrote a 36-page dissent stating that shelf registrations should not be permitted for offerings of equity securities and that a two-day notice period should be required for debt offerings not registered on Form S-3.[39]

The SEC again solicited comment on Rule 415 and its operation in order to provide those affected with one last opportunity to express their views before final action was taken.[40] In November

---

37. *See* Chapter 6.

38. SEC Release No. 33-6423 (September 2, 1982).

39. For an analysis and rebuttal of Commissioner Thomas's position, *see* B. Banoff, *Regulatory Subsidies, Efficient Markets, and Shelf Registration: An Analysis of Rule 415,* 70 Va. L. Rev. 135 (1984). For a critique of the Banoff article, *see* M. Fox, *Shelf Registration, Integrated Disclosure, and Underwriter Due Diligence: An Economic Analysis,* 70 Va. L. Rev. 1005 (1984). *See generally* ABA Committee on Federal Regulation of Securities, *Report of Task Force on Sellers' Due Diligence and Similar Defenses Under the Federal Securities Laws,* 48 Bus. Law. 1185 (1993).

40. SEC Release No. 33-6470 (June 9, 1983).

1983, the SEC adopted Rule 415 on a permanent basis, but in deference to the concerns expressed about the rule, it limited shelf registration to either "traditional" offerings or, in the case of "primary" offerings, to those made on Form S-3.[41] This limitation caused no great stir since most of the primary shelf filings that had been made since the adoption of the rule on a temporary basis had used this form.[42] The SEC also responded to concerns about due diligence and the quality of disclosure by expressing its conviction that new methods of "anticipatory" and "continuous" due diligence were being developed as an adequate substitute for traditional due diligence. Some of these methods, referred to by issuers during the hearings, included the appointment of a single law firm to act as underwriters' counsel, the holding of "drafting sessions" on 1934 Act reports in which prospective underwriters and their counsel could participate and the holding of "periodic due diligence sessions" between issuers and prospective underwriters either periodically or "at any time."

Commissioner Thomas stuck by her guns and continued to express the view that Rule 415 should not be applicable to primary offerings of equity securities. Chairman Shad filed a special concurring opinion in which he took issue with the SEC's inventory of techniques of "continuous" and "anticipatory" due diligence, finding them to be of "limited practical value" in view of the need for issuers and underwriters to spend "hundreds of thousands of hours annually" in meetings on the speculative possibility that an offering would occur. The chairman predicted that such meetings would soon be attended only by "junior observers, rather than qualified participants."

Expansion of Eligibility to Use Form S-3 and Form F-3

Notwithstanding the SEC's permanent adoption of Rule 415 in 1983, shelf registration would not have become a powerful

---

41. SEC Release No. 33-6499 (November 17, 1983).

42. The limitation did, however, raise the question whether continuous MTN offerings by issuers not eligible to use Form S-3 were "traditional" offerings or "primary" offerings. The SEC later confirmed their status as "traditional" offerings.

financing tool without an expansion of a U.S. issuer's ability to use Form S-3 and a non-U.S. issuer's ability to use Form F-3. As noted above, clause (x) of Rule 415 permits the registration of securities to be sold on a "continuous or delayed basis" but limits registration for this purpose to offerings on Form S-3 or Form F-3. An issuer not eligible to use these forms may register securities pursuant to clause (ix), which permits continuous offerings (such as MTNs) but not delayed offerings (such as periodic takedowns). Such an issuer will also not have the convenience of automatic updating by means of incorporating by reference its 1934 Act reports.

The SEC began in 1981 to lay the foundation for the use of Form S-3 to support shelf registration by republishing the new form for comment.[43] As originally proposed,[44] the predecessor to Form S-3 (like its immediate predecessor, Form S-16) would have been available for a primary offering only on condition that the offering be underwritten. If maintained, this requirement would have forced shelf offerings into an impractical long-form registration format with continuing updating obligations. Fortunately for the future of shelf registration, however, the SEC in 1981 followed the advice of commenters and decided not to repropose the requirement.

In October 1992, the SEC adopted amendments to Form S-3[45] that greatly expanded the number of companies eligible to use shelf registration for primary offerings. The amendments, among other things, reduced an issuer's required reporting history under the 1934 Act from 36 months to 12 months and reduced the equity "float" requirement from $150 million to $75 million. They also eliminated the three million share trading volume test. The form was also amended to include investment-grade asset-backed securities as an additional category of transactions eligible to use Form S-3 and, consequently, shelf registration.

The SEC adopted amendments to Form F-3 in April 1994[46] that expanded the use of Form F-3 and, consequently, shelf

---

43. SEC Release No. 33-6331 (August 6, 1981).
44. SEC Release No. 33-6235 (September 2, 1980).
45. SEC Release No. 33-6964 (October 22, 1992).
46. SEC Release No. 33-7053 (April 19, 1994).

registration for eligible non-U.S. issuers. The amendments shortened the minimum reporting history requirement from 36 months to 12 months (provided the issuer has filed at least one annual report) and reduced the minimum public float requirement from $300 million to $75 million.

As discussed in Chapter 6, there is an exemption from the NASD's filing requirements under its Corporate Financing Rule for securities registered on Form S-3 and Form F-3 and offered pursuant to Rule 415. Oddly enough, however, this exemption applies only if the issuer meets the standards for the use of the respective forms as they were in effect prior to October 21, 1992. The NASD believes in its wisdom that the premise of the exemption—that S-3 and F-3 issuers can be presumed to have enough bargaining power to resist unfair arrangements—may not be justified under the new standards adopted by the SEC in 1992.

The SEC's expansion of Form S-3 and Form F-3 as a vehicle for delayed or continuous offerings has been a principal driving force behind the shelf registration phenomenon.[47]

The Impact of Rule 415

In the end, the adoption of Rule 415 was inevitable. Issuers needed capital in large amounts and on a regular basis. Given increasingly volatile market conditions, there was a premium on speedy and reliable access to the markets during periods of perceived opportunity. Issuers and investment bankers were no longer willing to tolerate unpredictable delays arising from SEC administrative practices. Even those who most opposed Rule 415 because of its consequences for disclosure and verification agreed that issuers would, if the rule were not adopted, make increased use of the Eurodollar market where "bought deals" were the rule. Indeed, some of the larger firms that opposed

---

47. In June 2003 the SEC requested as part of its concept release on the use of ratings under the federal securities laws that the public comment on whether the SEC should abandon debt ratings as a criterion for the use of Form S-3 in favor of "investor sophistication or large size denomination criteria." SEC Release No. 33-8236 (June 4, 2003).

Rule 415 were nevertheless among those that found the rule most attractive because it enabled them to offer their clients options in both markets.

Important changes had taken place in the way that securities were distributed well before the adoption of Rule 415. One of the most significant developments was the action taken by the SEC in April 1978 in extending the availability of Form S-16 to underwritten primary offerings.[48] The result was to speed up the registration process, first to approximately one week and later to a matter of days. The old practices of allowing a month or more to elapse between the filing of a registration statement and its effective date and allocating upward of a week to form a syndicate and sell the issue fell by the wayside in the case of high-grade debt and equity securities. A consequence was a reduction in the amount of time available for underwriters to perform due diligence. The due diligence concerns expressed in the Rule 415 hearings were the same concerns that previously had been expressed in the context of Form S-16.[49]

The development in the Euromarket of "bought deals," deals in which underwriting commitments would be made with no prior marketing efforts, led to increasing pressure for more rapid access to the U.S. markets. In Europe, where there are no requirements that securities be sold pursuant to an effective registration statement, the traditional method of selling debt securities through underwriting syndicates following a marketing period largely had been replaced by instantaneous sales to banks or other financial institutions that would bid for the securities on a firm basis and resell them in whatever manner they chose.[50] Issuers thus avoided the market risk inherent in the former practice of pricing an issue after a two-week selling period.

As bought deals became increasingly prevalent in the Euromarket, U.S. investment bankers sought ways to fit this

---

48. SEC Release No. 33-5923 (April 10, 1978).

49. *See* C. Johnson, *Expanded Use of Form S-16; Guide 42,* Tenth Annual Institute on Securities Regulation 39 (Practising Law Institute Transcript 1979).

50. *See generally* N. Adam, *Behind the Bravado of the Bought Deal,* Euromoney, Aug. 1980.

concept within the framework of an offering registered under the 1933 Act.

The discipline of fixed-price offerings also began to erode before the adoption of Rule 415. Debt securities purchased in the Euromarket pursuant to bought deals generally are not reoffered at a fixed price. Instead, as stated in Morgan Stanley's February 2, 1982 letter to the SEC, sales are made first at discounted prices to large investors willing to act promptly, then the balance is hedged in the options or futures market, and a portion is offered to retail buyers at higher prices.

Although the NASD's *Papilsky* rules[51] prohibit sales at a discount in a fixed-price offering except to an NASD member (or certain foreign dealers) for services actually performed in the distribution of the securities, there is no requirement that a public offering of securities be made at a fixed price. If there is no agreement with the issuer to reoffer the securities at a fixed price or if the prospectus does not indicate that they are to be so offered, then the *Papilsky* rules do not apply. Indeed, there is nothing to prevent an investment banker from offering registered securities at different prices to institutions and retail purchasers.

The complaints voiced to the SEC about Rule 415's adverse consequences for disclosure and due diligence were therefore directed largely at the wrong target. Underwriters' ability to engage in due diligence investigations prior to an offering had already been weakened by the introduction of the integrated disclosure system and an added premium on speedy access to markets. It came to be questionable whether the underwriter any longer "sponsored" an issue in a meaningful way, as opposed to delivering pricing advice and distribution services. Changes in SEC review practices, volatile market conditions and severe competition among underwriters also adversely affected disclosure and due diligence.

An ABA task force summarized these developments:

> For underwriters, the effect of the changes described above was to accelerate the transition from "relationship"

---

51. Rules 2730, 2740 and 2750. *See* Chapter 6.

to "transactional" investment banking. The traditional underwritten public offering by a reporting company—sometimes referred to as that "high ceremony of capitalism"—degenerated in the space of a few years into a series of bargain-basement brawls, characterized by abbreviated and sporadic opportunities for investigation and successive sales by different underwriters of large amounts of securities on the basis of identical disclosure documents. The finely-honed prospectus—"the best record of our due diligence," in the view of many underwriters—was replaced by a multi-document "offering package" consisting of documents that had been filed by the issuer at varying times for varying purposes (e.g., periodic reporting, Form 8-K reporting, proxy solicitation) and large portions of which were beyond the underwriters' capacity to influence, that were often delivered constructively (i.e., not at all) to the buyer, and that especially in the case of continuous offerings were subject to automatic change whenever the issuer filed a 1934 Act report. Indeed, it was no longer clear what the underwriter's goal was to be in sorting out the accuracy of different documents prepared at different times.[52]

Whether these developments are viewed as beneficial to issuers or detrimental to the capital markets, they represented significant changes in the distribution process that had come about independently of Rule 415. These practices had been evolving in any event, but Rule 415 raised the consciousness of issuers to the possibilities of change. Investment bankers responded by intensifying their efforts to be innovative. They also realized that to compete effectively they must be willing to commit large amounts of capital. Growing capital requirements led to a renewed interest in public ownership by privately owned securities firms, an increase in public financing by the major firms (often at the holding company level under their own debt

---

52. ABA Committee on Federal Regulation of Securities, *Report of Task Force on Sellers' Due Diligence and Similar Defenses Under the Federal Securities Laws,* 48 Bus. Law. 1185, 1186–87 (1993).

shelf registration statements) and a willingness by a number of securities firms to be acquired by larger companies (not always in the securities business) that were in a position to provide needed capital.

One of the authors and his partner concluded in an article published shortly after Rule 415 was adopted on a temporary basis:

> Whether shelf registrations become the norm or most companies decide to "shelve the shelf rule," changes in traditional underwriting practices are likely to continue in the new rule 415 environment. Bought deals and other alternatives to fixed-price syndicated offerings did not require the adoption of rule 415. What really matters is the climate for change resulting from the financial community's reaction to the rule. Even if the SEC rescinds or amends rule 415 (and rescission seems unlikely), it cannot turn back the clock to the time when it was assumed without question that a fixed-price syndicated offering was the only proper way to distribute securities.[53]

How Rule 415 Works

If an issuer decides to file a shelf registration statement, it determines the dollar amount of securities to be registered and checks the box on the facing sheet of the registration statement to indicate that the filing is being made under Rule 415. The registration statement must contain the undertakings described below. The SEC may or may not review the document. If the registration statement covers an at-the-market offering of equity securities, other substantive requirements must be met.

- *Securities Covered by Rule 415*

Rule 415 permits securities to be registered under the 1933 Act for an offering to be made on a continuous or delayed basis

---

53. C. Johnson & K. Cote, *The New Shelf Registration Rule,* 15 Rev. Sec. Reg. 925, 934 (1982).

SHELF REGISTRATION (RULE 415)

in the future *if* the registered securities are specified in one of the eleven clauses of Rule 415(a)(1).

Some of these are traditional uses of shelf registration: (i) securities to be offered or sold by a person other than the issuer or an affiliate, (ii) securities to be offered and sold pursuant to a dividend or interest reinvestment plan or employee benefit plan, (iii) securities to be issued on the exercise of options, warrants or rights, (iv) securities to be issued on the conversion of other securities, (v) securities pledged as collateral, (vi) depositary receipts registered on Form F-6 and (viii) securities to be issued in business combinations.[54]

The most important categories of shelf-registered securities are specified in clause (ix), covering securities "the offering of which will be commenced promptly, will be made on a continuous basis and may continue for a period in excess of 30 days from the date of initial effectiveness," and in clause (x), covering securities "registered (or qualified to be registered) on Form S-3 or Form F-3 . . . which are to be offered and sold on a continuous or delayed basis" by or on behalf of the issuer or an affiliate.

Note that clause (x), which permits continuous or delayed offerings, is available only where the securities are registered or qualified to be registered on Form S-3 or Form F-3. If the securities are not eligible for Form S-3 or Form F-3, they may be offered on a continuous basis (e.g., in an MTN program) but not in sporadic "takedowns" from time to time.

The eligibility requirements of Form S-3 and Form F-3 are therefore important in terms of what securities may be offered on what basis. As an example, clause (vii) permits shelf registration of mortgage-related securities, but this excludes other categories of asset-backed securities such as those backed by credit card receivables and auto loans. The instructions to Form S-3, however, expressly make investment-grade asset-backed securities eligible to use Form S-3. Offerings of these securities

---

54. Clause (xi) covers common stock to be offered and sold on a delayed or continuous basis by an investment company that makes periodic repurchase offers.

are therefore eligible under clause (x) of Rule 415(a)(1) to be registered for offer and sale on a delayed as well as a continuous basis.

- *Amount of Securities Registered*

If securities are being registered for sale on a delayed or continuous basis (i.e., pursuant to clauses (viii), (ix), or (x)), Rule 415 limits the amount of securities that an issuer may register to those that it reasonably expects to sell within two years. The SEC will defer to the issuer's judgment in this respect, and it has not been known to second-guess an issuer that does not manage to sell all of the shelf registered securities within the two-year period. The expiration of the two-year period will not terminate the registration of securities that remain unsold.

The two-year limitation does not apply to offerings of mortgage-related securities pursuant to clause (vii). The limitation does apply, however, to offerings of securities backed by assets other than mortgages, for example, credit card or other receivables, because the staff believes that such a distinction "is consistent with the Congressional policy of facilitating the marketability of mortgages."[55] The limitation also applies to MTN programs and other traditional shelf offerings that "will be commenced promptly, will be made on a continuous basis and may continue for a period in excess of 30 days from the date of initial effectiveness." These may include, in the words of the 1983 release that adopted Rule 415 on a permanent basis, "customer purchase plans; exchange, rights, subscription and rescission offers; offers to employees, consultants or independent agents; offerings on a best efforts basis; tax shelter and other limited partnership interests; commodity funds; condominium rental pools; time sharing agreements; real estate investment trusts; farmers' cooperative organizations or others making distributions on a membership basis; and continuous debt sales by finance companies to their customers."[56]

---

55. SEC Division of Corporation Finance, *Manual of Publicly Available Telephone Interpretations* 75 (#9) (July 1997).

56. SEC Release No. 33-6499 (November 17, 1983).

SHELF REGISTRATION (RULE 415)

In the case of securities offered on a continuous or delayed basis, an issuer is required to disclose a dollar amount to be offered. Because of the continuous offering requirement of clause (ix), it is customary for such offerings to specify the terms and conditions of the securities being registered (typically MTNs), including various interest rate and currency options. In the case of issuers eligible to make offerings on a delayed basis pursuant to clause (x) of the rule, the practice as discussed below is to specify a dollar amount of generic debt and equity securities and describe various categories of securities that may be issued (without any obligation to allocate as among these categories).

In the case of a shelf registration statement covering common stock or preferred stock, the amount of securities to be offered may be specified in terms of the number of shares.

Item 512(a)(3) of Regulation S-K requires the issuer to undertake to file a post-effective amendment to deregister any securities that remain unsold at the termination of the offering. In a continuous offering, of course, the offering never really "terminates," and the authors are not aware of any issuer that has done so for reasons related to this requirement.[57]

As takedowns occur, it is obviously important for the issuer to keep track of its remaining capacity under the shelf and for counsel to verify that any takedown does not exceed the amount of registered securities remaining on the shelf.

Prior to the sale of all of the registered securities, the issuer may file a new registration statement covering additional securities to be sold from time to time. A new registration statement is subject to the uncertainties of SEC staff review, and it is therefore a good idea to file sufficiently in advance of the exhaustion of the old shelf that the issuer will not be inconvenienced by an inability to sell securities on favorable conditions. Rule 462(b) offers a "cushion" in this regard, permitting an issuer to

---

57. The SEC does not require deregistration in the case of an offering pursuant to clauses (viii) through (x) of Rule 415(a)(1), even where securities remain unsold at the end of a two-year period. SEC Division of Corporation Finance, *Manual of Publicly Available Telephone Interpretations* 83 (#43) (July 1997).

register by means of a new *and immediately effective* registration statement an additional amount of securities equal to not more than 20% of the dollar amount of securities remaining on the shelf immediately prior to the final takedown.[58]

The securities remaining from the prior registration statement and the newly registered securities—whether or not pursuant to Rule 462(b)—may be offered pursuant to a common prospectus under Rule 429. Additional securities may generally not be registered by means of a post-effective amendment to an existing registration statement.[59]

- *Type of Securities Registered ("Unallocated," "Generic" or "Universal" Shelf)*

Issuers registering securities on Form S-3 or Form F-3 may elect to register both debt and equity securities on the same shelf registration statement without specifying the principal amount of debt or the number of shares of equity securities being registered. Thus, an issuer registering securities "for the shelf" on Form S-3 or Form F-3 may disclose in the registration statement and base prospectus the various types of securities covered by the registration statement (both debt and equity), but it does not have to identify the specific amount of each category to be offered. This type of registration statement is variously referred to an "unallocated," "generic" or "universal" shelf.

Issuers were once reluctant to register common stock on a shelf basis because of the perceived "overhang" effect, particularly where a common stock offering might be dilutive. This concern has largely dissipated, partly because of the unallocated

---

58. Rule 462(b) could be read as permitting the immediate registration of a quantity of securities equal to 20% of the original filing, but the staff does not agree. See *id.* at 49 (#126).

59. Rule 413 under the 1933 Act provides:

> Except as provided in Sections 24(e)(1) and 24(f) of the Investment Company Act of 1940, the registration of additional securities of the same class as other securities for which a registration statement is already in effect shall be effected through a separate registration statement relating to the additional securities.

shelf technique and also because including common stock in a registration statement can mean that the issuer might offer convertible securities rather than common stock. (It is necessary to register common stock as part of the shelf in order to do a convertible offering even though, as discussed in Chapter 12, the deemed offering of the underlying common stock when the convertible securities are taken down does not reduce the amount of securities registered.)

There are limitations on the unallocated shelf technique. For example, an issuer that is eligible to use Form S-3 to sell investment-grade debt securities but that does not otherwise qualify for the use of Form S-3 (e.g., because of insufficient "float") may not include non-investment-grade securities such as its common stock among the securities registered on an unallocated basis.

Also, the use of the unallocated shelf is limited to sales pursuant to Rule 415(a)(1)(x), that is, to sales by the issuer or one of its subsidiaries or a person of which the issuer is a subsidiary. The technique is not available for secondary sales. (The regulatory reason for the limitation is obscure, and the SEC has received several recommendations that it be abolished.)

In either case, it is permissible to register the non-qualifying securities on the same unallocated shelf registration statement provided that the identity and amount of the non-qualifying securities is separately set forth on the cover page of the registration statement.

It is important to describe in the base prospectus included in an unallocated shelf registration statement a broad description of each type and class of securities proposed to be sold. This will permit a takedown to occur with the specific terms of the security and the details of the plan of distribution to be included in a prospectus supplement to be filed under Rule 424 within two business days after pricing. New securities cannot be added after the shelf registration statement has become effective.

Describing all the contemplated securities in a base prospectus can result in a long and unwieldy document. An unallocated shelf registration statement will sometimes include multiple base prospectuses in an effort to mitigate this problem.

Questions sometimes arise as to whether the terms of a particular security have been adequately foreshadowed in the base prospectus as to justify the mere filing of a prospectus supplement rather than a post-effective amendment. In connection with "novel or unique" securities or distribution methods that raise these questions, it may be prudent to consult with the SEC staff to ensure that it has no objections to the prospectus supplement approach.

- *Documentation*

As part of the initial registration of shelf-registered securities, basic documents are filed with the SEC. The base prospectus, which as discussed above should permit broad variations on the securities that can be issued, is prepared by the issuer and its counsel, and frequently with the collaboration of counsel designated by the issuer to represent future underwriters. The base prospectus, of course, forms the principal part of the registration statement.

In the case of debt or asset-backed securities, an open-ended indenture that permits the issuance of numerous types of debt or asset-backed securities is normally qualified under the 1939 Act and filed as an exhibit to the registration statement. In the case of preferred stock, a form of charter amendment or the board of directors' resolution required to establish the basic terms of the preferred stock is filed as an exhibit to the registration statement. In other cases, such as the registration of rights or warrants, the documents creating the securities are also filed as exhibits.

The form of underwriting agreement, if any, or the form of distribution agreement relating to MTNs is also included as an exhibit to the registration statement. The base prospectus should include a plan of distribution broad enough to cover every reasonably likely method by which the securities will be sold.

An issuer will usually try to satisfy itself that its documents are satisfactory to at least some of the underwriters with whom it expects to do business on the basis of the shelf registration statement. Occasionally, an underwriter will raise objections to a feature of one of the key documents, for example, to the "market out" clause of the underwriting agreement. If the issuer wants the underwriter to participate in its offerings, it may negotiate the offending clause. If the issuer believes that it has a large enough "stable" of underwriters who are satisfied with the documents as they stand, the issuer will refuse to negotiate. Of course, it may change its mind at some point in the future depending on the performance of the other underwriters.

When a financing opportunity arises, the issuer will be able to move quickly because of the availability of registered securities and pre-negotiated agreements. A terms agreement under the underwriting agreement previously filed with the SEC (or, alternatively, a terms agreement that incorporates the underwriting agreement) will be executed and delivered as the basis for the contract between the issuer and the underwriters who make a successful proposal. The terms of the new securities and the underwriting arrangements are set forth in a prospectus supplement that is delivered to investors together with the base prospectus, and the securities are issued pursuant to preestablished procedures with the underwriters or selling agent and, in the case of debt securities, the trustee. Although the prospectus supplement and, in some cases, final forms of the securities or related documents are filed with the SEC at the time of a "takedown," the SEC does not ordinarily review these filings.

- *Incorporation by Reference of 1934 Act Reports*

As noted above, the usefulness of shelf registration is greatly enhanced by an issuer's ability to use Form S-3 or Form F-3 and to incorporate by reference its reports filed under the 1934 Act.

Item 12 of Form S-3 and Item 6 of Form F-3 require the issuer to incorporate by reference into the prospectus the issuer's most recent annual report filed with the SEC (e.g., Form 10-K, Form 20-F or Form 40-F) and all other reports filed with the SEC since the end of the fiscal year covered by the annual report. The issuer must identify these reports in the prospectus. As noted below, some items in a Form 8-K are deemed to be "furnished" to the SEC and not "filed."

In addition, the form requires the issuer to state in the prospectus that all reports and proxy statements subsequently filed by the issuer under the 1934 Act will be deemed to be incorporated by reference into the prospectus. These reports include, of course, a U.S. or a foreign issuer's subsequent annual reports as well as a U.S. issuer's subsequent reports on Form 10-Q and Form 8-K (except to the extent that items on a Form 8-K are "furnished" and not "filed" with the SEC). They do not, however, include a foreign issuer's reports on Form 6-K since these are "furnished" and not "filed."

From a liability point of view, it is obviously important that the issuer and its underwriters know exactly what documents incorporated by reference can create liability under either Section 11 or Section 12(a)(2) of the 1933 Act. Counsel delivering a disclosure opinion must also know exactly what is being covered by that opinion.

Some companies that published "earnings releases" after the end of a fiscal period used to follow the practice of voluntarily filing these releases with the SEC as part of a Form 8-K. These companies and their counsel may have believed that the prospectus would be incomplete or misleading if it did not include the latest earnings information. On the other hand, these releases include at a minimum financial statements that have not yet been reviewed by the issuer's outside accountants, and they often also include statements by the issuer's officers about the past period's results and the issuer's prospects for the future that are difficult to verify. The result of filing such a release as part of a Form 8-K is to incorporate the release into the issuer's Form S-3 registration statement and to convert the issuer's potential Rule 10b-5 liability for the press release into Section 11 and Section 12(a)(2) liability for everyone involved in takedowns from the shelf.

The SEC has permitted some mandatory disclosures on Form 8-K to be "furnished" rather than "filed," which prevents them from being automatically incorporated into a Form S-3 registration statement. This is the case for Regulation FD disclosures under Item 7.01 of Form 8-K, and also for earnings releases required to be furnished under Item 2.02 of Form 8-K. These are not subject to incorporation by reference unless the issuer makes an affirmative election to do so.[60] In fact, an issuer may

---

60. *See* Instruction B(2) to Form 8-K.

SHELF REGISTRATION (RULE 415)

elect to bifurcate an earnings release so as to "file" any financial information as to which it has a sufficiently high comfort level and "furnish" the information in the release as to which its comfort level may be lower.[61]

When the SEC expanded in 2004 the number of events that would trigger a Form 8-K reporting obligation, it created a "safe harbor" under Rule 10b-5 for a failure to file a report required "solely" pursuant to certain items of Form 8-K. The items were those the SEC acknowledged required the making of "rapid materiality and similar judgments within the compressed . . . filing timeframe" imposed by the amendments.[62] The safe harbor does not extend to Section 11 liability if statements in the registration statement are rendered misleading because of the omission of the information required to be reported on Form 8-K.

Item 512(b) of Regulation S-K requires an issuer that is registering securities under Rule 415 to undertake, for the purpose of determining 1933 Act liability, that each filing of an annual report incorporated by reference will be deemed to be a new registration statement relating to the offered securities and that any subsequent offering of such securities will be deemed to be the initial bona fide offering thereof. The purpose of the undertaking is to "restart the clock" each time an annual report is filed for purposes of the statute of limitations applicable under Sections 11 and 12(a)(2).

The effect of the undertaking is also to make it clear that the issuer and other potential defendants have liability under Sections 11 and 12(a)(2) for each newly filed annual report. This is not unreasonable, since the annual report is the principal part of any registration statement on Form S-3.

The liability status of the issuer's other periodic reports—and prospectus supplements—is not so clear. First of all, as noted above, a foreign issuer's reports on Form 6-K are not "filed" so they are clearly not incorporated by reference. Second, even a U.S. issuer's quarterly reports on Form 10-Q are incorporated not into the registration statement but into the "prospectus." This should mean that there is no Section 11 liability for such reports even

---

61. *See* Instruction 3 to Item 2.02 of Form 8-K.
62. SEC Release 33-8400 (March 16, 2004).

though they can be the basis for liability under Section 12(a)(2) or Rule 10b-5. The same result should apply for prospectus supplements filed with the SEC under Rule 424(b).[63]

As noted in Chapter 3, timely filing of all 1934 Act reports during the past 12 months (with an exception for certain reports on Form 8-K) is generally a precondition to an issuer's use of Form S-3, including for purposes of a shelf registration statement. If the issuer is subsequently late in making a 1934 Act filing and does not obtain a waiver from the SEC, is it still able to effect takedowns from the effective shelf? There is no definitive SEC or staff statement on the subject, although the authors understand that the staff will informally advise that the registration statement will remain usable until the next Form 10-K is due. As of that time, in the staff's view, the undertaking about the filing of a Form 10-K as constituting a "new registration statement" in effect requires the issuer to meet the requirements of Form S-3. There is nothing explicit in the rules to support this position.

On the other hand, if a reporting issuer has made a recent acquisition (or if a "probable" acquisition is pending), Regulation S-X and Item 9.01 of Form 8-K require it to file specified financial statements. According to the instructions to Item 9.01 of Form 8-K, during any period in which the issuer has not filed the required financial statements, "offerings should not be made pursuant to effective registration statements" (with certain exceptions for non-financing transactions). Accordingly, takedowns from effective shelf registrations may not be possible during this period.[64]

---

63. In the Aircraft Carrier Release, the SEC noted the views of commentators (including the previous edition of this book) to the effect that Rule 424 prospectus supplements and forward-incorporated 1934 Act reports were not subject to Section 11 liability. It stated its disagreement with those views but proposed amendments to "eliminate any uncertainty." SEC Release No. 33-7606A (November 13, 1998), text at nn.75–76. The amendments were not adopted.

64. As noted in Chapter 7, an issuer in this position "should" not make private placements under Rule 505 or 506 where the purchasers include persons other than accredited investors. In addition, the SEC will not declare effective the issuer's new registration statements or any post-effective amendments.

SHELF REGISTRATION (RULE 415)

- *Use of Offering Material*

The question often arises whether the company and the underwriters may enhance the marketing effort by using a term sheet, a brochure or other supplementary selling literature. As we saw in Chapter 1, supplementary selling literature may be used without violating Section 5(b)(1) of the 1933 Act (the "free writing" privilege) if it is accompanied or preceded by a prospectus that meets the requirements of Section 10(a) of the 1933 Act, that is, a prospectus that contains all the information—including pricing information—required by the 1933 Act. A base prospectus does not usually contain sufficient information to meet this standard, although there have been exceptions (e.g., base prospectuses with pricing ranges set forth in grid form).

Offering material could be used after the prospectus supplement becomes available, but that defeats the purpose of offering material, which is to help gauge investor interest prior to pricing. Some issuers have resorted to filing offering material under cover of a Form 8-K. The theory is that the offering material becomes part of the prospectus when it is incorporated along with the Form 8-K into the prospectus. The downside of this technique is that the offering material remains a part of the prospectus, at least until the next filing of a Form 10-K. Some of these issuers, after the closing of the offering in question, have filed a new Form 8-K that purported to "expunge" the previous Form 8-K. The issuers in question purported to rely on Rule 412, under which statements in documents incorporated by reference are deemed to be modified or superseded by new information contained in a prospectus or a document later incorporated by reference. The SEC staff does not agree that Rule 412 permits an issuer to file a document to remove or expunge the information in the earlier Form 8-K, and it has stated that any attempt to do so would be "null and void."[65]

Of course, it remains open to the issuer and underwriters to include any offering material they please in the prospectus filed

---

65. SEC Division of Corporation Finance, *Current Issues and Rulemaking Projects* 66–67 (Nov. 14, 2000).

with the SEC under Rule 424(b). As discussed below, the SEC staff would likely take the position that the prospectus and offering material would create potential Section 11 liability, but this result is not so clear.

- *Undertaking to File Post-Effective Amendments in Certain Situations*

There are limits on the degree to which the SEC's rules permit a shelf registration statement to be updated by means of incorporation by reference of the issuer's 1934 Act filings. In certain situations (apart from the "convenience shelf" situation described below), the SEC insists on an opportunity to review new information before an offering can proceed, and in other situations the new information must be incorporated by reference in a particular manner.

Item 512(a) of Regulation S-K implements these SEC policies by requiring specific undertakings from issuers that file registration statements under Rule 415. These undertakings require that certain updating be accomplished by means of a post-effective amendment to the registration statement. Except in the case of the Rule 462(b) procedure mentioned above, post-effective amendments are subject to SEC review (which may require 48 hours or longer) and must be declared effective before the related prospectus may be used in confirming sales.

Pursuant to the undertakings, a post-effective amendment must be filed to incorporate information into the registration statement that is for the purpose of

- including any prospectus required by Section 10(a)(3) of the 1933 Act (which provides that any prospectus used more than nine months after the effective date of a registration statement must contain information as of a date not more than 16 months prior to its use);

- reflecting in the prospectus any facts or events arising after the effective date of the registration statement (or the most recent post-effective amendment) that, individually or in the aggregate, represent a "fundamental change" in the information set forth therein; and

- including any material information with respect to the plan of distribution not disclosed in the registration statement or any material change to such information.

Item 512 specifies that the first two undertakings do not apply to registration statements on Form S-3 or Form F-3 if the relevant information is contained in a 1934 Act report that is incorporated by reference in the registration statement.

The SEC has said that a "fundamental change" is something more than a "material change" and has given examples of the differences. It has stated that, while many variations and matters such as operating results, properties, business, product development, backlog, management, and litigation ordinarily would not be fundamental, major changes in the issuer's operations, such as significant acquisitions or dispositions, would require the filing of a post-effective amendment. Also, any change in the business or operations of the registrant that would necessitate a restatement of the financial statements may be a fundamental change. But as material changes, to say nothing of fundamental changes, will be included in the issuer's filed 1934 Act reports (with accompanying press releases), it has not been necessary for issuers or their counsel to trouble themselves with close calls as to what is fundamental rather than simply material.[66] Care should be taken that any 1934 Act report relied on

---

66. It should be noted that the "fundamental" as opposed to "material" dichotomy adopted by the SEC to determine when a post-effective amendment will be required flies in the face of the traditional analysis that a post-effective amendment should be used to change or correct a statement in an effective registration statement while a supplement should be used to reflect a development that has occurred after the registration statement has become effective. Professor Loss' classic example—taken from a 1934 FTC proceeding predating the formation of the SEC—is that if a registration statement discloses that the issuer owns 500 acres of timberland and a subsequent survey shows that it owns only 250 acres, then a post-effective amendment is required to correct the error. If, however, the registration statement correctly discloses that the issuer owns 500 acres, and after effectiveness, a forest fire destroys the timber on half of these acres, then a supplement filed under Rule 424 is the proper means of reflecting this material, perhaps fundamental, change in the registrant's affairs. 1 L. Loss & J. Seligman, *Securities Regulation* 562–63 (rev. 3d ed. 1998).

for this purpose, for example, a Form 8-K regarding an earnings release, is in fact incorporated by reference and not merely "furnished."

Whether or not a change is reflected in a post-effective amendment is important to the timing of a transaction. On the other hand, timing is not everything. It is still necessary to be sure that investors are informed about the change. Even if the issuer puts out a press release about a material change and files (rather than "furnishes") the information as part of a Form 8-K, the underwriters may still want the change to be described in the prospectus supplement. And if the circumstances warrant, the underwriters may decide to inform each prospective investor about the change prior to making sales.

Material changes in the plan of distribution may require a post-effective amendment whether or not they are described in a 1934 Act report (which would usually not be the case in any event). As originally adopted, the required undertaking ended with the words "including (but not limited to) any addition or deletion of a managing underwriter." Rule 405 broadly defines the term "managing underwriter," but the staff has construed it sensibly to cover only an underwriter who actually performs a management function. Primarily because of this undertaking, the early shelf registration statements named a number of potential managing underwriters.

The undertaking operated in a rather strange fashion. If a registration statement contemplated offerings directly by the issuer or through three named investment banking firms or underwriting syndicates managed by one or more of them, the members of a syndicate managed by any one or more of the designated firms could be named in a sticker, and a post-effective amendment would not be required. If a firm not previously named were to co-manage a syndicate with one or more of the named underwriters, no post-effective amendment would be required even if the new firm acted as the book-running manager. But if that firm acted as the sole manager of a subsequent offering, a post-effective amendment would be required even though it had been named in the previous supplement and even though its management of the earlier offering would have satisfied the SEC's rationale for requiring a post-effective amendment—namely, the need to create a "pause" in the process to "facilitate underwriter involvement with the registration statement when such a material change in the plan of distribution occurs."

What would happen if an unnamed firm initiated a "bought deal" and did not invite a named firm to act as a co-manager? Initially, the staff had no ready answer and determined to proceed on a case-by-case basis to resolve questions of this type.

When it acted in 1982 to extend the effective date of Rule 415,[67] the SEC noted that two principal interpretive questions had arisen in the course of administering the rule. These were (1) determining those circumstances in which a person would be deemed to be a managing underwriter and (2) whether it was necessary under particular circumstances to proceed by means of a post-effective amendment or a prospectus supplement. Recognizing that a post-effective amendment would often have adverse consequences for a transaction, the SEC amended Rule 415 to delete the requirement to undertake to file a post-effective amendment to reflect the addition or deletion of a managing underwriter. This action made it unnecessary to name any underwriters in the first place and afforded issuers the flexibility of doing deals quickly with whatever firm might come along and offer attractive terms.

As discussed above, issuers avoid problems under the third undertaking by describing the plan of distribution in the base prospectus in terms that are as broad as possible.

Another undertaking specifies that any post-effective amendment filed for the purpose of filing an annual report starts the clock running anew for purposes of the statute of limitations contained in Section 13 of the 1933 Act. As noted above, this is not an issue if the registration statement is on Form S-3 or Form F-3. Even as to these issuers, however, another undertaking achieves the same result as to each future annual report on Form 10-K or Form 20-F that is incorporated by reference into the registration statement.

---

67. SEC Release No. 33-6423 (September 2, 1982).

Unfortunately, the staff does not always regard the undertakings under Item 512(a) as exhausting the occasions that require a post-effective amendment. See the discussion below under "Non-Underwritten Registered Equity Secondaries," for example, regarding the addition or substitution of selling shareholders.

Shelf Filings by Foreign Governments or Political Subdivisions

Rule 415(b) excludes any registration statement filed by a foreign government or one of its political subdivisions. In addition, as discussed in Chapter 9, these issuers are not eligible to use Form F-3. Instead, they register their securities under Schedule B to the 1933 Act. They are not subject to the continuous reporting requirements of the 1934 Act unless they choose to list their securities on an exchange.

Nonetheless, the SEC has adopted procedures that allow "seasoned" foreign governments to file shelf registrations in a manner similar to that specified in Rule 415. Even before Rule 415 was first proposed, the Kingdom of Sweden was permitted to register for shelf debt securities to be sold from time to time in the United States. The base prospectus contained the same type of political, economic and statistical information contained in prospectuses previously used by the kingdom in selling its debt securities. The registration statement contemplated the filing by post-effective amendment of preliminary and final prospectus supplements, similar to a Form S-16 prospectus, for each issue. According to the correspondence with the SEC permitting the filing, the procedure was designed to provide Sweden with substantially the same benefits as a Form S-16 registrant.[68]

The SEC followed up with a release setting forth the views of the Division of Corporation Finance on the use of registration statements for delayed offerings by foreign governments.[69] In effect, the SEC invited other foreign governments that

---

68. SEC No-action Letter, *Kingdom of Sweden* (September 10, 1980).
69. SEC Release No. 33-6240 (September 10, 1980).

previously had filed registration statements to follow the same procedures as those developed for the Kingdom of Sweden.

In September 1982, at the same time that it extended the effectiveness of Rule 415, the SEC published a revised staff interpretation regarding foreign government shelf registration statements.[70] When the SEC adopted Rule 415 on a permanent basis in November 1983, it reaffirmed the September 1982 staff position and concluded that it allowed seasoned foreign governments to use the shelf registration procedure in a manner substantially similar to that specified in Rule 415.

The shelf procedure continued to be applicable to "seasoned" foreign governments and their political subdivisions, those that had registered securities (or guarantees of the securities of others) within the past five years and had not defaulted in the payment of principal or interest.[71] The original procedure required the annual filing of a registration statement of securities to be offered on a "firm commitment" basis during a period of 12 months from the effective date. Under the revised procedure, foreign governments could register an amount reasonably expected to be offered and sold within two years, the same amount that could be registered under Rule 415. The requirement of a firm commitment underwriting was later eliminated. The original procedure contemplated two supplements, a preliminary supplement and a final supplement that would contain the pricing information, and that the base prospectus containing the Schedule B information would accompany both the preliminary supplement and the final supplement. Under the revised procedure, if the registrant had previously furnished a person with a copy of its base prospectus, it need only deliver prospectus supplements to that person. The supplements were required

---

70. SEC Release No. 33-6424 (September 2, 1982).

71. This definition had first been established in SEC No-action Letter, *Republic of Venezuela* (November 24, 1980). An otherwise "non-seasoned" non-U.S. governmental issuer wishing to conduct a delayed or continuous offering may satisfy the seasoning requirement by first filing a registration statement for a discrete offering of securities. It may then file a shelf registration immediately following completion of the first offering.

to state that a copy of the base prospectus would be furnished promptly, without charge, on request.

The Division of Corporation Finance has no objection to an issuer's including in the base prospectus all the information included in the prospectus supplements under the original procedure except for "price, maturity, and related information." That information can be furnished by means of a Rule 424 sticker instead of in a post-effective amendment. A condition to using this procedure is that the base prospectus be "adequately disseminated to the public" a reasonable period of time before the offering.

The SEC has issued no-action letters to several "seasoned" Schedule B issuers[72] in which it has allowed these issuers to use a special procedure to update their registration statements and to comply with the disclosure requirements under the 1933 Act. Under this procedure, the issuer voluntarily files an annual report on Form 18-K and amendments to the annual report on Form 18-KA. These filings are then incorporated by reference into the issuer's Schedule B registration statements, including its shelf registrations.

The annual Form 18-K includes all information required by the form and any additional information required to be included in a Schedule B registration statement, together with any other information deemed material to investors. The Form 18-KA amendments are filed as necessary and include, for example, such information as the interim financial reports of the issuer, its annual budget and any additional information deemed necessary or appropriate for disclosure purposes.

When the registration statement is filed under Schedule B, the base prospectus incorporates by reference the most recently filed Form 18-K, including all amendments. Incorporation of the filed Form 18-K and any Form 18-KA effectively relieves the

---

72. E.g., *United Mexican States* (February 25, 1994), *Nacional Financiera, S.N.C.* (July 5, 1994), *Kreditanstalt für Wiederaufbau and Kfw Int'l Finance Inc.* (July 18, 1994), *Republic of Portugal* (July 22, 1994), *Japan Dev. Bank et al.* (August 3, 1994), *Ontario Hydro* (October 31, 1994), *Commonwealth of Australia* (April 4, 1995), *Government of Victoria and Treasury Corp. of Victoria* (June 23, 1995).

issuer of the need to file annual post-effective amendments to its shelf registration statement.

Conventional Debt and Preferred Stock Shelf Registration

A Rule 415 shelf registration is a vehicle ideally suited to issuers of investment-grade debt securities eligible to use Form S-3 or Form F-3 that seek access to the capital markets on a regular basis. It is also well suited to continuous MTN offerings, which will be examined later in this chapter.

Market overhang is not a significant factor for high-grade debt, and the ability to move quickly to take advantage of market windows is important in the debt market. The same can be said for straight preferred stock, and a significant number of issuers have registered preferred stock to be sold off the shelf. Rule 415 does not require an investment-grade rating as a condition to filing, but the rule has not been used as often by issuers of high-yield securities. Many of these issues are sold under Rule 144A, often on a one-shot basis with a heavy degree of marketing.

Once a company decides to file a shelf registration statement covering its debt securities or straight preferred stock, there are certain procedures to be put in place and numerous documents to be drafted. The key to the process is to provide for maximum flexibility and the ability to accomplish a takedown from the shelf in a matter of hours. If the proper structure is created, there should seldom be a need for any SEC involvement (such as a post-effective amendment) when the securities are sold.

If the company has a significant relationship with an investment banking firm, it may be helpful to bring it into the loop at an early stage to take advantage of its expertise. Many issuers will not do so in the interest of maintaining their own independence or in order to keep the playing field level for all potential underwriters.

It is strongly recommended that a law firm be designated as counsel for the underwriters or other purchasers of the securities. If a firm is appointed to act in this capacity, it should be allowed to participate in the establishment of the program. Such participation will facilitate the first takedown, which would otherwise be held up while counsel became familiar with the relevant disclosure and documentation.

- *Securities To Be Registered; "Convenience Shelf" Problem*

The company should review its financial needs and make a reasoned estimate of the amount of securities that it expects to sell over the next two years. While the SEC is not likely to second-guess a registrant, there is no reason to go overboard. Remember that the filing fee for a billion dollar shelf is $126,700 as of January 2004. On the other hand, a shelf that registers less than $500 million of debt securities is hardly worth the effort.

For many issuers, the two-year limitation is not relevant because they register each year only the amount of securities needed to support the annual funding plan approved by the board of directors or one of its committees.

The question sometimes arises whether immediate takedowns from a shelf registration statement are permitted. At one point, the SEC condemned the use of shelf registration for the purpose of "procedural convenience," that is, the ability to facilitate an immediate securities offering by having a registration statement become effective without all required information.[73] The SEC's objections lost much of their force with the adoption of Rule 430A, and the SEC has since confirmed that immediate takedowns are permissible. The registration statement at the time it becomes effective, however, must include all material information to the extent it is known or reasonably available to the issuer. "Accordingly, if an offering of securities is certain at the time the shelf registration statement becomes effective, the relevant information (e.g., description of securities, plan of distribution and use of proceeds) must be disclosed with respect to the securities subject to the immediate takedown . . . ."[74] In practice, this means that the prospectus supplement for the first takedown is filed with the registration statement, which becomes

---

73. SEC Release No. 33-6499 (November 17, 1983), text at n.31.

74. SEC Release No. 33-7168 (May 11, 1995), text following n.39. *See also* SEC Release No. 33-8419 (May 3, 2004), n.83.

SHELF REGISTRATION (RULE 415)

effective pursuant to Rule 430A. If the deal in fact proceeds within the Rule 430A time frame, all is well; if not, then the registration statement is a true shelf (i.e., a "delayed" offering), and the offering can proceed when the time is right without having to worry about the limitations of Rule 430A.

One still hears from time to time reports of SEC staff comments that takedowns within one or two days of effectiveness (or even a week) should be effected by means of a post-effective amendment. If a takedown is proposed shortly after effectiveness and counsel is being called on to render a disclosure opinion, he or she should inquire into what the issuer's intentions were at the time of effectiveness.

As discussed above, it is obviously important for the company to keep track of the registered securities taken down from the shelf and to "reload" its program by registering additional securities on a new registration statement before its ability to sell securities has been exhausted. Counsel must also verify that the securities taken down do not exceed the amount of registered securities still "on the shelf."

- *Plan of Distribution*

Rule 415 merely sets forth a procedure for registering securities. It does not mandate any particular method of distribution. Many issuers file shelf registrations with no intention of selling securities other than in conventional underwritings managed by their traditional investment banker. They have been successful in the past in raising funds in this fashion, and they see no reason to change simply because they are using a shelf registration statement. Although there is no longer any legal reason to name potential underwriters in the base prospectus, some issuers will name their traditional banker as a potential underwriter while maintaining the flexibility of using another firm. In a traditional type of underwritten transaction off a shelf, the deal will be structured, there will be price talk with potential purchasers, and the underwriters will build a book, all before an underwriting commitment is made.

For the more frequent issuers, the so-called "commodity" issuers of debt securities, the process is far less refined. An assistant treasurer may place phone calls to the capital markets desks of three or four underwriting houses and solicit bids for an amount of securities with a specified maturity. In some cases, the amount and maturity will be left open. A response will be expected within the hour. The firms will go through an exercise that they refer to as a "fire drill," calling on the resources of sales, trading and syndicate personnel in coming up with a bid. The best bid may not be the winner. Issuers have been known to shop bids.

The winning bidder will have entered into a bought deal—that is, it will have agreed to purchase the securities before beginning its marketing efforts. It may have tested the market a bit, but it will not have built a book before agreeing on a price. It may get together a group of large or small firms to join in a syndicate to spread the risk or improve marketing or to repay favors (whether owed by the winning bidder to these firms or, more frequently, by the issuer). But, in any case, it must scurry around and try to unload the securities at a profit. In all likelihood, the securities will wind up in the hands of a small number of institutional investors.

There is fierce competition for bought deals among the top originating firms. The spreads are thin. In some swap-driven transactions, underwriters have been known to bid with a negative spread in order to obtain the fee for arranging the currency or interest rate swap.

There have been bids that would appear to make little economic sense. The bidder may have been seeking to buy an introduction to a potential corporate client. Or it may have been trying to build its position in the published standings or "league tables."[75] It may be that its primary interest was in having its name appear in a tombstone advertisement along with a top-grade issuer.

In doing bought deals, the risk : reward ratio is weighted heavily on the risk side. Without an accurate forward calendar to rely on, underwriters are unable to gauge the potential supply of debt securities coming to market, an important consideration

---

75. One widely followed version of such tables is compiled periodically by *Investment Dealers' Digest*.

in making a pricing decision. Some bought deals have resulted in spectacular, well-publicized losses for the firms involved.

Deals may be done without an issuer soliciting bids. In the Rule 415 environment, issuers are besieged with creative financing proposals to be done off the shelf. Many of the ideas are good ones that fit the issuer's needs. This is one of the reasons why flexibility is essential, not only with respect to timing but also with respect to the terms of the securities. As stated in an article on innovative debt securities:

> It became customary for lawyers to receive urgent calls from investment bankers to the effect that "We have a purchaser for $20 million zero-coupon debt of X Corporation. Can this be done today off X Corporation's shelf?" Or "We have a swap for 100 million New Zealand dollars. Can New Zealand dollar denominated securities be issued under Y Corporation's shelf? And can we sell them in Europe in bearer form?" Perhaps neither shelf was drafted with zero-coupon or foreign currency denominated bearer debt securities expressly in mind, but with sufficient flexibility in the documents the transaction could go forward.[76]

Direct sales to institutional investors without the use of an underwriter has not become an accepted method of distribution. Perhaps issuers realize that if they bypass the traditional distribution channels, those channels may not be around when they need them. An exception that proves the rule was a Dutch auction in 1982 of $135 million of debt securities of Exxon Corporation.[77]

---

76. N. D. Slonaker & L. M. Wiltshire, *Innovative Debt Securities,* 20 Rev. Sec. & Comm. Reg. 89, 90 (1987).

77. The mechanics of a Dutch auction are described in a 1977 SEC no-action letter issued to a subsidiary of Exxon Corporation. Each bidder, including institutions and individuals as well as broker-dealers, indicates the amount of debt securities to be purchased and the yield. "After closing the invitation period, the bids are listed in ascending order of yields. The bid with the lowest yield is accepted first, and then other bids at successively higher

However the securities are marketed in fact, the plan of distribution set forth in the base prospectus should be drafted so broadly that the undertaking to file a post-effective amendment to reflect a material change in the plan of distribution will never come into play.

- *The Indenture and the Description of the Securities*

A single shelf registration statement may cover both senior and subordinated debt securities, and a single trustee may serve for the holders of both classes of securities unless and until there is a default.

Indentures for shelf programs should be open-ended. There should be no limitation on the amount of debt securities that may be issued thereunder. The indenture will set forth the terms and provisions that are common to all of the securities that may be issued. It should be drafted in such a way that when each series of debt is issued a supplemental indenture will not be required. Rather, the terms of each series should be permitted to be set forth in an officer's certificate delivered to the trustee. The variable terms also will be set forth in the body of the securities. The indenture should also anticipate the possible "reopening" of an issue as discussed later in this chapter.

The indenture should be drafted so broadly that any conceivable type of debt can be issued thereunder, including convertible and exchangeable securities. It should provide for original issue discount (OID) securities (zero coupon obligations or those bearing a rate of interest below market rates). In the case of a deep discount security, the full principal amount will not be payable on the acceleration of maturity (in the event of default or the operation of some other indenture provision), and the indenture should provide that, in such case, the amount

---

yields are accepted up to those bids with the highest yield required to reach the total amount of the offering. The highest accepted yield is the yield at which all of the bonds are awarded. Upon determination of the yield, the interest rate and price are fixed by the issuer. The securities will be awarded to the successful bidders at a uniform price based on the accepted yield." SEC No-action Letter, *Exxon Corporation* (May 9, 1977). *See also* SEC No-action Letter, *Salomon Brothers* (August 22, 1985).

payable will be as specified in the terms of the security. The indenture should provide that the securities may be issued in registered form or in bearer form with coupons attached. This will accommodate sales in the Euromarket and elsewhere outside of the United States. Provision should be made for obligations denominated in foreign currencies as well as U.S. dollars. The indenture should permit the issuance of floating rate obligations, as well as those with a fixed interest rate. It should be broad enough to allow puttable bonds and securities with extendible maturities as well as the possibility that the terms of the security may provide for non-cash payment at maturity or on redemption.

In dealing with separate series of obligations under a single indenture, care should be taken to ensure that action by the holders of debt of a particular series is sufficient in appropriate cases and that the holders of other series of debt need not be involved. For example, an amendment of the indenture should require the consent of the holders of a specified percentage of the debt securities of each series affected thereby. Likewise, in the event of default with respect to debt securities of a particular series, only the holders of that series of debt should have rights with respect to the declaration of acceleration, rescission of any declaration of acceleration and waiver of events of default.

The base prospectus will contain a description of the debt securities and the indenture or indentures under which they are to be issued. It will refer to the prospectus supplement for a description of the terms of the securities of the particular series to which it relates: their designation (e.g., by coupon and maturity); any limit on the aggregate principal amount; the percentage of their principal amount at which the securities will be issued and, in the case of original issue discount securities, the principal amount payable upon acceleration of maturity; the date or dates on which the securities will mature or the manner in which those dates are determined; the rate or rates per annum (which may be fixed or variable) at which the securities will bear interest, if any, or the method of determining the rate or rates; the date from which interest, if any, will accrue, the dates on which interest will be payable and the record dates for interest payment dates; the dates, if any, on which, and the price or prices at which, the securities will, pursuant to any mandatory sinking fund provisions, or may, pursuant to any optional sinking fund provisions, be redeemed by the issuer, and the other detailed sinking fund provisions; the date, if any, after which, and the price or prices at which, the securities may be redeemed at the option of the issuer or of the holder and the other detailed terms and provisions of any optional redemption, including any remarketing arrangements; whether any issue may be "reopened"; the form (registered or bearer or both) in which the securities may be issued and any restrictions applicable to the exchange of one form for another and to the offer, sale and delivery of the securities in either form; whether and under what circumstances the issuer will pay additional amounts in respect of any securities held by a person who is not a U.S. person in respect of specified taxes, assessments or other governmental charges and whether the issuer has the option to redeem affected securities rather than pay such additional amounts; whether the securities are to be issued initially or permanently in the form of a global security and, if so, the identity of the depositary for the global security; and the currency, currencies or currency units for which the securities may be purchased and in which they are payable.

One "moral hazard" that offsets to some degree the flexibility and other advantages of shelf registration is that the lawyers working on a transaction may be tempted to assume things that are not the case. The indenture for a transaction may have been filed with the SEC many years ago, following which it may have been reincorporated by reference into subsequent "reload" registration statements and served as the basis for issuing securities in a large number of takedowns. Also, the issuer may have been involved in one or more mergers since the original filing. A major bank holding company found itself a few years ago the victim of an expensive error regarding the indenture under which it issued two tranches of ten-year subordinated debt in the aggregate amount of $4.25 billion. The debt was intended to qualify as Tier 2 capital under the Federal Reserve Board's capital adequacy guidelines. These guidelines prohibit any right on the part of the debtholders to accelerate the debt for any reason other than bankruptcy. Unfortunately, the debt was issued under the shelf registration statement and indenture of a predecessor company—not a bank holding company—that had become the surviving company on the merger of the two companies. The predecessor company's indenture did not contain the mandated anti-acceleration provisions, without which the $4.25 billion of subordinated notes would not count as Tier 2 capital. The bank holding company eventually received the Fed's approval to count the notes as Tier 2 capital, but only on the condition that it create and pay into an escrow account the present value of five years of interest payments on the notes.

- *Preferred Stock*

Preferred stock must be authorized by the issuer's certificate of incorporation. The amount authorized must be a fixed amount, and it may be increased only by action of the board of directors, a stockholder vote and the filing of a certificate of amendment. A charter provision of the type that had been customary long before the adoption of Rule 415 that authorizes the issuance of preferred stock in series, with the terms of each series established by a board resolution, should provide the necessary flexibility for a preferred stock shelf program. The terms of each particular series must be set forth in a certificate of designation filed with the secretary of state of the state in which the issuer is incorporated. This requirement will not impede a takedown under a shelf, for the certificate of designation need only be filed prior to the closing at which the securities are issued.

- *Board Authorization*

Before a shelf program can be implemented, the issuer's board of directors must meet to authorize the issuance of the securities to be registered, the filing of the shelf registration statement, the execution of the indenture, and the other matters that customarily are found in a carefully prepared set of resolutions for a financing. A shelf program could not function, however, if it were necessary for the board to meet, even by telephone, each time securities are taken off the shelf. To permit expeditious takedowns, the board must delegate to a special committee, or preferably to specified officers, the authority to determine the amount of securities for each tranche and the terms of the securities to be sold.

When Rule 415 was first adopted, there was some question as to the extent to which boards of directors would be willing to give up control over specific issues of debt securities. As debt shelf registration statements have become commonplace, this concern has faded, and boards of major companies seem quite comfortable in delegating to senior officers discretion as to the timing, size and terms of debt issues. Lawyers practicing in the area of corporate finance likewise are comfortable that, as a matter of state law, a board of directors can delegate borrowing authority to individuals holding specified offices in the corporation and that these officers may be authorized by the board to redelegate this authority to subordinates under their direction. Indeed, in the case of MTNs, which are sold on a continuous basis, it is not unusual for the pricing of individual notes to be the responsibility of an employee other than a senior officer. The pricing of debt should be contrasted to the pricing of an issue of common stock. Most lawyers take the position that the pricing of a common stock issue may be delegated by the board only to the executive committee or to a special committee of directors authorized by statute. (This does not preclude delegation by reference to current market prices.)

The creation of a series of preferred stock requires action by the board of directors or at least a special committee of the board. This is because the applicable corporate statute will require a certificate of designation adopted by the board. Perhaps the board will allow the corporate officers to authorize a preferred stock tranche under the issuer's shelf registration, but any such action must be subject to formal corporate action before the stock can be issued.

- *Underwriting Documents*

All of the investment banking firms that are players in the shelf arena have in place master AAUs, so that no agreement need be signed by the underwriters when a syndicate is put together to take securities off the shelf. When Rule 415 first was adopted on a temporary basis and it was necessary for issuers to name a number of potential managing underwriters in order to avoid the delay inherent in a post-effective amendment, it became the custom to enter into a basic underwriting

SHELF REGISTRATION (RULE 415)

agreement with the underwriters named in the prospectus and to use a terms agreement for each takedown. The underwriting agreement with the form of terms agreement attached would be filed as an exhibit to the registration statement, and it was unnecessary to make a subsequent filing when the terms agreement was filled in and signed. In some cases, these underwriting agreements continue to operate.

An issuer that has not named underwriters in its shelf prospectus also will file a standard underwriting agreement as an exhibit to its registration statement, but it is not pre-signed. Rather, the underwriting agreement with the filled-in terms is signed at the time that the underwriters commit to purchase the securities. There is little difference in the two procedures. Whether the managing underwriter signs a terms agreement, having previously signed an underwriting agreement, or whether it signs an underwriting agreement with the terms attached, a single signature will be required when the takedown is made, and the transaction can be completed just as expeditiously whichever procedure is followed.

The terms of the underwriting agreement will be basically the same as those found in the issuer's pre-Rule 415 underwriting agreements. The closing will be set for three business days after the takedown from the shelf or such longer period as may be agreed to pursuant to the SEC's "T+3" rule (see Chapter 3). The standard legal opinions, comfort letter and officer's certificate will be required as conditions to closing. In the case of a bought deal, there may be no comfort letter at the time that the underwriting agreement is signed, but only at the closing. This differs from the standard practice in conventional underwritten offerings. The underwriting agreement will contain the usual indemnification and contribution provisions.

An "out" clause that has become quite customary in underwriting agreements for shelf programs that was not in vogue prior to the adoption of Rule 415 is one that allows the underwriters to terminate their commitment if the issuer's debt securities are downgraded by one of the rating agencies. Underwriting agreements may also permit the underwriters to terminate their obligation to purchase the securities if any facts come to their attention that lead them to believe that the prospectus is false or misleading. In straight debt or preferred offerings, it is quite common for the issuer to agree with the underwriters that it will not issue any similar securities under its shelf until the closing or the earlier sale of the securities by the underwriters. In the case of common stock or convertible offerings, the issuer may agree not to offer additional common stock or convertible securities for 30 or 90 days or longer, depending on the underwriters' estimate of the market impact of such an additional offering.

There have been some complaints that designated underwriters' counsel has little leverage in negotiating the terms of the form of underwriting agreement. This complaint simply reflects the fact that a lawyer has little leverage in negotiations if he or she does not have a client at the table. Some underwriters simply will not bid on an issuer's securities if they are unhappy with the underwriting terms (e.g., the "market out" or the indemnity or contribution provisions). If they would otherwise be interested in bidding, they will often inform the issuer of the source of their concern. The issuer may ignore this concern if it believes that enough other firms are participating to guarantee vigorous competition. If it concludes at some point that it can use the services of the excluded firm in order to reinvigorate competition, it may volunteer a modification that will bring the excluded firm back into the fold.

- *Use of Preliminary Prospectus*

Most shelf takedowns are effected without the use of a preliminary prospectus. Investors are usually familiar with the issuing company, and the securities are often "plain vanilla." Occasionally, however, the underwriters will recommend the use of a preliminary prospectus. The purpose may be to provide investors with an opportunity to study the terms of a novel or unusual type of security or the company may not have accessed the capital markets for some time. Or the company may have been through some difficult times that require an extensive discussion under "Recent Developments." Also, the underwriters may recommend an electronic roadshow, and as discussed in Chapter 3 the SEC staff has imposed the condition that an electronic roadshow is possible only if investors are provided with the prospectus for the transaction.

The preliminary prospectus takes the form of a "wrapper" around the base prospectus, and the combined document is made available to investors both electronically and in hard copy. It will be filed with the SEC under Rule 424(b)(5) not later than the second business day after it is first used.

At one time, the SEC staff was said to have reservations about whether a preliminary prospectus could be used in connection with a shelf registration. Rule 430, which is the rule that permits preliminary prospectuses, specifically states that a preliminary prospectus is deemed to meet the requirements of Section 10 of the 1933 Act—thus avoiding a violation of Section 5(b)(1) of the 1933 Act—only if it is used "prior to the effective date of the registration statement." The staff's concerns appear to have abated. On the other hand, it would have been difficult in any event for the staff to oppose the use of preliminary prospectuses in a shelf context. First, the SEC itself might think twice about a staff recommendation that would mean less disclosure for investors. Second, there are frequent references in SEC pronouncements to preliminary prospectuses in a shelf context. Third, there is the staff's own imposition of a prospectus delivery requirement as a condition to an electronic roadshow.

As discussed in Chapter 1, the SEC staff took the position during the Internet Bubble that underwriters could not rely on Rule 134 unless a preliminary prospectus were available. It is doubtful that this staff position can be understood to *require* the use of a preliminary prospectus as a condition to reliance on Rule 134 in other contexts, for example, offerings of fixed-income securities where the underwriters wish to communicate to investors written information about anticipated price, yield and maturity.

- *Disclosure and Due Diligence*

The ABA's Federal Regulation of Securities Committee appointed a task force in 1990 to study the effect of shelf registration, integrated disclosure and related developments on underwriters' ability to perform due diligence sufficient to sustain a defense under Section 11 or Section 12(a)(2) of the

1933 Act. In its report,[78] the task force described in depth the disclosure and due diligence process associated with shelf takedowns of investment grade debt securities:

> The issuers eligible to use Rule 415 for primary shelf offerings on a delayed basis are those eligible to use Forms S-3 and F-3 . . . . As such, the issuers for the most part are established companies about which there is relatively wide dissemination of the information contained in the 1934 Act reports. The debt securities of most shelf issuers are rated by the rating agencies.
>
> The buyers of shelf-registered debt securities are almost exclusively institutional investors. As in the secondary market, decisions to buy are made on the basis of yield (premium over Treasury securities of comparable maturity), rating information, and the name of the issuer. The name of the issuer is particularly important in the case of investors such as insurance companies with internal credit evaluation capabilities and well-defined procedures for approving issuers' securities for purchase. Where the investor has previously approved the name, securities of the issuer are treated more or less as commodities with yield and rating information becoming the key ingredients to a purchase decision. Where an issuer's name is relatively new or little-known in the debt markets, one or more investment banking firms may work with investors' credit analysts or investment committees to explain the issuer's credit and seek to have the name approved.
>
> The disclosure document for a shelf offering is the short-form basic prospectus contained in the registration statement, as supplemented at the time of the offering by a prospectus supplement that describes the offered securities and, to the extent necessary, updates previously

---

78. ABA Committee on Federal Regulation of Securities, *Report of Task Force on Sellers' Due Diligence and Similar Defenses Under the Federal Securities Laws*, 48 Bus. Law. 1185, 1218–24 (1993) (some footnotes omitted).

reported information concerning the issuer. The basic prospectus incorporates by reference the issuer's 1934 Act reports filed prior to and subsequent to the registration statement's effective date.

Although there is considerable variation, most prospectus/prospectus supplement combinations contain, at most, very abbreviated financial and business disclosure concerning the issuer. Frequently, the prospectus/prospectus supplement combination will contain only a table of selected financial information and a very brief business description. Less frequently there will be a management's discussion and analysis ["MD&A"] or an MD&A summary. Financial statements rarely are included. Accordingly, normally most, if not all, of the key information for an informed credit decision—the financial statements, the complete MD&A and the full description of the issuer's business—are in the incorporated documents. The incorporated documents are, of course, equally available to the buyers of the securities and the potential underwriters on an ongoing basis.

While practice varies, potential underwriters sometimes are invited to review and comment on shelf registration statements prior to their filing. In such cases, the underwriters have the opportunity to review, on a more traditional time schedule, the disclosures included and incorporated by reference in the registration statement and to make adjustments to the sum total of the disclosures contained therein through adjustments to the registration statement. Frequently, however, potential underwriters are not invited to participate in the filing of a shelf registration statement, and obviously they are not invited when they have not been identified (which very frequently is the case).

Following effectiveness of the shelf registration statement, there is considerable variation in the ongoing business relationships between the issuer and potential underwriters and in the access that is afforded underwriters to perform an ongoing investigation in anticipation of shelf takedowns. As to ongoing business relationships, there is a whole spectrum of possibilities. In some cases, the issuer of shelf-registered debt securities will tend to be in more or less continuous consultation with one or a small group of investment banking firms and, as market conditions warrant, sell a portion of the registered securities through one or more such firms on a negotiated basis. In other cases, the issuer will invite a relatively large number of investment banking firms (i) to make proposals from time to time with respect to the type of shelf-registered security that may be sold on favorable terms under current market conditions or (ii) bid, in an auction-like process, for a security identified in advance by the issuer. In still other cases, an issuer may respond favorably to an unsolicited proposal from an investment banking firm that may or may not have a pre-existing relationship with the issuer. Because market conditions change rapidly, the time between presentation of a proposal and a commitment to proceed can be a few hours or even minutes.

Importantly, the use of bid-like procedures has transformed shelf underwriting into a transaction-oriented business as opposed to a relationship-oriented business. Attendant to this, there is a reduced level of familiarity between many underwriters and issuers and, realistically, a substantially reduced level of influence that these underwriters may bring to bear on the disclosures made in the issuer's disclosure documents, particularly in the circumstance where the underwriter has not participated in the preparation of the registration statement or, as discussed *infra*, the incorporated documents. The underwriter functions less as a trusted adviser and more as a trader. Competition among underwriters is fierce and, realistically, issuers have little incentive to cooperate with any one underwriter who raises a disclosure concern or who insists on its "standard" documentation or closing conditions. Shelf takedowns may occur months after the effective date of the shelf registration statement, and there may be long periods when there are no offerings taken off a shelf registration statement. New underwriters may become involved, having no history with the issuer or the registration statement.

There is a range of practices by which issuers permit underwriters to conduct updating due diligence investigations following the effective date of the registration statement. Some issuers stay in relatively frequent communication with one or a small number of prospective underwriters for the purpose of providing them with a more or less continuous flow of information about the issuer and its financing needs. Frequent issuers may hold annual or even quarterly "due diligence" meetings with prospective underwriters. Other issuers provide prospective underwriters with relatively little information on a continuous basis, although the issuers' periodic reports under the 1934 Act are of course available for review. When a decision is reached to proceed with a particular offering, there is usually a "due diligence" conference call involving representatives of the issuer and of the underwriters (or, if there are many underwriters, the lead or managing underwriters). Where due diligence investigations were performed at the time of filing of the registration statement and at periodic intervals thereafter, this conference call may merely serve to update the underwriters with respect to the most current information. In circumstances where no investigation was performed at the time of filing of the registration statement and/or periodically thereafter, however, this conference call may serve as the underwriters' sole investigation, at least during the issuer's current reporting period. Underwriters are making more frequent use of their equity analysts and credit departments as a means of identifying "red flags" relating to a particular issuer.

Following effectiveness, identified potential underwriters sometimes may be invited to comment on drafts of documents prepared for the purpose of subsequent filing and incorporation by reference, although frequently and perhaps routinely they are not afforded this opportunity. As a practical matter, many issuers are unwilling to discuss unfiled draft 1934 Act reports with a group of potential underwriters out of concern that leaks of such information will occur and affect trading in the issuer's securities. While issuers may be willing to discuss draft reports with an underwriter with whom they have a long-term relationship, many issuers view the risk of such discussions with other potential underwriters as an unwarranted risk.

In the case of most issuers utilizing the shelf takedown method of distribution, the issuer or the prospective underwriters, assuming they are a relatively small and discrete group, will designate one law firm to act as counsel for the underwriters of the shelf-registered securities on the occasion of each particular offering. The underwriters of each particular offering are responsible for paying this law firm's fees and disbursements, including those associated with the "startup" and maintenance of the shelf facility. The use of one counsel typically serves to provide continuity throughout the life of the shelf registration. Designated underwriters' counsel may review and participate in the filing of the registration statement. On an ongoing basis, the designated counsel may or may not be afforded an opportunity to comment on drafts of the issuer's annual, quarterly and other reports before they are filed with the SEC. It will participate in any annual or quarterly "due diligence" meetings, if the issuer arranges for any, again at the expense of the underwriters of future takedowns. Counsel's activity in this regard will otherwise be confined to updating its document review at the time of a particular underwriting and participating in any "due diligence" conference call or meeting relating to the particular underwriting.

The continuity provided by designated underwriters' counsel serves an important "bridging" function in linking the due diligence efforts of successive underwriters. For example, where the underwriter of a particular takedown is an investment banking firm that has not acted recently as underwriter for the issuer, the underwriter naturally takes a degree of comfort from counsel's ability to describe, for example, the areas of investigation that received emphasis on prior offerings. The new underwriter is then able to allocate its due diligence resources accordingly.

There are severe limitations, however, on what counsel can do in the absence of an underwriting client. An underwriter is more often better equipped from the standpoint of business and financial expertise to identify the weak points in an issuer's business and financial condition and to assess the adequacy of an issuer's disclosure in this regard. And whatever counsel's degree of activity on a particular takedown or even between takedowns, it is still the underwriter that is exposed to liability and that has the burden of establishing a "due diligence" defense.

During the period between pricing and closing, the "winning" underwriter and its counsel may still conduct due diligence. As a practical matter, of course, the underwriter's only recourse if a disclosure problem is identified during this period is to decline to go forward, relying on such "outs" in the underwriting agreement as the absence of a clean opinion of issuer's counsel or underwriters' counsel. Underwriters are reluctant to pull deals, however, especially if significant effort has been invested in the transaction or there is a danger that the issuer might accuse the underwriter of reneging on its commitment. For this reason, an underwriter will call off the deal only in the event of a very clear and serious disclosure problem.

Although it may seem too obvious to require special mention, any inquiries made between pricing and closing are part of the underwriter's "investigation" for purposes of the due diligence defense. It is true that, as to underwriters, the accuracy of the registration statement is assessed for section 11 purposes as of the date of pricing (date of purchase by the underwriter), but this is irrelevant. What is important is that the underwriter retains the ability not to close if its inquiries turn up a significant disclosure problem.

Competition among prospective underwriters to offer the issuer the best "all-in" cost of funds on any particular offering has led to pressure on underwriters' compensation in shelf-registered debt offerings. The disclosed "spread" for a particular offering may not tell the whole story, given the possibility of market losses in the event that the security was priced away from the market. The frequent practice of "at-the-market" offerings, combined with the frequent use of swaps or other derivative products in connection with an offering, also makes it difficult to quantify the degree to which underwriters are making or losing money in shelf-registered offerings.

Pressure on underwriting compensation has also led to pressure on underwriters' ability to pay their counsel's fees. This has led, in turn, to a not undesirable review of what areas counsel reasonably should examine in a particular offering. In equity transactions, for example, counsel may no longer routinely do the work necessary to be able to give a validity opinion on all of the issuer's outstanding stock. Despite *BarChris*, even the reading of the issuer's and its subsidiaries' minute books is not immune from analysis on a cost-benefit basis.

In the Rule 415 environment of shelf-registered takedowns, underwriters face two practical problems in establishing a due diligence defense under section 11. The first problem relates to the opportunity for and scope of due diligence. When the issuer is in continuous consultation with one or a small group of potential underwriters prior to an offering, there sometimes will be time for the underwriters to perform a due diligence investigation of the issuer's current affairs prior to a take-down much in the same manner as would be done prior to a traditional "stand-alone" offering, even where significant time has elapsed from the time of filing of the registration statement or where new underwriters are involved. But other than in this fairly limited circumstance, when an issuer requests proposals from prospective underwriters, the deadlines are such that the prospective underwriters have little or no opportunity to perform "traditional" due diligence before responding to the request. Realistically, a prospective underwriter interested in making a proposal will be able to review the issuer's 1934 Act reports, consult its equity analyst who follows the issuer, check available information on the issuer's ratings, and assess the issuer's and its management's reputation for avoiding surprises. Of course, the issuer will as a condition of closing be responsible for confirming specific representations and warranties and for furnishing an opinion of its counsel and a "comfort letter" from its accountants; designated underwriters' counsel also will deliver an opinion. To the extent that the opinions cover disclosure matters, they are more qualified than in the case of matters such as due incorporation or the validity of the registered securities.

The task will be easier to the extent that the prospective underwriter has taken advantage of opportunities provided by the issuer for "continuous due diligence" or to the extent that designated underwriters' counsel has been able to review documents between offerings on behalf of underwriters to be designated in the future. (The value of such procedures varies: as was predicted during the debate that led up to the adoption of Rule 415, they suffer from a high degree of abstraction because of the absence of an actual offering and an actual client.) While it is possible to conduct these review procedures—and possibly conduct some face-to-face meetings with the issuer's management—after the underwriter agrees to "take down" the securities and prior to the closing of the transaction, whatever is discovered will have to be extraordinarily significant to justify the dissemination of supplemental disclosure (which will be strongly resisted by the issuer) or cancellation of the underwriter's commitment (which will—especially if issuer's counsel is able to "give the opinion"—expose the underwriter to accusations of reneging and the risk of litigation).

The second problem relates to the content of the registration statement and the underwriter's responsibilities for that content. Under section 11, the liability of the issuer, directors, signing officers and experts is measured as of the registration statement's effective date. Their responsibility with respect to subsequently filed and incorporated

1934 Act reports is presumably subject to section 12(2) [now Section 12(a)(2)]. Under section 11(d), the liability of a securities firm that becomes an underwriter after the effective date is measured at the time the securities firm becomes an underwriter, which may be months after the effective date. By this time the registration statement also will consist of subsequently filed and incorporated reports on Forms 10-Q and 8-K or, in the case of certain foreign private issuers, Form 6-K. Information contained in the registration statement may be out of date, and some such information will not have been updated in all cases by the subsequently filed and incorporated reports. Some information also will have been superseded by issuer announcements and analyst reports.

There is no clear test for the purpose of underwriters' due diligence as to what constitutes the "registration statement" for section 11 purposes at its "effective date," i.e., the date the underwriters become underwriters. In one case, the district court held that, for purposes of issuer liability, accuracy was to be "assessed as of the effective date of the allegedly misleading part of the Registration Statement. For most disclosures that date was . . . [the effective date], but for after-incorporated documents it was the date they were filed."[79] It is easier to express the distinction than it is to find it in practice, however, and underwriters still are forced in many cases to dissipate their limited due diligence resources on documents that no longer correspond to the "mix" of information on the basis of which investors buy the securities. Indeed, the idea of the "registration statement" as the defining document for liability and due diligence purposes is at odds with the SEC's premise of an "efficient capital market."

It should not be overlooked that the rating agencies play a key role in the success of a shelf program covering debt securities

---

79. *Wielgos v. Commonwealth Edison Co.,* 688 F. Supp. 331, 338–40 (N.D. Ill. 1988), *aff'd on other grounds,* 892 F.2d 509 (7th Cir. 1989).

or straight preferred stock. They have adapted their procedures to the realities of Rule 415. They will now assign a rating to all of an issuer's debt securities of a specified ranking, whereas in the days before Rule 415 they would only rate a specific issue. An issuer that expects to successfully carry on a shelf program must establish its credibility with the rating agencies and maintain an open line of communications with the persons responsible for its rating. Periodic rating agency presentations are essential. Investors rely on ratings. So do the people on the capital markets desk that buy the deals. In many respects, the analysis of the rating agencies is more important to them than whatever due diligence their firms may perform. This is one reason for the provision found in shelf underwriting agreements permitting termination in the event of a rating agency downgrade or watch-list action.

The question has been raised as to the obligation of underwriters' counsel to confer with an underwriter about to do a bought deal if there is a close call on an item of disclosure and the decision is made—by the issuer and its counsel and by underwriters' counsel—that the disclosure will not be made. The problem is more theoretical than real. Counsel should always be sure that his or her client is aware of any set of facts that gives rise to a close disclosure problem or, for that matter, any set of facts that is disclosed but that may have escaped the client's attention. But the client will not be interested in whether or not the set of facts is disclosed, provided that underwriters' counsel is still willing to render the usual disclosure opinion to the effect that anything that has to be disclosed has in fact been disclosed. Where underwriters' counsel believes that a disclosure should be made and the issuer does not agree, he or she always has the option of withholding or qualifying the disclosure opinion. In situations like this, however, it is important to remember who the real client is. It is probably not the underwriter's representative on the capital markets desk. Even if underwriters' counsel could catch such an individual's attention in the clamor of a trading room, he or she would be in no position to evaluate the business risk and decide whether or not to do the deal. In this instance, the person to contact is the firm's in-house investment banking counsel.

Medium-Term Note Programs

MTNs need not have medium terms. Indeed, the prospectuses under which they are sold generally provide that they may have maturities of from nine months to 30 years. MTN programs were first used by finance company subsidiaries of automobile manufacturers to "match fund" automobile loans to dealers and consumers with liabilities of similar maturities and were designed to fill the gap between commercial paper with its maximum maturity of nine months and the minimum practicable maturity of underwritten debt securities (usually in the area of three years).

MTNs were developed by the commercial paper departments of the investment banks, rather than by bankers working in their general corporate finance departments. This is why, even today, MTN programs are frequently promoted and administered by a specialty group within an investment banking firm, rather than by those bankers who would be called on to handle a standard underwritten offering of notes or debentures. MTNs are distinguished from other securities not so much by their terms but by the way that they are marketed using techniques familiar to commercial paper dealers. The settlement procedures for MTNs also have been borrowed from the world of commercial paper.

MTNs were first developed in the early 1970s when finance companies, traditional issuers of commercial paper, sought to extend the maturities of their paper in order to better match the maturities of their consumer and commercial loans. They came to their commercial paper dealers for help. It was clear that maturities could not be extended beyond 270 days while still relying on the Section 3(a)(3) exemption under which these companies had been issuing their commercial paper. So notes with longer maturities began to be issued in continuous Section 4(2) programs of the type described in Chapter 7. The next development came in the mid-1970s, when a number of finance companies persuaded the SEC to allow them to conduct their programs under a registration statement. As the notes were sold on a continuous basis, the very nature of the programs demanded a shelf registration statement.

Form S-16, the predecessor of Form S-3, was available for primary offerings only if there was a firm commitment underwriting. MTNs, for the most part, were originally sold on an agency basis, and accordingly, the issuers that registered their programs prior to the adoption of Form S-3 were required to file on Form S-1 or Form S-7. This proved to be cumbersome. The related prospectuses tended to be long and required the continuing expense of periodic revision and reprinting since current financial and other information could not be incorporated by reference to 1934 Act filings. The most common procedure followed was to set forth in the prospectus the interest rates for specified ranges, or "bands," of maturities and to change the rates as required by market conditions. Originally, the SEC required a post-effective amendment for this purpose, but in time it permitted interest rates to be changed with a sticker mailed after the fact for filing pursuant to Rule 424.

MTN programs normally provide the flexibility to issue securities with maturities that range from nine months to 30 years or more, although they are usually issued with maturities of two to five years. MTNs are generally sold on a principal or agency basis from a dealer's trading desk with three business-day settlement in same day funds. Payment of principal and interest due at maturity is made in same day funds. Book-entry only MTN programs, with payments through DTC, have become standard.

While the traditional MTN is a fixed-rate, non-redeemable senior debt security, almost all programs provide the flexibility to issue other types of debt securities (e.g., floating rate, zero coupon, amortizing, multicurrency or indexed MTNs). Many MTN programs now offer the flexibility to issue subordinated MTNs. For floating rate MTNs, the most common interest rate indices include LIBOR, bank prime rates, commercial paper composite rates, certificate of deposit composite rates, swap rates, federal funds rates and Treasury bill rates.[80] Many MTN

---

80. Since floating rate MTNs are often issued in connection with interest rate swaps, the interest rate indices for floating rate MTNs may be based on the definitional conventions of the International Swap Dealers Association, Inc.

programs permit takedowns that are denominated in non-U.S. currencies. Most MTN programs are rated investment-grade by at least one nationally recognized rating agency.

While finance companies were the initial users of MTN programs, such programs provide an easy means for many other types of issuers to access the capital markets. MTN programs have been developed to securitize mortgage loans (both fixed and floating rate) and other financial assets, including mortgage-backed securities. Equipment trust certificates have also been marketed on a continuous basis as MTNs.

Despite the availability of registration, some corporate issuers continue to sell MTNs in continuous Section 4(2) programs. Domestic banks and branches and agencies of foreign banks, have also relied on Section 3(a)(2) for note programs.[81]

Traditionally, bank financing had been effected on the holding company level, but as the rating agencies came to view some banks as stronger credits than their holding company parents, it made sense to have the bank as the obligor. Domestic banks and U.S. branches and agencies of foreign banks typically issue such debt obligations in the form of "bank notes" (which are bank-level debt instruments structured to resemble corporate MTNs) or as "deposit notes" (which closely resemble bank notes but are treated by the issuer as deposits for financial reporting and regulatory purposes).

- *Documentation*

Once established, an MTN program allows the issuer to offer and sell a wide range of debt securities, in varying amounts and maturities, without the need to go through the registration process for each issuance. Each sale requires only that (1) the terms of the sale be agreed on at pricing (this is frequently done orally with written confirmation) and, in the case of certain principal takedowns, that an update of the most recently delivered comfort letter, legal opinions and officers' certificate be provided,

---

81. As discussed in Chapter 1, U.S. branches and agencies of foreign banks may rely on Section 3(a)(2) for these programs. *See* SEC Release No. 33-6661 (September 23, 1986).

SHELF REGISTRATION (RULE 415)

(2) a copy of the existing prospectus and a pricing supplement relating to the sale be delivered to the purchaser, (3) an MTN, either in global or certificated form, be completed by the trustee or issuing and paying agent, as the case may be, on the issuer's instructions and (4) a copy of the pricing supplement be filed with the SEC under Rule 424.

Traditionally, the pricing supplement for an MTN offering would include specific selling price information only in the case of agency transactions. In the case of principal takedowns, the supplement might set forth an initial public offering price (subject to its being varied at the election of the broker-dealer) or it might simply state the price at which the broker-dealer had purchased the MTNs from the issuer and that the broker-dealer intended to reoffer the MTNs "at the market." Each purchaser would, of course, receive a confirmation setting forth the exact price paid by that purchaser.

An indenture must be qualified under the Trust Indenture Act of 1939 in respect of shelf-registered MTNs (except in the case of a non-U.S. governmental issuer registering pursuant to Schedule B of the 1933 Act). The trustee under an indenture can be qualified after the securities are registered under the 1933 Act, and it is possible to qualify an indenture with one trustee that relates to both senior and subordinated debt securities. There are two types of indenture normally used for MTN programs, one being restricted to MTNs and the other permitting the issuance of any type of debt security. Both are open-ended in that they do not limit the amount of debt securities that can be issued. The terms of both forms are generally standard, while certain provisions (such as the negative pledge and other covenants, events of default and consolidation and merger provisions) will vary depending on the issuer and its undertakings under outstanding borrowing documents.

One advantage of an indenture not restricted to MTNs is that it permits the issuance of many varieties of debt securities that are limited only in that they must be debt securities. This advantage, however, is available as a practical matter only to issuers eligible to use Form S-3 or Form F-3 since the offering would otherwise not be able to take advantage of delayed offerings under clause (x) of Rule 415(a)(1).

Each investment bank has its own form of agreement providing for the distribution of MTNs to or through one or more dealers by the issuer, although the forms used by the investment banks that participate most actively in the market have become similar in many respects. The issuer will enter into one distribution agreement that will be signed by all the investment banks it has appointed as dealers for the MTNs, and this agreement will govern all sales by these firms acting as principal or agent. The agreement contains basic representations and warranties by the issuer about its business, its financial condition and the MTN program; these representations and warranties will be deemed to be updated as of the time of each sale and issuance. Closing conditions, including officers' certificates, comfort letters and opinions of counsel, as well as the requirement for periodic delivery of officers' certificates, comfort letters and opinions of counsel, are specified. The agreement also contains indemnity and contribution undertakings by the issuer against liabilities arising out of any material misstatement or omission in the prospectus.

Because of the continuous nature and many variables of an MTN program, the issuer will provide for administrative procedures to clarify its role, that of the trustee or issuing and paying agent and the dealers in connection with the offer, sale, issuance, settlement and maturity of the MTNs. Other standard agreements required in connection with an MTN program include an Interest Calculation Agreement between the issuer and the calculation agent (usually the trustee or the issuing and paying agent) that calculates the interest on floating rate MTNs and an Exchange Agency Agreement between the issuer and the exchange rate agent (again, usually the trustee or the issuing and paying agent) that acts in connection with any currency exchange that may be required pursuant to the terms of any MTNs payable other than in U.S. dollars or with an option for payments in U.S. dollars.

- *Registration Under Rule 415*

MTN issuers eligible to use Form S-3 or Form F-3 may file a shelf registration statement under clause (x) of Rule 415(a)(1), permitting continuous or delayed offerings. MTN issuers not

SHELF REGISTRATION (RULE 415)

eligible to use Form S-3 or Form F-3 are limited to continuous offerings under clause (ix). There is more flexibility under clause (x) in being able to issue debt securities generally or even equity securities from a shelf registration statement that permits either continuous or delayed offerings. Moreover, the incorporation by reference advantage offered by Form S-3 and Form F-3 is significant in that it avoids the need for a lengthy prospectus and frequent post-effective amendments. Issuers have, to be sure, registered MTN programs on Form S-1 or Form F-1, but the process requires close coordination between the drafting of 1934 Act reports and the maintenance of the 1933 Act prospectus and registration statement.

It will be recalled that the SEC, in adopting Rule 415 on a permanent basis in 1983, limited the use of shelf registration for "primary" transactions to issuers eligible to use Form S-3. Other issuers could use shelf registration only for "traditional" transactions. MTN programs, of course, are both "traditional" and "primary." It did not take long for the SEC to question whether an issuer not eligible to use Form S-3 could use shelf registration for an MTN program.

A finance company subsidiary of a major insurance company had registered its MTN program on Form S-1 since it was not a 1934 Act reporting company at the time of the original filing. When the company filed its first annual post-effective amendment after the 1983 release, the SEC examiner questioned whether the notes could continue to be registered under Rule 415.

Counsel for the issuer and counsel for the agents were of the opinion that this continuous offering satisfied the requirements of subsection (ix) of the rule. The basis for this opinion was set forth in a letter to the examiner, which stated as follows:

> Before filing the Registration Statement Amendment, we, together with counsel for the prospective agents, gave careful consideration to the requirements of Release No. 33-6499. This offering is a traditional shelf registration under paragraph (a)(1)(ix) of revised Rule 415 as set forth and explained in Release No. 33-6499. Paragraph (a)(1)(ix) permits registration of securities "the offering of which will be commenced promptly, will be made on

a continuous basis and may continue for a period in excess of 30 days from the date of initial effectiveness." This type of offering is permitted whether or not the issuer qualifies for Form S-3. The Notes have been, and will continue to be, offered precisely in this manner. Of the $200,000,000 of Notes originally registered, an aggregate of $9,000,000 have been sold on a "best efforts basis" in four separate transactions through December 31, 1983, and the remaining $191,000,000 will be priced and sold from time to time with adjustments in pricing occurring as market conditions dictate, which may be weekly or daily. Such a pattern of continuous distribution of debt securities meets the requirements of paragraph (a)(1)(ix).

Release No. 33-6499 makes it clear that the Commission intended to limit the use of Rule 415 to primary offerings of securities qualified to be registered on Form S-3 or Form F-3 and to "traditional shelf offerings." In the mid-1970s, long before the adoption of Rule 415, the Commission began to permit offerings of debt securities pursuant to shelf registrations by finance companies and finance subsidiaries of industrial companies that borrowed frequently in the capital markets. A number of these companies filed shelf registration statements covering offerings from time to time of medium-term notes with varying maturities and interest rates. These offerings were made directly or through investment banking firms acting as agent or as principal. The distinguishing feature of these offerings was that they were made on a continuous basis rather than on a delayed basis as is often the case with Rule 415 filings.

Among the traditional shelf registration statements covering medium-term notes was a $200,000,000 medium-term note filing on Form S-7 made by Ford Motor Credit Company in March 1973. Other companies that filed for continuous offerings of medium-term notes prior to the adoption of Rule 415 were Clark Equipment Credit Company, Associates Corp. of North America, Commercial Credit Company, Sears Roebuck Acceptance Corporation,

Montgomery Ward Credit Corp. and General Motors Acceptance Corporation. The enclosed excerpt from *Moody's Bond Record* for December 1981 shows a separate grouping entitled "Medium-Term Notes (SEC Shelf Registrations)" demonstrating that this type of offering was widely used prior to the adoption of Rule 415.

The type of offering being made by the Issuer is exactly the type of traditional shelf registration that the Commission intended would continue after the adoption of the amendments to Rule 415. The purpose of offering in this manner is to enable the Issuer to match capital demands with portfolio holdings, an objective that the Commission recognized in Release No. 33-6499 requires the use of a shelf registration statement. If the Commission were to take the position, despite the clear language of paragraph (a)(1)(ix) of revised Rule 415, that the Issuer may not distribute the Notes in the manner contemplated, then the Issuer would be placed at a severe competitive disadvantage with respect to other finance companies and would, as a practical matter, be unable to offer the Notes publicly.

The amendment to the registration statement was declared effective with no further delay, and deals continued to be done off the issuer's shelf.

- *Procedures*

MTNs will be offered off the dealers' trading desks in much the same manner as commercial paper. The market for MTNs, like commercial paper, is investor driven. The dealers will continuously offer the MTNs through electronic posting procedures on a "maturity band" basis (e.g., 3% for maturities from two years to three years from date of sale), and within this maturity range the investor, the dealer and the issuer will tailor the exact maturity to specific investment and funding requirements. As in the case of shelf-registered debt securities, the investor is primarily interested in (other than maturity) rating information, the name of the issuer and the yield (premium over Treasury securities of comparable maturity). While the dealer's traditional obligation was to distribute the securities on a "best efforts" basis, the depth of the MTN marketplace and competitive pressures now usually result in dealers' taking down securities as principal on a more or less regular basis. Whether it is acting as agent or principal, the MTN dealer is generally regarded as an "underwriter" for Section 11 purposes.

The buyers of MTNs are to a large measure also the buyers of underwritten corporate debt securities, consisting of institutional investors such as banks and bank trust departments, insurance companies, pension funds, mutual funds, investment advisors, nonprofit corporations, state and local governments and corporations. The average transaction in an MTN program is usually in excess of $2 million.

- *Disclosure and Due Diligence*

The ABA task force report on sellers' due diligence defenses described the MTN disclosure and due diligence process as follows:[82]

> While the degree of disclosure about the issuer and its business, and the scope of its financial statements, that are actually contained in an MTN prospectus (as opposed to being incorporated by reference) vary among issuers, prospectuses used in very active MTN programs often contain only the ratio of earnings to fixed charges required by Item 3 of Form S-3 and rely entirely upon incorporated 1934 Act filings. Prospectuses seldom are distributed to prospective purchasers before they make an investment decision; rather, the supplemented prospectus is usually delivered with the confirmation.
>
> Agents for MTN programs operate on the basis of documentation that is similar to that used for Rule 415 shelf takedowns. The underwriting agreement often is referred to as a distribution agreement, to reflect the fact that it provides for the named agents to sell MTNs on

---

82. ABA Committee on Federal Regulation of Securities, *Report of Task Force on Sellers' Due Diligence and Similar Defenses Under the Federal Securities Laws,* 48 Bus. Law. 1185, 1226–27 (1993) (footnotes omitted).

a best efforts agency basis or to buy the MTNs as principal and resell them, usually "at the market." Because it is not practical to deliver closing documents at the time of each sale of MTNs, distribution agreements usually provide for an initial "paper" closing at which legal opinions, accountants' "comfort letters," officers' certificates and other traditional closing documents are delivered. The issuer's representations and warranties are deemed to be reaffirmed as of the time of each sale and settlement of an MTN. Additional legal opinions, comfort letters and officers' certificates are usually required on a periodic basis (generally each quarter) as the prospectus is amended, whether by the filing of 1934 Act documents that are incorporated by reference pursuant to Item 12 of Form S-3 or otherwise. Issuers agree to amend the prospectus as required and to alert the agents if disclosure problems arise.

Agents usually request the right to review the issuer's 1934 Act periodic reports before they are filed, but have little meaningful influence over the content of such filings. As a practical matter, their only option is to resign from the program. Agents' purchases as principal also are subject to customary termination provisions, such as material adverse changes in the issuer's business or financial condition, a downgrading of the securities or their being put on a "watch list" by a rating agency, and other "market outs." Indemnification and contribution agreements are identical to those contained in standard underwriting agreements.

Because each agent controls its own selling efforts and presents all offers within posted rates directly to the issuer, MTN programs usually do not have a "lead agent" or "lead manager" responsible for sponsoring and coordinating the offering. (If there is a lead agent, the designation only serves to determine the order of listing on the prospectus cover and in the tombstone advertisement and the style of the documentation.) Some issuers allow limited "reverse inquiry," i.e., an investor may be allowed to purchase MTNs from the issuer either directly or through a broker-dealer not designated as an agent in the prospectus.

Because agents must reckon with the possibility of losing a significant amount of MTN sales to "reverse inquiry" by investors or non-designated broker-dealers, they typically prevail upon the issuer to pay a portion of their expenses associated with the transaction. This usually includes the fees and disbursements (up to a predetermined amount) of the law firm that is designated by the issuer as "agents' counsel." Issuers correctly regard this expense as affecting their "all-in" cost of funds raised through the MTN program, and there is considerable pressure on law firms to keep down their quoted and actual charges. To the extent that counsel's charges exceed what the issuer is willing to reimburse, the agents of course must pick up the difference.

The initial due diligence investigation usually is conducted by designated agents' counsel and all agents. Additional due diligence sessions with the issuer and its representatives take place when the prospectus is periodically updated or 1934 Act documents are being prepared for filing and incorporation by reference. Despite the predictable schedule for the filing of an issuer's 1934 Act reports, the agents' need to maintain continuous sales under an ongoing program often imposes considerable time pressure on the agents and their counsel to review these reports and reach conclusions, if any, as to the adequacy of the issuer's disclosure. An agent's due diligence often is supplemented by its corporate credit department, which generally monitors the credit of issuers and even may establish position limits on principal purchases and secondary market positions.

- *Section 11(d)(1)*

As discussed in Chapter 3, Section 11(d)(1) of the 1934 Act prohibits the extension of credit by a broker-dealer on a new issue of securities. The restriction also applies to certain transactions in the after-market for a period of 30 days after the broker-dealer was a participant in the distribution of the securities.

A broker-dealer will be considered a participant in the distribution of a new issue so long as it continues to be "a party to an executory agreement to purchase or distribute such issue." The staff of the SEC took the position in 1986 that a broker-dealer acting as an agent in an MTN program could not extend credit on the notes, even those that were issued 30 days prior to the proposed extension of credit, on the theory that the distribution agreement constituted an executory agreement to distribute the notes.[83] Fortunately, the staff reversed its position in a 1990 no-action letter[84] in which it appeared to take the position that, because the financial terms of MTNs are tailored to the individual needs of customers, each tranche can be considered as a separate distribution under Section 11(d)(1).

As nonequity securities, dealers are entitled under Regulation T to extend "good faith" credit on MTNs. The maintenance rules of the SROs may impose higher margin requirements.

Common Stock Shelf Registration

- *Primary Offerings*

Issuers were quick to see the advantages of shelf registration as a vehicle for distributing debt securities, but they warmed more slowly to shelf registration as a vehicle for primary distributions of common stock. Rapid access to the market is generally less important for common stock offerings than for straight debt, and the advantages of a shelf registration may be outweighed by the detrimental effects of a large block of stock overhanging the market. Some companies, however, have adopted so-called "dribble plans" under which they sell common stock on a more or less continuous basis.

As noted earlier, some of the "overhang" concern may have been dissipated by the recent availability of the "universal" shelf registration statement that covers an amount of securities that

---

83. SEC No-action Letter, *Goldman, Sachs & Co.* (December 4, 1986).
84. *Kidder, Peabody & Co. Inc.* (August 16, 1990).

need not be allocated between debt and equity. Indeed, there have been "block trades" of common stock taken down from an issuer's shelf registration statement. There have also been "overnight" (or "drive-by") convertible securities offerings in which a securities firm commits to buy the securities from the issuer at a fixed price agreed on after the close of the market and then resells to institutional clients before the opening of the market on the next day. There is no roadshow and no book-building process. Obviously, the banker incurs a significant risk that it will be unable to resell the securities at a profit.

- *At-the-Market Equity Offerings*

Rule 415(a)(4) imposes additional requirements in the case of a shelf registration statement pertaining to an issuer's at-the-market offering of equity securities—that is, an offering "into an existing trading market for outstanding shares of the same class at other than a fixed price on or through the facilities of a national securities exchange or to or through a market maker otherwise than on an exchange." To effect this type of offering, the registrant must qualify for Form S-3 or Form F-3. Where voting stock is registered, the amount registered for the purpose of the at-the-market offering may not exceed 10% of the aggregate market value of the registrant's outstanding voting stock held by non-affiliates (calculated as of a date within 60 days prior to the date of filing).

Finally, the offering must be made through one or more named underwriters acting as principal or as agent for the issuer. In the case of at-the-market equity offerings, however, it is necessary to file a post-effective amendment naming the underwriter if no underwriter was named in the effective registration statement.[85]

- *Investment Companies*

Rule 415(b) makes shelf registration unavailable for certain investment company securities, including redeemable shares issued

---

85. SEC Division of Corporation Finance, *Manual of Publicly Available Telephone Interpretations* 74 (#7) (July 1997).

by an open-end mutual fund. Although mutual funds offer their shares on a continuous basis, they operate under their own set of rules promulgated under the 1940 Act. Rule 24f-2 under the 1940 Act permits open-end funds to register an indefinite number of shares and to file an annual notice showing the number of shares sold, accompanied by the requisite registration fee.

Closed-end funds are permitted to use Rule 415, but because they use Form N-2 to register their securities under the 1933 Act and the 1940 Act and are not eligible to use Form S-3, they do not come under clause (a)(1)(x) of Rule 415, which permits delayed offerings only by Form S-3 or Form F-3 issuers. Instead, certain fixed-income funds and "funds of hedge funds" have relied for their continuous offerings on clause (ix), which permits shelf filings for securities "the offering of which will be commenced promptly, will be made on a continuous basis and may continue for a period in excess of 30 days from the date of initial effectiveness." The continuous offerings made by these funds are not "at-the-market offerings" and thus are not subject to the limitations on such offerings discussed above. Rather, the shares are continuously offered at prices equal to the fund's then-current net asset value per share. Not only are the shares not offered at the market, but, as the prospectuses state, there is not expected to be any secondary trading market for the shares of these funds.[86]

Where continuous offerings have not been preceded by a firm commitment underwriting, a single prospectus has been used, even where there is first an invitation for subscriptions. Where there is a firm commitment underwriting, however, a separate prospectus is used for that offering and a newly dated prospectus is used for the continuous offering. In some cases, the original registration statement covering the underwritten offering does not cover the continuous offering, and a new

---

86. The SEC staff issued a no-action letter in 1998 permitting a closed-end fund to conduct a delayed offering under clause (x) on the condition that it send to shareholders and file with the SEC quarterly reports containing information complying in all material respects with the information required to be included in Form 10-Q. SEC No-action Letter, *Pilgrim America Prime Rate Trust* (May 1, 1998).

registration statement is subsequently filed for this purpose. In other cases, two forms of prospectus are included in a single registration statement that is used to register the shares for the underwritten offering (including the overallotment option) and the continuous offering.

Certain closed-end funds that make periodic repurchase offers pursuant to Rule 23c-3 under the 1940 Act are eligible to rely on subsection (xi) of Rule 415 to offer their shares on a continuous basis.

- *Non-Underwritten Registered Equity Secondaries*

As previously mentioned, shelf registrations frequently are used to cover offerings of outstanding common stock by control persons or statutory underwriters where sales are to be made from time to time at market prices current at the time of sale. These are traditional shelfs, and there are a number of legal issues and marketing considerations that arise in the context of this type of offering. While bought deals and large debt underwritings receive the press coverage and merit the tombstone advertisements, shelf secondaries continue to be handled in substantial volume with little if any publicity.

The prospectus delivery requirements of the 1933 Act can be satisfied in the case of a regular way sale on an exchange by delivering copies of the prospectus to the exchange pursuant to Rule 153. The theory is that physical delivery to the broker on the other side of the transaction is unnecessary because the broker can get a copy of the prospectus from the exchange library. Will the buying broker do so? Probably not. Will he even know that he is buying registered securities? Again, probably not.

Rule 153 is applicable only to transactions between brokers on an exchange. If the shares are being sold by means of a spot secondary after the close of the exchange or in a block trade, the securities firm handling the transaction will be dealing directly with the purchasers, and a copy of the prospectus must be delivered to them with their confirmation. (Of course, any institution whose mailroom receives a confirmation will usually forward the confirmation for processing while dropping the prospectus into the wastebasket.) In the case of a sale to another dealer through NASDAQ, or otherwise in the over-the-counter market, physical delivery of the prospectus is likewise required because Rule 153 currently applies only to transactions on an exchange.[87] When the dealer purchasing the shares receives the prospectus, must it redeliver it to its customer, assuming that it finds its way out of the mail room? The registered shares will simply become part of the dealer's inventory, indistinguishable from any other shares of the same issuer. As the dealer continues to make a market, there is no way of pointing to any particular shares in its inventory and saying that these are the registered shares and that they are being resold to an identified buyer. The fact of the matter is that the prospectus will not be redelivered to an ultimate investor but may also wind up in the wastebasket.[88]

A dealer that sells shares under a shelf registration statement for a control person or a statutory underwriter will itself be deemed an underwriter. It is customary for shelf prospectuses so to state. A dealer that buys the registered shares from the dealer handling the sale will not be deemed an underwriter so long as it is operating in the ordinary course of its business and has not entered into any special arrangements with the selling shareholders or the dealer on the sell side of the trade.

---

87. One of the authors proposed many years ago that the NASD adopt a rule similar to Rule 153 that would dispense with the need for over-the-counter dealers to deliver prospectuses among themselves. Joseph McLaughlin, *"Ten Easy Pieces" for the SEC*, 18 Rev. Sec. & Comm. Reg. 200, 201 (1985). Whatever difficulties may have existed at the time, there can hardly be any remaining valid objection to dispensing with such deliveries in view of the ready availability of prospectuses on EDGAR or by other electronic means, and the fact that every over-the-counter dealer by definition has access to a computer and a modem.

88. In its 1998 Aircraft Carrier Release, the SEC proposed to repeal Rule 153 for the principal reason that it would be unnecessary under the new prospectus delivery requirements proposed in that release. The SEC referred to Rule 153 as "contemplat[ing] that these prospectuses [delivered to an exchange] will then be taken or copied by the members of the exchange that are on the buy side of the transaction and delivered to the beneficial purchaser." SEC Release 33-7606A (November 13, 1998), text at n.441. Nothing in the rule contemplates such a redelivery obligation.

The SEC has addressed this issue in the context of primary at-the-market offerings under Rule 415. The following statement in the release reproposing Rule 415 sets forth principles that are equally applicable to secondary offerings:

> Accordingly, an exchange member or specialist effecting a transaction in the shelf-registered security with an underwriter who is in privity with the registrant generally would not be deemed to be an underwriter if the member or specialist performed its usual functions and had not entered into any special selling arrangements with the registrant or the underwriter. The same would be true in the case of an over-the-counter market maker who did not buy from the registrant. In a similar vein, a broker-dealer could solicit buy orders from its customers for a security subject to such a shelf registration statement without being deemed an underwriter of that security upon executing the trade, as long as such broker-dealer limited itself to its ordinary business activities and had no special arrangements with the underwriters or issuer.[89]

As previously noted, most of the early shelf offerings were handled as regular way brokerage transactions. When Form S-16 was first adopted in 1970, it was available for secondary offerings only if they were effected "in the regular way" on a stock exchange. Form S-16 was a convenient device for issuers required to file shelf registration statements to meet their obligations under registration rights agreements, and regular way sales were specified in these filings as the plan of distribution. In 1972, Form S-16 was amended to eliminate the requirement that sales be made only "in the regular way" on an exchange, thus opening the door for more efficient distribution methods for shelf offerings on Form S-16.

By the early 1970s, the major securities firms had established block trading departments and were committing large amounts of capital to facilitate trades of large blocks of stock. Today, block trades make up a major portion of the trading

---

89. SEC Release No. 33-6334 (August 6, 1981).

volume on the principal exchanges. If a firm is approached by a customer wishing to sell a substantial number of listed shares, say more than 10% of the daily trading volume, a block trade may be the most cost-effective method of effecting the sale. If there is institutional interest in the stock and the number of shares involved bears a reasonable relationship to that interest, then the firm's block trading department will be in a position to quickly and efficiently place the shares with institutional buyers, usually few in number. In most cases, the transaction price is set at a discount from the last sale price on the exchange. The firm lines up interest in the block and makes a firm bid to the seller. It sells the shares as agent, but will position a portion of the block if necessary to meet its commitment to its customer. The trade is crossed on the floor of the exchange and is printed on the tape.

The block trade became the preferred method of sale for outstanding shares covered by shelf registration statements, although off-board secondary offerings frequently were used for sales off the shelf where warranted by size or investor interest. In a spot secondary, other securities firms are invited to participate in the distribution, and a selling concession is offered.

Several securities firms have organized sales units that monitor shelf filings and approach the named sellers in an effort to convince them to use the services of the firm in selling their shares. A major part of the pitch would be the firm's distribution capacity and its willingness to commit its capital to make a firm bid.

A firm handling a shelf offering may enter into negotiations with the customer before the registration statement is filed, especially where the firm has a role in placing the securities with the customer or in advising on a merger or similar transaction in which the customer receives the shares. More often, the firm may be presented with a registration statement that has already been declared effective. If it does have the opportunity to participate in the drafting of the prospectus, the firm will have the advantage of ensuring that the plan of distribution is appropriately set forth. In some cases, the method of distribution will be known in advance and can be described with precision in the prospectus. In other cases, it may be advisable to draft the plan of distribution to provide for the widest latitude.

If a dealer is chosen to handle a sale after the registration statement has been declared effective, and if the plan of distribution does not contemplate the method of distribution that the dealer has proposed to its customer, then the issuer's undertakings pursuant to Item 512(a) of Regulation S-K will require it to file a post-effective amendment to the registration statement if the change to the plan of distribution is "material." Many issuers will be reluctant to file a post-effective amendment for this purpose, and there may be no contractual right on the part of the selling shareholder to require the issuer to do so.

Derivatives are often used to hedge or monetize common stock positions, and plans of distribution will often refer to the selling shareholders' having entered into forward or other derivative transactions with dealers who may deliver the prospectus when they make offsetting short sales of the common stock or, alternatively, long sales of common stock loaned, pledged or delivered to them by the selling shareholders.

Item 507 of Regulation S-K requires that each selling shareholder be named in the registration statement together with information on the selling shareholder's holdings of the registered class and any material relationship with the issuer. The SEC staff's position on adding or substituting selling shareholders has not been entirely consistent. A telephone interpretation states that selling shareholders may be added or substituted by filing a Rule 424(b) prospectus unless there are circumstances indicating that the change is material and on the assumption that the change does not involve increasing the securities registered or including shares from a transaction other than the one to which the original filing related.[90] The interpretation also stresses that the ability to reflect changes in selling shareholders by Rule 424 does not permit the omission of the names of known

---

90. SEC Division of Corporation Finance, *Manual of Publicly Available Telephone Interpretations* 39 (#81) (July 1997). Another telephone interpretation states that Rule 462(b) is available to file a new and immediately effective registration statement "in order to increase the number of shares or add selling shareholders, provided that no material information is newly disclosed by virtue of such increase or by virtue of the change in identity of selling shareholders." *Id.* at 49 (#127).

selling shareholders from the original filing. More recently, the staff appears to be treating this interpretation as being limited to the substitution of transferees of originally named sellers and requiring in all other situations the filing of a post-effective amendment to identify all sellers whose predecessor holders were not identified (subject to disclosure on a group basis where the group holds less than 1% of the class of securities).

A selling shareholder named in a resale shelf registration statement is still free to sell the registered shares by some other means, including Rule 144. Although the staff at one time took the opposite position, or required that the possibility of selling under Rule 144 be mentioned in the prospectus, it no longer attaches any conditions to a resale under Rule 144.

A firm selling common stock for a customer under circumstances that may make it a statutory underwriter should also be concerned about its potential liabilities under Section 11. Many firms will not act for a customer in this capacity unless the customer can deliver an indemnity agreement from the issuer. If the customer's shares originated in a private placement or in a merger or similar transaction, the customer or his or her counsel may have bargained for such an indemnity. The dealer will want to review the terms of the issuer's undertaking and bargain for the widest indemnity contemplated by those terms. If the indemnity does not measure up to the dealer's standards, it may decline to execute the transaction.

Indemnities, of course, are vulnerable to SEC or judicial scrutiny as well as to the issuer's possible insolvency. The dealer's better course of action is to try to establish a secondary defense by doing a reasonable amount of due diligence. The issuer is highly unlikely to be willing to afford the dealer an opportunity to ask questions—much less to make suggestions about the quality of the issuer's disclosure. There is no reason, however, why the dealer should not seek out its research analyst who follows the issuer to inquire about his or her views on the stock and on whether any surprises are expected to occur in the near future.[91]

---

91. *See* ABA Committee on Federal Regulation of Securities, *Report of Task Force on Sellers' Due Diligence and Similar Defenses Under the Federal Securities Laws,* 48 Bus. Law. 1185, 1229 (1993).

The Presumptive Underwriter Problem

Beginning in the 1960s, the SEC took the position that a purchaser of a relatively large amount of securities covered by a registration statement would be presumed to be an underwriter and thus required to redeliver a current prospectus in making resales.[92] The presumptive underwriter doctrine began as SEC lore (not law). It is alluded to in the 1969 *Wheat Report*.[93]

The theory was that a distribution of securities had not been completed while they were still in the hands of a large purchaser and that the disclosures required by the 1933 Act should be provided to the "ultimate" purchasers. Surely (went the theory) disclosure to the "ultimate" investors could not be avoided by registering securities for sale to a single institution that might turn around the next day and sell them to the public without delivering a prospectus. But where should the line be drawn? With respect to offerings of common stock, the traditional presumptive underwriter doctrine had been that anyone who purchased more than 10% of an offering would be deemed an underwriter unless the number of shares purchased was relatively small in relation to the number outstanding.[94] With respect to fixed-income securities, the SEC took a somewhat more liberal stance, and in one case, took a no-action position with respect to a purchaser of 14% of a registered offering of nonconvertible preferred stock.[95]

The presumptive underwriter doctrine generated considerable concern in the context of shelf offerings, particularly with respect to bought deals. Assume that an issuer filed a registration statement under Rule 415 covering $500 million of its debt securities to be sold in several tranches. If a single institutional investor bought an entire series of $100 million of debt through an underwriter, could it freely resell the securities at any time

---

92. See generally C. Nathan, *Presumptive Underwriters,* 8 Rev. Sec. Reg. 881 (1975).

93. *Wheat Report, supra* Chapter 1, note 29, at 272, note 22.

94. SEC No-action Letter, *Hercules, Inc.* (October 2, 1972).

95. SEC No-action Letter, *Jersey Central Power & Light Co.* (January 22, 1975).

without delivering a current prospectus? In applying the presumptive underwriter doctrine, should one look to the total amount of securities covered by the shelf registration statement or to the amount of securities sold in each discrete offering?

Lee B. Spencer, Jr., then the director of the SEC's Division of Corporation Finance, was determined to make Rule 415 work. In connection with the rule's adoption, he advised the financial community that the staff was no longer applying the presumptive underwriter doctrine, at least insofar as it embodied any automatic percentage test. Rather, he said, the staff would examine all of the facts and circumstances surrounding the purchase of a large block of securities to determine whether the purchaser should be deemed an underwriter in making resales. Among the circumstances to be considered were the amount of securities purchased in relation to the amount outstanding, whether the purchaser was likely to hold for the long pull, and the length of time that the securities were owned before the resale took place.

A determination of a purchaser's status as an underwriter would thus depend on subjective factors. The real thrust of the SEC's revised position was that it would not deem a purchaser an underwriter unless (with the benefit of hindsight) it appeared to be acting as a conduit for the issuer to avoid delivery of a current prospectus to the ultimate purchasers.

Institutions had lingering concerns despite Mr. Spencer's statement that "[w]e are going to give that doctrine the full funeral rites it so richly deserves."[96] In time, however, these concerns diminished, and institutions now purchase securities off the shelf with little, if any, fear that they will be considered underwriters in making resales. The SEC helped matters when it issued the American Council of Life Insurance no-action letter, in which Mr. Spencer agreed with counsel's view that "insurance companies and similar institutional investors generally should not be deemed underwriters under Section 2(11) with regard to

---

96. W. J. Williams, Jr., *Problems in the Application of the 1933 Act and Rules Thereunder to Shelf Offerings,* Fourteenth Annual Institute on Securities Regulation 117 (Practising Law Institute Transcript 1983).

the purchase of large amounts of registered securities provided such securities are acquired in the ordinary course of their business from the issuer or underwriter of those securities and such purchasers have no arrangement with any person to participate in the distribution of such securities."[97] The real comfort, however, has come from the fact that Rule 415 has operated for many years now without the SEC raising underwriter concerns with respect to resales of securities taken off the shelf.

Regulation M

For many years after the adoption of Rule 415, the SEC applied a "single distribution" analysis to shelf registration statements for purposes of its antimanipulation rules (primarily Rule 10b-6) discussed in Chapter 4. Under this approach, each takedown from a shelf was deemed to be part of a "distribution" for Rule 10b-6 purposes if the aggregate amount of securities registered on the shelf was sufficient to constitute a distribution for such purposes. The effect of this approach was that all participants in the distribution were subject to Rule 10b-6 for the life of the shelf, but with exceptions for certain bids or purchases outside specified "cooling-off" periods.

The SEC's "single distribution" analysis arose largely out of the SEC's concern, discussed earlier in this chapter, regarding shelf registration statements covering sales by numerous unaffiliated selling securityholders. Treating these sales as a single distribution, however, meant mandating coordination where there would otherwise be no reason for coordination. Recognizing that this approach was counterproductive, the SEC soon relaxed its position so that the restrictions of Rule 10b-6 ordinarily applied to an individual selling shelf stockholder only when that person was offering or selling securities from the shelf. A broker-dealer effecting such sales would be subject to the rule only where it was involved in a distribution based on the amount of securities that it was asked to sell (or foreseeably would be asked to

---

97. SEC No-action Letter, *American Council of Life Ins.* (May 10, 1983).

sell) as well as on the basis of the methods used to sell the securities.[98]

From the standpoint of issuers' offerings of shelf-registered securities, the primary significance of the single-distribution theory was that it was necessary to determine whether specific prospective underwriters had "continuing agreements" with the issuer to sell the registered securities. If so, the underwriter would be deemed to have commenced its participation in the distribution when it entered into the agreement and would be subject to Rule 10b-6 restrictions in respect of each takedown.

The SEC effected a major simplification of the rules in this area when it abandoned the single-distribution approach as part of its adoption of Regulation M in late 1996. Under the new approach, each takedown off a shelf is to be individually examined to determine whether the offering constitutes a distribution (i.e., whether the takedown satisfies the magnitude criterion and the special selling efforts and selling methods criterion). As to the second of these criteria, the Regulation M Release states that the issuer's description in the shelf registration statement of a variety of potential selling methods will not cause, by itself, any sales off the shelf to be treated as a distribution unless the underwriter "in fact uses special selling efforts or selling methods in connection with particular sales off the shelf, and the sales are of a magnitude sufficient to demonstrate the existence of a distribution."[99]

In the Regulation M Release, the SEC also confirmed its earlier position that "[i]n those situations where a broker-dealer sells shares on behalf of an issuer or selling security holder in ordinary trading transactions into an independent market (i.e., without any special selling efforts) the offering will not be considered a distribution and the broker-dealer will not be subject to Rule 101." It added a caveat, however, that the result would likely be different where the broker-dealer had a sales agency agreement that provided for "unusual transaction-based com-

---

98. SEC Release No. 34-23611 (September 11, 1986).
99. SEC Release No. 34-38067 (January 3, 1997), at n.47.

pensation," even if the securities were sold in ordinary trading transactions.[100]

Deep Discount and Zero Coupon Obligations

The yield on a debt security is a function of both the stated interest rate and the price at which the security is sold to the investor. Thus, non-convertible debt securities that are sold at a discount from their face amount may carry an interest rate below that which the market would require if they were sold at par. If a note with a specified rating and maturity would require a 6% interest rate to receive market acceptance if offered at par, then a 4% coupon would only be acceptable if the note were offered at a price sufficiently below par. The lower the interest rate, the greater must be the discount from the face amount.

The ultimate deep discount instrument is the zero coupon obligation, a debt security that bears no interest at all. Commercial paper is generally a zero coupon obligation, although it is not thought of as such. It generally does not bear interest but is sold to investors at a discount from its principal amount. Because of the short maturities of commercial paper, the discount is relatively small. Where long-term zero coupon obligations are issued, however, the discount from par will be substantial.

- *Tax Considerations*

If a debt security is sold to the public at a substantial discount, the original issue discount (OID) provisions of Sections 1271–1273 and Section 1275 of the Internal Revenue Code and the regulations thereunder will come into play.

• • *Definition of OID.* Publicly offered debt securities potentially subject to the OID provisions include any obligation with an original term of more than one year from the date of original issue other than U.S. savings bonds.

OID on these obligations is equal to the excess of the "stated redemption price at maturity" over the "issue price." The stated

---

100. *Id.* at text following nn.47 and 48. *See* the discussion in Chapter 4.

redemption price of a debt instrument is equal to the sum of all payments provided by the debt instrument other than "qualified stated interest" payments. The term "qualified stated interest" generally means stated interest that is unconditionally payable in cash or property (other than debt instruments of the issuer) at least annually at a single fixed rate. For example, in the case of a zero coupon obligation, the stated redemption price would be simply the stated face amount. However, varying rates of interest, or multiple payments of principal, bring more complex rules into play. The "issue price" of an obligation sold to the public for cash is the initial offering price to the public (excluding dealers and brokers) at which price a substantial amount of the debt instruments was sold. There is no guidance as to what is a "substantial amount," but most firms look to the price at which the first 10% or 20% of the obligations are sold.

OID may be ignored by holders if it is less than ¼ of 1% of the stated redemption price at maturity multiplied by the number of complete years to maturity.[101] For example, the holder of a ten-year bond with an issue price of more than $975.00 would not be subject to the OID rules. Note that, if a bond closing is on June 3, 2004, and the bond matures on June 1, 2014, the bond is only a nine-year bond for this purpose and, thus, an issue price of, say, $976.00 would make holders of the bond subject to the OID rules.

• • *Consequences of OID.* If OID exists, the holder must accrue currently, in all periods during which the obligation is held, the OID allocable to such periods. While the allocation of OID to particular periods is complex, it is basically a "constant yield" method from the issue date to the maturity date, with the yield being based on compounding at the close of each "accrual period." An "accrual period" may be of any length and may vary over the term of the instrument, provided that each accrual period is no longer than one year and each scheduled payment of principal and interest occurs either on the first or last day of

---

101. Issuers, however, can still take an interest deduction for the de minimis OID under Section 163 of the Internal Revenue Code.

an accrual period. If a holder purchases a debt instrument for an amount that is greater than its adjusted issue price as of the purchase date and less than or equal to the sum of all amounts payable on the debt instrument after the purchase date other than qualified stated interest, it will be able to reduce the amount of OID that it must include in its gross income with respect to such debt instrument for any taxable year (or portion thereof in which it holds the debt instrument) a proportionate amount of the excess properly allocable to the period. If a holder purchases a debt instrument for an amount that is greater than the sum of all amounts payable on the debt instrument after the purchase date other than qualified stated interest, then it will not be required to include any OID in income. If the holder purchases the bond for less than the issue price, plus accrued OID to date, the difference is not subject to the OID rules but instead is subject to the market discount rules. Any OID accrued by the holder increases its tax basis in the obligation.

• • *Reporting of OID.* An issuer is required to report OID accruing to a holder of its debt on Form 1099-OID in the same manner as interest. Of course, since the issuer has no way of knowing the price paid by a particular holder, the Form 1099-OID is only accurate as to a holder who has purchased the obligation at a price equal to or below the issue price, plus accrued OID to date. All other holders must make their own adjustments, based on their own purchase date and purchase price.

Regulations require the issuer, in the case of instruments that are not publicly offered, to legend a debt instrument by stating on the face of the instrument that the instrument has OID and either (i) set forth on the face of the debt instrument the issue price, the amount of OID, the issue date, the yield to maturity and certain other additional information in the case of certain types of instruments or (ii) provide the name or title and either the address or telephone number of a representative of the issuer who will, beginning no later than ten days after the issue date, promptly make available to holders on request the information described above.

In the case of instruments that are publicly offered and that have OID, the issuer must file an information return with the

Internal Revenue Service in the form prescribed by regulations.[102] The penalty for failure to comply, absent reasonable cause, is 1% of the aggregate issue price, not to exceed $50,000 per issue.

- *Bankruptcy and Events of Default*

If a bankruptcy proceeding is commenced in respect of the issuer of a deep discount or zero coupon obligation, the claim of the holder is limited under Section 502(b)(2) of the Bankruptcy Code to the initial public offering price of the obligation plus that portion of the OID that is amortized from the date of issue to the commencement of the bankruptcy proceeding. If there is an event of default under the terms of the obligation or the governing indenture and this is followed by an acceleration of the maturity of the obligation, the indenture will usually provide that the holders will receive an amount of principal equal to the sum of the initial public offering price plus that portion of OID attributable to the period from the date of issue to the date of acceleration.

- *Accounting Treatment*

Under U.S. GAAP, a holder of an obligation purchased with OID normally must report as an item of income for financial accounting purposes the portion of the discount attributable to the applicable reporting period. The calculation of this attributable income is made in accordance with the "interest method," which corresponds generally to the method provided by the Internal Revenue Code. The issuer reports amortization of debt discount as an item of interest expense on the same basis. The debt is carried on the issuer's balance sheet at par, less the unamortized debt discount, with appropriate details in the notes to its financial statements. The normal footnote presentation is to list all issues of long-term debt at their stated principal amounts and subtract the aggregate debt discount from the subtotal of the principal amounts to arrive at the net amount reflected

---

102. Form 8281, as revised to September 2002, is available on the IRS website at www.irs.gov/pub/irs-pdf/f8281.pdf.

on the balance sheet. An alternative presentation is to state the amount of discount separately for each issue.

- *Deep Discount Obligations*

There are cost savings to an issuer of deep discount debt securities. Less cash is taken in at the outset than would be the case if the debt were issued at par, but smaller periodic cash interest payments are required. Amortization of OID is a non-cash expense, but it is deductible for tax purposes.

With deep discount obligations, the holder receives cash based on the stated below-market interest rate but is taxed on the basis of that amount plus the amortized OID. A deep discount obligation can be structured so that the investor receives cash interest payments in an amount at least sufficient to cover the required tax payments.

Debt securities may be sold at a discount from their face amount not because the interest rate is below market but because the initial interest payment is deferred until a specified date in the future. Securities of this type can be used effectively by a company financing a leveraged buyout that needs all the cash that it can conserve in the early years, but projects that it will be able to pay interest at a market rate when it begins to realize the cost savings from the operating efficiencies that it plans to institute. Section 163(i) of the Internal Rvenue Code, relating to "applicable high yield discount obligations," imposes certain limits on this strategy.

- *Zero Coupon Obligations*

Zero coupon obligations are debt securities that do not bear any interest but, instead, are sold at a discount from par that is sufficient to provide the investor with a yield to maturity based on market rates at the time of issue. Because the holder must pay taxes even though it receives no cash until maturity, zero coupon obligations are designed primarily for the tax-deferred market—pension plans, IRAs and Keogh plans.

Notwithstanding the tax disadvantages, many taxpaying institutions and individuals look on zero coupon bonds as convenient vehicles for acting on their convictions as to the direction of interest rates. If such an investor believes that bond prices are about to rise, there is tremendous leverage in buying a 30-year zero at a very low price.

Zero coupon obligations are used by money managers to eliminate reinvestment risk. In the case of conventional interest-bearing investments, the holder bears the risk that future interest payments may be reinvestable only at a lower rate. With zero coupon obligations, this risk is eliminated. The rate at which accrued interest is compounded is determined at the time of issuance and is built into the amount of the discount. Investment managers seeking to "immunize" their portfolios are willing to accept a lower yield in return for this certainty and convenience. Another highly important feature of zero coupon obligations is call protection, which assures the permanence of the investment. These advantages inure to the benefit of the issuer in the form of lower borrowing costs.

Some of the advantages of zero coupon obligations were highlighted in a ditty sung some years ago at the annual dinner meeting of the investment banking division of a major underwriting firm. The words were sung to the melody of "The Battle Hymn of the Republic:"

> Mine eyes have seen the glory of the zero coupon bond;
> It saves the client basis points over current coupon ones;
> It gives the buyer call protection and reinvestment break;
> And the firm goes marching on.

In purchasing a zero coupon obligation with a long maturity, an investor must be satisfied that the issuer will be able to make payment when the obligation becomes due. In the case of an interest bearing obligation, the investor at least is receiving interest on a periodic basis. With a zero, the investor receives no cash until maturity. For this reason, there is virtually no market for non-convertible zeros that are not rated investment grade. (Convertible zero coupon bonds in the form of LYONs are discussed in Chapter 12.)

"Reopenings"

An issuer may decide to "reopen" an outstanding class of debt securities—that is, to offer securities that have terms identical to those of the outstanding securities. The issuer may take this step to improve liquidity in the outstanding securities, to relieve secondary market dislocations or to qualify the issue for an electronic trading platform.

From a shelf registration point of view, a reopening is nothing more than a routine takedown that requires fewer changes in the documents than is usually the case. The terms of the new security will literally be identical to those of the old security, including maturity date, coupon, interest payment dates, CUSIP number and so on, with the objective of achieving complete fungibility with the old securities. The only change will be the price at which the new securities are to be sold, since interest rates will almost invariably have changed since the old securities were issued.

If the debt securities are investment grade, Regulation M will not apply to bids for and purchases of the old securities during the distribution of the new securities. If they are less than investment-grade, however, Regulation M may apply to such bids and purchases because the old securities will be considered part of the same "class and series" as the new securities as a result of their being "identical" with the new securities.[103]

If interest rates have risen since the old securities were issued—or the issuer's creditworthiness has deteriorated—the new securities will have to be offered at a discount in order to justify the fact that they bear the same coupon as the old securities. Such a discount may be treated for tax purposes as OID, not only for the new securities but also for the old securities (since there will be no way to distinguish the new securities from the old securities). This is generally not an acceptable result.

If the reopening takes place within 13 days of the issue of the old securities to investors and as part of a common plan, a single transaction or a series of related transactions, and if the new securities have the "same credit and payment terms" as the old securities, then the new securities will be considered to be part of the same issue as the old securities.

---

103. *See* Chapter 4, "Regulation M—Covered Securities."

SHELF REGISTRATION (RULE 415)

If that is not the case, however, then it will be necessary to rely on recently amended Treasury Regulations[104] that prevent the OID problem from arising if the new securities are sold in "Qualified Reopenings." A reopening is a Qualified Reopening if

- the old securities are publicly traded,[105] and the new securities are issued with no more than a de minimis amount of OID (as discussed above, this is generally ¼ of 1% of the stated redemption price at maturity multiplied by the number of complete years until maturity), or

- the old securities are publicly traded, the reopening date is not more than six months after the issue date of the old securities and the new securities satisfy a "Yield Test." The Yield Test is satisfied if on the pricing date of the new securities (or any earlier "announcement date") the yield of the old securities based on their fair market value is not more than 110% of their yield on the date on which they were issued (or, if the old securities were issued with no more than a de minimis amount of OID, their coupon rate). The "announcement date" for this purpose is the later of (a) seven days before the pricing date for the new securities or (b) the date the issuer announced its intention to reopen through one or more media channels.

The regulations do not apply to contingent payment debt securities, so any reopening of these securities should be completed within the 13-day window in order to avoid any OID problem.

---

104. TD 8934 (December 29, 2000), *Reopening of Treasury Securities and Other Debt Obligations,* 66 Fed. Reg. 2811 (January 12, 2001).

105. "Publicly traded" means listed or quoted on a U.S. exchange, a designated foreign exchange or certain quotation systems or that are otherwise (with certain exceptions) "readily quotable."

Chapter 9

INTERNATIONAL FINANCINGS

The last 25 years have been marked by a dramatic growth in the size and importance of international securities markets. For many U.S. issuers, the markets outside the United States have become an important source of capital that they can tap relatively quickly and with a minimum of disclosure formalities. On the other hand, foreign issuers also frequently find it advantageous—for reasons we shall discuss—to offer or at least list their securities in the U.S. markets. Finally, many U.S. and foreign issuers have become accustomed to offering their securities in "global offerings" directed simultaneously to investors in the U.S. and offshore markets.

The fortunate beneficiary of the growth of international securities markets is the investor, for whom the U.S. and offshore markets are becoming, for many purposes, indistinguishable. On the equity side, U.S. and foreign investors alike have the capability of analyzing investments in markets around the world. On the fixed-income side, they monitor interest rate and currency developments as a basis for determining their relative involvement in dollar-denominated or non-dollar-denominated fixed-income investments. On both the equity and fixed-income sides, investors look to securities firms on a global basis to provide deep and liquid secondary markets in many securities as well as to offer the ability to hedge all or a portion of the risk inherent in a single instrument or market sector.

There are many reasons for the globalization of securities markets. A few might include the ability of investment bankers to access favorable financing opportunities for issuers in diverse markets; financial innovation and particularly the development of sophisticated devices to hedge against interest rate and currency risk; advances in communications and computer technology that make it possible for securities firms to "pass the book" around the world for trading purposes; the deregulation of exchange controls and capital markets; the introduction of the Euro among the member countries of the European Monetary Union; the development of book-entry clearance and settlement facilities; improved transparency and liquidity in the worldwide secondary markets; and the creation of global research capabilities by many of the world's leading securities firms.

The institutionalization of the securities markets has been a significant factor as well. There is increased interest on the part of portfolio managers, both domestic and foreign, in securities issued outside of their own countries, both for reasons of risk diversification and a search for superior returns. The growth of global investment companies that invest on a worldwide basis, as well as the introduction of numerous "country funds" (U.S. closed-end investment companies that invest in the securities markets of specific countries), have also contributed to the increase in holdings of foreign securities by U.S. investors.

The federal securities laws have their clearest application when an issuer—domestic or foreign—is offering securities within the United States. Their application has been less clear where the securities are offered, at least initially, outside the United States. In these cases, while the SEC has acknowledged that the federal securities laws are not intended to protect persons outside the United States, it has nevertheless worried that securities offered in an ostensibly "offshore" transaction may be intended to find their ultimate home in the United States.

This chapter will discuss the SEC's efforts over the last four decades to spell out the circumstances under which a U.S. or foreign issuer may make an "offshore" offering without violations of the registration requirements of the 1933 Act. It will also discuss the particular problems a foreign issuer must overcome when it wishes to make a registered public offering in the United States.[1] Finally, we will discuss the challenges of a "global" offering—that is, a public offering outside the United States together with a simultaneous public or private offering in the United States.

Offshore Offerings and the 1933 Act

- *Interest Equalization Tax*

As the European economy recovered in the years following World War II, a European capital market developed in the early 1960s that provided a source of funds for U.S. corporations. During the 1950s, the strength of the dollar in the foreign exchange markets caused U.S. goods to become less competitive, resulting in an outflow of dollars to Europe. At the same time, U.S. companies increased their overseas investment in manufacturing facilities. The sale of debt securities by foreign issuers in the U.S. market further contributed to the outflow of dollars. By the end of the 1950s, the U.S. balance of payment deficit had become a matter of concern, and in 1963 Congress imposed the Interest Equalization Tax (IET),[2] a tax on the value of foreign debt or equity securities acquired by U.S. persons.

The IET was designed to make foreign investment less attractive and thus to discourage foreign borrowing in the United States. The implementation of the IET caused non-U.S. borrowers to turn to the Euromarket as a source of funds. The money was there,

---

1. Of course, foreign issuers may take advantage of any available exemptions under the 1933 Act. For example, Chapter 7 describes private placements in the United States by U.S. and non-U.S. issuers.

2. Interest Equalization Tax Act of 1963–64, Pub. L. No. 88-563, 78 Stat. 809 (repealed 1976).

including the large pool of dollars that had grown from the dollar outflow during the preceding decade. These funds came to be known as "Eurodollars," dollars held by non-residents of the United States, usually on deposit with European banks and held by those banks in their New York branches, subsidiaries, or correspondent banks.

Continuing balance of payment deficits led to restrictions on overseas direct investment by U.S. corporations. Under controls imposed in 1968 and administered by the Office of Foreign Direct Investments, U.S. corporations were forced to finance their foreign operations in foreign markets. Eurobond issues by these companies increased from $527 million in 1967 to more than $1.9 billion in 1968.[3]

As U.S. issuers began to sell debt securities in the Euromarket, partly in response to the direct investment guidelines, questions arose as to the application of the 1933 Act to such transactions. The registration provisions of Section 5 of the 1933 Act apply to any offer or sale of a security involving interstate commerce or the use of the mails ("jurisdictional means") unless an exemption is available. Since "interstate commerce" is defined in Section 2(a)(7) of the 1933 Act to include "trade or commerce in securities or any transportation or communication relating thereto . . . between any foreign country and any State, Territory, or the District of Columbia," the registration provisions of the 1933 Act might be construed to reach any offer or sale of securities—even to foreign investors—if the offer or sale involved even incidental use (e.g., by the issuer or by underwriters) of U.S. jurisdictional means.

Although it might well have taken enforcement action in the event of a sale to dealers in a foreign country with a view to resale in the United States, the SEC had little inclination to test its jurisdiction where a domestic issuer effected a distribution exclusively abroad. The lore of the SEC going back to the early years of the 1933 Act included a vague theory to the effect that a Section 4(2) exemption would be available to this type of transaction in that the term "public offering" should be read to

---

3. F. G. Fisher, *International Bonds*, 1981, at 21.

mean "public offering in the United States." But prior to 1964, the SEC had not fully articulated its position, and as Eurodollar offerings proliferated, many felt that it was time for the SEC to do so.[4]

- *Release 33-4708*

In 1964, a presidential task force chaired by Henry H. Fowler delivered its Report on Promoting Increased Foreign Investment in United States Corporate Securities and Increased Foreign Financing for United States Corporations Operating Abroad (Fowler Task Force Report). One of the recommendations of the task force report was that the SEC clarify the circumstances under which 1933 Act registration would not be required in connection with public offerings of securities outside the United States to foreign purchasers. In response to this recommendation, the SEC on July 9, 1964 published Release No. 33-4708 in which it acknowledged that *"the registration requirements of Section 5 of the Act are primarily intended to protect American investors"* (emphasis added). The release then noted that the SEC

> had not taken any action for failure to register securities of United States corporations distributed abroad to foreign nationals, even though use of jurisdictional means may be involved in the offering. It is assumed in these situations that *the distribution is to be effected in a manner which will result in the securities coming to rest abroad.* . . . Apart from [a situation involving a distribution through a Canadian stock exchange that might be expected to flow into the hands of American investors or a situation involving an offer targeted toward American investors living abroad], . . . it is immaterial whether the offering originates from within or outside of the United States, whether domestic or foreign broker-dealers are involved and whether the actual mechanics of the

---

4. For a discussion of this subject with extensive citations, *see* Comment, *Extraterritorial Effect of the Registration Requirements of the Securities Act of 1933,* 24 Vill. L. Rev. 729 (1978–79).

distribution are effected within the United States, *so long as the offering is made under circumstances reasonably designed to preclude distribution or redistribution of the securities within, or to nationals of, the United States.* (Emphasis added.)

In response to another task force recommendation, the release also stated that the SEC would not integrate an offering made abroad with a simultaneous private placement in the United States of the same security. "Generally, transactions otherwise meeting the requirements of . . . [Section 4(2) of the 1933 Act] need not be integrated with simultaneous offerings being made abroad and, therefore, are not subject to the registration requirements of the Act solely because a foreign offering is being made concurrently with the American private placement which otherwise meets the standards of the exemption."

As noted above, the IET represented at the time of the publication of Release 33-4708 a significant economic disincentive for U.S. investors to acquire securities of foreign issuers. The SEC staff subsequently regarded the IET as a factor to be taken into account in deciding whether to grant no-action letters on the need to register offerings made abroad.[5] While the IET was in effect, the principles of Release 33-4708 were relied on primarily for sales abroad of Eurodollar obligations issued by a foreign finance subsidiary (or an "80-20" U.S. finance subsidiary) of a U.S. corporation, guaranteed by the parent and often convertible into the parent's common stock. Where the U.S. parent or a domestically incorporated subsidiary was the issuer of the obligations, an election could be made to have the obligations treated as those of a foreign issuer whose acquisition by a U.S. person would be subject to the IET.[6]

---

5. E.g., SEC No-action Letter, *Intercontinental Hotels Corp.* (August 11, 1971). Although Release 33-4708 specifically refers only to U.S. issuers, the SEC staff also applied it to offerings by foreign issuers. *See, e.g., Vizcaya International N.V.* (April 4, 1973), *Republic of Iceland* (March 19, 1971).

6. Committee on Taxation of International Finance and Investment of New York State Bar Association, Tax Section, *Report on International Finance Subsidiaries*, 28 Tax. L. Rev. 443, 509 (1973).

- *Debt Financings After Elimination of IET*

In January 1974, the IET was reduced to zero,[7] and one of Release 33-4708's important underpinnings was accordingly eliminated. With respect to a Eurodollar financing made shortly after the elimination of the IET in accordance with offering procedures that had then become standard, the SEC's staff took a no-action position on the offering itself but expressly refused to take a position as to when and under what circumstances the securities could be resold in the United States or to U.S. nationals.[8]

Securities lawyers soon developed elaborate procedures designed to substitute for the IET in meeting the objectives of Release 33-4708 regarding non-distribution of securities to U.S. investors. Many of these procedures were the subject of SEC no-action letters, including *Pacific Lighting Corporation* (June 13, 1974) and *The Singer Co.* (September 3, 1974). The procedures were considerably simplified in a no-action letter relating to *The Procter & Gamble Company* (February 21, 1985). By the mid-1980s, the substance of the procedures generally in effect (subject to variations as a result of the preferences of individual securities firms and their counsel and the circumstances of particular cases) could be summarized as follows:

1. *Invitation Telexes.* Invitation telexes to prospective underwriters and dealers stated that the securities to be distributed ("distribution securities") would not be registered under the 1933 Act and that they would not be offered, sold or delivered in the United States or to U.S. persons as part of the distribution.

2. *Contractual Restrictions.* Underwriters and dealers would agree (a) not to acquire distribution securities for the account of a U.S. person, (b) not to sell distribution securities in the U.S. or to U.S. persons (or to others for

---

7. Exec. Order No. 11,766 (1974), reprinted in [1974] U.S. Code Cong. & Ad. News 8260. The Interest Equalization Tax Act was repealed by the Tax Reform Act of 1976, Pub. L. No. 94-455, 90 Stat. 1520.

8. SEC No-action Letter, *Sperry Rand Corp.* (March 1, 1974). *See also* SEC No-action Letter, *American Motors Corp.* (January 24, 1974).

reoffering in the United States or to U.S. persons), (c) as to securities of the same class acquired otherwise than in connection with the distribution, not to offer or sell such securities in the U.S. or to U.S. persons prior to 90 days after completion of the distribution, as determined by the lead managing underwriter, (d) in connection with sales of distribution securities, to deliver confirmations stating (i) that the securities had not been registered under the 1933 Act, (ii) as to non-dealer purchasers, the substance of the foregoing restrictions and (iii) as to dealer purchasers, that the purchaser represented that it would comply with the foregoing restrictions and would deliver similar confirmations to persons to whom it sold the distribution securities.

3. *Disclosure.* The offering circular or prospectus would state (a) that the distribution securities were unregistered and could not be sold in the United States or to U.S. persons, (b) that the securities would initially be represented by a temporary global security exchangeable for definitive securities (i) not earlier than 90 days after the date certified by the lead managing underwriter as the date of completion of the distribution and (ii) on certification of non-U.S. beneficial ownership and (c) that non-complying offers or sales in the United States or to U.S. persons might violate U.S. law.

4. *"All-Sold" Telexes.* Underwriters and dealers would agree to confirm to the lead managing underwriter, on request, that they had sold all allotted securities in compliance with the foregoing restrictions.

5. *Delivery of Securities.* The securities would be initially represented by a temporary global security that would be exchangeable for definitive securities only under the circumstances described above.

6. *Press Releases and Advertising.* Press releases and tombstone advertisements would state that the securities had not been registered under the 1933 Act and that they could not be sold in the United States or to U.S. persons

as part of the distribution. Tombstones would customarily not be published until the closing date or such later time as the lead managing underwriter believed the distribution to have been completed.

Release 33-4708 did not contemplate international equity offerings,[9] and the SEC could be expected to be more concerned about the potential for resale of equity securities into the United States than in the case of debt offerings. Subsequent to the elimination of the IET, however, the SEC issued a number of no-action letters relating to equity offerings where it considered the procedures adequate to prevent illicitly unregistered resales into the United States.[10] These procedures became so well known that even foreign issuers making international equity offerings incorporated similar restrictions into their offering procedures, including complex confirmation delivery undertakings designed to avoid sales in the United States or to U.S. persons. Oddly enough, similar offerings of U.S. issuers did not always require these undertakings, but they did contemplate an absolute prohibition of U.S. sales for a period of one year as opposed to a 120-day prohibition for the non-U.S. issuers.

In 1985 the SEC issued a no-action letter to InfraRed Associates Inc.,[11] a U.S. issuer that proposed to make an initial public offering through a U.K. underwriting firm to investors

---

9. Because of the flow-back potential, the October 1972 sale in Japan of 700,000 shares of common stock of General Telephone & Electronics Corp. (the first equity offering by a U.S. company in Japan) was registered under the 1933 Act as well as under the Japanese securities law. Also, G.D. Searle & Co. registered all of the common stock that it offered outside of the United States in an October 24, 1974, exchange offer for shares of Gold Cross Hospital Supplies Limited, an English company.

10. E.g., SEC No-action Letter, *Foote, Cone & Belding Communications Inc.* (reconsidered June 21, 1976); SEC No-action Letter, *Hexalon Real Estate, Inc.* (July 1, 1977); SEC No-action Letter, *Sulpetro International, Ltd.* (August 25, 1977); SEC No-action Letter, *RSA Corp.* (January 3, 1978); SEC No-action Letter, *American Eastern Real Estate and Investment Corp.* (November 27, 1978).

11. SEC No-action Letter, *InfraRed Associates, Inc.* (October 14, 1985).

outside North America. The letter was issued after some negotiation, and it noted

> particularly that securities may be transferred to or for the benefit of North American persons only after a twelve month period following the end of the offering, and then only if (i) the securities are duly registered under the [1933] Act, and any applicable securities laws of any state of the United States ("State Act"); (ii) an exemption from registration under the [1933] Act and any applicable State Act is available and InfraRed has received an opinion of counsel to such effect reasonably satisfactory to it; or (iii) such securities are sold on the London Stock Exchange in accordance with procedures approved by the London Stock Exchange.

The *InfraRed* letter was unusual in implying the SEC staff's agreement that a specific method of resale was available to purchasers of the securities offered abroad.

- *Dissatisfaction with Release 33-4708*

By the mid-1980s, it was becoming apparent that Release 33-4708 had some serious conceptual shortcomings and that the procedures it had spawned were excessively complex, subject to breaking down in practice and designed primarily for the convenience of counsel in rendering legal opinions:

1. It was unclear exactly what the SEC had done in Release 33-4708. While the SEC acknowledged in the release and in subsequent no-action letters that it was possible to effect a foreign distribution without 1933 Act registration, it generally (with rare exceptions such as the *InfraRed* letter mentioned above) carefully reserved its position on when (if ever) the distributed securities could be resold in the United States or to U.S. persons. Because this uncertainty was built into the procedural structure, holders of (and would-be dealers in) securities distributed abroad in compliance with the release and the no-action letters were in some ways in a worse

position than holders of (and would-be dealers in) securities *illegally* distributed in the United States. At least, these securities could be resold in reliance on Section 4(3)(A) commencing 40 days after the commencement of the illegal distribution.

2. The definition of "U.S. person" for purposes of the release and the related procedures was customarily taken as "any national or resident of the United States, any corporation, partnership, or other entity created or organized in or under the laws of the United States or any political subdivision thereof, or any estate or trust that is subject to U.S. federal income taxation regardless of the source of its income." It was often difficult for underwriters and dealers to apply this definition to particular customers, for example, foreign branches of U.S. banks and insurance companies.[12] The definition was derived from tax requirements applicable in the fixed-income area, however, and it resisted attempts at modification despite its having no necessary relevance to the purposes of the 1933 Act. More important, it was becoming less clear that the 1933 Act should prevent U.S. persons located abroad from purchasing securities involved in offshore distributions. For one thing, it was difficult (if not impossible), in the case of equity securities listed on a foreign exchange (as in the case of the *InfraRed* letter), to prevent U.S. persons from simply purchasing the distributed securities in the secondary market. For another, prohibiting sales to U.S. persons had the potential for depriving U.S. investors of important opportunities.

3. Despite the premise of the release that the registration provisions of the 1933 Act are primarily concerned with the protection of U.S. investors, the release implied that offers and sales in the geographic United States are

---

12. The SEC took the position, however, that a branch or agency of a U.S. bank or insurance company operating outside of the United States for valid business reasons and subject to local regulation would not be viewed as a U.S. person and could thus be offered unregistered securities. SEC No-action Letter, *Foreign Agencies and Branches of United States Banks and Insurance Companies* (February 25, 1988).

prohibited. This leaves unclear the status of non-U.S. investors whose accounts are managed by U.S. investment advisors, U.S.-based international organizations and approaches to U.S. corporations regarding investments by their foreign affiliates.

4. On its face, the release set forth only an interpretation of the 1933 Act. While the release was codified in the Code of Federal Regulations, it was not clear that persons relying on the release could do so as if it were a "rule or regulation" within the meaning of Section 19(a) of the 1933 Act.[13]

5. The determination whether a distribution has been "completed" is customarily left to the lead manager of an issue, who must certify such completion as a condition of the exchange of temporary global securities for definitive securities. Obviously, the lead manager is at the mercy of the information provided by the underwriters. What would happen if an underwriter were to misrepresent the state of its position?

6. Also, counsel would customarily require as a condition of a legal opinion regarding the non-applicability of the registration provisions of the 1933 Act that the lead manager certify to such counsel one of (or some combination of) the propositions that (a) the lead manager has no reason to believe that the contractual restrictions would be disregarded so that a distribution would take place in the United States and (b) the lead manager was of the opinion that the offering was being made "under circumstances reasonably designed to preclude distribution or redistribution of the securities" in the United States or to U.S. persons. Responsible counsel obviously requires some factual basis for such an opinion, but it is

---

13. Section 19(a) of the 1933 Act protects persons from liability under the 1933 Act if they act in good faith in conformity with an SEC "rule or regulation." Compare *Gerstle v. Gamble-Skogmo, Inc.*, 478 F.2d 1281 (2d Cir. 1973), with *Colema Realty Corp. v. Bibow*, 555 F. Supp. 1030 (D. Conn. 1983).

not clear whether the requested certifications did not in effect beg the question as to which counsel was being asked to opine.

7. It was unclear under the release and the procedures whether a breakdown of the procedures in any one trade would "taint" the entire transaction.

- *Evolution of a Territorial Approach*

During the 1980s, the SEC began to take a new look at the growing internationalization of the capital markets with a view to ensuring that its rules did not unnecessarily impede multinational offerings. It came to recognize that the United States was facing serious competition from a largely unregulated transnational financial market. In its *1987 Internationalization Report*, the SEC staff noted that securities markets around the world were changing as foreign issuers expanded their use of U.S. capital markets, domestic issuers accessed foreign markets and both debt and equity offerings were made on an international basis. "As a result of these offerings," the staff observed, "the lines of demarcation between domestic and international capital markets are beginning to blur and domestic markets are facing serious competition from a largely unregulated, transnational financial market." In addition, questions concerning the reach of Section 5 of the 1933 Act had "resulted in complex and costly offering procedures to assure that registration provisions do not apply [to an offering], as well as the exclusion of United States persons from various offshore investment opportunities." At the same time, the ability of U.S. investors (particularly institutions) to purchase securities in foreign secondary markets meant that they were likely to be disadvantaged when the foreign issuers engaged in rights offerings or exchange offers.[14]

The fact that U.S. institutional investors were beginning to chafe at SEC policies relating to the jurisdictional reach of Section 5 was a new phenomenon in 1987. For example, Peter C. Clapman of College Retirement Equities Fund (CREF) stated to

---

14. *1987 Internationalization Report* at III-311.

the SEC at its 1987 roundtable on the internationalization of securities markets that CREF was being deprived of the opportunity to invest in attractive foreign new issues.[15] Investing in France was a case in point:

> The focus of the new issue problem now turns to France and the new privatization issues. These are issues of stock of companies presently owned by the French government being sold mostly to the French public, with a small amount of stock available to non-French citizens. Such stock has been and is likely to be attractively priced. It is difficult to obtain such stock. An American must take [the] initiative to find out about it—who the underwriters are. Because CREF has been in the French market since 1978, we should normally be able to acquire some shares. A limited amount is available to foreigners—but until now—not to Americans. Why? The French government and French issuers were concerned about doing a private placement with American institutions because of perceived fear of the SEC. Americans were, of course, free to buy in the aftermarket—after the benefits of the bargain were enjoyed by all others. Hopefully, the SEC will address this issue shortly. Until then, Americans will continue to have difficulty.

The SEC did address the issue and granted to CREF a no-action letter that made clear that equity securities issued as part of the French privatization program could be sold to U.S. institutions in reliance on the private placement exemption and that these institutions could freely resell the securities on the *Bourse* in Paris without inquiring as to the identity of the purchasers. The institutions would agree not to resell within the United States or knowingly to a U.S. national. The SEC's staff also agreed that the French issuers would not be required to comply

---

15. Statement of Peter C. Clapman, Senior Vice President and Associate General Counsel, Teachers Insurance & Annuity Association—College Retirement Equities Fund, to the SEC Roundtable on Internationalization of Securities Markets (February 17, 1987), *id.* at V B-115, 121.

with any additional procedures in the foreign offerings as a result of the U.S. private placement.[16]

In the *1987 Internationalization Report*, the SEC staff suggested that a territorial approach to the registration provisions of the 1933 Act would be consistent with its purpose and with "comity principles. . . . Such an approach recognizes the primacy of the laws in which a market is located. As investors choose their markets, they would choose the laws applicable to such markets."[17]

- *Adoption of Regulation S*

Regulation S was first proposed in June 1988.[18] As suggested in the *1987 Internationalization Report*, the proposed rule was based on a territorial approach to Section 5. "Under such an approach, the registration of securities is intended to protect the U.S. capital markets and all investors purchasing in the U.S. capital market, whether U.S. or foreign nationals. Principles of comity and reasonable expectations of participants in the global market justify reliance on laws applicable in jurisdictions outside the United States to define disclosure requirements for transactions effected offshore. . . . [T]his territorial approach to the application of the registration provisions would not affect the broad reach of the antifraud provisions of the federal securities laws."[19]

---

16. SEC No-action Letter, *College Retirement Equities Fund* (February 18, 1987). In a subsequent letter, the SEC confirmed the first CREF letter in regard to foreign issuers' rights offerings and exchange offers. SEC No-action Letter, *College Retirement Equities Fund* (June 4, 1987).

17. *1987 Internationalization Report* at III-317. The new approach had been foreshadowed in a November 1986 speech by the late Linda C. Quinn, then director of the SEC's Division of Corporation Finance. She observed that it may have been "appropriate before the Euromarket, London, Japan and others evolved into major markets, for the Commission to suggest that securities offered to a U.S. citizen anywhere in the world should comply with the Securities Act. But if this was ever warranted, it surely is not today."

18. SEC Release No. 33-6779 (June 10, 1988) (proposing release).

19. *Id.* (footnotes omitted). Unlike Release 33-4708, Regulation S recognizes no distinction between Canada and other parts of the world. The

Regulation S was adopted in final form in April 1990 with its territorial philosophy intact.[20]

• • *Subsequent SEC Concerns with "Abusive" Regulation S Transactions.* Preliminary Note 2 to Regulation S stated that neither the general statement nor any of the safe harbors is available "with respect to any transaction or series of transactions that, although in technical compliance with . . . [the] rules, is part of a plan or scheme to evade the registration provisions of the [1933] Act."

In mid-1995 the SEC published an interpretive release setting forth its views concerning "problematic practices" that had developed under Regulation S and requesting comment as to whether Regulation S should be amended "to limit its vulnerability to abuse."[21] The SEC stated that it had learned that some market participants were conducting placements of securities purportedly offshore under Regulation S "under circumstances that indicate that such securities are in essence being placed offshore temporarily to evade registration requirements with the result that the incidence of ownership of the securities never leaves the U.S. market, or that a substantial portion of the economic risk relating thereto is left in or is returned to the U.S. market during the restricted period, or that the transaction is such that there was no reasonable expectation that the securities could be viewed as actually coming to rest abroad." These transactions, the SEC concluded, were of the kind "that run afoul of Preliminary Note 2" and would therefore not be covered either by the general statement in Rule 901 or by the safe harbors in Rule 903.

The release went on to describe transactions such as "parking" securities with offshore affiliates of the issuer or a distributor,

---

proposing release stated that given the dramatic changes in the world capital markets since 1964, the SEC was no longer of the view that the Canadian markets should be singled out for special treatment under Section 5. *Id.* at n.64.

20. SEC Release No. 33-6863 (April 24, 1990) (Adopting Release). The rule had been reproposed for comment in SEC Release No. 33-6838 (July 11, 1989).

21. SEC Release No. 33-7190 (June 27, 1995).

the use of non-recourse promissory notes expected to be repaid with the proceeds of a resale of the Regulation S securities into the U.S. market, fees paid or discounts granted to induce the purchaser to hold the securities for the restricted period and short selling or other hedging having the effect of transferring the risk of ownership of the securities back to the U.S. market.

The SEC asked for comment on whether Regulation S should be amended in certain respects to deter the perceived abuses, and it eventually proposed amendments in early 1997.[22] It adopted final amendments in early 1998.[23] As discussed below, the 1998 amendments make it more difficult for U.S. reporting issuers to make offshore equity offerings in reliance on Regulation S.

• • *General Statement.* Regulation S consists of a general statement of the applicability of the registration provisions of the 1933 Act, and it also consists of two non-exclusive safe harbors for the extraterritorial offer, sale and resale of securities.

The general statement, contained in Rule 901, defines the terms "offer," "offer to sell," "sell," "sale" and "offer to buy" as used in Section 5 of the 1933 Act as including only "offers and sales that occur within the United States" and as not including offers and sales "that occur outside the United States." The Adopting Release states that the determination "as to whether a transaction is outside the United States will be based on the facts and circumstances of each case. If it can be demonstrated that an offer or sale of securities occurs 'outside the United States,' the registration provisions of the Securities Act will not apply, regardless of whether the conditions of the safe harbor are met. For a transaction to qualify under the General Statement, both the sale and the offer pursuant to which it was made must be outside the United States."[24]

---

22. SEC Release No. 33-7392 (Feb. 20, 1997).

23. SEC Release No. 33-7505 (Feb. 17, 1998).

24. As proposed, the general statement would have included a list of factors to be considered in determining whether an offer or sale occurred outside the United States. Commenters generally opposed such a list as more harmful than helpful. Adopting Release, text following n.28.

• • *Safe Harbors.* The general statement in Rule 901 can sometimes be useful, but issuers and underwriters generally prefer to rely on the two safe harbors made available by Regulation S.

The *issuer safe harbor* in Rule 903 deems certain offers or sales by an issuer or a distributor (or any affiliate or person acting on their behalf) to be outside the United States for purposes of Rule 901 (i.e., the general statement). It has three "channels" that are more or less restrictive, the severity of the restrictions depending on the likelihood that the offered securities will flow back into the United States.

The *resale safe harbor* in Rule 904 is available for certain offers and sales outside the United States by all persons other than those covered by Rule 903 (except for certain officers and directors of an issuer).

Each of the safe harbors is subject to two general conditions: there must be an "offshore transaction," and there may not be any "directed selling efforts" in the United States. On the other hand, "[o]ffers made in the United States in connection with contemporaneous registered offerings or offerings exempt from registration will not preclude reliance on the safe harbors."[25]

• • *Offshore Transaction.* An offer or sale of securities is made in an "offshore transaction" if (i) the offer is not made to a person in the United States (other than a distributor) and (ii) at the time the buy order is originated, the buyer is outside the United States or the seller and any person acting on his behalf reasonably believes that the buyer is outside the United States.

There are two alternatives to the second requirement. For purposes of the issuer safe harbor, it is sufficient if the transaction is executed in, on or through a physical trading floor of an established foreign securities exchange. For purposes of the resale safe harbor, it is sufficient if the transaction is executed in, on or through the facilities of a "designated foreign securities market"[26] and neither the seller nor any person acting on its

---

25. *Id.* at n.36.
26. As defined in Rule 902(b). The SEC or its staff have designated a total of 35 offshore markets as "designated offshore securities markets" for this purpose. Additional markets may be so designated by the Division of Corporation Finance, acting pursuant to delegated authority, on the basis of criteria specified in Rule 902(b).

behalf knows that the transaction has been pre-arranged with a buyer in the United States.

Notwithstanding these provisions, offers and sales of securities specifically targeted at identifiable groups of U.S. citizens abroad, such as members of the U.S. armed forces serving overseas, are not deemed to be made in offshore transactions. On the other hand, offers and sales to certain persons not considered to be "U.S. persons" (see below) are permitted even though these persons are physically located in the United States.

As noted in the Adopting Release, "[a]ctivities specifically excluded from the definition of directed selling efforts also will not be deemed offers in the United States" for purposes of the offshore transaction requirement.[27]

• • *Directed Selling Efforts.* The term "directed selling efforts" means "any activity undertaken for the purpose of, or that could reasonably be expected to have the effect of, conditioning the market in the United States for any of the securities being offered in reliance on . . . Regulation S." This is a subjective definition similar to the SEC's general approach to defining an "offer" for the purpose of Section 5 of the 1933 Act. As discussed in Chapter 3, an activity or communication must be analyzed for this purpose in terms of its audience, timing and content.

It may not be necessary to engage in subjective analysis if there is a relevant exception in the definition or an SEC staff position. In this connection, problems frequently arise relating to the Internet, foreign press-related activity, advertising, quotation services and research.

• • • *Internet Postings.* The definition of "directed selling efforts" is broad enough to include information posted on Internet websites. In a 1998 interpretive release,[28] the SEC rejected the notion that it should attempt to regulate any Internet offer of securities that could be accessed by U.S. residents.

---

27. Adopting Release at n.53.

28. *Use of Internet Web Sites to Offer Securities, Solicit Securities Transactions, or Advertise Investment Services Offshore*, SEC Release No. 33-7516 (March 23, 1998).

684   **CORPORATE FINANCE & THE SECURITIES LAWS**

Rather, the SEC's investor protection concerns could be best addressed through the implementation by issuers and financial services providers of "precautionary measures that are reasonably designed to ensure that offshore Internet offers are not targeted to persons in the United States or to U.S. persons." The measures deemed adequate to achieve this purpose would depend on all the facts and circumstances of any particular situation, but the release stated that the SEC would generally not consider an offshore Internet offer as targeted at the United States if:

In the case of a non-U.S. offeror, (1) the website included a prominent disclaimer making it clear that any offer was directed only to countries other than the United States,[29] and (2) the website offeror implemented procedures reasonably designed to guard against "sales" in the United States.[30]

The 1998 release emphasized that these procedures were not exclusive; rather, "other procedures that suffice to guard against sales to U.S. persons also can be used to demonstrate that the offer is not targeted to the United States." It also cautioned that no precautions might be sufficient if a solicitation appeared by its content to be targeted at U.S. persons (e.g., a solicitation that emphasized the availability of U.S. tax benefits).

The 1998 release acknowledged that U.S. persons might respond falsely to residence questions or use offshore nominees in order to participate in offshore offerings. If a U.S. person succeeded by these means in purchasing securities in an offshore offering, the SEC would not "view the Internet offer after the fact as having been targeted at the United States, absent indications that would put the issuer on notice that the purchaser was a U.S. person" (e.g., inconsistent statements, receipt of payment drawn on a U.S. bank, or provision of a U.S. taxpayer identification or social security number). If an issuer became

---

29. A general disclaimer would be insufficient. To be "meaningful," the disclaimer would have to appear in proximity to the offering material and would have to state either that the offer was not being made in the United States or list those countries in which it was being made.

30. The release stated that such procedures might include, for example, the website offeror's (or its underwriter's) obtaining a purchaser's address or telephone number prior to a sale.

aware that it had sold securities to U.S. persons, it would need to evaluate whether it should improve its procedures for the purpose of future offerings.

A non-U.S. issuer engaged in an offshore offering in reliance on Regulation S would not be deemed to be using "directed selling efforts" in the United States if it followed the foregoing procedures in connection with its Internet website.

Of course, many offshore offerings by foreign issuers have an exempt component in the United States (e.g., in reliance on a private placement exemption such as Regulation D or Rule 144A). The 1998 release cautioned that publicly accessible website postings may not be used as a means of locating investors to participate in a pending or imminent exempt U.S. offering. To prevent this from occurring, the release suggested that a non-U.S. issuer could either (1) permit unrestricted access to its website but not permit persons responding to participate in the exempt component, even if otherwise qualified to do so or (2) restrict access to persons who first provide non-U.S. identifying information. In any event, the website should not provide information on the exempt offering or hyperlink to such information.

In the case of a U.S. offeror, the 1998 release stated the SEC's belief that "additional precautions" are necessary because of such an issuer's substantial contacts with the United States, the stronger likelihood of flowback to the United States and the expectations of U.S. issuers and investors. These additional precautions would include "password-type procedures that are reasonably designed to ensure that only non-U.S. persons can obtain access to the offer" (e.g., persons seeking access would have to demonstrate to the issuer or intermediary that they are not U.S. persons). A footnote made clear that access could also be granted to persons who are eligible to buy in an exempt U.S. component.

• • • *Foreign Press-Related Activity*. In response to complaints by U.S. journalists that they were being excluded from foreign issuers' news conferences, Preliminary Note 7 to Regulation S specifically states that nothing in the regulation "precludes access by journalists for publications with a general circulation in the United States to offshore press conferences, press releases and meetings with company press spokespersons in which an offshore offering or tender offer is discussed, provided that the information is made available to the foreign and United States press generally and is not intended to induce purchases of securities by persons in the United States or tenders of securities by United States holders in the case of exchange offers."

Preliminary Note 7 has a subjective element that undermines its effectiveness in inducing issuers to make information about offshore offerings available to U.S. journalists,[31] notwithstanding a 1990 no-action letter[32] in which the staff stated that the SEC's rules "are not intended to limit or interfere with news stories or other bona fide journalistic activities, or otherwise hinder the flow of normal corporate news." Congress directed the SEC in the Improvements Act to address the applicability of the securities laws to foreign press conferences and foreign press releases. Even before the president signed the legislation, the SEC proposed in late 1996 the adoption of a new Rule 135e that would exempt certain offshore activities by U.S. and foreign issuers that involved "journalists." As adopted in late 1997, however, new Rule 135e applies only to foreign issuers. U.S. issuers will therefore have to continue to rely on Preliminary Note 7 and the staff's exhortations.

Rule 135e permits the foreign issuer (or a selling securityholder or a representative) to provide "journalists" with "access" to information that discusses a "present or proposed offering of securities" if the information is provided

- at a "press conference" held outside the United States;
- in meetings held outside the United States; or
- in "written press-related materials" released outside the United States.

There are two principal conditions to the rule. The first is that the offering is not being, or to be, conducted solely in the

---

31. The SEC issued a no-action letter in 1995 covering Deutsche Telekom AG's communications with the U.S. press in advance of its privitization and IPO. *See* SEC No-action Letter, *Deutsche Telekom AG* (June 13, 1995).

32. SEC No-action Letter, *Reuters Holding PLC* (March 6, 1990).

United States. This means that there is an intent to make a bona fide offering offshore. There is no need that any part of the offering be made, or intended to be made, in the United States.

The second condition is that access is provided both to U.S. and foreign journalists. This condition is sometimes a trap for the unwary, since some foreign issuers and their advisers continue to believe that they are complying with the SEC's wishes by refusing to invite the U.S. press to a press conference announcing a major transaction. On the other hand, the SEC adopted the rule in an effort to protect the U.S. financial press from just this type of discrimination, and a failure to invite the U.S. press will result in the loss of the exemption afforded by the rule.

Rule 135e covers "meetings" held outside the United States, and the Adopting Release states that this includes one-on-one interviews. According to the release, an issuer that grants an exclusive interview to a U.S. journalist must also grant an interview to a foreign journalist, unless it conducts a press conference—either before or after the interview—that both U.S. and foreign journalists are allowed to attend.

Conference calls are covered by the rule, but the Adopting Release states that the safe harbor protection is lost if even a single participant in the call is located in the United States.

The Adopting Release also states that the inclusion of research reports in written press-related materials covered by the rule does not cause the materials in the press package, including the research material, to lose the safe harbor protection.

An additional condition to the rule is that any press-related materials must contain specified legends, but this is required only if the materials relate to transactions in the United States. No purchase order or coupon may be included in the materials.

Communications covered by Rule 135e are not "offers" for the purpose of Section 5. Also, they do not constitute "directed selling efforts" for the purpose of Regulation S or a general solicitation or general advertising within the meaning of Regulation D.

The SEC staff has considerably undermined Rule 135e's usefulness by insisting on several occasions that an issuer include in its U.S. prospectus material information that is discussed or released abroad in reliance on the rule.

• • • *Notices of Unregistered Offerings.* Not long after the adoption of Regulation S, a listed U.S. company completed an offshore convertible debt offering in reliance on the new regulation. It not unreasonably concluded that its U.S. shareholders might want to know about the offering and accordingly filed a report of the transaction on Form 8-K. The SEC staff criticized the issuer in strong terms on the theory that the report on Form 8-K amounted to directed selling efforts in respect of the convertible offering.

The staff position was untenable from the beginning, and the SEC eventually amended the definition of "directed selling efforts" to exclude notices in accordance with Rule 135 or newly adopted Rule 135c.[33] These rules are discussed in Chapter 1.

• • • *Advertising.* The definition of "directed selling efforts" specifically includes the placement of an advertisement in a publication with a general circulation in the United States that refers to the Regulation S offering.[34] On the other hand, the definition also excludes certain forms of advertising. It is permissible to place an advertisement required to be published under U.S. or foreign law or regulation that contains no more information than legally required and contains a statement that the securities have not been registered under the 1933 Act and may not be offered or sold in the United States (or, if applicable, to a U.S. person) without registration or an exemption. It is also permissible to place a limited tombstone advertisement in a publication with a general circulation in the United States if less than 20% of the foreign publication's circulation (calculated by aggregating its U.S. and "comparable" non-U.S. editions) is in the United States.[35]

---

33. SEC Release No. 33-7053 (April 19, 1994).

34. A publication has a general circulation in the United States if it either (a) is printed primarily for distribution in the United States or (b) has had, during the preceding 12 months, an average circulation in the United States of 15,000 or more copies per issue. Where a foreign publication produces a separate edition with a general circulation in the United States, only the U.S. edition will be considered a publication with a general circulation in the United States if the affiliated non-U.S. editions together do not meet the definition when the U.S. edition is disregarded. Rule 902(c)(2).

35. Rule 902(c)(3)(iii)(C) specifies the permitted content of the tombstone, which the Adopting Release describes as similar to that permitted under

• • • *Quotations.* According to the Adopting Release, distribution in the United States of a broker-dealer's quotations for a security offered in reliance on Regulation S could be construed as directed selling efforts. Rule 902(c)(3)(v) provides, however, that this will not be the case with U.S. distribution of a foreign broker-dealer's quotations by a third-party system that distributes quotations "primarily in foreign countries" if two conditions are met: (1) that the system not permit transactions between foreign broker-dealers and persons in the United States and (2) that contacts not be initiated within the United States or with U.S. persons beyond those permitted under the SEC's safe harbor rule for foreign broker-dealers (i.e., Rule 15a-6 under the 1934 Act).

• • • *Research.* According to the Adopting Release, the "[d]istribution or publication in the United States of information, opinions or recommendations concerning the issuer or any class of its securities could constitute directed selling efforts, depending on the facts and circumstances." As to reporting issuers only, however, the Adopting Release in 1990 carved out of "directed selling efforts" the publication of information, opinions and recommendations that essentially meet the requirements of Rule 139(b) under the 1933 Act.[36]

For many years, the more liberal exemption under Rule 139(a) applicable to registered public offerings in the United States was simply not available for Regulation S offerings, even for issuers qualifying for Forms S-3 or F-3. Moreover, there was no relief whatsoever under Regulation S for non-reporting issuers.[37]

Rule 134. The rule also prescribes certain legends that must be included. For a discussion of what editions of a foreign publication are "comparable" for purposes of a tombstone advertisement, see the Adopting Release, text at n.55.

36. I.e., "reasonable regularity," "normal course of business," reference to a "substantial number" of other companies or a "comprehensive list" of recommended securities, no "materially greater space or prominence" and no more favorable opinion or recommendation.

37. Joseph McLaughlin, *"Directed Selling Efforts" Under Regulation S and the U.S. Securities Analyst*, 24 Rev. of Sec. & Comm. Reg. 117, 120 (1991).

The SEC corrected this anomaly in 1998, albeit in an unusual manner. In the Aircraft Carrier Release of that year,[38] it proposed a number of liberalizing amendments to the research rules as well as amendments to Regulation S and Rule 144A that would have permitted research material covered by Rules 138 and 139 (as the release proposed to amend those rules) notwithstanding the Regulation S prohibition against directed selling efforts and the Rule 144A prohibition against offers to non-QIBs. In the release, the SEC also criticized its own position in the Adopting Release and stated that, effective immediately, research could be published as described in current Rules 138 or 139 without constituting directed selling efforts under Regulation S.

The SEC did not adopt the research rule amendments proposed in the Aircraft Carrier Release, but the liberalized interpretation regarding directed selling efforts remains in effect.[39]

• • • *Miscellaneous Activities.* In the Adopting Release, the SEC tried to provide comfort that the prohibition on directed selling efforts would not prevent an "isolated, limited contact with the United States,"[40] the dissemination of "routine information of the character and content normally published by a company, and unrelated to a securities offering," the conduct of "bona fide journalistic activities" or the flow of "normal corporate news." It is also made clear in the Adopting Release that it is permissible to initiate selling efforts *from the United States* so long as they are directed abroad.

• • • *Registered or Exempt Offers Excluded.* As in the case of the requirement for an offshore transaction, discussed above, certain activity in the United States is not considered to constitute directed selling efforts. "Offering activities [in the

---

38. SEC Release No. 33-7606A (November 13, 1998).

39. The interpretation did not refer to Rule 144A, but it should be self-evident that research that does not constitute directed selling efforts should also not constitute an offer to a non-QIB.

40. Such a contact, however, might constitute an offer in the United States for purposes of the offshore transaction requirement. See Adopting Release, text following n.60.

United States] in contemporaneous registered offerings or offerings exempt from registration will not preclude reliance on the safe harbors."[41] This is the basis for the frequent transactions in which a public offering takes place abroad in reliance on Regulation S and a contemporaneous private placement takes place in the United States in reliance on Rule 144A or Regulation D.

• • • *Duration of Prohibition.* The prohibition on directed selling efforts applies for the entire period that the issuer, the distributors, their affiliates and any persons acting on their behalf are offering and selling the securities and for any additional "distribution compliance period" described below. Any violation of the prohibition on directed selling efforts by any of these persons precludes reliance on the safe harbor *by any person.*

• • *Issuer Safe Harbor.* Rule 903 provides a safe harbor for offers and sales of securities by an issuer, a distributor, their respective affiliates or any person acting on their behalf. A particular offering will be eligible to qualify for one of the three channels provided by the safe harbor. Each channel requires compliance with a set of conditions that are more or less restrictive according to the potential of the particular offering for flowback to the United States and the potential harm to investors if such flowback were to occur.[42]

• • • *Category 1 Transactions.* The conditions discussed above relating to the presence of an *offshore transaction* and the absence of *directed selling efforts* in the United States are the only conditions that must be met for Category 1 transactions, which are those referred to in Rule 903(b)(1). These transactions include

---

41. *Id.* at n.47.
42. In the case of offerings of debt securities that are fully and unconditionally guaranteed as to principal and interest by the issuer's parent company, Rule 903(b)(4) provides that the relevant category is determined by the status of the guarantee and not by the status of the guaranteed security.

- offerings by foreign issuers that reasonably believe at the start of their offering that there is no "substantial U.S. market interest" (popularly known as "SUSMI") in the security being offered;[43]

- "overseas directed offerings" by foreign issuers and, in certain cases, by U.S. issuers;[44]

- securities backed by the full faith and credit of a foreign government; and

- certain employee benefit plans of foreign issuers.

---

43. SUSMI exists with respect to a class of equity securities if U.S. exchanges and inter-dealer quotation systems constituted the single largest market for such securities in the last fiscal year (or the period since the issuer's incorporation) *or* 20% or more of all trading in such securities took place during such period on U.S. exchanges and inter-dealer quotation systems and less than 55% of such trading took place in or through the market facilities of a single foreign country.

SUSMI exists with respect to a class of debt securities if *all* of the following conditions apply: (a) the issuer's debt, preferred and asset-backed securities are held of record by 300 or more U.S. persons, (b) $1 billion or more of such securities is held of record by U.S. persons and (c) 20% or more of the outstanding amount of such securities is held of record by U.S. persons. Commercial paper exempt under Section 3(a)(3) is excluded from SUSMI calculations. Rule 902(j)(3).

44. An "overseas directed offering" is an offering of securities "directed into a single country other than the United States to the residents thereof and that is made in accordance with the local law and customary practices and documentation of such country." Rule 903(b)(1)(ii). U.S. issuers may take advantage of the overseas directed offering option only if the offering is limited to non-convertible debt, preferred stock or asset-backed securities that are denominated in a currency other than U.S. dollars and that are neither convertible into U.S. dollar-denominated securities nor linked to U.S. dollars in a manner that has the effect of converting the securities into U.S. dollar-denominated securities. On the other hand, the securities may be combined with interest rate or currency swaps that are "commercial in nature." Rule 903(b)(1)(ii)(B). The distinction between "linkages" and "swaps commercial in nature" is sometimes elusive in practice.

INTERNATIONAL FINANCINGS 693

Category 1 does not contemplate any distribution compliance period during which the offering is subject to the selling restrictions described below for Category 2 or Category 3 transactions. Out of an abundance of caution, however, some lawyers advise their clients in some Category 1 transactions to impose a 40-day distribution compliance period as a prophylactic measure.

• • • *Category 2 Transactions.* Category 2 includes transactions that are not eligible for Category 1 and that are any of the following:

— equity transactions by a reporting foreign issuer;[45]

— debt[46] transactions by a reporting issuer (U.S. or foreign); or

— debt transactions by a non-reporting foreign issuer.

Category 2 transactions require the imposition of specified selling restrictions as well as compliance with the two general conditions. In the case of reporting issuers, the selling restrictions "are designed to protect against an indirect unregistered public offering in the United States during the period the market is most likely to be affected by selling efforts offshore. In the event flowback of reporting issuers' securities does occur after the restricted period, the information relating to such securities publicly available under the Exchange Act generally should be sufficient to ensure investor protection." In the case of debt transactions by foreign issuers, the SEC expects the restrictions to provide adequate protection against an indirect U.S. distribution

---

45. A reporting foreign issuer means one that is obligated to file 1934 Act reports and that has filed all required 1934 Act reports for a period of 12 months prior to the Regulation S offering (or such shorter time the issuer was required to file reports). Foreign issuers that file pursuant to Rule 12g3-2(b) are not reporting issuers for Category 2 purposes. A foreign issuer for whose securities there is no SUSMI may, of course, proceed under Category 1.

46. "Debt" for Category 2 purposes includes non-participating preferred stock and asset-backed securities "because of the similarity of the market for these securities to the debt market." Adopting Release, text at nn.106–08.

"because of the generally institutional nature of the debt market and the trading characteristics of debt securities."[47]

The selling restrictions for Category 2 transactions include "offering restrictions" and restrictions on particular offers and sales ("transactional restrictions").

Offering restrictions are procedures intended to ensure compliance with the transactional restrictions and must be adopted for the entire offering by the issuer, the distributors, their affiliates and any persons acting on their behalf. The restrictions require distributors to agree that all their offers and sales will be made in accordance with the safe harbor, any other available exemption or pursuant to registration under the 1933 Act. In addition, all offering materials and documents (other than press releases) used in connection with offers and sales prior to the expiration of the restricted period must disclose that the securities have not been registered under the 1933 Act and may not be offered or sold in the United States or to a U.S. person (other than a distributor) unless registered or entitled to an exemption from registration. This disclosure must appear at specified places in the prospectus or offering circular and in all advertisements. Unlike the transactional restrictions, failure to implement the offering restrictions will preclude the availability of the safe harbor for *all* parties.

Since the 1998 amendments to Regulation S, it is also necessary in equity offerings by U.S. companies to obtain agreements from distributors (and to disclose in offering documents and advertisements) that hedging transactions may not be conducted except in compliance with the 1933 Act.

Transactional restrictions require that the securities sold under Regulation S prior to the expiration of a 40-day distribution compliance period (formerly the "restricted period") not be offered or sold to or for the benefit or account of a U.S. person. (No certification to this effect is required by Regulation S, although in the case of debt securities a certification may be required for tax purposes as discussed below.) In addition, a distributor selling securities to another distributor or to a dealer

---

47. Adopting Release, text following n.105.

or any person receiving a selling concession or similar compensation must include in any confirmation sent prior to the expiration of the 40-day period a notice stating that the purchaser is subject to the same restrictions on offers and sales that apply to the distributor.[48] Importantly, non-compliance with a transactional restriction precludes reliance on the safe harbor by the person who failed to comply as well as its affiliates and persons acting on their behalf, but such non-compliance does not affect anyone else's ability to rely on the safe harbor.[49]

The 40-day distribution compliance period is defined in Rule 902(f) as the period beginning on the later of the date on which the securities were first offered to persons other than distributors in reliance upon Regulation S or the date of closing of the offering. In the case of a continuous offering, the distribution compliance period commences "upon completion of the distribution, as determined and certified by the managing underwriter or person performing similar functions."[50] However, in the case of a continuous offering of non-convertible debt securities "in identifiable tranches" (e.g., MTNs), the distribution compliance period

---

48. Unlike the no-action letters issued under Release 33-4708, it is not necessary to seek to create a binding agreement to abide by the restrictions. Screen-based confirmations or other notices may be used, including a summary notice if all subscribers to a screen-based system are provided with a key that includes the full text of a notice. Adopting Release, text at n.129.

The question sometimes arises whether the transactional restrictions impose a complete ban on sales to U.S. persons or whether they should be read in tandem with the offering restrictions, which permit sales in reliance on an exemption. In other words, could a distributor (or a dealer who buys from a distributor) immediately sell the securities to a U.S. person—or even a person in the United States—by making a judgment about the person's sophistication and obtaining the person's agreement to treat the securities as restricted securities? Keeping in mind that Regulation S is only a safe harbor, nothing in the 1933 Act would appear to prevent this. On the other hand, a person planning to engage in such a transaction should examine carefully whether it is permitted under any applicable agreements, confirmations or notices.

49. Adopting Release at n.109.

50. Special conditions apply in the case of a continuous offering of securities to be acquired on the exercise of warrants.

for a tranche commences upon the manager's certification of the completion of the distribution of that tranche. Significantly, all offers and sales by a distributor of an unsold allotment are deemed to be made during the distribution compliance period. After the expiration of the period, the securities (other than unsold allotments) are no longer subject to restrictions.

The term "U.S. person" is defined in Rule 902(k). Unlike the no-action letters issued under Release 33-4708, residence in the United States rather than U.S. citizenship is the principal factor in determining the status of a natural person under Regulation S. Thus, as the Adopting Release illustrates, a French citizen resident in the United States is a U.S. person.

The following persons are "U.S. persons" for purposes of the transactional restrictions under Category 2:

- any natural person resident in the United States;
- any partnership or corporation organized or incorporated under the laws of the United States;
- any estate of which any executor or administrator is a U.S. person;
- any trust of which any trustee is a U.S. person;
- any agency or branch of a foreign entity located in the United States;
- any non-discretionary or similar account (other than an estate or trust) held by a dealer or other fiduciary for the benefit or account of a U.S. person;
- any discretionary or similar account (other than an estate or trust) held by a dealer or other fiduciary organized, incorporated or (if an individual) resident in the United States; and
- any partnership or corporation if (a) organized or incorporated under the laws of any foreign jurisdiction and (b) formed by a U.S. person principally for the purpose of investing in securities not registered under the 1933 Act, unless it is organized or incorporated, and owned, by accredited investors as defined in Regulation D who are not natural persons, estates or trusts.

Even if they fall within one of the above categories, the following are not U.S. persons:

- any discretionary account or similar account (other than an estate or trust) held for the benefit or account of a non-U.S. person by a dealer or other professional fiduciary[51] organized, incorporated or (if an individual) resident in the United States;

- any estate of which any professional fiduciary acting as executor or administrator is a U.S. person if (a) another executor or administrator who is not a U.S. person has sole or shared investment discretion with respect to the assets of the estate and (b) the estate is governed by foreign law;

- any trust of which any professional fiduciary acting as trustee is a U.S. person if (a) another trustee who is not a U.S. person has sole or shared investment discretion with respect to the assets of the trust and (b) no beneficiary of the trust (and no settlor of a revocable trust) is a U.S. person (note that the presence of U.S. persons as beneficiaries is irrelevant if there is no U.S. person acting as trustee);

- an employee benefit plan established and administered in accordance with the law of a foreign country and customary local practices and documentation;

- any agency or branch of a U.S. person located outside the United States if it operates for valid business reasons, is engaged in the banking or insurance business and is subject to "substantive" local banking or insurance regulation; and

- the International Monetary Fund, the World Bank, the Inter-American Development Bank, the Asian Develop-

---

51. The term "professional fiduciary" does not appear to contemplate more than that a person is in the business of managing money for accounts under circumstances that imply a fiduciary duty. Professional qualifications or registrations, e.g., under the Investment Advisers Act of 1940, would appear to be unnecessary, particularly in light of the fact that all "dealers" are automatically included.

ment Bank, the African Development Bank, the United Nations, and their agencies, affiliates and pension plans, and any other similar international organizations, their agencies, affiliates and pension plans.

Contacts with U.S. dealers or professional fiduciaries acting with investment discretion for the accounts of non-U.S. persons, in their capacities as such, and with multinational organizations excluded from the definition of U.S. person, are also excluded from the definition of "directed selling efforts." Offers and sales to such persons are also deemed to be made in offshore transactions.

Category 2 transactions do not require the imposition of any restrictions for the purpose of backing up the required agreements and notices. On the other hand, in connection with the deposit at DTC of the global certificate for a Regulation S offering of debt securities, there has been a practice for many years of issuing instructions that limit participation in the securities to two banks that maintain custody accounts at DTC for Clearstream and Euroclear and that in turn agree for the duration of the 40-day distribution compliance period to limit participation in the securities to persons holding through Clearstream and Euroclear. The theory of this practice, known as a "chill," has been that it makes it less likely that U.S. persons will be able to hold beneficial interests in the securities. There is no evidence that the practice was ever required or encouraged by the SEC or its staff.

Recently, the "chill" practice was criticized by both DTC and certain of its participants who were not participants in either Clearstream or Euroclear, and DTC announced in a notice dated May 13, 2003 that it would no longer honor 40-day "chill" requests.

• • • *Category 3 Transactions.* Category 3 includes all transactions not covered by Categories 1 or 2, including those presumed to be most at risk for flowback into the United States. Since 1998,[52] these include debt or equity offerings by non-reporting U.S. issuers

---

52. As discussed above, the SEC in 1998 amended Regulation S in an effort to curb what it viewed as "abusive" equity transactions by SEC-reporting U.S. companies. Essentially, it moved such transactions from Category 2 to the more restrictive Category 3.

INTERNATIONAL FINANCINGS

as well as equity offerings by U.S. reporting companies.[53] Category 3 also includes equity offerings by non-reporting foreign issuers where SUSMI exists for such securities, thus making Category 1 unavailable. Category 3 transactions must meet the general conditions relating to the presence of an offshore transaction and the absence of directed selling efforts and must comply with more extensive transactional restrictions than in the case of Category 2 transactions.

One such required transactional restriction is that any distributor selling securities to another distributor or to a dealer or any person receiving a selling concession or similar compensation must include in any confirmation sent prior to the expiration of the distribution compliance period (40 days or one year, as noted below) a notice stating that the purchaser is subject to the same restrictions on offers and sales that apply to the distributor.

In the case of debt securities, the required transactional restrictions also mandate that (a) any offer or sale prior to the end of a 40-day distribution compliance period not be made to a U.S. person or for the account or benefit of a U.S. person (other than a distributor) and (b) the securities be represented by a temporary global certificate that cannot be exchanged for definitive securities until the expiration of the 40-day restricted period and until certification of beneficial ownership of the securities by non-U.S. persons (or by any U.S. person who purchased the securities in an exempt transaction).

In the case of equity securities, the required transactional restrictions mandate that an offer or sale prior to the expiration of a *one-year* distribution compliance period[54] may not be made to a U.S. person or for the account or benefit of a U.S. person (other than a distributor). In addition, *all* of the following additional conditions must be satisfied:

- the purchaser (other than a distributor) must certify that it is not a U.S. person and is not acquiring the securities

---

53. These include securities offered and sold to non-U.S. employees through employee benefit plans and all offerings of convertible securities.

54. The one-year period is roughly the same as the one-year period required before restricted securities may be sold in the United States under the conditions specified in Rule 144.

for the account or benefit of a U.S. person (or that it acquired the securities pursuant to an exemption);

- the purchaser (other than a distributor) must agree to resell or hedge only in accordance with Regulation S, pursuant to registration under the 1933 Act or in reliance on an exemption;[55]

- in the case of a U.S. issuer, the securities must contain a legend to the effect that transfer or hedging is prohibited except in accordance with the provisions of Regulation S, pursuant to registration or in reliance on an exemption;[56] and

- the issuer is required by contract or charter or by-law document to refuse to register any transfer of securities not in accordance with the provisions of Regulation S (except that if the securities are in bearer form or foreign law prohibits such refusal, then other reasonable procedures may be implemented to prevent any impermissible transfer).

The 1998 amendments presented special difficulties for U.S. issuers of convertible securities. Unlike the "abusive" transactions identified by the SEC prior to 1998, these issuers were large, well-known companies that as a group had a long history of

---

55. As to hedging, the adopting release for the amendments noted that (a) issuers would be free to require purchasers not to engage in any hedging transactions, even if permissible, and (b) the SEC had earlier requested comment on whether and how to impose additional restrictions on the hedging of restricted securities. SEC Release No. 33-7505 at n.28, citing SEC Release No. 33-7391 (Feb. 20, 1997).

56. The SEC stated in the adopting release for the amendments that the legend requirement was not intended to require that securities be offered in certificated form. "Depending on the circumstances, the following alternatives, among others, may be sufficient to put holders on notice and prevent a public distribution into the United States: notices of the restrictions to investors on the confirmation or allotment telex, use of global securities held in a depository, and restrictions on trading in the United States through the use of restricted CUSIP numbers." SEC Release No. 33-7505 at n.31. This concession did not extend to the new requirement for contractual or charter or bylaw restrictions on transfer.

offshore convertible securities offerings. After the adoption of the 1998 amendments, it appeared that the only way these offerings could comply with the new transactional requirements was for the securities to be issued in definitive registered form rather than the customary book-entry form. This would have imposed additional costs, increased settlement risk and made the securities less attractive to offshore investors.

Accordingly, the SEC staff was requested to take a no-action position based on the assumption that the securities would be held in global form by a depository for a book-entry clearance facility, that they would be identified in CUSIP and similar data bases as restricted securities, that the offering circulars for the securities would require purchasers to make deemed representations regarding resales and hedging and that legends would be included on definitive securities issued prior to the expiration of the one-year distribution compliance period. The SEC staff issued the requested no-action advice, which covered exchangeable as well as convertible debt securities but inexplicably refused to apply the advice to the securities issuable on conversion.[57]

• • *New Rule 905*. As part of its 1998 effort to stamp out "abuses" involving equity securities of U.S. companies, the SEC also adopted a new Rule 905 as part of Regulation S. This rule specifies that equity securities of U.S. companies acquired in transactions subject to the conditions of either the general rule in Rule 901 or one of the safe harbors in Rule 903 are deemed to be "restricted securities" within the meaning of Rule 144—notwithstanding that they were publicly offered—and must be resold by any offshore purchaser in reliance on Regulation S, the registration requirements of the 1933 Act or an applicable exemption. The new rule is not retroactive, except for a provision that "codifies" the SEC's interpretive position that offshore

---

57. SEC No-action Letter, *Securities Act of 1933—Rule 903* (August 26, 1998). The SEC staff has also issued no-action letters permitting non-reporting U.S. companies to deviate from the Category 3 requirements when conducting IPOs under Regulation S in conjunction with listings on certain foreign exchanges. See, e.g., SEC No-action Letter, *European Association of Securities Dealers Automated Quotation N.V./S.A. ("EASDAQ")* (July 27, 1999).

resales of restricted securities do not "wash off" the applicable restrictions.

• • *Convertible Securities.* According to the Adopting Release, convertible securities are generally treated for purposes of the issuer safe harbor and the applicable restricted periods like the security into which they are convertible. However, if convertibility is delayed until after the expiration of the restricted period for the underlying securities, then the restricted period is determined solely by reference to the convertible security. "Thus, an offering of convertible debt securities by a foreign issuer with substantial U.S. market interest in its debt and equity securities would fall within the second category of the issuer safe harbor if the debt securities are not convertible for 13 months but would fall within the third issuer safe harbor category if the debt securities were convertible after 11 months."[58] For purposes of determining SUSMI, the measurement is made both by reference to the convertible security and the underlying security. If SUSMI exists in either case, it exists with respect to the convertible securities.

The issuance of common stock on conversion of debentures is exempt pursuant to Section 3(a)(9) of the 1933 Act, which exempts exchanges by an issuer with its own securityholders. According to the Adopting Release, where such a conversion takes place during the applicable restricted period, the securities issued on conversion will be restricted only for the remainder of the restricted period.[59]

• • *Private Placements in United States Concurrent with Public Offerings Abroad.* Like Release 33-4708 before it, Regulation S expressly contemplates that a private placement in the United States may take place at the same time as an offshore public offering in reliance on the safe harbor.[60] Also, a preliminary note to Regulation D states that Regulation S may be relied on for offers and sales of securities outside of the

---

58. Adopting Release, text following n.76.
59. *Id.* at n.75.
60. *Id.*, text at n.47.

United States even if coincident offers and sales are made in accordance with Regulation D inside the United States.

In recent years, it has become commonplace to provide for a U.S. private placement in connection with an international public offering of debt or equity securities. Sales in these private placements generally have been limited to institutions that qualify as QIBs under Rule 144A.

The Rule 144A portion of the transaction is generally coordinated by the managing underwriters, and individual underwriters and dealers are not permitted to sell any securities in the United States without coordinating with the managers.

Following the expiration of the distribution compliance period (if any) for an offering of debt in registered form (i.e., not in bearer form), the Regulation S securities held outside the United States will become freely saleable into the United States while the Rule 144A securities sold in the United States will remain "restricted" securities within the meaning of Rule 144 for a period of two years. To distinguish between the two classes of securities, issuers and underwriters usually arrange for a Regulation S global certificate to be deposited with a European clearing system, to be held on behalf of its participants or sub-custodians, and a second Rule 144A global certificate with a restrictive legend to be deposited in the United States with DTC (or its agent), to be held on behalf of DTC participants. The certificates will have different CUSIP and other identification numbers. Holders of the Rule 144A securities may sell to non-U.S. persons who wish to receive an interest in the Regulation S global certificate only if the bank acting as registrar receives a certificate that the buyer is a non-U.S. person and that the sale otherwise complies with Regulation S. The registrar may also provide a link between the European and U.S. clearing systems, including the making of entries in a register to reflect increases or decreases in the respective certificates as a result of secondary market activity.

An alternative procedure involves depositing both notes with DTC. In that case, holders of the Regulation S securities receive their interest in the Regulation S note by means of the European clearing systems' indirect participation in DTC. This procedure is less suitable for debt securities denominated in currencies other than U.S. dollars.

Obviously, if the holders of the Regulation S securities are contractually obligated for two years to sell the securities in the United States only pursuant to Rule 144A, the need to distinguish between the two classes disappears, and only one global certificate is necessary. This has the disadvantage, however, of limiting for two years the liquidity of the Regulation S securities.

• • *Resale Safe Harbor.* In addition to the safe harbor for issuer and distributor transactions, Regulation S provides a safe harbor for resales by persons other than the issuer, any distributor, any of their respective affiliates (except an officer or director who is an affiliate solely by virtue of such position) or any person acting on their behalf.

The resale safe harbor requires compliance with the general conditions requiring the presence of an offshore transaction and the absence of directed selling efforts in the United States by the seller, any affiliate or any person acting on their behalf. "Offshore transaction" for this purpose is defined, however, to require that the buyer be outside the United States or that the seller and any person acting on his or her behalf reasonably believe this to be the case. In the alternative, the transaction must be executed on or though a "designated offshore securities market"[61] without any knowledge on the part of the seller or any person acting on his or her behalf that the transaction has been pre-arranged with a buyer in the United States.

Additional conditions apply to resales by certain affiliates or securities professionals. If a person is an affiliate of an issuer or a distributor solely because he or she holds the position of an officer or director, then that person may rely on the resale safe harbor if he or she pays no more than the "usual and customary broker's commission that would be received by a person executing such transaction as agent."[62] A dealer or other person receiving selling compensation in connection with the offering may rely on the safe harbor to resell securities prior to the expiration of the restricted period if neither the seller nor any person acting on its behalf knows the offeree or buyer to

---

61. See note 26 *supra.*
62. Adopting Release, text at n.138.

INTERNATIONAL FINANCINGS   705

be a U.S. person[63] and if a confirmation or other notice of applicable restrictions is sent to any purchaser known to be another securities professional.

• • *Resales in the United States.* The Rule 904 resale safe harbor applies, of course, only to securities sold outside the United States. But when may a dealer effect a resale in the United States on behalf of a foreign customer who is selling securities that were offered abroad in reliance on Regulation S and where the applicable distribution compliance period has not yet expired?

As we have seen, an "end user" acquires Regulation S securities with "strings attached" only where the securities are Category 3 debt securities locked up in a temporary global certificate or where they are Category 3 equity securities with legends and transfer restrictions and the purchaser has been required to agree to resell the securities only pursuant to an exemption. In the case of equity securities of a U.S. issuer, the securities are also "restricted securities" under Rule 905.

Also, the dealer itself may also have been a distributor in the Regulation S transaction or it may have been informed by a distributor that it is subject to the same restrictions on resale as apply to a distributor.

Under any of these circumstances, public resales in the United States will be subject to significant practical obstacles as well as serious problems under the 1933 Act.

In any other circumstance, a customer is free to sell in the United States under the Section 4(1) exemption. The dealer would normally rely on the Section 4(3) exemption, but as discussed in Chapter 1 the exemption is not available for a 40-day period following the first public offering of the security by the issuer or an underwriter. An offshore offering under Regulation S is undoubtedly a public offering, and offering circulars customarily caution dealers that they might violate Section 5 of the 1933 Act if they effect resales of the Regulation S securities in the United States during the 40-day period following the offering.[64]

---

63. There is no "duty of inquiry." *Id.* at n.140.
64. There is no relief for reporting issuers under Rule 174(b) because the relief afforded by that rule is available only following an SEC-registered public offering.

Where the securities are offered abroad under the general rule or Category 1 or Category 2 and are additional securities of an outstanding class, however, it becomes difficult (and sometimes impossible) to distinguish the newly offered securities from the previously outstanding securities. For example, some foreign government securities are offered in identical tranches at regular intervals. Also, some debt securities are "reopened" subsequent to the original offering (see Chapter 8), and in common stock offerings it is impossible to distinguish the new shares from the old shares.

If a U.S. dealer receives a solicited order from a U.S. customer who wishes to buy securities of a foreign issuer, should the dealer worry about the possibility that the issuer may have engaged in a Regulation S public offering during the past 40 days and that, if so, it is theoretically possible that the securities that the dealer purchases for the customer may have been part of that offering? The statutory analysis is not clear, but it would be surprising if the dealer could not fill such an order, unless of course it or one of its affiliates pre-arranged for the order to be filled by a seller of the newly offered securities.

If the call is from a U.S. or foreign seller of securities of a foreign issuer, and the seller instructs the dealer to execute the order in the United States (or where the dealer knows that the best execution is available in the United States), should the dealer worry about the same possibility? Again, it would be surprising if the dealer could not fill such an order, but if the dealer knows that the customer bought securities of the same class in a Regulation S offering that took place within the last 40 days, it might consider inquiring whether the customer is selling new securities or old securities.

Tax Considerations in Offshore Debt Offerings

A U.S. issuer making an offshore offering of debt securities must take into account the requirements of U.S. tax law as well as Regulation S. The primary tax concerns relate to (a) the TEFRA sanctions on issuers and holders of bearer obligations sold to U.S. investors and (b) a U.S. issuer's obligation to make gross-up payments to compensate holders for the imposition of U.S. withholding taxes.

- *TEFRA Issuer and Holder Sanctions*

The Tax Equity and Fiscal Responsibility Act of 1982 (TEFRA) added Sections 163(f) and 4701 to the Internal Revenue Code, which provide sanctions for any company that issues obligations in bearer form[65] to U.S. persons (so-called "issuer sanctions"). The issuer sanctions deny the issuer a deduction for interest payments on such obligations (Section 163(f)(1)) and subject the issuer to an excise tax equal to the product of 1% of the obligation's principal amount and the number of calendar years from the date of issuance to maturity (Section 4701(a)). Interest payments on such obligations will also not qualify as "portfolio interest" exempt from U.S. withholding taxes (Sections 871(h)(2)(A) and 881(c)(2)(A)). The purpose of the issuer sanctions is to prevent U.S. taxpayers from acquiring bearer obligations, including those issued by governmental entities, thereby facilitating the avoidance of U.S. federal income taxes.

U.S. persons who hold such obligations are also subject to limitations under the U.S. income tax laws. These limitations include a prohibition on deducting losses incurred with respect to the obligation (Section 165(j)) and mandatory treatment of gains as ordinary income (Section 1287(a)) (so-called "holder sanctions").

Obligations are not required to be in registered form if they are issued by a natural person, are of a type not offered to the general public or have a maturity of not more than one year (Section 163(f)(2)(A)).

Also, Section 163(f)(2)(B) (commonly known as the "Eurobond exception")[66] provides an exception from the issuer sanctions for a bearer obligation that (a) is sold under arrangements reasonably designed to ensure that it will be sold (or resold in connection with its original issue) only to non-U.S.

---

65. In some cases, bearer obligations may be considered as being in registered form if they are deposited into an irrevocable custody arrangement maintained by an agent of the issuer as a book-entry system.

66. The term "Eurobond market" has come to be replaced by the term "international debt market," at least according to the International Primary Market Association.

persons, (b) the interest on which is payable only outside the United States and its possessions and (c) has a legend on its face that any U.S. person who holds the obligation will be subject to the holder sanctions described above. Prior to the adoption of Regulation S, an issuer could establish the Eurobond exception by following procedures designed to comply with Release 33-4708 and relying on an opinion of counsel that the 1933 Act was not applicable because the securities were intended for distribution to persons who were not U.S. persons.

• • *TEFRA D Rules.* Shortly after the SEC adopted Regulation S, Treasury Regulation 1.163-5(c)(2)(i)(D) established the "TEFRA D" exemption. Unlike the Eurobond exception that relied on SEC standards, the new exemption stands on its own for the purpose of determining when a bearer obligation is sold under arrangements reasonably designed to ensure that it will be sold (or resold in connection with its original issuance) only to non-U.S. persons. The exemption cannot be established simply by complying with Regulation S. Thus, the procedures for a Eurobond financing must be established with two sets of regulations in mind.

The first requirement for the establishment of the TEFRA D exemption is that neither the issuer nor any distributor may offer or sell the obligation during a 40-day restricted period to a person who is within the United States or its possessions or to a "U.S. person." A distributor must covenant that it will not do so and, if it establishes procedures reasonably designed to ensure that its employees are aware of the restrictions, will be deemed to satisfy the exemption's restrictions on offers and sales notwithstanding the occurrence of an inadvertent sale to a U.S. person. The 40-day restricted period is essentially the same as that provided for in Regulation S, including that it is deemed to continue while there is an unsold allotment, except that it is measured from the earlier of the closing date or the first date on which the obligation is offered to persons other than distributors. The definition of "U.S. person" differs from that in Regulation S. While Regulation S excludes citizens residing abroad from its definition of U.S. person, Section 7701 of the Internal Revenue Code defines a U.S. person to include any citizen of the United States.

Notwithstanding the tax definition of U.S. person, the TEFRA D exemption contains one substantial concession to the liberalized overseas sales provisions of Regulation S. Under certain circumstances, a bearer obligation can be sold to a U.S. person outside of the United States if that person buys and holds the obligation through a foreign branch of a U.S. financial institution, including a U.S. bank or securities firm. Direct sales to foreign branches of U.S. financial institutions are permitted as well, as are sales to international organizations such as the World Bank.

A second requirement of the TEFRA D exemption is that neither the issuer nor a distributor may deliver the obligation in definitive form within the United States in connection with a sale that occurred during the 40-day restricted period.

Finally, except in the case of certain offshore offerings targeted to a single foreign country, a certificate must be provided to the issuer on the earlier of the date of the first interest payment or the date of delivery by the issuer of the obligation in definitive form. The certificate must state that the obligation is owned by a non-U.S. person or by an exempt U.S. person, generally including a foreign branch of a U.S. financial institution and a U.S. person who acquired the obligation through a foreign branch of a U.S. financial institution and holds it there on the date of certification.

An obligation issued in bearer form may be converted to registered form in order to permit its resale into the United States or to a U.S. person. But once an obligation is in registered form, it may not be converted to bearer form for sale to a foreign person.

As noted above, debt obligations issued with a maturity of not more than one year are not subject to the issuer sanctions or holder sanctions.

• • *TEFRA C Rules.* Non-U.S. issuers may, as an alternative to the TEFRA D exemption, rely on the TEFRA C rules. The availability of these rules as an exemption from the issuer sanctions depends on the obligation being issued outside the United States by an issuer not significantly engaged in interstate commerce in the United States, as defined in the rules, with respect to the obligation. Certain activities including negotiation between the issuer and its underwriters and a prospective purchaser if either is in the United States or advertising or promotion of an obligation in the United States can be enough to disqualify the issuer from relying on the TEFRA C rules. There is no requirement of a certificate of non-U.S. beneficial ownership similar to that required under the TEFRA D rules, but there is also no safe harbor protection in the event of an inadvertent sale to a U.S. person.

- *Withholding Taxes and Gross-Up Obligations*

Compliance with the TEFRA D exemption will generally excuse a U.S. issuer from compliance with U.S. federal withholding tax, backup withholding tax and information reporting requirements. If an obligation with a maturity of 183 days or less is sold to a non-U.S. person, however, the obligation will be subject to backup withholding and information reporting unless the issuer receives from the beneficial owner a completed Internal Revenue Service Form W-8BEN (Certificate of Foreign Status of Beneficial Owner for U.S. Tax Withholding).

The issuer can avoid having to collect Form W-8BENs if the obligation is issued under specific guidelines. U.S. issuers in the Euromarket will nevertheless agree, subject to certain limitations and exceptions, to pay to a foreign holder of their debt securities such additional amounts as may be necessary so that every net payment of principal and interest on the securities, after deducting or withholding for or on account of any present or future U.S. tax or other governmental charge imposed upon the holder or by reason of the making of such payment, will be not less than the amount provided for in the obligations and the related coupons. This "gross-up" agreement protects the holder against a change in U.S. tax law that would subject it to a withholding tax. If it appears that the additional amount will be payable, the issuer will have the right to redeem the obligations.

Foreign Private Issuers and the U.S. Securities Laws

As we have seen, an issuer need not register its securities with the SEC or file reports with the SEC merely because it wishes to raise capital in the United States. Both U.S. and foreign companies raise large sums of money in the U.S. commercial paper market or in U.S. private placements without the need for SEC registration or reporting.

Many foreign companies have chosen, however, to enter the U.S. disclosure system as full reporting companies under the 1934 Act. This significant step gives the company access to the U.S. public securities markets, primary and secondary. It also permits the company to offer its securities as "currency" in the event of acquisitions in the United States, and it simplifies the process of offering equity-based compensation to its U.S.-based employees.

The SEC has offered foreign companies a number of "accommodations" designed to make it easier for them to enter the U.S. disclosure system. These include:

- permitting foreign companies to list their securities or make public offerings on the basis of their home country accounting principles (albeit with a "reconciliation" to U.S. GAAP);
- permitting foreign companies entering the United States for the first time to file their disclosure documents with the SEC on a confidential basis for the purpose of receiving the SEC staff's comments on these documents;
- relieving foreign private issuers from the U.S. requirements regarding proxies and insider trade reporting and short-swing profit recapture;
- relieving foreign companies from having to make quarterly reports to the SEC, substituting instead a requirement to furnish information to the SEC as and when it is made public in the home country; and
- permitting foreign companies to provide more limited information regarding compensation to their management and regarding their operating segments.

On the other hand, becoming a U.S. reporting company brings with it very nearly the full range of Sarbanes–Oxley requirements imposed on U.S. companies, including the requirement that the chief executive and chief financial officers certify their companies' periodic reports and financial statements. And many foreign companies are justifiably concerned with the litigation exposure that may accompany a listing on the NYSE or NASDAQ.

Finally, as we shall see, it is usually easier to enter the SEC disclosure system than to exit it.

- *Status as a "Foreign Private Issuer"*

The SEC's accommodations for foreign companies and the forms and rules for foreign companies apply only to those companies that are "foreign private issuers" under the SEC's rules. All foreign companies are foreign private issuers *unless* more than 50% of the company's outstanding voting securities are directly or indirectly owned of record by residents of the United States *and* any of the following three conditions is applicable:

- the majority of the executive officers or directors are U.S. citizens or residents;
- more than 50% of the assets of the issuer are located in the United States; or
- the business of the issuer is administered principally in the United States.[67]

The purpose of the definition is to make sure that companies that are essentially U.S. companies cannot take advantage of the relaxed disclosure and other accommodations that the SEC has reserved for genuine foreign companies. For example, some publicly held U.S. companies that have "inverted" their status by reincorporating in the Bahamas or similar jurisdictions are still treated for SEC purposes as U.S. companies.

Although the rules for this purpose refer to holders "of record," this is not the exclusive consideration. Since 1999,[68] the SEC rules have instructed foreign issuers to make inquiries of all of their holders of record who are brokers, dealers, banks

---

67. Rule 405 under the 1933 Act and Rule 3b-4 under the 1934 Act.
68. SEC Release No. 33-7745 (September 28, 1999).

or nominees in the United States, the issuer's home country and (if different) the country where the principal trading market is located. The purpose of the inquiry is to "look through" the intermediary for the purpose of identifying the country of residence of each separate account on whose behalf the intermediary is a holder of record. The issuer may rely "in good faith" on any estimate provided by its intermediaries.

The issuer is also chargeable with knowledge of any U.S. beneficial ownership that has been publicly reported or that has been privately communicated to the issuer. If the issuer is unable "after reasonable inquiry" to obtain information about the U.S. residence of an intermediary's accounts, it may presume that they are residents of the jurisdiction where the intermediary has its principal place of business.

As the SEC explained in 1999 when it applied the "look through" requirement to the definition of foreign private issuer, this "gives a better picture of whether or not a company incorporated outside the United States is entitled to the accommodations available to foreign private issuers under the federal securities laws."

- *American Depositary Receipts*

Before discussing the advantages and disadvantages of becoming a 1934 Act reporting company, we should focus on a traditional means by which foreign issuers have made their securities available to U.S. investors.

Nothing in the U.S. securities laws prevents a U.S. person from owning the "ordinary" shares of a foreign company. Direct ownership has historically been inconvenient, however, and the American Depositary Receipt (ADR) was developed to mitigate this inconvenience. An ADR is a negotiable receipt, resembling a stock certificate, that is issued by a U.S. bank to evidence "ordinary" shares of a foreign company that have been deposited with it and that are held at or by its branch office in the country of origin.[69]

---

69. The shares underlying ADRs are sometimes referred to as "American Depositary Shares" (ADSs). When an ADS represents a single share, there is

J.P. Morgan Chase & Co. takes credit for initiating and developing the ADR. It claims that its predecessor, Morgan Guaranty, issued the first ADR in 1927 for Selfridge's, a British retailer.[70] On the other hand, Irving Trust Company (now merged into The Bank of New York) testified to the SEC that it had been issuing ADRs against shares of Roan Antelope Copper Mines since 1926.[71]

A traditional advantage of ADRs is that they permit a U.S. investor to purchase in a U.S. market an interest in a foreign company's securities. The U.S. market's rules would govern how the ADRs are purchased and paid for, and the ADRs would be delivered to the customer's account or custodian in the same manner as any listed stock. The investor would have the advantage of being able to check at any time the U.S. dollar price of the ADRs. Sometimes, the investor would be able to avoid stamp or transfer taxes imposed in the foreign market.

Many of the practical advantages of ADRs are no longer as clear as they once were. Liquidity in the U.S. market, even on the NYSE, may be less than that on the local market (especially after the local market has closed). Also, a U.S. investor today can easily purchase a foreign company's ordinary shares by instructing its U.S. broker-dealer accordingly. The broker-dealer will purchase the shares in the local market through its foreign affiliate, which will hold them on behalf of the U.S. broker-dealer and the investor through a local depository. The U.S. broker-dealer will bill the U.S. investor for the U.S. dollar equivalent of the purchase

---

virtually no distinction between it and the share that it represents. When the ordinary shares trade in their local market at a price that is much higher or lower than a price to which U.S. investors are accustomed, the ADS may represent a fraction or a multiple of the ordinary share. However "conceptually accurate," most market participants ignore the distinction between ADRs and ADSs. See SEC Release No. 33-8287 (September 11, 2003).

70. *See American Depositary Receipts* on the J.P. Morgan Chase website (www.jpmorgan.com).

71. *Official Report of Proceedings Before the SEC in the Matter of Conference on American Depositary Receipts* 7 (June 20, 1955) [hereinafter ADR Proceedings].

price and will carry the shares in the customer's account, converting dividends into U.S. dollars as they are received (less withholding tax, if applicable). Alternatively, the broker-dealer will deliver the securities through the local depository to the investor's custodian bank. Of course, the local market's rules will govern how the securities are purchased and paid for.

Moreover, many foreign securities are traded in the United States in ordinary share form, without the use of ADRs. Because of similar clearance and settlement systems, Canadian shares have long traded in the United States without the use of ADRs. According to the SEC,[72] some Dutch and other issuers issue a class of "New York shares" rather than ADRs. And, more recently, some foreign companies have created "global share" arrangements, in which the same security is traded in multiple markets without the use of ADRs. According to the SEC, the first such arrangement was created in connection with Daimler-Benz' acquisition of Chrysler in 1998, and since that time Celanese AG, UBS AG and Deutsche Bank AG have established global share arrangements.

Even with the diminishing inconvenience of owning ordinary shares, ADRs remain the most common form in which foreign shares are traded in the United States.

• • *Types of ADR Facilities.* A foreign issuer that makes an SEC-registered public offering of its shares in the United States will usually do so by means of ADRs. A facility set up for this purpose is called a "Level 3" program.

A foreign company may also set up an ADR facility solely for the purpose of listing the ADRs on a U.S. exchange or having them quoted on NASDAQ. A facility set up for this purpose is called a "Level 2" program. Both Level 2 and Level 3 facilities require the filing of a Form 20-F with the SEC, which involves extensive disclosure and SEC review and triggers nearly the full range of Sarbanes–Oxley requirements.

Other ADR programs are set up at the "Level 1" stage—an ADR that trades in the over-the-counter "pink sheet" market.

---

72. SEC Release No. 33-8287 (September 11, 2003).

A facility at the Level 1 stage can be unsponsored or sponsored by the issuer. As the SEC explained in a September 2003 release,[73] an unsponsored facility is established by a depository acting on its own, usually in response to a perceived interest among U.S. investors in a particular foreign security that is not traded on the NYSE or NASDAQ. An unsponsored facility does not require the consent, participation or even acquiescence of the foreign issuer, except that the foreign issuer must at least be furnishing information to the SEC under Rule 12g3-2(b), discussed below. An unsponsored facility is "essentially a two-party contract between the depository and the ADR holders." The holders pay most or all of the related fees or costs. Unless the ADR provides otherwise, the depository has no obligation to pass on reports from the foreign company or to make it possible for ADR holders to exercise voting rights.

A sponsored facility is "effectively a three-party contract: it is established jointly by a deposit agreement between the foreign company . . . and the depository, with ADR holders as third-party beneficiaries. The foreign company generally bears some of the costs, such as dividend payment fees, but the ADR holders may pay other costs such as deposit and withdrawal fees." The depository will generally arrange for holders to exercise voting rights and to receive shareholder communications.

Whether or not a facility is sponsored by the foreign company has no bearing on the company's SEC reporting obligations. That is determined by whether or not the ADRs are to be listed, since listing requires that the issuer be a reporting company under the 1934 Act.

It is possible for a foreign company to be a reporting company under the 1934 Act without having listed its ADRs on the NYSE or NASDAQ. In that case, a depository could theoretically establish a Level 2 unsponsored facility, but the NYSE and NASDAQ will not list unsponsored ADRs.

Unsponsored ADR programs may be duplicated by rival depositories, and the SEC has raised no objections to this practice.

---

73. SEC Release No. 33-8287 (September 11, 2003). The references to the SEC in this discussion are to this release.

It has been concerned for some years, however, about the possibility of market disorder and investor confusion where sponsored and unsponsored programs exist side-by-side. In 1991, it summarized the staff's position as being that an unsponsored facility could not co-exist with a sponsored facility for the same deposited securities. "Thus, if a sponsored facility existed, no other depository could create another facility for the same securities. Similarly, if a sponsored facility were created after the establishment of one or more unsponsored ADR facilities, the depositories of the unsponsored facilities would effect a transfer of the deposited securities and the related ADR holders to the new sponsored facility and terminate their unsponsored facilities."[74]

In its September 2003 release, the SEC proposed an amendment to Form F-6 that would prevent the creation of unsponsored facilities where the issuer had already listed its ordinary shares in the United States. The SEC explained the proposal as intended to reduce investor confusion and to provide foreign companies with more control over the form in which their securities trade in the United States.

• • *1933 Act Status of ADR Facilities.* When the 1933 Act was adopted, a substantial number of ADR facilities were in place. The question then arose whether additional ADRs could be issued without going through the registration process. At that time, Section 3(a)(1) of the 1933 Act provided an exemption for securities that had been sold or disposed of by the issuer in a bona fide offer to the public prior to 60 days after the enactment of the statute. Early on, the SEC took the position that where an ADR facility had been established prior to the Section 3(a)(1) cutoff date and where prior to that date the offer to issue ADRs against a deposit of shares outstanding on that date had been made, registration of the ADRs was not required even though they were issued after the cutoff date.[75] The SEC also

---

74. SEC Release No. 33-6894 (May 23, 1991), text at nn.24–31. *See also* SEC Division of Corporation Finance, *Manual of Publicly Available Telephone Interpretations* 10 (# 9S) (March 1999).

75. R. E. Moxley, *The ADR: An Instrument of International Finance and a Tool of Arbitrage*, 8 Vill. L. Rev. 19, 29 (1962).

permitted the issuance of ADRs against shares issued by way of a stock dividend on shares outstanding prior to the cutoff date.[76] Subsequently, depository banks and their counsel persuaded members of the SEC's staff that, where underlying shares could be sold in the United States without registration in reliance on what is now the Section 4(1) exemption, they could be made the subject of ADRs on the theory that the ADRs themselves were entitled to the Section 3(a)(2) exemption as securities issued by a bank.[77]

The legal status of ADRs continued to be fuzzy into the mid-1950s. In 1955, Irving Trust Company announced that it would issue ADRs against 34 selected foreign securities.[78] When Guaranty Trust Company became aware of the new program, its counsel called the director of the Division of Corporation Finance to request an opinion similar to the one that was reported to have been given to Irving Trust. Later that day, the director advised counsel that he was concerned about various problems connected with the program and that the entire matter was to be brought before the SEC. He further stated that, until the SEC had taken some action, he regarded it inadvisable for a bank to proceed with a general issue of ADRs. When Irving Trust learned of this, it quite naturally was distressed. One can imagine the reaction of its officers to the fact that counsel for Guaranty Trust had mucked up its program by raising the issue with the SEC.

The next development was an all-day conference at the SEC on June 20, 1955 among four of the commissioners, members of the staff, representatives of the major New York City banks that issued ADRs and the banks' counsel. As a result of this conference and subsequent discussions with the staff, the SEC determined that ADRs were not entitled to the Section 3(a)(2) exemption. Instead, it adopted a simplified registration form that would enable banks to issue ADRs without undue difficulty or

---

76. ADR Proceedings, *supra* note 71, at 32.
77. *Id.* at 8 and 42.
78. *Id.* at 7.

expense.[79] The result was Form S-12,[80] which could be used to register ADRs on the deposit of the underlying shares into the deposit arrangement established for the program. The form was available only if the holder was entitled to withdraw the underlying securities at any time and where the underlying securities, if sold in the United States, would not be subject to the registration provisions of the 1933 Act. The form provided that the prospectus could be the ADR itself and that the only items of information required to be set forth were the terms of deposit, a description of any fees or charges that could be imposed on a holder, the name and address of the depository and a statement as to the availability for inspection of reports and communications emanating from the issuer of the underlying securities.

The form stated that the entity created by the agreement for the issuance of the ADRs was deemed to be the issuer of the ADRs for purposes of the 1933 Act. It provided that the registration statement was to be signed by the depository bank in the name and on behalf of this fictitious entity. But the form specifically stated that the depository itself would not be deemed an issuer, a person signing the registration statement or a person controlling an issuer. By this device, the SEC made the issuance of ADRs possible without subjecting the depository bank to potential liabilities under Section 11 of the 1933 Act.

In 1997, the SEC exempted listed ADRs from the requirement that they be separately registered under the 1934 Act.[81] The SEC explained the exemption, which equalized the 1934 treatment of listed and unlisted ADRs, as being "consistent with the Commission's view of ADRs as separate securities that provide a mechanism for investing in the underlying securities. . . . Moreover, eliminating the Section 12(b) registration requirement for ADRs will eliminate unintentional technical violations of the Exchange Act by issuers that register the underlying shares, but

---

79. Moxley, *supra* note 75, at 29.

80. SEC Release No. 33-3593 (November 17, 1955), proposed in SEC Release No. 33-3570 (August 31, 1955).

81. SEC Release No. 33-7431 (July 18, 1997).

neglect to register the ADRs under the Exchange Act by listing the ADRs on the cover page of the Exchange Act registration statement."

In view of the diminishing returns from the SEC's view of ADRs as separate securities requiring 1933 Act registration, one could argue that the SEC should simply exempt ADRs entirely. Especially in a Level 1 or 2 facility, where the underlying shares can be sold in the United States without registration in reliance on the exemptions provided by Section 4(1) and Section 4(3) of the 1933 Act, why should the ADRs representing them be subject to registration any more than the actual stock certificates? The functions performed by the depository bank are custodial and ministerial, and the holder of the ADR may take possession of the underlying shares at any time. If an ADR is a separate security, why not a monthly statement received from a brokerage firm showing the ownership of securities in a securities account and held by the broker in street name?

• • *Form F-6.* In 1983, the SEC adopted Form F-6 for registering ADSs represented by ADRs.[82] As in the case of Form S-12, the form is available where the holder of the ADRs is entitled to withdraw the deposited securities at any time (with certain permitted exceptions) and the deposited securities are offered or sold in a transaction registered under the 1933 Act or in an exempt transaction. The issuer of the deposited securities must be a foreign company reporting under Section 13(a) or Section 15(d) of the 1934 Act or an issuer exempt under Rule 12g3-2(b), unless the issuer concurrently files a registration statement on another form covering the deposited securities. As in the case of Form S-12, the prospectus may take the form of the ADR itself. Form F-6 must be signed by the depository bank and, in the case of sponsored facilities, by the foreign company, a majority of its directors, its principal chief executive,

---

82. SEC Release No. 33-6459 (March 18, 1983). Form S-12 clearly referred to the registration of the ADRs, and Form F-6 clearly refers to the registration of the depositary shares that are evidenced by the ADRs. The distinction, as the SEC admitted 20 years later, has no practical significance. *See supra* note 69.

financial and accounting officers and its authorized representative in the United States.

In 1991 the SEC requested information and comment on three principal regulatory concerns relating to the ADR market: (1) whether the substantive disclosure required by Form F-6 was sufficient for the protection of investors, (2) whether depositories and/or issuers of deposited securities should be required to assume responsibility for the disclosures in a Form F-6 registration statement and to accept 1933 Act liabilities for such disclosures and (3) what information regarding the ADRs themselves should be provided or made available to investors and which market participants should be responsible for providing or making available such information.[83] No rules were proposed or adopted as a result.

- *1934 Act Reporting Obligations of Foreign Companies*

The SEC's 1964 *Special Report of Special Study of Securities Markets* recommended that issuers of securities having 300 or more "equity securityholders of record and/or known beneficial holders" be made subject to Sections 13 (reporting requirements), 14 (proxy regulation) and 16 (insider trade reporting and short-swing profit recapture) of the 1934 Act. Until 1963, these requirements had applied only to issuers that had listed their securities with the NYSE or another exchange. The study did not consider the implications of this recommendation for foreign issuers whose unlisted securities were held by U.S. investors.

The Securities Acts Amendments of 1964 amended the 1934 Act to require for the first time that certain issuers register securities under the 1934 Act and comply with 1934 Act reporting requirements even though the issuers had not listed any securities on a national securities exchange and had not had a registration statement become effective under the 1933 Act. As it passed the Senate, the bill would have exempted all foreign securities (and related ADRs) from the registration and reporting requirements unless the SEC should find by rule or order that

---

83. SEC Release No. 33-6894 (May 23, 1991).

a "substantial public market" existed in the United States for the equity securities of an issuer (or class of issuers) and that continued exemption would not be "in the public interest or consistent with the protection of investors."[84] This approach was based on the premise that, while U.S. investors in foreign securities ought in principle be afforded the same protections as were provided for investors in domestic securities, their interests would be adversely affected if foreign securities could not trade at all in U.S. markets. The Senate approach also had the support of the SEC, which believed that enforcement of the registration and reporting requirements of the 1934 Act against foreign issuers outside the jurisdiction of the United States (at least those who had not voluntarily sought funds in the U.S. capital markets or a listing on an exchange) would present serious practical difficulties.[85]

On the House side, however, the Senate approach was politically unacceptable to a number of key legislators,[86] and the final legislation reversed the Senate position. As enacted, Section 12(g)(1) made no distinction between securities of foreign or domestic issuers, but Section 12(g)(3) authorized the SEC by rule or order to exempt any foreign security from the registration requirement.[87] The SEC also received broad power in new Section 12(h) to exempt securities from the provisions of Sections 12(g), 13, 14, 15(d) and 16 of the 1934 Act.

• • *Development of a Regulatory Compromise.* The SEC had opposed the House version of the bill because of what it saw as enforcement problems, as possible harm to existing trading markets in foreign securities and as a need for greater flexibility. Its first action was to exempt all foreign securities and related ADRs so that no foreign issuer would be required to

---

84. S. Rep. No. 88-379 at 29 (1963).

85. *Id.* at 29–31.

86. *See* the pungent colloquy between SEC Commissioner Manuel F. Cohen and Representative John D. Dingell of Michigan in *Hearings Before a Subcommittee of the Committee on Interstate and Foreign Commerce*, 88th Cong., 1st Sess. 1286 (1964).

87. H.R. Rep. No. 88-1418 at 11 (1964).

register until April 30, 1966 (in the case of an issuer whose fiscal year was the same as the calendar year).[88] During the next 14 months, the SEC studied how best to bring foreign issuers under the 1964 amendments. In November 1965, it noted that its study had "revealed continuing improvement in the reporting of financial and economic information by foreign issuers." Relying in part on this perceived improvement, the SEC at the same time proposed rules that would have required previously non-reporting and unlisted foreign issuers subject to Section 12(g) and having a class of securities held of record by 300 or more U.S. residents to register such securities on a new Form 20 by supplying "certain information, documents and reports which they are either required to make public abroad or which they transmit to their securityholders." (The computation of record holders was to include as separate holders the aggregate number of customers on whose behalf a broker-dealer, bank or other nominee held a foreign private issuer's securities; the nominee was "expected" to inform the issuer on request of the number of separate accounts.) The SEC justified the 300-holder breakpoint on the basis that "the existence of 300 holders resident in the United States indicates a sufficient public interest in a foreign security to warrant registration *by the issuer*" (emphasis added). ADRs were to be exempted but not the underlying shares.[89]

A proposed amendment to Rule 3a12-3—which exempted certain foreign issuers from Section 14 (proxy regulation) and Section 16 of the Act (insider trade reporting and short-swing profit recapture)—would have made these provisions wholly applicable to North American issuers (including Canadian and Mexican companies) as well as to foreign issuers having more than half of their stock held by U.S. residents or whose principal business was conducted in the United States. Other foreign issuers would have been exempt from the proxy solicitation rules only if they kept their U.S. solicitation efforts within prescribed limits. The SEC's rule package also contemplated a procedure

---

88. SEC Release No. 34-7427 (September 15, 1964).
89. SEC Release No. 33-7746 (November 16, 1965).

by which the SEC would identify foreign issuers it thought were subject to the registration requirement and invite them to state why registration was not required; non-responding issuers or those whose responses were unsatisfactory would be put on a "list," and broker-dealers would be required to inform their customers of the foreign issuers' non-compliance with the registration requirement.

Comments on the 1965 proposals—including comments from the U.K. and Canadian governments, supported by the International Law Committee of The Association of the Bar of the City of New York[90]—criticized them as improper under international law. The committee believed there was no problem under international law in an SEC requirement that foreign issuers comply with SEC regulations "to the extent that foreign issuers 'voluntarily' accept the jurisdiction of the Commission, for example, by listing their securities on a stock exchange in the United States or by publicly selling their securities in the United States." On the other hand, the committee noted that "[h]ow United States shareholders acquired their shares in these foreign issuers is irrelevant in determining the applicability of the Act—that is, the fact that United States persons acquired shares in the foreign corporation through their own actions and with no encouragement or assistance from the foreign corporation does not affect the applicability of the Act."

The committee cited Section 18(b) of the 1965 *Restatement (Second), Foreign Relations Law of the United States* as standing for the proposition that, as a matter of U.S. "municipal law," the United States could exercise its "legislative jurisdiction" over persons outside the United States who engaged in conduct that had a "substantial effect" within the United States and "a direct causal relationship." Merely having 300 shareholders in the United States did not, in the committee's view, meet this test. The committee drew an analogy to due process standards imposed by the U.S. Supreme Court on a state's attempt to assert personal jurisdiction over non-resident defendants. The committee believed a non-U.S. corporation, neither listing nor selling securities in the United

---

90. 21 *The Record* 240 (1966).

States, could not be subject to U.S. jurisdiction under the "standard" that looks to "some act by which [the foreign corporation] purposefully avails itself of the privilege of conducting activities within the forum state [asserting jurisdiction], thus invoking the benefits and protections of its laws."[91]

The committee was less concerned about the imposition on foreign issuers generally of registration and reporting requirements than it was about the potential application to foreign issuers—especially Canadian and other North American issuers—of the U.S. requirements regarding proxies (Section 14) and insider trade reporting and short-swing profit recapture (Section 16). As to the latter, it suggested that the SEC might "diminish the seriousness of the violation of international law" by adopting a rule that would exempt foreign "companies which voluntarily furnish [to the SEC] substantially the information required" by the SEC's proposed rules, "even though the fundamental problem of the extent of United States jurisdiction would remain."

Commenters also believed that the proposals would likely have the effect of retarding foreign countries from adopting improved corporate and securities laws. After extending the temporary exemption for foreign securities for another year,[92] the SEC requested foreign issuers subject to Section 12(g) and having more than 300 U.S. resident holders of equity securities to furnish it with certain home country information. In August 1966, the SEC published a list of 80 companies that it believed had complied with its request and a list of 32 companies that had not furnished information to the SEC pursuant to its request. It stated that it thought such lists would be "useful" to broker-dealers in making recommendations to their customers.[93]

In April 1966, the SEC adopted amendments to Rule 3a12-3 providing for full exemptions from Sections 14 and 16 for foreign issuers unless they were North American companies or what the SEC later referred to as "essentially United States companies" (i.e., companies that had more than 50% of their voting securities held

---

91. *Id.* at 251, quoting *Hanson v. Denckla*, 357 U.S. 235, 253 (1958).
92. SEC Release No. 34-7867 (April 21, 1966).
93. SEC Release No. 34-7934 (August 10, 1966).

of record directly or indirectly by U.S. residents *and* either their business was administered principally in the United States or 50% or more of their directors were U.S. residents).[94]

A year later, the SEC referred to the information provided by foreign issuers and its study of improvements in the reporting of financial information by foreign issuers. It concluded that "the continuing improvement in the quality of the information now being made public by foreign issuers, together with the improvement which may reasonably be expected to result from recent changes and current proposals for change in relevant requirements, warrants the provision of an exemption from Section 12(g) for those foreign companies which have not sought a public market for their securities in the United States through public offering or stock exchange listing."

The exemption—set forth in Rule 12g3-2(b)—required the foreign issuer to furnish to the SEC information it was required to make public abroad or transmit to its securityholders and to identify the information as being furnished for the purpose of claiming the exemption. This information would not be deemed "filed" with the SEC, and the issuer would, therefore, not be subject to potential civil liability under Section 18 of the 1934 Act. (There was no mention of Rule 10b-5.) Canadian and other North American issuers were eligible to take advantage of the new exemption.[95]

The SEC did not adopt proposed special rules for broker-dealers who dealt in foreign securities. It noted that information concerning certain foreign issuers might not be available in the United States and that broker-dealers should take this into consideration "in deciding whether they have a reasonable basis for recommending these securities to customers."[96]

---

94. SEC Release No. 34-7868 (April 21, 1966).

95. SEC Release No. 34-8066 (April 28, 1967). Professor Loss suggests that the SEC's shift "from the special registration procedure it had originally proposed [for foreign private issuers] to the technique of a conditional exemption" was "presumably for psychological reasons." 2 Loss & Seligman, *Securities Regulation* 824 (rev. 3d ed., 1999).

96. The history of the 1964 legislation makes clear, however, that if a foreign issuer subject to Section 12(g) does not comply with the SEC's

Only four years after the adoption of the Rule 12g3-2(b) exemption, the NASD initiated NASDAQ, its automated inter-dealer system for electronically disseminating quotations. By the early 1980s the SEC had come to the conclusion that "trading on NASDAQ is substantially the same as trading on an exchange,"[97] and it proposed in October 1982 an amendment to Rule 12g3-2(b) that would have made that rule's exemption unavailable for foreign private issuers whose securities were traded in NASDAQ.[98] In support of its proposal, the SEC cited an issuer's necessary involvement in applying for a NASDAQ "listing," the payment of fees and the meeting of specific standards as evidence of "voluntary" entry into the U.S. capital markets.[99] The effect of the proposal was to force affected foreign issuers to choose between registering their securities under Section 12(g) or "delisting" their securities from NASDAQ and leaving them to trade in the "pink sheets."

As might be expected, comment was overwhelmingly critical of the SEC proposal. Predicted consequences of a shift to "pink sheet" trading included "increased price spreads, decrease in information, price quotes not carried in newspapers, less liquid market[s] and fewer institutions in the market, absence of NASD surveillance, and delays in execution of transfers."[100] One commenter estimated that these factors could cause a price drop of 20%.

In view of these concerns, the SEC decided to strike a "pragmatic balance" and apply only prospectively its view that foreign issuers of NASDAQ securities should be regarded as

---

registration and reporting requirements, this will not of itself mean that trading in its securities in the United States will be illegal or that broker-dealers trading in these securities will have civil liability as a result. H.R. Rep. No. 88-1418 at 11.

97. SEC Release No. 33-6493 (October 6, 1983).

98. SEC Release No. 33-6433 (October 28, 1982).

99. The SEC candidly admitted, however, that many foreign issuers had in fact not taken any action in support of a NASDAQ listing for their securities; the relevant obligations had been undertaken, and the fees paid, by the depository banks that issued the related ADRs.

100. SEC Release No. 33-6493 (October 6, 1983).

"voluntarily seeking U.S. trading markets." It accordingly "grandfathered" indefinitely those non-Canadian foreign private issuers that were in compliance with the Rule 12g3-2(b) exemption as of October 5, 1983 and quoted in NASDAQ as of that date. Securities of Canadian issuers were "grandfathered" only until January 1986, in view of what the SEC described as "hot-issue" problems involving Canadian securities.

• • *Current "Trigger" for 1934 Act Registration.* As modified by SEC rules, the 1934 Act requires a foreign company to register a class of its unlisted equity securities with the SEC—or obtain the Rule 12g3-2(b) exemption—if the company has total assets of $10 million or more and the class is owned of record by 500 or more persons of whom 300 or more are resident in the United States.[101] The number of U.S. resident holders is calculated according to the same "look through" procedure described above for purposes of the definition of "foreign private issuer."

The Rule 12g3-2(b) exemption is not available if the foreign company's equity securities are traded on NASDAQ or on the NASD's OTC Bulletin Board. In both cases, full registration under the 1934 Act on Form 20-F is required. If not registered under the 1934 Act, the "pink sheets" are the only quotation medium in which a foreign company's shares or ADRs may be traded in the United States.

• • *Obtaining the Rule 12g3-2(b) Exemption.* Many foreign issuers have more than 300 U.S. resident holders of their equity securities and have never registered their securities with the SEC or taken advantage of the Rule 12g3-2(b) exemption. Many of these companies have probably never heard of the 1934 Act or its applicability to unlisted non-U.S. companies.

The SEC has limited means of requiring foreign companies to register or obtain an exemption. The jurisdictional debate preceding the adoption of Rule 12g3-2(b) has not been resolved, and the SEC probably has no desire to revive it.

---

101. Of course, there is also a "jurisdictional means" requirement that the issuer be engaged in interstate commerce or in a business affecting interstate commerce or that its securities be traded by use of the mails or by any means of interstate commerce.

INTERNATIONAL FINANCINGS

Notwithstanding, nearly 700 foreign companies had elected by mid-2004 to take advantage of the Rule 12g3-2(b) exemption. Some of these probably concluded that they could no longer deny that they had many U.S. shareholders and that it was not prudent in view of their substantial U.S. investment and operations to ignore the SEC's requirements. Others may have viewed Rule 12g3-2(b) as a means of raising their profile among U.S. investors, particularly since (as discussed above) obtaining the exemption is a condition to the availability of Form F-6 for an ADR facility.

Other foreign companies have voluntarily obtained the Rule 12g3-2(b) exemption as a means of satisfying the information requirement under Rule 144A(d)(4), thus permitting Rule 144A offerings without the preparation of a formal offering document.

Another collateral benefit of obtaining the Rule 12g3-2(b) exemption is that it satisfies the information requirement imposed by Rule 15c2-11 on broker-dealers that wish to publish quotations on, or make a market in, the foreign company's securities.

The procedure for obtaining the exemption is quite simple. The issuer sends a letter to the SEC requesting the exemption, describing the requirements under which it provides material information in its home country to the public, any exchange or its securityholders and furnishing a copy of each material communication it distributed since the beginning of its last fiscal year pursuant to such requirements. It also informs the SEC of the number of U.S. resident shareholders, the amount and percentage that they hold, how the securities were acquired and the date and circumstances of the most recent public distribution of securities by the issuer or any of its affiliates. (The purpose of this requirement is to identify for the SEC any distributions in the United States that should have been registered under the 1933 Act. The SEC takes failures to register securities under the 1933 Act much more seriously than failures to register under the 1934 Act.) Once the exemption is issued, the foreign company must furnish the SEC with copies of the required material communications "promptly" after they are distributed in the home country.

A foreign issuer is entitled to rely on the Rule 12g3-2(b) exemption notwithstanding the number of U.S. resident shareholders or the volume of trading in the U.S. "pink sheets." The rule states that the exemption should be obtained before a 1934 Act registration statement would be required, but the authors are not aware of any adverse consequences following from an admission in connection with a Rule 12g3-2(b) application that a foreign issuer has more than 300 U.S. resident shareholders.

As originally adopted, Rule 12g3-2(b) required a list identifying the information furnished and provided that, if the issuer had prepared an English translation or version of a document, it should furnish that translation or version rather than the original language document. A foreign language document nevertheless could satisfy the requirements of the rule. Some issuers shipped off to the SEC crates of foreign language documents with no identifying list.[102] The rule now states that foreign language documents are not required to be furnished. Rather, a foreign company must furnish English translations, summaries or descriptions of press releases and other communications distributed directly to securityholders.

Documents furnished to the SEC pursuant to the exemption are not required—indeed, are not allowed—to be electronically furnished under the SEC's EDGAR system. When the SEC extended the EDGAR requirement to foreign issuers in 2002, it rejected suggestions that documents furnished under Rule 12g3-2(b) be either required or permitted to be furnished electronically.[103] It justified its position on the basis that there was "less need" for electronic access to these documents, but it is clear that the SEC wanted to avoid creating the impression that Rule 12g3-2(b) permitted a "light" form of SEC registration.

Information provided to the SEC pursuant to the exemption is still deemed to be "furnished" rather than "filed" and not to be subject to the liabilities imposed by Section 18 of the 1934 Act, but the more potent liabilities imposed under Rule 10b-5 remain in full force.

---

102. Jennings & Marsh, *Securities Regulation* 1593–94 (6th ed. 1987).
103. SEC Release No. 33-8099 (May 14, 2002), text at n.100.

INTERNATIONAL FINANCINGS 731

- *Form 20-F*

Form 20-F is the registration form for the registration of a foreign private issuer's equity securities under the 1934 Act. It also sets forth the disclosure requirements for a foreign private issuer's annual report, which must be filed with the SEC within six months of the end of the issuer's fiscal year. The SEC adopted extensive revisions to Form 20-F in 1999 in order that it conform to the international disclosure standards endorsed by the International Organization of Securities Commission in September 1998.[104]

Some of the items of Form 20-F do not require responses if the form is being used as an annual report but do require responses if the form is being used for the purpose of an initial registration under the 1934 Act or for the purpose of a registered public offering under the 1933 Act.

As in the case of domestic issuers, the staff is prepared to meet with non-U.S. issuers and their advisors in a pre-filing conference for the purpose of discussing anticipated disclosure or accounting problems. In an effort to accommodate non-U.S. issuers, the SEC also informally permits first-time foreign issuers to make a "confidential" submission of the registration statement for the purpose of comment by the staff. Not only is such a submission confidential, since it does not appear in the public file, but the filing does not even require payment of the filing fee. The staff attempts to provide comments on such filings within the same 30-day period applicable to formal filings.

Item 1 of Form 20-F requires, except for an annual report, information about the issuer's directors and senior management, principal bankers, legal advisors (if required to be disclosed outside the United States) and auditors.

Item 2 requires, only in the case of a registered public offering, information about the offer and the expected timetable.

Item 3 calls for a summary of key information about the issuer's financial condition, capitalization and risk factors. In the

---

104. SEC Release No. 33-7745 (September 28, 1999). The SEC adopted technical corrections to Form 20-F in June 2001. SEC Release No. 33-7983 (June 11, 2001).

case of a securities offering, it also requires information about the issuer's capitalization and the intended use of proceeds.

Item 4 requires information about the issuer's business operations, its products or services and the factors that affect the business.

Item 5 requires disclosure regarding operating results, liquidity and capital, research and development and trend information similar to that required of a U.S. issuer in connection with MD&A. In addition, recent amendments require disclosure of off-balance sheet arrangements and a tabular disclosure of the issuer's contractual obligations.

Item 6 requires information regarding the issuer's directors and managers that will enable investors to assess these individuals' experience, qualifications and levels of compensation, as well as their relationships with the issuer.

Item 7 requires information on the issuer's major shareholders and other persons who may control the issuer, as well as information on transactions between such persons and the issuer and whether the terms of such transactions are fair to the issuer.

Items 8, 17 and 18 of Form 20-F specify the financial statements that must be included in the Form 20-F. These items are discussed below under "Financial Statements Requirements."

Item 9 requires information relevant to an offering or listing.

Item 10 requires information on legal matters relating to the issuer and its securities, in particular its equity securities, and a discussion of relevant tax considerations and summaries of certain material contracts.

Item 11 requires information intended to clarify the issuer's exposure to market risk associated with activities in derivative financial instruments, other financial instruments and derivative commodity instruments (as these categories are defined in the SEC's rules).

Item 12 requires a description of the securities being offered (if the Form 20-F is not being used only as an annual report), to the extent that they are not equity securities described under Item 10.

Other items of Form 20-F include requirements to disclose information about defaults, delinquencies and arrearages, material modifications to the rights of securityholders and the use of proceeds raised in an IPO.

New items recently added to Form 20-F as a result of Sarbanes–Oxley include requirements regarding the issuer's disclosure controls and procedures, its internal control over financial reporting, whether or not there is a member of the audit committee who is a "financial expert," whether or not it has a "code of ethics" for certain senior officers and information about the audit, audit-related, tax and other fees paid to its independent accountant.

In addition, the chief executive and chief financial officers of the foreign issuer must individually and personally certify the accuracy and completeness of the disclosure in the Form 20-F and the fairness of the financial presentation. They must also make specified statements regarding the issuer's "disclosure controls and procedures" and "internal control over financial reporting."

- *Financial Statement Requirements*

It is generally advisable to discuss any accounting questions with the SEC before the registration statement is filed, even on a "confidential" basis.[105] The SEC has in the past shown flexibility with non-U.S. issuers and required less than full compliance with some of the financial disclosure requirements where the issuer was able to demonstrate that historical compliance was impractical and that systems were in place that would assure future compliance.

- - *Formal Requirements.* Item 8 of Form 20-F, together with Items 17 and 18 discussed below, specify the financial statements that must be included, including the periods to be covered, the age of the financial statements and other information of a financial nature. Audited financial statements are generally required for the preceding three fiscal years, and selected financial information for the preceding five fiscal years. The earliest balance

---

105. *See* "Matters of Interest to Initial Filers" and "Draft Submissions" in SEC Division of Corporation Finance, *International Financial Reporting and Disclosure Issues* 11–14 (October 1, 2003). This compilation of staff positions is on the SEC's website.

sheet may be omitted if it is not required outside the United States. The audit must be performed in accordance with U.S. generally accepted auditing standards, and the auditor must comply with the SEC's independence standards. The financial statement information required may vary depending on whether the Form 20-F is being used as an annual report or in connection with a registered securities offering.

The last year of audited financial statements may not be older than 15 months[106] at the time of a securities offering or listing of securities. If the issuer is making its IPO (i.e., the issuer is not a public company either in the United States or in its home country), the audited financial statements may not be older than 12 months at the time the document is filed. The effect of these requirements is that some issuers may be prevented from making a securities offering or listing their securities at certain times of the year. For example, a calendar year issuer that ordinarily makes its financial statements available in April may be prevented from making a registered public offering after March 31 and until the financial statements become available. Under specified circumstances, the issuer may request that the SEC waive the 12-month requirement.

Item 8 also specifies the interim financial statements that must be furnished if the Form 20-F is being used for any purpose other than as an annual report.

• • *Reconciliation to U.S. GAAP.* Items 17 and 18 of Form 20-F specify the financial statement requirements for Form 20-F. In either case, the issuer is required to furnish financial statements for the same fiscal years required of a U.S. issuer. The statements must "disclose an information content substantially similar to financial statements that comply with United States generally accepted accounting principles and Regulation S-X." They may be prepared according to U.S. GAAP or, alternatively, on the basis of another "comprehensive body of accounting

---

106. Eighteen months in the case of securities offered on the exercise of outstanding rights granted to securityholders, a dividend or interest reinvestment plan or on the conversion or exercise of certain outstanding securities.

principles" if accompanied by a discussion of the material variations between the two systems, including a quantification of such material variations by means of a reconciliation in a specified format of net income and balance sheet line items.

The "reconciliation" requirement is a matter of particular concern to many non-U.S. issuers, even though Form 20-F requires first-time foreign private issuers to reconcile net income for only the two most recent fiscal years. In addition, the SEC determined in 1994 to accept (without reconciliation to U.S. GAAP) cash flow statements and information relating to hyperinflation and business combinations presented in accordance with standards of the International Accounting Standards Committee (now the International Accounting Standards Board).[107]

Despite these accommodations by the SEC, there remain many non-U.S. issuers that are reluctant to provide the U.S. GAAP reconciliation required for 1934 Act registration and, therefore, for an NYSE or NASDAQ listing or a registered public offering. For one thing, the reconciliation effort involves significant time and expense. For another, reconciled numbers can be confusing to the issuer's home country tax authorities, labor unions and shareholders.

Many non-U.S. issuers do provide U.S. GAAP reconciliations, of course. If these numbers were really of value to U.S. investors, one would expect considerable attention to be paid to the announcement of the U.S. GAAP numbers as well as to any possible effect of these numbers on the issuer's stock price. In fact, the authors are not aware of a single situation where this has been the case. Most non-U.S. issuers' stock prices are set by supply and demand in the home country, and analysts who follow non-U.S. issuers necessarily rely on the issuer's home country financial statements. U.S. investors necessarily follow suit, suggesting that the reconciled numbers are not really "material" in a conventional securities law sense. The same conclusion is suggested by the fact that non-U.S. issuers who offer securities to U.S. investors under Rule 144A are hardly ever called on to provide reconciled numbers, rather customarily furnishing only

---

107. SEC Release Nos. 33-7053 (April 19, 1994), 33-7117 (December 13, 1994) and 33-7119 (December 13, 1994).

a narrative discussion of the significant differences between home country accounting principles and U.S. GAAP.

There is considerable support internationally for the acceptance of international financial reporting standards (IFRS) (formerly international accounting standards) developed under the auspices of the International Accounting Standards Board. In fact, EU and U.S. companies listed in Europe that now report according to U.S. GAAP will be required by 2007 to report according to IFRS. The SEC and the FASB profess to be supportive of "convergence," and the FASB issued in December 2003 four exposure drafts in furtherance of this goal.

In the meantime, the SEC proposed in March 2004 to permit companies that elect IFRS for fiscal years beginning on or before January 1, 2007 to omit the earliest of the three years of required audited financial statements. On the other hand, it proposed to require such companies to present condensed U.S. GAAP financial information for the three most recent fiscal years in a level of detail comparable to that required of interim reports under SEC rules. It also proposed guidelines for reconciling IFRS financial statements to U.S. GAAP and for presenting certain required disclosures.[108]

• • *Geographic Market and Industry Segments.* The principal difference between Items 17 and 18 of Form 20-F is that Item 17 does not require the information on geographic market and industry segments called for by SFAS 131. (See the discussion in Chapter 5.) Form F-3 permits a foreign issuer to follow Item 17 if it is making a public offering of investment grade non-convertible debt securities, and the instructions to Form 20-F permit the foreign issuer to follow Item 17 if it is simply listing its securities without making a simultaneous public offering. In all other cases, the foreign issuer must comply with Item 18.

While Item 18 usually imposes a heavier burden on foreign issuers, compliance will afford issuers (if otherwise eligible) full access to the benefits of the short-form registration statements. In view of the full access that Item 18 affords, the SEC advises issuers in the general instructions to Form 20-F to consider the

---

108. SEC Release No. 33-8397 (March 11, 2004).

benefits of the availability of short-form registration statements in determining which financial statements to include in their annual reports.

- *Continuous Reporting Under the 1934 Act*

Once a foreign private issuer registers its securities under the 1934 Act by means of a Form 20-F, it becomes subject to the continuous reporting requirements of the 1934 Act. The applicable reporting forms for this purpose are an annual report on Form 20-F and interim reports on Form 6-K.[109] The annual report on Form 20-F is due to be filed within six months after the end of each fiscal year, but the foreign private issuer should file its financial statements within three months after the end of the fiscal year in order to avoid the possibility of a "blackout" in its ability to make a public offering of securities registered under the 1933 Act.

Interim reports are required on Form 6-K only for the purpose of "furnishing" to the SEC (not "filing") material information that the foreign issuer makes public in its home country or sends to a stock exchange or to its securityholders. The information must be sent to the SEC "promptly" after it is released in the home country.

Required reports must be electronically transmitted to the SEC by means of its EDGAR system. The SEC has been considering an extension of EDGAR filing hours to accommodate foreign issuers.

By registering a class of securities under the 1934 Act, an issuer ordinarily becomes subject to the reporting, proxy, Williams Act, insider reporting and short-swing profit recapture provisions of the 1934 Act, as well as to the Foreign Corrupt Practices Act. As discussed above, however, foreign issuers with a class of securities registered under the 1934 Act are exempted by the SEC's Rule 3a12-3 under the 1934 Act from the proxy

---

109. Canadian issuers that have securities listed on a U.S. exchange or quoted on NASDAQ, or that exceed the Section 12(g) threshold of equity securities held of record by U.S. residents, must also use these forms unless they are eligible to use Forms 40-F or 6-K (which apply only to certain Canadian issuers under the SEC's Multijurisdictional Disclosure System applicable to Canadian issuers).

provisions of Section 14 and from all provisions of Section 16 (insider reporting and short-swing profit recapture).

- *Listing on a U.S. Exchange or NASDAQ*

As discussed above, registration under the 1934 Act is necessary in order for a foreign company to list its securities on a U.S. exchange or NASDAQ. In addition, the foreign company must also meet the exchange's or NASDAQ's minimum listing standards (e.g., number of shareholders, number of shares publicly held, earnings and market capitalization), file a listing application, sign a listing agreement and agree to pay the required initial and continuing listing fees. Both the NYSE and NASDAQ are willing to work with foreign companies by applying their listing standards to a company's particular circumstances.

A listed company must continue to comply with minimum standards for listing as well as with the market's corporate governance and reporting requirements. NYSE rules automatically exempt listed foreign private issuers from all corporate governance requirements but require the inclusion in an annual report or on the issuer's website of a summary of any significant differences between home country and NYSE standards. NASD rules are similar, except that the exemption is not automatic.

There is no exemption from the Sarbanes–Oxley requirement that all listed companies have an independent audit committee. The SEC rules implementing this requirement make certain accommodatations for foreign private issuers.[110]

- *Sarbanes–Oxley Consequences for Foreign Reporting Companies*

Congress did not distinguish in Sarbanes–Oxley between U.S. and foreign companies reporting under the 1934 Act when it imposed broad new requirements for the purpose of restoring confidence and enhancing investor protection. Foreign companies urged the SEC, during its rulemaking effort to implement Sarbanes–Oxley, to create reasonable accommodations for foreign companies on some of the more intrusive provisions of the Act, but the SEC largely ignored these pleas.

---

110. Rule 10A-3 under the 1934 Act, adopted in SEC Release No. 33-8220 (April 9, 2003).

INTERNATIONAL FINANCINGS

Some of the Sarbanes–Oxley consequences of particular concern to foreign companies—whether or not listed on the NYSE or NASDAQ—include the following:

- required personal certifications by the chief executive and chief financial officers;
- management assessment of the company's internal control over financial reporting;
- a prohibition on personal loans to directors and executive officers, with exemptions only for U.S. banks and broker-dealers;[111]
- enhanced independence standards for auditors, as well as auditor registration with the PCAOB;
- forfeiture of certain officers' bonuses and trading profits in the event of certain restatements;
- disclosure requirements relating to the use of "non-GAAP financial measures";
- "up the ladder" reporting requirements for certain attorneys representing issuers; and
- enhanced whistleblower protections.

Like their U.S. counterparts, foreign companies can expect the SEC staff to review their 1934 Act periodic reports on a more regular and systematic basis as the SEC responds to Sarbanes–Oxley's requirement that it review each reporting company at least once every three years.

- *Exiting the Continuous Reporting System*

As a result of Sarbanes–Oxley, some foreign issuers began as early as 2002 to reexamine their decisions to become reporting companies in the United States. In some cases, the benefits of doing so had not been as great as anticipated. In all cases, however, the cost and effort to meet the new U.S. reporting and governance requirements had greatly increased.

---

111. The SEC has exempted certain non-U.S. banks from this prohibition. SEC Release No. 34-49616 (April 26, 2004).

Exiting the U.S. disclosure system is not so easily done, as some of these companies discovered. Delisting from the NYSE or NASDAQ is not difficult, but a foreign company cannot by delisting simply slip back into the Rule 12g3-2(b) exemption from 1934 Act registration and reporting. Paragraph (d)(1) of that exemption makes it unavailable for any company that during the past 18 months has had a class of securities registered under Section 12 of the 1934 Act or that has had a reporting obligation under Section 15(d) of the Act.

A foreign company seeking to exit the U.S. disclosure system must therefore demonstrate that it meets the requirement of Rule 12g-4(a)(2) that it have fewer than 300 U.S. shareholders of record (both ADRs and ordinary shares). In the case of foreign companies only, however, the method of counting record holders is modified to pick up all U.S.-resident beneficial owners on whose behalf any brokers, dealers, banks and nominees hold ADRs or ordinary shares. See the discussion above regarding the definition of "foreign private issuer."

The "look through" requirement makes it much more difficult for foreign companies to withdraw from the U.S. disclosure system. In fact, the only alternative may be to delist from the NYSE and NASDAQ, terminate the sponsored ADR facility and wait out the period of time it takes to get to fewer than 300 U.S. holders of record of ADRs and ordinary shares.[112]

Some companies have tried to encourage their U.S. holders to sell their ADRs, either back to the company or on an offshore exchange. These efforts can raise tender offer problems (see Chapter 13), and the SEC staff has on occasion raised other imaginative objections to such efforts.

- *Multijurisdictional Disclosure System*

In 1991, the SEC and the Canadian Securities Administrators adopted a multijurisdictional disclosure system (MJDS) for use

---

[112]. A group of European companies requested in February 2004 that the SEC relax the conditions under which a non-U.S. company can terminate its reporting obligations. Letter dated February 9, 2004 from European Association for Listed Companies and ten of its member organizations to William H. Donaldson, Chairman, SEC, The Secrurities Reporter 28 (Spring 2004).

by the United States and each of the provinces and territories of Canada.[113] The MJDS was developed to allow qualified companies in the United States and Canada to make public offerings and file periodic reports in both countries while being regulated only in their home country. The MJDS allows Canadian issuers to register securities under the 1933 Act by means of a Canadian prospectus (with certain additional U.S. disclosures) using a "wrap-around" 1933 Act registration form. These public offerings may be made in conjunction with a contemporaneous Canadian public offering or the public offering may be made only in the United States. The MJDS is available to Canadian private issuers and crown corporations.

Under the MJDS, specific registration forms are available for Canadian issuers. Form F-9 is used to register investment-grade debt securities, while Form F-10 is used to register equity or non-investment-grade debt securities. F-7 is used for rights offerings. Unlike Forms F-1, F-2 and F-3, the SEC staff will not review registration statements filed pursuant to the MJDS, absent special circumstances, and the confidential review procedure discussed above is therefore not available to MJDS issuers. Registration statements of MJDS issuers are effective immediately on filing or, for U.S.-only offerings registered on Forms F-9 and F-10, at some later date as specified by the Canadian issuer. The principal jurisdiction in Canada designated by the issuer is responsible for conducting any review of the filings.

On the other hand, the MJDS offering remains subject to the SEC's authority to issue a "stop order" under Section 8(d) of the 1933 Act if the SEC believes such an order is in the public interest and necessary for the protection of investors.

Shortly after the adoption of the MJDS for Canadian issuers, the SEC referred to the MJDS as a first step in responding to the internationalization of the capital markets and to the possibility of extending the MJDS concept to include foreign countries other

---

113. SEC Release No. 33-6902 (June 21, 1991); *National Policy Statement No. 45—Multijurisdictional Disclosure System*, 14 OSC Bull. 2889 (June 28, 1991).

than Canada. More recently, however, the staff has appeared to regard MJDS with less enthusiasm. There is no sign of the SEC extending MJDS to other countries.

- *1933 Act Registration for Foreign Private Issuers*

In November 1982, the SEC adopted an integrated disclosure system for foreign private issuers.[114] The 1933 Act registration forms for these issuers, Forms F-1, F-2 and F-3, roughly parallel Forms S-1, S-2 and S-3 in the domestic system. Form F-1 must be used where the issuer does not qualify for the use of either Form F-2 or Form F-3. To be eligible to use Form F-3, a foreign private issuer must either (a) be registering investment-grade debt securities (non-convertible debt securities rated in one of the four highest rating categories by at least one nationally recognized U.S. rating organization) or (b) have an aggregate market value worldwide of its common equity held by non-affiliates that is the equivalent of $75 million or more. It also must have been subject to, and must have complied with, the reporting requirements of the 1934 Act for at least 12 months prior to the filing of the registration statement. In addition, the registrant and its subsidiaries must not, since the end of the last fiscal year for which an annual report on Form 20-F has been filed, have failed to make any required preferred stock dividend or sinking fund payment or defaulted on payment of any material indebtedness or long-term lease rentals.

A majority-owned subsidiary of a foreign private issuer may use Form F-3 to register non-convertible securities even though the subsidiary does not itself meet the requirements of the form, if the parent is eligible to use Form F-3 and fully guarantees the securities as to principal and interest. This exception is useful in those cases where non-U.S. companies offer guaranteed securities through U.S. subsidiaries for tax, legal investment or other reasons.

As in the case of domestic issuers, the staff is prepared to meet with non-U.S. issuers and their advisors in a pre-filing conference for the purpose of discussing anticipated disclosure or

---

114. SEC Release No. 33-6437 (November 19, 1982).

accounting problems. As in the case of Form 20-F filings discussed above, the SEC also informally permits first-time foreign issuers to make a "confidential" filing of the registration statement for the purpose of comment by the staff.

Form F-4 is used for the 1933 Act registration of a foreign reporting company's securities issued in business combinations and registered exchange offers (e.g., Exxon Capital exchange offers) and roughly parallels Form S-4 in the U.S. domestic system.

As discussed above, a foreign private issuer selling its shares in a public offering directed to the U.S. market in the form of ADSs represented by ADRs must file a registration statement covering the underlying shares and must also cause the depository bank to file a registration statement on Form F-6 covering the ADSs. A foreign private issuer that is making a public offering of its debt securities in the United States must also file a registration statement on the appropriate form; in addition, it must qualify an indenture under the Trust Indenture Act of 1939.

In addition to the same persons that are required to sign the registration statement of a domestic issuer, the registration statement of a foreign private issuer must be signed by its authorized representative in the United States.[115] The forepart of the prospectus should set forth information concerning the enforceability in the issuer's home jurisdiction of civil liabilities under the federal securities laws. The prospectus also should state that substantially all of the issuer's directors and officers, and certain experts named in the registration statement, reside outside of the United States and, as a result, it may not be possible for investors to effect service of process within the United States on such persons.

- *1940 Act Exemptions for Foreign Banks, Insurance Companies and Finance Subsidiaries*

Foreign private issuers that are banks, insurance companies or finance subsidiaries may find that they fall under the 1940 Act's definition of an "investment company." Chapter 10 discusses

---

115. As a person signing the registration statement, the authorized representative is subject to liability under Section 11 of the 1933 Act.

available exemptions for public offerings by these issuers, and Chapter 7 discusses available exemptions for their private offerings.

Rights Offerings

As noted by the SEC in its 1991 release on cross-border rights offers,[116] while rights offerings are no longer common in the United States they are still used in many countries as a means of raising equity capital. Many countries, especially in the European Union, have corporation law or exchange listing requirements that require preemptive rights.

As the SEC has observed, however, U.S. shareholders are often unable to participate in rights offerings because of the requirements of the U.S. securities laws:

> U.S. investors, particularly those holding over-the-counter securities, are often excluded from or cashed out of[117] these rights offerings because of foreign issuers' reluctance to comply with the disclosure requirements and accounting rules applicable to Securities Act registration statements, or to incur the obligation to file periodic reports under the Exchange Act required of those who conduct public offerings in the United States. There have even been instances where foreign issuers which are already reporting companies under the Exchange Act have excluded their U.S. shareholders from rights offerings, purportedly because of concerns with U.S. processing time at both the federal and state levels.

---

116. SEC Release No. 33-6896 (June 4, 1991).

117. "Where there is a trading market for the rights in the issuer's home country, the issuer may cash out its U.S. shareholders by causing the rights that would otherwise be distributed to them to be sold in the open market on their behalf. U.S. investors that are cashed out generally do not receive the full benefit of the offering, however, as they are usually responsible for selling expenses and other transaction costs, including underwriters' commissions. Exchange rate fluctuations may also affect net proceeds." *Id.* at n.14.

The exclusion or cashing out of U.S. investors not only denies these investors a potentially valuable investment opportunity, but may also subject them to substantial dilution. Depository banks for American Depositary Receipts ("ADRs") estimate that in 1990 alone, U.S. investors that own foreign securities in the form of ADRs were excluded from more than 25 rights offerings and cashed out of approximately 60 such transactions.[118]

Cashing out or excluding U.S. investors from a rights offering can raise difficult questions under local corporate or securities laws requiring that all shareholders be treated on a non-discriminatory basis.

The cash-out procedure described above by the SEC has been around at least since 1947. "[O]n the principle that it is no sin to be practical, especially if the letter of the law can be satisfied at the same time, the SEC has permitted Canadian and other non-American corporations to send their subscription rights into this country with substantially the following legend attached":[119]

> The shares of the company are not registered under the United States Securities Act of 1933. The shares referred to in the annexed warrants are being offered in Canada but not in the United States of America. The offering to which the said warrants relates is not, and under no circumstances is to be construed as, an offering of any shares for sale in the United States of America, or the territories or possessions thereof, or as a solicitation therein of an offer to buy any of the said shares. The company will not accept subscriptions from any person, or his agent, who appears to be, or who the company has reason to believe is, a resident of the United States of America. The company is informed that there

---

118. *Id.* (some footnotes omitted).
119. 2 Loss & Seligman, *Securities Regulation* 760–61 n.43 (3d ed. 1989). The statement does not appear in the 1999 revision of this volume, but there is no evidence that the staff has changed its views.

is no objection to a United States shareholder selling this warrant in Canada.

The SEC stated in connection with a 1947 rights offering by Royal Dutch Petroleum Company that it would interpose no objection if brokers or dealers purchased subscription rights from U.S. residents and sold them outside of the United States.[120]

As noted above, the SEC issued a no-action letter to CREF in 1987 that made it clear that CREF and other U.S. institutional investors could exercise rights to purchase shares of foreign corporations as part of a U.S. private offering.[121] The CREF letter, of course, did not solve the problem for the non-institutional holder of foreign shares. Accordingly, in the 1991 release quoted above, the SEC proposed "[t]o facilitate the extension of rights offerings to U.S. investors and to encourage foreign authorities to prohibit discriminatory treatment of U.S. investors" by proposing a small issue exemption under Section 3(b) of the 1933 Act for specified equity rights offerings not exceeding $5 million in the United States. It also proposed a new registration form that would allow the use of home country disclosure documents in the case of larger equity rights offerings as well as a relaxation of the requirements for use of Form F-3 in connection with the registration of rights offerings and other specified transactions. The SEC explained the proposed relief as based on the premise that "the interests of those U.S. investors that have already made an investment in a foreign issuer, frequently on the bases [sic] solely of disclosure required by foreign law, would be better served by facilitating the extension of rights offerings of additional securities to them than by insisting on U.S. disclosure."[122]

According to a subsequent SEC release, 78 rights offerings were made between 1994 and 1998 to U.S. shareholders holding

---

120. SEC Release No. 33-3266 (November 25, 1947).
121. SEC No-action Letter, *College Retirement Equities Fund* (June 4, 1987).
122. *Id.*

ADRs or other receipts issued by a single depository bank. In 39% of these offerings, U.S. shareholders were excluded entirely. In the remaining offerings, the depository bank sold the rights and provided shareholders with the proceeds after deducting transaction and ADR cash distribution or issuance fees.[123]

In 1999, the SEC finally took action on the 1991 proposals and adopted a series of rules on cross-border tender and exchange offers, business combinations and rights offerings.[124] Under new Rule 801, equity securities issued in rights offerings by foreign private issuers are exempt from the registration requirements of the 1933 Act if as of the record date U.S. securityholders own 10% or less of the issuer's securities that are the subject of the rights offering.[125] In making this calculation, an issuer may exclude securities held by persons owning 10% or more of the outstanding securities.

U.S. ownership is determined on a residence basis as in the case of the definition of "foreign private issuer" discussed above.

The rights offering must permit U.S. holders to participate on equal terms with non-U.S. holders, with an exception for blue sky registration or qualification requirements. If the issuer publishes or disseminates an informational document, an English version of that document bearing specified cautionary legends must be furnished to U.S. holders. The rights may not be transferable by the U.S. holders except in accordance with Regulation S.

The issuer must file a notice with the SEC as well as a form appointing an agent for service of process in the United States. The notice to the SEC must include as an attachment a copy of

---

123. SEC Release No. 33-7759 at n.54 (October 22, 1999).

124. SEC Release No. 33-7759 (October 22, 1999).

125. Under new Rule 802, securities issued in exchange offers for foreign private issuers' securities and securities issued in business combinations will be exempt from the registration requirements of the 1933 Act (and, in the case of debt securities, the qualification requirements of the Trust Indenture Act of 1939) if U.S. securityholders own 10% or less of the subject class of securities.

any document, notice or other information disseminated to U.S. offerees. The U.S. antifraud and antimanipulation rules and civil liability provisions continue to apply to these transactions notwithstanding the new 1933 Act exemptions.[126]

Securities purchased in a rights offering exempt under Rule 801 are not restricted securities in the hands of U.S. holders unless the securities held by the holder as of the record date were restricted securities.

The adopting release for Rule 801 discusses the consequences of an Internet posting of information about an offshore rights offering (presumably one that is not exempt under Rule 801). It states that offshore rights offerings "fall squarely within" the SEC's 1998 guidance on the use of Internet websites in connection with offshore transactions.[127] The release suggests that offshore rights offerings require "special care" in connection with Internet postings because of U.S. investors' preexisting investment in and familiarity with the offeror's securities. It recommends procedures to prevent a website from inducing U.S. investors to participate indirectly in a non-exempt offer, including in a privately placed U.S. component.

Of course, even where the conditions of the CREF no-action letter are not present, U.S. institutions often find a way to participate in offshore rights offerings through accounts maintained with, and securities held through, foreign banks or foreign offices of U.S. banks and broker-dealers. In some cases, there may be no use of U.S. "jurisdictional means" in connection with such transactions, and in others Regulation S may provide a perfectly satisfactory exemption. In the adopting release for Rule 801, however, the SEC cautions that a website accessible in the United States "cannot be used to entice U.S. investors to participate in the offering offshore," even in reliance on Regulation S.

---

126. Section 12(a)(2) of the 1933 Act might be applicable to the rights offering since Rule 801 contemplates an exempt public offering of the rights and the underlying securities.

127. *See* SEC Release No. 33-7516 (March 23, 1998), discussed above under "Directed Selling Efforts."

Global Offerings by Foreign Corporations

Some challenging problems arise in connection with international offerings by foreign issuers where a portion of the shares are to be sold in the United States. These problems are particularly acute where the offering arises out of a foreign privatization and it becomes necessary to coordinate the mechanics of the home country offering, the international offering (outside the United States) and the U.S. offering. In this type of transaction, it is often necessary to accommodate certain aspects of the U.S. federal securities laws to offering practices customary outside the United States.

- *1933 Act Registration*

A decision that must be made by a foreign issuer and its legal advisors is the number of shares to be registered under the 1933 Act. Should the issuer register only those shares to be purchased by the U.S. underwriting syndicate, should a certain number of additional shares be registered to provide for the possibility of additional shares flowing into the United States or should the entire issue be registered?

In 1977, Her Majesty's government sold a large block of ordinary shares of The British Petroleum Company Limited (BP) by means of two underwritten offerings. The principal market for the shares was in London, although ADRs were also traded on the NYSE. On June 14, 1977, the government announced a share offering to the public in the United Kingdom and elsewhere outside North America, but reserved the right to withdraw some of the shares for an offering in the United States and Canada. Purchasers were required to represent that they were not North American persons. Several days after the termination of this offering, 13,357,000 ADSs representing an equal number of ordinary shares were offered in the United States and Canada under a prospectus dated June 27, 1977. These represented shares withdrawn from the offering outside of North America. In addition to the shares represented by ADRs, 13,339,000 of the 53,428,591 shares sold outside of North America were covered by the registration statement.

In 1979, there was a public offering of an even larger block of BP ordinary shares. This time, the offering was made only in the United Kingdom, although nationals and residents of other countries were not precluded from purchasing so long as they met certain conditions, including payment in pounds sterling. Although (unlike the sale in 1977) there was to be no offering in the United States, the shares were registered under the 1933 Act in view of the close relationship between the United Kingdom and the U.S. markets for the BP shares. This was a time when the SEC was less accommodating to foreign issuers than it is today, and one can imagine the discussions with the SEC's staff that led to the decision to register under the 1933 Act even though there was to be no U.S. distribution.

In the massive BP offering that took place in October 1987, the registration statement covered 670 million ordinary shares, 610.8 million shares representing those to be sold to underwriters for resale under ADRs to purchasers in the United States and Canada and an additional number of shares that, according to the facing sheet of the Form F-3, had been offered and sold outside the United States but that might be resold from time to time in the United States during the distribution. Here the decision was made to register some additional shares to cover sales in the United States in the after-market. The cost of registering the entire offering would have been prohibitive. As it was, the filing fee was $807,153.

The pattern has developed—at least where there is no preexisting substantial U.S. interest in the foreign shares and the primary market is expected to be abroad—of registering with the SEC the number of shares to be offered and sold in the United States plus an additional 10% to 15% of such shares. The primary purpose of registering shares in excess of those expected to be sold in the United States is to cover transfers from the international underwriters to the U.S. underwriters to meet varying levels of demand in different markets.[128] During

---

128. These transfers take place pursuant to marketing agreements that divide the offering into markets for which particular syndicates are responsible. The agreements also permit the global coordinator of the offering to move shares from one syndicate to another and generally to make determinations relating to the offering that are commonly performed by a book-running managing underwriter in the United States.

the first 40 days following the commencement of the offering, registration of the excess shares is also deemed (albeit by means of a considerable leap of faith) to cover for purposes of Section 4(3)(A) of the 1933 Act the resale of shares in the United States by non-U.S. dealers who purchase shares from non-U.S. investors in a foreign secondary market.

- *Form and Delivery of Prospectus*

Where all or part of a global offering is registered under the 1933 Act, the question arises whether the form or forms of prospectus covering sales outside the United States must be filed as part of the U.S. registration statement. Also, must a prospectus meeting the requirements of the 1933 Act be delivered to foreign purchasers?

Section 5(b)(1) of the 1933 Act could be read as requiring that if a registration statement is filed with respect to a security, the prospectus covering that security, wherever used, must meet the requirements of Section 10(a).

This issue arose in 1973 in connection with an offering exclusively to Japanese investors of shares of Fundamerica of Japan, Inc., a U.S. mutual fund organized to invest in U.S. securities. In discussions with the SEC staff, it was agreed that the fund need not register shares to be offered exclusively in Japan where resales to U.S. persons were prohibited. However, the Japanese Ministry of Finance insisted on registration under the 1933 Act as well as under the comparable Japanese statute.

This resulted in an apparent conflict between the U.S. requirement that a prospectus covering registered securities must comply with Section 10(a) of the 1933 Act and the Japanese requirement that only the statutory Japanese prospectus could be used in that country. To allow the offering to proceed, the SEC adopted Rule 434C,[129] which provided, in effect, that a prospectus required by the Japanese laws covering securities that are also registered under the 1933 Act is deemed to meet the requirements of Section 10(a) when the offering in Japan is to persons who are not nationals or residents of the United States. This rule was subsequently rescinded by the SEC as "unnecessary

---

129. SEC Release No. 33-5365 (February 7, 1973).

or obsolete" as part of a general overhaul of its regulations.[130] Apparently, no one then on the staff could figure out what this rule was all about and what purpose it served.

The technique is often used of including more than one form of prospectus in the registration statement. This is usually accomplished by including the form of cover page to be used abroad (e.g., with the names of the international syndicate managers in lieu of the U.S. managing underwriters) and other relevant portions of the international prospectus (e.g., the tax section and the section describing the international underwriters).

Even if a prospectus meets or is deemed to meet the requirements of the 1933 Act, is it necessary—as a matter of U.S. law—to deliver the prospectus to a foreign investor with or before the confirmation of sale? As a theoretical matter, the position could be taken that shares offered abroad are registered only for the purpose of sale into the United States and that, consistent with Regulation S, the SEC is not interested in extending the prospectus delivery requirements of Section 5 to transactions outside of the United States. As a practical matter, however, the answer is likely to be that U.S. underwriters will include a copy of the relevant prospectus when they confirm sales to non-U.S. buyers, while non-U.S. underwriters will comply only with the prospectus delivery requirements (if any) imposed by their home country and the home country of the buyer.

- *Section 11 Liability*

If a non-U.S. purchaser can identify his or her purchased shares as having been registered under the 1933 Act, does it follow that the non-U.S. purchaser has Section 11 remedies against the non-U.S. issuer, the U.S. and non-U.S. underwriters and all other persons named in Section 11? It can be argued that the provision of Section 11 that limits an underwriter's liability to the "total price at which the securities underwritten by him and distributed to the public were offered to the public" should be

---

130. SEC Release No. 33-6383 (March 3, 1982).

construed to refer to the public in the United States.[131] If the argument holds in this context, as it should, persons named in Section 11 as potential defendants should have no liability under that section to non-U.S. purchasers. The argument is weaker for avoiding liability under Section 12(a)(2), but the fact that such liability is limited to the "seller" should mean that the recourse of non-U.S. investors under that section will be limited to the foreign underwriters or dealers from whom they purchased.

- *Underwriting Practices*

Differences between underwriting practices in a foreign country and those in the United States can give rise to substantial difficulties as evidenced by the problems that arose in connection with the October 1987 global offering of BP shares by Her Majesty's government. Prior to the offering, the government owned approximately 31.5% of the outstanding BP shares, with the balance held by members of the public. The shares were traded in London in the form of ordinary shares and ADSs. In addition, ADSs were listed and traded on the NYSE in the form of ADRs. The shares also were traded on the Tokyo Stock Exchange. As part of its continuing program of privatization, Her Majesty's government determined to sell its remaining BP shares. At the same time, BP proposed to sell additional shares to the government, which would be included with its own holdings as part of the offering.

The worldwide combined offering had a value of approximately $13 billion. The plan was for the major portion of the shares to be sold to retail subscribers and eligible BP employees in the United Kingdom at a price representing a discount from the market price. Existing holders of BP shares and ADSs were also to be offered the opportunity to subscribe in the offering on a priority basis. A "pathfinder" prospectus was released in the United Kingdom on September 25, 1987, and registration statements were filed with the SEC on the same date. The

---

131. J. R. Stevenson & W. J. Williams, Jr., "United States Legal Aspects of International Securities Transactions," *A Lawyer's Guide to International Business Transactions*, Part III, Folio 5, 51 (2d ed. 1980).

remainder of the combined offering, designated the international offer, was to be made to institutions in the United Kingdom and through syndicates of underwriters in the United States, Canada, Japan and continental Europe.

The key dates in any equity offering in the United Kingdom are "impact day," "application day" and "allocation day." In the case of the retail offering of BP shares in the United Kingdom, impact day was October 15, 1987. At that time, the offering price was fixed and the retail offer commenced. Applications in the retail offering, together with payment, were required to be submitted by application day, which was October 28, 1987. The basis of the allocation was to be announced on October 30, 1987. The stockholder offer was to follow a slightly different schedule. Pursuant to that offer, holders of BP shares on September 30, 1987, and holders of ADSs on October 14, 1987, were to be offered the opportunity to subscribe at the same price as that fixed for the retail offer.

The combined offering was underwritten on impact day. At that time, the United Kingdom underwriters entered into a standby underwriting commitment covering the shares proposed to be sold in the retail offer, those to be sold to United Kingdom institutions, and those covered by the stockholder offer outside the United States, Canada and Japan. The international underwriters—including the U.S. underwriters, Goldman, Sachs & Co., Morgan Stanley & Co. Incorporated, Salomon Brothers Inc. and Shearson Lehman Brothers Inc.—entered into an underwriting agreement at the same time. This differed from the procedure followed in the 1977 BP offering where the U.S. underwriters did not commit until allocation day. In the case of the 1987 offering, the registration statement covering the shares to be purchased by the U.S. underwriters was not to become effective until after allocation day, almost two weeks after the underwriting agreement was signed.

The commitment was made on the basis of the price in pounds sterling with payment to be made in dollars, on the basis of the exchange rate on the date of closing. The underwriters were thus protected against exchange rate fluctuation. They were not protected, however, against a turn in the stock market. Their commitment was firm, and they were required to close even if

INTERNATIONAL FINANCINGS

the registration statement had not yet become effective. Pursuant to the underwriting agreement, the four U.S. underwriters had the authority to form a broad syndicate of underwriters in the United States, and these underwriters were to be substituted and take up a portion of the commitments of the four U.S. underwriters who signed the underwriting agreement.

Between the execution of the underwriting agreement and the date that the registration statement was to be declared effective, share prices in London and in other world markets fell dramatically, reaching a climax in the October 19 crash. Between the close of business on October 14, 1987, when the fixed price was established at 3.30 pounds sterling per share, a 6% discount from the closing price, the price of the BP shares in London fell from 3.52 pounds to 2.62 pounds at the close of business on October 29, 1987. During the same period, the price of an ADS on the NYSE fell from 69-3/4 to 55-3/4. The underwriters were faced with a disaster. There was no market out in the underwriting agreement, and there was no way that the U.S. underwriters would be able to form a syndicate of substitute underwriters to share the loss.

As reported in *The New York Times* on October 21, there was speculation in London that the BP offering might be withdrawn, but that morning the chancellor of the exchequer made a public statement that the deal would go forward on schedule, even though it was expected to result in losses to the underwriters of as much as 500 million pounds. On October 26, representatives of the underwriters met with government officials to urge them to postpone the sale. But Prime Minister Margaret Thatcher held firm, and the deal went forward. The U.S. underwriters proceeded to offer the shares pursuant to a prospectus dated October 30, 1987. The public offering price was substantially less than the price paid by them for the ADSs.

As a concession, on October 29, 1987, the chancellor of the exchequer announced that the Bank of England would make an offer to purchase installment payment shares at 70 pence per share. The offer was made on November 6, 1987, and was to extend at least until December 11, 1987. This would serve to limit the potential losses of the purchasers of the BP shares and ADSs and would help to provide an orderly after-market. The

SEC accommodated the offer by granting exemptions under the Williams Act and under Rules 10b-6 and 10b-7.

- *Foreign Publicity*

Under the 1933 Act, publicity in advance of or during a distribution of securities is strictly limited. A television program advertising a securities offering or a newspaper advertisement not meeting the requirements of Rule 134 would be viewed as attempts to condition the market and therefore as illegal prospectuses. Similarly, a news item inspired by the issuer may result in an illegal prospectus. This is generally not the case abroad. Articles in the press with respect to an issuer and a proposed offering of its securities frequently appear in London and in other markets, often inspired by press releases emanating from the issuer. Officers of foreign companies, unless properly advised, may have no qualms about talking to the press in anticipation of a securities offering.

These activities during a global offering, a portion of which is to be made in the United States, have been a matter of some concern to the staff of the SEC. In particular, foreign privatizations tend to be accompanied by extraordinary advertising campaigns in the home country, and some of this publicity inevitably finds its way into the United States where it may "condition the market." In addition, foreign publicity relating to tender offers may raise questions under the Williams Act.

Notwithstanding the sometimes aggressive publicity efforts associated with privatizations and related global offerings, many non-U.S. issuers persuaded themselves that they should adopt "self-help" measures to alleviate the SEC's perceived concern even with relatively routine publicity. Accordingly, these issuers would regularly exclude journalists for publications with a significant U.S. circulation (whether the publications were U.S.-based or foreign-based) from their press conferences, from meetings with issuer representatives and from press materials released offshore where a current or proposed securities offering or tender offer was to be discussed.

As discussed above under "Foreign Press-Related Activity," the SEC in 1997 adopted a new Rule 135e that permits a foreign issuer (or a selling securityholder or a representative) to provide "journalists" with "access" to information that discusses a present or proposed securities offering if the information is provided at an offshore press conference, offshore meetings or written press-related materials released outside the United States. The SEC staff has considerably undermined Rule 135e's usefulness by insisting on several occasions that an issuer include in its U.S. prospectus material information that is discussed or released abroad in reliance on the rule.

- *Foreign Research*

The distribution of research in connection with a securities offering is strictly controlled in the United States, but this is not the case in most of the rest of the world. In fact, it is quite common for non-U.S. underwriters to publish research reports prior to or even during a public offering. There is nothing wrong with "pre-deal" research from the standpoint of the U.S. securities laws so long as the research material can be prevented from being delivered into the United States. Assurances on this point are hard to come by, however, and U.S. underwriters understandably worry that foreign pre-deal research may leak into the United States. In that case, of course, the SEC may delay an offering or require the information to be included in the U.S. prospectus. The SEC staff has even required material information (e.g., earnings projections) to be included in the prospectus where the pre-deal research was accessible from the United States by means of an Internet website, even one in a language other than English.

U.S. underwriters are also concerned about the content of such research material, both from a theoretical point of view (false or misleading statements in the research material might encourage foreign investors to file lawsuits in U.S. courts) or a practical point of view (foreign underwriters may be achieving an unfair competitive advantage in making sales based on the research material).

Rules 138 and 139 under the 1933 Act provide significant relief for persons who wish to disseminate research reports on U.S. issuers that are involved in registered public offerings. In 1994 and 1995, the SEC amended both rules to extend their benefits to research on foreign private issuers without regard to their reporting history under the 1934 Act so long as their securities had traded for a period of at least 12 months on a "designated offshore securities market" as defined in Regulation S.[132]

The 1994 and 1995 amendments to Rules 138 and 139 did not benefit providers of research on privatization candidates, who by definition did not meet the 12-month seasoning requirement. On the other hand, the main function of research—to provide continuous information to investors about securities that are traded in the market—is by definition inapplicable to privatization candidates. The SEC might not have reacted favorably to a suggestion that it permit research on a privatization candidate prior to or during an initial public offering, but a 1996 no-action request on behalf of Deutsche Telekom AG[133] presented the question in a much more favorable context: that of research on an entire industry.

DTAG's letter pointed out that U.S. investors had a legitimate interest in receiving research on the global telecommunications industry and that such research would be incomplete unless it discussed DTAG. The letter proposed guidelines under which any prospective underwriter that had an established history of covering the telecommunications or a related industry could distribute research in the ordinary course of business to persons to whom such research had customarily been provided. The research would have to focus generally on the industry or specifically on one or more companies competing with or engaged in business ventures with DTAG and would have to avoid giving DTAG any materially greater space or prominence. The research would have to avoid detailed financial or business information relating to DTAG, financial projections (with certain exceptions), nonpublic information and any specific discussion of the proposed offering.

The SEC staff responded that it would not recommend enforcement action if prospective underwriters and other participating broker-dealers were to publish industry reports in conformity with the stated guidelines.

---

132. SEC Releases No. 33-7053 (April 19, 1994) and 33-7132 (February 1, 1995). On "designated offshore securities markets," *see supra* note 26.

133. SEC No-action Letter, *Deutsche Telekom AG* (June 14, 1996).

Rule 135e does not extend to analysts' reports. The significance of the rule, however, is probably less in its actual coverage than in its representing for all practical purposes an acknowledgment by the SEC that the evolution of communications technology and the blurring of geographic boundaries has progressed to the point where regulation of communications as "offers" under the federal securities laws is simply no longer feasible. And if this is true for international communications, it is undoubtedly also true for purely domestic communications such as corporate websites, broker-dealer research, electronic databases and other methods of disseminating information to the market place. The best solution may be a significant deregulation of "offers" in general.

- *Regulation M*

It will generally be the case, where a non-U.S. issuer is making a public offering in the United States, either that the issuer's securities already have an established trading market in the issuer's home country or that such a market rapidly develops following the commencement of the offering. The SEC staff has traditionally taken the position that its antimanipulation rules apply to trading activity *anywhere in the world* if a distribution is taking place in the United States. This position means, of course, that SEC rules such as Rule 101 could apply to bids and offers for the issuer's securities by distribution participants (or their affiliates) in the normal course of their business in the issuer's home country. SEC rules such as Rule 104 could also apply to stabilizing activity or to attempts (such as by means of research reports) to "induce" someone to purchase the issuer's securities, whether or not such activity was permitted in the home country. These rules are discussed in Chapter 4.

- *Installment Payment Offerings*

Securities sold in global offerings, particularly in connection with privatizations, often provide for installment payments by the purchasers of the securities. As discussed in Chapter 3, Section 11(d)(1) of the 1934 Act prohibits a broker-dealer from extending or arranging for the extension of credit "on" securities that are part of a "new issue" in the "distribution" of which the broker-dealer was a participant. By selling installment payment securities, a U.S. underwriter might be viewed as arranging an extension of credit in violation of this prohibition. Prior to the Federal Reserve Board's dramatic curtailing in 1996 of the corresponding prohibition on "arranging" activities in Regulation T, the SEC was willing to take a no-action position under Section 11(d)(1) in situations where the Federal Reserve Board would not raise objections under Regulation T.[134]

The SEC staff has issued a large number of no-action letters (and exemptive orders since the SEC received exemptive authority in the Improvement Act in 1996) permitting installment payment arrangements under specified circumstances.[135] The requesting letters appear to assume that installment receipts are "new issues" whether or not the underlying securities should be so regarded and also that Rule 144A sales are "distributions" for Section 11(d)(1) purposes. As discussed in Chapter 7, the purposes of Section 11(d)(1) make it improbable that it applies to sales to QIBs.

In some cases, the seller of the installment receipts may have a Regulation U problem if the installment receipts or the underlying shares are "margin stock" under Regulation U. In the past, the Federal Reserve Board has been willing to entertain requests for relief, particularly where the transaction involves a privatization and the portion of the offering sold in the United States is relatively small.

Sales in the United States by Foreign Governments and Their Political Subdivisions

Foreign governments and their political subdivisions frequently borrow in the U.S. capital markets through the issuance of debt securities. Although securities issued or guaranteed by

---

134. SEC No-action Letter, *British Petroleum Company p.l.c.* (October 1, 1987); SEC No-action Letter, *Morgan Stanley & Co. Inc.* (November 26, 1984) (British Telecommunications plc offering).

135. C. F. Rechlin, *Securities Credit Regulation* §8:4 n.3 (2d ed. 2003).

the United States and its instrumentalities are exempt from the registration requirements of the 1933 Act, a similar exemption is not afforded to securities issued or guaranteed by foreign governments.[136] At or about the time that the 1933 Act was adopted, American investors held more than $1.5 billion dollars of defaulted foreign government bonds,[137] and Congress could hardly have been expected to provide an exemption for these securities from the registration requirements of the new 1933 Act.

- *1933 Act Registration*

Section 7 of the 1933 Act requires any "foreign government, or political sub-division thereof" registering securities under the 1933 Act to follow the disclosure requirements of Schedule B to the 1933 Act. The SEC has never adopted registration forms for these issuers comparable to those it has adopted for private issuers, and non-U.S. governmental issuers therefore continue to be guided by the statutory disclosure requirements of Schedule B as well as by SEC review policy and the self-enforcing policing mechanisms of the securities markets.

The term "political subdivision" is not defined in the 1933 Act, and the SEC has not developed express criteria for determining whether or not a particular issuer is a "political subdivision" for purposes of Schedule B. The SEC has, however, issued a number of no-action letters and provided informal advice on Schedule B eligibility. These letters and informal

---

136. Section 304(a)(6) of the Trust Indenture Act of 1939 exempts from the provisions of that statute "any note, bond, debenture, or evidence of indebtedness issued or guaranteed by a foreign government or by a subdivision, department, municipality, agency, or instrumentality thereof."

137. According to a key Senate report, about $4.9 billion of foreign government securities were outstanding as of March 1, 1934, of which about $1.5 billion were in default. These securities included national governments, states, provinces, departments and municipalities. S. Rep. 1455 pursuant to S. Res. 84 (72d Cong.) and S. Res. 56 and S. Res. 97 (73d Cong.) (June 6, 1934), at 91.

advice suggest the following:

- First, the SEC is more likely to allow a non-U.S. issuer to file a Schedule B registration statement if the issuer is formed by governmental action for the purpose of performing governmental functions delegated to it, or if the issuer is formed pursuant to an agreement among countries to serve their joint interests. In some cases, however, the SEC may require that the registration statement also be signed by the government or governments for which the issuer is performing such functions.

- Second, the SEC has issued favorable letters only to issuers that in effect have the credit support of a government, either by operation of law or in the form of an unconditional guarantee or pursuant to call provisions applicable to subscribed but unpaid capital. In one case, this included back-to-back lending arrangements pursuant to which the government undertook to pay principal and interest on the same terms as the issuer's borrowing. In the case of an express guarantee, of course, the guarantee will have to be registered as a separate security, and the government will have to sign the registration statement.

- Third, each of the issuers in the favorable no-action letters had legal immunities and exemptions commonly associated with governmental bodies, agencies and instrumentalities.

Whether or not an issuer with an ambiguous status is entitled to follow Schedule B is usually discussed with the SEC in a pre-filing conference. At such a conference, the issuer should be prepared to provide the SEC with detailed information about the issuer and its relationship to a government.

Schedule B requires the disclosure of specified information about the issuer (including a governmental guarantor, if applicable), the offering and the underwriters. The required information includes the use of proceeds, the amount and nature of funded debt, any defaults on external debt within the past 20 years, receipts and expenditures, legal matters and information relating to the offering. Rules 490 through 493 modify certain Schedule B requirements applicable to outstanding debt, underwriting arrangements and legal matters.

The fact that Schedule B specifies only minimal disclosure does not mean that no other disclosure is required. Depending on the size and reputation of the country, its credit rating and how often it has come to the capital markets, underwriters and investors (and possibly the SEC staff) may expect substantial additional disclosure, including information regarding the country's geography, population and political system, economy, monetary system, foreign trade and balance of payments, foreign exchange, public finance, public debt and other relevant matters.

Take, for example, a recent registration statement covering debt securities to be publicly offered in the United States by the People's Republic of China. The base prospectus provided information on China's geography, population, governmental structure, international relations and membership in international organizations. It then described the country's economy, including economic objectives, major economic indicators, employment and wages, environment, foreign investment and securities markets. The prospectus discussed China's foreign trade and balance of payments, including its membership in the World Trade Organization. It provided information on the country's balance of payments and official international reserves. The prospectus described the country's public finances, including the budget process, revenues and expenditures (on-budget and off-budget) and plans for fiscal and tax reform. It included a section on China's legal system, including the role of the courts, access to the courts by foreign persons and the enforceability of foreign judgments and arbitration awards. As contemplated by Schedule B, the prospectus described China's internal and external public debt.

An issuer that qualifies for Schedule B but is not a government or political subdivision will provide additional information concerning its business, financial condition and results of operations. Although Schedule B does not require audited financial statements, the SEC usually requires such a Schedule B issuer to include in the registration statement any financial statements that it otherwise publishes. Reconciliation to U.S. GAAP is not required, but the SEC may require such explanation of the financial statements as it believes may be appropriate for U.S. investors.

- *Consent to Service and Sovereign Immunity*

It is customary for a foreign governmental issuer to appoint an agent in the United States on whom process may be served in an action based on the issuer's securities; however, this appointment does not usually extend to actions brought against the issuer under the securities laws. It is also customary for a foreign governmental issuer to waive its sovereign immunity, but again not with respect to alleged securities law violations.

The waiver of sovereign immunity in respect of the foreign governmental issuer's securities may not be strictly necessary. The Foreign Sovereign Immunities Act of 1976 (FSIA)[138] provides that a foreign government is not immune from the jurisdiction of U.S. courts in an action based on "a commercial activity carried on in the United States by the foreign state; or upon an act performed in the United States in connection with a commercial activity of the foreign state elsewhere; or upon an act outside the territory of the United States in connection with a commercial activity of the foreign state elsewhere and that act causes a direct effect in the United States." The FSIA defines "commercial activity" by reference to "the nature of the course of conduct or particular transaction or act, rather than by reference to its purpose," and the U.S. Supreme Court held in 1992 that a foreign state's issuance of debt obligations was "commercial activity" for purposes of enforcement under the FSIA of a breach-of-contract claim.[139] In the same case, the Court also

---

138. 28 U.S.C. §1605(a)(2) (2000).

139. *Republic of Argentina v. Weltover, Inc.*, 504 U.S. 607, 112 S. Ct. 2160 (1992).

held that a unilateral rescheduling of debt obligations payable in New York was sufficient to cause a "direct effect" in the United States.

There is no direct authority as to whether a foreign governmental issuer may claim sovereign immunity with respect to the federal securities laws. If the issuance of debt securities in the U.S. markets is "commercial activity" under the FSIA for purposes of a breach-of-contract action, it is difficult to see why the conclusion should be any different where the claim is based on, for example, insufficient disclosure. It is also possible that a foreign governmental issuer's registration of its securities under the 1933 Act might be held to constitute an implied waiver of any such immunity.

The following excerpt from a recent People's Republic of China base prospectus relates to jurisdictional matters:

> China is a foreign sovereign state. Consequently, it may be difficult for you to obtain or realize upon judgments of courts in the United States against China. China will irrevocably submit to the jurisdiction of any state or federal court in the Borough of Manhattan, The City of New York, in any suit, action or proceeding arising out of or based on the debt securities and/or warrants or the fiscal agency agreement brought by any holder (other than any action arising out of or based on United States federal or state securities laws). China has designated Bank of China New York Branch as its authorized agent to receive processes in any suit, action or proceeding arising out of the debt securities and/or warrants or the fiscal agency agreement. In addition, China will irrevocably waive, to the fullest extent permitted by law, any immunity, including foreign sovereign immunity, from jurisdiction to which it may otherwise be entitled in any action arising out of or based on these securities (other than any action arising out of or based on United States federal or state securities laws) brought in any state or federal court in the Borough of Manhattan, The City of New York, or in any competent court in China. China has not waived, and will not waive, its sovereign immunity with respect

to the assets necessary for the proper functioning of China as a sovereign power, including military assets, and real property and buildings and the contents thereof owned by the Ministry of Foreign Affairs and located outside China. Because China has not waived its sovereign immunity in connection with any action arising out of or based on United States federal or state securities laws, it will not be possible to obtain a United States judgment against China based on such laws unless a court were to determine that China is not entitled under the Foreign Sovereign Immunities Act of 1976 to sovereign immunity with respect to such an action. Furthermore, under the Foreign Sovereign Immunities Act of 1976, execution upon any property of China in the United States to enforce a judgment is limited to an execution upon property used for the commercial activity on which the claim is based, and China has not waived any immunity which may otherwise be available to it with respect to the execution of any judgment. China has been advised by its PRC counsel, the Law Department of the Ministry of Finance, that there is doubt as to the enforceability in China of any actions to enforce judgments of United States courts arising out of or based on the debt securities and/or warrants, including judgments arising out of or based on the civil liability provisions of United States federal or state securities laws, primarily because there is no treaty or other arrangement or basis for reciprocal enforcement of judgments between China and the United States. China has also been advised by its PRC counsel that there is doubt as to the enforceability in original actions brought in PRC courts of the civil liability provisions of United States federal or state securities laws. See "Description of Debt Securities—Governing Law and Consent to Service."

As noted in Chapter 8, the SEC has made the benefits of shelf registration available to "seasoned" foreign governmental entities.

- *1934 Act Registration and Reporting*

Section 15(d) of the 1934 Act, which applies the continuous reporting requirements to issuers that have sold securities under a registration statement, expressly excludes foreign governments and political subdivisions from its coverage. As governments do not issue equity securities—at least not so far—they will not be caught up by Section 12(g). A foreign government will, therefore, become subject to the registration and reporting requirements of the 1934 Act only if it voluntarily lists its debt securities on a national securities exchange or has them traded on NASDAQ. In that event, it would file a registration statement on Form 18 in connection with its listing application. Thereafter, it would file annually on Form 18-K. In the case of a sovereign issuer, these forms require disclosure regarding gold reserves, import and export information, and the balance of international payments for the most recent fiscal year. (As discussed in Chapter 8, a foreign governmental issuer may also decide voluntarily to file reports in order to facilitate shelf registration.)

Chapter 10

COMMERCIAL PAPER

"Commercial paper" generally refers to a short-term unsecured financing instrument that is used by more than 1,700 U.S. financial and non-financial companies as a flexible and lower-cost alternative to bank borrowing. Most paper is issued in reliance on the Section 3(a)(3) exemption in the 1933 Act.

Privately placed commercial paper (often referred to as "restricted" or "Section 4(2) paper"), including "extendible commercial paper," is discussed in Chapter 7. Asset-backed commercial paper is a relatively new instrument that is discussed in Chapter 14.

Buyers of commercial paper are almost exclusively institutional investors who are interested in a short-term and high-quality alternative to one of the other so-called "money market" instruments, namely, U.S. Treasury bills, discount notes of U.S. government agencies, negotiable certificates of deposit and bankers' acceptances. Commercial paper is particularly attractive to money market funds. Other important buyers of commercial paper are bank trust departments, insurance companies, pension funds, corporations and state and local governments.

Beginning in late 2000, after several decades of steady growth, the commercial paper market experienced its sharpest contraction in over 40 years. In particular, the market for non-financial commercial paper plummeted from a peak of $352 billion in August 2000 to an average of $151.5 billion by mid-2003. Part of the decline was no doubt attributable to reduced business demand for short-term financing, a desire on the part of some issuers to reduce dependence on commercial paper as a source of financing and the availability of attractive refinancing opportunities in the long-term debt markets. But investor anxiety about corporate accounting scandals and "headline risk" also played a major role in the market's contraction as evidenced by

- a sharp increase in the amount of asset-backed commercial paper outstanding as compared to unsecured commercial paper;
- several well-publicized situations in which commercial paper issuers were forced to withdraw from the commercial paper market;
- a doubling at the end of 2001 of the five-year average "spread" between the top-rated nonfinancial commercial paper and lower-rated paper; and
- an increase in the rating agencies' downgrades of commercial paper issuers, with the ratio of downgrades to upgrades reaching a 14-year high in 2002 of 11.9:1 for financial and non-financial issuers.[1]

Issuers in the U.S. commercial paper market have traditionally been highly rated borrowers. The role of the rating agencies increased dramatically following the Penn Central default in 1970. Their role further increased as money market funds became major purchasers of commercial paper; these funds are

---

1. Standard & Poor's Global Fixed Income Research, *U.S. Commercial Paper Looks to Improve in 2003* (December 23, 2002); and *U.S. Non-Financial Commercial Paper Levels Off* (May 21, 2003).

subject to the SEC's Rule 2a-7 under the 1940 Act, which restricts their ability to purchase lower-grade commercial paper.

As discussed below, Section 3(a)(3) of the 1933 Act exempts commercial paper with a maturity of up to nine months, but in practice maturities are generally concentrated in the range of from one to 45 days with an average of 30 days.[2]

As discussed in Chapter 7, commercial paper can also be issued on a private placement basis. There is no limit on the maturity of privately placed commercial paper, but maturities of up to 395 days are most common because of rules under the Investment Company Act of 1940 that limit the ability of money market funds to purchase paper with longer maturities than 397 days.

Commercial paper is commonly sold at a discount from the face or principal amount of the transaction, with the discount representing an interest component to be paid to the investor at maturity, but interest-bearing paper is being offered in increasing amounts. Traditionally, commercial paper took the form of a short-term negotiable promissory note issued in bearer form. Book-entry commercial paper was introduced by DTC in 1990 and quickly came to dominate the market.

The U.S. commercial paper market is primarily a U.S. dollar market, but programs have been established that are denominated in other currencies.

Characteristics of the Market

A money market had become established in New York City by the middle of the 19th century, but the commercial paper market really did not come into its own until the 1960s when monetary restraints restricted the availability and increased the cost of bank financing, thus forcing issuers to find alternative sources of short-term funds.

Direct issuers, as opposed to those that sell through dealers, accounted for roughly 30% of the market in mid-1996, as

---

2. Federal Reserve Release, *About Commercial Paper and Rate Calculations*, available at www.federalreserve.gov/releases/cp/about.htm.

measured by the amount of commercial paper outstanding. There are approximately 45 direct issuers that are, for the most part, large financial companies such as General Electric Capital Corporation. These issuers have commercial paper programs of sufficient size to justify the cost of establishing their own placement facilities. The remaining 70% represents the dealer market, where commercial paper is sold through dealers.

The dealer market consists principally of a few major players and a larger number of smaller investment and commercial banks. It is highly competitive. At one time, some dealers (notably Goldman, Sachs & Co.) insisted that an issuing client sell its paper exclusively through them. Other dealers, of course, tried to persuade issuers that their interests were better served by having two or more dealers compete on the basis of performance. Goldman Sachs changed its policy in late 1987, and multiple dealerships are now the rule.

High interest rates and volatility in the long-term bond market during the 1980s contributed to the growth of commercial paper as a financing alternative. A chief financial officer who is not willing to issue long-term debt securities at a fixed rate has the option of issuing floating rate obligations (or one of the more innovative financial instruments that have been developed in recent years) or of entering the commercial paper market. A commercial paper program can have the same economic effect as a long-term floating rate obligation. Although commercial paper notes have short maturities, in the typical program new notes are issued to replace maturing notes on a continuous basis. Thus, an issuer can maintain a fixed amount of paper outstanding for as long as it considers advisable and market conditions permit. If the market remains stable and the issuer's credit rating remains strong, the size of its commercial paper program can be increased or decreased at will (subject to the "current transactions" requirement discussed below).

Historically, commercial paper programs have had a cost advantage over bank borrowings. Another advantage is that loan covenants are not required in the establishment of a commercial paper program. There are also less tangible factors at work in an issuer's decision to tap the commercial paper market. For one thing, it is clearly advantageous to have the alternate source of funding that commercial paper represents. For another, a commercial paper program enables an issuer to broaden its investor base and to cultivate relationships with a wide range of institutional investors.

The market for commercial paper is largely institutional. The principal investors are money market funds, bank trust departments, insurance companies, foreign central banks, pension funds and other managed accounts, and corporate treasury departments. The proliferation of money market funds has been a significant factor in the growth of the commercial paper market. There are an estimated 10,000 buyers of commercial paper, with the most active 20% of accounts representing about 80% of the demand.

Maturities can be tailored to meet investor needs so that, for example, if an investor has $50 million that it wishes to invest for 23 days, it should be able to find one or more dealers that act for one or more issuers willing to sell 23-day paper. Conversely, an issuer that needs $50 million for 23 days can ordinarily obtain these funds by calling its dealers during the morning of the day on which it needs the funds. (Unlike bank borrowing facilities, commercial paper programs do not usually require advance notification.)

Credit Quality and the "Orderly Exit"

Investors in commercial paper rely heavily on ratings assigned by Moody's Investors Service, Standard & Poor's Corporation and Fitch Ratings Ltd.[3] Most commercial paper investors are interested in a high degree of safety of principal and have a very low tolerance for any type of risk. S&P reported in late 2002 that nearly 95% of the commercial paper rated by it was in the top or "A-1" category.[4]

In the past, those issuers that could not obtain a sufficiently high "stand-alone" rating were able to enhance the credit of their

---

3. Moody's highest commercial paper rating is P-1; Standard & Poor's is A-1, and Fitch's is F-1.

4. Standard & Poor's Global Fixed Income Research, *U.S. Commercial Paper Looks to Improve in 2003* (December 23, 2002), at 4.

paper with a bank letter of credit (less often, an insurance company surety bond was used for this purpose). The cost of credit enhancement has increased in recent years, and this technique has become less attractive.

Defaults on commercial paper have been rare in recent years, thanks in large part to the market's development of an "orderly exit" mechanism for weakening credits. As explained by Moody's, "a weakening of an issuer's credit quality is typically accompanied by a refusal by investors to roll over maturing CP, thus forcing the issuer from the market." A downgrade or "watch list" designation will accelerate the process: the SEC reported in 2003 on concerns that a "ratings cliff" existed in the commercial paper market, "such that a slight downgrade of an issuer's commercial paper rating can dramatically restrict its access to the U.S. money markets."[5] One reason for the "ratings cliff" may be that in the case of money market funds, who in the aggregate are major investors in commercial paper, SEC rules limit the amount of lower-rated commercial paper that they can carry. Also, the board of directors of a money market fund is required under Rule 2a-7(c)(5)(i) under the Investment Company Act of 1940 to reassess promptly whether a downgraded portfolio security "continues to present minimal credit risks." The reassessment is not required if the security is sold (or matures) within five business days of the downgrading.

As noted by Moody's, "the process that forces an issuer out of the CP market begins long before access to alternative forms of liquidity, such as bank lines, are denied." Issuers in this position must replace the maturing commercial paper with alternative and presumably less convenient and more expensive forms of financing that are more consistent with their declining fortunes.[6]

Most issuers maintain unused bank lines in an amount equal to their outstanding paper (subject to seasonal fluctuations) in order to demonstrate to the market and the rating agencies their ability to liquidate their commercial paper obligations should

---

5. SEC Release No. 33-8236, *Concept Release: Rating Agencies and the Use of Credit Ratings Under the Federal Securities Laws* (June 4, 2003).

6. Moody's Investors Service, *Commercial Paper Defaults and Rating Transitions, 1972–2000* (October 2000) at 17.

market conditions prevent refinancing through the issuance of new notes. Recently, Moody's has been publishing Liquidity Risk Assessments for major issuers of commercial paper. These describe and analyze the quality of a commercial paper issuer's liquidity position, addressing the question, "How would the issuer be able to cope with an abrupt loss of access to the capital and credit markets as a result of an adverse name-specific event?"[7]

In recent years, investors have become as much concerned about "headline risk" as about credit risk. Adverse news such as an announcement of an SEC investigation into an issuer's accounting, particularly when accompanied by reports of management misconduct, can lead to dealer and buyer resistance to rolling over the issuer's commercial paper or at least to a significant increase in the cost of maintaining the size of the program. In these situations, an issuer may be unwilling or unable to make a comprehensive public disclosure of what is going on. An orderly exit may be advisable under these circumstances since it is easier to bring the bank lenders up to date than to attempt to make full disclosure to the buyers of commercial paper.[8]

Issuers can be relentless in pressuring their dealers to inventory their commercial paper during periods of market stress. Dealers should resist such pressures. On the other hand, issuers are also relentless in pressuring their investment banks to provide a broad range of financing services, including bank lines of credit and sometimes the very lines that back up the issuer's commercial paper. A dealer that has yielded to the pressure to provide such lines may have a conflict of interest when it comes to deciding whether to recommend an orderly exit from the commercial paper market. Even if it makes the right decision, the dealer can expect allegations that it waited longer than it should have because of its reluctance to become the lender of last resort.

---

7. Moody's Investors Service, *Moody's Liquidity Risk Assessments—Q&A* (March 2002). As discussed in Chapters 3 and 5, the SEC has also been emphasizing the role of MD&A in describing the issuer's liquidity position.

8. Disclosures to bank lenders should be covered by the "duty of trust or confidence" exception in Regulation FD.

Dealers' Role

For those issuers that do not wish to administer their own programs, commercial paper dealers provide an important service. The sponsoring dealer provides advice in establishing the program and in dealing with the rating agencies. For an issuer entering the market for the first time, the dealer will seek to create investor interest through discussions between its sales force and representatives of potential buyers, written announcements or memoranda to investors and, in some cases, "road shows" or face-to-face meetings with groups of potential investors.

Commercial paper dealers generally act as principals. They purchase notes from issuers and resell them to investors. They do attempt, however, to line up purchasers in advance and will take into inventory only that amount of paper as is necessary to accommodate the financing needs of their issuer clients. Investors usually hold commercial paper to maturity, but dealers stand ready in practice to provide liquidity to those investors to whom they originally sold the paper. In recent years, both investors and dealers have been more willing to trade in the secondary market.

Dealers are compensated through a small markup (historically 1/8 of 1% per annum, but now often less for larger programs) on the paper they place with investors or, alternatively, by periodically charging a fee to the issuer based on the amount of commercial paper outstanding. Traditionally, dealers have looked on a commercial paper relationship with an issuer as a "door opener" to other investment banking assignments.

Traditionally, dealers in commercial paper performed their role without a formal agreement with the issuer. Dealer agreements have become more common, however, and The Bond Market Association, an industry trade group, has developed model forms of agreement for both Section 3(a)(3) and Section 4(2) programs.[9]

---

9. The model forms of agreement, which were amended in February 2004, are posted on the association's website at www.bondmarkets.com/Market/corporate.shtml#comm. Model forms for guaranteed programs were added in May 2004.

Acting as a commercial paper dealer is not without its risks. See "Liabilities on Default" below.

Mechanics

Transactions in the U.S. commercial paper market usually take place between 8:00 A.M. and 1:00 P.M., New York City time (the normal trading hours for most U.S. commercial paper), and transactions are settled by 3:00 P.M. on the same day. Purchases and payments at maturity are both effected in same day funds.

The mechanics of a commercial paper program are handled by an issuing and paying agent, which is usually a money center bank with a special department established to perform this function. The advent of book-entry commercial paper has largely eliminated the cumbersome and expensive procedures associated for so many years with physical notes.[10] In a book-entry environment, the issuing and paying agent issues and holds in custody for DTC a master note representing all the commercial paper issued or to be issued by the issuer. The amount of commercial paper represented by the master note will fluctuate with entries by the agent on the master note and into DTC's electronic system as new paper is issued and outstanding paper is paid at maturity. All commercial paper issued in book-entry form is tracked by DTC through CUSIP numbers, which are assigned by the CUSIP Service Bureau of Standard & Poor's Rating Services (a division of the McGraw Hill Companies, Inc.). DTC processes the operational aspects of a commercial paper program in accordance with an agreement, or "letter of representations," among the issuer, the issuing and paying agent and DTC.[11]

---

10. Book-entry programs usually allow for the issuance of physical commercial paper in the event of a disruption of the DTC system.

11. DTC and an industry trade group issued a discussion paper in March 2003 recommending improvements in the commercial paper settlement system.

1933 Act Considerations

Registration under the 1933 Act is impracticable in the case of short-term obligations that are being issued, repaid and replaced with new obligations on a continuous basis. The SEC registration fee is based on the offering price of the specific securities to be issued, rather than the maximum dollar amount to be outstanding at any one time, thus making the cost of registration prohibitive for commercial paper. For example, if a $200 million program were established and $200 million of 30-day notes were issued each month over a 24-month period, $4.8 billion of notes would have to be registered with a registration fee of nearly $400,000.[12] Thus, commercial paper is never registered under the 1933 Act but always is issued in reliance on one of the statutory exemptions from registration, usually the Section 3(a)(3) exemption available to most commercial paper.

As discussed in Chapter 7, commercial paper can also be issued in reliance on the Section 4(2) private offering exemption. Where the paper is backed by a letter of credit issued by a U.S. bank or a regulated domestic branch or agency of a foreign bank, it is exempt under Section 3(a)(2), which exempts securities guaranteed by a bank, whether or not it also is exempt under Section 3(a)(3). If commercial paper is exempt under any of these provisions, it also is exempt from the requirements of the Trust Indenture Act of 1939.

- *Section 3(a)(3) Commercial Paper Exemption*

Section 3(a)(3) exempts from the registration and prospectus delivery requirements of Section 5 of the 1933 Act:

> Any note, draft, bill of exchange, or banker's acceptance which arises out of a current transaction or the proceeds of which have been or are to be used for current transactions, and which has a maturity at the time of issuance of not

---

12. The fee would have been nearly $1.5 million before Congress began to reduce the registration fee payable under Section 6(b) of the 1933 Act. The current fee is posted from time to time on the SEC's website at www.sec.gov/info/edgar/feeamt.htm.

exceeding nine months, exclusive of days of grace, or any renewal thereof the maturity of which is likewise limited[.]

• • *SEC Release No. 33-4412.* In construing Section 3(a)(3), it is important to consider SEC Release No. 33-4412 (September 20, 1961), in which the SEC stated:

> The legislative history of the [1933] Act makes clear that Section 3(a)(3) applies only to prime quality negotiable commercial paper of a type not ordinarily purchased by the general public, that is, paper issued to facilitate well-recognized types of current operational business requirements and of a type eligible for discounting by Federal Reserve banks.

Although there is no difficulty in applying the nine-month maturity requirement, since most commercial paper has a maturity of less than 45 days, the SEC stated in this release that "obligations payable on demand or having provision for 'automatic roll over' " would not satisfy the nine-month standard. The fact that it is customary to issue new commercial paper to refinance maturing paper does not create a problem in this context since the roll-over is not automatic but is in the discretion of the issuer and its commercial paper dealer.[13]

• • *The Prime Quality Standard.* With respect to the "prime quality" standard, an investment grade rating from one or more of the recognized rating agencies should be sufficient. If an issuer defaults on its commercial paper, however, a court may well apply hindsight and hold that the obligations could not possibly have been of prime quality.[14] In some cases, the staff

---

13. Compare SEC No-action Letter, *A.G. Becker Paribas Inc.* (July 2, 1984), in which the staff of the SEC refused to approve an arrangement under which an issuer would have the option of issuing "delayed delivery" notes to the dealer at the maturity of the original paper. The staff viewed the arrangement as in effect allowing the issuer to extend the maturity of the original paper.

14. *See* the discussion below under "Liabilities on Default—Section 12(a)(1)."

of the SEC has concurred that the Section 3(a)(3) exemption is available even though the commercial paper is not rated.[15]

• • *Offers to the Public.* It is true that commercial paper is a type of instrument "not ordinarily purchased by the general public," but this does not mean that the paper must be privately offered if the Section 3(a)(3) exemption is to be available. Such a restriction would make Section 3(a)(3) redundant in view of the exemption in Section 4(2) for private offerings generally.[16] Suggestions to the contrary by the SEC have been based on the following quotation in SEC Release No. 33-4412:

> Thus the Senate Report on the Securities Act of 1933 explained the purpose of Section 3(a)(3) as follows:
>
> > Notes, drafts, bills of exchange, and banker's acceptances which are commercial paper and arise out of current commercial, agricultural, or industrial transactions, and which are not intended to be marketed to the public, are exempted. . . . It is not intended under the bill to require the registration of short-term commercial paper which, as is the usual practice, is made to mature in a few months and ordinarily is not advertised for sale to the general public. (S. Rep. No. 47 on S. 875, 73d Cong., 1st Sess. (1933), pp.3–4.)

The ellipses inserted by the SEC in the above-quoted portion of its release reflect the omission of the words "(sec. 2(a))," which referred to a provision in the rejected Senate bill that excluded the following from the definition of the term "security":

> Notes, drafts, bills of exchange, or banker's acceptances which are commercial paper and arise out of current

---

15. E.g., SEC No-action Letter, *Southeast Banking Corp.* (November 21, 1989); SEC No-action Letter, *Lyondell Petrochemical Co.* (July 19, 1989); SEC No-action Letter, *Russell Corp.* (September 22, 1988).

16. 3 Loss & Seligman, *Securities Regulation* 1214 n.195 (rev. 3d ed. 1999).

commercial, agricultural, or industrial transactions or the proceeds of which have been or are to be used for current commercial, agricultural, or industrial purposes *when such paper is not offered or intended to be offered for sale to the public.* (Emphasis added.)

The language of the Senate report, which the SEC stated was applicable to Section 3(a)(3), related not to Section 3(a)(3) in the form adopted, but rather to a different bill that expressly limited the commercial paper exclusion to paper that is not offered to the public. The deletion of this limitation from the 1933 Act as finally adopted indicates a legislative intent to exempt commercial paper meeting the Section 3(a)(3) tests whether or not it is offered to the public.

In an action against Perera Company, Inc., the SEC sought to enjoin the sale of short-term paper on the ground that the Section 3(a)(3) exemption was not available where sales are made to the general public. The defendant was a company engaged in the purchase and sale of foreign currency, and in the course of its business it sold its short-term notes to finance its currency purchases. The notes had maturities of less than nine months, and the SEC did not contend that they were issued to finance other than current transactions. However, the notes were sold in small denominations and were advertised for sale to the general public.

Relying on SEC Release No. 33-4412, the SEC took the position that notes that are sold on the public market do not come within the Section 3(a)(3) exemption, thereby excluding the notes issued by Perera. The defendant contended that, not only did its notes fall within the express language of Section 3(a)(3), but also the only language in SEC Release No. 33-4412 that supported the SEC's position was the above quotation from the Senate report on the bill that never passed. In a procedural decision relating to a protective order sought by the SEC to prevent the taking of the deposition of a staff member instrumental in formulating SEC Release No. 33-4412, the court stated that "the S.E.C. appears suspect in the formulation of the release in issue. . . ."[17]

---

17. *SEC v. Perera Co., Inc.*, 47 F.R.D. 535, 537 (S.D.N.Y. 1969).

Perera was not decided on its merits; rather, the defendant agreed to a settlement without admitting any violations.[18] Perera agreed that it would not sell its notes in denominations of less than $2,500 and that it would not make use of pamphlets, brochures or other written forms of solicitation or advertisements in the offer and sale of its notes, except that order forms could be sent to present and former holders of Perera notes and, in addition, could be enclosed with statements of account or statements of transactions in foreign exchange. It was stipulated that the order forms would state that the notes were not offered pursuant to a registration statement and would be accompanied by Perera's most recent financial statement.

The significance of this settlement is that, although Perera agreed to limit the form of written solicitations that it would use, it was not prevented from continuing to offer to the general public short-term promissory notes in denominations of at least $2,500. If the SEC had been correct in its contention that the Section 3(a)(3) exemption is not available for sales to the public, it could not properly have entered into such a stipulation.

Nevertheless, in deference to the SEC's views on "public" offerings of commercial paper under Section 3(a)(3), commercial paper generally is offered only to institutional investors and substantial individual investors. It usually is issued in minimum denominations of $100,000 or more to ensure that all purchasers are substantial commercial paper investors and thus not members of the general public. The SEC, however, has specifically taken a no-action position with respect to the sale of commercial paper in minimum denominations of $25,000, provided all of the provisions of the exemption are otherwise met.[19]

The SEC staff has taken a no-action position that permitted "limited advertising" of a commercial paper program.[20] General

---

18. [1969–1970 Transfer Binder] Fed. Sec. L. Rep. (CCH) ¶92,764 (S.D.N.Y. August 3, 1970).

19. SEC No-action Letter, *Merrill Lynch, Pierce, Fenner & Smith Inc.* (September 5, 1972). See also SEC No-action Letter, *Southeast Banking Corp* (November 21, 1989); SEC No-action Letter, *Hughes Supply, Inc.* (October 4, 1988).

20. SEC No-action Letter, *General Electric Capital Corp.* (July 13, 1994).

Electric Capital Corporation (GECC), then and now the largest direct issuer of commercial paper, reported to the SEC that it regularly received unsolicited calls from sophisticated institutional investors expressing an interest in purchasing commercial paper of GECC or its affiliates. The only way that it could reach these potential investors would be to retain one or more commercial paper dealers—at considerable cost—or to advertise. GECC discussed the Senate Report language quoted above and concluded that advertising would be consistent with the exemption so long as it appeared in *The Wall Street Journal* or in publications directed primarily at institutional investors and so long as the advertising stated that the commercial paper was offered only to sophisticated institutional investors. The staff took a no-action position. The authors do not understand the GECC letter to stand for the proposition that commercial paper must be offered and sold only to institutional investors; rather, the letter stands for the proposition that it may be prudent to impose such a limitation if one intends to advertise a program.

• • *Eligibility for Discounting.* In a letter dated February 20, 1980 to the general counsel of the Board of Governors of the Federal Reserve System, the then general counsel of the SEC stated that the SEC's staff was no longer requiring that commercial paper be eligible for discounting at a Federal Reserve Bank as a condition for granting no-action requests under Section 3(a)(3). Since the Federal Reserve Banks no longer discount commercial paper, this is not a surprising conclusion.

• • *The Current Transaction Test.* The "current transaction" test is the most difficult and subjective requirement to be applied in determining whether commercial paper is exempt under Section 3(a)(3). In SEC Release No. 33-4412, the SEC stated, in the context of its then requirement that the paper be of a type eligible for discounting, that, under the regulations of the Board of Governors of the Federal Reserve System, it was permissible to discount a negotiable note that

> has been issued, or the proceeds of which are to be used in producing, purchasing, carrying or marketing goods or in meeting current operating expenses of a commercial,

agricultural or industrial business, and which is *not* to be used for permanent or fixed investment, such as land, buildings, or machinery, *nor* for speculative transactions or transactions in securities (except direct obligations of the United States government) . . . [emphasis in original].

The SEC further stated in this release that the current transaction standard is not satisfied where the proceeds from the issuance of the paper

> are to be used for the discharge of existing indebtedness unless such indebtedness is itself exempt under Section 3(a)(3); the purchase or construction of a plant; the purchase of durable machinery or equipment; the funding of commercial real estate development or financing; the purchase of real estate mortgages or other securities; the financing of mobile homes or home improvements; or the purchase or establishment of a business enterprise.

• • *The Concept of Commercial Paper Capacity.* Since the publication of SEC Release No. 33-4412, the staff of the SEC has issued numerous no-action letters in which it has recognized that an issuer need not trace the proceeds of a commercial paper program into identifiable current transactions. Rather, the current transaction requirement will be satisfied so long as the amount of commercial paper outstanding at any one time does not exceed the dollar amount of current transactions eligible to be financed.

In taking no-action positions based on this formula approach, the SEC has not inquired into an issuer's cash or cash equivalents, its investment portfolio, or the size of its borrowings under bank lines. The principle has been firmly established that dollars are fungible and that there is no requirement that the proceeds from the sale of commercial paper be segregated for a particular purpose or that they be traceable to a particular use.

In 1986, the staff of the SEC's Division of Corporation Finance took the unusual step of expressly endorsing the balance sheet formula approach advocated by counsel in a no-action request

COMMERCIAL PAPER

and the related concept of "commercial paper capacity."[21] Normally, the staff will respond to a no-action request with a short statement that no enforcement action will be recommended, but in this case the staff went on to make the following observations:

> In reaching this conclusion, the Division concurs in your view that the balance sheet test as applied in your letter is an appropriate measure of commercial paper capacity. More specifically, we agree that:
>
> 1. The Company may measure its commercial paper capacity by determining the capital it has committed to current assets, as defined in your letter for the purposes of Section 3(a)(3), and to the expenses of operating its business over the preceding 12-month period. If the transaction giving rise to the asset is a current transaction, it may be funded with commercial paper.
>
> 2. Since the emphasis of the balance sheet test is on the capital committed to, or funds invested in, certain assets, what is important in measuring the Company's commercial paper capacity is not so much the means by which capital is committed but the current character of the underlying asset. Current transactions giving rise to specific assets on the balance sheet may be defined for purposes of Section 3(a)(3) by reference to the following concepts:
>
>   (a) Means of Commitment. Capital may be committed to Section 3(a)(3) current assets by means of purchasing as well as directly originating the funding vehicles;
>
>   (b) Characterization of Asset. The nature of the underlying asset determines the relevant time

---

21. SEC No-action Letter, *Westinghouse Credit Corp.* (May 5, 1986). *See also* SEC No-action Letter, *Lyondell Petrochemical Co.* (July 19, 1989) and SEC Division of Corporation Finance, Manual of Publicly Available Telephone Interpretations 7 (#20) (July 1997).

period for evaluating whether or not the asset is a current asset for commercial paper purposes;

(c) Portion Financing. The relevant current portion (for purposes of Section 3(a)(3)) of capital committed to an asset will be credited toward the Company's commercial paper capacity irrespective of whether it is the only portion, the next portion or the final or remaining portion of capital invested in such asset. Capital becomes a current asset on the balance sheet of the Company for Section 3(a)(3) purposes when its maturity is certain and close enough to payoff that it can be viewed as attributable to a current transaction.

The staff endorsed the commercial paper capacity concept in this no-action letter in the context of finance company paper. It is equally applicable to other types of issuers, however, as evidenced by subsequent no-action letters.

The importance of the commercial paper capacity concept cannot be overemphasized. It is the key to applying the current transaction test under Section 3(a)(3). Indeed, if it had been necessary to demonstrate that specific funds were allocated to a particular purpose, as originally had been feared,[22] the commercial paper market never would have grown in the dramatic fashion that it has.

The question sometimes arises how commercial paper capacity should be calculated in the case of a parent company and its subsidiaries. It seems clear that a parent company should be able to calculate its commercial paper capacity on a consolidated basis. It is more doubtful that subsidiaries that issue commercial paper should be able to calculate their commercial paper

---

22. A. H. Dean, *The Federal Securities Act: I*, *Fortune* (August 1933), at 51–52. Dean wrote: "Inasmuch as most corporations do not 'earmark' the proceeds arising from various sources, it may be difficult to prove that the proceeds of commercial paper have been or are to be used for current transactions."

capacity on the basis of their parent's or their affiliates' current transactions.

• • *Role of No-action Letters.* The concept of commercial paper capacity took on even greater importance when the SEC staff in the late 1980s determined not to issue further no-action letters on the subject of current transactions for Section 3(a)(3) purposes. Up to that time, the staff had issued literally scores of letters, many of which sought to extend "laundry lists" of purposes that had been approved in earlier letters. The authors understand the staff to have become concerned that these letters were getting out of hand. In addition, the staff became concerned during this period about the role of an issuer's bank lines in determining whether the issuer's commercial paper was of the requisite "prime quality."

The staff has not issued any no-action letters on the current transactions test since 1990. The older letters have not been withdrawn, however, and securities lawyers still consult them as a supplement to the "commercial paper capacity" test when preparing to advise clients about the availability of the Section 3(a)(3) exemption.

In the absence of a no-action letter covering a specific situation and especially in the event of doubt about the issuer's commercial paper capacity, it may be advisable to consider a "restricted" or "Section 4(2)" program in lieu of a Section 3(a)(3) program. As discussed in Chapter 7, restricted programs are relatively easy to establish and permit an issuer to use the proceeds of the program for any purpose. In addition, the cost of such programs is usually comparable to that of a Section 3(a)(3) program.

• • *Financing of Inventories and Accounts Receivable.* The financing of inventories and accounts receivable by an industrial or commercial enterprise has long been recognized by the SEC as satisfying the current transaction test. The following is a typical factual presentation in seeking a no-action letter on this basis:

> The proceeds from the sale of the Notes . . . will not exceed the amounts required to support current transactions. Accordingly, the amount of the Notes sold in reliance

upon Section 3(a)(3) and outstanding at any particular time will be limited to the sum of the Company's consolidated inventory and accounts receivable, which, at March 31, 1985, was $1.946 billion.[23]

• • *Payment of Operating Expenses.* The staff of the SEC has been willing to take no-action positions where it is represented that the commercial paper proceeds will be used to pay ordinary operating expenses. This use of proceeds does not lend itself to a balance sheet formula approach, but rather a formula based on past levels of operating expenses. In some cases, the operating expenses providing commercial paper capacity have been stated to be those for the preceding 12 months.[24]

Generally, where the payment of operating expenses is listed as a current transaction, other uses that do lend themselves to a balance sheet approach, such as the carrying of inventories and accounts receivable or short-term lending activities, also are cited in the no-action request.[25] In one case, the issuer stated in its request that, in addition to financing inventory and current accounts receivable, it would use the commercial paper proceeds to pay such operating expenses as "federal, state and local income, property, franchise and other taxes, salaries, legal accounting and audit expenses, travel expenses, and retirement benefits."[26] In another no-action request, the operating expenses to be financed were stated to include interest on indebtedness

---

23. SEC No-action Letter, *Atlantic-Richfield Co.* (July 22, 1985). *See also* SEC No-action Letter, *Johnston Coca-Cola Bottling Group, Inc.* (May 17, 1989); SEC No-action Letter, *Russell Corp.* (September 22, 1988); SEC No-action Letter, *American Crystal Sugar Co.* (November 13, 1987).

24. E.g., SEC No-action Letter, *The Black & Decker Corp.* (July 12, 1989); SEC No-action Letter, *United Cable Television Corp.* (December 30, 1987).

25. E.g., SEC No-action Letter, *Turner Broadcasting System, Inc.* (November 7, 1989); SEC No-action Letter, *Hughes Supply Inc.* (October 4, 1988).

26. SEC No-action Letter, *General Host Corp.* (February 3, 1986). *See also* SEC No-action Letter, *J.B. Hunt Transport, Inc.* (August 8, 1989).

and deposits and dividends on the outstanding common and preferred stock of the issuer or its subsidiaries.[27]

• • *Carrying Finance Company Receivables.* Finance companies, such as General Motors Acceptance Corporation and Ford Motor Credit Company, are major issuers of commercial paper, with billions of dollars of notes outstanding at any one time. The types of activities in which finance companies engage have long been recognized as satisfying the current transaction test, and most finance companies have not found it necessary to seek no-action letters from the staff of the SEC.

In SEC Release No. 33-401 (June 18, 1935), the SEC published an opinion of its then general counsel to the effect that the proceeds of commercial paper notes of the type normally issued by finance companies may be regarded as used for current transactions if the issuer is in the business of making loans on or purchasing notes, installment contracts or other evidences of indebtedness and the proceeds are used for such purposes in the usual course of business. This position was reaffirmed by the SEC in SEC Release No. 33-4412, in which it stated that "short-term paper issued by finance companies to carry their installment loans" is a type of security that has usually been considered to fall within the terms of Section 3(a)(3).[28]

• • *Lending Activities of U.S. Bank Holding Companies and Foreign Banks.* The staff of the SEC has issued numerous no-action letters relating to commercial paper issued by U.S. bank holding companies for the purpose of financing their own current operating requirements and the various lending activities of their banking subsidiaries.

---

27. SEC No-action Letter, *Southeast Banking Corp.* (November 21, 1989). *See also* SEC No-action Letter, *National Community Banks, Inc.* (July 13, 1989); SEC No-action Letter, *MNC Financial, Inc.* (September 9, 1988).

28. See also SEC No-action Letter, *Kerr-McGee Credit Corp.* (October 12, 1987); SEC No-action Letter, *Dana Credit Corp.* (May 16, 1986); SEC No-action Letter, *Westinghouse Credit Corp.* (May 5, 1986).

Bank holding companies, unlike their bank subsidiaries, may not rely on the Section 3(a)(2) exemption available to regulated banks. Examples of permitted uses applicable to bank holding companies include funding (whether directly or through participations) of commercial, consumer, construction and mortgage loans having maturities not greater than five years and factoring and capital goods financing. Commercial paper may be used to finance loans with remaining terms of five years or less even though their original terms may have been much longer. In addition, commercial paper proceeds may be used to carry long-term mortgage loans pending their packaging and sale to permanent mortgage investors.[29] Similar no-action letters have been issued to savings and loan associations.[30]

Many foreign banks have issued commercial paper in the United States in reliance on the Section 3(a)(3) exemption. For the most part, these banks have not sought no-action letters from the SEC but have relied on opinions of U.S. counsel as to the availability of the exemption. In the usual opinion of this type, counsel recites that the bank requires funds for its short-term lending activities, states the current dollar amount of commercial, consumer and other loans having maturities of not greater than five years, and concludes that the current transaction test will be met so long as the amount of commercial paper outstanding at any one time does not exceed the dollar amount of the bank's loans maturing within five years. In the usual case, qualified loans far exceed the amount of commercial paper proposed to be outstanding at any one time.[31]

• • *Financing of Leasing and Related Activities.* In the past, the staff of the SEC was willing to grant no-action letters that

---

29. *See* SEC No-action Letter, *Southeast Banking Corp.* (November 21, 1989); SEC No-action Letter, *National Westminster Bancorp Inc.* (September 29, 1989); SEC No-action Letter, *Huntington Bancshares Inc.* (May 1, 1987).

30. E.g., SEC No-action Letter, *Imperial Savings Assoc.* (September 21, 1988).

31. A no-action position was taken in this context in SEC No-action Letter, *Chase Manhattan Corp. (Canadian Subsidiary)* (July 2, 1984).

COMMERCIAL PAPER

were quite liberal with respect to the terms of leases proposed to be financed with the commercial paper proceeds. An example is a 1980 letter in which the staff took a no-action position where a leasing company represented that it intended to limit the amount of notes sold in reliance on the Section 3(a)(3) exemption and outstanding at any particular time to the amount of its operating expenses for the preceding 12 months plus the sum of its net investment in direct finance leases of non-permanent equipment with original terms of seven years or less; its investment in operating leases covering equipment that had an original estimated economic life of nine years or less; secured loans having original terms of seven years or less on equipment that had an original estimated economic life of nine years or less; interim financing loans for temporarily "warehousing" equipment; and "floor plan" loans to affiliated equipment dealers.[32]

Other early no-action letters covered commercial paper issued to finance the acquisition of equipment of a non-permanent nature to be leased or sold under conditional sale contracts for periods of up to five years and, in some cases, seven years.[33]

In 1985, the SEC's staff tightened up its position with respect to leasing activities.[34] A bank holding company, after discussion with the staff, undertook to exclude any leases with terms in excess of five years. This reflected the staff view that the terms of the underlying leases supporting commercial paper qualifying for the Section 3(a)(3) exemption should not exceed five years.[35] The staff also has issued letters relating to the interim

---

32. SEC No-action Letter, *GATX Leasing Corp.* (June 23, 1980).

33. SEC No-action Letter, *Cummins Financial, Inc.* (July 2, 1984); SEC No-action Letter, *Goldman, Sachs & Co.* (May 21, 1984); SEC No-action Letter, *Centerre Bancorporation* (November 7, 1983); SEC No-action Letter, *E.F. Hutton Credit Corp.* (September 11, 1983); SEC No-action Letter, *Greyhound Corp.* (March 12, 1982); SEC No-action Letter, *Seafirst Corp.* (February 14, 1980).

34. SEC No-action Letter, *Landmark Banking Corp.* (March 14, 1985).

35. SEC No-action Letter, *MNC Financial Inc.* (September 9, 1988).

financing of equipment to be leased to clients of leasing companies without any limitation on the term of the lease.[36]

• • *Financing of Insurance Operations.* A comprehensive discussion of the current transaction test as it applies to the business of insurance is found in correspondence between the SEC's staff and counsel for Nationale-Nederlanden N.V., a Dutch holding company whose subsidiaries are engaged primarily in the insurance business.[37] The insurance holding company's request stressed that the commercial paper was being issued to bridge short-term timing differences between the receipt of premiums and other operating revenues and current cash requirements. The request proposed a formula under which the commercial paper outstanding at any one time would not exceed 75% of the amount by which life insurance premiums receivable within the following nine months—together with the principal of, and interest on, loans and net rentals receivable during the same period—exceeded short-term indebtedness other than the commercial paper. The request went on to characterize the commercial paper as being issued in order to "premature" premiums and other revenues receivable within nine months.[38]

• • *Financing of Broker-Dealer Operations.* The staff has issued a number of no-action letters under Section 3(a)(3) to securities firms and their holding company parents. Current transactions in the securities industry have been considered to include the financing of receivables arising in connection with

---

36. SEC No-action Letter, *Evans Railcar Leasing Co.* (February 27, 1981); SEC No-action Letter, *Ryder Truck Rental, Inc.* (January 18, 1980); SEC No-action Letter, *Pullman Leasing Co.* (May 29, 1979).

37. SEC No-action Letter, *Nationale-Nederlanden N.V.* (August 28, 1981).

38. *See also* SEC No-action Letter, *Pacific Mutual Life Insurance Co.* (May 13, 1988); SEC No-action Letter, *The Travelers Corp. and The Travelers Insurance Co.* (November 4, 1982); SEC No-action Letter, *The Mutual Benefit Life Insurance Co.* (February 8, 1982); SEC No-action Letter, *Equitable Life Assurance Society of the United States* (April 7, 1980 and June 23, 1980).

COMMERCIAL PAPER

margin indebtedness owed by customers and accounts that are payable by other broker-dealers and financial institutions in connection with securities borrowed and failed to deliver.[39]

The staff also has taken a no-action position with respect to any and all receivables from customers, and not just margin indebtedness, where it was represented that these receivables are typically payable within one year.[40] The carrying of inventories of obligations issued or guaranteed by the U.S. government or its agencies and of money market instruments with maturities of not more than one year from the date of their purchase also have been considered current transactions within the meaning of Section 3(a)(3).[41] The carrying of inventories of other debt and equity securities, at least in amounts necessary to satisfy customers' orders, also has been considered a current transaction.[42]

As indicated above, the staff of the SEC has been willing to take no-action positions where it is represented that commercial paper proceeds will be used to pay ordinary operating expenses. Several of the no-action letters issued to securities firms refer to operating expenses such as payroll, employee travel, rent, and similar items, in addition to current items that can be derived from the balance sheet.[43] The *Merrill Lynch* letter also refers to such operating expenses as taxes, retirement benefits, legal, accounting and audit expenses and advertising costs.

---

39. SEC No-action Letter, *Morgan Keegan, Inc.* (November 10, 1986); SEC No-action Letter, *Robert W. Baird & Co. Inc.* (March 26, 1986); SEC No-action Letter, *Shearson/American Express Holdings Inc.* (June 11, 1984); SEC No-action Letter, *Shearson American Express Inc.* (October 4, 1982).

40. SEC No-action Letter, *Merrill Lynch & Co., Inc.* (May 17, 1985).

41. SEC No-action Letter, *Robert W. Baird & Co. Inc.* (March 26, 1986); SEC No-action Letter, *Morgan Keegan, Inc.* (November 10, 1986); SEC No-action Letter, *Merrill Lynch & Co., Inc.* (May 17, 1985).

42. SEC No-action Letter, *Morgan Keegan, Inc.* (November 10, 1986); SEC No-action Letter, *Merrill Lynch & Co., Inc.* (May 17, 1985).

43. SEC No-action Letter, *Morgan Keegan, Inc.* (November 10, 1986); SEC No-action Letter, *Robert W. Baird & Co. Inc.* (March 26, 1986).

• • *Investments in Money Market Obligations.* A number of issuers have instituted commercial paper programs to generate funds to invest in short-term money market obligations, including securities issued by the U.S. government or its agencies, bankers' acceptances, bank certificates of deposit and commercial paper of other issuers. Under certain market conditions, the yield that can be derived from investments in obligations of this type may be higher than the rate that the issuer must pay on its own commercial paper. In these cases, the maturities of the money market obligations are matched against the maturities of the commercial paper, thereby, in effect, creating an arbitrage.

In a series of no-action letters beginning in the early 1970s, the staff of the SEC approved the investment of commercial paper proceeds in money market obligations such as short-term certificates of deposit or commercial paper of other issuers. Initially, the no-action letters covered cases where the issuer periodically had excess liquidity and not where the issuer proposed to sell its commercial paper for the purpose of generating funds for investment in money market obligations.[44]

In 1976, the staff for the first time found the current transaction test to have been met where commercial paper was to be issued by a bank holding company to generate funds for investment.[45] There the holding company stated that it would invest the proceeds "in short-term direct obligations of the United States and in obligations of other issuers where the periods to maturities of such obligations from the dates of investment therein are not more than nine months." There was no suggestion that the investments would be made only to utilize temporary cash surpluses.[46]

---

44. *See, e.g.,* SEC No-action Letter, *Hospital Corp. of America* (August 20, 1979); SEC No-action Letter, *First Kentucky National Corp.* (June 21, 1976); SEC No-action Letter, *Horizon Bancorp* (May 3, 1976); SEC No-action Letter, *Texas American Bancshares, Inc.* (November 11, 1974); SEC No-action Letter, *The Fort Worth National Corp.* (January 3, 1973).

45. SEC No-action Letter, *BancOklahoma Corp.* (March 1, 1976).

46. See also SEC No-action Letter, *Pan American Banks Inc.* (May 28, 1984); SEC No-action Letter, *Crocker National Corp.* (November 15, 1982);

COMMERCIAL PAPER

In 1983, for the first time, the staff took a no-action position on the issuance of commercial paper by an industrial company for the express purpose of funding an arbitrage program.[47] The Kellogg Company, a manufacturer and marketer of convenience food products, stated in its no-action request that its current transactions might include investments in short-term financial instruments having a term to maturity at the time of purchase not in excess of 12 months, including U.S. government and federal agency obligations; municipal notes rated "AA" or better; certificates of deposit; bankers' acceptances and other commercial bank obligations; and commercial paper of other issuers having a rating of A-1, P-1, or F-1. The no-action request went on to state that the maturity of the commercial paper issued by Kellogg would "fall within five business days of any reset or other change in the interest rates of financial instruments . . . purchased or carried . . . with funds allocable to the proceeds of the Paper, or within five business days of the maturity dates of such instruments where such maturity dates have not been preceded by an interest rate change."

The staff took a similar no-action position the following year.[48] Counsel to the issuer stated that commercial paper notes would be issued as part of Gillette's "cash management program" and that the proceeds would be invested in

> high grade debt securities, United States and foreign bank time deposits, bankers' acceptances or bank certificates of deposit which, at the time of their purchase, have remaining maturities not in excess of twelve months or in certain diversified, open-end investment companies . . . which invest only in United States dollar denominated money market instruments[.]

SEC No-action Letter, *Interstate Financial Corp.* (October 11, 1982); SEC No-action Letter, *Exchange National Corp.* (February 8, 1982).

47. SEC No-action Letter, *Kellogg Co.* (October 7, 1983).
48. SEC No-action Letter, *The Gillette Co.* (May 15, 1984).

While taking a no-action position on the program in general, the staff expressly refused to take a no-action position on the investment in money market funds because interests in such investment companies are equity securities.

The staff also took a no-action position under Section 3(a)(3) with respect to a program initiated by Goldman, Sachs & Co. under which its commercial paper clients would invest all or a portion of the proceeds from the sale of their commercial paper in secured obligations of Goldman, Sachs with maturities matching the commercial paper notes, each obligation bearing interest at a rate equal to the discount rate at which the corresponding commercial paper note was issued plus a spread to be determined by agreement between the issuer and Goldman, Sachs.[49]

• • *Interim Construction Financing.* In SEC Release No. 33-4412, the SEC stated that the current transaction standard would not be satisfied where the proceeds from the sale of commercial paper were to be used for "permanent or fixed investment, such as land, buildings, or machinery" or for "the purchase or construction of a plant" or "the purchase of durable machinery or equipment." Subsequent to that release, however, the staff recognized that, under certain circumstances, interim financing of permanent improvements would qualify as a current transaction. In 1972, the staff granted a no-action letter under Section 3(a)(3) covering the interim financing of hotel construction when accompanied by a take-out commitment for permanent financing.[50] The staff then took a no-action position with respect to the use of proceeds by a real estate developer to finance building and land improvements accompanied "in most instances" by take-out commitments for permanent financing.[51]

In July 1979, a major commercial paper dealer applied for and was granted a generic no-action letter covering commercial paper to be issued to finance, on an interim basis, the construction of a plant or other capital assets where the construction period would not exceed three years, even in cases where there was

---

49. SEC No-action Letter, *Goldman, Sachs & Co.* (May 15, 1986).
50. SEC No-action Letter, *Marriott Corp.* (March 10, 1972).
51. SEC No-action Letter, *Kaiser Aetna* (February 7, 1974).

no take-out commitment for permanent financing.[52] Counsel argued in the no-action request that alternative methods of permanent financing—namely, bank borrowings under an existing line of credit, the use of internally generated funds or subsequently arranged financing—are as suitable as a take-out commitment for permanent financing to retire commercial paper. The staff agreed with respect to "internally generated funds or subsequently arranged financing in the case of issuers which, by virtue of their outstanding credit position, appear to clearly have the ability to retire the commercial paper as indicated."

Subsequently, the staff issued no-action letters covering commercial paper used to finance the construction of a common carrier pipeline system[53] and improvements to or extensions of an existing pipeline system.[54] In neither case was there a take-out commitment for permanent financing.

In the first case, it was represented to the staff that it was expected that the commercial paper would be retired with funds derived from operations or through the issuance of long-term debt obligations in the private placement market "within a reasonable period after the completion of the improvement or extension being financed, which period is not expected to exceed twelve months." In the other case, it was represented that the financial objective was that by the end of the construction period the debt portion of the capital cost of the pipeline would be financed by securities with the longest available maturities that could be obtained at acceptable interest rates and that, in any event, the issuer did not expect to issue any commercial paper to finance or refinance the construction costs of the pipeline after a specified date approximately two and one-half years after the date of the letter.

The staff also took a no-action position where it was represented that commercial paper issued to provide interim financing for restaurant development would be retired no later than 36

---

52. SEC No-action Letter, *A. G. Becker Inc.* (September 24, 1979).
53. SEC No-action Letter, *Cortez Capital Corp.* (August 18, 1982).
54. SEC No-action Letter, *Colonial Pipeline Co.* (September 18, 1981).

months after completion of the particular project being financed.[55] No-action requests by bank holding companies frequently included, among other uses of proceeds, loans for interim construction financing.[56]

Goldman, Sachs & Co., one of the largest commercial paper dealers, demonstrated in the early 1980s the usefulness of the commercial paper market as a source of construction financing by selling commercial paper to finance the construction of its headquarters building at 85 Broad Street in New York City. The same firm subsequently used commercial paper to finance the construction of another major building in 2000.

• • *Financing of Public Utility Operations.* For several decades, major electric and gas public utilities were engaged in continuous construction programs, including the construction of large nuclear facilities. Traditionally, public utilities had financed their construction programs through the sale of first mortgage bonds and equity securities with commercial paper providing interim financing.

In 1973, Consolidated Edison Company of New York, Inc., in seeking a no-action letter covering the issuance of commercial paper in an amount not to exceed its utility receivables and fuel inventory, specifically addressed the issue of tracing proceeds to construction. The utility's order from the New York State Public Service Commission made reference to so-called "arrearage" financing, in which short-term credit (bank loans or commercial paper) would be used to meet construction requirements with permanent financing undertaken to pay off the short-term debt only when the amount outstanding approached the magnitude of the desired permanent financing. Also, the utility's mortgage bond prospectus stated that the net proceeds from the

---

55. SEC No-action Letter, *McDonald's Corp.* (June 25, 1982). *See also* SEC No-action Letter, *Hawaiian Electric Industries, Inc.* (March 28, 1985); SEC No-action Letter, *Olympia & York Properties* (October 29, 1984, *reconsidered* November 20, 1984).

56. E.g., SEC No-action Letter, *National Westminster Bancorp Inc.* (September 29, 1989); SEC No-action Letter, *First Fidelity Bancorp.* (July 28, 1988).

sale of the bonds would be used in part "to repay from time to time at or before maturity short-term obligations incurred as a result of the Company's construction program." The no-action request conceded that it might be argued that the statements in the Public Service Commission order and the prospectus had identified the proceeds of the commercial paper as being used for plant construction, at least on a temporary basis, pending refunding through permanent financing. This did not present a problem to the SEC's staff, and a no-action letter was issued based on a formula tied to receivables and fuel inventory.[57]

The SEC staff has issued letters that permit a public utility or its holding company to issue commercial paper up to an amount equal to the greater of (a) 25% of consolidated operating revenues during the past 12 months or (b) the sum of receivables and fuel inventory.[58] Another formula that has been acceptable to the staff is to limit the amount of outstanding commercial paper to the greater of 25% of gross revenues for the past 12 months or 50% of gross revenues for the preceding six months.[59] Other utilities have been granted no-action letters where the request stated that the commercial paper would be issued to carry accounts receivable and fuel inventories, to meet current operating requirements and to finance construction on an interim basis.[60]

• • *Nuclear Fuel Financing.* A number of public utilities have financed nuclear fuel by leasing the fuel from a special

---

57. SEC No-action Letter, *Consolidated Edison Co. of New York, Inc.* (February 22, 1973).

58. SEC No-action Letter, *Hawaiian Electric Industries, Inc.* (March 28, 1985); SEC No-action Letter, *Dominion Resources, Inc.* (October 28, 1983); SEC No-action Letter, *Minnesota Power and Light Co.* (November 8, 1971).

59. SEC No-action Letter, *New Jersey Natural Gas Co.* (September 6, 1976).

60. SEC No-action Letter, *Peoples Gas Light and Coke Co.* (September 28, 1989); SEC No-action Letter, *Lee County Electric Cooperative, Inc.* (May 13, 1988); SEC No-action Letter, *PaineWebber Inc.* (October 21, 1985); SEC No-action Letter, *Public Service Co. of New Mexico* (June 29, 1984); SEC No-action Letter, *Tucson Electric Power Co.* (April 22, 1983).

purpose corporation or trust established to issue commercial paper. The proceeds from the commercial paper issued by the special purpose entity are used to purchase nuclear fuel materials in process or finished nuclear fuel assemblies and in some cases contract rights pertaining to nuclear fuel. Where nuclear fuel materials are purchased, the proceeds also are used to pay the costs of processing and fuel assembly fabrication.

The period from the acquisition of nuclear fuel materials through the expiration of the fuel's usefulness is known as the "nuclear fuel cycle," and the commercial paper proceeds are used to finance the fuel in various stages throughout this cycle. In the original no-action letters relating to nuclear fuel financing, it was stated that the nuclear fuel cycle (the period of time that the issuer would own the nuclear fuel in the reactor or the materials from which it was processed) would not exceed 60 months.[61]

Subsequently, the staff found acceptable financing over a nuclear fuel cycle that would normally be six and one-half years but initially would be 11.5 years because of delays in the construction of the nuclear facility.[62] Even later, the staff took a no-action position where it was represented that for an operating reactor the complete nuclear fuel cycle would be a period of between 61 and 85 months when reloading of the fuel is involved or a period of between 68 and 92 months when preparation of the initial core is involved.[63]

---

61. SEC No-action Letter, *Duke Power Co.* (August 9, 1979); SEC No-action Letter, *A.G. Becker Inc.* (January 16, 1978); SEC No-action Letter, *Lehman Commercial Paper Inc.* (October 3, 1977).

62. SEC No-action Letter, *Mid-Michigan Energy Co.* (September 8, 1980). *See also* SEC No-action Letter, *Illinois Power Co.* (March 6, 1981).

63. SEC No-action Letter, *Goldman, Sachs & Co.* (May 21, 1984). *See also* SEC No-action Letter, *Security Pacific Merchant Banking Group* (May 23, 1988), which contemplated a nuclear fuel cycle of between 48 and 84 months, and SEC No-action Letter, *Renaissance Energy Corp.* (December 29, 1989), in which note proceeds were to be used to purchase nuclear fuel for resale to The Detroit Edison Co.

• • *Acquisition Financing.* It is quite common to see references in the financial press and in rating agency reports to commercial paper being used to fund acquisitions or capital expenditures, presumably in reliance on the issuer's commercial paper capacity, either directly or for the purpose of repaying bank debt incurred for that purpose. SEC Release No. 33-4412 made clear that the current transaction standard is not satisfied where the proceeds from the issuance of commercial paper are to be used for the purchase or establishment of a business enterprise. Moreover, while interim financing of construction may satisfy Section 3(a)(3), the SEC staff's position on interim financing of acquisitions has not been consistent.[64]

On the other hand, an issuer that has sufficient inventories and accounts receivable to support a commercial paper program of a certain size should not be precluded from instituting or increasing such a program simply because it will use otherwise available funds to acquire another company. The *Consolidated Edison* letter discussed above strongly supports the position that a formula approach is acceptable even if the purpose or motive underlying the issuance of commercial paper is the financing of a noncurrent transaction.

The no-action letter most frequently cited in support of the proposition that a recent acquisition that requires financing should not affect the availability of an otherwise supportable Section 3(a)(3) exemption is a 1981 letter issued to Fluor Corporation covering a commercial paper program that it planned to institute shortly after it acquired St. Joe Minerals Corporation.[65] Whether or not a need to refinance the acquisition was a motivating factor in the establishment of the commercial

---

64. Three letters were issued in 1983 only after the requesting issuers deleted references to acquisition financing. SEC No-action Letters, *Liberty National Corp.* (May 6, 1983), *Continental Bancorp, Inc.* (February 17, 1983), *Florida Coast Banks, Inc.* (September 12, 1983). *But see Bank of Boston Corp.* (August 28, 1989) (approving as a current transaction the acquisition by a bank holding company of "banks and other entities" for a period ending on the earlier to occur of 270 days or the obtaining of permanent financing).

65. SEC No-action Letter, *Fluor Corp.* (December 18, 1981).

paper program is not evident from the text of the request. In the no-action request, however, it was stated quite clearly that the proceeds would not be segregated but would become part of Fluor's general funds and that accordingly it would not be practicable to trace specific dollars from the proceeds to specific applications. It was represented that the aggregate principal amount of commercial paper to be outstanding at any time would not exceed the sum of Fluor's consolidated accounts receivable, contract work in progress and inventories. The no-action request included a table setting forth on a combined basis the current asset accounts (more than $940 million) of Fluor and St. Joe as of various dates. In effect, the SEC staff took a no-action position with respect to a commercial paper program in the magnitude of close to $1 billion within months following a very major acquisition by Fluor.

It has since become quite common to see references in the financial press to issuers' using commercial paper for the "initial" funding of acquisitions and capital expenditures.

• • *Issuer's Repurchase of Securities.* An issuer should be entitled to rely on the Section 3(a)(3) exemption to issue commercial paper where it has sufficient commercial paper capacity and the proceeds will be used in part to finance a stock repurchase program. In *Bank of Boston Corp.* (available August 28, 1989), the staff approved as a current transaction in and of itself the financing of a stock repurchase program for a period ending on the earlier to occur of 270 days or the obtaining of permanent financing.

• • *Financing by Foreign Governmental Entities.* A foreign governmental entity may finance its short-term needs through the issuance of notes in the United States in reliance on Section 3(a)(3). In 1982, the City of Gothenburg, Sweden, received a no-action letter relating to short-term notes that it proposed to issue in order to finance the operation of a municipal electric utility.[66] In its request, the City's counsel referred to an unpublished 1962 exchange of correspondence with the SEC relating

---

66. SEC No-action Letter, *City of Gothenburg* (March 5, 1982).

to the City of Montreal. In that situation, the staff had advised that the exemption was not available because the notes to be sold would not be discountable by the Federal Reserve Bank (which it was then advised could only discount notes arising out of commercial transactions), and because certain of the proposed uses of the proceeds were not within the contemplation of the current transactions standard contained in Section 3(a)(3). Counsel argued that the Montreal precedent was not relevant because there the proceeds were to be applied to non-commercial purposes, such as the financing of maintenance of sidewalks, streets and public places, anticipation of tax revenues, and other purposes for which Montreal was authorized to borrow pending the sale of long-term obligations. Counsel stressed that in the case of Gothenburg the proceeds were to meet the current operating expenses of the city's public utility operations. The no-action letter was granted without any reference to these distinctions.

Two other no-action requests submitted on behalf of sovereign governments also stressed the commercial nature of the proposed use of proceeds. The request of the Kingdom of Denmark referred to certain state enterprises, including railways, the postal and telegraph services (which also provide long-distance telephone services), seaports, airports, forests, a ferry and the company through which trade between Denmark and Greenland is conducted. It was represented that Denmark would limit the amount of its commercial paper so that at no time would the aggregate amount outstanding exceed the sum of the then dollar equivalent of the current accounts receivable of these state enterprises, their depreciation and amortization charges for the preceding year, their inventories and their requirements for salaries, pension payments, rental and general office expenses. On this basis, the staff granted the no-action request.[67]

The staff subsequently issued a no-action letter to the Kingdom of Spain on the basis that the aggregate amount of commercial paper outstanding would not exceed the amount of the current advances to state enterprises engaged in such activities as

---

67. SEC No-action Letter, *Kingdom of Denmark* (May 13, 1985).

the operation of railroads, coal mining, metallurgy, maritime shipping, airline transportation and telecommunications. In addition, the outstanding paper would not exceed the sum of the U.S. dollar equivalents of these enterprises' accounts receivable, depreciation expenses and inventories and wage-related expenditures.[68]

In view of the advice by the general counsel of the SEC in 1980 that the staff no longer requires commercial paper to be eligible for discounting, there was no reason to have emphasized in these no-action requests the commercial nature of the use of proceeds. A foreign governmental issuer may issue short-term promissory notes in reliance on Section 3(a)(3) to finance current transactions, whether or not they are of a commercial nature. This is confirmed by a no-action letter issued in 1986 to Lehman Commercial Paper Incorporated allowing its sovereign clients to issue commercial paper to finance current governmental expenditures or to retain the proceeds as part of their foreign exchange reserves.[69]

Nothing in Section 3(a)(3) limits that exemption to programs that are designated as "commercial paper" or requires that an issuer elect to rely on that exemption. Indeed, it is not even necessary that the foreign governmental issuer ever have heard of Section 3(a)(3). In the normal situation, of course, a foreign governmental issuer of short-term debt obligations will not be selling these obligations into the United States. It is often the case, however, that U.S. securities firms wish to trade these obligations in the United States or to sell them to their U.S. customers. There is no reason why a dealer may not rely on the exemption for these purposes if it can confirm that the debt obligations meet the requirements of Section 3(a)(3) as described above. In this connection, it should be possible to verify the issuer's "commercial paper capacity" by reference to its public accounts.

---

68. SEC No-action Letter, *Kingdom of Spain* (August 1, 1985).

69. SEC No-action Letter, *Lehman Commercial Paper Inc.* (December 1, 1986).

- *Section 3(a)(2) Bank Support Exemption*

Commercial paper backed by letters of credit of domestic banks have long been viewed by the staff of the SEC as exempt under Section 3(a)(2) on the basis that letters of credit are in effect guarantees and that the commercial paper they support are therefore exempt as securities guaranteed by a bank.[70] It is immaterial for this purpose whether the letter of credit is attached to the notes or the bank issues a master letter of credit or whether the letter of credit runs to a depository bank or directly to the holders of the notes.[71]

Where commercial paper is backed by a letter of credit and is therefore exempt under Section 3(a)(2), there is no need to be concerned as to whether the current transaction test is satisfied. Nor is there a need to be concerned with the nine-month limitation of Section 3(a)(3), although for marketing reasons "Section 3(a)(2) paper" usually has the same terms and is sold in the same manner as Section 3(a)(3) paper.

Foreign banks' U.S. branches and agencies received numerous no-action letters to the effect that commercial paper backed by their letters of credit is also entitled to the Section 3(a)(2) exemption. These letters were issued on the premise that the nature and extent of the supervision in a particular state, and the manner in which the branch or agency is regulated, permitted reliance upon the Section 3(a)(2) exemption.[72]

---

70. SEC No-action Letter, *Underwood Neuhaus & Co. (Allied Bank of Texas)* (February 21, 1985); SEC No-action Letter, *Chase Manhattan Bank, N.A.* (July 2, 1979); SEC No-action Letter, *Security Pacific National Bank* (June 26, 1978 and October 2, 1978); SEC No-action Letter, *Mason-McDuffie* (June 20, 1975); SEC No-action Letter, *Chemical Bank/Lomas & Nettleton Mortgage Investors* (December 1, 1971); SEC No-action Letter, *United California Bank* (April 15, 1971).

71. SEC No-action Letter, *Goldman, Sachs & Co.* (July 10, 1978). For bankruptcy law reasons, however, letters of credit are usually direct-pay (i.e., the letter of credit bank pays holders of maturing commercial paper, and the issuer reimburses the bank through a reimbursement agreement).

72. SEC No-action Letter, *Fuji Bank Ltd.* (September 17, 1984); SEC No-action Letter, *The Toronto-Dominion Bank (Hiram Walker Commercial Paper, Inc.)* (July 6, 1984); SEC No-action Letter, *Industrial Bank of Japan,*

In a 1986 release,[73] the SEC reviewed the history of its no-action positions with respect to Section 3(a)(2) and formalized its position on the application of that section to securities issued or guaranteed by foreign banks' U.S. branches and agencies. It stated that the exemption would be available provided that the nature and extent of federal or state regulation and supervision of the particular branch or agency is "substantially equivalent" to that applicable to federal or state chartered domestic banks doing business in the same jurisdiction. The SEC stated that this determination was the responsibility of issuers and their counsel and that no-action letters on this subject would no longer be granted.

If a letter of credit is viewed as a security separate from the underlying obligation that it supports, then it must independently find its own exemption under the 1933 Act. In seeking a no-action letter with respect to letters of credit issued by the home office (not a branch or agency) of a bank based in the Netherlands to back short-term promissory notes issued by certain commercial and industrial customers, counsel took the position that the letters of credit should be exempt from registration based upon the Section 3(a)(3) exemption. Counsel assumed that the exemption under Section 3(a)(3) would be available for the notes alone and then framed the issue as whether the addition of the letter of credit supporting such notes would require registration of either the notes or the letter of credit. Counsel pointed out that no-action letters covering parent guarantees of a subsidiary's commercial paper had been granted on the basis that the essential characteristics of the guarantees were derived from the notes they supported.[74] Counsel argued that letters of credit issued by a foreign bank should be regarded in the same way.

Ltd. (*New York Agency*) (February 10, 1984); SEC No-action Letter, *National Westminster Bank, Ltd.* (November 30, 1981); SEC No-action Letter, *Mitsui Bank, Ltd.* (*New York Branch*) (November 30, 1981).

73. SEC Release No. 33-6661 (September 23, 1986).

74. *See* SEC No-action Letter, *U.S. Pioneer Electronics Corp.* (August 13, 1979); SEC No-action Letter, *Mitsui & Co. (Canada), Ltd.* (September 5, 1974).

In addition, counsel argued that the letters of credit viewed alone should qualify for the Section 3(a)(3) exemption in that they would have the same duration as the underlying notes and that, although not technically notes, they came within the spirit of the Section 3(a)(3) exemption. The staff took a no-action position, but subject to the condition that the commercial paper notes backed by the letters of credit would be limited to those issued by U.S. customers of the foreign bank.[75] In a subsequent letter issued to a bank in Finland, however, the staff took a no-action position even though it was stated that the bank's letters of credit would back commercial paper of U.S. and non-U.S. issuers.[76]

Commercial paper sometimes is backed by a surety bond written by an insurance company. In such cases, the commercial paper itself must be exempt under Section 3(a)(3) and the surety bond, if deemed a separate security, will be entitled to the exemption provided by Section 3(a)(8), which exempts "[a]ny insurance or endowment policy . . . issued by a corporation subject to the supervision of the insurance commissioner, bank commissioner, or any agency or officer performing like functions, of any State or Territory of the United States or the District of Columbia."[77] Unlike a letter of credit issued by a domestic bank or a domestic branch or agency of a foreign bank, a surety bond cannot create an exemption for underlying commercial paper that is not itself exempt.[78]

The disparity in treatment of obligations guaranteed by banks and those guaranteed by insurance companies drew complaints from the insurance industry, notwithstanding the fact that banks are extensively regulated on the federal level while insurance companies are regulated only on the state level. In Section 105

---

75. SEC No-action Letter, *Amsterdam-Rotterdam Bank N.V.* (October 14, 1980).

76. SEC No-action Letter, *Saastopankkien Keskus-Osake-Pankki* (October 24, 1988).

77. *See* SEC No-action Letter, *Lehman Commercial Paper Inc.* (October 3, 1977). *See also* SEC No-action Letter, *Financial Security Assurance Inc.* (October 24, 1988).

78. SEC No-action Letter, *Insurance Co. of North America* (September 26, 1983).

of the Government Securities Act of 1986,[79] however, Congress directed the SEC to conduct a study of the Section 3(a)(2) exemption, including its impact on competition between banks and insurance companies in providing financial guarantees. The SEC's report[80] recognized the existence of a competitive disparity and recommended that Congress eliminate the Section 3(a)(2) exemption for securities backed by bank guarantees and also grant general exemptive authority to the SEC. Congress did not act in response to the SEC report, and support for raising insurance company guarantees to the level of bank guarantees evaporated as several insurance companies began to encounter well-publicized financial difficulties.

- *Section 4(2) Continuous Private Placement Programs*

An issuer whose commercial paper does not meet the Section 3(a)(3) requirements and that is unable or unwilling to obtain a bank letter of credit may still take advantage of the commercial paper market by setting up a "restricted" or "Section 4(2)" commercial paper program. This type of program is discussed in Chapter 7.

Restricted commercial paper programs present special challenges for registered open-end investment companies, particularly money market funds. Because the SEC considers restricted securities to be "illiquid" assets, open-end investment companies must generally avoid investing more than 15% of their assets in such securities.[81] Money market funds are subject to a 10% limit.[82] On the other hand, the SEC permits an open-end

---

79. Pub. L. No. 99-571.

80. *Report by the United States Securities and Exchange Commission on the Financial Guarantee Market: The Use of the Exemption in Section 3(a)(2) of the Securities Act of 1933 for Securities Guaranteed by Banks and the Use of Insurance Policies to Guarantee Debt Securities* (August 28, 1987).

81. "The usual limit on aggregate holdings by an open-end investment company of illiquid assets is 15 percent of its net assets." Guide 4 of the Guides to Form N-1A, as amended in SEC Release No. IC-18612 (March 12, 1992).

82. SEC Letter dated December 9, 1992 to Matthew P. Fink, President, Investment Company Inst.

fund's directors to determine that Rule 144A and foreign securities are liquid. In a 1994 interpretive letter, the SEC staff concurred in a commercial paper dealer's views that a fund's board of directors might determine that non-Rule 144A "restricted" commercial paper was also liquid for purposes of the percentage limitation so long as it was rated in one of the two highest-rating categories. The board was also required to "consider the trading market for the specific security, taking into account all relevant factors."[83]

1940 Act Considerations

As discussed in Chapter 3, any issuer that holds significant amounts of "securities" as defined by the 1940 Act may find itself an "inadvertent investment company" for purposes of that statute. Among the commercial paper issuers most likely to be caught by the statute's definition are issuers of asset-backed securities, broker-dealers, banks and insurance companies. Finance subsidiaries may also meet the literal definition of an investment company.

The status under the 1940 Act of issuers of asset-backed securities, including asset backed commercial paper, is discussed in Chapter 14.

As for broker-dealers, banks and insurance companies, there are express exemptions in the 1940 Act for *U.S.* issuers engaged in these businesses as well as for their holding companies.[84] There are no statutory exemptions for *foreign* banks and insurance companies or for finance subsidiaries, and these entities have had to depend for relief on SEC exemptions and rulemaking.

---

83. SEC No-action Letter, *Merrill Lynch Money Markets, Inc.* (January 14, 1994).

84. 1940 Act §§3(c)(2), 3(c)(3), 3(c)(6). The SEC has taken the interpretive position that U.S. branches and agencies of foreign banks are "banks" for purposes of the 1940 Act for the limited purpose of issuing securities in the United States. SEC Release No. IC-17681 (August 17, 1990).

- *Foreign Banks and Insurance Companies*

In late 1978, a Swedish commercial bank entered the U.S. commercial paper market without seeking exemptive relief under the 1940 Act. Through a series of circumstances, the staff of the SEC became aware of this and questioned whether the bank might be deemed an investment company. When made aware of the problem, the bank withdrew from the market.

The 1940 Act question arises because the principal assets of commercial banks are consumer and commercial loans represented by some form of note or other evidence of indebtedness. If the evidences of indebtedness representing these loans were to be considered investment securities[85] and if they amounted to more than 40% of the bank's assets (which would almost always be the case), then the bank would be deemed an investment company unless it could demonstrate that it was primarily engaged in a business other than that of owning or holding such securities.

The status of foreign banks under the 1940 Act became something of a legal *cause célèbre* following the staff's challenge to the Swedish bank's commercial paper program. In February 1979, five New York City law firms submitted to the staff of the SEC a draft letter setting forth legal arguments to the effect that foreign commercial banks should not be deemed to be investment companies. This letter was prepared following a meeting between representatives of these firms and the SEC staff at which the legal issues were fully aired. The staff did not respond to the letter but advised that the best course for a foreign bank to follow would be to assume that it was an investment company (without so admitting) and to seek an exemption from the provisions of the 1940 Act pursuant to Section 6(c).

In April 1979, the SEC began granting exemptive orders permitting foreign banks or their finance subsidiaries to sell their debt securities in the United States without registering as investment companies under the 1940 Act. These exemptions became routine, and the SEC codified them in 1987 by adopting Rule

---

85. The status of bank loans as "securities" is far from self-evident (*see Reves v. Ernst & Young*, 494 U.S. 56 (1990), discussed in Chapter 1), but securities lawyers have not been inclined to challenge the SEC on this point.

COMMERCIAL PAPER

6c-9 (which also permitted the sale of non-voting preferred stock). Subsequently, the SEC granted a number of individual exemptive orders under Section 6(c) of the 1940 Act permitting foreign banks to sell their equity securities in the United States.

The SEC treated foreign insurance companies in similar fashion, granting individual exemptive orders permitting the sale of both debt and equity securities.

In 1990, the SEC proposed to extend the scope of Rule 6c-9 to cover foreign banks' equity securities and to exempt foreign insurance companies (and their finance subsidiaries) on the same basis as foreign banks and their finance subsidiaries.[86] In 1991, however, the SEC decided to adopt a new Rule 3a-6 that superseded Rule 6c-9 and specifically excluded foreign banks (as defined) and foreign insurance companies (as defined) from the 1940 Act's definition of investment company.[87]

Rule 3a-6 is discussed in Chapter 9. A side effect of the rule is that foreign banks' and insurance companies' holding companies are now also excluded from the definition of investment company under Rule 3a-1, and their finance subsidiaries are excluded under Rule 3a-5.

- *Finance Subsidiaries*

Most commercial paper programs established by foreign issuers have used a U.S. finance subsidiary to issue the commercial paper with an unconditional guarantee of the parent backing the subsidiary's obligation. The proceeds are advanced to the parent or to the parent's operating subsidiaries. U.S. finance subsidiaries are used primarily for marketing purposes, in view of the fact that certain institutional investors are limited by corporate policy or otherwise in the amount of foreign securities that they may purchase.

Rule 3a-5 under the 1940 Act is intended to exclude from the definition of investment company any issuer—whatever its legal form—that is organized primarily to finance the business operations of its parent company or a company controlled by

---

86. SEC Release No. IC-17682 (August 17, 1990).
87. SEC Release No. IC-18381 (November 4, 1991).

its parent company. If the finance subsidiary's debt securities or nonvoting preferred stock are "issued to or held by the public," they must be unconditionally guaranteed by the parent company.[88] In addition, at least 85% of the proceeds of the offering must be advanced to the parent company or a company controlled by the parent company "as soon as practicable" but in any event not more than six months after receipt of the proceeds. To avoid temptation, the rule limits the types of securities that the finance subsidiary may hold as temporary investments.

A guarantee of preferred stock need extend only to dividends that have been declared and, in the event of liquidation, to the lower of the liquidation preference plus accumulated and unpaid dividends or the subsidiary's remaining assets after the satisfaction of prior claims.[89] A support or "keepwell" agreement does not currently satisfy the "unconditional guarantee" condition of the rule, although the SEC has issued Section 6(c) exemptive orders in the case of support agreements where regulatory requirements prevented the parent companies from issuing guarantees.[90]

On the other hand, in view of the rule's requirement of a guarantee only for securities "issued to or held by the public," a guarantee is not required if the finance subsidiary sells its securities by means of a private placement,[91] including a transaction in reliance on Rule 144A,[92] or in an offshore offering pursuant to Regulation S.[93]

---

88. Rule 3a-5(a)(7) permits a parent company that is a foreign bank as defined in Rule 3a-6 to satisfy the guarantee requirement by issuing a letter of credit that meets specified conditions.

89. SEC No-action Letter, *Chieftain International Funding Corp.* (November 3, 1992).

90. SEC Release No. IC-15388 (October 31, 1986) (application); SEC Release No. IC-15430 (November 21, 1986) (order); SEC Release No. IC-14964 (February 28, 1986) (application); SEC Release No. IC-15014 (March 25, 1986) (order).

91. SEC No-action Letter, *PSEG Capital Corp.* (July 13, 1988).

92. SEC No-action Letter, *Sony Capital Corp.* (April 27, 1992).

93. SEC No-action Letter, *Societe Generale and SGA Societe Generale Acceptance N.V.* (February 14, 1992).

Oddly enough, Rule 3a-5 does not extend to direct subsidiaries of U.S. banks or insurance companies (as distinguished from indirect subsidiaries of their holding companies). It does extend to finance subsidiaries of foreign banks and insurance companies that are owned or controlled by foreign governmental entities.

In addition to Rule 3a-5, finance subsidiaries engaged exclusively in the issuance of notes with a maturity of no more than nine months may be eligible to claim an exclusion under Rule 3a-3. This exclusion is available, however, only if the parent company does not fall within the statutory definition of investment company or is excluded by Rule 3a-1.

Liabilities on Default

In the case of common stock or long-term debt obligations, there is always a risk that the value of the security may decline at any time because of earnings disappointments, rating changes or other adverse developments. An underwriter of common stock or long-term debt securities may face litigation risk under these circumstances. The underwriter may be comforted to some degree by the knowledge that the issuer will surely be a co-defendant in any litigation and even by a reasonable expectation that the issuer will pay the costs of defense and settlement pursuant to the usual indemnification arrangements.

The risk associated with a short-term obligation such as commercial paper is not that the value of the instrument will decline prior to maturity as the result of adverse developments. Rather, the risk is that the "orderly exit" mechanism described earlier will not work in time and that the issuer will be forced to default on outstanding paper. A default of this kind is usually quickly followed by a bankruptcy filing and the prospect of a total loss of principal for investors who are not accustomed to regarding commercial paper as an investment associated with risk of this kind.

In the event of a default by an issuer of commercial paper, holders will have to wait in line in bankruptcy court in order to recover anything from the issuer. Since commercial paper is typically unsecured, their place is at the end of the line (just before the holders of equity securities). If they believe their investment was induced by false or misleading disclosure, they may make claims against the rating agencies or the issuer's independent accountants.

If they purchased the paper from a dealer, however, the holders may believe that they have available an additional "deep pocket." The dealer's potential liability under these circumstances can be for the entire amount of the issuer's defaulted commercial paper. In the case of a multibillion dollar program, this can lead to a serious weakening of the dealer's own financial standing. It is this potential for catastrophic liability that motivates dealers to take pains to examine the 1933 Act status of their issuers' commercial paper programs, to monitor their issuers' creditworthiness and to urge the issuers to exit the market by drawing down on bank lines if there are signs of a deteriorating credit situation.

A dealer's potential liabilities can arise under Sections 12(a)(1) and 12(a)(2) of the 1933 Act, under Rule 10b-5, under corresponding provisions in state securities laws, or on the basis of common law fraud. Obviously, there are no Section 11 liabilities since commercial paper is not registered under the 1933 Act.

- *Section 12(a)(1)*

If commercial paper is sold without an available exemption from the registration requirements of Section 5 of the 1933 Act, then any purchaser may rescind the transaction as against any "seller" for a period of one year. Under the U.S. Supreme Court's decision in *Pinter v. Dahl*,[94] a dealer that passes title to the investor or that solicits the transaction for pecuniary reasons would appear to be a "seller" for this purpose.

It is therefore vital for a dealer to have confidence in the exemption under which it is selling the issuer's commercial paper. As we have seen, the Section 3(a)(3) exemption requires that the issuer use the proceeds of the sale of commercial paper for "current transactions." It is standard for a dealer at the commencement of a program to obtain an opinion from the issuer's counsel as to the availability of the exemption, but this opinion

---

94. 486 U.S. 622 (1988).

usually assumes that the proceeds will be used for stated purposes. Even if the opinion is required to be updated at future intervals, it is unlikely to provide specific factual comfort. Since a dealer has few alternative means of verifying that the issuer is in fact using the proceeds of the program for current transaction purposes, the dealer is necessarily at the issuer's mercy on this important part of the exemption.

It is not entirely clear that a court would visit the drastic rescission remedy on a dealer that had been lied to by an issuer about its use of the proceeds of the program for current transactions. On the other hand, it is clearly advisable for the dealer to take some precautions. In this connection, the concept of "commercial paper capacity" is again likely to be of significant help. A dealer can relatively easily—and therefore should—monitor an issuer's use of commercial paper against the information contained in the issuer's financial statements. And even though the concept of "commercial paper capacity" is based on SEC staff advice, a dealer ought to have a reasonable chance of persuading a court that the concept's origins and longevity make it eligible for the "good faith reliance" protection of Section 19(a) of the 1933 Act.[95]

Another potential vulnerability for the dealer lies in the Section 3(a)(3) exemption's dependence, at least under the SEC's Release 33-4412, on the "prime quality" of the commercial paper at the time of issuance. There are some cases under Rule 10b-5[96] that suggest a "Catch-22" outcome on this point: if an issuer of commercial paper defaults on the paper, then that paper could not have met the "prime quality" test at the time of its issuance.

Whatever the validity of these cases for Rule 10b-5 purposes, they should not control the availability of the 1933 Act exemption. It should be sufficient for the latter purpose that the paper

---

95. Compare *Gerstle v. Gamble-Skogmo, Inc.*, 478 F.2d 1281, 1293–94 (2d Cir. 1973), with *Colema Realty Corp. v. Bibow*, 555 F. Supp. 1030, 1040 (D. Conn. 1983).

96. *Zeller v. Bogue Electric Manufacturing Corp.*, 476 F.2d 795, 800 (2d Cir.), *cert. denied*, 414 U.S. 908 (1973). *See also Sanders v. John Nuveen & Co.*, 463 F.2d 1075, 1079 (7th Cir.), *cert. denied*, 409 U.S. 1009 (1972).

was rated "prime" at the time of its issuance by any of the major rating agencies and that the dealer had no reason to question that rating.

The vagaries of the Section 3(a)(3) exemption suggest that it would be in the interest of dealers to rely less on Section 3(a)(3) and more on Section 3(a)(2) and "restricted" or Section 4(2) programs. In particular, dealers can have a higher degree of confidence that 1933 Act exemptions are in fact available where the program is based on Rule 144A or procedures that parallel Regulation D. This does not mean, however, that a dealer cannot argue—even after an issuer's default—that a program should be regarded as having been entitled to a private placement exemption even where it was run for many years as a Section 3(a)(3) program. If the commercial paper was in fact sold to institutional accredited investors who did not (and were not likely to) act as underwriters in making resales, the program's entitlement to a private placement exemption may be sufficiently strong to withstand a rescission claim.

- *Antifraud Remedies*

Even if an exemption from 1933 Act registration can be established for the defaulted commercial paper, the dealer is still exposed to liability under the antifraud remedies. The scope of this liability will depend on the manner in which the commercial paper was offered and sold. The two major remedies are Section 12(a)(2) of the 1933 Act and Rule 10b-5 under the 1934 Act. In general, a dealer should prefer to be subject to liability only under Rule 10b-5, which requires reliance by the plaintiff as well as scienter (intentional or reckless misconduct) by the defendant. By contrast, Section 12(a)(2) is a negligence-based remedy.

Section 3(a)(2) commercial paper, for example, is expressly excluded from liability under Section 12(a)(2). A holder of defaulted Section 3(a)(2) commercial paper must therefore proceed under Rule 10b-5.

Under the U.S. Supreme Court's *Gustafson* decision, discussed in Chapters 5 and 7, the Section 12(a)(2) remedy applies only to public offerings. A dealer that has sold commercial paper under a private placement exemption should therefore be subject only to Rule 10b-5 liability. On the other hand, as suggested above for Section 12(a)(1) purposes, the fact that a program was conducted in ostensible reliance on the Section 3(a)(3) exemption should not foreclose the dealer from demonstrating retroactively that the paper was in fact offered other than "publicly." Whether this will be sufficient under *Gustafson* to limit the plaintiff to Rule 10b-5 remedies is, of course, an open question.

• • *Section 12(a)(2)*. Section 12(a)(2) permits a buyer of a security to rescind his purchase as against any person who offered or sold the security "by means of a prospectus or oral communication" that contained an untrue statement of material fact or omitted to state a material fact necessary in order to make the seller's statements, "in the light of the circumstances under which they were made, not misleading." The seller has a defense based on a showing that the seller did not know and, in the exercise of "reasonable care" could not have known, of the relevant untruth or omission. Since the enactment of the Reform Act, a plaintiff's recovery under Section 12(a)(2) is subject to reduction for any amount shown to be attributable to reasons unrelated to the asserted untruth or omission.

A claim under Section 12(a)(2) can take two forms in a commercial paper case. First, the plaintiff may rely on an allegedly false or misleading disclosure document used in connection with the sale. Second, the plaintiff can rely on asserted implied representations by the dealer to the effect that it believed that the commercial paper issuer was creditworthy *and* that this belief was based on a reasonable investigation.

The format of commercial paper disclosure documents can affect an investor's ability to make the first form of claim described above. For example, if the documents contain, refer to or incorporate by reference all or any of the issuer's 1934 Act reports, then the plaintiff may be able to find (with the aid of hindsight) some incorrect statement or an omission that made a statement misleading. The plaintiff's task is usually even easier if the dealer, in preparing the disclosure document, excerpted information from the issuer's public reports or edited or summarized some of this information. On the other hand, if the documents contain only "bare bones" information about the commercial paper program (size of program, denominations, form and ratings), with a reference to the issuer or its 1934 Act reports for further information, it will be much harder for the plaintiff to point to deficiencies in the document. It will also be harder for the investor to claim that the commercial paper was sold to him "by means of" a specific document or communication, which is an essential element of Section 12(a)(2), or on the basis of an implied recommendation by the dealer.

There appears to be a trend among dealers toward "bare bones" offering documents in commercial paper programs. There are probably two reasons why this did not happen at an earlier date. First, many dealers were influenced by the terms of the SEC's 1974 settlement of injunctive proceedings against Goldman, Sachs & Co. arising out of the Penn Central bankruptcy and commercial paper default.[97] These terms contemplated that the dealer would provide investors with information relating to the credit worthiness of the issuer. It was common knowledge at the time that the SEC's Division of Enforcement expected the settlement to establish a standard of commercial paper disclosure comparable to that required by the 1933 Act.

Second, the SEC began to amend its 1934 Act reporting forms in the early 1970s to require much more extensive information about an issuer's business and financial condition. The availability of informative 1934 Act reports made it easier for dealers to include these reports (or excerpts from the reports) as part of their commercial paper disclosure materials. The incentive to do so was probably influenced by the fact that investors did not have ready access to 1934 Act reports except from the issuer or an intermediary such as a dealer.

Conditions have changed significantly in the past few years regarding the availability of 1934 Act reports, which are now readily available to investors through electronic and other sources. Moreover, investors in commercial paper are typically sophisticated investors who have access to this information as well as the ability to analyze it and make their own credit judgments.

---

97. *SEC v. Goldman, Sachs & Co.*, SEC Litigation Rel. No. 6349 (May 2, 1974) (S.D.N.Y. Docket No. 74 Civ. 1916 (HRT)).

Finally, the market has come to rely to a much greater degree on the rating agencies.

Accordingly, disclosure documents for commercial paper programs are more likely to be limited to the "bare bones" of the program and to refer the investor to the issuer or an electronic data base for the issuer's 1934 Act and other public reports—and even the paper's current rating. This is especially the case if there are multiple dealers and the issuer is responsible for producing the disclosure documents. In these cases, there is not really a good reason for any dealer's name or logo to appear on the disclosure document. Unfortunately, many dealers cannot resist the temptation to see their name associated with that of the issuer.

The second form of Section 12(a)(2) exposure described above is more difficult for a dealer to mitigate. It is based on the concept that a dealer in commercial paper makes an implied representation regarding its belief in the issuer's creditworthiness and, further, that this belief is based on a reasonable investigation. To be sure, the determination of what is a "reasonable" investigation will depend on the facts.

In an extended series of cases decided between 1972 and 1981,[98] purchasers of defaulted commercial paper sued the dealer who had marketed it. At a time when the plaintiff's case was based on Rule 10b-5, a panel of the Seventh Circuit referred to the dealer as the "exclusive underwriter" of the paper and noted that:

> An underwriter's relationship with the issuer gives the underwriter access to facts that are not equally available to members of the public who must rely on published information. And the relationship between the underwriter and its customers implicitly involves a favorable recommendation of the issued security. Because the

---

98. *Sanders v. John Nuveen & Co., Inc.*, 524 F.2d 1064 (7th Cir. 1975) (*Sanders II*), *vacated and remanded on other grounds*, 425 U.S. 929 (1976), *on remand*, 554 F.2d 790 (7th Cir. 1977) (*Sanders III*), *reh'g denied*, 619 F.2d 1222 (7th Cir. 1980) (*Sanders IV*), *cert. denied*, 450 U.S. 1005 (1981).

public relies on the integrity, independence and expertise of the underwriter, the underwriter's participation significantly enhances the marketability of the security. And since the underwriter is unquestionably aware of the public's reliance on his participation in the sale of the issue, the mere fact that he has underwritten it is an implied representation that he has met the standards of his profession in his investigation of the issuer.[99]

Ultimately, the case became one under Section 12(a)(2) of the 1933 Act, but the Seventh Circuit adhered to the previous panel's conclusion (when the case was based on Rule 10b-5) that the dealer had not made a "reasonable investigation" of the issuer because it had not reviewed the issuer's tax returns and its accountant's work papers. In response to the dealer's argument that the previous panel had confused the "reasonable investigation" standard of Section 11 with the "reasonable care" defense of Section 12(a)(2), and that by so doing it had held the dealer to a standard higher than that imposed in a Section 11 case, the Seventh Circuit concluded that it could "find no significance in this difference in language [i.e., "reasonable investigation" as opposed to "reasonable care"] in the case at bar."[100] It also suggested that it did not regard it as "at all clear" that there was always a higher standard in a Section 11 case.[101]

The Supreme Court denied a writ of *certiorari* over a dissent by Justices Powell and Rehnquist, who noted that the SEC had filed a brief in the Seventh Circuit arguing that it would "undermine the Congressional intent . . . if the same degree of investigation were to be required to avoid potential liability whether or not a registration statement is required."[102] The dissenting Justices were particularly troubled by the Seventh Circuit's having "denied" the dealer the "right to rely on 'the authority of an expert' " —the issuer's auditors in this case—that it would

---

99. 524 F.2d at 1069–70 (footnotes omitted).
100. 619 F.2d at 1228.
101. *Id.*
102. 450 U.S. at 1009 (quoting Brief of SEC, filed in *Sanders III*).

have had if the commercial paper had been registered under the 1933 Act.[103]

In *University Hill Foundation v. Goldman, Sachs & Co.*,[104] one of the cases involving Penn Central's 1970 default on its commercial paper, Judge Lasker concluded that it would be "inappropriate to import wholesale to the commercial paper context" the duties imposed on an underwriter under Section 11. He also rejected a reading of *Sanders* as "establishing an inflexible rule that an investigation which fails to include firsthand verification of an issuer's financial condition is *per se* unreasonable." Rather, a commercial paper dealer's obligations under Section 12(a)(2) should be analyzed in terms of

> a close consideration of the facts of the relationship between Penn Central and Goldman, Sachs, the latter's access to information, the nature of the data it relied upon and the presence or absence of "warning signals." . . . Based on the role it played in marketing Penn Central notes, Goldman, Sachs' credit investigation must be judged by a fairly rigorous standard. . . . [I]t singlehandedly directed the entire distribution campaign and was the exclusive source of the notes for all would-be purchasers. Not only was its relationship to the Penn Central management, therefore, uniquely close, but its implicit warrant of the soundness of its basis for recommending the notes was correspondingly far greater than that of an ordinary broker-dealer. . . .[105]

---

103. *Id.* at 1009–10. The ABA Task Force on Sellers' Due Diligence Defenses and Similar Defenses under the Federal Securities Laws (of which one of the authors was co-chair) agreed with the dissenting Justices that *Sanders* should be confined to its facts and expressed the belief that the current Supreme Court would recognize the significant distinction between "reasonable investigation" and "reasonable care" that the words of the statute imply. 48 Bus. Law. 1185, 1238–39 (1993).

104. 422 F. Supp. 879 (S.D.N.Y. 1976).

105. *Id.* at 900–01.

Ultimately, Judge Lasker held that there had been sufficient "storm warnings" about Penn Central's financial condition that should have led Goldman, Sachs to make further inquiries, to require access to internal records and projections, and to verify them. Its failure to do so, the court concluded, made its ongoing credit investigation unreasonable and its representation to the purchaser untrue within the meaning of Section 12(a)(2).[106]

Of course, the market has changed a great deal since Judge Lasker's decision. Any given dealer is no longer the "exclusive source" of an issuer's paper, and even all the dealers as a group may not have a practical means of obtaining direct access to the issuer for the purpose of verifying the issuer's creditworthiness. Indeed, it may not be practical for a dealer to do more than periodically review publicly available rating and credit information about the issuer.

• • *Rule 10b-5.* Rule 10b-5 applies only to misstatements or omissions made in connection with the purchase or sale of a "security." Unlike the 1933 Act, Section 3(a)(10) of the 1934 Act specifically excludes from the definition of a security "any note which has a maturity at the time of issuance of not exceeding nine months." If the definition were applied literally, there could be no liability under Rule 10b-5 in a commercial paper case. As noted above, however, the Second Circuit has held that a short-term note is not excluded from Rule 10b-5 unless it meets the general notion of commercial paper reflected in SEC Release No. 33-4412, including the prime quality requirement. In view of the U.S. Supreme Court's recent emphasis on the text of federal statutes, the Second Circuit position may be open to question.[107]

---

106. *Id.* at 902. Under this analysis, a dealer that has breached its implied representation about the reasonableness of its credit investigation—which creates the false statement that Section 12(a)(2) requires—presumably does not get a second chance to argue the same point as an affirmative defense under Section 12(a)(2).

107. The courts that considered whether Penn Central notes were securities either did not reach the issue by finding no Section 10(b) liability or followed the criteria in SEC Release No. 33-4412 and found the notes lacking

From the dealer's point of view, it is not very important whether the plaintiff can bring a claim under Rule 10b-5 as well as under Section 12(a)(2). This was not the case, of course, when the statute of limitations for actions brought under Rule 10b-5 was thought to be longer than that allowed for Section 12(a)(2) actions. On the other hand, Rule 10b-5 is likely to be the only federal remedy available to a plaintiff for purposes of proceeding against non-"seller" potential defendants such as accountants or rating agencies. (This is not to say that such a plaintiff could not use Rule 10b-5 to reach the issuer of the commercial paper, but an issuer that cannot pay its commercial paper at maturity is likely to be in bankruptcy proceedings by the time litigation is commenced.)

---

in one or more respects and thus subject to the 1934 Act. *See Franklin Savings Bank of New York v. Levy,* 551 F.2d 521, 527–28 (2d Cir. 1977); *University Hill Foundation v. Goldman, Sachs & Co.,* 422 F. Supp. 879, 905 (S.D.N.Y. 1976); *Mallinckrodt Chem. Works v. Goldman, Sachs & Co.,* 420 F. Supp. 231, 239–41 (S.D.N.Y. 1976); *Alton Box Board Co. v. Goldman, Sachs & Co.,* 418 F. Supp. 1149, 1157–58 (E.D. Mo. 1976), *rev'd,* 560 F.2d 916 (8th Cir. 1977); *Welch Foods, Inc. v. Goldman, Sachs & Co.,* 398 F. Supp. 1393, 1397–99 (S.D.N.Y. 1974).

Chapter 11

INNOVATIVE FINANCING TECHNIQUES

Innovation in the financial markets is spurred in the first instance by competition among investment banking firms. While always fierce, this competition intensified during the 1980s and 1990s as a result of the Rule 415 environment and the breakdown in traditional investment banking relationships. More recently, competition has been stimulated by the introduction of sophisticated modeling techniques, the increased importance of hedge funds and other knowledgeable investors and an increased emphasis—not always for the better—on achieving financial reporting or tax objectives. Volatile markets also play an important role in forcing investment bankers to develop innovative debt and equity securities that will better serve the needs of potential issuers, whether or not traditional clients, as well as the interests of investors.

Even in times of relative stability, innovation remains the keynote of investment banking. The major firms have formed product development departments that work with securities lawyers to create new financial instruments. One way of enabling issuers to finance at a lower all-in cost is through the use of tax benefits, and for this reason tax counsel plays a significant role in the process. Good accounting advice is also essential, not only with a view to the current accounting rules but also with an eye on what may be on the horizon. The process is highly market-oriented with new products being designed not only to serve the needs of issuers but also to meet the demands of portfolio managers and other investors.

Innovative products often have long gestation periods during which the bankers, counsel and accountants explore various means of accomplishing companies' objectives. The process can involve considerable expense, which of course needs to be amortized once a product gets to the stage where it can be the subject of actual transactions. The cost of legal opinions, for example, may include an amount in respect of development cost.

There is a difference, of course, between keeping in mind the tax and accounting consequences of a transaction and arranging a transaction that has no purpose but to achieve tax or accounting objectives. As discussed in Chapter 5, investment banking firms have come to recognize that they cannot "turn a blind eye" to the financial reporting and other consequences of the transactions that they arrange for their issuer clients. It hardly pays to earn a fee or league table credit—or even be considered for "Deal of the Year" recognition—for a transaction that later explodes into a legal and reputational disaster.[1]

Investment bankers like to package new instruments in exotic formats with fancy names that are often formulated to create a catchy acronym. Merrill Lynch's Treasury Investment Growth Receipts were known as "TIGRs" and were followed by equity products such as "LYONS," "PRIDES" and "STRYPES." Other firms have comparable products and acronyms. The trademark bar has been an unintended beneficiary of Wall Street's creativity.[2]

---

1. *See* the proposed *Interagency Statement on Sound Practices Concerning Complex Structured Finance Activities,* SEC Release No. 34-49695 (May 14, 2004).

2. For a collection of products that have been "service marked" by investment banking firms, *see* Securities Industry Association, *Capital Markets Handbook* 1137–42 (John C. Burch, Jr. and Bruce S. Foerster eds., 5th ed. 2004).

INNOVATIVE FINANCING TECHNIQUES

Given the events of recent years, however, it goes without saying that too much creativity can backfire. Parmalat's use of an investment vehicle whose name could be roughly translated as "black hole" ranks alongside Sun Company's use in the 1970s of a vehicle called "L.H.I.W."[3]

The financial community's response to the changing needs of issuers and investors has, of course, not been limited to the development of innovative securities products. These products occupy only a portion of the spectrum of derivative products that Wall Street has developed in recent years. For example, swap contracts also play an important role for many issuers and investors, whether the contracts are keyed to interest or currency rates, credit standing or commodity or equity prices. Caps, floors and collars are also part of the corporate treasurer's and institutional investor's arsenals, along with options on commodities, currencies and equities. Exchange-traded futures and options provide additional alternatives for hedging risk.

The ABA Section on Business Law's Committee on Developments in Business Financing publishes annually a useful review of innovative financial products.

For any innovative product, there are certain key questions that the securities lawyer must address. These may arise from the point of view of the issuer of the product or from that of the broker-dealers who will be selling the product and maintaining a secondary market. To start with, all of the participants in the transaction are obviously interested in whether the product should be treated as a security within the meaning of the 1933 Act. As discussed in Chapter 1, the line between securities and non-securities is not always so clear. If the product is to be treated as a security, however, is it to be registered with the SEC? If not, what exemption is available? Is the product a futures contract or option subject to regulation by the CFTC under the Commodities Exchange Act? What disclosure obligations will arise, either regarding the issuer or the product itself?

---

3. Standing for "Let's hope it works." *Wellman v. Dickinson*, 475 F. Supp. 783 (S.D.N.Y. 1979), *aff'd*, 682 F.2d 355 (2d Cir. 1982), *cert. denied*, 460 U.S. 1069 (1983).

From the standpoint of the broker-dealer, how will the product be marketed, and what information will be supplied to the sales force? Are there any special suitability standards that should be applied as a matter of prudence or as required by the NASD[4] or another market on which the product is traded? If the product must be carried in inventory for a time, what will be the impact on the broker-dealer's regulatory net capital? Is the product eligible for margin credit? May it be the subject of repurchase agreement financing? How will transactions be cleared and settled?

From the issuer's standpoint, does it have systems in place that are adequate to measure its exposure under the product? Does the issuer plan to engage in any hedging activity as a result of the offering? How will the issuer treat the product and any related hedging activity for financial reporting and tax purposes?

Regulation Under the Commodity Exchange Act

Until just a few years ago, one of the principal legal challenges to innovative financing techniques was the possibility that an instrument might be subject to regulation as a futures contract under the Commodity Exchange Act (CEA). For example, beginning principally in June 1986 with an issue of oil indexed notes by The Standard Oil Company of Ohio, many issuers sold debt instruments where the amount of principal payable at maturity and/or the interest rate was tied to the performance of a commodity, a stock or bond index, a foreign currency or the rate of inflation. By providing the investor with a play on the price movement of the underlying commodity or index, the issuer could attach a lower fixed interest rate to the obligation.

Some of these so-called "hybrid" instruments raised the question whether they were the economic equivalent of commodity

---

4. NASD Rule 4420(f)(3) refers to NASDAQ's evaluating the "nature and complexity" of a product and contemplating the possibility of a circular to the NASD's membership providing guidance about compliance responsibilities and requirements. See, e.g., SEC Release 34-47350 (February 11, 2003) (approving NASDAQ's listing and trading of a "callable puttable common stock").

INNOVATIVE FINANCING TECHNIQUES

option contracts or futures contracts subject to the jurisdiction of the CFTC and thus prohibited as off-board transactions under the CEA.

- *Evolution of the Regulatory Structure*

Section 4(a) of the CEA provides that it is unlawful to enter into a commodity futures contract that is not made "on or subject to the rules of a board of trade which has been designated by the Commission as a 'contract market' for such commodity."

Futures contracts are contracts for the purchase or sale of a commodity for delivery at a specified time in the future at a price that is established when the contract is made. Both parties to the contract are obligated to fulfill the contract at the agreed price, but contracts providing for delivery may usually be closed out by paying the price differential. Thus, a speculator in commodity futures need not wind up with a pile of soybeans on his front lawn.

Futures contracts are undertaken principally to assume or shift price risk without transferring title to the underlying commodity. The contracts have standard terms. There are margin requirements, and clearing organizations match trades and guarantee counterparty performance.

Prior to the early 1970s, trading in the pits of the commodity exchanges was limited to trading in contracts for physical commodities—wheat, cotton, pork bellies, frozen concentrated orange juice, and the like. In 1974, the CEA was amended to broaden the definition of "commodity" to include not only agricultural commodities (except onions) but also all "services, rights, and interests in which contracts for future delivery are presently *or in the future* dealt in" (emphasis added). At the same time, Congress created the CFTC to assume the functions previously performed by the Department of Agriculture, functions that were no longer thought appropriate for the department as futures markets expanded beyond physical commodities into financial instruments.

During the 1970s, the Chicago Mercantile Exchange developed under the leadership of Leo Malamed a market for futures contracts on foreign currencies, Eurobonds, U.S. Treasury obligations and broad-based stock indices. A major event was the introduction in April 1982 of the S&P 500 futures contract, an instrument that played an important role in the "market break" of October 1987.[5] It was not long before other index futures contracts and stock index options came to be traded under the jurisdiction of the CFTC.

The status of financial products traded elsewhere than on the futures exchanges was often ambiguous. If an off-board product turned out to be a contract for future delivery of a commodity, the contract would be illegal. And the CEA had no exemption, similar to Section 4(2) of the 1933 Act or Section 3(c)(7) of the 1940 Act, for non-public transactions among sophisticated persons.

One example of such ambiguity led Congress in 1974 to add the "Treasury Amendment" to the CEA. The Department of the Treasury had been concerned that the definition of "commodity" was so broad as to make illegal off-board contracts for government securities and foreign currency or at least to make trading in these contracts subject to regulation by the CFTC. The amendment excluded from the CEA transactions in foreign currency, securities and other instruments unless such transactions involved a sale for future delivery on a board of trade. The scope of the exclusion became the subject of extensive litigation.

In 1980, the SEC and the CFTC became embroiled in a dispute over which agency had jurisdiction over options on GNMA pass-through certificates. While litigation was pending, the chairmen of the two agencies (John R. Shad of the SEC and Phillip Johnson of the CFTC) reached an accord to the effect that jurisdiction over options follows jurisdiction over the instruments on which the options are written. The SEC took jurisdiction over options on securities, and the CFTC took jurisdiction over options on futures contracts (including futures contracts based on securities indices). The courts, however, held that the agencies could not alter their jurisdiction by mutual agreement and that options on GNMA pass-throughs came within the jurisdiction of the CFTC.[6] Congress then passed legislation that codified the Shad–Johnson accord.

---

5. *See* T. Metz, *Black Monday* (1988).

6. *Chicago Board of Trade v. SEC*, 677 F.2d 1137 (7th Cir.), *vacated as moot*, 459 U.S. 1026 (1982).

The status of swaps under the CEA and also under the federal securities laws became an issue during the 1990s,[7] as did the ability of banks to engage in transactions involving instruments such as certificates of deposit that were indexed to commodities.

- *The Commodity Futures Modernization Act of 2000*

Many of these questions were clarified when Congress enacted the Commodity Futures Modernization Act of 2000 (CFMA).[8] This statute amended the CEA to provide exemptions and exclusions from the CEA's prohibition against OTC commodities transactions.

SEC–CFTC Jurisdiction. As amended by CFMA, the CEA does not apply to (and the SEC has exclusive jurisdiction over) options on securities or on any group or index of securities that is "narrow-based" as defined. On the other hand, the CEA does apply to (and the CFTC has exclusive jurisdiction over) contracts for future delivery based on a group or index of securities that is not narrow-based, as well as options on such contracts. The SEC and the CFTC have joint regulatory authority over futures contracts (and options on futures) based on one or more securities, including any narrow-based securities index.

Treasury Amendment. CFMA clarified the Treasury Amendment so as to exclude from the CEA transactions in foreign currency, government securities and certain other instruments unless the transaction involves a futures contract traded on a futures exchange. Unless executed by regulated financial institutions, however, the CEA applies to off-board retail transactions in foreign currency.

Excluded Derivative Transactions. Transactions in "excluded commodities"[9] are excluded from the CEA if the transactions involve only "eligible contract participants" and are not executed or traded on a trading facility (with certain exceptions for

---

7. *See, e.g., Procter & Gamble Co. v. Bankers Trust Co.*, 925 F. Supp. 1270 (S.D. Ohio 1996).

8. Pub. L. No. 106-554, 114 Stat. 2763 (2000).

9. An "excluded commodity" means (a) an interest rate, exchange rate, currency, security, security index, credit risk or measure, debt or equity instrument, index or measure of inflation, or other macroeconomic index or measure, (b) any other rate, differential, index, or measure of economic or commercial risk, return, or value that is either not based on the value of

electronic trading facilities). "Eligible contract participants" are specified financial institutions or individuals with specified minimum levels of total assets. For the first time, therefore, the CEA has an exemption similar to the 1933 Act's or 1940 Act's exemptions for large and sophisticated investors.

Hybrid Instruments. A "hybrid instrument" that is "predominantly a security" is excluded from all provisions of the CEA. A "hybrid instrument" for this purpose is a security having one or more payments indexed to the value of one or more commodities. A hybrid instrument is "predominantly" a security, and therefore regulated under the federal securities laws, if (A) the issuer of the hybrid instrument receives payment in full substantially contemporaneously with its delivery, (B) the purchaser or holder of the hybrid instrument is not required to make any payment to the issuer in addition to the purchase price, whether as margin, settlement payment or otherwise, during the life of the instrument or at maturity, (C) the instrument does not require the issuer to post margin on a mark-to-market basis[10] and (D) the instrument is not marketed as a futures contract (or option thereon) or commodity option.

An indexed debt security that satisfies these conditions is excluded from regulation by the CFTC, even if the security is sold to retail investors. Because non-exempt securities are "commodities," exchangeable securities and equity-linked notes must qualify for the hybrid instrument exclusion to achieve the legal certainty that they are not offered and sold in violation of the CEA. In determining whether a security qualifies as an excluded hybrid instrument, particular attention must be paid to (i) the disclosure and marketing materials, to ensure that the security is

---

a narrow group of commodities not described in clause (a) or is based solely on one or more commodities that have no cash market, (c) any economic or commercial index based on inputs that are not within the control of any party to the relevant agreement or (d) an occurrence, extent of an occurrence or contingency that is (i) not previously described, (ii) beyond the control of the parties to the relevant agreement and (iii) associated with a financial, commercial or economic consequence.

10. The issuer-related margining prohibition does not prevent an issuer of a secured debt instrument from increasing the amount of collateral it pledges for the benefit of the holder to secure its obligations under the debt instrument.

not marketed as a futures contract (or option thereon) or commodity option and (ii) whether there is an actively managed trading aspect of the commodity-indexation component, to ensure that the security is not subject to recharacterization as a CFTC-regulated commodity trading account or commodity pool, each triggering distinct registration and other regulatory requirements.[11]

Excluded Swap Transactions. Swaps related to non-agricultural commodities are excluded from the CEA if they are entered into between eligible contract participants, subject to individual negotiation by the parties and not executed or traded on a trading facility.[12]

Transactions in Exempt Commodities. The CEA does not apply, except for its antifraud and antimanipulation provisions, to transactions in "exempt commodities" if entered into between eligible contract participants and elsewhere than on a trading facility. Slightly broader exemptions apply for transactions in exempt commodities entered into on a principal-to-principal basis between "eligible commercial entities" and that are entered into on an electronic trading facility.

Exempt commodities include those that are neither "excluded commodities" (as discussed above) nor agricultural commodities. Examples include energy and metals derivatives.

---

11. The exclusion for hybrid instruments that are predominantly securities is similar to pre-CFMA exemptions set forth in Part 34 of the CFTC's regulations adopted in 1989 (17 C.F.R. Part 34) and the CFTC's 1989 Statutory Interpretation Concerning Certain Hybrid Instruments (54 *Federal Register* 1139 (CFTC, January 11, 1989)). The CFMA exclusion differs from the CFTC's two pre-CFMA exemptions in that the "predominance" test is now primarily determined by whether the hybrid instrument is a security or identified banking product, rather than based on complex mathematical formulaic tests that often required the assistance of an economist to apply. For a complete description of the pre-CFMA hybrid instrument exemptions, *see* Chapter 11 of the second edition of this book at pages 725–37.

12. Swaps that meet these conditions and others specified in the Gramm-Leach-Billey Act, whether or not they relate to securities, are also excluded by the CFMA from the 1933 Act and 1934 Act definitions of "security." Swaps excluded from the definition of security do not include those capable of characterization as options or forward contracts, those that relate to debt securities or certain transactions by issuers through underwriters for the purpose of raising capital.

Traditional Bank Products. CFMA also excludes from the CEA hybrid instruments that are "predominantly" identified banking products (as defined in Sections 206(a)(1)–(5) of the Gramm–Leach–Bliley Act), such as deposit instruments, loans, letters of credit, banker's acceptances and loan participations that are offered by U.S. depository institutions, foreign banks and branches and agencies of foreign banks, federal or state credit unions, Edge Act corporations and trust companies, or the subsidiaries of such entities that are regulated as if they were part of such entities, other than broker-dealers or futures commission merchants. The exclusion applies to any identified banking product that (A) an appropriate banking agency certifies was commonly offered in the United States by any such financial institution on or before December 5, 2000, under applicable banking law and (B) was not prohibited by the CEA or regulated by the CFTC as a futures contract (or option thereon) or commodity option on or prior to such date. Any newly developed banking product that is a hybrid instrument, that is, indexed to a commodity, is also excluded from the CEA if it is "predominantly a banking product" pursuant to criteria similar to those set forth above for hybrid instruments that are "predominantly a security." The CFTC must consult with and seek the Federal Reserve Board's concurrence before regulating such products, and in the event of litigation the court is to decide the issue without giving deference to the views of either the CFTC or the Federal Reserve Board.

State Law Preemption. Section 12(e)(2)(B) of the CEA preempts state gaming and bucket shop laws (other than antifraud provisions of general applicability) with respect to excluded hybrid instruments. CFMA also amended Section 28(a) of the 1934 Act to preempt the application of state gaming and bucket shop laws to any security that is "subject to" the 1934 Act, whether or not the security is traded on a securities exchange or otherwise traded pursuant to the rules of an SRO.

Debt Securities with Embedded Options

It sounds exotic to describe a debt security as having an "embedded option," but nothing could be simpler. A convertible security (as discussed in Chapter 12) contains an embedded "call" option in the form of a privilege on the part of the holder to convert the security into the issuer's common stock. Obviously, the holder will do so only if the value of the common stock received at the time of conversion is in excess of the principal amount of the debt security. At the same time, the holder is under no compulsion to convert just because this is the case. Rather, the holder may choose to defer conversion since the option represented by the conversion feature will continue—like other options—to have "time value."

All straight debt securities that permit the issuer to redeem the securities prior to their maturity date can also be said to have an embedded call option, that is, the issuer has a contractual right to "call" on the holders to deliver back the security in exchange for cash in the amount of the agreed-on redemption price. Presumably, the issuer will take advantage of this right if interest rates decline subsequent to the issuance of the security. In that case, the issuer will be able to borrow money more cheaply elsewhere and use the proceeds to redeem the more expensive debt securities. Of course, purchasers of debt securities are aware of this possibility, and they often bargain for protections such as a minimum number of years before the issuer may redeem the bonds, a redemption "premium" that makes it more expensive for the issuer to redeem the securities in the early years of their life and (on some occasions) a prohibition on redemption with the use of money borrowed at a cheaper cost.

More recently, companies have issued debt securities with embedded "put" options, that is, a privilege on the part of the holder to elect to deliver the security at agreed-on intervals in exchange for payment of the agreed-on "put" price. Presumably, the holder will take advantage of this right if interest rates increase subsequent to the issuance of the security. In that case, the holder will be able to reinvest elsewhere at a better rate the cash received from the issuer. Credit considerations may also play a role.

Options are seldom without cost, whether embedded or not. The purchaser of a convertible bond "pays" for the option on the common stock by accepting a lower coupon rate on the convertible securities. The issuer of a redeemable security pays for the right to redeem the bond by paying a higher coupon rate. The buyer of a "puttable" bond pays for the privilege by accepting a lower coupon rate.

When an issuer registers its convertible securities with the SEC under the 1933 Act, it also registers at the same time the securities into which the convertible securities are convertible. As discussed in Chapter 12, this is because the offering is deemed to involve the underlying securities as well as the convertible securities (at least if the convertible securities are immediately convertible). Even though the purchaser is also paying for the embedded call option represented by the conversion privilege (and even though options on securities are defined as securities for all purposes of the 1933 Act), no one has argued that the issuer should also be registering the embedded call option as a separate security. In this respect, the offering is unlike an offering that might be economically and functionally equivalent to a convertible security offering, for example, an offering of straight debt or preferred securities with attached warrants to purchase common stock, in which case (as discussed in Chapter 12) the warrants would have to be registered as a separate security. The difference, of course, is that the warrants will usually trade separately at some point, while the conversion feature in a convertible security usually remains embedded for the life of the security.

In the case of a redeemable security, the embedded option is really being purchased by the issuer from the purchaser of the redeemable security. More precisely, one might say that the issuer has "retained" the privilege of calling back the securities and paid for this privilege by paying a higher coupon rate. No one has suggested, however, that there would be any point in worrying about whether the holders' options should be registered under the 1933 Act.

In the case of puttable securities, the issuer is "selling" an option to the buyers of the securities. The question, therefore, arises whether the put should be separately registered along with the securities. As in the case of convertible securities, however, the option usually remains embedded for the life of the security. It would be pointless to register the put as a separate security.

There is no reason, however, why an issuer of redeemable securities should not be able to "detach" or "strip out" its right to redeem the securities. In a 1993 transaction, Safeway Inc. did precisely this in connection with the issuance of SEC-registered underwritten medium-term notes. Safeway's right to redeem the notes after two years was stripped out in the form of "option purchase rights" that were sold in a Rule 144A transaction to QIBs. Upon exercise of the option purchase rights and deposit of the principal amount of the notes, the QIBs would be deemed to have purchased the notes from the original holders of the notes (presumably in reliance on the Section 4(1) exemption). At this time, of course, the QIBs would be the owners of non-redeemable notes with a remaining life to maturity of eight years.

The fact that it was deemed necessary to sell the option purchase rights in a Rule 144A transaction suggests that the rights were assumed to be separate securities on their being stripped out of the notes. Indeed, it was necessary to persuade the SEC staff that there should be no "integration" between the public sale of the notes and the private sale of the rights. It is difficult, however, to see a separate security where the rights are stripped out by the issuer contemporaneously with the issuance of the notes and without any involvement, decision or payment by the original holders. It also helps that the notes were book-entry securities deposited with DTC, thus simplifying the purchase of the notes by the QIBs on exercise of the rights.

Safeway was also able to persuade the SEC staff that the deemed sale of the notes by the holders thereof to the QIBs who were exercising their option purchase rights was a secondary market transaction exempt under Section 4(1) and not a distribution by the issuer.[13]

The technique of "stripping out" the issuer's right to redeem debt securities has also been applied to municipal securities.

Inflation-Indexed Debt Securities

An early example of an inflation-indexed debt security was an issue of one-year Inflation Indexed Notes paying interest quarterly at the rate of 2.15% per annum sold by Federal National Mortgage

---

13. It was also necessary to persuade the staff that the transaction was a proper use of the issuer's shelf registration statement. The issuer took the position that the registration statement contemplated the sale of redeemable securities and that the option purchase rights should be viewed as an assignment of the redemption rights.

Association under an offering circular dated July 19, 1988. Under the terms of the instrument, the principal was revalued on each interest payment date with reference to the consumer price index.

In early 1997, the U.S. Treasury sold its first inflation-indexed bonds. These are formally known as Treasury Inflation-Indexed Securities but are more often referred to as Treasury Inflation-Protected Securities or "TIPS." The principal amount of these bonds is adjusted based on changes in the Consumer Price Index–Urban over time, while interest on the bonds accrues at a fixed rate based on the adjusted principal amount of the bonds. One of the disadvantages of TIPS is that the holder accrues phantom income for income tax purposes based on the increased principal amount that the holder will not receive until maturity.

Many corporate and quasi-governmental issuers and banks have also sold debt securities at interest rates—not principal amounts—that are linked to the Consumer Price Index–Urban. They are therefore more attractive for taxable investors.

Inflation-indexed debt securities are attractive for issuers whose revenues tend to rise with inflation, such as commodity producers or utilities. Other issuers may prefer to swap their way out of the inflation risk, and these issuers may find an inflation-indexed financing more cost effective than a straight debt financing, even after taking into account the cost of the swap.

Despite criticism from an advisory committee to the effect that TIPS were an expensive adjunct to the Treasury's funding operations, the amount of outstanding TIPS had increased by February 2004 to $187.5 billion or about 5% of outstanding Treasury debt.[14] Corporations and banks have also begun to issue inflation-indexed securities.

Retail-Oriented Issuer Debt Programs

Innovative financing techniques can involve the method of distribution as well as what is being distributed. One of the remarkable financing techniques developed over the past few years is the continuous sale by "household name" corporations

---

14. *See* the website of The Bond Market Association at www.bondmarkets.com/Research/TreasOutstandMO.shtml.

of their investment-grade notes to retail investors, often with the aid of Internet websites. General Motors Acceptance Corporation pioneered this technique in 1996 with its "SmartNotes." Other platforms include CoreNotes, which is operated by Merrill Lynch & Co. on behalf of Ford Motor Credit Company, Fannie Mae, Principal Life, The Bank of New York, The Gillette Company and other issuers; InterNotes, which is operated by InCapital LLC on behalf of Bank of America Corp., Boeing, CIT, Daimler Chrysler, Dow Chemical, GE Capital, Household Finance and other companies; and Direct Access Notes, which is operated by LaSalle Bank Corporation and ABN AMRO Financial Services, Inc. on behalf of GMAC's SmartNotes and ten other companies.

The websites for these offerings display a logo of the issuers whose securities are available for purchase, a "fact sheet" with publicly available information on each issuer, a rate chart for each issuer and a copy of the final prospectus. There is no need to limit the information to that permitted under the safe harbor of Rule 134 because the inclusion of a link to the final prospectus takes all the information out of the category of "prospectus" within the meaning of Section 2(a)(10)(a) and therefore prevents any Section 5(b)(1) violation.

The securities offered through the programs described above are usually available in minimum denominations of $1,000. In an effort to make corporate debt accessible to even larger numbers of retail investors, investment banks have been "repackaging" debt securities and offering them in $25 minimum denominations. Repackagings of this kind are discussed in Chapter 14.

In a variation on the theme, several large corporations also offer money market accounts. GE Financial's money market account, GE Interest Plus, grew from $3.7 billion at the start of 2003 to $5.3 billion by the end of the year; Ford's product, Ford Money Market, grew from $5.1 billion to $7.4 billion. Other companies offering similar programs include GMAC (DemandNotes) and Caterpillar (Cat Money Market Account).

Trust Preferred Securities

"Trust preferred securities" constitute a subset of a broader category of securities often referred to as "capital securities" or "Tier I Capital Products." The broader category includes a wide variety of securities issued by U.S. and non-U.S. banks subject to capital adequacy guidelines established by the Basel Committee as well as by their national regulators.

The 1988 Basel Accord divided bank capital for the first time into Tier 1 or core capital and Tier 2 or supplementary capital. In late 1996, the Federal Reserve Board approved U.S. bank holding companies' use of trust preferred securities as a means of adding to Tier 1 capital. And in 1998, the Basel Committee announced that it would consider it acceptable for banks to issue "innovative capital instruments" such as trust preferred securities for up to 15% of a bank's Tier 1 capital.[15]

There are many varieties of Tier 1 capital instruments, all of which seek to lower a bank's cost of capital by balancing the instrument's loss-bearing attributes against the bank's tax-saving objectives. Specifically, the instruments are treated for regulatory and rating purposes as the equivalent or near-equivalent of equity securities while the issuer hopes to achieve a tax deduction for payments on the securities (something that is not possible in the case of dividends on common or preferred stock).

Tax-deductible non-operating subsidiary preferred securities ("trust preferred") have become the most common form of innovative Tier 1 capital. A common form of this structure involves a bank holding company's issuance of a junior subordinated debt obligation to a grantor trust. Prior to FIN 46R (discussed below), the trust was treated for accounting purposes as the bank holding company's subsidiary. The trust, whose only asset is the bank holding company's debt obligation, issues its preferred securities to investors. The bank holding company guarantees the preferred securities to the extent of amounts that it pays on the debt obligation issued to the trust. The debt generally has a maturity of 30 years, and interest on the debt is deferrable for up to five consecutive years. The distributions on the trust preferred are cumulative but are payable only to the extent that the bank holding company pays interest on its debt obligation.

---

15. "Basle Committee and U.S. Regulatory Capital Guidelines Treatment of Innovative Tier 1 Capital Instruments" (February 2004), included as Appendix A to Sidley Austin Brown & Wood LLP, *Preferred and Capital Product Development: Focusing on Tier 1 Capital Products* (February 2004).

The effect of the transaction is that the bank holding company achieves Tier 1 capital treatment for regulatory purposes, a partial equity credit from the rating agencies and a tax deduction for its interest payments on the debt.

Although trust preferred securities resemble long-term equity capital, a leading rating agency has stated that it does not assign "an absolute percentage of 'equity credit'" to an instrument for analytic purposes. Rather, the agency views a specific instrument "within the context of the issuer's overall credit fundamentals."[16]

The Federal Reserve Board's approval in late 1996 of trust preferred securities as a means of adding to a bank holding company's Tier 1 capital was conditioned on a minimum five-consecutive-year deferral period on distributions to holders of the preferred securities. In addition, the intercompany loan was required to be subordinated to all other subordinated debt of the bank holding company and to have the "longest feasible maturity." The Board's approval took into consideration the fact that bank holding companies seldom (if ever) suspend their preferred dividends for as much as five years. In addition, other regulated entities such as insurance companies had been able to use similar securities for capital-boosting purposes.

Trust preferred securities received a serious blow in 2003 when the Financial Accounting Standards Board issued FIN 46, which has the consequence of requiring bank holding companies to deconsolidate their "subsidiary" trusts that issue the trust preferred securities.[17] In this event, the trust preferred securities might no longer qualify as Tier 1 capital. In May 2004 the Federal Reserve Board proposed rules that would allow the continued inclusion of trust preferred securities in Tier 1 capital, subject to stricter quantitative limits and qualitative standards.

---

16. Moody's Investors Service, *Moody's Assesses Hybrid Securities* (June 1996), at 7.

17. FIN 46 as revised in December 2003 (FIN 46R) must be applied for periods ending after December 15, 2003 unless a company is eligible for certain exceptions. See "Selected U.S. Bank Regulatory Issues Applicable to Innovative Capital Securities Offerings" (February 2004), included as Appendix B to Sidley Austin Brown & Wood LLP, *Preferred and Capital Product Development: Focusing on Tier 1 Capital Products* (February 2004).

Pending clarification of the status of trust preferred securities as Tier 1 capital, some issuers are reserving the right to redeem the securities if an event occurs that results in adverse consequences for Tier 1 capital treatment.

- *1933 Act Considerations*

In an SEC-registered transaction, the bank holding company will file a registration statement that will cover the trust preferred securities together with the related bank holding company debt securities and guarantees. The trust or trusts that will issue the trust preferred securities (the Trust) and the sponsoring bank holding company will sign the registration statement as co-registrants. Form S-3 will be used in reliance on the bank holding company's eligibility to use that form, the deemed status of the trust as a majority-owned subsidiary of the bank holding company and the deemed equivalence of the bank holding company's obligations to a guarantee of the trust preferred securities. Separate financial statements for the Trust will not be necessary in reliance on Rule 3-10(b) of Regulation S-X.

Trust preferred securities are frequently offered to QIBs pursuant to Rule 144A as well as to offshore investors in reliance on the safe harbor afforded by Regulation S. The question arises under Regulation S as to the "category" in which the offering belongs for purposes of determining the duration of the required "offering restrictions." If the preferred securities were regarded as equity securities of a non-reporting U.S. issuer—namely, the Trust—they would be Category 3 securities subject to a one-year restricted period and other conditions. This is an unreasonable result if the underlying debt securities would themselves be Category 2 securities subject to a 40-day restricted period. To be sure, Rule 903(c)(4) would permit non-participating preferred stock to be treated for this purpose as debt securities subject to Category 3, but this would still require compliance with some onerous conditions. A more promising solution is afforded by Rule 903(c)(5), which permits reliance on a parent company's guarantee of an issuer's "debt securities" to determine the appropriate category. The authors believe that trust preferred securities are similar enough to debt securities to justify reliance on this approach, but the point has not been raised with the SEC staff.

- *1934 Act Considerations*

The Trust does not have ongoing reporting and disclosure obligations under the 1934 Act in reliance on Rule 3-10(b) of Regulation S-X and Rule 12h-5 under the 1934 Act and the deemed equivalence of the bank holding company's obligations to a guarantee of the trust preferred securities.

Moreover, the Trust will not be viewed as subject to the 48-hour prospectus delivery obligation imposed by Rule 15c2-8(b) on underwriters of securities of non-reporting issuers. Again, the basis for this conclusion is the fact that investors are relying on the banking holding company's obligations and that the bank holding company is itself a reporting company.

- *1939 Act Considerations*

All of the following will be qualified as indentures under the Trust Indenture Act of 1939: (a) the Trust's declaration of trust, pursuant to which the trust preferred securities are issued, (b) the indenture pursuant to which the debt securities are issued and (c) the bank holding company's guarantee.

- *1940 Act Considerations*

The Trust will be exempt from the requirements of the 1940 Act in reliance on Rule 3a-5, a rule normally applied for the purpose of exempting finance subsidiaries. To qualify for Rule 3a-5, it is necessary to assume (among other things) that the Trust could be treated as a "corporation" and that the trust preferred securities could be treated as non-voting preferred stock issued by a "finance subsidiary." The SEC staff has acquiesced in these assumptions.[18]

- *Effects of Deconsolidation*

According to public remarks by members of the SEC staff, the conclusions described above regarding omission of the Trust's financial statements from the registration statement, its continuing 1934 Act reporting obligations and its ability to rely

---

18. *See, e.g.*, SEC No-action Letter, *Brown & Wood* (February 24, 2000).

on Rule 3a-5 under the 1940 Act appear to be surviving the Trust's deconsolidation as a result of FIN 46R.

- *"Securitization" of Trust Preferred Securities*

There are many banks and bank holding companies in the United States, and the great majority of them are smaller institutions that would find it challenging because of cost and the absence of a rating to issue trust preferred securities on their own. Some investment banks have for this reason "securitized" the trust preferred securities of a large number of bank issuers and re-offered Collateralized Debt Obligations based on the underlying trust preferred securities.[19]

In a recent transaction of this kind, Keefe Bruyette & Woods, Inc. and FTN Financial Capital Markets in March 2004 caused two issuing entities to be organized in the Cayman Islands and Delaware for the purpose of issuing $539.1 million aggregate principal amount of non-recourse 30-year notes in eight different series. The proceeds of the sale of the notes were used to purchase 69 "capital securities" from trust subsidiaries of 67 depository institution holding companies (PreTS) and subordinated debentures issued by trust subsidiaries of two additional depository institution holding companies and one financial services holding company. The offering document stated that the PreTS had been issued by the trust subsidiaries for the purpose of purchasing junior subordinated deferrable interest debentures issued by the affiliated holding company. The PreTS and the other securities were pledged to secure the notes.

None of the depository institutions nor their holding companies was identified in the offering document for the notes. Rather, a chart and map were provided showing the geographic distribution of the depository institutions among five U.S. regions and the aggregate principal amount of notes associated with each region.

The notes were offered in the United States exclusively to "qualified purchasers" (QPs) as defined in Section 2(a)(51) of

---

19. *See* Moody's Investors Service, *Moody's Approach to Rating U.S. Bank Trust Preferred Security CDOs* (April 14, 2004).

the 1940 Act in order to take advantage of the Section 3(c)(7) exemption (see Chapter 7). Depending on the seniority of the notes being purchased, the QPs had to be either QIBs, institutional accredited investors or accredited investors.

In 2003, Sandler O'Neill & Partners, LP and Keefe Bruyette & Woods, Inc. separately extended these securitized trust preferred offerings to insurance company issuers.

Custody Receipts (Old Bottles Waiting for New Wine)

From time to time, investment bankers come up with the idea of repackaging a security by means of a custody receipt, that is, the security will be deposited with a custodian and remarketed with some variations such as a larger or smaller size. We discussed in Chapter 9 the introduction of American Depository Receipts or ADRs as a more convenient way of buying and selling foreign stocks.

ADRs are separately registered with the SEC under the 1933 Act, but as we saw in Chapter 9 this is largely for historical reasons and does not result in the usual liabilities that attach to an issuer of a new security. Apart from the special case of ADRs, if a broker-dealer deposits a security with a custodian and then sells an interest in the security to its customers, has a new security been created? Has an investment company been created? There is a lot of history on this question that might be useful when the next such product is proposed.

For example, we discussed above the introduction of zero coupon bonds. Initially, these were corporate obligations, but it did not take long for someone to come up with the idea of a zero coupon U.S. Treasury obligation. Of course, no responsible government would issue an instrument that would saddle a future generation with a large balloon payment while the current generation received a free ride with respect to interest payments. But the right to receive the interest payment that comes due on a Treasury obligation 10, 15, or 20 years hence has all of the economic characteristics of a zero coupon obligation.

The Treasury and the Federal Reserve Bank of New York initially opposed the idea of stripping and selling Treasury coupons because of perceived disruptive market effects. The stripping that had taken place had been done on an informal ad hoc basis, and there was no secondary market for the stripped coupons.

In the middle of 1982, after months of study of the economic, tax and regulatory ramifications, Merrill Lynch announced a new program under which the interest and principal components of U.S. Treasury obligations would be sold separately to the public through the use of deposit receipts. By purchasing from Merrill Lynch an instrument called "Treasury Investment Growth Receipts" (or TIGRs), investors would be purchasing zero coupon Treasury obligations. Tax counsel advised Merrill Lynch that TIGRs would be taxed in the same way as any other zero coupon obligation. Merrill Lynch also received opinions of counsel that TIGRs were not securities separate and apart from the underlying Treasury obligations and, thus, were exempt from registration under Section 3(a)(2) of the 1933 Act, which exempts obligations of the United States, and that the custodial arrangement did not constitute an investment company under the 1940 Act.

Other investment banking firms quickly established deposit receipt programs based on the TIGR format. These included the Certificates of Accrual on Treasury Securities (CATS) program of Salomon Brothers and the Treasury Receipt (TR) program sponsored by Goldman, Sachs & Co. and others.

These programs were highly successful, not only for the investment banking firms and their clients, but also in terms of assisting the Treasury in marketing long-term obligations at more favorable rates than would otherwise have been available. The programs were so successful, in fact, that the Treasury, which had originally viewed stripping with skepticism, decided to "move in." In January 1985, the Secretary of the Treasury announced a new program, to be known as "Separate Trading of Registered Interest and Principal of Securities" (STRIPS), pursuant to which the principal and interest payments on certain Treasury securities would be made available for separate trading in the book-entry system. This program enabled investors to purchase Treasury obligation principal and interest payments in the secondary market as zero coupon securities, without the necessity of a custody arrangement.

STRIPS quickly eclipsed the private sector programs. Although the SEC staff never took a no-action position with respect to any of the Treasury stripping programs, it was asked to review subsequent stripping programs involving securities other than U.S. Treasury securities. In a 1989 no-action letter, the SEC staff agreed that receipts sold pursuant to a stripped coupon municipal bond program were subject to the MSRB's rules.[20] While this letter purported to express no view regarding whether the stripped coupon arrangement created a separate security, the conclusion that they constituted "municipal securities" under the 1934 Act necessarily determined that no separate security was created. Similarly, the conclusion reached in two subsequent letters that custodial receipts for municipal[21] and Small Business Administration[22] instruments were entitled to the Section 3(a)(2) exemption also necessarily implied that no separate security was created.[23] Each of these letters also stated that the receipt programs could be operated without registration of an investment company under the 1940 Act.

The conclusions set forth in these letters were conditioned on the program sponsor's obtaining an opinion of counsel that:

— owners of the stripped coupon securities would have all the rights and privileges of owners of the underlying municipal securities;

— each receipt holder, as the real party in interest, would have the right, upon default of the underlying municipal securities, to proceed directly and individually against the issuer of the securities; and

---

20. SEC No-action Letter, *Municipal Securities Rulemaking Board* (January 19, 1989).

21. SEC No-action Letter, *Merrill Lynch, Pierce, Fenner & Smith Inc.* (September 26, 1990). The stripped municipal securities were not redeemable prior to maturity and had no provision for acceleration of maturity on a default.

22. SEC No-action Letter, *Bear, Stearns & Co. Inc.* (January 28, 1992).

23. Another letter stated the agreement of the staffs of three SEC divisions that a custodial receipt program for Section 3(a)(2) exempt securities did not require 1933 Act registration, broker-dealer registration under Section 15(b) of the 1934 Act, or registration of an investment company under the 1940 Act. SEC No-action Letter, *CRT Government Securities, Ltd.* (August 4, 1992).

– the holder of a receipt would not be required to act in concert with other holders or the custodian.

The staff's conclusions also were conditioned on the program sponsor's obtaining an opinion of counsel to the effect that each receipt would represent the entire and undivided interest in the underlying instrument; the custodian bank would perform only clerical or ministerial services on behalf of the receipt holders; neither the custodian nor the sponsor would guarantee or otherwise enhance the creditworthiness of the underlying instrument or the receipt; the custodian would undertake to notify holders in the event of a default and to forward to them copies of all communications from the issuer of the underlying instrument;[24] the underlying instruments would not be considered assets of either the sponsoring firm or the custodian bank; and other factors would not be present, such as remarketing agreements, that would require the investors in the stripped coupon securities to rely on the sponsor or custodian or other third party to obtain the benefit of their investment.

The letters from the SEC staff emphasized that "the custodial arrangements generally are structured to ensure that the custodian's role is essentially passive and that in all material respects the receipt holder is the real party in interest and otherwise treated as the beneficial owner of an interest in the underlying . . . [instrument]." Some lawyers refer to the contemplated structure as being based on a "coat check" theory. For example, each of the staff's letters was conditioned on the issuer of the underlying instrument's not having "officially disavowed" any obligation to the receipt holders, a statement that in the staff's eyes would be the equivalent of a restaurant owner's having announced the right to abscond with the customers' coats.

Similar conditions have formed the basis for the no-action positions of the Division of Corporation Finance and the Division of Investment Management with respect to whether custodial receipts for bonds insured in the secondary market

---

24. Two of the letters limit such communications to those relating to defaults.

were securities required to be registered under the 1933 Act or gave rise to investment companies required to be registered under the 1940 Act.[25] The SEC staff has also issued a number of favorable no-action responses with respect to primary participation programs to which the issuer of the underlying security is a party.[26]

The letters referred to above involved underlying instruments issued by a single person. A 1993 no-action letter acquiesced in a receipt program involving substantially identical convertible preferred stock issued by approximately seven issuers in a "bundled" format, that is, each investor would acquire—in a private placement—a fixed portion of each issuer's preferred stock and, if the investor so elected, receipts evidencing the investor's interest in each issuer's preferred stock. The staff took a no-action position on the existence of an investment company subject to 1940 Act registration but stated its belief that the receipts might nevertheless be separate securities under the 1933 Act.[27]

As noted above, the no-action letters rely on the custodian's role as being "essentially passive." Problems can arise in the separate security and 1940 Act analysis if the custodian may be

---

25. SEC No-action Letter, *Financial Security Assurance Inc.* (March 30, 1988); SEC No-action Letter, *Financial Guaranty Insurance Company* (February 15, 1989).

26. SEC No-action Letter, *Best Products Co., Inc.* (February 11, 1980) (master note arrangement); SEC No-action Letter, *Prudential-American Securities Inc.* (January 26, 1975) (aggregation arrangement involving bankers' acceptances); SEC No-action Letter, *Blyth Eastman Dillon & Co.* (May 21, 1975) (commercial paper safekeeping and hypothecation plan); SEC No-action Letter, *Bankers Trust Co.* (July 4, 1972) (sale of depository receipts for underlying bankers' acceptances); SEC No-action Letter, *Keeling & Co., Inc.* (October 22, 1984) (certificates of participation in municipal leases); SEC No-action Letter, *Lincoln Federal Savings and Loan Association* (January 8, 1985) (pooling of customers' funds in money market deposit accounts); SEC No-action Letter, *E.F. Hutton & Co. Inc.* (March 28, 1985) (units of participation in FSLIC-insured certificates of deposit); SEC No-action Letter, *United Financial Banking Companies, Inc.* (May 11, 1988) (master note commercial paper program).

27. SEC No-action Letter, *Robertson, Stephens & Co.* (March 13, 1993).

called on to perform more than passive functions. The programs involving custodial receipts for components of stripped municipal bonds have been limited to those where the bonds have been defeased with U.S. Treasury obligations (thus making them virtually risk free) or, as discussed above, where high-grade bonds are not redeemable prior to maturity[28] and there is no provision for acceleration of maturity in the event of default. These limitations reduce the custodian's role as well as the risk of total loss that otherwise would be faced by the owner of a coupon component in the event of redemption or acceleration of maturity prior to the due date of the interest payment.

It goes without saying that it would not be feasible to strip corporate obligations unless the custodial arrangements provided for a restructuring of the rights of the holders of the certificates in the event of bankruptcy. In the absence of a provision of this type, the sale of a future interest payment makes sense only where the credit is ironclad. If, for example, a corporation were to file for bankruptcy or if its debt were accelerated as a result of a covenant violation, the future interest payment could simply disappear. Under the Bankruptcy Code, a claim for unmatured interest is not "allowable." There is always a risk in buying corporate obligations, but an investor should not accept the risk that its right to receive payment, in the event of the issuer's bankruptcy, may not even be allowable.

When TIGRs were first developed, the separate security analysis was viewed as precluding an arrangement whereby the custodian would be required to allocate proceeds in the event of bankruptcy, at least if the receipts were to be sold in the United States. The SEC has issued 1940 Act exemptive orders with respect to stripped bond custody receipt programs in which the custodian was provided with the power to allocate proceeds on acceleration in proportion to the relative present values of each outstanding receipt at the time of payment. The orders were conditioned on the receipts being offered in private placements

---

28. Alternatively, receipts could be sold representing only coupons due prior to the first call date.

only to institutional accredited investors in minimum amounts of $150,000.[29]

The SEC staff recently has appeared to be extremely cautious of new arrangements involving custody receipts, especially those involving multiple issuers of the underlying securities where the holder cannot withdraw individual securities.

Remarketings

Investment bankers have devised a variety of securities to provide risk-reducing alternatives to the issuance of fixed-rate, long-term debt in an uncertain interest rate environment. These securities—notes with extendible terms, obligations with adjustable interest rates, preferred stock with dividends reset through auction or remarketing procedures—have been customized to satisfy the needs of the issuer and the appetite of investors and typically rely on remarketing arrangements to facilitate the shifting of risk from one set of investors to another.

For example, extendible notes are those that have a fixed interest rate (or a specified spread over an index) for an initial period, say one or three years, at the end of which the issuer may reset the rate or spread for a specified period based on current market conditions. At this point, the issuer may have the option to redeem the notes at par, although redemption provisions will vary from instrument to instrument. After receiving notice of the new interest rate or spread and the new interest period, holders may elect to have the notes repurchased by the issuer at par.

Remarketings raise two interesting questions under the 1933 Act. The first is whether, if the terms of the securities are changed as a result of the remarketing, there is a "new" security that needs to be registered under the 1933 Act. The second is whether the issuer's involvement in the remarketing is sufficient to cause the dealer conducting the remarketing to be participating in a distribution for the issuer and therefore be an "underwriter." If either of these conclusions were to be reached, it might be

---

29. *See The First Boston Corp.*, SEC Release No. IC-15741 (May 15, 1987).

necessary to register the securities being remarketed or at least to deliver a current prospectus.

Extendible notes were first conceived in the early part of 1982, a time when many issuers were trying to bridge a period of anticipated high interest rates. They provided issuers with the opportunity to finance at short-term rates while retaining the flexibility to extend the financing if market conditions were favorable at the end of each reset period. It is true that the same objectives could be accomplished by simply issuing one- or three-year notes from time to time, but extendible notes are more economical in that there is only a one-time underwriting cost.

Xerox Credit Corporation was the first issuer to have its extendible notes reach the first extension date. Prior to the mailing of the rate differential notice to the holders of the notes, the corporation's general counsel wrote to the SEC seeking concurrence in his opinion that the annual rate-fixing would not require a new registration under the 1933 Act. He contended that the interest rate adjustment was a change in one term of the security accomplished in the manner expressly provided for at the time the security was issued and that accordingly the resetting of the interest rate should not be viewed as the issuance of a new security notwithstanding that the issuer would be required to repay the notes of any holder who did not accept the new rate. Even if it were viewed as the issuance of a new security, he argued, the transaction should be considered an exchange of securities with existing securityholders and thus exempt under Section 3(a)(9). The staff of the SEC agreed and issued the requested no-action letter, without indicating which argument it agreed with.[30]

As these instruments evolved, remarketing agreements became the norm to avoid the cost of redemption and to keep outstanding those securities that the investors did not elect to continue to hold under the revised terms. The securities permitted the issuer to elect to designate a purchaser (an investment banking firm) to purchase and remarket the securities. Although the securities were purchased by the investment banker, the staff of the SEC viewed the issuer's relationship to the transaction to be such as to require

---

30. SEC No-action Letter, *Xerox Credit Corp.* (June 16, 1983).

a new registration, just as would be the case if the issuer purchased the securities itself and reissued them. For an issuer that had in place a shelf registration covering a sufficient amount of debt securities, this would create no mechanical or timing problems, although the principal amount of securities being remarketed would be applied against the total amount registered and remaining available under the shelf. A post-effective amendment to the shelf would not be required if the method of distribution were set forth in sufficiently broad terms. No further action would be required under the 1939 Act in connection with the remarketing. If the issuer did not have a shelf in place, a new registration statement would be required.

Since the early extendible note transactions, instruments typically have been designed to avoid the necessity of registration by structuring the remarketing as a secondary offering on behalf of the holders of the securities who no longer desire to hold them at the new interest rate. Under this approach, the holders bear the risk that it will not be possible to remarket the securities at the new interest rate. In responses in 1984 to two no-action letter requests involving auction preferred stock, the SEC staff acquiesced in the view that a new registration statement or post-effective amendment would not be required in connection with dividend rate resets, although one issuer did agree to file pricing supplements to reflect each new interest rate and the other agreed to continue filing periodic 1934 Act reports notwithstanding any automatic suspension under Section 15(d) of its obligation to do so.[31]

A few years later, the issues were complicated by innovations in the remarketing process that contemplated not only a change in the dividend rate but also in terms such as the dividend period or the repricing mechanism or even an exchange of one security for another. Also, the remarketing agents were in some cases the affiliated broker-dealer arms of the issuers of the auction preferred stock. The SEC staff required a number of

---

31. SEC No-action Letter, *Simpson Thacher & Bartlett* (May 20, 1984); SEC No-action Letter, *City Capital Funding Inc.* (November 12, 1984).

issuers to agree to deliver prospectuses in the event of exchanges or where an affiliated broker-dealer was acting as remarketing agent, and it apparently in some cases held out the possibility that a new registration statement might be required.[32]

In 1993 and 1995, the SEC staff reviewed at least two registered transactions involving remarketed reset note programs and required neither registration nor delivery of a current prospectus at the time of the remarketing. Subsequent to this period, with the exception of remarketing arrangements involving mandatorily exchangeable securities as discussed below, it does not appear that any issuer was required to register remarketing transactions conducted by unaffiliated remarketing agents or to deliver a current prospectus in connection with such transactions.

In 1999, the SEC staff questioned remarketing arrangements involving synthetic put bonds. In these transactions, the issuer is required to repurchase the securities from the holders in the event of a failed remarketing. Some issuers in question agreed with the staff's request that the synthetic put bonds be registered at the time of the remarketing. Another agreed to do whatever might be required when the time for remarketing arrived.

In 2001, the SEC staff was asked about the reset and remarketing arrangements in connection with mandatorily exchangeable securities involving units consisting of notes and also of purchase contracts obligating the holder to buy the issuer's common stock at a specified price. The notes served as collateral for the holder's obligations under the purchase contracts, and the reset and remarketing arrangements were designed to facilitate the sale of the notes to provide funds for this purpose. The SEC staff is understood to have orally required the issuer to deliver a current prospectus at the time of the remarketing while agreeing that a new registration would not be required. Under the facts presented, the issuer would receive the proceeds of the remarketed notes as payment under the purchase contracts and

---

32. Miriam Bensman, *SEC Reopens Basic Question That Spurred Variable-Rate Preferred*, *Investment Dealers' Digest* (September 26, 1988), at 12–13. Presumably, the Section 3(a)(9) exemption was not available for the exchanges because the remarketing agent was being compensated for soliciting the exchanges.

issue its common stock—an excessive amount of issuer involvement in the SEC staff's view.

More recently, the SEC staff has focused on the issuer's involvement in the remarketing and rate reset process in the context of ABS, questioning the role of the administrator of an ABS issuer trust in performing such ministerial functions as selecting the swap counterparties eligible to bid on the interest rate swaps entered into in connection with the interest rate reset. In these situations, the staff appears to be insisting only on delivery of a current prospectus at the time of the remarketing and not on a new registration of the remarketed securities.

"Equity Line" Financing Arrangements

In an "equity line" arrangement, a company and one or more investors enter into an agreement under which the company may require the investors to purchase its securities (usually common stock). In other words, the company may elect to "put" its stock to the investors. Within the limits established by the agreement, it is the company's decision to give notice to the investors as to when and how many shares the investors will be required to purchase. The dollar value of the "line" is set forth in the agreement, but the actual number of shares will depend on the market price of the company's stock at the time it exercises its put.

- *1933 Act Issues*

The company will usually rely on the private placement exemption to issue the shares to the investors, but the investors will want to have freely tradable stock. The company will be obligated to register the stock for resale, but the SEC staff views this type of registration as an "indirect primary offering."[33] This means, according to the staff, that the company may register the stock before its exercise of the put only under the following conditions: the 1933 Act registration form used by the company must be the form it would use for a primary offering; the investors must be named as underwriters as well as selling shareholders;

---

33. SEC Division of Corporation Finance, *Current Issues and Rulemaking Projects* (March 31, 2001), at 11.

and, except for conditions outside the investors' control, they must be irrevocably bound to purchase the securities once the company exercises its put. This last condition means that they must not be in a position to make any further investment decision, including the ability to perform due diligence or to transfer their obligations under the equity line agreement.

If the above conditions for registration are not met, the staff position is that the company may still register the shares for resale if it is eligible to use Form S-3 or Form F-3 for a primary offering, if it complies with the "at-the-market" conditions of Rule 415(a)(4) and if it discloses in the prospectus "issues relating to the potential violation of Section 5 in connection with the private transaction." (Of course, it is not at all clear that there are any such violations.)

If the company wishes to register the stock as a primary offering, the staff will require it to meet the conditions for an "at-the-market" offering under Rule 415(a)(4). As a general matter, the staff will object to the company and the investors entering into the equity line agreement before effectiveness of the registration statement unless the investors are broker-dealers acting as underwriters.

- *1934 Act Issues*

Broker-dealers entering into an equity line agreement should be aware that this may give rise to an "open contractual commitment" to purchase all of the securities contemplated by the agreement, thus resulting in an immediate reduction of the broker-dealer's regulatory net capital under the SEC's Rule 15c3-1.

The SEC staff has also cautioned that equity line arrangements can give rise to questions under Regulation M and under the NASD's Corporate Financing Rule.

Short Sales and Equity Derivatives

The 2003 "deal of the year" in the financial institutions group sector was another case of old wine in new bottles. The Bank of New York (BONY) agreed in January 2003 to pay Credit Suisse First Boston $2 billion in cash to acquire Pershing LLC.

To raise the cash, it planned to issue $900 million in debt and $1.1 billion in common stock. The acquisition of Pershing was expected to close during the second quarter of 2003. BONY could wait to issue the stock until just before the closing, but this would mean running the risk of the market. It could sell the stock immediately, but this would be dilutive.

The solution was for BONY and the underwriters to enter into two forward sale agreements covering 40 million shares of common stock. The agreements provided for settlement on a date or dates as specified by BONY or otherwise within 12 months at an initial forward price of $25.11 per share. The forward price was subject to increase based on an interest factor and subject to decrease based on dividends prior to settlement. With the protection provided by the forward sale agreements, the underwriters borrowed 40 million shares of BONY common stock and sold them in a registered public offering pursuant to a BONY prospectus supplement dated January 29, 2003. The Pershing transaction closed on May 1, following which BONY issued 40 million shares to the underwriters who used these shares to close out their borrowings.

Under the forward sale agreements, BONY had the right to settle in cash if the Pershing deal did not close. In that event, the underwriters would buy 40 million shares in the open market with BONY paying any additional cost and keeping any savings.

The prospectus supplement covering the 40 million shares referred under "Validity of Common Stock" to BONY's counsel's opinion regarding the validity of the common stock *to be issued upon settlement of the forward sale agreements.* Of course, the purchasers in the January 2003 offering were buying shares that the underwriters had borrowed in the market. The opinion therefore covered the new shares BONY would issue to the underwriters after the closing of the Pershing acquisition. The underwriters would then return these new shares to the lenders, who would presumably reintroduce them into the market.[34]

---

34. The prospectus supplement also noted that BONY's counsel's legal opinion on the validity of the new shares would be conditioned on and subject to certain assumptions regarding future action by BONY "and other matters

As the 2003 BONY transaction illustrates, there is no reason why an issuer or a selling securityholder should not be able to deliver securities borrowed from another person. From the investor's point of view, after all, the origin of the securities being purchased is immaterial. It is no different in the secondary market, where any investor purchasing securities may in fact be purchasing securities that the seller has borrowed from another source.

The technique of agreeing to sell securities and meeting one's delivery obligation by the use of borrowed securities while retaining an equivalent "long" position is known as "selling short against the box." Its most common purpose is to postpone the realization of a taxable gain.

The 2003 BONY transaction had an antecedent in the November 1995 IPO of The Estée Lauder Company Inc., where two of the selling shareholders borrowed the shares they were selling from certain family members and family trusts.

In the BONY transaction, the underwriters did not consider themselves obligated to deliver a prospectus to the lenders of the shares when they repaid these loans with shares received from BONY. The agreement between BONY and the underwriters contained a covenant on the part of BONY that the new shares delivered to the lenders would be freely saleable without "further registration or other restrictions" under the 1933 Act. Delivery of a prospectus on repayment of a stock loan would be pointless since repayment of a stock loan is not a "sale" for purposes of Section 2(a)(3) of the 1933 Act. Moreover, the investment position of the stock lenders had not changed as a result of the transaction. Finally, 1933 Act liability had already attached to the identical number of shares sold in the registered offerings.

In October 2003, Microsoft Corporation offered certain of its eligible employees who held out-of-the-money stock options

---

which may affect the validity of the common stock but which cannot be ascertained on the date of the opinion." Presumably, this is a reference to the steps needed to be taken in connection with the issuance of and payment for the new shares at the time of settlement of the forward sale agreements, the non-modification of necessary corporate action and the absence of changes in applicable law.

and stock appreciation rights the opportunity to sell these to J.P. Morgan Securities Inc. at a price to be determined by reference to the market price of Microsoft common stock during an "averaging period" consisting of 15 trading days. J.P. Morgan would not retain the proceeds but would turn them over to Microsoft, which in turn agreed to amend the terms of the options from those under its employee stock option plans "to those typically found in equity option transactions entered into between sophisticated financial counterparties at arm's-length."

J.P. Morgan was expected to sell up to 635 million shares of Microsoft common stock under a Microsoft prospectus dated October 24, 2003 for the purpose of establishing its "desired hedge position" to offset its economic risk in connection with the purchase of the options. It would also make "additional sales pursuant to . . . [the] prospectus to comply with regulatory requirements. . . . The sale of these additional shares will not be made to establish a hedge position." According to the prospectus, J.P. Morgan also expected to purchase shares in the secondary market—in an amount "likely" to be "substantially more than half of the total number of shares sold under the registration statement"—on the same days on which it sold these "additional shares" in order to get back to its "desired hedge position." Why the two-way activity? One possible clue is that Microsoft's obligation to update the prospectus terminated at the end of a "prospectus delivery period," which was defined as the period ending on the date on which J.P. Morgan had delivered a prospectus in connection with the sale of the number of shares of common stock covered by the participating options. Microsoft and J.P. Morgan must have assumed (probably with good reason) that the SEC staff would raise no objection if J.P. Morgan thereafter sold Microsoft common stock for hedge adjustment purposes without delivering a prospectus.

J.P. Morgan's sales of Microsoft stock would include short sales using stock borrowed from lenders, and these stock loans would be closed out with stock acquired by J.P. Morgan on exercise of the options.

During the period in which J.P. Morgan was making sales, Microsoft agreed to make its chief financial or accounting officer available for bi-weekly telephone due diligence sessions. This was in recognition of the fact that the prospectus characterized J.P. Morgan as an underwriter of the shares that it was selling.

The Microsoft/J.P. Morgan transaction illustrates a problem that has bedeviled hedging transactions involving shares of common stock held by affiliates of the issuer or by persons in whose hands the shares are "restricted" within the meaning of Rule 144. If a dealer enters into a hedging transaction with such a person—for example, an option or a forward sale agreement—and subsequently makes short sales for the purpose of limiting its risk, these short sales must have an exemption under the 1933 Act. Assuming that the person owning the stock would not have Rule 144 available for his own sales, can the dealer enter into the hedging transaction and then go off and make short sales in reliance on the dealer exemption?

The dealer can do so if he is not an "underwriter." There are some obvious red flags indicating possible underwriter status in this type of situation. For example, passing along to the customer the economics of the dealer's short sales (e.g., by adjusting the price of the hedge) would suggest that the short sales are for the benefit of the customer. The fact that the customer had recently acquired his shares in a private placement would also be troubling, as would the borrowing of the customer's stock for the purpose of making delivery on the short sales.

A 1999 no-action letter issued to Goldman, Sachs & Co. (Goldman Sachs I) provided some comfort in this area.[35] Building on a 1979 SEC staff interpretation[36] that approved a Rule 144 short sale "against the box" if all conditions of Rule 144 were met at the time the short sale took place, Goldman Sachs I approved short sales by a dealer who was party to a variable share forward sale agreement with a control person or a holder of restricted stock. The short sales would have to meet all conditions of Rule 144, but after the dealer had sold into the public market the maximum

---

35. SEC No-action Letter, *Goldman, Sachs & Co.* (December 20, 1999).

36. SEC Release No. 33-6099 (August 2, 1979) (questions 80–82). The SEC staff applied similar reasoning in a 1991 interpretive letter permitting the Rule 144 sale of control or restricted securities through the exercise of a listed put option. SEC No-action Letter, *Bear Stearns & Co. Inc.* (April 4, 1991).

number of shares deliverable on settlement of the agreement, then the control or restricted shares pledged to Goldman Sachs under the agreement (and any shares returned to the customer after final settlement of the agreement) would not be treated as restricted securities. The letter necessarily implies that the dealer's hedging sales after the Rule 144 short sales would be ordinary trading transactions entitled to the Section 4(3) dealer's exemption.

In 2003, the SEC staff approved (Goldman Sachs II) transactions that in effect amounted to a registered version of the transactions covered by Goldman Sachs I.[37] Under Goldman Sachs II, once a company had registered the maximum number of shares deliverable to a dealer pursuant to a forward or option-based agreement and the dealer had delivered a prospectus in connection with sales of the maximum number of shares deliverable pursuant to the agreement, then the dealer could make further sales (e.g., "dynamic hedging" sales) during the life of the agreement without delivering a prospectus. The dealer could also deliver up to the same number of shares to close out open borrowings of the stock created in the course of hedging activities.

Goldman Sachs II offers companies some interesting capital-raising possibilities, including variable share forward agreements and synthetic convertible financing.[38] Essentially, the issuer can deal directly with a dealer and not concern itself with investors' reaction to the terms and conditions of a particular offering since investors' only role in the transaction will be to purchase the common stock sold short by the dealer after entering into the transaction with the issuer. For example, a company and a dealer can enter into a variable share forward sale obligating the company to sell, and the dealer to buy, a number of shares of the company's common stock on a specified date. Unlike the BONY transaction discussed above, the number of shares will not be fixed but will vary according to the performance of the company's

---

37. SEC No-action Letter, *Goldman, Sachs & Co.* (October 9, 2003).

38. *See* Michael D. Dayan, Glen A. Rae, Robert W. Reeder III and Leslie N. Silverman, "Raising Capital Through OTC Equity Derivatives: The Goldman, Sachs & Co. Interpretive Letter," 9 The Securities Reporter 2 (Spring 2004).

stock price. The terms of the deal may give the issuer a share in any appreciation in the stock price while the dealer will engage in short sales to establish and maintain its desired short position. Essentially, the issuer can achieve many of the benefits of a mandatory convertible issuance without having to engage in marketing efforts or negotiating with investors.

A company can also issue a debt instrument to one group of investors and at the same time sell warrants to another group of investors, thus putting itself in the same economic position as if it had issued a convertible security to one group of investors. Of course, market conditions will determine whether at any given time the genuine or synthetic convertible security is more advantageous to the company.

Finally, a company may be able to rely on Goldman Sachs II to negotiate more favorable terms with the owners of a closely held target company that it is about to acquire for stock. The owners may be willing to accept restricted stock for the sake of speed, but they will certainly demand registration rights even though they may not be interested in immediate sales because of the tax considerations that probably motivated them to ask for stock in the first place. On the other hand, they will also be interested in hedging their exposure to market risk. Just as BONY was able to hedge its exposure to the market during the period prior to the Pershing closing, the owners of the business being acquired may be able to enter into hedge transactions with dealers who will make short sales into the public markets. If the plan of distribution in the resale shelf registration statement so states, a prospectus supplement can cover the dealers' short sales as well as their long sales of stock pledged, loaned or delivered to them by the former owners of the target company in connection with their hedge transactions. And once the full amount of the registered stock has been sold under the resale registration statement, any further sales by the dealers to adjust their hedge may be made without delivery of a prospectus.

Goldman Sachs II included the following sample plan of distribution:

> The Company may enter into derivative transactions with third parties, or sell securities not covered by this

prospectus to third parties in privately negotiated transactions. If the applicable prospectus supplement indicates, in connection with those derivatives, the third parties may sell securities covered by this prospectus and the applicable prospectus supplement, including in short sale transactions. If so, the third party may use securities pledged by the Company or borrowed from the Company or others to settle those sales or to close out any related open borrowings of stock, and may use securities received from the Company in settlement of those derivatives to close out any related open borrowings of stock. The third party in such sale transactions will be an underwriter and, if not identified in this prospectus, will be identified in the applicable prospectus supplement (or a post-effective amendment).

The sample plan of distribution refers expressly to an issuer's lending its own stock to a dealer for the purpose of enabling the dealer to deliver that stock to settle short sales or to deliver that stock to persons from whom the dealer borrowed stock for the purpose of settling short sales. To be sure, the stock loans contemplated by Goldman Sachs II are in connection with the issuer's own derivative transaction, but there is no reason why an issuer should not be able to lend its registered stock to dealers for the purpose of making or closing out short sales. Issuers do not commonly encourage short sellers, of course, but situations do occur from time to time where issuers have been willing to make stock available to arbitragers or to hedge funds who purchase their convertible securities. It goes without saying that the same lending opportunities should be available to holders of control or restricted shares that have been registered with the benefit of a similar plan of distribution.

Finally, some of these techniques may be facilitated by the SEC's adoption of Regulation SHO, which as of January 2005 suspends the "tick" restriction on short sales in approximately 1,000 stocks and in other stocks outside normal trading hours.

Chapter 12

CONVERTIBLE, EXCHANGEABLE AND "LINKED" SECURITIES; WARRANTS

A company selling debt securities or preferred stock may be able to reduce its cost of funds by providing investors with an "equity kicker." There are many ways to do this. A long-standing technique is to issue securities that are convertible at the holder's election into the company's common stock. The conversion price will be set above the common stock's market price at the time of the offering. The convertibility feature is the economic equivalent of a call option on the common stock for the life of the convertible security. It therefore has value, and this value is reflected in the investor's willingness to accept a lower current return in the form of interest or dividend payments.

A company may be less concerned about lowering its costs than about demonstrating to its creditors or to the rating agencies that its convertible securities will in fact become equity securities rather than remain in the form of preferred stock or a debt obligation. The key to this treatment may be to issue mandatorily convertible securities, that is, securities that will become common stock whatever the price performance of the common stock in the open market or the preferences of the holder. The conversion may be triggered either because the issuer's common stock price exceeds a certain level or simply by the passage of a specified period of time. Unlike the buyer of traditional convertible securities, who in effect purchases a call option on the underlying common stock, the buyer of mandatorily convertible securities is in effect selling a put option to the issuer. Just as the buyer of traditional convertible securities expects to pay for the call option by receiving a lower current return, the buyer of mandatorily convertible securities expects to be compensated for the sale of the put option by receiving a higher current return.

A company may also "monetize" its common stock holdings in another company by issuing its debt securities or preferred stock that are exchangeable for the common stock of the other company. Even in the absence of such actual holdings, a company may issue securities that are "linked" to another company's securities or to a securities market index. The securities may provide for a current return to the investor that is higher than the return available on the underlying security and also for a payout at maturity, either in cash or securities, in an amount that depends on the performance of the linked security or market index.

Another financing alternative is the simultaneous issuance of debt securities with warrants to buy the issuer's common stock. Warrants are nothing more than a long-term call option on the underlying common stock. They will usually trade separately from the debt securities, will have a fixed life and will entitle the holders to purchase for cash a specified number of shares of common stock at the warrant exercise price.

Finally, a company may issue debt securities that are "linked" to another company's securities or to a securities market index or to certain credit events. The securities will provide for a cash payment to the investor depending on the performance of the linked security or market index or the occurrence or non-occurrence of the referenced credit events.

In the case of convertible or exchangeable securities, the company may reserve the right to call the securities for redemption at a fixed price. If the market price of the underlying security has increased by a sufficient amount, the call for redemption will effectively force the holders to exercise the conversion or exchange privilege so as not to lose the economic benefit of the increase in price.

The terms of convertible, exchangeable or linked debt securities will be set forth in an indenture or supplement to an indenture between the company and a bank acting as trustee. The terms of convertible, exchangeable or linked preferred stock will be set forth in a certificate of designation filed as a charter document. The terms of warrants will be set forth in a warrant agreement between the issuer and a warrant agent (usually a bank).

Convertible Securities

Holders of "plain vanilla" convertible securities are entitled to convert their securities at any time into shares of common stock at a specified conversion price. The conversion price, like the interest or dividend rate, will be determined at the time the securities are offered for sale. It will typically be fixed at a premium over the current market price of the common stock. Convertible securities are, therefore, sometimes described as a means of "issuing stock at a premium over market."

Because of the conversion privilege, the company will pay a lower interest or dividend rate than it would pay on a comparable "straight" debt or preferred security. In general, a lower conversion premium will tend to make up for a lower interest or dividend rate, and vice versa.

The market price of a convertible security will fluctuate with the price and volatility of the issuer's common stock as well as in response to the changing market environment for fixed-income securities. The influence of the common stock price on the price of the convertible security will be greater to the extent that the security is "in-the-money"—where the current market price of the underlying common stock exceeds the conversion price. In general, convertible securities neither appreciate nor depreciate quite in line with the equity markets. Holders of convertible securities may realize gains or losses either by selling the securities or by converting them and selling the common stock. Of course, early conversion means giving up some of the value of the embedded call option represented by the conversion privilege, and the fact is that most holders of convertible securities do not convert unless and until they are forced to do so.

- *Current Return*

The current interest or dividend rate can be fixed or floating. It can be zero or even a negative number. It can be unconditional or contingent.

In March 2002, Merrill Lynch & Co. sold $2 billion of 30-year Liquid Yield Option Notes (LYONs) convertible into its own shares. Contemporaneous reports said that this was the first floating-rate convertible debt issue. The notes were registered with the SEC and sold at 100% of their principal amount. Interest would accrue daily at a rate, to be reset every quarter, of two percentage points (i.e., 200 basis points) below Libor, with a zero floor and a 5.5% cap, but this interest would not be paid until maturity. Additional interest would become payable, but on a current basis, if the market price of the securities exceeded 120% of their accreted value.

In August 2003, Lockheed Martin sold $1 billion of 30-year floating rate convertible securities in a Rule 144A transaction. The securities were sold at 100% of their principal amount and paid current interest for five years at a rate of Libor less 25 basis points, with a zero floor. After five years, interest would continue to accrue at the same rate but would not be paid until maturity. Additional interest would become payable, but on a current basis, if the market price of the securities exceeded 120% of their accreted value.

The additional interest payable on the Merrill Lynch and Lockheed Martin securities is sometimes referred to as "contingent interest." One advantage of contingent interest—for the issuer—is that the issuer may be able to deduct for federal income tax purposes an amount of interest computed with reference to the higher rate it would pay on a comparable nonconvertible security.[1] Conversely, of course, the holder would have to include the higher amount in income.

Companies have also issued zero coupon convertible securities, typically at a discount. In these transactions, as in the Merrill Lynch and Lockheed Martin transactions discussed above, investors at least receive a return on their investment, even if it is not paid until some time in the future. But companies have also sold securities, sometimes referred to as "no-nos," in which investors have enjoyed neither a current coupon nor an accreting

---

1. There were reports in early 2004 that the Senate Finance Committee was considering a bill that would, among other things, limit the issuer's tax deduction to the actual yield on the convertible security.

principal amount. For example, Novellus Systems, Inc. in July 2001 sold at face amount $800 million of subordinated LYONs due 2031. Also, Yahoo Inc. in April 2003 sold at face amount $750 million of five-year zero coupon convertible senior notes. In purchasing the Novellus and Yahoo notes, one might assume that the investors were relying entirely on the prospect of an increase in the value of the underlying common stocks. On the other hand, given the volatility of Yahoo and Novellus common stock, hedge fund investors could use the notes as a platform for hedging strategies. One market observer described Yahoo's sale of the convertible notes as "monetizing volatility."

If investors are willing to accept zero return, why not a negative return? In 2002, Berkshire Hathaway sold units called "Negative 0.75% SQUARZ" in a Rule 144A transaction. The units consisted of a 3% note with a principal amount of $10,000 due in 2007, a warrant to purchase common stock at an exercise price of $10,000 and a fractional interest in stripped U.S. Treasury securities. The warrant was exercisable at a 15% premium, but holders were required to pay Berkshire Hathaway semiannual "installment payments" at a rate of 3.75% of the exercise price, thus resulting in an annual negative carry of 0.75%. The note and the stripped U.S. Treasury securities were pledged to Berkshire Hathaway to secure the obligation of the SQUARZ holders to make the warrant installment payments. Berkshire Hathaway subsequently registered the SQUARZ under the 1933 Act to permit resales by the initial investors.

- *Conversion Price*

The conversion price will be set at a level above the current market price of the underlying common stock. The premium must be at least 10% in a Rule 144A transaction involving a listed or NASDAQ stock. Prior to 2002, conversion premiums seldom exceeded 40%, but there have been several recent transactions with much higher premiums.

There is no end to the types of bells and whistles that can be attached to a convertible security. For example, a company may sell securities on a "contingent convertibility" basis where the securities are not immediately convertible and will not become convertible unless and until the underlying common stock reaches a specified level. The Merrill Lynch LYONs referred to above were convertible if the Merrill Lynch common stock traded for a specified period at more than 120% of the "accreted conversion price," that is, the original principal amount increased by the accrued but unpaid interest and divided by the number of shares of common stock issuable on conversion. Lockheed Martin's securities became convertible if the common stock traded for specified periods at 130% or more of the conversion price.

The conversion trigger may be fixed or it may decline over time. It may also be defined in a way that results in the investor not obtaining the benefit of the conversion privilege unless the stock appreciates by more than a specified amount.

Conversion rights may also be triggered by adverse credit developments, specified corporate events or the company's decision to call the securities for redemption.

"Contingently convertible" securities (also known as "co-cos") have an accounting advantage for the issuing company: in reporting earnings per share, the dilutive effect of the underlying shares is not recognized until the occurrence of one of the events that permits conversion. (The FASB took action in September 2004 to eliminate this advantage.) If the stock price rises, however, the company's earnings per share can be adversely affected.

Another way to counteract dilution is for the issuing company to use part of the proceeds of the sale of the convertible securities to purchase its stock in the open market. A more immediate goal of the buyback activity is usually to offset the short selling activity by hedge funds that buy the convertible securities and then short the underlying stock. (As discussed in Chapter 4, Rule 102 of Regulation M may prevent the company from repurchasing its stock during a distribution of its convertible securities unless the convertible securities are offered and sold exclusively to QIBs under Rule 144A.)

In some cases, the issuing company can mitigate dilution and hedge fund selling by entering into derivative transactions involving its common stock, often with the underwriter leading the convertible security transaction. One such technique is for the issuer to enter into a "call spread" under which it will purchase a call option that parallels the call option embedded in the convertible security and simultaneously sell a call option at a much higher "strike" or exercise price. The net effect is that the issuer obtains the benefit of a higher conversion premium. An ancillary benefit is that the counterparty on the call spread will usually hedge by purchasing stock in the open market, thus mitigating the effects of hedge funds' short sales.

Traditionally, the conversion price did not change over the life of the convertible securities, except to the extent that it was adjusted pursuant to antidilution provisions to reflect such events as stock splits, stock dividends, and distributions of rights or warrants that can result in the company selling common stock at less than the current market price. More recently, companies have attempted to provide investors with "downside protection" by agreeing to issue additional shares or reset the conversion price if the underlying security is selling below an agreed-on threshold. For example, Microsoft Corporation—which at the time paid no dividend on its common stock—publicly offered in December 1996 a series of 2-3/4% Convertible Exchangeable Principal-Protected Preferred Shares. This security offered investors a current return and the guarantee of receiving common stock or cash having a value not less than the value of the common stock on the issuance date of the preferred shares. In return, however, the investor's opportunity for equity appreciation was capped at 28%.

Providing downside protection for investors can be carried too far. In the case of the infamous "death spiral convertibles," companies issued convertible securities on terms that continually adjusted the conversion price downward. Hedge fund investors sold the stock short as the price declined and covered their short position with stock obtained on conversion. The more the stock fell, the more stock became issuable on conversion and the more stock could be sold short, thus driving the price even farther downward.

In some cases, the documents will provide that the company may lower the conversion price for a limited period of time, thus allowing it to induce conversions without calling the securities. This amounts to holding a "fire sale" for that period of time, and if a holder does not convert while the sale is going on, the conversion price of his securities will revert to the original level when the sale is over.[2]

Conversely, convertible securities can be issued under terms that include a "step-up" in the conversion price at stated intervals over the security's life.

Even without such features, an issuer—for example, an issuer of convertible preferred securities on which there are substantial dividend arrearages—may attempt to "induce" conversions by offering to holders the opportunity to convert and receive additional amounts of the underlying security. In other cases, the issuer will offer a cash payment to induce conversions.

A frequent reason for inducing conversions is to facilitate the issuance of a new convertible security. Often, the existing holders are hedge funds that are short the underlying stock. If the supply of "borrowable" stock is limited, the hedge funds may be unable to participate in the new offering unless the old issue is converted, thus making stock available to support short sales against the new issue.

In the case of convertible securities such as LYONs that are sold with OID, the terms of the LYONs typically provide that a holder that exercises the conversion privilege will not receive any cash payment representing accrued OID. The issuer's delivery to the converting holder of the number of shares of common stock into which the LYON is convertible will satisfy its obligation to pay the principal amount of the LYON, including the accrued OID attributable to the period from the date of issue to the conversion date. Thus, while the conversion rate (i.e., the number of shares of common stock into which each $1,000 face value of LYONs is convertible) remains fixed, the economic effect is that the conversion price increases as OID accrues. In other words, for conversion to make economic sense, the

---

2. SRO listing standards may specify the minimum number of days during which the fire sale must remain in effect. The SEC staff has taken the position that reductions of the conversion price of convertible securities constitute issuer tender offers for purposes of Rule 13e-4 and that the "offer" must therefore remain open for at least 20 business days. Induced conversions will still qualify for the Section 3(a)(9) exemption unless the issuer compensates a third party for soliciting conversions.

market price of the common stock must continuously increase to compensate for the accrual of OID.

- *Puts by Holder*

Holders of convertible securities that are sold with OID often have the right to put the securities back to the company at stated intervals or on the occurrence of such events as a change in control. For example, the Merrill Lynch LYONs referred to above gave the holder the right to put some or all of their securities to Merrill Lynch in the third and fifth year and thereafter at five-year intervals. Merrill Lynch could honor the put right with cash, common stock or a combination of the two. The holders of the Lockheed Martin securities referred to above had the right to put the securities to the issuer at five-year intervals, but Lockheed Martin had to honor the put right by the payment of cash.

In the Novellus transaction referred to above, the holders of the LYONs had the right to put the LYONs to the issuer at stated intervals beginning one year after their original issuance. The issuer could honor the put with cash or common stock or a combination of the two, except that it had to pay cash on the first put date. To secure its obligation to do so, the issuer agreed to deposit substantially all of the proceeds of the sale of the LYONs into a pledge account that would be used to purchase U.S. Treasury securities maturing on or before the first put date for an amount equal to the face value of the LYONs.

Put options at stated intervals can be dangerous for the issuing company if its stock price falls and especially if its credit deteriorates. Even if the company is permitted under the terms of the security to issue common stock in satisfaction of the holders' put right, this may be an unattractive option if it would cause excessive dilution. In other circumstances, the company may have no choice but to raise cash by selling new securities under unfavorable conditions. In 2001, however, Comcast met the challenge of an anticipated put of more than half of an outstanding issue of $1.2 billion of convertible securities by offering the holders the opportunity to put the securities to Comcast at the same time in the following year rather than having to wait until the next scheduled put date in 2003.

- *Cash or Stock on Conversion*

The distinguishing feature of a convertible security, as opposed to a cash-settled equity-linked security, has traditionally been that the company must issue new common stock to a holder who elects conversion. Recent transactions give the company the right to issue stock, cash or a combination of stock and cash.

- *Redemption*

Convertible securities, whether debentures or preferred stock, usually are redeemable, in whole or in part, at the option of the issuer. In the case of traditional current coupon convertible securities, the redemption price will decline over time. For example, where the coupon on the debenture is 3.75%, the indenture might provide that in the first year the redemption price will be par plus a premium of 3.75%. The redemption premium might decline incrementally over the next ten years, and the debentures might thereafter be redeemable at par. It is also possible that the indenture will not allow any redemption at the option of the issuer until the securities have been outstanding for a stated number of years or until the underlying stock has traded above a specified price level for a stated period of time or unless the issuer reimburses the holders for a specified number of lost interest payments. Alternatively, the issuer might agree to a "soft-call" provision that gives it the right to call the security at any time in the first three years if the underlying security rises a specified amount above the conversion price, a lesser amount in the second year and a lower amount in the third year. This provides flexibility to an issuer with high-growth expectations while compensating the investor as if the security had a certain number of years of "hard-call" protection. See below under "Calls for Redemption to Force Conversions."

- *M&A Transactions*

Indentures invariably provide for the contingency that the issuer will be acquired by another company. In the case of convertible securities, what is the effect on the conversion privilege of a merger, consolidation or sale of assets? The indenture should provide that the holders of the convertible securities will receive on conversion whatever the company's shareholders receive in the way of securities, property or cash exactly as if they had converted their securities immediately prior to the effective date of the merger, consolidation or sale of assets. Of course, the holders of the convertible securities may elect to convert at an earlier date, particularly if they want to be able to vote on the transaction.

Care must be taken that the provision is worded so as to operate effectively in the case of a reverse triangular merger, where a subsidiary of the acquiring company merges into the target company and the target company maintains its corporate identity. The drafter should avoid the language found in older indentures that excludes "a consolidation or merger in which the company is the continuing corporation."

The indenture should provide specifically for an acquisition transaction where the consideration payable to the holders of the common stock is cash. In the case of a cash acquisition, the holders of the convertible securities should be entitled to convert their securities only into cash. An indenture of Collins Radio Corporation was found to be ambiguous, and the case remanded for a jury determination of the parties' intent, where the applicable provision referred to conversion into "the kind and amount of shares of stock and other securities and property receivable upon such consolidation, merger, sale, conveyance, transfer or disposition," but did not refer specifically to cash. The result was remedied on rehearing (cash after all is property), but it is best to leave nothing to chance.[3]

The announcement of an acquisition, especially at a large premium, is normally good news for the target company's equity securityholders. On the other hand, hedge funds holding convertible securities may find such an announcement painful since, as noted above, they are often short the issuer's common stock. It has been reported that hedge funds have recently been bargaining for the inclusion in convertible securities of make-whole provisions that will protect them in the event of the issuer's being acquired.

- *1933 Act Considerations*

Common stock of a company issued on conversion of its debentures or preferred stock is exempt from registration under

---

3. *Broad v. Rockwell International Corp.*, 614 F.2d 418 (5th Cir. 1980), *rev'd on reh'g en banc*, 642 F.2d 929 (5th Cir. 1981).

Section 3(a)(9) of the 1933 Act in that it constitutes a "security exchanged by the issuer with its existing securityholders exclusively," where no remuneration is paid for soliciting the exchange. In other words, when the holder of the debenture or preferred stock surrenders it for conversion into shares of the issuer's common stock, an exchange of securities takes place and the Section 3(a)(9) exemption is applicable. The only instance in which this would not be the case is in the context of an underwritten call where the standby underwriters solicit conversions and a portion of their standby fee is considered to have been paid for making the solicitations.

A public offering of convertible securities requires registration of the underlying common stock if, as is customary, the securities are immediately convertible. The legal basis for this is found in the 1933 Act definitions of "offer" and "sale." Section 2(a)(3) provides (emphasis added):

> The issue or transfer of a right or privilege, when originally issued or transferred with a security, giving the holder of such security the right to convert such security into another security of the same issuer or of another person, or giving a right to subscribe to another security of the same issuer or of another person, *which right cannot be exercised until some future date*, shall not be deemed to be an offer or sale of such other security; but the issue or transfer of such other security upon the exercise of such right of conversion or subscription shall be deemed a sale of such other security.

By negative implication, the reverse is true. If a company offers debentures or preferred stock *immediately* convertible into common stock, it is deemed to be offering the underlying common stock at the same time. It should be stressed, however, that the common stock is registered only for purposes of the original distribution of the convertible securities and that registration of the common stock is not a prerequisite for the availability of the Section 3(a)(9) exemption when the securities are converted. The conversion is an exempt transaction.

But how long is "some future date"? Some might regard it as an evasion of the registration requirements for a company to issue a convertible security without registering the common stock in reliance on the conversion privilege's not commencing until, say, the day after the closing. For a significant period of time, the SEC staff regarded a three-month delay as adequate. The staff subsequently took the position that there had to be a one-year delay to justify not registering the common stock, but its reasoning has remained obscure. It is easy enough to register the common stock at the outset, so it is seldom necessary to delay conversion in an effort to avoid registration. In any event, Section 3(a)(9) will still exempt conversions whether or not the common stock is ever registered.

When a company files its 1933 Act registration statement covering convertible securities, the conversion price will not yet have been established and the company will therefore not know how many shares of common stock will be issuable on conversion. Accordingly, it is customary for the grid on the facing sheet of the registration statement that sets forth the amount of securities to be registered to contain a footnote reference providing for the registration of "such currently indeterminate number of shares of common stock as may be required for issuance on conversion of the debentures [or preferred stock] being registered hereunder." This will be sufficient to register the requisite number of shares of common stock. The actual number of shares into which the securities are originally convertible is not relevant in calculating the registration fee.

Some facing sheets will contain, in addition to the above-quoted footnote language, the words "including such additional shares as may be issuable as a result of adjustments to the conversion price." This additional language does no harm, but it is not required. First of all, the additional shares would be required to be registered only if the antidilution provisions of the indenture became operative while the debentures were still being distributed. The underlying common stock is registered only for purposes of the original distribution of the debentures in that, as discussed above, their issuance on conversion is exempt under Section 3(a)(9). But even if the antidilution provisions kicked in before the distribution was completed (which would certainly be unusual), Rule 416(a) would deem the additional shares of common stock to be registered.

Chapter 9 discusses 1933 Act considerations applicable to convertible securities issued in offshore transactions pursuant to Regulation S.

At one time, tax considerations required that a foreign finance subsidiary be the primary obligor on convertible debt securities sold abroad. A company organized under the laws of the Netherlands Antilles was customarily used for this purpose. The parent would guarantee the obligations, and the securities would be convertible into shares of common stock of the parent. The Section 3(a)(9) exemption was considered unavailable because of the lack of corporate identity between the parent issuer of the common stock and the subsidiary issuer of the debentures. In this type of transaction, it was customary to delay the conversion privilege for nine months and to register the underlying common stock on Form S-16 prior to the time that the debentures became convertible. A number of issuers that had been maintaining current registration statements to cover conversions of securities issued by foreign finance subsidiaries were able to convince the staff of the SEC that they should no longer be required to do so where a relatively small amount of securities was outstanding.

In the case of puttable convertible securities that give the issuer the right to honor the investor's put by delivering common stock or notes, the practice initially was to have the registration statement cover an indeterminate number of shares and an indeterminate principal amount of notes. Again, registration of these securities was for purposes of the original distribution of the securities, and it was not considered necessary to deliver a current prospectus in connection with the put procedures. But because the put is not exercisable until a date certain in the future, an analogy may be made to a delayed conversion feature and an argument constructed that the stock and notes issuable by the company to satisfy the put need not be registered in the first instance. The staff of the SEC eventually took the position that the stock and the notes need not be registered, and it became the practice not to register them.

- *1934 Act Issues*

Some years ago, the SEC staff took the position that a company's offer to purchase LYONs pursuant to the investor's repurchase option constituted an issuer tender offer for purposes of Rule 13e-4. As discussed in Chapter 13, this rule requires an issuer making a tender offer for its own equity securities to publish, send or give to securityholders the information required by certain items of Schedule 13e-4, including the consideration being offered in the tender offer. In a LYONs transaction, of course, it is not possible to specify at the outset the number of shares of common stock that persons tendering their LYONs will receive or the interest rate on the notes. The staff also took the position that the disclosure in the registration statement of the terms of the option provisions might constitute a public announcement of a tender offer within the meaning of what is now Rule 14e-5. This rule prohibits a person making a tender offer for an equity security from purchasing that security otherwise than pursuant to the tender offer from the time the offer is publicly announced until it expires. The typical LYON permits purchases of the subject securities prior to the publication of the number of shares to be issued to satisfy the put or the interest rate on the notes to be issued for that purpose.

In April 1989, the staff of the SEC issued a letter to Shoney's, Inc. in which the relief from Rule 13e-4 and the predecessor provisions to Rule 102 of Regulation M and to Rule 14e-5 took the form of no-action positions on each of the rules. The staff has rendered informal advice that if a transaction comes within the terms of the Shoney's no-action letter, it is not necessary to seek relief from the SEC.[4]

The staff positions described above included the view that the disclosure in the registration statement of the terms of the option provisions might constitute a bid for the LYONs during the period of their distribution, and the Shoney's no-action letter provided relief on this point. Under the Regulation M Release, however, neither the writing of a put option nor the maintenance of a short put position is deemed to be a continuing bid for the underlying security. This would suggest that the issuer's repurchase option should not constitute a bid for the LYONs or for the common stock and the notes (i.e., as "reference securities").

As discussed in Chapter 4, however, convertible securities do not qualify for an exemption from Regulation M even if they are investment-grade and even if the underlying securities qualify for the ADTV exemption.

---

4. SEC No-action Letter, *Shoney's, Inc.* (April 4, 1989).

- *Rule 144A Convertible Securities*

A significant part of the U.S. domestic market is represented by convertible securities offered and sold pursuant to Rule 144A. If the issuer does not have a current and effective shelf registration statement with sufficient capacity, Rule 144A offers more certainty in terms of timing than filing a registration statement with the SEC.[5] Also, as discussed in Chapter 4, there are exceptions under Rules 101 and 102 of Regulation M where Rule 144A convertible securities are offered and sold only to QIBs, but there are no exceptions for SEC-registered offerings of convertible securities even if they are investment-grade and even if the underlying common stock meets the ADTV test. As in the case of high-yield securities, underwriters are reluctant to risk being unable to make a market in the offered securities if the deal becomes "sticky," and this is often a sufficient reason to choose the Rule 144A procedure.

Many of these securities are sold to hedge funds, which are less interested in holding the securities as a long-term investment than in hedging by means of short sales of the underlying common stock. If the offering is registered under the 1933 Act (which, as noted in the preceding paragraph, is often not the case), such short sales raise no 1933 Act problems. As discussed in Chapter 7, short sales in the context of a Rule 144A offering raise some questions that have yet to be resolved.

Convertible securities sold under Rule 144A are frequently registered under the 1933 Act to permit resales by the original investors. The "Exxon Capital" or "A/B" exchange offer technique discussed in Chapter 7 is not available for convertible securities of U.S. issuers.

Exchangeable Securities

A company that owns shares of common stock of another publicly owned company may issue securities exchangeable at a fixed or formula price for all or a portion of those shares.

---

5. As discussed below, the SEC staff takes the position that Rule 144A is not available for mandatorily convertible or exchangeable securities.

CONVERTIBLE SECURITIES

These are called "exchangeable securities" to distinguish them from securities convertible into the issuing company's stock, but the financial press sometimes uses the terms "exchangeable" and "convertible" interchangeably.

The only difference between an exchangeable security and a convertible security is that, in the case of the former, holders are entitled to acquire stock of an entity other than the issuer of the exchangeable securities. Otherwise, the legal structure is substantially identical. The same antidilution provisions also apply, and the same potential exists for forcing exchanges by calling the securities for redemption.

A company may issue exchangeable securities if it has made an investment in the stock of another company and wishes to hold it in anticipation of an increase in its market price. While continuing to own the stock, the company may use it as a means of raising funds at favorable interest rates. If the investor company determines that it would be willing to sell the stock if the price increases to a certain level, then it makes economic sense for it to issue securities exchangeable for the stock at a price that would enable it to call the securities and force exchanges when the price of the stock reaches the target level.

- *Registration of the Underlying Securities*

    The transfer of stock to the holder of the securities on exercise of the exchange privilege does not qualify for the Section 3(a)(9) exemption because the issuer of the exchangeable securities and the issuer of the stock are different entities. The exchange transaction, however, will be exempted under Section 4(1) as a transaction by "any person other than an issuer, underwriter or dealer" unless one or both of the following conditions apply:

    – the common stock is a "restricted security" in the hands of the issuer of the exchangeable securities; or

    – subject to the possible exception discussed below, the issuer of the exchangeable securities is in a control relationship with the issuer of the underlying common stock.

If the stock is not a restricted security and a control relationship does not exist, then it is not necessary to register the common stock either in connection with the initial sale of the securities or in connection with the exchange of the securities for the underlying shares. Most exchangeable securities have been issued under these circumstances, usually on the basis of an opinion of counsel to the effect that the underlying shares are not restricted securities and that a control relationship does not exist between the issuer of the securities and the issuer of the underlying shares.

If the relationship between the issuer of the exchangeable securities and the issuer of the common stock is reasonably cordial, the issuer of the shares may be willing to register them. Of course, if a control relationship really exists, the issuer may simply be instructed to register. This, after all, is the real test of control: the power to compel registration. Of course, there may also be a registration rights agreement under which the issuer of the exchangeable securities may demand registration of the underlying shares.

Registration should not be burdensome if the issuer of the underlying shares is eligible to use Form S-3. Moreover, for purposes of the instructions to Form S-3, the exchangeable securities should be viewed as convertible securities, and if the issuer meets the reporting requirements then Form S-3 should be available to register securities to be offered on the exchange of outstanding exchangeable securities issued by an affiliate of the issuer, even if the issuer of the common stock does not meet the other tests for the use of Form S-3.

If registration is required, there will be two separate 1933 Act registration statements, one by the issuer of the exchangeable securities and the other by the issuer of the underlying securities. The two prospectuses are generally delivered as one document.

- *Avoiding Registration in Control Situations*

In 1971, International Paper Company obtained a no-action letter from the SEC permitting it to issue debentures exchangeable for common stock of C.R. Bard, Inc. without registration of the Bard shares, even though it owned 17% of the outstanding

Bard common stock.[6] The SEC previously had been unwilling to conclude that International Paper was not in a control relationship with Bard and expressed concerns as to whether International Paper should be deemed a statutory underwriter with respect to its Bard shares in that it had acquired them approximately two and one-half years previously in connection with the acquisition of a company that the staff considered to be in control of Bard.[7] International Paper had no representation on the board of directors of Bard; the family of Harris L. Willets owned more than 19% of the outstanding Bard common stock and was recognized to be in control; and, after a request to do so, Bard had refused to register the common stock underlying the exchangeable debentures. As part of its no-action request, International Paper agreed to relinquish its voting rights to the Bard common stock and to have the escrow agent agree to vote the shares in escrow in proportion to the votes cast by all other shareholders. The registration statement covering the International Paper debentures contained information with respect to Bard obtained from filings with the SEC under the 1934 Act. The debentures were not exchangeable for a year after issuance, and it was pointed out to the staff that at the time the debentures could be exchanged for Bard shares, International Paper would have held them for four years.

Relinquishing voting rights is only a means by which the absence of control can be established or at least reinforced. But assuming that there is a control relationship, is there any way of avoiding registration? One possibility would be to delay the exchange privilege. Under Section 2(a)(3) of the 1933 Act, the offer and sale of the exchangeable securities would not be deemed an offer or sale of the underlying shares if the exchange privilege "cannot be exercised until some future date." In that case, the underwriters of the exchangeable securities might not be underwriters of the common stock. Section 2(a)(11) of the 1933 Act defines the term "underwriter" to include any person who offers or sells for an issuer in connection with the distribution

---

6. SEC No-action Letter, *C.R. Bard, Inc.* (November 8, 1971).
7. SEC No-action Letters, *C.R. Bard, Inc.* (June 28, 1971 and October 4, 1971).

of any security, and for purposes of this definition, the term "issuer" includes a person in a control relationship with the issuer. If, however, the securities are not exchangeable for the common stock until some date in the future, it is clear that the common stock need not be registered to permit the underwriting of the securities.

An SEC staff telephone interpretation confirms this position, stating that the underlying securities need not be registered at the time of registering the exchangeable securities if the latter are not exchangeable within one year.[8]

If the exchange privilege is delayed, the question then arises whether the common stock must be registered at the time it is actually issued when the holder elects to exchange the exchangeable securities. The SEC staff telephone interpretation states that the underlying securities must be registered no later than the date by which the exchangeable securities become exchangeable. A strong argument can be made, however, that the common stock need not be registered to cover an exchange when the delayed exchange privilege becomes effective. The fact that the issuer of the securities may be in a control relationship with the issuer of the underlying shares is relevant only for purposes of determining whether the underwriters of the securities are also underwriters of the common stock underlying the securities. Under the 1933 Act, a controlling person is deemed an issuer only for purposes of defining who is an underwriter. But a controlling person may offer securities directly to the public without registration so long as there is no intermediary involved in the transaction who might be deemed an underwriter. This will be the case when the delayed exchange privilege becomes effective. At that point, no investment banking firm will be involved in the transaction and the issuer will be dealing directly with the public in exchanging the common stock for its securities. If this is a correct interpretation of the law, then registration of the common stock would not be required even when the securities become exchangeable.

---

8. SEC Division of Corporation Finance, *Manual of Publicly Available Telephone Interpretations* 5 (#9) (September 2001).

CONVERTIBLE SECURITIES

This analysis has not been tested with the staff of the SEC, and it is not supported by any no-action letters issued in the context of exchangeable securities or in the analogous context of subsidiary debt convertible into shares of its parent. But if the occasion should arise where there is a substantial question of control and the issuer of the shares underlying the securities is unwilling to register them, the possibility of a delayed exchange privilege and reliance on the Section 4(1) exemption for the actual exchanges could be the solution to the problem. Here a conference with the staff would be in order, but a no-action request should not be submitted unless there is reasonable assurance that the response will be favorable.

- *Disclosure About Issuer of Underlying Securities*

Whether or not the underlying security needs to be registered, the investor who buys an exchangeable security is making an investment decision about the underlying security. The question therefore arises whether, and to what extent, the prospectus for the exchangeable security should disclose information about the issuer of the underlying security.

An issuer would understandably be reluctant to include such disclosure, even if it were available from the linked issuer's public filings, because of its concern that it would become liable under Section 11 of the 1933 Act or otherwise for deficiencies in these filings. Accordingly, it became the practice for issuers of exchangeable securities to include only a very brief description of the underlying issuer's business, a reference to the availability of its filings under the 1934 Act and a history of the underlying issuer's stock price and (in some cases) dividend payments.

The SEC staff acquiesced for a number of years in this practice. It subsequently began to draw a distinction, however, between offerings in which the underlying issuer was eligible to register primary offerings of its securities for cash on Form S-3 or Form F-3 and those offerings in which this was not the case. In the SEC staff's view, complete financial statement and non-financial statement disclosure about the underlying issuer was material to investors at the time of the initial sale of the exchangeable securities and on a continuous basis until exchange or payment. Where the underlying issuer was not eligible to use Form S-3 or Form F-3, then the issuer of the exchangeable security would have to include in its prospectus all of the information about the underlying issuer that the latter would have to include in its own prospectus if it were to make an offering of its own.

In a 1996 no-action letter involving unaffiliated issuers of the two securities, the SEC staff stated that "[s]ince an investor's return on the Exchangeable Securities depends materially on the market performance of the Underlying Securities, holders of the Exchangeable Securities should be provided with full and fair disclosure about the issuer of the Underlying Securities in addition to that provided with respect to the issuer of the Exchangeable Securities." It was the staff's view, however, that complete disclosure was not required where there was "sufficient market interest and publicly available information" about the issuer of the underlying securities. In the staff's judgment, this was the case where the issuer of the underlying securities had a class of equity securities registered under the 1934 Act and either (a) was eligible to use Form S-3 or Form F-3 for a primary offering of non-investment-grade debt securities or (b) met a national securities exchange's listing criteria applicable to the underlying issuer in the case of a listing of equity-linked notes. In the case of the American Stock Exchange, for example, those criteria would require either (a) a minimum market capitalization of $3 billion and at least 2.5 million shares traded during the past 12 months, (b) a minimum market capitalization of $1.5 billion and at least 20 million shares traded during the past 12 months or (c) a minimum market capitalization of $500 million and at least 80 million shares traded during the past 12 months.

In addition, the issuer of the exchangeable securities would have to include in its 1933 Act registration statement (or prospectus or prospectus supplement) and periodic reports abbreviated information about the underlying issuer and the underlying securities. Such abbreviated information would include "[a] brief discussion of the business of the issuer" of the underlying securities, disclosure about the availability of its 1934 Act reports and "information concerning the market price" of the underlying securities.[9]

---

9. SEC No-action Letter, *Morgan Stanley & Co., Inc.* (June 24, 1996).

CONVERTIBLE SECURITIES

- *Liabilities and Due Diligence*

The issuer of the exchangeable securities, its directors and signing officers and any underwriters will have the usual Section 11 liabilities for disclosures and omissions relating to the exchangeable securities as well as any disclosures and omissions relating to the underlying securities. Underwriters may also have Section 12(a)(2) liability to purchasers of the exchangeable securities for any such disclosures and omissions.

The first defense for the issuer of the exchangeable securities and the underwriters is to exercise care in selecting those companies whose securities underlie the exchangeable securities. There is obviously a tension here between what is of interest to investors and what is likely to result in losses and litigation. The second defense is to limit the information in the registration statement (or prospectus or prospectus supplement) to the bare minimum needed to comply with the SEC staff's no-action position described above. Finally, at least for underwriters, there is the due diligence defense. Since an underwriter cannot expect the cooperation of the underlying issuer, it should do what is reasonable under the circumstances—including documenting any selection process regarding the underlying issuer, consulting with the responsible analyst for his or her views on the underlying issuer's common stock and otherwise inquiring into the existence of any "red flags" that should be investigated—or, if investigation is not feasible, should call for the offering to be abandoned.

In early 2003, UBS AG issued $19.5 million of its GOALS linked to the common stock of WorldCom, Inc. The prospectus supplement stated that, "[a]ccording to publicly available information, WorldCom, Inc. provides a broad range of communications services to both U.S. and non-U.S. based businesses and consumers." It also referred investors to WorldCom's reports filed with the SEC under the 1934 Act and set forth information on the market price of WorldCom stock since the first quarter of 1998. The prospectus supplement stated that neither UBS nor its affiliates were responsible for WorldCom's public disclosure of information, whether in SEC filings or otherwise, that WorldCom was in no way involved in the GOALS offering and that historical market prices should not be taken as an indication of future performance.

Investors in the GOALS eventually brought a class action against UBS and others under Section 11 of the 1933 Act, alleging that the market prices of WorldCom's stock in the prospectus supplement "were artificially inflated as a result of the wrongdoing of the non-UBS defendants, and were therefore materially false and misleading." The court granted UBS's motion to dismiss, holding that the plaintiffs had failed to identify any "statement (or omission) by UBS that related to the reliability of the stock prices as an indicator of WorldCom's financial health in either the past or the future."[10]

- *Communications with Underlying Issuer*

As noted above, neither the issuer of the exchangeable securities nor any underwriter will have any reason to expect the underlying issuer's cooperation in the due diligence effort. The underlying issuer has no prospect of economic benefit from the transaction, and it may even perceive the transaction as undermining its own ability to issue equity. The question remains whether an underwriter should ask the underlying issuer to cooperate, for example, by answering a few questions on the telephone or in a brief meeting. If there were no downside to this inquiry, it might be prudent to make it. On the other hand, the underlying issuer could easily, whether or not in good faith, sabotage the offering by suggesting that it was aware of material, adverse and undisclosed information that it was not yet prepared to disclose. In view of this potential interference with the offering from a person having no stake in it, and in view of the unlikelihood under the best of circumstances of obtaining the underlying issuer's cooperation, there appears to be no point in asking the underlying issuer to cooperate in the due diligence effort.[11] This does not mean, of course, that an underwriter

---

10. *In re WorldCom, Inc. Securities Litig. (In re PaineWebber GOALS Securities Litig.)*, 2004 U.S. Dist. LEXIS 39 (S.D.N.Y. January 16, 2004).

11. *Cf. Feit v. Leasco Data Proc. Eq. Corp.*, 332 F. Supp. 544, 581–83 (S.D.N.Y. 1971) (dealer-managers found to have established due diligence defense under Section 11 when facts indicated that officer of target company would not cooperate by providing data on "surplus surplus" and that an estimate should therefore not be included in the prospectus).

might not wish as a business courtesy to inform the underlying issuer of the planned offering in advance of its being publicly announced.

- *Listing; State Preemption; CEA Considerations*

Exchangeable securities are often listed on a national securities exchange or quoted on NASDAQ. As noted above, each of the NYSE, the AMEX and NASDAQ has detailed listing requirements for such securities.

Among the listing requirements is that the exchangeable security not exceed 5% of the total outstanding shares of a U.S. underlying security. Even stricter limitations apply if the underlying security is a non-U.S. security. The limitations may be waived by the listing SRO with the concurrence of the SEC staff, but such concurrence has been infrequent in recent years.

Prior to the CFMA, an important reason for listing was often the need to take advantage of the federal preemption of state gaming and bucket shop laws contained in Section 28(a) of the 1934 Act for instruments that were "traded pursuant to rules and regulations of a self-regulatory organization" filed with the SEC pursuant to Section 19(b) of the 1934 Act. The CFMA amended Section 28(a) to preempt the application of state gaming and bucket shop laws to any security that is "subject to" the 1934 Act, whether or not the security is traded on a securities exchange or otherwise traded pursuant to the rules of an SRO.

As discussed in Chapter 11, if exchangeable securities are excluded hybrid instruments under the CEA, then Section 12(e)(2)(B) of the CEA also preempts state gaming and bucket shop laws (other than antifraud provisions of general applicability).

- *Regulation M*

If the offering of the exchangeable security constitutes a "distribution" for Regulation M purposes, then the issuer and any participants in the distribution may become subject to the limitations on bids and purchases imposed by Rules 101 and 102, respectively, of Regulation M.

As discussed in Chapter 4, Rule 101 has an exception for non-convertible investment-grade debt. It is not clear whether exchangeable securities are "convertible" securities for the purposes of this exception, but it is probably safe to assume that the exception is not available. Rule 101 also has an exception for any "reference security" that meets an ADTV test. If the underlying securities meet the ADTV test, Rule 101 would not apply to transactions in those securities. But based on the analogous treatment of convertible securities discussed in Chapter 4, it may be that the exchangeable security itself does not qualify for any exception from Rule 101 even though its constituent "pieces" so qualify.

The issuer of the exchangeable security would not appear to be entitled to any exceptions under Rule 102 for the exchangeable security or the underlying security, but the issuer is not likely to be in the market for either of these securities while the distribution is in progress. And, of course, the issuer of the underlying security is probably not a participant in the distribution to any degree.

Mandatorily Convertible or Exchangeable or Cash-Settled Securities

Mandatorily convertible securities can offer issuers a number of advantages. In their most basic form, an issuer will issue a debt security or preferred stock that is mandatorily convertible within a specified number of years into the issuer's own common stock. The technique serves as a means of persuading a rating agency that the issuer will definitely receive equity capital within a specified number of years. It also offers the issuer a means of selling its common stock now at a minimum price. In return, the investor will expect to receive a higher return on the security than the investor can obtain from an investment in the common stock.

It is only a short step to issuing a debt security or preferred stock that is mandatorily convertible into (or, more precisely, exchangeable for) the common stock of another company in which the issuer is simply an investor. In this case, the issuer is using the mandatorily exchangeable security as a means of obtaining immediate cash—without having to pay any capital gains taxes—and at the same time ensuring that it will receive at least a minimum price for the underlying stock that it owns. This is sometimes referred to as "monetizing" a minority position in another company.

As a variation in these cases, the issuer may reserve the right to pay cash at the time of exchange in lieu of delivering actual shares, thereby giving it the option of retaining the shares indefinitely or even exposing itself to market risk if it decides to sell the shares prior to the security's maturity. Or the issuer may never have owned any of the underlying securities, as in those situations where a securities firm creates products for its customers by issuing mandatorily exchangeable securities and simultaneously establishes a hedge in the underlying securities.

- *Conversion into Company's Own Common Stock*

Essentially, mandatorily convertible securities involving a company's own stock offer the investor a higher dividend than that available on the issuer's common stock. In return, the investor accepts a cap on the common stock's appreciation potential. The product is similar from the investor's standpoint to a purchase of common stock and a simultaneous writing of a call option on the stock. The investor receives more income but limits its participation in a potential increase in the market price of the stock. At the same time, the issuer has the assurance that it will eventually be able to issue common stock on mandatory conversion within a specified period.

The investor's obligation to take the common stock, usually pursuant to a forward purchase agreement, is customarily secured by the investor's pledging the convertible security (or the debt portion if the security is in a bifurcated form) to the issuer.

Mandatorily convertible securities have been useful to issuers that have had to reduce the dividend on their common stock. In 1988, Avon Products, Inc. wanted to cut the generous dividend on its common stock without upsetting those of its shareholders for whom a high yield was important. In exchange for up to 25% of its common stock, it offered mandatorily convertible securities with a yield equivalent to the pre-cut common stock yield but with a cap on upside potential. In 1994, Times Mirror Company settled a lawsuit arising out of a proposed 80% cut in its dividend by agreeing to issue up to $350 million in mandatorily convertible securities. In 1995, Sun Company, Inc. wanted to avoid a major shift in its shareholder base as a consequence of its plans to cut its common stock dividend. It therefore offered its shareholders a choice between participation in an exchange offer of mandatorily convertible securities or in a Dutch auction tender offer for the common stock.

In 2003, Xerox Corporation offered and sold $800 million of mandatorily convertible preferred stock with a 6.25% dividend. The dividend was payable in cash, shares of Xerox common stock or a combination of the two. Shares used to pay the dividend would be delivered to the transfer agent to be sold on the holders' behalf, resulting in cash to be distributed to the holders in an amount equal to the dividend.

Mandatorily convertible debt securities received a boost in 2003 when the Internal Revenue Service issued Revenue Ruling 2003-97 confirming a company's ability to deduct interest payments notwithstanding the mandatory convertibility feature.

- *Exchange for Another Company's Common Stock*

An issuer may wish to "monetize" all or a portion of its holding in another publicly held company. It may do so by issuing a mandatorily exchangeable debt or preferred security that is automatically exchanged for the common stock of the other company, generally within three to five years. The issuer may intend that the stock be delivered or it may retain the right to pay the holders cash at maturity. For credit rating reasons, the issuer may commit to deliver cash only if it is able to raise the cash by selling its own equity securities within a specified period. The advantages of the transaction for the issuer are the immediate receipt of cash, the guarantee of a minimum price for its stock position in the other company and the deferral of capital gains taxes until the stock is actually delivered. The issuer may also retain an interest, depending on the price terms of the transaction, in the underlying stock's upside potential before maturity.

- *1933 Act Registration*

In the case of securities that are mandatorily convertible into the issuer's own securities, the SEC staff takes the position that the issuer must register the underlying securities at the time it sells the mandatorily convertible securities, whether or not they are convertible immediately or only after one year, because the investors make an investment decision about both securities when they buy the convertible security. In the case of securities mandatorily exchangeable for securities of another company, 1933 Act registration is not necessary if the underlying securities are not restricted securities and there is no control relationship between the issuer of the mandatorily convertible securities and the underlying issuer. Otherwise, the underlying securities must be registered at the time the exchangeable securities are registered for the reason, again, that the investor is in effect making a single investment decision to buy both securities.

- *Rule 144A*

The SEC staff has taken the position that because mandatorily convertible securities in effect require the investor to make an investment decision on the underlying security, then the "fungibility" requirement of Rule 144A is not met if the underlying security is listed or quoted in an automated inter-dealer quotation system such as NASDAQ. Eligibility is not affected, however, if the underlying security was not so listed or quoted at the time of its issuance.[12]

- *Disclosure*

The disclosure issues in the case of mandatorily convertible (i.e., exchangeable) securities are the same as those discussed above in connection with exchangeable securities.

- *Cash-Settled Equity-Linked Notes*

Many companies, especially securities firms, have issued debt obligations the return on which is primarily or even exclusively linked to the performance of a securities market index or a security issued by another company. These securities, sometimes referred to as "equity-linked notes," can be cash settled and take the idea of mandatorily exchangeable securities to its ultimate conclusion by dispensing with the need for any underlying

---

12. SEC No-action Letter, *Shearman & Sterling* (December 21, 1998).

securities. Of course, the issuer of the equity-linked note may choose to mitigate its risk by purchasing underlying securities in the open market.

Wells Fargo & Company sold an interesting equity-linked note to the public in April 2004 that was linked to the stock price of Station Casinos, Inc. The principal-protected notes had a 10-year maturity but could be called at stated redemption prices after three years, thus setting a cap on an investor's return.

Registration under the 1933 Act is obviously limited to the exchangeable securities since there are no actual underlying securities associated with the transaction. On the other hand, the disclosure, due diligence and listing issues are the same as those discussed above in connection with exchangeable securities.

- *Third-Party Monetizations (STRYPES)*

A company with a stock position that it would like to "monetize" may not be in a position to issue its own mandatorily convertible securities for that purpose. Nevertheless, such a company can still achieve its objectives if it can find another company willing to issue its securities that are mandatorily convertible into the securities held by the first company.

A popular vehicle for this purpose uses a security known as Structured Yield Product Exchangeable for Stock (STRYPES), developed by Merrill Lynch & Co. The basic STRYPES product is a Merrill Lynch debt security with a three- to five-year maturity that bears interest at a fixed rate, payable quarterly. It is discharged by the delivery of shares of the underlying security or, at the security owner's option, cash. The number of shares or the amount of cash is fixed by a formula based on the average price of the underlying security over a specified number of trading days prior to maturity. The holder has no choice but to receive the shares or cash; it therefore faces the possibility of a loss of principal. On the other hand, the holder is buying the shares at today's price and will receive an enhanced return over the period until maturity of the STRYPES.

The owner of the underlying shares realizes a number of advantages from the STRYPES transaction. It is "selling" the underlying shares at today's price, but the cash election makes it possible to retain the shares if it wishes to do so. It can also maintain voting rights, collect dividends and defer the payment of taxes.

The STRYPES issuer's obligation to deliver the underlying security or cash is hedged by entering into a forward purchase contract with the owner of the underlying security. The forward contract may be "pre-paid" (i.e., the owner of the underlying security receives cash up front) or settled at the maturity of the STRYPES. In the case of a pre-paid forward purchase, the issuer of the STRYPES will retain the present value of the coupon payments on the STRYPES, or the owner of the underlying security will agree to make periodic payments to the STRYPES issuer equal to the coupon payment on the STRYPES.

Depending on the owner's credit standing, the agreement may require the owner to pledge the underlying security as collateral for the owner's performance of its obligation to deliver the security or cash at the maturity of the STRYPES. The agreement will provide for antidilution adjustments similar to those associated with convertible securities.

• • *1933 Act Considerations.* The issuer of the STRYPES will usually register them on Form S-3. If, as is often the case, it is not certain that the owner of the underlying security is not in "control" of the issuer of the underlying security, or if the underlying securities are "restricted securities" within the meaning of Rule 144, it will also be necessary for the underlying security to be registered at the start of the transaction. In that case, each issuer will file its separate registration statement or take advantage of a previously filed and effective shelf registration. There will be a "stapled" prospectus that consists of a prospectus relating to the STRYPES that is attached to a prospectus for the underlying security. The STRYPES prospectus will include information about the STRYPES issuer that is consistent with a debt takedown by that issuer. The issuer of the underlying security will usually be eligible to use Form S-3 or Form F-3, in which case the information on this issuer contained in the STRYPES prospectus will be limited to a brief description of the issuer, recent market prices of the underlying security and a statement that the issuer is a reporting company under the 1934 Act whose filings are available from the SEC. There is also a reference to the attached prospectus of the issuer of the underlying security, but it is stated that the attached prospectus is not a part of the STRYPES issuer's prospectus or incorporated by reference therein.

The STRYPES issuer and the issuer of the underlying security will file their respective prospectuses with the SEC under Rule 424(b). After extensive discussions with the SEC, it is settled that there is no obligation to deliver a prospectus relating to the underlying securities at the time the STRYPES mature (so long as the issuer of the underlying securities has a class of securities registered under the 1934 Act throughout the life of the STRYPES).

If the underlying security is not a "restricted security" and its owner is not in "control" of its issuer, then Section 4(1) of the 1933 Act will make it unnecessary for the underlying security to be registered at the commencement of the transaction. In this case, the extent of disclosure in the STRYPES prospectus relating to the issuer of the underlying security will vary depending on marketing considerations.

• • *Liability Considerations.* The issuer of the STRYPES will normally not be concerned about civil liability for its own disclosure, but it may be less sure about its liability as an issuer for the disclosure provided to investors by the underlying issuer. None of this disclosure is included in the STRYPES issuer's registration statement, so there should at least be no question of Section 11 liability.

The underwriter of the STRYPES will certainly be deemed a "seller" of the underlying securities for purposes of Section 12(a)(2) liability. The underwriting agreement will call for representations and warranties, legal opinions and a comfort letter that are consistent with a secondary offering.

• • *Listing; State Preemption; CEA Considerations.* STRYPES are listed with the NYSE or AMEX or quoted on NASDAQ. As discussed above, each of the exchanges and NASDAQ has special listing standards for equity-linked debt securities, and STRYPES are considered to fall into that category.

The same state preemption and CEA considerations apply as in the case of exchangeable securities.

Debt/Stock Units

Companies have often made simultaneous offerings of their debt securities and common stock, and these have often been offered (at least initially) as units. Unlike an investor in convertible securities or even debt with warrants, the investor in debt/stock units becomes an immediate owner of both the debt and the stock. Each security is separately registered under the 1933 Act, and a separate filing fee is paid for each.

In late 2003, several companies began offering Income Deposit Securities (IDS). Based on a product developed in Canada, these securities consisted of a subordinated note in a specified principal amount together with a share of common stock. The issuer specified the initial fair market value of the debt and the stock, and each investor was deemed to have agreed to that allocation for purposes of establishing the investor's tax basis. The IDS were listed, often on the American and Toronto stock exchanges, and the common stock was separately listed. Holders could break up their IDS after 90 days from the date of offering and could recombine the debt and stock into IDS at any time.

Several IDS transactions permitted the issuer to defer interest payments on the subordinated note and to extend the maturity date of the subordinated note if the issuer ran into cash flow difficulties. Some observers criticized the product in early 2004 as not being suitable for some of the investors who found IDS most appealing.[13]

Stock Purchase Warrants

Stock purchase warrants are securities that entitle the holder to purchase from the issuer shares of its common stock at an agreed on cash price at any time prior to their expiration. Unlike a convertible or exchangeable debenture, where the conversion or exchange privilege is simply one of the terms of the instrument, warrants can be traded as separate securities. One of the drawbacks of warrants is that they require an "evergreen" prospectus that will be delivered to the holder on the exercise of his warrant.

- *Units of Debt Securities and Warrants*

An issuer can reduce its cost of funds when issuing debt securities by issuing units consisting of securities and warrants

---

13. *IDS Risks Seen,* Corporate Financing Week (April 19, 2004), at 4.

to purchase common stock of the issuer. The warrants will have a limited life (frequently five years), and the exercise price will be fixed at a premium to the market price of the common stock at the time of sale. The purchaser of the securities will have an equity play not unlike that afforded to a purchaser of convertible securities. The terms of the offering may be such that the warrants may not be separated from the securities prior to a specified date, or earlier if the managing underwriter determines that a separate trading market will not interfere with the success of the distribution of the units.

Warrants are issued under a warrant agreement with a bank or trust company acting as warrant agent. The warrants should contain antidilution provisions similar to those used for convertible securities and should also provide for the possibility of a merger or other acquisition involving the issuer.

When units are offered in reliance on Regulation S, the applicable restricted period for the units is determined by reference to the constituent security that triggers the longest restricted period. If the constituent securities can be separately traded immediately after issuance of the units, however, then separate restricted periods may be applied "to the extent feasible."[14]

- *Units of Common Stock and Warrants*

   Warrants are also frequently offered in units along with common stock. In this type of offering, both the warrants and the common stock must be registered, as must be the common stock underlying the warrants. If the warrants are exercisable on a "net share" basis for no additional consideration, Section 3(a)(9) will be available as an exemption for the issuance of the new common stock. Otherwise, the issuer must deliver to each holder exercising a warrant a prospectus meeting the requirements of Section 10(a) of the 1933 Act. If the issuer is not eligible to use Form S-3 for this purpose, it must maintain a current Form S-1 prospectus (at least while the warrants are in-the-money) until it is eligible to convert to a Form S-3 prospectus.

   If an issuer of warrants fails to keep its prospectus current, holders of the warrants may find themselves in the position of

---

14. SEC Release No. 33-6863 (April 24, 1990), text following n.77.

having the issuer refuse to honor exercises for fear of violating the 1933 Act. The holders of the warrants could not care less whether they are furnished a current prospectus, for their decision to exercise is solely a function of the market price of the underlying common stock in relation to the exercise price of the warrants. One securities trading firm found itself in a difficult position in 1983 when it built a short position in an issuer's common stock matched by a long position in the issuer's warrants. Although the prospectus continued to meet the requirements of Section 10(a) of the 1933 Act, material developments had occurred that had not yet been reflected in the prospectus.

Counsel for the issuer advised his client to refuse to honor the firm's exercise of its warrants until a post-effective amendment was filed and declared effective. This would take some time, and in the meantime the firm was caught in a short squeeze. The firm retained counsel, who was able to persuade counsel for the issuer to relent and permit the exercise of the warrants on the basis of the following legal opinion dated September 29, 1983:

> Trading Firm, Inc. ("TFI") has a 5,231,017 share short position in the Common Stock of XYZ, Inc. (the "Company") and owns Warrants entitling it to purchase 5,200,000 shares of Common Stock of the Company. The Warrants and the shares of Common Stock underlying the Warrants have been registered under the Securities Act of 1933 (the "Securities Act") pursuant to a registration statement which we are advised became effective on December 2, 1982. We are also advised that the Securities and Exchange Commission has not issued any stop order suspending the effectiveness of the registration statement. TFI wishes to exercise its Warrants and intends to use the shares of Common Stock purchased upon such exercise solely for the purpose of covering its short position. You have requested our opinion as to whether the issuance of 5,200,000 shares of Common Stock of the Company to TFI upon exercise of its Warrants will constitute a violation of the Securities Act in view of the fact that certain developments have occurred which render the prospectus relating to such Common Stock incomplete as of this time. We will assume, for purposes of this

opinion, that the prospectus currently omits to state certain material facts necessary in order to make the statements therein not misleading.

Notwithstanding such omission, it is our opinion that, under the circumstances, the issuance of 5,200,000 shares of Common Stock of the Company to TFI will not violate Section 5 of the Securities Act and thus will not subject the Company to liability under Section 12(1) of the Securities Act. Section 5(a) provides that unless a registration statement is in effect as to a security it shall be unlawful to use interstate commerce to sell such security. We have been advised that the registration statement is in effect with respect to the Common Stock to be issued in that the registration statement was declared effective on December 2, 1982, and no stop order has been issued. Section 5(b) makes it unlawful to cause a security to be carried in interstate commerce for the purposes of sale or for delivery after sale unless accompanied or proceeded by a prospectus that meets the requirements of Section 10(a) of the Securities Act. All that is required by Section 10(a) is that the prospectus shall contain the information contained in the registration statement and that if the prospectus is used more than nine months after the effectiveness of the registration statement, the information contained therein shall be as of a date not more than 16 months prior to such use so far as such information is known to the user of the prospectus or can be furnished by such user without unreasonable effort or expense. Section 10(a)(4) provides that there may be omitted from any prospectus any of the information required under Section 10(a) which the Securities and Exchange Commission may by rules or regulations designate as not necessary or appropriate in the public interest or for the protection of investors. We assume that at the time the registration statement became effective the prospectus contained the required information. Although the prospectus is to be used more than nine months after the effective date of the registration statement, the information therein, including the certified financial statements, is as of a date not more than 16 months prior to its use. In this connection we note that the certified financial statements are dated August 31, 1982.

You have asked us to address Section 10(c), which provides that a prospectus shall contain such other information as the Securities and Exchange Commission may by rules or regulations require as being necessary or appropriate in the public interest or for the protection of investors, and specifically Item 512 of Regulation S-K, which requires certain undertakings for Rule 415 offerings. We are advised that these undertakings are contained in the Company's registration statement. The relevant undertaking requires that a post-effective amendment be filed to reflect in a prospectus any facts or events representing a fundamental change in the information set forth in the registration statement. It is our opinion, based on the history of this undertaking and the release relating to its adoption, that it is essentially procedural in nature and is intended to address the issue of when a post-effective amendment, and not merely a prospectus supplement, is required when a prospectus is to be amended. The importance of the undertaking is that if the prospectus is amended to reflect facts or events which represent a fundamental change in the information set forth in the registration statement, then a post-effective amendment is required, but that if a prospectus is amended to reflect facts or events which do not represent a fundamental change, then a prospectus supplement is sufficient. The existence of the undertaking does not affect our conclusion that the prospectus continues to meet the requirements of Section 10(a) notwithstanding that it omits to state material facts necessary to make the statements therein not misleading.

Prospectuses must be updated to reflect material developments because a failure to do so could subject the issuer to liability under Section 12(2) of the Securities Act. Section 12(2) provides that any person who offers or sells a security in interstate commerce by means of a prospectus which omits to state a material fact necessary in order to make the statements therein not misleading shall be liable to the person purchasing the security. If the Company's prospectus does contain a material omission, then the Company would have potential liability to TFI in connection with the sale to it of the Common Stock, but for the fact that TFI has not and will not incur any loss. By creating a short position, TFI has in effect sold the (common Stock to be acquired upon exercise of its Warrants). TFI has assured us that the aggregate price at which the 5,200,000 shares of Common Stock were sold exceeds the aggregate cost of its Warrants plus the aggregate exercise price. Accordingly, the Company cannot be liable to TFI for any damages. The exercise of its Warrants will merely enable TFI to close out its short position, and the information or lack of information in the prospectus is irrelevant to it.

Calls for Redemption to Force Conversions

There are often strong economic incentives for a company to call for redemption of an issue of convertible securities or preferred stock with a view to forcing the conversion of these securities into common stock.

By way of illustration, assume that a company has outstanding 25 million shares of common stock and 5 million shares of convertible preferred stock. Each share of preferred stock is convertible into .6 of a share of common stock, and the preferred stock is redeemable at the option of the company at $20 per share plus accrued dividends. The annual cash dividend currently paid on the common stock is $.80 per share, and the annual preferential dividend on the preferred stock is $1 per share. If all outstanding preferred shares were converted, the annual dividend requirement for the 3 million additional common shares issuable on conversion would be only $2.4 million, as compared to $5 million for the existing preferred stock. The market price of the common stock is $40, and the preferred stock is trading at $25. Under these circumstances, the company might well consider calling its preferred stock for redemption with a view to forcing conversions into common stock.

The success of the call will depend on substantially all of the holders of the convertible securities electing to convert, rather than allowing their shares to be redeemed. Rationally, this should occur if immediately prior to the expiration of the conversion privilege the market value of .6 of a share of common stock exceeds the redemption price of a share of preferred stock plus accrued dividends. On the other hand, there are sometimes delays in receiving notices that are initially received by The Depository Trust Company as registered holder of the securities, retransmitted to one or possibly more layers of participating broker-dealers or banks and then retransmitted in turn to the actual holder. Finally, many holders are "sleepers" who neglect to take any action even after receiving timely notice.[15] Some broker-dealers will take action on behalf of a "sleeper" client to convert the client's securities if it is clearly in the client's interest to do so.

Assuming that the relevant charter provision requires a 30-day notice of redemption, that the conversion privilege terminates at the close of business on the business day next preceding the redemption date, and that once the call is made it cannot be rescinded, then there will be a market risk for at least 29 days. If there should be a substantial market decline during the redemption period, so that the market value of .6 of a share of

---

15. If convertible preferred stock or registered convertible debentures are called, a notice of redemption must be mailed to each holder of record on the date of the call. It is customary and advisable also to mail the notice to each transferee of record during the redemption period. In addition, the notice usually will be published in newspapers in major financial centers and in cities where there is a geographical concentration of holders of the called securities.

Although coupon debentures in bearer form have not been issued in the United States for many years, some older issues still may be outstanding. If such an issue is called, the company must follow the requirements of the indenture as to publication of notice. Consideration should be given to more extensive publication if necessary to provide reasonable notice. See *Van Gemert v. Boeing Co.*, 520 F.2d 1373 (2d Cir.), *cert. denied*, 423 U.S. 947 (1975); *Van Gemert v. Boeing Co.*, 553 F.2d 812 (2d Cir. 1977). See also A. B. Miller, *How to Call Your Convertibles*, Harv. Bus. Rev., May–June 1971, at 66.

common stock falls below the $20 redemption price of a share of preferred stock, plus accrued dividends (assumed to be $.10 per share), it is possible that none of the called securities will be converted, and the company could find itself in the position of being required to make a cash outlay of more than $100 million, which was not the point of the call. In this example, so long as the market price of a share of common stock (trading at $40 when the call was made) does not fall below $33.50, holders of preferred stock, on conversion, would receive common stock having a market value greater than the cash that would be received on redemption. In general, conversion would be advantageous if the common stock does not fall below that price.[16]

If, when the call is made, the spread between the conversion price and the market price of the common stock is sufficiently great that the risk of an unsuccessful call is minimal, the company might be willing to assume the risk of a market decline. But in a more marginal case, as in the above example, or in a period of uncertain market conditions, the company might look to its investment bankers to form a syndicate of standby purchasers to underwrite the risk.

- *Standby Arrangements*

In the case of an underwritten call, the investment banking firms acting as standby purchasers will agree to purchase any convertible securities properly tendered to them prior to the expiration of the conversion privilege at a price slightly in excess of the redemption price plus accrued dividends and to surrender the purchased convertible securities for conversion. In the above example, where the redemption price of a share of preferred stock is $20, plus accrued dividends of $.10 per share, the standby purchasers might agree to purchase preferred stock tendered to them at $20.25 per share.

---

16. In individual cases, tax considerations may be an added factor. Conversion will not result in taxable gain or loss. Gain or loss will be recognized for federal income tax purposes on redemption or sale of the convertible securities.

The effect of such an agreement is that, assuming adequate communication with the holders of the called securities apprising them of the available alternatives, the risk of a market decline is shifted from the company to the standby purchasers. If the price of the common stock should decline during the redemption period to a point at which a holder of preferred stock would find it in his best interests not to convert, it would still be advantageous for him to tender his preferred stock to the standby purchasers and receive the tender price of $20.25, rather than $20.10, the redemption price plus accrued dividends. As the standby purchasers are committed to surrender for conversion any preferred stock purchased by them, the company should be effectively protected against the risk of having to make a substantial cash outlay. The risk that the standby purchasers run is that they will realize less on the resale of the common stock acquired on conversion than the amount paid by them for the preferred stock purchased from tendering shareholders.

For assuming this risk, the standby purchasers will be paid a fee by the company. The amount of the fee will depend in part upon the degree of risk assumed, which in turn will depend on the spread between the market price of the common stock and the effective conversion price. The usual arrangement is for the standby purchasers to receive a standby fee based on a percentage of their maximum dollar commitment plus a take-up fee for shares of common stock actually acquired on conversion.

- *1933 Act Considerations*

As previously discussed, the issuance of common stock on conversion of publicly owned convertible securities or preferred stock is ordinarily exempt from registration under Section 3(a)(9). Prior to a 1978 amendment to Form S-16 (the short-form predecessor of Form S-3) that made registration economical for underwritten calls, it had been the universal practice to have the standby purchasers agree that they would not solicit conversions in order to ensure that the fees paid to them would not destroy the Section 3(a)(9) exemption.

Historically, the more difficult question had been the availability of an exemption from registration for resales of common stock issued to the standby purchasers on conversion of the convertible securities purchased by them. In this connection, it should be noted that the SEC has long taken the position that Section 3(a)(9) of the 1933 Act is a transaction exemption rather than an exemption for the securities issued on conversion. Accordingly, a seller of securities issued on conversion of an outstanding security (or in any other transaction exempted by Section 3(a)(9)) must find his own exemption under Section 4 or otherwise. The question then is whether the standby purchasers would be deemed to be "underwriters" as defined in Section 2(a)(11) of the 1933 Act in reselling to the public the stock acquired by them on conversion. This in turn would depend on whether their sales would constitute a "distribution."

Standby purchasers relied for many years on SEC no-action letters to proceed with unregistered resales of shares acquired on conversion. When it became clear that standby purchasers could be considered selling securityholders for purposes of Form S-16[17] (and, subsequently, for purposes of Form S-3), it became the practice to register the underlying securities to cover resales by the standby purchasers.

Originally, in the context of an underwritten call, a Form S-16 registration statement could be used only to cover resales by the standby purchasers, and not the issuance of stock on conversion of the outstanding convertible securities. The issuance of stock on conversion was required to be made under the Section 3(a)(9) exemption, and thus there could be no solicitation of conversions by the standby purchasers.

Eventually, it became possible to use Form S-16 and then Form S-3 to register shares for the purpose of solicited conversions. The prospectus included in the registration statement is mailed to holders of the convertible securities to cover the shares issued on conversion as well as being used to cover resales by the standby purchasers. Where this procedure is followed, the standby purchasers should be permitted to solicit conversions

---

17. SEC No-action Letter, *Salomon Brothers* (September 28, 1972).

while they stand ready to purchase any convertible securities tendered to them.[18]

When issuers began to register the common stock issuable on conversion of securities called for redemption, there was some concern that the customary form of redemption notice published in the financial press might be considered an illegal prospectus in that it did not conform strictly to Rule 134 under the 1933 Act. To avoid this problem, some issuers published their full Form S-16 prospectus in lieu of an abbreviated notice of redemption. In effect, the prospectus was the notice of redemption, and the notice of redemption was the prospectus. There is nothing to say that a prospectus must be in booklet form, and the prospectus filed as part of the Form S-16 registration statement was identical to the newspaper advertisement that would appear as soon as the registration statement became effective. It was all very neat and creative, but the practice never caught on; and, notwithstanding that shares are registered for the purpose of conversions, traditional notices of redemption continue to be published with no ill effects under the 1933 Act.[19]

---

18. In an administrative proceeding involving Blyth, Eastman Dillon & Co. Inc., SEC Release Nos. 34-10565 and 34-10566 (December 19, 1973), the firm and two of its registered representatives were censured by the SEC for alleged misuse of a shareholder list obtained in connection with a redemption standby. The SEC charged that the registered representatives improperly used the list to generate leads for new accounts and commission business, and in making calls to shareholders on the list, ostensibly to assist them in connection with the redemption, engaged in improper selling practices in recommending the purchase of securities. The questions raised in this proceeding as to the proper use of shareholder lists by investment bankers are in no way peculiar to redemption standbys. The same issues are involved if a shareholder list is furnished to an investment banker in connection with a tender offer, an exchange offer or a merger.

19. It should be noted that a redemption pursuant to the terms of the instrument creating or governing the securities being redeemed is not subject to the SEC's going private rule, Rule 13e-3, by virtue of the exception in subsection (g)(4). A similar exception from Rule 13e-4, the issuer tender offer rule, is provided by subsection (h)(1) thereof.

- *Redemptions and Regulation M*

The SEC staff has occasionally referred to redemptions of "in-the-money" convertible securities as potentially triggering a "distribution" for purposes of Regulation M of the underlying common stock. The theory is that the call for redemption will inevitably result in the issuance of the underlying common stock and that if the "magnitude" element is present the issuer's act in issuing the call will be sufficient to make up the "special selling efforts and selling methods" element.[20] Under this view, the issuer and its affiliated purchasers would have to cease bids for and purchases of the underlying common stock from the announcement of the call to the termination of the redemption period (or later, if a standby purchaser has an unsold long position).

An issuer may seek to redeem or induce conversions of an older convertible security while it is at the same time engaged in a "distribution" for Regulation M purposes of a new convertible security. Even if the call for redemption or the effort to induce conversions gives rise to a distribution of the underlying common stock, the distribution of the new convertible security can still proceed because the new convertible security is not a "reference security" for the common stock.

- *Lay-Offs*

It is customary for standby agreements to provide that the standby purchasers may (but are under no obligation to) purchase convertible securities in addition to those purchased pursuant to tenders in such amounts and at such prices as the purchasers may deem advisable and that all convertible securities so purchased will be converted into common stock.

The take-up fee usually will be payable in respect of any common stock acquired on conversion of convertible securities so purchased, as well as those purchased pursuant to tenders. As long as the price of the common stock holds firm, there is

---

20. The SEC staff takes a similar position regarding issuer efforts to encourage the exercise of warrants. Staff Legal Bulletin No. 9 at 4 (revised January 4, 2000).

little reason for the standby purchasers to buy convertible securities in the open market. But if weakness develops in the price of the common stock, the standby purchasers might wish to make short sales of the common stock, purchase convertible securities in the open market and use the shares acquired on conversion of those securities to deliver against their short sales. Such transactions during the redemption period would reduce the purchasers' risk in a manner similar to Shields Plan transactions effected in connection with underwritten rights offerings.[21]

Prior to the adoption of Regulation M, it was necessary to deal with the fact that Rule 10b-6 prohibited purchases of convertible securities in the open market because these represented "rights to purchase" the common stock being distributed. For many years, the SEC granted exemptions that permitted such purchases so long as they were effected in accordance with Rule 10b-8, which applied to rights offerings. The need for exemptions disappeared in 1983, when Rule 10b-8 was amended to make it expressly applicable to convertible securities called for redemption pursuant to a standby underwriting agreement.[22] Of course, the lengthy history of SEC regulation of "lay-off" activities in connection with rights offerings and standby underwritings came to an end in late 1996 when the SEC adopted Rules 101 and 102, neither of which applies to "rights to purchase" a covered security.

Expiring Warrants

Just as an issuer of convertible securities may have a fire sale by reducing the conversion price for a period of time in order to encourage conversions, a company that has outstanding warrants that are about to expire may sweeten the terms in an effort to induce holders to exercise. This is sometimes referred to as a "warrant flush" or a "flush-out."

Prior to the adoption of Regulation M, the SEC staff was willing to grant exemptions under Rule 10b-6 to permit transactions

---

21. *See* Chapter 13.
22. SEC Release No. 34-19565 (March 4, 1983).

subject to Rule 10b-8 restrictions designed to facilitate the exercise of warrants that were about to expire. Of course, there is no need under Regulation M to obtain such an exemption since neither Rule 101 nor Rule 102 applies to purchases of "rights to purchase," such as warrants.

If the exercise price of warrants is to be reduced for a temporary period, SRO listing standards may specify the minimum number of days during which the reduction must remain in effect. The SEC staff has taken the position that reductions of the exercise price of warrants constitute issuer tender offers for purposes of Rule 13e-4 and that the "offer" must therefore remain open for at least 20 business days.[23]

---

23. SEC Release No. 33-7422 (June 10, 1997), text at and in nn.25 and 36); SEC No-action Letter, *Heritage Entertainment, Inc.* (May 11, 1987).

Chapter 13

TRANSACTIONS WITH SECURITYHOLDERS: STOCK REPURCHASES, DEBT RESTRUCTURINGS AND RIGHTS OFFERINGS

In this chapter, we discuss transactions in which companies deal directly with their own securityholders for the purpose of changing their capital structure or raising additional funds.

A company may wish to reduce the amount of its outstanding common stock. This can be done through open market purchases, privately negotiated purchases or by means of a tender offer. A company's management or an affiliate may decide to take it private. A tender offer or statutory merger would be the general means by which such a buyout (leveraged or otherwise) would be accomplished.

A company may decide that it is advantageous to eliminate high coupon debt securities or to reduce the amount of its outstanding debt. It may be possible to do so simply by calling all or a portion of the securities for redemption. If this is not permitted under the governing indenture, purchases in the open market may be the answer, at least if the securities are not widely held. If there is widespread ownership and the company wishes to retire all or most of the issue, a cash tender offer may be the best approach. If the company does not have sufficient funds on hand or wishes to preserve its cash, it may choose to offer a new debt or equity security, or a package of debt and equity securities, in exchange for the outstanding debt security that it wishes to eliminate. An exchange offer or cash tender offer may be coupled with a consent solicitation designed to eliminate burdensome covenants, or a consent solicitation may be made independently of a debt restructuring.

In some cases, a company may decide to increase its capital by means of a rights offering, or, as it is also called, a "subscription offering," in which it offers additional shares of common or preferred stock, or in some cases convertible securities, directly to its existing securityholders rather than to the general public through underwriters.

Stock Repurchases

As the SEC has noted, "[i]ssuers repurchase their stock for many legitimate business reasons."[1] Some of these reasons include offsetting the dilution arising from acquisitions or from stock purchase, stock option, dividend reinvestment or similar plans, increasing earnings per share or eliminating smaller holdings and thus reducing servicing costs. Prior to the reduction of federal income tax rates on corporate dividends, stock repurchases also represented a more tax-efficient way of returning capital to shareholders. Particularly in times of market stress, stock repurchases also provide much-needed liquidity.

During the 1980s and into the bull market from 1994 through mid-2000, public companies repurchased their common stock in record amounts. There was particularly concentrated activity during the October 1987 market break, the debt market crisis of August through October 1998 and following the events of September 11, 2001. On the other hand, announcements of stock repurchases declined in 2001 and 2002. Fluctuations in stock repurchases occur for many reasons, including not only changes in market conditions but also changes in tax or accounting rules, e.g., those relating to "greenmail," pooling-of-interest

---

1. SEC Release No. 34-46980 (December 10, 2002) (proposing amendments to Rule 10b-18).

treatment of acquisitions, expense treatment of stock options and the tax rates applicable to dividends and capital gains.[2]

Public companies may also "go private," some because they conclude that public ownership and the pressure to increase performance in each quarter stand in the way of long-term growth and others because of concern about the increased costs since Sarbanes–Oxley of remaining a public company.

- *Corporate Law Considerations*

State law must be examined before a company embarks on a stock repurchase program. For example, Section 160(a)(1) of the Delaware General Corporation Law provides that a corporation may purchase its own shares except when its capital is impaired or when the purchase would result in an impairment of capital (unless the shares are retired and the capital of the corporation reduced). Unless retired, repurchased shares become treasury shares, which cannot be voted and cannot be counted in computing the number of shares necessary for a quorum.

Indentures and loan agreements must be reviewed to ensure that the proposed repurchase of stock will not violate any financial covenants. The usual covenant restricting the payment of dividends restricts stock repurchases as well.

Stock repurchases may be made for any proper corporate purpose, and the courts ordinarily will not second-guess the business judgment of the board. Press releases announcing stock repurchase programs frequently state that the shares being acquired will be used for stock options or acquisitions. Such a statement makes little sense inasmuch as authorized but unissued shares are usually available for this purpose. What really is being said is that shares are being repurchased so that shares can be issued under stock options or for acquisitions without diluting earnings per share.

---

2. Letter dated February 27, 2003 from Charles J. Plohn, Jr., Merrill Lynch, Pierce, Fenner & Smith Inc. to Jonathan G. Katz, Secretary, Securities and Exchange Commission, commenting on SEC Release No. 34-46980 (December 10, 2002) (proposing amendments to Rule 10b-18).

One company announced that it was making a tender offer to partially offset the number of shares that would otherwise be outstanding on a fully diluted basis assuming conversion of a new class of preferred stock proposed to be issued to an ESOP. Most amusing are the press releases that state that the shares are being acquired because, given the current market price of the shares, their purchase "is an attractive investment in comparison to alternative investment opportunities." A reduction of a company's capital base hardly can be viewed as an "investment." Perhaps the most straightforward reason that can be given in the usual case is that the board considers the purchase to be "a prudent use of the company's cash balances and debt capacity" while at the same time keeping the shareholders happy.

- *Rule 10b-5 Considerations*

Care must be taken to ensure that the company does not purchase its stock at a time when it is aware of material nonpublic information that could have a favorable impact on the price of its stock. Many companies impose "blackout periods" on their repurchase activity at times when such information might exist, for example, before the end of a fiscal quarter until after the announcement of earnings for that quarter.

The SEC's Rule 10b5-1, adopted in 2000, offers the possibility of an issuer's continuation of purchases notwithstanding its possession of material nonpublic information if it makes sure that the company employee controlling the program does not have access to the information or if its agreement with the broker-dealer acting as repurchasing agent provides for Rule "10b5-1 Plan Periods" during which repurchases take place pursuant to a binding contract, instruction or plan.

- *Purchases in the Open Market*

Purchases of common stock from time to time in the open market have an advantage over a tender offer in that they do not require the company to offer a premium over the current market price. The purchases are effected on an exchange or in the over-the-counter market at prevailing market prices.

These transactions raise a number of regulatory issues. First, the purchases must be made in such a way that the acquisition program does not constitute a tender offer under federal and state securities laws. The purchases must not be manipulative. Most of the major brokerage firms have trading desks that specialize in stock repurchase programs. To ensure that a program is conducted properly in accordance with all applicable regulations, it is advisable to call on a specialist to handle the purchases.

• • *Avoiding a "Tender Offer."* If a company makes a tender offer for its shares, it must comply with the applicable tender offer rules. Open market purchases, being unstructured, by their very nature cannot conform to the requirements relating to the conduct of tender offers. A stock repurchase program, however, may take on the appearance of a tender offer, and care should be taken to ensure that it is not actually a tender offer. For the most part, these programs have been conducted in a manner that does not raise concerns under the tender offer rules.

The 1934 Act does not define the term "tender offer." Attempts by the courts and the SEC to come up with an acceptable definition have been unsuccessful. Consequently, subjective considerations will be taken into account in determining whether a tender offer has been made. The SEC has suggested that the courts look to the following eight factors in determining the existence of a tender offer: whether there is an active and widespread solicitation of public securityholders; whether the solicitation is made for a substantial percentage of the issuer's securities; whether the offer is made at a premium over the prevailing market price; whether the terms of the offer are firm rather than negotiable; whether the offer is contingent on the tender of a fixed minimum number and perhaps subject to the ceiling of a fixed maximum number of securities to be purchased; whether the offer is open for only a limited period of time; whether the offerees are subjected to pressure to sell; and whether public announcements of a purchasing program precede or accompany a rapid accumulation of large amounts of the target company's securities.

The SEC's eight-factor test was first adopted by a court in 1979 in *Wellman v. Dickinson*.[3] The eight factors also were

---

3. 475 F. Supp. 783 (S.D.N.Y. 1979), *aff'd*, 682 F.2d 355 (2d Cir. 1982), *cert. denied*, 460 U.S. 1069 (1983).

discussed in *SEC v. Carter Hawley Hale Stores, Inc.*[4] There Carter Hawley Hale, without complying with the rules governing issuer tender offers, repurchased over 50% of its outstanding common stock in the open market in response to a tender offer by The Limited. The Court of Appeals evaluated the SEC's eight-factor test and found that the repurchase program did not constitute a tender offer, despite the existence of one of the eight factors (a large percentage of stock was accumulated following a public announcement). It should be noted that the district court arrived at the same conclusion despite its finding that two of the eight factors were present (pressure on shareholders to sell and a large accumulation of stock following a public announcement). While it is clear that not all of the eight factors must be present for there to be a tender offer, it remains unclear precisely how many of the factors must be present for a purchase program to constitute a tender offer.

In *Crane Co. v. Harsco Corp.*,[5] it was held that a target company's purchase of its own stock from arbitragers in an attempt to block a tender offer was not itself a tender offer by the target company to the arbitragers. The payment of a premium for the shares was the only one of the eight factors present, and this, standing alone, was not sufficient to make the transaction a tender offer.

In *Hanson Trust PLC v. SCM Corp.*,[6] the court held that there was no tender offer where Hanson Trust purchased 25% of the outstanding common stock of SCM Corporation in open market and privately negotiated transactions immediately after Hanson terminated its tender offer for a large percentage of SCM's stock. The court rejected the SEC's eight-factor test. Instead, its analysis turned on the fact that the sellers of SCM stock to Hanson were knowledgeable, sophisticated investors

---

4. 760 F.2d 945 (9th Cir. 1985).

5. 511 F. Supp. 294 (D.C. Del. 1981).

6. 774 F.2d 47 (2d Cir. 1985). For a more recent case finding that open market and privately negotiated purchases did not amount to a tender offer within the meaning of the Williams Act, *see Gorman v. Coogan*, 2004 U.S. DIST. LEXIS 301 (D. Me. 2004).

TRANSACTIONS WITH SECURITYHOLDERS 917

selling, for the most part, in private transactions and thus not in need of the protection afforded by the tender offer rules.

The fundamental concern of the courts has been to prevent offers that put pressure on shareholders leading them to make uninformed, ill-considered decisions to sell. Offering a premium for a limited time can contribute to such pressure, especially if the offer is not limited to sophisticated investors. On the other hand, it should be possible to avoid a tender offer if a stock repurchase program is limited to open-market transactions. Even in these situations, it is still important for the purchaser and the securities dealer responsible for executing the transactions to be in agreement as to how the transactions will be executed.

• • *Rule 10b-18.* The increased demand for an issuer's stock created by a stock repurchase program may result in an increase in the market price. Indeed, this may be an unspoken reason for instituting such a program. There is nothing wrong with issuer repurchases that have the effect of shoring up the price of the stock as long as the purchases are not manipulative. At one time, the SEC was rather concerned over issuer repurchases. The sense was that the temptations to manipulate were there, and the SEC should keep up its guard.

A device once used by the SEC to maintain control over stock repurchases had its basis in a rather strained interpretation of former Rule 10b-6. The SEC took the position that if a company had an issue of convertible securities outstanding, it was engaged in a continuous distribution of the underlying stock for purposes of former Rule 10b-6, at least if the convertibles were in-the-money. Thus, if the company wished to purchase its own stock, it would have to obtain an exemptive order. These orders were readily granted, but they were granted subject to a set of standard conditions designed to ensure that the purchases did not unduly affect the price of the stock.

In 1982, former Rule 10b-6 was amended to provide that it did not apply to purchases of a security solely because the issuer or a subsidiary had outstanding securities convertible into or exchangeable for that security. At the same time, the SEC adopted Rule 10b-18, which codified the standard conditions and provided all issuers with a safe harbor in which to conduct stock repurchase programs without fear of being accused of manipulation.[7] The SEC amended Rule 10b-18 in late 2003 in order to "simplify and update the safe harbor provisions in light of market developments since the Rule's adoption."[8] In May 2004 the SEC's Division of Market Regulation published its response to Frequently Asked Questions regarding Rule 10b-18.[9]

• • • *"Rule 10b-18 Purchases."* The safe harbor of Rule 10b-18 is available only for "Rule 10b-18 purchases," which mean purchases (including bids or limit orders that would result in such purchases) of an issuer's common stock[10] by or for the issuer or any affiliated purchaser.[11] Under certain conditions, a broker-dealer can rely on the safe harbor to purchase common stock for purposes of resale to the issuer in a "riskless principal" transaction.[12]

---

7. SEC Release No. 34-19244 (November 17, 1982).

8. SEC Release No. 34-48766 (November 10, 2003) (hereafter the 2003 Adopting Release).

9. Available on the SEC's website at www.sec.gov/divisions/marketreg/r10b18faq0504.htm ("2004 FAQ").

10. The safe harbor applies only to purchases of common stock or equivalent interests such as depositary shares. It does not apply to purchases of other securities, even those related to common stock. 2004 FAQ #2.

11. An "affiliated purchaser" is a person who acts directly or indirectly in concert with the issuer for the purpose of acquiring the issuer's securities or who is an affiliate who directly or indirectly controls the issuer's purchases, whose purchases are controlled by the issuer or whose purchases are under common control with those of the issuer. Broker-dealers who effect Rule 10b-18 purchases and officers and directors of the issuer who participate in authorizing Rule 10b-18 purchases are not necessarily affiliated purchasers. References to "issuers" in this discussion of Rule 10b-18 should be understood to include "affiliated purchasers."

The SEC staff stated in 2004 FAQ #19 that a target company became an "affiliated purchaser" of the acquiring company with respect to purchase of the acquiror's stock after the signing of the merger agreement.

12. The broker-dealer's purchase as principal (the offsetting transaction) must be for the purpose of satisfying a previously received buy order from the issuer and must be at the same price as the sale to the issuer (exclusive of transaction costs). Only the offsetting transaction must be reported to the

Rule 10b-18 purchases do not include purchases by an issuer or affiliated purchaser effected during the applicable Rule 102 restricted period when the issuer or affiliated purchaser is distributing (within the meaning of Regulation M) the issuer's common stock or any other security for which the common stock is a reference security. Accordingly, such purchases by the issuer or an affiliated purchaser are not protected by Rule 10b-18 even if they are entitled to one of the exceptions to Rule 102 (e.g., exception 6 for unsolicited purchases). This does not make such purchases illegal, of course, but the underwriters are likely to be understandably suspicious of such purchases just prior to pricing. Moreover, if an underwriter's price-influencing activity can be illegal (see the discussion in Chapter 4 of the C.O.M.B. incident), why not similar activity by an issuer or an affiliated purchaser?

Purchases during a third-party tender offer are not covered by the safe harbor, nor are purchases pursuant to an issuer tender offer (whether or not subject to Rule 13e-4, discussed below) or, except as discussed below under "Conditions to Availability of Safe Harbor," purchases during the pendency of a merger, acquisition or similar transaction involving a recapitalization.

Rule 10b-18 purchases also do not include purchases made for an employee benefit plan or stock ownership plan by a trustee or other person independent of the issuer. An independent agent can be presumed to be interested solely in getting the best price for the plan and to have no incentive to drive up the price of the stock. The agent will be deemed to be independent of the issuer under the standards specified in Rule 100 of Regulation M—namely, that it is not an affiliate of the issuer and neither the issuer nor any affiliate of the issuer exercises any direct or indirect control or influence over the price, amount, timing or manner of purchases, or the selection of a broker other than the agent itself. The issuer will not be deemed to have such control or influence solely because it revises not more than once in

---

market. Also, the broker-dealer must have procedures adequate to ensure, among other things, that the issuer's order is received before the offsetting transaction takes place and that the offsetting transaction is allocated within 60 seconds of its execution.

any three-month period the source of the shares to fund the plan, the basis for determining the amount of its contributions to the plan, or the basis for determining the frequency of its allocations to the plan, or any formula specified in the plan that determines the amount of shares to be purchased by the agent.

• • • *Scope of Safe Harbor.* If the rule's conditions are met, Rule 10b-18 purchases will not be deemed to violate the anti-manipulation provisions of Section 9(a)(2) of the 1934 Act (see Chapter 4) or Section 10(b) or Rule 10b-5 "solely" by reason of the time, price or amount of such purchases or the number of broker-dealers used to effect such purchases.

As a safe harbor, however, Rule 10b-18 has a number of hidden rocks. First of all, a Preliminary Note to the rule states that the safe harbor is not available for repurchases that are made in technical compliance with the rule but that are part of a "plan or scheme" to evade the securities laws. Second, the SEC made it clear in the 2003 Adopting Release that repurchases can meet all the conditions of the safe harbor and still violate the antifraud or antimanipulation provisions of the 1934 Act (a) if the issuer engages in repurchases while it possesses material nonpublic information or (b) if the repurchases are fraudulent or manipulative "when viewed in the totality of the facts and circumstances surrounding the repurchases (i.e., facts and circumstances in addition to the volume, price, time and manner of the repurchases)."[13]

The 2003 Adopting Release states that the SEC decided against "extend[ing] the safe harbor to issuer repurchases effected outside the United States" because it did not believe that "a workable rule could be created for universal application both inside *and* outside the United States, without unnecessarily complicating or undermining the utility of the safe harbor." It also noted that there was no practical way for it to adequately monitor the impact of an issuer's repurchase activity outside the United States. As adopted, Rule 10b-18 does not by its terms exclude purchases that take place outside the United States, but

---

13. 2003 Adopting Release, text at nn.5, 24.

it may be difficult to apply the safe harbor's conditions to purchases in foreign markets.

• • • *Conditions to Availability of Safe Harbor.* In order for the safe harbor to be available to an issuer or affiliated purchaser on any given day, all of the following conditions must be met on that day:

- Purchases must be made from or through only one broker or dealer on any single day. This condition does not apply to purchases that are not solicited by the issuer and its affiliated purchasers. Purchases are not necessarily considered solicited merely because they take place after the issuer's disclosure and announcement of its repurchase program.[14] If more than one of the issuer and its affiliated purchasers are repurchasing on any one day they must all use the same broker-dealer, but different broker-dealers may be used during the regular trading session and an after-hours trading session. Issuers cannot use a broker-dealer and an electronic communications network (ECN) or other alternative trading system (ATS) at the same time, but a broker-dealer used by the issuer on any given day may "access ECN or other ATS liquidity" on behalf of the issuer on that day.

    Does the "single broker-dealer" condition mean that privately negotiated purchases are not eligible for the safe harbor? The staff so concluded in a 1984 no-action letter,[15] in which it also observed that privately negotiated purchases generally present little potential for manipulative abuse and therefore do not require the protection of a safe harbor. An issuer could strengthen its claim to the safe harbor by interposing a broker-dealer between it and the seller in a private transaction, but such transactions (e.g., accelerated share repurchases and forward contracts) are typically with broker-dealers.

---

14. "Whether a transaction has been solicited necessarily depends on the facts and circumstances of each case." 2004 FAQ #24.

15. SEC No-action Letter, *General Electric Co.* (August 3, 1984).

Many companies prefer to work with several broker-dealers on their buyback programs and periodically rotate the responsibility for executing repurchases.

- Purchases must not constitute the opening (regular way) purchase reported in the consolidated reporting system. If the stock has an ADTV value of $1 million or more and a public float of $150 million or more, the purchase must not be made during the first or last 10 minutes of the primary trading session of the market where the purchase is made. Other stocks may not be purchased during the first or last 30 minutes of such session. Under specified conditions, Rule 10b-18 purchases may be made during an after-hours trading session.

- The purchase must be made at a price that does not exceed the highest independent bid or the last independent transaction price, whichever is higher, either (a) quoted or reported in the consolidated system at the time the purchase is made or (b) displayed and disseminated on any exchange or inter-dealer quotation system that displays at least two priced quotations for the stock. For all other securities, purchases must be made at a price no higher than the highest independent bid obtained from three independent dealers.[16]

- The number of shares purchased on any day may not exceed 25% of the prior four weeks' ADTV for the stock. The 2003 amendments to Rule 10b-18 eliminated the previous exemption for block trades[17] but permitted

---

16. The SEC rejected as "premature" proposals to permit the pricing condition to be met where stock is purchased on the basis of a "passive" pricing system (such as the volume-weighted average price).

17. The term "block" means a quantity of stock that either has a purchase price of $200,000 or more, is at least 5,000 shares and has a purchase price of at least $50,000, or is at least 20 round lots and totals 150% or more of ADTV (or 1/10 of 1% of the issuer's float if trading volume is unavailable). A block does not include any amount that a broker-dealer has accumulated as principal for sale to the issuer or affiliated person if the issuer or affiliated purchaser knows or has reason to know that it was accumulated for this purpose.

blocks to be included in computing ADTV. Also, the amended rule permits—as an alternative volume test—a single block purchase on a single day no more than "once each week" if no other safe harbor purchases are made on that day and the block purchase is not included when calculating the stock's ADTV.

A modified volume test applies during the pendency of a merger, acquisition or similar transaction involving a recapitalization where the consideration is other than cash or involves a valuation period. Because of its belief that an issuer had "considerable incentive" to support or raise the price of its common stock to facilitate such a transaction, the SEC had proposed suspending the availability of Rule 10b-18 for purchases during the pendency of the transaction. For companies that make frequent acquisitions or that make acquisitions with extended periods for regulatory review, this would have reduced or eliminated the availability of Rule 10b-18. After considering comments on the proposal, the SEC decided to amend Rule 10b-18 so as to impose a modified volume test during the period from the time of public announcement of the transaction to the earlier of the completion of the transaction or the completion of the vote by the target's shareholders. The modified test permits purchases to be treated as "Rule 10b-18 purchases" and to be eligible for the safe harbor during this period where (a) the volume of such purchases on a given day does not exceed the lesser of 25% of the stock's four-week ADTV or the issuer's average daily Rule 10b-18 purchases during the three-week period preceding the date of announcement, (b) the issuer's block purchases under Rule 10b-18 during this period do not exceed the "average size and frequency" of the issuer's block purchases during the three full calendar months preceding the date of announcement and (c) the purchases are not otherwise restricted or prohibited (e.g., as a result of Regulation M). Obviously, the effect of the modified volume test is to permit repurchases in an amount consistent

---

Nor does it include stock that a broker-dealer sells short to the issuer or affiliated purchaser if the issuer or affiliated purchaser knows or has reason to know that the sale is a short sale.

with past practice but to make it difficult to increase the amount of such activity during the pendency of a merger or similar transaction.

• • • *Relaxed Conditions During Marketwide Trading Suspensions.* In 1999, the SEC adopted amendments to Rule 10b-18 to expand the safe harbor to cover certain transactions taking place in the trading session following a marketwide trading suspension (or "circuit breaker").

Following the events of September 11, 2001, the SEC used its emergency authority under Section 12(k)(2) of the 1934 Act to relax the timing and volume conditions of Rule 10b-18 for the first five business days after reopening of the U.S. equities and option markets.[18] In doing so, the SEC acknowledged that issuer repurchases "can represent an important source of liquidity during times of market volatility." The SEC subsequently extended the emergency relief for an additional five business days and, following the cessation of emergency conditions, used its exemptive authority under Section 36 to extend the relief to October 12, 2001.[19]

The 2003 amendments to Rule 10b-18 provide relief from the time-of-trade and volume conditions of the safe harbor during the trading session following a marketwide trading suspension, which includes a marketwide trading halt of more than 30 minutes imposed either by an SRO pursuant to a circuit breaker or by the SEC pursuant to its emergency powers.

• • • *Purchases Outside the Safe Harbor.* Like any safe harbor rule, it is not possible to "violate" Rule 10b-18. The only consequence of a bid or purchase outside the limitations of the rule is that the safe harbor is unavailable in the event of an allegation that the bid or purchase violated Section 9(a)(2) of the 1934 Act or Rule 10b-5. Rule 10b-18 expressly provides that non-conforming bids and purchases do not create a presumption that there was such a violation. Nevertheless, many issuers try to conform their stock repurchases to the limitations of

---

18. SEC Release No. 34-44791 (September 14, 2001).

19. SEC Release No. 34-44827 (September 21, 2001) and 34-44874 (September 28, 2001).

the rule and require broker-dealers acting on their behalf to do the same.

••• *Short Sales by Broker-Dealers.* Some broker-dealers are willing to offer blocks to the issuer on a short sale basis. One of the advantages of this technique is that it gives the issuer an assured means of quickly purchasing the desired amount of stock at an acceptable price. One of the disadvantages is that the issuer's purchase may be outside the safe harbor of Rule 10b-18 because, as noted above, securities that an issuer knows or has reason to know are being sold short are not considered "blocks" for purposes of the limited exclusion in Rule 10b-18 from that rule's volume restrictions.

The issuer may nevertheless be willing to proceed because of the unlikelihood that a block trade, especially one executed outside normal trading hours, could in and of itself constitute manipulation. Practice is not uniform as to whether the broker-dealer conforms its covering transactions to Rule 10b-18, particularly where the price paid by the issuer for the stock sold short is a function of the price eventually paid by the broker-dealer in its covering transactions. Practice is also not uniform as to whether the broker-dealer considers itself free to continue covering its short position during periods where the issuer, because of unannounced material information, would consider itself disabled from making direct repurchases.

- *Using Derivatives*

Several companies have supplemented their stock repurchase programs by selling put options or by engaging in other derivative transactions.

Put warrants can be attractive because the premium that a company receives for the sale of the warrants is tax-free and will effectively reduce the average cost of the stock repurchase program, whether or not the warrants are ever exercised. An SEC no-action letter issued in 1991 to the Chicago Board Options Exchange (CBOE)[20] addressed several securities law issues

---

20. SEC No-action Letter, *Chicago Board Options Exchange* (February 22, 1991).

arising in connection with an issuer's sale of standardized put options.

A buyer of a put warrant hopes, of course, that the market price of the issuer's stock will fall below the exercise price of the put warrant, thus permitting the holder to purchase the stock in the market and then require the issuer to repurchase it at the higher price. The issuer should be indifferent to this result, assuming that it really wishes to repurchase its stock at the exercise price.

The CBOE letter addressed both 1933 Act and 1934 Act questions. On the 1933 Act side, the request letter noted that questions might be raised under Section 5 of the 1933 Act because such a transaction might be construed as a "sale" of the issuer's stock, given the breadth of the relevant definitions in Section 2(a)(3) of the 1933 Act. It argued against this result, however, on the basis that the transaction was "an ordinary, open-market transaction unrelated to any effort by the issuer to offer or sell, or to solicit offers to buy, its own stock." The staff took a no-action position without addressing CBOE's arguments under Section 2(a)(3).

Standardized options are, of course, formally issued by the Options Clearing Corporation and registered under the 1933 Act. One could therefore take the position that an issuer writing standardized puts on its own stock was simply engaging in a transaction in another person's security. Would the result be different in the case of non-standardized options? One would think not, since an issuer's writing of a put option remains far from any attempt on its part to offer or sell, or to solicit offers to buy, its stock. The activity should therefore not constitute a "sale" under Section 2(a)(3) of the 1933 Act, but it is just as easy to structure the sale of the put options as a private placement.

The CBOE letter also addressed 1934 Act issues under the antimanipulation, issuer tender offer and issuer stock repurchase rules. The SEC staff granted exemptions under former Rules 10b-6 and 10b-7 to deal with the possible characterization of the puts as "continuing bids" by the issuer for its common stock. (Such relief would not be necessary under Regulation M, which replaced Rules 10b-6 and 10b-7 in early 1997.) In addition, the staff granted an exemption under Rule 13e-4 to make harmless any characterization of the issuer puts as an issuer tender offer. It also took a no-action position under Rule 13e-1 to permit the issuer to purchase stock on exercise of the put during the pendency of a third-party tender offer. CBOE did not request, and the SEC did not grant, any relief under Rule 10b-13 on the theory that the issuer could control its own tender offers so as not to create a conflict with its obligation to purchase stock on exercise of a put.

The SEC relief was conditioned on the issuer's writing only standardized out-of-the-money put options on a U.S. options market. The puts written by the issuer on any day would be limited to the extent to which the issuer would have been allowed to purchase stock on that day under Rule 10b-18's volume limitation (without regard to the block exclusion). Also, the issuer could write puts only through one broker-dealer on any given day, and it could not participate in the opening rotation for such puts or within 30 minutes before the close of trading in the principal market for the stock. Finally, the staff assumed that the issuer would not engage in any transactions for the purpose of creating actual or apparent trading in, or raising or depressing the price of, its securities.

To the extent an issuer sells puts to a broker-dealer, of course, the broker-dealer may wish to hedge its investment by purchasing stock in the open market. Should the broker-dealer follow any or all of the conditions of Rule 10b-18 in effecting such purchases? Should the issuer require the broker-dealer to follow any or all of such conditions? Should the broker-dealer suspend purchases when the issuer would suspend purchases (e.g., prior to announcements that are likely to increase the stock price)? As noted above in connection with the discussion of the functionally similar practice of broker-dealers' shorting significant amounts of stock to an issuer in furtherance of its repurchase program, practice is not uniform in this regard.

An issuer need not stop at put options to supplement a stock repurchase program. It may also purchase call options on its stock, thus locking in for the life of the option the right to buy a specific number of shares for a specific price. By combining the sale of put options with the purchase of call options, usually on an OTC basis with a broker-dealer as the counterparty, it may achieve a low-cost or zero-cost "collar"—that is, the right to purchase its stock at prices within a desired range. The settlement terms may call for "gross" or "net" share delivery or for a cash payment. In some of these transactions, the broker-dealer may hedge its obligations by buying or selling the issuer's stock in the open market. In the case of purchases by the broker-dealer, the same questions arise as discussed above. In the case of sales, particularly where the broker-dealer is to settle in cash with the issuer, interesting questions arise as to whether the broker-dealer has become an "underwriter" or whether it can still rely on the Section 4(3) dealer's exemption.

- *Disclosure of Stock Repurchases*

When it adopted the original version of Rule 10b-18 in 1982, the SEC noted that it had considered requiring issuers to make a prior public disclosure before repurchasing more than 2% of their stock during a 12-month period. The SEC decided against imposing such requirements, stating that "the obligation to disclose information concerning repurchases of an issuer's stock should depend on whether the information is material under the circumstances, regardless of whether such purchases are made as part of a program authorized by a company's board of directors or otherwise."[21]

By the time the SEC amended Rule 10b-18 in 2003, it had become customary for issuers to announce stock repurchase programs. Broker-dealers engaged to effect stock repurchases also expected the issuer to announce its plans to buy back its stock. In fact, the SEC referred in adopting the 2003 amendments to studies demonstrating a rise in issuers' stock prices after public announcements and to evidence that some issuers had failed to follow through on buybacks after making public announcements. Simultaneously with but independent of the amendments to Rule 10b-18, the SEC in 2003 therefore adopted a new Item 703 of Regulation S-K to require disclosure of *all* issuer repurchases of equity securities registered under the 1934 Act.

---

21. SEC Release No. 34-19244 (November 17, 1982), text at nn.8 and 9.

For U.S. issuers, each quarterly report on Form 10-Q must include a table showing purchases[22] in each month covered by the report and each annual report on Form 10-K must include a table showing purchases in each month during the issuer's fourth quarter.[23] The table must show (a) the total number of shares purchased in each month (including whether pursuant to publicly announced repurchase programs, tender offers or otherwise and the nature of the transactions), (b) the average price paid per share, (c) the total number of shares purchased as part of publicly announced plans or programs (including the date of announcement, the amount approved, the expiration date (if any) and each plan or program that has expired or that the issuer does not intend to pursue) and (d) the maximum number (or approximate dollar value) of shares that may yet be purchased under the plans or programs.

The disclosure requirements apply to all purchases, including purchases by means of tender offers, and they apply to all open-market purchases whether or not they are made in accordance with the conditions of Rule 10b-18.

- *Cash Tender Offers*

If a company wishes to acquire a sufficiently large block of its own or another company's stock, a cash tender offer may be the best means of accomplishing its objective. Tender offers can take several forms, and they are strictly regulated under the 1934 Act.

- - *Tender Offer Mechanics.* A tender offer usually is commenced with a mailing of the offer to shareholders and the publication of a summary advertisement of the offer in *The Wall*

---

22. "Purchase" is not separately defined in Item 703. The statutory definition in Section 3(a)(13) of the 1934 Act includes agreements to purchase, suggesting that forward purchase agreements must be reported. Unexercised puts and calls are probably not required to be reported under Item 703, especially given the express reference in the instructions to including in the table "purchases . . . in satisfaction of the company's obligations upon exercise of outstanding put options issued by the company."

23. For foreign private issuers, the annual report on Form 20-F must include a table showing purchases in each month during the year covered by the report.

Street Journal. The offer will specify the maximum number of shares that the maker of the offer will accept for purchase and the period of time that the offer will remain open. The offer may be made at a fixed price representing, in most cases, a premium over the current market price.

A company offering to purchase a large number of its own shares may do so at a price determined through a modified "Dutch auction" process.[24] In a modified Dutch auction tender offer, the offeror fixes the number of shares it will purchase and sets a range of prices at which holders may tender their shares. The purchase price will be the highest price that will allow the company to buy all of the shares for which it has solicited tenders or such smaller number of shares as are actually tendered. In effect, the market tells the company what the price should be, rather than the company telling the market. This may increase the chance that the offer will be successful.

In a modified Dutch auction, the price band usually is relatively narrow. In addition, the SEC requires an offeror to state a reasonable price range for the offer, which the SEC views as no more than 15% of the minimum price. Alternatively, if the most recent stock price prior to the commencement of the offer is above the minimum price, the reasonable range is determined on the basis of the most recent stock price. For example, Aftermarket Technology Corp. offered on December 16, 2003 to purchase up to approximately 2.6 million of its shares for a price not greater than $15.75 and not less than $13.00 per share. While this represented a range of more than 21%, the last reported sale price for the stock prior to the announcement and commencement of the offer was $13.75. On this basis, the range was less than 15%.

A company making a tender offer frequently will retain a securities firm to act as "dealer-manager" to assist it in soliciting tenders. During the early to mid-1980s, it was customary to

---

24. Traditionally, the staff of the SEC has not permitted modified "Dutch auction" procedures for tender offers by third parties. It has permitted these procedures, however, in a tender offer by a company's ESOP. SEC No-action Letter, *Kettle Restaurants, Inc. Employee Stock Ownership Plan and Kettle Restaurants, Inc.* (February 18, 1989).

provide that any dealer through whom shares were tendered would be entitled to a fee for each share tendered through it. Letters of transmittal contained a space in which tendering shareholders could designate the dealer entitled to the fee. The payment of fees to soliciting dealers fell into disuse during the late 1980s and early 1990s but has more recently been used again as a means of increasing the chances of success of the tender offer without having to pay a higher premium. Currently, the SEC staff's unwritten policy is that a broker-dealer may not receive fees as a soliciting dealer for shares that it tenders for its own account. The staff position is that allowing the broker-dealer to receive a fee would violate the "all holders" and "best price" requirements discussed below.

It is also important for the company to hire an information agent to coordinate the distribution of tender offer materials to brokers, follow up to ensure that the materials are forwarded to beneficial owners, and stand ready to answer questions from shareholders.

• • *Regulation of Issuer Tender Offers.* Tender offers in general and related matters are regulated by the SEC pursuant to authority granted under Sections 13(d), 13(e), 14(d), 14(e), and 14(f) of the 1934 Act. These sections, which were enacted in 1968, are known as the "Williams Act" after former Senator Harrison ("Pete") Williams of New Jersey.

Section 13(d) requires a filing (a Schedule 13D or under certain conditions a Schedule 13G), and supplemental filings to reflect changes, by any person or group acquiring more than 5% of a class of voting equity securities registered under Section 12 of the 1934 Act (or securities of certain insurance companies or closed-end investment companies registered under the 1940 Act). It has no application to tender offers. Section 13(e) makes it unlawful for an issuer that has a class of equity securities registered under Section 12 or that is a registered closed-end investment company to purchase any equity securities issued by it in contravention of SEC rules. Purchases by affiliates are treated as purchases by the issuer itself. Section 14(d) governs third-party tender offers. Section 14(e) is a general antifraud provision applicable to all tender offers.

Rule 13e-4 is the basic rule governing tender offers for any class of equity security by the issuer or an affiliate.[25] The rule governs exchange offers as well as cash tender offers, so that if an issuer offered a debt security in exchange for shares of its common stock it would have to comply with Rule 13e-4 as well as the 1933 Act and the 1939 Act. The issuer must file with the SEC, as soon as practicable on the day the tender offer is commenced, a tender offer statement on Schedule TO. It must report any material change in the information set forth in the schedule by promptly filing an amendment to the schedule and must file a final amendment to report the results of the tender offer. The rule provides that the commencement of the offer is the day on which the "means to tender" (i.e., the transmittal form or a statement regarding how the transmittal form may be obtained) is "first published, sent or given" to securityholders. Schedule TO requires the payment of a fee as specified in the SEC's Rule 0-11(b).[26]

Written pre-commencement communications, from and including the first public announcement of the issuer tender offer, must be filed with the SEC under cover of Schedule TO as soon as practicable on the date of the communication. Such communications must advise shareholders to read the tender offer statement when it becomes available and how to obtain the tender offer statement and other filed documents from the SEC's website.

The filed Schedule TO must set forth information required by the specified items of Regulation M-A, including a summary term sheet (written in "plain English"), basic information about the issuer (which is also, of course, the "subject company" for purposes of the schedule), the material terms of the transaction (including the number and class of securities sought in the offer,

---

25. Rule 13e-1 requires an issuer to make an SEC filing containing specified information if it proposes to purchase any of its equity securities while a third-party tender offer is in progress for any class of the issuer's equity securities.

26. The fee is currently $126.70 per million dollars of securities to be acquired. The SEC posts its current filing fees on its website at www.sec.gov/info/edgar/feeamt.htm.

the type and amount of consideration, the scheduled expiration date, whether and how the offer could be extended, withdrawal dates, procedures for tendering and withdrawing, the manner of payment and pro rationing procedures), agreements involving the subject company's securities, the purposes of the transaction, the source and amount of funds for the transaction, specified insiders' interest in and recent transactions in the subject company's securities and the identity of persons retained to make solicitations or recommendations. Financial statements must be provided "if material," but the instructions to Item 10 of Schedule TO state that financial statements are not considered material in the case of an issuer tender offer if the consideration consists solely of cash, the offer is not subject to any financing condition and either the issuer is an SEC-reporting company or the offer is for all outstanding securities of the subject class. The schedule must also disclose any material arrangements with or among specified insiders as well as any material regulatory requirements or legal proceedings. Disclosure materials must be filed as exhibits, along with specified other documents.

An issuer tender offer may be disseminated to shareholders by making adequate publication in a newspaper or newspapers on the date of commencement of the issuer tender. "Long-form" publication—that is, the summary term sheet and the remaining information required to be stated in Schedule TO (except for exhibits) or a fair and adequate summary of the information—is permitted but is expensive. It is more common to publish a summary advertisement containing specified information and providing information on how to obtain more detailed information regarding the tender offer as well as a letter of transmittal. Alternatively, the issuer may disseminate the offer through shareholder lists or clearing agencies and their participants, in which case the issuer must contact brokers named in the clearing agency listing and make inquiry as to the number of beneficial owners for whom they are holding shares. This is done by means of a so-called "brokers' search letter." The issuer must furnish the brokers with a sufficient number of copies of the tender offer and agree to reimburse them promptly for their reasonable expenses incurred in forwarding the tender offer to beneficial owners.

An instruction to the rule states that "adequate publication . . . may require publication in a newspaper with a national circulation, a newspaper with metropolitan or regional circulation, or a combination of the two, depending on the facts and circumstances involved."

The tender offer, unless withdrawn, must remain open for at least 20 business days from its commencement and for at least ten business days from the date that notice of an increase or decrease in the percentage of the class of securities being sought or in the consideration offered or the dealer's soliciting fee is first published, sent or given to securityholders. The acceptance for payment of additional securities not to exceed 2% of the class outstanding is not deemed to be an increase for this purpose. The terms of the offer must permit securities to be withdrawn at any time during the period that the offer remains open and, if not yet accepted for payment, after the expiration of 40 business days from the commencement of the offer.

If the tender offer is for less than all of the outstanding equity securities of a class, and if a greater number of securities is tendered than the issuer is bound or willing to purchase, the securities must be purchased as nearly as may be pro rata, disregarding fractions, according to the number of securities tendered by each securityholder. There are exceptions to this requirement, however. The issuer may accept all securities tendered by persons who own an aggregate of not more than a specified number which is less than 100 shares, and who tender all their securities, before prorating securities tendered by others. In addition, if the terms of the offer permit, the issuer may accept by lot securities tendered by securityholders who tender all securities held by them and who, when tendering their securities, elect to have either all or none or at least a minimum amount or none accepted, if the issuer first accepts all securities tendered by securityholders who do not so elect.

In the event the issuer increases the consideration offered after the tender offer has commenced, it must pay the increased consideration to all securityholders whose securities are accepted for payment. Promptly after the termination or withdrawal of the tender offer, the issuer must either pay the consideration offered or return the tendered securities.

Rule 14e-5 (formerly Rule 10b-13) bars the issuer and dealer-manager or any of their affiliates from purchasing the equity securities that are the subject of a tender offer (or any related securities) except pursuant to the tender offer. The prohibition, which is subject to certain exceptions, applies from the time of public announcement of the offer until its expiration. Rule 13e-4(f)(6) also prohibits such purchases until the expiration of at least ten business days after the date of termination.

In one of the most hotly contested takeover battles of the 1980s, T. Boone Pickens, Jr. sought to acquire Unocal Corporation by means of a coercive two-step front-loaded tender offer. The Unocal board, deeming the offer inadequate, authorized an issuer tender offer, designed to thwart the Pickens offer, that was directed to all shareholders except the Pickens group. The Delaware court held that a corporation may deal selectively with its shareholders in making a tender offer, provided the directors do not act out of a sole or primary purpose to entrench themselves in office. The court found that the corporation's response was neither unlawful nor unreasonable given the nature of the threat. The directors were found to be disinterested despite the fact that they tendered their own shares in response to the Unocal offer. The court stated that the efforts of the board to protect the shareholders by providing an alternative to an inadequate offer would have been ineffective if those seeking to take over the corporation had been permitted to participate in the tender offer. In addition, the court noted that the offeror's activities with respect to other transactions justified an inference that its principal objective was greenmail.[27]

In response to this holding, the SEC amended Rule 13e-4 in 1986 so that no issuer or affiliate may make a tender offer unless it is open to all holders of the class of securities subject to the tender offer ("all holders" requirement) and the consideration paid to any securityholder pursuant to the tender offer is the highest consideration paid to any other securityholder ("best price" requirement).[28]

---

27. *Unocal Corp. v. Mesa Petroleum Co.*, 493 A.2d 946 (Del. 1985).
28. SEC Release No. 34-23421 (July 11, 1986).

Rule 13e-4(h)(5) excludes from the rule's provisions any "odd-lot" tender offer by an issuer, which is an offer that is directed to holders of less than 100 shares. The rule's "all holders" and "best price" requirements still apply, however, except that an issuer may exclude participants in an employee benefit plan and may pay for tendered shares "on the basis of a uniformly applied formula based on the market price of the subject security." With the deletion in late 1996 of a record date requirement,[29] the rule now permits issuers to conduct odd-lot offers on a continuous, extended or periodic basis. In the same release, the SEC also granted a class exemption from what was then Rule 10b-13 (now Rule 14e-5) to permit an issuer conducting an odd-lot tender offer to purchase the subject securities otherwise than pursuant to the offer, and that exemption is continued in the current rule. Also, as noted in Chapter 4, Rule 102 permits an issuer to purchase odd-lots while engaged in a distribution of the same security.

• • *Going Private Transactions.* Purchases of equity securities by the issuer or an affiliate, whether by tender offer or otherwise, may give rise to a "going private" transaction subject to Rule 13e-3 if the purpose or likely effect of the purchases is to cause any class of equity securities of the issuer subject to Section 12(g) or Section 15(d) of the 1934 Act to be held of record by fewer than 300 persons or to cause a class of the issuer's equity securities to be delisted from an exchange or to be no longer authorized for quotation on NASDAQ.[30] Section 3(a)(11) of the 1934 Act defines the term "equity security" to include not only stock but also any security convertible into common or preferred stock.

Going-private transactions that result in the termination of a company's reporting obligations under the 1934 Act also result in freeing a company from nearly the full range of requirements imposed by Sarbanes–Oxley. Some surveys reported in 2004 a

---

29. SEC Release No. 33-7376 (December 20, 1996).

30. A going private transaction also can result from a proxy or consent solicitation involving a merger, recapitalization or similar transaction with an affiliate, a sale of assets to an affiliate or a reverse stock split involving the purchase of fractional share interests.

significant increase in going-private transactions in the 16 months following the enactment of Sarbanes–Oxley as compared to the 16 months preceding its enactment. It is too early to tell whether this increase amounts to a trend or, if so, whether it will continue.

Going-private transactions are regulated by Rule 13e-3, which the SEC adopted in response to perceived inequities and the potential for coercion and overreaching involved in corporate freezeouts and other going private transactions.[31] The final version of the rule emphasized disclosure concerning the fairness of a going private transaction rather than a demonstration that the transaction was indeed fair to the company's shareholders.

Rule 13e-3 refers to a transaction or "series of transactions," and thus open market purchases made in anticipation of or in furtherance of a tender offer or other going private transaction may be caught up under the rule.[32] For example, the SEC in late 2003 settled an enforcement action based on allegations that respondents increased their ownership in a company from 19.1% to 56.8% in a "series of transactions" over five months for the purpose of acquiring control of the company and taking it private without complying with Rule 13e-3.[33]

A Rule 13e-3 transaction requires the filing with the SEC of a transaction statement on Schedule 13E-3. In the case of an issuer tender offer, this will be filed at the same time as the Schedule TO. The additional disclosures required by Schedule 13E-3 will be disseminated to shareholders as part of the tender offer statement. These disclosures include a statement as to whether the issuer or affiliate filing the statement reasonably believes that the transaction is fair or unfair to unaffiliated securityholders. One can search in vain for a Schedule 13E-3 that says outright that the shareholders are being injured, but technically this would satisfy the filer's disclosure obligation.

A statement, however, that the issuer has no reasonable belief as to the fairness of the transaction is not adequate disclosure. The filer must discuss in reasonable detail the material factors

---

31. SEC Release No. 34-16075 (August 2, 1979).
32. SEC Release No. 34-17719 (April 13, 1981). This release discusses the principal interpretative questions that had theretofore arisen under Rule 13e-3.
33. *SEC v. Wilkerson*, Litigation Release No. 18427 (October 27, 2003).

on which the belief as to fairness is based and, to the extent practicable, the weight assigned to each factor. The schedule must state whether or not the filer has received a report, opinion or appraisal from an outside party with respect to the transaction, including any fairness opinion by an investment banking firm. If there is such a document, the schedule must identify its author, describe the author's qualifications and how the author was selected, disclose any material relationships of the author with the issuer or its affiliates and summarize the report, opinion or appraisal. A copy of the document must be filed as an exhibit and made available for inspection and copying at the issuer's or affiliate's principal executive offices. The schedule may but need not state that a copy will be sent to any shareholder.

• • *Short Tendering of Securities; Rule 14e-4.* If a tender offer is for less than all of the issuer's shares, tenders from shareholders will be subject to proration. In that event, a shareholder wishing to dispose of all of his shares will not be able to do so at the tender price. He may sell in the open market any shares that he tenders and that are not accepted, but the market price will probably not be as high as the tender price. Alternatively, the shareholder may in lieu of tendering sell all of his shares in the open market while the tender offer is still pending. In that case, the market price will reflect the influence of the tender offer with a discount for the risk of proration. The amount of the discount will reflect the activity of arbitragers, who will be at work in the market buying shares at prices that take that risk into account.

If one could tender more shares than one owned, this would increase the proportion of one's shares that would be accepted in the partial tender offer. Because tenders usually require a guarantee by a broker-dealer that the tendering shareholder will in fact deliver the tendered shares, market professionals could have an advantage over ordinary shareholders in tendering more shares than they owned. Since 1968, the SEC has sought to promote equality of opportunity and risk for all tendering shareholders by a rule originally known as Rule 10b-5 and now known as Rule 14e-4.

In its current form, Rule 14e-4 prohibits anyone from tendering into a partial tender offer unless he has a net long position[34] in the tendered security equal to or greater than the amount tendered. The net long position must exist at the time of tender and must be maintained through the end of the proration period or period during which securities are accepted by lot (including any extensions of such period). The person tendering must also actually tender the tendered securities within the period specified in the offer. The requirement of a net long position may be fulfilled by a net long position in an equivalent security where the person tendering acquires the subject security by conversion or otherwise and then tenders the tendered securities within the period specified in the offer.

A person such as a broker-dealer who tenders for a customer must do so either knowing that the subject security is in the customer's account or on the basis of a reasonable belief that he owns the subject security or an equivalent security and will promptly deliver the subject security or an equivalent security.

The current rule therefore prohibits the techniques used in the past of "short tendering" (tendering more shares than one owns) or "hedged tendering" (tendering shares but at the same time hedging against the possibility that all tendered shares may not be accepted).[35]

---

34. A net long position is the excess of a person's long position over his short position in the same security. A "long position" is the amount that a person owns (including securities loaned to another) or has the right to receive pursuant to a binding purchase contract or an exercised standardized call option or on the basis of an equivalent security. A "short position" for purposes of the rule is the amount that the person has sold or borrowed or on which the person has written a non-standardized call option or granted any other right pursuant to which his shares may be tendered by another person. A person is also considered to be short shares that the person is obligated to deliver on exercise of a standardized call option written on or after the beginning of the tender offer if the exercise price of the option is lower than the tender offer price (i.e., where the person having the right to exercise the option is likely to do so).

35. Prior to its amendment in 1990, ambiguities in the rule had led to a well-known decision by the Second Circuit involving an arbitration award. *Merrill Lynch, Pierce, Fenner & Smith, Inc. v. Bobker*, 808 F.2d 930 (2d Cir. 1986). The tendering customer in this case was a stockholder of Phillips Petroleum Company and tendered all of his 4,000 shares into a partial tender offer by the issuer. Before the proration date, the customer entered an order for

At one time, the rule also prohibited "multiple tendering," that is, tendering the same securities into more than one partial tender at the same time. The SEC dropped this prohibition in 1990 with the explanation that such tendering did not lessen a shareholder's risk at the expense of other shareholders with respect to any particular partial offer.

Debt Restructurings

Companies that issue debt securities during periods of high interest rates may seek to eliminate them or to reduce the amount outstanding through various means, including redemption in accordance with the terms of the indenture, open market purchases, negotiated purchases, tender offers and exchange offers. If interest rates have declined since the time that the securities were originally issued, they will be trading at a premium over par. But the premium may not fully reflect the decline in interest rates for a number of reasons, including the company's ability to redeem the securities or the existence of a sinking fund provision under which a portion of the securities can be redeemed at par. Under these circumstances, a repurchase of the securities, even at a premium over their principal amount, may be a practical step in the company's efforts to reduce the average cost of its debt.

If, on the other hand, the securities are trading below par, perhaps because interest rates have increased, the issuer may make a tender offer at a premium over the market price, thus retiring indebtedness at less than the principal amount with a corresponding increase in shareholders' equity resulting from

---

the short sale of 2,000 shares. When his broker's compliance department canceled the short sale, he commenced an arbitration proceeding claiming that his tender and his short sale were independent transactions. The arbitrators' award of damages was upheld by the Court of Appeals as not in "manifest disregard of the law." In supporting its view of Bobker's short sale as an independent transaction, the court said that it "amounted to a separate gamble." It noted that the rule did not at the time of the tender define the term "net long" and refused to grant deference to the SEC's interpretation of the term as applied to Bobker's short sale because it viewed the SEC's interpretation as being inconsistent with the purpose of the rule and as lacking a rational basis.

the recognition of income. Some issuers of high-yield bonds were able to avoid default only through an exchange of new securities with manageable terms for the securities that were about to go into default.

A company's objective in restructuring its debt usually is a reduction in financing costs. But other factors may come into play. A stronger balance sheet and a resulting enhanced credit rating may be the goal. The issuer's principal objective may be the elimination of onerous financial covenants, in which case it may seek to acquire the securities through a cash tender offer or an exchange offer and at the same time make a consent solicitation aimed at modifying the covenants applicable to all of the securities, even those that are not tendered or exchanged.

- *Redemptions*

Whether or not a debt security may be called for redemption will depend on the terms of the governing indenture. Some obligations will have absolute call protection, particularly if they have a relatively short maturity. Zero coupon obligations, which are marketed as a means to eliminate reinvestment risk, generally are not redeemable by the issuer. Other obligations may provide limited call protection. They may be non-redeemable for five years, for ten years, or for some other specified period of time. Some debt securities are redeemable immediately on issuance. If debt is redeemable at the option of the issuer, the redemption price will be structured to protect the holder's yield to maturity. This is often done by requiring the payment of a "make-whole" amount. Alternatively, the redemption price may include a premium equal to the stated interest rate that will be scaled down over the term of the instrument until the final year, or perhaps the last five years, at which time redemption may be effected at par.

Although the question is less important today, debt securities—even if they were immediately redeemable—might be "non-refundable" for some number of years from the time of issuance; they could not be redeemed during that period with the proceeds of lower-cost debt securities. Non-refunding provisions vary from deal to deal and have been the subject of litigation. If there is a non-refunding provision, a call for redemption during the relevant period must be considered with great care. On the other hand, the courts have been relatively lenient to issuers in construing these provisions and have permitted them to trace the source of funds in appropriate cases.

In *Franklin Life Insurance Co. v. Commonwealth Edison Co.*,[36] a redemption of preferred stock purporting to be funded out of a common stock issue was challenged in a class action as violating the issuer's certificate of designation, which provided that the preferred stock could not be redeemed through refunding, directly or indirectly, by or in anticipation of the incurring of any debt or the issuance of any shares ranking prior to or on a parity with the preferred stock at an interest or dividend cost less than the dividend cost of the preferred stock. The holders claimed that the preferred stock could not be redeemed so long as the company was borrowing more per year than it repaid at an interest cost below the dividend cost of the preferred stock. The court rejected this theory and held that the proper interpretation of the non-refunding provision required an examination of the "source of the funds actually used to achieve the redemption" without regard to the issuer's other borrowing activities.

Another court arrived at a similar result in *Morgan Stanley & Co. Inc. v. Archer Daniels Midland Co.*[37] Archer Daniels had outstanding an issue of debentures that by the terms of the indenture could not be redeemed with funds raised from the issuance of indebtedness at an interest cost of less than 16.06% per annum. The debentures were redeemed out of the proceeds of an issue of common stock. Morgan Stanley alleged that, in addition to the common stock offering, Archer Daniels had made several recent debt offerings at an interest cost of less than 16.06% and accordingly the debentures had been indirectly refunded through lower cost borrowings. Citing *Franklin Life*, the court agreed with the company's position that the indenture had not been violated because the direct source of the funds used for the redemption was the sale of the common stock. The court also indicated that cash on hand could be used for a redemption without regard to other arguably unrelated borrowings.

---

36. 451 F. Supp. 602 (S.D. Ill. 1978), *aff'd*, 598 F.2d 1109 (7th Cir.), *cert. denied*, 444 U.S. 900 (1979).

37. 570 F. Supp. 1529 (S.D.N.Y. 1983).

An issuer seeking to redeem obligations during a non-refunding period in reliance on the *Franklin Life* and *Morgan Stanley* cases must take care to segregate "clean cash" (e.g., funds on hand or the proceeds of an offering not covered by the refunding provision) from the "tainted" proceeds of a lower-cost issuance of securities that are covered by the refunding provision. An issuer in this posture is treading on thin ice. It may well be inviting litigation, and the 30-day notice period customarily required for redemptions provides sufficient time for a litigant to mount an attack. The risk of a court fight, even though it ultimately may be defended successfully, may be a sufficient reason to choose another route. Moreover, the issuer's credibility in the debt market is a factor to be taken into account. If a company is perceived to being playing fast and loose with the holders of its debt securities, the acceptance of its securities in the marketplace may be substantially impaired.

An issuer seeking an early redemption of debt must take into account the antifraud provisions of the securities laws. For example, even where an electric utility's redemption of bonds had been held by a state court to have been authorized under the indenture, an appellate court still found itself able to affirm a jury verdict to the effect that the prospectus under which the bonds were sold had "omitted material facts that would have adequately disclosed [the utility's] right to call the bonds, in violation of Rule 10b-5(b)."[38] Moreover, it is probably no defense to such a federal antifraud claim that the indenture or the terms of the security purport to restrict or eliminate the holder's right to sue. Such a provision may be given effect insofar as the holder's *contractual* claims are concerned, but an extension of the provision to the holder's rights under the 1933 and 1934 Acts would conflict with the antiwaiver provisions of those statutes.[39]

---

38. *Harris v. Union Electric Co.*, 787 F.2d 355 (8th Cir. 1986), *cert. denied*, 479 U.S. 823 (1986). *Cf. Lucas v. Florida Power & Light Co.*, 575 F. Supp. 552 (S.D. Fla. 1983), *aff'd*, 765 F.2d 1039 (11th Cir. 1985).

39. *McMahan & Co. v. Wherehouse Entertainment, Inc.*, 65 F.3d 1044 (2d Cir. 1995), *cert. denied*, 116 S. Ct. 1678 (1996).

Can an issuer avoid a nonrefunding provision by making a tender offer with "tainted" lower-cost financing while simultaneously announcing its intention to redeem any untendered securities with "clean cash"? In 1992, James River Corporation of Virginia made a tender offer for its $250 million of outstanding 10.75% 30-year debentures that it had issued in 1988. The indenture provided that the debentures could not be redeemed for ten years with the proceeds of "moneys borrowed" at a lower interest cost. The tender price was $1,093.75 per debenture, just over the redemption price of $1,086 per debenture. The holders tendered $245 million of the debentures, which the company purchased with $200 million from the sale of its 6.75% medium-term notes and $45 million from the sale of preferred stock. It then redeemed the remaining debentures with additional funds from the preferred stock offering.

Holders of debentures sued the issuer and the dealer-manager in state court, claiming breach of contract in that the transaction amounted to a simultaneous tender and call (STAC) that coerced them into tendering their debentures. In a 5–4 decision, the Supreme Court of Alabama affirmed the grant of summary judgment for the issuer and the dealer-manager. The majority found that the tender offer and the call were separate transactions permitted by the indenture and that any economic pressure exerted on the holders was "legitimate." It also held that the issuer had no duty to disclose to the holders that it had insufficient "clean cash" on hand to finance the tender offer.[40]

If debt securities are to be redeemed, the procedures set forth in the indenture must be strictly adhered to. Under the typical indenture, notice of redemption must be given not less than 30 nor more than 60 days prior to the date fixed for redemption. If less than all of the securities are to be redeemed, the selection of securities to be redeemed will be made by the trustee on a pro rata basis or by lot, or by such other method as the trustee deems fair and appropriate. Notice of redemption is given by mail to the holders at their addresses as they appear on the register maintained by the trustee.

---

40. *Mutual Savings Life Ins. Co. et al. v. James River Corp. of Virginia and Merrill Lynch, Pierce, Fenner & Smith Inc.,* 716 So. 2d 1172 (Ala. 1998).

TRANSACTIONS WITH SECURITYHOLDERS 945

- *Open Market Purchases*

Debt securities may be acquired by the issuer in the open market without regard to the redemption provisions of the indenture. These are consensual transactions between the holders and the issuer, and the indenture provisions simply do not apply. The same is true of a tender offer. Thus, if an issuer feels constrained by a non-refunding provision in its indenture, purchases in the open market or through a tender offer may be the way to accomplish its objective. Open market purchases may be the best and cheapest route if the issuer is not seeking to repurchase an entire issue or if it is known that the debt is in the hands of a limited number of holders. (Some privately placed debt securities restrict repurchases by the issuer except on a pro rata basis, and the existence of any such restriction should be investigated before any purchases are made.)

If the issuer decides to embark on a program of open market purchases, it must take care that its purchases do not constitute a tender offer. The same considerations are applicable here as in the case of a common stock repurchase program. Although Rule 13e-4 is applicable only to tender offers for equity securities, Section 14(e) and Rules 14e-1, 14e-2, and 14e-3 thereunder are applicable to all tender offers, including those for straight debt securities. Rule 14e-1(a), which requires a tender offer to be held open for 20 business days, is usually the provision that causes the most difficulty.

In some respects, greater care must be taken to avoid the tender offer trap when repurchasing debt securities than when repurchasing common stock. Common stock can be purchased from time to time on an exchange or in the over-the-counter market with little risk of the purchases being viewed as a tender offer, but debt repurchases often require direct dealings with the holders of the securities.

To reduce the risk that open market purchases will be viewed as a tender offer, certain procedures should be followed. It probably will make sense to effect the purchases through the securities firm that managed the underwriting in which the securities were sold. That firm's institutional salesmen are in the best position to contact the customers to whom they sold the securities in the first place. The firm should be furnished with a list of securityholders in order to supplement its own knowledge of where the securities are held. If only a portion of the issue is to be reacquired, the objective should be to obtain that amount from the smallest number of institutional holders in order to avoid the appearance of a general solicitation.

From a compliance standpoint, the firm should limit the number of holders to be solicited in the first instance. The number will depend on the distribution of ownership. If it is necessary to contact additional holders, this should be done on a controlled and supervised basis, rather than by simply turning the sales force loose. The sales force should be instructed to apply no pressure on the holders of the securities, to set no limit on the time that the holder has to make a decision, and to be prepared to negotiate the purchase price subject to the issuer's approval.

- *Cash Tender Offers*

If the issuer is seeking to purchase the entire issue and the securities are held by more than a limited number of investors, then a cash tender offer may be the most effective way to accomplish the issuer's purposes. As in the case of a tender offer for equity securities, notice will be given by mailing or distributing tender offer materials to all registered holders. The notice may be supplemented by a press release and sometimes by a summary notice in a newspaper of national circulation. Unlike the substantial premium that may be paid in a common stock tender offer, the price offered by the issuer in a debt tender offer usually represents a relatively modest premium over the market price of the securities sought to be acquired. The issuer may condition the offer upon the valid tender of a specified minimum aggregate principal amount of the issue.

As stated above, debt tender offers are subject to less stringent regulation than tender offers for equity securities. Rule 13e-4 is not applicable, and no filing with the SEC is required. Rule 14e-1 does apply, however, unless the offer is for exempted securities,[41] securities issued by certain Canadian issuers[42] or

---

41. *See* Rule 14d-1(a).
42. *See* Rule 14d-1(b).

securities issued by foreign governments and their political subdivisions.[43]

Rule 14e-1 requires tender offers to be held open for at least 20 business days from the date that the tender offer is first published or sent to securityholders and for at least ten business days from the date that notice is given of an increase or decrease in the percentage of the class of securities being sought or the consideration offered or the dealers' soliciting fee. The 20-day and ten-day requirements would be impractical in the case of fixed-price debt tender offers, and the SEC staff in 1986 provided no-action relief in the case of issuer tender offers for nonconvertible investment-grade debt securities.[44] The conditions in the no-action letters are that the offer be for "any and all" nonconvertible debt securities of a particular series,[45] be open to all holders of those securities, be conducted in a manner designed to afford all holders a reasonable opportunity to participate, including dissemination of the offer on an "expedited basis" where the tender offer is open for a period of less than ten calendar days, and not be made in anticipation of or in response to other tender offers for the issuer's securities.

In taking this no-action position, the staff took into account the economic realities of debt tender offers as represented to it in the no-action requests. Thus, in the *Merrill Lynch* letter it stated:

> Issuer Debt Tender Offers invariably involve the retirement of high coupon debt during periods when relatively lower interest rates prevail. Generally, the retirement of debt is closely preceded, accompanied, or followed by a refunding issue of debt that takes advantage of lower

---

43. *See* Rule 3a12-3(a).

44. SEC No-action Letter, *Merrill Lynch, Pierce, Fenner & Smith Inc.* (July 2, 1986); SEC No-action Letter, *Goldman, Sachs & Co.* (March 26, 1986); SEC No-action Letter, *Salomon Brothers, Inc.* (March 12, 1986). The SEC staff did not make clear until 1990 that the 1986 no-action relief was available only where the debt was investment-grade. SEC No-action Letter, *Salomon Brothers, Inc.* (September 28, 1990).

45. The offer may still be conditioned on the tender of a minimum amount of securities.

interest rates to reduce the average cost to the issuer of its debt. If market conditions render it economic for an issuer to refinance its high coupon debt in this manner, it is generally advantageous for an issuer to refinance as much of its outstanding high coupon debt as possible. As a result, Issuer Debt Tender Offers are usually for any and all outstanding debt of the class or series subject to the offer. In this regard, there may be instances in which an issuer, for economic and financial reasons, may wish to condition the Issuer Debt Tender Offer upon the valid tender of a minimum aggregate principal amount of the debt subject to the offer. The success of the refinancing depends upon maintaining the desired relationships (i) between the principal amount of debt retired in the tender offer and the principal amount of the refunding issue, and (ii) between the cost to the issuer of the debt retirement and the refunding issue.

Based on Merrill Lynch's experience, Issuer Debt Tender Offers are generally held open for a period of seven to ten calendar days depending on a number of factors, including the percentage of debt held by individual debtholders and the principal amount of debt that the issuer desires to retire. Extending the period during which an Issuer Debt Tender Offer remains open increases the likelihood that interest rates will increase or decrease during the tender offer period. Both the issuer and its debtholders will be exposed to additional interest rate risk in those circumstances. Because interest rates can move against a debtholder during the tender offer period and since a debtholder often does not have withdrawal rights, a debtholder has a disincentive to tender his debt early. As a result, if interest rates decline during the tender offer period, the issuer may retire much less debt than it intended. If, on the other hand, interest rates rise during the tender offer period, the issuer may retire many bonds but at a price higher than is justified by interest rates prevailing at that time. In either case, the issuer will be confronted with a substantial potential mismatch between the principal amount of debt it retires and the principal amount of debt it has issued, or intends to issue, in the refunding.

Because an extension of the tender offer period also increases the uncertainty as to the principal amount of debt to be refinanced, an issuer will be less likely to commence refunding operations at or prior to the commencement of its tender offer. This will create interest rate risk on the refunding side of the refinancing. If interest rates continue to rise during the tender offer period, the debt refinancing, if not done in advance, could become particularly costly to the issuer, since the increased refunding costs that the issuer will incur will not be offset by a corresponding decrease in the cost to the issuer of retiring its debt.

There are several choices open to an issuer that is required to hold an Issuer Debt Tender Offer open for more than the customary seven to ten calendar days. An issuer may elect to price the tender offer on the basis of prevailing interest rates and accept the increased risk that the tender offer will be unsuccessful (if interest rates decline) or that the refunding will be more expensive than expected (if interest rates rise). Alternatively, an issuer may elect to increase the premium it offers to debtholders in order to provide a cushion against declining interest rates—thus increasing the cost to it of retiring its debt.

On the other hand, an issuer may decide not to refinance its debt by means of a tender offer and, instead, may elect to engage in an open market repurchase program or request a securities dealer to short debt to it. In either case, purchases of the issuer's debt will be privately negotiated. Under such circumstances, debtholders are less likely to receive equal treatment, and it is unlikely that an individual noninstitutional debtholder will be contacted and afforded an opportunity to receive a repurchase premium.

The staff concluded:

> The Division believes that Issuer Debt Tender Offers for any and all non-convertible debt securities of a particular

class or series may present considerations that differ from any and all or partial issuer tender offers for a class or series of equity securities. For example, because of the modest premiums typically offered in an Issuer Debt Tender Offer, it is not clear that participation in the tender offer by individual non-institutional debtholders would be materially increased by requiring that the tender offer be held open for twenty business days.

- *Fixed-Spread Cash Tender Offers*

In 1990, the SEC staff was asked to provide no-action relief from the 20-business-day and ten-business-day requirements of Rule 14e-1 in connection with an issuer cash tender offer for debt securities where the price was to be determined on each day during the tender offer period by reference to a stated fixed spread over the then-current yield on a specified benchmark U.S. Treasury security determined as of the date, or the date preceding the date, of tender.

The staff took a no-action position subject to the conditions that the offer (i) be an offer for cash for any and all non-convertible, investment-grade debt of a particular class or series, (ii) be open to all record and beneficial holders of that class or series of debt, (iii) provide that information regarding the benchmark U.S. Treasury security would be reported each day in a daily newspaper of national circulation, (iv) be conducted in a manner designed to afford all record and beneficial holders of that class or series of debt a reasonable opportunity to participate in the tender offer, and, in the case of an offer conducted in reliance on the 1986 no-action letter, dissemination of the tender offer would be made on an expedited basis, (v) provide that all tendering holders of that class or series of debt be paid promptly for their tendered securities after such securities are accepted for payment and (vi) not be made in anticipation of or in response to other tender offers for the issuer's securities.[46]

---

46. SEC No-action Letter, *Salomon Brothers, Inc.* (October 1, 1990).

In July 1993, the SEC staff extended the above position to permit issuers to conduct debt tender offers using a fixed-spread pricing methodology in which the nominal purchase price is calculated by reference to a stated fixed spread over the most current yield on a benchmark U.S. Treasury security determined *at the time* that the securityholder tenders the debt security (a "real-time fixed-spread offering") rather than by reference to the yield on a benchmark U.S. Treasury security as of a specified time on the date, or date preceding the date, of the tender offer as permitted in the 1990 no-action letter. Real-time fixed price offerings apply a fixed spread to arrive at a series of nominal purchase prices, but the nominal purchase prices do not remain constant but change with any movements in the benchmark U.S. Treasury security.[47]

The 1993 letter is subject to the following conditions over and above those specified in the 1990 letter: (a) the tender offer must identify the specific benchmark U.S. Treasury security to be used and specify the fixed spread to be added to the yield on the benchmark U.S. Treasury security, (b) the tender offer must state the nominal purchase price that would have been payable based on the applicable reference yield immediately preceding the commencement of the tender offer, (c) the tender offer must indicate a daily newspaper of general circulation that will provide the closing yield of the benchmark U.S. Treasury security on each day of the tender offer, (d) the tender offer must indicate the electronic reference source to be used during the tender offer to establish the current yield on the benchmark U.S. Treasury security (i.e., Telerate, Bloomberg, Cantor Fitzgerald, etc.), (e) the tender offer must describe the methodology used to calculate the purchase price for the tendered securities and (f) the tender offer must indicate that the current yield on the benchmark U.S. Treasury security and the resulting nominal purchase price of the debt securities is accessible on a real-time basis by either calling the dealer-manager collect or through an

---

47. SEC No-action Letter, *Merrill Lynch, Pierce, Fenner & Smith Inc.* (July 19, 1993).

"800" telephone number, if established for the tender offer. In addition to the above conditions, the SEC requires the dealer-manager to maintain records showing the date and time of each tender, the current yield on the benchmark U.S. Treasury security at the time of each tender and the purchase price of the tendered securities based on that yield. The dealer-manager must also send a confirmation of the transaction to tendering securityholders no later than the next business day after the tender.

The SEC staff's no-action relief under Rule 14e-1 for issuer debt tender offers has so far been limited to offers for securities that are investment-grade debt securities and to offers that are for "any and all" of the securities for which the offer is made. The staff has been willing in some instances, however, to grant oral relief in connection with offers for non-investment-grade or split-rated securities. In at least one offer that was not "all or any," the staff has also granted oral relief from the ten-day requirement of Rule 14e-1(b).

- *Premium Payable to Tendering Holder*

A company tendering for its debt securities may encourage tenders by offering to pay an "early tender premium" to holders who tender before a specified deadline. For example, Cox Communications, Inc. launched a tender offer on August 26, 2003 for any and all of approximately $1.8 billion principal amount (at maturity) of its outstanding discount debentures. The offer was for $495 per debenture and was to expire on September 23, 2003. Holders who tendered on or before September 9 were eligible to receive an early tender premium of $15 per debenture. To the extent that the falling away of the early tender premium on September 9 amounted to a change in the consideration offered, the offer would still comply with Rule 14e-1(b) because it would not expire until September 23.

- *Issuer Recommendation*

Rule 14e-2 does not contain an express exemption for issuer tender offers. This rule provides that, no later than ten business days from the date a tender offer is first made, the subject company shall publish, send or give to securityholders a statement disclosing that it recommends acceptance or rejection of the bidder's tender offer, expresses no opinion and is remaining neutral toward the bidder's tender offer or is unable to take a position with respect to the bidder's tender offer. It can be argued that the definitions of the terms "bidder" and "subject company" in Rule 14d-1 and plain common sense lead to the conclusion that Rule 14e-2 is not applicable to issuer tender offers. It is more prudent, however, for the issuer to state its position or lack of a position. Typically, the tender offer materials will contain a statement that the issuer makes no recommendation that holders of debt securities tender or refrain from tendering and that such holders must make their own decision as to whether to tender securities and, if so, how many securities to tender.

It used to be necessary to obtain an exemption under the SEC's former Rule 10b-6 if an issuer engaged in a "distribution" of new debt securities at or about the same time as it made a tender offer for outstanding debt securities of the same "class and series."[48] As discussed in Chapter 4, the SEC's new Rules 101 and 102—the successor rules to Rule 10b-6—no longer apply to securities of the same class and series unless they are "identical in all of their terms" to those being distributed.

- *Exchange Offers*

As part of a capital restructuring, a company may offer to exchange new debt securities for outstanding debt securities that it wishes to retire. Or it may offer equity securities, or a package of debt and equity, in exchange for existing debt. The exchange offer may include a cash amount payable to the holder.

In making an exchange offer to existing securityholders, an issuer may retain a dealer-manager to solicit exchanges or it may decide to go it alone. If a dealer is paid a fee for soliciting exchanges, the exchange offer will not be exempt from registration under Section 3(a)(9). On the other hand, an issuer that is in financial difficulty or that wishes to reduce its interest costs

---

48. E.g., SEC No-action Letter, *Playtex FP Group Inc.* (December 19, 1988).

may be willing to go to the trouble and expense of registration in order to enhance the potential success of its exchange offer by using the services of a dealer-manager. If the issuer does decide to register, the registration statement must be filed on Form S-4.

On the other hand, a registered exchange offer may not be a viable option. For example, an issuer may not be able to comply with the SEC's financial statement requirements, possibly because of a recent acquisition or even because its financial statements have been restated or its auditors have withdrawn their opinion on the financial statements. In late 2002, Qwest Communications International Inc. found itself in a precarious situation and decided to launch an *exempt* exchange offer for nearly $13 billion of its outstanding securities. The offer was limited to QIBs and institutional accredited investors in reliance on the private placement exemption (see Chapter 7) and to persons outside the United States in reliance on Regulation S (see Chapter 9).

• • *Section 3(a)(9).* Section 3(a)(9) under the 1933 Act exempts from registration "any security exchanged by the issuer with its existing securityholders exclusively where no commission or other remuneration is paid or given directly or indirectly for soliciting such exchange."

• • • *Issuer Identity Requirement.* For Section 3(a)(9) to be available, both the security issued and the security surrendered in exchange must be those of the same issuer. This is frequently called the "issuer identity requirement." Thus, as a general rule, if an issuer offers its common stock in exchange for debt securities issued by its wholly owned subsidiary, the Section 3(a)(9) exemption cannot be relied on.

The issuer identity requirement is not absolute, however, especially in the area of guaranteed securities or other securities having multiple issuers. The Division of Corporation Finance's *Manual of Telephone Interpretations* states that "the Division has agreed that a parent may rely on the Section 3(a)(9) exemption to issue its own securities to holders of a wholly-owned subsidiary's debt securities supported by the parent's full and unconditional guarantee."[49] The staff has also taken a no-action position where a subsidiary proposed to offer its obligations guaranteed by its parent in exchange for its outstanding debt securities that did not have the benefit of a parent guarantee (although the staff concluded that the parent guarantee had to be registered).[50]

The SEC has also taken no-action positions under Section 3(a)(9) with respect to small amounts of common stock of parent companies issuable on conversion of long-outstanding securities of subsidiaries involving a parent guarantee on the basis of representations that "as a practical matter" the exchange involves securities of a single issuer[51] or that as an "economic reality" the guarantee and the underlying obligation constitute securities of the same issuer.[52] The staff has also acquiesced in the use of Section 3(a)(9) to exempt securities issued by a post-merger entity in exchange for securities issued by a pre-merger entity where the post-merger entity had in connection with the merger become a joint and several obligor on the old securities.[53] The same theory has been applied to foreign sovereign debt.[54] And, not surprisingly, the staff has also taken a no-action position permitting the holding company of a savings bank to rely on Section 3(a)(9) in exchanging new debt securities that were joint and several obligations of the holding company and the savings bank, where the securities taken in exchange were also joint and several obligations of the same two entities.[55]

---

49. SEC Division of Corporation Finance, *Manual of Telephone Interpretations* #2S (March 1999).

50. SEC No-action Letter, *Union Planters Corp.* (January 10, 1983).

51. SEC No-action Letter, *Baxter Travenol Laboratories, Inc.* (July 8, 1983).

52. SEC No-action Letter, *American Motors Corp.* (July 8, 1982). See also SEC No-action Letter, *National Can Corp.* (September 22, 1983).

53. E.g., SEC No-action Letter, *W.R. Grace & Co.* (July 25, 1988).

54. SEC No-action Letter, *Federal Republic of Germany* (April 8, 1994).

55. SEC No-action Letter, *First Liberty Financial Corp.* (July 23, 1991).

The staff also took a no-action position where Norlin Corporation and its essentially "mirror-image" wholly owned subsidiary made a joint exchange offer of Norlin warrants and debentures of the subsidiary for outstanding debt securities of the subsidiary that had been guaranteed by Norlin.[56] There the position was taken that Norlin was offering its warrants in exchange for its guarantee and its subsidiary was offering its new obligations in exchange for its outstanding primary obligations. In another instance, where an acquired company's debentures became convertible into cash and debt securities of the acquiring company and the acquiring company guaranteed the debentures, the staff agreed that Section 3(a)(9) could be relied on for conversions.[57] Because the acquiring company would be liable on the acquired company's debentures, it was viewed as the issuer of those debentures as well as of the debt securities issuable upon conversion.

It is not clear whether the word "exclusively" in Section 3(a)(9) modifies the word "exchanged" as well as the phrase "with its existing securityholders." The SEC has taken the position that it does.[58] The consequence of requiring that the exchange be "exclusively" with existing securityholders can be illustrated as follows. Suppose a company offers to exchange a new issue of debentures for outstanding debentures and at or about the same time sells some of the new debentures for cash to non-holders of the old debentures. Under the SEC's interpretation, there is a possibility that the Section 3(a)(9) exemption would not be available for the exchange offer. The concurrent cash sale would destroy the exclusivity of the exchange. If, however, the issue of securities to the non-holders could be viewed as a separate "issue," either because of its timing or purpose, then the exchange offer would be exempt under Section 3(a)(9).[59]

---

56. SEC No-action Letter, *ECL Industries, Inc. and Norlin Corp.* (December 16, 1985).
57. SEC No-action Letter, *Daisy Systems Corp.* (April 10, 1989).
58. SEC Release No. 33-2029 (August 8, 1939).
59. *Id.*

The interpretation makes little sense. The existence of a concurrent cash sale of securities of the same class and series as those offered in an otherwise-exempt exchange offer does not affect in the slightest the need or lack of need on the part of the exchanging securityholders for the protections afforded by the 1933 Act.

• • • *Exclusivity Requirement.* One thing that "exclusively" clearly means is that Section 3(a)(9) will not be available if securityholders of the issuer are required to give up anything other than their securities. An offer of new securities in exchange for existing securities plus a cash payment from the tendering securityholders would not be an exempt transaction. There is an exception, however. Rule 149 provides:

> The term "exchanged" in Section 3(a)(9) shall be deemed to include the issuance of a security in consideration of the surrender by the existing securityholders of the issuer, of outstanding securities of the issuer, notwithstanding the fact that the surrender of the outstanding securities may be required by the terms of the plan of exchange to be accompanied by such payment in cash by the securityholder as may be necessary to effect an equitable adjustment, in respect of dividends or interest paid or payable on the securities involved in the exchange, as between such securityholder and other securityholders of the same class accepting the offer of exchange.

In the request for the no-action letter issued to ECL Industries, Inc. and Norlin Corporation, it was explained that the exchange offer provided that tendering holders of old debentures would not be entitled to the November interest payment or any other interest accruing on their old debentures after November 15, 1985. By accepting the exchange offer, holders of old debentures would affirmatively waive their right to receive these payments. Tendering holders of old debentures who became holders after the October 31, 1985 record date for the November interest payment would be required to pay ECL Industries $45 for each $1,000 principal amount of debentures tendered to reimburse it for the November interest payment that it would be required to make to those persons who were holders on the record date but who subsequently sold their debentures in the open market.

The request set forth an example of how this would work. Assume that two debentureholders, *A* and *B,* had acquired their debentures two days before the October 31 record date. On November 2, *B* sells his debentures to *C. A* and *C* subsequently tender. *A* thereby waives his right to the November interest payment, but as *C* was not a holder on the record date no interest is payable to him and he has nothing to waive. He is not entitled, so the argument went, to waive on *B*'s behalf the interest payment due to him as the holder on the record date. Presumably, the price paid by *C* to *B* for his debentures was reduced to reflect the fact that they were purchased after the record date, and thus it was argued that it was only fair to require *C* to reimburse the company, thereby placing him on a parity with *A,* who did not purchase at a reduced price.

The no-action request pointed to two prior instances where the staff had taken no-action positions where tendering securityholders were required to relinquish their right to unpaid accrued interest.[60] It contended that the requirement that certain tendering debentureholders make a $45 payment for each $1,000 principal amount of debentures tendered represented an "equitable adjustment" in respect of interest payments within the meaning of Rule 149. The staff granted the no-action request without commenting on this analysis.

• • • *No Paid Solicitation.* We have already noted the condition to Section 3(a)(9) that there be no paid solicitation. As originally enacted, Section 3(a)(9) prohibited the payment of remuneration "in connection with such exchange" rather than "for soliciting such exchange." The 1934 amendments to the

---

60. SEC No-action Letter, *Barnett Winston Investment Trust* (October 11, 1977); SEC No-action Letter, *Geoscience Technology Services Corp.* (May 14, 1976). *See also* SEC No-action Letter, *NJB Prime Investors* (May 14, 1976); SEC No-action Letter, *Conrad Precision Industries, Inc.* (August 28, 1973); SEC No-action Letter, *Wright Air Lines, Inc.* (August 23, 1973).

1933 Act substituted the present language to codify the interpretation of the Federal Trade Commission that the payment of expenses—such as engraving costs, clerical costs and payments to third persons for services in effecting but not promoting the exchange—would not render the exemption unavailable.

The exemption is not lost because cash or other consideration along with the securities is issued to the holders making the exchange. This is clear from the language of Section 3(a)(9), as this additional consideration is not paid for solicitation. Rule 150 eliminates any doubt by providing that the term "commission or other remuneration" in Section 3(a)(9) does not include "payments made by the issuer, directly or indirectly, to its securityholders in connection with an exchange of securities for outstanding securities, when such payments are part of the terms of the offer of exchange."

An issuer may rely on Section 3(a)(9) in an offer to acquire its debentures for cash or for new debentures and cash at the option of the tendering debentureholder.[61] If the issuer makes a cash tender offer for its outstanding preferred stock and, prior to such offer, extends offers to certain substantial holders to take common stock in exchange for their preferred shares, the cash offer will not affect the availability of the exemption for the swap.[62]

As in the case of cash tender offers, information agents are retained in connection with exchange offers to perform certain ministerial functions. The payment of the information agent's fee will not cause the exemption to be lost. In the ECL Industries/Norlin correspondence, the staff of the SEC was advised that the services of The Carter Organization had been enlisted to do no more than to notify debentureholders of the appropriate details of the exchange offer; to confirm the accuracy of their addresses; to ascertain by telephone whether debentureholders have received the offering circular and understand the mechanics of tendering; to answer questions relative thereto; to ascertain what action the debentureholders plan to take and communicate

---

61. SEC No-action Letter, *Barnett Winston Investment Trust* (February 9, 1978).

62. SEC No-action Letter, *Clevepak Corp.* (March 23, 1984).

this information to the company; to remind debentureholders of deadlines; and to communicate with the back office personnel of brokers, banks and nominees who hold securities for others to make sure that the offering circular and the accompanying materials are forwarded properly and to urge them to check with the beneficial owners to ascertain whether they have received the materials and understand the mechanics of the offer. The Carter Organization was instructed that it could not make any recommendation regarding the tender of debentures and that, if it was asked for advice, it should respond that it was not authorized to give investment advice and that the debentureholder should consult his own advisors or contact appropriate officers of the company.

The compensation payable to The Carter Organization was not contingent on the number of debentures tendered for exchange, but was based on the number of debentureholders. In approving this arrangement, the staff acted consistently with earlier no-action positions.[63] If, however, a proxy solicitation firm were retained to convey management's recommendations to the securityholders, the exemption would not be available.[64]

Communications between a company's officers and its securityholders advising them of the merits of an exchange offer will not destroy the Section 3(a)(9) exemption so long as the communications are incidental to the officers' regular duties and no special compensation is paid to them for performing this function.[65] Also, the staff of the SEC raised no objection where exchanges were to be solicited by the advisor of an investment

---

63. SEC No-action Letter, *Mortgage Investors of Washington* (October 8, 1980); SEC No-action Letter, *Hamilton Brothers Petroleum Corp.* (August 14, 1978); SEC No-action Letter, *Barnett Winston Investment Trust* (February 9, 1978); SEC No-action Letter, *Valhi, Inc.* (October 15, 1976); SEC No-action Letter, *The Carter Organization* (April 7, 1975); SEC No-action Letter, *Georgeson & Co.* (June 11, 1973).

64. SEC No-action Letter, *Stokely-Van Camp, Inc.* (April 29, 1983).

65. SEC No-action Letter, *Hamilton Brothers Petroleum Corp.* (August 14, 1978); SEC No-action Letter, *Chris-Craft Industries, Inc.* (October 9, 1972).

trust.[66] The issuer may hire an investment banking firm to act as its financial advisor in structuring the exchange offer. But the firm may not solicit exchanges lest its advisory fee be viewed as an indirect payment for promoting the exchange.

The basic authority on the role of a financial advisor was found for many years in no-action correspondence between counsel for Dean Witter & Co., Inc. and the staff of the SEC.[67] Counsel's first letter to the SEC asked whether its client could receive a fixed fee from a company offering its debt securities in exchange for outstanding stock without destroying the Section 3(a)(9) exemption if its services were limited to consultation and advice to the company regarding the terms of the offer, including the terms of the debt securities to be issued; advice regarding the preparation of the offering circular, letter of transmittal, shareholder letter and other documents; the delivery of the offering documents to brokers, banks and nominees for distribution to beneficial shareholders; the rendering of an opinion concerning the fairness of the exchange to the shareholders of the company; and telephone contacts with the shareholders during which the investment banker's personnel would inquire whether they had received the offering materials and during which they would respond to questions asked by shareholders, provided their response was confined to the information contained in the documentation sent to shareholders. The staff replied that it was of the view that the performance of these services by the investment banker, "particularly the expression of an opinion by it concerning the fairness of the proposed exchange coupled with subsequent telephone discussions of the exchange with shareholders," would raise serious doubts as to the availability of the Section 3(a)(9) exemption.

Counsel asked for clarification of the staff's position to determine whether Section 3(a)(9) would be rendered unavailable if its client performed all of the described services, plus being

---

66. SEC No-action Letter, *Barnett Winston Investment Trust* (February 9, 1978).

67. SEC No-action Letters, *Dean Witter & Co., Inc.* (December 23, 1974 and February 24, 1975).

named in the offering circular as the dealer-manager for the exchange offer, but did not have its personnel communicate directly with the company's shareholders. Counsel also asked whether its client could perform all of these services, including the limited communications with shareholders, if there were excluded from the offering circular the description of its fairness opinion. The staff replied that the exemption provided by Section 3(a)(9) would not be rendered unavailable if the dealer-manager were to provide all of the described services other than the proposed communications with shareholders. However, the answer to the second question was negative. The staff stated, "In our view, there is an inconsistency on the surface in the proposition that representatives of a firm which has expressed an opinion (whether publicly disclosed or not) on the fairness of a proposed exchange may initiate contacts with the securityholders voting [*sic*] on the exchange and express wholly impartial views on questions raised by those securityholders."

Counsel did not ask, and the staff did not address, the question whether the investment banking firm could contact shareholders in the limited manner described if it did not render a fairness opinion. The staff limited its responses to the questions asked. In a subsequent no-action letter, however, the staff agreed that an investment banking firm acting as financial advisor could answer unsolicited inquiries directed to it concerning the terms of an exchange offer, within the confines of the information set forth in the offering materials.[68]

In later no-action letters, the staff appears to have relaxed its position to the degree that it has acquiesced in an issuer's financial advisor's participation in meetings and telephone conversations with the legal and financial adviser to a committee of holders of the outstanding securities that were to be the subject of the exchange offer. In one such letter, these meetings took place before the commencement of the offer,[69] and in another the meetings took place after the commencement of the

---

68. SEC No-action Letter, *Mortgage Investors of Washington* (October 8, 1980).

69. SEC No-action Letter, *Seaman Furniture Co., Inc.* (October 10, 1989).

offer.[70] The issuer's financial advisor would not be named as a dealer-manager in offering documents, would not deliver any fairness opinion and would not communicate directly with any holders on substantive matters. Moreover, its fee would not be contingent on the success of the exchange offer, and the committee itself would not solicit exchanges.

It is not clear to what extent the more recent no-action letters depend on the issuer's weak financial condition. In any event, many lawyers believe that it is dangerous to have securities sales representatives engage in discussions with customers regarding an exchange offer with respect to which their firm is acting as financial advisor in reliance on Section 3(a)(9). It may be unrealistic to expect these representatives to limit their responses to their customers' questions to the information that is contained in the documents. It is also quite likely that any holder contacted would inquire as to the recommendations of the firm or its representative. If the response must be that the firm cannot recommend exchanges, this could have a negative—and not merely a neutral—effect on the holder's inclination to exchange. Nonetheless, it is not uncommon for a financial advisor to a company making an exchange offer, where it has not rendered a fairness opinion, to permit its personnel to perform the services normally performed by an information agent and to refer any substantive inquiries to specified officers of the issuer.

Under the blue sky laws of a few states, an issuer will be required to register as a dealer if it offers its securities directly and not through a registered dealer. To avoid this problem in the case of an exchange offer, it is customary for the mailing to securityholders resident in those states to go out under the name of a registered dealer. If a dealer is paid a flat fee for performing this service and does not make any recommendation or other solicitation regarding the exchange offer, the Section 3(a)(9) exemption will be available despite the dealer's involvement.[71]

---

70. SEC No-action Letter, *International Controls Corp.* (August 6, 1990).

71. SEC No-action Letter, *ECL Industries, Inc. and Norlin Corp.* (December 16, 1985); SEC No-action Letter, *Mortgage Investors of Washington* (October 8, 1980); SEC No-action Letter, *Barnett Winston Investment Trust*

• • • *Shareholder Votes; Trust Indenture Act; Resales of Exchanged Securities.* Section 3(a)(9) may be relied on in a transaction, such as a reclassification of securities, that is effected by means of a shareholder vote rather than through a voluntary exchange. Rule 145 provides that an "offer" or "sale" occurs when there is submitted to securityholders a plan or agreement under which they are asked to approve, on the basis of what in substance is a new investment decision, the exchange of a new or different security for their existing securities. However, a transaction for which a statutory exemption is otherwise available, including one exempt under Section 3(a)(9), is not affected by Rule 145. This is made perfectly clear in the preliminary note to Rule 145.[72]

Even if an exchange offer is exempt from registration under Section 3(a)(9), if debt securities are offered in the exchange, an indenture must be qualified under the 1939 Act. Section 304(a)(4)(A) of the 1939 Act exempts most securities exempted from the provisions of the 1933 Act, but not those exempted by Section 3(a)(9). If the issuer does not have a qualified open-ended indenture, the exchange offer may commence after the filing of the application for qualification of the indenture without waiting for the actual qualification of the indenture.[73]

Finally, it is important to keep in mind that Section 3(a)(9) only provides the issuer with an exemption from the registration and prospectus delivery requirements. It has nothing to say about the ability of the person receiving the exchanged securities to resell them. Such persons must find their own exemptions, and in the ordinary case they will be able to make use of the Section 4(1) or Section 4(3) exemptions.

• • *Tender Offer and Going Private Rules.* An exchange offer is a tender offer. Thus, if the securities being sought in an exchange offer are equity securities, including convertible

---

(February 9, 1978); SEC No-action Letter, *Western Pacific Industries, Inc.* (available October 11, 1976).

72. *See also* SEC Release No. 33-5463 (February 28, 1974); SEC No-action Letter, *Valhi, Inc.* (October 15, 1976).

73. SEC No-action Letter, *Mississippi Chemical Corp.* (November 25, 1988).

debentures, the issuer must comply with the issuer tender offer requirements of Rule 13e-4.[74] In addition, if equity securities are to be acquired, the exchange offer may constitute a going private transaction, in which case the issuer will be required to comply with Rule 13e-3.

The SEC has recognized, however, that exchange offers in which securityholders "are permitted to maintain an equivalent or enhanced equity interest" are outside the purpose of Rule 13e-3.[75] Accordingly, Rule 13-e(g)(2) provides an exemption if the securityholders are offered or receive only an equity security that (i) has substantially the same rights as the equity security to be surrendered in exchange, including voting, dividend, redemption and liquidation rights (except that this requirement is deemed to be satisfied if unaffiliated securityholders are offered common stock), (ii) is registered pursuant to Section 12 of the 1934 Act (or reports are required to be filed by the issuer pursuant to Section 15(d) of the 1934 Act) and (iii) is either listed on a national securities exchange or authorized to be quoted on NASDAQ if the security to be surrendered was either so listed or quoted. For the exception to be available, all securityholders must be offered the same form of consideration.[76]

The substantially equivalent test is met if the security offered in exchange is common stock. Thus, if a company offers shares of its common stock in exchange for its outstanding convertible debentures, Rule 13e-3 will not be applicable provided that the registration or reporting test and the listed or quoted test are also met.[77]

---

74. The SEC staff has taken the position, however, that a company did not have to comply with Rule 13e-4 when it made a tender offer for its debt securities exchangeable for less than 5 percent of an unaffiliated company's common stock. To the extent the debt securities were equity securities, they were issued by another company. To the extent the offer was a tender offer for less than 5 percent of the other company's common stock, it was not subject to Regulation 14D. The offer was, however, subject to Regulation 14E. SEC Division of Corporation Finance, *Manual of Telephone Interpretations* 203 (#17) (July 1997).

75. SEC Release No. 34-16075 (August 2, 1979).

76. SEC Release No. 34-17719 (April 13, 1981).

77. SEC No-action Letter, *Instrument Systems Corp.* (February 19, 1983).

A 1988 no-action letter issued to Savin Corporation is pertinent to the scope of the subsection (g)(2) exemption.[78] The no-action request described an offer to exchange convertible preferred stock for zero coupon convertible senior subordinated notes, an existing class of convertible preferred stock and several issues of straight debt securities. Counsel pointed out that the substantially equivalent requirement is satisfied if unaffiliated securityholders are offered common stock and argued that this was the case because the preferred stock offered in exchange for the outstanding equity securities was immediately convertible into common stock. Counsel referred to Rule 13d-3 under the 1934 Act, which provides that a person is deemed to be the beneficial owner of a security that, within 60 days, he has the right to acquire through the conversion of another security, and to Rule 16a-2(b), which then defined beneficial ownership of a security to include owning a security presently convertible into that security. Counsel contended that, if the convertibility feature of the new preferred stock is sufficient to make its holders the beneficial owners of the underlying common stock, it was logical to conclude that the requirements of the exemption had been met. Counsel argued, in the alternative, that the new convertible preferred shares afford the holders of the outstanding equity securities not only substantially similar rights but substantially enhanced rights. The staff took a no-action position without specifying which of counsel's alternative arguments it considered the more convincing.

The substantially similar test was found to be satisfied in the case of an exchange offer by Trans World Airlines, Inc. of new convertible debentures for outstanding convertible debentures.[79] It was represented that the new debentures were similar to the old debentures in that both were entitled to annual interest payments, were convertible into common stock of the airline's parent, had sinking fund requirements, were subordinated to senior debt and had the same remedies on default and

---

78. SEC No-action Letter, *Savin Corp.* (June 28, 1988).
79. SEC No-action Letter, *Trans World Airlines, Inc.* (November 2, 1980).

substantially the same indenture modification provisions. While the new debentures varied from the old debentures with respect to interest rates and conversion ratios, the variations were designed to provide tendering holders of old debentures with a security having a value that represented a slight premium over the market price of the old debentures at the time of the exchange offer.

• • *Regulation M and 14e-5.* If an exchange offer involves a "distribution" of the offered security for purposes of Regulation M (see Chapter 4), then the dealer-manager and the issuer must refrain from bids for and purchases of the offered security unless they are permitted under an exception to Rule 102 or Rule 101, respectively. For example, neither rule's restrictions will apply if the offered security is an investment-grade debt security or preferred stock. Rule 101 will not apply to the dealer-manager in the case of common stock that meets the $1 million ADTV/$150 million public float standard, but the issuer has no such exception under Rule 102. When applicable, the rules' restrictions commence on the mailing of the exchange offer prospectus and continue until the conclusion of the offer.

The former Rule 10b-6 also applied to bids for and purchases of the securities sought to be acquired pursuant to the exchange offer, on the theory that these were "rights to purchase" the offered security. As discussed in Chapter 4, however, Rule 101 no longer applies to any "rights to purchase" the securities being distributed.

On the other hand, if the exchange offer is for an equity security, then Rule 14e-5 also becomes applicable. This rule precludes any person making a cash tender offer or exchange offer for an equity security from purchasing such security or any security immediately convertible into or exchangeable for such security.

If neither Rule 101 nor Rule 14e-5 applies to an exchange offer, it is now possible for a dealer-manager to assist in the distribution by making lay-offs of the offered securities, against which it may purchase and exchange outstanding securities. This activity was formerly prohibited by Rule 10b-8, which was rescinded by the SEC on the adoption of Regulation M.

- *Consent Solicitations*

Indentures generally permit financial covenants to be amended or waived with the consent of the holders of a specified percentage of the principal amount of outstanding securities. But holders of senior securities cannot be expected to agree to relaxing a financial covenant unless they receive some benefit in return. If a consent solicitation is part of a tender offer or exchange offer, the ability to participate in the offer may provide sufficient incentive. In the case of a stand-alone consent solicitation, however, some incentive must be provided to induce securityholders to go along with the indenture modification.[80]

An example of a consent solicitation tied to a tender offer is the offer to purchase and consent solicitation made on February 28, 1989 for two outstanding issues of convertible debentures of Catalyst Energy Corporation. The offer was made by an affiliate of the company that had provided substantially all of the financing for an earlier acquisition by Merrimac Corporation of the entire equity interest in Catalyst. The debentures sought to be acquired were convertible into the amount of cash paid by Merrimac for each Catalyst share. There was a limited market for the debentures, and the consideration offered was based on the rate of return acceptable to the purchaser. The indentures were to be amended to eliminate or modify numerous restrictive covenants, including a restriction on dividends and financial tests as a condition to mergers.

The offer provided that holders of debentures wishing to accept the tender offer must consent to the proposed amendments. The consent form was part of the letter of transmittal pursuant to which tenders were to be made. Under each of the indentures, the consent of the holders of a majority of the outstanding

---

80. In the case of any indenture modification, consideration must be given to whether the changes are sufficiently substantial as to give rise for 1933 Act purposes to the issuance of a new security in exchange for the security being modified. *See* Felicia Smith, *Applicability of the Securities Act of 1933 and the Trust Indenture Act of 1939 to Consent Solicitations to Amend Trust Indentures*, 35 Howard L.J. 343, 360–80 (1992). Even if this is the case, however, the "exchange" may still be exempt (as discussed above in the context of exchange offers) under Section 3(a)(9).

debentures was sufficient to effect the amendments. The materials mailed to debentureholders made clear that holders who did not tender would be bound by the amendments and could be adversely affected by them. In this consent solicitation, as in others, a record date was not set to determine those entitled to consent. Transferees could consent to the same extent as the holders to whom the offer was initially made. A similar offer to purchase and consent solicitation was made by Union Pacific Corporation for the debt securities of Southern Pacific Rail Corporation on September 5, 1996. This offer and solicitation was made in connection with the acquisition of Southern Pacific by Union Pacific.

In 1994, the SEC staff granted relief from the ten-day requirement of Rule 14e-1(b) where the issuer wished to combine its debt tender offer with a consent solicitation and was unwilling to commit to accept debt securities on a fixed-spread basis prior to the time it would have a meaningful indication of whether its consent solicitation had been successful. The no-action position permitted the company to purchase securities at a price set on the business day immediately preceding the expiration date on the basis of a spread defined at the commencement of the offer.[81]

A company may provide added incentive to its holders to tender their securities *and* to furnish the requested consent by offering not only cash for the securities but also a cash payment for the consent. For example, Rio Algom Limited launched an offer on November 5, 2003 for any and all of its $150 million of outstanding debentures for cash, based on a fixed spread over a U.S. Treasury security of comparable maturity, plus a cash fee of $35 for each debenture as to which holders furnished a valid consent to the elimination of substantially all relevant financial covenants. The offer expired on December 5, but the opportunity to collect the $35 consent fee expired on November 19. As in the case of the early tender premium discussed above, the expiration of the opportunity to collect the consent fee could be viewed as a change in the consideration being offered to

---

81. SEC No-action Letter, *The Times Mirror Co.* (November 15, 1994).

holders, but the fact that the tender offer continued until December 5 satisfied the ten-day "extension" requirement of Rule 14e-1(b).

May a company extend the opportunity to collect a consent fee without extending the expiration date of the tender offer? The authors understand that the SEC staff has allowed companies to extend the consent payment deadline by up to five additional business days without extending the expiration date of the tender offer. As a result, a "10/10" structure—ten business days with a consent fee and ten business days without a consent fee—could be amended to a "15/5" structure or 15 days with a consent fee and five days without. But if the company extends the consent fee period beyond the fifteenth day, then it must extend the offer so that there are at least five business days between the consent fee deadline and the expiration of the offer.

In the case of a consent solicitation unrelated to a tender offer or exchange offer, there must be some incentive to consent. In a May 13, 1983 request by Fleet Financial Group, Inc. for waivers of a covenant prohibiting the incurrence or assumption of senior indebtedness having a maturity of more than three years unless a capitalization ratio was met, the company agreed that if sufficient waivers were obtained, the rate of interest on all of the debentures would be increased from 8.25% to 9.25%. In most solicitations, however, only those who consent receive the benefits.

For example, in a January 13, 2003 solicitation, Usinor offered holders of its $300 million of debt securities due August 1, 2006 the sum of $1.25 per $1,000 principal amount as a fee for consenting to amendments to the relevant indenture that would permit the delivery to holders of information regarding Usinor's parent company in lieu of information regarding Usinor. Holders who did not consent would not receive the fee but would be bound by the amendments if at least two-thirds of the holders agreed to the changes.

The consent fee need not be payable in cash or by means of an increase in the relevant interest rate. In 1986, Eastern Air Lines, Inc. solicited proxies from the holders of an issue of its convertible debt securities, offering holders who agreed to certain amendments the choice of receiving for each $1,000 principal amount either $35 in cash or $125 in ticket vouchers, applicable toward up to 50% of the price of an Eastern Air Lines ticket purchased before a specified date. The consent payment was conditioned, of course, on a successful proxy solicitation and amendment. As in the case of the Usinor consent solicitation, holders who did not give a proxy would not receive the consent payment but would be bound by the amendments if approved.

In the case of the Eastern proxy solicitation, the scheduled meeting date set the time frame within which proxies had to be received, although Eastern reserved the right to postpone the meeting if sufficient proxies were not received. Where there is no meeting, but consents are solicited, it is customary to provide that the consent payment will be made to all holders who consent within a specified time period and that, if the requisite consents are not received by the end of the solicitation period, the company will extend the solicitation period as in the case of a tender or exchange offer. Alternatively, the company may continue to accept consents in the order received and make corresponding consent payments until the requisite consents are obtained or the company elects to terminate the solicitation.

For example, Itel Corporation made a consent solicitation on July 3, 1986, that provided for the acceptance of, and payment of the consent payment of $10 per $1,000 of principal amount with respect to all consents received by the close of business on July 17, 1986. The company reserved the right, until the requisite majority approval was received, to accept in the order received (on a daily basis), any consents received after July 17, 1986, but on or before July 31, 1986. Consent solicitations made by Catalyst Energy Corporation on February 26, 1987, and by BCI Holdings Corporation on May 21, 1987, contained no outside limit on the length of time that the consent solicitation could be kept open.

Sometimes the issuer and its financial advisor will underestimate what it takes to bring in the necessary consents. In the case of the BCI consent solicitation, the original offer to the holders of four separate issues of debt securities called for a cash payment of $2.50 for each $1,000 of securities consenting to the amendment. On June 15, 1987, four days before the initial termination date, the company made a second mailing in which it stated that, on the basis of discussions with certain major holders of its debt securities, it had determined to make changes in the indenture amendments and in the terms of the solicitation proposed in the May 21, 1987 consent solicitation statement, including an increase in the consent payment to $12.50 per $1,000 for its senior notes and $10 per $1,000 for its other debt securities.

Consent solicitations have been the subject of litigation. In *Katz v. Oak Industries Inc.*,[82] the plaintiff sought to enjoin the consummation of an exchange offer and consent solicitation made by Oak Industries to the holders of various issues of its long-term debt. Oak Industries was in deep financial trouble. It had managed to negotiate a deal with Allied-Signal, Inc. for the sale of its materials segment and for an equity investment by Allied-Signal.

Allied-Signal was unwilling to commit to the cash infusion unless Oak Industries reduced its long-term debt by 85%. In order to complete the transaction with Allied-Signal, it was necessary for Oak Industries to eliminate the financial covenants in its indentures. Thus, the company offered to exchange common stock for certain of its debt securities and cash payment certificates for others, the latter being payable after the closing of the sale of the materials segment to Allied-Signal. The offer required that tendering securityholders consent to amendments to the indentures governing the tendered securities in order to remove the financial covenants that they contained.

The plaintiff contended that the exchange offer and consent solicitation was a "coercive" device that, under the circumstances, constituted a breach of a contractual obligation to act in good faith that Oak Industries owed to the holders of its debt securities. The plaintiff argued that no free choice was provided to the holders by the exchange offer and consent solicitation. Under the terms of the offer, so went the argument, a rational securityholder was "forced" to tender and consent. Failure to do so would face a holder with the risk of owning a security stripped of all financial covenant protections and for which it was likely

---

82. 508 A.2d 873 (Del. Ch. 1986).

that there would not be a ready market. A reasonable holder, it was suggested, could not possibly accept those risks and thus was coerced to accept the offer and consent to the indenture modifications. It was argued that the linking of the offer to purchase with the granting of a consent interfered with the mechanism for effecting amendments agreed to in the indentures.

Chancellor Allen concluded that the relevant test was whether it was apparent from the provisions of the indentures that the contracting parties—had they negotiated with the exchange offer and consent solicitation in mind—would have expressly agreed to prohibit contractually the linking of the giving of consent with the purchase and sale of the security. The chancellor placed substantial weight on the fact that the inducement to consent was made on the same terms to all holders of the securities affected and concluded that, while it was clear that Oak Industries had fashioned the exchange offer and consent solicitation in a way designed to encourage consents, he could not conclude that the offer violated the intendment of any of the express contractual provisions considered or that its structure and timing breached any implied obligation of good faith and fair dealing.

The Eastern Air Lines proxy solicitation also was challenged in court.[83] Here the amendment proposed to be voted on would relax certain financial covenants and thus permit Eastern to pay dividends or make other payments to its shareholders. It would enable Eastern to effect its merger with Texas Air Corporation in a transaction involving the payment, following the merger, of a $1.75 per share cash dividend by the merged entity to Texas Air, which would then be its sole shareholder. The plaintiff claimed that in offering consideration only in exchange for a consent (rather than offering consideration that would flow to every debentureholder if the amendments were approved, without regard to how any one holder voted on the amendments) Eastern had embarked on a course that violated public policy and constituted a breach of an implied contractual term requiring it to deal fairly and in good faith with the holders of its securities.

---

83. *Kass v. Eastern Air Lines, Inc.*, Del. Ch., Civ. Action Nos. 8700, 8701, and 8711 (slip op. November 14, 1986).

The first theory asserted by the plaintiff was that Eastern's offer of a consent payment constituted "vote buying" and that vote buying in any context was a legal wrong. The chancellor found that however wrong vote buying may be in a political context, and despite a line of Delaware cases arguably prohibiting in the stockholder context the transfer of voting power for consideration (except as part of a transfer of the underlying share),[84] there was insufficient authority to support a conclusion that public policy precluded Eastern from offering an inducement to consent and limiting that inducement to those who grant the consent.

The implied contract argument put forth by the plaintiff was given the same treatment as in *Oak Industries*. Again, the fact that the consideration was offered to all consenting holders turned the tide in favor of the defendant. The chancellor stated that "had Eastern not made its offer to all bondholders on the same terms, but had it privately paid money to sufficient holders to carry the election, one would, without more, feel some confidence in concluding, provisionally at least, that such conduct was so inconsistent with the concept of voting implied by the amendment provision that it constituted a violation of what must have been the reasonable expectation of the contracting parties."

An attempt to enjoin the consent solicitation by BCI Holdings Corporation likewise failed.[85] Citing *Oak Industries* and *Eastern Air Lines*, the court held that the consent solicitation did not violate any public policy against vote buying nor any implied term of the indenture. The court also noted that a separate ground for dismissal was the plaintiff's failure to satisfy a contractual condition precedent to the commencement of an action, namely, the provision of the indentures that the holders of a majority of the securities must request the trustee to

---

84. *Chew v. Inverness Mgt. Corp.*, 352 A.2d 426 (Del. Ch. 1976); Hall v. Isaacs, 146 A.2d 602 (Del. 1958), *aff'd in part*, 163 A.2d 288 (Del. Ch. 1960); *Macht v. Merchants Mortgage & Credit Co.*, 194 A. 19 (Del. Ch. 1937).

85. *Pisik v. BCI Holdings Corp.*, N.Y. Sup. Ct. Index No. 14593/87 (slip op. June 5, 1987).

commence the action, offer to indemnify the trustee and afford the trustee 60 days to comply. The court observed that this standard indenture provision had been upheld consistently as a reasonable restriction on the freedom of action of individual bondholders.

When-Issued Trading and Arbitrage

If a dealer-manager and other soliciting dealers were permitted to sell securities offered in exchange and purchase the outstanding securities sought to be acquired, they would be playing a role not unlike that played by securities firms that engage in risk arbitrage (more recently known as "event arbitrage") in connection with exchange offers, mergers and cash tender offers. In accordance with the SEC's current views, a securities firm may either act as a soliciting dealer in connection with such transactions or act as an arbitrager. It may not do both.

A securities dealer engaged in risk arbitrage will seek to make a profit on the disparity that exists between the market price of a security and the value, whether in securities or cash, being offered for it in an exchange offer, a merger or a cash tender offer. For example, in the case of a merger, the acquiring company may propose to exchange one share of its common stock with a market value of $20 per share for each share of common stock of the target company with a market value of $15 per share. Theoretically, the market value of the two securities should come into line if there were certainty that the merger would be consummated. Because of the uncertainties that may exist as a result of regulatory questions, the opposition of the target company's management, the validity of shark repellents, the outcome of a shareholder vote (if one is called for) or any number of other factors, a share of the target company's stock may trade at a price that is less than the share-equivalent of the acquiring company's stock to be issued in the merger. Arbitragers will purchase shares of the target company in the highly educated expectation that the merger will be consummated and that they will ultimately realize the discrepancy in price. At the same time, they may lock in the value of the stock to be issued in the merger by making short sales or by dealing in call options.

- *When-Issued Trading*

Certain legal questions relating to when-issued trading and the activities of arbitragers are covered in two no-action letters issued by the staff of the SEC for the benefit of certain NYSE member firms that engaged in risk arbitrage on a regular basis.[86] A merger or other Rule 145 transaction, an exchange offer by one company for the securities of another public company or an exchange offer to existing securityholders using the services of a dealer-manager will require registration under the 1933 Act. The question then arises whether an arbitrager may sell the securities to be registered at the time the transaction is announced and prior to the effectiveness of the registration statement. The answer to this question will depend on whether the securities are of a class that is already outstanding and traded or whether they are of a class that is not outstanding, such as, for example, a new class of preferred stock or a new issue of debentures.

Under the terms of the *Cleary, Gottlieb* letters, where the securities to be issued are of a class that is outstanding and traded, they may be sold short by an arbitrager as soon as the terms of the transaction are announced and before the registration statement is effective, if the following four requirements are met:

- The short sales involved in the proposed arbitrage activities will not be considered or marked "short exempt," that is, exempt from the prohibitions of Section 10(a) of the 1934 Act and Rule 10a-1(a) thereunder by virtue of the arbitrage exemption under Rule 10a-1(e)(7).

- The arbitrager will not acquire 10% or more of the securities being registered.

- In the case of exchange offers, the arbitrager will not sign a soliciting dealer's agreement or accept any fee payable to soliciting dealers whether or not it executes such an agreement.

---

86. SEC No-action Letters, *Cleary, Gottlieb, Steen & Hamilton* (February 11, 1973, and March 18, 1973). *See also* SEC No-action Letter, *Crocker National Corp.* (October 16, 1975); SEC No-action Letter, *King's Department Stores, Inc.* (March 12, 1975).

– The arbitrager will not have any agreement or understanding with the issuer or any other participant in the distribution.

If the securities to be issued are of a class not previously outstanding, sales in arbitrage transactions will of necessity be made on a when-issued basis. Such sales may not be made until after the registration statement becomes effective.

With respect to when-issued trading in a security to be issued in a Section 3(a)(9) transaction, the Section 4(3) dealer's exemption will be available where the ultimate issuance will be pursuant to an exempt exchange.[87] But when-issued trading may not begin in a debt security to be issued pursuant to a Section 3(a)(9) exemption from registration until application has been made to qualify the indenture under the 1939 Act. It is not necessary to wait until the indenture is actually qualified.[88]

After terminating its arbitrage activity, a dealer may execute a soliciting dealer's agreement, tender for its own account securities acquired in arbitrage transactions and receive the soliciting dealer's fee (if any) with respect to the securities tendered.[89] Under

---

87. *See* L. Loss & R. Vernon, *When-Issued Securities Trading in Law and Practice*, 54 Yale L.J. 741, 782–86 (1945). *See also* FTC Release No. 33-97 (December 28, 1933); SEC Release No. 33-646 (February 3, 1936).

88. SEC No-action Letter, *Skadden, Arps, Slate, Meagher & Flom* (March 12, 1986). This no-action position was based on counsel's analysis of Section 304(b) of the 1939 Act and reversed the SEC's prior position that when-issued trading was prohibited prior to the qualification of an indenture. The letter is also authority for the proposition that when-issued trading in anticipation of a Section 3(a)(9) transaction is permitted under the 1933 Act. *See also* SEC No-action Letter, *Mississippi Chemical Corp.* (June 23, 1989).

89. SEC No-action Letter, *OAK Industries Inc.* (December 22, 1976); SEC No-action Letter, *Hospital Affiliates, Inc.* (January 2, 1975). The authors understand the SEC staff's position to be that the "best price" and "all holders" rules prevent a dealer from accepting a soliciting fee for its proprietary securities in connection with a cash tender offer. This position probably also applies to exchange offers. On the other hand, the staff is not believed to have abandoned its previous position that an arbitrager may receive a soliciting dealer's fee in connection with a cash tender offer. SEC Release No. 34-9395 (November 24, 1971).

the *Cleary, Gottlieb* letters, such a dealer may not make short sales of the securities offered in the exchange offer prior to the effective date of the registration statement, even though the offered securities are of a class already outstanding and traded. This makes little sense, but it is one of the conditions set forth in the correspondence. In a 1976 telephone conversation with a member of the SEC's staff, the senior author was advised that this condition had been volunteered by counsel, perhaps in an effort to ensure that the arbitrager was not an underwriter, and that preeffective short sales by an arbitrager should be permitted even if he subsequently receives a soliciting dealer's fee.[90]

- *Borrowing Stock from Control Persons*

Arbitragers have raised the question from time to time whether certificates borrowed to cover short sales pending completion of a transaction can be borrowed from a person in a control relationship with the issuer. Assume that a company is offering to issue shares of its common stock in exchange for an issue of its outstanding debt securities. An arbitrager wishes to make short sales of the common stock, purchase the equivalent in debt securities and make the exchange for its own account. Pending the completion of the exchange, it must borrow common stock certificates to deliver on the settlement date for the short sale. There is a scarcity of certificates in the normal borrowing channels, but the arbitrager has reason to believe that it can borrow the requisite certificates from the founder and principal shareholder of the issuer.

The SEC staff is not inclined to issue a no-action letter on the subject. As a matter of legal analysis, however, if the borrowed certificates are replaced with certificates representing stock of the same class (which may be the certificates received in the exchange offer and need not be the identical certificates borrowed), the borrowing and delivery of certificates provided by a controlling shareholder should not create any problems under the 1933 Act. Although a controlling shareholder may sell his or her shares through a broker in a public unregistered transaction only pursuant

---

90. Memorandum dated January 16, 1976, in senior author's files.

TRANSACTIONS WITH SECURITYHOLDERS 979

to Rule 144, this transaction does not involve a sale by the controlling shareholder. The only sale will be the sale made by the arbitrager acting for its own account. For purposes of the 1933 Act, a distinction should be made between shares and the pieces of paper that are used to evidence them. After the controlling shareholder has loaned his certificates to the arbitrager, he will continue to own the same number of shares. In this context, the reference in Section 5(a)(2) of the 1933 Act to "delivery after sale" should be read to refer to a sale by the controlling shareholder and not to an exempt sale by another person to whom he merely has made a certificate loan.

As discussed in Chapter 11, a more reliable means of making control stock available to arbitragers and other persons who need to borrow stock for the purpose of making short sales may be to register the stock for that purpose.

Rights Offerings

Many years ago, rights offerings with standby underwriters were a preferred method by which U.S. corporations raised new equity capital. Today they are far less common, especially in large size, with the exceptions in recent years of closed-end investment companies, companies emerging from Chapter 11 reorganizations and some financial services companies. In the international sphere, however, many European and Japanese companies continue to rely heavily on this financing technique. As noted in Chapter 9, foreign companies may either register their shares under the 1933 Act to permit their rights offerings to be made to shareholders in the United States or take advantage of relatively recent exemptions to permit the offering to be made to U.S. shareholders.

If the shareholders of a corporation have preemptive rights,[91] the corporation will not be able to sell new common stock (or in

---

91. A preemptive right is simply the right of an existing shareholder to subscribe for his proportionate share of a new issue of equity securities. Whether or not a particular corporation's shareholders have preemptive rights is a question of state law. Under Section 622 of the New York Business

some cases securities convertible into common stock) directly to underwriters for resale to the public. Rather, it will have to offer the new securities first to its existing shareholders and hold the offer open for a reasonable period of time. Fortunately, preemptive rights are seldom encountered these days. No corporation wishes to be in the position of being forced into a rights offering as a legal requirement.

- *Mechanics*

Rights offerings of common stock usually are made at a discount from the market. The offering is made by issuing rights certificates (also referred to as "subscription warrants") to shareholders of record on a specified date. The certificates evidence the right to subscribe for one additional share for a specified number of shares held of record on that date. Thus, a company with 100 million shares of common stock outstanding might issue to shareholders rights to subscribe for one additional share for each ten shares held of record, thereby offering an additional ten million shares to increase its equity capital by 10%. In our example, a holder of 100 shares would be issued a warrant representing 100 rights to subscribe. As ten rights are required to purchase one additional share, with the 100 rights represented by his warrant, the holder could buy ten shares at the $18 subscription price.

Corporation Law, for example, holders of common stock have a preemptive right as to any new issue of common stock, or securities convertible into common stock, unless the certificate of incorporation provides otherwise or the corporation was organized after February 22, 1998. The general rule does not apply to shares offered to effect a business combination, pursuant to employee stock options or convertible securities, or with respect to treasury shares. The certificate of incorporation may extend preemptive rights beyond those otherwise provided by statute.

The Delaware General Corporation Law provides in Section 102(b)(3) that stockholders do not have any preemptive right to subscribe to an additional issue of stock or to any security convertible into such stock unless that right is expressly granted in the certificate of incorporation or such right existed on July 3, 1967 and has not been changed or terminated by appropriate action.

The NYSE requires listed companies to send a written notice to shareholders at least ten days in advance of the proposed record date. The record date will usually be the effective date of the company's 1933 Act registration statement covering the new securities (assuming the company does not have an effective shelf registration statement that includes the possibility of a rights offering). The record date is important not only for purposes of determining who is eligible to participate in the rights offering but also because trading in the listed security will be on an "ex-rights" basis commencing on the second business day prior to the record date. In order to prevent confusion if there is a delay in the effectiveness of the 1933 Act registration statement, the NYSE recommends that the effective date occur well in advance of the record date. It also recommends that the company's board of directors establish the record date as a specified date "or such later date as registration under the Securities Act of 1933 shall become effective."[92]

For rights to have value, they must be transferable. Rights will be traded on the exchange on which the issuer's common stock is listed or in the over-the-counter market if the shares are not listed on an exchange. A holder may sell his rights and receive cash to compensate for his diluted position in the company if he does not wish to subscribe for the shares offered to him at a price below the market. The price at which rights are purchased and sold will depend on market forces, including the relationship between the subscription price and the current market price of the stock.

In a rights offering, holders may be given a so-called "step-up privilege." The way that a step-up privilege works is that if one is issued a warrant that is not evenly divisible by the subscription ratio, in the above example if it is not evenly divisible by ten, if he fully exercises the rights evidenced by his or her warrant, he may subscribe for one additional full share in lieu of a fractional share without furnishing any additional rights. A holder of a warrant evidencing fewer than ten rights would be entitled to subscribe for one full share without furnishing any

---

92. NYSE, Listed Company Manual ¶703.03.

additional rights. For example, if a shareholder owns 105 shares of stock and there is a one-for-ten rights offering, he would receive rights to subscribe for ten shares, but because he owns another five shares he may subscribe for 11 shares.

Holders are also frequently given an over-subscription privilege, in which case the holder of a warrant who has fully exercised his basic subscription privilege and the step-up privilege, if any, may subscribe for an additional number of shares, usually not more than the aggregate number of shares subscribed for by him pursuant to the basic subscription privilege and the step-up privilege. The over-subscription privilege will be subject to allotment, so that if there are not enough unsubscribed shares to cover all over-subscriptions, shares will be allotted pro rata among those who exercised the over-subscription privilege as nearly as practicable in proportion to the shares they requested under that privilege. Another formula for allotment is the ratio that the rights exercised by each person exercising the over-subscription privilege bears to the total number of rights exercised by all persons exercising the over-subscription privilege.

After the record date and the effectiveness of the 1933 Act registration statement, the subscription agent (usually the company's transfer agent) will mail a warrant and a final prospectus to each shareholder of record. There are no strict rules as to the period for which the subscription offer must be left open. Where there are preemptive rights, state law usually will provide for a reasonable time as determined by the board of directors. The NYSE, however, requires that the date on which rights terminate should be at least 16 days after the mailing of the warrants. This can be reduced to 14 days if special mailing arrangements are used.

- *The Role of the Investment Banker*

A company making a rights offering is subject to the risk that its financing efforts will be unsuccessful if the price of its common stock declines during the subscription period. In the above example, the issuer wishes to raise $180 million by selling 10 million shares of common stock at a subscription price of $18 per share. The issuer may need this amount to finance a new plant or for some other specific corporate purpose. But the subscription offer will be open for several weeks, and holders of rights will often wait until the last day before deciding whether to subscribe. They may decide not to subscribe and let their rights lapse if the market price of the common stock declines sufficiently. If the market price of the common stock is on the decline, there probably will be substantial sales of rights. If the market price of the stock were to decline below the subscription price, there would be few, if any, subscriptions and the rights would have no value.

The issuer has two choices. It can set the subscription price sufficiently below the market price so that the risk that the price of its common stock will fall below the subscription price is remote. Here an issuer may be willing to assume the risk of the market. Many issuers, however, in order to ensure the receipt of the proceeds required for their particular financing purposes, will retain an investment banking firm to form an underwriting syndicate that will agree to purchase at the subscription price any shares not subscribed for on the exercise of rights and the over-subscription privilege. Under such an arrangement, the risk of a decline in the market price of the shares is shifted from the issuer to the underwriters.

As compensation for their commitments, the underwriters will be paid a flat standby fee, plus a per share amount for each unsubscribed share purchased by them after the subscription offer expires and for each share purchased by them on the exercise of rights which they purchase in the open market. The standby fee may be viewed as an insurance premium paid by the issuer for the certainty that all shares offered will be sold.

The underwriters may be required to purchase shares at the end of the subscription period even if the market price remains strong. Although this is not likely to occur where there is an over-subscription privilege, there are always a number of shareholders who will lose their warrants or for some other reason will fail to exercise or sell their rights. These are the so-called "sleepers." In such circumstances, the underwriters will be purchasing at the subscription price, which is less than the current market price, without having to purchase any rights. This will result in a profit to the underwriters. The underwriting agreement has often provided that any profit realized by the underwriters on the sale of unsubscribed shares will be split with the issuer on a 50–50 basis.

- *1933 Act Registration*

A rights offering by a publicly held company requires registration of the offered securities under the 1933 Act. After the adoption of the 1933 Act, there was some question whether or not this was the case.[93] Efforts were made to include in the 1934 amendments to the 1933 Act an exemption for offerings to shareholders.[94] These efforts proved unsuccessful.

Although it is necessary to register the securities being offered for subscription, it is not necessary to register the warrants mailed to shareholders or the rights that they represent, notwithstanding that transferable subscription rights are securities. The reason is that the rights are not offered or sold to the shareholders, but are granted to them for no consideration. The only circumstance under which rights might be registered is if a controlling shareholder wishes to sell his rights rather than exercise them. In this case, the requisite number of rights would be registered and a statement would be included in the prospectus that it may be used to cover sales of rights by an identified controlling person.

Securities offered pursuant to rights can be registered on Form S-3 if the registrant has been a reporting company under the 1934 Act for at least 12 months and has been timely in its filing obligations during the preceding 12 calendar months. The instructions to the form specifically provide that if the registrant requirements are met, Form S-3 can be used to register securities to be offered "upon the exercise of outstanding rights granted by an issuer of the securities to be offered, if such rights are

---

93. A. H. Dean, *The Federal Securities Act: I*, Fortune, August 1933, at 97. Mr. Dean stated that according to street custom and the English precedents, the issuance by a corporation of additional stock to its own stockholders is not considered a public offering, but that language in the conference report would indicate otherwise.

94. A. H. Dean, *As Amended: The Federal Securities Act*, Fortune, September 1934, at 82.

granted on a *pro rata* basis to all existing security holders of the class of securities to which the rights attach."

If, at the end of the subscription period, the standby underwriters acquire and resell unsubscribed shares, then they must deliver a prospectus supplemented to disclose the results of the subscription offering. Item 512(c) of Regulation S-K requires the following undertaking in a registration statement covering securities offered pursuant to rights:

> The undersigned registrant hereby undertakes to supplement the prospectus, after the expiration of the subscription period, to set forth the results of the subscription offer, the transactions by the underwriters during the subscription period, the amount of unsubscribed securities to be purchased by the underwriters, and the terms of any subsequent reoffering thereof. If any public offering by the underwriters is to be made on terms differing from those set forth on the cover page of the prospectus, a post-effective amendment will be filed to set forth the terms of such offering.

- *Shields Plan*

In 1947, a special committee of the Investment Bankers Association, of which a partner in Shields & Co. was chairman, recommended a new technique to reduce the underwriters' risks in handling standby commitments for rights offerings. This was the so-called "Shields Plan."

The technique involves sales by the underwriting syndicate of the securities offered for subscription (so-called "lay-offs"), purchases of rights in the open market, and the exercise of rights (or purchases pursuant to the standby commitment) to cover the sales. These activities take place during the subscription period and enable the managing underwriter, on behalf of the syndicate, to place shares with investors prior to the expiration of the subscription offer, thus avoiding the need to wait until after the expiration of the subscription period to determine the number of shares that the syndicate will be required to purchase. If, during the subscription period, the market price declines, lay-offs may be made to protect against further declines.

Shields Plan activities were formerly governed by Rule 10b-8, which was rescinded as part of the SEC's adoption in late 1996 of Regulation M. Rule 10b-8 regulated the underwriters' bids for and purchase of rights and, in so doing, exempted such bids and purchases from Rule 10b-6 (which prohibited bids for and purchases of "rights to purchase" the securities being distributed). As discussed above, Rule 101 no longer regulates bids for and purchases of "rights to purchase" the securities being distributed.

Rule 10b-8 also independently regulated, however, the underwriters' sale of securities obtained on their exercise of rights. Such sales were expressly permitted by Rule 10b-6, so there was no need to rely on Rule 10b-8 for an exemption. The rule regulated the lay-off price on the theory that the underwriters might otherwise manipulate upward the market price of the offered security in order to guarantee the success of the rights offering.

The fact that Rule 10b-8 has been repealed does not mean, of course, that the SEC may not still treat conduct formerly prohibited by the rule as a violation of Rule 10b-5. On the other hand, the SEC repealed the rule on the theory that the prohibited conduct was not an efficient way to manipulate the market. This admission would appear to require egregious misconduct in order to expose an underwriter to the threat of enforcement proceedings under Rule 10b-5.

- *Dealer-Manager Plan*

In some cases, a rights offering has been made without any standby arrangements but with an investment banking firm retained to manage the distribution. The issuer pays a commission to any broker or dealer whose name appears on any warrant that is exercised. As under the Shields Plan, the dealer-manager may sell shares short and then cover by buying and exercising rights. This is known as the "dealer-manager" plan or the "Columbia Gas Plan."

Chapter 14

ASSET-BACKED SECURITIES

Asset-backed securities (ABS) are securities the payments on which are derived primarily from the cash flow generated by a pool of assets supporting the securities. The underlying assets are usually financial assets, such as mortgage loans or credit card receivables, which by their terms require payments on a regular basis.[1] The more common ABS are similar to amortizing debt securities in that interest is payable on a periodic basis and principal is paid from time to time, depending on the structure of the security.

The timing of the payment of principal of an ABS is often dependent on the timing of collections of principal (or cash flow treated as principal) of the underlying assets. The inherent unpredictability of the timing of such principal collections and, therefore, the timing of related payments of principal of the

---

1. As used in this chapter, the term "ABS" is a security backed by a pool of any type of asset, including first mortgage loans. As commonly used in the market place, the term "mortgage-backed security" (MBS) means a security backed by a pool of first mortgage loans, while the term ABS means a security backed by a pool of any other type of asset (including second mortgage loans and home equity loans).

ABS, is one major feature that sets ABS apart from other debt securities. The other major distinguishing feature is that the issuer of ABS is normally not an actively managed entity for which a balance sheet and income statement are relevant to an investment decision. The issuer is rather a passive entity that merely owns the underlying assets and only requires servicing, performed by a third party, to collect the cash flows due on those assets.

Common to almost all securitizations is the legal separation of the credit risk of the Sponsor (defined below) from the cash flow of the assets being securitized, with the result that the credit rating of the related ABS is based on the creditworthiness of those assets and the legal structure of the securitization and is not normally affected by the financial condition of the Sponsor. If a Sponsor ever becomes subject to Title 11 of the United States Code (the Bankruptcy Code), the transfer of the assets from the Sponsor to the Depositor (defined below) is intended to hold up as "true sale"—that is, a transfer that succeeded in removing the assets from the Sponsor's bankruptcy estate.

The size and importance of the ABS market is enormous. At the end of 2002, there were $6.2 trillion of ABS outstanding of which $4.7 trillion were mortgage-backed securities. The ABS market was therefore larger than the U.S. Treasury securities market ($3.2 trillion) or the $4 trillion corporate bond market.[2]

The basic framework of the securities laws, which was developed prior to the creation of the ABS market, is designed to accommodate offerings of debt obligations and equity securities of corporate and other entities that are actively managed. In contrast, the essential elements of an ABS are (i) the nature and quality of the underlying assets, (ii) the timing of the receipt of the cash flows from those assets and (iii) the structure for distributing those cash flows to the securityholders. In other words, trying to accommodate ABS and the securities laws has for many years been a classic example of attempting to fit a "square peg in a round hole."

---

2. U.S. Census Bureau, *Statistical Abstract of the United States: 2003* (2003), at 754.

The regulatory gap was filled for years for public ABS offerings by an unwieldy combination of SEC rules for the use of Form S-3 by ABS issuers, staff no-action letters, interpretive statements and SEC staff comments made on specific transactions during the 1933 Act registration process. Securities industry trade associations, the major Sponsors, investment banks and lawyers engaged in discussions for many years among themselves and with the SEC staff regarding the possibility of an overhaul of SEC rules that would rationalize and formalize the SEC's regulation of ABS offerings and periodic reporting requirements.[3] In response to the SEC's Aircraft Carrier Release in late 1998, part of which asked for comment on the ABS registration process, an American Bar Association group proposed to the SEC a comprehensive regulatory scheme for such offerings.[4]

In May 2004, the SEC for the first time proposed new and amended rules and forms to address comprehensively the registration, disclosure and reporting requirements for ABS under the 1933 Act and the 1934 Act.[5] The SEC's Proposed Rules largely update and codify—but in some cases modify—the current ABS regulatory scheme and consist of a new Regulation AB (a subpart of Regulation S-K), new general rules under the 1933 Act and amendments to Form S-3, Form 10-K and Form 8-K to accommodate these rules and forms to ABS transactions.

The SEC expresses its concern in the Proposing Release that the absence of a standard set of disclosure requirements for ABS transactions has led to the inclusion in ABS filings of "undue boilerplate language," an "accumulation of unnecessary detail," "legalistic recitations of transaction terms" and "duplicative or uninformative disclosure that obscures material information." Also, disclosures may have been carried over from other filings

---

3. In addition, a task force consisting of representatives from the SEC, the Department of the Treasury and the Office of Federal Housing Enterprise Oversight delivered a report in January 2003 on disclosure practices related to mortgage-backed securities. The report is on the SEC's website at www.sec.gov/news/studies/mortgagebacked.htm.

4. The 1999 ABA letter is on the SEC's website at www.sec.gov/rules/proposed/s73098/liftin1.htm.

5. SEC Release No. 33-8419 (May 3, 2004) (Proposing Release).

without consideration of their relevance to a particular transaction. The Proposing Release therefore urges ABS transaction participants to regard the Proposed Rules as an opportunity to reevaluate the manner and content of disclosure so as to reduce or eliminate disclosure that is neither required, material nor useful to investors and to emphasize disclosure that is relevant, clear and understandable.

The proposals have not been adopted as of this writing, and it remains to be seen whether any part of them will be controversial or whether they will in large part be adopted as proposed. Our discussion in this chapter will describe the Proposed Rules and point out significant changes from the current regulatory treatment of ABS. Unless otherwise specified, rule references are to the Proposed Rules.

Basic Structure of an Asset-Backed Transaction

To help understand the application of the securities laws to ABS, it will be useful to set forth a basic structure and to define the entities and documents involved. A company (defined in the Proposed Rules as the "Sponsor") with a portfolio of receivables that it has originated, or purchased from another originator, may wish to sell those receivables for any of a number of reasons. It may need the liquidity provided by the sale proceeds, it may want to improve its balance sheet by applying the sale proceeds to pay down debt, it may want to generate earnings or, if it is a regulated entity such as a bank, it may want to remove assets from its balance sheet against which it would otherwise have to maintain regulatory capital. Because the underlying assets in a securitization are intended to be isolated from the credit risk of the Sponsor, the cost of funding the assets through a securitization (i.e., the weighted average yield on the ABS) will often be lower than the cost of borrowing by the Sponsor to fund those same assets. Lastly, many Sponsors with good credit ratings may securitize assets to diversify the types of funding available to them.

- *Conventional Securitizations*

In a typical securitization, the Sponsor sells or contributes the assets to a wholly owned "bankruptcy remote" subsidiary (defined in the Proposed Rules as the "Depositor"), which in turn transfers the assets to a special purpose vehicle (SPV), which is often a trust, and receives in return the ABS issued by the SPV. The ABS are simultaneously sold to investors, usually through underwriters, with the net proceeds going to the Depositor. The Depositor in turn uses the net proceeds to pay the Sponsor for the purchased assets.

The SPV contracts with the Sponsor or a third party to act as servicer of the assets. The servicer can be terminated on the occurrence of certain defaults in its performance of servicing obligations. Because substitute servicers for most asset types are available to replace defaulting servicers, the financial condition of the servicer is normally not material to the investor. Item 1107 of proposed Regulation AB includes a requirement, however, to disclose information regarding the servicer's financial condition "where it could have a material impact on one or more aspects of servicing of the pool assets and where those aspects could materially impact pool performance." In the Proposing Release, the SEC stated that this item would not require "general financial information" on the servicer; rather, it would require disclosure of "particular information that could have a material impact as described."

The basic documents normally involved in a securitization are (i) a purchase agreement pursuant to which the assets are sold by the Sponsor to the Depositor, (ii) a sale and servicing agreement pursuant to which the assets are sold by the Depositor to the SPV and that obligates the servicer to service the assets on the SPV's behalf and (iii) the agreement governing the issuance of the ABS, pursuant to which the trustee is also appointed.

In a securitization, the collections on the assets are applied to make distributions of interest and principal on the ABS (the so-called "waterfall"). Many securitizations have multiple classes of securities, or "tranches" in the jargon of the market. Tranching may be used to create classes with different maturities or to create internal credit enhancement for a transaction by subordinating one or more classes to other classes. In maturity tranching, Class A receives all distributions of principal until the Class A principal balance is reduced to zero, then Class B receives all distributions of principal until the Class B principal balance is reduced to zero, and so on. Maturity tranching also has the effect of credit enhancing the classes that are paid first. In credit tranching, Class A receives the amount due it on each distribution date. Class B also receives the amount due it, but only to the extent that there are sufficient collections remaining after the required amount has been distributed to Class A. The variations on these basic themes are endless. In addition, classes of ABS may be structured to pay interest only or principal only or to defer the distribution of interest by adding accrued interest to the principal balance for some period of time. This flexibility allows investment bankers to structure classes specifically addressing the investment needs of their clients. The realization of the intended results of a structure, especially in the case of maturity tranching, often depends on the payment speeds of the underlying assets.

- *Asset-Backed Commercial Paper*

A large segment of the asset-backed market consists of asset-backed commercial paper. Asset-backed commercial paper is commonly issued by "commercial paper conduit vehicles" which are entities set up to purchase receivables or receivables-backed securities from one or more Sponsors. The commercial paper is payable from the cash flow generated by this diverse pool of receivables, as well as from bank liquidity facilities backing the commercial paper programs. In addition, the commercial paper often has credit support in the form of either bank letters of credit or insurance policies issued by monoline insurers. A recent variation on this product is "extendible" asset-backed commercial paper, which has some of the features of extendible commercial paper discussed in Chapter 7.

- *New Asset Classes*

Companies and investment bankers are continually coming up with ideas for new classes of assets to be securitized and sold to investors. In 1997, $55 million of ABS based on rock musician David Bowie's recording and publishing royalties were sold in a private placement, and this transaction led to several other deals based on intellectual property rights. ABS transactions based on student loans and lease payments are commonplace, but recent years have seen actual or proposed transactions based on less common assets such as truck-driving-school loans and leases of tanker jets to the U.S. Air Force. Sports team revenues have been securitized on several occasions, beginning with a European soccer team and most recently for 19 major league baseball teams based on their broadcast revenues, media contracts and other revenues.

Another recent ABS transaction was based on a pool consisting of a European pharmaceutical manufacturer's royalty interests and contingent payments in 13 biopharmaceutical products. Recent years have also seen "whole business securitizations," where the ABS are backed by the cash flows from an operating business (e.g., £210 million of "death bonds" issued in 2003 and backed by revenues from a chain of funeral parlors in the United Kingdom). And a major international bank was reported in 2003 to have securitized the cash flow from 65 private equity funds in order to raise new money and also to reduce its exposure to this sector.

New asset classes require new answers to old questions. From a technical point of view, do the assets qualify as ABS for registration on Form S-3? If not, the transaction may have to be registered with the SEC by means of a stand-alone registration statement. Or the transaction may have to be done privately, but even in a private transaction the requirements of the Investment Company Act have to be taken into account. Will attempts to educate investors about new asset classes amount to gun-jumping as discussed in Chapter 1? And, of course, new asset classes mean new due diligence and disclosure challenges.

1933 Act Considerations

- *Who Is the Registrant?*

As described above, the ABS evidence either an obligation of or interest in the SPV, which issues the ABS as a formal matter. Under Rule 191, however, for 1933 Act purposes the issuer of publicly offered ABS is the Depositor, and the amended Forms S-1 and S-3 would specify that the registration statement must be signed by the Depositor. Prior to the Proposed Rules, the Depositor was the registrant only if the SPV was a trust as in the basic structure described above. If the SPV was a corporation, then it was the registrant. The distinction was based on the definition of "issuer" in Section 2(a)(4) of the 1933 Act, which states that "with respect to certificates of interest . . . in an unincorporated investment trust not having a board of directors . . . , the term 'issuer' means the persons performing the acts and assuming the duties of Depositor or manager pursuant to the provisions of the trust or other agreement." Under the Proposed Rules, the SPV's form is irrelevant.

Rule 191 preserves the distinction that the Depositor is the issuer only in its capacity as Depositor to the SPV as the issuing entity. Moreover, the Depositor is deemed to be a different issuer for each SPV for which it acts as Depositor as well as for its own securities. The SEC's position on this latter point goes back to the first 1933 Act-registered offering of ABS: the offering of mortgage pass-through certificates by Bank of America in 1977.[6]

- *Definition of ABS*

Prior to the Proposed Rules, the SEC's rules defined ABS only for purposes of registering ABS on Form S-3. Under the Proposed Rules, the definition is important for many purposes and has therefore been moved from Form S-3 to Item 1101 of Regulation AB. On the other hand, not all ABS are eligible to be registered on Form S-3.

ABS are defined in Item 1101 as "a security that is primarily serviced by the cash flows of a discrete pool of receivables or other financial assets, either fixed or revolving, that by their terms convert into cash within a finite time period, plus any rights or other assets designed to assure the servicing or timely distributions of proceeds to the security holders; provided that in the case of financial assets that are leases, those assets may convert to cash partially by the cash proceeds from the disposition of the physical property underlying such leases."[7]

---

6. In that registration process, the SEC rejected the proposition that if Bank of America were the registrant, then the mortgage pass-through certificates would be exempt securities of a bank under Section 3(a)(2).

7. Item 1101 also imposes two conditions that the Proposing Release says "always have been implied." These are that the issuer of ABS must be an SPV, that is, a passive entity whose activities are limited to the ABS transaction, and that neither the Depositor nor the SPV may be an investment company.

The definition is substantially the same as in the preexisting Form S-3 except for the proviso relating to leases.

The definition contemplates assets that require payments to be made over a finite period. There is no requirement that the payments be made on a regular basis or that they have principal and interest components (e.g., a trade receivable is eligible). On the other hand, the definition would presumably not extend to a transaction supported by natural resource assets, such as petroleum products or timber, since such assets, while they can be sold for cash, do not *by their terms* produce cash flow. The definition would also presumably not extend to a transaction based on assets, such as certain revolving lines of credit, that do not have a maturity date.[8]

New asset classes often present novel questions regarding their characterization as ABS or the availability of Form S-3, and it is sometimes necessary to discuss the eligibility question with the SEC staff well in advance of filing a registration statement.

Non-performing assets (as characterized in the transaction documents or in the Sponsor's policies, whichever standard is more restrictive) may not be included in the pool at the time of issuance of the ABS, and delinquent assets (30 days or more past due) may not constitute 50% or more of the original asset pool. In addition, in order for the ABS to be eligible for registration on Form S-3, delinquent assets must not amount to 20% or more of the original asset pool.

If leases are included in the pool, the portion of cash flow anticipated from residual values must not constitute 60% or more of the original asset pool (in the case of auto leases)[9] or 50%

---

8. "Synthetic" securitizations are also not covered by the definition. These are transactions in which payments are determined based on an external reference asset or on an external equity or commodity or other index. According to the Proposing Release, these do not meet the basic requirement of the ABS definition that payments be based primarily on the performance of the financial assets in a pool. The Proposing Release contrasts swaps or other derivatives entered into to reduce or alter risk or to provide credit enhancement but where the return on the ABS is still based primarily on the performance of the financial assets in the pool. Proposing Release at n.62.

9. Automobile leases include motorcycle leases but not leases "for leisure craft such as watercraft or snowmobiles." Proposing Release at n.72.

or more (in the case of all other leases). In the case of leases other than auto leases, Form S-3 requires that the portion of cash flow anticipated from residual values must not constitute 20% or more of the original asset pool.

The ABS definition's requirement of a "discrete" pool of assets has three exceptions. First, additional assets may be added to a "master trust" where the expanding pool backs both past and future ABS issuances by the master trust. Second, a portion of the proceeds of the ABS offering may be set aside for the future acquisition of pool assets (a prefunding account). Third, a portion of the cash flow from the asset pool may be recycled and used to acquire new pool assets instead of being paid out to investors (the so-called "revolving period").

A prefunding account for ABS may not exceed 50% of the proceeds of the offering, and the prefunding period may not extend more than one year from the initial issuance of the ABS. In order to qualify for Form S-3, the prefunding account may not exceed 25% of the proceeds of the offering. The additional assets acquired during a revolving period may not exceed 50% of the proceeds of the offering if fixed receivables or other non-revolving financial assets are to be acquired, and the duration of the revolving period for such assets may not exceed more than one year from the initial issuance of the ABS. To be eligible for registration on Form S-3, the limit for the additional assets acquired during the revolving period is 25%.

In a prefunded securitization, the Depositor sells an aggregate principal amount of ABS that is greater than the aggregate principal amount of assets transferred to the SPV at the time of issuance of the ABS, with the intention of transferring additional assets in the amount of such differential to the SPV over a predetermined period (known as the "prefunding period") after such issuance. Net proceeds from the offering in the amount of such differential are deposited in a "prefunding account" and are thereafter applied to the purchase price of assets acquired during the prefunding period. Pending such application, such net proceeds are invested in interim investments that satisfy the definition of financial assets. If the amount in the prefunding account has not been fully applied to the purchase of assets by the end of the prefunding period, the balance is distributed as principal to securityholders.

Sponsors may decide to use a prefunding mechanism for the purpose of lowering the cost of the securitization by spreading the same amount of costs over a larger securitization the size of which has been increased by the amount in the prefunding account or, if they believe that interest rates are rising, to lock in a lower yield for the portion of the ABS supported by the amount in the prefunding account. The prefunding mechanism is normally available only to Sponsors that have an established record of stable origination standards, as both the rating agency and the investment bankers will require substantial assurance that the assets originated after closing will have terms and credit quality substantially similar to those of the assets transferred to the SPV at the closing.[10]

In a 1992 release, the SEC took the position that the definition of ABS (then included in Form S-3) did not encompass securities issued in structured financings for a single obligor or a group of related obligors. The Proposal Release abandons this position and states that such securities may be treated as ABS so long as the underlying assets are registered (if registration is required as discussed below under "Registration of Underlying Pool Assets") and disclosure is provided as discussed below under "Disclosure Requirements."

- *Form S-1 and Form S-3*

Under the Proposed Rules, ABS transactions would be registered only on Form S-1 or on Form S-3. Foreign ABS transactions would also be limited to these forms, and Form S-11 would no longer be available to register ABS.

As noted above, some transactions meet the definition of ABS but are not eligible to be registered on Form S-3. In the

---

10. The asset pool may change for other reasons without infringing the "discrete pool" requirement, for example, where assets are substituted as a result of a breach of standard representations and warranties. According to the Proposing Release, these pool composition changes are covered by the definition's reference to "rights or other assets designed to assure the servicing or timely distribution of proceeds to the security holders" and do not require a separate exception from the "discrete pool" requirement. Proposing Release at n.74.

absence of any such disqualifying characteristics, Form S-3 eligibility requires that the ABS be rated investment-grade.

The Proposing Release states that it has been existing staff policy that a Depositor's other ABS transactions must have complied with applicable 1934 Act reporting obligations during the prior 12 months in order for a new ABS transaction to be eligible to be filed on Form S-3, and the Proposed Rules extend this requirement to other ABS transactions by the same Sponsor. Taken literally, this eligibility requirement could be extremely onerous, especially for Sponsors of transactions registered under "rent-a-shelf" programs where the 1934 Act reporting obligations for particular transactions are carried out by the third-party originator or servicer of the related pool assets.

As discussed above, the Proposed Rules treat the Depositor as the issuer for 1933 Act purposes. Accordingly, an ABS registration statement on Form S-1 or Form S-3 must be signed by the Depositor and the individuals specified in Section 6(a) of the 1933 Act.

Form S-1 is not really a practical alternative to Form S-3, since shelf registration and incorporation by reference are essential to most ABS transactions. If a transaction cannot be registered on Form S-3, there may be no alternative but to rely on a private placement exemption. Accordingly, some commenters on the Proposed Rules made the novel suggestion that Form S-3 be available for all MBS and also for all other transactions if the ABS are offered only to investors having specified qualifications.

- *Registration of Underlying Pool Assets*

Where the underlying assets consist of home mortgages, student loans, auto loans, credit card receivables and similar assets, the question of separately registering these assets under the 1933 Act never arises. But where the asset pool contains non-exempt securities, such as corporate debt securities backing a Collateralized Debt Obligation (CDO), these may have to be separately registered under the 1933 Act along with the related ABS. Rule 190 codifies staff policy in this area (often referred to as "repackaging") by stating that registration will be required unless the underlying securities would be freely tradable by the Depositor *and* neither the issuer of the underlying securities nor any of its

ASSET-BACKED SECURITIES

affiliates is involved or has an interest in the ABS transaction or is affiliated with the Sponsor, Depositor, SPV or underwriter of the ABS transaction. The first condition will not be met if the underlying securities consist of restricted securities (e.g., privately placed securities where the Rule 144(k) two-year period has not run) or if the ABS offering is part of the distribution of the underlying securities (e.g., where the underlying securities are part of an unsold allotment from a prior registered transaction).

An ABS offering may involve a Sponsor, Depositor or underwriter that was an underwriter or affiliate of an underwriter in the prior registered offering of the underlying securities, but where these securities were subsequently purchased for the purposes of the ABS transaction. Rule 190 continues a prior staff "bright line" test to the effect that registration of the underlying securities will not be required where these have been purchased at arm's length in the secondary market at least three months after the last sale of any unsold allotment or subscription by the affiliated underwriter.

ABS transactions may also have underlying securities that are themselves ABS. For example, the Depositor or another entity affiliated with the Sponsor often retains the subordinated (and usually unrated) class or classes from a securitization. Often, the Depositor or such other entity may wish to liquefy its portfolio of these retained classes by securitizing them (referred to as a "resecuritization"). Investors purchase the higher rated class or classes that are issued in the resecuritization, and the Depositor normally takes back the subordinated class or classes, which provide internal credit enhancement for the higher rated classes. In addition, a broker or dealer may purchase any type of debt security or ABS in the secondary market and securitize those securities.

In these situations, if the underlying ABS are required to be registered, they may be registered in the same registration statement under which the newly issued ABS are being registered. As a practical matter, this approach is available only when the Depositor is resecuritizing subordinated classes created and retained by it because, while the Depositor (or an affiliated Sponsor) would be willing to sign the registration statement in respect of its underlying ABS, any unrelated issuer of the underlying securities would be understandably reluctant to sign the resecuritization registration statement.[11]

If registration of the underlying securities is required, Rule 190 specifies the steps that must be taken. These include the filing of a post-effective amendment to the registration statement under which the underlying securities were offered, if necessary in order to amend the plan of distribution to cover the ABS transaction, and the simultaneous delivery of a prospectus for the underlying securities together with the prospectus for the ABS.[12] If the ABS transaction is registered on Form S-3, then the offering of the underlying securities must be eligible to be registered under Form S-3 or Form F-3 as a primary offering of such securities (this condition is necessary, in the SEC's view, to prevent the offering of non-shelf-eligible underlying securities through a shelf-eligible ABS offering).

Prior staff policy in this area had relied on Rule 140 as a basis for requiring registration of the underlying securities. The Proposed Rules do not explicitly rely on Rule 140.

- *Disclosure Requirements*

In the seminal Bank of America offering referred to above, the SEC and the parties to the transaction worked to develop disclosure appropriate for that securitization, the basic substance of which has guided disclosure for ABS offerings up to the present.

Disclosure in respect of ABS has, of course, evolved since the Bank of America offering, especially as ABS supported by assets other than mortgage loans have come to be offered in the marketplace. The evolution has taken place through the process of the SEC staff's comments on filings and registrants' responses to such comments.

---

11. Resecuritization may be effected under a shelf registration statement; however, there are no SEC rules for adding a new registrant to an effective registration statement.

12. Certain disclosure and delivery conditions do not apply if the underlying securities consist of an interest in an asset pool established for legal or administrative purposes (e.g., a "titling" or "origination" trust in connection with auto lease transactions).

Regulation AB sets forth a comprehensive "principles-based" disclosure format for ABS transactions. The SEC stated in the Proposing Release that it did not believe it was practical or effective to draft detailed disclosure guides for each asset type that might be securitized.

Some of the key elements of disclosure under Regulation AB are the following:

Sponsors. Item 1104 requires a general discussion of the Sponsor's experience in securitizing assets of any type, as well as a more detailed discussion of the Sponsor's experience in and overall procedures for originating or acquiring and securitizing assets of the type to be included in a current transaction. Information regarding the size, composition and growth of the Sponsor's portfolio of assets of the type to be securitized and information or factors related to the Sponsor that may be material to an analysis of the origination or performance of the pool assets, such as whether any prior securitizations originated by the Sponsor have defaulted or experienced an early amortization triggering event, should be included to the extent material.

Other relevant information includes the Sponsor's credit-granting or underwriting criteria for the asset types being securitized (and the extent to which they have changed), the extent to which the Sponsor outsources to third parties any of its origination or purchasing functions and the extent to which the Sponsor relies on securitization as a funding source.

Item 1104 also calls for disclosure of three years of "static pool" or "vintage" delinquency and loss data indicating how groups or pools of assets—such as those originated at different intervals—are performing over time. The Proposing Release states that "[b]y presenting comparisons between originations at similar points in the assets' lives, such data allow the detection of patterns that may not be evident from overall portfolio numbers and thus may reveal a more informative picture of material elements of portfolio performance and risk." If material, the information must be provided on a pool level basis with respect to prior securitized pools involving the same asset type established by the Sponsor during the relevant period. In addition, to the extent material, static pool data should be presented separately according to factors such as asset term, asset type, yield, payment rates, geography or ranges of credit scores or other applicable measures of obligor credit quality.

If the pool assets have not been originated by the nominal Sponsor, as is typical of "rent-a-shelf" ABS transactions, then Item 1109 calls for similar information about any single originator or any group of affiliated originators that has originated or is expected to originate 10% or more of the pool assets. Item 1109 does not require static pool data under these circumstances.

SPV (Issuing Entity). Item 1106 calls for information about the SPV (referred to in the Proposed Rules as the "issuing entity"). The sale or transfer of the pool assets to the SPV must be described as well as the creation and status of any security interest in the pool assets. The amount paid for the pool assets must be disclosed together with the principles followed or to be followed in determining that amount, the persons making that determination and their relationship to the other participants in the transaction.

Servicers. Item 1107 calls for information on the entire servicing function applicable to the ABS being registered, including a clear description of the roles, responsibilities and oversight requirements of the servicing function and the parties involved. Where subservicers or multiple servicers are involved, separate information is required for each master servicer, each affiliated servicer, each unaffiliated servicer that services 10% or more of pool assets and any other servicer, such as a special servicer, that performs work-outs, foreclosures or other material aspects of the servicing of pool assets.

Disclosure must be provided for each relevant servicer of the general character of its business and how long it has been servicing assets, the material terms of the servicing agreement and the servicer's duties regarding the ABS and the arrangements for a servicer's resignation or removal and for a successor servicer. As noted above, the servicer's financial statements need not be provided, but information about the servicer's financial condition might be necessary if it could have a material impact on one or more aspects of servicing.

Pool Assets. Item 1110 requires a description of pool assets, including the type or type of pool assets, the material characteristics of the asset pool, delinquency and loss information, sources of pool cash flow, representations and warranties and repurchase obligations regarding pool assets, third-party claims on pool assets and the terms under which assets may be added to, substituted for or removed from the pool.

Significant Obligors of Pool Assets. A "significant obligor" is an obligor, a property or a lessee (or a group of related obligors, properties or lessees) related to a pool asset or pool assets that make up 10% or more of the asset pool. Item 1111 requires information about significant obligors, including the selected financial data required by Item 301 of Regulation S-K if the pool assets related to the obligor make up 10% or more but less than 20% of the asset pool. If the pool assets related to the obligor make up 20% or more of the pool, then the obligor's financial statements as required by Regulation S-X (with some exceptions) must be included.

Transaction Structure. Item 1112 requires information about the type or types of ABS that may be offered, a clear description of the flow of funds for the transaction, an itemized list of all estimated fees and expenses to be paid or payable out of the cash flows for the transaction, information on collections and distributions and arrangements for any "clean up" call or other optional or mandatory redemption of the ABS if the principal balance of the asset pool or ABS declines to a specified level. The Proposing Release cautions that a base prospectus for shelf-registered ABS should fully describe the types of offerings contemplated by the registration statement; takedowns involving features not described in the base prospectus may require a new registration statement or a post-effective amendment.

Credit Enhancement and Other Support. Item 1113 requires a description of all external or internal sources of credit enhancement or other support, including external credit enhancement of pool assets or the ABS (e.g., bond insurance, letters of credit or guarantees), mechanisms to ensure timely payment of the ABS (e.g., liquidity or lending facilities), derivatives used to reduce or alter risk (e.g., interest rate or currency swaps or credit default swaps related to the assets in the pool) and internal credit enhancement structured into the transaction (e.g., subordination provisions, overcollateralizations, reserve accounts, cash collateral or spread accounts).

The Proposing Release notes the possibility that credit enhancement may raise questions as to whether a separate security is involved that needs to be separately registered. It draws a distinction between a guarantee of the ABS, which would create a separate security required to be registered under the 1933 Act, and a guarantee of the underlying assets.

Of course, external enhancements that are themselves exempted securities are not required to be separately registered. A surety bond issued by an insurer is normally within the exemption for insurance policies provided in Section 3(a)(8) of the 1933 Act, and a letter of credit provided by a domestic bank is normally within the exemption for bank securities provided in Section 3(a)(2) of the 1933 Act.[13]

Even if credit enhancement does not result in a separate security required to be registered, it may require additional disclosure if it is significant in amount and is provided by a single person or group of affiliated persons. Item 1113 requires that if a person or group of affiliated persons is liable or contingently liable to provide payments representing 10% or more of the cash flow supporting any offered class of ABS, then additional descriptive and financial information must be provided. As in the case of significant obligors (discussed above), the additional financial information may consist of selected financial data or full financial statements depending on the amount of cash flow supporting any ABS class.

Item 1113 would base the triggering event for disclosure on payments that the enhancement provider is liable or contingently liable to provide. Valuation of the enhancement, such as for swaps or other derivatives, would not be the relevant test. The manner of calculating the relevant percentage levels for payments from swaps or other derivatives is not clearly set forth in the Proposed Rules or the Proposing Release.

Alternative Methods of Presenting Third-Party Financial Information. In the case of a significant obligor, Item 1100(c) permits the ABS prospectus to refer the investor to the third party's required financial information or to incorporate such information by reference into the ABS prospectus. In the case of a significant enhancement provider, Item 1100(c) permits

---

13. *See* SEC Release No. 33-6661 (September 23, 1986) for factors affecting the determination whether the exemption provided in Section 3(a)(2) is applicable to the obligation of a U.S. branch of a non-U.S. bank.

incorporation by -reference as an alternative to including the information in the ABS prospectus. Both alternatives are based on prior no-action letters issued by the SEC staff and are subject to conditions.

Incorporation by reference is permitted if the third party has filed all required 1934 Act reports during the past 12 months, such reports include the relevant financial statements and the ABS prospectus (a) describes any and all material changes to the incorporated information that have occurred since its filing and (b) states that all documents subsequently filed by the third party shall be deemed to be incorporated by reference. The incorporation by reference alternative would be available even where the ABS transaction was being registered on Form S-1. An instruction to Item 1100(c) points out that all applicable consents would be required to be furnished for the material incorporated by reference.

Referring the investor to the third party's information is the second alternative for presenting third-party financial information, but it is available only where the third-party is a significant obligor. The Proposing Release acknowledges that incorporating third-party information by reference presents practical difficulties in obtaining required consents or in evaluating the information of an uncooperative third party, but these considerations are obviously not as compelling where the third party is providing credit enhancement. The alternative contemplates a reference in the ABS prospectus to the significant obligor's 1934 Act reports on file with the SEC along with a statement of how to access those reports. The significant obligor may not be involved in the ABS transaction or be an affiliate of a participant in the ABS transaction. In addition, one of the following conditions must be met: (i) the significant obligor must be eligible to use Form S-3 or Form F-3 for a primary offering of non-investment-grade securities (i.e., have a $75 million public float), (ii) the significant obligor must meet specified registrant requirements of Form S-3 or Form F-3 *and* its securities included in the asset pool must be non-convertible investment-grade securities, (iii) a parent or subsidiary of the significant obligor guarantees the securities included in the asset pool and the information requirements of Regulation S-X and the eligibility requirements of Form S-3 or

Form F-3 are met, (iv) the significant obligor is a U.S. government-sponsored enterprise meeting specified requirements or (v) the significant obligor's securities included in the asset pool are themselves ABS and the significant obligor is a 1934 Act reporting entity that has been current in its reporting obligations for at least 12 months.[14]

An ABS issuer relying on the "reference" alternative must undertake that if the significant obligor ceases to meet the above conditions, then the ABS issuer will either provide the required information or terminate the transaction or the affected portion of the transaction—that is, either distribute or sell the disqualified underlying security. The Proposing Release states that it will not be acceptable to permit the security to remain in place for a "reasonable time," as some current transactions permit.

- *Offering Materials*

• • *ABS Informational and Computational Materials.* By some reports, more than 95% of ABS are held by institutional investors. Institutions will not buy ABS unless they are able to form an understanding of how a particular ABS will perform under various scenarios based on different assumptions as to the rate of principal payments on the underlying assets (including voluntary prepayments by the underlying obligors and prepayments as a result of liquidation on default) and losses on liquidation of underlying assets as a result of default. The yield and weighted average life of an ABS will change, sometimes significantly, depending on such assumptions.

Investors may request the underwriter to create "cash flow runs" and yield tables for scenarios designated by the investors or prepare their own materials on the basis of information provided by the underwriter. Such materials, which are generally referred to as "computational materials," are now more often created by investors on Bloomberg or with the assistance of

---

14. Item 1100(c) does not continue a prior staff position that also required that the significant obligor under these circumstances have a public float of $75 million.

ASSET-BACKED SECURITIES

software provided by Intex Solutions, Inc. In either case, the underwriter provides the structural and collateral information that serves as the basis for the investors' computations.

Computational materials can be voluminous, and therefore cannot realistically be orally transmitted, and they may be tailored to the requests of particular prospective buyers. Consequently, they are normally not suitable for inclusion in the prospectus. In some cases, the structure of the proposed ABS will be changed to satisfy the requirements of a prospective buyer after the buyer has completed its analysis of the computational materials.

Computational materials used prior to the delivery of the related final prospectus—if created by the Sponsor or underwriters—are likely to be considered written materials that offer the ABS for sale and therefore a prospectus within Section 2(a)(10) of the 1933 Act, the use of which, absent some relief, would violate Section 5(b)(1) of the 1933 Act. As discussed in Chapter 1, Rule 134 can be of assistance in permitting some basic factual information to be disseminated in writing, but nothing as elaborate as computational materials.

In 1994, the SEC issued two no-action letters[15] that, in effect, permit the use of computational materials (including information as to (i) the structure of the related ABS and (ii) the assets themselves) prior to the delivery of a final prospectus, subject to the satisfaction of the conditions stated in the requesting letters. One of these conditions is that the computational materials must be filed with the SEC for incorporation by reference into the registration statement covering the related ABS.[16]

Rule 167 codifies the "concept" underlying the no-action letters. The rule applies to "ABS informational and computational material," which Item 1101(a) defines as a written

---

15. SEC No-action Letters, *Kidder Peabody Acceptance Corp. I* (May 20, 1994) and *Public Securities Association* (May 27, 1994). *See also* SEC No-action Letter, *Public Securities Association* (March 9, 1995) (providing similar relief for "structural term sheets" and "collateral term sheets").

16. In the case of a registration on Form S-3, the filing may be made by means of a current report on Form 8-K. Because Form S-1 and Form S-11 do not permit incorporation by reference, the filing must be made by means of a post-effective amendment.

communication consisting solely of one or some combination of the following:

- a brief summary of the structure of an ABS offering;
- descriptive factual information regarding the pool assets;
- static pool data, as "referenced" in the applicable items of Regulation AB; and
- statistical information displaying the investment characteristics of the ABS under specified prepayment, interest rate, loss or other hypothetical scenarios (e.g., the results of interest rate sensitivity analyses), the cash flows associated with specified prepayment speeds and the financial impact of losses based on a variety of assumptions.[17]

As noted above, it has become more common since the no-action letters for underwriters to provide investors with data regarding structure or underlying assets that the investors can use to conduct their own analytics and computations with the assistance of third-party services. The Proposing Release states that "if the investor analytics or third-party service simply allow an investor to perform its own calculations based on collateral and structural inputs and models provided by the issuer or underwriter, only the inputs, models and other information provided by the issuer or underwriter would constitute ABS informational and computational material." The Proposing Release hedges on this point, however, in the event of any affiliation between the third party and the issuer or underwriter or in the event of unspecified compensation arrangements.[18]

The Proposal Release states that "loan level" information may be provided under the prior no-action letters and would continue to be permissible under Rule 167. It cautions, however, that issuers and underwriters should be mindful of any privacy, consumer

---

17. One benefit of the new defined term is that it would no longer be necessary to characterize specific material as falling under the no-action letters' overlapping descriptions of term sheets and computational materials.

18. Proposing Release, text at n.191.

ASSET-BACKED SECURITIES

protection or other regulatory requirements regarding the disclosure of individual information, "especially given that in most cases the data must be publicly filed" with the SEC (as discussed below).

The Proposing Release cautions against the use of "inappropriate legends or disclaimers" in such material, for example, those regarding accuracy or completeness and statements requiring investors to read or to acknowledge that they have read any disclaimers or legends or the ABS registration statement.

As in the prior no-action letters, Rule 167 requires that ABS informational and computational material be filed with the SEC. Rule 426 specifies how the filing is to be made:

- The material is to be filed on Form 8-K and is deemed to be a part of the ABS registration statement (and thus subject to Section 11 liability) as of the earlier of its filing date or the date of filing of the Rule 424(b) prospectus for the ABS offering.

- Material must only be filed to the extent that it is provided at any time to an investor that has "indicated to the underwriter that it will purchase" all or a portion of the class of ABS to which the materials relate, in which case all materials provided to that investors must be filed. Material provided to other investors need be filed only to the extent that it is provided after the establishment of the final terms of all classes of the ABS offering.

- Material must be filed by the later of the due date for the filing of the Rule 424(b) prospectus for the ABS offering or two business days after it is first used. It would no longer be necessary to refrain from confirming the sale of ABS until the material has been filed.

- Data may be aggregated and filed in consolidated form if there is no omission of any information required to be filed and if the presentation does not make the information misleading.

- Material need not be filed if it relates to abandoned structures, if it does not contain any new or different information from material previously filed or if it is entitled to some other exemption.

- Revised Rule 311 of Regulation S-T requires that material be filed by means of the SEC's EDGAR system, but executable code used by a program to read the material is not to be filed.

The effect of the filing is to impose the applicable 1933 Act liabilities for such materials on the Depositor (as the 1933 Act issuer), its signing persons and the underwriters. Consequently, an issuer may request that an underwriter indemnify it in respect of material inaccuracies in the computational materials created by that underwriter. The underwriter will not indemnify the issuer for information about the structure of the transaction or for any inaccuracy resulting from any inaccuracies in the information about the underlying assets furnished by the Sponsor to the underwriter for the purpose of creating the computational materials, since the issuer is able to verify such information. If there is a syndicate of underwriters in the offering, the lead underwriter often develops one set of computational materials that may be used by any member of the syndicate. At present, there does not appear to be a market standard as to whether the underwriter who develops the computational materials should indemnify the other underwriters for any material inaccuracies in the computational materials. It is fairly common, however, for the Sponsor to indemnify the underwriters for liabilities arising from any inaccuracies in the information regarding the underlying assets (such as interest rates and original and remaining terms to maturity) on the basis of which the calculations in the computational materials are made.

The Proposal Release justifies the continuation of the filing requirement for ABS informational and computational material by reference to the SEC's rules on communications in the business combination context, which also require that certain communications be filed. This reference, however, is at odds with public statements by the staff made prior to the publication of the Proposal Release. Those statements acknowledged the difference between a situation in which an issuer disseminates information about a business combination to equally situated investors and a situation in which many different underwriters are disseminating ABS-related information to investors who are making different assumptions about the investment characteristics of the securities.

The Proposal Release also states that the SEC is still studying the possibility of broader reforms to the registration process under the 1933 Act, including potential reforms to the restrictions regarding communications at or about the time of a registered offering. It requests comments on whether Rule 134 should be amended to accommodate ABS offerings and also states that additional reforms involving ABS will be considered in connection with such broader reforms.

Rule 167 also requires that the ABS informational and computational material, in addition to being filed with the SEC, contain the SEC file number for the related ABS registration statement. The material must also urge the investor to read the transaction documents filed or to be filed with the SEC and explain how to obtain such documents.

In providing that the rule may be relied on by any participant in the transaction, Rule 167 reflects the SEC's expansive view of the universe of persons who can be liable for a Section 5 violation. It should be clear that an underwriter that sends out offering material in violation of Section 5 does not create any liability for the issuer or any other underwriter.

• • *Access to Loan Files.* In the case of a securitization in which the individual assets have high balances or are not originated on a uniform basis (e.g., commercial mortgage loans), prospective investors may wish to review the related loan files and make their own decisions as to the creditworthiness and security of the assets. More recently, some investors have been concerned about whether loans in the pool could be characterized as "predatory."

Loan files, in a very technical sense, may be written communications that offer the related ABS for sale and may therefore come within the definition of "prospectus" in Section 2(a)(10) of the 1933 Act. Consequently, in the view of some practitioners, access to loan files prior to the delivery of a final prospectus could be a violation of Section 5 of the 1933 Act. For this reason, many issuers of ABS do not allow prospective purchasers of registered ABS access to the loan files relating to such securities.

As discussed below, a particular series of ABS may have one or more publicly offered classes as well as one or more privately placed classes. In a private placement, the delivery of written materials other than the offering memorandum does not result in a Section 5 violation. An issue arises, however, if a prospective buyer in a securitization with both publicly and privately offered classes is interested in purchasing some of the private classes and some of the public classes. The related loan files are relevant to both the public classes and the private classes. Access to the loan files, while permissible in respect of the private classes, could under the analysis set forth above still result in a Section 5 violation in respect of the public classes. In this situation, some issuers have granted access to the loan files only to prospective purchasers who agree not to purchase any of the publicly offered classes.

- *Prospectus Delivery Considerations*

 • • *Rule 15c2-8(b)*. The SEC stated in May 1995 that, if no preliminary prospectus is distributed in connection with a takedown from an ABS shelf registration statement, it then interpreted Rule 15c2-8(b) of the 1934 Act to require that broker-dealers deliver the final prospectus for the takedown at least 48 hours prior to sending a confirmation for the sale of the related ABS.[19] The SEC staff subsequently provided no-action relief from the 48-hour rule for issuances of ABS so long as the amount in the prefunding account, if any, is not greater than 25% of the aggregate principal amount of the securities.[20]

The no-action relief recognized that the structuring process for ABS (which, as discussed above in the context of ABS informational and computational materials, often involves a dialogue between the issuer and prospective buyers) and the assembling of the underlying assets and the related information for the prospectus take place throughout the offering process, even up to a few days before closing, making it difficult to comply with

---

19. SEC Release No. 33-7168 (May 11, 1995), at n.80.
20. SEC No-action Letter, *Public Securities Association* (December 15, 1995).

the 48-hour rule. The SEC's relief was extended on three occasions and finally extended indefinitely in December 2000.[21]

The Proposed Rules would amend Rule 15c2-8(b) to exclude investment-grade ABS registered on Form S-3. The limitation on the prefunding account would be eliminated since it is now one of the eligibility criteria for the use of Form S-3. The Proposing Release explains the failure to propose relief for ABS registered on Form S-1 as attributable to the SEC's belief that investors in such securities should be entitled to more time and information.

• • *Post-Offering Delivery Requirements; Availability of Materials through Electronic Media.* Because the issuer of ABS (in the basic structure example, the SPV) is often newly created at the time of issuance and, therefore, not subject to the reporting requirements of Section 13 or 15(d) of the 1934 Act, the applicable prospectus delivery period under Section 4(3) of the 1933 Act is 90 days.[22] During this period, dealers making a market in the ABS will not, absent an exemption, distribute written materials that might come within the definition of "prospectus" in respect of such security without first delivering a current final prospectus.

ABS investors receive, often on a monthly basis, servicing reports that describe the performance of the related asset pool (e.g., information as to principal collections, delinquencies, losses, etc.). Servicing reports arguably come within the definition of "prospectus" and could constitute a Section 5(b)(1) violation if delivered during the 90-day period to a buyer who receives the reports before receiving the final prospectus. The possibility of this occurring was low when servicing reports were delivered in paper form only to holders of the related ABS. More recently, servicing reports have been posted on electronic, online financial information services available to the investment community at large. An issuer or dealer with knowledge that servicing reports are available online to the investment community

---

21. SEC No-action Letter, *The Bond Market Association* (December 15, 2000).

22. In practice, even issuers such as master trusts, which issue more than one series of ABS and therefore may be subject to such reporting requirements after the first issuance, use a 90-day prospectus delivery period.

could be deemed to have delivered the servicing report to a prospective buyer. Issuers who put their servicing reports online may avoid this problem by making both the servicing report and the final prospectus available on the online service and linking the servicing report to an electronic version of the final prospectus.[23] Another way of analyzing the problem is to apply by analogy the SEC's long-standing position discussed in Chapter 3 that normal corporate reports to investors do not constitute "gun-jumping."

Servicing reports and other performance-related information are no less important to holders of privately placed ABS. In fact, dealers may be less willing to bid on Rule 144A ABS if they are not able to receive this information promptly and on a regular basis. Electronic display of such information runs the risk of being considered an "offer" to non-QIBs in the case of Rule 144A securities or a "general solicitation" in the case of Regulation D securities. A password or other device for restricting access to QIBs or institutional accredited investors would solve the problem, but passwords and similar devices are often cumbersome. It would be more straightforward to use a simple restrictive legend that would state clearly that the information is made available only for use by persons eligible to purchase the related securities, but the SEC staff has not yet confirmed the acceptability of such a procedure.

It is generally understood that the SEC staff is considering the issues discussed above as part of its study of broader 1933 Act reform.

• • *Market-Maker Prospectuses.* As discussed in Chapter 1, the SEC takes the position that the Section 4(3) dealer's exemption is not available for transactions in which the dealer is an affiliate of the issuer. The theory of this position is that a dealer, according to the definition in Section 2(a)(12), is a person who deals in securities issued "by another person," and an issuer is not deemed by the SEC to be "another person" with respect to its affiliates. While this analysis may be somewhat less than persuasive, there is a policy basis for the position: when a person

---

23. SEC Release No. 33-7233 (October 5, 1995), illus. 15.

controlled by the issuer resells a security of the issuer, the resale by that person may not be far removed in substance from a primary issuance by the issuer, thus justifying the delivery of what has come to be called a "market-maker prospectus."

In the context of ABS, however, the substantive reason for requiring a market-maker prospectus in the secondary trading activities of a dealer affiliated with the issuer is not always present. The situation normally arises in a "conduit" securitization in which the Depositor is an affiliate of the dealer and purchases assets from a Sponsor with servicing responsibilities who may or may not be an affiliate of the Depositor. If the Sponsor is not an affiliate of the Depositor and the dealer, the SEC will not require the use of a market-maker prospectus in secondary trades by the dealer in the related ABS. The theory is that because the Depositor and the dealer are not affiliates of the Sponsor, they most likely do not have any access to information about the related asset pool beyond the servicing reports that are generally available to investors. However, if they are affiliates of the Sponsor with servicing responsibilities, the theory is that the Depositor and dealer have sufficient access to information about the asset pool to permit them to supplement the prospectus to the extent necessary to comply with Section 10 of the 1933 Act.

The Proposing Release suggests that pool composition tables may be required to keep the information in a market-making or remarketing prospectus current in addition to periodic distribution reports that may be incorporated by reference into Form S-3 prospectuses.[24] It is also generally understood that the SEC staff is considering issues relating to market-making prospectuses as part of its study of broader 1933 Act reform.

- *Research Materials*

Rule 139 provides a safe harbor in the determination as to whether, with respect to a security registered or proposed to be registered under the 1933 Act, written information, recommendations or opinions about that security (collectively referred to as "research reports") put out by an underwriter or prospective

---

24. Proposal Release at n.86.

underwriter of that security will be considered to constitute an offer for sale or an offer to sell that security for purposes of Section 2(a)(10) of the 1933 Act and, therefore, a prospectus. Absent the relief provided by Rule 139, the delivery of a research report about an issuer to a purchaser of the issuer's securities in a public offering prior to the purchaser's receipt of the related final prospectus could constitute a violation of Section 5.

Investment banks that deal in ABS normally distribute research reports concerning particular ABS, particular types of underlying assets or particular structures used in securitizations. Rule 139, however, only applies to a registrant that is required to file reports pursuant to Section 13 or 15(d) of the 1934 Act. The issuer of an ABS (i.e., the SPV), however, is not formed in many securitizations until the issuance of its ABS.[25] Consequently, such issuers may not qualify for Rule 139, and research reports distributed prior to the availability of such an issuer's final prospectus may pose the risk of a Section 5 violation. In addition, Rule 139 requires that the publication in which the research report is contained be published with reasonable regularity, and this requirement is sometimes difficult to satisfy with respect to a new asset type.

Because of the industry's difficulties in publishing research on ABS, a trade association now known as The Bond Market Association but then known as the Public Securities Association (PSA) entered into discussions with the SEC staff with a view to obtaining interpretive relief. In a letter dated February 7, 1997,[26] the staff responded with interpretive advice to the effect that the publication or distribution by a broker or dealer of information, an opinion or a recommendation with respect to investment-grade ABS (as defined for purposes of Form S-3 eligibility) would not be deemed, for purposes of Section 2(a)(10) or Section 5(c) of the 1933 Act, to constitute an offer

---

25. In addition, because institutions buy substantially all ABS and the number of holders of a class or series is usually fewer than 300, issuers often deregister such securities after the end of the fiscal year in which the securities were issued. *See* Section 15(d) of the 1934 Act.

26. SEC No-action Letter, *Dissemination of Research Materials Relating to Asset-Backed Securities* (February 7, 1997).

for sale or an offer to sell ABS registered or proposed to be registered under the 1933 Act.

Rule 139a would codify the no-action relief as a non-exclusive safe harbor. Under the new rule, the publication or distribution by a broker or dealer of information, an opinion or a recommendation with respect to ABS eligible to be registered on Form S-3 will not be deemed an offer for sale or an offer to sell such ABS registered or to be registered under the 1933 Act (referred to as Registered Securities), even though the broker or dealer is or will be a participant in the distribution of the Registered Securities, if the following conditions are met:

- The broker or dealer must have previously published or distributed with reasonable regularity information, opinions or recommendations relating to ABS[27] backed directly (or, with respect to securitizations of other securities, indirectly) by substantially similar collateral as that directly or indirectly backing the ABS that are the subject of the information, opinion or recommendation that is to be distributed.

- If the Registered Securities have not yet been offered or are part of an unsold allotment or subscription, the information, opinion or recommendation must not (a) identify the Registered Securities, (b) give greater prominence to specific structural or collateral-related attributes of the Registered Securities than it gives to the same attributes of other ABS that it mentions or (c) contain any ABS informational and computational material. Consistent with the 1997 no-action letter, the Proposing Release states that this condition is consistent with, and would not by itself prevent, the dissemination of a research piece that focuses on a single topic, such as

---

27. Rule 139a refers to the prior publication of research on ABS eligible to be registered on Form S-3. This may be a mistake, since there is no logical reason why the prior publication of research on ABS backed by similar collateral but not eligible to be registered on Form S-3 should not be part of the "track record" that the condition seeks to establish.

a single collateral attribute, collateral source, structural attribute or market sector.

- If the material published by the broker or dealer identifies a specific ABS of a specific issuer and specifically recommends that such ABS be purchased, sold or held by persons receiving such material, then a recommendation as favorable or more favorable as to such ABS must have been published by the broker or dealer in the last publication of such broker or dealer addressing such ABS prior to the commencement of its participation in the distribution of the Registered Securities. (PSA's 1997 request letter stated its understanding that this condition was limited to "exhortations to purchase, sell or hold a specific [ABS] of a specific issuer, not general comments regarding relative investment merits.")

- Sufficient information must be available from one or more public sources to provide a reasonable basis for the view expressed by the dealer with respect to the ABS that are the subject of the information, opinion or recommendation. (PSA's 1997 request letter stated that the purpose of this condition was to encourage broker-dealers to publish information, opinions or recommendations on ABS that are issued by entities affiliated with other broker-dealers.)

- If the material published by the broker or dealer identifies ABS backed directly or indirectly by substantially similar collateral as that directly or indirectly backing the Registered Securities and specifically recommends that such ABS be preferred over other ABS backed by different types of collateral, then the material must explain in reasonable detail the reasons for such preference.

Consistent with the position taken in the 1997 no-action letter, the Proposing Release states that in the case of a multitranche offering of ABS, each tranche would be treated as a different Registered Security.

The Proposing Release notes that the SEC staff is considering issues relating to research reports as part of its study of broader 1933 Act reform.

ASSET-BACKED SECURITIES 1019

- *Integration*

The principle of integration of separate securities offerings is discussed in Chapter 7. An issuer of a particular series of ABS containing multiple classes may often sell some classes publicly and some privately. Because classes that are rated below investment-grade cannot be sold under a shelf registration, they are often sold privately to avoid the time and expense of registering them under a stand-alone registration statement. Occasionally, a particular buyer requires that its purchase of a class be done on a private placement basis. Practitioners are virtually unanimous in the view that the differentiation of separate classes of a particular series of ABS, by virtue of their relative subordination, their expected maturity dates or any other substantive structural feature, is sufficient to avoid integration of any such classes even though all of the classes are sold at one time.

Integration concerns are sometimes also expressed when the prospectus for registered ABS describes lower-rated classes in the same transaction that are being offered on a private placement basis. The Proposing Release notes that the lower-rated classes may provide important structural support for the registered ABS and that a description of such classes "in this manner" would not raise general solicitation issues with respect to the private placement of the lower-rated classes.[28]

- *Due Diligence*

The due diligence review for an ABS offering must be tailored to the type of asset being securitized and the degree of future activity of the Sponsor (e.g., just servicing a static pool of assets *versus* also originating assets that will be transferred to the SPV from time to time after the issuance of the ABS). Such a review normally focuses on the following matters:

(i) the underwriting procedures of the Sponsor in originating the asset, including, if applicable, credit checks, appraisal and income verification;

---

28. Proposing Release at n.125.

(ii) the servicing procedures of the Originator/Servicer, including billing and collection methods, pursuit of delinquent accounts and realization on collateral;

(iii) compliance of documents creating the assets with applicable law, especially consumer protection laws;

(iv) proper licensing of the Sponsor; and

(v) procedures for perfecting a security interest in any collateral.

In the case of assets for which the Sponsor is not using form documents known to comply with local law (e.g., first mortgage documents developed by the Federal National Mortgage Association and the Federal Home Loan Mortgage Corporation), item (iii) is often verified by requiring local opinions of counsel as to such compliance in a representative number of states.

In connection with most securitizations, the underwriter normally requires a comfort letter from the registrant's accountants that reflects the following:

(i) specified procedures performed by the accountants pursuant to which information on the computer tape containing various information (e.g., interest rate, maturity date, type of collateral, etc.) about the underlying assets (from which tape (the so-called "pool tape") the information about the assets that appears in the prospectus is derived) is checked against the same information in the related loan files, and

(ii) (a) comparison of information in the prospectus about the assets to information on the pool tape and recomputation of such information, (b) comparison of loss, delinquency and, in some cases, prepayment information appearing in the prospectus to the records of the Sponsor and (c) recomputation of yield tables and tables showing declining principal balances of classes on the basis of various prepayment assumptions.

The procedures performed by the accountants will vary depending on the type of asset being securitized.

- *Rule 144A(d)(4) Information*

In transfers of privately placed ABS pursuant to Rule 144A, what information is to be provided in satisfaction of the minimum information condition found in Rule 144A(d)(4)? As discussed above, balance sheets and income statements are not relevant to an SPV. In the release that adopted Rule 144A, the SEC stated that the financial statements and other information specified in Rule 144A(d)(4) should be understood in the case of ABS "to mandate provision of basic, material information concerning the structure of the securities and distributions thereon, the nature, performance and servicing of the assets supporting the securities, and any credit enhancement mechanism associated with the securities."

It is also not immediately clear who the "issuer" is for purposes of the information requirement of Rule 144A(d)(4). In the same release, the SEC stated that the "issuer" in the case of ABS means for purposes of the information requirement "the servicer of the assets or trustee of the trust having title to the mortgage loans or other assets." Also, in connection with a 1990 interpretive letter,[29] the SEC staff was asked to approve an arrangement under which "the issuer (or Depositor of the trust issuer) will cause the trustee to deliver" the required information. The staff stated that it concurred with the view that paragraph (d)(4) of Rule 144A does not "preclude the parties by contract from identifying the person from whom . . . [the required information] may be obtained."

1934 Act Considerations

The current periodic reporting forms under the 1934 Act are not easily applied to ABS for the same reason that the current disclosure requirements under the 1933 Act are not easily applied. In response to this mismatch, the SEC and its staff have over the years issued exemptive orders and provided no-action relief to permit ABS issuers to file 1934 Act reports on a modified basis.

---

29. SEC No-action Letter, *Mortgage-Backed and Asset-Backed Securities—Securities Act Release No. 6862—The Rule 144A Release* (November 29, 1990).

For example, ABS issuers do not file quarterly reports on Form 10-Q. Rather, they file under cover of Form 8-K distribution reports that set forth the payments and performance of the assets in the pool and payments on the ABS. ABS issuers file a modified Form 10-K that consists principally of the servicer's statement of compliance with its servicing obligations and a report by an independent accountant regarding compliance with specified servicing criteria. ABS issuers are permitted to file a modified form of certification pursuant to Section 302 of Sarbanes–Oxley, and ABS issuers are exempt from the "internal control over financial reporting" requirements of Section 404 of Sarbanes–Oxley.

The Proposed Rules purport to codify the basic modified reporting system for ABS issuers. The key elements are as follows:

In lieu of continuing to use Form 8-K as the vehicle for filing distribution reports, the SEC would introduce a new Form 10-D for this purpose. The reports on Form 10-D would be required to be filed within 15 days after each required distribution date on the ABS as specified in the transaction documents. The Proposing Release states the SEC's belief that the Depositor or the servicer is in a better position than the trustee with respect to the possession, responsibility and awareness of the information called for by Form 10-D, and the SEC proposes that the Form 10-D be signed by the Depositor or servicer rather than by the trustee.

The Form 10-D would have to provide the information required by Item 1119 of Regulation AB and attach as an exhibit the distribution report delivered to the trustee or to the ABS holders pursuant to the transaction documents. Taken together, the Form 10-D and the distribution report must contain all the information required by Item 1119. That information would include (i) relevant flow of funds information, including fees and expenses, (ii) distributions accrued and paid on the ABS, (iii) the amount of excess cash flow or excess spread, (iv) beginning and ending principal balances of the ABS, (v) interest rates, if variable, (vi) beginning and ending balances of transactions accounts and account activity during the period, (vii) amounts drawn on any credit enhancement or other support, (viii) updated pool composition information, (ix) delinquency and loss information for the period, (x) breaches of material representations, warranties or covenants and (xi) information on new issuances of ABS backed by the same pool and on any pool asset additions, removals or substitutions, including whether there were any material changes in origination, acquisition or selection standards.

Form 8-K would specify which of its recently adopted "triggers" apply to ABS. These would include entering into or terminating a definitive agreement that is material to the ABS transaction, including an agreement to which the issuer is not a party (e.g., a servicing agreement) and other specified items. Some new ABS-relevant triggers would be added, including (i) the required filing of any ABS informational and computational material, (ii) any change of servicer or trustee, (iii) any change in credit enhancement or other external support, (iv) failure to make a required distribution, (v) sales of additional ABS backed by the same pool and (vi) any previously unreported variation of more than 5% in the composition of the pool between the time of issuance of the ABS and the description of the pool in the final Rule 424(b) prospectus. The Proposal Release states that the limited safe harbor for Rule 10b-5 liability would be available for a failure to report any change in credit enhancement or other external support, but not otherwise, and then only if the change were reported in the next Form 10-D. A late filing as to such a change would also not affect the Form S-3 eligibility of other ABS transactions established by the same Sponsor or Depositor so long as the Form 8-K reporting obligations are current at the time of a new filing.

Form 10-K would specify the disclosure requirements for ABS issuers, which would be based on Regulation AB, and codify the Section 302 Sarbanes–Oxley certification for ABS issuers. The issuer would respond to Items 4, 5, 9, 9B, 12 (portion) and 15 of Form 10-K, as well as specified items of Regulation AB.

The annual report on Form 10-K would continue to require a report of compliance with the servicing agreement. It will also include a report on compliance with specified servicing criteria. Because there are few existing criteria for evaluating servicing, and because the most widely used standards were designed to be applicable only to mortgages and may not be suitable for the full range of ABS servicing, the SEC is proposing its own disclosure-based servicing criteria that would form the basis for an assessment and assertion as to material compliance with such criteria (or disclosure as to non-compliance).

The requirement would also be continued of obtaining a public accountant attestation, which under the Proposed Rules would cover the new servicing criteria statement, and of including the attestation and the statement in the annual report on Form 10-K.

The certification required by Section 302 of Sarbanes–Oxley applies to Form 10-Ks filed by ABS issuers, but the SEC currently provides (and the Proposed Rules would continue to provide) for a form of certification that is tailored to the circumstances of ABS issuers. The Proposed Rules require the certification to be signed by the Depositor if the Depositor signs the report on Form 10-K or by the servicer if the servicer signs the report on behalf of the issuing entity.

An ABS registrant's 1934 Act reporting obligations are normally triggered by Section 15(d) of the 1934 Act. The Proposed Rules would codify a "longstanding interpretive position that no annual or other reports need be filed [by an ABS issuer] pursuant to Section 15(d) until the first bona fide sale in a takedown of securities under the registration statement."

Section 15(d) reporting obligations are automatically suspended if the ABS are held of record by fewer than 300 investors at the beginning of a fiscal year (other than the year of issuance). SEC Rule 15d-6 requires an issuer whose reporting obligations have been suspended to inform the SEC by filing a Form 15. Some issuers choose to continue to file reports notwithstanding the suspension of the obligation to do so.

Rule 10b-10(a)(7) requires broker-dealers to disclose in confirmations for transactions in ABS that the yield to the investor may vary according to the rate of principal prepayments on the underlying assets and that information as to minimum estimated yield, weighted average life and prepayment assumptions underlying yield will be furnished on written request.

As discussed in Chapter 3, Section 11(d)(1) of the 1934 Act prohibits the extension, or the arrangement for the extension, of credit by a broker or dealer on a security (other than an exempted security) which is part of a public distribution in which the broker or dealer participated as a selling member within 30 days prior to such credit transaction. The distribution continues with respect to a particular broker or dealer until it has sold its allotment of the security. The staff has taken a no-action position that in the context of the distribution of a multiclass issuance of ABS, each class of such ABS is a separate security for purposes of Section 11(d)(1).[30]

1940 Act Considerations

The definition of "investment company" in Section 3(a)(1) of the 1940 Act includes any person that is primarily engaged in the business of investing and reinvesting in securities, as well as any person engaged in the business (whether primarily or not) of investing in or holding investment securities (as defined) and more than 40% of whose assets consist of such investment securities. Assets that generate cash flow may, at least under certain circumstances, come within the definition of "security" in Section 2(a)(36) of the 1940 Act, which includes, among other items, evidences of indebtedness. In the SEC's view, the definition extends even to commercial and consumer loans. Consequently, absent an exemption, most SPVs that issue ABS would come within the definition of "investment company" in Section 3(a)(1) of the 1940 Act because their primary activity of acquiring and holding cash flow assets amounts to engaging in the business of investing in securities.

Registering an SPV as an investment company under the 1940 Act is not a practical possibility since the 1940 Act is a pervasive regulatory scheme that is incompatible with the operation of most types of entities other than true investment companies. For example, 1940 Act provisions would likely limit the ability of the Sponsor to engage in certain transactions with the SPV and, moreover, would limit the SPV's ability to issue ABS

---

30. SEC No-action Letter, *Bear, Stearns & Co. Inc.* (August 29, 1994).

at all because of restrictions on the ability of registered investment companies to issue debt.

Prior to the adoption of Rule 3a-7, SPVs issuing ABS relied on the exemptions provided in Section 3(c)(5) of the 1940 Act. These exemptions worked well for asset types within the terms of the exemption, so long as the assets were whole receivables of specified types (i.e., not participations or other fractional interests in the receivables). Early on in the securitization of mortgage loans, investment bankers began securitizing mortgage-backed securities guaranteed by government agencies. As long as the mortgage-backed security represented the whole pool of underlying mortgage loans, the SEC would apply the exemption by looking through the mortgage-backed security to the underlying whole mortgage loans. With limited exceptions, if the mortgage-backed security represented only a fractional interest in the pool of mortgage loans, then there was no look-through. If a majority of the mortgage-backed securities represented "whole pools," then, subject to certain other composition requirements developed by the SEC in various no-action letters, Section 3(c)(5)(C) was satisfied.

Assembling a majority of whole pools for a securitization was burdensome and expensive. Investment bankers obtained exemptive orders from the SEC exempting securitizations that did not satisfy the Section 3(c)(5)(C) test, but the process was time consuming and the orders had to be amended if a newly developed structure did not satisfy all of the conditions of the relevant order. In addition, new asset types that did not come within Section 3(c)(5) were continually being securitized. One such example was the securitization of credit card receivables. While Section 3(c)(5)(A) excludes from the 1940 Act issuers holding receivables and other obligations representing the sale of merchandise, insurance or services, the exclusion would not accommodate, for example, credit card cash advances.

The "private placement" exemption in Section 3(c)(1), which was historically the only alternative, is basically too confining. Section 3(c)(7) of the 1940 Act provides greater flexibility than Section 3(c)(1) in that it imposes a sophistication test as an alternative to a numerical limit on buyers. However, as discussed in Chapter 7, Section 3(c)(7) also permits only private placements.

ASSET-BACKED SECURITIES 1027

The SEC responded to this bottleneck in 1992 by adopting Rule 3a-7, which "was intended to exclude virtually all structured financings from the definition of investment company, subject to certain conditions."[31] An issuer (i.e., an SPV) that satisfies the conditions of the Rule will not be deemed to be an investment company. The Rule provides that:

- the issuer must acquire and hold "eligible assets" (described below), may engage in activities related thereto and must not issue redeemable securities. The definition of redeemable security has a long interpretive history starting with SEC staff interpretations under Section 3(c)(5);

- the issuer's securities must be paid primarily out of cash flow on its eligible assets;

- the issuer's fixed-income securities that are rated investment-grade may be sold to anyone; other types of its securities may only be sold to institutional accredited investors or qualified institutional buyers; "fixed-income" securities for this purpose are securities that have either a principal amount or, subject to certain limitations, provide for the payment of interest on a principal amount (which may be a notional amount) or any combination of such features;

- the issuer may acquire and dispose of its eligible assets only in accordance with the documents governing its securities and only if such dispositions are not made for the purpose of recognizing gains and decreasing losses resulting from changes in market value (i.e., no active management of the issuer's assets as would be typical of an investment company); and

- except in the case of an issuer of commercial paper exempt pursuant to Section 3(a)(3) of the 1933 Act, a non-affiliated trustee meeting the requirements of

---

31. SEC Release No. IC-19105 (November 19, 1992). As will be discussed in the text, the SEC staff has more recently interpreted Rule 3a-7 in a relatively restrictive fashion. Thus, Section 3(c)(5) is still sometimes used as a basis for an exemption when it is available.

Section 26(a)(1) of the 1940 Act must be appointed and receive a perfected security interest or ownership interest in the eligible assets.

The definition of "eligible assets" in Rule 3a-7 is quite similar to the definition of "financial assets" in current Form S-3. With respect to the requirement that eligible assets "by their terms convert into cash within a finite period of time," the SEC staff has taken no-action positions that cumulative preferred stock[32] and auction rate preferred stock[33] do not satisfy this requirement. As a related matter, the securities issued by the SPV must, as indicated above, be based on the cash flow from eligible assets. Securities whose payments derived from changes in the market value of such assets do not qualify.

As with financial assets under current Form S-3, eligible assets include rights and assets designed to ensure the servicing or timely distribution of proceeds to securityholders. This language picks up credit and liquidity enhancements, cash flow enhancements and collateral securing the cash flow asset.[34]

The SEC takes the position that an issuer relying on Rule 3a-7 may only engage in acquiring and holding eligible assets (and in activities related thereto).[35] Consequently, an issuer cannot hold both eligible assets and "hard" assets unless the hard assets are ancillary or incidental to holding the eligible assets, although an issuer holding only hard assets would not be an investment company.

As noted above, the Proposed Rules expand the definition of ABS to include securitizations backed by leases where part of the cash flows backing the ABS is to come from the disposal of the residual asset underlying the lease. The Proposed Rules do not extend to Rule 3a-7. Indeed, the Proposing Release states specifically that the application of the 1940 Act to ABS transactions is

---

32. SEC No-action Letter, *Brown & Wood* (February 24, 1994).

33. SEC No-action Letter, *Donaldson, Lufkin & Jenrette Securities Corp.* (September 23, 1994).

34. SEC Release IC-19105 (November 19, 1992).

35. SEC No-action Letter, *Citicorp Securities Inc.* (August 4, 1995); SEC Release IC-19105 (November 19, 1992).

beyond its scope. It does confirm, however, that "an ABS transaction that relies on Rule 3a-7 must comply with the conditions of that rule regardless of whether the issuer may register the offering of its asset-backed securities on Form S-3 or S-1." The Proposing Release encourages pre-filing conferences with the SEC staff to discuss questions or issues that may arise regarding the availability of Rule 3a-7 or other exemptions under the 1940 Act.

Some issuers of ABS create classes that may be purchased by money market funds pursuant to Rule 2a-7 of the 1940 Act, a complex SEC rule that governs the operations of such funds. The remaining maturity of a class of ABS eligible for purchase by a money market fund may not exceed 397 days (computed from the trade date rather than from the settlement date). In addition, the securities must be rated in one of the two highest short-term rating categories or, in the case of ABS having only a long-term rating, be of comparable quality to securities having such a short-term rating. In order to "shorten" the remaining term of a floating rate or variable rate ABS, the issuer may structure the security with a demand feature that allows the securityholder to give notice and thereafter unconditionally receive, at a time not later than 397 days after such notice, its unamortized cost for the security plus accrued interest. In some cases, the demand feature is a put right issued by a third party; in other cases, it is a right to commence receiving principal distributions from collections on the issuer's underlying assets, which collections, in the absence of the exercise of the demand feature, would be applied by the issuer to purchase new underlying assets. The credit of the provider of a third-party demand feature also may be used to satisfy the Rule's rating requirements if certain conditions are met.

Money market funds must also satisfy certain issuer diversification requirements in Rule 2a-7. In general, the issuer of an ABS is the related SPV. Under certain circumstances, however, the issuer of certain of the assets underlying the ABS may be the issuer for purposes of the diversification determination.[36]

---

36. Rule 2a-7(c)(4)(vi)(A)(4).

Other Considerations

- *Bankruptcy*

Most rated securitizations are structured so that the insolvency of the Sponsor will not interrupt the distribution of the cash flow from the underlying assets to the securityholders. In the context of a Sponsor subject to the Bankruptcy Code, this means that the underlying assets must not be part of the Sponsor's bankruptcy estate pursuant to Section 541(a) of the Bankruptcy Code. If the assets were part of the bankruptcy estate, the cash flow from the assets would be subject to the automatic stay provisions of Section 362 of the Bankruptcy Code, therefore delaying distributions to the securityholders for some period of time. In rated securitizations, the rating agencies usually[37] require a "true sale" legal opinion to the effect that the assets will not be part of the bankruptcy estate of the Sponsor.[38]

As noted above, the Sponsor often transfers the assets to the Depositor, which in turn transfers the assets to the SPV. The true sale opinion is often given only as to the transfer from the Sponsor to the Depositor, since the Depositor may retain some subordinated interest in the SPV, which may be viewed as a retention of recourse on the assets and, if large enough, make it difficult to give a true sale opinion as to the transfer from the Depositor to the SPV. In many cases, the rating agencies

---

37. In the case of transfers by banks, which are not subject to the Bankruptcy Code, the rating agencies require an opinion that the transfer is either (i) a sale, (ii) a transfer for security, with the resulting security interest being a perfected, first priority security interest or (iii) a transaction covered by a rule of the Federal Deposit Insurance Corporation (12 C.F.R. §360.6) to the effect that the FDIC, as conservator or receiver, will not treat property as part of the depository institution's estate if it has been transferred in a securitization that satisfies certain conditions. In the view of the rating agencies, in such a case the insolvency proceedings applicable to banks will not interrupt cash flow distributions to securityholders.

38. If such an opinion could not be given, the ABS might well not be rated higher than the credit rating of the Sponsor, thus defeating one of the main purposes of a securitization—namely, achieving a higher credit rating for the ABS and a correspondingly lower cost of funds for the transaction.

ASSET-BACKED SECURITIES

also require an opinion to the effect that a bankruptcy court would not substantively consolidate the assets of the Depositor with the bankruptcy estate of the Sponsor, which would have the effect of nullifying any true sale to the Depositor by pulling the assets back into the estate of the Sponsor and therefore subjecting them to the automatic stay.

Both the Depositor and the SPV issuer of the ABS are normally "bankruptcy-remote" in that they have no liabilities that are not related to the ABS and are therefore not likely to enter into bankruptcy.

The absence of controlling court decisions on when a "true sale" has occurred in the context of an ABS transaction led Congress recently to consider creating a legislative safe harbor defined by objective criteria under which certain ABS-related transfers would not be included within a debtor's bankruptcy estate. Unfortunately, the legislation became tarred with the Enron brush and was not enacted.

- *Accounting Issues*

As noted at the outset of this Chapter, many ABS transactions are premised on the ability of the Sponsor to remove the securitized assets and related debt from its balance sheet. The FASB's issuance in 2003 of FIN 46R has created significant uncertainties about the proper accounting for some ABS structures.

- *Tax Issues*

The SPV is normally structured so as not to be subject to tax. Any tax at the SPV level could erode the cash flow from the assets so that securityholders would not receive the amounts due to be distributed to them. Special, complex federal income tax laws such as the REMIC legislation have been enacted to provide tax treatment pursuant to which there will not be a tax at the SPV level. The offering materials will discuss these tax considerations at length.

- *1939 Act*

If publicly offered ABS are in the form of notes, the notes must be issued pursuant to an indenture qualified under the 1939 Act unless an exemption is available. If the ABS are in the form of pass-through or other certificates evidencing an interest in a trust that is acting as the SPV, the governing agreement for the certificates need not be qualified under the 1939 Act because either (i) the certificates will be equity securities (i.e., they merely evidence an interest in the trust that entitles them to receive cash distributions to the extent of collections on the underlying assets and there is no default mechanism) or (ii) if the trust contains more than one underlying asset, the exemption in Section 304(a)(2) of the 1939 Act for "any certificate of interest or participation in two or more securities having substantially different rights and privileges" is applicable.

- *SMMEA*

The Secondary Mortgage Market Enhancement Act[39] was enacted in 1984 to improve the marketability of "mortgage related-securities." A mortgage-related security, as defined in Section 3(a)(41) of the 1934 Act, must be rated in one of the top two investment grades and be supported by cash flows from first lien mortgages on real estate on which is located a residential or commercial structure (including manufactured housing that is personal property under state law and stock allocated to a dwelling unit in a residential cooperative housing corporation). The underlying mortgage loans must be originated by certain lenders subject to governmental supervision. A mortgage-backed security that otherwise qualifies as a mortgage-related security but is backed in part by a prefunding account will not be a mortgage-related security until the prefunding account has been entirely disbursed.

The SMMEA legislation made mortgage-related securities legal investments for institutional investors otherwise limited by law as to their investments to the same extent that obligations issued or guaranteed as to principal and interest by the United States are authorized investments under such laws. Such legal investment status could be overridden by states prior to October 4, 1991, and 21 states did so to some extent. In addition, SMMEA increased the ability of federally chartered Depository institutions to

---

39. P.L. No. 98-440, 98 Stat. 1689.

purchase mortgage-related securities. It also preempted the application of the registration provisions under state securities laws to the extent such provision was not overridden by a state prior to October 4, 1991.

- *Legal Investment Considerations*

Absent the legal investment preemption in SMMEA, the legal investment authority for regulated institutions investing in ABS is often unclear. If the ABS are pass-through securities, the investor may sometimes look through to the underlying assets and determine whether it can invest in such assets. If the securities are notes, many legal investment laws require the satisfaction of historical debt coverage ratios, which may be impossible in the case of a newly formed SPV. Many regulated institutions may have to rely on "basket" clauses to establish legality.

- *Preemption of State Securities Registration*

As amended by the Improvement Act, Section 18 of the 1933 Act exempts "covered securities" from the registration provisions of state securities laws. While ABS are not within the definition of covered securities, any securities sold to "qualified purchasers" will be covered securities. The SEC is given the authority to define qualified purchasers, and in late 2001 it proposed (but has not yet adopted) a definition based on the definition of "accredited investor" in Regulation D under the 1933 Act.

The House Commerce Committee report on the bill that became the Improvement Act states that the committee expected the SEC to craft regulations for qualified purchasers that would implement Congress' intention that ABS and other structured offerings be regulated exclusively by the federal government.[40] Without a federal definition of qualified purchasers, however, sales of ABS must rely on institutional or investment-grade exemptions provided by state law.

---

40. H.R. Report No. 104-622, 104th Cong., 2d Sess. at 31 (1996).

- *Underwriting*

ABS underwriting practices have been spared the scandals associated in recent years with corporate underwritings, particularly IPOs. An industry group, the American Securitization Forum, has nevertheless recommended "minimum standards" and "best practices" for ABS underwriters.[41]

- *NASD Considerations*

Publicly offered ABS rated in one of the top four rating categories are not subject to the filing requirements of the NASD's Corporate Financing Rule discussed in Chapter 6.[42] Even if the Depositor and one of the underwriters are affiliates, the QIU and other requirements of the NASD's Rule 2720 do not apply if the ABS being distributed is rated in one of the four highest rating categories.[43]

---

41. The recommendations are at the organization's website at www.americansecuritization.com/docs/ABS_Synd_Best_Practice.pdf.

42. NASD Conduct Rule 2710(b)(7)(E).

43. NASD Conduct Rule 2720(b)(1)(C)(v).

Index

[References are to page numbers.]

A

AAU. *See* Agreement among underwriters
Abbreviated registration forms
  F-2, 18, 741, 742
  F-3, 14, 18, 204, 205, 502, 561-563, 585, 586, 591, 594, 597, 603, 605, 606, 609, 622, 635, 636, 638, 645, 689, 741, 742, 746, 750, 856, 885, 886, 895, 1000, 1005
  F-6, 591, 711, 720, 721, 729, 743
  S-2, 17, 127, 128, 129, 130, 131, 204, 742
  S-3, 14, 17, 99, 121, 127, 128-131, 143, 192, 204, 205, 214, 268, 330, 346, 372, 402, 554, 561-563, 582-586, 591, 594, 595, 597, 598, 599, 600, 603, 605, 609, 622, 633, 635-638, 641, 644, 645, 689, 742, 842, 856, 882, 885, 886, 895, 898, 905, 906, 984, 989, 993, 994, 995, 996, 997, 998, 1000, 1005, 1013, 1017, 1023, 1028, 1029
  S-16 (rescinded), 17, 587, 606, 633, 648, 905, 906
"A/B" exchange offer, 555, 880
ABN AMRO Financial Services, Inc., 839
ABS, 506
Acceleration of effectiveness of registration statement, 18, 401

Accounting support fees (PCAOB), 93
Accounting treatment
  asset-backed securities, 1031
  comfort letters, 104, 367, 1020
  deep discount and zero coupon obligations, 659
  derivatives, 362
  due diligence, 351
  expertizing of selected financial data, 313
  GAAP, 659
    continuous offering of medium-term notes, 528
    foreign issue financial statement, 734
    Rule 144A transactions, 510, 511
    Schedule B, 764
  liabilities, 308, 312
Accounts receivable
  commercial paper current transaction test, 787, 793
Accredited investor, 482–493, 518, 519, 526, 529
  defined, 490
  institutional accredited investor, 492, 494
  sophistication of, 493
Acquisitions. *See also* Arbitrage; Merger
  financing, commercial paper current transaction test, 801
  and leveraged buyouts, 660

restricted period, 259
and Rule 145, 40
shelf registrations covering, 566
Actions
for damages, 308, 314
for rescission, 815, 817
Adjustable rate debt securities. *See*
Convertible securities; Notes
Adjustable rate preferred stock. *See*
Preferred stock
ADR. *See* American depositary receipts
ADS. *See* American depositary receipts
ADTV, 922
calculation of, 269
defined, 268
test, 879, 880, 890
ADTV security
defined, 268
Advertising, 133. *See also* Gun-jumping
commercial paper, 782
global offerings, 756
private offerings, 481, 487
Regulation S, 688
road shows, electronic and
otherwise, 191
tombstone, 37
unregistered distribution securities,
672
Advisory Committee on the Capital
Formation and Regulatory
Processes, 61
Affiliate
affiliated purchaser, 257, 293
defined, 419
to issuer of asset-backed securities,
1014, 1034
obligor, 1003
purchases by, 931
resale safe harbor, 704
and Rule 144, 47
Affiliated broker-dealers, 29
Affiliated Fund, Inc., 446
Affiliated purchasers, 257, 293
African Development Bank, 51, 698
After-market transactions, 25
after-market purchases, 250, 251

Agent dealer as, 520
medium-term notes, 639–642
remarketing, 853, 854
Agreement among underwriters
(AAU), 71
authority to borrow, 82
calamity or crisis, termination in
event of, 114
claims against underwriters, 83
discussion, 71
disruptions of market, 114, 115
exculpation of manager, 84
first-day market orders in IPOs,
proposed restrictions, 76
indemnification provisions, 84,
111, 112
hostilities, pending or threatened, 114
internal counsel, opinion
responsibility of, 101, 102
legal work, division of responsibility,
101–103
manager's authority, 74
market out provision, 115
miscellaneous provisions, 84
NASD provisions, 83, 454
outside counsel, opinion
responsibility of, 101, 102
overallotment and stabilization
authority, 77
payment and delivery, 82
penalty clause, 79
"pot" sales, 75
price maintenance, 74
retention and "pot" sales, 75
returned shares, 76
settlement of syndicate accounts, 85
shares returned to underwriters, 76
shelf registration, 618
stabilization, 279
termination of price and other
restrictions, 85
trading restrictions, 78
underwriters' questionnaire, 73
underwriting agreement, 86
Agriculture, Department of, 829
AICPA, 370

INDEX

Aircraft Carrier Release, 30, 31, 33, 61, 62, 196, 208, 506, 690, 989
  safe harbor rules, 31
Alcohol or repeal stocks, 234
Allen, Chancellor, 973
All-holders requirement, 931, 935
Allied Chemical Corporation, 571
Allied-Signal, Inc., 972
Allocations, of securities to underwriters, 75
Alloyd Co., Inc. case, 314
Alternative trading system (ATS), 921
Amendments
  post-effective, 593, 602–606, 614, 637
  prospectus, 27
  to registration statements, 97, 602
American Bar Association, 989
  due diligence report, 306
  Federal Regulation of Securities Committee of the Section on Business Law, 306
  review of innovative financial products, 827
American Council of Life Insurance, no-action letter, 653
American depositary receipts (ADRs), 56, 515, 715, 719, 720, 845
  BP global offering, 753
  defined, 713
  facilities, types and status of, 717, 740
  global offerings, 749
  Form F-6, 501, 720
  Form S-12, 601, 720
  1933 Act status of ADR facilities, 717
  1934 Act amendments, foreign issuer exemption, 740
  registration of, 56
  rights offerings, 744
  Rule 144A, 514, 515
  shelf registration, 563
  types of ADR facilities, 715
American International Franchises, Inc., 476
American Life Insurance Company of New York, 217
American Marietta, 565, 567

American Stock Exchange (AMEX), 137, 138, 472, 566, 576, 577, 886, 889
American Securitization Forum, 1034
Analysts. *See also* Research
  presentations to, 134
  role in securities offerings, 146
Andrews, Kurth, Campbell & Jones, 388
Annual reports
  and gun-jumping, 134
  during registration process, 134
  at road shows, 192
Anti-dilution provisions, 870, 877, 895
  exchangeable security, 881
Antifraud provisions of securities laws
  early redemption of debt, 943
  remedies, commercial paper liabilities on default, 816
  short tendering, 938
  tender offers, 931
Anti-manipulation provisions, 299. *See also* Manipulative practices
Anti-rebate rules of stock exchanges, 445
Antitrust
  fixed price offerings in underwriting agreement, 86
  investment banking industry and, 68, 86
Anti-underwriter precautions, 493
A.P. Montgomery & Co., Inc., 297
Arbitrage, 978, 979
  event arbitrage, 975
  no-action letter, 976
  program funding, commercial paper current transaction test, 795
  risk arbitrage, 975
  and when-issued trading, 975
Archer Daniels Midland Company case, 942
Arning, John
  and Penn Central offering, 378
Arvida Corporation, 375
Asian Development Bank Act, 51, 697–698
  asset-backed securities, 56
  accounting issues, 1031

bankruptcy, 1030
basic structure, 987, 988, 990
classes of assets, 992
commercial paper, 992
conventional securitizations, 990
defined, 987, 994
delinquent assets, 995
disclosure requirements, 1000
  challenges, 993
  credit enhancement and other support, 1003
  pool assets, 1002, 1003
  servicers, 1002
  significant obligors of pool assets, 1003
  sponsors, 1001
  SPV (issuing entity), 1002
  structure of transaction, 1003
  third-party financial information, presenting, 1004
elements of, 988
issuers, as investment company, 809
legal investment considerations, 1033
NASD considerations, 1034
new asset classes, 992, 993
  1933 Act considerations, 993
  applicable form, 993
  computational materials, 1006
  credit enhancement, 1003
  disclosure requirements, 1000
  due diligence, 1019
  electronic media, availability of materials through, 1013
  Form S-1, 997
  Form S-3, 997
  informational materials, 1006
  integration, 1019
  loan files, access to, 1011
  market-maker prospectuses, 1014
  offering materials, 1006
  post-offering delivery requirements, 1013
  prefunding accounts, 996, 1032
  prospectus delivery considerations, 1012
  registrant, 993
  registration of underlying pool assets, 998
  research materials, 1015
  resecuritization, 999
  Rule 144A(d)(4) information, 1021
  underlying pool assets, registration of, 998
1934 Act considerations, 1021
1939 Act considerations, 1031
1940 Act considerations, 1025
non-performing assets, 995
other considerations, 1030
pool of assets, 995, 996
  disclosure requirements, 1002, 1003
  obligors of, 1003
  registration of underlying assets, 998
preemption of state securities registration, 1033
prefunded securitization, 996
proposed new and amended rules, 989
registration, disclosure, and reporting requirements, 989
Secondary Mortgage Market Enhancement Act (SNMEA), 1032
size and importance of market, 988
tax issues, 1031
timing of principal payments, 987
transfer of assets, 988
underwriting, 1034
vs. other debt securities, 987, 988
Associates Corp. of North America, 638
ATS. *See* Alternative trading system (ATS)
At-the-market equity offerings, 628, 635, 641, 644
Attorneys. *See* Lawyers
Auction, Dutch. *See* Preferred stock
Auction, electronic, 179
Audit committee, 334, 340
Auditors. *See* Accounting treatment
Average daily trading volume (ADTV), 147, 148
Avon Products, Inc., 891
Avis, 227

INDEX

B

Backup withholding, 710
Bahamas, 712
Balance of Payments Release
 No. 33-4708, 669, 674, 708
Bangor & Aroostook Railroad, 327
Bangor-Punta Corp., 327
Bank. *See also* Foreign banks;
 Investment banking;
 Qualified institutional buyer
 bankers' acceptance
  exemption from registration and
  prospectus delivery, 778
 bank holding companies
  commercial paper current
  transaction test, 789, 794
 bank securities, 1933 Act
  exemptions, 54–55
 bank support exemption, commercial
  paper, 805
 as investment company, 810
 as QIB, 503
Bank lines, 527, 528
Bank of America, 839, 994, 1000
Bank of Boston Corp, 802
Bank of England, 755
Bank of New York (BONY), 714, 839,
 856, 857, 858, 862
Bankruptcy, 616
 asset-backed securities, 1030
 deep discount or zero coupon
  obligation, 659
 exemption, 60
Bankruptcy Code, 850
 reorganization under, 60
Bankruptcy-remote, 1031
BarChris case, 323, 328, 335, 380, 628
BarChris Construction Corp., 340
Barrett & Company, 240
Basel Accord, 840
Basket transactions, 273, 1033
Bateman Eichler, Hill Richards,
 Incorporated, 539
BCI Holdings Corporation, 974
Beaman, Middleton, 4, 462

Bearer obligations, 706
Beating the gun. *See* Gun-jumping
Bent, Maury 386
Berenger case, 238
Berkshire Hathaway, 869
Berle, A.A. Jr., 239
Bespeaks caution doctrine, 170, 310, 319
Best efforts offering underwriting
 documents, 66
Best-price requirement, 931, 935
Better Business Bureau, 420
Bevan, David, 376
Beverly Hills Hotel, 388
Beverly Wilshire Hotel, 388
Bidding, competitive
 Public Utility Holding Company Act
 of 1935, 119
Black Box no-action letter, 547
Black Monday. *See* Crash
Blackout periods, 914
 on research reports, 207
Blind pool offering, 210
Block purchases, 923
Block trades, 922, 923
 Trading Practice Rules, 251, 252, 953
 shelf registration, 648, 649
 Trading Practice Rules, short sales,
 925
Bloomberg, 506, 951, 1006
Bloomberg reports, 200
Blue sky laws
 blue sky survey by underwriter, 126
 exchange offers, 963
 first enactment in Kansas, 3
 private offerings, 495
 public offering registration
  exemptions, 137
 Regulation D, 495
 stock exchange listing, 137, 138
 underwriting agreement covenants, 97
Board of directors
 due diligence, 324
 shelf registration authorization, 617
Bobker case, 939
Boeing, 839
Bond Market Association, 559, 776, 1016

Bonds. *See also* Notes
  Eurobonds, 707, 829
  high yield
    exchange, debt restructurings, 941
    industrial development, 52
  Moody's Bond Record
    medium-term notes, shelf
      registration, 639
  mortgage bond prospectus,
    798, 799
  municipal, 51
Book-entry system,
  commercial paper, 777
Book-runners
  joint book-runners, 71
Borden Chemicals and Plastics Limited
  Partnership, 90
Borrowing authority, underwriting
  agreement, 82
Bought deals
  shelf registration, 612, 646
Bourse, 678
Bowie, David, 992
Bretton Woods Agreements Act, 51
Bring downs, 552
British Petroleum Company Limited,
  749, 753
Broker-dealer
  affiliated broker-dealers, 29
  asset-backed securities, 1014,
    1018, 1024
  calls for redemptions to force
    conversions, 903
  commercial paper, 771, 772, 776,
    792, 793, 814, 821, 822, 823
  dealer-manager plan
    rights offerings, 986
  dealer's exemption, 28, 43
  as distribution participants, 257
  exchange offer, 962
  fees, arbitrage and when-issued
    trading, 977
  foreign securities, 740
  hot issue sales, 428
  innovative financing techniques, key
    questions, 827, 828
  as investment company, 809
  joint back office (JBO) broker-dealer,
    432
  limited business broker-dealer, 433
  MTN program documentation, 634
  not underwriter, 203
  as prospective underwriters, 257
  QIBs, 502
  quotations, Regulation S, 689
  rights offerings, 986
  shelf registration, 646, 647, 655
  short sales by, 925
  when-issued trading and arbitrage,
    975
  written confirmation, 22
Brokers' search letter, 933
Brown, Scott v., 238
Brown, United States v., 238, 240
Brown & Wood letter, 30
Bruns, Nordeman case, 252, 253
Buckeye Pipeline Corporation, 375
Bulky documents
  review of, 353
Business prospects, 113
Byrnes case, 23

C

Call options. *See* Options
Calls for redemption to force
  conversions, 902, 902
Canada, 436, 715, 723, 725, 897
  Montreal, commercial paper
    exemption, 803
  multijurisdictional disclosure system,
    740
  subscription offers, 745
Cantor Fitzgerald, 951
Capital formation. *See* Advisory
  Committee on the Capital Formation
  and Regulatory Processes; Securities
  Act Concepts and Their Effects on
  Capital formation
Capsule business description
  prospectus, 145

INDEX 1041

Carl M. Loeb, Rhoades & Co.,
  et al., 32
Carter, Judge, 302
Carter Hawley Hale Stores, Inc., 916
Carter Organization, The, 959
Cary, William J., 577
Cash-settled securities, 890. *See also*
  Convertible securities
Cash tender offer. *See* Tender offer
Castro, Fidel, 113
Catalyst Energy Corporation, 968, 971
Caterpillar, Inc., 164, 340, 839
Cat Money Market Account, 839
CATS. *See* Certificates; Stripped
  Treasury obligations
Cayman Islands, 844
CBOE. *See* Chicago Board Option
  Exchange
CEA. *See* Commodity Exchange Act
Celanese AG, 715
Certificate loan, 979
Certificates. *See also* Equipment trust
  certificates
  asset-backed securities, 1032
  Certificates of Accrual on Treasury
    Securities (CATS), 846
  certification requirement
    TEFRA D issuer sanctions, 706,
      707, 710
  equipment trust, 57
  global certificates, 106
  mortgage pass-through, 884
  of deposit, 57. *See also* Indexed debt
    instruments
    commercial paper current
      transaction test, 794
    sale by Merrill Lynch, 10
  of designation
    redemption of preferred
      stock, 942
  of incorporation
    preferred stock shelf program, 617
  of interest, issuer defined, 994
  officers' certificate, 103
Certificates of Accrual on Treasury
  Securities (CATS) program, 846

CFMA. *See* Commodity Futures
  Modernization Act of 2000
CFTC. *See* Commodity
Chancellor of the exchequer, British
  Petroleum offering, 755
Change in size of deal, 208
Change of circumstances doctrine, 474,
  475
Channel stuffing, 361
Charitable organizations, securities
  exempt, 60
Checklists
  and due diligence, 337
Chemical Bank, 381
Chicago Board Options Exchange
  (CBOE), 925, 927
Chicago Mercantile Exchange, 829
Chill practice (DTC), 698
China, People's Republic of, public
  offering, 763, 765
Chinese Walls, 218
Chris-Craft case, 326
Chris-Craft Industries, 35
Chrysler, 715
CIT, 839
Citicorp, 582
Civil liabilities. *See* Liabilities
Claims
  against underwriters, 83
Clapman, Peter C., 677
Clark, Justice, 470, 471
Clark Equipment Credit
  Company, 638
Clean cash, 944
Clearing organizations, 829
Clearstream, 698
Cleary, Gottlieb, 976, 978
Clemenceau, 354
Closed-end investment companies and
  Rule 415, 645
Closing
  underwriting agreement provisions,
    101, 106
Co-cos, 870
Cohen, Benjamin V., 4, 462
Cohen, Manuel F., 46, 565, 567, 572

Cohen, Milton H., 16
Collateral
　shelf registration, 573
Collateralized Debt Obligation (CDO), 844, 998
College Retirement Equities Fund (CREF), 677, 678, 746, 748
Collins Radio Corporation, 875
Columbia Gas Plan, 986
C.O.M.B. Co., 301–304, 919
Comcast, 873
Comfort letter
　due diligence, 367
　negative assurance, 104
　negotiation of, 367
　review, multiple layers of, 105
　securitization, 1020
　underwriting agreement, 104
Comment letters on registration statements, 188
Commercial activity
　defined, under FSIA, 764, 765
Commercial Credit Company, 638
Commercial paper. *See also* Investment
　accounts receivable, financing of, 787
　acquisition financing, 801
　asset-backed, 992, 1027
　backed by surety bond, 807
　bank holding companies, lending activities of, 789
　bank support exemption, 805
　bare bones offering documents, 817, 819
　book-entry, 777
　broker-dealer operations, financing of, 792
　capacity, 784
　construction financing, interim, 796
　continuous offering procedures, 516
　continous private placement programs, 808
　credit quality, 776
　current transaction test, 783, 784. *See also* Current transaction test
　dealers' role, 776
　default, 779
　　liabilities on. *See* liabilities on default, *this heading*
　defined, 769
　denominations, 781, 782
　discount, 771, 783
　exempt securities, 54
　extendible commercial paper, 527, 528
　finance company receivables, carrying of, 789
　foreign banks, lending activities of, 789
　foreign governmental entities, financing by, 802
　integration with private offering, 524
　interim construction financing, 796
　inventories, financing of, 787
　issuer's repurchase of securities, 802
　leasing and related activities, financing of, 790
　lending activities of U.S. bank holding companies and foreign banks, 789
　liabilities on default, 813
　　antifraud remedies, 816
　　Rule 10b-5, 819, 822
　　Section 12(a)(1), 814
　　Section 12(a)(2), 814, 817
　market characteristics, 771
　maturity, 771, 779
　mechanics of, 777
　money market obligations, investments in, 794
　1933 Act considerations, 778
　　SEC Release 33-4412, 779, 780
　　Section 3(a)(2) bank support exemption, 54, 55, 805
　　Section 3(a)(3) exemption, 778
　　Section 4(2) continuous private placement programs, 808
　1940 Act considerations, 809
　　finance subsidiaries, 811
　　foreign banks and insurance companies, 810

INDEX

no-action letters, role of, 787
nuclear fuel financing, 799
operating expenses, payment of, 788
"orderly exit," 773
prime quality standard, 779
public offerings, 780
public utility operations, financing of, 798
repurchase of securities by issuer, 802
restricted commercial paper, 523, 527
restricted program, 808
rollover, 779
SEC Release 33-4412, 779, 780
Section 4(2) continuous private placement program, 808
Commodity
  commodity futures contract. *See* Futures contract
  defined, 829
  hybrid instrument rules, 832
  jurisdiction over indexed debt instruments, 830
  commodity option, hybrid instruments. *See* Indexed debt instruments
Common enterprise, as element of definition of investment contract, 10
Commodity Exchange Act (CEA), 541, 828, 829, 830, 831, 832, 833, 834
  regulation under, 828
    evolution of regulatory structure, 829
Commodity Futures Modernization Act of 2000 (CFMA), 11, 831
  bank products, traditional, 834
  derivative transactions
    excluded transactions, 831
    exempt commodities, transactions in, 833
  hybrid instruments, 832
  preemption, state law, 834
  SEC-CFTC jurisdiction, 830, 831
  state law preemption, 834
  swap transactions
    excluded transactions, 833

traditional bank products, 834
Treasury amendment, 831
Common stock
  equity securities, offering of, 514
  fair market price, 455
  liabilities on default, 813
  and mandatorily convertible securities, 890
    exchange for another company's common stock, 892
    into company's own common stock, 891
  Rule 144A offering of equity securities, 514
  shelf registration, 561, 566, 643
Commonwealth Edison Company case, 942
Communications. *See also* Gun-jumping
  exchange offer, 960
  offering process, communications during, 30
    communications not deemed a prospectus, 36
  timing of, 33
  websites, 132–133
    website or Internet, 132
Communications Satellite Corporation, 176
Companies Act, England, 4
Compensation
  excessive compensation, 412, 439
  NASD rules, 403, 439
  underwriters, 81, 408
Competitive bidding
  Public Utility Holding Company Act of 1935, 119
  and Trading Practice Rules, 256, 257
  and stabilization, 279–283
Comptroller of the Currency
  exempt securities, 56
ConAgra Inc., 300–304
Conditional dealer undertakings. *See* Notes
Conditional offer to buy, 176

Conduct rules, 83, 116. *See also* Rules of Fair Practice; National Association of Securities Dealers
Confidential documents
 review of, 353
Confidentiality
 correspondence to/from SEC staff, 190
 foreign issuers, registration statement filing, 731, 743
 request, 185
Confirmation
 prospectus delivery, 21
Conflicts of interest, 146–147
Consent
 global consents, 216
 informed consent, means of obtaining, 216
 revocation of, 216, 217
 solicitations, 968
Consent solicitation, 969
Consolidated Edison Company of New York, 117, 798, 801
Construction financing
 commercial paper current transaction test, 796
Consumer loans. *See* Loans
Continental Tobacco Company, 476
Contingently convertible securities, 870
Continuous offerings, 486
 procedures, 516
Continuous private placement programs, 516
 continuous offering procedures, restricted commercial paper, 516
 continuous offering procedures, restricted MTNs, 528
 integration, 524
Continuous reporting
 under 1934 Act, 737
  exiting the continuous reporting system, 739
Contribution
 indemnification, underwriting agreement, 107

Control
 control person
  affiliate of the issuer, 919
  borrowing stock from, 978
  defined, 320
  issuer, deemed as, 884
 defined, 46–47
Controls and procedures
 private offerings, 541
Convertible securities, 867. *See also* Common stock; Debentures; Exchange; Exchangeable securities; Preferred stock
 calls for redemptions to force conversions, 902
 lay-offs, 908
 1933 Act considerations, 905
 Regulation M, and redemptions, 908
 standby arrangements, 904
 cash on conversion, 874
 conversion price, 869
 current return, 867
 equity kicker, 865
 vs. exchangeable securities, 880. *See also* Exchangeable securities
 listing, 894
 LYONs, 868
 M&A transactions, 874
 mandatorily convertible or exchangeable or cash-settled securities, 890
 disclosure, 893
 due diligence, 894
 equity kicker, 865
 equity-linked notes, cash-settled, 893
 exchange for another company's common stock, 892
 into company's own common stock, 891
 listing, 894
 1933 Act registration, 892
 1934 Act issues, 878
 puts by holder, 873
 redemption, 874

INDEX

Rule 144A, 893
  third-party monetizations
    (STRYPES), 894
  1933 Act considerations, 875, 905
  1934 Act issues, 878
  puts by holder, 873
  redemption, 874
  Regulation S issuer safe harbor
    and, 702
  Rule 144A convertible securities, 880
  stock on conversion, 874
Cooke, Jay, 68
Corcoran, Thomas G., 4, 462
CoreNotes, 839
Corporate financing
  antitrust immunity, 415
  exemptions, 401
    applications for, 415
  filing requirements, 398
  "included in underwriting
    compensation," 408
      "profit-sharing" allegations, 411
  issuer's role in pricing IPOs,
    proposed enhancements, 96, 416
  items of value, 403
  lockup agreements, 406
  pricing information, submission
    of, 403
  pricing IPOs, issuer's role in, 416
  proceeds directed to member, 414
  "profit-sharing" allegations, 411
  request for underwriting activity
    report, 403
  review of, 397
  standards of fairness, 412
  underwriting compensation, included
    in, 408
      "profit-sharing" allegations, 411
  unfair underwriting arrangements, 413
Corporate Financing Rule, (NASD),
  83, 856
Corporate governance, 334
Counsel. *See* Lawyers
Country funds, 666
Court-approved exchanges
  exempt, 59

Covenants
  affirmative, private placements, 534
  and consent solicitations, 968
  stock repurchases, 912
  underwriting agreement, 97
Covered securities
  defined, 248, 266
Cox Communications, Inc., 952
Crane Company case, 916
Crash
  of 1929, 3, 233
  of 1987, 115, 755
  securities litigation and, 1
Cravath, Swaine & Moore, 5
C.R. Bard, Inc., 882, 883
Credit
  card, receivables, 1026
  enhancement
    and guarantees, 184, 1004
    asset-backed securities, 1003,
      1022, 1023
  extension, 852
    asset-backed securities, 1024
    installment payment securities, 759
    medium-term notes, 643
    1934 Act, 223, 1024
    Regulation T, 521, 760
    Section 11(d)(l), 223–229
  keepwell agreement, 812
  rating. *See* Rating
  regulation
    Regulation T, 95, 96, 521
    Section 11(d)(l) and new issues,
      223
Credit risk, 775
Credit Suisse First Boston, 856
Credit tranching, 992
CREF. *See* College Retirement Equities
  Fund
Critical accounting estimates, 367
Cross-border activity, 31
Cross-border transactions. *See*
  Foreign; Global offerings by
  foreign corporations; International
  financing; Offshore offerings and
  the 1933 Act

Crowell-Collier case, 472, 537
Cul-de-sac structure, 174, 175, 182, 183
Currency
    exchange warrants. *See also*
        Warrants currency swaps as
        securities, 10
    swaps, 445
Current transaction test. *See also*
    Commercial paper
    acquisition financing, 801
    broker-dealer operations, 792
    capacity, 784
    carrying finance company
        receivables, 789
    commercial paper exemption, 783
    foreign governmental entities, 802
    insurance operations, 792
    interim construction financing, 796
    inventories and account receivable, 787
    issuer's repurchase of securities, 802
    leasing and related activities, 790
    lending activities of U.S. bank
        holding companies and foreign banks, 789
    money market obligations, 794
    no-action letters, role of, 787
    nuclear fuel financing, 799
    payment of operating expenses, 788
    public utility operations, 798
    role of no-action letters, 787
Custodial arrangements
    ADRs, 714

D

Dahl case, 814
Daimler Chrysler, 839
Damage remedy, 308, 314
Dealer. *See* Broker-dealer
"Deal sites," 146, 181
Dean, Arthur H., 4, 379, 464
Dean Witter & Co.
    transactions with securityholders, 961
Death spiral convertibles, 871

Debentures
    exchange offer, 956, 967
    tender offer consent solicitations, 968
Debt restructuring
    cash tender offer, 946
    discussion, 940
    exchange offers, 953
        exclusivity requirement, 957
        issuer identity requirement, 954
        no paid solicitation, 958
        Regulation M, 967
        resales of exchanged securities, 964
        Rule 14e-5, 967
        shareholder votes, 964
        Trust Indenture Act, 964
    fixed-spread cash tender offers, 950
    open market purchases, 945
    premium payable to tendering holder, 952
    redemptions, 941
    tender offers
        and going private rules, 964
        issuer recommendation, 952
Debt securities. *See also* Indexed debt
    instruments; Innovative financing
    techniques; Notes
    asset-backed securities, 987–1034
    debt financing
        after IET elimination, 671
        hybrids. *See* Indexed debt instruments
    embedded options, 834
    inflation-indexed, 837
    Rule 144A transactions, 511
    shelf registration, 609
Debt/stock units, 896
Deduction. *See* Tax considerations
Deep discount and zero coupon obligations
    accounting treatment, 659
    bankruptcy, 659
    deep discount obligations, 660
    default, events of, 659
    tax considerations, 656
        bankruptcy and default events, 659
        OID consequences, 657

INDEX 1047

OID definition, 656
OID reporting, 658
zero coupon obligation defined, 656
zero coupon obligations, 660
Default
  commercial paper, 779
  commercial paper issuer liabilities, 813
  deep discount or zero coupon obligation, 659
  underwriting agreement, 116
Deficiency letters. *See* Comment letters on registration statements
Delaware
  General Corporation Law, 913
Delayed delivery contracts, 94
Delivery
  prospectus
    asset-backed securities, 1012, 1013
    dealers' delivery of final prospectus, after market transactions, 25
    delivery of final prospectus with confirmation, 21
    delivery of final prospectus with security, 25
    "free-writing" privilege, 24
    global offerings, 751
    operation of requirement, 20
    preliminary prospectus, 21
    private placement exemption, 459
    problems, 211
    shelf registration, 646
  registration and prospectus, 11
  short tendering of securities, 938
  unregistered distribution securities, 672
Demand Notes, 839
de minimis transactions, 274
Denman, Justice, 470
Denmark
  commercial paper, 803
Department of Agriculture, 829
Deposit notes, 634
Depository instruments, hybrids. *See* Indexed debt instruments
Depository Trust Company (DTC), The, 106, 107, 494, 509, 522, 633, 903

Depreciation in value, 309
Derivatives
  due diligence, 362
  innovations, 827
  market risk and, 361
  Regulation M prohibitions, 267
Designated orders, 81, 446, 453
Deutsche Bank AG, 715
Dickinson case, 915
Dietrich, Noah, 387
Digital Equipment Corp., 371
Diligence. *See* Due diligence
Direct Access Notes, 839
Directors. *See also* Board of directors
  liabilities, 308
  outside directors, liability of, 311
  questionnaire, due diligence, 346
Disclosure. *See also* Advertising; Notice; Prospectus; Registration
  asset-backed securities, 1000
    credit enhancement, 1003
    key disclosure elements, 1001
    1934 Act considerations, 1021
    prefunding accounts, 996
  commercial paper documents, 817, 818, 819
  derivatives, 362
  documents, Chinese Walls, 218
  equity-linked note, 893
  integrated disclosure system, 1, 7, 621
  medium-term note shelf registration, 640
  multijurisdictional, foreign securities, 740
  officers' and directors' questionnaire, 366
  overview, 1
  philosophy, 1933 Act, 7
  private offerings, 493
  Regulation M, 266–271
  SEC-registered offerings by foreign private issuers, 731
  shelf registration, 621

Task Force on Disclosure
    Simplification, SEC, 61
  to ultimate purchasers, 652
  unregistered distribution securities, 672
Discount. *See also* Deep discount and
    zero coupon obligations
  commercial paper, 771, 783
  obligations. *See* Deep discount and
    zero coupon obligations; Original
    issue discount to underwriting
    syndicate members and
    nonmembers, 75
Discretionary accounts
  and securities of NASD members, 450
Disqualification
  Regulation D, 495
Distributions. *See also* Distributions
    (Trading Practice Rules)
  common stock, shelf registration, 643
  completion, 676
  defined, 248, 251
  fixed-price, 440
  medium-term notes, 636, 640
  methods, block trade, 648, 649
  Papilsky rules, 440
  process
    dealing with gun-jumping
      problems, 195
    e-mail and other electronic
      communications, 198
    press coverage, 200
    rating agencies, 202
    research coverage, 203
    restricted period, 259
    road shows, 191
    and shelf registration, 562, 611
  public, asset-backed securities, 1025
  sample plan of, 862–863
  T + 3 settlement date and prospectus
    delivery problems, 211
Distributions (Trading Practice Rules).
  See also Distributions; Manipulative
  Practices
  affiliated purchasers, 257
  background, 231
  basket transactions, 273

covered securities, 266
debt restructuring, exchange
  offers, 953
defined, 248, 251, 252
de minimis transactions, 274
discussion, 575, 578
exceptions, 270–278
exchange offers, 953, 967
international financings, 759
Jaffee case, 251 n.56
manipulation outside Trading
  Practice Rules, 300
manipulative practices, 231–304
overhaul of Trading Practice Rules,
  245
participant, 255
passive market making, 278
put warrants, 925
Regulation M
  exceptions, 270–278
  problems, 208
  restricted period, 259
  rights offerings, 986
  shelf registration, 255
  short sales covered with registered
    securities, 291, 292
  stabilization, 279–290
  termination of restrictions, 259
  trading restrictions for issuers and
    selling securityholders, 292–295
  unsolicited transactions, 271
Dividends, 912
Documentation. *See also* Forms;
  Registration; Schedules
  asset-backed securities, 991
  commercial paper, 817, 818, 819
  document review. *See* Due diligence
  medium-term notes
    shelf registration, 634, 640
  shelf registration, 596
Doescher, N. Gregory, 376
Dollar BILS. *See* Indexed debt
  instruments
Donaldson, Lufkin & Jenrette, Inc., 417
Douglas Aircraft Co., Inc., 218
Dow Chemical, 839

INDEX

Downgrading of rating as out in shelf underwriting agreements, 619
Drexel & Co., BarChris case, 324
Drexel Burnham Lambert Incorporated
manipulative practices, 301–302
Dribble plans, 643
DTC *See* Depository Trust Company
Due diligence, 158, 888
   accounting matters, 354. *See also* financial statement due diligence, *this heading*
   administrative proceedings, SEC, 322
   analyst's role, 342
   asset-backed securities, 1019
   BarChris case, 323, 328, 380
   basic document review, 344
   "bring-down" due diligence, 371
   bulky documents, review of, 353
   checklists, 337
   Chris-Craft case, 326
   comfort letters, negotiation of, 367
   confidential documents, review of, 353
   corporate governance, 334
   defined, 305
   derivatives, 361
      market risk and, 361
   disclosure matters, legal review, 339
   documentation, 344, 353, 372
   due diligence out, 552
   equity-linked notes, 893
   exchangeable securities, 887
   "expertization," maximizing, 351
   facilities, visits to, 352
   financial statement due diligence
      critical accounting estimates, 367
      derivatives and market risk, 361
      MD&A adequacy, 366
      meeting focused on, 356
      non-GAAP financial measures, 364
      off-balance sheet entities, 367
      other areas for inquiry, 366
      preparing for, 355
      related-party transactions, 366
      revenue recognition, 360
      SEC's formal requirements for financial statements, 359
      segment disclosure, 365
   financial statement of issuer, effect of transaction on, 332
   forward-looking statements, 351
   Gustafson case, 512, 513
   high-risk ventures, 321
   Hughes Tool Company IPO, 382
   importance of continuing to closing date, 371
   industry review, 341, 347
   issuer's financial statement, effect of transaction on, 332
   issuer's website, 344
   judicial interpretations, 321
   Leasco Data Processing case, 325
   legal review, 337, 339
   management integrity, 331
   medium-term notes, 640
   meetings, 352
   negotiation of comfort letters, 367
   negotiation of underwriting agreement, 353
   officers' and directors' questionnaire, 346
   opinion matters, legal review, 337
   and Penn Central, 374
   principal officers, meetings, with, 352
   private offerings, 512
   procedures, 331
   prospective underwriters, 628
   questionnaires from officers, directors, other persons, 346
   questions to ask, 329
   registration statement review, 347
   review of confidential or bulky documents, 353
   Richmond case, 322
   Rule 144A equity offering, 514
   SEC administrative proceedings, 322
   SEC and judicial interpretations, 321
   Section 11 action, 308

Section 12(a)(2) claim, 11, 24, 314,
  370, 814, 817
shelf registration, 584, 621, 625
staffing, 335
standards, 329
summary judgment, 328
underwriting agreement, negotiation
  of, 353
visits to principal facilities, 352
website of issuer, 344
Dulles, John Foster, 4
Dutch auction, 67, 930
  modified Dutch auction, 67, 930
Dutch auction preferred stock. *See*
  Preferred stock
Dutch auction tender offer, 892
Dynegy Inc., 333

E

Earnings statement and projections
  covenants, 98
  due diligence, 343
Eastern Air Lines, Inc., 970, 971
EBITDA, 356
E-brokers, 174, 177
Eckersley, Howard, 383
ECL Industries, Inc., 957, 959
E-dealers, 174
EDGAR. *See* Electronic media
E.F. Hutton & Company, 540
Electronic auctions, 179
Electronic communications, 198
  dangers of, 198
  methods of communication, 67
Electronic communications network
  (ECN), 921
Electronic delivery
  of prospectus, 30
Electronic documents
  hidden text or comments, 374
Electronic media
  asset-backed securities, 1013
  Electronic Data Gathering Analysis
    and Retrieval (EDGAR) system,
    128, 186, 344, 551, 730, 737, 1010

medium-term note offerings, 639
  prospectus, 214
  QIB, 505
  road shows, 191
  trading, PORTAL, 509
  shareholder communication, 132
  use of, 484
Electronic prospectus, 180
Electronic roadshow, 620
Electronic underwriting, 38, 196
Elevator music, 157, 161
Elliott & Company, 472
E-mail, 19, 20, 38, 198, 199, 200
Embedded option. *See* Options
Emerging Issues Task Force, 356
Employee benefit plans, 436
Employee Retirement Income Security
  Act of 1974, 491
Employees
  offers and sales to, 49
Enron Corporation, 333
Equipment trust certificates
  exempt securities, 57
  as MTN, 634
Equity kicker, 865
Equity-linked notes. *See* Notes
Ernst & Young, 8
Estée Lauder Company Inc.,
  The, 858
Euro, 666
Eurobonds, 829
  exception, issuer sanctions,
    707, 708
  TEFRA D rules, 708
Euroclear, 698
Eurocommercial paper. *See*
  Commercial paper
Eurodollar obligations
  interest equalization tax, 668
European Monetary Union, 666
Event arbitrage, defined, 975
Evergreen
  registration statement, 554
Excess investor demand for IPO, 210
Exchange. *See also* Convertible
  securities; Currency exchange
  warrants; Debt restructuring;

INDEX

Debentures; National exchange listing; Preferred stock
  court or government approved, exempt, 59
  early manipulative practices, 232
  exchange agency agreement medium-term notes, 636
  with existing securityholders exemption, 58
  offer, 953
    dealer manager, 975
    "Exxon Capital" or "A/B" exchange offer, 555
    and private offerings, 555
    restricted period, 259
  prospectus delivery, 574
  rates, and stabilization, 289
Exchangeable securities, 890. *See also* Convertible securities
  CEA considerations, 889
  communications with underlying issuer, 888
  control situations, avoiding registration in, 882
  disclosure about issuer of underlying securities, 885
  due diligence, 887
  liabilities, 887
  listing, 889
  preemption, 889
  registration of underlying securities, 881, 882
  Regulation M., 889
  state preemption, 889
Exchanges
  court or government approved exchanges of securities, conditions for, 59
Exclusively
  defined, 957
Executive Jet Aviation, 381
Executor, indemnification of underwriters by, 109
Exempt securities (1933 Act). *See, also* Private offering exemption under 1933 Act
  bankruptcy, 60

bank securities, 54
charitable organizations, 60
commercial paper, 57, 778, 802, 805
Comptroller of the Currency, 56
equipment trust certificates, 57
FNMA, 51
hybrid instruments, 832
insurance contracts, 58
municipal obligations, 51
notes, 778, 780, 781
other exemptions, 60
thrift institutions, 57
U.S. government obligations, 49
Exempt transactions (1933 Act)
  court or government approved exchanges, 59
  dealer's exemption, 25, 43
  employees, offers and sales to, 49
  exchange offers, 953
  exchanges with existing securityholders, 58
  private placements, 42
  Rule 144, 47
  Section 4, 42, 49
  trading transactions, 42
  underwriters, 44
  when-issued trading, 975
Expertization, maximizing, 351
Expertized information in registration statement, 313
Expiring warrants. *See* Warrants
Extendible notes. *See* Credit; Notes
Extension of credit. *See* Credit
Extraterritorial application of 1933 Act. *See* International financing; Offshore offerings and the 1933 Act
"Exxon Capital" exchange offer, 555, 743, 880
Exxon Corporation, 613

F

Facts-and-circumstances test, 31
Family resemblance test
  Reves case, 8

Fannie Mae, 51, 839. *See also* Federal National Mortgage Association
Faulkner, Dawkins & Sullivan case, 23
Federal Home Loan Mortgage Corporation
documents, 1020
Federal National Mortgage Association (FNMA)
documents, 1020
exempt securities, 51
inflation-indexed debt securities, 837
Federal Reserve
bank
discount, commercial paper exemption, 783, 803
Board, 83, 616, 840, 841, 834
delayed delivery contracts and Regulation T, 95
Regulation K, 83;
trust preferred securities, 840
Federal Reserve Bank of New York, 333, 845
Federal Trade Commission, 5, 959
Fee. *See also* Commission; Compensation
accounting support fees, 93
rights offerings, 983
standby purchase, 788
Feline PRIDES, 854
Fictitious transactions. *See* Manipulative practices
Fiduciaries
directed selling effort exclusion, 698
Filing requirements. *See also* Forms; Registration; Schedules
NASD, 398
FIN 45, 161
FIN 46, 161, 841
FIN 46R, 840, 1031
Finance. *See also* Innovative financing techniques
company
carrying receivables, current transaction test, 789
subsidiary, commercial paper, 811
Financial Accounting Standards Board, 841

Financial statements
asset-backed securities, 1004, 1021
credit enhancer, 1021
due diligence, 350
meeting focused on, 356
preparing for, 355
expertization, 313
formal requirements, SEC's, 359
international financing, 734
geographic market and industry segments, 736
interim financial information, 734
reconciliation to U.S. GAAP, 734
revenue recognition, 360
Financial Covenants Reference Manual, 533
Financial services holding company, 29
Firewalls
between analysts and bankers, 150, 166
First Amendment
commercial speech, 205
First Boston Corporation, The, 35, 327, 375, 376
First National City Bank, 381
First-time registrant. *See* Initial public offering
Fitch Ratings Ltd., 773
Fixed-income securities, 36, 37, 1027
Fixed interest rate notes. *See* Notes
Fixed price offerings
Euromarket, 588
and NASD, 440
provisions, 86
Fleet Financial Group, Inc., 970
Fletcher, Duncan U., 233
Flippers
defined, 90
Flipping, 79
by institutions vs. retail customers, 80
Floating rate obligations. *See* Notes; Preferred stocks
Float test, 129, 130, 268, 269
Fluor Corporation, 801
FNMA. *See* Federal National Mortgage Association
Forced calls. *See* Underwriting

INDEX 1053

Ford Money Market, 839
Ford Motor Company, 72, 839
Ford Motor Credit Company, 638, 789, 839
Forecasts. *See* Forward-looking information; Projections
Foreign
 banks
  commercial paper current transaction test, 790
  commercial paper issuance, 790
  exemptions under 1940 Act, 743
  Section 3(a)(2) exemption, 54, 55, 805
  significant holdings and investment company status, 809
  underwriting by, 83
 bonds, sovereign transactions in, 277
 broker-dealers, 83
 companies
  registration under 1934 Act, current "trigger," 728
  regulatory compromise, development of, 722
  reporting obligations, under 1934 Act, 721
  rights offerings, 979
  Rule 12g3-2(b) exemption, obtaining, 728
 debt or equity securities acquired by U.S. persons, interest equalization tax, 667
 finance subsidiaries, 1940 Act exemptions for, 743
 governments and political subdivisions
  commercial paper current transaction test, 802
  consent to service and sovereign immunity, 764, 765
  1933 Act coverage, 711
  1933 Act registration, 741
  sales in the United States, 741, 760
  shelf registration, 606

 insurance companies, 1940 Act exemptions for, 743
 investment
  discouraging, 667
  interest equalization tax, 667
 issuers
  foreign private issuer, status as, 712
  global offerings by, 749–760
  markets. *See* Offshore offerings
  private issuers. *See* International financing
  sovereign bonds, transactions in, 277
  underwriters, 83
Foreign Corrupt Practices Act, 737
Foreign issuers
 first-time issuers, confidential filing for, 731, 743
Foreign press-related activity, 685
Foreign Sovereign Immunities Act of 1976 (FSIA), 764, 766
Forms (1933 Act)
 144, 48
 D, 496
 F-1, 14, 18, 637, 742
 F-2, 18, 741, 742
 F-3, 14, 18, 204, 205, 402, 561–563, 585, 586, 591, 594, 597, 603, 605, 606, 609, 622, 635, 636, 638, 645, 689, 741, 742, 746, 750, 856, 885, 886, 895, 1000, 1005
 F-4, 743
 F-6, 591, 717, 720, 721, 729, 743
 F-7, 741
 F-9, 741
 F-10, 741
 S-1, 14, 17, 127, 346, 359, 633, 637, 742, 898, 993, 997, 998, 1005, 1029
 S-2, 17, 127, 128, 129, 130, 131, 204, 742
 S-3, 14, 17, 99, 121, 127, 128–131, 143, 192, 204, 205, 214, 268, 330, 346, 372, 402, 554, 561–563, 582–586, 591, 594, 595, 597, 598, 599, 600, 603, 605, 609, 622, 633, 635–638, 641, 644, 645, 689, 742, 842, 856, 885, 886, 895, 898, 905,

906, 984, 989, 993, 994, 995, 996,
997, 998, 1000, 1005, 1013, 1017,
1023, 1028, 1029
S-4, 130, 743, 954
S-7 (rescinded), 17, 633, 638
S-8, 572
S-11, 997
S-12, 719, 720
S-14, 570, 571, 573
S-16 (rescinded), 17, 587, 606, 633,
648, 905, 906
W-8BEN, 710
Forms (1934 Act)
6-K, 36, 598, 599, 630, 737
8-K, 36, 99, 128, 344, 364, 538, 597,
598, 599, 600, 601, 630, 688, 989,
1009, 1022, 1023
10-D (proposed), 1022, 1023
10-K, 17, 98, 128, 165, 269, 330,
344, 359, 480, 597, 600, 601, 605,
929, 989, 1022, 1023, 1024
10-Q, 98, 128, 165, 344, 370, 480,
599, 630, 929, 1022
15, 1024
18-K, 608, 767
18-KA, 608
20-F, 597, 605, 728, 731–733, 737, 742
40-F, 597
Schedule 13D, 931
Schedule 13E-3, 937
Schedule TO, 932
Forms (1940 Act)
N-2, 645
Fortune magazine, 581
Fortune 500 review, 360, 365,
366, 367
Forward-looking information, 157, 162,
164, 170
forward-looking statements, 310, 351
safe harbors, 310, 316, 319
IPO, 166
MD&A, 164
safe harbor, 167
Forward sale agreements, 857
Fowler Task Force Report, 669
France, investment in, 678

Francom, George A., 385, 388
Frankel, Judge, *Papilski* case, 446
Frankfurter, Felix, 4, 7, 462
Franklin Life Insurance Company
case, 942
Fraud. *See* Antifraud provisions of
securities laws
Freddie Mac, 51
Free-riding. *See also* National
Association of Securities Dealers,
Inc. (NASD)
early NASD and SEC responses
to, 424
hot issue markets, 83, 423
Free-writing privilege, 24, 25
Freezeouts, 937
Friends-and-family programs, 140
FTA Financial Capital Markets, 844
Fuller, Lon, 564
Fundamerica of Japan, Inc., 751
Fungibility, 506, 507
Futures contract. *See also* Indexed debt
instruments
CFTC jurisdiction, 829–834
commodity futures contract
commodity defined, 829, 830
futures contract defined, 829
unlawful where not subject to
contract market rules, 829
defined, 829

G

GE Capital, 839
GE Financial, 839
GE Interest Plus, 839
Generally accepted accounting
principles (GAAP), 162, 359, 366,
711, 736. *See also* Non-GAAP
financial measures (NGFM)
continuous offering of medium term
notes, 528
reconciliation to, foreign issuer
financial statements, 734
Rule 144A transactions, 512, 515

INDEX

General Electric Capital Corporation, 782–783, 839
General Motors Acceptance Corporation, 639, 789, 839
Generic shelf, 594
Gillette Company, 795, 839
Global certificates, 106, 703
Global offerings by foreign corporations. *See also* Foreign; International financing; Offshore offerings and the 1933 Act
  ADRs, 745
  foreign publicity, 756
  foreign research, 757
  form and delivery of prospectus, 751
  installment payment offerings, 759
  Japanese investors, 751
  1987 British Petroleum offering, 753
  1933 Act registration, 749
  Regulation M, 759
  Section 11 liability, 752
  underwriting practices, 753
Global settlements, 124, 146, 150, 166, 343
Global share arrangements, 715
Globus case
  underwriting indemnity agreements, 108
Glore Forgan, Wm. R. Staats, Inc., and Penn Central offering, 375
GOALS offering, 887
GNMA. *See* Government National Mortgage Association
Going private transactions (Rule 13e-3)
  adoption of rule, 936
  tender offers, 936, 964
Goldman, Henry, 69
Goldman, Sachs & Co., 846, 860, 861, 862, 863
  commercial paper, 796, 798, 818, 821, 822
  shelf registrations, 580, 581
  underwriting syndication, 68, 69
  underwriting agreement, BP offering, 753
Goldman Sachs Money Markets Inc., 526

Goodwill, 305
Google Inc., 67, 132, 193, 345
  electronic auction, 181
  electronic prospectus, 217
Government. *See also* Foreign
  approved exchanges, exempt, 59
  obligations, exempted securities, 49
Government National Mortgage Association (GNMA), 830
  exempt securities, 50
  pass-through certificates, jurisdictional dispute, 830
Gramm-Leach-Bliley Act, 834
Great Southwest Corporation, 375
Great Sweet Grass case, 570
Greenmail, 912, 935
Green Shoe Manufacturing Company, 89
Green Shoe option, 77, 78, 88, 107, 261, 262
  extra-wide shoe, 91
  overallotments in excess of amount of option, 90
  refreshing the shoe, 262
  size of, 89, 90
  time limit on exercise, 90
  underwriter protection, 78
Gross-up obligations
  TEFRA D regulations, 706–709
Guarantees. *See also* Credit; Representations; Warranties
  bank securities, 54
  commercial paper, 778, 805
  municipal obligations, 51
  1940 Act exemption, 812
  U.S. government, 49
Guaranty Trust Company, 718
Guide 4, shelf registration, 578
Guide 53, shelf registration, 577, 578
Gun-jumping, 20, 30, 202, 548
  annual reports, 132
  discussion, 30
  email, 19, 20, 38, 198, 199, 200
  presentations to securities analysts, 134
  problems, dealing with, 195
  product advertisements, 133
  questions, securities registration, 131

restricted lists, 136
Rule 134, 36, 140, 907
Rule 135, 33–36, 131
Rule 137, 203
Rule 138, 204
Rule 139, 205, 1016
source of problem, 31
websites, information on, 132, 344
Gustafson case, 314, 316, 512, 817
Gutfreund, John H., 582

H

Hanson Trust PLC case, 916
Harden case, 422
Harsco case, 916
Harvard Law School, 564
Hazel Bishop case, 574
Headline risk, 775
Healy, Commissioner, 243
Hearst, Randolph, Sr., 386
Hedge funds, 90, 488, 489, 870, 871, 875, 880
Hedged tendering, 939
Hedging transactions, 650, 681, 694, 701, 895
Henderson, A.I., 5
High coupon debt securities, repurchase agreements, 911
High yield bonds. *See* Bonds
Hill, Charles, 378
Hill York Corp. case, 476
Hirschfeld case, 475
Holiday Inns of America, Inc., 567
Holliday, Raymond M., 383
Hot issue markets, 423
  definition of hot issue, 427
  excessive compensation for other services, proposed restrictions on, 439
  free-riding and withholding, 426
  "spinning," proposed restrictions on, 437
  ways of exploiting, 423–440

Household Finance, 839
Howey case, 10
Hughes, Howard R., Sr., 382–389
Hughes Tool Company, The, 341, 382–389
Hybrid instruments, 828, 832. *See also* Indexed debt instruments
Hyperlinks, use of, 174, 179, 182, 183

I

Implications of the Growth of Hedge Funds, 488, 489
Improvement Act. *See* National Securities Markets Improvement Act of 1996
Inadvertent investment companies, 219
InCapital LLC, 839
Income Deposit Securities (IDS), 897
Incorporation by reference, 14, 15, 127, 128, 365, 895, 998
Increasing rate notes. *See* Notes
Indemnification. *See* Underwriting
Indenture
  asset-backed securities, 1031
  corporate law considerations, 913
  debt restructuring, 942, 943
  exchange offer, 968
  medium-term notes, 635
  shelf registration, 614
  trust preferred securities, 839
Independence issues, 357
Index. *See* Indexed debt instruments; Stock indexes
Indexed debt instruments. *See also* Commodity
  CFTC jurisdiction, 830
  inflation-indexed debt securities, 837
Indirect primary offering, 855
Industrial development bonds and Rule 131, 52
Industrial Electronic Hardware Corp, 566

INDEX

Industry review
  due diligence considerations, 341
Inflation-indexed debt securities, 837
InfraRed Associates Inc., 673
Initial public offering (IPO), 2, 67, 171
  analyst's due diligence role, 342
  excess investor demand for IPO, 210
  first-day market orders, proposed restriction on, 76
  friends and family, amount reserved for, 140
  getting organized and other preliminary matters, 125
  the Hughes Tool Company offering, 382
  investor demand for IPO, 210
  issuer-directed shares, 138
  lock-up agreements related to. *See* Lock-up agreements
  pricing
    enhancement of issuer's role, 96, 416, price range, 171
    transparency in, 97
  registration and distribution process, 121
  reneged IPO allocations, 77
  restricted lists, 136
  stock exchange listing, blue sky considerations, 137
  tracking system, 79
Innovative financing techniques
  Commodity Exchange Act, regulation under. *See* Commodity Exchange Act
  Commodity Futures Modernization Act, regulation under. *See* Commodity Futures Modernization Act of 2000
  custody receipts, 845
  debt securities with embedded options, 834
  equity derivatives, 856
  "equity line" financing arrangements, 855
    1933 Act issues, 855

    1934 Act issues, 856
  inflation-indexed debt securities, 837
  remarketings, 851
  retail-oriented issuer debt programs, 838
  short sales and equity derivatives, 856
  trust preferred securities, 839
Insider information
  Chinese Walls, 218
  purchases in the open market, 914
Installment payment offerings, 759
Institutions. *See* Banks; Foreign; Qualified institutional buyers
Institutional investors
  accredited institutional investors, 492, 494
  asset-backed securities, 1932
  as commercial paper buyers, 769
  continuous private placement programs, 516
  direct sales, 613
  pressure by, *Papilsky* rules, 443
  qualified institutional buyer, 502–505
  shelf registration, 622
Insurance
  companies
    guarantees, commercial paper considerations, 807
    as investment companies, 809
  contracts, exempt securities, 58
  operations, commercial paper, current transaction test, 792
Integrated disclosure system. *See also* Disclosure
  development of, 15
  and due diligence, 621
  overview, 1, 7
Integration. *See also* Private offering exemption under 1933 Act
  asset-backed securities, 1019
  commercial paper and private offering, 524
  Regulation D sales, 497

Integrity of management, 332
  and due diligence, 331
Inter-American Development Bank Act,
  51, 697
Intercontinental Hotel, Managua,
  383, 384
Interest calculation agreement,
  medium-term notes, 636
Interest equalization tax, 667, 670, 671
Interest rate swaps
  as securities, 10
International Bank for Reconstruction
    and Development (the World Bank)
  exclusion as U.S. person, 697
  exempted securities, 51
International financing
  continuous reporting under 1934
    Act, 737
  financial statement requirements, 733
    formal requirements, 733
    geographic market and industry
      segments, 736
    interim financial information, 734,
      736
    reconciliation to U.S.
      GAAP, 734
  foreign private issuer, 712
  global offerings by foreign
    corporations, 749–760
  globalization of securities markets, 666
  multijurisdictional disclosure
    system, 740
  offshore offerings and the 1933 Act,
    667–706. *See also* Offshore
    offerings and the 1933 Act
  subscription or rights offers,
    744–748
Internationalization Report, 1987,
  SEC, 679
International Law Committee of the
  Association of the Bar of the City of
  New York, 724
International Monetary Fund
  exclusion as U.S. person, 697
International Organization of Securities
  Commissions, 731

International Paper Company, 882, 883
International Stock Exchange in
  London, 674
International Telephone & Telegraph
  Company, 227
Internet
  auctions, 146
  communications, 132
  "deal sites," 181
  electronic auctions, 179
  offerings and notices, 483
  offshore offerings, postings on
    Internet, 683, 748
  "online" offerings, 174
  publicity, 198
Internet Bubble, 37, 38, 96, 140, 146,
  174, 177, 196, 202, 306, 342, 396,
  411, 416, 439
  bursting of, 1, 2, 146
  lock-up agreements and, 100
  losses during, 76
Internet IPO, 306
InterNotes, 839
Interstate commerce
  1933 Act registration provisions, 668
  security registration and prospectus
    delivery requirements, 11
Interstate Commerce Commission, 58,
  375, 382
Interviews
  of investment banker, 487
In-the-money convertible securities, 908
Intrastate offering exemption, 60
Inventories
  financing, current transaction test, 787
Investigation. *See* Due diligence
Investment
  account held by underwriter, 264
  banking
    asset-backed securities, 1016
    equity-linked notes, 893
    industry review, 341
    innovation, 825–863
    medium-term note distribution, 636
    NASD membership, 391
    NYSE membership, 391

INDEX 1059

rights offerings, 982, 986
selection, 122
standby arrangements, 904
company
  defined, 1025
  inadvertent and transient, 219
  asset-backed securities issuer as, 809
  bank as, 809
  broker-dealer as, 809
  common stock shelf registration, 644
  finance subsidiary as, 811
  foreign bank as, 809
  holder of significant amount of securities, 809
contract, as a security, 58
foreign, discouraging, 667
rating, prime quality standard commercial paper, 779
risks, registration statement, 143
Investment Bankers Association, 985
Investment Bankers Code, 394, 442
Investment Bankers Conference Committee, 394
Investment Bankers Conference, Inc., 394
Investment Company Act of 1940, 339, 405, 407, 558, 774, 993
  asset-backed securities, 1025
  exemptions, 1026
  trust preferred securities, 839
Investment contract, as security, 11
Investment-grade debt securities shelf registration, 609
Investment-grade exception, 277, 280
Investor
  accredited, defined, 490
  effect of 1933 Act on, 60
IPO. *See* Initial public offering
IPONET, 484, 485
Irving, Clifford, 384
Irving Trust Company, 714
Issuer
  asset-backed securities, 993, 1002, 1014, 1016, 1019, 1021, 1027, 1028, 1029

commercial paper, rating, 770
foreign private issuer, status as, 712
innovative financing techniques, key questions, 827, 828
issuer-directed shares, 138
liability, STRYPES, 896
prospective, selecting the investment banker, 122
repurchase of securities, 802
safe harbor (Regulation S), 680, 681, 682, 702
sanctions, TEFRA, 706–710
tender offer regulation
  basic Rule 13e-4, 932
  going private rules, 964
  offer to purchase LYONS, 878
  open market purchases, 945
  put warrants, 925
trading restrictions, 292
Itel Corporation, 971
Items of value, 404
Ivey, J. Courtney, 384

J

Jaffe case, 251 n.56
James River Corporation, 944
James Talcott Inc., 324
Johnson & Johnson, 228
Johnson, J. Seward, 228
Johnson, Phillip, 830
Joint back office (JBO) broker-dealers, 432
Joint book-runners, 71
Jones, Ralph L., 389
J.P. Morgan Securities Inc., 859, 860
Junk bonds. *See* Bonds
Jurisdiction
  over persons outside the U.S., 724
  SEC-CFTC jurisdiction, 831

K

Kaiser-Frazer Corporation, 243
Katz case, 972

Keefe Bruyette & Woods Inc., 844, 845
Keep-well agreements. *See* Credit enhancement
Kellogg Company, The, 795
"Key indicators," MD&A, 153
Kidder Peabody & Co., 241
Kleinwort Sons & Co., 69

L

Laddering, 249
Landis, James M., 4, 5, 462
LaSalle Bank Corporation, 839
Lasker, Judge, regarding Penn Central offer, 821, 822
Lawyers. *See also* American Bar Association
  as counsel for shelf registration, 609, 611
  innovative financing techniques, key questions, 827, 828
  legal review, due diligence, 337, 339
  providing continuity, 626
Lay-offs
  calls for redemption to force conversions, 908
  exchange offers, 967
  and Rule 10b-8, 986
  Shields plan, 985
Lead manager, 97
Lead underwriter
  selecting, 123
League table credit, 71, 332, 826
Leasco Data Processing case, 325
Leasing
  commercial paper current transaction test, 790
  nuclear fuel, commercial paper current transaction test, 799
Legal counsel. *See* Lawyers
Legal investment considerations, asset-backed securities, 1033
Legal review
  disclosure matters, 339
  opinion matters, 337

Legends, restrictive, 535
Lehman Brothers, 69, 325
Lehman Commercial Paper Incorporated, 802
Lehman, Philip, 69
Leland Stanford case, 570 n.15
Leness, George, 388
Letters of credit. *See also* Commercial paper
  commercial paper exemption, 805
Leveraged buy-outs. *See* Acquisitions
LexisNexis, 345
L.H.I.W., 827
Liabilities
  controlling persons, 320
  on default, commercial paper, 813
  exchangeable securities, 887
  outside directors, 311
  Rule 10b-5, 317
  under Section 11 of the 1933 Act, 308, 328, 348, 372
    ADRs, 719
    commercial paper, 820
    due diligence, 627, 630
    global offerings, 752
    MTN agent, 640
    as of registration statement's effective date, 629, 630
    STRYPES, 896
  under Section 12(a)(2) of the 1993 Act
    due diligence, 314
    exempted securities, 11
    statutory bases, 307
    third-party monetizations, 896
Libor, 868
Limited partnership offerings, 537
Linked securities, 866
Liquidity, 159
Liquidity Risk Assessments, 775
Liquid yield option notes. *See* Notes
Listing, national exchanges. *See* National exchange listing
Lively case, 475

INDEX

Loans
  certificate loan, 979
  commercial, as security, 9
  commercial paper current transaction test, 789
  significant holder as investment company, 809
Lockheed Martin, 868, 870, 873
Lockup, 407
Lock-up agreements, 100
  corporate financing, review of, 406
  extension of lock-up, 101
  hedging or collaring of locked-up shares, 100
  modification of, 100
  underwriting agreement, 99
London Stock Exchange, 674
Look-through procedure, ADRs, 713, 728
Lord, Abbett & Co., 446
Loss, Louis, 68
LYONS. *See* Notes

M

MAAU. *See* Master agreement among underwriters (MAAU)
Mail fraud, 238
Mail or interstate commerce as basis for jurisdiction, 11, 25, 214, 668
Malamed, Leo, 829
Maloney Act, 394
Management integrity
  due diligence, 331
Management's discussion and analysis (MD&A), 102, 151, 355, 357, 366, 370
  additional information available to management, 155–157
  adequacy of, 366
  Caterpillar proceeding, 164
  content and focus, 153
    analysis, 155
    "key indicators," 153
    materiality, 154
    material trends and uncertainties, 154
  contractual obligations, tabular disclosure of, 162
  critical accounting estimates, 162
  due diligence, 351, 354, 366
  focus. *See* content and focus, *this heading*
  forward-looking function of, 164
  fresh look, 152
  liquidity and capital resources, 159
  off-balance sheet arrangements, 161
  participants in development, review and revision of MD&A, 158
  presentation, 152
  purpose of, 164
  registration statements, 150
  relevant information, identification of, 157
  requirements for, 151, 152
  responsibility for preparation of, 157
  results of operations, 160
  shelf registration considerations, 623
  tabular disclosure of contractual obligations, 162
Managing underwriter
  defined, 604
  handling restricted periods, 259
  investment account, 264
  liabilities and due diligence, 305
  request for underwriting activity report, 403
  selection, 125
  stabilization, 280
Mandatorily convertible instruments. *See* Convertible securities
Manipulative practices. *See also* Distributions (Trading Practice Rules); Short sale; Stabilization (Trading Practice Rules)
  Subscription offers
  anti-manipulation rules
    background, 231
    effects of Section 9, 238
    global offerings, 759

the next twenty years, 239
SEC, 181, 577
shelf registration, 654
trading practice rules, 231
covering short sales with registered
 securities, 296
disclosure, SRO notification and
 recordkeeping, 278
early prohibitions, 232
 adoption of original trading
  practice rules, 244
 Fletcher Committee
  investigation, 233
 subsequent revisions of trading
  practice rules, 244
 Wall Street's response, 235
excepted activities
 basket transactions, 273
 foreign sovereign bonds,
  transactions in, 277
 odd lot transactions, 271, 936
 passive market-making and
  stabilization transactions, 271
 research, 270
 transactions among distribution
  participants, 274
 transactions in foreign sovereign
  bonds, 277
 transactions in Rule 144A
  securities, 277
 transactions in the securities being
  distributed or offered as
  principal, 275
 unsolicited transactions, 271
manipulation outside the trading
 practice rules, 300
problems under trading practice
 rules, 295
passive market making, 278
Regulation M
 adoption, 246
 affiliated purchasers, 257
 basic outline, 248
 basic prohibitions, 248
 convertible securities, 889
 covered securities, 266

distribution participant, 255
distributions, 251, 759
equity offerings during restricted
 period, 208
excepted activities, 270
excepted securities, 268
global offerings by foreign
 corporations, 759
gun jumping, restricted lists, 136
investment account, 264
Jaffee case, 251 n.56
manipulative practices, 232, 246, 290
1983 definition of distribution, 252
1994 Concept Release, 253
problems, 208
prospectus disclosure, SRO
 notification, and
 recordkeeping, 266
restricted period, beginning of, 259
restricted period, termination,
 259
Rule 101–basic outline and
 prohibitions, 248
shelf registrations, 255, 654
stabilization. *See* Stabilization
stock repurchases, put warrants, 925
stock repurchases, Rule 10b-18,
 928, 929
trading practice rules, 232
trading restrictions for issuers and
 selling securityholders, 292
Marcus case, 535
Margin
 indebtedness
  commercial paper current
   transaction test, 793
 marginable securities, 229
Market
 asset-backed securities, 1014
 competitive bidding, 118
 open market purchase
  debt securities, 945
  described, 914
  going private transactions, 936
  tender offer considerations, 915,
   945, 949

INDEX 1063

passive market making, 271
price, Rule 10b-18, 917
stabilization, 282–290
Market Axess Inc., 183
Market crashes, and securities litigation, 1
Market-maker
  delivery of prospectus when affiliated with issuer, 29
  prospectus, 29
Market-making resales, 29
Market orders
  prohibition for first trading day following IPO, 76
Master agreement among underwriters (MAAU), 65
Material adverse change clause, 113
Material changes, 372
Materiality, 154
  defined, 349
Material trends and uncertainties, 154
Maturity tranching, 992
May Day and abolition of fixed commission rates, 444
McLean, Judge
  BarChris opinion, 323, 325, 335
MD&A. *See* Management's discussion and analysis
Media, 487. *See also* Electronic media
Medina, Harold R., 68, 69, 86
Medium-term notes (MTNs), 306, 523, 643
  closing, 636
  commercial paper program, 527
  continuous offering procedures, 528
  development, 632
  documentation, 634
  floating rate, 633
  shelf registration, 632
    documentation, 634, 640
    indenture, 635
    procedures, 639
    registration under Rule 415, 636

Membership
  NASD, 391, 414
  NYSE, 391
Merger. *See also* Acquisitions
  arbitrage, 975
  Rule 145, 40
  statutory, 911
Merrill Lynch
  cash tender offers, 947
  CD Program, 10
  commercial paper current transaction test, 793
  liquid yield option notes, 868
  STRYPES, 894
  Treasury Investment Growth Receipts (TIGRs), 826
Merrill Lynch & Co., Inc., 868, 870, 873, 826, 839, 894
  LYONS, 826, 868
Merrill Lynch, Pierce, Fenner & Smith Incorporated, 417
  Chinese Walls, 218
  due diligence, 383
Merrimac Corporation, 968
Micro-Moisture Controls, Inc. case, 570
Microsoft Corporation, 858, 859, 860, 871
Milken, Michael, 301
Minutes of meetings, 340
  due diligence review, 338, 340
Misstatements and omissions, 339
Modified Dutch auction, 67
Moley, Raymond S., on securities legislation, 4
Monetization. *See* Convertible securities
Money market
  accounts, 839
  cumulative preferred stock. *See* Preferred stock
  funds
    and asset-backed securities, 1029
    restricted commercial paper program, 808
  instruments, commercial paper current transaction test, 793

Montgomery Ward Credit Corp., 639
Montreal, city of, 803
Moody's Investors Service, 278, 430, 773, 774, 775
Morgan Guaranty Trust Company, ADR initiation, 714
Morgan Stanley & Co. Incorporated, 67, 580, 581, 588, 754, 942
Mortgage-backed securities, 1026, 1032
Mortgage-related securities, 1032, 1033
Mortgage pass-through certificates, 994
MTNs. *See* Medium-term notes
Multijurisdictional disclosure system (MJDS)
  Canada and U.S., 740
Multiple tendering, 940
Municipal bonds
  exempt securities, 51
  NASD filing not required, 402
Mutual fund
  fixed commission rates, 445
  global offerings, 751
  NASD filing exemption, 402
  shelf registration, 645

N

Naked shorts, 90
NASD. *See* National Association of Securities Dealers, Inc.
NASDAQ. *See* National Association of Securities Dealers Automated Quotations
NASD Regulation, Inc. (NASDR) operation, 392
National Association of Securities Dealers, Inc. (NASD), 8, 342. *See also* Self-regulatory organizations
  background, 391
  compensation, excessive, for other services
    proposed restrictions on, 439
  Conduct Rules, 392, 396
  conflicts of interest, 417
  Corporate Financing Department, 396
  corporate financing review, 397
  defined, 391
  exemptions, 401
  filing
    exemption for asset-backed securities, 1034
    fees, IPO, 126
    requirements, 398
  free-riding and withholding, 423
    definition of hot issue, 423, 427
    general exemptions, 434
    hot issue, defined, 427
    hot issue markets, 423
    issuer-directed securities, 436
    interpretation, 426
    NASD and SEC response, 424
    "new issues" vs. "hot issues," 430
    normal investment practice, 428
    preconditions for sale, 434
    restricted persons, 432, 428
    Rule 2790, impact of. *See* Rule 2790, this *heading*
    special study observations on free-riding, 425
  hot issue markets, 423
    Rule 2790, impact of. *See* Rule 2790, this *heading*
  issuer-directed securities, 436
  items of value, 403
  manipulative practices, notification, 290
  member, 414
  and NASDAQ, 392
  OTC Bulletin Board, 728
  Papilsky case, 446
  Papilsky rules, 396, 440
    analysis, 448
    background, 442
    pressures by institutions, 443
    related persons, transactions with, 396, 457, 458
    Rule 2730, 396, 454, 455, 456
    Rule 2740, 396, 448, 454, 457
    Rule 2750, 396, 457, 458
    selling commissions, discounts, other allowances, 396, 448, 454, 457
    trade, securities taken in, 396, 454, 455, 456

INDEX

proceeds directed to a member, 414
prohibitions on discounts or selling
  concessions to nonunderwriter
  members, 75
registration with SEC, 391
Rule 2720, 417
Rule 2790, 429
  antidilution provisions, 437
  exemptions, general, 434
  issuer-directed securities, 436
  "new issues" rather than "hot
    issues," applicability to, 430
  other exemptive relief, 437
  preconditions for sale, 434
  prohibitions of, 431
  restricted persons, 432
  standby purchasers, 437
Rules of Fair Practice, 392, 395
short sales, 296
signoff, and registration statement, 401
"spinning," proposed restrictions
  on, 437
standards of fairness, 412
underwriting syndicate provisions, 81
unfair underwriting arrangements, 413
National Association of Securities
  Dealers Automated Quotations
  (NASDAQ), 114, 129, 130, 507, 712,
  715, 767, 889
  ADR listing, 715
  exchange offers, 965
  foreign issuers, 738, 739, 740
  foreign shares, 715
  going private transactions, 936
  initial public offering, 137
  operation, 392
  passive market making, 278
  prospectus delivery, 647
  restricted period duration, 259
  Rule 144A, 514
Nationale-Nederlanded N.V., 792
National securities exchange listing.
  See also National Association of
  Securities Dealers Automated
  Quotations
  American Stock Exchange, 137, 138,
    472, 566, 576, 577

IPO, stock exchange listing, 137
New York Stock Exchange, 137, 233,
  272, 292, 300–302, 391, 976, 982
National Industrial Recovery Act,
  394, 442
National Securities Markets
  Improvement Act of 1996, 138, 497,
  686, 1033
Negative assurance, 102
  comfort letters, 104
Negative causation defense, 309
Negative return, 869
Negotiated rates. *See* May Day
Negotiating underwriting agreement
  and comfort letter, 367
  due diligence, 353, 367
Netherlands Antilles, 878
New issue
  defined, 430
New-issue market, 2
New issues, and extension of credit, 223
Newsletters, 487
New York Central railroad merger, 375
New York Insurance Law, 535
New York shares, 715
New York Society of Security
  Analysts, 135
New York Stock Exchange (NYSE),
  114, 137, 144, 233–236, 272, 286,
  287, 292, 300–302, 342, 391, 712,
  889, 976, 981, 982
  record date, 981
New York Times, 201, 755
NGFM. *See* Non-GAAP financial
  measures (NGFM)
NIMP. *See* Shearson Lehman
Non-accredited investor, 493
Non-convertible securities. *See also*
  Convertible securities
  continuous offer, Regulation S,
    695, 696
  trading restrictions, 293
Non-GAAP financial measures
  (NGFM), 356, 364, 365
Norfolk & Western railroad, 375
Norlin Corporation, 956
Normal investment practice, 428

North American Securities
  Administrators Association, 496
Northway case, 349
Notes
  asset-backed securities, 1033
  bank notes vs. deposit notes, 634
  equity-linked, 832, 893, 1033
  liquid yield option notes (LYONS),
    826, 868, 878, 879
  medium-term
    closing, 636
    commercial paper program, 527
    continuous offering procedures, 528
    development, 632
    floating rate, 633
    shelf registration, 632, 636, 639, 640
  public offerings, 1933 Act
    exemption, 780, 781
  as securities, 9
Notice
  asset-backed securities, 1029
  cash tender offer, 946
  of proposed registered offerings, 33
  of proposed unregistered offerings,
    35, 688
  QIB, 508
  of redemption, 907
  Regulation D, 495
  SRO, manipulative practices, 290
Novellus Systems, Inc., 869, 873
NYSE. *See* New York Stock Exchange
NYSE/NASD Advisory Committee, 76,
  79, 96, 100, 140, 210, 417, 438
Nuclear fuel
  commercial paper current transaction
    test, 799
Number of offerees, 488

O

Oak Industries Inc. case, 972
October 19, 1987, market collapse.
  See Crash
Odd-lot dealer, 271
Off-balance sheet arrangements, 161

Off-balance sheet entities, 367
Off-balance sheet monetization. *See*
  Convertible securities
Offerees, number of, 488
Offers and sales. *See also* Global
  offerings by foreign corporations;
  Manipulative practices; Public
  offering; Unit offerings
  at-the-market equity offerings,
    628, 644
  commercial paper, 780
  common stock
    shelf registration, 643
  communications during offering
    process, 30
  to employees, 49
  fixed price, *Papilsky* rules, 440
  global offerings by foreign
    corporations, 749–760
  gun-jumping questions, 131
  offer defined, 876
  offering documents
    asset-backed securities, 1006
    commercial paper, 817, 818
  offering process
    communications during, 30
    online offerings, 38
  offering restrictions, preferred
    securities, 842
  offshore offerings and the 1933 Act,
    667
  oral vs. written, 19, 191
  product advertisements, 133
  public, commercial paper, 780
  registered securities, 19
  registration and distribution
    process, 121
  restricted periods, 259
  sale defined, 876
  sales following private placements,
    shelf registration, 567
  sales representatives, designation, 542
  Securities Act of 1933, 39
  securities analyst, role in offerings, 146
  secondary, 579
  selling. *See also* Short sales

INDEX

allocations, 75
concession, 81
defense of seller, 317, 640
trading restrictions, 292
shelf offerings, 330
stabilization and related activities, 280
Office of the Comptroller of the Currency. *See* Comptroller of the Currency
Officers
certificate, 634
as to closing, 614
terms of sale,
due diligence meetings, 352
indemnification claim, 110
questionnaire, due diligence, 346
Offshore offerings and the 1933 Act. *See also* Foreign; International financing; Offers and sales
debt financing after elimination of IET, 671
foreign private issuers and U.S. securities laws, 710
ADR facilities, status of, 717
ADR facilities, types of, 715
ADRs, 713
continuous reporting, exiting reporting system, 739
continuous reporting under the 1934 Act, 737
disclosure, 731
foreign banks, insurance companies, finance subsidiaries, 1940 Act exemptions, 743
foreign reporting companies, Sarbanes-Oxley consequences for, 738
Form F-6, 720
Form 20-F, 731
listing on U.S. exchange or NASDAQ, 738
multijurisdictional disclosure system, 740
registration under 1933 Act, 742
registration under 1934 Act, current "trigger" for, 728

regulatory compromise, development of, 722
reporting obligations of foreign companies under 1934 Act, 721
Rule 12g3-2(b) exemption, 728
status as foreign private issuer, 712
types of ADR facilities, 715
1933 Act registration, 729
interest equalization tax, 667
press-related communications, 36
purchasers, Rule 144A ADR facilities, 515
Regulation S
"abusive" transactions, subsequent SEC concerns, 680
adoption, 679
advertising, 688
Category 1 transactions, 691
Category 3 transactions, 698
Category 2 transactions, 693
convertible securities, 702
directed selling efforts, 683
duration of prohibition, 691
exempt offers excluded, 690
foreign press-related activity, 685
general statement, 681
Internet postings, 683
issuer safe harbor, 691
miscellaneous activities, 690
notices of unregistered offerings, 688
offshore transaction, 682
private placements in U.S. concurrent with public offerings abroad, 702
quotations, 689
registered or exempt offers excluded, 690
resale safe harbor, 704
resales in U.S., 705
research, 689
safe harbors, 680, 571, 682, 691
U.S. person defined, 696
unregistered offerings, notices of, 688

Release 33-4708, 669, 708
  dissatisfaction, 674
  tax considerations in offshore debt offerings, 706
  TEFRA C rules, 709
  TEFRA D rules, 709
  TEFRA issuer and holder sanctions, 708–709
  withholding taxes and gross-up considerations, 710
  territorial approach, 677
  U.S. sales by foreign governments and their political subdivisions, 741
O'Herron, Jonathan, 376
OID. *See* Original issue discount
Oil indexed notes, 828
On-demand registration, 62
Online offerings, 38, 146, 174
Open-ended indentures and shelf registration, 614
Open-end funds, 645
Open-end mutual funds, 645
Open market purchase, 78. *See also* Market
Operating expenses
  commercial paper current transaction test, 793
  payment, and commercial paper current transaction test, 788
Opinions. *See* Lawyers
Options. *See also* Commodity; Futures contract
  embedded, 834
    registration, 836
    hybrid instruments, 832
    jurisdiction, 830, 831
    purchase rights, 836, 837
    stock option plans, shelf registration, 572
Options Clearing Corporation, 926
Oral communications, 316
Oral offers, and 1933 Act, 19, 191
Original issue discount (OID)
  accrual period, 657
  consequences, 657
  deep discount obligations, 656
  defined, 656
  reporting, 658
Outside directors
  liability of, 311
Overallotment option, 89
  Regulation M treatment, 262
  underwriting syndicates, 77
Overallotments, 77, 78, 89, 107. *See also* Green shoe option, 89
Overhang
  common stock distribution, 643
Over-the-counter market, 137, 394
Overtrading, 441, 443, 445, 454

P

Pacific Lighting Corporation, 671
Pacific Stock Exchange, 301
Papilsky
  application to shelf registration considerations, 583, 588
  the *Papilsky* case, 446
  rules, 83, 322, 440
    analysis, 448
    background, 440, 441, 446
    fixed-price offerings, 440, 450
    pressures by institutions, 443
    Rule 2730, 454
    Rule 2740, 448
    Rule 2750, 457
Paris stock exchange, 678
Parmalat, 827
Partnerships
  investment partnerships, 428, 432
Passive market making, 271, 278
Pass-through certificate
  asset-backed securities, 1032, 1033
  GNMA, jurisdictional dispute, 830
Payment and delivery
  underwriting agreement, 82
Pecora, Ferdinand D., 233
Penalty
  bid, 91, 290
    abuse of, 79
    stabilization, 291
  clause, underwriting syndicate, 79

INDEX

Penn Central
　commercial paper default, 818, 821
　due diligence, 374
　shelf registration, 582
Penn Central Transportation Co., 375
Pennsylvania railroad merger, 375
Perera Company, Inc. case, 781
Periodic reports 1934 Act, 15, 16
PERLS. *See* Indexed debt instruments
Pershing LLC, 856, 857, 862
Pickens, T. Boone, Jr., 935
Pierson, Heldring & Pierson, 376
Pink herring, 37
Pink sheet trading, 715, 727, 728
Pinter case, 814
PIPE. *See* Private investment, public equity (PIPE) transaction
Plain English, 142, 143, 307, 350, 932
　Plain English Handbook: How to Create Clear SEC Disclosure Documents, A, 142
Plants, due diligence visits, 352
Pledged securities
　shelf registration, 572
Political subdivision. *See* Foreign
Pooling. *See* Manipulative practices
Pooling and servicing agreement. *See* Asset-backed securities
Pooling-of-interest acquisition treatment, 913
PORTAL, 494, 509, 515. *See also* Private offering exemption under 1933 Act
Post-effective amendments, 172, 180, 209, 606, 644, 899, 1000
　Green Shoe option and, 91
　to registration statements, 593, 602–606, 614, 637
　to shelf, 853
Post-filing issues
　dealing with gun-jumping problems, 195
　deal size, changes in, 208
　legal issues, 191–218
Pot orders, 75
Pot sales, 75

Pot, syndicate account, 75
Powell, Justice, dissenting opinion in *Sanders* case, 820
Preemption, 834, 889, 896, 1033
　of state gaming and bucket shop laws, 889
　of state securities registration
　　asset-backed securities, 1033
Preexisting relationships, 519
　individual private placements, 538
　number of offerees, 541
Preferred stock
　auction rate, 1028
　authorization, 617
　　calls for redemptions to force conversions, 902
　　lay-offs, 908
　　1933 Act considerations, 905
　　standby arrangements, 904
　convertible, 764
　cumulative, 1028
　exchange for another company's common stock, 892
　exchangeable for common, 866
　holding considerations and investment company status, 812
　shelf registration, 596, 609
　trust preferred securities
　　generally, 839
　　1933 Act considerations, 842
　　1934 Act considerations, 843
　　1939 Act considerations, 843
　　1940 Act considerations, 843
Prefunding accounts
　asset-backed securities, 996, 1013, 1032
Preliminary prospectus, 171, 172, 620, 621
　recirculation of amended prospectus, 190
Premium
　cash tender offer, 946
Pre-sale reports, 202
Presentations for securities analysts. *See* Gun-jumping
Press coverage, 200. *See also* Gun-jumping

Press-related activity
  offshore offerings, and foreign press, 685
Press releases
  international financing, 672
  stock repurchases, 913
Presumptive underwriter, 652. *See also* Underwriter
Price
  amendment, 209, 209, 210
  information
    registration statement, 191
  IPO pricing, transparency in, 97
  price maintenance agreements, among underwriters, 74
  pricers. *See* Underwriter
  supplement, medium-term note, 635
Pricing committee, 96, 97
PRIDES, 826
Prime quality standard commercial paper, 779
Principal Life, 839
Principal protection, 57
Private investment companies (Section 3(c)(7), 558
Private investment, public equity (PIPE) transaction, 547, 557
Private offering exemption under 1933 Act (Section 4(2))
  commercial paper, 516, 520, 808
  continuous offering procedures for restricted commercial paper, 516
  continuous private placement programs, 516
  restricted medium-term notes, 528
  Crowell-Collier case, 471
  designation of participating sales representatives, 542
  early administrative interpretations, 463
  equity-linked notes, 893
  and exchange offer, 555
  exemption from registration and prospectus delivery requirements, 459
  "Exxon Capital" or "A/B" exchange offer, 555

extendible commercial paper, 527
integration, 524
legislative history, 461
PORTAL system of NASD, 509, 515, 531
pre-Rule 146 developments, 474
private placement procedures, 510
procedures and controls, 541
  qualified offerees, designation of, 542
  qualified offerees, solicitation of, 543
  qualified sales representatives, 542
  solicitation of qualified offerees, 543
and public filings, 549
QIB status, 502
  DTC, 509
  fungibility, 506
  information requirement, 507
  notice, 508
  PORTAL, 509
  resales, 509
  screen-based and other offers, 505
Ralston Purina case, 467–471
registration, concurrent or future, 552
registration rights agreement, 553
Regulation D, 481
  accredited investors, 490
  anti-underwriter precautions, 493
  express exclusions, 482
  general solicitation and prior relationships, 538
  general solicitation or advertising, 482
  general solicitation prohibition, future of, 489
  informational access and disclosure, 493
  integration, 497
  Internet offerings and notices, 483
  interviews, 487
  media, 487
  newsletters, 487
  nature and number of purchasers, 490
  notice, disqualification blue sky requirements, 495

INDEX

number of offerees, 488
placements with individual
   investors, 537
potential ineligibility of certain
   reporting companies, 538
procedures and controls, 541
qualified offerees, designation and
   solicitation of, 542, 543
qualified sales representatives,
   designation of, 542
resales, 495
restrictive legends, 494
screen-based solicitation, 523
substantial compliance rule, 500
related private placements and
   private offerings, 543
   concurrent or future
      registration, 552
   exchange offer, 555
   public filings, 544, 549
   registration rights agreement, 553
   short sales into public
      market, 557
Rule 144A, 501, 510
   debt offering, 511
   equity securities, offering of, 514
Rule 146, 476
secondary private placements, 536
short sales into public market
   afterward, 557
stand-alone institutional
   placements, 531
   availability of Section 4(2)
      exemption, 535
   investment representations, 534
   procedures, 533
Private offerings. *See also* Offers and
   sales; Private offering exemption
   under 1933 Act
commercial paper, 780
investment banker selection, 122
registration, concurrent or future, 552
registration rights agreement, 553
short sales into public market after
   private offering, 557
Private Placement Enhancement
   Project, 532
Private Placement Process
   Enhancements, 533
Private placements
   asset-backed securities, 1012,
      1021, 1026
   memorandum, 533
   model forms, 532
   procedures, 533
   related private placements and public
      offerings, 543
   shares issued upon conversions, 568
   shelf registration, 565
      sales following private
         placements, 567
   simultaneous with foreign
      offering, 670
   in U.S., concurrent with public
      offerings abroad, 702
Private Securities Litigation Reform
   Act of 1995, 167, 317, 319
Procter & Gamble Company, The, 671
Projections. *See also* Forward-looking
   information
   IPO, 166
Promissory notes
   foreign governments, commercial
      paper and, 802
   integration, 524
Prospective underwriter. *See* Underwriter
Prospectus. *See also* Forms;
   Registration
ADR, 720
ADS, 720
Allied Chemical Corporation, 571
asset-backed securities, 1000, 1003,
   1007, 1011, 1012, 1013, 1014,
   1015, 1016, 1020
calls for redemption to force
   conversions, 907
circulation, 190
communications not deemed a
   prospectus, 36
"deal sites," 181
definition, 22
delivery, 15, 20
   after-market transactions, 25
   asset-backed securities, 1012

block trade, 648, 649
dealers' delivery, after-market transactions, 25
electronic delivery, 30
market-makers' delivery of prospectus, when affiliated with issuer, 29
1933 Act Section 3(a)(3) commercial paper exemption, 778
operation of requirement, 20
private placement exemption, 459
problems, 211
requirements, 1933 Act, 11
updating the prospectus, 27
with registered security, 25
electronic, 214
electronic auctions, 179
equity linked security, 894
evergreen, 897
final prospectus, 22, 25
defined, 22, 25
form and delivery, global offerings by foreign corporations, 751
"free-writing" privilege, 24
illegal, 24
Internet, posting, 174
IPOs, 171
Judge Weinstein's criticism, 350
market maker prospectus, 29, 30, 1015
"online" offerings, 174
preliminary, 21, 25, 190, 620
shelf registration, 597, 619, 620
standby arrangements, 906
STRYPES, 895
summary, 145
supplement, shelf registration, 622, 623
swap eligibility, 456
Proxy statements, 128
Prudent man test. *See* Due diligence
Public Company Accounting Oversight Board (PCAOB), 8, 358, 359
Public filing
private offerings and, 544, 549, 902

Public float, 129, 130, 268, 269
Publicity. *See* Advertising
Publicly held corporation. *See also* Going private transactions; Offers and sales; Public offering
rights offerings, 984
Public offering. *See also* Offers and sales
asset-backed securities, 1031
abroad, concurrent with U.S. private placements, 702
commercial paper, 780
convertible securities, 876
defined, 398
exchange requirements, 396
filing exemption for asset-backed securities, 1034
Section 12(a)(2) claim, 314
Public Securities Association (PSA), 1016
Public utilities
nuclear fuel, commercial paper current transaction test, 799
operations, commercial paper current transaction test, 798
Public Utility Holding Company Act of 1935, 119, 402
Purchase. *See also* Stock repurchase programs
agreement. *See also* Underwriting
purchaser
affiliated, 257, 293
nature and number, 490
defined, 249
underwriting agreement provision, 106
Put, investor. *See* Investor puts
Put options. *See* Options
Puttable convertible securities, 878
Put warrants. *See* Stock repurchase programs

Q

QIB. *See* Qualified institutional buyer
QIU procedures, 418

INDEX

Qualified independent underwriters (QIU)
See Underwriter
Qualified institutional buyer (QIB), 281, 505, 703, 870, 954
   and asset-backed securities, 1014
   exempt transactions, 277
   private medium-term note programs, 529
   Regulation T, 521
   Rule 144A, 501
   status, 502
Qualified purchasers (QPs), 559, 844
   defined, 559
Quantitative information
   disclosure alternatives for, 362
Questionnaire
   to officers and directors, due diligence, 346, 366
Quiet periods, 147, 148
Quinn, Linda C., 679
Quotations. *See also* National Association of Securities Dealers Automated Quotations
   Regulation S, 689
Qwest Communications International Inc., 954

R

Raffensperger, Hughes & Co., Inc., 422
Ralston Purina case, 460, 467–471, 476
Rating. *See* Moody's Standard & Poor's
   agency, 202
      shelf registration, 630, 631
   credit rating
      trust preferred securities, 839
      issuer of commercial paper, 770
Ratings cliff, 774
Rayburn, Sam, 4
Reacquired securities, registering for sale, 12
Reallowance. *See* Debt restructuring
Recapitalization. *See* Debt restructuring
Recapture
   of commissions, 445–447
Reciprocal commission business, 445
Recirculation of preliminary prospectus, 190
Record date, NYSE, 981
Record keeping
   due diligence, 344, 354
   manipulative practices, 290
   Regulation M, 266
Redemption. *See also* Debt restructuring; stock repurchase programs; Underwriting
   calls for redemption to force conversions, 902
   lay-offs, 908
   1933 Act considerations, 905
   Regulation M, 908
   standby arrangements, 904
   debt restructuring, 941
   hard-call protection, 874
   notice, by mail, 944
   soft-call provision, 874
   30-day notice, 903
Red herring. *See* Prospectus
Reference security
   defined, 248, 266
Refinancing. *See* Debt restructuring
Registered offerings, notice of, 33
Registration. *See also* Shelf registration
   ADS, 713
   asset-backed securities, 993
   current or future, with private offering, 552
   exchangeable securities, 881
   exemption, exchange offers, 832
   foreign private issuers, 710, 720, 742
   Green Shoe option, securities covered by, 91
   LYONS, 772
   multijurisdictional disclosure system, 740
   NASD, 391
   1933 Act, 9
      convertible securities, 836
      effectiveness, 18
      and embedded options, 836

foreign governments and political
subdivisions, 741
global offerings, 749
mandatorily convertible
securities, 892
rights offerings, 984
waiting period, 19
1933 Act exemptions
convertible securities, 875
1934 Act
foreign private issuers, 737
foreign government issuer
coverage exemptions, 743
90-day undertakings, 573
on-demand registration, 62
preemption of state securities
registration, 1033
private offering
with concurrent or future
registration, 552
registration rights agreement, 553
process. *See also* Distribution
annual reports during, 132, 134
dealing with gun-jumping
problems, 195
issuer-directed shares, 138
post-filing issues, 191–218
presentations to securities
analysts, 134
registration statement, 141
restricted lists, 136
road shows, 191
role of securities analyst, 146
public offering of convertible
securities, 876
reopenings, 661
requirements
1933 Act, 11
private placement exemption, 459
Section 3(a)(3) exemption,
commercial paper, 778
rights agreement, private offerings, 553
sale involving interstate commerce,
668
statement, 15. *See also* Forms

acceleration of effectiveness,
18, 401
annual reports, 132, 134
anti-dilution provision, 877
asset-backed securities, 999, 1000,
1003, 1019
Chinese Walls, 218
circulation of prospectus, 190
confidential treatment, 185
contents, 14
convertible securities, 876
delaying amendments, 18
due diligence review, 347
effective date, 18
EDGAR filing, 186
exchangeable securities, 882
filing, 127
firm commitment basis, 607
first draft preparation, 126
foreign issue accounting
questions, 734
foreign private issuer, 736
form of, 127
Form S-16, 17
forward-looking, 351
global offering, 749, 751
guarantees and credit
enhancement, 184
integrated disclosure system,
development of, 15
management's discussion and
analysis, 150. *See also*
Management's discussion and
analysis (MD&A)
merger or exchange, 976
NASD filing, 398
officers' and directors'
questionnaire, 346
operation of the registration
requirement, 13
other selected issues, 146
plain English, 141
post-effective amendment, 98,
593, 602–606, 614, 637
preparation of, 141

INDEX

presentations to securities analysts, 134
product advertisements, 133
projections and other forward-looking information, 166
prospectus, 645
prospectus summary, 145
registration for a purpose, 12
responding to comments, 188
review by SEC staff, 18, 185
review of confidential or bulky documents, 353
risk factors, 143
SEC comments, 188
SEC staff review process, 18, 185
Section 11 action, 308, 348, 351, 368
selective review, 186
shelf registration. *See* Shelf registration
shelf updating, 602
STRYPES, 895
underwritten call, 905, 906
waiting period, 19

Regulations
A, 60
AB, 991, 994, 1001, 1023
AC, 149
C, 580
D, 60, 460, 481–490, 492, 493, 494, 506, 535, 537, 538, 541, 549, 685, 687, 691, 702, 816, 1014
FD, 170, 192, 483, 598
G, 364, 365
K, 83
M, 101, 147, 148, 251, 266, 269, 290, 295, 299, 662, 856, 870, 879, 880, 908, 909, 910, 919, 926
  adoption, 246
  affiliated purchasers, 257
  basic prohibitions, 248
  convertible securities, 870
  covered securities, 266
  debt restructurings, 967
  distribution participant, 255
  distributions, 248, 759
  equity offerings during restricted period, 208
  exchange offers, 967
  excepted activities, 270
  excepted securities, 268
  exchangeable securities, 889
  global offerings by foreign corporations, 759
  gun-jumping, restricted lists, 136
  investment account, 264
  Jaffee case, 251 n.56
  manipulative practices, 232, 246, 290
  problems, 208
  prospectus disclosure, SRO notification, and recordkeeping, 278
  redemption and, 908
  restricted period, duration, 259
  restricted period, termination, 259
  shelf registration, 255, 654
  stabilization, 271
  stock repurchases, put warrants, 925
  stock repurchases, Rule 10b-18, 919
  trading practice rules, 232
M-A, 932
S, 204, 281, 315, 430, 679, 680–683, 685, 687, 689, 690, 691, 694–696, 701–706, 708, 709, 747, 842, 877, 901, 954
S-K, 14, 17, 73, 91, 104, 110, 143, 151, 161, 180, 185, 209, 290, 321, 347, 351, 362, 364, 367, 406, 411, 580, 593, 599, 602, 650, 928, 985, 989, 1003
S-T, 186, 1010
S-X, 184, 359, 538, 600, 734, 1003, 1005
T, 86, 229, 521, 643, 760
Rehnquist, Justice
  dissenting opinion in *Sanders* case, 820
Reinvestment risk, zero coupon obligations, 941

Related-party transactions, 334, 340, 366
Related persons, Rule 2750, 457
Reliance Insurance Company, 325, 326
Reliance on misstatements and 1933 Act Section 11, 308
Remarketed preferred stock. *See* Preferred stock
Remarketing
  agent. *See* Agent
  agreements, extendible notes, 851, 852
  arrangements
    put bonds and, 854
Renewable notes. *See* Notes
Rent-a-shelf programs, 998, 1002
Reopenings
  qualified reopening, 663
Reorganization
  plan of, 60
Repackaging, 845
  of debt securities, 839
Repeal stocks, 234
Reporting. *See also* Forms; Registration; Tax considerations
  continuous, foreign government issuer, 737
Representations. *See also* Guarantees; Warranties
  as due diligence aid, 91
  medium-term notes, 636, 641
  new representations, addition of, 83
  underwriting agreement, 91
    representations by selling securityholders, 94
  updating of, 94
Repurchase. *See* Stock repurchase programs
Reputation, 305
Resale, 495
  of exchanged securities, 964
  Regulation S safe harbor, 704
  restrictions, private offerings, 495
  Rule 144A, 502
  safe harbor, 682, 704
Rescission of securities sale
  reliance on oral misstatement, 815, 816

Research
  asset-backed securities, 1015
  global offerings by foreign corporations, 757
  manipulative practices, 270
  reports, gun-jumping, 38
Research analyst
  conflicts of interest, 146–150
  due diligence, role of, 343
Research materials
  electronic means, receipt by, 208
Research reports
  conflicts of interest in preparation of, 146–150
Resecuritization, 999
Reservation of securities for dealers and institutions, 76
Restatement (Second), Foreign Relations Law of the United States, 724
Restricted
  lists, prior to offering, 136
  persons, NASD, free-riding and withholding, 428
  securities, under Rule 144, 47
Restrictive covenants. *See* Covenants
Restrictive legends, 494, 704
Restructuring debt. *See* Debt restructuring
Retail-oriented issuer debt programs, 838
Returned shares, 76
  disposition of, 76
Revenue Act of 1932, 70
Revenue recognition, 360
Reverse triangular merger, 875
Reves case, 8
Review of registration statements
  by SEC
    comment letters, 188
    selective review, 186
Rex case, 238
Richmond case, 322, 323
Rickard, James H., 383
Rights offerings. *See* Subscription offers
Rights to purchase, 910
Rio Algom Limited, 969
Risk arbitrage. *See* Arbitrage

INDEX 1077

Risk factors
   risk-reward ratio in bought deals, 612
   stated in registration statement, 143
   zero coupon obligations, 941
Roadshow
   distribution of material, 192, 193
      Section 11 liability for, 193
   electronic roadshow, 191, 193
   post-filing, 191
Roan Antelope Copper Mines, 714
Robert Wood Johnson Foundation, 228
Rollover of commercial paper, 779
Roosevelt, Franklin D., 1–4, 442
Royal Dutch Petroleum Company, 746
Rules (1933 Act)
   130, 14 n.24
   131, 52
   133 (rescinded), 41, 565, 570
   134, 36–38, 140, 178, 179, 183, 621, 756, 907, 1011
   134(b), 36, 37
   134(d), 176, 178
   135, 33–35, 131, 135, 688
   135c, 35, 482, 489, 506, 688
   135e, 36, 483, 489, 686, 687
   137, 203
   138, 204, 506, 757, 690, 1016
   139, 101, 147, 148, 205, 207, 506, 757, 1015, 1016
   139(a), 206
   139(b), 206
   139a, 1017
   141, 315
   142, 466
   144, 41, 47–49, 309, 475, 495, 509, 567, 569, 570, 651, 701, 860, 895, 979
   144(k), 495, 509, 515, 999
   144A, 42, 71, 277, 281, 307, 460, 494, 501–510, 521, 523, 528–531, 538, 556, 557, 560, 609, 685, 690, 691, 703, 704, 735, 816, 837, 842, 868, 869, 880, 1014, 1021
   144A(d)(4), 729, 1021
   145, 40, 41, 569, 964, 976
   146 (rescinded), 474, 476–481, 517, 520
   147, 60
   149, 957, 958
   150, 959
   151, 58
   153, 26, 574, 646
   154 (rescinded), 570
   155 (rescinded), 569
   158, 98, 311
   174(b), 26
   174(d), 26
   176, 322
   264(c), 209
   401(g), 131
   405, 19 n.37, 46, 349, 604
   406, 185
   408, 348
   415. *See* Shelf registration
   415(a)(1), 635, 636
   416(a), 877
   421(b), 142
   421(d), 142
   424, 189, 608, 633
   424(b), 88, 119, 172, 180, 209, 210, 1009, 1023
   426, 1009
   429, 594
   430, 20, 21, 37
   430A, 18, 87, 88, 172, 208, 209, 291, 610
   430A(a), 172
   434, 212
   434C (rescinded), 751
   457(a), 172
   457(o), 172
   462(b), 172, 210
   473, 18
   482, 20 n.39
   501, 481
   501(c)(1)(iv), 490
   502, 481
   502(a), 497, 498
   502(c), 482, 487
   502(d), 493
   503, 482, 495, 496

504, 60, 482
505, 482
506, 482, 483, 488, 495, 496
506(b), 490
506(b)(2)(i), 490
506(b)(2)(ii), 493507, 496
508, 500
701, 49
2710, 403
2720, 401
Rules (1934 Act)
3a12-3, 723, 725, 737
10a-1(a), 976
10a-1(d)(7), 976
10b-2, 576
10b-4, 814–816
10b-5, 102, 156, 165, 196, 219, 251, 299, 317, 319, 322, 323, 512, 551, 598, 599, 730, 815, 816, 819, 820, 822, 823, 914, 938, 986, 1023
10b-5(b), 943
10b-6. *See* Distributions (Regulation M)
10b-7. *See* Stabilization (Regulation M)
10b-8, 909, 910, 967, 986
10b-10, 22
10b-10(a)(7), 1024
10b-13, 935
10b-18, 295, 917, 918, 919, 920, 925, 927, 928
10b-21, 297–298, 299
10b-21(T), 298
10b5-1, 219
11d-1, 223–229
11d-1(e), 224, 225
12g3-2(b), 506, 507, 720, 726, 727, 728, 729, 730, 740
12g-4(a)(2), 740
13d-3, 966
13e-3, 936, 937, 965
13e-4, 878, 879, 910, 919, 926, 932, 945, 965
13e-4(f)(6), 935
14d-1, 953
14e-1, 945, 947, 952

14e-1(a), 945
14e-1(b), 952, 969, 970
14e-2, 945, 952, 953
14e-3, 219, 945
14e-4, 938
14e-5, 879, 935, 967
15a-6, 689
15c2-8, 21, 22, 190
15c2-8(b), 21, 843, 1012, 1013
15c2-11, 729
15c2-12, 53, 54
15c3-1, 856
15c6-1, 212
15d-6, 1024
16a-2(b), 866, 966
17a-2, 292
20b-10, 22
Rules (1935 Act)
50, 119
Rules (1940 Act)
2a-7, 1029
3a-1, 811, 813
3a-3, 813
3a-5, 811, 813, 843, 844
3a-6, 811
3a-7, 1026, 1027, 1028, 1029
3a-8, 221, 222
6c-9, 811
Rules of Fair Practice
NASD, 392, 424

S

SAB 99, 357
SAB 101, 360, 361
Safe harbor
  asset-backed securities, research materials, 1015
  forward-looking statements, 167
  Regulation S, 680, 682, 702, 704, 842
  statutory, 170
  stock repurchase programs, 918–923
  trading restrictions, 295

INDEX

St. Joe Minerals Corporation, 801
Sale, defined, 876
Sales. *See* Offers and sales
Sales credits
   allocation of, 75
   tying of, to actual sales, 76
Salomon Brothers, 846
   dual underwriting syndicates, 754
   Rule 415 hearings, 581
Sanctions
   TEFRA D issuer sanctions, 708–709
Sandler O'Neill & Partners, LP, 845
S&P. *See* Standard & Poor's
   Corporation
Sarbanes–Oxley Act, 1, 8, 148, 159,
   161, 186, 307, 312, 317, 334, 345,
   346, 357, 367, 711, 715, 733, 738,
   739, 913, 1022, 1023, 1024
   corporate governance reforms, 334
   foreign companies, effect on, 739
   foreign reporting companies, effect
     on, 738
SAS 42, 351
SAS 100, 370
Savin Corporation, 966
Schedules
   13D filing, 931
   13E-3, 937
   13G, 931
   A, 14, 185
   B, 606, 607, 608, 761–763
   E, NASD, 401
   TO, 932–933, 937
Schering-White Laboratories, 571
Scienter
   and Rule 10b-5, 246, 320
   and Rule 10b-6, 246
   and 1933 Act Section 17(a), 320
SCM Corporation case, 916
Scott case, 238
Screen-based and other offers, 505
   password-protected display, 505
   QIB, 505
   violating dealer agreement, 523
Screen shots, 180, 181
Sears, Roebuck & Co., 69

Sears Roebuck Acceptance
   Corporation, 638
SEC. *See* Securities and Exchange
   Commission
Secondary markets, 2, 29
   secondary market trading, 77
Secondary Mortgage Market
   Enhancement Act of 1984
   (SMMEA), 1032
Section 11. *See* Securities Exchange
   Act of 1934
Securities. *See also* Asset-backed
   securities; Hybrid instruments;
   Innovative financing techniques;
   Manipulative practices
   ADRs, 713
   asset-backed securities, 987–1034
   at-the-market equity offerings, 644
   as collateral, shelf registration, 572
   bank, exemptions, 54
   defined, 8, 1025
   derivative. *See* Derivatives
   description, shelf registration, 614
   distribution. *See also* Underwriting
     syndicates
   exempted, 49
   fixed-income, 1027
   fungibility, 506
   investment-grade debt securities, 609
   issuer-directed
     IPO, 138
   markets, globalization, 666
   mortgage-related, 1032, 1033. *See
     also* Mortgage backed securities
   notes as, 9
   offers and sales, 19
   preemption from state registration
     laws, 1033
   prohibited transactions exceptions, 270
   redeemable, 1027
   restricted, under Rule 144, 47
   restricted lists prior to offering, 136
   taken in trade, 455
   unregistered distribution
     securities, 672
   unsold allotments, 27

Securities Act of 1933
  after-market transaction, 25
  commercial paper, 778
    Section 3(a)(2) exemption, 805
    Section 3(a)(3) exemption, 778
    Section 4(2) exemption, 808
  disclosure philosophy, 7
  enactment, 5
  exempt securities. *See* Exempt securities
  exempted transactions. *See* Exempted transactions
  future of act, 60
  gun-jumping, 30–33
  history of act, 3
  market crashes, 1
  offers and sales, 39
    of registered securities, 19
    Rule 145, 40
    spin-offs, 39
  offshore offerings. *See* Offshore offerings and the 1933 Act
  offshore press-related communications, 36
  overview, 3, 7
  registration and prospectus delivery requirements, 11
    delivery of final prospectus with confirmation, 21
    delivery of final prospectus with registered security, 25
    Forms S-1, S-2, S-1, and S-3, 17
    "free-writing" privilege, 24
    global offerings, 751
    operation of registration requirement, 13
    preliminary prospectus, 21
    registration for a purpose, 12
    unsold allotments, 27
    updating the prospectus, 27
  registration statement effective date, 18
  research reports, 38
  rights offerings, 984
  Rule 134, 36
  Rule 135c, 35
  Rule 135, 33
  Rule 135e, 36
  SEC concept release, Securities Act Concepts and Their Effects on Capital Formation, 61
  Section 2(a)(1), 8, 9
  Section 2(a)(3), 858, 883, 926
  Section 2(a)(10), 1001, 1007
  Section 2(a)(10)(a), 179
  Section 3(a)(1), 717
  Section 3(a)(2), 49, 51, 52, 54, 57, 805, 1004
  Section 3(a)(3), 523, 528
  Section 3(a)(8), 1004
  Section 3(a)(9), 60, 953–964
  Section 3(a)(10), 60
  Section 4 exemptions, 42, 45
  Section 5, 11, 174, 179, 195, 196, 200, 202, 705, 1011, 1012
  Section 5(a)(2), 979
  Section 5(b)(1), 621, 1007
  Section 7, 14
  Section 10, 22, 179, 182, 621
  Section 10(a), 601, 898, 899, 900
  Section 10(b), 280
  Section 10(c), 901
  Section 11 liability, 102, 201, 209, 322, 351, 421, 422, 550, 598, 602, 885, 887, 888, 1009
    ADRs, 719
    commercial paper, 820
    disclosure-based remedy, 11
    documenting due diligence, 372
    early settlement of case, 328
    expertized material, 351
    non-U.S. purchaser, 752
    statutory bases for liability, 307
    STRYPES, 896
  Section 11(c), 5
  Section 11(e), 309
  Section 11(f), 112
  Section 12(a)(1), 196, 551
  Section 12(a)(2), 11, 52, 102, 314, 316, 322, 598, 600, 630, 814, 816, 887
  Section 12(b), 128
  Section 12(g), 128
  Section 12(g)(1), 722

INDEX 1081

Section 13, 312
Section 15(d), 128
Section 17, 11
Section 17(a), 323
securities issued or guaranteed by foreign governments, 742
security defined, 11
senate report, commercial paper, 780
STRYPES, 895
trust preferred securities, 842
Securities analyst
  conflicts of interest, 146–150
  independence, steps to promote, 148, 149
  role in securities offerings, 146–150
Securities and Exchange Commission (SEC), 6
  anti-manipulation rules, 577, 759
  Chief Accountant, Office of, 6
  concept release, Securities Act Concepts and Their Effects on Capital Formation, 61
  Corporation Finance, Division of, 6, 7
  creation, 5
  distribution definition, 252
  divisions and departments of, 6
  due diligence role, 321
  Enforcement Division, 6
  General Counsel, Office of, 6
  Guide 4, 578
  Guide 53, 577
  history, 6
  interpretive letters, 7
  Investment Management Division, 6
  Market Regulation, Division of, 6, 7
  1933 Act Section 5 enforcement, 11
  1987 Internationalization Report, 679
  no-action letters by staff, 7
  offices, location of, 7
  registration forms, 14
    Form S-1, 14
  registration statement comments, 188
  registration statement review process, 185
  Release 33-4412, 779, 780, 783
  Release 33-4708, 669, 674, 708

response to free-riding, 424
Rule 10b-5, 317–320
Rule 135e, 756, 757, 759
Rule 137, 203
Rule 138, 204
Rule 144, 475
Rule 146, 474, 476, 476
Rule 24f-2, 645
Securities Act Concepts and Their Effects on Capital Formation, SEC concept release, 61
selective review of registration statements, 186
Special Study of Securities Markets, 423
Securities Exchange Act of 1934
  antimanipulation, 236
  asset-backed securities, 1021–1025
  continuous reporting for foreign private issuers, 737
  enactment, 6
  foreign companies, reporting obligations of, 721
  NASD registration with SEC, 391
  periodic report filing, 15
  registration and reporting, foreign private issuer coverage exemptions, 743
  registration "trigger," 728
  Rule 10b-5, 317
  Rule 10b-6A, 246
  Rule 10b-10, 22
  Section 3(a)(10), 8
  Section 9, 236
  Section 9(a), 251
  Section 9(a)(2), 299
  Section 11(d)(l), 223–229, 560, 642, 759
  Section 12(k)(2), 924
  Section 13(a), 720
  Section 15(b)(8), 391 Section 15(d), 720, 1024
  Section 18, 730
  Section 19(b), 889
  Section 28(a), 889

shelf registration, 575
trust preferred securities, 843
Securitization transactions, 307
Securities Investor Protection Act (SIPA)
    underwriting agreement, 117
Security
    defined, 56
Securityholders
    exchanges, exempt, 58
    trading restrictions, 292
Sedlmayr, Julius H. ("Dooley"), 384
Segment disclosure, 365
Segregation
    of broker-dealer functions, 223, 224
    of proceeds, commercial paper and
        private placements, 524, 525
Selected dealers agreement, 117
Self-insurance activity, 366
Self-regulatory organizations. *See also*
    National Association of Securities
    Dealers, Inc. (NASD); New York
    Stock Exchange (NYSE)
    manipulative practices,
        notification, 290
    NASD as, 391
    NYSE as, 391
    Regulation M, 278
    sanctions, 393
Seller's defenses
    due diligence, medium-term
        notes, 640
    Section 12(a)(2) claim, 314
Selling. *See* Offers and sales
Sensitivity analysis, 362, 363
Separate security, 52
Separate Trading of Registered Interest
    and Principal of Securities
    (STRIPS), 846
Servicing reports, asset-backed
    securities, 1013, 1014, 1022
Settlement date, T+3, 211
SFAS 5, 341
SFAS 131, 365
Shad, John R., 830
Shad-Johnson accord, 830
Shares returned to underwriters, 76

Shearson Lehman Brothers Inc.,
    300–302, 304, 754
Shelf registration, 128, 299, 300
    advantages of, 19
    asset-backed securities, 1000, 1002
    at-the-market equity offerings, 644
    block trades, 648, 649
    common stock, 643
        at-the-market equity offerings, 644
        investment companies, 644
        non-underwritten registered equity
            secondaries, 646
        primary offerings, 643
    continuous acquisition programs, 566
    conventional debt and preferred
        stock, 609, 617
        board authorization, 617
        "convenience shelf" problem, 610
        disclosure and due diligence, 621
        distribution plan, 611
        indenture and description of
            securities, 614
        preliminary prospectus, use of, 620
        securities to be registered, 610
        underwriting documents, 618
    deep discount and zero coupon
        obligations. *See* Deep discount
        and zero coupon obligations
    documentation, 596
    due diligence, 621–631
    evolution, 564
    expansion of Form S-3 and Form F-3
        eligibility, 584
    foreign governments or political
        subdivisions, 606
    further developments, 579
    generic shelf, 594
    Guide 4, 578
    Hazel Bishop case, 574
    investment companies, 644
    medium-term notes
        disclosure and due diligence, 640
        documentation, 634
        due diligence, 640
        procedures, 639
        programs, 632

INDEX

registration under Rule 415, 636
  Section 11(d)(1), 642
90-day undertakings, 573
pledged securities, 572
presumptive underwriter problem, 652
prospectus, 645
Regulation M, 255, 654
reloading the shelf, 563
reopenings, 661
resales following Rule 133
  transactions, 569
Rule 10b-6, 654, 655
Rule 415
  adoption, 528, 579
  amount of securities registered, 592
  covered securities, 590
  filing exemption, 401
  generic shelf, 594
  how Rule 415 works, 590
  impact, 586
  incorporation by reference, of 1934 Act reports, 597
  offering material, use of, 601
  offering price, 75
  operation, 590
  post-effective amendment, filing of, 602
  post-effective amendment vs. prospectus supplement, 119
  prospectus supplement for bid filing, 119
  and traditional syndicate practices, 66–67
  types of securities registered, 594
  unallocated shelf, 594
  universal shelf, 594
sales following private placements, 567
SEC Section 11 liability, 627–630, 640
secondary offerings, 579
shares issued upon conversions of privately placed securities, 568
shelf updating procedures, 602
statement
  disclosures, 621
  Rule 415 effect, 590

stock options plans, 572
and STRYPES, 895
swaps, 628
takedowns, 593, 595, 611, 620
traditional, 565
types of securities registered, 594
unallocated shelf, 594
underwriters' stock and warrants, 569
universal shelf, 594
use, 561
Shelf takedowns, 306, 307, 331
Sherman Act. *See* Antitrust
Shields Plan, 909, 985–986. *See also* Subscription offers
Shingle theory approach, 323
Shoe. *See* Green Shoe option; Overallotment option
Shoney's, Inc., 879
Short-form registration statements. *See* Abbreviated registration forms
Short sale, 78, 89, 299, 557, 650, 681, 856, 859, 860, 871, 880. *See also* Offers and sales
  against the box, 858, 860
  arbitrage, 976–978
  block trade, 923, 925
  by broker-dealers, 925
  covering with registered securities, 296
  lay-offs, 909, 985
  overallotments, 77
  private offering followed by short sales into public market, 557
Short tendering. *See* Tender offer
Short-term notes. *See* Commercial paper
Shreve, Charles E., 566
Silicon Valley, 423
Simultaneous tender and call (STAC), 944
Singer Company, The, 671
Single broker-dealer condition, 921
Sinking funds, 616
Size of deal, changes in, 208
Slack, Tom, 388
Small Business Administration instruments, 847
SmartNotes, 839

Smith, Winthrop R., 387
SMMEA. *See* Secondary Mortgage Market Enhancement Act of 1984
Solicitation, *see also* Advertising; Manipulative practices
  consent, 968
  electronic media, 505
  exchange offers, 953
  fees, arbitrage and when-issued trading, 977
  general solicitation, 505
    exclusion of certain communications, 482
    future of prohibition, 489 and prior relationships, 538
  private offerings, 482
  qualified offerees, 452
  rights offerings, 982
  tender offers, 930, 933
Somoza, Anastasio, 383
Southern Pacific Rail Corporation, 969
Spain, commercial paper, 803
Special purpose vehicle (SPV), 991
Special Report of Special Study of Securities Markets, 721
Special Study of Securities Markets, 423, 425
Spencer, Lee B. Jr., 653
"Spinning," 396, 400
  proposed restrictions on, 437
Spin-offs, 39
  unregistered spin-offs, 40
  valid business purpose for, 40
SPINS. *See* Indexed debt instruments
Sports Arenas, Inc., 567
Spread, underwriting, 80
SQUARZ, 869
Stabilization
  adjustments to bid, 289
  after security starts to trade, 286
  before security starts to trade, 286
  defined, 280
  disclosure and record keeping, 290
  effect of exchange rates, 289
  excepted securities, 280
  general rules, 282
  Hazel Bishop case, 57–578
  increasing or reducing bid, 288
  initiating
    no market, 284
    principal market closed, 285
    principal market open, 284
  international financings, Regulation M, 759
  maintaining or carrying over bid, 288
  manipulative practices, 231, 271, 279
  mechanics, 281
  outside U.S., 289
  prices at which stabilization may take place, 283
    adjustments to stabilizing bid, 289
    before offering price determined, 287
    effect of exchange rates, 289
    increasing or reducing stabilizing bid, 288
    maintaining or carrying over stabilizing bid, 288
    no market for security, 284
    principal market closed, 285
    principal market open, 284
  problems, 295
  put warrants, 926
  Regulation M, 271
  transactions, 91
Staffing, and due diligence, 335
Staff Legal Bulletin No. 3, 59
Staff Legal Bulletin No. 7, 142, 144, 145
Staff Legal Bulletin No. 10, 249, 250
Standard & Poor's Corporation, 57, 420, 773
  commercial paper ratings, 773
  rating, 278
  S&P 500 futures contract, 829
  S&P Index, 57
Standard Oil Company, The, 828
Standards. *See also* Due diligence; Fairness
  due diligence, 329
  of fairness, NASD, 412
  NASD conduct rules, 392, 396

INDEX

prime quality, commercial paper, 779
reasonable care, 817
Standby arrangements
  discussion, 904
  lay-offs, 909
  prospectus, 906
  standby purchase fee, 905
  underwriters, 905
Stand-off agreements. *See* Lock-up agreements
State securities laws. *See also* Blue sky laws
  preemption from registration, 1033
Statute of limitations
  civil actions, 312, 317
Stock. *See* Securities
Stock dividends. *See* Dividend
Stock exchange listing. *See* National exchange listing
Stock market crash. *See* Crash
Stock offering. *See* Offers and sales
Stock options. *See* Options
Stock purchase warrants. *See* Warrants
Stock repurchase programs, 915. *See also* Going private transactions
  cash tender offers, 929
  corporate law considerations, 913
  debt restructuring, 940
  derivatives, using, 925
  disclosure of repurchases, 928
  discussion, 911, 912
  open market, purchases in, 911, 914
  privately negotiated purchases, 911
  put warrants, 925, 926
    1933 Act considerations, 926
    1934 Act considerations, 926
  Rule 10b-5 considerations, 914
  Rule 10b-18, 917
  Rule 10b-18 purchases, 918
  safe harbor, 918–924
    conditions to availability of, 921
    marketwide trading suspensions, relaxed conditions during, 924
    purchases outside safe harbor, 924
    scope of, 920
  short sales by broker-dealers, 925

tender offer, 911
  avoiding tender offer, 915
  eight-factor test, 915
  going private transactions, 936
  mechanics, 929
  rules, 915
  short tendering of securities, 938, 939
Stock splits
  public offering, 126
  Section 11(d)(1) of 1934 Act, 227
Stop transfer instructions, 475, 478
Story issuers, 532
Stride Rite shoes, 89
Stripped bond custody receipt programs, 850
  Stripped Treasury obligations, 826, 845, 846, 869
Stripping corporate obligations, 850
Stripping out issuer's right to redeem securities, 836, 837
STRIPS, 846
Structured financing vehicles
  asset-backed securities, 1027
Structured Yield Product Exchangeable for Stock (STRYPES), 826, 894
  CEA considerations, 896
  discussion, 894
  liability considerations, 896
  listing, 896
  1933 Act considerations, 895
  prospectus, 895
  state preemption, 896
STRYPES. *See* Structured yield product exchangeable for stock
Student loans, 992
Subdivision. *See* Foreign; Offshore offerings and the 1933 Act
Subordinated notes. *See* Notes
Subscription offers. *See also* Shields Plan
  ADRs, 745
  Canada, 745
  cash-out procedure, 745
  College Retirement Equities Fund, 746

cross-border rights offers, 744
dealer-manager plan, 986
disclosures, 746
discussion, 980
European Union directive, 744
investment banker's role, 982, 986
lay-offs, 908
mechanics, 744–748, 980
1933 Act registration, 984
over-subscription privilege, 982
to raise equity capital, 744
record date, 982
Royal Dutch Petroleum Company, 746
Shields plan, 985
transactions with securityholders, 978, 979
use, 744
Subsidiaries
finance, foreign banks, 810, 811
Substantial compliance rule Regulation D, 500
Substantial U.S. market interest (SUSMI), 692, 702
Suitability standards, 76, 419, 425, 426, 492
Sullivan & Cromwell, 5, 375, 376
Summa Corporation, 383
Summary judgment
due diligence case, 328
Sunbeam Gold Mines case, 470
Sun Company, Inc., 827, 892
Supplementary selling literature, 25
Supplements to prospectus. *See* Prospectus
Support agreements. *See* Credit
Surety bond
commercial paper exemption, 807
Surveys, blue sky, and legal investment, 126
SUSMI. *See* Substantial U.S. market interest
Suspension of trading, 924
Swaps, 11, 831, 833
bought deals, 612
credit default swaps, 1003
currency, asset-backed securities, 1003
interest rate, 1003
Rule 2730, 454
as securities, 10, 833
shelf registration, 612, 628
Sweden
bank as investment company, 810
shelf registration, 607
Syndicates. *See* Underwriting

T

Take-up fee
standby arrangements, 908
Task Force on Disclosure Simplification
SEC, 61
Tax considerations. *See also* Withholding
asset-backed securities, 1031
trust preferred securities, 840
deep discount and zero coupon obligations, 656
interest equalization, 667
offshore offerings and the 1933 Act, 706
shelters, 538
short sales against the box, 858
U.S. person defined, 675
withholding
hot issue markets, 423
TEFRA D sanctions, 706–710
Tax Equity and Fiscal Responsibility Act of 1983 (TEFRA)
TEFRA D issuer sanctions, 706–710
Taylor, E.K., 378
T. Boone Pickens, 935
TEFRA D sanctions
issuers of bearer obligations sold to U.S. investors, 706–709
Telecommunications
global, U.S. interest, 758
Telerate, 951
Tender offer
avoidance of, 915
brokers' search letter, 933

INDEX 1087

cash, 929, 946
consent solicitations, 968
debt, 946
    no-action letter, 955
discussion, 911
exchange, 954
fixed-spread cash tender offers, 950
    no-action letter, 950
going private, 936, 964
hedged tendering, 939
issuer debt, 945
    issuer recommendation, 952
issuer recommendation, 952
mechanics of, 929
modified Dutch auction, 930
non-convertible debt securities,
    no-action letter, 947
vs. open market purchase, 945
regulation of, 931, 945, 964
Rule 14e-4, 938–940
rules, 915
short tendering of securities,
    938–940
third-party, 931
Termination
    of price and other restrictions, in
        AAU, 85
    restricted period, 259
    stabilizing arrangements and trading
        restrictions, 85
    tender offer, 934
    underwriting agreement, 85, 112
Terms agreement. *See* Underwriting
Territorial approach of Regulation S, 679
Terrorist activity, 114, 115
Texas Air Corporation, 973
Thatcher, Margaret, 755
Third-party monetizations
    (STRYPES), 894
    CEA considerations, 896
    liability considerations, 896
    listing, 896
    1933 Act considerations, 895
    preemption, 896
Thomas, Barbara, 583, 584
Thompson, Houston, 4, 461

Thompson-Starrett Companies, Inc., 577
Thrift institutions
    exemptions, 57
Tie-in agreement, 249
TIGRs. *See* Stripped Treasury
    obligations; Treasury Investment
    Growth Receipts (TIGRs)
Timbers, Judge, 327
Times Mirror Company, 891
Tokyo Stock Exchange, 753
Tombstone. *See* Advertising; *Wall
    Street Journal, The*
TOPrS. *See* Merrill Lynch
Toronto stock exchange, 897
Tower Amendment, The, 53
TRs. *See* Stripped Treasury obligations
T+3, T+4, or T+5 settlements,
    211, 212
Trading
    foreign. *See* Offshore offerings and
        the 1933 Act
    markets, institutionalization, 666
    restrictions
        issuers and selling
            securityholders, 292
        underwriting syndicates, 78
    suspension, 114
    transactions, 1933 Act exemption, 42
Trading Practice Rules. *See* Regulation
    M, Rules 105-b, 105-7 and 105-8
Tranching
    asset-backed securities, 991, 992, 1018
Transactions
    with securityholders, 911
    transactional restrictions, Regulation
        S, 694
Transfer
    agents, 127
    stop-transfer instructions, 475, 478
    transferable share repurchase rights.
        See Stock repurchase programs
Transient investment companies, 219
Transmittal letter
    to SEC, 189
TransWorld Airlines, Inc., 966
Treanor, James A., 241

Treasury. *See* U.S. Treasury
Treasury Investment Growth Receipts (TIGRs), 697, 705, 710, 712, 826, 846
Treasury obligations, stripped. *See* Stripped Treasury obligations
Treasury Receipt (TR) program, 846
Trust. *See also* Equipment trust certificates
   Trust Indenture Act of 1939, 6, 74, 635, 743, 843, 964, 1032
   trust originated preferred securities. *See* Preferred stock
Trust-preferred securities, 202
Truth in Securities, Revisited, 16
TSC Industries case, 349
TWA stock financing deal, 386

U

UBS AG, 715
Unaudited financial information, 314
Uncoordinated distributions, 574
Underpricing, 416
Undertakings
   indemnification of officers and directors, 110
   qualified independent underwriters, 421
   Rule 430A offerings, 87
   subscription offers, 985
Underwriter. *See also* Underwriting
   affiliated purchaser trading restrictions, 293
   anti-manipulation, 256
   asset-backed securities, 1008, 1010, 1015, 1020, 1034
   compensation, 403, 408, 411
   competition, 624
   counsel for, shelf registration, 609
   defined, 883, 884
   due diligence, 627
      equity-linked notes, 893
   exchangeable securities, 887
   exclusive, 819
   fee, 126
   lead
      selecting, 123
   liability, 45, 259. *See also* Liabilities
      on default, 813
      potential, of qualified independent underwriters, 420
   managing or lead defined, 604
      handling restricted periods, 259
      investment account, 264
      liabilities and due diligence, 305
      restricted lists, 136
      selection, 123, 125
      stabilization, 281
   manipulative practices and market activities during distributions, 231–300
   1933 Act exemption, 44
   presumptive underwriter problem, 652
   "profit-sharing" allegations, 411
   prospective, 257, 628
   qualified independent underwriters, potential liabilities, 420
   questionnaire, 73
   rights offerings, 982
   shelf registration, 626, 645, 646
   standby commitments, reducing risk, 985
   standby purchasers as underwriters, 905
   stock and warrants, shelf registration, 569
   STRYPES, 896
   subsequent purchaser as, 521
   unnamed in shelf registration, 619
Underwriting
   activity report, 403
   agreements. *See also* Agreement among underwriters
      BP global offering, 753
      comfort letters, 104
      conditions, 101
      contribution, 111
      covenants, 97
      default, 116
      defined, 65, 86

INDEX

delayed delivery contracts, 94
"Green Shoe" option, 88
indemnification, 84, 107
issuers' role in pricing IPOs,
 proposed enhancement, 96, 416
lock-up agreements, 99
medium-term notes, 640
negotiations, due diligence,
 353, 367
overallotment and stabilization, 77
purchase and sale; closing, 106
representations and warranties, 91
Rule 430A, 87
several commitments, 87
and shelf registration, 596, 619, 620
STRYPES, 896
termination of underwriting
 agreement, at underwriters'
 election, 112, 619
timing and risk, 88
unfair, NASD rules, 397, 412, 413
updating the prospectus, 28
best efforts, 66
conflicts of interest, 417
differences, BP global offering, 753
documents
 agreement among underwriters
  (AAU), 72–86
 background, 65
 competitive bidding, 118
 post-1933 Act procedures, 70
 price maintenance, 74
 selected dealers agreement, 117
 selling allocations, 75
 shelf registration, 618
 the underwriting agreement, 86–117
global offerings by foreign
 corporations, 753
NASD filing, 398
NASD regulation, 392
restricted periods, 259
Rule 2720, 417
spread
 components, 80
standby, rights offerings, 985
syndicate

after World War II, 72
asset-backed securities, 1010
background, 66
BP global offering, 754
components of spread, 80
control, 78
covering short sales with
 registered securities, 296
early arrangements, 68
intersyndicate agreements, 66
penalty clause, 79
pre-1933 Act procedures, 68
prior to World War I, 69
rights offerings, 985
shelf registration, 618
trading restrictions, 78, 261
unsuccessful offering, 263
underwritten calls
 layoffs, 909
 1933 Act registration, 905
 redemption, 903
 standby arrangements, 904
Unfair underwriting arrangements, 413
Uniform Commercial Code negotiable
 instruments, 521
Uniform Practice Code, 85
Union Pacific Corporation, 969
Union Texas Natural Gas
 Corporation, 571
United Cigar Manufacturers, 69
United Kingdom, 724, 993. *See also*
 British Petroleum Company
 Limited; Companies Act; Foreign;
 International financing; London
 Stock Exchange
United Nations
 exclusion as U.S. person, 698
U.S. Bank Holding Company Act, 83
U.S. person
 defined, 675, 696
 transactions in Rule 144A
  securities, 277
U.S. Treasury. *See also* Stripped
 Treasury obligations
 benchmark security, 951, 952
 obligations, 829

1089

exempted securities, 49
futures contract market, 829
security, fixed-spread cash tender offers, 950
stock registration, 12
Unit offerings
 common stock and warrants, 898
 debt securities and warrants, 897
 debt/stock units, 895
Universal Match Corporation, 568
University Hill Foundation case, 821
Unocal Corporation, 935
Unregistered offerings
 notice of, 35, 688
Usinor, 970, 971
Unsolicited transactions. *See* Advertising; Manipulative practices; Solicitation
Utilities. *See* Public utilities

V

Value at risk (VAR) disclosures, 362, 363
Value Line Fund, Inc. case, 535
Variable coupon renewable notes. *See* Notes
Virtual companies, 11
Virtual shares, purchase of, 11
Virtual stock exchange, 11
Visits to principal facilities due diligence, 352
Volume limitations
 stock repurchase programs, 923

W

Wabash railroad, 375
Waiting period, 486
 1933 Act registration statement, 19
Waldron, Clarence A., 385, 388
Wall Street Journal articles and references, 67, 98, 200, 201, 783, 929–930

Warranties. *See also* Certificates; Guarantees; Representations
 medium-term notes, 636, 641
 underwriting agreement, 91
Warrants. *See also* Currency exchange warrants; Stock indexes
 antidilution, 898
 with common stock, 898
 debt securities and, 897
 discussion, 866
 exchange offer, no-action letter, 956
 expiring, 909
 put warrants, stock repurchase programs, 925
 rights offerings, 981, 984
 stock purchase warrants
  and common stock, 898
  defined, 897
  units of common stock and warrants, 898
  units of debt securities and warrants, 897
 underwriters' shelf registration, 569
 unit sale, 898
Wash sale prohibition, 236
Washington Water Power Company, The, 291
Website communications, 132, 344
 gun-jumping issues, 132–133, 344
 password-protected website, 484, 485, 486
 retail-oriented issuer debt programs, 839
Weinstein, Judge, against prospectuses, 350
Weis Securities, Inc., 117
Wellman case, 915
Wells Fargo & Company, 894
West, Milton H. Jr., 385
Wheat Report, 16, 34, 203, 652
When-issued trading
 control persons, borrowing stock from, 978
 discussion, 975, 976
 no-action letter, 976
Whistleblower protections, 739

INDEX

Whitehead, John C., 581
White Weld & Co., 325
Whitney, Richard, NYSE President, 235
Whole business securitizations, 993
Willets, Harris L., 883
Williams Act, 737, 756, 931
Williams, Harrison, 931
Williams, William J., Jr, 374
Wit Capital Corporation, 174, 175, 176, 177, 181
Withholding. *See* Tax considerations
Wolfe, Block, Schorr and Solis-Cohen case, 491 n.59
Woolsey, Judge (stock manipulation), 238
World Bank, 697. *See also* International Bank for Reconstruction and Development
WorldCom, Inc., 887, 888
World Trade Organization, 763
Written offers. *See* Offers and sales

X

Xerox Corporation, 892
Xerox Credit Corporation, 852

Y

Yahoo Inc., 869
Yield test, 663

Z

Zero coupon obligations. *See also* Deep discount and zero coupon obligations
   convertible stock, exchange offer, 966
   defined, 656, 660
   redemption, 941
   risk, 941